LEARNSMART ADVANTAGE WORKS

LEARNSMART

A	B	C	D	
30.5%	33.5%	22.6%	8.7%	4.7%

A	B	C	D	
19.3%	38.6%	28.0%	9.6%	4.5%

Without LearnSmart

More C students earn B's

*Study: 690 students / 6 institutions

Over 20%
more students pass the class with LearnSmart

*A&P Research Study

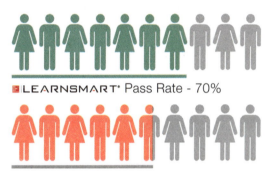

LEARNSMART Pass Rate - 70%

Without LearnSmart Pass Rate - 57%

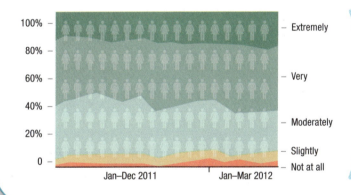

- Extremely
- Very
- Moderately
- Slightly
- Not at all

Jan–Dec 2011   Jan–Mar 2012

More than 60%
of all students agreed LearnSmart was a very or extremely helpful learning tool

*Based on 750,000 student survey responses

> **AVAILABLE** *ON-THE-GO*

http://bit.ly/LS4Apple

http://bit.ly/LS4Droid

How do you rank against your peers?

What you know (green) and what you still need to review (yellow), based on your answers.

Let's see how confident you are on the questions.

Contemporary Management

Management

Ninth Edition

Gareth R. Jones

Jennifer M. George
Jesse H. Jones Graduate School of Business
Rice University

CONTEMPORARY MANAGEMENT, NINTH EDITION

Published by McGraw-Hill Education, 2 Penn Plaza, New York, NY 10121. Copyright © 2016 by McGraw-Hill Education. All rights reserved. Printed in the United States of America. Previous editions © 2014, 211, and 2009. No part of this publication may be reproduced or distributed in any form or by any means, or stored in a database or retrieval system, without the prior written consent of McGraw-Hill Education, including, but not limited to, in any network or other electronic storage or transmission, or broadcast for distance learning.

Some ancillaries, including electronic and print components, may not be available to customers outside the United States.

This book is printed on acid-free paper.

1 2 3 4 5 6 7 8 9 0 DOR/DOR 1 0 9 8 7 6 5

ISBN 978-0-07-771837-4
MHID 0-07-771837-2

Senior Vice President, Products & Markets: *Kurt L. Strand*
Vice President, General Manager, Products & Markets: *Michael Ryan*
Vice President, Content Design & Delivery: *Kimberly Meriwether David*
Managing Director: *Susan Gouijnstook*
Director, Management and Organizational Behavior: *Michael Ablassmeir*
Product Developer: *Jane Beck*
Marketing Manager: *Elizabeth Trepkowski*
Director of Development: *Ann Torbert*
Director, Content Design & Delivery: *Terri Schiesl*
Program Manager: *Mary Conzachi*
Content Project Managers: *Danielle Clement, Bruce Gin*
Buyer: *Michael R. McCormick*
Design: *Matt Backhaus*
Content Licensing Specialist: *Keri Johnson*
Cover Image: *© Robert Churchill/Getty Images*
Compositor: *Laserwords Private Limited*
Printer: *R. R. Donnelley*

All credits appearing on page or at the end of the book are considered to be an extension of the copyright page.

Library of Congress Cataloging-in-Publication Data

Jones, Gareth R.
    Contemporary management / Gareth R. Jones, Jennifer M. George.—Ninth edition.
      pages cm
    ISBN 978-0-07-771837-4 (alk. paper)
    1. Management. I. George, Jennifer M. II. Title.
  HD31.J597 2016
  658–dc23

                        2014031868

The Internet addresses listed in the text were accurate at the time of publication. The inclusion of a website does not indicate an endorsement by the authors or McGraw-Hill Education, and McGraw-Hill Education does not guarantee the accuracy of the information presented at these sites.

www.mhhe.com

BRIEF CONTENTS

Part One

Management

Chapter 1
Managers and Managing 2

Chapter 2
The Evolution of Management Thought 32

Chapter 3
Values, Attitudes, Emotions, and Culture: The Manager as a Person 60

Part Two

The Environment of Management

Chapter 4
Ethics and Social Responsibility 90

Chapter 5
Managing Diverse Employees in a Multicultural Environment 122

Chapter 6
Managing in the Global Environment 156

Part Three

Decision Making, Planning, and Strategy

Chapter 7
Decision Making, Learning, Creativity, and Entrepreneurship 184

Chapter 8
The Manager as a Planner and Strategist 214

Chapter 9
Value Chain Management: Functional Strategies for Competitive Advantage 246

Part Four

Organizing and Controlling

Chapter 10
Managing Organizational Structure and Culture 276

Chapter 11
Organizational Control and Change 312

Chapter 12
Human Resource Management 344

Part Five

Leading Individuals and Groups

Chapter 13
Motivation and Performance 378

Chapter 14
Leadership 412

Chapter 15
Effective Groups and Teams 442

Part Six

Managing Critical Organizational Processes

Chapter 16
Promoting Effective Communication 474

Chapter 17
Managing Conflict, Politics, and Negotiation 508

Chapter 18
Using Advanced Information Technology to Increase Performance 534

CREDITS 562

INDEX 610

   NAMES 610

   ORGANIZATIONS 618

   GLOSSARY/SUBJECTS 622

CONTENTS

Part One | Management

Chapter 1 — Managers and Managing 2

A MANAGER'S CHALLENGE
Hitting the Mark at Alcon Entertainment 3

Topics

Overview 5

What Is Management? 5

  Achieving High Performance: A Manager's Goal 5

  Why Study Management? 6

Essential Managerial Tasks 7

  Planning 7

  Organizing 9

  Leading 10

  Controlling 10

  Performing Managerial Tasks: Mintzberg's Typology 10

Levels and Skills of Managers 11

  Levels of Management 11

  Managerial Skills 14

Recent Changes in Management Practices 17

  Restructuring and Outsourcing 17

  Empowerment and Self-Managed Teams 19

Challenges for Management in a Global Environment 20

  Building Competitive Advantage 20

  Maintaining Ethical and Socially Responsible Standards 22

  Managing a Diverse Workforce 24

  Utilizing IT and E-Commerce 25

  Practicing Global Crisis Management 25

Chapter 2 — The Evolution of Management Thought 32

A MANAGER'S CHALLENGE
Simplification and Excellence at General Electric 33

Topics

Overview 35

Scientific Management Theory 35

  Job Specialization and the Division of Labor 36

  F. W. Taylor and Scientific Management 37

  The Gilbreths 39

Administrative Management Theory 40

  The Theory of Bureaucracy 40

  Fayol's Principles of Management 42

Behavioral Management Theory 46

  The Work of Mary Parker Follett 46

  The Hawthorne Studies and Human Relations 47

  Theory X and Theory Y 48

Management Science Theory 50

Organizational Environment Theory 51

  The Open-Systems View 51

  Contingency Theory 52

Examples

Manager as a Person
Dennis Corsi: Flying High
at Armstrong Consultants   8

Managing Globally
Insourcing Is Out at GE's
Appliance Division   18

Ethics in Action
Apple Makes Sure Its Suppliers
Don't Fall Too Far from the Tree   23

Ethics in Action
Digging Deep to Promote
Workplace Safety   26

Management in Action

Summary and Review   27

Management in Action   28
Topics for Discussion and Action   28
Building Management Skills   28
Managing Ethically   29
Small Group Breakout Exercise   29
Exploring the World Wide Web   29
Be the Manager   29
New York Magazine, Case in
the News: Elon Musk Is in
an Empire State of Mind   30

Examples

Ethics in Action
McDonald's and Human Rights   38

Manager as a Person
John D. Rockefeller   40

Management Insight
Jim Collins: *Good to Great*   46

Management in Action

Summary and Review   54

Management in Action   55
Topics for Discussion and Action   55
Building Management Skills   55
Managing Ethically   56
Small Group Breakout Exercise   56
Exploring the World Wide Web   57
Be the Manager   57
The Wall Street Journal Case in the
News: Deutsche Bank Found
Inappropriate Communication
between Staffer, Central Bank
Salesperson Was Placed on
Leave in March   57

Chapter 3

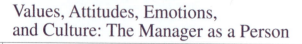

Values, Attitudes, Emotions, and Culture: The Manager as a Person 60

A MANAGER'S CHALLENGE

Jess Lee's Determination and Broad Interests Lead to the Top at Polyvore 61

Topics

Overview 63

Enduring Characteristics: Personality Traits 63
The Big Five Personality Traits 63
Other Personality Traits That Affect Managerial Behavior 67

Values, Attitudes, and Moods and Emotions 68
Values: Terminal and Instrumental 69

Attitudes 70
Moods and Emotions 74

Emotional Intelligence 76

Organizational Culture 78
Managers and Organizational Culture 78
The Role of Values and Norms in Organizational Culture 80
Culture and Managerial Action 83

Chapter 4

Ethics and Social Responsibility 90

A MANAGER'S CHALLENGE

Michelle Obama's Challenge to Kids across America: Let's Move! 91

Topics

Overview 93

The Nature of Ethics 93
Ethical Dilemmas 93
Ethics and the Law 93
Changes in Ethics over Time 94

Stakeholders and Ethics 95
Stockholders 96
Managers 96
Ethics and Nonprofit Organizations 98
Employees 99
Suppliers and Distributors 99
Customers 100
Community, Society, and Nation 102
Rules for Ethical Decision Making 103
Why Should Managers Behave Ethically? 105

Ethics and Social Responsibility 107
Societal Ethics 107
Occupational Ethics 109
Individual Ethics 110
Organizational Ethics 111

Approaches to Social Responsibility 114
Four Different Approaches 115
Why Be Socially Responsible? 116
The Role of Organizational Culture 116

Examples

Manager as a Person
Kevin Plank's Openness to Experience and Conscientiousness Pay Off at Under Armour 65

Ethics in Action
Telling the Truth at Gentle Giant Moving 69

Ethics in Action
Protecting the Environment and Jobs at Subaru of Indiana Automotive 72

Management Insight
Emotions as Triggers for Changes in Organizations 75

Management in Action

Summary and Review 85

Management in Action 86
Topics for Discussion and Action 86
Building Management Skills 86
Managing Ethically 86
Small Group Breakout Exercise 87
Exploring the World Wide Web 87
Be the Manager 87
The Wall Street Journal Case in the News: After Apple, Tackling Poverty 88

Examples

Ethics in Action
Safety in the Garment Industry 99

Ethics in Action
Cleaning up the Soap Market 101

Ethics in Action
Finding Diamonds in a Rough Ethical Landscape 108

Ethics in Action
TOMS One for One: Identify a Need and Then a Product 113

Management in Action

Summary and Review 117

Management in Action 119
Topics for Discussion and Action 119
Building Management Skills 119
Managing Ethically 119
Small Group Breakout Exercise 120
Exploring the World Wide Web 120
Be the Manager 120
Bloomberg Businessweek Case in the News: Missed Alarms and 40 Million Stolen Credit Card Numbers: How Target Blew It 121

Chapter 5

Managing Diverse Employees in a Multicultural Environment 122

A MANAGER'S CHALLENGE

PricewaterhouseCoopers Effectively Manages Diversity in Multiple Ways 123

Topics

Overview 125

The Increasing Diversity of the Workforce and the Environment 125
  Age 126
  Gender 127
  Race and Ethnicity 128
  Religion 129
  Capabilities/Disabilities 129
  Socioeconomic Background 130
  Sexual Orientation 131
  Other Kinds of Diversity 132

Managers and the Effective Management of Diversity 133
  Critical Managerial Roles 133
  The Ethical Imperative to Manage Diversity Effectively 136
  Effectively Managing Diversity Makes Good Business Sense 137

Perception 138
  Factors That Influence Managerial Perception 139
  Perception as a Determinant of Unfair Treatment 140
  Overt Discrimination 142

How to Manage Diversity Effectively 144
  Steps in Managing Diversity Effectively 144

Sexual Harassment 148
  Forms of Sexual Harassment 148
  Steps Managers Can Take to Eradicate Sexual Harassment 149

Chapter 6

Managing in the Global Environment 156

A MANAGER'S CHALLENGE

Getting Global Right on the Internet 157

Topics

Overview 158

What Is the Global Environment? 158

The Task Environment 159
  Suppliers 159
  Distributors 162
  Customers 163
  Competitors 163

The General Environment 165
  Economic Forces 166
  Technological Forces 166
  Sociocultural Forces 167
  Demographic Forces 167
  Political and Legal Forces 168

The Changing Global Environment 169
  The Process of Globalization 170
  Declining Barriers to Trade and Investment 172
  Declining Barriers of Distance and Culture 173
  Effects of Free Trade on Managers 174

The Role of National Culture 175
  Cultural Values and Norms 175
  Hofstede's Model of National Culture 175
  National Culture and Global Management 177

Examples

Focus on Diversity
Preventing Discrimination
Based on Sexual Orientation 131

Focus on Diversity
Effectively Managing Diversity
at Sodexo and Principal
Financial Group 134

Ethics in Action
Disabled Employees Make
Valuable Contributions 140

Management Insight
Top Execs Improve Their
Understanding of the Front Line 145

Management in Action

Summary and Review 150

Management in Action 151
Topics for Discussion and Action 151
Building Management Skills 151
Managing Ethically 151
Small Group Breakout Exercise 152
Exploring the World Wide Web 152
Be the Manager 152
The Wall Street Journal Case in
the News: Do You Know Your
Hidden Work Biases? 153

Examples

Managing Globally
Watering Down the Supply Chain 162

Managing Globally
Leveraging London for Leadership 170

Management Insight
Cultural Differences That Expatriates
Face in International Business 178

Management in Action

Summary and Review 179

Management in Action 180
Topics for Discussion and Action 180
Building Management Skills 180
Managing Ethically 180
Small Group Breakout Exercise 181
Exploring the World Wide Web 181
Be the Manager 181
Bloomberg BusinessWeek
Case in the News: In Trade Talks,
It's Countries versus Companies 182

Chapter 7

Decision Making, Learning, Creativity, and Entrepreneurship   184

A MANAGER'S CHALLENGE

Decision Making and Learning at 1-800-Flowers.com 185

Topics

Overview	187
The Nature of Managerial Decision Making	187
Programmed and Nonprogrammed Decision Making	188
The Classical Model	191
The Administrative Model	191
Steps in the Decision-Making Process	194
Recognize the Need for a Decision	195
Generate Alternatives	195
Assess Alternatives	196
Choose among Alternatives	198
Implement the Chosen Alternative	198
Learn from Feedback	198
Cognitive Biases and Decision Making	200

Prior Hypothesis Bias	200
Representativeness Bias	200
Illusion of Control	200
Escalating Commitment	201
Be Aware of Your Biases	201
Group Decision Making	201
The Perils of Groupthink	202
Devil's Advocacy and Dialectical Inquiry	202
Diversity among Decision Makers	203
Organizational Learning and Creativity	203
Creating a Learning Organization	204
Promoting Individual Creativity	205
Promoting Group Creativity	205
Entrepreneurship and Creativity	206
Entrepreneurship and New Ventures	207
Intrapreneurship and Organizational Learning	208

Chapter 8

The Manager as a Planner and Strategist   214

A MANAGER'S CHALLENGE

Toys"R"Us Is Not Playing Around When It Comes to Planning 215

Topics

Overview	216
Planning and Strategy	217
The Nature of the Planning Process	217
Why Planning Is Important	218
Levels of Planning	218
Levels and Types of Planning	219
Time Horizons of Plans	221
Standing Plans and Single-Use Plans	221
Scenario Planning	221
Determining the Organization's Mission and Goals	222
Defining the Business	222
Establishing Major Goals	223

Formulating Strategy	224
SWOT Analysis	224
The Five Forces Model	227
Formulating Business-Level Strategies	227
Low-Cost Strategy	228
Differentiation Strategy	228
"Stuck in the Middle"	228
Focused Low-Cost and Focused Differentiation Strategies	229
Formulating Corporate-Level Strategies	231
Concentration on a Single Industry	232
Vertical Integration	233
Diversification	234
International Expansion	237
Planning and Implementing Strategy	241

Examples

Focus on Diversity
Programmed Decision Making
at UPS   188

Manager as a Person
Curbing Overconfidence   190

Ethics in Action
Helping to Ensure Decisions
Contribute to Sustainability   197

Management Insight
Decision Making and Learning
from Feedback at GarageTek   199

Management in Action

Summary and Review   209

Management in Action   210
Topics for Discussion and Action   210
Building Management Skills   210
Managing Ethically   210
Small Group Breakout Exercise   211
Exploring the World Wide Web   211
Be the Manager   211
The New York Times Case in
the News: For Many Older
Americans, an Enterprising Path   212

Examples

Manager as a Person
Mary Barra Faces GM's Problems   225

Management Insight
Redbox and Netflix versus
Blockbuster   229

Management Insight
Getting Walked All Over
in the Shoe Business   232

Management Insight
PepsiCo: Would You Like a Snack
with That Beverage?   235

Managing Globally
Joint Venture Is a Sweet Deal for
Sugar Production and Distribution   240

Management in Action

Summary and Review   241

Management in Action   243
Topics for Discussion and Action   243
Building Management Skills   243
Managing Ethically   243
Small Group Breakout Exercise   244
Exploring the World Wide Web   244
Be the Manager   244
Bloomberg Businessweek Case
in the News: How the Average
McDonald's Makes Twice as
Much as Burger King   245

Chapter 9

Value Chain Management: Functional Strategies for Competitive Advantage   246

A MANAGER'S CHALLENGE

Ready for Takeoff? Increasing Airlines' Boarding Efficiency 247

Topics

Overview   249

Functional Strategies, the Value Chain, and Competitive Advantage   249

    Functional Strategies and Value Chain Management   250

Improving Responsiveness to Customers   252

    What Do Customers Want?   253

    Managing the Value Chain to Increase Responsiveness to Customers   253

    Customer Relationship Management   255

Improving Quality   256

    Total Quality Management   257

Improving Efficiency   261

    Facilities Layout, Flexible Manufacturing, and Efficiency   261

    Just-in-Time Inventory and Efficiency   263

    Self-Managed Work Teams and Efficiency   264

    Process Reengineering and Efficiency   264

    Information Systems, the Internet, and Efficiency   265

Improving Innovation   266

    Two Kinds of Innovation   266

    Strategies to Promote Innovation and Speed Product Development   266

Chapter 10

Managing Organizational Structure and Culture   276

A MANAGER'S CHALLENGE

Three Studios, Three Cultures, One Company 277

Topics

Overview   278

Designing Organizational Structure   279

    The Organizational Environment   279

    Strategy   280

    Technology   280

    Human Resources   281

Grouping Tasks into Jobs: Job Design   282

    Job Enlargement and Job Enrichment   282

    The Job Characteristics Model   283

Grouping Jobs into Functions and Divisions: Designing Organizational Structure   285

    Functional Structure   285

    Divisional Structures: Product, Market, and Geographic   287

    Matrix and Product Team Designs   291

Coordinating Functions and Divisions   293

    Allocating Authority   294

    Integrating and Coordinating Mechanisms   298

Organizational Culture   300

    Where Does Organizational Culture Come From?   302

    Strong, Adaptive Cultures versus Weak, Inert Cultures   304

Examples

Management Insight
Bread in the e-Commerce
Fast Lane 254

Management Insight
Vendor Relationships Key to
TJX's Store Offerings 257

Management Insight
Everything's Coming up Roses
in One Texas Town 260

Management Insight
Workspace Company Redefines
Its Own Workspace Philosophy,
Putting Its Money Where Its
Mouth Is 262

Management Insight
Legos Doesn't Play Around
When It Comes to Quality 270

Management in Action

Summary and Review 271

Management in Action 273
Topics for Discussion and Action 273
Building Management Skills 273
Managing Ethically 273
Small Group Breakout Exercise 274
Exploring the World Wide Web 274
Be the Manager 274
Bloomberg Businessweek Case
in the News: Maybe March
Madness Boosts (Rather Than
Kills) U.S. Productivity 275

Examples

Management Insight
Giving Wendy's a New Image 283

Managing Globally
Engineering across the World 289

Management Insight
The Miami Dolphins' Team-First
Culture 291

Manager as a Person
Satya Nardella, Microsoft's
New CEO 297

Manager as a Person
Marissa Mayer Shakes Up Yahoo! 301

Management in Action

Summary and Review 305

Management in Action 307
Topics for Discussion and Action 307
Building Management Skills 307
Managing Ethically 308
Small Group Breakout Exercise 307
Exploring the World Wide Web 309
Be the Manager 309
Bloomberg Businessweek Case
in the News: Panasonic Revives as
Other Japanese Tech Giants Falter 310

Chapter 11

Organizational Control and Change

312

A MANAGER'S CHALLENGE

The Zappos Holacracy 313

Topics

Overview	314
What Is Organizational Control?	315
The Importance of Organizational Control	315
Control Systems and IT	318
The Control Process	319
Output Control	323
Financial Measures of Performance	323
Organizational Goals	325
Operating Budgets	326
Problems with Output Control	327

Behavior Control	327
Direct Supervision	327
Management by Objectives	328
Bureaucratic Control	329
Problems with Bureaucratic Control	331
Clan Control	333
Organizational Change	334
Lewin's Force-Field Theory of Change	335
Evolutionary and Revolutionary Change	336
Managing Change	336

Chapter 12

Human Resource Management

344

A MANAGER'S CHALLENGE

Treating Employees Well Leads to Satisfied Customers and Low Turnover at the Four Seasons 345

Topics

Overview	347
Strategic Human Resource Management	347
Overview of the Components of HRM	348
The Legal Environment of HRM	351
Recruitment and Selection	353
Human Resource Planning	353
Job Analysis	355
External and Internal Recruitment	356
The Selection Process	358

Training and Development	361
Types of Training	361
Types of Development	362
Transfer of Training and Development	363
Performance Appraisal and Feedback	364
Types of Performance Appraisal	364
Who Appraises Performance?	366
Effective Performance Feedback	368
Pay and Benefits	369
Pay Level	369
Pay Structure	369
Benefits	370
Labor Relations	371
Unions	371
Collective Bargaining	372

Examples

Management Insight
Email at Work 316

Management Insight
The Four Control Steps in
Afghanistan 321

Management Insight
Quantitative Skills in the
Job Market 325

Ethics in Action
Netflix: Freedom and
Responsibility 332

Management Insight
How Philanthrofits Help Users
Help Charities 334

Managing Globally
Changing Online Retailing
with Virtusize 338

Management in Action

Summary and Review 340

Management in Action 341
Topics for Discussion and Action 341
Building Management Skills 341
Managing Ethically 341
Small Group Breakout Exercise 342
Exploring the World Wide Web 342
Be the Manager 342
Bloomberg Businessweek Case
in the News: How Chick-fil-
A Spent $50 Million to Change
Its Grilled Chicken 343

Examples

Management Insight
Recruitment and Selection
and Training and Development
at Zappos 349

Managing Globally
Managing Human Resources
at Semco 350

Managing Globally
Recent Trends in Outsourcing 354

Information Technology Byte
Fog Creek Software's Approach
to Recruiting 356

Management in Action

Summary and Review 372

Management in Action 374
Topics for Discussion and Action 374
Building Management Skills 374
Managing Ethically 374
Small Group Breakout Exercise 375
Exploring the World Wide Web 375
Be the Manager 375
The Wall Street Journal Case
in the News: Amazon Recruits
Face "Bar Raisers" 376

Chapter 13

Motivation and Performance 378

A MANAGER'S CHALLENGE

High Motivation Rules at the SAS Institute 379

Topics

Overview 381

The Nature of Motivation 381

Expectancy Theory 384
    Expectancy 385
    Instrumentality 386
    Valence 386
    Bringing It All Together 387

Need Theories 389
    Maslow's Hierarchy of Needs 389
    Alderfer's ERG Theory 390
    Herzberg's Motivator-Hygiene Theory 391
    McClelland's Needs for Achievement, Affiliation, and Power 392
    Other Needs 392

Equity Theory 392
    Equity 393
    Inequity 393
    Ways to Restore Equity 393
    Equity and Justice in Organizations 395

Goal-Setting Theory 395

Learning Theories 396
    Operant Conditioning Theory 397
    Social Learning Theory 399

Pay and Motivation 401
    Basing Merit Pay on Individual, Group, or Organizational Performance 402
    Salary Increase or Bonus? 403
    Examples of Merit Pay Plans 404

Chapter 14

Leadership 412

A MANAGER'S CHALLENGE

Jim Whitehurst Leads Red Hat 413

Topics

Overview 415

The Nature of Leadership 415
    Personal Leadership Style and Managerial Tasks 415
    Leadership Styles across Cultures 417
    Power: The Key to Leadership 418
    Empowerment: An Ingredient in Modern Management 421

Trait and Behavior Models of Leadership 421
    The Trait Model 421
    The Behavior Model 422

Contingency Models of Leadership 424
    Fiedler's Contingency Model 425
    House's Path–Goal Theory 427
    The Leader Substitutes Model 428
    Bringing It All Together 429

Transformational Leadership 430
    Being a Charismatic Leader 431
    Stimulating Subordinates Intellectually 431
    Engaging in Developmental Consideration 431
    The Distinction between Transformational and Transactional Leadership 432

Gender and Leadership 432

Emotional Intelligence and Leadership 433

Examples

Managing Globally
Seeking Intrinsic Motivation in
Far-Flung Places   382

Management Insight
Motivating and Retaining
Employees at The Container Store   386

Management Insight
How Enterprise Rent-A-Car
Motivates Employees   388

Management Insight
Training Spurs Learning at
Stella & Dot   397

Management in Action

Summary and Review   404

Management in Action   406
Topics for Discussion and Action   406
Building Management Skills   406
Managing Ethically   407
Small Group Breakout Exercise   407
Exploring the World Wide Web   407
Be the Manager   408
INC. Case in the News: You Can
Buy Employee Happiness. But
Should You?   408

Examples

Ethics in Action
Servant Leadership at
Zingerman's   416

Manager as a Person
Gregory Maffei and Expert Power   420

Management Insight
Consideration at Costco   423

Focus on Diversity
Admitting a Mistake Helps Small
Business Leader   434

Management in Action

Summary and Review   435

Management in Action   436
Topics for Discussion and Action   436
Building Management Skills   436
Managing Ethically   437
Small Group Breakout Exercise   437
Exploring the World Wide Web   438
Be the Manager   438
Bloomberg Businessweek Case
in the News: "Don't Mess This Up."
How Lego Finally Trusted Warner
Bros. to Bring Its Minifigs to the
Big Screen   438

Chapter 15

Effective Groups and Teams

442

A MANAGER'S CHALLENGE

Teams Innovate at W.L. Gore 443

Topics

Overview 445

Groups, Teams, and Organizational Effectiveness 445

Groups and Teams as Performance Enhancers 446

Groups, Teams, and Responsiveness to Customers 446

Teams and Innovation 447

Groups and Teams as Motivators 448

Types of Groups and Teams 449

The Top Management Team 449

Research and Development Teams 449

Command Groups 450

Task Forces 450

Self-Managed Work Teams 450

Virtual Teams 452

Friendship Groups 453

Interest Groups 453

Group Dynamics 454

Group Size, Tasks, and Roles 454

Group Leadership 457

Group Development over Time 458

Group Norms 459

Group Cohesiveness 462

Managing Groups and Teams for High Performance 465

Motivating Group Members to Achieve Organizational Goals 465

Reducing Social Loafing in Groups 466

Helping Groups to Manage Conflict Effectively 468

Chapter 16

Promoting Effective Communication

474

A MANAGER'S CHALLENGE

Encouraging Effective Communication and Collaboration at Salesforce.com 475

Topics

Overview 477

Communication and Management 477

The Importance of Good Communication 478

The Communication Process 479

The Role of Perception in Communication 480

The Dangers of Ineffective Communication 481

Information Richness and Communication Media 482

Face-to-Face Communication 482

Spoken Communication Electronically Transmitted 484

Personally Addressed Written Communication 485

Impersonal Written Communication 487

Communication Networks 488

Communication Networks in Groups and Teams 488

Organizational Communication Networks 490

External Networks 491

Information Technology and Communication 491

The Internet 491

Intranets 491

Groupware and Collaboration Software 492

Communication Skills for Managers 495

Communication Skills for Managers as Senders 495

Communication Skills for Managers as Receivers 497

Understanding Linguistic Styles 498

Examples

Information Technology Byte
Pizza Teams Innovate at Amazon   447

Management Insight
Self-Managed Teams at Louis
Vuitton and Nucor Corporation   451

Ethics in Action
Leadership in Teams at
ICU Medical   457

Management Insight
Teams Benefit from Deviance
and Conformity at IDEO   461

Management in Action

Summary and Review   468

Management in Action   469
Topics for Discussion and Action   469
Building Management Skills   469
Managing Ethically   470
Small Group Breakout Exercise   470
Exploring the World Wide Web   470
Be the Manager   471
The Wall Street Journal Case
in the News: The Team Can
See You Now   471

Examples

Managing Globally
Global Communication for Global
Innovation at GE Healthcare   478

Management Insight
Knowing When Face-to-Face
Communication Is Called For   483

Ethics in Action
Monitoring Email and Internet Use   487

Information Technology Byte
Collaborating with Wikis   494

Management in Action

Summary and Review   501

Management in Action   503
Topics for Discussion and Action   503
Building Management Skills   503
Managing Ethically   503
Small Group Breakout Exercise   504
Exploring the World Wide Web   504
Be the Manager   504
The Wall Street Journal Case
in the News: "Help! I'm on a
Conference Call"   505

Chapter 17   Managing Conflict, Politics, and Negotiation   508

A MANAGER'S CHALLENGE

Indra Nooyi Collaborates and Builds Alliances at PepsiCo 509

Topics

Overview   511

Organizational Conflict   511

  Types of Conflict   512

  Sources of Conflict   514

  Conflict Management Strategies   516

Negotiation   519

  Distributive Negotiation and Integrative Bargaining   519

Strategies to Encourage Integrative Bargaining   520

Organizational Politics   521

  The Importance of Organizational Politics   522

  Political Strategies for Gaining and Maintaining Power   522

  Political Strategies for Exercising Power   525

Chapter 18   Using Advanced Information Technology to Increase Performance   534

A MANAGER'S CHALLENGE

What's a Wearable? 535

Topics

Overview   536

Information and the Manager's Job   537

  Attributes of Useful Information   537

  What Is Information Technology?   538

  Information and Decisions   539

  Information and Control   539

  Information and Coordination   541

The IT Revolution   542

  The Effects of Advancing IT   542

  IT and the Product Life Cycle   542

  The Network of Computing Power   545

Types of Management Information Systems   548

The Organizational Hierarchy: The Traditional Information System   548

Transaction-Processing Systems   549

Operations Information Systems   549

Decision Support Systems   550

Artificial Intelligence and Expert Systems   550

Enterprise Resource Planning Systems   551

E-Commerce Systems   553

The Impact and Limitations of Information Technology   555

  Strategic Alliances, B2B Network Structures, and IT   555

  Flatter Structures and Horizontal Information Flows   556

Credits   562

Index   610

  Names   610

  Organizations   618

  Glossary/Subjects   622

Examples

Ethics in Action
The U.S. Labor Department
and Big Home Builders Clash   513

Managing Globally
Understanding Other Cultures   517

Ethics in Action
Building Alliances at The
Nature Conservancy   524

Ethics in Action
El Faro Estate Coffee Benefits
Multiple Stakeholders   528

Management in Action

Summary and Review   529

Management in Action   530

Topics for Discussion and Action   530

Building Management Skills   530

Managing Ethically   530

Small Group Breakout Exercise   531

Exploring the World Wide Web   531

Be the Manager   531

The New York Times Case in
the News: Advocates for Workers
Raise the Ire of Business   532

Examples

Management Insight
Using "Big Data"   540

Information Technology Byte
What Happened to Windows XP?   544

Management Insight
Accessing and Storing Data   545

Information Technology Byte
ERP Helps Custom Profile   552

Information Technology Byte
PeopleG2 Goes Virtual   557

Management in Action

Summary and Review   558

Management in Action   559

Topics for Discussion and Action   559

Building Management Skills   559

Managing Ethically   559

Small Group Breakout Exercise   560

Exploring the World Wide Web   560

Be the Manager   560

Bloomberg Businessweek Case
in the News: Twitter and Amazon
Go Hashtag Shopping and
Solve a Problem No One Ever Had   561

PREFACE

Since the eighth edition of *Contemporary Management* was published, our book has strengthened its position as a leader in the management market. This tells us that we continue to meet the expectations of our existing users and attract many new users to our book. It is clear that most management instructors share with us a concern for the need to continuously introduce new and emerging issues into the text and its examples to ensure that cutting-edge issues and new developments in the field of contemporary management are addressed.

In the new ninth edition of *Contemporary Management,* we continue with our mission to provide students the most current and up-to-date account of the changes taking place in the world of business management. The fast-changing domestic and global environment continues to pressure organizations and their managers to find new and improved ways to respond to changing events in order to maintain and increase their performance. More than ever, events around the globe, rapid changes in technology, and economic pressures and challenges show how fast the success and even survival of companies can change. For example, the increasing complexity of the exchanges between global companies has profoundly affected the management of both large and small organizations. Today there is increased pressure on managers to find new management practices that can increase their companies' efficiency and effectiveness and ability to survive and prosper in an increasingly competitive global environment.

In revising our book, we continue our focus on making our text relevant and interesting to today's students—something that we know from instructor and student feedback engages them and encourages them to make the effort necessary to assimilate the text material. We continue to mirror the changes taking place in management practices by incorporating recent developments in management theory and research into our text and by providing vivid, current examples of how managers of companies large and small have responded to the changes taking place. Indeed, we have incorporated many new and contemporary examples in the new edition illustrating how founders, managers, and employees in a variety of types of organizations respond to the opportunities and challenges they face. These examples drive home to students how essential it is for them to develop a rich understanding of management theory and research and the ability to apply what they have learned in organizational settings.

The number and complexity of the strategic, organizational, and human resource challenges facing managers and all employees have continued to increase throughout the 2010s. In most companies, managers at all levels are playing catch-up as they work toward meeting these challenges by implementing new and improved management techniques and practices. Today relatively small differences in performance between companies, such as in the speed at which they can bring new products or services to market or in how they motivate their employees to find ways to improve performance or reduce costs, can combine to give one company a significant competitive advantage over another. Managers and companies that use proven management techniques and practices in their decision making and actions increase their effectiveness over time. Companies and managers that are slower to implement new management techniques and practices find themselves at a growing competitive disadvantage that makes it even more difficult to catch up. Thus many industries have widening gaps between weaker competitors and the most successful companies, whose performance reaches new heights because their managers have made better decisions about how to use a company's resources in the most efficient and effective ways. In the rapidly changing and dynamic environment facing organizations today, effective managers recognize the vital role that creativity and innovation play in successfully anticipating and responding to these changes as well as seizing the potential opportunities that they bring while mitigating the threats.

The challenges facing managers continue to mount as changes in the global environment, such as increasing global outsourcing and rising commodity prices, impact organizations large and small. In the ninth edition, we discuss recent developments in global outsourcing and examine the many managerial issues that must be addressed when millions of functional jobs in information technology, customer service, and manufacturing are sent to countries overseas. Similarly, increasing globalization means managers must respond to major differences in the legal rules and regulations and ethical values and norms that prevail in countries around the globe. Many companies and their managers, for example, have been accused of ignoring "sweatshop" working conditions under which the products they sell are manufactured abroad.

Moreover, the revolution in information technology (IT) has transformed how managers make decisions across all levels of a company's hierarchy and across all its functions and global divisions. The ninth edition of our book continues to address these ongoing challenges as IT continues to evolve rapidly, especially in the area of mobile digital devices such as smartphones and tablet computers that can access ever more sophisticated software applications that increase their functionality. Other major challenges we continue to expand on in the new edition include the impact of the steadily increasing diversity of the workforce on companies, and how this increasing diversity makes it imperative for managers to understand how and why people differ so they can effectively manage and reap the many benefits of diversity. Similarly, across all functions and levels, managers and employees must continuously search out ways to "work smarter" and increase performance. Using new IT to improve all aspects of an organization's operations to boost efficiency and customer responsiveness is a vital part of this process. So too is the continuing need to innovate and improve the quality of goods and services, and the ways they are produced, to allow an organization to compete effectively. We have significantly revised the ninth edition of *Contemporary Management* to address these challenges to managers and their organizations.

Major Content Changes

Once again, encouraged by the increasing number of instructors and students who use each new edition of our book, and based on the reactions and suggestions of both users and reviewers, we have revised and updated our book in the following ways. First, just as we have included pertinent new research concepts in each chapter, so too have we been careful to eliminate outdated or marginal management concepts. As usual, our goal has been to streamline our presentation and keep the focus on the changes that have been taking place that have the most impact on managers and organizations. Our goal is to avoid presenting students with excessive content in too many and too long chapters just for the sake of including outmoded management theory. In today's world of instant sound bites, video uploading, text messaging, and tweets, providing the best content is much more important than providing excessive content—especially when some of our students are burdened by time pressures stemming from the need to work long hours at paying jobs and fulfilling personal commitments and obligations.

Second, we have added significant new management content and have reinforced its importance by using many new relevant small and large company examples that are described in the chapter opening cases titled "A Manager's Challenge"; in the many boxed examples featuring managers and employees in companies both large and small in each chapter; and in the new "Case in the News" closing cases.

Chapter 1, for example, contains new and updated material on the way changes in IT and the products and services that result from it are affecting competition among companies. The chapter includes a new opening case about the way Scott Parish, Alcon's CFO and COO, is helping Alcon successfully overcome challenges brought on by constantly changing technology and difficult economic times. It also contains an updated discussion of insourcing, as opposed to outsourcing, and why some companies are bringing jobs back to the United States from abroad to increase performance. Additionally, the coverage of ethics and social responsibility has been updated. New examples of global crisis management have been added that examine

the Haiyan Typhoon disaster as well as the consequences surrounding the Upper Big Branch South Mine explosion in West Virginia. Chapter 2 has updated coverage of changing manufacturing practices across industries and of the way traditional management theories, such as Theory X and Theory Y, have been modified to suit changing work conditions today.

Chapter 3 updates material about the manager as a person and the way personal characteristics of managers (and all members of an organization) influence organizational culture and effectiveness. There is also new in-text discussion of recent trends in job satisfaction in the United States. Also included is a discussion of how emotions can be triggers for change in organizations and a new "Manager as a Person" feature on Kevin Plank, founder and CEO of Under Armour.

Chapter 4, "Ethics and Social Responsibility," provides updated material about the unethical and illegal behaviors of managers from various industries. We have updated our coverage of the many issues involved in acting and managing ethically throughout the book. We also discuss new issues in ethics and ethical dilemmas and provide conceptual tools to help students understand better how to make ethical decisions. We highlight issues related to worker safety, environmental responsibility, and regulations to protect consumer safety. Finally, we have updated coverage of the ethics of nonprofits and their managers as well as how formerly ethical companies, such as General Motors, began to behave in unethical ways in order to boost their returns to shareholders and benefit their managers. The ethical exercise at the end of every chapter continues to be a popular feature of our book.

Chapter 5, "Managing Diverse Employees in a Multicultural Environment," focuses on the effective management of the many faces of diversity in organizations for the good of all stakeholders. We have updated and expanded the text material and examples for such issues as age, gender, race and ethnicity, socioeconomic background, disabilities, and sexual orientation. We also discuss ways to effectively manage diversity and include an updated discussion of women's earnings in comparison to men's earnings. Methods to prevent discrimination and sexual harassment in an era when many companies face discrimination lawsuits involving hundreds of millions of dollars are also considered. The chapter provides expanded coverage of the way managers can take advantage of the increasing diversity of the population and workforce to reap the performance benefits that stem from diversity while ensuring that all employees are treated fairly and are not discriminated against.

Chapter 6 contains an integrated account of forces in both the domestic and global environments. It has also been revised and updated to reflect the way increasing global competition and free trade have changed the global value creation process. The chapter uses updated examples from the fashion industry, electronics industry, and automotive industry to illustrate these issues. It also has an updated discussion of issues related to global outsourcing and of the movement to insource production back to the United States as well as to find ways for companies to become powerful suppliers to emerging leading global companies in China and other countries. Finally, it continues to update the treatment of the changing dynamics of global competition—particularly in relation to how newly dominant global companies have developed successful new strategies to customize products to the tastes of customers in countries abroad.

Chapter 7, "Decision Making, Learning, Creativity, and Entrepreneurship," discusses these vital processes in organizations and their implications for managers and all employees. The chapter opens with a new "A Manager's Challenge" discussion of Jim McCann of 1-800-Flowers.com, highlighting his entrepreneurial path and the many decisions and learning opportunities he experienced along the way. We include a discussion of the position of chief sustainability officer and examine how managers can make decisions to help ensure decisions contribute to sustainability. Also, we continue our discussion of social entrepreneurs who seek creative ways to address social problems to improve well-being by, for example, reducing poverty, increasing literacy, and protecting the natural environment. More generally, we discuss how managers in organizations large and small can improve decision making, learning, and creativity in their organizations. For example, we discuss ways of curbing overconfidence in decision making and how to use contests and rewards to encourage creativity and give examples of companies that use them.

As in the last edition, Chapter 8 focuses on corporate-, global-, and business-level strategies, and Chapter 9 discusses functional strategies for managing value chain activities. These two chapters make clear the links between the different levels of strategy while maintaining a strong focus on managing operations and processes. Chapter 8 continues the discussion of planning and levels of strategy, which focuses on how companies can use vertical integration and related diversification to increase long-term profitability. It also includes updated examples of business-level strategy that focuses on the importance of low-cost strategies in a world in which the prices of many products are falling or under pressure because of recession and increased global competition, or because companies like Toys"R"Us and Redbox are finding new strategies to reach customers more cost-effectively. In Chapter 9 we continue to explore how companies can develop new functional-level strategies to improve efficiency, quality, innovation, and responsiveness to customers. For example, in addition to coverage of TQM, including the Six Sigma approach, we include a discussion of the importance of customer relationship management and the need to retain customers during hard economic times. We focus on the ways various airlines have developed new functional strategies.

Chapters 10 and 11 offer updated coverage of organizational structure and control and discuss how companies have confronted the need to reorganize their hierarchies and ways of doing business as the environment changes and competition increases. In Chapter 10, for example, we discuss how companies such as Pixar Animation Studios and the Walt Disney Company have reorganized to improve their domestic performance. We also discuss how the Meritage Hospitality Group has changed its approach to hiring and training employees. Because of hard economic times, we continue to give updated examples that show how companies are designing global organizational structure and culture to improve performance. In Chapter 11 we continue this theme by looking at how companies are changing their control systems to increase efficiency and quality, for example. More generally, how to use control systems to increase quality is a theme throughout the chapter.

We have updated and expanded our treatment of the many ways in which managers can effectively manage and lead employees in their companies. For example, Chapter 12 includes an updated discussion of how treating employees well can lead to exceptional customer service. The chapter also discusses best practices to recruit and attract outstanding employees, the importance of training and development, pay differentials, and family-friendly benefit programs. In addition, there is treatment of the use of background checks by employers, the use of forced ranking systems in organizations, and issues concerning excessive CEO pay and pay comparisons between CEOs and average workers and statistics on U.S. union membership. Chapter 13 continues coverage of prosocially motivated behavior, including examples of people who are motivated to benefit others. It also discusses the many steps managers can take to create a highly motivated workforce and the importance of equity and justice in organizations.

Chapter 14 highlights the critical importance of effective leadership in organizations and factors that contribute to managers being effective leaders, including a discussion of servant leadership. There is a discussion of how managers with expert power need to recognize that they are not always right. The chapter also addresses how emotional intelligence may help leaders respond appropriately when they realize they have made a mistake, and it gives updated examples of leadership in a variety of organizations. Expanded and updated coverage of the effective management of teams, including virtual teams, is provided in Chapter 15, which opens with a new "A Manager's Challenge" on teams at W. L. Gore. The chapter also covers the problems that arise because of a lack of leadership in teams.

Chapter 16 includes coverage of effective communication and how, given the multitude of advances in IT, it is important to create opportunities for face-to-face communication. There is also information on the ethics of monitoring email and Internet use, including statistics on increased Internet use in the United States. Finally, there is also a discussion of social networking sites and why some managers attempt to limit employees' access to them while at work. Chapter 17 includes an updated discussion of the vital task of effectively managing conflict and politics in organizations and how to negotiate effectively on a global level. There are many new examples of how managers can create a collaborative work context and avoid competition between individuals and groups.

Chapter 18 has been updated to discuss the changing nature of companywide total computing solutions—including a new opening case that discusses how managers are using the latest technology like wearables to measure employee performance. There is also an updated discussion of the nature of bricks and mortar and mobile server computers and how "server farms" can be used to connect to mobile digital devices such as tablet computers and smartphones to enhance competitive advantage. Recent developments in mobile and tablet computing and their many uses in global communication and coordination are also a focus of discussion—as is the growing competition between global IT suppliers.

We feel confident that the major changes we have made to the ninth edition of *Contemporary Management* reflect the changes that are occurring in management and the workplace; we also believe they offer an account of management that will stimulate and challenge students to think about their future as they look for opportunities in the world of organizations.

Unique Emphasis on Contemporary, Applied Management

In revising our book, we have kept at the forefront the fact that our users and reviewers are supportive of our attempts to integrate contemporary management theories and issues into the analysis of management and organizations. As in previous editions, our goal has been to distill new and classic theorizing and research into a contemporary framework that is compatible with the traditional focus on management as planning, leading, organizing, and controlling but that transcends this traditional approach.

Users and reviewers report that students appreciate and enjoy our presentation of management—a presentation that makes its relevance obvious even to those who lack exposure to a real-life management context. Students like the book's content and the way we relate management theory to real-life examples to drive home the message that

management matters both because it determines how well organizations perform and because managers and organizations affect the lives of people inside and outside the organization, such as employees, customers, and shareholders.

Our contemporary approach has led us to discuss many concepts and issues that are not addressed in other management textbooks, and it is illustrated by the way we organize and discuss these management issues. We have gone to great lengths to bring the manager back into the subject matter of management. That is, we have written our chapters from the perspective of current or future managers to illustrate, in a hands-on way, the problems and opportunities they face and how they can effectively meet them. For example, in Chapter 3 we provide an integrated treatment of personality, attitudes, emotions, and culture; in Chapter 4, a focus on ethics from a student's and a manager's perspective; and in Chapter 5, an in-depth treatment of effectively managing diversity and eradicating sexual harassment. In Chapters 8 and 9, our integrated treatment of strategy highlights the multitude of decisions managers must make as they perform their most important role—increasing organizational efficiency, effectiveness, and performance.

Our applied approach can also be clearly seen in the last three chapters of the book, which cover the topics of promoting effective communication; managing organizational conflict, politics, and negotiation; and using information technology in ways that increase organizational performance. These chapters provide a student-friendly, behavioral approach to understanding the management issues entailed in persuasive communication, negotiation, and implementation of advanced information systems to build competitive advantage.

Flexible Organization

Another factor of interest to instructors is how we have designed the grouping of chapters to allow instructors to teach the chapter material in the order that best suits their needs. For example, the more micro-oriented instructor can follow Chapters 1 through 5 with Chapters 12 through 16 and then use the more macro chapters. The more macro-oriented professor can follow Chapters 1 and 2 with Chapters 6 through 11, jump to 16 through 18, and then use the micro chapters, 3 through 5 and 12 through 15.

Our sequencing of parts and chapters gives instructors considerable freedom to design the course that best suits their needs. Instructors are not tied to the planning, organizing, leading, and controlling framework, even though our presentation remains consistent with this approach.

ACKNOWLEDGMENTS

Finding a way to integrate and present the rapidly growing literature about contemporary management and make it interesting and meaningful for students is not an easy task. In writing and revising the various drafts of *Contemporary Management,* we have been fortunate to have the assistance of several people who have contributed greatly to the book's final form. First, we are grateful to Michael Ablassmeir, our director, for his ongoing support and commitment to our project and for always finding ways to provide the resources that we needed to continually improve and refine our book. Second, we are grateful to Andrea Scheive, our development editor, for so ably coordinating the book's progress; and to her and Elizabeth Trepkowski, our senior marketing manager, for giving us concise and timely feedback and information from professors and reviewers that have allowed us to shape the book to the needs of its intended market. We also thank Matt Backhaus for executing an awe-inspiring design; Danielle Clement for coordinating the production process; and Iliya Atanasov (Rice University) for his assistance with research. We are also grateful to the many colleagues and reviewers who gave us useful and detailed feedback and perceptive comments and valuable suggestions for improving the manuscript.

Producing any competitive work is a challenge. Producing a truly market-driven textbook requires tremendous effort beyond simply obtaining reviews of a draft manuscript. Our goal was simple with the development of *Contemporary Management:* to be the most customer-driven principles of management text and supplement package ever published! With the goal of exceeding the expectations of both faculty and students, we executed one of the most aggressive product development plans ever undertaken in textbook publishing. Hundreds of faculty have taken part in developmental activities ranging from regional focus groups to manuscript and supplement reviews and surveys. Consequently, we're confident in assuring you and your students, our customers, that every aspect of our text and support package reflects your advice and needs. As you review it, we're confident that your reaction will be, "They listened!"

We extend our special thanks to the faculty who gave us detailed chapter-by-chapter feedback during the development of the ninth edition:

Kelly Barbour-Conerty, Parkland College

Jason W. Coleman, Wesley College

Joy Colarusso, Daytona State College

Renee Y. Cooper, Fashion Institute of Technology

Rusty Juban, Southeastern Louisiana University

Deanna R. Knight, Daytona State College

Cynthia J. Lanphear, University of the Ozarks

Joyce Lopez, Missouri State University

Troy V. Mumford, Colorado State University

Eren Ozgen, Troy University, Dothan Campus

Frederick J. Slack, Indiana University of Pennsylvania

Warren Stone, University of Arkansas at Little Rock

Laurie Taylor-Hamm, California State University, Fresno

William K. Wesley, Golden Gate University

And our thanks also go to the faculty who contributed greatly to the fourth, fifth, sixth, seventh, and eighth editions of *Contemporary Management:*

Jerry Alley, Aspen University

M. Ruhul Amin, Bloomsburg University of Pennsylvania

Gerald Baumgardner, Pennsylvania College of Technology

Charles W. Beem, Bucks County Community College

James D. Bell, Texas State University

Danielle R. Blesi, Hudson Valley Community College

Susan Blumen, Montgomery College Department of Business and Economics

Jennifer P. Bott, Ball State University

Edwin L. Bowman, Principal, Manhattanville College, Purchase, NY

Charley Braun, Marshall University

Reginald Bruce, College of Business, University of Louisville

Murray Brunton, Central Ohio Technical College

Judith G. Bulin, Monroe Community College, Rochester, New York

Barry Bunn, Valencia Community College

Gerald Calvasina, Southern Utah University

Bruce H. Charnov, Hofstra University

Jay Christensen-Szalanski, University of Iowa

Cheryl Cunningham, Embry-Riddle Aeronautical University–Daytona Beach

Brad Cox, Midlands Technical College

Marian Cox Crawford, University of Arkansas–Little Rock

Teresa A. Daniel, Marshall University

Thomas W. Deckelman, Owens Community College

Richard S. DeFrank, University of Houston

Fred J. Dorn, University of Mississippi

D. Harold Doty, University of Southern Mississippi

Max E. Douglas, Indiana State University

Sandra Edwards, Northeastern State University

Stewart W. Edwards, Northern VA Community College–Annandale

William Eichenauer, Northwest State Community College

Scott Elston, Iowa State University

Richard Estrella, California Polytechnic University

Valerie Evans, Kansas State University

Bagher Fardanesh, Piaget Consulting

Andrea Foster, John Tyler Community College

Travis Lee Hayes, Chattanooga State Technical Community College

Samuel Hazen, Tarleton State University

Kim Hester, Arkansas State University

Anne Kelly Hoel, University of Wisconsin–Stout

Robert C. Hoell, Georgia Southern University

Irene Joanette-Gallio, Western Nevada College

Jim Glasgow, Instructor, Villanova School of Business

Monica Godsey, PhD, University of Nebraska

Selina Griswold, The University of Toledo

Kathy Hastings, Greenville Technical College

Perry Hidalgo, Gwinnett Technical College

Carol Larson Jones, Cal Poly Pomona, California

Coy A. Jones, The University of Memphis

Gwendolyn Jones, University of Akron

Kathleen Jones, University of North Dakota

Jordan J. Kaplan, Long Island University School of Business

Joanne E. Kapp, Siena College

Renee N. King, Eastern Illinois University

Mike Knudstrup, Florida Southern College

Susan Kowalewski, D'Youville College

Jim Long, Southwestern Oklahoma State University

Margaret Lucero, Texas A&M–Corpus Christi

Nicholas Mathys, DePaul University

Daniel W. McAllister, University of Nevada–Las Vegas

Christy McLendon Corey, University of New Orleans

Chrisann Merriman, University of Mary Hardin–Baylor

Douglas L. Micklich, Illinois State University

Sandra Jeanquart Miles, Murray State University

Carol T. Miller, Community College of Denver

Don C. Mosley Jr., University of South Alabama

Clive Muir, Stetson University

Bahaudin G. Mujtaba, Nova Southeastern University

Jane Murtaugh, College of DuPage

Nanci D. Newstrom, Eastern Illinois University

Catherine Nowicki, International Business College

John Overby, The University of Tennessee at Martin

Karen Overton, Houston Community College

Fernando A. Pargas, James Madison University

Marc Pendel, Miller College of Business, Ball State University

Susan A. Peterson, Scottsdale Community College

Gary Renz, Webster University

L. Jeff Seaton, University of Tennessee–Martin

Gregory J. Schultz, Carroll University

Marc Siegall, California State University–Chico

Michaeline Skiba, Monmouth University–Leon Hess Business School

Fred Slack, Indiana University of Pennsylvania

Randi L. Sims, Nova Southeastern University

M. James Smas, Kent State University

Gerald Smith, University of Northern Iowa

Marjorie Smith, Mountain State University

Susan D. Steiner, The University of Tampa

Cynthia L. Sutton, Metropolitan State College of Denver

Sabine Turnley, Kansas State University

Isaiah O. Ugboro, North Carolina A&T State University

Velvet Weems, Landingham, Kent State University

John Weiss, Daytona State College

Elizabeth Wilson, Georgia Southwestern State University

Please note that these lists do not include the more than 160 faculty members who reviewed or contributed to earlier editions of the text.

Finally, we are grateful to two incredibly wonderful children, Nicholas and Julia, for being all that they are and for the joy they bring to all who know them.

Gareth R. Jones

Jennifer M. George
Jesse H. Jones Graduate School of Business
Rice University

Rich and Relevant Examples

An important feature of our book is the way we use real-world examples and stories about managers and companies to drive home the applied lessons to students. Our reviewers praised the sheer range and depth of the rich, interesting examples we use to illustrate the chapter material and make it come alive. Moreover, unlike boxed material in other books, our boxes are seamlessly integrated into the text; they are an integral part of the learning experience and are not tacked on or isolated from the text itself. This is central to our pedagogical approach.

A Manager's Challenge opens each chapter, posing a chapter-related challenge and then discussing how managers in one or more organizations responded to that challenge. These vignettes help demonstrate the uncertainty and excitement surrounding the management process.

Our box features are not traditional boxes; that is, they are not disembodied from the chapter narrative. These thematic applications are fully integrated into the reading. Students will no longer be forced to decide whether or not to read boxed material. These features are interesting and engaging for students while bringing the chapter contents to life.

Additional in-depth examples appear in boxes throughout each chapter. **Management Insight** boxes illustrate the topics of the chapter, while the **Ethics in Action, Managing Globally, Focus on Diversity, and Information Technology Byte** boxes examine the chapter topics from each of these perspectives.

Further emphasizing the unique content covered in Chapter 3, "Values, Attitudes, Emotions, and Culture: The Manager as a Person," the **Manager as a Person** boxes focus on how real managers brought about change within their organizations. These examples allow us to reflect on how individual managers dealt with real-life, on-the-job challenges related to various chapter concepts.

Small Business Examples To ensure that students see the clear connections between the concepts taught in their Principles of Management course and the application in their future jobs in a medium-sized or small business, Jones and George have included a number of examples of the opportunities and challenges facing founders, managers, and employees in small businesses.

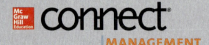 **McGraw-Hill Connect Management**

Less managing . . . More teaching . . . Greater learning . . .

McGraw-Hill Connect Management is an online assignment and assessment solution that connects students with the tools and resources they need to achieve success. With Connect Management, students can engage with their coursework anytime, anywhere, enabling faster learning, more efficient studying, and higher retention of knowledge. It also offers faculty powerful tools that make managing assignments easier, so instructors can spend more time teaching.

Features

SmartBook™. Fueled by LearnSmart—SmartBook is the first and only adaptive reading experience available today. Distinguishing what students know from what they don't, and honing in on concepts they are most likely to forget, SmartBook personalizes content for each student in a continuously adapting reading experience. Reading is no longer a passive and linear experience, but an engaging and dynamic one where students are more likely to master and retain important concepts, coming to class better prepared. Valuable reports show instructors how students are progressing through textbook content, which is useful for shaping in-class time or assessment. As a result of the adaptive reading experience found in SmartBook, students are more likely to retain knowledge, stay in class, and get better grades.

Interactive Applications. Interactive Applications offer a variety of automatically graded exercises that require students to apply key concepts. Whether the assignment includes a drag and drop, video case, sequence, or case analysis, these applications provide instant feedback and progress tracking for students and detailed results for the instructor.

Manager's Hot Seat. This interactive, video-based application puts students in the manager's hot seat and builds critical thinking and decision-making skills and allows students to apply concepts to real managerial challenges. Students watch as 15 real managers apply their years of experience when confronting unscripted issues such as bullying in the workplace, cyber loafing, globalization, intergenerational work conflicts, workplace violence, and leadership versus management.

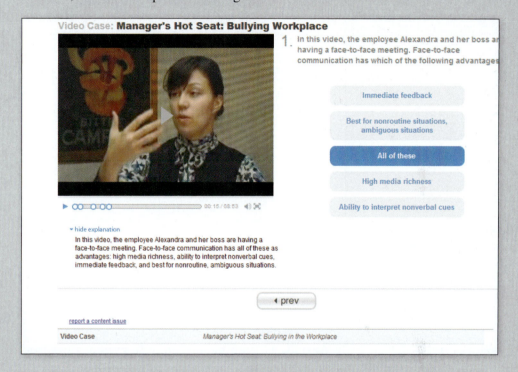

Video Case 1: Office Romance: Groping for Answers
Video Case 2: Ethics: Let's Make a Fourth Quarter Deal
Video Case 3: Negotiation: Thawing the Salary Freeze
Video Case 4: Privacy: Burned by the Firewall?
Video Case 5: Whistle Blowing: Code Red or Red Ink?
Video Case 6: Change: More Pain Than Gain
Video Case 7: Partnership: The Unbalancing Act
Video Case 8: Cultural Differences: Let's Break a Deal
Video Case 9: Project Management: Steering the Committee
Video Case 10: Diversity: Mediating Morality
Video Case 11: Personal Disclosure: Confession Coincidence
Video Case 12: Virtual Workplace: Out of the Office Reply
Video Case 13: Listening Skills: Yeah, Whatever
Video Case 14: Diversity in Hiring: Candidate Conundrum
Video Case 15: Working in Teams: Cross-Functional Dysfunction

Insight. Connect Insight is a powerful data analytics tool that allows instructors to leverage aggregated information about their courses and students to provide a more personalized teaching and learning experience.

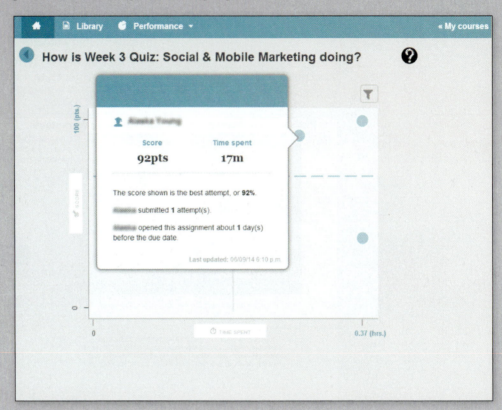

Smart Grading. When it comes to studying, time is precious. Connect Management helps students learn more efficiently by providing feedback and practice material when they need it, where they need it. When it comes to teaching, your time also is precious. The grading function enables you to

• Have assignments scored automatically, giving students immediate feedback on their work and side-by-side comparisons with correct answers.

• Access and review each response; manually change grades or leave comments for students to review.

• Reinforce classroom concepts with practice tests and instant quizzes.

Simple Assignment Management. With Connect Management, creating assignments is easier than ever, so you can spend more time teaching and less time managing. The assignment management function enables you to

• Create and deliver assignments easily with selectable end-of-chapter questions and test bank items.

• Streamline lesson planning, student progress reporting, and assignment grading to make classroom management more efficient than ever.

• Go paperless with the eBook and online submission and grading of student assignments.

Instructor Library. The Connect Management Instructor Library is your repository for additional resources to improve student engagement in and out of class. You can select and use any asset that enhances your lecture. The Connect Management Instructor Library includes

- Instructor's Manual
- PowerPoint files
- Test Bank
- Management Asset Gallery
- eBook
- Connect IM

McGraw-Hill Connect Plus Management. McGraw-Hill reinvents the textbook learning experience for the modern student with Connect Plus Management. Connect Plus features the following

- An integrated eBook.
- All Connect assignments and tools, which provide a dynamic link between your assignment and chapter content.
- A powerful search function to pinpoint and connect key concepts in a snap.

For more information about Connect, go to www.mcgrawhillconnect.com, or contact your local McGraw-Hill sales representative.

 **Tegrity Campus:** Lectures 24/7. Tegrity Campus is a service that makes class time available 24/7 by automatically capturing every lecture in a searchable format for students to review when they study and complete assignments. With a simple one-click start-and-stop process, you capture all computer screens and corresponding audio. Students can replay any part of any class with easy-to use browser-based viewing on a PC or Mac.

Educators know that the more students can see, hear, and experience class resources, the better they learn. In fact, studies prove it. With Tegrity Campus, students quickly recall key moments by using Tegrity Campus's unique search feature. This search helps students efficiently find what they need, when they need it, across an entire semester of class recordings. Help turn all your students' study time into learning moments immediately supported by your lecture. Lecture Capture enables you to

- Record and distribute your lecture with a click of button.
- Record and index PowerPoint presentations and anything shown on your computer so it is easily searchable, frame by frame.
- Offer access to lectures anytime and anywhere by computer, iPod, or mobile device.
- Increase intent listening and class participation by easing students' concerns about note taking.

Lecture Capture will make it more likely you will see students' faces, not the tops of their heads. To learn more about Tegrity, watch a two-minute Flash demo at http://tegritycampus.mhhe.com.

 **Create.** Craft your teaching resources to match the way you teach! With McGraw-Hill Create, www.mcgrawhillcreate.com, you can easily rearrange chapters, combine material from other content sources, and quickly upload content you have written, like your course syllabus or teaching notes. Find the content you need in Create by searching through thousands of leading McGraw-Hill textbooks. Arrange your book to fit your teaching style. Create even allows you to personalize your book's appearance by selecting the cover and adding your name, school, and course information. Order a Create book and you'll receive a complimentary print review copy in three to five business days or a complimentary electronic review copy (eComp) via e-mail in about one hour. Go to www.mcgrawhillcreate.com today and register. Experience how McGraw-Hill Create empowers you to teach your students your way.

The **Best** of **Both Worlds**

McGraw-Hill Higher Education and Blackboard have teamed up. What does this mean for you?

1. **Your life simplified.** Now you and your students can access McGraw-Hill's Connect™ and Create™ right from within your Blackboard course—all with one single sign-on. Say goodbye to the days of logging in to multiple applications.

2. **Deep integration of content and tools.** Not only do you get single sign-on with Connect™ and Create™, you also get deep integration of McGraw-Hill content and content engines right in Blackboard. Whether you're choosing a book for your course or building Connect™ assignments, all the tools you need are right where you want them—inside of Blackboard.

3. **Seamless gradebooks.** Are you tired of keeping multiple gradebooks and manually synchronizing grades into Blackboard? We thought so. When a student completes an integrated Connect™ assignment, the grade for that assignment automatically (and instantly) feeds your Blackboard grade center.

4. **A solution for everyone.** Whether your institution is already using Blackboard or you just want to try Blackboard on your own, we have a solution for you. McGraw-Hill and Blackboard can now offer you easy access to industry-leading technology and content, whether your campus hosts it, or we do. Be sure to ask your local McGraw-Hill representative for details.

Instructor Resources

Multiple high-quality, fully integrated resources are available to make your teaching life easier:

- **The Instructors Manual (IM)** includes thorough coverage of each chapter. New in this edition, we offer two versions of the IM, for newer and experienced faculty. Included in both versions are the appropriate level of theory, recent application or company examples, teaching tips, PowerPoint references, critical discussion topics, and answers to end-of-chapter exercises.

- **The PowerPoint (PPT)** slides provide comprehensive lecture notes, video links, and company examples not found in the textbook. There will be instructor media enhanced slides as well as notes with outside application examples.

- **The Test Bank** includes 100-150 questions per chapter, in a range of formats and with a greater-than-usual number of comprehension, critical thinking, and application (or scenario-based) questions. It's tagged by learning objective, Bloom's Taxonomy levels, and AACSB compliance requirements.

- **EZ Test,** McGraw-Hill's flexible and easy-to-use electronic testing program, allows instructors to create tests from book-specific items. It accommodates a wide range of question types, and instructors may add their own questions. Multiple versions of the test can be created, and any test can be exported for use with course management systems such as WebCT or BlackBoard.
- **EZ Test Online,** available at www.eztestonline.com, allows you to access the test bank virtually anywhere at any time, without installation, and to administer EZ Test-created exams and quizzes online, providing instant feedback for students.
- **The Online Learning Center (OLC),** located at www.mhhe.com/jones-george9e, offers downloadable resources for instructors. In the instructors' portion of the OLC, which is password-protected, instructors can access all of the teaching resources described above.

McGraw-Hill Customer Care Contact Information

At McGraw-Hill, we understand that getting the most from new technology can be challenging.

That's why our services don't stop after you purchase our products. You can email our product specialists 24 hours a day, seven days a week, to get product training online. Or you can search our knowledge bank of frequently asked questions on our support website. For customer support, call 800-331-5094 or visit www.mhhe.com/support. One of our technical support analysts will be able to assist you in a timely fashion.

Assurance of Learning Ready

Many educational institutions today are focused on the notion of assurance of learning, an important element of many accreditation standards. *Contemporary Management* is designed specifically to support your assurance of learning initiatives with a simple yet powerful solution.

Each chapter in the book begins with a list of numbered learning objectives, which appear throughout the chapter as well as in the end-of-chapter assignments. Every Test Bank question for *Contemporary Management* maps to a specific chapter learning objective in the textbook. Each Test Bank question also identifies topic area, level of difficulty, Bloom's Taxonomy level, and AACSB skill area. You can use our Test Bank software, EZ Test and EZ Test Online, or Connect Management to easily search for learning objectives that directly relate to the learning objectives for your course. You can then use the reporting features of EZ Test to aggregate student results in a similar fashion, making the collection and presentation of Assurance of Learning data simple and easy.

AACSB Statement

McGraw-Hill Education is a proud corporate member of AACSB International. Understanding the importance and value of AACSB accreditation, *Contemporary Management* recognizes the curricula guidelines detailed in the AACSB standards for business accreditation by connecting selected questions in the Test Bank to the general knowledge and skill guidelines in the AACSB standards.

The statements contained in *Contemporary Management* are provided only as a guide for the users of this textbook. The AACSB leaves content coverage and assessment within the purview of individual schools, the mission of the school, and the faculty. While *Contemporary Management* and the teaching package make no claim of any specific AACSB qualification or evaluation, we have within *Contemporary Management* labeled selected questions according to six of the general knowledge and skills areas.

AUTHORS

Gareth Jones currently offers pro bono advice on solving management problems to nonprofit organizations in Houston, Texas. He received his BA in Economics/Psychology and his PhD in Management from the University of Lancaster, U.K. He was formerly Professor of Management in the Graduate School of Business at Texas A&M University and earlier held teaching and research appointments at Michigan State University, the University of Illinois at Urbana-Champaign, and the University of Warwick, UK.

He continues to pursue his research interests in strategic management and organizational theory and his well-known research that applies transaction cost analysis to explain many forms of strategic and organizational behavior. He also studies the complex and changing relationships between competitive advantage and information technology in the 2010s.

He has published many articles in leading journals of the field, and his research has appeared in the *Academy of Management Review,* the *Journal of International Business Studies,* and *Human Relations.* An article about the role of information technology in many aspects of organizational functioning was published in the *Journal of Management.* One of his articles won the *Academy of Management Journal's* Best Paper Award, and he is one of the most cited authors in the *Academy of Management Review.* He is, or has served, on the editorial boards of the *Academy of Management Review,* the *Journal of Management,* and *Management Inquiry.*

Gareth Jones has used his academic knowledge to craft leading textbooks in management and three other major areas in the management discipline: organizational behavior, organizational theory, and strategic management. His books are widely recognized for their innovative, contemporary content and for the clarity with which they communicate complex, real-world issues to students.

Jennifer George is the Mary Gibbs Jones Professor of Management and Professor of Psychology in the Jesse H. Jones Graduate School of Business at Rice University. She received her BA in Psychology/Sociology from Wesleyan University, her MBA in Finance from New York University, and her PhD in Management and Organizational Behavior from New York University. Prior to joining the faculty at Rice University, she was a professor in the Department of Management at Texas A&M University.

Professor George specializes in organizational behavior and is well known for her research on mood and emotion in the workplace, their determinants, and their effects on various individual and group-level work outcomes. She is the author of many articles in leading peer-reviewed journals such as the *Academy of Management Journal,* the *Academy of Management Review,* the *Journal of Applied Psychology, Organizational Behavior and Human Decision Processes, Journal of Personality and Social Psychology, Organization Science,* and *Psychological Bulletin.* One of her papers won the Academy of Management's Organizational Behavior Division Outstanding Competitive Paper Award, and another paper won the *Human Relations* Best Paper Award. She is, or has been, on the editorial review boards of the *Journal of Applied Psychology, Academy of Management Journal, Academy of Management Review, Administrative Science Quarterly, Journal of Management, Organizational Behavior and Human Decision Processes, Organization Science, International Journal of Selection and Assessment,* and *Journal of Managerial Issues;* was a consulting editor for the *Journal of Organizational Behavior;* was a member of the SIOP *Organizational Frontiers Series* editorial board; and was an associate editor of the *Journal of Applied Psychology.* She is a fellow in the Academy of Management, the American Psychological Association, the American Psychological Society, and the Society for Industrial and Organizational Psychology and a member of the Society for Organizational Behavior. She also has coauthored a textbook titled *Understanding and Managing Organizational Behavior.*

Contemporary
Management

CHAPTER 1

Managers and Managing

Learning Objectives

After studying this chapter, you should be able to:

LO1-1 Describe what management is, why management is important, what managers do, and how managers use organizational resources efficiently and effectively to achieve organizational goals.

LO1-2 Distinguish among planning, organizing, leading, and controlling (the four principal managerial tasks), and explain how managers' ability to handle each one affects organizational performance.

LO1-3 Differentiate among three levels of management, and understand the tasks and responsibilities of managers at different levels in the organizational hierarchy.

LO1-4 Distinguish between three kinds of managerial skill, and explain why managers are divided into different departments to perform their tasks more efficiently and effectively.

LO1-5 Discuss some major changes in management practices today that have occurred as a result of globalization and the use of advanced information technology (IT).

LO1-6 Discuss the principal challenges managers face in today's increasingly competitive global environment.

A MANAGER'S CHALLENGE

Hitting the Mark at Alcon Entertainment

How does management change with technology? Scott Parish is the chief financial officer and chief operating officer of Alcon Entertainment, a Los Angeles—based entertainment production company. Alcon was started in 1997 by film producers (and former business students) Broderick Johnson and Andrew Kosove, who remain Alcon's chief executive officers (CEOs). Since its humble beginnings in a rented apartment, the company has grown into a respected and profitable enterprise, making hit movies such as *The Blind Side, P.S., I Love You,* and *What to Expect When You're Expecting.*

Parish left a successful career in logistics and transportation to pursue his dream of working in the motion picture industry. Relocating from Mississippi to California, he took an hourly administrative job at a film production company to learn about the craft. By taking the initiative to develop his understanding of the entertainment business from the ground up, Parish was able to rise in management over the years. Now as a member of Alcon's top team, he is credited with helping grow Alcon from a boutique film company into a respected creator of not just films but television shows and music as well.

However, maintaining Alcon's growth is a significant challenge in a turbulent and changing entertainment business. Managers like Scott Parish must economically produce valuable content that earns profits. Film creation is a complex process. It can take years to shepherd a film from inception to distribution before audiences. As a result, significant planning is invested into production long before the cameras roll. Parish and Alcon's leadership team are constantly on the lookout for innovative ideas that give them an edge at the box office, and must identify and produce ideas that have a strong potential to connect with an intended audience.

Andrew Kosove, co-CEO of Alcon Entertainment, and Scott Parish, COO and CFO. Parish left a career in logistics to learn the motion picture industry from the ground up. Now he is part of the top management team that runs a successful film, TV, and music company.

Once viable ideas are obtained and screened, Parish must obtain funding for projects that can cost $40 to $80 million each.[1] Financing films often means coordinating with outside investors, so Parish and his team must be able to explain complex film production processes to those unacquainted with the film business. These outside investors represent important stakeholders in the film production process.

After representing Alcon to investors and obtaining needed financing, Parish must build the right team to produce and market new hit films. This means negotiating with and retaining the services of directors and a cast who can help turn concepts into reality. Missteps at this stage of a film's development can be highly detrimental to its eventual success, and Parish and his team must also balance the needs of Hollywood superstars against the creative demands of directors to create products audiences will pay to see and enjoy. Hollywood talent is notoriously difficult to manage, so Parish must negotiate and align the interests of the company with the talent it retains to help make films.

In addition to the challenges of managing film production in a competitive environment, Parish is helping lead Alcon in an entertainment industry being transformed by technological and economic change. Consumers increasingly prefer to watch content digitally, so Alcon has evolved to broaden the ways it distributes content. Previously, film production companies like Alcon worked with movie theaters and brick-and-mortar retailers to sell content. Although these distribution channels are still being used, Alcon's content can now be found digitally on streaming subscription services such as Netflix, for download on Amazon Prime, and on other services.[2] Alcon also retains the rights to its films, meaning it earns residual income from its catalog of film projects. With changing consumer tastes and a recession that has limited consumers' disposable income, managers like Parish are challenged to find new ways of ensuring profitable content creation and distribution.

In a larger sense, the ease of transferring digital content has made digital piracy more prevalent, posing a significant threat to the entertainment industry. Piracy occurs when third parties distribute copyrighted materials that they do not own to others without permission from the copyright holder, typically for commercial gain. However, entertainment production companies receive revenues only when their content is purchased by retailers or consumers, meaning piracy has the potential to undermine the production of new movies, music, and television. Indeed, Alcon now adjusts its revenue projections to reflect the threats of piracy. However, the company is not responding passively to this new managerial challenge, but is taking action to mitigate the distribution and use of pirated content.

For example, in conjunction with other major studios and entertainment production companies, Alcon has responded to this new economic and technological reality by mobilizing support for CreativeFuture, an industry coalition designed to mitigate digital piracy on the web by informing and educating policymakers and consumers about the long-term effects of digital piracy on the sustainability of the entertainment industry.[3]

Running an entertainment company is difficult work. Managers like Scott Parish must help their companies stay creative and create profitable content in an industry rapidly evolving amid changing consumer tastes and technological change. This requires managers to represent the interests of the organization to the public and an increasingly complex array of external stakeholders.

Overview

Managing today's organizations is a complex affair, and seasoned leaders like Scott Parish face multiple challenges from within and outside of their organizations. To make decisions and lead others successfully, managers must possess a complex set of skills, knowledge, and abilities that help them interpret cues from the environment and respond accordingly.

In this chapter we consider what managers do and the skills, knowledge, and abilities they must possess to lead their organizations effectively. We also identify the different kinds of managers that organizations rely on to help guide them. Finally, we consider some of the challenges that managers must overcome to help their organizations prosper.

What Is Management?

When you think of a manager, what kind of person comes to mind? Do you think of an executive like Scott Parish, who helps direct his company? Or do you see a manager at a fast-food restaurant, who engages directly with employees and customers? Perhaps you think of a foreman at a manufacturing company? Regardless of how we view managers, they all share important characteristics. First, they all work in organizations. **Organizations** are collections of people who work together and coordinate their actions to achieve a wide variety of goals or desired future outcomes.[4] Second, as managers, they are the people responsible for supervising and making the most of an organization's human and other resources to achieve its goals.

Management, then, is the planning, organizing, leading, and controlling of human and other resources to achieve organizational goals efficiently and effectively. An organization's *resources* include assets such as people and their skills, know-how, and experience; machinery; raw materials; computers and information technology; and patents, financial capital, and loyal customers and employees.

organizations Collections of people who work together and coordinate their actions to achieve a wide variety of goals or desired future outcomes.

management The planning, organizing, leading, and controlling of human and other resources to achieve organizational goals efficiently and effectively.

LO1-1

Describe what management is, why management is important, what managers do, and how managers use organizational resources efficiently and effectively to achieve organizational goals.

organizational performance A measure of how efficiently and effectively a manager uses resources to satisfy customers and achieve organizational goals.

efficiency A measure of how well or how productively resources are used to achieve a goal.

Achieving High Performance: A Manager's Goal

One of the key goals that organizations try to achieve is to provide goods and services that customers value and desire. Scott Parish's principal goal is to manage Alcon so that it creates a continuous stream of new and improved entertainment content—enjoyable films, television shows, and music—that customers are willing to buy. Like other entertainment companies, Alcon also seeks projects that have potential to grow into film or television franchises, encouraging repeat business. Likewise, the principal goal of fast-food managers is to produce tasty and convenient food that customers enjoy and come back to buy. Finally, manufacturing managers must balance the quality needs of their consumers against the pressure to be cost-effective.

Organizational performance is a measure of how efficiently and effectively managers use available resources to satisfy customers and achieve organizational goals. Organizational performance increases in direct proportion to increases in efficiency and effectiveness, as Figure 1.1 shows. What are efficiency and effectiveness?

Efficiency is a measure of how productively resources are used to achieve a goal.[5] Organizations are efficient when managers minimize the amount of input resources (such as labor, raw materials, and component parts) or the amount of time needed to produce a given output of goods or services. For example, McDonald's develops ever more efficient fat fryers that not only reduce the amount of oil used in cooking, but also speed up the cooking of french fries. UPS develops new work routines to reduce delivery time, such as instructing drivers to leave their truck doors open when going short distances.

To encourage efficiency, Scott Parish has changed the way Alcon compensates many of its actors. Previously, film production companies paid actors using guaranteed compensation and without consideration of a movie's success. They would recoup the cost of making a movie only if it had adequate performance at the box office. Unfortunately, that meant film producers like Alcon held all of the risk.

Figure 1.1

Efficiency, Effectiveness, and Performance in an Organization

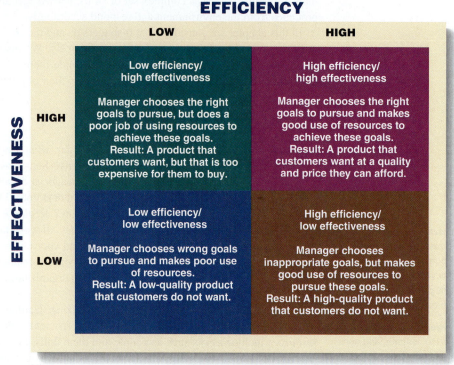

High-performing organizations are efficient *and* effective.

As an alternative, Parish has linked actor compensation to a film's success.[6] This new compensation method means fewer dollars are risked if a film flops. However, for actors, the new compensation model means they can earn far more than a flat sum of guaranteed compensation. Thus, when a film succeeds, both Alcon and its actors realize the gains. This new compensation model encourages both parties to work efficiently. Alcon also strives to build good relationships and trust with its actors, which in turn brings goodwill toward the organization.

effectiveness A measure of the appropriateness of the goals an organization is pursuing and the degree to which the organization achieves those goals.

Effectiveness is a measure of the *appropriateness* of the goals that managers have selected for the organization to pursue and the degree to which the organization achieves those goals. Organizations are effective when managers choose appropriate goals and then achieve them. Some years ago, for example, managers at McDonald's decided on the goal of providing breakfast service to attract more customers. The choice of this goal has proved smart: Sales of breakfast food now account for more than 30 percent of McDonald's revenues and are still increasing. Parish's goal is to create a continuous flow of innovative entertainment products that resonate with audiences. High-performing organizations such as Apple, McDonald's, Walmart, Intel, Home Depot, Accenture, and Habitat for Humanity are simultaneously efficient and effective. Effective managers are those who choose the right organizational goals to pursue and have the skills to utilize resources efficiently.

Why Study Management?

The dynamic and complex nature of modern work means that managerial skills are in demand. Organizations need individuals like you who can understand this complexity, respond to environmental contingencies, and make decisions that are ethical and effective. Studying management helps equip individuals to accomplish each of these tasks.

In a broader sense, individuals generally learn through personal experience (think the "school of hard knocks") or the experiences of others. By studying management in school, you are exposing yourself to the lessons others have learned. The advantage of such social learning is that you are not bound to repeat the mistakes others have made in the past. Furthermore, by studying and practicing the behaviors of good managers and high-performing companies, you will equip yourself to help your future employer succeed.

The economic benefits of becoming a good manager are also impressive. In the United States, general managers earn a median wage of $95,000, with a projected growth rate in job openings of 8 percent and 14 percent between now and 2022.[7]

Finally, learning management principles can help you make good decisions in non-work contexts. If you're coaching a child's baseball team, organizing a charity 5K run, planning your financial budget, or starting a new business, good management principles will help you understand others, make quality decisions, and improve your personal success.

Essential Managerial Tasks

The job of management is to help an organization make the best use of its resources to achieve its goals. How do managers accomplish this objective? They do so by performing four essential managerial tasks: *planning, organizing, leading,* and *controlling.* The arrows linking these tasks in Figure 1.2 suggest the sequence in which managers typically perform them. French manager Henri Fayol first outlined the nature of these managerial activities around the turn of the 20th century in *General and Industrial Management,* a book that remains the classic statement of what managers must do to create a high-performing organization.[8]

Managers at all levels and in all departments—whether in small or large companies, for-profit or not-for-profit organizations, or organizations that operate in one country or throughout the world—are responsible for performing these four tasks, which we look at next. How well managers perform these tasks determines how efficient and effective their organizations are.

Planning

To perform the **planning** task, managers identify and select appropriate organizational goals and courses of action; they develop *strategies* for how to achieve high performance. The three steps involved in planning are (1) deciding which goals the organization will pursue, (2) deciding what strategies to adopt to attain those goals, and (3) deciding how to allocate

LO1-2

Distinguish among planning, organizing, leading, and controlling (the four principal managerial tasks), and explain how managers' ability to handle each one affects organizational performance.

planning Identifying and selecting appropriate goals; one of the four principal tasks of management.

Figure 1.2
Four Tasks of Management

Planning
Choose appropriate organizational goals and courses of action to best achieve those goals.

Organizing
Establish task and authority relationships that allow people to work together to achieve organization goals.

Leading
Motivate, coordinate, and energize individuals and groups to work together to achieve organizational goals.

Controlling
Establish accurate measuring and monitoring systems to evaluate how well the organization has achieved its goals.

organizational resources to pursue the strategies that attain those goals. How well managers plan and develop strategies determines how effective and efficient the organization is—its performance level.[9]

As an example of planning in action, consider Alcon's new venture into television. Co-CEOs Broderick Johnson and Andrew Kosove are aiming to take Alcon's expertise in film production and apply it to television audiences by producing and distributing quality original programming. Movie and television production have many features in common, but operate on different economic models. Films are produced and distributed with partners to reach theater audiences, whereas television shows are produced and offered for channels to distribute to cable and satellite audiences.

To help navigate these new waters, Alcon hired Sharon Hall, formerly of Sony Pictures Television. One of Hall's foremost priorities will be finding ways to create television content that will support and reinforce Alcon's film business.[10] For example, successful films may be parlayed into television series. Likewise, television shows can be used as a creative vehicle to build audience interest in potential film projects.

However, Alcon will be entering a highly competitive market. There are more television stations and shows today than ever before, and competition is fierce to build and maintain audience interest. Thus Alcon will need to shape its planning into an effective business strategy, which is a cluster of decisions concerning what organizational goals to pursue, what actions to take, and how to use resources to achieve these goals.

Alcon originally produced one film at a time,[11] with an emphasis on reducing costs and maximizing efficiency in filmmaking. This constituted a low-cost strategy—a way of obtaining customers by making decisions that allow an organization to produce goods or services more cheaply than its competitors so it can charge lower prices than they do. This low-cost strategy allowed Alcon to weather sometimes disappointing box office results. Alcon's low-cost strategy contrasts with a differentiation strategy, in which organizations seek to create highly innovative products that appeal to different types of consumers.[12] Another manager passionate about his industry is Dennis Corsi, who is profiled in the "Manager as a Person" box.

Manager as a Person

Dennis Corsi: Flying High at Armstrong Consultants

Each day over 2 million people fly within America's large network of nearly 20,000 commercial and general aviation airports. In fact, an estimated 87,000 flights operate in American skies daily. Most people probably don't consider the amazing amount of work required to plan, develop, and maintain such a comprehensive airport system. In the middle of this development are managers like Dennis Corsi, president of Armstrong Consultants, a Colorado-based airport engineering firm. Corsi is a pilot and former member of the U.S. Air Force. The knowledge and experience he has amassed over the years, coupled with his managerial talent, have helped Armstrong become a leader in the region.[13]

Headquartered along the western slope of Colorado in Grand Junction, Armstrong Consultants works to help general and commercial aviation airports plan, engineer, and construct facilities that meet the needs of their customers. Airports receive revenues primarily when aircraft land and refuel at their facilities. However, as aircraft have different landing, takeoff, and taxiing requirements, Armstrong must offer the right mix of facilities to accommodate the needs of pilots. For example, some small propeller aircraft can use grass airport runways as short as 600 feet, while other business jets require paved runways exceeding one mile in length and over 100 feet wide. Thus managers at engineering companies like Armstrong help airports understand and accommodate these different needs. This is where Corsi's 23 years of experience in aviation and time spent managing more than 250 airport projects come in handy.[14] He has become knowledgeable about the industry from having inspected airfield facilities, and recommends corrective actions when needed.

Like other forms of transportation, airports are also highly regulated. They must comply with an intimidating mix of local, state, and federal regulations that specify how they can operate.[15] Managers like Corsi help their clients coordinate with local, state, and federal agencies to comply with highly complex regulations. Armstrong itself has completed more than 1,000 airport improvement projects, which amounts to 30 to 40 projects each year that must comply with all kinds of regulatory issues.[16] Aviation is also marked by significant technological change and changing consumer needs. For example, aviation companies began producing very light jets, such as the Cessna Mustang, in the last decade. These jets require a different set of facilities than traditional (larger) business jets. Managers like Corsi have to work hard to stay ahead of the curve, refining their expertise to provide valued insight to clients. Companies like Armstrong also benefit from building and maintaining strong relationships with regulatory agencies, such as the Federal Aviation Administration, which help guide the activities of client airports.

The process of airport planning and engineering is challenging—something Corsi understands well. For example, before facilities are constructed or modified, airports must obtain adequate funding, typically through a combination of local and federal government grants that are financed by aviation fuel taxes.[17] Airports then develop forecasts that help inform the types of traffic they expect, including an estimation of economic impacts. These forecasts act as inputs for facility engineering plans, which are developed to guide the use and development of airfield facilities. However, before amending facilities, airports must also obtain adequate state and federal environmental clearances to ensure that their activities do not damage the natural environment. This includes surveying the area around an airport, estimating light and sound emissions, testing air and water, and forecasting potential impacts to the region. Only then can construction commence at an airport, which presents its own set of challenges.

To help airports with this daunting process, Armstrong retains a staff of engineers, planners, environmental specialists, and construction managers. Corsi must be able to understand the complexities of each of these functional areas, and coordinate their activities for multiple clients at once.

Armstrong's clients are also widely dispersed through the western United States, and driving is often dangerous along treacherous mountain roads. To mitigate the danger, Armstrong maintains a small fleet of aircraft to give it better access to clients, and Corsi often flies to client meetings.

Organizing

organizing Structuring working relationships in a way that allows organizational members to work together to achieve organizational goals; one of the four principal tasks of management.

organizational structure A formal system of task and reporting relationships that coordinates and motivates organizational members so they work together to achieve organizational goals.

Organizing is structuring working relationships so organizational members interact and cooperate to achieve organizational goals. Organizing people into departments according to the kinds of job-specific tasks they perform lays out the lines of authority and responsibility between different individuals and groups. Managers must decide how best to organize resources, particularly human resources.

The outcome of organizing is the creation of an **organizational structure**, a formal system of task and reporting relationships that coordinates and motivates members so they work together to achieve organizational goals. Organizational structure determines how an organization's resources can be best used to create goods and services. As Alcon has grown in size and scope, they have faced the issue of how to structure the company and maintain their core values. The company that once made one movie per year now produces content in film, television, and music. This requires coordinating the activities of a larger workforce working on multiple projects in different markets. Managers like Scott Parish also have the difficult task of maintaining the "filmmaking friendly" culture that helped Alcon grow and thrive. Finally, Parish must work to ensure that each of Alcon's new businesses are working together toward their common objective, and doing so in a cost-effective manner. We examine the organizing process in detail in Chapters 10 through 12.

Leading

leading Articulating a clear vision and energizing and enabling organizational members so they understand the part they play in achieving organizational goals; one of the four principal tasks of management.

An organization's *vision* is a short, succinct, and inspiring statement of what the organization intends to become and the goals it is seeking to achieve—its desired future state. In **leading**, managers articulate a clear organizational vision for the organization's members to accomplish, and they energize and enable employees so everyone understands the part he or she plays in achieving organizational goals. Leadership involves managers using their power, personality, influence, persuasion, and communication skills to coordinate people and groups so their activities and efforts are in harmony. Leadership revolves around encouraging all employees to perform at a high level to help the organization achieve its vision and goals. Another outcome of leadership is a highly motivated and committed workforce. Alcon's employees appreciate the core values and stability of their leadership, which has contributed toward their success as a workforce. Likewise, because he worked his way up from an administrative role to a leadership position, Scott Parish is better able to relate to his employees. We discuss the issues involved in managing and leading individuals and groups in Chapters 13 through 16.

Controlling

controlling Evaluating how well an organization is achieving its goals and taking action to maintain or improve performance; one of the four principal tasks of management.

In **controlling**, the task of managers is to evaluate how well an organization has achieved its goals and to take any corrective actions needed to maintain or improve performance. For example, managers monitor the performance of individuals, departments, and the organization as a whole to see whether they are meeting desired performance standards. Scott Parish learned early in his career about the importance of monitoring performance to ensure that his organization realized its profit objectives. When these goals fall short, Parish and the Alcon management team must find ways to improve performance.

Ken Chenault, pictured here, is the chairman[18] and CEO of American Express Company. Promoted in 1997, he climbed the ranks from its Travel Related Services Company thanks to his even temper and unrelenting drive. Respected by colleagues for his personality, most will say they can't remember him losing his temper or raising his voice. His open-door policy for subordinates allows him to mentor AmEx managers and encourages all to enter and speak their minds.

The outcome of the control process is the ability to measure performance accurately and regulate organizational efficiency and effectiveness. To exercise control, managers must decide which goals to measure—perhaps goals pertaining to productivity, quality, or responsiveness to customers—and then they must design control systems that will provide the information necessary to assess performance—that is, determine to what degree the goals have been met. The controlling task also helps managers evaluate how well they themselves are performing the other three tasks of management—planning, organizing, and leading—and take corrective action.

Cost control is a delicate practice in Hollywood due to contingencies that affect the production of film, television, and music content. Artist personal and schedule demands, changes in creative direction, and even the weather can affect content production costs, representing a challenge for Parish and Alcon's team. However, innovative compensation schemes, core values, and stable and respected leadership help give Alcon an advantage relative to peers.

The four managerial tasks—planning, organizing, leading, and controlling—are essential parts of a manager's job. At all levels in the managerial hierarchy, and across all jobs and departments in an organization, effective management means performing these four activities successfully—in ways that increase efficiency and effectiveness.

Performing Managerial Tasks: Mintzberg's Typology

So far, our discussion of management has presented it as an orderly process in which individuals carefully weigh information before making the best possible decision. Henry Mintzberg was one of the first to show that management is often chaotic, marked by quick decisions in a tense and sometimes emotional environment. Quick, immediate reactions to situations, rather than deliberate thought and reflection, are an important aspect of managerial action.[19] Henry Mintzberg, a professor at McGill University, has spent most of his life researching management in an attempt to help organizations better achieve their goals in an ethical manner. Some of his most important research examined the different roles that managers play in organizations, and directly informs our discussion in this chapter. Often managers are overloaded with responsibilities and do not have time to analyze every nuance of a situation; they therefore make decisions in uncertain conditions not knowing which outcomes will be best.[20] Moreover, top managers face constantly changing situations, and a decision that seems right today may prove to be wrong tomorrow. The range of problems that managers face is enormous; managers usually must handle many problems simultaneously; and they often must make snap decisions using the intuition and experience gained through their careers to perform their jobs to the best of their abilities.[21] Henry Mintzberg, by following managers and observing what they actually *do* hour by hour and day by day, identified 10 kinds of specific roles, or sets of job responsibilities, that capture the dynamic nature of managerial work.[22] He grouped these roles according to whether the responsibility was primarily decisional, interpersonal, or informational; they are described in Table 1.1.

Given the many complex, difficult job responsibilities managers have, it is no small wonder that many claim they are performing their jobs well if they are right just half of the time.[23] And it is understandable that many experienced managers accept failure by their subordinates as a normal part of the learning experience and a rite of passage to becoming an effective manager. Managers and their subordinates learn from both their successes and their failures.

Levels and Skills of Managers

To perform the four managerial tasks efficiently and effectively, organizations group or differentiate their managers in two main ways—by level in hierarchy and by type of skill. First, they differentiate managers according to their level or rank in the organization's hierarchy of authority. The three levels of managers are first-line managers, middle managers, and top managers—arranged in a hierarchy. Typically first-line managers report to middle managers, and middle managers report to top managers.

Second, organizations group managers into different departments (or functions) according to their specific job-related skills, expertise, and experiences, such as a manager's engineering skills, marketing expertise, or sales experience. A **department**, such as the manufacturing, accounting, engineering, or sales department, is a group of managers and employees who work together because they possess similar skills and experience or use the same kind of knowledge, tools, or techniques to perform their jobs. Within each department are all three levels of management. Next we examine why organizations use a hierarchy of managers and group them, by the jobs they perform, into departments.

department A group of people who work together and possess similar skills or use the same knowledge, tools, or techniques to perform their jobs.

LO1-3

Differentiate among three levels of management, and understand the tasks and responsibilities of managers at different levels in the organizational hierarchy.

first-line manager A manager who is responsible for the daily supervision of nonmanagerial employees.

Levels of Management

Organizations normally have three levels of management: first-line managers, middle managers, and top managers (see Figure 1.3). Managers at each level have different but related responsibilities for using organizational resources to increase efficiency and effectiveness.

At the base of the managerial hierarchy are **first-line managers**, often called *supervisors*. They are responsible for daily supervision of the nonmanagerial employees who perform the specific activities necessary to produce goods and services. First-line managers work in all departments or functions of an organization.

Examples of first-line managers include the supervisor of a work team in the manufacturing department of a car plant, the head nurse in the obstetrics department of a hospital, and the chief mechanic overseeing a crew of mechanics in the service function of a new car dealership. At Alcon, first-line managers are often directors who work creatively with talent to produce quality entertainment content. One key to management here is building trust between Alcon's top management and the directors it relies on to create new content.

Table 1.1

Managerial Roles Identified by Mintzberg

Type of Role	Specific Role	Examples of Role Activities
Decisional	Entrepreneur	Commit organizational resources to develop innovative goods and services; decide to expand internationally to obtain new customers for the organization's products.
	Disturbance handler	Move quickly to take corrective action to deal with unexpected problems facing the organization from the external environment, such as a crisis like an oil spill, or from the internal environment, such as producing faulty goods or services.
	Resource allocator	Allocate organizational resources among different tasks and departments of the organization; set budgets and salaries of middle and first-level managers.
	Negotiator	Work with suppliers, distributors, and labor unions to reach agreements about the quality and price of input, technical, and human resources; work with other organizations to establish agreements to pool resources to work on joint projects.
Interpersonal	Figurehead	Outline future organizational goals to employees at company meetings; open a new corporate headquarters building; state the organization's ethical guidelines and the principles of behavior employees are to follow in their dealings with customers and suppliers.
	Leader	Provide an example for employees to follow; give direct commands and orders to subordinates; make decisions concerning the use of human and technical resources; mobilize employee support for specific organizational goals.
	Liaison	Coordinate the work of managers in different departments; establish alliances between different organizations to share resources to produce new goods and services.
Informational	Monitor	Evaluate the performance of managers in different tasks and take corrective action to improve their performance; watch for changes occurring in the external and internal environments that may affect the organization in the future.
	Disseminator	Inform employees about changes taking place in the external and internal environments that will affect them and the organization; communicate to employees the organization's vision and purpose.
	Spokesperson	Launch a national advertising campaign to promote new goods and services; give a speech to inform the local community about the organization's future intentions.

middle manager A manager who supervises first-line managers and is responsible for finding the best way to use resources to achieve organizational goals.

Supervising the first-line managers are **middle managers**, responsible for finding the best way to organize human and other resources to achieve organizational goals. To increase efficiency, middle managers find ways to help first-line managers and nonmanagerial employees better use resources to reduce manufacturing costs or improve customer service. To increase effectiveness, middle managers evaluate whether the organization's goals are appropriate and suggest to top managers how goals should be changed. Often the suggestions that middle

Figure 1.3
Levels of Managers

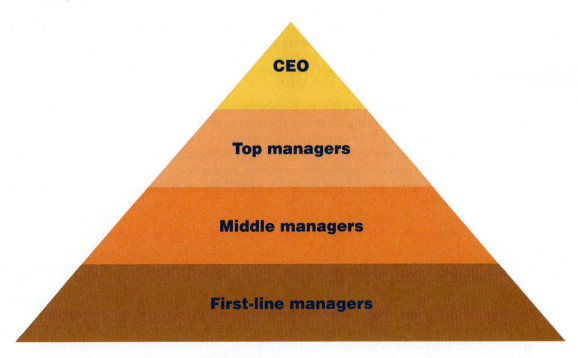

managers make to top managers can dramatically increase organizational performance. A major part of the middle manager's job is developing and fine-tuning skills and know-how, such as manufacturing or marketing expertise, that allow the organization to be efficient and effective. Middle managers make thousands of specific decisions about the production of goods and services: Which first-line supervisors should be chosen for this particular project? Where can we find the highest-quality resources? How should employees be organized to allow them to make the best use of resources?

Behind a first-class sales force, look for the middle managers responsible for training, motivating, and rewarding the salespeople. Behind a committed staff of high school teachers, look for the principal who energizes them to find ways to obtain the resources they need to do outstanding and innovative jobs in the classroom.

In contrast to middle managers, **top managers** are responsible for the performance of *all* departments.[24] They have *cross-departmental responsibility*. Top managers establish organizational goals, such as which goods and services the company should produce; they decide how the different departments should interact; and they monitor how well middle managers in each department use resources to achieve goals.[25] Top managers are ultimately responsible for the success or failure of an organization, and their performance (like that of Alcon's television president, Sharon Hall) is continually scrutinized by people inside and outside the organization, such as other employees and investors.[26]

The *chief executive officer (CEO)* is a company's most senior and important manager, the one all other top managers report to. Today the term *chief operating officer* (COO) often refers to top managers, such as Scott Parish, who are being groomed to assume CEO responsibilities when the current CEO retires, leaves the company, or assumes other responsibilities. Together the CEO and COO are responsible for developing good working relationships among the top managers of various departments (manufacturing and marketing, for example); usually these top managers have the title "vice president." A central concern of the CEO is the creation of a smoothly functioning **top management team**, a group composed of the CEO, the COO, and the vice presidents most responsible for achieving organizational goals.[27] Alcon's CEOs, Andrew Kosove and Broderick Johnson, are working to build such a team.

The relative importance of planning, organizing, leading, and controlling—the four principal managerial tasks—to any particular manager depends on the manager's position in the managerial hierarchy.[28] The amount of time managers spend planning and organizing

top manager A manager who establishes organizational goals, decides how departments should interact, and monitors the performance of middle managers.

top management team A group composed of the CEO, the COO, the president, and the heads of the most important departments.

resources to maintain and improve organizational performance increases as they ascend the hierarchy (see Figure 1.4).[29] Top managers devote most of their time to planning and organizing, the tasks so crucial to determining an organization's long-term performance. The lower that managers' positions are in the hierarchy, the more time the managers spend leading and controlling first-line managers or nonmanagerial employees.

LO1-4

Distinguish between three kinds of managerial skill, and explain why managers are divided into different departments to perform their tasks more efficiently and effectively.

conceptual skills The ability to analyze and diagnose a situation and to distinguish between cause and effect.

Managerial Skills

Both education and experience enable managers to recognize and develop the personal skills they need to put organizational resources to their best use. Alcon co-CEOs Andrew Kosove and Broderick Johnson realized from the start that they lacked the experience and expertise in marketing, operations, and planning to guide the company alone. Thus they recruited experienced managers from other companies, such as Sony Television and New Regency, to help build the company. Research has shown that education and experience help managers acquire and develop three types of skills: *conceptual, human,* and *technical.*[30]

Conceptual skills are demonstrated in the general ability to analyze and diagnose a situation and to distinguish between cause and effect. Top managers require the best conceptual skills because their primary responsibilities are planning and organizing.[31] Managers like Scott Parish must constantly identify new opportunities and mobilize organizational resources to take advantage of those opportunities.

Formal education and training are important in helping managers develop conceptual skills. Business training at the undergraduate and graduate (MBA) levels provides many of the conceptual tools (theories and techniques in marketing, finance, and other areas) that managers need to perform their roles effectively. The study of management helps develop the skills that allow managers to understand the big picture confronting an organization. The ability to focus on the big picture lets managers see beyond the situation immediately at hand and consider choices while keeping in mind the organization's long-term goals.

Today continuing management education and training, including training in advanced IT, are an integral step in building managerial skills because new theories and techniques are constantly being developed to improve organizational effectiveness, such as total quality

Figure 1.4

Relative Amount of Time That Managers Spend on the Four Managerial Tasks

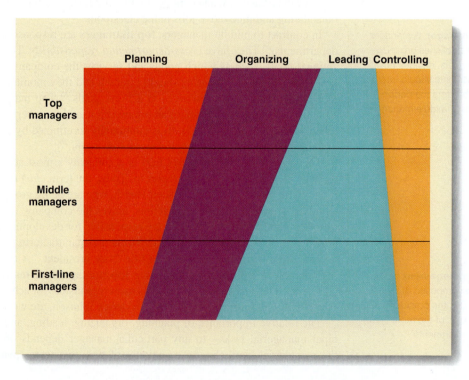

management, global supply chain management, and cloud computing and virtual business-to-business (B2B) networks. A quick scan through a magazine such as *Bloomberg Businessweek* or *Fortune* reveals a host of seminars on topics such as advanced marketing, finance, leadership, and human resources management that are offered to managers at many levels in the organization, from the most senior corporate executives to middle managers. Microsoft, IBM, Oracle, and many other organizations designate a portion of each manager's personal budget to be used at the manager's discretion to attend management development programs.

In addition, organizations may wish to develop a particular manager's abilities in a specific skill area—perhaps to learn an advanced component of departmental skills, such as international bond trading, or to learn the skills necessary to implement total quality management. The organization thus pays for managers to attend specialized programs to develop these skills. Indeed, one signal that a manager is performing well is an organization's willingness to invest in that manager's skill development. Similarly, many nonmanagerial employees who are performing at a high level (because they have studied management) are often sent to intensive management training programs to develop their management skills and to prepare them for promotion to first-level management positions.

human skills The ability to understand, alter, lead, and control the behavior of other individuals and groups.

Human skills include the general ability to understand, alter, lead, and control the behavior of other individuals and groups. The ability to communicate, to coordinate, and to motivate people, and to mold individuals into a cohesive team distinguishes effective from ineffective managers. Managers like Scott Parish require a high level of human skills to motivate and reward their people.

Like conceptual skills, human skills can be learned through education and training, as well as be developed through experience.[32] Organizations increasingly use advanced programs in leadership skills and team leadership as they seek to capitalize on the advantages of self-managed teams.[33] To manage personal interactions effectively, each person in an organization needs to learn how to empathize with other people—to understand their viewpoints and the problems they face. One way to help managers understand their personal strengths and weaknesses is to have their superiors, peers, and subordinates provide feedback about their job performance. Thorough and direct feedback allows managers to develop their human skills.

technical skills The job-specific knowledge and techniques required to perform an organizational role.

Technical skills are the *job-specific* skills required to perform a particular type of work or occupation at a high level. Examples include a manager's specific manufacturing, accounting, marketing, and IT skills. Managers need a range of technical skills to be effective. The array of technical skills managers need depends on their position in their organizations. The manager of a restaurant, for example, may need cooking skills to fill in for an absent cook, accounting and bookkeeping skills to keep track of receipts and costs and to administer the payroll, and aesthetic skills to keep the restaurant looking attractive for customers.

As noted earlier, managers and employees who possess the same kinds of technical skills typically become members of a specific department and are known as, for example, marketing managers or manufacturing managers.[34] Managers are grouped into different departments because a major part of a manager's responsibility is to monitor, train, and supervise employees so their job-specific skills and expertise increase. Obviously this is easier to do when employees with similar skills are grouped into the same department because they can learn from one another and become more skilled and productive at their particular jobs.

Figure 1.5 shows how an organization groups managers into departments on the basis of their job-specific skills. It also shows that inside each department, a managerial hierarchy of first-line, middle, and top managers emerges. These managers work together on similar tasks in departments. For example, middle and front-line managers may specialize in areas such as marketing and sales, human resource management, accounting, engineering, or production. When the head of manufacturing finds that she has no time to supervise computer assembly, she may recruit experienced manufacturing middle managers from other companies to assume this responsibility.

core competency The specific set of departmental skills, knowledge, and experience that allows one organization to outperform another.

Today the term **core competency** is often used to refer to the specific set of departmental skills, knowledge, and experience that allows one organization to outperform its competitors. In other words, departmental skills that create a core competency give an organization a *competitive advantage*. Dell, for example, was the first PC maker to develop a core competency in materials management that allowed it to produce PCs at a much lower cost than its competitors—a major source of competitive advantage. Google is well known for its core competency in research and development (R&D) that allows it to innovate new products and

Figure 1.5

Types and Levels of Managers

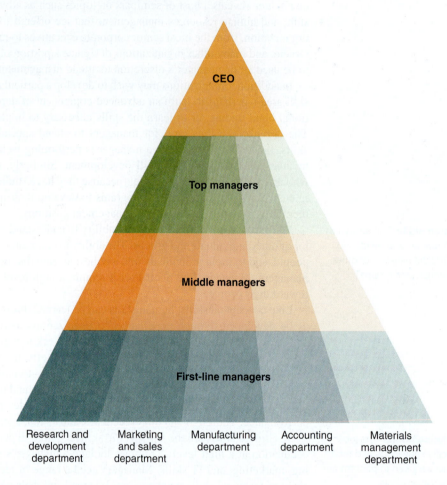

CEO

Top managers

Middle managers

First-line managers

| Research and development department | Marketing and sales department | Manufacturing department | Accounting department | Materials management department |

services at a faster rate than its competitors. From computerized glasses to self-driving cars, Google has been pioneering the development of technology for the masses.

Effective managers need all three kinds of skills—conceptual, human, and technical—to help their organizations perform more efficiently and effectively. The absence of even one type of managerial skill can lead to failure. One of the biggest problems that people who start small businesses confront, for example, is their lack of appropriate conceptual and human skills. Someone who has the technical skills to start a new business does not necessarily know how to manage the venture successfully. Similarly, one of the biggest problems that scientists or engineers who switch careers from research to management confront is their lack of effective human skills. Ambitious managers or prospective managers are constantly in search of the latest educational contributions to help them develop the conceptual, human, and technical skills they need to perform at a high level in today's changing and increasingly competitive global environment.

Developing new and improved skills through education and training has become a priority for both aspiring managers and the organizations they work for. Many people are enrolling in advanced management courses, and many companies, such as Microsoft, GE, and IBM, have established their own colleges to train and develop their employees and managers at all levels. Every year these companies put thousands of their employees through management programs designed to identify the employees who the company believes have the competencies that can be developed to become its future top managers. Most organizations closely link promotion to a manager's ability to acquire the competencies a particular company believes are important.[35] At Apple and 3M, for example, the ability to successfully lead a new product development team is viewed as a vital requirement for promotion; at Accenture and IBM, the ability to attract and retain clients is viewed as a skill its consultants must possess. We discuss the various kinds of skills managers need to develop in most of the chapters of this book.

Recent Changes in Management Practices

The tasks and responsibilities of managers have been changing dramatically in recent years. Two major factors that have led to these changes are global competition and advances in information technology (IT). Stiff competition for resources from organizations both at home and abroad has put increased pressure on all managers to improve efficiency and effectiveness. Increasingly, top managers are encouraging lower-level managers to look beyond the goals of their own departments and take a cross-departmental view to find new opportunities to improve organizational performance. Modern IT gives managers at all levels and in all areas access to more and better information and improves their ability to plan, organize, lead, and control. IT also gives employees more job-related information and allows them to become more skilled, specialized, and productive.[36]

Restructuring and Outsourcing

To utilize IT to increase efficiency and effectiveness, CEOs and top management teams have been restructuring organizations and outsourcing specific organizational activities to reduce the number of employees on the payroll and make more productive use of the remaining workforce.

restructuring Downsizing an organization by eliminating the jobs of large numbers of top, middle, and first-line managers and nonmanagerial employees.

Restructuring involves simplifying, shrinking, or downsizing an organization's operations to lower operating costs, as Dell, Nokia, and Xerox have been forced to do. The continuing recession that started in 2009 has forced most companies—large and small, and profit and nonprofit—to find ways to reduce costs because their customers are spending less money, so their revenues decrease. Restructuring can be done by eliminating product teams, shrinking departments, and reducing levels in the hierarchy, all of which result in the loss of large numbers of jobs of top, middle, or first-line managers, as well as nonmanagerial employees. Modern IT's ability to improve efficiency has increased the amount of downsizing in recent years because IT makes it possible for fewer employees to perform a given task. IT increases each person's ability to process information and make decisions more quickly and accurately, for example. U.S. companies are spending over $100 billion a year to purchase advanced IT that can improve efficiency and effectiveness. We discuss the many dramatic effects of IT on management in Chapter 18 and throughout this book.

Restructuring, however, can produce some powerful negative outcomes. It can reduce the morale of remaining employees, who worry about their own job security. And top managers of many downsized organizations realize that they downsized too far when their employees complain they are overworked and when increasing numbers of customers complain about poor service.[37]

outsourcing Contracting with another company, usually abroad, to have it perform an activity the organization previously performed itself.

Outsourcing involves contracting with another company, usually in a low-cost country abroad, to have it perform a work activity the organization previously performed itself, such as manufacturing, marketing, or customer service. Outsourcing increases efficiency because it lowers operating costs, freeing up money and resources that can be used in more effective ways—for example, to develop new products.

Low-cost global competition dramatically increased outsourcing at the turn of the century. In 2013 nearly 2.6 million U.S. jobs were outsourced offshore. India, Indonesia, and China were rated as the best outsourcing countries. Companies primarily reported offshore outsourcing to control costs and gain access to unavailable resources while freeing up internal ones.[38] Tens of thousands of high-paying IT jobs have also moved abroad, to countries like India and Russia, where programmers work for one-third the salary of those in the United States. Dell employs over 12,000 customer service reps in India, for example.[39]

Large for-profit organizations today typically employ 10–20 percent fewer people than they did 10 years ago because of restructuring and outsourcing. Ford, IBM, AT&T, HP, Dell, and DuPont are among the thousands of organizations that have streamlined their operations to increase efficiency and effectiveness. The argument is that the managers and employees who have lost their jobs will find employment in new and growing U.S. companies where their skills and experience will be better utilized. For example, the millions of manufacturing jobs that have been lost overseas will be replaced by higher-paying U.S. jobs in the service sector that are made possible because of the growth in global trade. At the same time, many companies have experienced growing problems with outsourcing in the 2010s, and the move to insource jobs (that is, to bring them back to the United States) has been increasing as discussed in the following "Managing Globally" feature.

Insourcing Is Out at GE's Appliance Division

Making headlines by calling outsourcing an "outdated business model,"[40] General Electric CEO, Jeff Immelt, is betting on the benefits of insourcing. After trying to sell its barely breathing, iconic appliance manufacturing operation located in Louisville, Kentucky, just four years ago, the CEO has changed course and invested $1 billion to revive it. The story of the about-face illustrates a quickening current in industry: Bring jobs back to domestic shores.

Built in the 1950s, GE's famed Appliance Park is a massive manufacturing compound that boasts six factory buildings, a power plant, a dedicated fire department, and its own zip code. In its heyday, around the early 1970s, Appliance Park employed 23,000 workers and churned out more than 60,000 appliances a week. In many ways, it stood alongside Detroit as an American pillar of manufacturing.

But as with many businesses, and for reasons inside and outside its control, it couldn't sustain the growth. It became more beneficial for the company to produce many of its appliances overseas to take advantage of lower wage rates and liberal trade policies. The hustle and bustle at the facility started to decline in the 1980s, 1990s, and 2000s, to the point where barely a hum of 1,863 employees turned out a trickle of product in 2011. It seemed that GE's appliance division had outsourced itself almost to oblivion, as did the majority of American manufacturing firms over the same period.[41]

However, several factors have brought jobs back to domestic shores over the past two years, creating what has become known as America's "manufacturing renaissance." First, high energy prices abroad have made shipping many products, such as appliances, expensive. Second, increasing wage rates and strengthened currencies in nations like China have made labor less competitive compared with American wage rates. Third, many states have enacted regulations that are more "business friendly," further reducing costs. Finally, American labor has continued to increase in productivity, meaning average U.S. workers produce more at an increasingly competitive wage rate. These factors have precipitated increased demand for American workers, bringing many jobs back to the States from abroad.

In GE's case, the reason to keep jobs on American soil is more about innovation than anything else. Whereas a product's life cycle—refrigerators, microwaves, stoves, for example—might previously have lasted, on average, seven years, innovations in technology today, especially computer technology, have sped up the cycle to two or three years. Smarter versions with neater tricks and gadgets are both on the rise and in demand. It no longer makes sense to set up operations overseas when products have shorter life cycles—the savings just aren't there.

A notable example of new product technology is the GE GeoSpring water heater. This innovative product uses ambient air to heat water with about 40 percent of the electricity of a traditional water heater. It can also be controlled using a smartphone. The GeoSpring's technological differentiation is one reason why GE decided to produce it in Louisville. Specifically, a key concern was that the product would be copied by competitors in China, reducing the competitive advantage GE hoped to gain through this innovation.

GE has revived a few of its other manufacturing lines—dishwashers and refrigerators, for instance—and has started making some of the component parts for those lines as well. It is also producing frontloading washers and dryers, which it has never made in the United States. GE and many other companies are finding that the benefits of keeping everything in-house—design, manufacturing, sales, marketing—under one roof, rather than in different locations far away from each other, ensures the highest-quality product and the conditions to foster innovation.

How is Appliance Park today? Having just celebrated its 60-year anniversary in September 2013, GE estimated that by year-end 2014, 75 percent of the revenue from its appliance business would come from its U.S. operations. Its rebound since 2012 has been impressive. "This investment isn't just a physical transformation, but also a demonstration of American productivity and ingenuity," said GE Appliances President and CEO Chip Blankenship.[42]

Empowerment and Self-Managed Teams

LO 1-5

Discuss some major changes in management practices today that have occurred as a result of globalization and the use of advanced information technology (IT).

empowerment The expansion of employees' knowledge, tasks, and decision-making responsibilities.

The second principal way managers have sought to increase efficiency and effectiveness is by empowering lower-level employees and moving to self-managed teams. **Empowerment** is a management technique that involves giving employees more authority and responsibility over how they perform their work activities. The way in which John Deere, the well-known tractor manufacturer, empowered its employees illustrates how this technique can help raise performance. The employees who assemble Deere's vehicles possess detailed knowledge about how Deere products work. Deere's managers realized these employees could become persuasive salespeople if they were given training. So groups of these employees were given intensive sales training and sent to visit Deere's customers and explain to them how to operate and service the company's new products. While speaking with customers, these newly empowered "salespeople" also collect information that helps Deere develop new products that better meet customers' needs. The new sales jobs are temporary; employees go on assignment but then return to the production line, where they use their new knowledge to find ways to improve efficiency and quality.

Some employees who assemble John Deere tractors are also given intensive sales training so they can visit customers and explain how to operate and service John Deere products.

Often companies find that empowering employees can lead to so many kinds of performance gains that they use their reward systems to promote empowerment. For example, Deere's moves to empower employees were so successful that the company negotiated a new labor agreement with its employees to promote empowerment. The agreement specifies that pay increases will be based on employees' learning new skills and completing college courses in areas such as computer programming that will help the company increase efficiency and quality. Deere has continued to make greater use of teams throughout the 2010s, and its profits have soared because its competitors cannot match its user-friendly machines that are the result of its drive to respond to its customers' needs.

self-managed team A group of employees who assume responsibility for organizing, controlling, and supervising their own activities and monitoring the quality of the goods and services they provide.

IT is being increasingly used to empower employees because it expands employees' job knowledge and increases the scope of their job responsibilities. Frequently IT allows one employee to perform a task that was previously performed by many employees. As a result, the employee has more autonomy and responsibility. IT also facilitates the use of a **self-managed team**, a group of employees who assume collective responsibility for organizing, controlling, and supervising their own work activities.[43] Using IT designed to give team members real-time information about each member's performance, a self-managed team can often find ways to accomplish a task more quickly and efficiently. Moreover, self-managed teams assume many tasks and responsibilities previously performed by first-line managers, so a company can better utilize its workforce.[44] First-line managers act as coaches or mentors whose job is not to tell employees what to do but to provide advice and guidance and help teams find new ways to perform their tasks more efficiently.[45] Using the same IT, middle managers can easily monitor what is happening in these teams and make better resource allocation decisions as a result. We discuss self-managed teams in more detail in Chapters 2, 10, and 15.

Challenges for Management in a Global Environment

Because the world has been changing more rapidly than ever before, managers and other employees throughout an organization must perform at higher and higher levels.[46] In the last 20 years, rivalry between organizations competing domestically (in the same country) and globally (in countries abroad) has increased dramatically. The rise of **global organizations**, organizations that operate and compete in more than one country, has pressured many organizations to identify better ways to use their resources and improve their performance. The successes of the German chemical companies Schering and Hoechst, Italian furniture manufacturer Natuzzi, Korean electronics companies Samsung and LG, Brazilian plane maker Embraer, and Europe's Airbus Industries are putting pressure on companies in other countries to raise their level of performance to compete successfully against these global organizations.

Even in the not-for-profit sector, global competition is spurring change. Schools, universities, police forces, and government agencies are reexamining their operations because looking at how activities are performed in other countries often reveals better ways to do them. For example, many curriculum and teaching changes in the United States have resulted from the study of methods that Japanese and European school systems use. Similarly, European and Asian hospital systems have learned much from the U.S. system—which may be the most effective, though not the most efficient, in the world.

Today managers who make no attempt to learn from and adapt to changes in the global environment find themselves reacting rather than innovating, and their organizations often become uncompetitive and fail.[47] Five major challenges stand out for managers in today's world: building a competitive advantage, maintaining ethical standards, managing a diverse workforce, utilizing new information systems and technologies, and practicing global crisis management.

global organizations
Organizations that operate and compete in more than one country.

LO 1-6

Discuss the principal challenges managers face in today's increasingly competitive global environment.

Building Competitive Advantage

competitive advantage
The ability of one organization to outperform other organizations because it produces desired goods or services more efficiently and effectively than they do.

What are the most important lessons for managers and organizations to learn if they are to reach and remain at the top of the competitive environment of business? The answer relates to the use of organizational resources to build a competitive advantage. **Competitive advantage** is the ability of one organization to outperform other organizations because it produces desired goods or services more efficiently and effectively than its competitors. The four building blocks of competitive advantage are superior *efficiency; quality; speed, flexibility,* and *innovation;* and *responsiveness to customers* as Figure 1.6 shows.

Figure 1.6

Building Blocks of Competitive Advantage

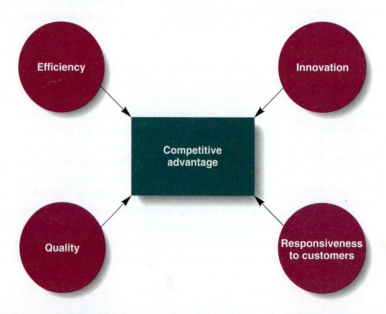

Organizations increase their efficiency when they reduce the quantity of resources (such as people and raw materials) they use to produce goods or services. In today's competitive environment, organizations continually search for new ways to use their resources to improve efficiency. Many organizations are training their workforces in the new skills and techniques needed to operate heavily computerized assembly plants. Similarly, cross-training gives employees the range of skills they need to perform many different tasks; and organizing employees in new ways, such as in self-managed teams, lets them make good use of their skills. These are important steps in the effort to improve productivity. Japanese and German companies invest far more in training employees than do American or Italian companies.

Managers must improve efficiency if their organizations are to compete successfully with companies operating in Mexico, China, Malaysia, and other countries where employees are paid comparatively low wages. New methods must be devised either to increase efficiency or to gain some other competitive advantage—higher-quality goods, for example—if outsourcing and the loss of jobs to low-cost countries are to be prevented.

The challenge from global organizations such as Korean electronics manufacturers, Mexican agricultural producers, and European design and financial companies also has increased pressure on companies to develop the skills and abilities of their workforces in order to improve the quality of their goods and services. One major thrust to improving quality has been to introduce the quality-enhancing techniques known as *total quality management (TQM)*. Employees involved in TQM are often organized into quality control teams and are responsible for finding new and better ways to perform their jobs; they also must monitor and evaluate the quality of the goods they produce. We discuss ways of managing TQM successfully in Chapter 9.

Today companies can win or lose the competitive race depending on their *speed*—how fast they can bring new products to market—or their *flexibility*—how easily they can change or alter the way they perform their activities to respond to actions of their competitors. Companies that have speed and flexibility are agile competitors: Their managers have superior planning and organizing abilities; they can think ahead, decide what to do, and then speedily mobilize their resources to respond to a changing environment. We examine how managers can build speed and flexibility in their organizations in later chapters. Agile companies are adept at responding to changes in their environments, including change from technological, regulatory, and economic sources. For example, entertainment companies like Alcon are seeking ways to more economically produce their content amid tightening margins and smaller audiences. One way Alcon is responding to this pressure is by expanding into music production that will support its film and television production endeavors. Producing music "in-house" reduces cost, providing Alcon with maximum flexibility to use music as it sees fit. Rather than enable other competitors to profit on future music royalties, Alcon also retains the rights to its music, keeping the company agile and competitive.

innovation The process of creating new or improved goods and services or developing better ways to produce or provide them.

Innovation, the process of creating new or improved goods and services that customers want or developing better ways to produce or provide goods and services, poses a special challenge. Managers must create an organizational setting in which people are encouraged to be innovative. Typically innovation takes place in small groups or teams; management decentralizes control of work activities to team members and creates an organizational culture that rewards risk taking. Innovation doesn't happen by itself; companies have to devote resources that enable innovation. These investments are a delicate balancing act. Consider Google. In 2004 Google was praised for its 80/20 work allocation, where 20 percent of an employee's time was given to work on individual "pet projects." Consumer hits such as Gmail came from this program. But the company recently announced that it was suspending the 80/20 program due to productivity concerns. Google had banked on the idea that slack time would enable individuals to innovate, but economic realities and productivity needs meant a change in how it structured employee work. Instead of a more autonomous approach to innovation, Google is now relying on its Google X lab as a formal means of maintaining a competitive edge.[48]

Organizations compete for customers with their products and services, so training employees to be responsive to customers' needs is vital for all organizations, but particularly for service organizations. Retail stores, banks, and hospitals, for example, depend entirely on their employees to perform behaviors that result in high-quality service at a reasonable cost.[49] As many countries (the United States, Canada, and Switzerland are just a few) move toward a more service-based economy (in part because of the loss of manufacturing jobs to China, Malaysia, and other countries with low labor costs), managing behavior in service organizations is becoming increasingly important. Many organizations are empowering their customer service employees and giving them the authority to take the lead in providing high-quality customer service. As noted previously, empowering nonmanagerial employees and creating self-managed teams change the role of first-line managers and lead to more efficient use of organizational resources.

Sometimes the best efforts of managers to revitalize their organization's fortunes fail; and faced with bankruptcy, the directors of these companies are forced to appoint a new CEO who has a history of success in rebuilding a company. **Turnaround management** is the creation of a new vision for a struggling company using a new approach to planning and organizing to make better use of a company's resources and allow it to survive and eventually prosper—something Apple's Steve Jobs excelled at. It involves developing radical new strategies such as how to reduce the number of products sold or change how they are made and distributed, or close corporate and manufacturing operations to reduce costs. Organizations that appoint turnaround CEOs are generally experiencing a crisis because they have become inefficient or ineffective; sometimes this is because of poor management over a continuing period, and sometimes it occurs because a competitor introduces a new product or technology that makes their own products unattractive to customers. Japanese technology firm Sony once dominated the market with a high-visibility brand. In fact, Sony was at the forefront of e-reader technology 10 years ago with its Librie, the first e-book reader with an electronic ink display. However, Sony was unable to successfully commercialize this technological breakthrough, and rival Amazon now commands the e-reader market with its Kindle devices and apps. Although Sony has had a distinctive competency in technological innovation, it will need strong leadership to help it develop the ability to commercialize its innovations in a fiercely competitive technology sector.[50]

Achieving a competitive advantage requires that managers use all their skills and expertise, as well as their companies' other resources, to find new and improved ways to improve efficiency, quality, innovation, and responsiveness to customers. We revisit this theme often as we examine the ways managers plan strategies, organize resources and activities, and lead and control people and groups to increase efficiency and effectiveness.

Maintaining Ethical and Socially Responsible Standards

Managers at all levels, especially after the recent economic crisis, are under considerable pressure to make the best use of resources to increase the level at which their organizations perform.[51] For example, top managers feel pressure from shareholders to increase the performance of the entire organization to boost its stock price, improve profits, or raise dividends. In turn, top managers may pressure middle managers to find new ways to use organizational resources to increase efficiency or quality and thus attract new customers and earn more revenues—and then middle managers hit on their department's supervisors.

Pressure to increase performance can be healthy for an organization because it leads managers to question how the organization is working, and it encourages them to find new and better ways to plan, organize, lead, and control. However, too much pressure to perform can be harmful.[52] It may induce managers to behave unethically, and even illegally, when dealing with people and groups inside and outside the organization.[53]

A purchasing manager for a nationwide retail chain, for example, might buy inferior clothing as a cost-cutting measure or ignore the working conditions under which products are made to obtain low-priced products. These issues faced the managers of companies that made footwear and clothing in the 1990s, when customers learned about the sweatshop conditions in which garment and shoe workers around the world labored. Today companies such as Nike, Walmart, and Apple are trying to stop sweatshop practices and prevent managers abroad from adopting work practices that harm their workers. They now employ hundreds of inspectors who police the factories overseas that make the products they sell and who can terminate contracts with suppliers when they behave in an unethical or illegal way. Nevertheless, in a 2010 report Apple revealed that its investigations showed that sweatshop conditions still existed in some of the factories it used abroad. Apple said that at least 55 of the 102 factories were ignoring Apple's rule that staff cannot work more than 60 hours a week, for example. Apple is continuing its efforts to reduce these abuses.[54]

Similarly, to secure a large foreign contract, a sales manager in a large company, such as in the defense or electronics industry, might offer bribes to foreign officials to obtain lucrative contracts—even though this is against the law. For example, cosmetics manufacturer

---

turnaround management
The creation of a new vision for a struggling company based on a new approach to planning and organizing to make better use of a company's resources and allow it to survive and prosper.

Avon recently announced that it will pay $89–132 million to settle a U.S. bribery probe into its development of new markets. Avon is the world's largest direct sales cosmetics manufacturer, and is not alone. Companies like Siemens, KBR/Halliburton, and BAE Systems have all settled bribery probes for amounts exceeding $400 million each.[55]

The issue of social responsibility, discussed in Chapter 4, centers on deciding what obligations a company has toward the people and groups affected by its activities—such as employees, customers, or the cities in which it operates. Some companies have strong views about social responsibility; their managers believe they should protect the interests of others. But some managers may decide to act in an unethical way and put their own interests first, hurting others in the process. A recent example showing why managers must always keep the need to act in an ethical and socially responsible way at the forefront of their decision making is profiled in the following "Ethics in Action" feature, which discusses Apple and the companies it contracts with overseas to make its iPhones and other products.

Ethics in Action

Apple Makes Sure Its Suppliers Don't Fall Too Far from the Tree

As a worldwide producer of technology, Apple has to coordinate with suppliers throughout the globe. Many of these suppliers have standards of work that differ significantly from Western expectations, including the use of child labor, workweeks exceeding 60 hours, and work environments that are physically and psychologically crippling.

Apple got into some hot water recently over complaints of excessive work hours, sex discrimination, and other serious abuses at some of its Chinese facilities.[56] It also came under fire for not carefully monitoring work conditions at supplier factories in other parts of the globe, specifically those that mine what are known as "conflict minerals." Such minerals—tantalum, gold, tungsten, and tin, for example—are considered "conflict minerals" because they are found in politically unstable countries such as the Democratic Republic of Congo and other African nations. Tantalum, in particular, is a much-needed component in cell phone production. The issue of mining in conflict zones has become important enough that in 2012 the Dodd-Frank Act required U.S. companies to disclose whether their production materials come from such countries and to file a report with Securities and Exchange Commission.[57]

Apple suppliers at work in Foxconn Technology Group's Shenzen plant in China. Because of complaints of excessive work hours, sex discrimination, and other abuses at Chinese facilities, Apple has changed how it monitors its suppliers to ensure health and safety guidelines are followed.

Apple responded to these events by stepping up its supplier compliance and monitoring efforts. Each year, the company publishes an annual Report of Supplier Responsibility that is available to the public. In the 2014 report, Apple listed the extensive measures it is taking to ensure that workers throughout its supply chain are treated fairly and safely. It is conducting routine and surprise audits (451 in 2013) of suppliers, interviewing workers, reviewing financial statements, and monitoring production practices. Apple is also monitoring environmental conditions to ensure that companies support good health and wellness for their employees. Suppliers who fail to meet Apple's standards risk the loss of its business.

The 2014 report showed significant improvement in many areas. Specifically, the company reported that 95 percent of supplier factories adhere to a less than 60-hour workweek and none of its suppliers mined for minerals in war zone countries. In addition, Apple started its own Clean Water Program that reuses and recycles water at 13 supplier locations to keep use of this precious resource to a minimum.[58]

A company touted for its meticulous attention to detail and quality has to ensure that it extends that attention throughout its supply chain.

Managing a Diverse Workforce

A major challenge for managers everywhere is to recognize the ethical need and legal requirement to treat human resources fairly and equitably. Today the age, gender, race, ethnicity, religion, sexual preference, and socioeconomic composition of the workforce presents new challenges for managers. To create a highly trained and motivated workforce, as well as to avoid lawsuits, managers must establish human resource management (HRM) procedures and practices that are legal and fair and do not discriminate against any organizational members.[59] Today most organizations understand that to motivate effectively and take advantage of the talents of a diverse workforce, they must make promotion opportunities available to each and every employee.[60] Managers must recognize the performance-enhancing possibilities of a diverse workforce, such as the ability to take advantage of the skills and experiences of different kinds of people.[61] Accenture provides a good example of a company that has utilized the potential of its diverse employees.

Accenture is a global management consulting company that serves the IT needs of thousands of client companies located in over 120 countries around the world. A major driving force behind Accenture's core organizational vision is to manage and promote diversity in order to improve employee performance and client satisfaction. At Accenture, managers at all levels realize consultants bring distinct experiences, talents, and values to their work, and a major management initiative is to take advantage of that diversity to encourage collaboration between consultants to improve the service Accenture provides to each of its clients. Because Accenture's clients are also diverse by country, religion, ethnicity, and so forth, it tries to match its teams of consultants to the attributes of its diverse clients.

Global consulting company Accenture employs a diverse workforce whose talents, values, and experiences match those of the clients they serve.

Accenture provides hundreds of diversity management training programs to its consultants each year using its 13 teams of global human capital and diversity experts, who collaborate to create its programs. Accenture also encourages each of its consultants to pursue opportunities to "work across different geographies, workforces, and generations to create agile global leaders."[62] Thirty-five percent of its workforce is composed of women, including 25 percent of its Global Management Committees and 3 of 10 corporate board members. Accenture also works to accommodate individuals with disabilities, as well as promoting an inclusionary environment for lesbian, gay, bisexual, and transgender employees.[63] The firm also provides diversity training programs to its suppliers and prospective suppliers around the world to show them how diversity can increase their efficiency and effectiveness. In all these ways, Accenture uses its expertise in managing diversity to promote individual and organizational performance—one reason it has become the most successful and fast-growing consultancy company in the world.

Managers who value their diverse employees not only invest in developing these employees' skills and capabilities but also succeed best in promoting performance over the long run. Today more organizations are realizing that people are their most important resource and that developing and protecting human resources is the most important challenge for managers in a competitive global environment. Kevin Rollins, a former CEO of Dell, commented, "I've seen firsthand the power of a diverse workforce. Leveraging the similarities and differences of all team members enables Dell to develop the best products, provide a superior customer experience, and contribute in meaningful ways to the communities where we do business."[64] And as Takahiro Moriguchi of Union Bank of California said when accepting a national diversity award for his company when he was its CEO, "By searching for talent from among the disabled, both genders, veterans, gay, all ethnic groups and all nationalities, we gain access to a pool of ideas, energy, and creativity as wide and varied as the human race itself."[65] We discuss the many issues surrounding the management of a diverse workforce in Chapter 5.

Utilizing IT and E-Commerce

As we have discussed, another important challenge for managers is to continually utilize efficient and effective new IT that can link and enable managers and employees to better perform their jobs—whatever their level in the organization. One example of how IT has changed the jobs of people at all organizational levels comes from UPS, where the average UPS driver makes 120 deliveries a day, and figuring out the quickest way to navigate all of those stops is a problem with economic implications for the shipping company. UPS estimates that a driver with 25 packages could choose from 15 trillion trillion different routes! To help it navigate these difficult roads, UPS relies on ORION—its On-Road Integrated Optimization and Navigation. ORION is designed to blend GPS navigation and learning to help drivers optimize their routes. Of course UPS drivers must also balance promised delivery times, traffic, and other factors into their decisions, meaning ORION is a critical technological competency helping UPS work effectively and efficiently. To date, UPS estimates that it has saved 85 million miles and 100 million minutes due to ORION and other technologies.[66]

Increasingly, new kinds of IT enable not just individual employees but also self-managed teams by giving them important information and allowing virtual interactions around the globe using the Internet. Increased global coordination helps improve quality and increase the pace of innovation. Microsoft, Hitachi, IBM, and most companies now search for new IT that can help them build a competitive advantage. The importance of IT is discussed in detail in Chapters 16 and 18, and throughout the text you will find examples of how IT is changing the way companies operate.

Practicing Global Crisis Management

Today another challenge facing managers and organizations is global crisis management. The causes of global crises or disasters fall into two main categories: natural causes and human causes. Crises that arise because of natural causes include the hurricanes, tsunamis, earthquakes, famines, and diseases that have devastated so many countries in the 2000s; hardly any country has been untouched by their effects. In 2013 the Philippines were hit by Typhoon Haiyan, the strongest recorded storm ever to make landfall. The typhoon killed over 6,000 people and injured scores more. Although many nations and businesses rallied to help the people of the Philippines, critical roads and infrastructure remain unrepaired, deeply affecting the Filipino economy.

Meanwhile, human-created crises result from factors such as industrial pollution, inattention to employee safety, the destruction of natural habitat or environment, and geopolitical tension and terrorism, including war. Human-created crises, such as global warming due to emissions of carbon dioxide and other gases, may intensify the effects of natural disasters. For example, increasing global temperatures and acid rain may have increased the intensity of hurricanes, led to unusually strong rains, and contributed to lengthy droughts. Scientists believe that global warming is responsible for the rapid destruction of coral reefs, forests, animal species, and the natural habitat in many parts of the world. The shrinking polar ice caps are expected to raise the sea level by a few critical inches.

Increasing geopolitical tensions, which reflect increased globalization, have upset the balance of world power as nations jockey to protect their economic and political interests. For example, the Ukraine's ouster of its Russian-backed president resulted in a swift military response from Russia in the Crimea region. Similar instability can be found elsewhere, and results in the need for managers who can interpret and respond to often unpredictable contingencies in a global marketplace.

Finally, industrial pollution and limited concern for the health and safety of workers have become increasingly significant problems for companies and countries. Companies in heavy industries such as coal and steel have polluted millions of acres of land around major cities in eastern Europe and Asia; billion-dollar cleanups are necessary. The 1986 Chernobyl nuclear power plant meltdown released over 1,540 times as much radiation into the air as occurred at Hiroshima; over 50,000 people died as a result, while hundreds of thousands more have been affected. In the area of worker health and safety, one example of a company whose managers paid too little attention to preventing crises is the company that ran the Upper Big Branch South Mine in West Virginia, which is discussed in the following "Ethics in Action" feature.

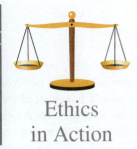

Ethics
in Action

Digging Deep to Promote Workplace Safety

In 2010 a coal mine called the Upper Big Branch South Mine exploded in West Virginia. Twenty-nine miners were killed in a massive explosion. The tragic accident shocked and saddened the entire country and brought the issue of mine safety to the national forefront. Massey Energy, the company that managed the mine, was cited at fault by the Mine Health and Safety Administration (MHSA), which is part of the U.S. Department of Labor. MHSA's report blamed Massey's lax oversight and management practices as the underlying cause of the tragedy.[67] The Governor's Independent Investigation Panel, set up by the governor of West Virgina, Joe Manchin III, also faulted Massey.[68]

To get some context, coal mining is one of the most dangerous jobs in the world. Coal is located deep underground, so miners often work in cramped quarters sometimes several miles below the earth's surface, where conditions are inhospitable. Miners have to build shafts (roads) that provide access and allow extraction. Managing the construction of these underground roads is critical to ensure that they support the heavy industrial equipment needed to get the coal out. As coal is extracted, potentially explosive methane gas is released into the air, where it interacts with coal dust. Air quality must be monitored and maintained to reduce the potential for explosions.

A sudden inundation of methane gas is believed to have started the Upper Big Branch mine explosion, but MHSA went even further in its report, sending the blame to Massey's top management. Joseph A. Main, Assistant Secretary at MSHA, wrote, "Every time Massey sent miners into the UBB Mine, Massey put those miners' lives at risk. Massey management created a culture of fear and intimidation in their miners to hide their reckless practices. [This] report brings to light the tragic consequences of a corporate culture that values production over people."[69]

Specific violations cited by MHSA against Massey were its management policies of intimidating miners, its warning of impending inspections in advance, and its not disclosing known hazards in the mine in official reports. Two other investigations found that worn and broken equipment, including clogged and broken water sprayers, contributed to the blast.[70]

The GIIP report also concluded that management at Massey was to blame: "The April 5, 2010, explosion was not something that happened out of the blue, an event that could not have been anticipated or prevented. It was, to the contrary, a completely predictable result for a company that ignored basic safety standards and put too much faith in its own mythology."[71] Massey CEO Don Blankenship was fired in 2014 with the release of a documentary asserting that MSHA pressured his company to install an adequate ventilation system at the mine. This was the first time the company had publicly taken a strong defensive stance.

Massey's management overlooked critical information that would have potentially reduced the risk of an explosion, and the lack of leadership and careful control led to a tragic disaster. Massey Energy was acquired by Alpha Natural Resources, which settled a $210 million agreement to provide restitution to families and fund mine safety research. In January 2014 West Virginia Governor Earl Ray Tomblin released an 85-page report detailing new regulations and resources to promote safety in mines. These actions highlight the importance of partnership between industry and government.

Indeed, mine safety reflects a long history of coordinated efforts of mining companies, labor organizations, local communities, and government. In 1910 Congress created the U.S. Bureau of Mines, which was charged with investigating accidents, advising industry, conducting production and safety research, and educating workers (and their management) on best practices on avoiding and handling accidents. Additional legislation has been enacted to protect miners, including the Federal Coal Mine Health and Safety Act of 1969, the Federal Mine Safety and Health Act of 1977, and the Mine Improvement and New Emergency Response Act of 2006.[72]

MSHA works to help companies create and maintain a safe working environment for miners. Today it reports that accident injury rates have dropped to historic lows thanks to safer equipment and better safety programs, as well as "more cooperative attitude[s] toward safety issues by the mining industry, labor and government."[73] Still, greater efforts must be made to ensure that American mining is as safe as possible for miners and their families.

Management has an important role to play in helping people, organizations, and countries respond to global crises; such crises provide lessons in how to plan, organize, lead, and control the resources needed to both forestall and respond effectively to a crisis. Crisis management involves making important choices about how to (1) create teams to facilitate rapid decision making and communication, (2) establish the organizational chain of command and reporting relationships necessary to mobilize a fast response, (3) recruit and select the right people to lead and work in such teams, and (4) develop bargaining and negotiating strategies to manage the conflicts that arise whenever people and groups have different interests and objectives. How well managers make such decisions determines how quickly an effective response to a crisis can be implemented, and it sometimes can prevent or reduce the severity of the crisis itself.

Summary and Review

WHAT IS MANAGEMENT? A manager is a person responsible for supervising the use of an organization's resources to meet its goals. An organization is a collection of people who work together and coordinate their actions to achieve a wide variety of goals. Management is the process of using organizational resources to achieve organizational goals effectively

LO1-1 and efficiently through planning, organizing, leading, and controlling. An efficient organization makes the most productive use of its resources. An effective organization pursues appropriate goals and achieves these goals by using its resources to create goods or services that customers want.

LO1-2 **MANAGERIAL TASKS** The four principal managerial tasks are planning, organizing, leading, and controlling. Managers at all levels of the organization and in all departments perform these tasks. Effective management means managing these activities successfully.

LO1-3, 1-4 **LEVELS AND SKILLS OF MANAGERS** Organizations typically have three levels of management. First-line managers are responsible for the day-to-day supervision of nonmanagerial employees. Middle managers are responsible for developing and utilizing organizational resources efficiently and effectively. Top managers have cross-departmental responsibility. Three main kinds of managerial skills are conceptual, human, and technical. The need to develop and build technical skills leads organizations to divide managers into departments according to their job-specific responsibilities. Top managers must establish appropriate goals for the entire organization and verify that department managers are using resources to achieve those goals.

LO1-5 **RECENT CHANGES IN MANAGEMENT PRACTICES** To increase efficiency and effectiveness, many organizations have altered how they operate. Managers have restructured and downsized operations and outsourced activities to reduce costs. Companies are also empowering their workforces and using self-managed teams to increase efficiency and effectiveness. Managers are increasingly using IT to achieve these objectives.

LO1-6 **CHALLENGES FOR MANAGEMENT IN A GLOBAL ENVIRONMENT** Today's competitive global environment presents many interesting challenges to managers. One of the main challenges is building a competitive advantage by increasing efficiency; quality; speed, flexibility, and innovation; and customer responsiveness. Other challenges include behaving in an ethical and socially responsible way toward people inside and outside the organization, managing a diverse workforce, utilizing new IT, and practicing global crisis management.

Management in Action

Topics for Discussion and Action

Discussion

1. Describe the difference between efficiency and effectiveness, and identify real organizations that you think are, or are not, efficient and effective. **[LO1-1]**

2. In what ways can managers at each of the three levels of management contribute to organizational efficiency and effectiveness? **[LO1-3]**

3. Identify an organization that you believe is high-performing and one that you believe is low-performing. Give five reasons why you think the performance levels of the two organizations differ so much. **[LO1-2, 1-4]**

4. What are the building blocks of competitive advantage? Why is obtaining a competitive advantage important to managers? **[LO1-5]**

5. In what ways do you think managers' jobs have changed the most over the last 10 years? Why have these changes occurred? **[LO1-6]**

Action

6. Choose an organization such as a school or a bank; visit it; then list the different organizational resources it uses. How do managers use these resources to maintain and improve its performance? **[LO1-2, 1-4]**

7. Visit an organization, and talk to first-line, middle, and top managers about their respective management roles in the organization and what they do to help the organization be efficient and effective. **[LO1-3, 1-4]**

8. Ask a middle or top manager, perhaps someone you already know, to give examples of how he or she performs the managerial tasks of planning, organizing, leading, and controlling. How much time does he or she spend in performing each task? **[LO1-3]**

9. Like Mintzberg, try to find a cooperative manager who will allow you to follow him or her around for a day. List the roles the manager plays, and indicate how much time he or she spends performing them. **[LO1-3, 1-4]**

Building Management Skills

Thinking about Managers and Management [LO1-2, 1-3, 1-4]

Think of an organization that has provided you with work experience and the manager to whom you reported (or talk to someone who has had extensive work experience); then answer these questions:

1. Think about your direct supervisor. Of what department is he or she a member, and at what level of management is this person?

2. How do you characterize your supervisor's approach to management? For example, which particular management tasks and roles does this person perform most often? What kinds of management skills does this manager have?

3. Do you think the tasks, roles, and skills of your supervisor are appropriate for the particular job he or she performs? How could this manager improve his or her task performance? How can IT affect this?

4. How did your supervisor's approach to management affect your attitudes and behavior? For example,

how well did you perform as a subordinate, and how motivated were you?

5. Think about the organization and its resources. Do its managers use organizational resources effectively? Which resources contribute most to the organization's performance?

6. Describe how the organization treats its human resources. How does this treatment affect the attitudes and behaviors of the workforce?

7. If you could give your manager one piece of advice or change one management practice in the organization, what would it be?

8. How attuned are the managers in the organization to the need to increase efficiency, quality, innovation, or responsiveness to customers? How well do you think the organization performs its prime goals of providing the goods or services that customers want or need the most?

Managing Ethically [LO1-1, 1-3]

Think about an example of unethical behavior that you observed in the past. The incident could be something you experienced as an employee or a customer or something you observed informally.

Questions

1. Either by yourself or in a group, give three reasons why you think the behavior was unethical. For example, what rules or norms were broken? Who benefited or was harmed by what took place? What was the outcome for the people involved?

2. What steps might you take to prevent such unethical behavior and encourage people to behave in an ethical way?

Small Group Breakout Exercise [LO1-2, 1-3, 1-4]

Opening a New Restaurant

Form groups of three or four people, and appoint one group member as the spokesperson who will communicate your findings to the entire class when called on by the instructor. Then discuss the following scenario:

You and your partners have decided to open a large full-service restaurant in your local community; it will be open from 7 a.m. to 10 p.m. to serve breakfast, lunch, and dinner. Each of you is investing $50,000 in the venture, and together you have secured a bank loan for $300,000 to begin operations. You and your partners have little experience in managing a restaurant beyond serving meals or eating in restaurants, and you now face the task of deciding how you will manage the restaurant and what your respective roles will be.

1. Decide what each partner's managerial role in the restaurant will be. For example, who will be responsible for the necessary departments and specific activities? Describe your managerial hierarchy.

2. Which building blocks of competitive advantage do you need to establish to help your restaurant succeed? What criteria will you use to evaluate how successfully you are managing the restaurant?

3. Discuss the most important decisions that must be made about (a) planning, (b) organizing, (c) leading, and (d) controlling to allow you and your partners to use organizational resources effectively and build a competitive advantage.

4. For each managerial task, list the issues to solve, and decide which roles will contribute the most to your restaurant's success.

Exploring the World Wide Web [LO1-2]

Go to the Curb Records website at www.curb.com, click on "About Us," and then go to Mike Curb's biography. Feel free to peruse his personal website, and search this website for information that describes his approach to planning, organizing, leading, and controlling Curb Records. What is his approach to managing? What values help define him as a manager?

Be the Manager [LO1-2, 1-5]

Problems at Achieva

You have just been called in to help managers at Achieva, a fast-growing Internet software company that specializes in business-to-business (B2B) network software. Your job is to help Achieva solve some management problems that have arisen because of its rapid growth.

Customer demand to license Achieva's software has boomed so much in just two years that more than 50 new software programmers have been added to help develop a new range of software products. Achieva's growth has been so swift that the company still operates informally, its organizational structure is loose and flexible, and programmers are encouraged to find solutions to problems as they go along. Although this structure worked well in the past, you have been told that problems are arising.

There have been increasing complaints from employees that good performance is not being recognized in the organization and that they do not feel equitably treated. Moreover, there have been complaints about getting managers to listen to their new ideas and to act on them. A bad atmosphere is developing in the company, and recently several talented employees left. Your job is to help Achieva's managers solve these problems quickly and keep the company on the fast track.

Questions

1. What kinds of organizing and controlling problems is Achieva suffering from?

2. What kinds of management changes need to be made to solve them?

New York Magazine, Case in the News [LO1-1, 1-2, 1-6]

Elon Musk Is in an Empire State of Mind

There's a trend in tech these days of trying to own as little as possible. Companies like Uber and Airbnb have become billion-dollar behemoths by employing what's called the "platform-only" model, which involves outsourcing the messy work of owning cars and operating hotels to a network of "independent contractors." These companies have learned that doing business as a middleman is much easier than being a full-service supplier—just build the software that matches buyers and sellers, take a cut of each transaction, and get out of the way.

Elon Musk, the billionaire entrepreneur behind SpaceX and Tesla Motors, is taking the opposite tack.

Musk's solar-panel company, SolarCity, announced this week that it is acquiring Silevo, a maker of high-quality solar panels. Until now, SolarCity had bought cheap photovoltaic panels from outside suppliers and leased them to customers at a markup. Now it's going to start making its own, at one of the largest solar-panel factories in the world.

Musk used to be known primarily as an inventor. But these days, he's in his empire-building phase, taking on the less flashy work of building the infrastructure required to support all his crazy inventions at scale. His car company, Tesla Motors, is building a "gigafactory" for electric-car batteries in a to-be-determined state in the southwest U.S., which will power its electric vehicles as well as those of competitors. SolarCity plans to plant its manufacturing flag in Buffalo, New York, expanding a Silevo factory that was already in progress there. Being in Buffalo will give the company a foothold on the east coast, and, it hopes, allow SolarCity to keep up with increasing demand for solar panels. Naturally, Governor Cuomo is crowing, calling the merger a "landmark investment and economic game-changer taking place in the new western New York."

Why Buffalo? Well, as with much of the green-energy industry to date, SolarCity's decision comes down to government subsidies. New York State has already committed to spending $225 million on a high-tech complex in the city, at the site of the former Republic Steel mill, where the Silevo plant-in-progress is located. The state is hammering out additional subsidies and perks for the new factory, which could create as many as a thousand jobs in the Buffalo region and make New York state an important locus of green-energy innovation.

Musk's manufacturing push comes at an odd time in the solar-energy industry. Prices on solar panels have been falling for years, in part owing to an influx of Chinese manufacturers that flooded the market with cheap panels. SolarCity has been hoovering up these panels and leasing them out at a markup to its American customers. But now, it wants to out-China China, and bring the economics of solar-panel installation even further in its favor. "If we do the manufacturing ourselves and take advantage of some different technology, our costs will be lower," Peter Rive, Musk's cousin and SolarCity's co-founder, told *Bloomberg Businessweek.* Saving on panel production costs will be especially important if, as expected by many, the solar-power industry loses some of its more generous forms of government subsidy in the coming years.

Eventually, Musk and Rive hope to raise Silevo's production capacity to 1,000 megawatts. (It's currently at 32.) And they hope that the combined SolarCity-Silevo will be able to fix one of the big problems with today's solar-panel market—too much supply, too little demand—by making it as easy and cost-efficient as possible for people to get solar panels installed on their homes. SolarCity is already installing one out of every three solar panels in the U.S., and it hopes to become even more dominant in the years ahead by doing essentially what Tesla wants to do for cars: control every step of the manufacturing and sales process, and make the barriers to entry as low as possible.

"What we are trying to address is not the lay of the land today," the company wrote in a blog post, "but how we see the future developing. Without decisive action to lay the groundwork today, the massive volume of affordable, high efficiency panels needed for unsubsidized solar power to outcompete fossil fuel grid power simply will not be there when it is needed."

It's a risky bet for Musk and SolarCity. It's also a bet for Governor Cuomo, who could face repercussions if the Buffalo solar push doesn't go as expected. California has been subsidizing solar-panel installations for years, and while a significant portion of the state's energy now comes from solar, progress has taken longer than expected, and critics of the industry's setbacks have been numerous.

Cuomo has already proven he's a Musk fan — earlier this year, he helped broker a deal that allowed Tesla to keep its retail locations in New York amid pressure from automotive dealers to shut them down. And by sponsoring the Buffalo energy complex, he gets the best of both worlds _ the promise of hundreds of new manufacturing jobs in upstate New York, where the unemployment rate is hovering around 8 percent, and the appearance of having built a tech-friendly innovation zone in a time when every city wants one.

Plus, with SolarCity building panels in Buffalo, New York will get a front-row seat for Musk's "build it and they will come" approach to infrastructure creation. Which is proving to be the hottest ticket around.

Questions for Discussion

1. What management challenges is Elon Musk facing as he prepares SolarCity to make its own solar panels?

2. How is Elon Musk responding to these challenges?

3. Search the web. How is SolarCity performing?

CHAPTER 2

The Evolution of Management Thought

Learning Objectives

After studying this chapter, you should be able to:

LO2-1 Describe how the need to increase organizational efficiency and effectiveness has guided the evolution of management theory.

LO2-2 Explain the principle of job specialization and division of labor, and tell why the study of person–task relationships is central to the pursuit of increased efficiency.

LO2-3 Identify the principles of administration and organization that underlie effective organizations.

LO2-4 Trace the changes in theories about how managers should behave to motivate and control employees.

LO2-5 Explain the contributions of management science to the efficient use of organizational resources.

LO2-6 Explain why the study of the external environment and its impact on an organization has become a central issue in management thought.

Simplification and Excellence at General Electric

What is the best way to maintain a competitive edge? More than ever before, companies must learn how to adapt and remain competitive in a changing global marketplace. General Electric is one example. It is a highly diversified global company that makes everything from lightbulbs and refrigerators to locomotives and aircraft engines. It also has finance businesses, and it runs power plants.

The company was created in 1892 from the merger of two companies: the Edison General Electric Company and the Thomas-Houston Company. (It is the only company included in the original 1896 Dow Jones Industrial Index that is still included today.) Thomas Edison and Charles Coffin pioneered the development of the incandescent lightbulb, which heats a filament wire, using electricity, until it emits light. The filament is protected from oxidation by a glass bulb that contains inert gas or a vacuum. General Electric was not the first company to produce and sell such bulbs and related electrical equipment. However, Edison and Coffin used their combined expertise and patents to produce practical, affordable lightbulbs relatively easily, which gave them a competitive advantage.

Originally General Electric produced lightbulbs and related electrical equipment at its headquarters in Schenectady, New York. Over the years it has expanded to serve customers in more than 160 nations with a lineup of multiple businesses and several hundred products. To do this, General Electric draws on the talents of more than 300,000 employees.

General Electric's birth as a merger established a pattern for quick growth by diversifying its businesses through merger and acquisition of other firms, as well as

CEO Jeffrey Immelt has been trying to change GE's competitive position by simplifying its operations and focusing on manufacturing physical products.

developing new business portfolios. In 1911 GE bought the National Electric Lamp Association, which strengthened its distribution and product portfolio. A few short years later, in 1919, GE formed the Radio Corporation of America (RCA). RCA was intended to operate as a retailer for General Electric's radios, but grew into a large business of its own. Since then General Electric has diversified into aircraft engines, computers, medical technology, entertainment, wind power, appliances, and even petroleum extraction products. It also maintains financial stakes in banking and finance.

One challenge inherent in this growth is the incredible complexity of managing multiple businesses in different industries across the globe. As businesses like General Electric grow in size and scope, they often become cumbersome to manage. To be consistent across its operations, these businesses can become highly formalized and bureaucratic. This management style enables the company to maintain control over its operations. However, it can also impede the company's ability to respond to changing market dynamics and competitive realities. Because General Electric competes in multiple industries, it must work hard to stay flexible in the face of multiple competitors.

Large companies also struggle to maintain a competitive edge with innovation because new products or offerings must be approved by layers of formal bureaucracy, which slows down the process. Since companies often compete to bring products to market first, the size and formal bureaucracy of an organization can be a stumbling block. For example, even though a General Electric engineer, Edward Hammer, developed the spiral compact fluorescent light (CFL) in the 1970s, General Electric's management decided to shelve the project due to cost concerns.

Today incandescent bulbs are being phased out in favor of CFLs, and GE has lost ground to competitors like Philips.

It is in this competitive environment that General Electric CEO Jeffrey Immelt noted the need for GE to change. First, Immelt cited the importance of embracing a culture of simplification and manufacturing excellence. He is steering the company toward a focus on the manufacture of physical products, and a reduction in its lines of business. He noted that customers demand smarter and faster service. With regard to simplification, Immelt said, "The biggest risks at GE are the inability to seize market opportunities. Simplification is making us more competitive."[1] He also commented, "This is not a reorganization or an initiative. Rather, it defines the way we make decisions, work together, and work with our customers. We are focused on efficiency, speed, and market impact. We are driving decisions closer to markets and making our teams accountable for outcomes, not process."[2]

One effort to simplify General Electric involves reducing the firm's exposure to risk in economic markets. GE Capital is the financial arm of the corporation, and it took on risky bets that hurt its parent company during the recent economic downturn. Immelt and General Electric's managers are working to divest its financial assets so that the firm has less exposure to economic risk. For example, GE Capital recently sold a Swiss subsidiary that had a successful initial public offering. Normally, companies like General Electric would be pursuing these start-up firms, but managers like Immelt realize that such acquisitions can distract the company from its core businesses.

General Electric has also divested other businesses, including insurance and media. In 2013 Comcast purchased General

Electric's remaining stake in NBCUniversal, an entertainment production company. Although NBCUniversal is profitable, Immelt and General Electric's management believed that the business did not reflect the manufacturing core GE wanted to spend its energies and resources on. These divestitures have changed General Electric's focus to businesses such as aircraft engines and refining equipment, and have helped the company simplify its management processes.[3]

Time will tell whether these actions change General Electric's competitive position, but GE is betting on changes in management to help move the company forward in the next century.

Overview

As this sketch of the evolution of management thinking at General Electric suggests, changes in management practices occur as managers, theorists, researchers, and customers look for ways to increase how efficiently and effectively products can be made. The driving force behind the evolution of management theory is the search for better ways to use organizational resources to make goods and services. Advances in management thought typically occur as managers and researchers find better ways to perform the principal management tasks: planning, organizing, leading, and controlling human and other organizational resources.

In this chapter we examine how management thought has evolved in modern times and the central concerns that have guided ongoing advances in management theory. First we examine the so-called classical management theories that emerged around the turn of the 20th century. These include scientific management, which focuses on matching people and tasks to maximize efficiency, and administrative management, which focuses on identifying the principles that will lead to the creation of the most efficient system of organization and management. Next we consider behavioral management theories developed both before and after World War II; these focus on how managers should lead and control their workforces to increase performance. Then we discuss management science theory, which developed during World War II and has become increasingly important as researchers have developed rigorous analytical and quantitative techniques to help managers measure and control organizational performance. Finally, we discuss changes in management practices from the middle to the late 20th century and focus on the theories developed to help explain how the external environment affects the way organizations and managers operate.

By the end of this chapter you will understand how management thought and theory have evolved over time. You will also understand how economic, political, and cultural forces have affected the development of these theories and how managers and their organizations have changed their behavior as a result. In Figure 2.1 we summarize the chronology of the management theories discussed in this chapter.

Scientific Management Theory

The evolution of modern management began in the closing decades of the 19th century, after the industrial revolution had swept through Europe and America. In the new economic climate, managers of all types of organizations—political, educational, and economic—were trying to find better ways to satisfy customers' needs. Many major economic, technical, and cultural changes were taking place at this time. The introduction of steam power and the development of sophisticated machinery and equipment changed how goods were produced, particularly in the weaving and clothing industries. Small workshops run by skilled workers who produced hand-manufactured products (a system called *crafts production*) were being replaced by large factories in which sophisticated machines controlled by hundreds or even thousands of unskilled or semiskilled

Figure 2.1
The Evolution of Management Theory

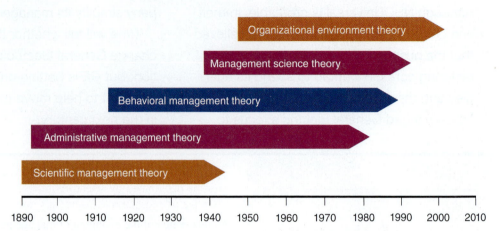

workers made products. For example, raw cotton and wool, which in the past had been spun into yarn by families or whole villages working together, were now shipped to factories where workers operated machines that spun and wove large quantities of yarn into cloth.

Owners and managers of the new factories found themselves unprepared for the challenges accompanying the change from small-scale crafts production to large-scale mechanized manufacturing. Moreover, many managers and supervisors in these workshops and factories were engineers who had only a technical orientation. They were unprepared for the social problems that occur when people work together in large groups in a factory or shop system. Managers began to search for new techniques to manage their organizations' resources, and soon they began to focus on ways to increase the efficiency of the worker–task mix.

Job Specialization and the Division of Labor

Initially management theorists were interested in why the new machine shops and factory system were more efficient and produced greater quantities of goods and services than older crafts-style production operations. Nearly 200 years before, Adam Smith had been one of the first writers to investigate the advantages associated with producing goods and services in factories. A famous economist, Smith journeyed around England in the 1700s studying the effects of the industrial revolution.[4] In a study of factories that produced various pins or nails, Smith identified two different manufacturing methods. The first was similar to crafts-style production, in which each worker was responsible for all the 18 tasks involved in producing a pin. The other had each worker performing only one or a few of these 18 tasks.

Smith found that the performance of the factories in which workers specialized in only one or a few tasks was much greater than the performance of the factory in which each worker performed all 18 pin-making tasks. In fact, Smith found that 10 workers specializing in a particular task could make 48,000 pins a day, whereas those workers who performed all the tasks could make only a few thousand.[5] Smith reasoned that this performance difference occurred because the workers who specialized became much more skilled at their specific tasks and as a group were thus able to produce a product faster than the group of workers who each performed many tasks. Smith concluded that increasing the level of **job specialization**— the process by which a division of labor occurs as different workers specialize in tasks— improves efficiency and leads to higher organizational performance.[6]

Armed with the insights gained from Adam Smith's observations, other managers and researchers began to investigate how to improve job specialization to increase performance. Management practitioners and theorists focused on how managers should organize and control the work process to maximize the advantages of job specialization and the division of labor.

job specialization The
process by which a division
of labor occurs as different
workers specialize in different
tasks over time.

Frederick W. Taylor, founder of scientific management, and one of the first people to study the behavior and performance of people at work.

scientific management
The systematic study of relationships between people and tasks for the purpose of redesigning the work process to increase efficiency.

F. W. Taylor and Scientific Management

Frederick W. Taylor (1856–1915) is best known for defining the techniques of **scientific management**, the systematic study of relationships between people and tasks for the purpose of redesigning the work process to increase efficiency. Taylor was a manufacturing manager who eventually became a consultant and taught other managers how to apply his scientific management techniques. Taylor believed that if the amount of time and effort that each worker expends to produce a unit of output (a finished good or service) can be reduced by increasing specialization and the division of labor, the production process will become more efficient. According to Taylor, the way to create the most efficient division of labor could best be determined by scientific management techniques rather than by intuitive or informal rule-of-thumb knowledge. Based on his experiments and observations as a manufacturing manager in a variety of settings, he developed four principles to increase efficiency in the workplace:

- Principle 1: *Study the way workers perform their tasks, gather all the informal job knowledge that workers possess, and experiment with ways of improving how tasks are performed.*

To discover the most efficient method of performing specific tasks, Taylor studied in great detail and measured the ways different workers went about performing their tasks. One of the main tools he used was a time-and-motion study, which involves the careful timing and recording of the actions taken to perform a particular task. Once Taylor understood the existing method of performing a task, he then experimented to increase specialization. He tried different methods of dividing and coordinating the various tasks necessary to produce a finished product. Usually this meant simplifying jobs and having each worker perform fewer, more routine tasks, as at the pin factory or on a car assembly line. Taylor also sought to find ways to improve each worker's ability to perform a particular task—for example, by reducing the number of motions workers made to complete the task, by changing the layout of the work area or the type of tools workers used, or by experimenting with tools of different sizes.

- Principle 2: *Codify the new methods of performing tasks into written rules and standard operating procedures.*

Once the best method of performing a particular task was determined, Taylor specified that it should be recorded so this procedure could be taught to all workers performing the same task. These new methods further standardized and simplified jobs—essentially making jobs even more routine. In this way efficiency could be increased throughout an organization.

- Principle 3: *Carefully select workers who possess skills and abilities that match the needs of the task, and train them to perform the task according to the established rules and procedures.*

To increase specialization, Taylor believed workers had to understand the tasks that were required and be thoroughly trained to perform the tasks at the required level. Workers who could not be trained to this level were to be transferred to a job where they were able to reach the minimum required level of proficiency.[7]

- Principle 4: *Establish a fair or acceptable level of performance for a task, and then develop a pay system that rewards performance above the acceptable level.*

To encourage workers to perform at a high level of efficiency, and to give them an incentive to reveal the most efficient techniques for performing a task, Taylor advocated that workers benefit from any gains in performance. They should be paid a bonus and receive some percentage of the performance gains achieved through the more efficient work process.[8]

By 1910 Taylor's system of scientific management had become nationally known and in many instances was faithfully and fully practiced.[9] However, managers in many organizations chose to implement the new principles of scientific management selectively. This decision ultimately resulted in problems. For example, some managers using scientific management obtained increases in performance, but rather than sharing performance gains with workers through bonuses as Taylor had advocated, they simply increased the amount of work that each worker was expected to do. Many workers experiencing the reorganized work system found that as their performance increased, managers required that they do more work for the same pay. Workers also learned that performance increases often meant fewer jobs and a greater threat of layoffs because fewer workers were needed. In addition, the specialized, simplified jobs were often monotonous and repetitive, and many workers became dissatisfied with their jobs.

Scientific management brought many workers more hardship than gain and a distrust of managers who did not seem to care about workers' well-being.[10] These dissatisfied workers resisted attempts to use the new scientific management techniques and at times even withheld their job knowledge from managers to protect their jobs and pay. It is not difficult for workers to conceal the true potential efficiency of a work system to protect their interests. Experienced machine operators, for example, can slow their machines in undetectable ways by adjusting the tension in the belts or by misaligning the gears.

Unable to inspire workers to accept the new scientific management techniques for performing tasks, some organizations increased the mechanization of the work process. For example, one reason why Henry Ford introduced moving conveyor belts in his factory was the realization that when a conveyor belt controls the pace of work (instead of workers setting their own pace), workers can be pushed to perform at higher levels—levels that they may have thought were beyond their reach. Charlie Chaplin captured this aspect of mass production in one of the opening scenes of his famous movie *Modern Times* (1936). In the film Chaplin caricatured a new factory employee fighting to work at the machine-imposed pace but losing the battle to the machine. Henry Ford also used the principles of scientific management to identify the tasks that each worker should perform on the production line and thus to determine the most effective division of labor to suit the needs of a mechanized production system.

From a performance perspective, the combination of the two management practices—(1) achieving the right worker–task specialization and (2) linking people and tasks by the speed of the production line—makes sense. It produces the huge cost savings and dramatic output increases that occur in large organized work settings. For example, in 1908 managers at the Franklin Motor Company using scientific management principles redesigned the work process, and the output of cars increased from 100 cars a *month* to 45 cars a *day;* workers' wages, however, increased by only 90%.[11] From other perspectives, however, scientific management practices raise many concerns. Some companies, like McDonald's in the accompanying "Ethics in Action" feature, have codified management practices to protect workers.

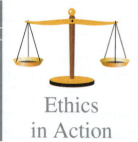

Ethics
in Action

McDonald's and Human Rights

When most individuals think about McDonald's, they might think of a Big Mac, McChicken Sandwich, or perhaps Ronald McDonald, the lovable clown. Human rights probably would be far down the list.

However, McDonald's, like other global companies, has faced increased scrutiny about the way its employees are treated. McDonald's estimates that one in eight Americans has worked for the fast-food giant. Public figures such as Sharon Stone, Jay Leno, Shania Twain, Rachel McAdams, and Pink have been employed at McDonald's.

Fast-food work is not well paid, and it sometimes places employees in uncomfortable and stressful situations. In one recent case, a McDonald's franchise owner in Pennsylvania faced charges for requiring his foreign workers to live in expensive company-owned housing while underpaying them.[12]

In response to the increased scrutiny, the McDonald's corporation recently issued a report on the sustainability and corporate responsibility of its businesses.[13] The

McDonald's corporation operates approximately 35,000 restaurants worldwide. Of these, 80 percent are owned by independent businesses or franchisees. This means that McDonald's has only indirect control over the majority of its restaurants. Yet the company has put in place a number of managerial controls designed to help ensure that all McDonald's employees are treated humanely and fairly.[14]

For example, McDonald's has hired a global chief compliance officer to ensure that its businesses comply with local and international regulations regarding the treatment of employees. This officer maintains a staff that travels to stores throughout the world to interview employees and ensure that each restaurant is complying with the standards the company has developed. McDonald's also conducts training on humane treatment of employees. Finally, McDonald's maintains a hotline for employees to report instances of mistreatment. To ensure that employees are not afraid to report violations, the company has a "nonretaliation policy" that protects employees from retaliation by management.[15]

McDonald's hopes that these policies and controls will ensure that its employees are treated well, and that any human rights violations will be quickly reported.

The Gilbreths

Two prominent followers of Taylor were Frank Gilbreth (1868–1924) and Lillian Gilbreth (1878–1972), who refined Taylor's analysis of work movements and made many contributions to time-and-motion study.[16] Their aims were to (1) analyze every individual action necessary to perform a particular task and break it into each of its component actions, (2) find better ways to perform each component action, and (3) reorganize each of the component actions so that the action as a whole could be performed more efficiently—at less cost in time and effort.

The Gilbreths often filmed a worker performing a particular task and then separated the task actions, frame by frame, into their component movements. Their goal was to maximize the efficiency with which each individual task was performed so that gains across tasks would add up to enormous savings of time and effort. Their attempts to develop improved management principles were captured—at times quite humorously—in the movie *Cheaper by the Dozen,* a new version of which appeared in 2004, which depicts how the Gilbreths (with their 12 children) tried to live their own lives according to these efficiency principles and apply them to daily actions such as shaving, cooking, and even raising a family.[17]

Eventually the Gilbreths became increasingly interested in the study of fatigue. They studied how physical characteristics of the workplace contribute to job stress that often leads to fatigue and thus poor performance. They isolated factors that result in worker fatigue, such as lighting, heating, the color of walls, and the design of tools and machines. Their pioneering studies paved the way for new advances in management theory.

In workshops and factories, the work of the Gilbreths, Taylor, and many others had a major effect on the practice of management. In comparison with the old crafts system, jobs in the new system were more repetitive, boring, and monotonous as a result of the application of scientific management principles, and workers became increasingly dissatisfied. Frequently the management of work settings became a game between workers and managers: Managers tried to initiate work practices to increase performance, and workers tried to hide the true potential efficiency of the work setting to protect their own well-being.[18] The story of how Rockefeller built Standard Oil is another illustration of the same kind of management thinking (see the accompanying "Manager as a Person" feature).

This scene from *Cheaper by the Dozen* illustrates how "efficient families," such as the Gilbreths, use formal family courts to solve problems of assigning chores to different family members and to solve disputes when they arise.

John D. Rockefeller

On July 8, 1839, John D. Rockefeller was born. As a child, he showed an aptitude for finance. He earned money doing odd jobs, and he was able to save $50. Then, instead of spending the money, Rockefeller lent it to a farmer at a 7 percent interest rate.[19] This transaction was the beginning of Rockefeller's career.

In 1855, at the age of 16, Rockefeller attended Folsom's Commercial College, where he studied accounting and banking, among other subjects. That same year, he began seeking work in Cleveland, Ohio, as a clerk or accountant.[20] Eventually he landed a job as an assistant bookkeeper.[21] Rockefeller's mathematical ability and conscientiousness soon gained him additional responsibilities at his company. This included helping manage the company's supply chain and attempting to optimize the profit from moving freight.

At the age of 19, Rockefeller created a commodities partnership with Maurice Clark. The American Civil War began in 1861, and prices and demand for commodities soared. Rockefeller's exposure to rail shipping showed him the potential of railroads as a mode of transferring freight, and the importance of petroleum as a commodity. In 1862 Rockefeller entered the industry for which he would become famous: oil refining. As he learned the business, he devoted a significant amount of energy to increasing the efficiency of his refineries.

In February 1865 Rockefeller bought out his partners and then hired his brother, William, to help manage the operation, which he called the "Standard Works." He set up his business so that the refinery increased the scope and efficiency of production to develop and maintain economies of scale.[22]

In 1870 Rockefeller, along with his associates, founded the Standard Oil Company of Ohio.[23] At the time of its creation, the Standard Oil Company of Ohio serviced about 10 percent of the oil market. That same year, Rockefeller began implementing his vision to unite the area's oil producers and consolidate the industry. He handled negotiations with rival firms himself.

By 1872 Rockefeller had acquired nearly all the oil refineries in Cleveland. Inefficient operations were closed, while Rockefeller worked to improve the quality of the rest. By 1879, just eight years after its creation, Standard Oil had grown to managing almost 90 percent of the oil refining business. The business would make Rockefeller among the wealthiest men of his day. In response, Rockefeller gave most of his fortune away to charitable groups before his death.[24]

Administrative Management Theory

LO2-3

Identify the principles of administration and organization that underlie effective organizations.

administrative management The study of how to create an organizational structure and control system that leads to high efficiency and effectiveness.

Side by side with scientific managers like Rockefeller studying the person–technology mix to increase efficiency, other managers and researchers were focusing on **administrative management**, the study of how to create an organizational structure and control system that leads to high efficiency and effectiveness. *Organizational structure* is the system of task and authority relationships that controls how employees use resources to achieve the organization's goals. Two of the most influential early views regarding the creation of efficient systems of organizational administration were developed in Europe: Max Weber, a German sociology professor, developed one theory; and Henri Fayol, the French manager who developed the model of management introduced in Chapter 1, developed the other.

The Theory of Bureaucracy

Max Weber (1864–1920) wrote at the turn of the 20th century, when Germany was undergoing its industrial revolution.[25] To help Germany manage its growing industrial enterprises while it was striving to become a world power, Weber developed the principles of

Figure 2.2
Weber's Principles of Bureaucracy

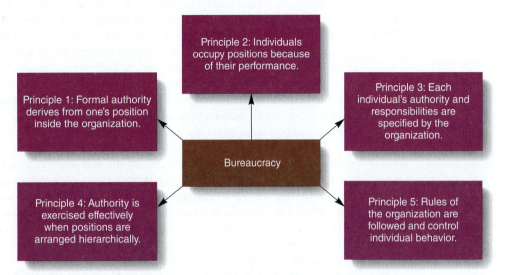

Principle 2: Individuals occupy positions because of their performance.

Principle 1: Formal authority derives from one's position inside the organization.

Principle 3: Each individual's authority and responsibilities are specified by the organization.

Bureaucracy

Principle 4: Authority is exercised effectively when positions are arranged hierarchically.

Principle 5: Rules of the organization are followed and control individual behavior.

bureaucracy A formal system of organization and administration designed to ensure efficiency and effectiveness.

authority The power to hold people accountable for their actions and to make decisions concerning the use of organizational resources.

bureaucracy—a formal system of organization and administration designed to ensure efficiency and effectiveness. A bureaucratic system of administration is based on the five principles summarized in Figure 2.2:

- Principle 1: *In a bureaucracy, a manager's formal authority derives from the position he or she holds in the organization.*

Authority is the power to hold people accountable for their actions and to make decisions concerning the use of organizational resources. Authority gives managers the right to direct and control their subordinates' behavior to achieve organizational goals. In a bureaucratic system of administration, obedience is owed to a manager not because of any personal qualities—such as personality, wealth, or social status—but because the manager occupies a position that is associated with a certain level of authority and responsibility.[26]

- Principle 2: *In a bureaucracy, people should occupy positions because of their performance, not because of their social standing or personal contacts.*

This principle was not always followed in Weber's time and is often ignored today. Some organizations and industries are still affected by social networks in which personal contacts and relations, not job-related skills, influence hiring and promotional decisions.

- Principle 3: *The extent of each position's formal authority and task responsibilities, and its relationship to other positions in an organization, should be clearly specified.*

When the tasks and authority associated with various positions in the organization are clearly specified, managers and workers know what is expected of them and what to expect from each other. Moreover, an organization can hold all its employees strictly accountable for their actions when they know their exact responsibilities.

- Principle 4: *Authority can be exercised effectively in an organization when positions are arranged hierarchically, so employees know whom to report to and who reports to them.*[27]

Managers must create an organizational hierarchy of authority that makes it clear who reports to whom and to whom managers and workers should go if conflicts or problems arise. This principle is especially important in the armed forces, FBI, CIA, and other organizations that deal with sensitive issues involving possible major repercussions. It is vital that managers at high levels of the hierarchy be able to hold subordinates accountable for their actions.

Max Weber developed the principles of bureaucracy during Germany's burgeoning industrial revolution to help organizations increase their efficiency and effectiveness.

- Principle 5: *Managers must create a well-defined system of rules, standard operating procedures, and norms so they can effectively control behavior within an organization.*

rules Formal written instructions that specify actions to be taken under different circumstances to achieve specific goals.

standard operating procedures (SOPs) Specific sets of written instructions about how to perform a certain aspect of a task.

norms Unwritten, informal codes of conduct that prescribe how people should act in particular situations and are considered important by most members of a group or organization.

Rules are formal written instructions that specify actions to be taken under different circumstances to achieve specific goals (for example, if A happens, do B). **Standard operating procedures (SOPs)** are specific sets of written instructions about how to perform a certain aspect of a task. A rule might state that at the end of the workday employees are to leave their machines in good order, and a set of SOPs would specify exactly how they should do so, itemizing which machine parts must be oiled or replaced. **Norms** are unwritten, informal codes of conduct that prescribe how people should act in particular situations and are considered important by most members of a group or organization. For example, an organizational norm in a restaurant might be that waiters should help each other if time permits.

Rules, SOPs, and norms provide behavioral guidelines that increase the performance of a bureaucratic system because they specify the best ways to accomplish organizational tasks. Companies such as McDonald's and Walmart have developed extensive rules and procedures to specify the behaviors required of their employees, such as "Always greet the customer with a smile." For example, Walmart, the world's largest retailer, automatically tracks inventory levels of products at its stores. When inventory is too low, the retailer sends an automatic request to a supplier to purchase an item and have it shipped. These items are then routed as efficiently as possible to the store where they are needed. Thus Walmart incorporates bureaucratic controls in its operations to make employees as efficient as possible.[28]

Weber believed organizations that implement all five principles establish a bureaucratic system that improves organizational performance. The specification of positions and the use of rules and SOPs to regulate how tasks are performed make it easier for managers to organize and control the work of subordinates. Similarly, fair and equitable selection and promotion systems improve managers' feelings of security, reduce stress, and encourage organizational members to act ethically and further promote the interests of the organization.[29]

If bureaucracies are not managed well, however, many problems can result. Sometimes managers allow rules and SOPs, "bureaucratic red tape," to become so cumbersome that decision making is slow and inefficient and organizations cannot change. When managers rely too much on rules to solve problems and not enough on their own skills and judgment, their behavior becomes inflexible. A key challenge for managers is to use bureaucratic principles to benefit, rather than harm, an organization.

Fayol's Principles of Management

Henri Fayol (1841–1925) was the CEO of Comambault Mining. Working at the same time as Weber, but independently, Fayol identified 14 principles (summarized in Table 2.1) that he believed essential to increase the efficiency of the management process.[30] We discuss these principles in detail here because, although they were developed at the turn of the 20th century, they remain the bedrock on which much of recent management theory and research is based. In fact, as the "Management Insight" feature following this discussion suggests, modern writers such as well-known management guru Jim Collins continue to extol these principles.

DIVISION OF LABOR   A champion of job specialization and the division of labor for reasons already mentioned, Fayol was nevertheless among the first to point out the downside of too much specialization: boredom—a state of mind likely to diminish product quality, worker initiative, and flexibility. As a result, Fayol advocated that workers be given more job duties to perform or be encouraged to assume more responsibility for work outcomes—a principle increasingly applied today in organizations that empower their workers. Modern grocery stores like Publix use division of labor in their operations. For example, in the bakery and deli, employees focus on creating cakes, pies, and ready-to-eat meals. In the meat section, a butcher provides fresh cuts of poultry and beef. In the produce section, workers place fresh vegetables and fruits. Shelf stockers ensure that store shelves have the products customers want. Finally, customer service employees help customers bag, purchase, and carry groceries out to their automobiles. By using division of labor, Publix employees are able to develop expertise they might not otherwise gain.[31]

Table 2.1
Fayol's 14 Principles of Management

Division of labor Job specialization and the division of labor should increase efficiency, especially if managers take steps to lessen workers' boredom.

Authority and responsibility Managers have the right to give orders and the power to exhort subordinates for obedience.

Unity of command An employee should receive orders from only one superior.

Line of authority The length of the chain of command that extends from the top to the bottom of an organization should be limited.

Centralization Authority should not be concentrated at the top of the chain of command.

Unity of direction The organization should have a single plan of action to guide managers and workers.

Equity All organizational members are entitled to be treated with justice and respect.

Order The arrangement of organizational positions should maximize organizational efficiency and provide employees with satisfying career opportunities.

Initiative Managers should allow employees to be innovative and creative.

Discipline Managers need to create a workforce that strives to achieve organizational goals.

Remuneration of personnel The system that managers use to reward employees should be equitable for both employees and the organization.

Stability of tenure of personnel Long-term employees develop skills that can improve organizational efficiency.

Subordination of individual interests to the common interest Employees should understand how their performance affects the performance of the whole organization.

Esprit de corps Managers should encourage the development of shared feelings of comradeship, enthusiasm, or devotion to a common cause.

AUTHORITY AND RESPONSIBILITY Like Weber, Fayol emphasized the importance of authority and responsibility. Fayol, however, went beyond Weber's formal authority, which derives from a manager's position in the hierarchy, to recognize the *informal* authority that derives from personal expertise, technical knowledge, moral worth, and the ability to lead and to generate commitment from subordinates. (The study of authority is the subject of recent research into leadership, discussed in Chapter 14.)

unity of command A reporting relationship in which an employee receives orders from, and reports to, only one superior.

UNITY OF COMMAND The principle of **unity of command** specifies that an employee should receive orders from, and report to, only one superior. Fayol believed that *dual command,* the reporting relationship that exists when two supervisors give orders to the same subordinate, should be avoided except in exceptional circumstances. Dual command confuses subordinates, undermines order and discipline, and creates havoc within the formal hierarchy of authority. Assessing any manager's authority and responsibility in a system of dual command is difficult, and the manager who is bypassed feels slighted and angry and may be uncooperative in the future. For example, the U.S. Army maintains unity of command for its soldiers. Clearly defined ranks range from private to five-star general, and each soldier answers to a commanding officer with a higher rank. While operating in the field, it is critical that soldiers understand their objectives, and consistent unity of command enables each soldier to know exactly whom he or she should follow to get the job done.[32]

line of authority The chain of command extending from the top to the bottom of an organization.

LINE OF AUTHORITY The **line of authority** is the chain of command extending from the top to the bottom of an organization. Fayol was one of the first management theorists to point out the importance of limiting the length of the chain of command by controlling the number of levels in the managerial hierarchy. The more levels in the hierarchy, the longer communication takes between managers at the top and bottom and the slower the pace of planning and organizing. Restricting the number of hierarchical levels to lessen these communication problems lets an organization act quickly and flexibly; this is one reason for the recent trend toward restructuring (discussed in Chapter 1).

Fayol also pointed out that when organizations are split into different departments or functions, each with its own hierarchy, it is important to allow middle and first-line managers in each department to interact with managers at similar levels in other departments. This interaction helps speed decision making because managers know each other and know whom to go to when problems arise. For cross-departmental integration to work, Fayol noted the importance of keeping one's superiors informed about what is taking place so that lower-level decisions do not harm activities taking place in other parts of the organization. One alternative to cross-departmental integration is to create cross-departmental teams controlled by a team leader (see Chapter 1).

CENTRALIZATION   Fayol also was one of the first management writers to focus on **centralization**, the concentration of authority at the top of the managerial hierarchy. Fayol believed authority should not be concentrated at the top of the chain of command. One of the most significant issues that top managers face is how much authority to centralize at the top of the organization and what authority to decentralize to managers and workers at lower hierarchical levels. This important issue affects the behavior of people at all levels in the organization.

If authority is very centralized, only managers at the top make important decisions and subordinates simply follow orders. This arrangement gives top managers great control over organizational activities and helps ensure that the organization is pursuing its strategy, but it makes it difficult for the people who are closest to problems and issues to respond to them in a timely manner. It also can reduce the motivation of middle and first-line managers and make them less flexible and adaptable because they become reluctant to make decisions on their own, even when doing so is necessary. They get used to passing the buck. The pendulum is now swinging toward decentralization as organizations seek to empower middle managers and create self-managed teams that monitor and control their own activities both to increase organizational flexibility and to reduce operating costs and increase efficiency. The U.S. Department of State is responsible for maintaining diplomatic relations between America and nearly 180 other nations. Although the Department of State operates embassies and consulates throughout the world, the Secretary of State is based at its headquarters in Washington, DC, so that major policy decisions are centralized.[33]

UNITY OF DIRECTION   Just as there is a need for unity of command, there is also a need for **unity of direction**, the singleness of purpose that makes possible the creation of one plan of action to guide managers and workers as they use organizational resources. An organization without a single guiding plan becomes inefficient and ineffective; its activities become unfocused, and individuals and groups work at cross-purposes. Successful planning starts with top managers working as a team to craft the organization's strategy, which they communicate to middle managers, who decide how to use organizational resources to implement the strategy.

EQUITY   As Fayol wrote, "For personnel to be encouraged to carry out their duties with all the devotion and loyalty of which they are capable, they must be treated with respect for their own sense of integrity, and equity results from the combination of respect and justice."[34] **Equity**—the justice, impartiality, and fairness to which all organizational members are entitled—is receiving much attention today; the desire to treat employees fairly is a primary concern of managers. (Equity theory is discussed in Chapter 13.)

ORDER   Like Taylor and the Gilbreths, Fayol was interested in analyzing jobs, positions, and individuals to ensure that the organization was using resources as efficiently as possible. To Fayol, **order** meant the methodical arrangement of positions to provide the organization with the greatest benefit and to provide employees with career opportunities that satisfy their needs. Thus Fayol recommended the use of organizational charts to show the position and duties of each employee and to indicate which positions an employee might move to or be promoted into in the future. He also advocated that managers engage in extensive career

centralization The concentration of authority at the top of the managerial hierarchy.

unity of direction The singleness of purpose that makes possible the creation of one plan of action to guide managers and workers as they use organizational resources.

equity The justice, impartiality, and fairness to which all organizational members are entitled.

order The methodical arrangement of positions to provide the organization with the greatest benefit and to provide employees with career opportunities.

planning to help ensure orderly career paths. Career planning is of primary interest today as organizations increase the resources they are willing to devote to training and developing their workforces.

INITIATIVE   Although order and equity are important means to fostering commitment and loyalty among employees, Fayol believed managers must also encourage employees to exercise **initiative**, the ability to act on their own without direction from a superior. Used properly, initiative can be a major source of strength for an organization because it leads to creativity and innovation. Managers need skill and tact to achieve the difficult balance between the organization's need for order and employees' desire for initiative. Fayol believed the ability to strike this balance was a key indicator of a superior manager.

initiative The ability to act on one's own without direction from a superior.

DISCIPLINE   In focusing on the importance of **discipline**—obedience, energy, application, and other outward marks of respect for a superior's authority—Fayol was addressing the concern of many early managers: how to create a workforce that was reliable and hardworking and would strive to achieve organizational goals. According to Fayol, discipline results in respectful relations between organizational members and reflects the quality of an organization's leadership and a manager's ability to act fairly and equitably.

discipline Obedience, energy, application, and other outward marks of respect for a superior's authority.

REMUNERATION OF PERSONNEL   Fayol proposed reward systems including bonuses and profit-sharing plans, which are increasingly used today as organizations seek improved ways to motivate employees. Convinced from his own experience that an organization's payment system has important implications for organizational success, Fayol believed effective reward systems should be equitable for both employees and the organization, encourage productivity by rewarding well-directed effort, not be subject to abuse, and be uniformly applied to employees. PayScale Incorporated is a company dedicated to helping its clients effectively compensate their employees. The company works with highly competitive IT customers to track employee performance and effectively reward talent, increasing employee morale and productivity while reducing employee attrition.[35]

STABILITY OF TENURE OF PERSONNEL   Fayol also recognized the importance of long-term employment, and this idea has been echoed by contemporary management gurus such as Tom Peters, Jeff Pfeffer, and Jim Collins. When employees stay with an organization for extended periods, they develop skills that improve the organization's ability to use its resources.

SUBORDINATION OF INDIVIDUAL INTERESTS TO THE COMMON INTEREST
The interests of the organization as a whole must take precedence over the interests of any individual or group if the organization is to survive. Equitable agreements must be established between the organization and its members to ensure that employees are treated fairly and rewarded for their performance and to maintain the disciplined organizational relationships so vital to an efficient system of administration.

ESPRIT DE CORPS   As this discussion of Fayol's ideas suggests, the appropriate design of an organization's hierarchy of authority and the right mix of order and discipline foster cooperation and commitment. Likewise, a key element in a successful organization is the development of **esprit de corps**, a French expression that refers to shared feelings of comradeship, enthusiasm, or devotion to a common cause among members of a group. Esprit de corps can result when managers encourage personal, verbal contact between managers and workers and encourage communication to solve problems and implement solutions. (Today the term *organizational culture* is used to refer to these shared feelings; this concept is discussed at length in Chapter 3.)

esprit de corps Shared feelings of comradeship, enthusiasm, or devotion to a common cause among members of a group.

Some of the principles that Fayol outlined have faded from contemporary management practices, but most have endured. The characteristics of successful organizations that Jim Collins presents in his best-selling book *Good to Great* (2001) are discussed in the following "Management Insight."

Management Insight

Jim Collins: *Good to Great*

In his book *Good to Great,* Jim Collins, noted consultant and business coach, reports on a case study of firms with exemplary performance. He is seeking to shed light on the factors that contributed to these firms' rise to excellence.[36] Collins says that several principles predict a firm's success.[37]

The first is that of Level 5 leadership. These leaders possess great humility but also an intense professional will. Although Level 5 leadership is applicable to all levels of the organization, Collins proposes that its application only by top managers is enough to raise an organization from mediocrity to greatness.

Second, Collins argues that having the right people in place is more important than establishing the values and strategy of the firm. Firms should focus on hiring the right people, and getting rid of the wrong people, to move firms in an upward trajectory.

Third, Collins says that confrontation and conflict are important drivers of decision success. Thus it is critical for managers to establish a climate of trust where information can be readily shared. Furthermore, Collins asserts that attempting to motivate others is wrong because the right employees will be self-motivated—rewards may actually be counterproductive.

Fourth, Collins argues for the Hedgehog Principle, which says that companies should stick to what they know; companies should do what they can excel at, make money at, and be passionate about. Fifth, Collins says that great companies are disciplined companies. Here *discipline* means adhering to only those opportunities that accommodate the Hedgehog Principle. Opportunities that violate the Hedgehog Principle should be avoided.

Sixth, *Good to Great* proposes that great companies do not chase technological fads, but instead seek incremental improvements in technology that complement core businesses. According to Collins, great companies pursue incremental change and improvement instead of radical change.

LO2-4

Trace the changes in theories about how managers should behave to motivate and control employees.

As this insight into contemporary management suggests, the basic concerns that motivated Fayol continue to inspire management theorists.[38] The principles that Fayol and Weber set forth still provide clear and appropriate guidelines that managers can use to create a work setting that efficiently and effectively uses organizational resources. These principles remain the bedrock of modern management theory; recent researchers have refined or developed them to suit modern conditions. For example, Weber's and Fayol's concerns for equity and for establishing appropriate links between performance and reward are central themes in contemporary theories of motivation and leadership.

Behavioral Management Theory

Because the writings of Weber and Fayol were not translated into English and published in the United States until the late 1940s, American management theorists in the first half of the 20th century were unaware of the contributions of these European pioneers. American management theorists began where Taylor and his followers left off. Although their writings were different, these theorists all espoused a theme that focused on **behavioral management**, the study of how managers should personally behave to motivate employees and encourage them to perform at high levels and be committed to achieving organizational goals.

behavioral management The study of how managers should behave to motivate employees and encourage them to perform at high levels and be committed to the achievement of organizational goals.

The Work of Mary Parker Follett

If F. W. Taylor is considered the father of management thought, Mary Parker Follett (1868–1933) serves as its mother.[39] Much of her writing about management and about the way managers should behave toward workers was a response to her concern that Taylor was

Mary Parker Follett, an early management thinker who advocated, "Authority should go with knowledge . . . whether it is up the line or down."

ignoring the human side of the organization. She pointed out that management often overlooks the multitude of ways in which employees can contribute to the organization when managers allow them to participate and exercise initiative in their everyday work lives.[40] Taylor, for example, never proposed that managers should involve workers in analyzing their jobs to identify better ways to perform tasks or should even ask workers how they felt about their jobs. Instead he used time-and-motion experts to analyze workers' jobs for them. Follett, in contrast, argued that because workers know the most about their jobs, they should be involved in job analysis and managers should allow them to participate in the work development process.

Follett proposed that "authority should go with knowledge . . . whether it is up the line or down." In other words, if workers have the relevant knowledge, then workers, rather than managers, should be in control of the work process itself, and managers should behave as coaches and facilitators—not as monitors and supervisors. In making this statement, Follett anticipated the current interest in self-managed teams and empowerment. She also recognized the importance of having managers in different departments communicate directly with each other to speed decision making. She advocated what she called "cross-functioning": members of different departments working together in cross-departmental teams to accomplish projects—an approach that is increasingly used today.[41]

Fayol also mentioned expertise and knowledge as important sources of managers' authority, but Follett went further. She proposed that knowledge and expertise, and not managers' formal authority deriving from their position in the hierarchy, should decide who will lead at any particular moment. She believed, as do many management theorists today, that power is fluid and should flow to the person who can best help the organization achieve its goals. Follett took a horizontal view of power and authority, in contrast to Fayol, who saw the formal line of authority and vertical chain of command as being most essential to effective management. Follett's behavioral approach to management was very radical for its time.

The Hawthorne Studies and Human Relations

Probably because of its radical nature, Follett's work was unappreciated by managers and researchers until quite recently. Most continued to follow in the footsteps of Taylor and the Gilbreths. To increase efficiency, they studied ways to improve various characteristics of the work setting, such as job specialization or the kinds of tools workers used. One series of studies was conducted from 1924 to 1932 at the Hawthorne Works of the Western Electric Company.[42] This research, now known as the *Hawthorne studies,* began as an attempt to investigate how characteristics of the work setting—specifically the level of lighting or illumination—affect worker fatigue and performance. The researchers conducted an experiment in which they systematically measured worker productivity at various levels of illumination.

The experiment produced some unexpected results. The researchers found that regardless of whether they raised or lowered the level of illumination, productivity increased. In fact, productivity began to fall only when the level of illumination dropped to the level of moonlight—a level at which workers could presumably no longer see well enough to do their work efficiently.

The researchers found these results puzzling and invited a noted Harvard psychologist, Elton Mayo, to help them. Mayo proposed another series of experiments to solve the mystery. These experiments, known as the *relay assembly test experiments,* were designed to investigate the effects of other aspects of the work context on job performance, such as the effect of the number and length of rest periods and hours of work on fatigue and monotony.[43] The goal was to raise productivity.

During a two-year study of a small group of female workers, the researchers again observed that productivity increased over time, but the increases could not be solely attributed to the effects of changes in the work setting. Gradually the researchers discovered that, to some degree, the results they were obtaining were influenced by the fact that the researchers themselves had become part of the experiment. In other words, the presence of the researchers was affecting the results because the workers enjoyed receiving attention and being the subject of study and were willing to cooperate with the researchers to produce the results they believed the researchers desired.

Subsequently it was found that many other factors also influence worker behavior, and it was not clear what was actually influencing the Hawthorne workers' behavior. However, this particular effect—which became known as the Hawthorne effect—seemed to suggest that workers' attitudes toward their managers affect the level of workers' performance. In particular, the significant finding was that each manager's personal behavior or leadership approach can affect performance. This finding led many researchers to turn their attention to managerial behavior and leadership. If supervisors could be trained to behave in ways that would elicit cooperative behavior from their subordinates, productivity could be increased. From this view emerged the human relations movement, which advocates that supervisors be behaviorally trained to manage subordinates in ways that elicit their cooperation and increase their productivity.

The importance of behavioral or human relations training became even clearer to its supporters after another series of experiments—the *bank wiring room experiments*. In a study of workers making telephone switching equipment, researchers Elton Mayo and F. J. Roethlisberger discovered that the workers, as a group, had deliberately adopted a norm of output restriction to protect their jobs. Workers who violated this informal production norm were subjected to sanctions by other group members. Those who violated group performance norms and performed above the norm were called "ratebusters"; those who performed below the norm were called "chiselers."

The experimenters concluded that both types of workers threatened the group as a whole. Ratebusters threatened group members because they revealed to managers how fast the work could be done. Chiselers were looked down on because they were not doing their share of the work. Work group members disciplined both ratebusters and chiselers to create a pace of work that the workers (not the managers) thought was fair. Thus a work group's influence over output can be as great as the supervisors' influence. Because the work group can influence the behavior of its members, some management theorists argue that supervisors should be trained to behave in ways that gain the goodwill and cooperation of workers so that supervisors, not workers, control the level of work group performance.

One implication of the Hawthorne studies was that the behavior of managers and workers in the work setting is as important in explaining the level of performance as the technical aspects of the task. Managers must understand the workings of the informal organization, the system of behavioral rules and norms that emerge in a group, when they try to manage or change behavior in organizations. Many studies have found that as time passes, groups often develop elaborate procedures and norms that bond members together, allowing unified action either to cooperate with management to raise performance or to restrict output and thwart the attainment of organizational goals.[44] The Hawthorne studies demonstrated the importance of understanding how the feelings, thoughts, and behavior of work group members and managers affect performance. It was becoming increasingly clear to researchers that understanding behavior in organizations is a complex process that is critical to increasing performance.[45] Indeed, the increasing interest in the area of management known as organizational behavior, the study of the factors that have an impact on how individuals and groups respond to and act in organizations, dates from these early studies.

Theory X and Theory Y

Several studies after World War II revealed how assumptions about workers' attitudes and behavior affect managers' behavior. Perhaps the most influential approach was developed by Douglas McGregor. He proposed two sets of assumptions about how work attitudes and behaviors not only dominate the way managers think but also affect how they behave in organizations. McGregor named these two contrasting sets of assumptions *Theory X* and *Theory Y* (see Figure 2.3).[46]

THEORY X According to the assumptions of Theory X, the average worker is lazy, dislikes work, and will try to do as little as possible. Moreover, workers have little ambition and wish to avoid responsibility. Thus the manager's task is to counteract workers' natural

Hawthorne effect The finding that a manager's behavior or leadership approach can affect workers' level of performance.

human relations movement A management approach that advocates the idea that supervisors should receive behavioral training to manage subordinates in ways that elicit their cooperation and increase their productivity.

informal organization The system of behavioral rules and norms that emerge in a group.

organizational behavior The study of the factors that have an impact on how individuals and groups respond to and act in organizations.

Theory X A set of negative assumptions about workers that leads to the conclusion that a manager's task is to supervise workers closely and control their behavior.

Figure 2.3

Theory X versus Theory Y

THEORY X	THEORY Y
The average employee is lazy, dislikes work, and will try to do as little as possible.	Employees are not inherently lazy. Given the chance, employees will do what is good for the organization.
To ensure that employees work hard, managers should closely supervise employees.	To allow employees to work in the organization's interest, managers must create a work setting that provides opportunities for workers to exercise initiative and self-direction.
Managers should create strict work rules and implement a well-defined system of rewards and punishments to control employees.	Managers should decentralize authority to employees and make sure employees have the resources necessary to achieve organizational goals.

Source: From D. McGregor, The Human Side of Enterprise. Copyright © McGraw-Hill Companies, Inc. Reprinted with permission.

tendencies to avoid work. To keep workers' performance at a high level, the manager must supervise workers closely and control their behavior by means of "the carrot and stick"— rewards and punishments.

Managers who accept the assumptions of Theory X design and shape the work setting to maximize their control over workers' behaviors and minimize workers' control over the pace of work. These managers believe workers must be made to do what is necessary for the success of the organization, and they focus on developing rules, SOPs, and a well-defined system of rewards and punishments to control behavior. They see little point in giving workers autonomy to solve their own problems because they think the workforce neither expects nor desires cooperation. Theory X managers see their role as closely monitoring workers to ensure that they contribute to the production process and do not threaten product quality. Henry Ford, who closely supervised and managed his workforce, fits McGregor's description of a manager who holds Theory X assumptions.

THEORY Y   In contrast, **Theory Y** assumes that workers are not inherently lazy, do not naturally dislike work, and, if given the opportunity, will do what is good for the organization. According to Theory Y, the characteristics of the work setting determine whether workers consider work to be a source of satisfaction or punishment, and managers do not need to closely control workers' behavior to make them perform at a high level because workers exercise self-control when they are committed to organizational goals. The implication of Theory Y, according to McGregor, is that "the limits of collaboration in the organizational setting are not limits of human nature but of management's ingenuity in discovering how to realize the potential represented by its human resources."[47] It is the manager's task to create a work setting that encourages commitment to organizational goals and provides opportunities for workers to be imaginative and to exercise initiative and self-direction.

When managers design the organizational setting to reflect the assumptions about attitudes and behavior suggested by Theory Y, the characteristics of the organization are quite different from those of an organizational setting based on Theory X. Managers who believe workers are motivated to help the organization reach its goals can decentralize authority and give more control over the job to workers, both as individuals and in groups. In this setting, individuals and groups are still accountable for their activities; but the manager's role is not to control employees but to provide support and advice, to make sure employees have the resources they need to perform their jobs, and to evaluate them on their ability to help the organization meet its goals. Henri Fayol's approach to administration more closely reflects the assumptions of Theory Y rather than Theory X. Companies like 3M, Apple, and Google exemplify those that follow Theory Y and the principles embedded in the HP Way.

Theory Y A set of positive assumptions about workers that leads to the conclusion that a manager's task is to create a work setting that encourages commitment to organizational goals and provides opportunities for workers to be imaginative and to exercise initiative and self-direction.

Herb Kelleher, former CEO and chairman of Southwest Airlines, built a company known for customer service by following an open door policy and giving employees flexible job descriptions and significant discretion in interacting with customers.

Southwest Airlines has long been the darling of the airline industry, and Southwest's leadership cites their Theory Y culture as a driving force. Inspired by former CEO and Chairman Herb Kelleher, Southwest Airlines emphasizes a culture of fun, creativity, and camaraderie.[48] Southwest employees note how Kelleher maintained an open-door policy of contact, which enabled him to stay in touch with problems facing the airline and find solutions faster.

Employees have highly flexible job descriptions that enable them to chip in and help where needed. Unlike many of its competitors, which use highly regimented and formalized employee roles, Southwest employees are encouraged to help solve problems where they see them. Thus it's not uncommon to see a Southwest manager helping move passenger luggage into aircraft or check in passengers at a gate.

Southwest also gives its employees significant discretion, enabling them to solve problems quickly. In an industry dominated by tight schedules and narrow windows to resolve problems, these actions enable employees to serve customers better.

Finally, Southwest Airlines views its unions as partners rather than adversaries. It works with independent unions to ensure that employees are compensated and treated fairly, and routinely solicits input from its employees on how to improve operations.[49] As a result of this innovative culture dominated by Theory Y thinking, Southwest Airlines has become the most consistently profitable company among its American competitors.

Management Science Theory

LO2-5

Explain the contributions of management science to the efficient use of organizational resources.

management science theory An approach to management that uses rigorous quantitative techniques to help managers make maximum use of organizational resources.

Management science theory is a contemporary approach to management that focuses on the use of rigorous quantitative techniques to help managers make maximum use of organizational resources to produce goods and services. In essence, management science theory is a contemporary extension of scientific management, which, as developed by Taylor, also took a quantitative approach to measuring the worker–task mix to raise efficiency. There are many branches of management science; and IT, which is having a significant impact on all kinds of management practices, is affecting the tools managers use to make decisions.[50] Each branch of management science deals with a specific set of concerns:

- *Quantitative management* uses mathematical techniques—such as linear and nonlinear programming, modeling, simulation, queuing theory, and chaos theory—to help managers decide, for example, how much inventory to hold at different times of the year, where to locate a new factory, and how best to invest an organization's financial capital. IT offers managers new and improved ways of handling information so they can make more accurate assessments of the situation and better decisions.

- *Operations management* gives managers a set of techniques they can use to analyze any aspect of an organization's production system to increase efficiency. IT, through the Internet and through growing B2B networks, is transforming how managers acquire inputs and dispose of finished products.

- *Total quality management (TQM)* focuses on analyzing an organization's input, conversion, and output activities to increase product quality.[51] Once again, through sophisticated software packages and computer-controlled production, IT is changing how managers and employees think about the work process and ways of improving it.

- *Management information systems (MISs)* give managers information about events occurring inside the organization as well as in its external environment—information that is vital for effective decision making. IT gives managers access to more and better information and allows more managers at all levels to participate in the decision-making process.

All these subfields of management science, enhanced by sophisticated IT, provide tools and techniques that managers can use to help improve the quality of their decision making and increase efficiency and effectiveness. For example, Toyota applied management science theory with its "Toyota Production System" (TPS). The TPS emphasizes continuous improvement in quality and the reduction of waste through learning. TPS was a major catalyst for the "lean revolution" in global manufacturing, and manufacturing companies worldwide have embraced this philosophy and adapted it for their own operations.[52] We discuss many important developments in management science theory thoroughly in this book. In particular, Chapter 9, "Value Chain Management: Functional Strategies for Competitive Advantage," focuses on how to use operations management and TQM to improve quality, efficiency, and responsiveness to customers. And Chapter 18, "Using Advanced Information Technology to Increase Performance," describes the many ways managers use information systems and technologies to improve their planning, organizing, and controlling functions.

Organizational Environment Theory

LO2-6

Explain why the study of the external environment and its impact on an organization has become a central issue in management thought.

An important milestone in the history of management thought occurred when researchers went beyond the study of how managers can influence behavior within organizations to consider how managers control the organization's relationship with its external environment, or **organizational environment**—the set of forces and conditions that operate beyond an organization's boundaries but affect a manager's ability to acquire and utilize resources. Resources in the organizational environment include the raw materials and skilled people that an organization requires to produce goods and services, as well as the support of groups, including customers who buy these goods and services and provide the organization with financial resources. One way of determining the relative success of an organization is to consider how effective its managers are at obtaining scarce and valuable resources.[53] The importance of studying the environment became clear after the development of open-systems theory and contingency theory during the 1960s.

organizational environment The set of forces and conditions that operate beyond an organization's boundaries but affect a manager's ability to acquire and utilize resources.

open system A system that takes in resources from its external environment and converts them into goods and services that are then sent back to that environment for purchase by customers.

The Open-Systems View

One of the most influential views of how an organization is affected by its external environment was developed by Daniel Katz, Robert Kahn, and James Thompson in the 1960s.[54] These theorists viewed the organization as an **open system**—a system that takes in resources from its external environment and converts or transforms them into goods and services that are sent back to that environment, where they are bought by customers (see Figure 2.4).

At the *input stage* an organization acquires resources such as raw materials, money, and skilled workers to produce goods and services. Once the organization has gathered the necessary resources, conversion begins. At the *conversion stage* the organization's workforce, using appropriate tools, techniques, and machinery, transforms the inputs into outputs of finished goods and services such as cars, hamburgers, or flights to Hawaii. At the *output stage* the organization releases finished goods and services to its external environment, where customers purchase and use them to satisfy their needs. The money the organization obtains from the sales of its outputs allows the organization to acquire more resources so the cycle can begin again.

The system just described is said to be open because the organization draws from and interacts with the external environment in order to survive; in other words, the organization is open to its environment. A **closed system**, in contrast, is a self-contained system that is not affected by changes in its external environment. Organizations that operate as closed systems, that ignore the external environment, and that fail to acquire inputs are likely to experience **entropy**, which is the tendency of a closed system to lose its ability to control itself and thus to dissolve and disintegrate.

closed system A system that is self-contained and thus not affected by changes occurring in its external environment.

entropy The tendency of a closed system to lose its ability to control itself and thus to dissolve and disintegrate.

Management theorists can model the activities of most organizations by using the open-systems view. Manufacturing companies like Ford and General Electric, for example, buy inputs such as component parts, skilled and semiskilled labor, and robots and computer-controlled manufacturing equipment; then at the conversion stage they use their manufacturing

Figure 2.4

The Organization as an Open System

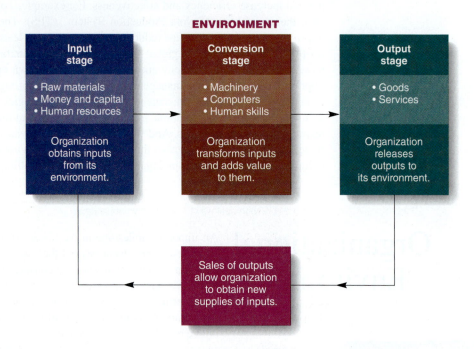

skills to assemble inputs into outputs of cars and appliances. As we discuss in later chapters, competition between organizations for resources is one of several major challenges to managing the organizational environment.

Researchers using the open-systems view are also interested in how the various parts of a system work together to promote efficiency and effectiveness. Systems theorists like to argue that the whole is greater than the sum of its parts; they mean that an organization performs at a higher level when its departments work together rather than separately. **Synergy**, the performance gains that result from the *combined* actions of individuals and departments, is possible only in an organized system. The recent interest in using teams combined or composed of people from different departments reflects systems theorists' interest in designing organizational systems to create synergy and thus increase efficiency and effectiveness.

synergy Performance gains that result when individuals and departments coordinate their actions.

Contingency Theory

contingency theory The idea that the organizational structures and control systems managers choose depend on (are contingent on) characteristics of the external environment in which the organization operates.

Another milestone in management theory was the development of **contingency theory** in the 1960s by Tom Burns and G. M. Stalker in Britain and Paul Lawrence and Jay Lorsch in the United States.[55] The crucial message of contingency theory is that *there is no one best way to organize:* The organizational structures and the control systems that managers choose depend on (are contingent on) characteristics of the external environment in which the organization operates. According to contingency theory, the characteristics of the environment affect an organization's ability to obtain resources; and to maximize the likelihood of gaining access to resources, managers must allow an organization's departments to organize and control their activities in ways most likely to allow them to obtain resources, given the constraints of the particular environment they face. In other words, how managers design the organizational hierarchy, choose a control system, and lead and motivate their employees is contingent on the characteristics of the organizational environment (see Figure 2.5).

An important characteristic of the external environment that affects an organization's ability to obtain resources is the degree to which the environment is changing. Changes in the organizational environment include changes in technology, which can lead to the creation of new products (such as Blu-ray discs) and result in the obsolescence of existing products (VHS tapes); the entry of new competitors (such as foreign organizations that compete for available resources); and unstable economic conditions. In general, the more quickly the organizational

Figure 2.5
Contingency Theory of Organizational Design

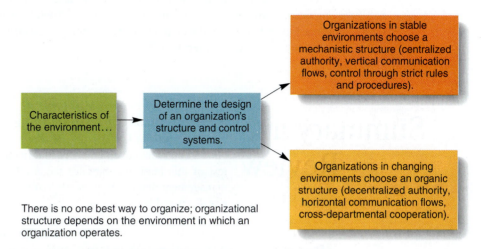

There is no one best way to organize; organizational structure depends on the environment in which an organization operates.

environment is changing, the greater are the problems associated with gaining access to resources, and the greater is managers' need to find ways to coordinate the activities of people in different departments to respond to the environment quickly and effectively.

MECHANISTIC AND ORGANIC STRUCTURES Drawing on Weber's and Fayol's principles of organization and management, Burns and Stalker proposed two basic ways in which managers can organize and control an organization's activities to respond to characteristics of its external environment: They can use a *mechanistic structure* or an *organic structure*.[56] As you will see, a mechanistic structure typically rests on Theory X assumptions, and an organic structure typically rests on Theory Y assumptions.

When the environment surrounding an organization is stable, managers tend to choose a mechanistic structure to organize and control activities and make employee behavior predictable. In a **mechanistic structure**, authority is centralized at the top of the managerial hierarchy, and the vertical hierarchy of authority is the main means used to control subordinates' behavior. Tasks and roles are clearly specified, subordinates are closely supervised, and the emphasis is on strict discipline and order. Everyone knows his or her place, and there is a place for everyone. A mechanistic structure provides the most efficient way to operate in a stable environment because it allows managers to obtain inputs at the lowest cost, giving an organization the most control over its conversion processes and enabling the most efficient production of goods and services with the smallest expenditure of resources. McDonald's restaurants operate with a mechanistic structure. Supervisors make all important decisions; employees are closely supervised and follow well-defined rules and standard operating procedures.

In contrast, when the environment is changing rapidly, it is difficult to obtain access to resources, and managers need to organize their activities in a way that allows them to cooperate, to act quickly to acquire resources (such as new types of inputs to produce new kinds of products), and to respond effectively to the unexpected. In an **organic structure**, authority is decentralized to middle and first-line managers to encourage them to take responsibility and act quickly to pursue scarce resources. Departments are encouraged to take a cross-departmental or functional perspective, and cross-functional teams composed of people from different departments are formed. As in Mary Parker Follett's model, the organization operates in an organic way because authority rests with the individuals, departments, and teams best positioned to control the current problems the organization is facing. As a result, managers in an organic structure can react more quickly to a changing environment than can managers in a mechanistic structure. However, an organic structure is generally more expensive to operate because it requires that more managerial time, money, and effort be spent on coordination. So it is used only when needed—when the organizational environment is unstable and rapidly changing.[57] Google, Apple, and IBM are examples of companies that operate with organic structures. For example, at Apple, all employees have the opportunity

mechanistic structure An organizational structure in which authority is centralized, tasks and rules are clearly specified, and employees are closely supervised.

organic structure An organizational structure in which authority is decentralized to middle and first-line managers and tasks and roles are left ambiguous to encourage employees to cooperate and respond quickly to the unexpected.

to provide and receive feedback from management, and even junior-level designers receive input from Apple executives. By employing an organic managerial structure, Apple is able to clarify exactly what is expected of employees and to ensure that its employees are making needed progress on the company's objectives. Apple's management is also able to stay abreast of technological developments and changing competitive conditions that bear on the company's products and services.[58]

Summary and Review

In this chapter we examined the evolution of management theory and research over the last century. Much of the material in the rest of this book stems from developments and refinements of this work. Indeed, the rest of this book incorporates the results of the extensive research in management that has been conducted since the development of the theories discussed here.

LO2-1, 2-2   SCIENTIFIC MANAGEMENT THEORY   The search for efficiency started with the study of how managers could improve person–task relationships to increase efficiency. The concept of job specialization and division of labor remains the basis for the design of work settings in modern organizations. New developments such as lean production and total quality management are often viewed as advances on the early scientific management principles developed by Taylor and the Gilbreths.

LO2-3   ADMINISTRATIVE MANAGEMENT THEORY   Max Weber and Henri Fayol outlined principles of bureaucracy and administration that are as relevant to managers today as they were when developed at the turn of the 20th century. Much of modern management research refines these principles to suit contemporary conditions. For example, the increasing interest in the use of cross-departmental teams and the empowerment of workers are issues that managers also faced a century ago.

LO2-4   BEHAVIORAL MANAGEMENT THEORY   Researchers have described many different approaches to managerial behavior, including Theories X and Y. Often the managerial behavior that researchers suggest reflects the context of their own historical eras and cultures. Mary Parker Follett advocated managerial behaviors that did not reflect accepted modes of managerial behavior at the time, and her work was largely ignored until conditions changed.

LO2-5   MANAGEMENT SCIENCE THEORY   The various branches of management science theory provide rigorous quantitative techniques that give managers more control over each organization's use of resources to produce goods and services.

LO2-6   ORGANIZATIONAL ENVIRONMENT THEORY   The importance of studying the organization's external environment became clear after the development of open-systems theory and contingency theory during the 1960s. A main focus of contemporary management research is to find methods to help managers improve how they use organizational resources and compete in the global environment. Strategic management and total quality management are two important approaches intended to help managers make better use of organizational resources.

Management in Action

Topics for Discussion and Action

Discussion

1. Choose a fast-food restaurant, a department store, or some other organization with which you are familiar, and describe the division of labor and job specialization it uses to produce goods and services. How might this division of labor be improved? **[LO2-1, 2-2]**

2. Apply Taylor's principles of scientific management to improve the performance of the organization you chose in topic 1. **[LO2-2]**

3. In what ways are Weber's and Fayol's ideas about bureaucracy and administration similar? How do they differ? **[LO2-3]**

4. Which of Weber's and Fayol's principles seem most relevant to the creation of an ethical organization? **[LO2-4, 2-6]**

5. How are companies using management science theory to improve their processes? Is this theory equally applicable for manufacturing and service companies? If so, how? **[LO2-4, 2-5]**

6. What is contingency theory? What kinds of organizations familiar to you have been successful or unsuccessful in dealing with contingencies from the external environment? **[LO2-6]**

7. Why are mechanistic and organic structures suited to different organizational environments? **[LO2-4, 2-6]**

Action

8. Question a manager about his or her views of the relative importance of Fayol's 14 principles of management. **[LO2-3, 2-4]**

9. Visit at least two organizations in your community, and identify those that seem to operate with a Theory X or a Theory Y approach to management. **[LO2-4]**

Building Management Skills

Managing Your Own Business [LO2-2, 2-4]

Now that you understand the concerns addressed by management thinkers over the last century, use this exercise to apply your knowledge to developing your management skills.

Imagine that you are the founding entrepreneur of a software company that specializes in developing games for home computers. Customer demand for your games has increased so much that over the last year your company has grown from a busy one-person operation to one with 16 employees. In addition to yourself, you employ six software developers to produce the software, three graphic artists, two computer technicians, two marketing and sales personnel, and two secretaries. In the next year you expect to hire 30 new employees, and you are wondering how best to manage your growing company.

1. Use the principles of Weber and Fayol to decide on the system of organization and management that you think will be most effective for your growing organization. How many levels will the managerial hierarchy of your organization have? How much authority will you decentralize to your subordinates? How will you establish the division of labor between subordinates? Will your subordinates work alone and report to you or work in teams?

2. Which management approach (for example, Theory X or Y) do you propose to use to run your organization? In 50 or fewer words write a statement describing the management approach you believe will motivate and coordinate your subordinates, and tell why you think this style will be best.

Managing Ethically [LO2-3, 2-4]

How Unethical Behavior Shut Down a Meatpacking Plant

By all appearances the Westland/Hallmark Meat Co. based in Chico, California, was considered to be an efficient and sanitary meatpacking plant. Under the control of its owner and CEO, Steven Mendell, the plant regularly passed inspections by the U.S. Dept. of Agriculture (USDA). Over 200 workers were employed to slaughter cattle and prepare the beef for shipment to fast-food restaurants such as Burger King and Taco Bell. Also, millions of pounds of meat the plant produced yearly were delivered under contract to one of the federal government's most coveted accounts: the National School Lunch Program.[59]

When the Humane Society turned over a videotape (secretly filmed by one of its investigators who had taken a job as a plant employee) to the San Bernardino County District Attorney showing major violations of health procedures, an uproar followed. The videotape showed two workers dragging sick cows up the ramp that led to the slaughterhouse using metal chains and forklifts, and shocking them with electric prods and shooting streams of water in their noses and faces. Not only did the tape show inhumane treatment of animals, but it also provided evidence that the company was flouting the ban on allowing sick animals to enter the food supply chain—something that federal regulations explicitly outlaw because of concerns for human health and safety.

Once the USDA was informed that potentially contaminated beef products had entered the supply chain—especially the one to the nation's schools—it issued a notice for the recall of the 143 million pounds of beef processed in the plant over the last two years, the largest recall in history. In addition, the plant was shut down as the investigation proceeded. CEO Steven Mendell was subpoenaed to appear before the House Panel on Energy and Commerce Committee. He denied that these violations had taken place and that diseased cows had entered the food chain. However, when panel members demanded that he view the videotape that he claimed he had not seen, he was forced to acknowledge that inhumane treatment of animals had occurred.[60] Moreover, federal investigators turned up evidence that as early as 1996 the plant had been cited for overuse of electric prods to speed cattle through the plant and had been cited for other violations since, suggesting that these abuses had been going on for a long period.

Not only were consumers and schoolchildren harmed by these unethical actions, but the plant itself was permanently shut down and all 220 workers lost their jobs. In addition, the employees directly implicated in the video were prosecuted and one, who pleaded guilty to animal abuse, was convicted and sentenced to six months' imprisonment.[61] Clearly, all the people and groups affected by the meatpacking plant have suffered from its unethical and inhumane organizational behaviors and practices.

Questions

1. Use the theories discussed in the chapter to debate the ethical issues involved in the way the Westland/Hallmark Meat Co. business operated.

2. Also use the theories to discuss the ethical issues involved in the way the meatpacking business is being conducted today.

3. Search the web for changes occurring in the meatpacking business.

Small Group Breakout Exercise [LO2-6]

Modeling an Open System

Form groups of three to five people, and appoint one group member as the spokesperson who will communicate your findings to the class when called on by the instructor. Then discuss the following scenario:

Think of an organization with which you are all familiar, such as a local restaurant, store, or bank. After choosing an organization, model it from an open-systems perspective. Identify its input, conversion, and output processes; and identify forces in the external environment that help or hurt the organization's ability to obtain resources and dispose of its goods or services.

Exploring the World Wide Web [LO2-3, 2-6]

Explore General Electric's corporate history (https://www.ge.com/about-us/history). Locate and read each module on the company's history, and then respond to the following questions:

1. What do you think precipitated General Electric's growth strategy based on merger and acquisition?

2. How were early acquisitions and mergers related to one another?

3. What challenges face General Electric's current leadership team?

Be the Manager [LO2-2, 2-4]

How to Manage a Hotel

You have been called in to advise the owners of an exclusive new luxury hotel. For the venture to succeed, hotel employees must focus on providing customers with the highest-quality customer service possible. The challenge is to devise a way of organizing and controlling employees that will promote high-quality service, that will encourage employees to be committed to the hotel, and that will reduce the level of employee turnover and absenteeism—which are typically high in the hotel business.

Questions

1. How do the various management theories discussed in this chapter offer clues for organizing and controlling hotel employees?

2. Which parts would be the most important for an effective system to organize and control employees?

The Wall Street Journal Case in the News [LO2-4, 2-6]

Deutsche Bank Found Inappropriate Communication between Staffer, Central Bank Salesperson Was Placed on Leave in March

A top Deutsche Bank saleswoman was placed on leave last month after the German bank found what it regarded as inappropriate communication between her and Singapore's central bank, according to a person familiar with the matter, marking a significant new twist in the yearlong global investigation into the currency market.

Kai Lew, a director of sales at Deutsche Bank in London tasked with handling central bank clients, was put on leave because the bank—the biggest currency dealer in the world—concluded that she had communicated improperly with the Monetary Authority of Singapore, or MAS, this person said.

She is one of roughly 30 employees at nine banks who have been fired or suspended as part of a burgeoning global investigation into possible manipulation of currency markets, and the first in sales rather than trading. At the time her suspension was first reported, March 31, the reasons for the move were unclear.

Lew couldn't be reached for comment. The MAS said it "does not comment on its dealings with individual financial institutions." Deutsche Bank said it "has received requests for information from regulatory authorities that are investigating trading in the foreign exchange market. The bank is

cooperating with those investigations, and will take disciplinary action with regards to individuals if merited."

The allegation makes the MAS the second central bank to be drawn into the case. The Bank of England last month said it had suspended a staff member and hired an outside law firm to perform an independent investigation into its employees' conduct.

The MAS itself is among a growing list of central banks and regulators that has said it is investigating potential manipulation of the foreign exchange markets. After finding Lew's communications with the MAS and deciding to put her on leave, Deutsche Bank executives called MAS officials to inform them of their findings, according to the person familiar with the matter.

The exact nature of Lew's communication with the MAS isn't clear. Traders from other banks have been disciplined in recent months for a variety of allegedly improper communication, primarily with traders at rival banks. The communication has ranged from sharing market-sensitive information to lewd banter, according to people familiar with the banks' findings.

Communication between bank employees and officials at central banks is common. Central banks rely on real-time intelligence from the financial industry to understand what is happening in the markets.

But with the global regulatory investigation into currency trading mushrooming and focusing in part on inappropriate sharing of information, some banks have started clamping down on that long-standing practice, industry officials say.

"The amount of information they [central banks] are getting from us has collapsed," said a senior executive at a large global bank.

By volume, central banks are typically small players in the currency market. The benchmark industry survey from the Bank for International Settlements last year noted that they contributed less than 1 percent of average daily trading volumes in April 2013.

Still, some bankers say central banks can command a special place in the market because of their dual role as an authority and a client.

"It starts with the fear factor," one banker said. "Are central banks even really clients? They regulate us as well as being clients. They can shut us down. They are special."

Central banks buy and sell currencies for a range of reasons, including direct intervention to weaken or strengthen their currencies under their monetary policy mandate, or trades on behalf of national pension funds or other stores of sovereign wealth. Most also monitor the market in their home currency in a regulatory capacity simply to check that market conditions are orderly.

This, bankers say, also muddies the usual relationship between a bank and its client. "We don't know if they are seeking to keep their currency steady or if they are rebalancing their official reserves," the banker said. "That puts traders and sales people in a potential conflict."

Source: Katie Martin, "Deutsche Bank Found Inappropriate Communication Between Staffer, Central Bank," *The Wall Street Journal,* April 9, 2014. Copyright © 2014 Dow Jones & Company, Inc. Reproduced with permission via Copyright Clearance Center.

Questions for Discussion

1. Under what conditions is it acceptable for a company to monitor its employees' communications?

2. How would you feel if your employer monitored your communications?

3. Are there alternatives to keeping such a close eye on employees? If so, what?

CHAPTER 3

Values, Attitudes, Emotions, and Culture: The Manager as a Person

Learning Objectives

After studying this chapter, you should be able to:

LO3-1 Describe the various personality traits that affect how managers think, feel, and behave.

LO3-2 Explain what values and attitudes are and describe their impact on managerial action.

LO3-3 Appreciate how moods and emotions influence all members of an organization.

LO3-4 Describe the nature of emotional intelligence and its role in management.

LO3-5 Define organizational culture and explain how managers both create and are influenced by organizational culture.

A MANAGER'S CHALLENGE

Jess Lee's Determination and Broad Interests Lead to the Top at Polyvore

What does it take to rise to the top in Silicon Valley? In her early thirties, Jess Lee's rise to the top at Polyvore, a fashion and style social commerce site and company, is a testament to her determination, hard work, persistence, broad interests, originality, and willingness to take risks. When she was growing up in Hong Kong, Lee loved to draw and thought she'd like to write and draw Japanese *manga* comics when she grew up (her "fun fact" on the Polyvore website notes that she likes to draw and has more than 1,000 comic books). Her parents had other ideas, and as an entrepreneur who operated a translation organization from their house, her mother instilled in her a sense of the value of being in charge of what you do.[1]

Lee attended Stanford University, where she received a degree in computer science. She had planned on becoming an engineer and had a job lined up when she received a phone call from a Google recruiter inviting her to interview for their associate product manager program. While interviewing at Google, Lee spoke with Marisa Mayer (who was an executive at Google prior to becoming president and CEO of Yahoo). Lee told Mayer she wasn't sure if she wanted to work at Google because she already had another offer and had planned to be an engineer. Mayer advised Lee to choose what she thought would be the most challenging position. Always up for a challenge, Lee decided to join Google and has not looked back since.[2]

As a product manager working on Google Maps, Lee realized that it was important for the engineers she worked with to hold her in high regard.[3] While her computer science background certainly helped, so did her

Jess Lee of Polyvore, a fashion and style social commerce website and company. Her ambition, hard work, and persistence, combined with dedication to users and employees, have helped make Polyvore one of the five best websites for one-stop online shopping.

hard work, determination, and persistence. While she was working at Google, one of her friends introduced her to the Polyvore website. With her love of art and fashion, Lee became hooked on the site, which enables users to build sets or collages of products from over 42 million images that typically combine clothing, fashion, and household goods into artistic compilations.[4] Spending an hour or two on the site each evening, Lee decided to let Polyvore's founders know that she liked the site but also give them suggestions for improvements and complaints and problems she had with the site. Her understanding , attention to detail, and close connection to Polyvore and its users made an impression on the founders, who suggested that perhaps she would like to correct all the problems she had uncovered as a Polyvore employee.[5] After a meeting for coffee, the deal was sealed and Lee became a product manager at Polyvore.[6]

Always open to new experiences, Lee engaged in all manner of tasks to help Polyvore create a great user experience, ranging from coding and management to sales. She also undertook a lot of responsibilities at Polyvore that she had never done before, providing challenges and opportunities for learning. In recognition of her dedication and contributions to Polyvore, the founders first decided to make Lee a cofounder and then decided to appoint her CEO.[7] Under her leadership, Polyvore became profitable. Although she is somewhat introverted, Lee has found her own leadership style that works well at Polyvore.[8]

Over 20 million people visit the Polyvore site each month, and the average purchase from a visit to the site is $220.[9] Polyvore earns revenue through affiliate advertising: All products on the site have links to pages where the products can be purchased, and when these links lead to sales, Polyvore receives affiliate fees.[10] Polyvore also earns revenues from native advertising.[11]

Three values are key to Polyvore's culture. One of these values, "delight the user," focuses on the user experience.[12] As a fan and dedicated user of Polyvore before she joined the firm, Lee knows how important the user experience is and seeks to provide users with outstanding products and make sure that they enjoy their time on the site. When users create sets, Polyvore collects information on how they use the site, the brands and styles they like, and how they put them together into sets. Another value, "do a few things well," speaks to Polyvore's approach of keeping everything simple.[13] By focusing on what is really important and doing it well while removing tangential activities, Polyvore focuses on high quality and attention to detail.[14]

A third value in Polyvore's culture, "make an impact," describes the sense of accomplishment that has always been important to Lee and that she encourages all employees to experience.[15] Each month an employee is named "employee of the month" and can spend $500 on something for the company or its employees such as a foosball table, a very large beanbag chair, or lunch for all employees from a food truck.[16]

An art lover herself, Lee prides herself on providing users with the technology and the site to express their own creativity through the sets they create. Using an analogy from painting, she suggests that Polyvore provides users with a blank canvas on which they can express their creativity.[17]

Time.com recently named Polyvore one of the five best sites for online shopping on a single site (in other words, one-stop shopping). More specifically, Polyvore was named "Best for Virtual Window Shopping" because users can see collections of products in sets created by other users as well as look through Polyvore's collection of products.[18]

Always open to new experiences and challenges, Lee sees Polyvore expanding beyond fashion, being available on more kinds of devices, and also expanding internationally. Her ambition, hard work, determination, and persistence, combined with her dedication to Polyvore's users and employees, show that Polyvore is in good hands as it seeks to expand.[19]

Overview

Like people everywhere, Jess Lee has her own distinctive personality, values, ways of viewing things, and personal challenges and disappointments. In this chapter we focus on the manager as a feeling, thinking human being. We start by describing enduring characteristics that influence how managers work and how they view other people, their organizations, and the world around them. We also discuss how managers' values, attitudes, and moods play out in organizations, shaping organizational culture. By the end of this chapter, you will appreciate how the personal characteristics of managers influence the process of management in general—and organizational culture in particular.

Enduring Characteristics: Personality Traits

personality traits Enduring tendencies to feel, think, and act in certain ways.

All people, including managers, have certain enduring characteristics that influence how they think, feel, and behave both on and off the job. These characteristics are **personality traits**: particular tendencies to feel, think, and act in certain ways that can be used to describe the personality of every individual. It is important to understand the personalities of managers because their personalities influence their behavior and their approach to managing people and resources.

Some managers are demanding, difficult to get along with, and highly critical of other people. Other managers may be as concerned about effectiveness and efficiency as highly critical managers but are easier to get along with, are likable, and frequently praise the people around them. Both management styles may produce excellent results, but their effects on employees are quite different. Do managers deliberately decide to adopt one or the other of these approaches to management? Although they may do so part of the time, in all likelihood their personalities account for their different approaches. Indeed, research suggests that the way people react to different conditions depends, in part, on their personalities.[20]

The Big Five Personality Traits

We can think of an individual's personality as being composed of five general traits or characteristics: extraversion, negative affectivity, agreeableness, conscientiousness, and openness to experience.[21] Researchers often consider these the Big Five personality traits.[22] Each of them can be viewed as a continuum along which every individual or, more specifically, every manager falls (see Figure 3.1).

Some managers may be at the high end of one trait continuum, others at the low end, and still others somewhere in between. An easy way to understand how these traits can affect a person's approach to management is to describe what people are like at the high and low ends of each trait continuum. As will become evident as you read about each trait, no single trait is

Figure 3.1

The Big Five Personality Traits

Managers' personalities can be described by determining which point on each of the following dimensions best characterizes the manager in question:

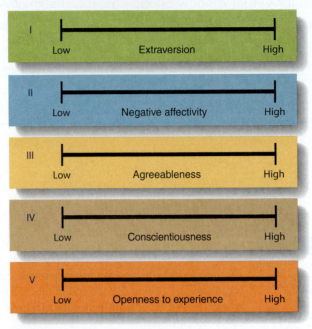

right or wrong for being an effective manager. Rather, effectiveness is determined by a complex interaction between the characteristics of managers (including personality traits) and the nature of the job and organization in which they are working. Moreover, personality traits that enhance managerial effectiveness in one situation may impair it in another.

EXTRAVERSION **Extraversion** is the tendency to experience positive emotions and moods and feel good about oneself and the rest of the world. Managers who are high on extraversion (often called *extraverts*) tend to be sociable, affectionate, outgoing, and friendly. Managers who are low on extraversion (often called *introverts*) tend to be less inclined toward social interactions and to have a less positive outlook. Being high on extraversion may be an asset for managers whose jobs entail especially high levels of social interaction. Managers who are low on extraversion may nevertheless be highly effective and efficient, especially when their jobs do not require much social interaction. Their quieter approach may enable them to accomplish quite a bit of work in limited time. See Figure 3.2 for an example of a scale that can be used to measure a person's level of extraversion.

extraversion The tendency to experience positive emotions and moods and to feel good about oneself and the rest of the world.

NEGATIVE AFFECTIVITY **Negative affectivity** is the tendency to experience negative emotions and moods, feel distressed, and be critical of oneself and others. Managers high on this trait may often feel angry and dissatisfied and complain about their own and others' lack of progress. Managers who are low on negative affectivity do not tend to experience many negative emotions and moods and are less pessimistic and critical of themselves and others. On the plus side, the critical approach of a manager high on negative affectivity may sometimes spur both the manager and others to improve their performance. Nevertheless, it is probably more pleasant to work with a manager who is low on negative affectivity; the better working relationships that such a manager is likely to cultivate also can be an important asset.

negative affectivity The tendency to experience negative emotions and moods, to feel distressed, and to be critical of oneself and others.

AGREEABLENESS **Agreeableness** is the tendency to get along well with others. Managers who are high on the agreeableness continuum are likable, tend to be affectionate, and care about other people. Managers who are low on agreeableness may be somewhat distrustful of others, unsympathetic, uncooperative, and even at times antagonistic. Being high on

agreeableness The tendency to get along well with other people.

Figure 3.2

Measures of Extraversion, Agreeableness, Conscientiousness, and Openness to Experience

Listed below are phrases describing people's behaviors. Please use the rating scale below to describe how accurately each statement describes *you*. Describe yourself as you generally are now, not as you wish to be in the future. Describe yourself as you honestly see yourself, in relation to other people you know of the same sex as you are and roughly your same age.

1	2	3	4	5
Very inaccurate	Moderately inaccurate	Neither inaccurate nor accurate	Moderately accurate	Very accurate

_____ **1.** Am interested in people.

_____ **2.** Have a rich vocabulary.

_____ **3.** Am always prepared.

_____ **4.** Am not really interested in others.*

_____ **5.** Leave my belongings around.*

_____ **6.** Am the life of the party.

_____ **7.** Have difficulty understanding abstract ideas.*

_____ **8.** Sympathize with others' feelings.

_____ **9.** Don't talk a lot.*

_____ **10.** Pay attention to details.

_____ **11.** Have a vivid imagination.

_____ **12.** Insult people.*

_____ **13.** Make a mess of things.*

_____ **14.** Feel comfortable around people.

_____ **15.** Am not interested in abstract ideas.*

_____ **16.** Have a soft heart.

_____ **17.** Get chores done right away.

_____ **18.** Keep in the background.*

_____ **19.** Have excellent ideas.

_____ **20.** Start conversations.

_____ **21.** Am not interested in other people's problems.*

_____ **22.** Often forget to put things back in their proper place.*

_____ **23.** Have little to say.*

_____ **24.** Do not have a good imagination.*

_____ **25.** Take time out for others.

_____ **26.** Like order.

_____ **27.** Talk to a lot of different people at parties.

_____ **28.** Am quick to understand things.

_____ **29.** Feel little concern for others.*

_____ **30.** Shirk my duties.*

_____ **31.** Don't like to draw attention to myself.*

_____ **32.** Use difficult words.

_____ **33.** Feel others' emotions.

_____ **34.** Follow a schedule.

_____ **35.** Spend time reflecting on things.

_____ **36.** Don't mind being the center of attention.

_____ **37.** Make people feel at ease.

_____ **38.** Am exacting in my work.

_____ **39.** Am quiet around strangers.*

_____ **40.** Am full of ideas.

* Item is reverse-scored: 1 = 5, 2 = 4, 4 = 2, 5 = 1
Scoring: Sum responses to items for an overall scale.
      Extraversion = sum of items 6, 9, 14, 18, 20, 23, 27, 31, 36, 39
      Agreeableness = sum of items 1, 4, 8, 12, 16, 21, 25, 29, 33, 37
      Conscientiousness = sum of items 3, 5, 10, 13, 17, 22, 26, 30, 34, 38
      Openness to experience = sum of items 2, 7, 11, 15, 19, 24, 28, 32, 35, 40

Source: L. R. Goldberg, Oregon Research sInstitute, http://ipip.ori.org/ipip/. Reprinted with permission.

agreeableness may be especially important for managers whose responsibilities require that they develop good, close relationships with others. Nevertheless, a low level of agreeableness may be an asset in managerial jobs that actually require that managers be antagonistic, such as drill sergeants and some other kinds of military managers. See Figure 3.2 for an example of a scale that measures a person's level of agreeableness.

conscientiousness The tendency to be careful, scrupulous, and persevering.

CONSCIENTIOUSNESS **Conscientiousness** is the tendency to be careful, scrupulous, and persevering.[23] Managers who are high on the conscientiousness continuum are organized and self-disciplined; those who are low on this trait might sometimes appear to lack direction and self-discipline. Conscientiousness has been found to be a good predictor of performance in many kinds of jobs, including managerial jobs in a variety of organizations.[24]

Entrepreneurs who found their own companies, like Jess Lee (a cofounder of Polyvore profiled in "A Manager's Challenge"), often are high on conscientiousness, and their persistence and determination help them to overcome obstacles and turn their ideas into successful new ventures. Figure 3.2 provides an example of a scale that measures conscientiousness.

openness to experience
The tendency to be original, have broad interests, be open to a wide range of stimuli, be daring, and take risks.

OPENNESS TO EXPERIENCE   Openness to experience is the tendency to be original, have broad interests, be open to a wide range of stimuli, be daring, and take risks.[25] Managers who are high on this trait continuum may be especially likely to take risks and be innovative in their planning and decision making. Jess Lee, discussed in this chapter's "A Manager's Challenge," has always been open to new challenges, learning opportunities, and things she hasn't done before—a testament to her high level of openness to experience. Managers who are low on openness to experience may be less prone to take risks and more conservative in their planning and decision making. In certain organizations and positions, this tendency might be an asset. The manager of the fiscal office in a public university, for example, must ensure that all university departments and units follow the university's rules and regulations pertaining to budgets, spending accounts, and reimbursements of expenses. Figure 3.2 provides an example of a measure of openness to experience.

Some successful entrepreneurs who start their own businesses are high on openness to experience and conscientiousness, which has contributed to their accomplishments as entrepreneurs and managers, as is true of Kevin Plank, founder, CEO, and chairman of the board of Under Armour.[26]

Manager as a Person

Kevin Plank's Openness to Experience and Conscientiousness Pay Off at Under Armour

When Kevin Plank was a walk-on fullback football player at the University of Maryland in the 1990s, he often became annoyed that his T-shirt was soaked and weighted down with sweat. Always an original thinker, he wondered why athletic apparel couldn't be make out of some kind of polyester blend that would help athletes' and sports aficionados' muscles stay cool while wicking away, and not holding, moisture from sweat.[27] As he was finishing his undergraduate studies at Maryland, he started experimenting with different fabrics, testing their durability, comfort, and water resistance with the help of a local tailor. A prototype of Under Armour's first product—the 0039 compression shirt—was developed.[28]

Upon graduation from the University of Maryland, Plank was offered a position at Prudential Life Insurance. An entrepreneur at heart willing to risk everything to pursue his bold ideas, Plank realized that accepting a secure position with an insurance company would have driven him nuts. So he turned down the Prudential offer and mustered his determination to sell his innovative T-shirt.[29] With little business training or experience, and a lot of perseverance and discipline, Plank pursued the makings of what would become a major competitor of Nike 16 years later with net revenues over $2.3 billion in 2013.[30] Entering and succeeding in the competitive sports apparel industry dominated by huge players like Nike with vast resources and a widely recognized brand would seem like an impossible feat even for a seasoned businessperson with access to capital. With around $20,000 in the bank and the resolve to turn his idea into a viable venture, Plank succeeded against all odds.[31]

Kevin Plank began by selling his innovative T-shirts from the trunk of his car. Under Armour is now a global company, producing and selling sports and fitness apparel, shoes, and accessories. His success demonstrates how taking risks, while also being determined and disciplined, can lead to success against tough odds.

Very outgoing and confident, Plank used his network of athletic contacts from playing on teams in high school, military school, and the University of Maryland to get the word out about the shirt.[32] From the various teams he had played on, he was familiar enough with around 40 NFL players to contact them and tell them about the shirt. Living out of his car with his trunk full of shirts, Plank drove around to training camps and schools to show athletes and managers his new product. Teaming up with two partners, Plank began running his business from the basement of his grandmother's house in the Georgetown area of Washington, DC, with the help of a $250,000 small business loan. As business and orders picked up, Under Armour outgrew the basement and set up shop on Sharp Street in Baltimore.[33] The rest has literally been history.

Under Armour currently produces and sells apparel, shoes, and accessories for women, men, and youth for athletics, sports, outdoor activities, and fitness.[34] Under Armour is a global company with 6,000 employees, operating in North America, Europe, the Middle East, Africa, Asia, and Latin America though most employees work in the United States.[35]

Under Armour is currently headquartered in what used to be the 400,000-square-foot Tide Point complex where Procter & Gamble used to manufacture detergent in Baltimore.[36] Some of the original names of the facilities like Joy and Cheer remain and seem aptly fit for a company like Under Armour.[37] Under Armour has made major contributions to help Baltimore's depressed economy, including employing over 2,000 people in the Baltimore area. Clearly Plank demonstrates that being original, daring, and taking risks while at the same time being highly determined, disciplined, and persevering can help managers and entrepreneurs succeed against tough odds. As Plank puts it, "There's an entrepreneur right now, scared to death . . . Get out of your garage and go take a chance, and start your business."[38]

Successful managers occupy a variety of positions on the Big Five personality trait continua. One highly effective manager may be high on extraversion and negative affectivity; another equally effective manager may be low on both these traits; and still another may be somewhere in between. Members of an organization must understand these differences among managers because they can shed light on how managers behave and on their approach to planning, leading, organizing, or controlling. If subordinates realize, for example, that their manager is low on extraversion, they will not feel slighted when their manager seems to be aloof because they will realize that by nature he or she is simply not outgoing.

Managers themselves also need to be aware of their own personality traits and the traits of others, including their subordinates and fellow managers. A manager who knows that he has a tendency to be highly critical of other people might try to tone down his negative approach. Similarly, a manager who realizes that her chronically complaining subordinate tends to be so negative because of his personality may take all his complaints with a grain of salt and realize that things probably are not as bad as this subordinate says they are.

In order for all members of an organization to work well together and with people outside the organization, such as customers and suppliers, they must understand each other. Such understanding comes, in part, from an appreciation of some fundamental ways in which people differ from one another—that is, an appreciation of personality traits.

Other Personality Traits That Affect Managerial Behavior

Many other specific traits in addition to the Big Five describe people's personalities. Here we look at traits that are particularly important for understanding managerial effectiveness: locus of control; self-esteem; and the needs for achievement, affiliation, and power.

internal locus of control
The tendency to locate responsibility for one's fate within oneself.

LOCUS OF CONTROL People differ in their views about how much control they have over what happens to and around them. The locus of control trait captures these beliefs.[39] People with an **internal locus of control** believe they themselves are responsible for their own fate; they see their own actions and behaviors as being major and decisive determinants of important outcomes such as attaining levels of job performance, being promoted, or being turned down for a choice job assignment. Some managers with an internal locus of control see the success of a whole organization resting on their shoulders. One example is Jess Lee in "A Manager's Challenge." An internal locus of control also helps to ensure ethical behavior and decision making in an organization because people feel accountable and responsible for their own actions.

external locus of control The tendency to locate responsibility for one's fate in outside forces and to believe one's own behavior has little impact on outcomes.

People with an **external locus of control** believe that outside forces are responsible for what happens to and around them; they do not think their own actions make much of a difference. As such, they tend not to intervene to try to change a situation or solve a problem, leaving it to someone else.

Managers need an internal locus of control because they *are* responsible for what happens in organizations; they need to believe they can and do make a difference, as does Jess Lee at Polyvore. Moreover, managers are responsible for ensuring that organizations and their members behave in an ethical fashion, and for this as well they need an internal locus of control—they need to know and feel they can make a difference.

self-esteem The degree to which individuals feel good about themselves and their capabilities.

SELF-ESTEEM **Self-esteem** is the degree to which individuals feel good about themselves and their capabilities. People with high self-esteem believe they are competent, deserving, and capable of handling most situations, as does Jess Lee. People with low self-esteem have poor opinions of themselves, are unsure about their capabilities, and question their ability to succeed at different endeavors.[40] Research suggests that people tend to choose activities and goals consistent with their levels of self-esteem. High self-esteem is desirable for managers because it facilitates their setting and keeping high standards for themselves, pushes them ahead on difficult projects, and gives them the confidence they need to make and carry out important decisions.

need for achievement The extent to which an individual has a strong desire to perform challenging tasks well and to meet personal standards for excellence.

need for affiliation The extent to which an individual is concerned about establishing and maintaining good interpersonal relations, being liked, and having other people get along.

need for power The extent to which an individual desires to control or influence others.

NEEDS FOR ACHIEVEMENT, AFFILIATION, AND POWER Psychologist David McClelland has extensively researched the needs for achievement, affiliation, and power.[41] The **need for achievement** is the extent to which an individual has a strong desire to perform challenging tasks well and to meet personal standards for excellence. People with a high need for achievement often set clear goals for themselves and like to receive performance feedback. The **need for affiliation** is the extent to which an individual is concerned about establishing and maintaining good interpersonal relations, being liked, and having the people around him or her get along with one another. The **need for power** is the extent to which an individual desires to control or influence others.[42]

Research suggests that high needs for achievement and for power are assets for first-line and middle managers and that a high need for power is especially important for upper-level managers.[43] One study found that U.S. presidents with a relatively high need for power tended to be especially effective during their terms of office.[44] A high need for affiliation may not always be desirable in managers because it might lead them to try too hard to be liked by others (including subordinates) rather than doing all they can to ensure that performance is as high as it can and should be. Although most research on these needs has been done in the United States, some studies suggest that these findings may also apply to people in other countries such as India and New Zealand.[45]

Taken together, these desirable personality traits for managers—an internal locus of control, high self-esteem, and high needs for achievement and power—suggest that managers need to be take-charge people who not only believe their own actions are decisive in determining their own and their organizations' fates but also believe in their own capabilities. Such managers have a personal desire for accomplishment and influence over others.

LO3-2
Explain what values and attitudes are and describe their impact on managerial action.

Values, Attitudes, and Moods and Emotions

What are managers striving to achieve? How do they think they should behave? What do they think about their jobs and organizations? And how do they actually feel at work? We can find some answers to these questions by exploring managers' values, attitudes, and moods.

Values, attitudes, and moods and emotions capture how managers experience their jobs as individuals. *Values* describe what managers are trying to achieve through work and how they think they should behave. *Attitudes* capture their thoughts and feelings about their specific jobs and organizations. *Moods and emotions* encompass how managers actually feel when they are managing. Although these three aspects of managers' work experience are highly personal, they also have important implications for understanding how managers behave, how they treat and respond to others, and how, through their efforts, they help contribute to organizational effectiveness through planning, leading, organizing, and controlling.

Values: Terminal and Instrumental

terminal value A lifelong goal or objective that an individual seeks to achieve.

instrumental value A mode of conduct that an individual seeks to follow.

norms Unwritten, informal codes of conduct that prescribe how people should act in particular situations and are considered important by most members of a group or organization.

value system The terminal and instrumental values that are guiding principles in an individual's life.

The two kinds of personal values are *terminal* and *instrumental*. A **terminal value** is a personal conviction about lifelong goals or objectives; an **instrumental value** is a personal conviction about desired modes of conduct or ways of behaving.[46] Terminal values often lead to the formation of **norms**, which are unwritten, informal codes of conduct, such as behaving honestly or courteously, that prescribe how people should act in particular situations and are considered important by most members of a group or organization.

Milton Rokeach, a leading researcher in the area of human values, identified 18 terminal values and 18 instrumental values that describe each person's value system.[47] By rank ordering the terminal values from "1 (most important as a guiding principle in one's life)" to "18 (least important as a guiding principle in one's life)" and then rank ordering the instrumental values from 1 to 18, people can give good pictures of their **value systems**—what they are striving to achieve in life and how they want to behave.[48]

Several of Rokeach's terminal values seem to be especially important for managers such as *"a sense of accomplishment (a lasting contribution)"*, *"equality (brotherhood, equal opportunity for all)"*, and *"self-respect (self-esteem)."*[49] A manager who thinks a sense of accomplishment is of paramount importance might focus on making a lasting contribution to an organization by developing a new product that can save or prolong lives, as is true of managers at Medtronic (a company that makes medical devices such as cardiac pacemakers), or by opening a new foreign subsidiary. A manager who places equality at the top of his or her list of terminal values may be at the forefront of an organization's efforts to support, provide equal opportunities to, and capitalize on the many talents of an increasingly diverse workforce.

Other terminal values are likely to be considered important by many managers, such as *"a comfortable life (a prosperous life)"*, *"an exciting life (a stimulating, active life)"*, *"freedom (independence, free choice)"*, and *"social recognition (respect, admiration)."*[50] The relative importance that managers place on each terminal value helps explain what they are striving to achieve in their organizations and what they will focus their efforts on.

Several of Rokeach's instrumental values seem to be important modes of conduct for managers, such as being *"ambitious (hardworking, aspiring)"*, *"broad-minded (open-minded)"*, *"capable (competent, effective)"*, *"responsible (dependable, reliable)"*, and *"self-controlled (restrained, self-disciplined)."*[51] Moreover, the relative importance a manager places on these and other instrumental values may be a significant determinant of actual behaviors on the job. A manager who considers being *"imaginative (daring, creative)"*[52] to be highly important, for example, is more likely to be innovative and take risks than is a manager who considers this to be less important (all else being equal). A manager who considers being *"honest (sincere, truthful)"*[53] to be of paramount importance may be a driving force for taking steps to ensure that all members of a unit or organization behave ethically, as indicated in the following "Ethics in Action" box.

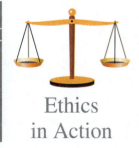

Ethics
in Action

Telling the Truth at Gentle Giant Moving

Gentle Giant Moving Company, based in Somerville, Massachusetts, was founded by Larry O'Toole in 1980 and now has over $28 million in revenues and offices in multiple states.[54] Gentle Giant opened its newest office, Chicago Movers–Gentle Giant Moving & Storage, in 2013 in Chicago, Illinois.[55] Although moving is undoubtedly hard work and many people would never think about having a career in this industry, Gentle Giant's unique culture and approach to managing people have not only contributed to the company's success but also give its employees satisfying careers. For example,

At Gentle Giant Moving Company, employees are given leadership training, access to company outings, and the opportunity to advance to management positions.

when Ryan Libby was in college, he worked for Gentle Giant during one of his summer vacations to make some extra money. After graduating from college, he was the assistant manager for the Providence, Rhode Island, Gentle Giant Office. Now Libby is branch manager for Providence.[56] As he puts it, "First it was just a paycheck, and it kind of turned into a long-term career."[57]

Libby is just the kind of employee O'Toole seeks to hire—employees who start out driving moving trucks and eventually move into management positions running offices. Whereas some moving companies hire a lot of temporary help in the summer to meet seasonal demand, 60 percent of Gentle Giant employees are employed full-time.[58] Because the demand for moving services is lower in the winter, Gentle Giant uses this time to train and develop employees. Of course new employees receive training in the basics of moving: packing, lifting, and carrying household goods safely. However, employees looking to advance in the company receive training in a host of other areas ranging from project management, communication, problem solving, and customer relations to leadership. An overarching goal of Gentle Giant's training efforts is inculcating in employees the importance of honesty. According to O'Toole, "We really emphasize that what matters most to us is telling the truth."[59]

Training benefits Gentle Giant's employees, customers, and the company as a whole. About one-third of the company's office and management employees started out driving moving trucks. Customers are satisfied because employees are capable, honest, and professional. And the company has continued to grow, prosper, and receive recognition in the business press as well as awards. For example, Gentle Giant was named one of the 15 Top Small Workplaces by *The Wall Street Journal* in collaboration with Winning Workplaces (a nonprofit organization that focuses on helping small and medium-size companies improve their work environments).[60]

Having fun and getting to know each other as people are also important at Gentle Giant.[61] The company holds parties and arranges outings for employees to sporting events, amusement parks, and other local attractions. Most workdays, O'Toole takes an employee out to lunch. Some college athletes are attracted to work for Gentle Giant because they see moving as a way to keep fit while at the same time having the opportunity to grow and develop on the job and move into a managerial position if they desire.[62]

All in all, managers' value systems signify what managers as individuals are trying to accomplish and become in their personal lives and at work. Thus managers' value systems are fundamental guides to their behavior and efforts at planning, leading, organizing, and controlling.

Attitudes

attitude A collection of feelings and beliefs.

An **attitude** is a collection of feelings and beliefs. Like everyone else, managers have attitudes about their jobs and organizations, and these attitudes affect how they approach their jobs. Two of the most important attitudes in this context are job satisfaction and organizational commitment.

job satisfaction The collection of feelings and beliefs that managers have about their current jobs.

JOB SATISFACTION **Job satisfaction** is the collection of feelings and beliefs that managers have about their current jobs.[63] Managers who have high levels of job satisfaction generally like their jobs, feel they are fairly treated, and believe their jobs have many desirable features or characteristics (such as interesting work, good pay and job security, autonomy, or nice coworkers). Figure 3.3 shows sample items from two scales that managers can use to measure job satisfaction. Levels of job satisfaction tend to increase as one moves up

Figure 3.3

Sample Items from Two Measures of Job Satisfaction

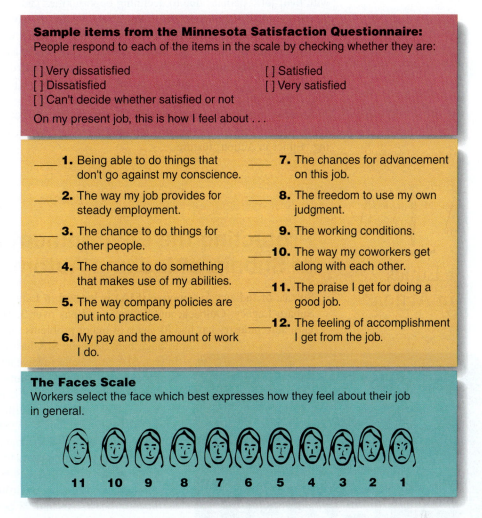

Sample items from the Minnesota Satisfaction Questionnaire:
People respond to each of the items in the scale by checking whether they are:

[ ] Very dissatisfied   [ ] Satisfied
[ ] Dissatisfied   [ ] Very satisfied
[ ] Can't decide whether satisfied or not

On my present job, this is how I feel about . . .

_____ **1.** Being able to do things that don't go against my conscience.

_____ **2.** The way my job provides for steady employment.

_____ **3.** The chance to do things for other people.

_____ **4.** The chance to do something that makes use of my abilities.

_____ **5.** The way company policies are put into practice.

_____ **6.** My pay and the amount of work I do.

_____ **7.** The chances for advancement on this job.

_____ **8.** The freedom to use my own judgment.

_____ **9.** The working conditions.

_____ **10.** The way my coworkers get along with each other.

_____ **11.** The praise I get for doing a good job.

_____ **12.** The feeling of accomplishment I get from the job.

The Faces Scale
Workers select the face which best expresses how they feel about their job in general.

11   10   9   8   7   6   5   4   3   2   1

Source: D.J. Weiss et al., *Manual for the Minnesota Satisfaction Questionnaire.* Copyrighted by the Vocational Psychology Research, University of Minnesota; copyright © 1975 by the American Psychological Association. Adapted by permission of R.B. Dunham and J.B. Brett.

the hierarchy in an organization. Upper managers, in general, tend to be more satisfied with their jobs than entry-level employees. Managers' levels of job satisfaction can range from very low to very high.

One might think that in tough economic times, when unemployment is high and layoffs are prevalent, people who have jobs might be relatively satisfied with them. However, this is not necessarily the case. For example, in December 2009 the U.S. unemployment rate was 10 percent, 85,000 jobs were lost from the economy, and the underemployment rate (which includes people who have given up looking for jobs and those who are working part-time because they can't find a full-time position) was 17.3 percent.[64] During these recessionary conditions, job satisfaction levels in the United States fell to record lows.[65]

The Conference Board has been tracking levels of U.S. job satisfaction since 1987, when 61.1 percent of workers surveyed indicated that they were satisfied with their jobs.[66] In 2009 only 45 percent of workers surveyed indicated that they were satisfied with their jobs, an all-time low for the survey.[67] Some sources of job dissatisfaction include uninteresting work, lack of job security, incomes that have not kept pace with inflation, and having to spend more money on health insurance. For example, three times as many workers in 2009 had to contribute to paying for their health insurance and had rising levels of contributions compared to 1980. Only 43 percent of workers thought their jobs were secure in 2009 compared to 59 percent in 1987. In the 2000s, average household incomes adjusted for inflation declined.[68]

Of all age groups, workers under 25 were the most dissatisfied with their jobs in 2009. More specifically, approximately 64 percent of workers in this age group were dissatisfied with their jobs, perhaps due to declining opportunities and relatively low earnings. Around 22 percent of all respondents didn't think they would still have the same job in a year.[69]

In 2012, 47.3 percent of U.S. workers indicated that they were satisfied with their jobs on the Conference Board survey.[70] This was the seventh year in a row in which less than one-half of Americans were satisfied with their jobs.[71] Factors contributing to levels of satisfaction/dissatisfaction in 2012 included potential for growth on the job, interesting work, communication, recognition, workload, and work–life balance.[72]

Some organizations have combined a concern about protecting the environment with a concern about preserving workers' jobs and avoiding layoffs, as illustrated in the accompanying "Ethics in Action" feature.

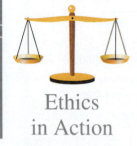

Ethics in Action

Protecting the Environment and Jobs at Subaru of Indiana Automotive

Subaru of Indiana Automotive (SIA) is located in Lafayette, Indiana; produces the Subaru Legacy, Outback, and Tribeca; and has over 3,700 employees.[73] While the U.S. auto industry has had its share of major problems ranging from massive layoffs to huge bankruptcies, SIA has never laid off employees.[74] In fact, SIA employees receive annual raises, premium-free health care, substantial amounts of overtime work, financial counseling, the option of earning a Purdue University degree at the production facility, and pay for volunteer work. While approximately 46,000 auto jobs have been lost in Indiana and several auto manufacturing plants have shut down in the state, SIA appears to be thriving.[75]

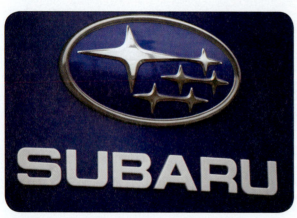

Subaru of Indiana, unlike many auto manufacturers, is thriving, perhaps due to its environmental philosophy, combined with a commitment to reducing worker injuries and promoting worker health.

At the same time, SIA has been on an uncompromising mission to protect the environment and save money by eliminating waste. Around 98 percent of the waste at SIA is recycled or composted with considerable efficiencies and cost savings.[76] An on-site broker manages bids for recycled metals, glass, plastic, and paper. Only about 2 percent of waste is incinerated, and this is done locally at an operation that converts waste to fuel. Suppliers are encouraged to minimize packaging, which enables SIA to get better deals from them, and boxes and containers shipping parts and materials back and forth from Japan to Indiana are reused, cutting costs. Scrap from welding is sold in copper auctions. Executive Vice President Tom Easterday estimates that SIA saves over $5 million per year from its efforts to eliminate waste, recycle, and compost.[77]

SIA combines its minimal environmental impact philosophy with a commitment to reducing worker injuries and promoting worker health.[78] For example, rather than inspecting the quality of welds by taking cars apart as was customary, SIA now uses ultrasonic technology to check welds. This change reduced worker injuries from jackhammers and metals waste and results in a process that is more effective, quicker, and less expensive. SIA has a free on-site gym with wellness and weight loss programs.[79] Workers receive bonuses for identifying unnecessary packaging and processes, which can cut costs and be a source of rebates from suppliers, with the top bonus being a brand new Subaru Legacy. All these costs savings are used for further plant investments and overtime pay.[80]

SIA's relentless quest for efficiency in terms of reducing waste/protecting the environment and increasing productivity on the assembly line puts a lot of pressure on employees, who are expected to work long hours.[81] Nonetheless, they know that their jobs are secure, and they receive overtime pay and premium-free health insurance. When the Japanese earthquake in 2011 forced the plant to slow down because of disruptions in the supply of parts from Japan, SIA continued to pay all its employees their full wages to volunteer in the local community. Thus it is not surprising that there are about 10 applicants for each open position at SIA. Clearly SIA has demonstrated that it is possible to protect the environment and protect jobs to the benefit of all.[82]

organizational citizenship behaviors (OCBs) Behaviors that are not required of organizational members but that contribute to and are necessary for organizational efficiency, effectiveness, and competitive advantage.

In general, it is desirable for managers to be satisfied with their jobs, for at least two reasons. First, satisfied managers may be more likely to go the extra mile for their organization or perform **organizational citizenship behaviors (OCBs)**—behaviors that are not required of organizational members but that contribute to and are necessary for organizational efficiency, effectiveness, and competitive advantage.[83] Managers who are satisfied with their jobs are more likely to perform these "above and beyond the call of duty" behaviors, which can range from putting in long hours when needed to coming up with truly creative ideas and overcoming obstacles to implement them (even when doing so is not part of the manager's job), or to going out of one's way to help a coworker, subordinate, or superior (even when doing so entails considerable personal sacrifice).[84]

A second reason why it is desirable for managers to be satisfied with their jobs is that satisfied managers may be less likely to quit.[85] A manager who is highly satisfied may never even think about looking for another position; a dissatisfied manager may always be on the lookout for new opportunities. Turnover can hurt an organization because it causes the loss of the experience and knowledge that managers have gained about the company, industry, and business environment.

A growing source of dissatisfaction for many lower-level and middle managers, as well as for nonmanagerial employees, is the threat of unemployment and increased workloads from organizational downsizings and layoffs. Organizations that try to improve their efficiency through restructuring and layoffs often eliminate a sizable number of first-line and middle management positions. This decision obviously hurts the managers who are laid off, and it also can reduce the job satisfaction levels of managers who remain. They might fear being the next to be let go. In addition, the workloads of remaining employees often increase dramatically as a result of restructuring, and this can contribute to dissatisfaction.

How managers and organizations handle layoffs is of paramount importance, not only for the layoff victims but also for employees who survive the layoff and keep their jobs.[86] Showing compassion and empathy for layoff victims, giving them as much advance notice as possible about the layoff, providing clear information about severance benefits, and helping layoff victims in their job search efforts are a few of the ways in which managers can humanely manage a layoff.[87] For example, when Ron Thomas, vice president of organizational development for Martha Stewart Living Omnimedia, had to lay off employees as a result of closing the organization's catalog business, he personally called all the catalog businesses he knew to find out about potential positions for laid-off employees.[88] Efforts such as Thomas's to help layoff victims find new jobs can contribute to the job satisfaction of those who survive the layoff. As Thomas puts it, "If you handle a restructuring well, the word gets out that you're a good place to work . . . if we post a job opening today, we'll get 1,500 résumés tomorrow."[89]

Unfortunately, when the unemployment rate is high, laid-off employees sometimes find it difficult to find new jobs and can remain jobless for months.[90] For small businesses, the decision to lay off employees and communicating that decision can be especially painful because managers often have developed close personal relationships with the people they have to let go, know their families, and fear what will happen to them with the loss of a steady income.[91] Shelly Polum, vice president for administration at Ram Tool, a small family-owned manufacturing company in Grafton, Wisconsin, broke down in tears in her office after she had to let employees know they were being laid off.[92] When Charlie Thomas, vice president of Shuqualak Lumber in Shuqualak, Mississippi, had to announce layoffs of close to a quarter of his employees, he wrote a speech that he could not get through without stopping and retreating to his office to pull himself together. As he put it, "I couldn't get it out . . . It just killed my soul."[93] As these managers realize, being laid off can be devastating for employees and their families.

organizational commitment
The collection of feelings and
beliefs that managers have
about their organization as a
whole.

ORGANIZATIONAL COMMITMENT   **Organizational commitment** is the collection of feelings and beliefs that managers have about their organization as a whole.[94] Managers who are committed to their organizations believe in what their organizations are doing, are proud of what these organizations stand for, and feel a high degree of loyalty toward their organizations. Committed managers are more likely to go above and beyond the call of duty to help their company and are less likely to quit.[95] Organizational commitment can be especially strong when employees and managers truly believe in organizational values; it also leads to a strong organizational culture.

Organizational commitment is likely to help managers perform some of their figurehead and spokesperson roles (see Chapter 1). It is much easier for a manager to persuade others both inside and outside the organization of the merits of what the organization has done and is seeking to accomplish if the manager truly believes in and is committed to the organization.

Do managers in different countries have similar or different attitudes? Differences in the levels of job satisfaction and organizational commitment among managers in different countries are likely because these managers have different kinds of opportunities and rewards and because they face different economic, political, and sociocultural forces in their organizations' general environments. Levels of organizational commitment from one country to another may depend on the extent to which countries have legislation affecting firings and layoffs and the extent to which citizens of a country are geographically mobile.

LO3-3

Appreciate how moods and emotions influence all members of an organization.

mood A feeling or state of mind.

Moods and Emotions

Just as you sometimes are in a bad mood and at other times are in a good mood, so too are managers. A **mood** is a feeling or state of mind. When people are in a positive mood, they feel excited, enthusiastic, active, or elated.[96] When people are in a negative mood, they feel distressed, fearful, scornful, hostile, jittery, or nervous.[97] People who are high on negative affectivity are especially likely to experience negative moods. People's situations or circumstances also determine their moods; however, receiving a raise is likely to put most people in a good mood regardless of their personality traits. People who are high on negative affectivity are not always in a bad mood and people who are low on extraversion still experience positive moods.[98]

emotions Intense, relatively short-lived feelings.

Emotions are more intense feelings than moods, are often directly linked to whatever caused the emotion, and are more short-lived.[99] However, once whatever has triggered the emotion has been dealt with, the feelings may linger in the form of a less intense mood.[100] For example, a manager who gets very angry when a subordinate has engaged in an unethical behavior may find his anger decreasing in intensity once he has decided how to address the problem. Yet he continues to be in a bad mood the rest of the day, even though he is not directly thinking about the unfortunate incident.[101]

Research has found that moods and emotions affect the behavior of managers and all members of an organization. For example, research suggests that the subordinates of managers who experience positive moods at work may perform at somewhat higher levels and be less likely to resign and leave the organization than the subordinates of managers who do not tend to be in a positive mood at work.[102] Other research suggests that under certain conditions creativity might be enhanced by positive moods, whereas under other conditions negative moods might push people to work harder to come up with truly creative ideas.[103] Recognizing that both mood states have the potential to contribute to creativity in different ways, recent research suggests that employees may be especially likely to be creative to the extent that they experience both mood states (at different times) on the job and to the extent that the work environment is supportive of creativity.[104]

Other research suggests that moods and emotions may play an important role in ethical decision making. For example, researchers at Princeton University found that when people are trying to solve difficult personal moral dilemmas, the parts of their brains that are responsible for emotions and moods are especially active.[105]

More generally, emotions and moods give managers and all employees important information and signals about what is going on in the workplace.[106] Positive emotions and moods signal that things are going well and thus can lead to more expansive, and even playful, thinking. Negative emotions and moods signal that there are problems in need of attention and areas for improvement. So when people are in negative moods, they tend to be more detail-oriented and focused on the facts at hand.[107] Some studies suggest that critical thinking and devil's advocacy may be promoted by a negative mood, and sometimes especially accurate judgments may be made by managers in negative moods.[108]

As indicated in the accompanying "Management Insight" feature, emotions can sometimes be the impetus for important changes in an organization.

Management Insight

Emotions as Triggers for Changes in Organizations

In our personal lives, intense emotional experiences can often be triggers for changes for the better. For example, the fear that accompanies a near-miss auto accident may prompt a driver to slow down and leave more time to get to destinations. Embarrassment experienced from being underprepared for a major presentation might prompt a student to be more prepared in the future. Anger over being treated poorly can sometimes help people get out of bad personal relationships.

Interestingly enough, some managers and organizations are using emotions to prompt needed changes. For example, the CEO of North American Tool, Curt Lansbery, was dismayed that employees weren't contributing as much as they could to their 401(k) retirement plans because the company had a matched contribution plan whereby it contributed a percentage of an employee's contribution.[109] North American Tool makes industrial cutting machinery and each year has an annual 401(k) enrollment meeting. Lansbery decided to bring a bag full of money to the next meeting that equaled the amount of money employees did not receive the prior year because they did not contribute the maximum to their 401(k) plans. He dumped the money on a table and told the employees that this really should be their money, not the company's.[110] The negative feelings that this invoked in employees—there's a bunch of money that should be ours and is not—prompted many more to maximize their 401(k) contributions for the coming year and reap the benefits of the matched contribution plan.[111]

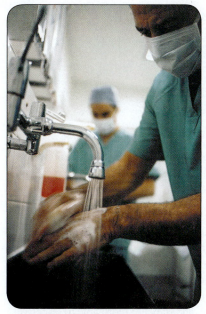

At one hospital, disgust at a screensaver on computers showing unwashed hands covered with bacteria led doctors and other health professionals to better comply with hand washing procedures. Repeated hand washing by medical staff is a key contributor to avoiding preventable bacterial infections acquired in hospitals and to saving lives.

Dr. Leon Bender and other colleagues at Cedars-Sinai Medical Center were concerned that doctors and nurses weren't washing their hands as often as they should.[112] Repeated hand-washing by medical staff is a key contributor to keeping patients free of secondary bacterial infections; avoiding these kinds of preventable bacterial infections acquired in hospitals can save patients' lives. Despite their efforts to encourage more hand washing in the Center, their compliance rates with standards was around 80 percent. The Center was due for an inspection during which a minimum compliance rate of 90 percent was needed.[113]

After lunch one day, a group of around 20 doctors and staff were requested by the Center's epidemiologist to put their hands on an agar plate.[114] After the agar plates were cultured, they showed that the doctors' and administrators' hands were coated with bacteria. Photos of the cultured plates were circulated and one was made into a screen saver for the computers on the hospital's networks. The disgust experienced by everyone who saw the screen saver and the photos was a powerful impetus for change, and compliance with hand-washing protocols increased to close to 100 percent and remained at a high level.[115] You can see how emotions can be useful triggers for needed changes in organizations.[116]

Managers and other members of an organization need to realize that how they feel affects how they treat others and how others respond to them, including their subordinates. For example, a subordinate may be more likely to approach a manager with a somewhat unusual but potentially useful idea if the subordinate thinks the manager is in a good mood. Likewise, when managers are in very bad moods, their subordinates might try to avoid them at all costs. Figure 3.4 is an example of a scale that can measure the extent to which a person experiences positive and negative moods at work.

Figure 3.4

A Measure of Positive and Negative Mood at Work

People respond to each item by indicating the extent to which the item describes how they felt at work during the past week on the following scale:

1 = Very slightly or not at all	4 = Quite a bit
2 = A little	5 = Very much
3 = Moderately	

____ **1.** Active		____ **7.** Enthusiastic	
____ **2.** Distressed		____ **8.** Fearful	
____ **3.** Strong		____ **9.** Peppy	
____ **4.** Excited		____ **10.** Nervous	
____ **5.** Scornful		____ **11.** Elated	
____ **6.** Hostile		____ **12.** Jittery	

Scoring: Responses to items 1, 3, 4, 7, 9, and 11 are summed for a positive mood score; the higher the score, the more positive mood is experienced at work. Responses to items 2, 5, 6, 8, 10, and 12 are summed for a negative mood score; the higher the score, the more negative mood is experienced at work.

Source: A.P. Brief, M.J. Burke, J.M. George, B. Robinson, and J. Webster, "Should Negative Affectivity Remain an Unmeasured Variable in the Study of Job Stress?" *Journal of Applied Psychology* 72 (1988), 193–98; M.J. Burke, A.P. Brief, J.M. George, L. Roberson, and J. Webster, "Measuring Affect at Work: Confirmatory Analyses of Competing Mood Structures with Conceptual Linkage in Cortical Regulatory Systems," *Journal of Personality and Social Psychology* 57 (1989), 1091–102.

Emotional Intelligence

emotional intelligence
The ability to understand and manage one's own moods and emotions and the moods and emotions of other people.

In understanding the effects of managers' and all employees' moods and emotions, it is important to take into account their levels of emotional intelligence. **Emotional intelligence** is the ability to understand and manage one's own moods and emotions and the moods and emotions of other people.[117] Managers with a high level of emotional intelligence are more likely to understand how they are feeling and why, and they are more able to effectively manage their feelings. When managers are experiencing stressful feelings and emotions such as fear or anxiety, emotional intelligence lets them understand why and manage these feelings so they do not get in the way of effective decision making.[118]

Emotional intelligence also can help managers perform their important roles such as their interpersonal roles (figurehead, leader, and liaison).[119] Understanding how your subordinates feel, why they feel that way, and how to manage these feelings is central to developing strong interpersonal bonds with them.[120] Moreover, emotional intelligence has the potential to contribute to effective leadership in multiple ways[121] and can help managers make lasting contributions to society. For example, Bernard (Bernie) Goldhirsh founded *Inc.* magazine in 1979, a time when entrepreneurs received more notoriety than respect, if they were paid attention at all.[122] Goldhirsh was an entrepreneur himself at the time, with his own publishing company. He recognized the vast contributions entrepreneurs could make to society, creating something out of nothing, and also realized firsthand what a tough task entrepreneurs faced.[123] His emotional intelligence helped him understand the challenges and frustrations entrepreneurs like himself faced and their need for support.

When Goldhirsh founded *Inc.*, entrepreneurs had few sources to which they could turn for advice, guidance, and solutions to management problems. *Inc.* was born to fill this gap and give entrepreneurs information and support by profiling successful and unsuccessful entrepreneurial ventures, highlighting management techniques that work, and providing firsthand accounts of how successful entrepreneurs developed and managed their businesses.[124]

Goldhirsh's emotional intelligence helped him recognize the many barriers entrepreneurs face and the emotional roller coaster of staking all one has on an idea that may or may not work. Goldhirsh believed that helping society understand the entrepreneurial process through *Inc.* magazine not only helped entrepreneurs but also enlightened bankers, lawmakers, and the public at large about the role these visionaries play, the challenges they face, and the support their ventures depend on.[125]

Emotional intelligence helps managers understand and relate well to other people.[126] It also helps managers maintain their enthusiasm and confidence and energize subordinates to help the organization attain its goals.[127] Recent theorizing and research suggest that emotional intelligence may be especially important in awakening employee creativity.[128] Managers themselves are increasingly recognizing the importance of emotional intelligence. An example of a scale that measures emotional intelligence is provided in Figure 3.5.

Figure 3.5

A Measure of Emotional Intelligence

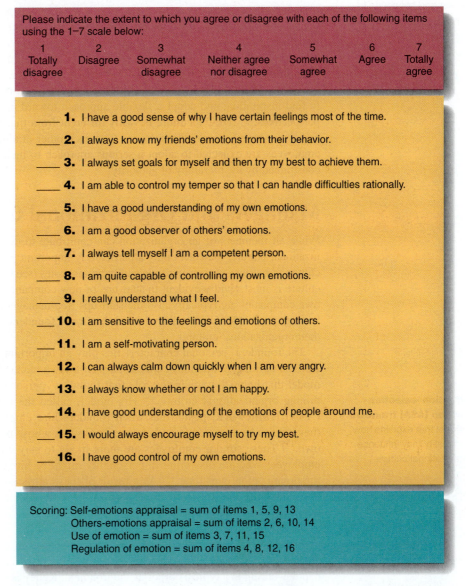

Please indicate the extent to which you agree or disagree with each of the following items using the 1–7 scale below:

1	2	3	4	5	6	7
Totally disagree	Disagree	Somewhat disagree	Neither agree nor disagree	Somewhat agree	Agree	Totally agree

_____ 1. I have a good sense of why I have certain feelings most of the time.

_____ 2. I always know my friends' emotions from their behavior.

_____ 3. I always set goals for myself and then try my best to achieve them.

_____ 4. I am able to control my temper so that I can handle difficulties rationally.

_____ 5. I have a good understanding of my own emotions.

_____ 6. I am a good observer of others' emotions.

_____ 7. I always tell myself I am a competent person.

_____ 8. I am quite capable of controlling my own emotions.

_____ 9. I really understand what I feel.

_____ 10. I am sensitive to the feelings and emotions of others.

_____ 11. I am a self-motivating person.

_____ 12. I can always calm down quickly when I am very angry.

_____ 13. I always know whether or not I am happy.

_____ 14. I have good understanding of the emotions of people around me.

_____ 15. I would always encourage myself to try my best.

_____ 16. I have good control of my own emotions.

Scoring: Self-emotions appraisal = sum of items 1, 5, 9, 13
Others-emotions appraisal = sum of items 2, 6, 10, 14
Use of emotion = sum of items 3, 7, 11, 15
Regulation of emotion = sum of items 4, 8, 12, 16

Source: David J. Weiss, et al., Manual for the Minnesota Satisfaction Questionnaire. Copyright © Vocational Psychology Research, University of Minnesota; Adapted by permission of Randall B. Dunham and J.B. Brett. Copyright © 1975 by the American Psychological Association.

Organizational Culture

LO3-5

Define organizational culture and explain how managers both create and are influenced by organizational culture.

organizational culture
The shared set of beliefs, expectations, values, norms, and work routines that influence how individuals, groups, and teams interact with one another and cooperate to achieve organizational goals.

Personality is a way of understanding why all managers and employees, as individuals, characteristically think and behave in different ways. However, when people belong to the same organization, they tend to share certain beliefs and values that lead them to act in similar ways.[129] **Organizational culture** comprises the shared set of beliefs, expectations, values, norms, and work routines that influence how members of an organization relate to one another and work together to achieve organizational goals. In essence, organizational culture reflects the distinctive ways in which organizational members perform their jobs and relate to others inside and outside the organization. It may, for example, be how customers in a particular hotel chain are treated from the time they are greeted at check-in until they leave; or it may be the shared work routines that research teams use to guide new product development. When organizational members share an intense commitment to cultural values, beliefs, and routines and use them to achieve their goals, a *strong* organizational culture exists.[130] When organizational members are not strongly committed to a shared system of values, beliefs, and routines, organizational culture is weak.

The stronger the culture of an organization, the more one can think about it as being the "personality" of an organization because it influences the way its members behave.[131] Organizations that possess strong cultures may differ on a wide variety of dimensions that determine how their members behave toward one another and perform their jobs. For example, organizations differ in how members relate to each other (formally or informally), how important decisions are made (top-down or bottom-up), willingness to change (flexible or unyielding), innovation (creative or predictable), and playfulness (serious or serendipitous). In an innovative design firm like IDEO Product Development in Silicon Valley, employees are encouraged to adopt a playful attitude toward their work, look outside the organization to find inspiration, and adopt a flexible approach toward product design that uses multiple perspectives.[132] IDEO's culture is vastly different from that of companies such as Citibank and ExxonMobil, in which employees treat each other in a more formal or deferential way, employees are expected to adopt a serious approach to their work, and decision making is constrained by the hierarchy of authority.

Managers and Organizational Culture

While all members of an organization can contribute to developing and maintaining organizational culture, managers play a particularly important part in influencing organizational culture[133] because of their multiple and important roles (see Chapter 1). How managers create culture is most vividly evident in start-ups of new companies. Entrepreneurs who start their own companies are typically also the start-ups' top managers until the companies grow and become profitable. Often referred to as the firms' founders, these managers literally create their organizations' cultures.

attraction–selection–attrition (ASA) framework
A model that explains how personality may influence organizational culture.

The founders' personal characteristics play an important role in the creation of organizational culture. Benjamin Schneider, a well-known management researcher, developed a model that helps to explain the role that founders' personal characteristics play in determining organizational culture.[134] His model, called the **attraction–selection–attrition (ASA) framework**, posits that when founders hire employees for their new ventures, they tend to be attracted to and choose employees whose personalities are similar to their own.[135] These similar employees are more likely to stay with the organization. Although employees who are dissimilar in personality might be hired, they are more likely to leave the organization over time.[136] As a result of these attraction, selection, and attrition processes, people in the organization tend to have similar personalities, and the typical or dominant personality profile of organizational members determines and shapes organizational culture.[137]

For example, when David Kelley became interested in engineering and product design challenges in the late 1970s, he realized that who he was as a person meant he would not be happy working in a typical corporate environment. Kelley is high on openness to experience, driven to go where his interests take him, and not content to follow others' directives. Kelley recognized that he needed to start his own business, and with the help of other Stanford-schooled engineers and design experts, IDEO was born.[138]

IDEO employees brainstorming—informal communication, casual attire, and flexibility are all hallmarks of this organization.

From the start, IDEO's culture has embodied Kelley's spirited, freewheeling approach to work and design—from colorful and informal workspaces to an emphasis on networking and communicating with as many people as possible to understand a design problem. No project or problem is too big or too small for IDEO; the company designed the Apple Lisa computer and mouse (the precursor of the Mac) and the Palm as well as the Crest Neat Squeeze toothpaste dispenser and the Racer's Edge water bottle.[139] Kelley hates rules, job titles, big corner offices, and all the other trappings of large traditional organizations that stifle creativity. Employees who are attracted to, are selected by, and remain with IDEO value creativity and innovation and embrace one of IDEO's mottos: "Fail often to succeed sooner."[140]

Although ASA processes are most evident in small firms such as IDEO, they also can operate in large companies.[141] According to the ASA model, this is a naturally occurring phenomenon to the extent that managers and new hires are free to make the kinds of choices the model specifies. However, while people tend to get along well with others who are similar to themselves, too much similarity in an organization can impair organizational effectiveness. That is, similar people tend to view conditions and events in similar ways and thus can be resistant to change. Moreover, organizations benefit from a diversity of perspectives rather than similarity in perspectives (see Chapter 5). At IDEO Kelley recognized early on how important it is to take advantage of the diverse talents and perspectives that people with different personalities, backgrounds, experiences, and education can bring to a design team. Hence IDEO's design teams include not only engineers but others who might have a unique insight into a problem, such as anthropologists, communications experts, doctors, and users of a product. When new employees are hired at IDEO, they meet many employees who have different backgrounds and characteristics; the focus is not on hiring someone who will fit in but, rather, on hiring someone who has something to offer and can "wow" different kinds of people with his or her insights.[142]

In addition to personality, other personal characteristics of managers shape organizational culture; these include managers' values, attitudes, moods and emotions, and emotional intelligence.[143] For example, both terminal and instrumental values of managers play a role in determining organizational culture. Managers who highly value freedom and equality, for example, might be likely to stress the importance of autonomy and empowerment in their organizations, as well as fair treatment for all. As another example, managers who highly value being helpful and forgiving might not only tolerate mistakes but also emphasize the importance of organizational members' being kind and helpful to one another.

Managers who are satisfied with their jobs, are committed to their organizations, and experience positive moods and emotions might also encourage these attitudes and feelings in others. The result would be an organizational culture emphasizing positive attitudes and feelings. Research suggests that attitudes like job satisfaction and organizational commitment can be affected by the influence of others. Managers are in a particularly strong position to engage in social influence given their multiple roles. Moreover, research suggests that moods and emotions can be contagious and that spending time with people who are excited and enthusiastic can increase one's own levels of excitement and enthusiasm.

The Role of Values and Norms in Organizational Culture

Shared terminal and instrumental values play a particularly important role in organizational culture. *Terminal values* signify what an organization and its employees are trying to accomplish, and *instrumental values* guide how the organization and its members achieve organizational goals. In addition to values, shared norms also are a key aspect of organizational culture. Recall that norms are unwritten, informal rules or guidelines that prescribe appropriate behavior in particular situations. For example, norms at IDEO include not being critical of others' ideas, coming up with multiple ideas before settling on one, and developing prototypes of new products.[144]

Managers determine and shape organizational culture through the kinds of values and norms they promote in an organization. Some managers, like David Kelley of IDEO, cultivate values and norms that encourage risk taking, creative responses to problems and opportunities, experimentation, tolerance of failure in order to succeed, and autonomy.[145] Top managers at organizations such as Microsoft and Google encourage employees to adopt such values to support their commitment to innovation as a source of competitive advantage.

Other managers, however, might cultivate values and norms that tell employees they should be conservative and cautious in their dealings with others and should consult their superiors before making important decisions or any changes to the status quo. Accountability for actions and decisions is stressed, and detailed records are kept to ensure that policies and procedures are followed. In settings where caution is needed—nuclear power stations, oil refineries, chemical plants, financial institutions, insurance companies—a conservative, cautious approach to making decisions might be appropriate.[146] In a nuclear power plant, for example, the catastrophic consequences of a mistake make a high level of supervision vital. Similarly, in a bank or mutual fund company, the risk of losing investors' money makes a cautious approach to investing appropriate.

Managers of different kinds of organizations deliberately cultivate and develop the organizational values and norms that are best suited to their task and general environments, strategy, or technology. Organizational culture is maintained and transmitted to organizational members through the values of the founder, the process of socialization, ceremonies and rites, and stories and language (see Figure 3.6).

Figure 3.6
Factors That Maintain and Transmit Organizational Culture

VALUES OF THE FOUNDER   From the ASA model just discussed, it is clear that founders of an organization can have profound and long-lasting effects on organizational culture. Founders' values inspire the founders to start their own companies and, in turn, drive the nature of these new companies and their defining characteristics. Thus an organization's founder and his or her terminal and instrumental values have a substantial influence on the values, norms, and standards of behavior that develop over time within the organization.[147] Founders set the scene for the way cultural values and norms develop because their own values guide the building of the company, and they hire other managers and employees who they believe will share these values and help the organization to attain them. Moreover, new managers quickly learn from the founder what values and norms are appropriate in the organization and thus what is desired of them. Subordinates imitate the style of the founder and, in turn, transmit their values and norms to their subordinates. Gradually, over time, the founder's values and norms permeate the organization.[148]

A founder who requires a great display of respect from subordinates and insists on proprieties, such as formal job titles and formal dress, encourages subordinates to act in this way toward their subordinates. Often a founder's personal values affect an organization's competitive advantage. For example, McDonald's founder Ray Kroc insisted from the beginning on high standards of customer service and cleanliness at McDonald's restaurants; these became core sources of McDonald's competitive advantage. Similarly, Bill Gates, the founder of Microsoft, pioneered certain cultural values in Microsoft. Employees are expected to be creative and to work hard, but they are encouraged to dress informally and to personalize their offices. Gates also established a host of company events such as cookouts, picnics, and sports events to emphasize to employees the importance of being both an individual and a team player.

SOCIALIZATION   Over time, organizational members learn from each other which values are important in an organization and the norms that specify appropriate and inappropriate behaviors. Eventually organizational members behave in accordance with the organization's values and norms—often without realizing they are doing so.

organizational socialization
The process by which newcomers learn an organization's values and norms and acquire the work behaviors necessary to perform jobs effectively.

Organizational socialization is the process by which newcomers learn an organization's values and norms and acquire the work behaviors necessary to perform jobs effectively.[149] As a result of their socialization experiences, organizational members internalize an organization's values and norms and behave in accordance with them not only because they think they have to but because they think these values and norms describe the right and proper way to behave.[150]

At Texas A&M University, for example, all new students are encouraged to go to "Fish Camp" to learn how to be an "Aggie" (the traditional nickname of students at the university). They learn about the ceremonies that have developed over time to commemorate significant events or people in A&M's history. In addition, they learn how to behave at football games and in class and what it means to be an Aggie. As a result of this highly organized socialization program, by the time new students arrive on campus and start their first semester, they have been socialized into what a Texas A&M student is supposed to do, and they have relatively few problems adjusting to the college environment.

Most organizations have some kind of socialization program to help new employees learn the ropes—the values, norms, and culture of the organization. The military, for example, is well known for the rigorous socialization process it uses to turn raw recruits into trained soldiers. Organizations such as the Walt Disney Company also put new recruits through a rigorous training program to teach them to perform well in their jobs and play their parts in helping Disneyland visitors have fun in a wholesome theme park. New recruits at Disney are called "cast members" and attend Disney University to learn the Disney culture and their parts in it. Disney's culture emphasizes the values of safety, courtesy, entertainment, and efficiency, and these values are brought to life for newcomers at Disney University. Newcomers also learn about the attraction area they will be joining (such as Adventureland or Fantasyland) at Disney University and then receive on-the-job socialization in the area itself from experienced cast members.[151] Through organizational socialization, founders and managers of an organization transmit to employees the cultural values and norms that shape the behavior of organizational members. Thus the values and norms of founder Walt Disney live on today at Disneyland as newcomers are socialized into the Disney way.

CEREMONIES AND RITES Another way in which managers can create or influence organizational culture is by developing organizational ceremonies and rites—formal events that recognize incidents of importance to the organization as a whole and to specific employees.[152] The most common rites that organizations use to transmit cultural norms and values to their members are rites of passage, of integration, and of enhancement (see Table 3.1).[153]

Rites of passage determine how individuals enter, advance within, and leave the organization. The socialization programs developed by military organizations (such as the U.S. Army) or by large accountancy and law firms are rites of passage. Likewise, the ways in which an organization prepares people for promotion or retirement are rites of passage.

Rites of integration, such as shared announcements of organizational successes, office parties, and company cookouts, build and reinforce common bonds among organizational members. IDEO uses many rites of integration to make its employees feel connected to one another and special. In addition to having wild "end-of-year" celebratory bashes, groups of IDEO employees periodically take time off to go to a sporting event, movie, or meal, or sometimes go on a long bike ride or for a sail. These kinds of shared activities not only reinforce IDEO's culture but also can be a source of inspiration on the job (for example, IDEO has been involved in making movies such as *The Abyss* and *Free Willy*). One 35-member design studio at IDEO led by Dennis Boyle has bimonthly lunch fests with no set agenda—anything goes. While enjoying great food, jokes, and camaraderie, studio members often end up sharing ideas for their latest great products, and the freely flowing conversation that results often leads to creative insights.[154]

A company's annual meeting also may be used as a ritual of integration, offering an opportunity to communicate organizational values to managers, other employees, and shareholders.[155] Walmart, for example, makes its annual stockholders' meeting an extravagant ceremony that celebrates the company's success. The company often flies thousands of its highest-performing employees to its annual meeting at its Bentonville, Arkansas, headquarters for a huge weekend entertainment festival complete with star musical performances. Walmart believes that rewarding its supporters with entertainment reinforces the company's high-performance values and culture. The proceedings are shown live over closed-circuit television in all Walmart stores so all employees can join in the rites celebrating the company's achievements.[156]

Rites of enhancement, such as awards dinners, newspaper releases, and employee promotions, let organizations publicly recognize and reward employees' contributions and thus strengthen their commitment to organizational values. By bonding members within the organization, rites of enhancement reinforce an organization's values and norms.

Stories and language also communicate organizational culture. Stories (whether fact or fiction) about organizational heroes and villains and their actions provide important clues about values and norms. Such stories can reveal the kinds of behaviors that are valued by the organization and the kinds of practices that are frowned on.[157] At the heart of McDonald's rich culture are hundreds of stories that organizational members tell about founder Ray Kroc. Most of these stories focus on how Kroc established the strict operating values and norms that are at the heart of McDonald's culture. Kroc was dedicated to achieving perfection in McDonald's quality, service, cleanliness, and value for money (QSC&V), and these four central values permeate McDonald's culture. For example, an often retold story

Table 3.1
Organizational Rites

Type of Rite	Example of Rite	Purpose of Rite
Rite of passage	Induction and basic training	Learn and internalize norms and values
Rite of integration	Office Christmas party	Build common norms and values
Rite of enhancement	Presentation of annual award	Motivate commitment to norms and values

describes what happened when Kroc and a group of managers from the Houston region were touring various restaurants. One of the restaurants was having a bad day operationally. Kroc was incensed about the long lines of customers, and he was furious when he realized that the products customers were receiving that day were not up to his high standards. To address the problem, he jumped up and stood on the front counter to get the attention of all customers and operating crew personnel. He introduced himself, apologized for the long wait and cold food, and told the customers they could have freshly cooked food or their money back—whichever they wanted. As a result, the customers left happy; and when Kroc checked on the restaurant later, he found that his message had gotten through to its managers and crew—performance had improved. Other stories describe Kroc scrubbing dirty toilets and picking up litter inside or outside a restaurant. These and similar stories are spread around the organization by McDonald's employees. They are the stories that have helped establish Kroc as McDonald's "hero."

Because spoken language is a principal medium of communication in organizations, the characteristic slang or jargon—that is, organization-specific words or phrases—that people use to frame and describe events provides important clues about norms and values. "McLanguage," for example, is prevalent at all levels of McDonald's. A McDonald's employee described as having "ketchup in his or her blood" is someone who is truly dedicated to the McDonald's way—someone who has been completely socialized to its culture. McDonald's has an extensive training program that teaches new employees "McDonald's speak," and new employees are welcomed into the family with a formal orientation that illustrates Kroc's dedication to QSC&V.

The concept of organizational language encompasses not only spoken language but how people dress, the offices they occupy, the cars they drive, and the degree of formality they use when they address one another. For example, casual dress reflects and reinforces Microsoft's entrepreneurial culture and values. Formal business attire supports the conservative culture found in many banks, which emphasizes the importance of conforming to organizational norms such as respect for authority and staying within one's prescribed role. When employees speak and understand the language of their organization's culture, they know how to behave in the organization and what is expected of them.

At IDEO, language, dress, the physical work environment, and extreme informality all underscore a culture that is adventuresome, playful, risk taking, egalitarian, and innovative. For example, at IDEO, employees refer to taking the consumers' perspective when designing products as "being left-handed." Employees dress in T-shirts and jeans, the physical work environment continually evolves and changes depending on how employees wish to personalize their workspace, no one "owns" a fancy office with a window, and rules are almost nonexistent.[158]

Culture and Managerial Action

While founders and managers play a critical role in developing, maintaining, and communicating organizational culture, this same culture shapes and controls the behavior of all employees, including managers themselves. For example, culture influences how managers perform their four main functions: planning, organizing, leading, and controlling. As we consider these functions, we continue to distinguish between top managers who create organizational values and norms that encourage creative, innovative behavior and top managers who encourage a conservative, cautious approach by their subordinates. We noted earlier that both kinds of values and norms can be appropriate depending on the situation and type of organization.

PLANNING Top managers in an organization with an innovative culture are likely to encourage lower-level managers to participate in the planning process and develop a flexible approach to planning. They are likely to be willing to listen to new ideas and to take risks involving the development of new products. In contrast, top managers in an organization with conservative values are likely to emphasize formal top-down planning. Suggestions from lower-level managers are likely to be subjected to a formal review process, which can significantly slow decision making. Although this deliberate approach may improve the quality of decision making in a nuclear power plant, it can have unintended consequences. In the past, at conservative IBM, the planning process became so formalized that managers spent most of their time assembling complex slide shows and overheads to defend their current positions rather than thinking about what they should do to keep IBM abreast of the changes taking place in the computer industry. When former CEO Lou Gerstner took over, he used every means at his disposal to abolish this culture, even building a brand-new campus-style headquarters to change managers' mind-sets. IBM's culture underwent further changes initiated by its next CEO, Samuel Palmisano, who is now chairman of the board.[159]

ORGANIZING   What kinds of organizing will managers in innovative and in conservative cultures encourage? Valuing creativity, managers in innovative cultures are likely to try to create an organic structure—one that is flat, with few levels in the hierarchy, and one in which authority is decentralized so employees are encouraged to work together to solve ongoing problems. A product team structure may be suitable for an organization with an innovative culture. In contrast, managers in a conservative culture are likely to create a well-defined hierarchy of authority and establish clear reporting relationships so employees know exactly whom to report to and how to react to any problems that arise.

LEADING   In an innovative culture, managers are likely to lead by example, encouraging employees to take risks and experiment. They are supportive regardless of whether employees succeed or fail. In contrast, managers in a conservative culture are likely to use management by objectives and to constantly monitor subordinates' progress toward goals, overseeing their every move. We examine leadership in detail in Chapter 14 when we consider the leadership styles that managers can adopt to influence and shape employee behavior.

CONTROLLING   The ways in which managers evaluate, and take actions to improve, performance differ depending on whether the organizational culture emphasizes formality and caution or innovation and change. Managers who want to encourage risk taking, creativity, and innovation recognize that there are multiple potential paths to success and that failure must be accepted for creativity to thrive. Thus they are less concerned about employees' performing their jobs in a specific, predetermined manner and in strict adherence to preset goals and more concerned about employees' being flexible and taking the initiative to come up with ideas for improving performance. Managers in innovative cultures are also more concerned about long-term performance than short-term targets because they recognize that real innovation entails much uncertainty that necessitates flexibility. In contrast, managers in cultures that emphasize caution and maintenance of the status quo often set specific, difficult goals for employees, frequently monitor progress toward these goals, and develop a clear set of rules that employees are expected to adhere to.

The values and norms of an organization's culture strongly affect the way managers perform their management functions. The extent to which managers buy into the values and norms of their organization shapes their view of the world and their actions and decisions in particular circumstances. In turn, the actions that managers take can have an impact on the performance of the organization. Thus organizational culture, managerial action, and organizational performance are all linked together.

While our earlier example of IDEO illustrates how organizational culture can give rise to managerial actions that ultimately benefit the organization, this is not always the case. The cultures of some organizations become dysfunctional, encouraging managerial actions that harm the organization and discouraging actions that might improve performance.[160] Corporate scandals at large companies like Enron, Tyco, and WorldCom show how damaging a dysfunctional culture can be to an organization and its members. For example, Enron's arrogant, "success at all costs" culture led to fraudulent behavior on the part of its top managers.[161] Unfortunately hundreds of Enron employees paid a heavy price for the unethical behavior of these top managers and the dysfunctional organizational culture. Not only did these employees lose their jobs, but many also lost their life savings in Enron stock and pension funds, which became worth just a fraction of their value before the wrongdoing at Enron came to light. We discuss ethics and ethical cultures in depth in the next chapter.

Summary and Review

LO3-1

ENDURING CHARACTERISTICS: PERSONALITY TRAITS Personality traits are enduring tendencies to feel, think, and act in certain ways. The Big Five general traits are extraversion, negative affectivity, agreeableness, conscientiousness, and openness to experience. Other personality traits that affect managerial behavior are locus of control, self-esteem, and the needs for achievement, affiliation, and power.

LO3-2, 3-3, 3-4   **VALUES, ATTITUDES, AND MOODS AND EMOTIONS**   A terminal value is a personal conviction about lifelong goals or objectives; an instrumental value is a personal conviction about modes of conduct. Terminal and instrumental values have an impact on what managers try to achieve in their organizations and the kinds of behaviors they engage in. An attitude is a collection of feelings and beliefs. Two attitudes important for understanding managerial behaviors include job satisfaction (the collection of feelings and beliefs that managers have about their jobs) and organizational commitment (the collection of feelings and beliefs that managers have about their organizations). A mood is a feeling or state of mind; emotions are intense feelings that are short-lived and directly linked to their causes. Managers' moods and emotions, or how they feel at work on a day-to-day basis, have the potential to impact not only their own behavior and effectiveness but also those of their subordinates. Emotional intelligence is the ability to understand and manage one's own and other people's moods and emotions.

LO3-5   **ORGANIZATIONAL CULTURE**   Organizational culture is the shared set of beliefs, expectations, values, norms, and work routines that influence how members of an organization relate to one another and work together to achieve organizational goals. Founders of new organizations and managers play an important role in creating and maintaining organizational culture. Organizational socialization is the process by which newcomers learn an organization's values and norms and acquire the work behaviors necessary to perform jobs effectively.

Management in Action

Topics for Discussion and Action

Discussion

1. Discuss why managers who have different types of personalities can be equally effective and successful. **[LO3-1]**

2. Can managers be too satisfied with their jobs? Can they be too committed to their organizations? Why or why not? **[LO3-2]**

3. Assume that you are a manager of a restaurant. Describe what it is like to work for you when you are in a negative mood. **[LO3-3]**

4. Why might managers be disadvantaged by low levels of emotional intelligence? **[LO3-4]**

Action

5. Interview a manager in a local organization. Ask the manager to describe situations in which he or she is especially likely to act in accordance with his or her values. Ask the manager to describe situations in which he or she is less likely to act in accordance with his or her values. **[LO3-2]**

6. Watch a popular television show, and as you watch it, try to determine the emotional intelligence levels of the characters the actors in the show portray. Rank the characters from highest to lowest in terms of emotional intelligence. As you watched the show, what factors influenced your assessments of emotional intelligence levels? **[LO3-4]**

7. Go to an upscale clothing store in your neighborhood, and go to a clothing store that is definitely not upscale. Observe the behavior of employees in each store as well as the store's environment. In what ways are the organizational cultures in each store similar? In what ways are they different? **[LO3-5]**

Building Management Skills

Diagnosing Culture   **[LO3-5]**

Think about the culture of the last organization you worked for, your current university, or another organization or club to which you belong. Then answer the following questions:

1. What values are emphasized in this culture?

2. What norms do members of this organization follow?

3. Who seems to have played an important role in creating the culture?

4. In what ways is the organizational culture communicated to organizational members?

Managing Ethically   **[LO3-1, 3-2]**

Some organizations rely on personality and interest inventories to screen potential employees. Other organizations attempt to screen employees by using paper-and-pencil honesty tests.

Questions

1. Either individually or in a group, think about the ethical implications of using personality and interest inventories to screen potential employees. How might this practice be unfair to potential applicants? How might organizational members who are in charge of hiring misuse it?

2. Because of measurement error and validity problems, some relatively trustworthy people may "fail" an honesty test given by an employer. What are the ethical implications of trustworthy people "failing" honesty tests, and what obligations do you think employers should have when relying on honesty tests for screening?

Small Group Breakout Exercise

Making Difficult Decisions in Hard Times [LO3-2, 3-3, 3-4, 3-5]

Form groups of three or four people, and appoint one member as the spokesperson who will communicate your findings to the whole class when called on by the instructor. Then discuss the following scenario:

You are on the top management team of a medium-size company that manufactures cardboard boxes, containers, and other cardboard packaging materials. Your company is facing increasing levels of competition for major corporate customer accounts, and profits have declined significantly. You have tried everything you can to cut costs and remain competitive, with the exception of laying off employees. Your company has had a no-layoff policy for the past 20 years, and you believe it is an important part of the organization's culture. However, you are experiencing mounting pressure to increase your firm's performance, and your no-layoff policy has been questioned by shareholders. Even though you haven't decided whether to lay off employees and thus break with a 20-year

tradition for your company, rumors are rampant in your organization that something is afoot, and employees are worried. You are meeting today to address this problem.

1. Develop a list of options and potential courses of action to address the heightened competition and decline in profitability that your company has been experiencing.

2. Choose your preferred course of action, and justify why you will take this route.

3. Describe how you will communicate your decision to employees.

4. If your preferred option involves a layoff, justify why. If it doesn't involve a layoff, explain why.

Exploring the World Wide Web [LO3-1, 3-2, 3-5]

Go to IDEO's website (www.ideo.com) and read about this company. Try to find indicators of IDEO's culture that are provided on the website. How does the design of the website itself, and the pictures and words it contains,

communicate the nature of IDEO's organizational culture? What kinds of people do you think would be attracted to IDEO? What kinds of people do you think would be likely to be dissatisfied with a job at IDEO?

Be the Manager [LO3-1, 3-2, 3-3, 3-4, 3-5]

You have recently been hired as the vice president for human resources in an advertising agency. One problem that has been brought to your attention is the fact that the creative departments at the agency have dysfunctionally high levels of conflict. You have spoken with members of each of these departments, and in each one it seems that a few members of the department are creating all the

problems. All these individuals are valued contributors who have many creative ad campaigns to their credit. The high levels of conflict are creating problems in the departments, and negative moods and emotions are much more prevalent than positive feelings. What are you going to do to both retain valued employees and alleviate the excessive conflict and negative feelings in these departments?

The Wall Street Journal Case in the News [LO3-1, 3-2, 3-3, 3-4]

After Apple, Tackling Poverty

More than a decade ago, James Higa was one of Steve Jobs's trusted advisers at Apple, helping lead thorny negotiations with music record labels and ultimately paving the way for the iTunes store.

Today he faces an arguably more difficult challenge.

On the first floor of a sun-drenched, airy room that could easily pass for one of the city's many startup pads, Higa is tackling the Bay Area's socio-economic problems. He is one of the first residents of the just-launched Invention Hub, an incubator for local jobs that is designed to bring together tech companies, nonprofits, and San Francisco's underprivileged.

The former Apple executive is among a growing group of techies seeking to bridge a widening income gap in San Francisco, riddled by rising home prices and persistent poverty.

In recent months, business leaders have started to speak out. At a technology awards show, startup investor Ron Conway, sometimes described as the "godfather of Silicon Valley," implored the audience to donate more time and money and to work closely with schools and nonprofits. He also encouraged entrepreneurs to rally behind sf.citi, his political advocacy group for the tech community.

Next week, San Francisco Mayor Ed Lee is cohosting a brainstorming session, alongside local enterprise software company Zen Desk, to discuss the revitalization of the city and reveal a new mobile app called Link-SF, designed to connect the homeless with "lifesaving services."

But as Silicon Valley's wealth balloons—punctuated last week by Facebook's $19 billion acquisition of 55-person startup WhatsApp—many citizens here are wondering why techies aren't doing more.

Higa, who comes from the "land of plenty" after spending years at Apple's 1 Infinite Loop, says he is asking the same. "We try to aspire to change the world, but if we can't even change our backyards, how can we aspire to change the world?" he said.

Higa, who is typically reserved—a reflection of Apple's discreet culture—split his time between Indiana and Japan growing up. After graduating from Stanford University, he became a photographer and met Jobs in 1984 during a photo assignment for Apple. Jobs, then 29, hired him immediately, placing him in the original Mac Group as part of the marketing team. Most of his career would closely track Jobs, from Apple to NeXT Computer and back to Apple, where he stayed until the summer of 2012, about eight months after Jobs's passing.

Since leaving Apple, Higa has continued to advise tech startups as a mentor-in-residence at Index Ventures, but now devotes the bulk of his time to philanthropy. In large part, he was inspired by what he sees as the ever-widening income gap in San Francisco.

He is the executive director of the Philanthropic Ventures Foundation, a nonprofit group that gives small grants to local causes, amounting to roughly $12 million a year. Higa also spends much of his time leaning on his connections in tech and philanthropy to push for greater collaboration between the disparate parts of the Bay Area community.

The new office is a testament to that. The Invention Hub—which officially opened on Tuesday in San Francisco's Dog Patch neighborhood next to a new luxury apartment complex—is a collaborative workspace led by Not for Sale, a human trafficking nonprofit, and its sister company, Just Business, which invests and incubates for-profit companies with a social good component.

The 7,000-square-foot building will also have space for Higa's nonprofit group PVF, a backer of Not For Sale, and a six-month training program that will teach job skills to local victims of human trafficking. The current class will learn how to become baristas from coffee company Amor Perfecto (a Just Business company) and learn skills necessary for internships at companies. Juniper, Salesforce.com, and Blue Bottle have agreed to provide internships to some graduates of the program.

As a founding partner of the Invention Hub, Higa will continue to help establish job connections in the industry and organize regular brainstorming sessions with the tech community to take on other issues, such as rising evictions, said David Batstone, a cofounder of Not for Sale. Higa is particularly focused on spreading the word to mid-to-large-sized startups with 50 or more employees that will need nontechnical help, such as those delivering goods and services across the Bay Area.

The hope is that the combination of these elements will create new jobs and begin to change how tech companies operate within their neighborhoods.

It is a unique setup, but more nonprofits in the city are trying to adopt Silicon Valley's practices. Just a few miles north, Tipping Point, another local philanthropy, has created its own incubator, called the T Lab, where it brings in professionals, including engineers and designers, to tackle specific social problems.

Not everyone, however, is convinced such actions will create a big enough dent here. Carlos Rivera, a communications coordinator for the Service Employees International

Union Local 1021, a labor union, says job programs will help some, but he wants to see bigger sacrifices from tech, such as donating the money they get from tax breaks. "It's a step in the right direction but not enough," he said.

Higa is unfazed by the criticism.

He says he's reminded of his projects at Apple, most of which started very small before becoming billion-dollar businesses. The initial iTunes group, for example, started as five people.

"My work has always been about finding the Northwest Passage," said Higa, referring to a historical sea route that connects the Atlantic and Pacific oceans. "But when you can find a way, then the railroads comes in, the city comes in, and then you're on to the next wilderness."

Source: Evelyn M. Rusli, "After Apple, Tackling Poverty: Ex-Aid to Jobs Pushes Social Change," *The Wall Street Journal,* February 26, 2014. Copyright © 2014 Dow Jones & Company, Inc. Reproduced with permission via Copyright Clearance Center.

Questions for Discussion

1. What personality traits do you think James Higa is high on?

2. What terminal and instrumental values do you think might be especially important to him?

3. What moods and emotions do you think he is likely to experience?

4. Do you think he is high or low on emotional intelligence? Why do you think this?

CHAPTER 4

Ethics and Social Responsibility

Learning Objectives

After studying this chapter, you should be able to:

LO4-1   Explain the relationship between ethics and the law.

LO4-2   Differentiate between the claims of the different stakeholder groups that are affected by managers and their companies' actions.

LO4-3   Describe four rules that can help companies and their managers act in ethical ways.

LO4-4   Discuss why it is important for managers to behave ethically.

LO4-5   Identify the four main sources of managerial ethics.

LO4-6   Distinguish among the four main approaches toward social responsibility that a company can take.

A MANAGER'S CHALLENGE

Michelle Obama's Challenge to Kids across America: Let's Move!

Can ethical and socially responsible management be good for the bottom line?
Childhood obesity has become a growing concern in the United States. According to the U.S. government, about 33 percent of children are overweight or obese. In African American and Latino communities, the numbers are even higher—nearly 40 percent.[1] To help combat the problem, First Lady Michelle Obama started the Let's Move! campaign to end childhood obesity in a generation's time.[2]

There are several causes for the rising numbers of overweight children. Children used to play outside more, where they would run around and burn calories. However, with television and video games providing enticing entertainment, children now have less active options for playing. Also, the faster pace at which life is lived often shrinks the time available to prepare and eat healthful, nutritionally balanced meals. Children now eat about three snacks per day, compared to one per day 30 years ago. Portion sizes for both food and beverages also have become much larger.[3] (Witness former New York City Mayor Michael Bloomberg's famous attempt to try to outlaw supersized drinks in the Big Apple.) Sugars and fats are much more prevalent in foods, and what we eat today is more processed than ever before, sapping our kids (and us) of vital nutrients.

Being overweight is unhealthy, especially in children. It may lead to serious health problems in childhood, such as Type 2 diabetes or heart disease. In addition to health risks, being overweight or obese can make children the targets of social discrimination. And the chances that a child will "grow out of it" are slim—obese children are likely to become obese adults.

So to bring awareness and activism to the problem, Mrs. Obama's campaign targets not just parents and caregivers, but the community at large too. Let's Move! has five pillars, as stated on letsmove.gov:

1. Creating a healthy start for children.
2. Empowering parents and caregivers.
3. Providing healthful food in schools.
4. Improving access to healthful, affordable foods.
5. Increasing physical activity.

Mrs. Obama says the movement will continue even after her husband leaves office and she is no longer First Lady. Some of the accomplishments of the movement so far include the MyPlate and MiPlato icon,

First Lady Michelle Obama tends the White House garden with a group of children as part of the *Let's Move* campaign to end childhood obesity.

which makes it easy to understand healthful food choices; the closing of city streets to create "play streets" where children can be active without worrying about traffic; and higher standards for nutrition and fitness in schools.

But what about the food industry? How does it play a role in the problem, and what can the Let's Move! campaign do about it? Let's Move! coincides with the Partnership for a Healthier America (PHA), an organization that was created at the same time but is separate from Let's Move! PHA works with the government and Let's Move! on industry-specific solutions to fight obesity. Partnership for a Healthier America aims to bring together leaders from all sectors to reduce childhood obesity.

But for the private sector, many of the Let's Move! campaign actions would appear to be bad for business. For example, in February 2014 the White House and the Department of Agriculture laid out new restrictions on the advertisements of unhealthful food and sugary drinks in U.S. schools. "If you can't sell it, you ought not to be able to market it," U.S. Agriculture Secretary Tom Vilsack said.[4]

Yet the beverage industry was on board with the changes. Following the announcement of the ban in advertising of sugary drinks in schools, the American Beverage Association issued a statement from its president, Susan Neely, stating, "Mrs. Obama's efforts to continue to strengthen school wellness make sense for the well-being of our schoolchildren. . . . We look forward to working with the USDA on their proposed rule to align food and beverage signage in schools with the new regulations as the next logical next step."[5]

Many food companies also have joined the Let's Move! campaign. For example, Darden, which owns popular restaurant chains like Olive Garden and Red Lobster, has pledged to offer a fruit or vegetable and low-fat milk with every kid's meal. It also is working to reduce the amount of calories and sodium in its menu items by 20 percent over the next 10 years. Walmart committed to lowering the cost of fruits, vegetables, and other healthful options and to work with manufacturers to reduce the amount of sugar and sodium in categories throughout the store.

In October 2009 more than 40 organizations and companies launched the Healthy Weight Commitment Foundation with the goal of reducing childhood obesity. In 2010 the Healthy Weight Commitment Foundation agreed with Let's Move! and the Partnership for a Healthier America to cut 1.5 trillion calories in food products over the next five years. The companies planned to develop lower-calorie options, reduce calories in existing products, and make portion sizes smaller. In January 2014 an independent evaluator announced that the Healthy Weight Commitment Foundation had exceeded its goal and removed 6.4 trillion calories from food products.

Why did companies join the Let's Move! campaign? Being socially responsible can help the bottom line. As the demand for more healthful food items is increasing, studies are being conducted to see how companies are faring. According to the Hudson Institute, "better-for-you" foods made up about 40 percent of the sales for the companies studied, but created 70 percent or more in sales growth over a four-year span. The study defined "better-for-you" foods as those with no, low, or reduced calories. The Hudson Institute report concludes that "sound strategic planning with a commitment to growing sales of better-for-you foods is just good business."[6]

Overview

As the Let's Move! campaign illustrates, management decision making can have far- reaching implications. The Let's Move! campaign may be targeted at children, but the campaign affects parents, schools, food and beverage companies, and many others. But globally, nations, companies, and managers differ enormously in their commitment to these people, or *stakeholders*—various groups of people who may benefit or be harmed by how managers make decisions that affect them. Managers of some companies make the need to behave ethically toward stakeholders their main priority. Managers of other companies pursue their own self-interest at the expense of their stakeholders and do harm to them—such as the harm done to the millions of people around the world who work in dangerous, unsanitary conditions or who work for a pittance.

In this chapter we examine the obligations and responsibilities of managers and the companies they work for toward the people and society that are affected by their actions. First we examine the nature of ethics and the sources of ethical problems. Next we discuss the major stakeholder groups that are affected by how companies operate. We also look at four rules or guidelines managers can use to decide whether a specific business decision is ethical or unethical. Finally we consider the sources of managerial ethics and the reasons why it is important for a company to behave in a socially responsible manner. By the end of this chapter you will understand the central role of ethics in shaping the practice of management and the life of a people, society, and nation.

The Nature of Ethics

Suppose you see a person being mugged. Will you act in some way to help even though you risk being hurt? Will you walk away? Perhaps you might not intervene, but will you call the police? Does how you act depend on whether the person being mugged is a fit male, an elderly person, or a homeless person? Does it depend on whether other people are around so you can tell yourself, "Oh well, someone else will help or call the police. I don't need to"?

Ethical Dilemmas

ethical dilemma The quandary people find themselves in when they have to decide if they should act in a way that might help another person or group even though doing so might go against their own self-interest.

The situation just described is an example of an **ethical dilemma**, the quandary people find themselves in when they have to decide if they should act in a way that might help another person or group and is the right thing to do, even though doing so might go against their own self-interest.[7] A dilemma may also arise when a person has to choose between two different courses of action, knowing that whichever course he or she selects will harm one person or group even while it may benefit another. The ethical dilemma here is to decide which course of action is the lesser of two evils.

People often know they are confronting an ethical dilemma when their moral scruples come into play and cause them to hesitate, debate, and reflect upon the rightness or goodness of a course of action. Moral scruples are thoughts and feelings that tell a person what is right or wrong; they are a part of a person's ethics. **Ethics** are the inner guiding moral principles, values, and beliefs that people use to analyze or interpret a situation and then decide what is the right or appropriate way to behave. Ethics also indicate what is inappropriate behavior and how a person should behave to avoid harming another person.

ethics The inner guiding moral principles, values, and beliefs that people use to analyze or interpret a situation and then decide what is the right or appropriate way to behave.

The essential problem in dealing with ethical issues, and thus solving moral dilemmas, is that no absolute or indisputable rules or principles can be developed to decide whether an action is ethical or unethical. Put simply, different people or groups may dispute which actions are ethical or unethical depending on their personal self-interest and specific attitudes, beliefs, and values—concepts we discussed in Chapter 3. How are we and companies and their managers and employees to decide what is ethical and so act appropriately toward other people and groups?

LO4-1

Explain the relationship between ethics and the law.

Ethics and the Law

The first answer to this question is that society as a whole, using the political and legal process, can lobby for and pass laws that specify what people can and cannot do. Many different kinds of laws govern business—for example, laws against fraud and deception and laws governing how companies can treat their employees and customers. Laws also specify what sanctions or punishments will follow if those laws are broken. Different groups in society lobby for which laws should be passed based on their own personal interests and beliefs about right and wrong. The group that can summon the most support can pass laws that align with its interests and beliefs. Once a law is passed, a decision about what the appropriate behavior is with regard to a person or situation is taken from the personally determined ethical realm to the societally determined legal realm. If you do not conform to the law, you can be prosecuted; and if you are found guilty of breaking the law, you can be punished. You have little say in the matter; your fate is in the hands of the court and its lawyers.

In studying the relationship between ethics and law, it is important to understand that *neither laws nor ethics are fixed principles* that do not change over time. Ethical beliefs change as time passes; and as they do so, laws change to reflect the changing ethical beliefs of a society. It was seen as ethical, and it was legal, for example, to acquire and possess slaves in ancient Rome and Greece and in the United States until the late 19th century. Ethical views regarding whether slavery was morally right or appropriate changed, however. Slavery was made illegal in the United States when those in power decided that slavery degraded the meaning of being human. Slavery makes a statement about the value or worth of human beings and about their right to life, liberty, and the pursuit of happiness. And if we deny these rights to other people, how can we claim to have any natural rights to these things?

Moreover, what is to stop any person or group, that becomes powerful enough to take control of the political and legal process, from enslaving us and denying us the right to be free and to own property? In denying freedom to others, one risks losing it oneself, just as stealing from others opens the door for them to steal from us in return. "Do unto others as you would have them do unto you" is a common ethical or moral rule that people apply in such situations to decide what is the right thing to do.

Changes in Ethics over Time

There are many types of behavior—such as murder, theft, slavery, rape, and driving while intoxicated—that most people currently believe are unacceptable and unethical and should therefore be illegal. However, the ethics of many other actions and behaviors are open to dispute. Some people might believe a particular behavior—for example, smoking tobacco or possessing guns—is unethical and so should be made illegal. Others might argue that it is up to the individual or group to decide if such behaviors are ethical and thus whether a particular behavior should remain legal.

As ethical beliefs change over time, some people may begin to question whether existing laws that make specific behaviors illegal are still appropriate. They might argue that although a specific behavior is deemed illegal, this does not make it unethical and thus the law should be changed. In 48 states, for example, it is illegal to possess or use marijuana (cannabis). To justify this law, it is commonly argued that smoking marijuana leads people to try more dangerous drugs. Once the habit of taking drugs has been acquired, people can get hooked on them. More powerful drugs such as heroin and other narcotics are addictive, and most people cannot stop using them without help. Thus the use of marijuana, because it might lead to further harm, is an unethical practice.

It has been documented medically, however, that marijuana use can help people with certain illnesses. For example, for cancer sufferers who are undergoing chemotherapy and for those with AIDS who are on potent medications, marijuana offers relief from many treatment side effects, such as nausea and lack of appetite. Yet in the United States it is illegal in many states for doctors to prescribe marijuana for these patients, so their suffering continues. Since 1996, however, 15 states have made it legal to prescribe marijuana for medical purposes; nevertheless, the federal government has sought to stop such state legislation. The U.S. Supreme Court ruled in 2005 that only Congress or the states could decide whether medical marijuana use should be made legal, and people in many states are currently lobbying for a relaxation of state laws against its use for medical purposes.[8] In Canada there has been a widespread movement to decriminalize marijuana. While not making the drug legal, decriminalization removes the threat of prosecution even for uses that are not medically related and allows the drug to be taxed. Initiatives are under way in several states to decriminalize the possession of small amounts

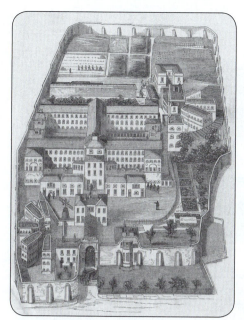

Coldbath Fields Prison, London, circa 1810. The British criminal justice system around this time was severe: a person could be executed for 350 different crimes, including sheep stealing. As ethical beliefs change over time, so do laws.

of marijuana for personal use as well as to make it more widely available to people legally for medical purposes. A major ethical debate is currently raging over this issue in many states and countries.

The important point to note is that while ethical beliefs lead to the development of laws and regulations to prevent certain behaviors or encourage others, laws themselves change or even disappear as ethical beliefs change. In Britain in 1830 a person could be executed for over 350 different crimes, including sheep stealing. Today the death penalty is no longer legal in Britain. Thus both ethical and legal rules are *relative:* No absolute or unvarying standards exist to determine how we should behave, and people are caught up in moral dilemmas all the time. Because of this we have to make ethical choices.

The previous discussion highlights an important issue in understanding the relationship between ethics, law, and business. Throughout the 2010s many scandals plagued major companies such as J.P. Morgan Chase, HSBC, Standard Chartered Bank, ING, Barclays, and Capital One. Managers at some of these companies engaged in risky trades, interest rate manipulation, illegal trade facilitation, drug money laundering, and deception of customers.

In other cases no laws were broken, yet outrage was expressed over perceptions of unethical actions. One example of this is the Occupy Wall Street movement, a protest that began on September 17, 2011, in a park close to New York City's Wall Street financial district. The movement was prompted in part by the perceived unethical influence of the financial services sector on the government. On its web page (occupywallstreet.org), the organization says it is "fighting back against the corrosive power of major banks and multinational corporations over the democratic process, and the role of Wall Street in creating an economic collapse that has caused the greatest recession in generations." It also raised issues of social and economic inequality.

Some of the goals of this protest were to reduce the influence of corporations on government and allow a more balanced distribution of income. While the protesters did not allege that what financial institutions were doing was illegal, they asserted that the actions of financial institutions were not congruent with ethical business practices.

In 2011 President Barack Obama commented on Occupy Wall Street's concerns about the way policies are influenced by the financial sector: "It expresses the frustrations that the American people feel that we had the biggest financial crisis since the Great Depression, huge collateral damage all throughout the country, all across Main Street. And yet you're still seeing some of the same folks who acted irresponsibly trying to fight efforts to crack down on abusive practices that got us into this problem in the first place."[9]

Stakeholders and Ethics

Just as people have to work out the right and wrong ways to act, so do companies. When the law does not specify how companies should behave, their managers must decide the right or ethical way to behave toward the people and groups affected by their actions. Who are the people or groups that are affected by a company's business decisions? If a company behaves in an ethical way, how does this benefit people and society? Conversely, how are people harmed by a company's unethical actions?

The people and groups affected by how a company and its managers behave are called its stakeholders. **Stakeholders** supply a company with its productive resources; as a result, they have a claim on and a stake in the company.[10] Because stakeholders can directly benefit or be harmed by its actions, the ethics of a company and its managers are important to them. Who are a company's major stakeholders? What do they contribute to a company, and what do they claim in return? Here we examine the claims of these stakeholders—stockholders; managers; employees; suppliers and distributors; customers; and community, society, and nation-state as Figure 4.1 depicts.

stakeholders The people and groups that supply a company with its productive resources and so have a claim on and a stake in the company.

Figure 4.1

Types of Company Stakeholders

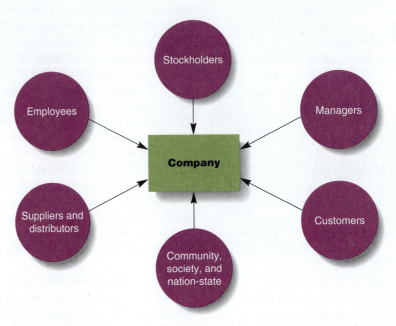

LO4-2

Differentiate between the claims of the different stakeholder groups that are affected by managers and their companies' actions.

Stockholders

Stockholders have a claim on a company because when they buy its stock or shares they become its owners. When the founder of a company decides to publicly incorporate the business to raise capital, shares of the stock of that company are issued. This stock grants its buyers ownership of a certain percentage of the company and the right to receive any future stock dividends. For example, in 2005 Microsoft decided to pay the owners of its 5 billion shares a special dividend payout of $32 billion. Bill Gates received $3.3 billion in dividends based on his stockholding, and he donated this money to the Bill and Melinda Gates Foundation, to which he has reportedly donated over $28 billion to date, with the promise of much more to come; and Warren Buffet committed to donate at least $30 billion to the Gates Foundation over the next decade. The two richest people in the world have decided to give away a large part of their wealth to serve global ethical causes—in particular to address global health concerns such as malnutrition, malaria, tuberculosis, and AIDS. Gates is also donating about $1.8 billion to the Gates Foundation to help eradicate polio as part of the Polio Eradication & Endgame Strategic Plan 2013–2018.[11]

Stockholders are interested in how a company operates because they want to maximize the return on their investment. Thus they watch the company and its managers closely to ensure that management is working diligently to increase the company's profitability.[12] Stockholders also want to ensure that managers are behaving ethically and not risking investors' capital by engaging in actions that could hurt the company's reputation. No company wants the reputation described by the Occupy Wall Street protesters, who alleged that business organizations value money over people and work in the self-interest of a privileged few. However, experts warn businesses not to ignore the movement. Harvard bloggers say the persistence of Occupy Wall Street is "a signal that there is authentic, deep-seated unhappiness with the failings of the U.S. economic system. It's an indicator that economic inequality is perceived as an important issue—one requiring businesses' immediate attention."[13]

Managers

Managers are a vital stakeholder group because they are responsible for using a company's financial, capital, and human resources to increase its performance and thus its stock price.[14] Managers have a claim on an organization because they bring to it their skills, expertise, and experience. They have the right to expect a good return or reward by investing their human

Rajat Kumar Gupta, former Goldman Sachs board member, exits federal court in New York after being convicted of insider trading and sentenced to two years in prison.

capital to improve a company's performance. Such rewards include good salaries and benefits, the prospect of promotion and a career, and stock options and bonuses tied to company performance.

Managers are the stakeholder group that bears the responsibility to decide which goals an organization should pursue to most benefit stakeholders and how to make the most efficient use of resources to achieve those goals. In making such decisions, managers frequently must juggle the interests of different stakeholders, including themselves.[15] These sometimes difficult decisions challenge managers to uphold ethical values because some decisions that benefit certain stakeholder groups (managers and stockholders) harm other groups (individual workers and local communities). For example, in economic downturns or when a company experiences performance shortfalls, layoffs may help cut costs (thus benefiting shareholders) at the expense of the employees laid off. Many U.S. managers have recently faced this difficult decision. Until the 2009 financial crisis sent unemployment soaring over 10 percent, on average about 1.6 million U.S. employees out of a total labor force of 140 million were affected by mass layoffs each year; and over 3 million jobs from the United States, Europe, and Japan have been outsourced to Asia since 2005. Layoff decisions are always difficult: They not only take a heavy toll on workers, their families, and local communities but also mean the loss of the contributions of valued employees to an organization. In 2014 Michelin North America (Canada) announced it would slash 500 jobs from its Granton tire plant over the next 18 months. The company was Nova Scotia's largest private manufacturer.[16]

As we discussed in Chapter 1, managers must be motivated and given incentives to work hard in the interests of stockholders. Their behavior must also be scrutinized to ensure they do not behave illegally or unethically, pursuing goals that threaten stockholders and the company's interests.[17] Unfortunately we have seen in the 2010s how easy it is for top managers to find ways to ruthlessly pursue their self-interest at the expense of stockholders and employees because laws and regulations are not strong enough to force them to behave ethically.

In a nutshell, the problem has been that in many companies corrupt managers focus not on building the company's capital and stockholders' wealth but on maximizing their own personal capital and wealth. In an effort to prevent future scandals, the Securities and Exchange Commission (SEC), the government's top business watchdog, has begun to rework the rules governing a company's relationship with its auditor, as well as regulations concerning stock options, and to increase the power of outside directors to scrutinize a CEO. The SEC's goal is to outlaw many actions that were previously classified as merely unethical. For example, companies are now forced to reveal to stockholders the value of the stock options they give their top executives and directors and when they give them these options; this shows how much such payments reduce company profits. Managers and directors can now be prosecuted if they disguise or try to hide these payments. In the 2010s the SEC announced many new rules requiring that companies disclose myriad details of executive compensation packages to investors; already the boards of directors of many companies have stopped giving CEOs perks such as free personal jet travel, membership in exclusive country clubs, and luxury accommodations on "business trips." Also, in 2010 Congress passed new laws preventing the many unethical and illegal actions of managers of banks and other financial institutions that led to the 2009 financial crisis. One of these regulations, the "Volcker Rule," seeks to reduce the chances that banks will put depositors' money at risk.[18]

Indeed, many experts argue that the rewards given to top managers, particularly the CEO and COO, grew out of control in the 2000s. Top managers are today's "aristocrats," and through their ability to influence the board of directors and raise their own pay, they have amassed personal fortunes worth hundreds of millions of dollars. For example, according to a study by the Federal Reserve, U.S. CEOs now get paid about 600 times what the average worker earns, compared to about 40 times in 1980—a staggering increase. In 2014 the median

CEO pay was $8.64 million.[19] We noted in Chapter 1 that besides their salaries, top managers often receive tens of millions in stock bonuses and options—even when their companies perform poorly.

Is it ethical for top managers to receive such vast amounts of money from their companies? Do they earn it? Remember, this money could have gone to shareholders in the form of dividends. It could also have reduced the huge salary gap between those at the top and those at the bottom of the hierarchy. Many people argue that the growing disparity between the rewards given to CEOs and to other employees is unethical and should be regulated. CEO pay has skyrocketed because CEOs are the people who set and control one another's salaries and bonuses; they can do this because they sit on the boards of other companies as outside directors. Others argue that because top managers play an important role in building a company's capital and wealth, they deserve a significant share of its profits. Some recent research has suggested that the companies whose CEO compensation includes a large percentage of stock options tend to experience big share losses more often than big gains, and that on average, company performance improves as stock option use declines.[20] The debate over how much money CEOs and other top managers should be paid is still raging, particularly because the financial crisis beginning in 2009 showed how much money the CEOs of troubled financial companies earned even as their companies' performance and stock prices collapsed. For example, Countrywide Mortgage, which pioneered the subprime business, suffered losses of over $1.7 billion in 2007, and its stock fell 80 percent; yet its CEO Angelo Mozilo still received $20 million in stock awards and sold stock options worth $121 million before the company's price collapsed.

Ethics and Nonprofit Organizations

The issue of what is fair compensation for top managers is not limited to for-profit companies; it is one of many issues facing nonprofits. The many ethics scandals that have plagued companies in the 2010s might suggest that the issue of ethics is important only for profit-seeking companies, but this would be untrue. There are almost 2 million private nonprofit charitable and philanthropic organizations in the United States, and charges that their managers have acted in unethical and even illegal ways have grown in the 2010s. For example, many states and the federal government are investigating the huge salaries that the top executives of charitable institutions earn.

One impetus for this was the revelation that the NYSE, which is classified as a charitable organization, paid its disgraced top executive Richard A. Grasso over $187 million in pension benefits. It turns out that over 200 nonprofits pay their top executives more than $1 million a year in salary, and the boards of trustees or directors of many of these organizations also enjoy lavish perks and compensation for attendance at board meetings. And unlike for-profit companies, which are required by law to provide detailed reports of their operations to their shareholders, nonprofits do not have shareholders, so the laws governing disclosure are far weaker. As a result, the board and its top managers have considerable latitude to decide how they will spend a nonprofit's resources, and little oversight exists.

To remedy this situation, many states and the federal government are considering new laws that would subject nonprofits to strict Sarbanes-Oxley-type regulations that force the disclosure of issues related to managerial compensation and financial integrity. There are also efforts in progress to strengthen the legal power of the IRS to oversee nonprofits' expenditures so that it has more authority to examine how these organizations spend their resources on managerial and director compensation and perks.

Experts hope that the introduction of new rules and regulations to monitor and oversee how nonprofits spend their funds will result in much more value being created from the funds given by donors. After all, every cent that is spent administering a nonprofit is a cent not being used to help the people or cause for which the money was intended. Ethical issues are involved because some badly run charities spend 70 cents of every dollar on administration costs. And charges have been leveled against charities such as the Red Cross for mishandling the hundreds of millions of dollars they received in donations after Hurricane Katrina struck; changes have been made in the Red Cross to address these issues. Clearly the directors and managers of all organizations need to carefully consider the ethical issues involved in their decision making.

Employees

A company's employees are the hundreds of thousands of people who work in its various departments and functions, such as research, sales, and manufacturing. Employees expect to receive rewards consistent with their performance. One principal way that a company can act ethically toward employees and meet their expectations is by creating an occupational structure that fairly and equitably rewards employees for their contributions. Companies, for example, need to develop recruitment, training, performance appraisal, and reward systems that do not discriminate against employees and that employees believe are fair.

Suppliers and Distributors

No company operates alone. Every company is in a network of relationships with other companies that supply it with the inputs (such as raw materials, components, contract labor, and clients) that it needs to operate. It also depends on intermediaries such as wholesalers and retailers to distribute its products to the final customers. Suppliers expect to be paid fairly and promptly for their inputs; distributors expect to receive quality products at agreed-upon prices. Once again, many ethical issues arise in how companies contract and interact with their suppliers and distributors. Important issues concerning safety specifications are governed by the contracts a company signs with its suppliers and distributors, for example; however, lax oversight can have tragic consequences, as the accompanying "Ethics in Action" feature shows.

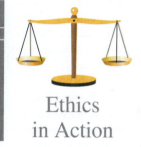

Ethics in Action

Safety in the Garment Industry

Why did more than 150 international brands and retailers, including Abercrombie & Fitch, American Eagle Outfitters, Fruit of the Loom, and PVH, sign the Accord on Fire and Building Safety in Bangladesh in 2013? The accord is a five-year agreement stating that the signing companies and organizations commit to meet the minimum safety standards for the textile industry in Bangladesh.

Could it be that the buying power of consumers in their mid-twenties—consumers very concerned about the plight of the global worker—encouraged brands and retailers to sign the agreement? Sébastien Breteau, founder and chief executive officer of AsiaInspection, a quality control service provider of supplier audits, product inspections, and lab testing for consumer goods and food importers, believes young people have raised awareness of social accountability in global supply chain management. "This generation cares a lot about transparency," he said. "They want to know that what they are buying doesn't kill the planet."[21] This means that organizations who do not monitor their suppliers carefully risk paying a steep price with young consumers.

Several industrial accidents in 2013 catalyzed social accountability in global supply chain management, according to Breteau's firm. Probably the most tragic of the tipping points was the collapse of the Rana Plaza in Dhaka, Bangladesh. The collapse of the eight-story commercial building killed 1,132 workers and injured more than 2,500 on April 24, 2013. The day before the collapse, building inspectors had found cracks in the structure and warned business owners to evacuate. A few shops and a bank heeded the warning, but owners of garment factories in the building ordered employees to come to work. The collapse was the deadliest disaster in the history of the garment industry worldwide.

There are parallels between the collapse of Rana Plaza and a tragedy in the history of American garment factories. In 1911 a fire destroyed the Triangle Shirtwaist Factory and killed 146 garment workers. The factory was on the top floors of a building in Greenwich Village, New York City. When the fire broke out, workers found the exit doors locked from the outside, a common practice at the time to stop theft and unauthorized breaks. Many workers died by jumping out the windows to escape the flames. The outrage that followed the Triangle fire was a catalyst for change in factory conditions, much like the outrage that followed the Rana Plaza collapse. In the aftermath of the fire, the Factory Investigating Commission was formed and, much like the Accord on Fire and Building Safety in Bangladesh, began factory inspections. Many factories in New York City were found to have the same conditions that caused the Triangle fire, such as flammable materials, locked exit doors, and inadequate fire alarms and fire suppression systems. Between 1911 and 1913, 60 new laws were passed to improve factory conditions.

In March 2014 engineering teams organized through the Accord issued inspection reports on 10 Bangladesh factories. The reports indicated many factories did not have adequate fire alarm and sprinkler systems and that some fire exits were locked.[22] Also, many factories had dangerously high weight loads on floors, which is believed to be a cause of the Rana Plaza collapse.

Following the Rana Plaza collapse, clients of the Breteau's inspection firm have become less reluctant to commit to the creation and enforcement of programs to audit factory working conditions. "Suddenly, we saw a switch in our clients' attitude to social accountability," according to Breteau. "They became very serious about running audit programs through their supply chains."[23] The company's audit programs include quality management standards according to the ISO 9001 or U.S. C-TPAT standards, social compliance according to SA 8000 standards, and ethical trading according to Sedex Ethical Trade Audits.

Will this change in attitudes toward social accountability in global supply chains have a lasting impact? *Forbes* blogger Robert Bowman, managing editor of SupplyChainBrain, a website and magazine covering global supply chains, names several reasons why retailers have failed to take aggressive action to stop unsafe working conditions in the past. From the retailers' point of view, it can be difficult to keep track of complex supply chains. Multiple layers of suppliers and subcontractors in some supply chains make it complicated to know exactly how and where goods are being produced, Bowman says. From the consumer's point of view, shocking revelations of poor labor practices cause temporary indignation. After headlines and media stories about sweatshops and safety violations, shoppers quickly return to being indifferent about how clothing is produced, Bowman says. However, the shocking collapse of Rana Plaza and the resulting signatures on the Accord on Fire and Building Safety in Bangladesh bode well for real change in global supply chain ethics.

Many other issues depend on business ethics. For example, numerous products sold in U.S. stores have been outsourced to countries that do not have U.S.-style regulations and laws to protect the workers who make these products. All companies must take an ethical position on the way they obtain and make the products they sell. Commonly this stance is published on a company's website. Table 4.1 presents part of the Gap's statement about its approach to global ethics (www.gapinc.com).

Customers

Customers are often regarded as the most critical stakeholder group because if a company cannot attract them to buy its products, it cannot stay in business. Thus managers and employees must work to increase efficiency and effectiveness in order to create loyal customers and attract new ones. They do so by selling customers quality products at a fair price and providing good after-sales service. They can also strive to improve their products over time and provide guarantees to customers about the integrity of their products like the Soap Dispensary, profiled in the accompanying "Ethics in Action" feature.

Table 4.1

Some Principles from the Gap's Code of Vendor Conduct

As a condition of doing business with Gap Inc., each and every factory must comply with this Code of Vendor Conduct. Gap Inc. will continue to develop monitoring systems to assess and ensure compliance. If Gap Inc. determines that any factory has violated this Code, Gap Inc. may either terminate its business relationship or require the factory to implement a corrective action plan. If corrective action is advised but not taken, Gap Inc. will suspend placement of future orders and may terminate current production.

I. General Principles

Factories that produce goods for Gap Inc. shall operate in full compliance with the laws of their respective countries and with all other applicable laws, rules, and regulations.

II. Environment

Factories must comply with all applicable environmental laws and regulations. Where such requirements are less stringent than Gap Inc.'s own, factories are encouraged to meet the standards outlined in Gap Inc.'s statement of environmental principles.

III. Discrimination

Factories shall employ workers on the basis of their ability to do the job, without regard to race, color, gender, nationality, religion, age, maternity, or marital status.

IV. Forced Labor

Factories shall not use any prison, indentured, or forced labor.

V. Child Labor

Factories shall employ only workers who meet the applicable minimum legal age requirement or are at least 14 years of age, whichever is greater. Factories must also comply with all other applicable child labor laws. Factories are encouraged to develop lawful workplace apprenticeship programs for the educational benefit of their workers, provided that all participants meet both Gap Inc.'s minimum age standard of 14 and the minimum legal age requirement.

VI. Wages & Hours

Factories shall set working hours, wages, and overtime pay in compliance with all applicable laws. Workers shall be paid at least the minimum legal wage or a wage that meets local industry standards, whichever is greater. While it is understood that overtime is often required in garment production, factories shall carry out operations in ways that limit overtime to a level that ensures humane and productive working conditions.

Ethics
in Action

Cleaning up the Soap Market

Soap consumption is not as clean a business as you might think. First, soap is often packaged in plastic, and that's beyond the bar: dishwashing detergent, clothing detergent, shampoos, body washes, liquid hand soaps—they're all in plastic containers. With over 33 million tons of plastic being discarded yearly by Americans, only about 14 percent is recycled or sent to waste-to-energy facilities. The rest goes to landfills, where it may leak pollutants into the soil and water, or into the ocean, where an estimated 100 million tons of plastic debris already threatens the health of marine life.[24]

Second, many soaps have chemicals that contain suspected or known carcinogens (cancer-causing agents). One study of 25 household products found that many of their fragrances emitted hazardous chemicals.[25] One such chemical is triclosan, which is commonly found in soap products. Triclosan is toxic to aquatic plants and animals. When it reacts with chlorine in water, it can cause cancer, nerve disorders, and immune system disorders. It also contributes to antibiotic resistance in bacteria that causes infection in humans.

To combat the dirty residue of soap consumption, stores like the Soap Dispensary in Vancouver, Canada, are popping up. The Soap Dispensary is a refill store specializing in soaps, household cleaners, and personal care products that are not harmful to

At the Soap Dispensary in Vancouver, owner Linh Truong sells biodegradable household and personal products free from fillers, dyes, and perfumes. Customers bring their own containers to refill over and over again, and Linh tracks the savings to the environment with each bottle refilled.

humans or the environment. Instead of harsh chemicals, the Soap Dispensary's products are selected to be as free as possible from fillers, dyes, and synthetic perfumes. The products are also biodegradable and animal cruelty–free, and some are vegan certified.

Customers bring their own containers back to the store again and again to refill instead of throwing them away, or they can pay a small deposit fee to obtain a reusable container from the store. The store also sells ingredients customers can use to make their own soaps (as well as other products) and conducts classes to teach customers how to make them at home. Classes range from simple soap making to using cloth diapers to composting to aromatherapy. Besides soap, the store sells nonplastic cleaning supplies, reusable razors, natural beeswax candles, repurposed fabric, and other environmentally friendly items.

Linh Truong and Stewart Lampe, owners of the Soap Dispensary, estimate that in the first two years of the store's existence, it has kept more than 8,000 plastic containers from being thrown away.

The store also has provided a venue where customers can purchase locally made products. Among the local brands sold at the Soap Dispensary are Curiosities Tallow Soap and Sadie's Soap. Curiosities Tallow Soap's ingredients include beef fat collected from local butcher shops, and Sadie's Soap's ingredients include hops from locally crafted beer.[26] These locally made soaps and their locally acquired ingredients make a short supply chain that is easier on the environment than a national or international one. When locally owned businesses provide supplies for other locally owned businesses, less fuel and other energy is spent on transportation, creating less pollution in the environment.[27]

The Soap Dispensary tracks the savings to the environment of each bottle refilled, which Truong uses to inspire her customers to keep conserving. Refill stores like the Soap Dispensary make a difference by focusing on one feasible aspect of sustainability. Truong also achieves her mission of reducing waste by encouraging her suppliers to switch to more sustainable packaging and by washing out some delivery containers to return to suppliers for reuse.

"Refilling soap is just one way to do it," she said. "It's just the art of shifting consumers' mentality. Once you start that shift, it can be applied to lots of other things in their lives, and also to how a business is run."[28]

Community, Society, and Nation

The effects of the decisions made by companies and their managers permeate all aspects of the communities, societies, and nations in which they operate. *Community* refers to physical locations like towns or cities or to social milieus like ethnic neighborhoods in which companies are located. A community provides a company with the physical and social infrastructure that allows it to operate; its utilities and labor force; the homes in which its managers and employees live; the schools, colleges, and hospitals that serve their needs; and so on.

Through the salaries, wages, and taxes it pays, a company contributes to the economy of its town or region and often determines whether the community prospers or declines. Similarly, a company affects the prosperity of a society and a nation and, to the degree that a company is involved in global trade, all the countries it operates in and thus the prosperity of the global economy. We have already discussed the many issues surrounding global outsourcing and the loss of jobs in the United States, for example.

Although the individual effects of the way each McDonald's restaurant operates might be small, for instance, the combined effects of how all McDonald's and other fast-food companies do business are enormous. In the United States alone, over 500,000 people work in the fast-food industry, and many thousands of suppliers like farmers, paper cup manufacturers, builders, and so on depend on it for their livelihood. Small wonder then that the ethics of the fast-food business are scrutinized closely. This industry was the major lobbyer against attempts to raise the national minimum wage (which was raised to $7.25 an hour in 2009, where it remains in 2014 up from $5.15—a figure that had not changed since 1997), for example, because a higher minimum wage would substantially increase its operating costs. However, responding to protests about chickens raised in cages where they cannot move, McDonald's—the largest egg buyer in the United States—issued new ethical guidelines concerning cage size and related matters that its egg suppliers must abide by if they are to retain its business. What ethical rules does McDonald's use to decide its stance toward minimum pay or minimum cage size?

Business ethics are also important because the failure of a company can have catastrophic effects on a community; a general decline in business activity affects a whole nation. The decision of a large company to pull out of a community, for example, can threaten the community's future. Some companies may attempt to improve their profits by engaging in actions that, although not illegal, can hurt communities and nations. One of these actions is pollution. For example, many U.S. companies reduce costs by trucking their waste to Mexico, where it is legal to dump waste in the Rio Grande. The dumping pollutes the river from the Mexican side, but the U.S. side of the river is increasingly experiencing pollution's negative effects.

Rules for Ethical Decision Making

When a stakeholder perspective is taken, questions on company ethics abound.[29] What is the appropriate way to manage the claims of all stakeholders? Company decisions that favor one group of stakeholders, for example, are likely to harm the interests of others.[30] High prices charged to customers may bring high returns to shareholders and high salaries to managers in the short run. If in the long run customers turn to companies that offer lower-cost products, however, the result may be declining sales, laid-off employees, and the decline of the communities that support the high-priced company's business activity.

When companies act ethically, their stakeholders support them. For example, banks are willing to supply them with new capital, they attract highly qualified job applicants, and new customers are drawn to their products. Thus ethical companies grow and expand over time, and all their stakeholders benefit. The results of unethical behavior are loss of reputation and resources, shareholders selling their shares, skilled managers and employees leaving the company, and customers turning to the products of more reputable companies.

When making business decisions, managers must consider the claims of all stakeholders.[31] To help themselves and employees make ethical decisions and behave in ways that benefit their stakeholders, managers can use four ethical rules or principles to analyze the effects of their business decisions on stakeholders: the *utilitarian, moral rights, justice,* and *practical* rules (Figure 4.2).[32] These rules are useful guidelines that help managers decide on the appropriate way to behave in situations where it is necessary to balance a company's self-interest and the interests of its stakeholders. Remember, the right choices will lead resources to be used where they can create the most value. If all companies make the right choices, all stakeholders will benefit in the long run.[33]

utilitarian rule An ethical decision is a decision that produces the greatest good for the greatest number of people.

UTILITARIAN RULE The utilitarian rule is that an ethical decision is a decision that produces the greatest good for the greatest number of people. To decide which is the most ethical course of business action, managers should first consider how different possible courses of business action would benefit or harm different stakeholders. They should then choose the course of action that provides the most benefits, or, conversely, the one that does the least harm, to stakeholders.[34]

The ethical dilemma for managers is this: How do you measure the benefit and harm that will be done to each stakeholder group? Moreover, how do you evaluate the rights of different stakeholder groups, and the relative importance of each group, in coming to a decision? Because stockholders own the company, shouldn't their claims be held above those of employees? For example, managers might face a choice of using global outsourcing to reduce costs and lower prices or continuing with high-cost production at home. A decision to use global outsourcing benefits shareholders and customers but will result in major layoffs that will harm employees and the communities in which they live. Typically, in a capitalist society such as the United States, the interests of shareholders are put above those of employees, so

Figure 4.2
Four Ethical Rules

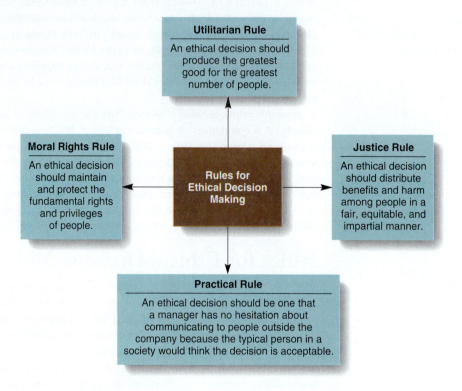

Utilitarian Rule

An ethical decision should produce the greatest good for the greatest number of people.

Moral Rights Rule

An ethical decision should maintain and protect the fundamental rights and privileges of people.

Rules for Ethical Decision Making

Justice Rule

An ethical decision should distribute benefits and harm among people in a fair, equitable, and impartial manner.

Practical Rule

An ethical decision should be one that a manager has no hesitation about communicating to people outside the company because the typical person in a society would think the decision is acceptable.

LO4-3

Describe four rules that can help companies and their managers act in ethical ways.

moral rights rule An ethical decision is one that best maintains and protects the fundamental or inalienable rights and privileges of the people affected by it.

production will move abroad. This is commonly regarded as being an ethical choice because in the long run the alternative, home production, might cause the business to collapse and go bankrupt, in which case greater harm will be done to all stakeholders.

MORAL RIGHTS RULE   Under the **moral rights rule**, an ethical decision is one that best maintains and protects the fundamental or inalienable rights and privileges of the people affected by it. For example, ethical decisions protect people's rights to freedom, life and safety, property, privacy, free speech, and freedom of conscience. The adage "Do unto others as you would have them do unto you" is a moral rights principle that managers should use to decide which rights to uphold. Customers must also consider the rights of the companies and people who create the products they wish to consume.

From a moral rights perspective, managers should compare and contrast different courses of business action on the basis of how each course will affect the rights of the company's different stakeholders. Managers should then choose the course of action that best protects and upholds the rights of *all* stakeholders. For example, decisions that might significantly harm the safety or health of employees or customers would clearly be unethical choices.

The ethical dilemma for managers is that decisions that will protect the rights of some stakeholders often will hurt the rights of others. How should they choose which group to protect? For example, in deciding whether it is ethical to snoop on employees, or search them when they leave work to prevent theft, does an employee's right to privacy outweigh an organization's right to protect its property? Suppose a coworker is having personal problems and is coming in late and leaving early, forcing you to pick up the person's workload. Do you tell your boss even though you know this will probably get that person fired?

justice rule An ethical decision distributes benefits and harms among people and groups in a fair, equitable, or impartial way.

JUSTICE RULE   The **justice rule** is that an ethical decision distributes benefits and harms among people and groups in a fair, equitable, or impartial way. Managers should compare and contrast alternative courses of action based on the degree to which they will fairly or equitably distribute outcomes to stakeholders. For example, employees who are similar in their level of skill, performance, or responsibility should receive similar pay; allocation of outcomes should not be based on differences such as gender, race, or religion.

The ethical dilemma for managers is to determine the fair rules and procedures for distributing outcomes to stakeholders. Managers must not give people they like bigger raises than they give to people they do not like, for example, or bend the rules to help their favorites. On the other hand, if employees want managers to act fairly toward them, then employees need to act fairly toward their companies by working hard and being loyal. Similarly, customers need to act fairly toward a company if they expect it to be fair to them—something people who illegally copy digital media should consider.

PRACTICAL RULE   Each of these rules offers a different and complementary way of determining whether a decision or behavior is ethical, and all three rules should be used to sort out the ethics of a particular course of action. Ethical issues, as we just discussed, are seldom clear-cut, however, because the rights, interests, goals, and incentives of different stakeholders often conflict. For this reason many experts on ethics add a fourth rule to determine whether a business decision is ethical: The **practical rule** is that an ethical decision is one that a manager has no hesitation or reluctance about communicating to people outside the company because the typical person in a society would think it is acceptable. A business decision is probably acceptable on ethical grounds if a manager can answer yes to each of these questions:

practical rule An ethical decision is one that a manager has no reluctance about communicating to people outside the company because the typical person in a society would think it is acceptable.

1. Does my decision fall within the accepted values or standards that typically apply in business activity today?
2. Am I willing to see the decision communicated to all people and groups affected by it— for example, by having it reported in newspapers or on television?
3. Would the people with whom I have a significant personal relationship, such as family members, friends, or even managers in other organizations, approve of the decision?

Applying the practical rule to analyze a business decision ensures that managers are taking into account the interests of all stakeholders.[35] After applying this rule, managers can judge if they have chosen to act in an ethical or unethical way, and they must abide by the consequences.

LO4-4

Discuss why it is important for managers to behave ethically.

Why Should Managers Behave Ethically?

Why is it so important that managers, and people in general, should act ethically and temper their pursuit of self-interest by considering the effects of their actions on others? The answer is that the relentless pursuit of self-interest can lead to a collective disaster when one or more people start to profit from being unethical because this encourages other people to act in the same way.[36] More and more people jump onto the bandwagon, and soon everybody is trying to manipulate the situation to serve their personal ends with no regard for the effects of their action on others. This is called the "tragedy of the commons."

Suppose that in an agricultural community there is common land that everybody has an equal right to use. Pursuing self-interest, each farmer acts to make the maximum use of the free resource by grazing his or her own cattle and sheep. Collectively all the farmers overgraze the land, which quickly becomes worn out. Then a strong wind blows away the exposed topsoil, so the common land is destroyed. The pursuit of individual self-interest with no consideration of societal interests leads to disaster for each individual and for the whole society because scarce resources are destroyed.[37] Consider digital piracy: The tragedy that would result if all people were to steal digital media would be the disappearance of music, movie, and book companies as creative people decided there was no point in working hard to produce original songs, stories, and so on.

We can look at the effects of unethical behavior on business activity in another way. Suppose companies and their managers operate in an unethical society, meaning one in which stakeholders routinely try to cheat and defraud one another. If stakeholders expect each other to cheat, how long will it take them to negotiate the purchase and shipment of products? When they do not trust each other, stakeholders will probably spend hours bargaining over fair prices, and this is a largely unproductive activity that reduces efficiency and effectiveness.[38] The time and effort that could be spent improving product quality or customer service are lost to negotiating and bargaining. Thus unethical behavior ruins business commerce,

Figure 4.3

Some Effects of Ethical and Unethical Behavior

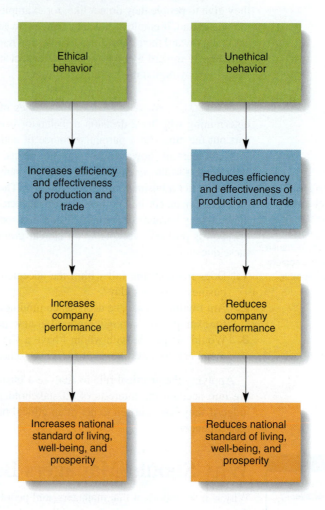

and society has a lower standard of living because fewer goods and services are produced, as Figure 4.3 illustrates.

On the other hand, suppose companies and their managers operate in an ethical society, meaning stakeholders believe they are dealing with others who are basically moral and honest. In this society stakeholders have a greater reason to trust others. **Trust** is the willingness of one person or group to have faith or confidence in the goodwill of another person, even though this puts them at risk (because the other might act in a deceitful way). When trust exists, stakeholders are likely to signal their good intentions by cooperating and providing information that makes it easier to exchange and price goods and services. When one person acts in a trustworthy way, this encourages others to act in the same way. Over time, as greater trust between stakeholders develops, they can work together more efficiently and effectively, which raises company performance (see Figure 4.3). As people see the positive results of acting in an honest way, ethical behavior becomes a valued social norm, and society in general becomes increasingly ethical.

As noted in Chapter 1, a major responsibility of managers is to protect and nurture the resources under their control. Any organizational stakeholders—managers, workers, stockholders, suppliers—who advance their own interests by behaving unethically toward other stakeholders, either by taking resources or by denying resources to others, waste collective resources. If other individuals or groups copy the behavior of the unethical stakeholder, the rate at which collective resources are misused increases, and eventually few resources are available to produce goods and services. Unethical behavior that goes unpunished creates incentives for people to put their unbridled self-interests above the rights of others.[39] When this happens, the benefits that people reap from joining together in organizations disappear quickly.

trust The willingness of one person or group to have faith or confidence in the goodwill of another person, even though this puts them at risk.

An important safeguard against unethical behavior is the potential for loss of reputation.[40] **Reputation**, the esteem or high repute that people or organizations gain when they behave ethically, is an important asset. Stakeholders have valuable reputations that they must protect because their ability to earn a living and obtain resources in the long run depends on how they behave.

If a manager misuses resources and other parties regard that behavior as being at odds with acceptable standards, the manager's reputation will suffer. Behaving unethically in the short run can have serious long-term consequences. A manager who has a poor reputation will have difficulty finding employment with other companies. Stockholders who see managers behaving unethically may refuse to invest in their companies, and this will decrease the stock price, undermine the companies' reputations, and ultimately put the managers' jobs at risk.[41]

All stakeholders have reputations to lose. Suppliers who provide shoddy inputs find that organizations learn over time not to deal with them, and eventually they go out of business. Powerful customers who demand ridiculously low prices find that their suppliers become less willing to deal with them, and resources ultimately become harder for them to obtain. Workers who shirk responsibilities on the job find it hard to get new jobs when they are fired. In general, if a manager or company is known for being unethical, other stakeholders are likely to view that individual or organization with suspicion and hostility, creating a poor reputation. But a manager or company known for ethical business practices will develop a good reputation.[42]

In summary, in a complex, diverse society, stakeholders, and people in general, need to recognize they are part of a larger social group. How they make decisions and act not only affects them personally but also affects the lives of many other people. Unfortunately, for some people, the daily struggle to survive and succeed or their total disregard for others' rights can lead them to lose that bigger connection to other people. We can see our relationships to our families and friends, to our school, church, and so on. But we must go further and keep in mind the effects of our actions on other people—people who will be judging our actions and whom we might harm by acting unethically. Our moral scruples are like those "other people" but are inside our heads.

Ethics and Social Responsibility

Some companies, like GlaxoSmithKline, Bristol Myers Squib, Prudential Insurance, Whole Foods, and Blue Cross–Blue Shield, are known for their ethical business practices.[43] Other companies, such as PAC and Enron, which are now out of business, or WorldCom, Tyco, and Siemens, which have been totally restructured, repeatedly engaged in unethical and illegal business activities. What explains such differences between the ethics of these companies and their managers?

There are four main determinants of differences in ethics between people, employees, companies, and countries: *societal* ethics, *occupational* ethics, *individual* ethics, and *organizational* ethics—especially the ethics of a company's top managers.[44] (See Figure 4.4.)

Societal Ethics

Societal ethics are standards that govern how members of a society should deal with one another in matters involving issues such as fairness, justice, poverty, and the rights of the individual. Societal ethics emanate from a society's laws, customs, and practices and from the unwritten values and norms that influence how people interact with each other. People in a particular country may automatically behave ethically because they have *internalized* (made a part of their morals) certain values, beliefs, and norms that specify how they should behave when confronted with an ethical dilemma.

Societal ethics vary among societies. Countries like Germany, Japan, Sweden, and Switzerland are known as being some of the most ethical countries in the world, with strong values about social order and the need to create a society that protects the welfare of all their citizens. In other countries the situation is different. In many economically poor countries bribery is standard practice to get things done—such as getting a telephone installed or a contract

Figure 4.4
Sources of Ethics

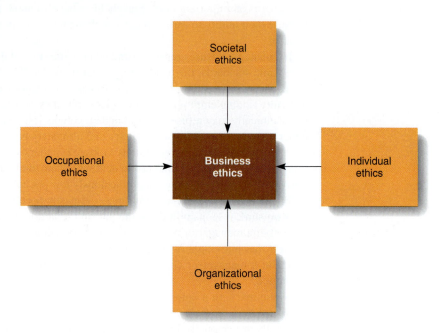

awarded. In the United States and other economically advanced countries, bribery is considered unethical and has been made illegal.

German engineering firm Siemens reported its involvement in a price-fixing cartel in Brazil so that it could build the Sao Paolo Metro.[45] Brazil ranks 72nd out of 177 countries in the corruption perceptions index compiled by Transparency International.[46] However, that perception could soon change. In 2014 Brazil began imposing harsh penalties on any organization operating in Brazil that engages in corruption through its Law to Combat Corruption. The 2014 World Cup in June 2014 and the 2016 Olympic Games will be held in Brazil. Contractors for those events will be subject to following the new law.[47]

Countries also differ widely in their beliefs about appropriate treatment for their employees. In general, the poorer a country is, the more likely employees are to be treated with little regard. One issue of concern is how an organization uses the resources of another country. The accompanying "Ethics in Action" feature discusses how the jewelry company Tiffany works to be ethical in its sourcing.

Ethics
in Action

Finding Diamonds in a Rough Ethical Landscape

Tiffany & Co., an American multinational luxury jewelry and specialty retailer, has a stated commitment to "obtaining precious metals and gemstones and crafting our jewelry in ways that are socially and environmentally responsible." On its website the company recognizes the challenges of living up to that commitment. According to the company, the biggest concern is the impact of large, industrial-scale mining activities. These concerns include air, water and soil contamination, the destruction of cultural sites, and human rights abuses.

"I would like to think that the majority of consumers are genuinely concerned about ethical sourcing," says Michael J. Kowalski, chairman of the Board and CEO. ". . . .I do believe that Tiffany customers trust, either explicitly or through assumption, that Tiffany—as part of our brand promise—has in fact attended to those concerns. . . . For many of our customers those promises may be implicit, but it makes them no less real. And should we fail to deliver on those promises, the damage to our brand will most certainly be real."[48]

The company, along with the Jewelers of America and other organizations, has founded the Initiative for Responsible Mining Assurance (IRMA) to help ensure that ethical mining practices are followed. IRMA is creating a certification system for environmentally and socially responsible mining, which it plans to implement in 2015. The vision statement of IRMA calls for practices that "respect human rights and aspirations of affected communities, provide safe, healthy and respectful workplaces, avoid or minimizes harm to the environment and leave positive legacies."[49] IRMA believes that most negative social and environmental impacts can be avoided if responsible mining practices are followed. These practices include careful choice of mine location to preserve ecologically and culturally significant areas, reduction of environmental impact from habitat loss and pollution, informed consent of indigenous peoples for mining, health and safety provisions, and transparency in revenue and corporate governance.[50]

In other ethical sourcing efforts, Tiffany & Co. purchases diamonds only from countries that use the Kimberley Process Certification Scheme (KPCS). This process was established by a United Nations General Assembly Resolution to stop the smuggling of "conflict diamonds" or diamonds that are sold to support violence, war efforts, or other malevolent activities. While the company believes the Kimberley Process has made a difference, it would like to see the definition of "conflict diamonds" expanded to include diamond-related human rights abuses.[51]

". . .While we certainly have a deep moral commitment to act responsibly—a commitment which emanates not just from myself or the senior management group but from all our Tiffany colleagues around the world—we also believe we have a business imperative to act responsibly," Kowalski said. "We have always prided ourselves on managing Tiffany & Co. for the long term. Witness our storied 177-year history. And over the long term, we have no doubt whatsoever that consumers will increasingly demand responsible behavior, and that effectively meeting that demand will be a source of brand differentiation and ultimately lead to the creation of long-term shareholder value."[52]

Occupational Ethics

occupational ethics
Standards that govern how members of a profession, trade, or craft should conduct themselves when performing work-related activities.

Occupational ethics are standards that govern how members of a profession, trade, or craft should conduct themselves when performing work-related activities.[53] For example, medical ethics govern how doctors and nurses should treat their patients. Doctors are expected to perform only necessary medical procedures and to act in the patient's interest, not their own self-interest. The ethics of scientific research require that scientists conduct their experiments and present their findings in ways that ensure the validity of their conclusions. Like society at large, most professional groups can impose punishments for violations of ethical standards.[54] Doctors and lawyers can be prevented from practicing their professions if they disregard professional ethics and put their own interests first.

Within an organization, occupational rules and norms often govern how employees such as lawyers, researchers, and accountants should make decisions to further stakeholder interests. Employees internalize the rules and norms of their occupational group (just as they do those of society) and often follow them automatically when deciding how to behave. Because most people tend to follow established rules of behavior, people frequently take ethics for granted. However, when occupational ethics are violated, such as when scientists fabricate data to disguise the harmful effects of products, ethical issues come to the forefront. For example, in 2014 Toyota said it had deceived "U.S. consumers by concealing and making deceptive statements about two safety issues involving its vehicles."[55] Millions of Toyota and Lexus vehicles had problems with unintended acceleration. As part of the $1.2 billion

Table 4.2

Some Failures in Professional Ethics

For manufacturing and materials management managers:

- Releasing products that are not of a consistent quality because of defective inputs.

- Producing product batches that may be dangerous or defective and harm customers.

- Compromising workplace health and safety to reduce costs (for example, to maximize output, employees are not given adequate training to maintain and service machinery and equipment).

For sales and marketing managers:

- Knowingly making unsubstantiated product claims.

- Engaging in sales campaigns that use covert persuasive or subliminal advertising to create customer need for the product.

- Marketing to target groups such as the elderly, minorities, or children to build demand for a product.

- Having ongoing campaigns of unsolicited junk mail, spam, door-to-door, or telephone selling.

For accounting and finance managers:

- Engaging in misleading financial analysis involving creative accounting or "cooking the books" to hide salient facts.

- Authorizing excessive expenses and perks to managers, customers, and suppliers.

- Hiding the level and amount of top management and director compensation.

For human resource managers:

- Failing to act fairly, objectively, and in a uniform way toward different employees or kinds of employees because of personal factors such as personality and beliefs.

- Excessively encroaching on employee privacy through non-job-related surveillance or personality, ability, and drug testing.

- Failing to respond to employee observations and concerns surrounding health and safety violations, hostile workplace issues, or inappropriate or even illegal behavior by managers or employees.

settlement with the Justice Department, Toyota's procedures and practices will be assessed by an independent monitor. As of early 2014 it was the largest criminal penalty ever levied against a U.S. automobile company.[56] Table 4.2 lists some failures or lapses in professional ethics according to type of functional manager.

Individual Ethics

individual ethics Personal standards and values that determine how people view their responsibilities to others and how they should act in situations when their own self-interests are at stake.

Individual ethics are personal standards and values that determine how people view their responsibilities to other people and groups and thus how they should act in situations when their own self-interests are at stake.[57] Sources of individual ethics include the influence of one's family, peers, and upbringing in general. The experiences gained over a lifetime—through membership in social institutions such as schools and religions, for example—also contribute to the development of the personal standards and values that a person uses to evaluate a situation and decide what is the morally right or wrong way to behave. However, suppose you are the son or daughter of a mobster, and your upbringing and education take place in an organized crime context; this affects how you evaluate a situation. You may come to believe that it is ethical to do anything and perform any act, up to and including murder, if it benefits your family or friends. These are your ethics. They are obviously not the ethics of the wider society and so are subject to sanction. In a similar way, managers and employees in an organization may come to believe that actions they take to promote or protect their organization are more important than any harm these actions may cause other stakeholders. So they behave unethically or illegally, and when this is discovered, they also are sanctioned—as happened to New York's cab drivers.

In 2009 the New York City taxi commission, which regulates cab fares, began an investigation after it found that one cab driver from Brooklyn, Wasim Khalid Cheema, overcharged 574 passengers in just one month. The taxi drivers' scheme, the commission said, involved 1.8 million rides and cost passengers an average of $4 to $5 extra per trip. The drivers pressed a button on the taxi's payment meter that categorized the fare as a Code No. 4, which is charged for trips outside the city to Nassau or Westchester and is twice the rate of Code No. 1, which is charged for rides within New York City limits. Passengers can see which rate is being charged by looking at the meter, but few bother to do so; they rely on the cab driver's honesty.

After the commission discovered the fraud, it used GPS data, collected in every cab, to review millions of trips within New York City and found that in 36,000 cabs the higher rates were improperly activated at least once; in each of about 3,000 cabs it was done more than 100 times; and 35,558 of the city's roughly 48,000 drivers had applied the higher rate. This scheme cost New York City riders more than $8 million plus all the higher tips they paid as a result of the higher charges. The fraud ranks as one of the biggest in the taxi industry's history, and New York City Mayor Michael R. Bloomberg said criminal charges could be brought against cab drivers.

As a result of the scandal, a notification system in taxicabs now alerts passengers if the higher rate is activated. The message is displayed on a television screen in the back seat of the cab and encourages riders to call the city to report any suspected abuse. Also, officials said taxi companies would eventually be forced to use meters based on a GPS system that would automatically set the charge based on the location of the cab, and drivers would no longer be able to manually activate the higher rate—and cheat their customers. In 2011, 630 taxi drivers had their licenses revoked.

In general, many decisions or behaviors that one person finds unethical, such as using animals for cosmetics testing, may be acceptable to another person. If decisions or behaviors are not illegal, individuals may agree to disagree about their ethical beliefs, or they may try to impose their own beliefs on other people and make those ethical beliefs the law. In all cases, however, people should develop and follow the ethical criteria described earlier to balance their self-interests against those of others when determining how they should behave in a particular situation.

Organizational Ethics

organizational ethics
The guiding practices and beliefs through which a particular company and its managers view their responsibility toward their stakeholders.

Organizational ethics are the guiding practices and beliefs through which a particular company and its managers view their responsibility toward their stakeholders. The individual ethics of a company's founders and top managers are especially important in shaping the organization's code of ethics. Organizations whose founders had a vital role in creating a highly ethical code of organizational behavior include UPS, Procter & Gamble, Johnson & Johnson, and the Prudential Insurance Company. Johnson & Johnson's code of ethics—its credo—reflects a well-developed concern for its stakeholders (see Figure 4.5). Company credos, such as that of Johnson & Johnson, are meant to deter self-interested, unethical behavior; to demonstrate to managers and employees that a company will not tolerate people who, because of their own poor ethics, put their personal interests above the interests of other organizational stakeholders and ignore the harm they are inflicting on others; and to demonstrate that those who act unethically will be punished.

Managers or workers may behave unethically if they feel pressured to do so by the situation they are in and by unethical top managers. People typically confront ethical issues when weighing their personal interests against the effects of their actions on others. Suppose a manager knows that promotion to vice president is likely if she can secure a $100 million contract, but getting the contract requires bribing the contract giver with $1 million. The manager reasons that performing this act will ensure her career and future, and what harm would it do anyway? Bribery is common and she knows that, even if she decides not to pay the bribe, someone else surely will. So what to do? Research seems to suggest that people who realize they have the most at stake in a career sense or a monetary sense are the ones most likely to act unethically. And it is exactly in this situation that a strong code of organizational ethics can help people behave in the right or appropriate way. *The New York Times* detailed code of ethics, for example, was crafted by its editors to ensure the integrity and honesty of its journalists as they report sensitive information.

If a company's top managers consistently endorse the ethical principles in its corporate credo, they can prevent employees from going astray. Employees are much more likely to act unethically when a credo does not exist or is disregarded. Arthur Andersen, for example, did not follow its credo at all; its unscrupulous partners ordered middle managers to shred records

Figure 4.5
Johnson & Johnson's Credo

Our Credo

We believe our first responsibility is to the doctors, nurses and patients, to mothers and fathers and all others who use our products and services. In meeting their needs everything we do must be of high quality. We must constantly strive to reduce our costs in order to maintain reasonable prices. Customers' orders must be serviced promptly and accurately. Our suppliers and distributors must have an opportunity to make a fair profit.

We are responsible to our employees, the men and women who work with us throughout the world. Everyone must be considered as an individual. We must respect their dignity and recognize their merit. They must have a sense of security in their jobs. Compensation must be fair and adequate, and working conditions clean, orderly and safe. We must be mindful of ways to help our employees fulfill their family responsibilities. Employees must feel free to make suggestions and complaints. There must be equal opportunity for employment, development and advancement for those qualified. We must provide competent management, and their actions must be just and ethical.

We are responsible to the communities in which we live and work and to the world community as well. We must be good citizens — support good works and charities and bear our fair share of taxes. We must encourage civic improvements and better health and education. We must maintain in good order the property we are privileged to use, protecting the environment and natural resources.

Our final responsibility is to our stockholders. Business must make a sound profit. We must experiment with new ideas. Research must be carried on, innovative programs developed and mistakes paid for. New equipment must be purchased, new facilities provided and new products launched. Reserves must be created to provide for adverse times. When we operate according to these principles, the stockholders should realize a fair return.

Johnson & Johnson

Source: © Johnson & Johnson. Used with permission.

that showed evidence of their wrongdoing. Although the middle managers knew this was wrong, they followed the orders because they responded to the personal power and status of the partners and not the company's code of ethics. They were afraid they would lose their jobs if they did not behave unethically, but their actions cost them their jobs anyway.

Top managers play a crucial role in determining a company's ethics. It is clearly important, then, that when making appointment decisions, the board of directors should scrutinize the reputations and ethical records of top managers. It is the responsibility of the board to decide whether a prospective CEO has the maturity, experience, and integrity needed to head a company and be entrusted with the capital and wealth of the organization, on which the fate of all its stakeholders depends. Clearly a track record of success is not enough to decide whether a top manager is capable of moral decision making; a manager might have achieved this success through unethical or illegal means. It is important to investigate prospective top managers and examine their credentials. Although the best predictor of future behavior is often past behavior, the board of directors needs to be on guard against unprincipled executives who use unethical means to rise to the top of the organizational hierarchy. For this reason it is necessary that a company's directors continuously monitor the behavior of top executives. In the 2000s this increased scrutiny has led to the dismissal of many top executives for breaking ethical rules concerning issues such as excessive personal loans, stock options, inflated expense accounts, and even sexual misconduct. As illustrated in the accompanying "Ethics in Action" feature, the tone set by the founder and leader of an organization can set its ethical tone and business model.

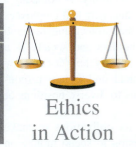

Ethics in Action

TOMS One for One: Identify a Need and Then a Product

One for One. That is the trademark at TOMS. In 2006 the company began selling shoes, but for every pair of shoes purchased, it gave a pair of new shoes to a person in need. In 2011 the company did the same with eyeglasses, donating a pair of glasses for every pair of sunglasses and optical frames purchased. In 2014 the company got into the coffee business, and is donating one week of water to one person for every bag of coffee purchased.

How can TOMS afford to do this? It is estimated that the TOMS shoes cost $9 to manufacture. The "best sellers" in the shoe area on the TOMS website cost $48. Another best seller on the website is a $179 pair of sunglasses. Twelve ounces of TOMS coffee beans cost $12.99, almost the same price as 16 ounces of Starbucks coffee beans.

TOMS operates by identifying a global need and creating a product to help address it. It began when Blake Mycoskie, TOMS founder, was traveling in Argentina and found that many children had no shoes. In response, he established a company that donates a pair of shoes for every purchased pair of shoes. Since then more than 10 million pairs of shoes have been purchased, and 10 million pairs have been donated. TOMS are sold at more than 500 stores globally and on TOMS.com.

The next global need he identified was eyesight. TOMS partnered with the Seva Foundation to provide eyeglasses and surgeries to the 284 million people who are visually impaired in the world.[58] Whenever a pair of TOMS sunglasses or optical frame is purchased, help is given to restore sight and support sustainable community-based eye care programs. More than 150,000 people have received eyeglasses or surgery through the One for One program since 2011. TOMS sunglasses, made in Italy, have three hand-painted stripes that symbolize the three elements of One for One: the buyer, the person being helped, and TOMS.[59]

In 2014 the global need identified was clean water. Mycoskie announced that the company would apply its One for One business model to help provide clean drinking water. To do so, TOMS went into the coffee business. For every bag of TOMS beans sold, a person in need will get clean water for a week. TOMS is partnering with Water for People, an international charity based in Denver, to deliver the water to the regions from which the beans will be sourced, including Peru, Honduras, Rwanda, Malawi, and Guatemala.

TOMS founder Blake Mycoskie. In his One for One program, every time a product is bought the company donates one to fill a global need. He began with shoes, and has expanded his business model to include eyeglasses and optical frames to support community-based eye care programs. In 2014 TOMS entered the coffee roasting business to help supply clean drinking water.

When announcing the launch of TOMS Roasting Co., Mycoskie reflected on the One for One model of doing business. "In the last seven years, we've seen the incredible impact our customers can have on communities around the world," he said. "We've learned a lot through our Shoe and Sight Giving about what truly transforms communities in need—and it was important that the next One for One support economic opportunity."[60]

Approaches to Social Responsibility

LO4-6

Distinguish among the four main approaches toward social responsibility that a company can take.

social responsibility The way a company's managers and employees view their duty or obligation to make decisions that protect, enhance, and promote the welfare and well-being of stakeholders and society as a whole.

A company's ethics are the result of differences in societal, organizational, occupational, and individual ethics. In turn, a company's ethics determine its stance or position on social responsibility. A company's stance on **social responsibility** is the way its managers and employees view their duty or obligation to make decisions that protect, enhance, and promote the welfare and well-being of stakeholders and society as a whole.[61] As we noted earlier, when no laws specify how a company should act toward stakeholders, managers must decide the right, ethical, and socially responsible thing to do. Differences in business ethics can lead companies to diverse positions or views on their responsibility toward stakeholders.

Many kinds of decisions signal a company's beliefs about its obligations to make socially responsible business decisions (see Table 4.3). The decision to spend money on training and educating employees—investing in them—is one such decision; so is the decision to minimize or avoid layoffs whenever possible. The decision to act promptly and warn customers when a batch of defective merchandise has been accidentally sold is another one. Companies that try to hide such problems show little regard for social responsibility. In the past both GM and Ford tried to hide the fact that several of their vehicles had defects that made them dangerous to drive; the companies were penalized with hundreds of millions of dollars in damages for their unethical behavior, and today they move more quickly to recall vehicles to fix problems. In 2014 General Motors CEO Mary Barra admitted that the automaker did not react fast enough when fault was found with an ignition switch that triggered the recall of 1.62 million cars worldwide.[62] On the other side, also in 2014, Fitbit voluntarily recalled its activity tracking wrist band, the Fitbit Force, due to skin rash issues. The company offered to send consumers a return kit and promised a reimbursement check or exchange within two to six weeks of receipt.[63] The way a company announces business problems or admits its mistakes provides strong clues about its stance on social responsibility.

Table 4.3

Forms of Socially Responsible Behavior

Managers are being socially responsible and showing their support for their stakeholders when they

- Provide severance payments to help laid-off workers make ends meet until they can find another job.

- Give workers opportunities to enhance their skills and acquire additional education so they can remain productive and do not become obsolete because of changes in technology.

- Allow employees to take time off when they need to and provide health care and pension benefits for employees.

- Contribute to charities or support various civic-minded activities in the cities or towns in which they are located. (Target and Levi Strauss both contribute 5 percent of their profits to support schools, charities, the arts, and other good works.)

- Decide to keep open a factory whose closure would devastate the local community.

- Decide to keep a company's operations in the United States to protect the jobs of American workers rather than move abroad.

- Decide to spend money to improve a new factory so it will not pollute the environment.

- Decline to invest in countries that have poor human rights records.

- Choose to help poor countries develop an economic base to improve living standards.

Four Different Approaches

obstructionist approach
Companies and their managers choose *not* to behave in a socially responsible way and instead behave unethically and illegally.

The strength of companies' commitment to social responsibility can range from low to high (see Figure 4.6). At the low end of the range is an **obstructionist approach**, in which companies and their managers choose *not* to behave in a socially responsible way. Instead they behave unethically and often illegally and do all they can to prevent knowledge of their behavior from reaching other organizational stakeholders and society at large. Managers at the Manville Corporation adopted this approach when they sought to hide evidence that asbestos causes lung damage; so too did tobacco companies when they sought to hide evidence that cigarette smoking causes lung cancer. In 2010 it was revealed that the managers of Lehman Brothers, whose bankruptcy helped propel the 2008–2009 financial crisis, used loopholes in U.K. law to hide billions of dollars of worthless assets on its balance sheet to disguise its poor financial condition. The fall of Lehman Brothers has been recorded in several films, including the 2009 British television film *The Last Days of Lehman Brothers,* the 2011 American independent film *Margin Call,* and the 2011 HBO movie *Too Big to Fail.* It is also referenced in the 2010 animated film *Despicable Me.* In that film the criminal mastermind Gru goes into a building called the "Bank of Evil," which displays a small banner with the words "Formerly Lehman Brothers."

Top managers at Enron also acted in an obstructionist way when they prevented employees from selling Enron shares in their pension funds while they sold hundreds of millions of dollars' worth of their own Enron stock. Most employees lost all their retirement savings. Senior partners at Arthur Andersen who instructed their subordinates to shred files chose an obstructionist approach that caused not only a loss of reputation but devastation for the organization and for all stakeholders involved. These companies are no longer in business.

defensive approach
Companies and their managers behave ethically to the degree that they stay within the law and strictly abide by legal requirements.

A **defensive approach** indicates at least some commitment to ethical behavior.[64] Defensive companies and managers stay within the law and abide strictly by legal requirements but make no attempt to exercise social responsibility beyond what the law dictates; thus they can and often do act unethically. These are the kinds of companies, like Computer Associates, WorldCom, and Merrill Lynch, that gave their managers large stock options and bonuses even as company performance was declining rapidly. The managers are the kind who sell their stock in advance of other stockholders because they know their company's performance is about to fall. Although acting on inside information is illegal, it is often hard to prove because top managers have wide latitude regarding when they sell their shares. The founders of most dot-com companies took advantage of this legal loophole to sell billions of dollars of their dot-com shares before their stock prices collapsed. When making ethical decisions, such managers put their own interests first and commonly harm other stakeholders.

accommodative approach
Companies and their managers behave legally and ethically and try to balance the interests of different stakeholders as the need arises.

An **accommodative approach** acknowledges the need to support social responsibility. Accommodative companies and managers agree that organizational members ought to behave legally and ethically, and they try to balance the interests of different stakeholders so the claims of stockholders are seen in relation to the claims of other stakeholders. Managers adopting this approach want to make choices that are reasonable in the eyes of society and want to do the right thing.

This approach is the one taken by the typical large U.S. company, which has the most to lose from unethical or illegal behavior. Generally, the older and more reputable a company, the more likely its managers are to curb attempts by their subordinates to act unethically.

Figure 4.6
Four Approaches to Social Responsibility

Source: Reprinted with permission of Johnson & Johnson.

Large companies like GM, Intel, DuPont, and Dell seek every way to build their companies' competitive advantage. Nevertheless, they rein in attempts by their managers to behave unethically or illegally, knowing the grave consequences such behavior can have on future profitability. Sometimes they fail, however, such as in 2013 when SAC Capital Advisors (among others) agreed to pay $1.8 billion and plead guilty to criminal insider trading charges. It was the biggest insider trading settlement in history.[65]

proactive approach
Companies and their managers actively embrace socially responsible behavior, going out of their way to learn about the needs of different stakeholder groups and using organizational resources to promote the interests of all stakeholders.

Companies and managers taking a **proactive approach** actively embrace the need to behave in socially responsible ways. They go out of their way to learn about the needs of different stakeholder groups and are willing to use organizational resources to promote the interests not only of stockholders but also of the other stakeholders such as their employees and communities. U.S. steelmaker Nucor is one such company. In 1977 its visionary CEO Ken Iverson announced that throughout its history Nucor had never laid off one employee, and even though a major recession was raging, it did not plan to start now. In 2009 Nucor CEO Daniel R. DiMicco announced that Nucor again would not start layoffs despite the fact its steel mills were operating at only 50 percent of capacity (compared to 95 percent just months earlier) because customers had slashed orders due to the recession. While rivals laid off thousands of employees, Nucor remained loyal to its employees. However, even though there were no layoffs, both managers and employees took major cuts in pay and bonuses to weather the storm together, as they always had, and they searched for ways to reduce operating costs so they would all benefit when the economy recovered, and by 2012 their sacrifice paid off: Nucor was doing well again. By January 2014 it was reporting above-expected earnings per share.[66]

Proactive companies are often at the forefront of campaigns for causes such as a pollution-free environment; recycling and conservation of resources; the minimization or elimination of the use of animals in drug and cosmetics testing; and the reduction of crime, illiteracy, and poverty. For example, companies like McDonald's, Google, Green Mountain Coffee, Whole Foods, and Target all have reputations for being proactive in the support of stakeholders such as their suppliers or the communities in which they operate.

Why Be Socially Responsible?

Several advantages result when companies and their managers behave in a socially responsible manner. First, demonstrating its social responsibility helps a company build a good reputation. Reputation is the trust, goodwill, and confidence others have in a company that lead them to want to do business with it. The rewards for a good company reputation are increased business and improved ability to obtain resources from stakeholders.[67] Reputation thus can enhance profitability and build stockholder wealth; and behaving responsibly socially is the economically right thing to do because companies that do so benefit from increasing business and rising profits.

A second major reason for companies to act responsibly toward employees, customers, and society is that, in a capitalist system, companies as well as the government, have to bear the costs of protecting their stakeholders, providing health care and income, paying taxes, and so on. So if all companies in a society act responsibly, the quality of life as a whole increases.

Moreover, how companies behave toward their employees determines many of a society's values and norms and the ethics of its citizens, as already noted. It has been suggested that if all organizations adopted a caring approach and agreed that their responsibility is to promote the interests of their employees, a climate of caring would pervade the wider society. Experts point to Japan, Sweden, Germany, the Netherlands, and Switzerland as countries where organizations are highly socially responsible and where, as a result, crime, poverty, and unemployment rates are relatively low, literacy rates are relatively high, and sociocultural values promote harmony between different groups of people. Business activity affects all aspects of people's lives, so how business behaves toward stakeholders affects how stakeholders behave toward business. You "reap what you sow," as the adage goes.

The Role of Organizational Culture

Although an organization's code of ethics guides decision making when ethical questions arise, managers can go one step further by ensuring that important ethical values and norms are key features of an organization's culture. For example, Herb Kelleher and Coleen Barrett created Southwest Airlines' culture in which promoting employee well-being is a main company priority; this translates into organizational values and norms dictating that layoffs should be avoided and employees should share in the profits the company makes.[68] Google, UPS, and Toyota are among the many companies that espouse similar values. When ethical values and norms such as these are part of an organization's culture, they help organizational members resist self-interested action because they recognize that they are part of something bigger than themselves.[69]

Managers' roles in developing ethical values and standards in other employees are important. Employees naturally look to those in authority to provide leadership, just as a country's citizens look to its political leaders, and managers become ethical role models whose behavior is scrutinized by subordinates. If top managers are perceived as being self-interested and not ethical, their subordinates are not likely to behave in an ethical manner. Employees may think that if it's all right for a top manager to engage in dubious behavior, it's all right for them too, and for employees this might mean slacking off, reducing customer support, and not taking supportive actions to help their company. The actions of top managers such as CEOs and the president of the United States are scrutinized so closely for ethical improprieties because their actions represent the values of their organizations and, in the case of the president, the values of the nation.

ethics ombudsperson
A manager responsible for communicating and teaching ethical standards to all employees and monitoring their conformity to those standards.

Managers can also provide a visible means of support to develop an ethical culture. Increasingly, organizations are creating the role of ethics officer, or **ethics ombudsperson**, to monitor their ethical practices and procedures. The ethics ombudsperson is responsible for communicating ethical standards to all employees, designing systems to monitor employees' conformity to those standards, and teaching managers and employees at all levels of the organization how to respond to ethical dilemmas appropriately.[70] Because the ethics ombudsperson has organizationwide authority, organizational members in any department can communicate instances of unethical behavior by their managers or coworkers without fear of retribution. This arrangement makes it easier for everyone to behave ethically. In addition, ethics ombudspeople can provide guidance when organizational members are uncertain about whether an action is ethical. Some organizations have an organizationwide ethics committee to provide guidance on ethical issues and help write and update the company code of ethics.

Ethical organizational cultures encourage organizational members to behave in a socially responsible manner. One company epitomized in the past as a prime example of an ethical, socially responsible firm was Johnson & Johnson (J&J). The ethical values and norms in Johnson & Johnson's culture, along with its credo, have guided its managers to make the right decision in difficult situations for decades.

Summary and Review

LO4-1

THE NATURE OF ETHICS   Ethical issues are central to how companies and their managers make decisions, and they affect not only the efficiency and effectiveness of company operations but also the prosperity of the nation. The result of ethical behavior is a general increase in company performance and in a nation's standard of living, well-being, and wealth.

An ethical dilemma is the quandary people find themselves in when they have to decide if they should act in a way that might help another person or group and is the right thing to do, even though it might go against their own self-interest. Ethics are the inner guiding moral principles, values, and beliefs that people use to analyze or interpret a situation and then decide what is the right or appropriate way to behave.

Ethical beliefs alter and change as time passes, and as they do so laws change to reflect the changing ethical beliefs of a society.

LO4-2, 4-4   **STAKEHOLDERS AND ETHICS**   Stakeholders are people and groups who have a claim on and a stake in a company. The main stakeholder groups are stockholders, managers, employees, suppliers and distributors, customers, and the community, society, and nation. Companies and their managers need to make ethical business decisions that promote the well-being of their stakeholders and avoid doing them harm.

LO4-3, 4-5   To determine whether a business decision is ethical, managers can use four ethical rules to analyze it: the utilitarian, moral rights, justice, and practical rules. Managers should behave ethically because this avoids the tragedy of the commons and results in a general increase in efficiency, effectiveness, and company performance. The main determinants of differences in a manager's, company's, and country's business ethics are societal, occupational, individual, and organizational.

LO4-6   ETHICS AND SOCIAL RESPONSIBILITY   A company's stance on social responsibility is the way its managers and employees view their duty or obligation to make decisions that protect, enhance, and promote the welfare and well-being of stakeholders and society as a whole.

There are four main approaches to social responsibility: obstructionist, defensive, accommodative, and proactive. The rewards from behaving in a socially responsible way are a good reputation, the support of all organizational stakeholders, and thus superior company performance.

Management in Action

Topics for Discussion and Action

Discussion

1. What is the relationship between ethics and the law? **[LO4-1]**

2. Why do the claims and interests of stakeholders sometimes conflict? **[LO4-2]**

3. Why should managers use ethical criteria to guide their decision making? **[LO4-3]**

4. As an employee of a company, what are some of the most unethical business practices that you have encountered in its dealings with stakeholders? **[LO4-4]**

5. What are the main determinants of business ethics? **[LO4-5]**

Action

6. Find a manager and ask about the most important ethical rules he or she uses to make the right decisions. **[LO4-3]**

7. Find an example of (a) a company that has an obstructionist approach to social responsibility and (b) one that has an accommodative approach. **[LO4-6]**

Building Management Skills

Dealing with Ethical Dilemmas   [LO4-1, 4-4]

Use the chapter material to decide how you, as a manager, should respond to each of the following ethical dilemmas:

1. You are planning to leave your job to go work for a competitor; your boss invites you to an important meeting where you will learn about new products your company will be bringing out next year. Do you go to the meeting?

2. You're the manager of sales in an expensive sports car dealership. A young executive who has just received a promotion comes in and wants to buy a car that you know is out of her price range. Do you encourage the executive to buy it so you can receive a big commission on the sale?

3. You sign a contract to manage a young rock band, and that group agrees to let you produce their next seven records, for which they will receive royalties of 5 percent. Their first record is a smash hit and sells millions. Do you increase their royalty rate on future records?

Managing Ethically   [LO4-3, 4-5]

Apple Juice or Sugar Water?

In the early 1980s Beech-Nut, a maker of baby foods, was in grave financial trouble as it strove to compete with Gerber Products, the market leader. Threatened with bankruptcy if it could not lower its operating costs, Beech-Nut entered an agreement with a low-cost supplier of apple juice concentrate. The agreement would save the company over $250,000 annually when every dollar counted. Soon one of Beech-Nut's food scientists became concerned about the quality of the concentrate. He believed it was not made from apples alone but contained large quantities of corn syrup and cane sugar. He brought this information to the attention of top managers at Beech-Nut, but they were obsessed with the need to keep costs down and chose to ignore his concerns. The company continued to produce and sell its product as pure apple juice.[71]

Eventually investigators from the U.S. Food and Drug Administration (FDA) confronted Beech-Nut with evidence that the concentrate was adulterated. The top managers issued denials and quickly shipped the remaining stock of apple juice to the market before their inventory could be seized. The scientist who had questioned the purity of the apple juice had resigned from Beech-Nut, but he decided to blow the whistle on the company. He told the FDA that Beech-Nut's top management had known of the problem with the concentrate and had acted to maximize company profits rather than to inform customers about the additives in the apple juice. In 1987 the company pleaded guilty to charges that it had deliberately sold adulterated juice and was fined over $2 million. Its top managers were also found guilty and were sentenced to prison terms. The company's reputation was ruined, and it was eventually sold to Ralston Purina, now owned by Nestlé, which installed a new management team and a new ethical code of values to guide future business decisions.

Questions

1. Why is it that an organization's values and norms can become too strong and lead to unethical behavior?

2. What steps can a company take to prevent this problem—to stop its values and norms from becoming so inwardly focused that managers and employees lose sight of their responsibility to their stakeholders?

Small Group Breakout Exercise

Is Chewing Gum the "Right" Thing to Do? [LO4-1, 4-3]

Form groups of three or four people, and appoint one member as the spokesperson who will communicate your findings to the class when called on by the instructor. Then discuss the following scenario:

In the United States the right to chew gum is taken for granted. Although it is often against the rules to chew gum in a high school classroom, church, and so on, it is legal to do so on the street. If you possess or chew gum on a street in Singapore, you can be arrested. Chewing gum has been made illegal in Singapore because those in power believe it creates a mess on pavements and feel that people cannot be trusted to dispose of their gum properly and thus should have no right to use it.

1. What makes chewing gum acceptable in the United States and unacceptable in Singapore?

2. Why can you chew gum on the street but not in a church?

3. How can you use ethical principles to decide when gum chewing is ethical or unethical and if and when it should be made illegal?

Exploring the World Wide Web [LO4-2, 4-5]

Check out *Fortune's* list of the 50 World's Most Admired Companies (http://money.cnn.com/magazines/fortune/most-admired/). *Fortune* puts this list together each year based on ratings from executives, directors, and analysts.

1. Select a company on the list and go to that company's web page. How would you describe the company's organizational ethics?

2. What do you believe are the occupational ethics of the people who work at the company?

Be the Manager [LO4-3]

Creating an Ethical Code

You are an entrepreneur who has decided to go into business and open a steak and chicken restaurant. Your business plan requires that you hire at least 20 people as chefs, waiters, and so on. As the owner, you are drawing up a list of ethical principles that each of these people will receive and must agree to when he or she accepts a job offer. These principles outline your view of what is right or acceptable behavior and what will be expected both from you and from your employees.

Create a list of the five main ethical rules or principles you will use to govern how your business operates. Be sure to spell out how these principles relate to your stakeholders; for example, state the rules you intend to follow in dealing with your employees and customers.

Bloomberg Businessweek Case in the News [LO4-2, 4-4]

Missed Alarms and 40 Million Stolen Credit Card Numbers: How Target Blew It

The biggest retail hack in U.S. history wasn't particularly inventive, nor did it appear destined for success. In the days prior to Thanksgiving 2013, someone installed malware in Target's (TGT) security and payments system designed to steal every credit card used at the company's 1,797 U.S. stores. At the critical moment—when the Christmas gifts had been scanned and bagged and the cashier asked for a swipe—the malware would step in, capture the shopper's credit card number, and store it on a Target server commandeered by the hackers.

On November 30 the hackers had set their traps and had just one thing to do before starting the attack: plan the data's escape route. As they uploaded exfiltration malware to move stolen credit card numbers—first to staging points spread around the United States to cover their tracks, then into their computers in Russia—FireEye, a malware detection tool, spotted them. Target's team of security specialists in Bangalore got an alert and flagged the security team in Minneapolis. And then . . . nothing happened.

For some reason Minneapolis didn't react to the sirens. *Bloomberg Businessweek* spoke to more than 10 former Target employees familiar with the company's data security operation, as well as eight people with specific knowledge of the hack and its aftermath, including former employees, security researchers, and law enforcement officials. The story they tell is of an alert system, installed to protect the bond between retailer and customer, that worked beautifully. But then Target stood by as 40 million credit card numbers—and 70 million addresses, phone numbers, and other pieces of personal information—gushed out of its mainframes.

When asked to respond to a list of specific questions about the incident and the company's lack of an immediate response to it, Target Chairman, President, and Chief Executive Officer Gregg

Steinhafel issued an e-mailed statement: "Target was certified as meeting the standard for the payment card industry (PCI) in September 2013. Nonetheless, we suffered a data breach. As a result, we are conducting an end-to-end review of our people, processes and technology to understand our opportunities to improve data security and are committed to learning from this experience. While we are still in the midst of an ongoing investigation, we have already taken significant steps, including beginning the overhaul of our information security structure and the acceleration of our transition to chip-enabled cards. However, as the investigation is not complete, we don't believe it's constructive to engage in speculation without the benefit of the final analysis."

In testimony before Congress, Target has said that it was only after the U.S. Department of Justice notified the retailer about the breach in mid-December that company investigators went back to figure out what happened. What it hasn't publicly revealed: Poring over computer logs, Target found FireEye's alerts from November 30 and more from December 2, when hackers installed yet another version of the malware. Not only should those alarms have been impossible to miss, they went off early enough that the hackers hadn't begun transmitting the stolen card data out of Target's network. Had the company's security team responded when it was supposed to, the theft that has since engulfed Target, touched as many as one in three American consumers, and led to an international hunt for the hackers never would have happened at all.

On November 30, according to a person who has consulted on Target's investigation but is not authorized to speak on the record, the hackers deployed their custom code, triggering a FireEye alert that indicated unfamiliar malware: "malware.binary." Details soon followed, including addresses for the servers where the hackers wanted

their stolen data to be sent. As the hackers inserted more versions of the same malware (they may have used as many as five, security researchers say), the security system sent out more alerts, each the most urgent on FireEye's graded scale, says the person who has consulted on Target's probe.

The breach could have been stopped there without human intervention. The system has an option to automatically delete malware as it's detected. But according to two people who audited FireEye's performance after the breach, Target's security team turned that function off. Edward Kiledjian, chief information security officer for Bombardier Aerospace, an aircraft maker that has used FireEye for more than a year, says that's not unusual. "Typically, as a security team, you want to have that last decision point of 'what do I do,'" he says. But, he warns, that puts pressure on a team to quickly find and neutralize the infected computers.

Source: Michael Riley, Ben Elgin, Dune Lawrence and Carol Matlack, "Missed Alarms and 40 Million Stolen Credit Card Numbers: How Target Blew It," *Bloomberg Business Week,* March 13, 2014. Used with permission of Bloomberg L.P. Copyright © 2014. All rights reserved.

Questions for Discussion

1. Who are the stakeholders in the Target breach?

2. What is the responsibility of each stakeholder group in the breach?

3. Target Chairman, President, and Chief Executive Officer Gregg Steinhafel is quoted as saying that Target was certified as meeting the legal standard. Does being in compliance with the law and other standards negate any charges of unethical behavior on Target's behalf?

4. What can Target do to prove it will act ethically in the future and to regain the trust of its customers?

121

CHAPTER 5

Managing Diverse Employees in a Multicultural Environment

Learning Objectives

After studying this chapter, you should be able to:

LO5-1 Discuss the increasing diversity of the workforce and the organizational environment.

LO5-2 Explain the central role that managers play in the effective management of diversity.

LO5-3 Explain why the effective management of diversity is both an ethical and a business imperative.

LO5-4 Discuss how perception and the use of schemas can result in unfair treatment.

LO5-5 List the steps managers can take to effectively manage diversity.

LO5-6 Identify the two major forms of sexual harassment and how they can be eliminated.

What steps can organizations take to effectively manage an increasingly diverse workforce? By all counts, the diversity of the workforce is increasing. Effectively managing diversity is more than just ensuring that diverse members of organizations are treated fairly (itself a challenging task). When diversity is effectively managed, organizations can benefit from the diverse perspectives, points of view, experiences, and knowledge bases of their diverse members to produce better goods and services and be responsive to their increasingly diverse customer bases.

Extolling the benefits of effectively managing diversity is one thing; taking real and tangible steps to ensure that an organization continuously improves in this regard is another. Both organization-wide initiatives and the steps that each individual manager takes to effectively manage diversity have the potential for substantial payoffs in terms of both improved organizational effectiveness and maintaining a satisfied, committed, and motivated workforce.

Consider the steps that Pricewaterhouse-Coopers (PwC), one of the largest private companies in the United States with revenues over $32 billion and over 180,000 employees, has taken to effectively manage diversity.[1] PwC evolved from an accounting firm that Samuel Lowell Price founded in London in 1849. In 1854 William Cooper started his accounting firm, also in London, which eventually became Cooper Brothers. In 1865 Holyland and Waterhouse teamed up with Price, and the name of the partnership changed to Price, Waterhouse, & Co.

Cooper Brothers & Co. joined forces with McDonald, Currie and Co. from Canada and Lybrand, Ross Brothers & Montgomery from the United States to become Coopers and Lybrand in 1957. In 1982 the Price Waterhouse World Firm was created, and 16 years later in 1998, Price Waterhouse and Cooper & Lybrand merged worldwide to become PricewaterhouseCoopers.[2]

PwC renders audit and assurance, tax, and consulting services to clients in over 155 countries.[3] PwC's commitment to the effective management of diversity starts at the top and extends throughout the firm. Bob Moritz, chairman and senior partner of the U.S. firm of PwC and a PwC global network leadership team member, has long been an enthusiastic supporter and proponent of the effective management of diversity.[4] A long-tenured member of PwC, Moritz learned some valuable

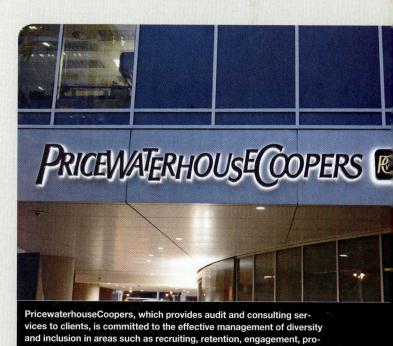

PricewaterhouseCoopers, which provides audit and consulting services to clients, is committed to the effective management of diversity and inclusion in areas such as recruiting, retention, engagement, promotion, and cross-cultural mentoring.

diversity lessons early in his career when he spent three years in PwC Tokyo assisting U.S. and European financial services firms doing business in Japan with audit and advisory services. Working in Japan opened Moritz's eyes to a host of diversity-related issues—what it felt like to be in the minority, to not speak the native language, and to experience discrimination. It also made him appreciate the value of cultural diversity, diversity of thought, and building trusting relationships with people who might be different from you on a number of dimensions.[5] As Moritz puts it, "Diverse and unexpected pools of talent are emerging around the world. To succeed in today's global economy requires organizations to have an inclusive culture the enables them to attract and retain diverse talent."[6]

Moritz gets together with diversity resource groups on a quarterly basis and ensures that executives and partners are working toward diversity and inclusion goals in a variety of areas such as recruiting and retention, engagement, promotions, and cross-cultural mentoring. All U.S. employees (the majority of whom are in management positions) are involved in mentoring programs (such as mentoring for newcomers, peer mentoring, and reverse mentoring), and over half of these mentoring relations involve a cross-cultural dyad.[7]

Maria Castañón Moats is an assurance partner at PwC and its chief diversity officer, leading its diversity strategy and initiatives.[8] She believes that effectively managing diversity includes providing all employees with the chance to have a successful career and that everyone needs to work to understand people who are different from themselves and help each other to thrive. Diverse employees also help PwC to innovatively meet the needs of diverse clients.[9]

At PwC, multiple dimensions of diversity are valued and effectively managed including ethnicity, gender, race, sexual orientation, religion, physical ability, and generation. A key focus of PwC's diversity initiatives is providing and maintaining an inclusive environment whereby diverse individuals not only feel welcome and supported but also have the opportunity to succeed and thrive. Thus initiatives focus on ensuring that PwC has a good pipeline for hiring diverse employees and that these employees can make valuable contributions and achieve early success in their careers with PwC. Providing ongoing opportunities for development and advancement is also key, along with having a diverse leadership base.[10]

Initiatives and resources are in place for a variety of minority and majority employees. For example, working parents are supported in numerous ways such as through paid parental leave, child care provisions (discounts for child care, a nanny resource/referral service, and backup child care for emergencies), adoption assistance and leave, parenting circles, and groups for working parents. As another example, GLBT (gay, lesbian, bisexual, and transgender) professionals are supported in multiple ways and have social networking and networking circles as well as access to full domestic partner benefit coverage and tax equalization. In fact, PwC is the only Big Four accounting firm that has a gay and lesbian partner advisory board composed of openly gay/lesbian partners, which advises PwC on GLBT concerns and issues and also focuses on career development.[11]

Over 35 percent of newly hired employees at PwC are minorities (Latino/Hispanic, Native American, Black/African-American, Asian/Pacific Islander, or multicultural), and PwC actively strives to ensure that these valuable employees are retained and advance in the firm. Diversity circles are professional forums whereby members of these and other diversity groupings can make contact with each other and provide learning, development, and mentoring experiences. The circles also give employees role models as they seek to advance in their careers. One of the most recent diversity circles that has been established at PwC is the Special Needs Caregivers Circle, which seeks to provide a support network for professionals who have a disability or special need or have someone in their personal lives with a special need or disability.[12]

Recognizing that many employees, at some point in their careers and lives, need or want flexibility to balance professional demands with their personal lives, PwC has a variety of flexible work arrangement that employees can take advantage of. PwC also helps employees determine which type of flexible work arrangement might best meet their professional and personal needs.[13]

This is just a sampling of the many diversity-related endeavors PwC has undertaken and continues to pursue. Perhaps it is not surprising that PwC has achieved national recognition for its diversity initiatives.[14] For example, in 2013 PwC was ranked second in *DiversityInc*'s "Top 50 Companies for Diversity."[15] PwC continues to strive to effectively manage diversity in multiple ways for the good of its employees, its clients, the firm itself, and other stakeholders.[16]

Overview

As indicated in "A Manager's Challenge," effective management of diversity means more than hiring diverse employees. It means learning to appreciate and respond appropriately to the needs, attitudes, beliefs, and values that diverse people bring to an organization. It also means correcting misconceptions about why and how various kinds of employee groups differ from one another and finding the most effective way to use the skills and talents of diverse employees.

In this chapter we focus on the effective management of diversity in an environment that is becoming increasingly diverse in all respects. Not only are the diversity and integration of the global workforce increasing, but suppliers and customers are also becoming increasingly diverse. Managers need to proactively manage diversity to attract and retain the best employees and effectively compete in a global environment. For example, managers at the audit and consulting firm Deloitte & Touche have instituted a program to encourage minority suppliers to compete for its business, and the firm sponsors schools and colleges that supply a stream of well-trained recruits.[17]

Sometimes well-intentioned managers inadvertently treat various groups of employees differently, even though there are no performance-based differences between them. This chapter explores why differential treatment occurs and the steps managers and organizations can take to ensure that diversity, in all respects, is effectively managed for the good of all organizational stakeholders.

Diversity dissimilarities or differences among people due to age, gender, race, ethnicity, religion, sexual orientation, socioeconomic background, education, experience, physical appearance, capabilities/disabilities, and any other characteristic that is used to distinguish between people.

The Increasing Diversity of the Workforce and the Environment

One of the most important management issues to emerge over the last 40 years has been the increasing diversity of the workforce. **Diversity** is dissimilarities—differences—among people due to age, gender, race, ethnicity, religion, sexual orientation, socioeconomic background, education, experience, physical appearance, capabilities/disabilities, and any other characteristic that is used to distinguish between people (see Figure 5.1).

Diversity raises important ethical issues and social responsibility issues (see Chapter 4). It is also a critical issue for organizations—one that if not handled well can bring an organization to its knees, especially in our increasingly

Figure 5.1

Sources of Diversity in the Workplace

global environment. There are several reasons why diversity is such a pressing concern and an issue both in the popular press and for managers and organizations:

- There is a strong ethical imperative in many societies that diverse people must receive equal opportunities and be treated fairly and justly. Unfair treatment is also illegal.

- Effectively managing diversity can improve organizational effectiveness.[18] When managers effectively manage diversity, they not only encourage other managers to treat diverse members of an organization fairly and justly but also realize that diversity is an important organizational resource that can help an organization gain a competitive advantage.

- There is substantial evidence that diverse individuals continue to experience unfair treatment in the workplace as a result of biases, stereotypes, and overt discrimination.[19] In one study, résumés of equally qualified men and women were sent to high-priced Philadelphia restaurants (where potential earnings are high). Though equally qualified, men were more than twice as likely as women to be called for a job interview and more than five times as likely to receive a job offer.[20] Findings from another study suggest that both women and men tend to believe that women will accept lower pay than men; this is a possible explanation for the continuing gap in pay between men and women.[21]

Other kinds of diverse employees may face even greater barriers. For example, the federal Glass Ceiling Commission Report indicated that African Americans have the hardest time being promoted and climbing the corporate ladder, that Asians are often stereotyped into technical jobs, and that Hispanics are assumed to be less well educated than other minority groups.[22] (The term **glass ceiling** alludes to the invisible barriers that prevent minorities and women from being promoted to top corporate positions.)[23]

Before we can discuss the multitude of issues surrounding the effective management of diversity, we must document just how diverse the U.S. workforce is becoming.

glass ceiling A metaphor alluding to the invisible barriers that prevent minorities and women from being promoted to top corporate positions.

Age

According to data from the U.S. Census Bureau and the CIA's World Fact Book, the median age of a person in the United States is the highest it has ever been, 37.6 years.[24] Moreover, by 2030 it is projected that close to 20 percent of the U.S. population will be 65 or over.[25] The Age Discrimination in Employment Act of 1967 prohibits age discrimination.[26] Although we discuss

Table 5.1

Major Equal Employment Opportunity Laws Affecting Human Resources Management

Year	Law	Description
1963	Equal Pay Act	Requires that men and women be paid equally if they are performing equal work.
1964	Title VII of the Civil Rights Act	Prohibits discrimination in employment decisions on the basis of race, religion, sex, color, or national origin; covers a wide range of employment decisions, including hiring, firing, pay, promotion, and working conditions.
1967	Age Discrimination in Employment Act	Prohibits discrimination against workers over the age of 40 and restricts mandatory retirement.
1978	Pregnancy Discrimination Act	Prohibits discrimination against women in employment decisions on the basis of pregnancy, childbirth, and related medical decisions.
1990	Americans with Disabilities Act	Prohibits discrimination against disabled individuals in employment decisions and requires that employers make accommodations for disabled workers to enable them to perform their jobs.
1991	Civil Rights Act	Prohibits discrimination (as does Title VII) and allows for the awarding of punitive and compensatory damages, in addition to back pay, in cases of intentional discrimination.
1993	Family and Medical Leave Act	Requires that employers provide 12 weeks of unpaid leave for medical and family reasons, including paternity and illness of a family member.

federal employment legislation in more depth in Chapter 12, major equal employment opportunity legislation that prohibits discrimination among diverse groups is summarized in Table 5.1.

The aging of the population suggests managers need to be vigilant to ensure that employees are not discriminated against because of age. Moreover, managers need to ensure that the policies and procedures they have in place treat all workers fairly, regardless of their ages. Additionally, effectively managing diversity means employees of diverse ages are able to learn from each other, work well together, and take advantage of the different perspectives each has to offer.

Gender

Women and men both have substantial participation rates in the U.S. workforce (approximately 55.6 percent of the U.S. workforce is male and 44.4 percent female),[27] yet women's median weekly earnings are estimated to be $706 compared to $860 for men.[28] Thus the gender pay gap appears to be as unfortunately real as the glass ceiling. According to the nonprofit organization Catalyst, which studies women in business, while women compose about 51.5 percent of the employees in managerial and professional positions,[29] only around 14.6 percent of executive officers in the 500 largest U.S. companies (that is, the *Fortune* 500) are women, and only 8.1 percent of the top earner executive officers are women.[30] These women, such as Virginia Rometty, CEO of IBM, and Indra Nooyi, CEO of PepsiCo, stand out among their male peers and often receive a disparate amount of attention in the media. (We address this issue later when we discuss the effects of being salient.) Women are also very underrepresented on boards of directors—they currently hold 16.9 percent of the board seats of *Fortune* 500 companies.[31] However, as Sheila Wellington, former president of Catalyst, indicates, "Women either control or influence nearly all consumer purchases, so it's important to have their perspective represented on boards."[32]

Additionally, research conducted by consulting firms suggests that female executives outperform their male colleagues in skills such as motivating others, promoting good communication, turning out high-quality work, and being good listeners.[33] For example, the

A female executive enjoying the company plane is not as rare a sight today as it used to be; nevertheless, the glass ceiling remains a real barrier to women in the business workforce.

Hagberg Group performed in-depth evaluations of 425 top executives in a variety of industries, with each executive rated by approximately 25 people. Of the 52 skills assessed, women received higher ratings than men on 42 skills, although at times the differences were small.[34] Results of a study conducted by Catalyst found that organizations with higher proportions of women in top management positions had significantly better financial performance than organizations with lower proportions of female top managers.[35] Another study conducted by Catalyst found that companies with three or more women on their boards of directors performed better in terms of returns on equity, sales, and invested capital than companies with fewer or no women on their boards.[36] Studies such as these make one wonder why the glass ceiling continues to hamper the progress of women in business (a topic we address later in the chapter).

Race and Ethnicity

The U.S. Census Bureau distinguished between the following races in the 2010 census: American Indian or Alaska Native; Asian Indian; black, African American, or Negro; Chinese; Filipino; Japanese; Korean; Vietnamese; other Asian; Native Hawaiian; Guamanian or Chamorro; Samoan; Other Pacific Islander; white; and other races.[37] Although *ethnicity* refers to a grouping of people based on some shared characteristic such as national origin, language, or culture, the U.S. Census Bureau treats ethnicity in terms of whether a person is Hispanic, Latino, or of Spanish origin or not.[38] Hispanics, also referred to as Latinos, are people whose origins are in Spanish cultures such as those of Cuba, Mexico, Puerto Rico, and South and Central America. Hispanics can be of different races.[39] According to a recent poll, most Hispanics prefer to be identified by their country of origin (such as Mexican, Cuban, or Salvadoran) rather than by the overarching term *Hispanic*.[40]

The racial and ethnic diversity of the U.S. population is increasing quickly, as is the diversity of the workforce.[41] According to the U.S. Census Bureau, approximately one of every three U.S. residents belongs to a minority group (is not a non-Hispanic white).[42] More specifically, 16.3 percent of the population is Hispanic or Latino, 83.7 percent of the population is not Hispanic or Latino, and 63.7 percent of the population is white alone (that is, white and not Hispanic or Latino).[43] For those individuals self-identifying one race in the 2010 U.S. census, approximately 72.4 percent of the population is white, 12.6 percent is black or African American, 0.9 percent is American Indian or Alaska Native, 4.8 percent is Asian, 0.2 percent is Native Hawaiian and other Pacific Islander, and 6.2 percent is another race; 2.9 percent of the population self-identified two or more races.[44] According to projections released by the U.S. Census Bureau, the composition of the U.S. population in 2050 will be quite different from its composition today; in 2050 the U.S. population is projected to be 54 percent minority.[45]

The increasing racial and ethnic diversity of the workforce and the population as a whole underscores the importance of effectively managing diversity. Statistics compiled by the Bureau of Labor Statistics suggest that much needs to be done in terms of ensuring that diverse employees have equal opportunities. For example, median weekly earnings for black men are approximately 75.1 percent of median earnings for white men; median weekly earnings for black women are approximately 83.9 percent of median earnings for white women.[46] In the remainder of this chapter, we focus on the fair treatment of diverse employees and explore why this is such an important challenge and what managers can do to meet it. We begin by taking a broader perspective and considering how increasing racial and ethnic diversity in an organization's environment (such as customers and suppliers) affects decision making and organizational effectiveness.

At a general level, managers and organizations are increasingly being reminded that stakeholders in the environment are diverse and expect organizational decisions and actions to reflect this diversity. For example, the NAACP (National Association for the Advancement of Colored People) and Children Now (an advocacy group) have lobbied the entertainment industry to increase the diversity in television programming, writing, and producing.[47] The need for such increased diversity is more than apparent. For example, while Hispanics make up 17 percent of the U.S. population (or 53 million potential TV viewers), less than 5 percent of the characters in prime-time TV shows are Hispanics, according to a study conducted by Children Now.[48] Moreover, less than 5 percent of the evening network TV news stories are reported by Hispanic correspondents, according to the Center for Media and Public Affairs.[49]

Pressure is mounting on networks to increase diversity for a variety of reasons revolving around the diversity of the population as a whole, TV viewers, and consumers. For example, home and automobile buyers are increasingly diverse, reflecting the increasing diversity of the population as a whole.[50] Moreover, managers have to be especially sensitive to avoid stereotyping different groups when they communicate with potential customers. For example, Toyota Motor Sales USA made a public apology to the Reverend Jesse Jackson and his Rainbow Coalition for using a print advertisement depicting an African-American man with a Toyota RAV4 sport utility image embossed on his gold front tooth.[51]

Religion

Title VII of the Civil Rights Act prohibits discrimination based on religion (as well as based on race/ethnicity, country of origin, and sex; see Table 5.1 and Chapter 12). In addition to enacting Title VII, in 1997 the federal government issued "The White House Guidelines on Religious Exercise and Expression in the Federal Workplace."[52] These guidelines, while technically applicable only in federal offices, also are frequently relied on by large corporations. The guidelines require that employers make reasonable accommodations for religious practices, such as observances of holidays, as long as doing so does not entail major costs or hardships.[53]

A key issue for managers in religious diversity is recognizing and being aware of different religions and their beliefs, with particular attention being paid to when religious holidays fall. For example, critical meetings should not be scheduled during a holy day for members of a certain faith, and managers should be flexible in allowing people to have time off for religious observances. According to Lobna Ismail, director of a diversity training company in Silver Spring, Maryland, when managers acknowledge, respect, and make even small accommodations for religious diversity, employee loyalty is often enhanced. For example, allowing employees to leave work early on certain days instead of taking a lunch break or posting holidays for different religions on the company calendar can go a long way toward making individuals of diverse religions feel respected and valued as well as enabling them to practice their faith.[54] According to research conducted by the Tanenbaum Center for Interreligious Understanding in New York, while only about 23 percent of employees who feel they are victims of religious discrimination actually file complaints, about 45 percent of these employees start looking for other jobs.[55]

Capabilities/Disabilities

The Americans with Disabilities Act (ADA) of 1990 prohibits discrimination against persons with disabilities and also requires that employers make reasonable accommodations to enable these people to effectively perform their jobs. On the surface, few would argue with the intent of this legislation. However, as managers attempt to implement policies and procedures to comply with the ADA, they face a number of interpretation and fairness challenges.

On one hand, some people with real disabilities warranting workplace accommodations are hesitant to reveal their disabilities to their employers and claim the accommodations they deserve.[56] On the other hand, some employees abuse the ADA by seeking unnecessary accommodations for disabilities that may or may not exist.[57] Thus it is perhaps not surprising that the passage of the ADA does not appear to have increased employment rates significantly for those with disabilities.[58] A key challenge for managers is to promote an environment in which employees needing accommodations feel comfortable disclosing their need and, at the same time, to ensure that the accommodations not only enable those with disabilities to effectively perform their jobs but also are perceived to be fair by those not disabled.[59]

In addressing this challenge, often managers must educate both themselves and their employees about the disabilities, as well as the real capabilities, of those who are disabled. For example, during a Disability Awareness Week, administrators at the University of Notre

Dame sought to increase the public's knowledge of disabilities while also heightening awareness of the abilities of persons who are disabled.[60] The University of Houston conducted a similar program called "Think Ability."[61] According to Cheryl Amoruso, director of the University of Houston's Center for Students with Disabilities, many people are unaware of the prevalence of disabilities as well as misinformed about their consequences.[62] She suggests, for example, that although students may not be able to see, they can still excel in their coursework and have successful careers.[63] Accommodations enabling such students to perform up to their capabilities are covered under the ADA.

The ADA also protects employees with acquired immune deficiency syndrome (AIDS) from being discriminated against in the workplace. AIDS is caused by the human immunodeficiency virus (HIV) and is transmitted through sexual contact, infected needles, and contaminated blood products. HIV is not spread through casual nonsexual contact. Yet out of ignorance, fear, or prejudice, some people wish to avoid all contact with anyone infected with HIV. Infected individuals may not necessarily develop AIDS, and some individuals with HIV are able to remain effective performers of their jobs while not putting others at risk.[64]

AIDS awareness training can help people overcome their fears and also give managers a tool to prevent illegal discrimination against HIV-infected employees. Such training focuses on educating employees about HIV and AIDS, dispelling myths, communicating relevant organizational policies, and emphasizing the rights of HIV-positive employees to privacy and an environment that allows them to be productive.[65] The need for AIDS awareness training is underscored by some of the problems HIV-positive employees experience once others in their workplace become aware of their condition.[66] Moreover, organizations are required to make reasonable accommodations to enable people with AIDS to effectively perform their jobs.

Thus managers have an obligation to educate employees about HIV and AIDS, dispel myths and the stigma of AIDS, and ensure that HIV-related discrimination is not occurring in the workplace. For example, Home Depot has provided HIV training and education to its store managers; such training was sorely needed given that over half of the managers indicated it was the first time they had the opportunity to talk about AIDS.[67] Moreover, advances in medication and treatment mean that more infected individuals are able to continue working or are able to return to work after their condition improves. Thus managers need to ensure that these employees are fairly treated by all members of their organizations.[68] And managers and organizations that do not treat HIV-positive employees in a fair manner, as well as provide reasonable accommodations (such as allowing time off for doctor visits or to take medicine), risk costly lawsuits.

Socioeconomic Background

The term *socioeconomic background* typically refers to a combination of social class and income-related factors. From a management perspective, socioeconomic diversity (and in particular diversity in income levels) requires that managers be sensitive and responsive to the needs and concerns of individuals who might not be as well off as others. U.S. welfare reform in the middle to late 1990s emphasized the need for single mothers and others receiving public assistance to join or return to the workforce. In conjunction with a strong economy, this led to record declines in the number of families, households, and children living below the poverty level, according to the 2000 U.S. census.[69] However, the economic downturns in the early and late 2000s suggest that some past gains that lifted families out of poverty have been reversed. In a strong economy, it is much easier for poor people with few skills to find jobs; in a weak economy, when companies lay off employees in hard times, people who need their incomes the most are unfortunately often the first to lose their jobs.[70] And in recessionary times, it is difficult for laid-off employees to find new positions. For example, in December 2009 there were an average of 6.1 unemployed workers for every open position.[71]

According to statistics released by the US Census Bureau, the official poverty rate in the United States in 2012 was 15.0 percent or 46.5 million people; in 2009 the poverty rate was 14.3 percent or 43.6 million people.[72] The Census Bureau relies on predetermined threshold income figures, based on family size and composition, adjusted annually for inflation, to determine the poverty level. Families whose income falls below the threshold level are considered poor.[73] For example, in 2012 a family of four was considered poor if their annual income fell below $23,492.[74] When workers earn less than $15 per hour, it is often difficult, if not impossible, for them to meet their families' needs.[75] Moreover, increasing numbers of families are facing the challenge of finding suitable child care arrangements that enable the adults to work long hours and/or through the night to maintain an adequate income level. New information technology has led to more businesses operating 24 hours a day, creating real challenges for workers on the night shift, especially those with children.[76]

Hundreds of thousands of parents across the country are scrambling to find someone to care for their children while they are working the night shift, commuting several hours a day, working weekends and holidays, or putting in long hours on one or more jobs. This has led to the opening of day-care facilities that operate around the clock as well as to managers seeking ways to provide such care for children of their employees. For example, the Children's Choice Learning Center in Las Vegas, Nevada, operates around the clock to accommodate employees working nights in neighboring casinos, hospitals, and call centers. Randy Donahue, a security guard who works until midnight, picks his children up from the center when he gets off work; his wife is a nurse on the night shift.[77]

Judy Harden, who focuses on families and child care issues for the United Workers Union, indicates that the demands families are facing necessitate around-the-clock and odd-hour child care options. Many parents simply do not have the choice of working at hours that allow them to take care of their children at night and/or on weekends, never mind when the children are sick.[78] Some parents and psychologists feel uneasy having children separated from their families for so much time and particularly at night. Most agree that, unfortunately for many families, this is not a choice but a necessity.[79]

Socioeconomic diversity suggests that managers need to be sensitive and responsive to the needs and concerns of workers who may be less fortunate than themselves in terms of income and financial resources, child care and elder care options, housing opportunities, and existence of sources of social and family support. Moreover—and equally important—managers should try to give such individuals opportunities to learn, advance, and make meaningful contributions to their organizations while improving their economic well-being.

Sexual Orientation

According to research conducted by Gary Gates of the Williams Institute at the UCLA School of Law, approximately 3.5 percent of adults in the United States, or 9 million U.S. residents, self-identify as lesbian, gay, bisexual, or transgender (LGBT).[80] Although no federal law prohibits discrimination based on sexual orientation, 21 states and the District of Columbia have such laws, and a 1998 executive order prohibits sexual orientation discrimination in civilian federal offices.[81] Moreover, an increasing number of organizations recognize the minority status of LGBT employees, affirm their rights to fair and equal treatment, and provide benefits to same-sex partners of gay and lesbian employees.[82] For example, a vast majority of *Fortune* 500 companies prohibit discrimination based on sexual orientation, and a majority of the *Fortune* 500 provide domestic partner benefits.[83] As indicated in the accompanying "Focus on Diversity" feature, managers can take many steps to ensure that sexual orientation is not used to unfairly discriminate among employees.

Focus on Diversity

Preventing Discrimination Based on Sexual Orientation

Although gays and lesbians have made great strides in attaining fair treatment in the workplace, much more needs to be done. In a study conducted by Harris Interactive Inc. (a research firm) and Witeck Communications Inc. (a marketing firm), over 40 percent of gay and lesbian employees indicated that they had been unfairly treated, denied a promotion, or pushed to quit their jobs because of their sexual orientation.[84] Given continued harassment and discrimination despite the progress that has been

Danish employees of Microsoft raise awareness at Copenhagen's annual Gay Pride Parade. Corporate backing, such as that displayed here, can go a long way toward making sure workplaces are safe and respectful for everyone.

made,[85] many gay and lesbian employees fear disclosing their sexual orientation in the workplace and thus live a life of secrecy. While there are a few openly gay top managers, such as David Geffen, cofounder of Dream-Works SKG, and Allan Gilmour, former vice chairman and CFO of Ford and currently a member of the board of directors of DTE Energy Holding Company, many others choose not to disclose or discuss their personal lives, including long-term partners.[86]

Thus it is not surprising that many managers are taking active steps to educate and train their employees about issues of sexual orientation. S.C. Johnson & Sons, Inc., maker of Raid insecticide and Glade air fresheners in Racine, Wisconsin, provides mandatory training to its plant managers to overturn stereotypes; and Merck & Co., Ernst & Young, and Toronto-Dominion Bank all train managers in how to prevent sexual orientation discrimination.[87] Other organizations such as Lucent Technologies, Microsoft, and Southern California Edison send employees to seminars conducted at prominent business schools. And many companies such as Raytheon, IBM, and Lockheed Martin assist their gay and lesbian employees through gay and lesbian support groups.[88] Recently Boeing, Google, Yahoo, Chevron, JP Morgan Chase, Goldman Sachs Group, and Bank of America were among the 304 companies recognized as Best Places to Work 2014 for gay, lesbian, bisexual, and transgender employees by the Human Rights Campaign, a nonprofit organization that advocates for the civil rights of LGBT people.[89]

The Chubb Group of Insurance Companies, a property and casualty insurance company, gives its managers a two-hour training session to help create work environments that are safe and welcoming for lesbian, gay, bisexual, and transgender (LGBT) people.[90] The sessions are conducted by two Chubb employees; usually one of the trainers is straight and the other is gay. The sessions focus on issues that affect a manager's ability to lead diverse teams, such as assessing how safe and welcoming the workplace is for LGBT people, how to refer to gay employees' significant others, and how to respond if employees or customers use inappropriate language or behavior. The idea for the program originated from one of Chubb's employee resource groups. Managers rate the program highly and say they are better able to respond to the concerns of their LGBT employees while creating a safe and productive work environment for all.[91] In 2014 the Chubb Group was also recognized as one of the Best Places to Work by the Human Right Campaign.[92]

Other Kinds of Diversity

Other kinds of diversity are important in organizations, are critical for managers to deal with effectively, and also are potential sources of unfair treatment. For example, organizations and teams need members with diverse backgrounds and experiences. This is clearly illustrated by the prevalence of cross-functional teams in organizations whose members might come from various departments such as marketing, production, finance, and sales (teams are covered in depth in Chapter 15). A team responsible for developing and introducing a new product, for example, often needs the expertise of employees not only from research and design and engineering but also from marketing, sales, production, and finance.

Other types of diversity can affect how employees are treated in the workplace. For example, employees differ from each other in how attractive they are (based on the standards of the cultures in which an organization operates) and in body weight. Whether individuals are attractive, unattractive, thin, or overweight in most cases has no bearing on their job performance unless they have jobs in which physical appearance plays a role, such as modeling. Yet sometimes these physical sources of diversity affect advancement rates and salaries. A study published in the *American Journal of Public Health* found that highly educated obese women earned approximately 30 percent less per year than women who were not obese and men (regardless of whether or not the men were obese).[93] Clearly managers need to ensure that all employees are treated fairly, regardless of their physical appearance.

Managers and the Effective Management of Diversity

The increasing diversity of the environment—which, in turn, increases the diversity of an organization's workforce—increases the challenges managers face in effectively managing diversity. Each of the kinds of diversity just discussed presents a particular set of issues managers need to appreciate before they can respond to them effectively. Understanding these issues is not always a simple matter, as many informed managers have discovered. Research on how different groups are currently treated and the unconscious biases that might adversely affect them is vital because it helps managers become aware of the many subtle and unobtrusive ways in which diverse employee groups can come to be treated unfairly over time. Managers can take many more steps to become sensitive to the ongoing effects of diversity in their organizations, take advantage of all the contributions diverse employees can make, and prevent employees from being unfairly treated.

LO5-2

Explain the central role that managers play in the effective management of diversity.

Critical Managerial Roles

In each of their managerial roles (see Chapter 1), managers can either promote the effective management of diversity or derail such efforts; thus they are critical to this process. For example, in their interpersonal roles, managers can convey that the effective management of diversity is a valued goal and objective (figurehead role), can serve as a role model and institute policies and procedures to ensure that all organizational members are treated fairly (leader role), and can enable diverse individuals and groups to coordinate their efforts and cooperate with each other both inside the organization and at the organization's boundaries (liaison role). Table 5.2 summarizes ways in which managers can ensure that diversity is effectively managed as they perform their different roles.

Table 5.2

Managerial Roles and the Effective Management of Diversity

Type of Role	Specific Role	Example
Interpersonal	Figurehead	Conveys that the effective management of diversity is a valued goal and objective.
	Leader	Serves as a role model and institutes policies and procedures to ensure that diverse members are treated fairly.
	Liaison	Enables diverse individuals to coordinate their efforts and cooperate with one another.
Informational	Monitor	Evaluates the extent to which all employees are treated fairly.
	Disseminator	Informs employees about diversity policies and initiatives and the intolerance of discrimination.
	Spokesperson	Supports diversity initiatives in the wider community and speaks to diverse groups to interest them in career opportunities.
Decisional	Entrepreneur	Commits resources to develop new ways to effectively manage diversity and eliminate biases and discrimination.
	Disturbance handler	Takes quick action to correct inequalities and curtail discriminatory behavior.
	Resource allocator	Allocates resources to support and encourage the effective management of diversity.
	Negotiator	Works with organizations (e.g., suppliers) and groups (e.g., labor unions) to support and encourage the effective management of diversity.

Given the formal authority that managers have in organizations, they typically have more influence than rank-and-file employees. When managers commit to supporting diversity, as is the case at PwC in "A Manager's Challenge," their authority and positions of power and status influence other members of an organization to make a similar commitment.[94] Research on social influence supports such a link: People are likely to be influenced and persuaded by others who have high status.[95]

Consider the steps that managers at Sodexo and Principal Financial Group have taken to effectively manage diversity as profiled in the accompanying "Focus on Diversity" feature.

Focus on Diversity

Effectively Managing Diversity at Sodexo and Principal Financial Group

Managers at Sodexo, Inc., a major food and facilities management company serving over 15 million consumers per day in businesses, health care facilities, schools and universities, and government agencies, take many steps to ensure that diversity is effectively managed.[96] Sodexo encourages managers to interact with diverse groups to gain a better appreciation and understanding of their experiences. When Ron Bond attended a meeting of the Women's Food Service Forum with some of his female coworkers, he stood out as one of the few men in attendance among 1,500 women. Thinking back on his own experiences when, for example, he started out his career and women were rare in the management ranks, Bond gained a deeper appreciation of what it means to be different in a group or organization. As he suggested, "That's a profound experience . . . I can begin to feel what it must have felt like to be different."[97]

Sodexo provides employees and managers with extensive diversity training, encourages managers to mentor and coach employees who are different from themselves, and bases 25 percent of top managers' bonuses on their performance on diversity initiatives, including hiring and training diverse employees.[98] Managers are encouraged to sponsor affinity groups for employees that differ from themselves. For example, Bond sponsored the women's affinity group, which provided a forum for female employees to connect with each other and address their mutual concerns (such as a lactation room so new mothers can pump breast milk). Sponsoring such groups helps managers become aware of and address concerns of some employee groups they might never have thought of otherwise. Bond realized that having a lactation room was "just one of those things I'd never thought about."[99]

Lorna Donatone managed a unit of Sodexo that provides food services for cruise companies. Of Swedish and German ancestry and raised in Nebraska, she sponsored Sodexo's Latino affinity group and discovered a better way to serve her unit's customers. Donatone learned to rely more on more bilingual materials to promote the services she provided to cruise companies and their customers. As senior vice president and global chief diversity officer for Sodexo Dr. Rohini Anand indicated, "To really engage people, you have to create a series of epiphanies and take leaders through those epiphanies."[100]

Sodexo's effective management of diversity has not gone unnoticed in the business community, and the company and its diverse employees have received numerous awards and recognition for their diversity initiatives.[101] Frequently ranked as a best place to work for diverse employees by magazines such as *DiversityInc.*,

Magic Johnson and Sodexo president and CEO George Chavel present Northwestern University student Sarah Suh with the Stephen J. Brady STOP Hunger scholarship at Sodexo's Diversity Business Leadership Summit in Chicago in 2013.

Working Mother, and *Latina Style,* Sodexo was ranked first in *DiversityInc.*'s listing of "The Top 50 Companies for Diversity" in 2013.[102]

Principal Financial Group, headquartered in Des Moines, Iowa, operates in a vastly different industry: financial products, services, and insurance.[103] Yet Principal Financial also has been recognized for its effective management of diversity.[104] To ensure that opportunities are open for diverse employees, Principal has offered its employees flexible work schedules since 1974—decades before many other companies provided this option. And employees who take advantage of this and other benefits, such as having 12 weeks off work after the birth of a child, do not find their career progress hampered as is sometimes the case at other companies.[105]

When Valarie Vest was a regional client service director at Principal and on her second maternity leave, her supervisors called to offer her a promotion to a position that included more responsibility, more travel, and relocation to a different city. They thought she was the best candidate for the position and let her decide if she wanted to take it. She was delighted to accept the position, which included managing 10 employees.[106]

Principal seeks to hire diverse employees and then gives them the resources and opportunities to help them reach their potential while helping Principal achieve its goals. These resources and opportunities include, but are not limited to, mentoring programs, multicultural celebrations, on-site child care, development programs, and domestic partner benefits.[107] Additionally, there are a variety of employee resource groups that all employees can join to network, engage in career development activities, and become involved in the community.[108]

Sodexo and Principal Financial Group are among the growing numbers of companies that are reaping the benefits of an increasingly diverse workforce.

When managers commit to diversity, their commitment legitimizes the diversity management efforts of others.[109] In addition, resources are devoted to such efforts, and all members of an organization believe that their diversity-related efforts are supported and valued. Consistent with this reasoning, top management commitment and rewards for the support of diversity are often cited as critical ingredients in the success of diversity management initiatives.[110] Additionally, seeing managers express confidence in the abilities and talents of diverse employees causes other organizational members to be similarly confident and helps reduce any prejudice they may have as a result of ignorance or stereotypes.[111]

Two other important factors emphasize why managers are so central to the effective management of diversity. The first factor is that women, African Americans, Hispanics, and other minorities often start out at a slight disadvantage due to how they are perceived by others in organizations, particularly in work settings where they are a numerical minority. As Virginia Valian, a psychologist at Hunter College who studies gender, indicates, "In most organizations women begin at a slight disadvantage. A woman does not walk into the room with the same status as an equivalent man, because she is less likely than a man to be viewed as a serious professional."[112]

The second factor is that research suggests that slight differences in treatment can accumulate and result in major disparities over time. Even small differences—such as a small favorable bias toward men for promotions—can lead to major differences in the number of male and female managers over time.[113] Thus while women and other minorities are sometimes advised not to make "a mountain out of a molehill" when they perceive they have been unfairly treated, research conducted by Valian and others suggests that molehills (slight differences in treatment based on irrelevant distinctions such as race, gender, or ethnicity) can turn into mountains over time (major disparities in important outcomes such as promotions) if they are ignored.[114] Once again, managers have the obligation, from both an ethical and a business perspective, to prevent any disparities in treatment and outcomes due to irrelevant distinctions such as race or ethnicity.

LO5-3

Explain why the effective management of diversity is both an ethical and a business imperative.

The Ethical Imperative to Manage Diversity Effectively

Effectively managing diversity not only makes good business sense (which is discussed in the next section) but also is an ethical imperative in U.S. society. Two moral principles guide managers in their efforts to meet this imperative: distributive justice and procedural justice.

distributive justice
A moral principle calling for fair distribution of pay, promotions, and other organizational resources based on meaningful contributions that individuals have made and not personal characteristics over which they have no control.

DISTRIBUTIVE JUSTICE   The principle of **distributive justice** dictates fair distribution of pay, promotions, job titles, interesting job assignments, office space, and other organizational resources among members of an organization. These outcomes should be distributed according to the meaningful contributions that individuals have made to the organization (such as time, effort, education, skills, abilities, and performance levels) and not irrelevant personal characteristics over which individuals have no control (such as gender, race, or age).[115] Managers have an obligation to ensure that distributive justice exists in their organizations. This does not mean that all members of an organization receive identical or similar outcomes; rather, it means that members who receive more favorable outcomes than others have made substantially higher or more significant contributions to the organization.

Is distributive justice common in organizations in corporate America? Probably the best way to answer this question is to say things are getting better. Fifty years ago, overt discrimination against women and minorities was common; today organizations are inching closer toward the ideal of distributive justice. Statistics comparing the treatment of women and minorities with the treatment of other employees suggest that most managers need to take a proactive approach to achieve distributive justice in their organizations.[116] For example, across occupations, women consistently earn less than men (see Table 5.3) according to data collected by the U.S. Bureau of Labor Statistics.[117] Even in occupations dominated by women, such as sales and office occupations, men tend to earn more than women.[118]

In many countries, managers have not only an ethical obligation to strive to achieve distributive justice in their organizations but also a legal obligation to treat all employees fairly. They risk being sued by employees who believe they are not being fairly treated. That is precisely what six African-American Texaco employees did when they experienced racial bias and discrimination.[119]

procedural justice A moral principle calling for the use of fair procedures to determine how to distribute outcomes to organizational members.

PROCEDURAL JUSTICE   The principle of **procedural justice** requires that managers use fair procedures to determine how to distribute outcomes to organizational members.[120] This principle applies to typical procedures such as appraising subordinates' performance, deciding who should receive a raise or a promotion, and deciding whom to lay off when an organization is forced to downsize. Procedural justice exists, for example, when managers (1) carefully appraise a subordinate's performance; (2) take into account any environmental obstacles to high performance beyond the subordinate's control, such as lack of supplies,

Table 5.3

Median Weekly Earnings for Full-Time Workers by Sex and Occupation in 2013

Occupation	Men	Women	Women's Earnings as a Percentage of Men's
Management, professional, and related	$1,349	$973	72
Service	555	452	81
Sales and office	756	615	81
Natural resources, construction, and maintenance	757	578	76
Production, transportation, and material moving	674	498	74

Source: "Household Data; Annual Averages; 39. Median Weekly Earnings of Full-Time Wage and Salary Workers by Detailed Occupation and Sex," http://www.bls.gov/cps/cpsaat39.htm, April 1, 2014.

machine breakdowns, or dwindling customer demand for a product; and (3) ignore irrelevant personal characteristics such as the subordinate's age or ethnicity. Like distributive justice, procedural justice is necessary not only to ensure ethical conduct but also to avoid costly lawsuits.

Effectively Managing Diversity Makes Good Business Sense

Diverse organizational members can be a source of competitive advantage, helping an organization provide customers with better goods and services.[121] The variety of points of view and approaches to problems and opportunities that diverse employees provide can improve managerial decision making. Suppose the Budget Gourmet frozen food company is trying to come up with creative ideas for new frozen meals that will appeal to health-conscious, time-conscious customers tired of the same old frozen fare. Which group do you think is likely to come up with the most creative ideas: a group of white women with marketing degrees from Yale University who grew up in upper-middle-class families in the Northeast or a racially mixed group of men and women who grew up in families with varying income levels in different parts of the country and attended a variety of geographically dispersed business schools? Most people would agree that the diverse group is likely to have a wider range of creative ideas. Although this example is simplistic, it underscores one way in which diversity can lead to a competitive advantage.

Just as the workforce is becoming increasingly diverse, so too are the customers who buy an organization's goods or services. In an attempt to suit local customers' needs and tastes, organizations like Target often vary the selection of products available in stores in different cities and regions.[122]

Diverse members of an organization are likely to be attuned to what goods and services diverse segments of the market want and do not want. Automakers, for example, are increasingly assigning women to their design teams to ensure that the needs and desires of female customers are taken into account in new car design.

For Darden Restaurants, the business case for diversity rests on market share and growth. Darden seeks to satisfy the needs and tastes of diverse customers by providing menus in Spanish in communities with large Hispanic populations.[123] Similarly, market share and growth and the identification of niche markets led Tracey Campbell to cater to travelers with disabilities.[124] She heads InnSeekers, a telephone and online listing resource for bed and breakfasts. Nikki Daruwala works for the Calvert Group in Bethesda, Maryland, a mutual fund that emphasizes social responsibility and diversity. She indicates that profit alone is more than enough of an incentive to effectively manage diversity. As she puts it, "You can look at an automaker. There are more women making decisions about car buying or home buying . . . $3.72 trillion per year are spent by women."[125]

Another way that effective management of diversity can improve profitability is by increasing retention of valued employees, which decreases the costs of hiring replacements for those who quit as well as ensures that all employees are highly motivated. In terms of retention, given the current legal environment, more and more organizations are attuned to the need to emphasize the importance of diversity in hiring. Once hired, if diverse employees think they are being unfairly treated, however, they will be likely to seek opportunities elsewhere. Thus recruiting diverse employees has to be followed with ongoing effective management of diversity to retain valued organizational members.

If diversity is not effectively managed and turnover rates are higher for members of groups who are not treated fairly, profitability will suffer on several counts. Not only are the future contributions of diverse employees lost when they quit, but the organization also has to bear the costs of hiring replacement workers. According to the Employment Management Association, on average it costs more than $10,000 to hire a new employee; other estimates are significantly higher. For example, Ernst & Young estimates it costs about $1,200,000 to replace 10 professionals, and the diversity consulting firm Hubbard & Hubbard estimates replacement costs average one-and-a-half times an employee's annual salary.[126] Moreover, additional costs from failing to effectively manage diversity stem from time lost due to the barriers diverse members of an organization perceive as thwarting their progress and advancement.[127]

Effectively managing diversity makes good business sense for another reason. More and more, managers and organizations concerned about diversity are insisting that their suppliers also support diversity.[128]

Finally, from both business and ethical perspectives, effective management of diversity is necessary to avoid costly lawsuits such as those settled by Advantica (owner of the Denny's chain) and the Coca-Cola Company. In 2000 Coca-Cola settled a class action suit brought by African-American employees at a cost of $192 million. The damage such lawsuits cause goes beyond the monetary awards to the injured parties; it can tarnish a company's image. One positive outcome of Coca-Cola's 2000 settlement is the company's recognition of the need to commit additional resources to diversity management initiatives. Coca-Cola is increasing its use of minority suppliers, instituting a formal mentoring program, and instituting days to celebrate diversity with its workforce.[129] These efforts have paid off, and Coca-Cola has appeared on *DiversityInc.*'s list of the "Top 50 Companies for Diversity."

In 2013 Merrill Lynch agreed to settle a racial discrimination lawsuit, brought by 700 black brokers, which spent around eight years in the U.S. federal court system; the settlement cost was $160,000,000.[130] After the suit was initially filed, Merrill Lynch was bought by Bank of America. As part of the settlement, Merrill Lynch agreed to change its policies, take proactive steps to ensure that discrimination does not take place, and ensure that black brokers have fair opportunities to be successful. This three-year initiative is being overseen by a committee composed of black brokers.[131] Also in 2013, Bank of America agreed to settle a discrimination lawsuit brought by female employees of Merrill Lynch for $39 million; from around 1998 to 2013, Merrill Lynch paid close to $500,000,000 to settle discrimination claims.[132] As part of the settlement, Merrill Lynch consented to alter its policies to help ensure that women have fair opportunities to be successful.[133] Initiatives undertaken as result of both of these lawsuits should help ensure that Merrill Lynch effectively manages diversity.

By now it should be clear that effectively managing diversity is a necessity on both ethical and business grounds. This brings us to the question of why diversity presents managers and all of us with so many challenges—a question we address in the next section on perception.

Perception

perception The process through which people select, organize, and interpret what they see, hear, touch, smell, and taste to give meaning and order to the world around them.

Most people tend to think that the decisions managers make in organizations and the actions they take are the result of objective determination of the issues involved and the surrounding situation. However, each manager's interpretation of a situation or even of another person is precisely that—an interpretation. Nowhere are the effects of perception more likely to lead to different interpretations than in the area of diversity. This is because each person's interpretation of a situation, and subsequent response to it, is affected by his or her own age, race, gender, religion, socioeconomic status, capabilities, and sexual orientation. For example, different managers may see the same 21-year-old black male, gay, gifted, and talented subordinate in different ways: One may see a creative maverick with a great future in the organization, while another may see a potential troublemaker who needs to be watched closely.

Perception is the process through which people select, organize, and interpret sensory input—what they see, hear, touch, smell, and taste—to give meaning and order to the world around them.[134] All decisions and actions of managers are based on their subjective perceptions. When these perceptions are relatively accurate—close to the true nature of what is actually being perceived—good decisions are likely to be made and appropriate actions taken. Managers of fast-food restaurant chains such as McDonald's, Pizza Hut, and Wendy's accurately perceived that their customers were becoming more health-conscious in the 1980s and 1990s and added salad bars and low-fat entries to their menus. Managers at Kentucky Fried Chicken, Jack-in-the-Box, and Burger King took much longer to perceive this change in what customers wanted.

One reason why McDonald's is so successful is that its managers go to great lengths to make sure their perceptions of what customers want are accurate. McDonald's has over 21,000 restaurants outside the United States that generate billions of dollars in annual revenues.[135] Key to McDonald's success in these diverse markets are managers' efforts to perceive accurately a country's culture and taste in food and then to act on these perceptions. For instance, McDonald's serves veggie burgers in Holland and black currant shakes in Poland.[136]

When managers' perceptions are relatively inaccurate, managers are likely to make bad decisions and take inappropriate actions, which hurt organizational effectiveness. Bad decisions concerning diversity for reasons of age, ethnicity, or sexual orientation include (1) not hiring qualified people, (2) failing to promote top-performing subordinates, who subsequently may take their skills to competing organizations, and (3) promoting poorly performing managers because they have the same "diversity profile" as the manager or managers making the decision.

Factors That Influence Managerial Perception

Several managers' perceptions of the same person, event, or situation are likely to differ because managers differ in personality, values, attitudes, and moods (see Chapter 3). Each of these factors can influence how someone perceives a person or situation. An older middle manager who is high on openness to experience is likely to perceive the recruitment of able young managers as a positive learning opportunity; a similar middle manager who is low on openness to experience may perceive able younger subordinates as a threat. A manager who has high levels of job satisfaction and organizational commitment may perceive a job transfer to another department or geographic location that has very different employees (age, ethnicity, and so on) as an opportunity to learn and develop new skills. A dissatisfied, uncommitted manager may perceive the same transfer as a demotion.

schema An abstract knowledge structure that is stored in memory and makes possible the interpretation and organization of information about a person, event, or situation.

Managers' and all organizational members' perceptions of one another also are affected by their past experiences with and acquired knowledge about people, events, and situations—information that is organized into preexisting schemas. **Schemas** are abstract knowledge structures stored in memory that allow people to organize and interpret information about a person, an event, or a situation.[137] Once a person develops a schema for a kind of person or event, any newly encountered person or situation that is related to the schema activates it, and information is processed in ways consistent with the information stored in the schema. Thus people tend to perceive others by using the expectations or preconceived notions contained in their schemas.[138] Once again, these expectations are derived from past experience and knowledge.

People tend to pay attention to information that is consistent with their schemas and to ignore or discount inconsistent information. Thus schemas tend to be reinforced and strengthened over time because the information attended to is seen as confirming the schemas. This also results in schemas being resistant to change.[139] This does not mean schemas never change; if that were the case, people could never adapt to changing conditions and learn from their mistakes. Rather, it suggests that schemas are slow to change and that a considerable amount of contradictory information needs to be encountered for people to change their schemas.

Schemas that accurately depict the true nature of a person or situation are functional because they help people make sense of the world around them. People typically confront so much information that it is not possible to make sense of it without relying on schemas. Schemas are dysfunctional when they are inaccurate because they cause managers and all members of an organization to perceive people and situations inaccurately and assume certain things that are not necessarily true.

gender schemas Preconceived beliefs or ideas about the nature of men and women and their traits, attitudes, behaviors, and preferences.

Psychologist Virginia Valian refers to inaccurate preconceived notions of men and women as gender schemas. **Gender schemas** are a person's preconceived notions about the nature of men and women and their traits, attitudes, behaviors, and preferences.[140] Research suggests that among white middle-class Americans, the following gender schemas are prevalent: Men are action-oriented, assertive, independent, and task-focused; women are expressive, nurturing, and oriented toward and caring of other people.[141] Any schemas such as these—which assume that a single visible characteristic such as gender causes a person to possess specific traits and tendencies—are bound to be inaccurate. For example, not all women are alike and not all men are alike, and many women are more independent and task-focused than men. Gender schemas can be learned in childhood and are reinforced in a number of ways in society. For instance, while young girls may be encouraged by their parents to play with toy trucks and tools (stereotypically masculine toys), boys generally are not encouraged, and sometimes are actively discouraged, from playing with dolls (stereotypically feminine toys).[142] As children grow up, they learn that occupations dominated by men have higher status than occupations dominated by women.

Perception as a Determinant of Unfair Treatment

Even though most people would agree that distributive justice and procedural justice are desirable goals, diverse organizational members are sometimes treated unfairly, as previous examples illustrate. Why is this problem occurring? One important overarching reason is inaccurate perceptions. To the extent that managers and other members of an organization rely on inaccurate information such as gender schemas to guide their perceptions of each other, unfair treatment is likely to occur.

stereotype Simplistic and often inaccurate beliefs about the typical characteristics of particular groups of people.

Gender schemas are a kind of **stereotype**, which is composed of simplistic and often inaccurate beliefs about the typical characteristics of particular groups of people. Stereotypes are usually based on a visible characteristic such as a person's age, gender, or race.[143] Managers who allow stereotypes to influence their perceptions assume erroneously that a person possesses a whole host of characteristics simply because the person happens to be an Asian woman, a white man, or a lesbian, for example. African-American men are often stereotyped as good athletes; Hispanic women as subservient.[144] Obviously there is no reason to assume that every African-American man is a good athlete or that every Hispanic woman is subservient. Stereotypes, however, lead people to make such erroneous assumptions. A manager who accepts stereotypes might, for example, decide not to promote a highly capable Hispanic woman into a management position because the manager thinks she will not be assertive enough to supervise others.

A recent study suggests that stereotypes might hamper the progress of mothers in their organizations when they are seeking to advance in positions that are traditionally held by men. According to the study, based on gender stereotypes, people tend to view mothers as less competent in terms of skills and capabilities related to advancing in such positions.[145]

People with disabilities might also be unfairly treated due to stereotypes.[146] Although the ADA requires (as mentioned previously) that organizations provide disabled employees with accommodations, employment rates of people with disabilities have declined in recent years. As profiled in the accompanying "Ethics in Action" feature, a number of organizations have not only provided employment opportunities for disabled adults but also have benefited from their valuable contributions.[147]

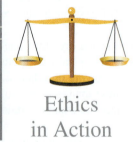

Ethics in Action

Disabled Employees Make Valuable Contributions

Some large organizations like McDonald's, Walmart, Home Depot, and Walgreens actively recruit disabled employees to work in positions such as cashiers, maintenance workers, greeters, shelf stockers, and floor workers that help customers find items. Home Depot, for example, works with a nonprofit agency called Ken's Krew, Inc., founded by parents of disabled adults, to recruit and place disabled employees in its stores.[148] Thus far, working with Ken's Krew has enabled Home Depot to recruit and place disabled adults in over 60 of its stores.[149]

Often, when given the opportunity, disabled employees make valuable contributions to their organizations. Walgreens opened an automated distribution center in Anderson, South Carolina, in which more than 40 percent of its 264 employees are disabled.[150] For disabled employees like Harrison Mullinax, who has autism and checks in merchandise to be distributed to drugstores with a bar code scanner, having a regular job is a godsend. Randy Lewis, senior vice president of distribution and logistics at Walgreens, thought about hiring workers with disabilities when Walgreens was considering using technology to increase automation levels in a distribution center. Lewis, the father of a young adult son who has autism, was aware of how difficult it can be for

Working through his training as a greeter, Jamie Heal embraces his job at Walmart with gusto. His new found independence became a catalyst for life changes (going by the name Cameron was one) as well as a deeper sense of self-respect.

young adults like his son to find employment. Various accommodations were made, like redesigning workstations and computer displays to suit employees' needs, and employees received appropriate training in how to do their jobs. Some days, disabled employees are actually the most productive in the center. As Lewis puts it, "One thing we found is they can all do the job. . . . What surprised us is the environment that it's created. It's a building where everybody helps each other out."[151]

Walgreens is a large organization, but small organizations also have benefited from the valuable contributions of disabled employees. Habitat International Inc., founded by current CEO David Morris and his father Saul over 30 years ago, is a manufacturer and contractor of indoor–outdoor carpet and artificial grass and a supplier to home improvement companies like Lowe's and Home Depot.[152] Habitat's profits have steadily increased over the years, and the factory's defect rate is less than 0.5 percent.[153]

Morris attributes Habitat's success to its employees, 75 percent of whom have either a physical or a mental disability or both.[154] Habitat has consistently provided employment opportunities to people with disabilities such as Down syndrome, schizophrenia, or cerebral palsy.[155] The company has also hired the homeless, recovering alcoholics, and non-English-speaking refugees from other countries. And these employees were relied on by plant manager Connie Presnell when she needed to fill a rush order by assigning it to a team of her fastest workers.[156] Habitat pays its employees regionally competitive wages and has low absence and turnover rates. Employees who need accommodations to perform their jobs are provided them, and Habitat has a highly motivated, satisfied, and committed workforce.[157]

While Habitat has actually gained some business from clients who applaud its commitment to diversity, Habitat's ethical values and social responsibility have also led the company to forgo a major account when stereotypes reared their ugly heads. Several years ago CEO Morris dropped the account of a distribution company because its representatives had made derogatory comments about his employees. Although it took Habitat two years to regain the lost revenues from this major account, Morris had no regrets.[158] Habitat's commitment to diversity and fair treatment is a win–win situation; the company is thriving, and so are its employees.[159]

bias The systematic tendency to use information about others in ways that result in inaccurate perceptions.

Inaccurate perceptions leading to unfair treatment of diverse members of an organization also can be due to biases. **Biases** are systematic tendencies to use information about others in ways that result in inaccurate perceptions. Because of the way biases operate, people often are unaware that their perceptions of others are inaccurate. There are several types of biases.

The *similar-to-me effect* is the tendency to perceive others who are similar to ourselves more positively than we perceive people who are different.[160] The similar-to-me effect is summed up by the saying "Birds of a feather flock together." It can lead to unfair treatment of diverse employees simply because they are different from the managers who are perceiving them, evaluating them, and making decisions that affect their future in the organization.

Managers (particularly top managers) are likely to be white men. Although these managers may endorse the principles of distributive and procedural justice, they may unintentionally fall into the trap of perceiving other white men more positively than they perceive women and minorities. This is the similar-to-me effect. Being aware of this bias as well as using objective information about employees' capabilities and performance as much as possible in decision making about job assignments, pay raises, promotions, and other outcomes can help managers avoid the similar-to-me effect.

Social status—a person's real or perceived position in a society or an organization—can be the source of another bias. The *social status effect* is the tendency to perceive individuals with high social status more positively than we perceive those with low social status. A high-status person may be perceived as smarter and more believable, capable, knowledgeable, and responsible than a low-status person, even in the absence of objective information about either person.

The salience effect focuses extra attention on a person who stands out from the group mold. Part of being a good manager includes being aware of these sorts of tendencies and actively working against them.

Imagine being introduced to two people at a company holiday party. Both are white men in their late 30s, and you learn that one is a member of the company's top management team and the other is a supervisor in the mailroom. From this information alone, you might assume that the top manager is smarter, more capable, more responsible, and even more interesting than the mailroom supervisor. Because women and minorities have traditionally had lower social status than white men, the social status effect may lead some people to perceive women and minorities less positively than they perceive white men.

Have you ever stood out in a crowd? Maybe you were the only man in a group of women; or maybe you were dressed formally for a social gathering, and everyone else was in jeans. Salience (that is, conspicuousness) is another source of bias. The *salience effect* is the tendency to focus attention on individuals who are conspicuously different from us. When people are salient, they often feel as though all eyes are watching them, and this perception is not far from the mark. Salient individuals are more often the object of attention than are other members of a work group, for example. A manager who has six white subordinates and one Hispanic subordinate reporting to her may inadvertently pay more attention to the Hispanic in group meetings because of the salience effect. In "A Manager's Challenge," Bob Moritz of PwC experienced salience firsthand when he lived and worked in Japan for three years.

Individuals who are salient are often perceived to be primarily responsible for outcomes and operations and are evaluated more extremely in either a positive or a negative direction.[161] Thus when the Hispanic subordinate does a good job on a project, she receives excessive praise, and when she misses a deadline, she is excessively chastised.

Overt Discrimination

overt discrimination
Knowingly and willingly denying diverse individuals access to opportunities and outcomes in an organization.

Inaccurate schemas and perceptual biases can lead well-meaning managers and organizational members to unintentionally discriminate against others. On the other hand, **overt discrimination**, or knowingly and willingly denying diverse individuals access to opportunities and outcomes in an organization, is intentional and deliberate. Overt discrimination is both unethical and illegal. Unfortunately, just as some managers steal from their organizations, others engage in overt discrimination.

Overt discrimination is a clear violation of the principles of distributive and procedural justice. Moreover, when managers are charged with overt discrimination, costly lawsuits can ensue. Organizations ranging from the Adam's Mark chain of luxury hotels, Texaco, and Ford Motor Company to Johnson & Johnson, BellSouth, Coca-Cola, Merrill Lynch, the National Football League, General Electric, Walmart, and Nike either have settled or face pending lawsuits alleging overt workplace discrimination.[162] Whereas in the past, lawsuits due to overt workplace discrimination focused on unfair treatment of women and minority group members, given the aging of the U.S. workforce, increasing numbers of discrimination cases are being brought by older workers who believe they were unfairly dismissed from their jobs due to their age.[163]

Despite all the advances that have been made, allegations of overt discrimination based on gender, race, age, and other forms of diversity continue to occur in the United States. For example, Nike settled a class action lawsuit filed on behalf of 400 African-American employees of its Chicago Niketown store.[164] Employees claimed that managers used racial slurs when referring to African-American employees and customers, gave African-American employees lower-paying jobs, made unwarranted accusations of theft, and had security personnel monitor employees and customers based on race.[165] Although Nike denied the allegations, as part of the settlement, Nike agreed to pay current and former employees $7.6 million and also agreed to promote effective management of diversity, partly by providing diversity training to all managers and supervisors in the store.[166]

Overt discrimination continues to be a problem in other countries as well. For example, although Japan passed its first Equal Employment Opportunity Law in 1985 and Japanese women are increasingly working in jobs once dominated by men, professional Japanese women have continued to find it difficult to advance in their careers and assume managerial positions.[167] Women make up almost half of the Japanese workforce, but only around 10 percent of managerial positions in business and government are occupied by women, according to the International Labor Organization agency of the United Nations.[168]

According to the United Nations Development Program's gender empowerment measure, which assesses the participation of women in a country's politics and economy, Japan is the most unequal of the world's wealthy nations when it comes to women.[169] Takako Ariishi witnessed women's struggle in Japan firsthand. As an employee of a family-owned manufacturing business that supplies parts to Nissan,[170] Ariishi was fired by her own father (who was then president of the company) when she had a son (her father claimed that her son would be his successor as president). Nonetheless, when Ariishi's father died, she took over as company president. Her company is one of 160 Nissan suppliers in Japan, and the heads of these companies meet twice a year; Ariishi is the only woman among the 160 presidents, and the first time the group met, she was asked to wait in a separate room with the secretaries. Miiko Tsuda, an employee of a tutoring company, indicated that she is paid less than her male coworkers, and she is often asked to push elevator buttons and make tea for male coworkers. Only 5 of the company's 300 management employees are women.[171]

Overt discrimination also can be a potential problem when in comes to layoff decisions. Organizational restructurings, a weak economy, and the recession that began in December 2007[172] led to record numbers of U.S. employees being laid off from 2007 to 2010. Although it is always a challenge for managers to decide who should be let go when layoffs take place, some laid-off employees felt that factors that should be irrelevant to this tough decision played a role in the layoffs at their former employers. And while many workers who believe they were unfairly discriminated against do not pursue legal remedies, some filed lawsuits alleging discrimination in layoff decisions.

Age-related discrimination complaints have been at record highs in recent times.[173] According to a press release issued in 2012 by the EEOC, "The number of age discrimination charges filed with the Commission increased by 50% since 2000."[174] Although this might be due to the fact that there were more older employees in the workforce than in previous years, David Grinberg, speaking on behalf of the EEOC, suggests that the rise in age discrimination allegations could also be due to the fact that older workers tend to be paid more and have better benefits.[175] For example, Joan Zawacki, in her late 50s, was laid off from her position as a vice president at the Cartus division of Realogy Corp. after having worked at the company for over 30 years. According to Zawacki, senior managers such as herself were told to discreetly talk with older workers in a friendly manner and suggest that they inquire with human resources about early retirement packages while protecting the jobs of younger workers. Zawacki indicates that she was laid off after not having convinced an older employee in her department to retire. A company spokesperson disputed the allegations in Zawacki's age discrimination lawsuit. In addition, over 90 employees at the Lawrence Livermore National Laboratory have filed complaints alleging age discrimination in layoffs. Eddy Stappaerts, a 62-year-old senior scientist who had worked at the lab for 11 years and has a PhD from Stanford University, says, "A week before I was laid off, my boss said my contributions were essential."[176] He alleges that some of the work he did was given to a younger employee.[177]

Some women laid off from their jobs in the financial industry filed lawsuits alleging gender discrimination. Laid-off female executives at Citigroup, Merrill Lynch, Bank of America, and Bank of Tokyo have claimed that gender played a role in their firings.[178] In some cases the women had done very well in their early years with the firms, were transferred to less desirable positions after becoming pregnant and taking maternity leaves, and ultimately were let go. Some of these women suggest that they were laid off even though they were just as qualified as men who were able to keep their jobs.[179]

Four former human resource managers at Dell filed a class action lawsuit alleging that Dell's massive layoffs discriminated against women and employees over age 40 and that women were unfairly treated in pay and promotions.[180] Dell agreed to settle the lawsuit for $9.1 million while not admitting any wrongdoing.[181] Although many companies charged with discrimination allege that no discrimination took place, these are matters for the courts to decide.[182]

How to Manage Diversity Effectively

Various kinds of barriers arise to managing diversity effectively in organizations. Some barriers originate in the person doing the perceiving; others are based on the information and schemas that have built up over time concerning the person being perceived. To overcome these barriers and effectively manage diversity, managers (and other organizational members) must possess or develop certain attitudes and values and the skills needed to change other people's attitudes and values.

Steps in Managing Diversity Effectively

LO5-5

List the steps managers can take to effectively manage diversity.

Managers can take a number of steps to change attitudes and values and promote the effective management of diversity. Here we describe these steps, some of which we have referred to previously (see Table 5.4).

SECURE TOP MANAGEMENT COMMITMENT As we mentioned earlier in the chapter, top management's commitment to diversity is crucial for the success of any diversity-related initiatives. Top managers need to develop the correct ethical values and performance- or business-oriented attitudes that allow them to make appropriate use of their human resources.

STRIVE TO INCREASE THE ACCURACY OF PERCEPTIONS One aspect of developing the appropriate values and attitudes is to take steps to increase the accuracy of perceptions. Managers should consciously attempt to be open to other points of view and perspectives, seek them out, and encourage their subordinates to do the same.[183] Organizational members who are open to other perspectives put their own beliefs and knowledge to an important reality test and will be more inclined to modify or change them when necessary. Managers should not be afraid to change their views about a person, issue, or event; moreover, they should encourage their subordinates to be open to changing their views in the light of disconfirming evidence. Additionally, managers and all members of an organization should strive to avoid making snap judgments about people; rather, judgments should be made only when sufficient and relevant information has been gathered.[184]

Table 5.4
Promoting the Effective Management of Diversity

- Secure top management commitment.
- Increase the accuracy of perceptions.
- Increase diversity awareness.
- Increase diversity skills.
- Encourage flexibility.
- Pay close attention to how employees are evaluated.
- Consider the numbers.
- Empower employees to challenge discriminatory behaviors, actions, and remarks.
- Reward employees for effectively managing diversity.
- Provide training utilizing a multipronged, ongoing approach.
- Encourage mentoring of diverse employees.

INCREASE DIVERSITY AWARENESS   It is natural for managers and other members of an organization to view other people from their own perspective because their own feelings, thoughts, attitudes, and experiences guide their perceptions and interactions. The ability to appreciate diversity, however, requires that people become aware of other perspectives and the various attitudes and experiences of others. Many diversity awareness programs in organizations strive to increase managers' and workers' awareness of (1) their own attitudes, biases, and stereotypes and (2) the differing perspectives of diverse managers, subordinates, coworkers, and customers. Diversity awareness programs often have these goals:[185]

- Providing organizational members with accurate information about diversity.

- Uncovering personal biases and stereotypes.

- Assessing personal beliefs, attitudes, and values and learning about other points of view.

- Overturning inaccurate stereotypes and beliefs about different groups.

- Developing an atmosphere in which people feel free to share their differing perspectives and points of view.

- Improving understanding of others who are different from oneself.

Sometimes simply taking the time to interact with someone who is different in some way can increase awareness. When employees and managers are at social functions or just having lunch with a coworker, often the people they interact with are those they feel most comfortable with. If all members of an organization make an effort to interact with people they ordinarily would not, mutual understanding is likely to be enhanced.[186]

In large organizations, top managers are often far removed from entry-level employees—they may lack a real understanding and appreciation for what these employees do day in and day out, the challenges and obstacles they face, and the steps that can be taken to improve effectiveness. Recognizing this fact, some managers have taken concrete steps to improve their understanding of the experiences, attitudes, and perspectives of frontline employees, as indicated in the accompanying "Management Insight" feature.

Top Execs Improve Their Understanding of the Front Line

Management Insight

A growing number of organizations are implementing programs whereby top managers spend time performing the jobs of frontline employees to improve their understanding of the challenges these employees face and ways to improve their working conditions.[187] For example, DaVita Inc.,[188] a major provider of kidney dialysis services in the United States, has a program called "Reality 101" through which senior executives who have never worked in a dialysis clinic spend time working as clinic technicians. Dialysis helps patients whose kidneys are not working properly to eliminate waste from their bloodstream. Treatments last around four hours, and patients often require multiple treatments per week.[189]

Carolyn Kibler, a senior executive at DaVita who oversaw 48 clinics and around 750 employees, gained a much better understanding of the challenges technicians face, the nature of their jobs, and how best to manage them as a result of her participation in Reality 101. A former nurse, Kibler was surprised at how physically and emotionally demanding the job was and the high levels of stress it entailed. She also gained a real appreciation of the high levels of empathy technicians have for their patients—trying to make them as comfortable as possible, helping them deal with their frustrations, and mourning the loss of those who die as a result of their often multiple medical problems.[190]

An executive meets with those who report to her to gain a better understanding of their jobs and the challenges they face.

Realizing how hard technicians work and how hectic and stressful the clinics can be, Kibler became more understanding when paperwork was submitted late due to staff shortages, gave positive feedback to those who might have to miss meetings or conference calls to treat patients, tried to avoid giving clinics last-minute requests and deadlines for reports, and was more forthcoming with praise for clinic staff. More fully appreciating how patient care is the top priority and the nature of work on the clinic floor, Kibler was also more sensitive to how her own initiatives might affect these frontline employees and the patients they serve. As she indicated, "I am more conscious of the power of my words and my actions and the impact they have down in the organization."[191]

As part of its "Now Who's Boss Day," senior executives at Loews Hotels perform entry-level jobs one day per year to appreciate and understand the challenges in these jobs and ways to make performing them easier while improving customer service.[192] This program originated when Loews Hotels then CEO and current chairman Jonathan Tisch[193] took part in a reality TV show called *Now Who's Boss?* and performed the jobs of pool attendant, housekeeper, and bellman at a Florida hotel. He perspired so much in the polyester uniform people in these jobs were required to wear that he changed the uniform. As a result of another manager's experience in the trenches, handlebars were installed on room service carts so they weren't as difficult to push.[194]

Clearly the jobs frontline employees perform are essential for organizational functioning. When top managers, who are far removed from these jobs, gain a better understanding of these jobs and the employees who perform them, they are in a better position to manage them effectively.

INCREASE DIVERSITY SKILLS   Efforts to increase diversity skills focus on improving how managers and their subordinates interact with each other and improving their ability to work with different kinds of people.[195] An important issue here is being able to communicate with diverse employees. Diverse organizational members may have different communication styles, may differ in their language fluency, may use words differently, may differ in the nonverbal signals they send through facial expressions and body language, and may differ in how they perceive and interpret information. Managers and their subordinates must learn to communicate effectively with one another if an organization is to take advantage of the skills and abilities of its entire workforce. Educating organizational members about differences in ways of communicating is often a good starting point.

Diversity education can help managers and subordinates gain a better understanding of how people may interpret certain kinds of comments. Diversity education also can help employees learn how to resolve misunderstandings. Organizational members should feel comfortable enough to "clear the air" and solve communication difficulties and misunderstandings as they occur rather than letting problems grow and fester without acknowledgment.

ENCOURAGE FLEXIBILITY   Managers and their subordinates must learn how to be open to different approaches and ways of doing things. This does not mean organizational members have to suppress their personal styles. Rather, it means they must be open to, and not feel threatened by, different approaches and perspectives and must have the patience and flexibility needed to understand and appreciate diverse perspectives.[196]

To the extent feasible, managers should also be flexible enough to incorporate the differing needs of diverse employees. Earlier we mentioned that religious diversity suggests that people of certain religions might need time off for holidays that are traditionally workdays in the United States; managers need to anticipate and respond to such needs with flexibility (perhaps letting people skip the lunch hour so they can leave work early). Moreover, flexible work hours, the option to work from home, and cafeteria-style benefit plans (see Chapter 12) are just a few of the many ways in which managers can respond to the differing needs of diverse employees while enabling those employees to be effective contributors to an organization.

PAY CLOSE ATTENTION TO HOW ORGANIZATIONAL MEMBERS ARE EVALUATED   Whenever feasible, it is desirable to rely on objective performance indicators (see Chapter 12) because they are less subject to bias. When objective indicators are not available or are inappropriate, managers should ensure that adequate time and attention are focused on the evaluation of employees' performance and that evaluators are held accountable for their evaluations.[197] Vague performance standards should be avoided.[198]

CONSIDER THE NUMBERS   Looking at the numbers of members of different minority groups and women in various positions, at various levels in the hierarchy, in locations that differ in their desirability, and in any other relevant categorizations in an organization can tell managers important information about potential problems and ways to rectify them.[199] If members of certain groups are underrepresented in particular kinds of jobs or units, managers need to understand why this is the case and resolve any problems they might uncover.

EMPOWER EMPLOYEES TO CHALLENGE DISCRIMINATORY BEHAVIORS, ACTIONS, AND REMARKS   When managers or employees witness another organizational member being unfairly treated, they should be encouraged to speak up and rectify the situation. Top managers can make this happen by creating an organizational culture (see Chapter 3) that has zero tolerance for discrimination. As part of such a culture, organizational members should feel empowered to challenge discriminatory behavior, whether the behavior is directed at them or they witness it being directed at another employee.[200]

REWARD EMPLOYEES FOR EFFECTIVELY MANAGING DIVERSITY   If effective management of diversity is a valued organizational objective, then employees should be rewarded for their contributions to this objective.[201] For example, after settling a major race discrimination lawsuit, Coca-Cola Company now ties managers' pay to their achievement of diversity goals. Examples of other organizations that do so include American Express and Bayer Corporation.[202]

PROVIDE TRAINING UTILIZING A MULTIPRONGED, ONGOING APPROACH
Many managers use a multipronged approach to increase diversity awareness and skills in their organizations; they use films and printed materials supplemented by experiential exercises to uncover hidden biases and stereotypes. Sometimes simply providing a forum for people to learn about and discuss their differing attitudes, values, and experiences can be a powerful means of increasing awareness. Also useful are role-plays that enact problems resulting from lack of awareness and show the increased understanding that comes from appreciating others' viewpoints. Accurate information and training experiences can debunk stereotypes. Group exercises, role-plays, and diversity-related experiences can help organizational members develop the skills they need to work effectively with a variety of people. Many organizations hire outside consultants to provide diversity training, in addition to utilizing their own in-house diversity experts.[203]

United Parcel Service (UPS), a package delivery company, developed an innovative community internship program to increase the diversity awareness and skills of its managers and, at the same time, benefit the wider community. Upper and middle managers participating in the program take one month off the job to be community interns.[204] They work in community organizations helping people who in many instances are very different from themselves—such organizations include a detention center in McAllen, Texas, for Mexican immigrants; homeless shelters; AIDS centers; Head Start programs; migrant farmworker assistance groups; and groups aiming to halt the spread of drug abuse in inner cities.

Interacting with and helping diverse people enhances the interns' awareness of diversity because they experience it firsthand. Bill Cox, a UPS division manager who spent a month in the McAllen detention center, summed up his experience of diversity: "You've got these [thousands of] migrant workers down in McAllen . . . and they don't want what you have. All they want is an opportunity to earn what you have. That's a fundamental change in understanding that only comes from spending time with these people."[205]

Many managers who complete the UPS community internship program have superior diversity skills as a result of their experiences. During their internships, they learn about different cultures and approaches to work and life; they learn to interact effectively with people whom they ordinarily do not come into contact with; and they are forced to learn flexibility because of the dramatic differences between their roles at the internship sites and their roles as managers at UPS.

ENCOURAGE MENTORING OF DIVERSE EMPLOYEES   Unfortunately African Americans and other minorities continue to be less likely to attain high-level positions in their organizations; and for those who do attain them, the climb up the corporate ladder typically takes longer than it does for white men. David Thomas, a professor at the Harvard Business School, has studied the careers of minorities in corporate America. One of his major conclusions is that mentoring is very important for minorities, most of whom have reached high levels in their organizations by having a solid network of mentors and contacts.[206] **Mentoring** is a process by which an experienced member of an organization (the mentor) provides advice and guidance to a less experienced member (the protégé) and helps the less experienced member learn how to advance in the organization and in his or her career.

According to Thomas, effective mentoring is more than providing instruction, offering advice, helping build skills, and sharing technical expertise. Of course these aspects of mentoring are important and necessary. However, equally important is developing a high-quality, close, and supportive relationship with the protégé. Emotional bonds between a mentor and a protégé can enable a protégé, for example, to express fears and concerns, and sometimes even reluctance to follow a mentor's advice. The mentor can help the protégé build his or her confidence and feel comfortable engaging in unfamiliar work behaviors.[207]

mentoring A process by which an experienced member of an organization (the mentor) provides advice and guidance to a less experienced member (the protégé) and helps the less experienced member learn how to advance in the organization and in his or her career.

Sexual Harassment

LO5-6

Identify the two major forms of sexual harassment and how they can be eliminated.

Sexual harassment seriously damages both the people who are harassed and the reputation of the organization in which it occurs. It also can cost organizations large amounts of money. In 1995, for example, Chevron Corporation agreed to pay $2.2 million to settle a sexual harassment lawsuit filed by four women who worked at the Chevron Information Technology Company in San Ramon, California. One woman involved in the suit said she had received violent pornographic material through the company mail. Another, an electrical engineer, said she had been asked to bring pornographic videos to Chevron workers at an Alaska drill site.[208] More recently, in 2001 TWA spent $2.6 million to settle a lawsuit that alleged female employees were sexually harassed at JFK International Airport in New York. According to the EEOC, not only was sexual harassment tolerated at TWA, but company officials did little to curtail it when it was brought to their attention.[209]

Unfortunately the events at Chevron and TWA are not isolated incidents.[210] In 2011 two lawsuits were filed against American Apparel and its founder and CEO, Dov Charney, alleging sexual harassment.[211] Of the 607 women surveyed by the National Association for Female Executives, 60 percent indicated that they had experienced some form of sexual harassment.[212] In a survey conducted by the Society for Human Resource Management of 460 companies, 36 percent of the companies indicated that, within the last 24 months, one or more employees claimed that they had been sexually harassed.[213] Sexual harassment victims can be women or men, and their harassers do not necessarily have to be of the opposite sex.[214] However, women are the most frequent victims of sexual harassment, particularly those in male-dominated occupations or those who occupy positions stereotypically associated with certain gender relationships, such as a female secretary reporting to a male boss. Though it occurs less frequently, men can also be victims of sexual harassment. For instance, several male employees at Jenny Craig filed a lawsuit claiming they were subject to lewd and inappropriate comments from female coworkers and managers.[215] Sexual harassment is not only unethical; it is also illegal. Managers have an ethical obligation to ensure that they, their coworkers, and their subordinates never engage in sexual harassment, even unintentionally.

Forms of Sexual Harassment

There are two basic forms of sexual harassment: quid pro quo sexual harassment and hostile work environment sexual harassment. **Quid pro quo sexual harassment** occurs when a harasser asks or forces an employee to perform sexual favors to keep a job, receive a promotion, receive a raise, obtain some other work-related opportunity, or avoid receiving negative consequences such as demotion or dismissal.[216] This "Sleep with me, honey, or you're fired" form of harassment is the more extreme type and leaves no doubt in anyone's mind that sexual harassment has taken place.[217]

quid pro quo sexual harassment Asking for or forcing an employee to perform sexual favors in exchange for receiving some reward or avoiding negative consequences.

hostile work environment sexual harassment Telling lewd jokes, displaying pornography, making sexually oriented remarks about someone's personal appearance, and other sex-related actions that make the work environment unpleasant.

Hostile work environment sexual harassment is more subtle. It occurs when organizational members face an intimidating, hostile, or offensive work environment because of their sex.[218] Lewd jokes, sexually oriented comments or innuendos, vulgar language, displays of pornography, displays or distribution of sexually oriented objects, and sexually oriented remarks about one's physical appearance are examples of hostile work environment sexual harassment.[219] A hostile work environment interferes with organizational members' ability to perform their jobs effectively and has been deemed illegal by the courts. Managers who engage in hostile work environment harassment or allow others to do so risk costly lawsuits for their organizations. For example, in February 2004 a federal jury awarded Marion Schwab $3.24 million after deliberating on her sexual harassment case against FedEx.[220] Schwab was the only female tractor-trailer driver at the FedEx facility serving the Harrisburg International Airport vicinity in Middletown, Pennsylvania, from 1997 to 2000. During that period she was the target of sexual innuendos, was given inferior work assignments, and was the brunt of derogatory comments about her appearance and the role of women in society. On five occasions the brakes on her truck were tampered with. The federal EEOC sued FedEx, and Schwab was part of the suit.[221]

The courts have recently recognized other forms of hostile work environment harassment, in addition to sexual harassment. For example, in June 2006 a California jury awarded $61 million in punitive and compensatory damages to two FedEx Ground drivers. The drivers, who are of Lebanese descent, indicated that they faced a hostile work environment and high levels of stress because a manager harassed them with racial slurs for two years.[222]

Steps Managers Can Take to Eradicate Sexual Harassment

Managers have an ethical obligation to eradicate sexual harassment in their organizations. There are many ways to accomplish this objective. Here are four initial steps managers can take to deal with the problem:[223]

- *Develop and clearly communicate a sexual harassment policy endorsed by top management.* This policy should include prohibitions against both quid pro quo and hostile work environment sexual harassment. It should contain (1) examples of types of behavior that are unacceptable, (2) a procedure for employees to use to report instances of harassment, (3) a discussion of the disciplinary actions that will be taken when harassment has taken place, and (4) a commitment to educate and train organizational members about sexual harassment.

- *Use a fair complaint procedure to investigate charges of sexual harassment.* Such a procedure should (1) be managed by a neutral third party, (2) ensure that complaints are dealt with promptly and thoroughly, (3) protect and fairly treat victims, and (4) ensure that alleged harassers are fairly treated.

- *When it has been determined that sexual harassment has taken place, take corrective actions as soon as possible.* These actions can vary depending on the severity of the harassment. When harassment is extensive, prolonged, of a quid pro quo nature, or severely objectionable in some other manner, corrective action may include firing the harasser.

- *Provide sexual harassment education and training to all organizational members, including managers.* The majority of *Fortune* 500 firms currently provide this education and training for their employees. Managers at DuPont, for example, developed DuPont's "A Matter of Respect" program to help educate employees about sexual harassment and eliminate its occurrence. The program includes a four-hour workshop in which participants are given information that defines sexual harassment, sets forth the company's policy against it, and explains how to report complaints and access a 24-hour hotline. Participants watch video clips showing actual instances of harassment. One clip shows a saleswoman having dinner with a male client who, after much negotiating, seems about to give her company his business when he suddenly suggests that they continue their conversation in his hotel room. The saleswoman is confused about what to do. Will she be reprimanded if she says no and the deal is lost? After watching a video, participants discuss what they have seen, why the behavior is inappropriate, and what organizations can do to alleviate the problem.[224] Throughout the program, managers stress to employees that they do not have to tolerate sexual harassment or get involved in situations in which harassment is likely to occur.

Barry S. Roberts and Richard A. Mann, experts on business law and authors of several books on the topic, suggest a number of additional factors that managers and all members of an organization need to keep in mind about sexual harassment:[225]

- Every sexual harassment charge should be taken seriously.

- Employees who go along with unwanted sexual attention in the workplace can be sexual harassment victims.

- Employees sometimes wait before they file complaints of sexual harassment.

- An organization's sexual harassment policy should be communicated to each new employee and reviewed with current employees periodically.

- Suppliers and customers need to be familiar with an organization's sexual harassment policy.

- Managers should give employees alternative ways to report incidents of sexual harassment.

- Employees who report sexual harassment must have their rights protected; this includes being protected from any potential retaliation.

- Allegations of sexual harassment should be kept confidential; those accused of harassment should have their rights protected.

- Investigations of harassment charges and any resultant disciplinary actions need to proceed in a timely manner.

- Managers must protect employees from sexual harassment from third parties they may interact with while performing their jobs, such as suppliers or customers.[226]

Summary and Review

LO5-1 **THE INCREASING DIVERSITY OF THE WORKFORCE AND THE ENVIRONMENT** Diversity is dissimilarity or differences among people. Diversity is a pressing concern for managers and organizations for business and ethical reasons. There are multiple forms of diversity such as age, gender, race and ethnicity, religion, capabilities/disabilities, socioeconomic background, sexual orientation, and physical appearance.

LO5-2, 5-3 **MANAGERS AND THE EFFECTIVE MANAGEMENT OF DIVERSITY** Both the workforce and the organizational environment are increasingly diverse, and effectively managing this diversity is an essential component of management. In each of their managerial roles, managers can encourage the effective management of diversity, which is both an ethical and a business imperative.

LO5-4 **PERCEPTION** Perception is the process through which people select, organize, and interpret sensory input to give meaning and order to the world around them. It is inherently subjective. Schemas guide perception; when schemas are based on a single visible characteristic such as race or gender, they are inaccurate stereotypes that lead to unfair treatment. Unfair treatment also can result from biases and overt discrimination.

LO5-5 **HOW TO MANAGE DIVERSITY EFFECTIVELY** Managers can take many steps to effectively manage diversity. Effective management of diversity is an ongoing process that requires frequent monitoring.

LO5-6 **SEXUAL HARASSMENT** Two forms of sexual harassment are quid pro quo sexual harassment and hostile work environment sexual harassment. Steps that managers can take to eradicate sexual harassment include development and communication of a sexual harassment policy endorsed by top management, use of fair complaint procedures, prompt corrective action when harassment occurs, and sexual harassment training and education.

Management in Action

Topics for Discussion and Action

Discussion

1. Discuss why violations of the principles of distributive and procedural justice continue to occur in modern organizations. What can managers do to uphold these principles in their organizations? **[LO5-2, 5-3, 5-4, 5-5]**

2. Why are workers who test positive for HIV sometimes discriminated against? **[LO5-1, 5-4]**

3. Why would some employees resent accommodations made for employees with disabilities that are dictated by the Americans with Disabilities Act? **[LO5-1, 5-4]**

4. Discuss the ways in which schemas can be functional and dysfunctional. **[LO5-4]**

5. Discuss an occasion when you may have been treated unfairly because of stereotypical thinking. What stereotypes were applied to you? How did they result in your being treated unfairly? **[LO5-4]**

6. How does the similar-to-me effect influence your own behavior and decisions? **[LO5-4]**

7. Why is mentoring particularly important for minorities? **[LO5-5]**

8. Why is it important to consider the numbers of different groups of employees at various levels in an organization's hierarchy? **[LO5-5]**

9. Think about a situation in which you would have benefited from mentoring but a mentor was not available. What could you have done to try to get the help of a mentor in this situation? **[LO5-5]**

Action

10. Choose a *Fortune* 500 company not mentioned in the chapter. Conduct research to determine what steps this organization has taken to effectively manage diversity and eliminate sexual harassment. **[LO5-2, 5-5, 5-6]**

Building Management Skills

Solving Diversity-Related Problems **[LO5-1, 5-2, 5-3, 5-4, 5-5, 5-6]**

Think about the last time that you (1) were treated unfairly because you differed from a decision maker on a particular dimension of diversity or (2) observed someone else being treated unfairly because that person differed from a decision maker on a particular dimension of diversity. Then answer these questions:

1. Why do you think the decision maker acted unfairly in this situation?

2. In what ways, if any, were biases, stereotypes, or overt discrimination involved in this situation?

3. Was the decision maker aware that he or she was acting unfairly?

4. What could you or the person who was treated unfairly have done to improve matters and rectify the injustice on the spot?

5. Was any sexual harassment involved in this situation? If so, what kind was it?

6. If you had authority over the decision maker (that is, if you were his or her manager or supervisor), what steps would you take to ensure that the decision maker stops treating people unfairly?

Managing Ethically **[LO5-1, 5-2, 5-3, 5-5]**

Some companies require that their employees work long hours and travel extensively. Employees with young children, employees taking care of elderly relatives, and employees who have interests outside the workplace sometimes find that their careers are jeopardized if they try to work more reasonable hours or limit their work-related travel. Some of these employees feel that it is unethical for their managers to expect so much of them in the workplace and not understand their needs as parents and caregivers.

Questions

1. Either individually or in a group, think about the ethical implications of requiring long hours and extensive amounts of travel for some jobs.

2. What obligations do you think managers and companies have to enable employees to have balanced lives and meet nonwork needs and demands?

Small Group Breakout Exercise

Determining If a Problem Exists [LO5-1, 5-2, 5-3, 5-4, 5-5]

Form groups of three or four people, and appoint one member as the spokesperson who will communicate your findings to the whole class when called on by the instructor. Then discuss the following scenario:

You and your partners own and manage a local chain of restaurants, with moderate to expensive prices, that are open for lunch and dinner during the week and for dinner on weekends. Your staff is diverse, and you believe that you are effectively managing diversity. Yet on visits to the different restaurants you have noticed that your African-American employees tend to congregate together and communicate mainly with each other. The same is true for your Hispanic employees and your white employees.

You are meeting with your partners today to discuss this observation.

1. Discuss why the patterns of communication that you observed might be occurring in your restaurants.
2. Discuss whether your observation reflects an underlying problem. If so, why? If not, why not?
3. Discuss whether you should address this issue with your staff and in your restaurants. If so, how and why? If not, why not?

Exploring the World Wide Web [LO5-1, 5-2, 5-3, 5-5, 5-6]

Go to the U.S. government websites that deal with employment issues, diversity, and sexual harassment, such as the websites of the Equal Employment Opportunity Commission (EEOC) and the Bureau of Labor Statistics. After reviewing these websites, develop a list of tips to help managers effectively manage diversity and avoid costly lawsuits.

Be the Manager [LO5-1, 5-2, 5-3, 5-4, 5-5]

You are Maria Herrera and have been recently promoted to the position of director of financial analysis for a medium-sized consumer goods firm. During your first few weeks on the job, you took the time to have lunch with each of your subordinates to try to get to know them better. You have 12 direct reports who are junior and senior financial analysts who support different product lines. Susan Epstein, one of the female financial analysts you had lunch with, made the following statement: "I'm so glad we finally have a woman in charge. Now, hopefully things will get better around here." You pressed Epstein to elaborate, but she clammed up. She indicated that she didn't want to unnecessarily bias you and that the problems were pretty self-evident. In fact, Epstein was surprised that you didn't know what she was talking about and jokingly mentioned that perhaps you should spend some time undercover, observing her group and their interactions with others.

You spoke with your supervisor and the former director, who had been promoted and had volunteered to be on call if you had any questions. Neither man knew of any diversity-related issues in your group. In fact, your supervisor's response was, "We've got a lot of problems, but fortunately that's not one of them."

What are you going to do to address this issue?

The Wall Street Journal Case in the News

Do You Know Your Hidden Work Biases? [LO5-1, 5-2, 5-3, 5-4, 5-5]

Everyone has hidden biases. For Denise Russell Fleming, a vice president at **BAE Systems** Inc., they include overlooking quieter colleagues during meetings. "I may have not made the best decisions" because of inadequate input from introverts, she says, adding that she tends to favor more talkative personalities.

As they struggle to diversify their workforces, big businesses are teaching staffers to recognize that "unconscious bias"—or an implicit preference for certain groups—often influences important workplace decisions.

BAE, a major defense contractor, is among the growing number of U.S. corporations offering training programs aimed at overcoming these hidden biases. As many as 20 percent of large U.S. employers with diversity programs now provide unconscious bias training, up from 2 percent five years ago, and that figure could hit 50 percent in five years, says Margaret Regan, head of FutureWork Institute, a diversity consultancy.

"It is the most requested and popular diversity topic now," says Regan, whose firm recently instructed 2,000 **Microsoft** managers about unconscious bias.

Everyone unwittingly favors certain types of people based on their upbringing, experience, and values because human beings need bias to survive, diversity experts say. For example, you might prefer fellow graduates of your alma mater. Left unchecked on the job, though, unconscious bias can affect hiring, assignments, promotions, evaluations, and dismissals.

BAE requires that all 1,600 middle managers and executives take a two-hour class about unconscious bias. The company partly credits the management training for an increase in the number of women and people of color targeted for advancement last year. Its experience also illustrates the advantages and drawbacks of the approach.

The training, designed by diversity consultants Cook Ross Inc., was aimed at getting managers to identify where bias crept into their thought processes rather than blaming anyone for the scarcity of women and minorities in top spots.

"I don't want you to feel guilty about any biases that you have," trainer Melissa Lambert told Fleming and nine others at an Arlington, Virginia, class late last year.

During the next two hours, attendees watched brief videos, participated in partner exercises, and discussed research summaries to understand why bosses make employment decisions that inadvertently give preference to tall individuals, thin ones, those without arm tattoos, or extroverts.

"It's a blind spot," Lambert observed. The trick is to "hit the pause button and question things" before you act, she said.

The training also exposed some internal tension. Midway through the session, a participant complained that colleagues didn't take her seriously because she was only 24 years old.

So-called millennials, young adults born since 1981, "don't want to work for what they get," and they expect to move up quickly merely because they completed college, retorted Diane Parisi, a 41-year-old vice president with two young subordinates.

In the workplace, Parisi admitted afterward, the bias she expressed probably "caused me to paint millennials with a broader negative brush than I should."

A typical one-day course for 50 people costs an average of $2,000 to $6,000, estimates Howard Ross, founder of Cook Ross. **Dow Chemical, Google, Pfizer,** and PricewaterhouseCoopers have also recently trained numerous staffers to spot hidden biases.

More than 13,000 of Google's roughly 46,000 global staffers attended

a workshop in 2013 that emphasized "situations where the influence of unconscious bias might be especially bad," such as performance reviews, a Google spokeswoman says.

Dow has trained 800 of its 4,600 managers worldwide since 2011—and seen the number of women in professional positions rise from 29.7 percent to 32.4 percent in that time. Unconscious bias training played a strong role in that gain, says Johanna Soderstrom, a human resources vice president at the large chemicals maker. At **Microsoft** the training helps hold leaders "accountable for building a diverse culture," a spokeswoman says.

Unconscious bias training arose from the Implied Association Test, a measure of hidden stereotypes invented in 1994 by Tony Greenwald, a University of Washington psychology professor. The online version has been taken more than 15 million times since its 1998 introduction, with most test takers showing a preference for white people, according to Brian Nosek, a codeveloper.

Greenwald warns that unconscious bias training often "is just window dressing" that fails to alter work practices. "You don't go to a class and next week, everything changes," adds Linda Hudson, chief executive of BAE, the U.S. arm of **BAE Systems** PLC.

Nonetheless, diversity specialists say, companies that pair training with such tactics as joint interviews of applicants and requirements that candidate slates include diverse prospects tend to see faster improvement.

BAE launched its unconscious bias training amid a multipronged push to bring more women and minorities into its managerial ranks.

Among the efforts Hudson spearheaded in 2011: A woman or a person of color now participates in interview panels for potential middle managers and executives. The hiring panels previously "had a tendency to select white males," recalls Bridgette A. Weitzel, BAE's chief talent officer. Between May 2011 and May 2013, BAE says, the number of women and people of color in senior management rose by nearly 10 percent.

As for Fleming, the class forced her to recognize that unconscious biases "are part of who I am," she remarked later.

She has begun giving her staffers advance notice about difficult meeting topics "so there will be more time for the more introspective folks to assimilate their thoughts." The executive also hopes to switch to "blind" résumés—documents without an applicant's name or address.

Source: J.S. Lublin, "Do You Know Your Hidden Work Biases," *The Wall Street Journal*, January 10, 2014. Copyright © 2014 Dow Jones & Company, Inc. Reproduced with permission via Copyright Clearance Center.

Questions for Discussion

1. What potential roles do unconscious biases play in the workplace?

2. Why is understanding unconscious biases important for the effective management of diversity?

3. What are the potential advantages of providing managers with diversity training related to unconscious biases?

4. Should nonmanagerial employees receive training related to unconscious biases? Why or why not?

CHAPTER 6

Managing in the Global Environment

Learning Objectives

After studying this chapter, you should be able to:

LO6-1 Explain why the ability to perceive, interpret, and respond appropriately to the global environment is crucial for managerial success.

LO6-2 Differentiate between the global task and global general environments.

LO6-3 Identify the main forces in the global task and general environments, and describe the challenges that each force presents to managers.

LO6-4 Explain why the global environment is becoming more open and competitive, and identify the forces behind the process of globalization that increase the opportunities, complexities, challenges, and threats managers face.

LO6-5 Discuss why national cultures differ and why it is important that managers be sensitive to the effects of falling trade barriers and regional trade associations on the political and social systems of nations around the world.

A MANAGER'S CHALLENGE

Getting Global Right on the Internet

How should managers think about globalization on the Internet? Being a global organization is one thing; having a global presence on the Internet is another. Many organizations do not have a truly global website. For organizations selling goods on the Internet, the checkout process alone is full of challenges. Users who want to buy something will typically be directed to an online checkout form to fill out with shipping and billing information. These forms alone present challenges. For example, when asking customers for information, a U.S. company's website form might ask for the person's "last name." In other cultures, the last name is called the "family name" or "surname." Also, in many cultures, last names are much longer than many Western names and require more spaces in the website's form.[1]

Then there's the name of the checkout area on the website. What do you call the place where a customer can store the names of goods until they are purchased? In the United States, Amazon uses the term "shopping cart" in its checkout process. In the United Kingdom, it uses the phrase "shopping basket."[2]

There are other concerns to be addressed in the checkout process, including having users select their country or region versus using geolocation, offering support via phone, providing billing and shipping information that is country or region specific, and specifying acceptable payment platforms such as Paypal or Visa.[3]

The 2014 Web Globalization Report Card from Global by Design provides input into the challenges of globalizing a website.[4] The 180-page report describes the best and worst practices in website globalization and ranks the best and worst sites. It praises companies at the top of the list, including Google, Hotels.com, and Facebook, for their efforts at localization. These efforts include using local images instead of stock photos, having culture-specific content, and using language that is not only translated but also culturally nuanced. The 25 companies whose websites ranked at the top of the list supported an average of 50 languages. Use of a global design template also helped company web pages score near the top of the list. While localization is important, the report stresses the importance of a consistent look across countries.

Amazon.cn's exhibit in Shanghai, China, in 2012.

At the other end of the list are those who received poor scores, including big names like Walmart and Budweiser. Their shortcomings, according to the report card, were often the opposite of what the best companies did right. Not every website with a low score did all of these things wrong, but they did some combination of poor practices that put them toward the bottom of the list. Many fell short on localization, especially on language translation. Many did not have or had inconsistent "global gateways" to local websites. Another big problem was the lack of a global design template.[5]

"Lack of global consistency is an issue with many websites." John Yunker, author of the Web Globalization Report Card, said in a blog post about the report. "That is, each country web team appears to have gone off on its own and created a website from scratch instead of working across company to share common design templates and resources."[6]

Overview

Top managers of a global company like Nokia operate in an environment where they compete with other companies for scarce and valuable resources. Managers of companies large and small have found that to survive and prosper in the 21st century most organizations must become **global organizations** that operate and compete not only domestically, at home, but also globally, in countries around the world. Operating in the global environment is uncertain and unpredictable because it is complex and changes constantly.

If organizations are to adapt successfully to this changing environment, their managers must learn to understand the forces that operate in it and how these forces give rise to opportunities and threats. In this chapter we examine why the environment, both domestically and globally, has become more open, vibrant, and competitive. We examine how forces in the task and general environments affect global organizations and their managers. By the end of this chapter, you will appreciate the changes that are taking place in the environment and understand why it is important for managers to develop a global perspective as they strive to increase organizational efficiency and effectiveness.

global organization An organization that operates and competes in more than one country.

LO6-1

Explain why the ability to perceive, interpret, and respond appropriately to the global environment is crucial for managerial success.

What Is the Global Environment?

The **global environment** is a set of forces and conditions in the world outside an organization's boundary that affect how it operates and shape its behavior.[7] These forces change over time and thus present managers with *opportunities* and *threats*. Some changes in the global environment, such as the development of efficient new production technology, the availability of lower-cost components, or the opening of new global markets, create opportunities for managers to make and sell more products, obtain more resources and capital, and thereby strengthen their organization. In contrast, the rise of new global competitors, a global economic recession, or an oil shortage poses threats that can devastate an organization if managers are unable to sell its products. The quality of managers' understanding of forces in the global environment and their ability to respond appropriately to those forces, such as Sony's managers' ability to make and sell the electronic products that customers around the world want to buy, are critical factors affecting organizational performance.

In this chapter we explore the nature of these forces and consider how managers can respond to them. To identify opportunities and threats caused by forces in the environment, it is helpful for managers to distinguish between the *task environment* and the more encompassing *general environment* (see Figure 6.1).

LO6-2

Differentiate between the global task and global general environments.

global environment The set of global forces and conditions that operates beyond an organization's boundaries but affects a manager's ability to acquire and utilize resources.

Figure 6.1
Forces in the Global Environment

task environment The set of forces and conditions that originates with suppliers, distributors, customers, and competitors and affects an organization's ability to obtain inputs and dispose of its outputs. These forces and conditions influence managers daily.

general environment The wide-ranging global, economic, technological, sociocultural, demographic, political, and legal forces that affect an organization and its task environment.

The **task environment** is the set of forces and conditions that originates with global suppliers, distributors, customers, and competitors; these forces and conditions affect an organization's ability to obtain inputs and dispose of its outputs. The task environment contains the forces that have the most *immediate* and *direct* effect on managers because they pressure and influence managers daily. When managers turn on the radio or television, arrive at their offices in the morning, open their mail, or look at their computer screens, they are likely to learn about problems facing them because of changing conditions in their organization's task environment.

The **general environment** includes the wide-ranging global, economic, technological, sociocultural, demographic, political, and legal forces that affect the organization and its task environment. For the individual manager, opportunities and threats resulting from changes in the general environment are often more difficult to identify and respond to than are events in the task environment. However, changes in these forces can have major impacts on managers and their organizations.

The Task Environment

Forces in the task environment result from the actions of suppliers, distributors, customers, and competitors both at home and abroad (see Figure 6.1). These four groups affect a manager's ability to obtain resources and dispose of outputs daily, weekly, and monthly and thus have a significant impact on short-term decision making.

suppliers Individuals and organizations that provide an organization with the input resources it needs to produce goods and services.

Suppliers

Suppliers are the individuals and companies that provide an organization with the input resources (such as raw materials, component parts, or employees) it needs to produce goods

LO6-3

Identify the main forces in the global task and general environments, and describe the challenges that each force presents to managers.

and services. In return, the suppliers receive payment for those goods and services. An important aspect of a manager's job is to ensure a reliable supply of input resources.

For example, consider Dell Computer. Dell has many suppliers of component parts such as microprocessors (Intel and AMD) and disk drives (Quantum and Seagate Technologies). It also has suppliers of preinstalled software, including the operating system and specific applications software (Microsoft and Adobe). Dell's providers of capital, such as banks and financial institutions, are also important suppliers. Cisco Systems and Oracle are important providers of Internet hardware and software for dot-coms.

Dell has several suppliers of labor. One source is the educational institutions that train future Dell employees and therefore provide the company with skilled workers. Another is trade unions, organizations that represent employee interests and can control the supply of labor by exercising the right of unionized workers to strike. Unions also can influence the terms and conditions under which labor is employed. Dell's workers are not unionized; when layoffs became necessary because of the financial crisis and recession beginning in 2009, Dell had few problems in laying off workers to reduce costs. In organizations and industries where unions are strong, however, such as the transportation industry, an important part of a manager's job is negotiating and administering agreements with unions and their representatives.

Changes in the nature, number, or type of suppliers produce opportunities and threats to which managers must respond if their organizations are to prosper. For example, a major supplier-related threat that confronts managers arises when suppliers' bargaining positions are so strong that they can raise the prices of the inputs they supply to the organization. A supplier's bargaining position is especially strong when (1) the supplier is the sole source of an input and (2) the input is vital to the organization.[8] For example, for 17 years G. D. Searle was the sole supplier of NutraSweet, the artificial sweetener used in most diet soft drinks. Not only was NutraSweet an important ingredient in diet soft drinks, but it also was one for which there was no acceptable substitute (saccharin and other artificial sweeteners raised health concerns). Searle earned its privileged position because it invented and held the patent for NutraSweet, and patents prohibit other organizations from introducing competing products for 17 years. As a result, Searle was able to demand a high price for NutraSweet, charging twice the price of an equivalent amount of sugar; and paying that price raised the costs of soft drink manufacturers such as Coca-Cola and PepsiCo. When Searle's patent expired, many other companies introduced products similar to NutraSweet, and prices fell.[9] In the 2000s Splenda, which was made by McNeil Nutritionals, owned by Tate & Lyle, a British company, replaced NutraSweet as the artificial sweetener of choice, and NutraSweet's price fell further; Splenda began to command a high price from soft drink companies.[10]

However, a new sweetener introduced in 2008 has been gaining market share on Splenda. The noncaloric, natural sweetener Truvia moved to the number 2 position by 2014.[11]

In contrast, when an organization has many suppliers for a particular input, it is in a relatively strong bargaining position with those suppliers and can demand low-cost, high-quality inputs from them. Often an organization can use its power with suppliers to force them to reduce their prices, as Dell frequently does. Dell, for example, is constantly searching for low-cost suppliers abroad to keep its PC prices competitive. At a global level, organizations can buy products from suppliers overseas or become their own suppliers by manufacturing their products abroad.

It is important that managers recognize the opportunities and threats associated with managing the global supply chain. On one hand, gaining access to low-cost products made abroad represents an opportunity for U.S. companies to lower their input costs. On the other hand, managers who fail to use low-cost overseas suppliers create a threat and put their organizations at a competitive disadvantage.[12] Levi Strauss, for example, was slow to realize that it could not compete with the low-priced jeans sold by Walmart and other retailers, and it was eventually forced to close all its U.S. jean factories and outsource manufacturing to low-cost overseas suppliers to cut the price of its jeans to a competitive level. Now it sells its low-priced jeans in Walmart. The downside to global outsourcing is, of course, the loss of millions of U.S. jobs, an issue we have discussed in previous chapters.

A common problem facing managers of large global companies such as Ford, Sony, and Dell is managing the development of a global supplier network that will allow their companies to keep costs down and quality high. For example, Boeing's 777 jet was originally built using many components from over 500 global suppliers; eight Japanese suppliers made parts for the 777 fuselage, doors, and wings.[13] Boeing chose these suppliers because they were the best in the world at performing their particular activities, and Boeing's goal was to produce a high-quality final product.[14] Pleased with the outcome, Boeing decided to outsource a greater percentage of components to global suppliers when it designed the new Boeing 787 Dreamliner; however, many serious problems delayed the introduction of the new aircraft for several years.

The purchasing activities of global companies have become increasingly complicated as a result of the development of a whole range of skills and competencies in different countries around the world. It is clearly in companies' interests to search out the lowest-cost, best-quality suppliers. IT and the Internet are continually making it easier for companies to coordinate complicated long-distance exchanges involving the purchasing of inputs and the disposal of outputs—something Sony has taken advantage of as it trims the number of its suppliers to reduce costs.

global outsourcing The purchase or production of inputs or final products from overseas suppliers to lower costs and improve product quality or design.

Global outsourcing occurs when a company contracts with suppliers in other countries to make the various inputs or components that go into its products or to assemble the final products to reduce costs. For example, Apple contracts with companies in Taiwan and China to make inputs such as the chips, batteries, and LCD displays that power its digital devices; then it contracts with outsourcers such as Foxconn to assemble its final products—such as iPods, iPhones, and iPads. Apple also outsources the distribution of its products around the world by contracting with companies such as FedEx or DHL.

Global outsourcing has grown enormously to take advantage of national differences in the cost and quality of resources such as labor or raw materials that can significantly reduce manufacturing costs or increase product quality or reliability. Today such global exchanges are becoming so complex that some companies specialize in managing other companies' global supply chains. Global companies use the services of overseas intermediaries or brokers, which are located close to potential suppliers, to find the suppliers that can best meet the needs of a particular company. They can design the most efficient supply chain for a company to outsource the component and assembly operations required to produce its final products. Because these suppliers are located in thousands of cities in many countries, finding them is difficult. Li & Fung, based in Hong Kong, is one broker that has helped hundreds of major U.S. companies to outsource their component or assembly operations to suitable overseas suppliers, especially suppliers in mainland China.[15]

Although outsourcing to take advantage of low labor costs has helped many companies perform better, in the 2010s its risks have also become apparent, especially when issues such as reliability, quality, and speed are important. In 2012 General Electric moved the production of its hybrid water heater from China to Kentucky due to rising wages in China and increasing transportation costs. Moving production back to the United States also gave the company more control over the product quality. When all the savings were taken into account, the Kentucky plant was able to produce a better product at a lower price than the plant in China.[16] Apple also brought the manufacture of its next generation of personal computers to the United States. The new Mac Pro is being manufactured in Austin, Texas.[17] On the other hand, some companies do not outsource manufacturing; they prefer to establish their own assembly operations and factories in countries around the world to protect their proprietary technology. For example, most global automakers own their production operations in China to retain control over their global decision making and keep their operations secret. An interesting example of how organizations have tried to control what happens in their supply chains is discussed in the accompanying "Managing Globally" feature.

The purchasing activities of global companies have become increasingly complicated. Hundreds of suppliers around the world produce parts for Boeing's new 787 Dreamliner.

Watering Down the Supply Chain

How much water did it take to manufacture the outfit you are wearing right now? The textile industry has a huge water footprint. First it takes water to grow cotton, the material that accounts for 90 percent of the textile industry's use of natural fibers.[18] One estimate suggests that nearly 400 gallons of water are needed to produce each cotton T-shirt.[19] The farming of cotton accounts for 2.6 percent of annual global water usage[20] and is the largest water consumption factor in the supply chain of the textile industry.[21] And it's not just quantity. Cotton production has a direct impact on water quality through the use of pesticides, herbicides, and fertilizers.[22]

Second, problems continue beyond the growing of raw materials. The textile industry uses and pollutes water while dyeing fabrics. It can take more than 6 gallons of water to dye one T-shirt.[23] The polyester apparel industry alone uses 2.4 trillion gallons of water a year.[24] Fabric treatment, rinsing, and dyeing account for about 20 percent of global industrial water pollution.[25] Dye houses in China and India have been accused of overuse of local water supplies as well as dumping toxic wastewater into local water supplies.[26] In response to concerns about the use and pollution of water to make fabric and garments, several manufacturers have sought no-water and reduced-water ways of working in their supply chains.

In 2014 Levi Strauss & Co. made more than 100,000 pairs of jeans using 100 percent recycled water in China. This batch alone saved about 3 million gallons of water and was in addition to the 203 million gallons the company's Water<Less jeans brand had already saved.[27] The company plans to retrofit facilities in Nicaragua and South Asia to recycle water in the production process as well.

Nike and Adidas also are cutting back on water use in their supply chains by using a new process that dyes polyester without using water or chemicals. The process, developed by DyeCoo Textile Systems in the Netherlands, dyes fabric by turning carbon dioxide into a liquid by putting it under extreme pressure. As the carbon dioxide cools, it turns back into a gas that can be recycled and used again.[28] The first garment produced by Nike using the process was the running singlet worn by Kenyan marathoner Abel Kirui in the 2012 Olympics. The company began selling products manufactured using the process in 2014 under the name Nike ColorDry.[29] Adidas also started waterless dyeing in 2012, producing a limited collection of 50,000 T-shirts with the Yeh Group, which owns a textile mill in Thailand.[30]

Nike COO Eric Sprunk said, "NIKE, Inc., innovates not only in the design of our products but also in how they are made. We see sustainability and business growth as complementary, and our strategy is to prioritize relationships with factory groups that demonstrate a desire to invest in sustainable practices and technologies. Our collaboration with Far Eastern and DyeCoo, to develop and scale the ColorDry process, is an important milestone on our path toward manufacturing innovation."[31]

Distributors

distributors Organizations that help other organizations sell their goods or services to customers.

Distributors are organizations that help other organizations sell their goods or services to customers. The decisions managers make about how to distribute products to customers can have important effects on organizational performance. For example, package delivery companies such as Federal Express, UPS, and the U.S. Postal Service have become vital distributors for the millions of items bought online and shipped to customers by dot-com companies both at home and abroad.

The changing nature of distributors and distribution methods can bring opportunities and threats for managers. If distributors become so large and powerful that they can control customers' access to a particular organization's goods and services, they can threaten the organization by demanding that it reduce the prices of its goods and services.[32] For example, the huge retail distributor Walmart controls its suppliers' access to millions of customers and thus can demand that its suppliers reduce their prices to keep its business. If an organization such as Procter & Gamble refuses to reduce its prices, Walmart might respond by buying products only from Procter & Gamble's competitors—companies such as Unilever and Colgate. To reduce costs, Walmart also has used its power as a distributor to demand that all its suppliers adopt a new wireless radio frequency scanning technology to reduce the cost of shipping and stocking products in its stores; otherwise it would stop doing business with them.[33]

In 2014 the Bridgestone Corporation joined more than two dozen Japanese automotive suppliers who had already pled guilty to conspiring to fix the prices of parts sold to automakers. The Tokyo-based company was accused of conspiring to allocate sales, prearrange bids, and fix prices of parts sold.[34] It paid a $425 million criminal fine, higher than the fines given the other suppliers due to a previous price-fixing conviction. The multiyear investigation was the largest criminal investigation by the Justice Department's Antitrust Division.

Customers

customers Individuals and groups that buy the goods and services an organization produces.

Customers are the individuals and groups that buy the goods and services an organization produces. For example, Dell's customers can be segmented into several distinct groups: (1) individuals who purchase PCs for home use, (2) small companies, (3) large companies, and (4) government agencies and educational institutions. Changes in the number and types of customers or in customers' tastes and needs create opportunities and threats. An organization's success depends on its responsiveness to customers—whether it can satisfy their needs. In the PC industry, customers are demanding smaller computers, longer battery life, new apps, and lower prices—and PC makers must respond to the changing types and needs of customers, such as by introducing smarter systems that recognize voice commands instead of requiring bulky keyboards.[35] A school, too, must adapt to the changing needs of its customers. For example, if more Spanish-speaking students enroll, additional classes in English as a second language may need to be scheduled. A manager's ability to identify an organization's main customer groups, and make the products that best satisfy their particular needs, is a crucial factor affecting organizational and managerial success.

The most obvious opportunity associated with expanding into the global environment is the prospect of selling goods and services to millions or billions of new customers, as Amazon.com's CEO Jeff Bezos discovered when he expanded his company's operations in many countries.[36] Similarly, Accenture and Cap Gemini, two large consulting companies, established regional operating centers around the globe, and they recruit and train thousands of overseas consultants to serve the needs of customers in their respective world regions.

Today many products have gained global customer acceptance. This consolidation is occurring both for consumer goods and for business products and has created enormous opportunities for managers. The worldwide acceptance of Coca-Cola, Apple iPods, McDonald's hamburgers, and Samsung smartphones is a sign that the tastes and preferences of customers in different countries may not be so different after all.[37] Likewise, large global markets exist for business products such as telecommunications equipment, electronic components, and computer and financial services. Thus Cisco and Siemens sell their telecommunications equipment; Intel, its microprocessors; and Oracle and SAP, their business systems management software, to customers all over the world.

Competitors

competitors Organizations that produce goods and services that are similar to a particular organization's goods and services.

One of the most important forces an organization confronts in its task environment is competitors. **Competitors** are organizations that produce goods and services similar and comparable to a particular organization's goods and services. In other words, competitors are organizations trying to attract the same customers. Dell's competitors include other domestic PC makers (such as Apple and HP) as well as overseas competitors (such as Sony and Toshiba in Japan, Lenovo, the Chinese company that bought IBM's PC division, and Acer, the Taiwanese company that bought Gateway). Similarly, dot-com stockbroker E*Trade has other competitors such as Ameritrade, Scottrade, and Charles Schwab.

Rivalry between competitors is potentially the most threatening force managers must deal with. A high level of rivalry typically results in price competition, and falling prices reduce customer revenues and profits. In the early 2000s competition in the PC industry became intense because Dell was aggressively cutting costs and prices to increase its global market share.[38] IBM had to exit the PC business after it lost billions in its battle against low-cost rivals, and Gateway and HP also suffered losses while Dell's profits soared. By 2006, however, HP's fortunes had recovered because it had found ways to lower its costs and offer stylish new PCs, and Apple was growing rapidly, so Dell's profit margins shrank. In 2009 HP overtook Dell to become the largest global PC maker. However, it did not hold onto the lead. At the end of 2013 Lenovo overtook HP for the top spot, pushing Dell to number 3. Dell plans to continue the rivalry with a new strategic focus on consumer PCs in emerging markets.[39]

potential competitors Organizations that presently are not in a task environment but could enter if they so choose.

Although extensive rivalry between existing competitors is a major threat to profitability, so is the potential for new competitors to enter the task environment. **Potential competitors** are organizations that are not presently in a task environment but have the resources to enter if they so choose. In 2010 Amazon.com, for example, was not in the furniture or large appliance business, but it could enter these businesses if its managers decided it could profitably sell such products online—and in 2012 it did sell furniture and large appliances. When new competitors enter an industry, competition increases and prices and profits decrease—as furniture and electronic stores such as Best Buy have discovered as they battle Amazon.com.

barriers to entry Factors that make it difficult and costly for an organization to enter a particular task environment or industry.

BARRIERS TO ENTRY   In general, the potential for new competitors to enter a task environment (and thus increase competition) is a function of barriers to entry.[40] **Barriers to entry** are factors that make it difficult and costly for a company to enter a particular task environment or industry.[41] In other words, the more difficult and costly it is to enter the task environment, the higher are the barriers to entry. The higher the barriers to entry, the fewer the competitors in an organization's task environment and thus the lower the threat of competition. With fewer competitors, it is easier to obtain customers and keep prices high.

economies of scale Cost advantages associated with large operations.

Barriers to entry result from three main sources: economies of scale, brand loyalty, and government regulations that impede entry (see Figure 6.2). **Economies of scale** are the cost advantages associated with large operations. Economies of scale result from factors such as manufacturing products in very large quantities, buying inputs in bulk, or making more effective use of organizational resources than do competitors by fully utilizing employees' skills and knowledge. If organizations already in the task environment are large and enjoy significant economies of scale, their costs are lower than the costs that potential entrants will face, and newcomers will find it expensive to enter the industry. Amazon.com, for example, enjoys significant economies of scale relative to most other dot-com companies because of its highly efficient distribution system.[42]

brand loyalty Customers' preference for the products of organizations currently existing in the task environment.

Brand loyalty is customers' preference for the products of organizations currently in the task environment. If established organizations enjoy significant brand loyalty, a new entrant will find it difficult and costly to obtain a share of the market. Newcomers must bear huge advertising costs to build customer awareness of the goods or services they intend to

Figure 6.2

Barriers to Entry and Competition

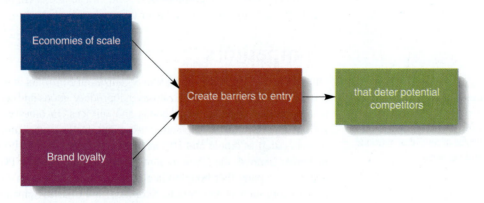

An O-bento lunch. Now that Japan can import rice from the United States, Japanese rice farmers, who cannot compete against lower-priced imports, have been forced to leave fields idle or grow less profitable crops.

provide.[43] Today Google, Amazon.com, and eBay enjoy a high level of brand loyalty and have some of the highest website hit rates, which allows them to increase their marketing revenues.

In some cases, *government regulations* function as a barrier to entry at both the industry and the country levels. Many industries that were deregulated, such as air transport, trucking, utilities, and telecommunications, experienced a high level of new entry after deregulation; this forced existing companies in those industries to operate more efficiently or risk being put out of business. At the national and global levels, administrative barriers are government policies that create barriers to entry and limit imports of goods by overseas companies. Japan is well known for the many ways in which it attempts to restrict the entry of overseas competitors or lessen their impact on Japanese firms. Japan has come under intense pressure to relax and abolish regulations such as those governing the import of rice, for example.

The Japanese rice market, like many other Japanese markets, was closed to overseas competitors until 1993 to protect Japan's thousands of high-cost, low-output rice farmers. Rice cultivation is expensive in Japan because of the country's mountainous terrain, and Japanese consumers have always paid high prices for rice. Under overseas pressure, the Japanese government opened the market; but overseas competitors are allowed to export to Japan only 8 percent of its annual rice consumption to protect its farmers.

In the 2000s, however, an alliance between organic rice grower Lundberg Family Farms of California and the Nippon Restaurant Enterprise Co. found a new way to break into the Japanese rice market. Because there is no tariff on rice used in processed foods, Nippon converts the U.S. organic rice into "O-bento," an organic hot boxed lunch packed with rice, vegetables, chicken, beef, and salmon, all imported from the United States. The lunches, which cost about $4 compared to a Japanese rice bento that costs about $9, are sold at railway stations and other outlets throughout Japan and have become very popular. A storm of protest from Japanese rice farmers arose because the entry of U.S. rice growers forced them to leave their rice fields idle or grow less profitable crops. Other overseas companies are increasingly forming alliances with Japanese companies to find new ways to break into the high-priced Japanese market, and little by little, Japan's restrictive trade practices are being whittled away.

In summary, intense rivalry among competitors creates a task environment that is highly threatening and makes it increasingly difficult for managers to gain access to the resources an organization needs to make goods and services. Conversely, low rivalry results in a task environment where competitive pressures are more moderate and managers have greater opportunities to acquire the resources they need to make their organizations effective.

The General Environment

Economic, technological, sociocultural, demographic, political, and legal forces in the general environment often have important effects on forces in the task environment that determine an organization's ability to obtain resources—effects that managers may not be aware of. For example, the sudden, dramatic upheavals in the mortgage and banking industry that started in 2007 were brought about by a combination of the development of complex new financial lending instruments called derivatives; a speculative boom in commodities and housing prices; and lax government regulation that allowed unethical bankers and financial managers to exploit the derivatives to make immense short-term profits. These events triggered the economic crisis that peaked in 2008 but continued to ripple through the world economy for years causing stock markets around the world to plummet, devastating the retirement savings of hundreds of millions of ordinary people, and causing layoffs of millions of employees as companies slashed their workforces because customers reduced their spending.

The implication is clear: Managers must continuously analyze forces in the general environment because these forces affect ongoing decision making and planning. How well managers can perform this task determines how quickly an organization can respond to the changes taking place. Next we discuss the major forces in the general environment and examine their impact on an organization's task environment.

Economic Forces

economic forces Interest rates, inflation, unemployment, economic growth, and other factors that affect the general health and well-being of a nation or the regional economy of an organization.

Economic forces affect the general health and well-being of a country or world region. They include interest rates, inflation, unemployment, and economic growth. Economic forces produce many opportunities and threats for managers. Low levels of unemployment and falling interest rates give people more money to spend, and as a result organizations can sell more goods and services. Good economic times affect the supply of resources that become easier or more inexpensive to acquire, and organizations have an opportunity to flourish. High-tech companies enjoyed this throughout the 1990s when computer and electronics companies like Sony made record profits as the global economy boomed because of advances in IT and growing global trade.

In contrast, worsening macroeconomic conditions, like those in the 2010s, pose a major threat because they reduce managers' ability to gain access to the resources their organizations need to survive and prosper. Profit-seeking organizations such as hotels and retail stores have fewer customers during economic downturns; hotel rates dropped by 14 percent in 2009 compared to 2008, for example, just as retail sales plunged. Nonprofits such as charities and colleges also saw donations decline by more than 20 percent because of the economic downturn.

Poor economic conditions make the environment more complex and managers' jobs more difficult and demanding. Companies often need to reduce the number of their managers and employees, streamline their operations, and identify ways to acquire and use resources more efficiently and effectively. Successful managers realize the important effects that economic forces have on their organizations, and they pay close attention to what is occurring in the economy at the national and regional levels to respond appropriately.

Technological Forces

technology The combination of skills and equipment that managers use in designing, producing, and distributing goods and services.

technological forces Outcomes of changes in the technology managers use to design, produce, or distribute goods and services.

Technology is the combination of tools, machines, computers, skills, information, and knowledge that managers use to design, produce, and distribute goods and services; **technological forces** are outcomes of changes in that technology. The overall pace of technological change has accelerated greatly in the last decades because technological advances in microprocessors and computer hardware and software have spurred technological advances in most businesses and industries. The effects of changing technological forces are still increasing in magnitude.[44]

Technological forces can have profound implications for managers and organizations. Technological change can make established products obsolete—for example, cathode-ray tube (CRT) computer monitors and televisions (such as Sony's Trinitron), bound sets of encyclopedias, and newspapers and magazines—forcing managers to find new ways to satisfy customer needs. Although technological change can threaten an organization, it also can create a host of new opportunities for designing, making, or distributing new and better kinds of goods and services. In 2014 AMD launched processors with powerful graphics capabilities for games and high-performance apps. The chips use Heterogeneous System Architecture (HSA) to speed up PCs. Innovations like these continue the IT revolution that has spurred demand for all kinds of new digital computing devices and services and has affected the competitive position of all high-tech companies.[45]

Changes in IT are altering the nature of work itself within organizations, including that of the manager's job. Today telecommuting, videoconferencing, and text messaging are everyday activities that let managers supervise and coordinate geographically dispersed employees. Salespeople in many companies work from home offices and commute electronically to work. They communicate with other employees through companywide electronic communication networks using tablet PCs and smartphones to orchestrate "face-to-face" meetings with coworkers across the country or globe.

Sociocultural Forces

sociocultural forces Pressures emanating from the social structure of a country or society or from the national culture.

Sociocultural forces are pressures emanating from the social structure of a country or society or from the national culture, such as the concern for diversity, discussed in the previous chapter. Pressures from both sources can either constrain or facilitate the way organizations operate and managers behave. **Social structure** is the traditional system of relationships established between people and groups in a society. Societies differ substantially in social structure. In societies that have a high degree of social stratification, there are many distinctions among individuals and groups. Caste systems in India and Tibet and the recognition of numerous social classes in Great Britain and France produce a multilayered social structure in each of those countries. In contrast, social stratification is lower in relatively egalitarian New Zealand and in the United States, where the social structure reveals few distinctions among people. Most top managers in France come from the upper classes of French society, but top managers in the United States come from all strata of American society.

social structure The traditional system of relationships established between people and groups in a society.

Societies also differ in the extent to which they emphasize the individual over the group. Such differences may dictate how managers need to motivate and lead employees.

national culture The set of values that a society considers important and the norms of behavior that are approved or sanctioned in that society.

National culture is the set of values that a society considers important and the norms of behavior that are approved or sanctioned in that society. Societies differ substantially in the values and norms they emphasize. For example, in the United States individualism is highly valued, but in Korea and Japan individuals are expected to conform to group expectations.[46] National culture, discussed at length later in this chapter, also affects how managers motivate and coordinate employees and how organizations do business. Ethics, an important aspect of national culture, were discussed in detail in Chapter 4.

Social structure and national culture not only differ across societies but also change within societies over time. In the United States, attitudes toward the roles of women, sex, marriage, and gays and lesbians changed in each past decade. Many people in Asian countries such as Hong Kong, Singapore, Korea, and even China think the younger generation is far more individualistic and "American-like" than previous generations. Currently, throughout much of Eastern Europe, new values that emphasize individualism and entrepreneurship are replacing communist values based on collectivism and obedience to the state. The pace of change is accelerating.

Individual managers and organizations must be responsive to changes in, and differences among, the social structures and national cultures of all the countries in which they operate. In today's increasingly integrated global economy, managers are likely to interact with people from several countries, and many managers live and work abroad. Effective managers are sensitive to differences between societies and adjust their behavior accordingly.

Managers and organizations also must respond to social changes within a society. In the last decades, for example, Americans have become increasingly interested in their personal health and fitness. Managers who recognized this trend early and took advantage of the opportunities that resulted from it were able to reap significant gains for their organizations, such as organic food delivery services. The organic produce industry has been growing for the past decade, even during the recession, due to people's interest in chemical-free food.[47] Many organizations have begun to offer weekly home delivery to customers.[48] PepsiCo used the opportunity presented by the fitness trend and took market share from archrival Coca-Cola by being the first to introduce diet colas and fruit-based soft drinks. Then Quaker Oats made Gatorade the most popular energy drink, and now others like Red Bull, Monster, and Rockstar are increasing in popularity. The health trend, however, did not offer opportunities to all companies; to some it posed a threat. Tobacco companies came under intense pressure due to consumers' greater awareness of negative health impacts from smoking. The rage for "low-carb" foods in the 2000s increased demand for meat and protein, and bread and doughnut companies such as Kraft and Krispy Kreme suffered—until the ongoing recession boosted the sale of inexpensive products such as macaroni and cheese and dry dinner mix.

demographic forces Outcomes of changes in, or changing attitudes toward, the characteristics of a population, such as age, gender, ethnic origin, race, sexual orientation, and social class.

Demographic Forces

Demographic forces are outcomes of changes in, or changing attitudes toward, the characteristics of a population, such as age, gender, ethnic origin, race, sexual orientation, and social class. Like the other forces in the general environment, demographic forces present managers with opportunities and threats and can have major implications for organizations. We examined the nature of these challenges in depth in our discussion of diversity in Chapter 5.

Today most industrialized nations are experiencing the aging of their populations as a consequence of falling birth and death rates and the aging of the baby boom generation. Consequently, the absolute number of older people has increased substantially, which has generated opportunities for organizations that cater to older people, such as the home health care, recreation, and medical industries, which have seen an upswing in demand for their services. The aging of the population also has several implications for the workplace. Most significant are a relative decline in the number of young people joining the workforce and an increase in the number of active employees who are postponing retirement beyond the traditional age of 65. Indeed, the continuing financial crisis in the 2010s has made it impossible for millions of older people to retire because their savings have been destroyed. These changes suggest that organizations need to find ways to motivate older employees and use their skills and knowledge—an issue that many Western societies have yet to tackle.

Political and Legal Forces

political and legal forces
Outcomes of changes in laws and regulations, such as deregulation of industries, privatization of organizations, and increased emphasis on environmental protection.

Political and legal forces are outcomes of changes in laws and regulations. They result from political and legal developments that take place within a nation, within a world region, or across the world and significantly affect managers and organizations everywhere. Political processes shape a nation's laws and the international laws that govern the relationships between nations. Laws constrain the operations of organizations and managers and thus create both opportunities and threats.[49] For example, throughout much of the industrialized world there has been a strong trend toward deregulation of industries previously controlled by the state and privatization of organizations once owned by the state such as airlines, railways, and utility companies. However, deregulation came under fire following the subprime mortgage crisis of 2007 and the resulting recession. Nobel Prize–winning economist Paul Krugman blamed global financial deregulation for, among other things, unstable economies in India, Brazil, Indonesia, South Africa, and Turkey in 2013.[50]

Another important political and legal force affecting managers and organizations is the political integration of countries that has been taking place during the last decades.[51] Increasingly, nations are forming political unions that allow free exchange of resources and capital. The growth of the European Union (EU) is one example: Common laws govern trade and commerce between EU member countries, and the European Court has the right to examine the business of any global organization and to approve any proposed mergers between overseas companies that operate inside the EU. For example, Microsoft's anticompetitive business practices came under scrutiny, and it was fined hundreds of millions for its uncompetitive practice of bundling its Internet Explorer web browser with its software. As part of its agreement with the European Court, Microsoft agreed that, beginning in 2010, it would ship its Windows 7 software with a choice of 10 web browsers (such as Chrome, Safari, and Mozilla). Also, in 2012, after months of delay, the court allowed the merger between Motorola and Google to proceed although the court was also investigating Google for possible anticompetitive online advertising practices. In 2014 there are ongoing negotiations between the United States and the European Union concerning the Transatlantic Trade and Investment Partnership (TTIP). The agreement would lower trade barriers to make it easier for organizations in the European Union and the United States to buy and sell each other's goods and services.[52]

Indeed, international agreements to abolish laws and regulations that restrict and reduce trade between countries have been having profound effects on global organizations. The falling legal trade barriers create enormous opportunities for companies to sell goods and services internationally. But by allowing overseas companies to compete in a nation's domestic market for customers, falling trade barriers also pose a serious threat because they increase competition in the task environment. For example, the Obama administration has been negotiating for the United States to join the Trans Pacific Partnership, a trade agreement whose possible members include Australia, Canada, Singapore, Brunei, Japan, Chile, Mexico, New Zealand, Malaysia, Peru, and Vietnam. The partnership may allow the United States to break into the Japanese rice market. Australia and New Zealand hope the trade agreement will open up the market for their dairy products. However, American car companies, sugar producers,

LO6-4

Explain why the global environment is becoming more open and competitive, and identify the forces behind the process of globalization that increase the opportunities, complexities, challenges, and threats managers face.

and textile makers have expressed concern about increased foreign competition if the United States joins the pact.[53] Public Citizen, a nonprofit consumer advocacy organization, believes the Trans Pacific Partnership will provide organizations with incentives to offshore their facilities, which will harm manufacturing industries in the United States.[54]

Deregulation, privatization, and the removal of legal barriers to trade are just a few of the many ways in which changing political and legal forces can challenge organizations and managers. Others include increased emphasis on environmental protection and the preservation of endangered species, increased emphasis on workplace safety, and legal constraints against discrimination on the basis of race, gender, or age. Managers face major challenges when they seek to take advantage of the opportunities created by changing political, legal, and economic forces.

The Changing Global Environment

The 21st century has banished the idea that the world is composed of distinct national countries and markets that are separated physically, economically, and culturally. Managers need to recognize that companies compete in a truly global marketplace, which is the source of the opportunities and threats they must respond to. Managers continually confront the challenges of global competition such as establishing operations in a country abroad, obtaining inputs from suppliers abroad, or managing in a different national culture.[55] (See Figure 6.3.)

In essence, as a result of falling trade barriers, managers view the global environment as open—that is, as an environment in which companies are free to buy goods and services from, and sell goods and services to, whichever companies and countries they choose. They also

Figure 6.3

The Peters Projection World Map shows the accurate area of landmasses. Africa appears much larger here than in many conventional maps. In today's open global environment, this large continent is starting to take on an increasingly important role.

are free to compete against each other to attract customers around the world. All large companies must establish an international network of operations and subsidiaries to build global competitive advantage. Coca-Cola and PepsiCo, for example, have competed aggressively for decades to develop the strongest global soft drink empire, just as Toyota and Honda have built hundreds of car plants around the world to provide the vehicles that global customers like.

In this section we first explain how this open global environment is the result of globalization and the flow of capital around the world. Next we examine how specific economic, political, and legal changes, such as the lowering of barriers to trade and investment, have increased globalization and led to greater interaction and exchanges between organizations and countries. Then we discuss how declining barriers of distance and culture have also increased the pace of globalization, and we consider the specific implications of these changes for managers and organizations. Finally we note that nations still differ widely from each other because they have distinct cultural values and norms and that managers must appreciate these differences to compete successfully across countries.

The Process of Globalization

globalization The set of specific and general forces that work together to integrate and connect economic, political, and social systems *across* countries, cultures, or geographical regions so that nations become increasingly interdependent and similar.

Perhaps the most important reason why the global environment has become more open and competitive is the increase in globalization. **Globalization** is the set of specific and general forces that work together to integrate and connect economic, political, and social systems across countries, cultures, or geographic regions. The result of globalization is that nations and peoples become increasingly interdependent because the same forces affect them in similar ways. The fates of peoples in different countries become interlinked as the world's markets and businesses become increasingly interconnected. And as nations become more interdependent, they become more similar to one another in the sense that people develop a similar liking for products as diverse as cell phones, iPods, blue jeans, soft drinks, sports teams, Japanese cars, and foods such as curry, green tea, and Colombian coffee. One outcome of globalization is that more women are joining the ranks of leadership. To help women transition to leadership positions, Ernst and Young, a multinational organization, has begun a special global program, as the accompanying "Managing Globally" feature describes.

Managing Globally

Leveraging London for Leadership

The 2012 London Olympics were a watershed moment for female athletes. For the first time ever, every country sending athletes to the games had women on the team, and women were able to participate in all sports.

"Coming out of London there was so much momentum around women. . . . It reinforced to us that women are an emerging market. The leadership potential that exists in these elite athletes is so consistent with our beliefs in somehow trying to unlock the potential to foster more women's economic empowerment and leadership," said Beth Brooke, global vice chair of regulatory and public policy for Ernst and Young.[56]

Between the 2012 London Olympics and the 2016 Rio Olympics, Ernst & Young is working to create a network of retired elite female athletes, former Olympians, and top female leaders and to encourage female athletes to pursue powerful careers after retiring from sports. Ernst & Young member firm Ernst & Young Terco is a sponsor of the Rio games.[57]

The background of this global network involved a study by Ernst & Young in May 2013 that confirmed a connection between sports and leadership. The study included a survey of 821 female senior managers and executives at companies around the world with annual revenues in excess of $250 million. Results found that almost all female leaders played sports at some point in their lives.[58]

More specifically, 96 percent of the women surveyed with board-level jobs played sports at the primary, secondary, postsecondary, or college level. The women in the

Beth Brooke, global vice chair of regulatory and public policy at Ernst and Young, is leading a drive to recruit female athletes because their confidence, high standards, discipline, and team experience may make them excellent business leaders.

study agreed that experience in playing sports leads to positive behaviors in the workplace, especially teamwork. Of the study respondents, 72 percent said that there seemed to be a correlation between playing, or having played, sports, and teamwork. Also, 76 percent said that behaviors and techniques from sports can be adopted to improve team performance in the workplace. While the study does not conclude that every athlete will become a strong organizational leader, it does conclude that sports can help women develop leadership skills that will serve organizations well.[59]

Ernst and Young's survey confirms the findings of a 2002 survey of more than 400 senior women executives commissioned by Mass-Mutual Financial Group and Oppenheimer, which found 80 percent or more of those surveyed had participated in an organized sport growing up and that the majority of those surveyed believed sports helped them to become more disciplined and built their leadership skills.[60] Beyond the results of these two surveys, there's anecdotal evidence. For example, Brazilian President Dilma Rousseff played volleyball. Basketball players who became high-level leaders include Mondolēz International CEO Irene Rosenfeld, former U.S. Secretary of State Hillary Clinton, and DuPont CEO Ellen Kullman.[61]

These women found success after their sports careers ended, but that is not always the case. Ernst and Young contends that many female athletes encounter difficulties in moving their success from the playing field to the corporate office.[62] The Women Athletes Global Leadership Network has three steps designed to make that transition easier and increase the impact of female leadership:[63]

1. Bringing together former elite athletes, former Olympians, and women in Ernst and Young's business network to form mentoring relationships and provide opportunities.
2. Using multimedia platforms to tell inspirational stories of women who found participation in sports to be important to their success.
3. Conducting research about the relationship between women's participation in sports and their leadership skills as well as their effect on global education, health, and development.

"Ernst & Young has seen the power of diversity and inclusion, and we want to build a better working world by expanding opportunities for women leaders. With their inherent confidence, high standards, discipline, and experience in working as a team, female athletes have tremendous value for businesses like ours, governments, and NGOs around the world," said Brooke, a Title IX scholarship recipient herself. "We have a long history of convening networks, helping female entrepreneurs scale their companies, and driving the global dialogue around the advancement of women. The impact of women at the London games was historic, and we want to continue this momentum by helping transform elite female athletes into exceptional leaders."[64]

But what drives or spurs globalization? What makes companies like IKEA, Toyota, or Microsoft want to venture into an uncertain global environment? The answer is that the path of globalization is shaped by the ebb and flow of *capital*—valuable wealth-generating assets or resources that people move through companies, countries, and world regions to seek their greatest returns or profits. Managers, employees, and companies like IKEA and Sony are motivated to try to profit or benefit by using their skills to make products customers around the world want to buy. The four principal forms of capital that flow between countries are these:

- *Human capital:* the flow of people around the world through immigration, migration, and emigration.
- *Financial capital:* the flow of money capital across world markets through overseas investment, credit, lending, and aid.

- *Resource capital:* the flow of natural resources, parts, and components between companies and countries, such as metals, minerals, lumber, energy, food products, microprocessors, and auto parts.

- *Political capital:* the flow of power and influence around the world using diplomacy, persuasion, aggression, and force of arms to protect the right or access of a country, world region, or political bloc to the other forms of capital.

Most of the economic advances associated with globalization are the result of these four capital flows and the interactions between them, as nations compete on the world stage to protect and increase their standards of living and to further the political goals and social causes that are espoused by their societies' cultures. The next sections look at the factors that have increased the rate at which capital flows between companies and countries. In a positive sense, the faster the flow, the more capital is being utilized where it can create the most value, such as people moving to where their skills earn more money, or investors switching to the stocks or bonds that give higher dividends or interest, or companies finding lower-cost sources of inputs. In a negative sense, however, a fast flow of capital also means that individual countries or world regions can find themselves in trouble when companies and investors move their capital to invest it in more productive ways in other countries or world regions—often those with lower labor costs or rapidly expanding markets. When capital leaves a country, the results are higher unemployment, recession, and a lower standard of living for its people.

Declining Barriers to Trade and Investment

One of the main factors that has speeded globalization by freeing the movement of capital has been the decline in barriers to trade and investment, discussed earlier. During the 1920s and 1930s many countries erected formidable barriers to international trade and investment in the belief that this was the best way to promote their economic well-being. Many of these barriers were high tariffs on imports of manufactured goods. A **tariff** is a tax that a government imposes on goods imported into one country from another. The aim of import tariffs is to protect domestic industries and jobs, such as those in the auto or steel industry, from overseas competition by raising the price of these products from abroad. In 2009, for example, the U.S. government increased the tariffs on vehicle tires imported from China to protect U.S. tire makers from unfair competition. The elevated tariffs expired in 2012, and in 2013 the passenger tire imports from China increased by 55.8 percent to 46 million units, an all-time high.[65]

tariff A tax that a government imposes on imported or, occasionally, exported goods.

The reason for removing tariffs is that, very often, when one country imposes an import tariff, others follow suit and the result is a series of retaliatory moves as countries progressively raise tariff barriers against each other. In the 1920s this behavior depressed world demand and helped usher in the Great Depression of the 1930s and massive unemployment. Beginning with the 2009 economic crisis, the governments of most countries have worked hard in the 2010s not to fall into the trap of raising tariffs to protect jobs and industries in the short run because they know the long-term consequences of this would be the loss of even more jobs. Governments of countries that resort to raising tariff barriers ultimately reduce employment and undermine the economic growth of their countries because capital and resources will always move to their most highly valued use—wherever that is in the world.[66]

GATT AND THE RISE OF FREE TRADE   After World War II, advanced Western industrial countries, having learned from the Great Depression, committed themselves to the goal of removing barriers to the free flow of resources and capital between countries. This commitment was reinforced by acceptance of the principle that free trade, rather than tariff barriers, was the best way to foster a healthy domestic economy and low unemployment.[67]

free-trade doctrine The idea that if each country specializes in the production of the goods and services that it can produce most efficiently, this will make the best use of global resources.

The **free-trade doctrine** predicts that if each country agrees to specialize in the production of the goods and services that it can produce most efficiently, this will make the best use of global capital resources and will result in lower prices.[68] For example, if Indian companies are highly efficient in the production of textiles and U.S. companies are highly efficient in the production of computer software, then, under a free-trade agreement, capital would move to India and be invested there to produce textiles, while capital from around the world would flow to the United States and be invested in its innovative computer software companies.

Consequently, prices of both textiles and software should fall because each product is being produced where it can be made at the lowest cost, benefiting consumers and making the best use of scarce capital. This doctrine is also responsible for the increase in global outsourcing and the loss of millions of U.S. jobs in textiles and manufacturing as capital has been invested in factories in Asian countries such as China and Malaysia. However, millions of U.S. jobs have also been created because of new capital investments in the high-tech, IT, and service sectors, which in theory should offset manufacturing job losses in the long run.

Historically, countries that accepted this free-trade doctrine set as their goal the removal of barriers to the free flow of goods, services, and capital between countries. They attempted to achieve this through an international treaty known as the General Agreement on Tariffs and Trade (GATT). In the half-century since World War II, there have been eight rounds of GATT negotiations aimed at lowering tariff barriers. The last round, the Uruguay Round, involved 117 countries and succeeded in lowering tariffs by over 30 percent from the previous level. It also led to the dissolving of GATT and its replacement by the World Trade Organization (WTO), which continues the struggle to reduce tariffs and has more power to sanction countries that break global agreements.[69] On average, the tariff barriers among the governments of developed countries declined from over 40 percent in 1948 to about 3 percent today,[70] causing a dramatic increase in world trade.[71]

Declining Barriers of Distance and Culture

Historically, barriers of distance and culture also closed the global environment and kept managers focused on their domestic market. The management problems Unilever, the huge British-based soap and detergent maker, experienced at the turn of the 20th century illustrate the effect of these barriers.

Founded in London during the 1880s by William Lever, a Quaker, Unilever had a worldwide reach by the early 1900s and operated subsidiaries in most major countries of the British Empire, including India, Canada, and Australia. Lever had a very hands-on, autocratic management style and found his far-flung business empire difficult to control. The reason for Lever's control problems was that communication over great distances was difficult. It took six weeks to reach India by ship from England, and international telephone and telegraph services were unreliable.

Another problem Unilever encountered was the difficulty of doing business in societies that were separated from Britain by barriers of language and culture. Different countries have different sets of national beliefs, values, and norms, and Lever found that a management approach that worked in Britain did not necessarily work in India or Persia (now Iran). As a result, management practices had to be tailored to suit each unique national culture. After Lever's death in 1925, top management at Unilever lowered or *decentralized* (see Chapter 10) decision-making authority to the managers of the various national subsidiaries so they could develop a management approach that suited the country in which they were operating. One result of this strategy was that the subsidiaries grew distant and remote from one another, which reduced Unilever's performance.[72]

Since the end of World War II, a continuing stream of advances in communications and transportation technology has worked to reduce the barriers of distance and culture that affected Unilever and all global organizations. Over the last decades, global communication has been revolutionized by developments in satellites, digital technology, the Internet and global computer networks, and video teleconferencing that allow transmission of vast amounts of information and make reliable, secure, and instantaneous communication possible between people and companies anywhere in the world.[73] This revolution has made it possible for a global organization—a tiny garment factory in Li & Fung's network or a huge company such as IKEA or Unilever—to do business anywhere, anytime, and to search for customers and suppliers around the world.

One of the most important innovations in transportation technology that has opened the global environment has been the growth of commercial jet travel. New York is now closer in travel time to Tokyo than it was to Philadelphia in the days of the 13 colonies—a fact that makes control of far-flung international businesses much easier today than in William Lever's era. In addition to speeding travel, modern communications and transportation technologies have also helped reduce the cultural distance between countries. The Internet and its millions of websites facilitate the development of global communications networks and media that are helping to create a worldwide culture that in some cases has diluted unique national cultures. Moreover, television networks such as CNN, MTV, ESPN, BBC, and HBO can now be received in many countries, and Hollywood films are shown throughout the world.

Effects of Free Trade on Managers

The lowering of barriers to trade and investment and the decline of distance and culture barriers have created enormous opportunities for companies to expand the market for their goods and services through exports and investments in overseas countries. The shift toward a more open global economy has created not only more opportunities to sell goods and services in markets abroad but also the opportunity to buy more from other countries. For example, apparel maker Ralph Lauren was heavily criticized when it was discovered that the uniforms it made for the 2012 U.S. Olympics team were made in China. Americans were not ready for their team uniforms to be bought from another country. For the 2014 Olympics, the Ralph Lauren uniform for the U.S. team was made in the United States. A manager's job is more challenging in a dynamic global environment because of the increased intensity of competition that goes hand in hand with the lowering of barriers to trade and investment.

REGIONAL TRADE AGREEMENTS   The growth of regional trade agreements, such as the North American Free Trade Agreement (NAFTA), and more recently the Central American Free Trade Agreement (CAFTA), also presents opportunities and threats for managers and their organizations. In North America, NAFTA, which became effective in 1994, had the aim of abolishing the tariffs on 99 percent of the goods traded between Mexico, Canada, and the United States by 2004. Although it did not achieve this lofty goal, NAFTA has removed most barriers on the cross-border flow of resources, giving, for example, financial institutions and retail businesses in Canada and the United States unrestricted access to the Mexican marketplace. After NAFTA was signed, there was a flood of investment into Mexico from the United States, as well as many other countries such as Japan. Walmart, Costco, Ford, and many major U.S. retail chains expanded their operations in Mexico; Walmart, for example, is stocking many more products from Mexico in its U.S. stores, and its Mexican store chain is also expanding rapidly.

The establishment of free-trade areas creates an opportunity for manufacturing organizations because it lets them reduce their costs. They can do this either by shifting production to the lowest-cost location within the free-trade area (for example, U.S. auto and textile companies shifting production to Mexico) or by serving the whole region from one location rather than establishing separate operations in each country. Some managers, however, view regional free-trade agreements as a threat because they expose a company based in one member country to increased competition from companies based in the other member countries. NAFTA has had this effect; today Mexican managers in some industries face the threat of head-to-head competition against efficient U.S. and Canadian companies. But the opposite is true as well: U.S. and Canadian managers are experiencing threats in labor-intensive industries, such as the flooring tile, roofing, and textile industries, where Mexican businesses have a cost advantage.

There are many regional trade agreements around the world. For example, the African Union was founded in 1999. Its purpose is both political and economic. Its goals include removing any remnants of colonization and apartheid, as well as creating cooperation for development.[74] Complementing the role of the African Union is the Southern African Development Community, an economic community whose members include Angola, South Africa, Botswana, Zambia, Democratic Republic of Congo, Seychelles, Lesotho, Madagascar, Mauritius, Malawi, Namibia, Mozambique, Swaziland, Tanzania, and Zimbabwe. This intergovernmental organization's goals include socioeconomic development and poverty eradication.[75] Another trade agreement is the Cooperation Council for the Arab States of the Gulf. This agreement was made among several countries, including Qatar, Oman, Bahrain, the United Arab Emirates, Kuwait, and Saudi Arabia. As a part of the agreement, countries cooperate on several issues, including regional cooperation and economic relations with others.[76] All these trade agreements are designed to allow managers to take advantage of opportunities that other members of the agreements can provide.

The Role of National Culture

Despite evidence that countries are becoming more similar because of globalization and that the world may become "a global village," the cultures of different countries still vary widely because of vital differences in their values, norms, and attitudes. As noted earlier, national culture includes the values, norms, knowledge, beliefs, moral principles, laws, customs, and other practices that unite the citizens of a country.[77] National culture shapes individual behavior by specifying appropriate and inappropriate behavior and interaction with others. People learn national culture in their everyday lives by interacting with those around them. This learning starts at an early age and continues throughout their lives.

Cultural Values and Norms

values Ideas about what a society believes to be good, right, desirable, or beautiful.

The basic building blocks of national culture are values and norms. **Values** are beliefs about what a society considers to be good, right, desirable, or beautiful—or their opposites. They provide the basic underpinnings for notions of individual freedom, democracy, truth, justice, honesty, loyalty, social obligation, collective responsibility, the appropriate roles for men and women, love, sex, marriage, and so on. Values are more than merely abstract concepts; they are invested with considerable emotional significance. People argue, fight, and even die over values such as freedom or dignity.

For example, antigovernment demonstrations broke out in the Ukraine after President Viktor Yanukovych chose a $15 billion bailout from Russia to help the country get back on its feet instead of a European trade and political offer. After months of bloody demonstrations, the Parliament voted Yanukovych out of power in February 2014.[78] Part of the problem is that some Ukrainian citizens consider themselves Russians while other feel closer to their European roots. Likewise, events in Egypt that led to President Hosni Mubarak stepping down in 2011 reflected a desire in the country to draft a new constitution and hold elections.[79]

norms Unwritten, informal codes of conduct that prescribe how people should act in particular situations and are considered important by most members of a group or organization.

Norms are unwritten, informal codes of conduct that prescribe appropriate behavior in particular situations and are considered important by most members of a group or organization. They shape the behavior of people toward one another. Two types of norms play a major role in national culture: mores and folkways. **Mores** are norms that are considered to be of central importance to the functioning of society and to social life. Accordingly, the violation of mores brings serious retribution. Mores include proscriptions against murder, theft, adultery, and incest. In many societies mores have been enacted into law. Thus all advanced societies have laws against murder and theft. However, there are many differences in mores from one society to another.[80] In the United States, for example, drinking alcohol is widely accepted; but in Saudi Arabia consumption of alcohol is viewed as a serious violation of social mores and is punishable by imprisonment.

mores Norms that are considered to be central to the functioning of society and to social life.

folkways The routine social conventions of everyday life.

Folkways are the routine social conventions of everyday life. They concern customs and practices such as dressing appropriately for particular situations, good social manners, eating with the correct utensils, and neighborly behavior. Although folkways define how people are expected to behave, violation of folkways is not a serious or moral matter. People who violate folkways are often thought to be eccentric or ill-mannered, but they are not usually considered immoral or wicked. In many countries, strangers are usually excused for violating folkways because they are unaccustomed to local behavior; but if they repeat the violation, they are censured because they are expected to learn appropriate behavior. Hence the importance of managers working in countries abroad to gain wide experience.

LO6-5

Discuss why national cultures differ and why it is important that managers be sensitive to the effects of falling trade barriers and regional trade associations on the political and social systems of nations around the world.

Hofstede's Model of National Culture

Researchers have spent considerable time and effort identifying similarities and differences in the values and norms of different countries. One model of national culture was developed by Geert Hofstede.[81] As a psychologist for IBM, Hofstede collected data on employee values and norms from more than 100,000 IBM employees in 64 countries. Based on his research, Hofstede developed five dimensions along which national cultures can be placed.[82]

individualism A worldview that values individual freedom and self-expression and adherence to the principle that people should be judged by their individual achievements rather than by their social background.

INDIVIDUALISM VERSUS COLLECTIVISM   The first dimension, which Hofstede labeled "individualism versus collectivism," has a long history in human thought. **Individualism** is a worldview that values individual freedom and self-expression and adherence to the principle that people should be judged by their individual achievements rather than by their social background. In Western countries, individualism usually includes admiration for personal success, a strong belief in individual rights, and high regard for individual entrepreneurs.[83]

collectivism A worldview that values subordination of the individual to the goals of the group and adherence to the principle that people should be judged by their contribution to the group.

In contrast, **collectivism** is a worldview that values subordination of the individual to the goals of the group and adherence to the principle that people should be judged by their contribution to the group. Collectivism was widespread in communist countries but has become less prevalent since the collapse of communism in most of those countries. Japan is a noncommunist country where collectivism is highly valued.

Collectivism in Japan traces its roots to the fusion of Confucian, Buddhist, and Shinto thought that occurred during the Tokugawa period in Japanese history (1600–1870s).[84] A central value that emerged during this period was strong attachment to the group—whether a village, a work group, or a company. Strong identification with the group is said to create pressures for collective action in Japan, as well as strong pressure for conformity to group norms and a relative lack of individualism.[85]

Managers must realize that organizations and organizational members reflect their national culture's emphasis on individualism or collectivism. Indeed, one of the major reasons why Japanese and American management practices differ is that Japanese culture values collectivism and U.S. culture values individualism.[86]

power distance The degree to which societies accept the idea that inequalities in the power and well-being of their citizens are due to differences in individuals' physical and intellectual capabilities and heritage.

POWER DISTANCE   By **power distance** Hofstede meant the degree to which societies accept the idea that inequalities in the power and well-being of their citizens are due to differences in individuals' physical and intellectual capabilities and heritage. This concept also encompasses the degree to which societies accept the economic and social differences in wealth, status, and well-being that result from differences in individual capabilities.

Societies in which inequalities are allowed to persist or grow over time have *high power distance.* In high-power-distance societies, workers who are professionally successful amass wealth and pass it on to their children, and, as a result, inequalities may grow over time. In such societies, the gap between rich and poor, with all the attendant political and social consequences, grows very large. In contrast, in societies with *low power distance,* large inequalities between citizens are not allowed to develop. In low-power-distance countries, the government uses taxation and social welfare programs to reduce inequality and improve the welfare of the least fortunate. These societies are more attuned to preventing a large gap between rich and poor and minimizing discord between different classes of citizens.

Advanced Western countries such as the United States, Germany, the Netherlands, and the United Kingdom have relatively low power distance and high individualism. Economically poor Latin American countries such as Guatemala and Panama, and Asian countries such as Malaysia and the Philippines, have high power distance and low individualism.[87] These findings suggest that the cultural values of richer countries emphasize protecting the rights of individuals and, at the same time, provide a fair chance of success to every member of society.

achievement orientation A worldview that values assertiveness, performance, success, and competition.

nurturing orientation A worldview that values the quality of life, warm personal friendships, and services and care for the weak.

ACHIEVEMENT VERSUS NURTURING ORIENTATION   Societies that have an **achievement orientation** value assertiveness, performance, success, competition, and results. Societies that have a **nurturing orientation** value the quality of life, warm personal relationships, and services and care for the weak. Japan and the United States tend to be achievement-oriented; the Netherlands, Sweden, and Denmark are more nurturing-oriented.

uncertainty avoidance The degree to which societies are willing to tolerate uncertainty and risk.

UNCERTAINTY AVOIDANCE   Societies as well as individuals differ in their tolerance for uncertainty and risk. Societies low on **uncertainty avoidance** (such as the United States and Hong Kong) are easygoing, value diversity, and tolerate differences in personal beliefs and actions. Societies high on uncertainty avoidance (such as Japan and France) are more rigid and skeptical about people whose behaviors or beliefs differ from the norm. In these societies, conformity to the values of the social and work groups to which a person belongs is the norm, and structured situations are preferred because they provide a sense of security.

long-term orientation A worldview that values thrift and persistence in achieving goals.

short-term orientation A worldview that values personal stability or happiness and living for the present.

LONG-TERM VERSUS SHORT-TERM ORIENTATION   The last dimension that Hofstede described is orientation toward life and work.[88] A national culture with a **long-term orientation** rests on values such as thrift (saving) and persistence in achieving goals. A national culture with a **short-term orientation** is concerned with maintaining personal stability or happiness and living for the present. Societies with a long-term orientation include

Taiwan and Hong Kong, well known for their high rate of per capita savings. The United States and France have a short-term orientation, and their citizens tend to spend more and save less.

National Culture and Global Management

Differences among national cultures have important implications for managers. First, because of cultural differences, management practices that are effective in one country might be troublesome in another. General Electric's managers learned this while trying to manage Tungsram, a Hungarian lighting products company GE acquired for $150 million. GE was attracted to Tungsram, widely regarded as one of Hungary's best companies, because of Hungary's low wage rates and the possibility of using the company as a base from which to export lighting products to western Europe. GE transferred some of its best managers to Tungsram and hoped it would soon become a leader in Europe. Unfortunately many problems arose.

One problem resulted from major misunderstandings between the American managers and the Hungarian workers. The Americans complained that the Hungarians were lazy; the Hungarians thought the Americans were pushy. The Americans wanted strong sales and marketing functions that would pamper customers. In the prior command economy, sales and marketing activities were unnecessary. In addition, Hungarians expected GE to deliver Western-style wages, but GE came to Hungary to take advantage of the country's low wage structure.[89] As Tungsram's losses mounted, GE managers had to admit that, because of differences in basic attitudes between countries, they had underestimated the difficulties they would face in turning Tungsram around. Nevertheless, by 2001 these problems had been solved, and the increased efficiency of GE's Hungarian operations made General Electric a major player in the European lighting market, causing it to invest another $1 billion.[90]

Often management practices must be tailored to suit the cultural contexts within which an organization operates. An approach effective in the United States might not work in Japan, Hungary, or Mexico because of differences in national culture. For example, U.S.-style pay-for-performance systems that emphasize the performance of individuals might not work well in Japan, where individual performance in pursuit of group goals is the value that receives emphasis.

Managers doing business with individuals from another country must be sensitive to the value systems and norms of that country and behave accordingly. For example, Friday is the Islamic Sabbath. Thus it would be impolite and inappropriate for a U.S. manager to schedule a busy day of activities for Saudi Arabian managers on a Friday.

A culturally diverse management team can be a source of strength for an organization participating in the global marketplace. Compared to organizations with culturally homogeneous management teams, organizations that employ managers from a variety of cultures have a better appreciation of how national cultures differ, and they tailor their management systems and behaviors to the differences.[91] Indeed, one advantage that many Western companies have over their Japanese competitors is greater willingness to create global teams composed of employees from different countries around the world who can draw on and share their different cultural experiences and knowledge to provide service that is customized to the needs of companies in different countries. For example, because IT services account for more than half of IBM's $90 billion annual revenues, it has been searching for ways to better use its talented workforce to both lower costs and offer customers unique, specialized kinds of services that its competitors cannot. IBM has developed several kinds of techniques to accomplish this.[92]

In the 2000s, IBM created "competency centers" around the world staffed by employees who share the same specific IT skill. Most of IBM's employees are concentrated in competency centers located in the countries in which IBM has the most clients and does the most business. These employees have a wide variety of skills, developed from their previous work experience, and the challenge facing IBM is to use these experts efficiently. To accomplish this, IBM used its own IT expertise to develop sophisticated software that allows it to create self-managed teams composed of IBM experts who have

Computer technicians at work in a server room. IBM's competency centers customize teams of workers who can manage their own tasks.

the optimum mix of skills to solve a client's particular problems. First, IBM programmers analyze the skills and experience of its 80,000 global employees and enter the results into the software program. Then they analyze and code the nature of a client's specific problem and input that information. IBM's program matches each specific client problem to the skills of IBM's experts and identifies a list of "best fit" employees. One of IBM's senior managers narrows this list and decides on the actual composition of the self-managed team.

Once selected, team members, from wherever they happen to be in the world, assemble as quickly as possible and go to work analyzing the client's problem. Together, team members use their authority. This new IT lets IBM create an ever-changing set of global self-managed teams that form to develop the software and service packages necessary to solve the problems of IBM's global clients. At the same time, IBM's IT also optimizes the use of its whole talented workforce because each employee is placed in his or her "most highly valued use"—that is, in the team where the employee's skills can best increase efficiency and effectiveness. There are a lot of factors involved in working for a global organization. The accompanying "Management Insight" feature describes how managers might educate themselves about some of the issues.

Management Insight

Cultural Differences That Expatriates Face in International Business

Where in the world would you like to be an expatriate? The annual Expat Explorer Survey by HSBC Bank International could help you decide. The survey ranks the best places in the world to be an expatriate worker. The results are available on the company's website (www.expatexplorer.hsbc.com) and can help people understand what it will be like to be an expatriate in different countries.

The HSBC site also allows users to submit tips based on their expatriate experiences. For example, a former expatriate named Matt provides a list of five "Things to Do before Relocating to China."

1. Make a temporary visit and get a gut feeling for whether China is the right place.
2. Work to gain an understanding of the culture and the language.
3. Make friends via social media or other means before arrival.
4. Take sufficient supplies of items like contact lenses and other Western products that may be difficult to obtain on the mainland.
5. Be mentally and physically sound when you arrive.[93]

Tips provided by an expatriate named Farrah on child health care in the Netherlands begin with "You no longer have a pediatrician. Accept that."[94]

Other information on the site is more general. For example, France, Germany, South Africa, Singapore, and New Zealand are rated highly for raising children. France, Belgium, Germany, and Taiwan get high marks for health care access and quality. When it comes to earning disposable income, the Cayman Islands, Switzerland, Bahrain, Thailand, Qatar, Taiwan, Russia, and Vietnam are the top ranked.

The HSBC survey ranks countries based on experience, economics, and raising children abroad. The economics factor includes income, disposable income, and host economic satisfaction. The experience factor includes a long list of issues from entertainment and work–life balance to local culture and making local friends to local weather and learning the local language. The raising children factor also includes a long list of issues from quality and cost of child care to access to better education to children learning a new language.

While the factors in the survey can be chosen to tailor a list of the best countries for an individual expatriate, the survey does rank the countries from best to worst. Among the "best" countries on the three factors are China, Switzerland, the Cayman Islands, Bahrain, and Singapore. The "worst" countries on the three factors include France, Spain, the United Kingdom, Italy, and Ireland.[95] The United States ranked 12th out of 24 due to poor scores on experience and economics.[96]

Another interesting finding of the most recent Expat Explorer report is that expatriates living in markets or economies that are classified as "emerging" or "frontier" were more optimistic about the state of the economy and business opportunities than were expatriates in other countries. Emerging markets were defined as BRIC countries—Brazil, Russia, India, and China. Frontier economies were defined as VITM countries—Vietnam, Indonesia, Turkey, and Mexico. The report found 93 percent of expatriates in BRIC countries and 68 percent of expatriates in VITM countries reported being satisfied with the local economy's condition versus 56 percent of expatriates from other places in the world who reported satisfaction with the local economy.[97]

The HSBC site also contains tips and advice for expatriates that were compiled from survey responses. One post lists "great ways to make friends with the locals:"

1. Take part in social events, join a club, or volunteer with a charity.
2. Learn the language and go to places where locals hang out.
3. Do not turn down an invitation to an event for the first six months of your assignment.
4. If you have children, join a youth organization such as a school group.
5. Interact with people as much as possible.[98]

Other topics of survey response compilations include tips for getting a car, finding a school for your children, arranging your paperwork, getting through immigration, settling in, and avoiding homesickness.[99]

There are several lists on how to adapt to life in the United States, with tips such as eating half your meals in restaurants immediately and packing the extra to take home to avoid gaining weight,[100] learning the names of the cuts of meat at the butcher shop because the cut described as a brisket in the United States is a different part of the cow than that of the British brisket,[101] eating the local food, "especially fried chicken in the South,"[102] learning to use or at least understand various sports metaphors such as "to punt" or "a Hail Mary,"[103] and recognizing that Americans are very task oriented and will want to get right to business before getting to know their coworkers.[104]

The site contains a disclaimer that the content on the site is the opinion of users and is not verified by HSBC.

Summary and Review

LO6-1 **WHAT IS THE GLOBAL ENVIRONMENT?**   The global environment is the set of forces and conditions that operates beyond an organization's boundaries but affects a manager's ability to acquire and use resources. The global environment has two components: the task environment and the general environment.

LO6-2, 6-3 **THE TASK ENVIRONMENT**   The task environment is the set of forces and conditions that originates with global suppliers, distributors, customers, and competitors and influences managers daily. The opportunities and threats associated with forces in the task environment

LO6-2, 6-3 become more complex as a company expands globally.

THE GENERAL ENVIRONMENT   The general environment comprises wide-ranging global economic, technological, sociocultural, demographic, political, and legal forces that affect an organization and its task environment.

LO6-4, 6-5 **THE CHANGING GLOBAL ENVIRONMENT**   In recent years there has been a marked shift toward a more open global environment in which capital flows more freely as people and companies search for new opportunities to create profit and wealth. This has hastened the process of globalization. Globalization is the set of specific and general forces that work together to integrate and connect economic, political, and social systems across countries, cultures, or geographic regions so that nations become increasingly interdependent and similar. The process of globalization has been furthered by declining barriers to international trade and investment and declining barriers of distance and culture.

Management in Action

Topics for Discussion and Action

Discussion

1. Why is it important for managers to understand the forces in the global environment that are acting on them and their organizations? **[LO6-1]**

2. Which organization is likely to face the most complex task environment—a biotechnology company trying to develop a cure for cancer or a large retailer like The Gap or Macy's? Why? **[LO6-2, 6-3]**

3. The population is aging because of declining birth rates, declining death rates, and the aging of the baby boom generation. What might some of the implications of this demographic trend be for (a) a pharmaceutical company and (b) the home construction industry? **[LO6-1, 6-2, 6-3]**

4. How do political, legal, and economic forces shape national culture? What characteristics of national culture do you think have the most important effect on how successful a country is in doing business abroad? **[LO6-3, 6-5]**

5. After the passage of NAFTA, many U.S. companies shifted production operations to Mexico to take advantage of lower labor costs and lower standards for environmental and worker protection. As a result, they cut their costs and were better able to survive in an increasingly competitive global environment. Was their behavior ethical—that is, did the ends justify the means? **[LO6-4]**

Action

6. Choose an organization and ask a manager in that organization to list the number and strengths of forces in the organization's task environment. Ask the manager to pay particular attention to identifying opportunities and threats that result from pressures and changes in customers, competitors, and suppliers. **[LO6-1, 6-2, 6-3]**

Building Management Skills

Analyzing an Organization's Environment [LO6-1, 6-2, 6-3]

Pick an organization with which you are familiar. It can be an organization in which you have worked or currently work or one that you interact with regularly as a customer (such as the college you are attending). For this organization do the following:

1. Describe the main forces in the global task environment that are affecting the organization.

2. Describe the main forces in the global general environment that are affecting the organization.

3. Explain how environmental forces affect the job of an individual manager within this organization. How do they determine the opportunities and threats that its managers must confront?

Managing Ethically [LO6-4, 6-5]

Home Depot Inc. misjudged the market in China. The world's largest home improvement chain entered the market in China in 2006 and decided to leave six years later. It was not able to sell its do-it-yourself brand to the Chinese. "China is a do-it-for-me market, not a do-it-yourself market, so we have to adjust," a Home Depot spokeswoman said.[105] Cheap labor in China means many people can hire someone else to do home improvement work for them.

Also, apartment-based living in China meant there was not much demand for products such as lumber.[106]

Questions

1. What could Home Depot have done to avoid its mistake?

2. In what cultures might Home Depot find better success?

Small Group Breakout Exercise

How to Enter the Copying Business [LO6-1, 6-2]

Form groups of three to five people, and appoint one group member as the spokesperson who will communicate your findings to the whole class when called on by the instructor. Then discuss the following scenario:

You and your partners have decided to open a small printing and copying business in a college town of 100,000 people. Your business will compete with companies like FedEx Kinko's. You know that over 50 percent of small businesses fail in their first year, so to increase your chances of success, you have decided to perform a detailed analysis of the task environment of the copying business to discover what opportunities and threats you will encounter.

1. Decide what you must know about (a) your future customers, (b) your future competitors, and (c) other critical forces in the task environment if you are to be successful.

2. Evaluate the main barriers to entry into the copying business.

3. Based on this analysis, list some steps you would take to help your new copying business succeed.

Exploring the World Wide Web [LO6-2, 6-3, 6-4]

Go to www.greatplacetowork.com and click on "World's Best Multinationals" under Best Companies. Take a look at the list for this year.

1. Find a company on the list that is based in a country other than your home country. How has that company had to adapt to become a global organization?

2. What are the forces in the global task environment and in the global general environment that affect the organization?

3. What criteria are used to select the great places to work? Do you agree that these criteria are what make an organization a great place to work?

Be the Manager [LO6-1, 6-2]

The Changing Environment of Retailing

You are the new manager of a major clothing store that is facing a crisis. This clothing store has been the leader in its market for the last 15 years. In the last three years, however, two other major clothing store chains have opened, and they have steadily been attracting customers away from your store—your sales are down 30 percent. To find out why, your store surveyed former customers and learned that they perceive your store as not keeping up with changing fashion trends and new forms of customer service. In examining how the store operates, you found out that the 10 purchasing managers who buy the clothing and accessories for the store have been buying from the same clothing suppliers and have become reluctant to try new ones. Moreover, salespeople rarely, if ever, make suggestions for changing how the store operates, and they don't respond to customer requests; the culture of the store has become conservative and risk-averse.

Questions

1. Analyze the major forces in the task environment of a retail clothing store.

2. Devise a program that will help other managers and employees to better understand and respond to their store's task environment.

Bloomberg BusinessWeek Case in the News [LO6-1, 6-4, 6-5]

In Trade Talks, It's Countries versus Companies

Beginning in the 1950s, trade negotiators evolved an elegant solution to a vexing problem: the risk that poor countries would seize the oil fields, mines, and factories of Western corporations that operated within their borders. Fearful of nationalization or other harsh treatment, multinationals were holding back on investment. Everyone lost.

The answer was to include language in treaties specifying that disputes between investors and governments would be settled by independent arbitrators, not courts in the country where a disagreement arose. That gave corporations confidence that their projects were safe and helped unleash trillions of dollars' worth of cross-border investment. Today there are about 3,000 treaties between countries that provide for such arbitration.

Yet that fix is now the subject of a bitter disagreement between corporations and governments that's impeding progress on two of the biggest free-trade treaties ever, both involving the United States: the Trans-Pacific Partnership (TPP) and the Transatlantic Trade and Investment Partnership (TTIP).

The problem is that to many people, arbitration looks profoundly undemocratic. Countries that sign the treaties give away a lot: The arbitration panels are unelected tribunals of three experts (usually lawyers, one chosen by each side and one picked by mutual consent or a third party) that are empowered to overrule a nation's highest authorities. The panels have come under attack from environmental groups, labor unions, and developing nations including Venezuela, Ecuador, and South Africa.

Opponents point to several disputes currently in arbitration where corporations are invoking treaties for protection from local laws. Philip Morris International(PM) has brought a case in Hong Kong challenging Australia's plain-packaging law for cigarettes. The tobacco company says the law prevents it from marketing its brand, in violation of a treaty between Australia and Hong Kong. Sweden's Vattenfall, which operates nuclear plants in Germany, is seeking compensation for the country's planned phaseout of electricity generation from nuclear power, which it says breaks the countries' bilateral investment treaty. Lone Pine Resources, a U.S. company that has licenses to produce natural gas from beneath the St. Lawrence River in Quebec, wants to be compensated by Canada for a moratorium on fracking in the province.

Lori Wallach, director of Global Trade Watch, a Ralph Nader organization, has called the arbitration system "a quiet, slow-moving coup d'état." Democratic Senator Sherrod Brown of Ohio, a prominent arbitration critic, said in an e-mail message that the "mere threat of costly litigation" can have a chilling effect on legitimate regulation, such as on tobacco.

To see how arbitration can squeeze a country, consider the case of a lead and zinc smelting operation in South America called Doe Run Perú. The Peruvian government demanded a costly waste cleanup. U.S. billionaire Ira Rennert, who owned Doe Run Perú for more than a decade through Renco Group, said the government's escalating cleanup demands forced the unit into bankruptcy in violation of the U.S.–Peru trade promotion agreement of 2006. Renco asked a panel of arbitrators to force Peru to pay it $800 million. It also said the country, which once owned the operation, should be liable for any damages arising from a pending lawsuit in federal court in St. Louis alleging that it sickened more than 700 Peruvian children. The case is ongoing.

The voices of opposition are becoming harder to ignore. In January, in response to criticism of the arbitration clauses now standard in nearly every agreement, the European Commission announced a halt to negotiations with the United States on the arbitration provisions of TTIP, the ambitious effort to open more trade and investment between the United States. and the European Union. The commission reaffirmed it was committed to including arbitration in the treaty, but said it wanted a 90-day break for "public consultation" to hear people's views. A high-profile campaign by opponents could complicate talks long after the listening period ends.

For the U.S. government and other backers of arbitration, a bigger blow came in mid-March when the German government—which has been a staunch supporter of investor–state dispute settlements—said it decided to push for excluding it from TTIP. "Special investment protection rules are not necessary in an accord between the USA and EU," the German economy ministry said in a statement. It said the rules were unnecessary because "both partners have adequate legal protection" for foreign investors in their courts. The Germans said they'd OK a treaty if the final text addresses their concerns on arbitration.

The Vattenfall challenge to Germany's nuke moratorium may have brought home the pitfalls of arbitration, says Pia Eberhardt, a researcher with Corporate Europe Observatory, which tracks corporate lobbying of the EU. Via e-mail, the press office for EU trade policy said Europe would make sure the investment provisions "fully enshrine democratic principles."

Australia and Malaysia are leading similar opposition to strong arbitration provisions in the TPP, a 12-nation trade and investment pact.

The United States can't afford to drop arbitration from the big Pacific and Atlantic trade deals because that would send the wrong signal for future agreements, says Sean Heather, vice president for global regulatory cooperation at the U.S. Chamber of Commerce. China, which is beginning to negotiate investment treaties with the United States and Europe, could argue that its pacts shouldn't have to include arbitration, either. That would leave investors in China relying on their governments to intervene with the Chinese government, or, worse, depending on fair treatment in Chinese courts.

Some of the opposition to investor–state arbitration is clearly overheated. It's one thing for a company to make an outrageous claim against a government and quite another to win. Companies win or settle about half their cases. (Notably, they've never won against the United States.) The arbitration agreement the United States wants to include in the Atlantic and Pacific trade pacts wouldn't give companies a free pass to pollute or break foreign laws. And companies couldn't claim that any law or regulation they dislike constitutes a "taking" of their property for which they deserve compensation. Arbitration hearings and documents would be open to the public. Still, lots of people have trouble with the idea of giving anyone as much power as the arbitrators have. "They're supreme court justices for the world," says Gus Van Harten, a professor at York University's Osgoode Hall Law School in Toronto. "Only they're not judges, and you don't know who they are."

Source: Peter Coy, Brian Parkin and Andrew Martin, "In Trade Talks, It's Countries vs. Companies," *Bloomberg Business Week,* March 20, 2014. Used with permission of Bloomberg L.P. Copyright © 2014. All rights reserved.

Questions for Discussion

1. Why do you believe trade treaties include arbitration clauses?

2. Would you support the continuation of arbitration clauses in trade treaties?

3. Search the web to see the latest on the Trans-Pacific Partnership.

CHAPTER 7

Decision Making, Learning, Creativity, and Entrepreneurship

Learning Objectives

After studying this chapter, you should be able to:

LO7-1 Understand the nature of managerial decision making, differentiate between programmed and nonprogrammed decisions, and explain why nonprogrammed decision making is a complex, uncertain process.

LO7-2 Describe the six steps managers should take to make the best decisions, and explain how cognitive biases can lead managers to make poor decisions.

LO7-3 Identify the advantages and disadvantages of group decision making, and describe techniques that can improve it.

LO7-4 Explain the role that organizational learning and creativity play in helping managers to improve their decisions.

LO7-5 Describe how managers can encourage and promote entrepreneurship to create a learning organization, and differentiate between entrepreneurs and intrapreneurs.

Why are decision making and learning the keys to entrepreneurial success?

All managers must make decisions day in and day out under considerable uncertainty. And sometimes those decisions come back to haunt them if they turn out poorly. Sometimes even highly effective managers make bad decisions. And factors beyond a manager's control, such as unforeseen changes in the environment, can cause a good decision to result in unexpected negative consequences. Effective managers recognize the critical importance of making decisions on an ongoing basis as well as learning from prior decisions.

Decision making and learning have been key to Jim McCann's success in building a small florist shop into a global business with $1 billion in 2013 revenues headquartered in Carle Place, New York.[1] In fact, learning and decision making have been mainstays for McCann throughout his life and career. As a child growing up in Queens, New York, McCann learned about plumbing, electrical work, and woodworking from his father, who had a small painting business. While he was bartending at night and going to college in the day, a friend let him know about an opportunity to work evenings in a group home for teenage boys. McCann decided to seize this opportunity, and while continuing to go to college in the day, he worked and slept (in his own room) in the St. John's Home for Boys in Queens. McCann was a psychology major and learned a lot from working and living with 10 teenage boys.[2] When he graduated, he continued to work at the home in administration for 14 years.[3]

McCann continued to bartend at night to make some extra money for his family, and one of his customers told him that he was planning on selling a small flower shop.[4] McCann thought he might like to learn that business and buy the shop, so he asked the customer if he could work in the shop a couple of weekends to see what it was like.[5] McCann ending up buying the store for $10,000, continued to work at the home for boys, and learned the flower business—and the rest has made history.[6]

Lifelong learning and good decision making have been crucial to the success of 1-800-Flowers.com Inc. James McCann, Chairman and CEO, bartended, worked in the administration of a group home for boys, got a degree in psychology, and then built a small florist shop into a billion-dollar global business.

When he bought the store, he decided he wanted to somehow turn it into a larger organization.[7] So he kept looking for additional opportunities to buy or open up flower shops. Ten years later he had over 20 flower stores and quit his job at the home for boys to work full-time on his flower shop business (by now his siblings were also working in the business).[8]

In the late 1980s McCann happened to hear a commercial on the radio for 1-800-Flowers, the first company that enabled customers to call a toll-free number to order flowers.[9] McCann decided to see if he could be a distributor for this company, called them, and became the florist for New York; this helped expand his business. However, over time, McCann stopped getting orders from this source of customers. McCann went to Dallas where the company was based and found out that although its owners had raised about $10 million in funding, they had ceased operating because of a lack of business.[10]

McCann decided to try to buy the business with his savings from his own business, while saving money by not involving lawyers, accountants, or bankers in the transaction.[11] He offered the owners $2 million for their 800 flower business and they accepted. Soon after, McCann discovered that in buying the business, he had become responsible for the $7 million in debt that the business had accrued and that his decision to buy 1-800-Flowers amounted to a big mistake.[12]

Determined to turn around this mistake, McCann turned his store in Queens into a telemarketing firm for flowers, but business was lackluster.[13] He tried to assuage his debtors while figuring out how to turn the business around. While on a trip to Dallas, he seized an opportunity to expand his business presented to him by Larry Zarin, who was marketing Kellogg's Nutri-Grain.[14] Zarin and McCann agreed that they would put advertisements on boxes of Nutri-Grain indicating that if customers bought the cereal, they could buy a dozen roses from 1-800-Flowers for $14.99. To their amazement, they received 30,000 orders for flowers, didn't have the floral capacity across the United States to fill them, and so created a box to ship flowers overnight via FedEx. And the rest has been history. A similar promotion worked with Zales jewelry stores, helping make the company known across the country (its network of florists is called BloomNet).[15]

In the early 1990s McCann and his brother and partner, Chris, decided they wanted to put their business online.[16] They met with Steve Case, one of the cofounders of AOL, and Ted Leonsis, and they were the first organization to have an online transaction over AOL. In the early days on the Internet, 1-800-Flowers.com had considerable competition. The company went public in 1999 and raised funds to create a better technological platform. By 2013 revenues had grown to $1 billion (including $200 million from franchises).[17]

Jim and Chris McCann and other managers at 1-800-Flowers.com continue to make decisions and learn to this day. 1-800-Flowers.com has become active in the social-mobile-local retail space and sells gifts for all occasions as well as flowers.[18] For example, 1-800-Flowers.com was the first organization to sell gifts on Facebook beginning at $5.[19] Clearly, learning and decision making have been crucial ingredients for the entrepreneurial success story behind 1-800-Flowers.com.[20]

Overview

"A Manager's Challenge" illustrates how decision making and learning are an ongoing challenge for managers that can profoundly influence organizational effectiveness. McCann's decision to seize an opportunity and buy a small flower shop and his subsequent decisions along the way have had a dramatic effect on his business.[21] The decisions managers make at all levels in companies large and small can change the growth and prosperity of these companies and the well-being of their employees, customers, and other stakeholders. Yet such decisions can be difficult to make because they are fraught with uncertainty.

In this chapter we examine how managers make decisions, and we explore how individual, group, and organizational factors affect the quality of the decisions they make and ultimately determine organizational performance. We discuss the nature of managerial decision making and examine some models of the decision-making process that help reveal the complexities of successful decision making. Then we outline the main steps of the decision-making process; in addition, we explore the biases that may cause capable managers to make poor decisions both as individuals and as members of a group. Next we examine how managers can promote organizational learning and creativity and improve the quality of decision making throughout an organization. Finally we discuss the important role of entrepreneurship in promoting organizational creativity, and we differentiate between entrepreneurs and intrapreneurs. By the end of this chapter you will appreciate the critical role of management decision making in creating a high-performing organization.

> **LO7-1**
>
> Understand the nature of managerial decision making, differentiate between programmed and nonprogrammed decisions, and explain why nonprogrammed decision making is a complex, uncertain process.

The Nature of Managerial Decision Making

Every time managers act to plan, organize, direct, or control organizational activities, they make a stream of decisions. In opening a new restaurant, for example, managers have to decide where to locate it, what kinds of food to provide, which people to employ, and so on. Decision making is a basic part of every task managers perform. In this chapter we study how these decisions are made.

As we discussed in the last three chapters, one of the main tasks facing a manager is to manage the organizational environment. Forces in the external environment give rise to many opportunities and threats for managers and their organizations. In addition, inside an organization managers must address many opportunities and threats that may arise as organizational resources are used. To deal with these opportunities and threats, managers must make decisions—that is, they must select one solution from a set of alternatives. **Decision making** is the process by which managers respond to opportunities and threats by analyzing the options and making determinations, or *decisions,* about specific organizational goals and courses of action. Good decisions result in the selection of appropriate goals and courses of action that increase organizational performance; bad decisions lower performance.

Decision making in response to opportunities occurs when managers search for ways to improve organizational performance to benefit customers, employees, and other stakeholder groups. In "A Manager's Challenge," Jim McCann seized the opportunities to buy a flower shop and expand his business in multiple ways including going online. *Decision making in response to threats* occurs when events inside or outside the organization adversely affect organizational performance and managers search for ways to increase performance.[22] Decision making is central to being a manager, and whenever managers engage in planning, organizing, leading, and controlling—their four principal tasks—they are constantly making decisions.

Managers are always searching for ways to make better decisions to improve organizational performance. At the same time they do their best to avoid costly mistakes that will hurt organizational performance. Examples of spectacularly good decisions include Martin Cooper's decision to develop the first cell phone at Motorola and Apple's decision to develop the iPod.[23] Examples of spectacularly bad decisions include the decision by managers at NASA and Morton Thiokol to launch the *Challenger* space shuttle—a decision that killed six astronauts in 1986—and the decision by NASA to launch the *Columbia* space shuttle in 2003, which killed seven astronauts.

decision making The process by which managers respond to opportunities and threats by analyzing options and making determinations about specific organizational goals and courses of action.

Programmed and Nonprogrammed Decision Making

Regardless of the specific decisions a manager makes, the decision-making process is either programmed or nonprogrammed.[24]

PROGRAMMED DECISION MAKING **Programmed decision making** is a *routine, virtually automatic* process. Programmed decisions are decisions that have been made so many times in the past that managers have developed rules or guidelines to be applied when certain situations inevitably occur. Programmed decision making takes place when a school principal asks the school board to hire a new teacher whenever student enrollment increases by 40 students; when a manufacturing supervisor hires new workers whenever existing workers' overtime increases by more than 10 percent; and when an office manager orders basic office supplies, such as paper and pens, whenever the inventory of supplies drops below a certain level. Furthermore, in the last example, the office manager probably orders the same amount of supplies each time.

This decision making is called *programmed* because office managers, for example, do not need to repeatedly make new judgments about what should be done. They can rely on long-established decision rules such as these:

- *Rule 1:* When the storage shelves are three-quarters empty, order more copy paper.
- *Rule 2:* When ordering paper, order enough to fill the shelves.

Managers can develop rules and guidelines to regulate all routine organizational activities. For example, rules can specify how a worker should perform a certain task, and rules can specify the quality standards that raw materials must meet to be acceptable. Most decision making that relates to the day-to-day running of an organization is programmed decision making. Examples include deciding how much inventory to hold, when to pay bills, when to bill customers, and when to order materials and supplies. Programmed decision making occurs when managers have the information they need to create rules that will guide decision making. There is little ambiguity involved in assessing when the stockroom is empty or counting the number of new students in class.

As profiled in the accompanying "Focus on Diversity" feature, effectively training new employees is essential to reap the benefits of programmed decision making.

Focus on Diversity

Programmed Decision Making at UPS

UPS is unrivaled in its use of programmed decision making. Practically all the motions, behaviors, and actions that its drivers perform each day have been carefully honed to maximize efficiency and minimize strain and injuries while delivering high-quality customer service. For example, a 12-step process prescribes how drivers should park their trucks, locate the package they are about to deliver, and step off the truck in 15.5 seconds (a process called "selection" at UPS).[25] Rules and routines such as these are carefully detailed in UPS's "340 Methods" manual (UPS actually has far more than 340 methods). Programmed decision making dictates where drivers should stop to get gas, how they should hold their keys in their hands, and how to lift and lower packages.[26]

When programmed decision making is so heavily relied on, ensuring that new employees learn tried-and-true routines is essential. UPS has traditionally taught new employees with a two-week period of lectures followed by practice.[27] In the 2000s, however, managers began to wonder if they needed to alter their training methods to suit their new Generation Y trainees (Generation Y typically refers to people born after 1980), who were not so keen on memorization and drills.[28] Generation Y trainees seemed to require more training time to become effective drivers (90–180 days compared to a typical average of 30–45 days), and quit rates for new drivers had increased.[29]

Given the fundamental importance of performance programs for UPS operations, managers decided to try to alter the training new hires receive so it would be better received by Generation Y trainees. In the late 2000s, UPS opened an innovative Landover, Maryland, training center called UPS Integrad, which has over 11,000 square feet and cost over $30 million to build and equip. Integrad was developed over a three-year period through a collaborative effort of over 170 people, including UPS top managers (many of whom started their careers with UPS as drivers), teams from Virginia Tech and MIT, animators from the Indian company Brainvisa, and forecasters from the Institute for the Future with the support of a grant from the Department of Labor for $1.8 million.[30] Results thus far suggest that Integrad training results in greater driver proficiency and fewer first-year accidents and injuries.[31]

Training at Integrad emphasizes hands-on learning.[32] For example, at Integrad a UPS truck with transparent sides is used to teach trainees selection so they can actually see the instructor performing the steps and then practice the steps themselves rather than trying to absorb the material in a lecture. Trainees can try different movements and see, with the help of computer diagrams and simulations, how following UPS routines will help protect them from injury and how debilitating work as a driver can be if they do not follow routines. Video recorders track and document what trainees do correctly and incorrectly so they can see it for themselves rather than relying on feedback from an instructor, which they might question. As Stephen Jones, Director of International Training & Development at UPS,[33] indicates, "Tell them what they did incorrectly, and they'll tell you, 'I didn't do that. You saw wrong.' This way we've got it on tape and they can see it for themselves."[34]

At Integrad, trainees get practice driving in a pseudo town that has been constructed in a parking lot.[35] They also watch animated demonstrations on computer screens, participate in simulations, take electronic quizzes, and receive scores on various components that are retained in a database to track learning and performance. Recognizing that Generation Y trainees have a lot of respect for expertise and reputation, older employees also are brought in to facilitate learning at Integrad. For example, long-time UPS employee Don Petersik, who has since retired from UPS,[36] trained facilitators at Integrad and shared stories with them to reinforce the UPS culture—such as the time he was just starting out as a preloader and, unknown to him, the founder of UPS, Jim Casey, approached him and said, "Hi, I'm Jim. I work for UPS."[37] As Petersik indicated, "What's new about the company now is that our teaching style matches your learning styles."[38] Clearly, when learning programmed decision making is of utmost importance, as it is at UPS, it is essential to take into account diversity in learning styles and approaches.

NONPROGRAMMED DECISION MAKING Suppose, however, managers are not certain that a course of action will lead to a desired outcome. Or in even more ambiguous terms, suppose managers are not even sure what they are trying to achieve. Obviously rules cannot be developed to predict uncertain events.

nonprogrammed decision making Nonroutine decision making that occurs in response to unusual, unpredictable opportunities and threats.

Nonprogrammed decision making is required for these *nonroutine* decisions. Nonprogrammed decisions are made in response to unusual or novel opportunities and threats. Nonprogrammed decision making occurs when there are no ready-made decision rules that managers can apply to a situation. Rules do not exist because the situation is unexpected or uncertain and managers lack the information they would need to develop rules to cover it. Examples of nonprogrammed decision making include decisions to invest in a new technology, develop a new kind of product, launch a new promotional campaign, enter a new market, expand internationally, or start a new business as did Jim McCann in "A Manager's Challenge."

intuition Feelings, beliefs, and hunches that come readily to mind, require little effort and information gathering, and result in on-the-spot decisions.

How do managers make decisions in the absence of decision rules? They may rely on their **intuition**—feelings, beliefs, and hunches that come readily to mind, require little effort and information gathering, and result in on-the-spot decisions.[39] Or they may make **reasoned judgments**—decisions that require time and effort and result from careful information gathering, generation of alternatives, and evaluation of alternatives. "Exercising" one's judgment

reasoned judgment A decision that requires time and effort and results from careful information gathering, generation of alternatives, and evaluation of alternatives.

Nonprogrammed decision making covers areas with no previous benchmarks or rubrics, such as seen in this photo.

is a more rational process than "going with" one's intuition. For reasons that we examine later in this chapter, both intuition and judgment often are flawed and can result in poor decision making. Thus the likelihood of error is much greater in nonprogrammed decision making than in programmed decision making.[40] In the remainder of this chapter, when we talk about decision making, we are referring to *nonprogrammed* decision making because it causes the most problems for managers and is inherently challenging.

Sometimes managers have to make rapid decisions and don't have time to carefully consider the issues involved. They must rely on their intuition to quickly respond to a pressing concern. For example, when fire chiefs, captains, and lieutenants manage firefighters battling dangerous, out-of-control fires, they often need to rely on their expert intuition to make on-the-spot decisions that will protect the lives of the firefighters and save the lives of others, contain the fires, and preserve property—decisions made in emergency situations entailing high uncertainty, high risk, and rapidly changing conditions.[41] In other cases managers do have time to make reasoned judgments, but there are no established rules to guide their decisions, such as when deciding whether to proceed with a proposed merger.

Regardless of the circumstances, making nonprogrammed decisions can result in effective or ineffective decision making. As indicated in the accompanying "Manager as a Person" feature, managers have to be on their guard to avoid being overconfident in decisions that result from either intuition or reasoned judgment.

Manager as a Person

Curbing Overconfidence

Should managers be confident in their intuition and reasoned judgments?[42] Decades of research by Nobel Prize winner Daniel Kahneman, his longtime collaborator the late Amos Tversky, and other researchers suggests that managers (like all people) tend to be overconfident in the decisions they make, whether based on intuition or reasoned judgment.[43] And with overconfidence comes failure to evaluate and rethink the wisdom of the decisions one makes and failure to learn from mistakes.[44]

Kahneman distinguishes between the intuition of managers who are truly expert in the content domain of a decision and the intuition of managers who have some knowledge and experience but are not true experts.[45] Although the intuition of both types can be faulty, that of experts is less likely to be flawed. This is why fire captains can make good decisions and why expert chess players can make good moves, in both cases without spending much time or deliberating carefully on what, for non-experts, is a complicated set of circumstances. What distinguishes expert managers from those with limited expertise is that the experts have extensive experience under conditions in which they receive quick and clear feedback about the outcomes of their decisions.[46]

Unfortunately managers who have some experience in a content area but are not true experts tend to be overly confident in their intuition and their judgments.[47] As Kahneman puts it, "People jump to statistical conclusions on the basis of very weak evidence. We form powerful intuitions about trends and about the replicability of results on the basis of information that is truly inadequate."[48] Not only do managers, and all people, tend to be overconfident about their intuition and judgments, but they also tend not to learn from mistakes. Compounding this undue optimism is the human tendency to be overconfident in one's own abilities and influence over unpredictable events. Surveys have found that the majority of people think they are above average, make better decisions, and are less prone to making bad decisions than others (of course it is impossible for most people to be above average on any dimension).[49]

Examples of managerial overconfidence abound. Research has consistently found that mergers tend to turn out poorly—postmerger profitability declines, stock prices drop, and so forth. For example, Chrysler had the biggest profits of the three largest automakers in the United States when it merged with Daimler; the merger was a failure and both Chrysler and Daimler would have been better off if it never had happened.[50] One would imagine that top executives and boards of directors would learn from this research and from articles in the business press about the woes of merged companies (such as the AOL–Time Warner merger and the Hewlett-Packard–Compaq merger).[51] Evidently not. Top managers seem to overconfidently believe that they can succeed where others have failed.[52] Similarly, whereas fewer than 35 percent of new small ventures succeed as viable businesses for more than five years, entrepreneurs, on average, tend to think that they have a 6 out of 10 chance of being successful.[53]

Jeffrey Pfeffer, a professor at Stanford University's Graduate School of Business, suggests that managers can avoid the perils of overconfidence by critically evaluating the decisions they have made and the outcomes of those decisions. They should admit to themselves when they have made a mistake and really learn from their mistakes (rather than dismissing them as flukes or situations out of their control). In addition, managers should be leery of too much agreement at the top. As Pfeffer puts it, "If two people agree all the time, one of them is redundant."[54]

The classical and administrative decision-making models reveal many of the assumptions, complexities, and pitfalls that affect decision making. These models help reveal the factors that managers and other decision makers must be aware of to improve the quality of their decision making. Keep in mind, however, that the classical and administrative models are just guides that can help managers understand the decision-making process. In real life the process is typically not cut-and-dried, but these models can help guide a manager through it.

The Classical Model

classical decision-making model A prescriptive approach to decision making based on the assumption that the decision maker can identify and evaluate all possible alternatives and their consequences and rationally choose the most appropriate course of action.

One of the earliest models of decision making, the **classical model**, is *prescriptive,* which means it specifies how decisions *should* be made. Managers using the classical model make a series of simplifying assumptions about the nature of the decision-making process (see Figure 7.1). The premise of the classical model is that once managers recognize the need to make a decision, they should be able to generate a complete list of *all* alternatives and consequences and make the best choice. In other words, the classical model assumes managers have access to *all* the information they need to make the **optimum decision**, which is the most appropriate decision possible in light of what they believe to be the most desirable consequences for the organization. Furthermore, the classical model assumes managers can easily list their own preferences for each alternative and rank them from least to most preferred to make the optimum decision.

optimum decision The most appropriate decision in light of what managers believe to be the most desirable consequences for the organization.

The Administrative Model

administrative model An approach to decision making that explains why decision making is inherently uncertain and risky and why managers usually make satisfactory rather than optimum decisions.

James March and Herbert Simon disagreed with the underlying assumptions of the classical model of decision making. In contrast, they proposed that managers in the real world do *not* have access to all the information they need to make a decision. Moreover, they pointed out that even if all information were readily available, many managers would lack the mental or psychological ability to absorb and evaluate it correctly. As a result, March and Simon developed the **administrative model** of decision making to explain why decision making is always an inherently uncertain and risky process—and why managers can rarely make decisions in the manner prescribed by the classical model. The administrative model is based on three important concepts: *bounded rationality, incomplete information,* and *satisficing.*

Figure 7.1

The Classical Model of Decision Making

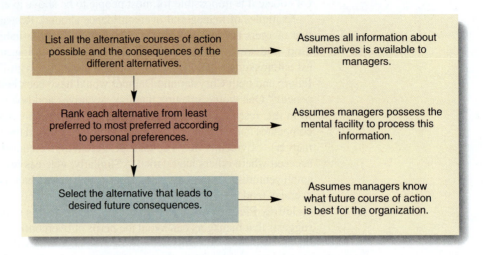

BOUNDED RATIONALITY   March and Simon pointed out that human decision-making capabilities are bounded by people's cognitive limitations—that is, limitations in their ability to interpret, process, and act on information.[55] They argued that the limitations of human intelligence constrain the ability of decision makers to determine the optimum decision. March and Simon coined the term **bounded rationality** to describe the situation in which the number of alternatives a manager must identify is so great and the amount of information so vast that it is difficult for the manager to even come close to evaluating it all before making a decision.[56]

INCOMPLETE INFORMATION   Even if managers had unlimited ability to evaluate information, they still would not be able to arrive at the optimum decision because they would have incomplete information. Information is incomplete because the full range of decision-making alternatives is unknowable in most situations, and the consequences associated with known alternatives are uncertain.[57] In other words, information is incomplete because of risk and uncertainty, ambiguity, and time constraints (see Figure 7.2).

RISK AND UNCERTAINTY   As we saw in Chapter 6, forces in the organizational environment are constantly changing. **Risk** is present when managers know the possible outcomes of a particular course of action and can assign probabilities to them. For example, managers in the biotechnology industry know that new drugs have a 10 percent probability of successfully passing advanced clinical trials and a 90 percent probability of failing. These probabilities

bounded rationality Cognitive limitations that constrain one's ability to interpret, process, and act on information.

risk The degree of probability that the possible outcomes of a particular course of action will occur.

Figure 7.2

Why Information Is Incomplete

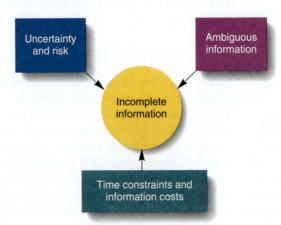

reflect the experiences of thousands of drugs that have gone through advanced clinical trials. Thus when managers in the biotechnology industry decide to submit a drug for testing, they know that there is only a 10 percent chance that the drug will succeed, but at least they have some information on which to base their decision.

uncertainty Unpredictability.

When **uncertainty** exists, the probabilities of alternative outcomes *cannot* be determined and future outcomes are *unknown*. Managers are working blind. Because the probability of a given outcome occurring is not known, managers have little information to use in making a decision. For example, in 1993, when Apple Computer introduced the Newton, its personal digital assistant (PDA), managers had no idea what the probability of a successful product launch for a PDA might be. Because Apple was the first to market this totally new product, there was no body of well-known data that Apple's managers could draw on to calculate the probability of a successful launch. Uncertainty plagues most managerial decision making.[58] Although Apple's initial launch of its PDA was a disaster due to technical problems, an improved version was more successful.

ambiguous information Information that can be interpreted in multiple and often conflicting ways.

AMBIGUOUS INFORMATION   A second reason why information is incomplete is that much of the information managers have at their disposal is **ambiguous information**. Its meaning is not clear—it can be interpreted in multiple and often conflicting ways.[59] Take a look at Figure 7.3. Do you see a young woman or an old woman? In a similar fashion, managers often interpret the same piece of information differently and make decisions based on their own interpretations.

TIME CONSTRAINTS AND INFORMATION COSTS   The third reason why information is incomplete is that managers have neither the time nor the money to search for all possible alternative solutions and evaluate all the potential consequences of those alternatives. Consider the situation confronting a Ford Motor Company purchasing manager who has one month to choose a supplier for a small engine part. There are 20,000 potential suppliers for this part in the United States alone. Given the time available, the purchasing manager cannot contact all potential suppliers and ask each for its terms (price, delivery schedules, and so on). Moreover, even if the time were available, the costs of obtaining the information, including the manager's own time, would be prohibitive.

satisficing Searching for and choosing an acceptable, or satisfactory, response to problems and opportunities, rather than trying to make the best decision.

SATISFICING   March and Simon argued that managers do not attempt to discover every alternative when faced with bounded rationality, an uncertain future, unquantifiable risks, considerable ambiguity, time constraints, and high information costs. Rather, they use a strategy known as **satisficing**, which is exploring a limited sample of all potential alternatives.[60]

Figure 7.3

Ambiguous Information: Young Woman or Old Woman?

When managers satisfice, they search for and choose acceptable, or satisfactory, ways to respond to problems and opportunities rather than trying to make the optimal decision.[61] In the case of the Ford purchasing manager's search, for example, satisficing may involve asking a limited number of suppliers for their terms, trusting that they are representative of suppliers in general, and making a choice from that set. Although this course of action is reasonable from the perspective of the purchasing manager, it may mean that a potentially superior supplier is overlooked.

March and Simon pointed out that managerial decision making is often more art than science. In the real world, managers must rely on their intuition and judgment to make what seems to them to be the best decision in the face of uncertainty and ambiguity.[62] Moreover, managerial decision making is often fast-paced; managers use their experience and judgment to make crucial decisions under conditions of incomplete information. Although there is nothing wrong with this approach, decision makers should be aware that human judgment is often flawed. As a result, even the best managers sometimes make poor decisions.[63]

Steps in the Decision-Making Process

LO7-2

Describe the six steps managers should take to make the best decisions, and explain how cognitive biases can lead managers to make poor decisions.

Using the work of March and Simon as a basis, researchers have developed a step-by-step model of the decision-making process and the issues and problems that managers confront at each step. Perhaps the best way to introduce this model is to examine the real-world nonprogrammed decision making of Scott McNealy at a crucial point in Sun Microsystems' history. McNealy was a founder of Sun Microsystems and was the chairman of the board of directors until Sun was acquired by Oracle in 2010.[64]

In early August 1985, Scott McNealy, then CEO of Sun Microsystems[65] (a hardware and software computer workstation manufacturer focused on network solutions), had to decide whether to go ahead with the launch of the new Carrera workstation computer, scheduled for September 10. Sun's managers had chosen the date nine months earlier when the development plan for the Carrera was first proposed. McNealy knew it would take at least a month to prepare for the September 10 launch, and the decision could not be put off.

Customers were waiting for the new machine, and McNealy wanted to be the first to provide a workstation that took advantage of Motorola's powerful 16-megahertz 68020 microprocessor. Capitalizing on this opportunity would give Sun a significant edge over Apollo, its main competitor in the workstation market. McNealy knew, however, that committing to the September 10 launch date was risky. Motorola was having production problems with the 16-megahertz 68020 microprocessor and could not guarantee Sun a steady supply of these chips. Moreover, the operating system software was not completely free of bugs.

If Sun launched the Carrera on September 10, the company might have to ship some machines with software that was not fully operational, was likely to crash the system, and utilized Motorola's less powerful 12-megahertz 68020 microprocessor instead of the 16-megahertz version.[66] Of course Sun could later upgrade the microprocessor and operating system software in any machines purchased by early customers, but the company's reputation would suffer. If Sun did not go ahead with the September launch, the company would miss an important opportunity.[67] Rumors were circulating in the industry that Apollo would be launching a new machine of its own in December.

McNealy clearly had a difficult decision to make. He had to decide quickly whether to launch the Carrera, but he did not have all the facts. He did not know, for example, whether the microprocessor or operating system problems could be resolved by September 10; nor did he know whether Apollo was going to launch a competing machine in December. But he could not wait to find these things out—he had to make a decision. We'll see what he decided later in the chapter.

Many managers who must make important decisions with incomplete information face dilemmas similar to McNealy's. Managers should consciously follow six steps to make a good decision (see Figure 7.4).[68] We review these steps in the remainder of this section.

Figure 7.4

Six Steps in Decision Making

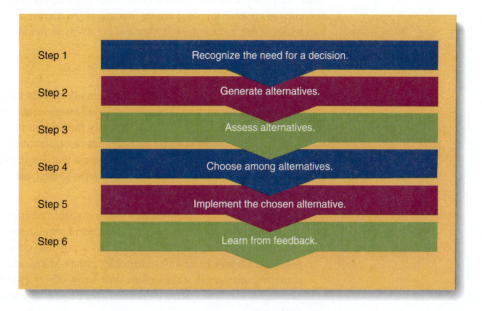

Recognize the Need for a Decision

The first step in the decision-making process is to recognize the need for a decision. Scott McNealy recognized this need, and he realized a decision had to be made quickly.

Some stimuli usually spark the realization that a decision must be made. These stimuli often become apparent because changes in the organizational environment result in new kinds of opportunities and threats. This happened at Sun Microsystems. The September 10 launch date had been set when it seemed that Motorola chips would be readily available. Later, with the supply of chips in doubt and bugs remaining in the system software, Sun was in danger of failing to meet its launch date.

The stimuli that spark decision making are as likely to result from the actions of managers inside an organization as they are from changes in the external environment.[69] An organization possesses a set of skills, competencies, and resources in its employees and in departments such as marketing, manufacturing, and research and development. Managers who actively pursue opportunities to use these competencies create the need to make decisions. Managers thus can be proactive or reactive in recognizing the need to make a decision, but the important issue is that they must recognize this need and respond in a timely and appropriate way.[70]

Generate Alternatives

Having recognized the need to make a decision, a manager must generate a set of feasible alternative courses of action to take in response to the opportunity or threat. Management experts cite failure to properly generate and consider different alternatives as one reason why managers sometimes make bad decisions.[71] In the Sun Microsystems decision, the alternatives seemed clear: go ahead with the September 10 launch or delay the launch until the Carrera was 100 percent ready for market introduction. Often, however, the alternatives are not so obvious or so clearly specified.

One major problem is that managers may find it difficult to come up with creative alternative solutions to specific problems. Perhaps some of them are used to seeing the world from a single perspective—they have a certain "managerial mind-set." Many managers find it difficult to view problems from a fresh perspective. According to best-selling management author Peter Senge, we all are trapped within our personal mental models of the world—our ideas about what is important and how the world works.[72] Generating creative alternatives to solve problems and take advantage of opportunities may require that we abandon our existing mind-sets and develop new ones—something that usually is difficult to do.

The importance of getting managers to set aside their mental models of the world and generate creative alternatives is reflected in the growth of interest in the work of authors such as Peter Senge and Edward de Bono, who have popularized techniques for stimulating problem solving and creative thinking among managers.[73] Later in this chapter, we discuss the important issues of organizational learning and creativity in detail.

Assess Alternatives

Once managers have generated a set of alternatives, they must evaluate the advantages and disadvantages of each one.[74] The key to a good assessment of the alternatives is to define the opportunity or threat exactly and then specify the criteria that *should* influence the selection of alternatives for responding to the problem or opportunity. One reason for bad decisions is that managers often fail to specify the criteria that are important in reaching a decision.[75] In general, successful managers use four criteria to evaluate the pros and cons of alternative courses of action (see Figure 7.5):

1. *Legality:* Managers must ensure that a possible course of action will not violate any domestic or international laws or government regulations.

2. *Ethicalness:* Managers must ensure that a possible course of action is ethical and will not unnecessarily harm any stakeholder group. Many decisions managers make may help some organizational stakeholders and harm others (see Chapter 4). When examining alternative courses of action, managers need to be clear about the potential effects of their decisions.

3. *Economic feasibility:* Managers must decide whether the alternatives are economically feasible—that is, whether they can be accomplished given the organization's performance goals. Typically managers perform a cost–benefit analysis of the various alternatives to determine which one will have the best net financial payoff.

4. *Practicality:* Managers must decide whether they have the capabilities and resources required to implement the alternative, and they must be sure the alternative will not threaten the attainment of other organizational goals. At first glance an alternative might seem economically superior to other alternatives; but if managers realize it is likely to threaten other important projects, they might decide it is not practical after all.

Figure 7.5

General Criteria for Evaluating Possible Courses of Action

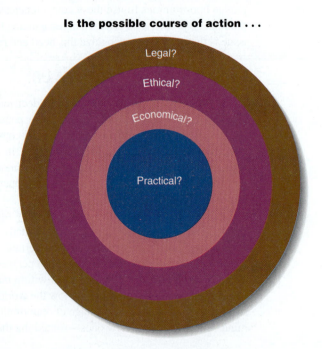

Is the possible course of action . . .

Legal?

Ethical?

Economical?

Practical?

Often a manager must consider these four criteria simultaneously. Scott McNealy framed the problem at hand at Sun Microsystems quite well. The key question was whether to go ahead with the September 10 launch date. Two main criteria were influencing McNealy's choice: the need to ship a machine that was as "complete" as possible (the *practicality* criterion) and the need to beat Apollo to market with a new workstation (the *economic feasibility* criterion). These two criteria conflicted. The first suggested that the launch should be delayed; the second, that the launch should go ahead. McNealy's actual choice was based on the relative importance that he assigned to these two criteria. In fact, Sun Microsystems went ahead with the September 10 launch, which suggests that McNealy thought the need to beat Apollo to market was the more important criterion.

Some of the worst managerial decisions can be traced to poor assessment of the alternatives, such as the decision to launch the *Challenger* space shuttle, mentioned earlier. In that case, the desire of NASA and Morton Thiokol managers to demonstrate to the public the success of the U.S. space program in order to ensure future funding (*economic feasibility*) conflicted with the need to ensure the safety of the astronauts (*ethicalness*). Managers deemed the economic criterion more important and decided to launch the space shuttle even though there were unanswered questions about safety. Tragically, some of the same decision-making problems that resulted in the *Challenger* tragedy led to the demise of the *Columbia* space shuttle 17 years later, killing all seven astronauts on board.[76] In both the *Challenger* and the *Columbia* disasters, safety questions were raised before the shuttles were launched; safety concerns took second place to budgets, economic feasibility, and schedules; top decision makers seemed to ignore or downplay the inputs of those with relevant technical expertise; and speaking up was discouraged.[77] Rather than making safety a top priority, decision makers seemed overly concerned with keeping on schedule and within budget.[78]

As indicated in the accompanying "Ethics in Action" feature, to help ensure that decisions meet the *ethicalness* criteria, some organizations have created the position of chief sustainability officer.

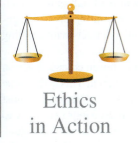

Ethics in Action

Helping to Ensure Decisions Contribute to Sustainability

Some large organizations have added the position of chief sustainability officer to their ranks of top managers reporting to the chief executive officer or chief operating officer. Chief sustainability officers are typically concerned with helping to ensure that decisions that are made in organizations conserve energy and protect the environment.[79] For example, Scott Wicker is the first chief sustainability officer for UPS.[80] Wicker leads a team that presides over a sustainability directors committee and a sustainability working committee focused on developing performance indicators and goals pertaining to sustainability to guide decision making.[81]

Linda Fisher is the vice president of DuPont Safety, Health & Environment and chief sustainability officer at DuPont. Before she joined DuPont, she held a variety of positions related to sustainability, including the position of deputy administrator of the Environmental Protection Agency.[82] Fisher leads efforts at DuPont to make decisions that help to reduce energy consumption, toxins and carcinogens in the air, and greenhouse gas emissions and help DuPont's customers reduce their environmental footprints. Protecting both the environment and human safety is a priority for Fisher and DuPont.[83]

Beatriz Perez is the chief sustainability officer for Coca-Cola, leading a global office of sustainability.[84] While Coca-Cola has over 500 different brands yielding over 3,500 products, sustainability is a companywide initiative centered around major goals and initiatives.[85] These goals include water conservation and returning to the environment the water that Coca-Cola consumes in making its products, reducing packaging waste and increasing recycling, and protecting the environment from pollution by, for example, using hybrid trucks, having energy-efficient manufacturing facilities, and improving the sustainability of refrigeration methods.[86] Clearly, ensuring that decisions contribute to sustainability means much more than simply complying with legal requirements. Having chief sustainability officers with dedicated teams and offices focused on sustainability might be a step in the right direction.

Choose among Alternatives

Once the set of alternative solutions has been carefully evaluated, the next task is to rank the various alternatives (using the criteria discussed in the previous section) and make a decision. When ranking alternatives, managers must be sure *all* the information available is brought to bear on the problem or issue at hand. As the Sun Microsystems case indicates, however, identifying all *relevant* information for a decision does not mean the manager has *complete* information; in most instances, information is incomplete.

Perhaps more serious than the existence of incomplete information is the often-documented tendency of managers to ignore critical information, even when it is available. We discuss this tendency in detail later when we examine the operation of cognitive biases and groupthink.

Implement the Chosen Alternative

Once a decision has been made and an alternative has been selected, it must be implemented, and many subsequent and related decisions must be made. After a course of action has been decided—say, to develop a new line of women's clothing—thousands of subsequent decisions are necessary to implement it. These decisions would involve recruiting dress designers, obtaining fabrics, finding high-quality manufacturers, and signing contracts with clothing stores to sell the new line.

Although the need to make subsequent decisions to implement the chosen course of action may seem obvious, many managers make a decision and then fail to act on it. This is the same as not making a decision at all. To ensure that a decision is implemented, top managers must assign to middle managers the responsibility for making the follow-up decisions necessary to achieve the goal. They must give middle managers sufficient resources to achieve the goal, and they must hold the middle managers accountable for their performance. If the middle managers succeed in implementing the decision, they should be rewarded; if they fail, they should be subject to sanctions.

Learn from Feedback

The final step in the decision-making process is learning from feedback. Effective managers always conduct a retrospective analysis to see what they can learn from past successes or failures. Managers who do not evaluate the results of their decisions do not learn from experience; instead they stagnate and are likely to make the same mistakes again and again.[87] To avoid this problem, managers must establish a formal procedure with which they can learn from the results of past decisions. The procedure should include these steps:

1. Compare what actually happened to what was expected to happen as a result of the decision.
2. Explore why any expectations for the decision were not met.
3. Derive guidelines that will help in future decision making.

Managers who always strive to learn from past mistakes and successes are likely to continuously improve the decisions they make. A significant amount of learning can take place when the outcomes of decisions are evaluated, and this assessment can produce enormous benefits. Learning from feedback is particularly important for entrepreneurs who start their own businesses, as profiled in the accompanying "Management Insight" feature.

Management Insight

Decision Making and Learning from Feedback at GarageTek

Decision making has been an ongoing challenge for Marc Shuman, founder and president of GarageTek, headquartered in Melville, New York.[88] Since founding his company less than 15 years ago,[89] he has met this challenge time and time again, recognizing when decisions need to be made and learning from feedback about prior decisions.

The interior of a garage showing a GarageTek custom system designed to organize storage capacity and uses for home garage space. The franchise has experienced its ups and downs, but, thanks to good management, business continues to grow.

Shuman was working with his father in a small business, designing and building interiors of department stores, when he created and installed a series of wall panels with flexible shelving for a store to display its merchandise. When he realized that some of his employees were using the same concept in their own homes to organize the clutter in their basements and garages, he recognized that he had a potential opportunity to start a new business, GarageTek, designing and installing custom garage systems to organize and maximize storage capacities and uses for home garage space.[90] A strong housing market at the time, the popularity of closet organizing systems, and the recognition that many people's lives were getting busier and more complicated led him to believe that home owners would be glad to pay someone to design and install a system that would help them gain control over some of the clutter in their lives.[91]

Schuman decided to franchise his idea because he feared that other entrepreneurs were probably having similar thoughts and competition could be around the corner.[92] Within three years GarageTek had 57 franchises in 33 states, contributing revenues to the home office of around $12 million. While this would seem to be an enviable track record of success, Shuman recognized that although many of the franchises were succeeding, some were having serious problems. With the help of a consulting company, Shuman and home office managers set about trying to figure out why some franchises were failing. They gathered detailed information about each franchise: the market served, pricing strategies, costs, managerial talent, and franchisee investment. From this information, Shuman learned that the struggling franchises tended either to have lower levels of capital investment behind them or to be managed by nonowners.[93]

Shuman learned from this experience. He now has improved decision criteria for accepting new franchisees to help ensure that their investments of time and money lead to a successful franchise.[94] Shuman also decided to give new franchisees much more training and support than he had in the past. New franchisees now receive two weeks of training at the home office that culminates in their preparing a one-year marketing and business plan;[95] on-site assistance in sales, marketing, and operations; a multivolume training manual; a sales and marketing kit; and access to databases and GarageTek's intranet. Franchisees learn from each other through monthly conference calls and regional and national meetings.[96]

By 2014 GarageTek had franchises covering 60 markets in the United States and also had expanded overseas into the United Kingdom, Australia, New Zealand, South Africa, and Russia.[97] And Shuman continues to make decisions day in and day out; in his words, "We're not, by any stretch, done."[98]

Cognitive Biases and Decision Making

In the 1970s psychologists Daniel Kahneman and the late Amos Tversky suggested that because all decision makers are subject to bounded rationality, they tend to use **heuristics**, which are rules of thumb that simplify the process of making decisions.[99] Kahneman and Tversky argued that rules of thumb are often useful because they help decision makers make sense of complex, uncertain, and ambiguous information. Sometimes, however, the use of heuristics can lead to systematic errors in the way decision makers process information about alternatives and make decisions. **Systematic errors** are errors that people make over and over and that result in poor decision making. Because of cognitive biases, which are caused by systematic errors, otherwise capable managers may end up making bad decisions.[100] Four sources of bias that can adversely affect the way managers make decisions are prior hypotheses, representativeness, the illusion of control, and escalating commitment (see Figure 7.6).

heuristics Rules of thumb that simplify decision making.

systematic errors Errors that people make over and over and that result in poor decision making.

Prior Hypothesis Bias

Decision makers who have strong prior beliefs about the relationship between two variables tend to make decisions based on those beliefs *even when presented with evidence that their beliefs are wrong*. In doing so, they fall victim to **prior hypothesis bias**. Moreover, decision makers tend to seek and use information that is consistent with their prior beliefs and to ignore information that contradicts those beliefs.

prior hypothesis bias A cognitive bias resulting from the tendency to base decisions on strong prior beliefs even if evidence shows that those beliefs are wrong.

Representativeness Bias

Many decision makers inappropriately generalize from a small sample or even from a single vivid case or episode; these are instances of the **representativeness bias**. Consider the case of a bookstore manager in the southeast United States who decided to partner with a local independent school for a "Book Day": Students and parents from the school would be encouraged to buy books at the bookstore as a fund-raiser for the school, and the bookstore would share a small portion of proceeds from these sales with the school. After quite a bit of planning, the Book Day generated lackluster sales and publicity for the store. When other public and independent schools approached the manager with similar proposals for fund-raising and Book Days, the manager declined based on her initial bad experience. As a result, she lost real opportunities to expand sales and gain word-of-mouth advertising and publicity for her store; her initial bad experience was the result of an inadvertent scheduling snafu at the school, whereby a key lacrosse game was scheduled the same day as the Book Day.

representativeness bias A cognitive bias resulting from the tendency to generalize inappropriately from a small sample or from a single vivid event or episode.

Illusion of Control

Other errors in decision making result from the **illusion of control**, which is the tendency of decision makers to overestimate their ability to control activities and events. Top managers seem particularly prone to this bias. Having worked their way to the top of an organization, they tend to have an exaggerated sense of their own worth and are overconfident about their ability to succeed and to control events.[101] The illusion of control causes managers to overestimate the odds of a favorable outcome and, consequently, to make inappropriate decisions. As mentioned earlier, most mergers turn out unfavorably; yet time and time again, top managers overestimate their abilities to combine companies with vastly different cultures in a successful merger.[102]

illusion of control A source of cognitive bias resulting from the tendency to overestimate one's own ability to control activities and events.

Figure 7.6

Sources of Cognitive Bias at the Individual and Group Levels

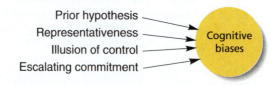

Escalating Commitment

Having already committed significant resources to a course of action, some managers commit more resources to the project *even if they receive feedback that the project is failing*.[103] Feelings of personal responsibility for a project apparently bias the analysis of decision makers and lead to this escalating commitment. The managers decide to increase their investment of time and money in a course of action and even ignore evidence that it is illegal, unethical, uneconomical, or impractical (see Figure 7.5). Often the more appropriate decision would be to cut their losses and run.

Consider the case of Mark Gracin, who owns a landscape company in the southwest United States. Gracin had a profitable business doing general landscape work (such as mowing grass, picking up leaves, and fertilizing) for home owners in a large city. To expand his business into landscape design, he hired a landscape designer, advertised landscape design services in local newspapers, and gave his existing customers free design proposals for their front and back yards. After a few months, Gracin had no landscape design customers. Still convinced that landscape design was a great way to expand his business despite this negative feedback, he decided he needed to do more. He rented a small office for his landscape designer (who used to work from her own home office) to work from and meet with clients, hired an assistant for the designer, had a public relations firm create promotional materials, and started advertising on local TV. These efforts also did not generate sufficient interest in his landscape design services to offset their costs. Yet Gracin's escalating commitment caused him to continue to pour money into trying to drum up business in landscape design. In fact, Gracin reluctantly decided to abandon his landscape design services only when he realized he could no longer afford their mounting costs.

Be Aware of Your Biases

How can managers avoid the negative effects of cognitive biases and improve their decision-making and problem-solving abilities? Managers must become aware of biases and their effects, and they must identify their own personal style of making decisions.[104] One useful way for managers to analyze their decision-making style is to review two decisions that they made recently—one decision that turned out well and one that turned out poorly. Problem-solving experts recommend that managers start by determining how much time to spend on each of the decision-making steps, such as gathering information to identify the pros and cons of alternatives or ranking the alternatives, to make sure they spend sufficient time on each step.[105]

Another recommended technique for examining decision-making style is for managers to list the criteria they typically use to assess and evaluate alternatives—the heuristics (rules of thumb) they typically employ, their personal biases, and so on—and then critically evaluate the appropriateness of these different factors.

Many individual managers are likely to have difficulty identifying their own biases, so it is often advisable for managers to scrutinize their own assumptions by working with other managers to help expose weaknesses in their decision-making style. In this context, the issue of group decision making becomes important.

Group Decision Making

Many (or perhaps most) important organizational decisions are made by groups or teams of managers rather than by individuals. Group decision making is superior to individual decision making in several respects. When managers work as a team to make decisions and solve problems, their choices of alternatives are less likely to fall victim to the biases and errors discussed previously. They are able to draw on the combined skills, competencies, and accumulated knowledge of group members and thereby improve their ability to generate feasible alternatives and make good decisions. Group decision making also allows managers to process more information and to correct one another's errors. And in the implementation phase, all managers affected by the decisions agree to cooperate. When a group of managers makes a decision (as opposed to one top manager making a decision and imposing it on subordinate managers), the probability that the decision will be implemented successfully increases. (We discuss how to encourage employee participation in decision making in Chapter 14.)

Some potential disadvantages are associated with group decision making. Groups often take much longer than individuals to make decisions. Getting two or more managers to agree to the same solution can be difficult because managers' interests and preferences are often different. In addition, just like decision making by individual managers, group decision making can be undermined by biases. A major source of group bias is *groupthink*.

The Perils of Groupthink

groupthink A pattern of faulty and biased decision making that occurs in groups whose members strive for agreement among themselves at the expense of accurately assessing information relevant to a decision.

Groupthink is a pattern of faulty and biased decision making that occurs in groups whose members strive for agreement among themselves at the expense of accurately assessing information relevant to a decision.[106] When managers are subject to groupthink, they collectively embark on a course of action without developing appropriate criteria to evaluate alternatives. Typically a group rallies around one central manager, such as the CEO, and the course of action that manager supports. Group members become blindly committed to that course of action without evaluating its merits. Commitment is often based on an emotional, rather than an objective, assessment of the optimal course of action.

The decision President Kennedy and his advisers made to launch the unfortunate Bay of Pigs invasion in Cuba in 1962, the decisions made by President Johnson and his advisers from 1964 to 1967 to escalate the war in Vietnam, the decision made by President Nixon and his advisers in 1972 to cover up the Watergate break-in, and the decision made by NASA and Morton Thiokol in 1986 to launch the ill-fated *Challenger* shuttle—all were likely influenced by groupthink. After the fact, decision makers such as these who may fall victim to groupthink are often surprised that their decision-making process and outcomes were so flawed.

When groupthink occurs, pressures for agreement and harmony within a group have the unintended effect of discouraging individuals from raising issues that run counter to majority opinion. For example, when managers at NASA and Morton Thiokol fell victim to groupthink, they convinced each other that all was well and that there was no need to delay the launch of the *Challenger* space shuttle.

Devil's Advocacy and Dialectical Inquiry

devil's advocacy Critical analysis of a preferred alternative, made in response to challenges raised by a group member who, playing the role of devil's advocate, defends unpopular or opposing alternatives for the sake of argument.

The existence of cognitive biases and groupthink raises the question of how to improve the quality of group and individual decision making so managers make decisions that are realistic and are based on thorough evaluation of alternatives. Two techniques known to counteract groupthink and cognitive biases are devil's advocacy and dialectic inquiry (see Figure 7.7).[107]

Devil's advocacy is a critical analysis of a preferred alternative to ascertain its strengths and weaknesses before it is implemented.[108] Typically one member of the decision-making group plays the role of devil's advocate. The devil's advocate critiques and challenges the

Figure 7.7

Devil's Advocacy and Dialectical Inquiry

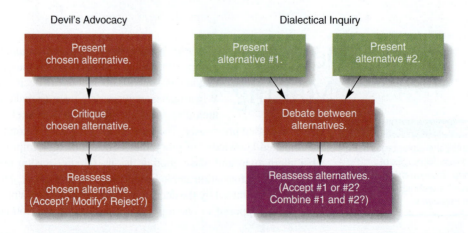

way the group evaluated alternatives and chose one over the others. The purpose of devil's advocacy is to identify all the reasons that might make the preferred alternative unacceptable. In this way, decision makers can be made aware of the possible perils of recommended courses of action.

dialectical inquiry Critical analysis of two preferred alternatives in order to find an even better alternative for the organization to adopt.

Dialectical inquiry goes one step further. Two groups of managers are assigned to a problem, and each group is responsible for evaluating alternatives and selecting one of them.[109] Top managers hear each group present its preferred alternative, and then each group critiques the other's position. During this debate, top managers challenge both groups' positions to uncover potential problems and perils associated with their solutions. The goal is to find an even better alternative course of action for the organization to adopt.

Both devil's advocacy and dialectical inquiry can help counter the effects of cognitive biases and groupthink.[110] In practice, devil's advocacy is probably easier to implement because it involves less managerial time and effort than does dialectical inquiry.

Diversity among Decision Makers

LO7-4

Explain the role that organizational learning and creativity play in helping managers to improve their decisions.

Another way to improve group decision making is to promote diversity in decision-making groups (see Chapter 5).[111] Bringing together managers of both genders from various ethnic, national, and functional backgrounds broadens the range of life experiences and opinions that group members can draw on as they generate, assess, and choose among alternatives. Moreover, diverse groups are sometimes less prone to groupthink because group members already differ from each other and thus are less subject to pressures for uniformity.

Organizational Learning and Creativity

The quality of managerial decision making ultimately depends on innovative responses to opportunities and threats. How can managers increase their ability to make nonprogrammed decisions that will allow them to adapt to, modify, and even drastically alter their task environments so they can continually increase organizational performance? The answer is by encouraging organizational learning.[112]

organizational learning The process through which managers seek to improve employees' desire and ability to understand and manage the organization and its task environment.

Organizational learning is the process through which managers seek to improve employees' desire and ability to understand and manage the organization and its task environment so employees can make decisions that continuously raise organizational effectiveness.[113] A **learning organization** is one in which managers do everything possible to maximize the ability of individuals and groups to think and behave creatively and thus maximize the potential for organizational learning to take place. At the heart of organizational learning is **creativity**, which is the ability of a decision maker to discover original and novel ideas that lead to feasible alternative courses of action. Encouraging creativity among managers is such a pressing organizational concern that many organizations hire outside experts to help them develop programs to train their managers in the art of creative thinking and problem solving.

learning organization An organization in which managers try to maximize the ability of individuals and groups to think and behave creatively and thus maximize the potential for organizational learning to take place.

creativity A decision maker's ability to discover original and novel ideas that lead to feasible alternative courses of action.

Get off email and lose the desk! Giving yourself and your employees the time and space to know that contributions off the beaten track are valued increases the ability to think outside the box.

Creating a Learning Organization

How can managers foster a learning organization? Learning theorist Peter Senge identified five principles for creating a learning organization (see Figure 7.8):[114]

1. For organizational learning to occur, top managers must allow every person in the organization to develop a sense of *personal mastery*. Managers must empower employees and allow them to experiment, create, and explore what they want.

2. As part of attaining personal mastery, organizations need to encourage employees to develop and use *complex mental models*—sophisticated ways of thinking that challenge them to find new or better ways of performing a task—to deepen their understanding of what is involved in a particular activity. Here Senge argued that managers must encourage employees to develop a taste for experimenting and risk taking.[115]

3. Managers must do everything they can to promote group creativity. Senge thought that *team learning* (learning that takes place in a group or team) is more important than individual learning in increasing organizational learning. He pointed out that most important decisions are made in subunits such as groups, functions, and divisions.

4. Managers must emphasize the importance of *building a shared vision*—a common mental model that all organizational members use to frame problems or opportunities.

5. Managers must encourage *systems thinking* (a concept drawn from systems theory, discussed in Chapter 2). Senge emphasized that to create a learning organization, managers must recognize the effects of one level of learning on another. Thus, for example, there is little point in creating teams to facilitate team learning if managers do not also take steps to give employees the freedom to develop a sense of personal mastery.

Building a learning organization requires that managers change their management assumptions radically. Developing a learning organization is neither a quick nor an easy process. Senge worked with Ford Motor Company to help managers make Ford a learning organization. Why would Ford want this? Top management believed that to compete successfully Ford must improve its members' ability to be creative and make the right decisions.

Increasingly, managers are being called on to promote global organizational learning. For example, managers at Walmart have used the lessons derived from its failures and successes in one country to promote global organizational learning across the many countries in which it now operates. When Walmart entered Malaysia, it was convinced customers there would respond to its one-stop shopping format. It found, however, that Malaysians enjoy the social experience of shopping in a lively market or bazaar and thus did not like the impersonal efficiency of the typical Walmart store. As a result, Walmart learned the importance of designing store layouts to appeal specifically to the customers of each country in which it operates.

When purchasing and operating a chain of stores in another country, such as the British ASDA chain, Walmart now strives to retain what customers value in the local market while taking advantage of its own accumulated organizational learning. For example, Walmart improved ASDA's information technology used for inventory and sales tracking in stores and enrolled ASDA in Walmart's global purchasing operations, which has enabled the chain to pay less for certain products, sell them for less, and, overall, significantly increase sales.

Figure 7.8

Senge's Principles for Creating a Learning Organization

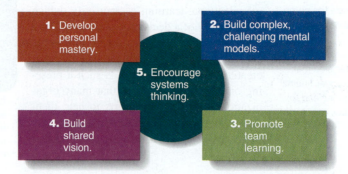

At the same time Walmart empowered local ASDA managers to run the stores; as the president of ASDA indicates, "This is still essentially a British business in the way it's run day to day."[116] Clearly global organizational learning is essential for companies such as Walmart that have significant operations in multiple countries.

Promoting Individual Creativity

Research suggests that when certain conditions are met, managers are more likely to be creative. People must be given the opportunity and freedom to generate new ideas.[117] Creativity declines when managers look over the shoulders of talented employees and try to "hurry up" a creative solution. How would you feel if your boss said you had one week to come up with a new product idea to beat the competition? Creativity results when employees have an opportunity to experiment, to take risks, and to make mistakes and learn from them. And employees must not fear that they will be looked down on or penalized for ideas that might at first seem outlandish; sometimes those ideas yield truly innovative products and services.[118] Highly innovative companies such as Google, Apple, and Facebook are well known for the wide degree of freedom they give their managers and employees to experiment and develop innovative goods and services.[119]

Once managers have generated alternatives, creativity can be fostered by giving them constructive feedback so they know how well they are doing. Ideas that seem to be going nowhere can be eliminated and creative energies refocused in other directions. Ideas that seem promising can be promoted, and help from other managers can be obtained.[120]

Top managers must stress the importance of looking for alternative solutions and should visibly reward employees who come up with creative ideas. Being creative can be demanding and stressful. Employees who believe they are working on important, vital issues are motivated to put forth the high levels of effort that creativity demands. Creative people like to receive the acclaim of others, and innovative organizations have many kinds of ceremonies and rewards to recognize creative employees.

Employees on the front line are often in a good position to come up with creative ideas for improvements but may be reluctant to speak up or share their ideas. To encourage frontline employees to come up with creative ideas and share them, some managers have used contests and rewards.[121] Contests and rewards signal the importance of coming up with creative ideas and encourage employees to share them. Examples of companies that have benefited from contests and rewards for creativity include Hammond's Candies in Denver, Colorado; Borrego Solar Systems in San Diego, California; and Infosurv in Atlanta, Georgia.

Promoting Group Creativity

To encourage creativity at the group level, organizations can use group problem-solving techniques that promote creative ideas and innovative solutions. These techniques can also prevent groupthink and help managers uncover biases. Here we look at three group decision-making techniques: *brainstorming*, the *nominal group technique*, and the *Delphi technique*.

BRAINSTORMING *Brainstorming* is a group problem-solving technique in which managers meet face-to-face to generate and debate a wide variety of alternatives from which to make a decision.[122] Generally from 5 to 15 managers meet in a closed-door session and proceed like this:

- One manager describes in broad outline the problem the group is to address.

- Group members share their ideas and generate alternative courses of action.

- As each alternative is described, group members are not allowed to criticize it; everyone withholds judgment until all alternatives have been heard. One member of the group records the alternatives on a flip chart.

- Group members are encouraged to be as innovative and radical as possible. Anything goes; and the greater the number of ideas put forth, the better. Moreover, group members are encouraged to "piggyback" or build on each other's suggestions.

- When all alternatives have been generated, group members debate the pros and cons of each and develop a short list of the best alternatives.

Brainstorming is useful in some problem-solving situations—for example, when managers are trying to find a name for a new perfume or car model. But sometimes individuals working alone can generate more alternatives. The main reason for the loss of productivity in brainstorming appears to be **production blocking**, which occurs because group members cannot always simultaneously make sense of all the alternatives being generated, think up additional alternatives, and remember what they were thinking.[123]

production blocking A loss of productivity in brainstorming sessions due to the unstructured nature of brainstorming.

nominal group technique A decision-making technique in which group members write down ideas and solutions, read their suggestions to the whole group, and discuss and then rank the alternatives.

NOMINAL GROUP TECHNIQUE   To avoid production blocking, the **nominal group technique** is often used. It provides a more structured way of generating alternatives in writing and gives each manager more time and opportunity to come up with potential solutions. The nominal group technique is especially useful when an issue is controversial and when different managers might be expected to champion different courses of action. Generally a small group of managers meets in a closed-door session and adopts the following procedures:

- One manager outlines the problem to be addressed, and 30 or 40 minutes are allocated for group members, working individually, to write down their ideas and solutions. Group members are encouraged to be innovative.

- Managers take turns reading their suggestions to the group. One manager writes all the alternatives on a flip chart. No criticism or evaluation of alternatives is allowed until all alternatives have been read.

- The alternatives are then discussed, one by one, in the sequence in which they were proposed. Group members can ask for clarifying information and critique each alternative to identify its pros and cons.

- When all alternatives have been discussed, each group member ranks all the alternatives from most preferred to least preferred, and the alternative that receives the highest ranking is chosen.[124]

delphi technique A decision-making technique in which group members do not meet face-to-face but respond in writing to questions posed by the group leader.

DELPHI TECHNIQUE   Both the nominal group technique and brainstorming require that managers meet to generate creative ideas and engage in joint problem solving. What happens if managers are in different cities or in different parts of the world and cannot meet face-to-face? Videoconferencing is one way to bring distant managers together to brainstorm. Another way is to use the **Delphi technique**, which is a written approach to creative problem solving.[125] The Delphi technique works like this:

- The group leader writes a statement of the problem and a series of questions to which participating managers are to respond.

- The questionnaire is sent to the managers and departmental experts who are most knowledgeable about the problem. They are asked to generate solutions and mail the questionnaire back to the group leader.

- A team of top managers records and summarizes the responses. The results are then sent back to the participants, with additional questions to be answered before a decision can be made.

- The process is repeated until a consensus is reached and the most suitable course of action is apparent.

LO7-5

Describe how managers can encourage and promote entrepreneurship to create a learning organization, and differentiate between entrepreneurs and intrapreneurs.

Entrepreneurship and Creativity

entrepreneur An individual who notices opportunities and decides how to mobilize the resources necessary to produce new and improved goods and services.

Entrepreneurs are individuals who notice opportunities and decide how to mobilize the resources necessary to produce new and improved goods and services. Entrepreneurs make all of the planning, organizing, leading, and controlling decisions necessary to start new business ventures. Thus entrepreneurs are an important source of creativity in the organizational world. These people, such as David Filo and Jerry Yang (founders of Yahoo!), make vast fortunes when their businesses succeed. Or they are among the millions of people who start new business ventures only to lose their money when they fail. Despite the fact that many small businesses fail in the first three to five years, many men and women in today's workforce want to start their own companies.[126]

social entrepreneur An individual who pursues initiatives and opportunities and mobilizes resources to address social problems and needs in order to improve society and well-being through creative solutions.

Social entrepreneurs are individuals who pursue initiatives and opportunities to address social problems and needs to improve society and well-being, such as reducing poverty, increasing literacy, protecting the natural environment, or reducing substance abuse.[127] Social entrepreneurs seek to mobilize resources to solve social problems through creative solutions.[128]

Many managers, scientists, and researchers employed by companies engage in entrepreneurial activity, and they are an important source of organizational creativity. They are involved in innovation, developing new and improved products and ways to make them, which we describe in detail in Chapter 9. Such employees notice opportunities for either quantum or incremental product improvements and are responsible for managing the product development process. These individuals are known as **intrapreneurs** to distinguish them from entrepreneurs who start their own businesses. But in general, entrepreneurship involves creative decision making that gives customers new or improved goods and services.

intrapreneur A manager, scientist, or researcher who works inside an organization and notices opportunities to develop new or improved products and better ways to make them.

There is an interesting relationship between entrepreneurs and intrapreneurs. Many managers with intrapreneurial talents become dissatisfied if their superiors decide neither to support nor to fund new product ideas and development efforts that the managers think will succeed. What do intrapreneurial managers who feel they are getting nowhere do? Often they decide to leave their current organizations and start their own companies to take advantage of their new product ideas! In other words, intrapreneurs become entrepreneurs and found companies that often compete with the companies they left. To avoid losing these individuals, top managers must find ways to facilitate the entrepreneurial spirit of their most creative employees. In the remainder of this section we consider issues involved in promoting successful entrepreneurship in both new and existing organizations.

Entrepreneurship and New Ventures

The fact that a significant number of entrepreneurs were frustrated intrapreneurs provides a clue about the personal characteristics of people who are likely to start a new venture and bear all the uncertainty and risk associated with being an entrepreneur.

CHARACTERISTICS OF ENTREPRENEURS   Entrepreneurs are likely to possess a particular set of the personality characteristics we discussed in Chapter 3. First, they are likely to be high on the personality trait of *openness to experience,* meaning they are predisposed to be original, to be open to a wide range of stimuli, to be daring, and to take risks. Entrepreneurs also are likely to have an *internal locus of control,* believing that they are responsible for what happens to them and that their own actions determine important outcomes such as the success or failure of a new business. People with an external locus of control, in contrast, would be unlikely to leave a secure job in an organization and assume the risk associated with a new venture.

Entrepreneurs are likely to have a high level of *self-esteem* and feel competent and capable of handling most situations—including the stress and uncertainty surrounding a plunge into a risky new venture. Entrepreneurs are also likely to have a high *need for achievement* and have a strong desire to perform challenging tasks and meet high personal standards of excellence.

ENTREPRENEURSHIP AND MANAGEMENT   Given that entrepreneurs are predisposed to activities that are somewhat adventurous and risky, in what ways can people become involved in entrepreneurial ventures? One way is to start a business from scratch. Taking advantage of modern IT, some people start solo ventures or partnerships.

When people who go it alone succeed, they frequently need to hire other people to help them run the business. Michael Dell, for example, began his computer business as a college student and within weeks had hired several people to help him assemble computers from the components he bought from suppliers. From his solo venture grew Dell Computer.

entrepreneurship The mobilization of resources to take advantage of an opportunity to provide customers with new or improved goods and services.

Some entrepreneurs who start a new business have difficulty deciding how to manage the organization as it grows; **entrepreneurship** is *not* the same as management. Management encompasses all the decisions involved in planning, organizing, leading, and controlling resources. Entrepreneurship is noticing an opportunity to satisfy a customer need and then deciding how to find and use resources to make a product that satisfies that need. When an entrepreneur has produced something customers want, entrepreneurship gives way to management because the pressing need becomes providing the product both efficiently and effectively. Frequently a founding entrepreneur lacks the skills, patience, and experience to engage in the difficult and challenging work of management. Some entrepreneurs find it hard to delegate authority because they are afraid to risk their company by letting others manage it. As a result they become overloaded and the quality of their decision making declines. Other entrepreneurs lack the detailed knowledge necessary to establish state-of-the-art information systems and technology or to create the operations management procedures that are vital to increase the efficiency of their organizations' production systems. Thus, to succeed, it is necessary to do more than create a new product; an entrepreneur must hire managers who can create an operating system that will let a new venture survive and prosper.

Intrapreneurship and Organizational Learning

The intensity of competition today, particularly from agile small companies, has made it increasingly important for large established organizations to promote and encourage intrapreneurship to raise their level of innovation and organizational learning. As we discussed earlier, a learning organization encourages all employees to identify opportunities and solve problems, thus enabling the organization to continuously experiment, improve, and increase its ability to provide customers with new and improved goods and services. The higher the level of intrapreneurship, the higher will be the level of learning and innovation. How can organizations promote organizational learning and intrapreneurship?

PRODUCT CHAMPIONS   One way to promote intrapreneurship is to encourage individuals to assume the role of **product champion**, a manager who takes "ownership" of a project and provides the leadership and vision that take a product from the idea stage to the final customer. 3M, a company well known for its attempts to promote intrapreneurship, encourages all its managers to become product champions and identify new product ideas. A product champion becomes responsible for developing a business plan for the product. Armed with this business plan, the champion appears before 3M's product development committee, a team of senior 3M managers who probe the strengths and weaknesses of the plan to decide whether it should be funded. If the plan is accepted, the product champion assumes responsibility for product development.

product champion A manager who takes "ownership" of a project and provides the leadership and vision that take a product from the idea stage to the final customer.

SKUNKWORKS   The idea behind the product champion role is that employees who feel ownership for a project are inclined to act like outside entrepreneurs and go to great lengths to make the project succeed. Using skunkworks and new venture divisions can also strengthen this feeling of ownership. A **skunkworks** is a group of intrapreneurs who are deliberately separated from the normal operation of an organization—for example, from the normal chain of command—to encourage them to devote all their attention to developing new products. The idea is that if these people are isolated, they will become so intensely involved in a project that development time will be relatively brief and the quality of the final product will be enhanced. The term *skunkworks* was coined at the Lockheed Corporation, which formed a team of design engineers to develop special aircraft such as the U2 spy plane. The secrecy with which this unit functioned and speculation about its goals led others to refer to it as "the skunkworks."

skunkworks A group of intrapreneurs who are deliberately separated from the normal operation of an organization to encourage them to devote all their attention to developing new products.

REWARDS FOR INNOVATION   To encourage managers to bear the uncertainty and risk associated with the hard work of entrepreneurship, it is necessary to link performance to rewards. Increasingly companies are rewarding intrapreneurs on the basis of the outcome of the product development process. Intrapreneurs are paid large bonuses if their projects succeed, or they are granted stock options that can make them millionaires if their products sell well. Both Microsoft and Google, for example, have made hundreds of their employees multimillionaires as a result of the stock options they were granted as part of their reward packages. In addition to receiving money, successful intrapreneurs can expect to receive promotion to the ranks of top management. Most of 3M's top managers, for example, reached the executive suite because they had a track record of successful intrapreneurship. Organizations must reward intrapreneurs equitably if they wish to prevent them from leaving and becoming outside entrepreneurs who might form a competitive new venture. Nevertheless, intrapreneurs frequently do so.

Summary and Review

LO7-1 **THE NATURE OF MANAGERIAL DECISION MAKING** Programmed decisions are routine decisions made so often that managers have developed decision rules to be followed automatically. Nonprogrammed decisions are made in response to situations that are unusual or novel; they are nonroutine decisions. The classical model of decision making assumes that decision makers have complete information; are able to process that information in an objective, rational manner; and make optimum decisions. March and Simon argued that managers exhibit bounded rationality, rarely have access to all the information they need to make optimum decisions, and consequently satisfice and rely on their intuition and judgment when making decisions.

LO7-2 **STEPS IN THE DECISION-MAKING PROCESS** When making decisions, managers should take these six steps: recognize the need for a decision, generate alternatives, assess alternatives, choose among alternatives, implement the chosen alternative, and learn from feedback.

LO7-2 **COGNITIVE BIASES AND DECISION MAKING** Most of the time managers are fairly good decision makers. On occasion, however, problems can result because human judgment can be adversely affected by the operation of cognitive biases that result in poor decisions. Cognitive biases are caused by systematic errors in the way decision makers process information and make decisions. Sources of these errors include prior hypotheses, representativeness, the illusion of control, and escalating commitment. Managers should undertake a personal decision audit to become aware of their biases and thus improve their decision making.

LO7-3 **GROUP DECISION MAKING** Many advantages are associated with group decision making, but there are also several disadvantages. One major source of poor decision making is groupthink. Afflicted decision makers collectively embark on a dubious course of action without questioning the assumptions that underlie their decision. Managers can improve the quality of group decision making by using techniques such as devil's advocacy and dialectical inquiry and by increasing diversity in the decision-making group.

LO7-4 **ORGANIZATIONAL LEARNING AND CREATIVITY** Organizational learning is the process through which managers seek to improve employees' desire and ability to understand and manage the organization and its task environment so employees can make decisions that continuously raise organizational effectiveness. Managers must take steps to promote organizational learning and creativity at the individual and group levels to improve the quality of decision making.

LO7-5 **ENTREPRENEURSHIP** Entrepreneurship is the mobilization of resources to take advantage of an opportunity to provide customers with new or improved goods and services. Entrepreneurs start new ventures of their own. Intrapreneurs work inside organizations and manage the product development process. Organizations need to encourage intrapreneurship because it leads to organizational learning and innovation.

Management in Action

Topics for Discussion and Action

Discussion

1. What are the main differences between programmed decision making and nonprogrammed decision making? **[LO7-1]**

2. In what ways do the classical and administrative models of decision making help managers appreciate the complexities of real-world decision making? **[LO7-1]**

3. Why do capable managers sometimes make bad decisions? What can individual managers do to improve their decision-making skills? **[LO7-1, 7-2]**

4. In what kinds of groups is groupthink most likely to be a problem? When is it least likely to be a problem? What steps can group members take to ward off groupthink? **[LO7-3]**

5. What is organizational learning, and how can managers promote it? **[LO7-4]**

6. What is the difference between entrepreneurship and intrapreneurship? **[LO7-5]**

Action

7. Ask a manager to recall the best and the worst decisions he or she ever made. Try to determine why these decisions were so good or so bad. **[LO7-1, 7-2, 7-3]**

8. Think about an organization in your local community or your university, or an organization that you are familiar with, that is doing poorly. Now think of questions managers in the organization should ask stakeholders to elicit creative ideas for turning around the organization's fortunes. **[LO7-4]**

Building Management Skills

How Do You Make Decisions? [LO7-1, 7-2, 7-4]

Pick a decision you made recently that has had important consequences for you. It may be your decision about which college to attend, which major to select, whether to take a part-time job, or which part-time job to take. Using the material in this chapter, analyze how you made the decision:

1. Identify the criteria you used, either consciously or unconsciously, to guide your decision making.

2. List the alternatives you considered. Were they all possible alternatives? Did you unconsciously (or consciously) ignore some important alternatives?

3. How much information did you have about each alternative? Were you making the decision on the basis of complete or incomplete information?

4. Try to remember how you reached the decision. Did you sit down and consciously think through the implications of each alternative, or did you make the decision on the basis of intuition? Did you use any rules of thumb to help you make the decision?

5. In retrospect, do you think your choice of alternative was shaped by any of the cognitive biases discussed in this chapter?

6. Having answered the previous five questions, do you think in retrospect that you made a reasonable decision? What, if anything, might you do to improve your ability to make good decisions in the future?

Managing Ethically [LO7-3]

Sometimes groups make extreme decisions—decisions that are either more risky or more conservative than they would have been if individuals acting alone had made them. One explanation for the tendency of groups to make extreme decisions is diffusion of responsibility. In a group, responsibility for the outcomes of a decision is spread among group members, so each person feels less than fully accountable. The group's decision is extreme because no individual has taken full responsibility for it.

Questions

1. Either alone or in a group, think about the ethical implications of extreme decision making by groups.

2. When group decision making takes place, should members of a group each feel fully accountable for outcomes of the decision? Why or why not?

Small Group Breakout Exercise

Brainstorming [LO7-3, 7-4]

Form groups of three or four people, and appoint one member as the spokesperson who will communicate your findings to the class when called on by the instructor. Then discuss the following scenario:

You and your partners are trying to decide which kind of restaurant to open in a centrally located shopping center that has just been built in your city. The problem confronting you is that the city already has many restaurants that provide different kinds of food at all price ranges. You have the resources to open any type of restaurant. Your challenge is to decide which type is most likely to succeed.

Use brainstorming to decide which type of restaurant to open. Follow these steps:

1. As a group, spend 5–10 minutes generating ideas about the alternative restaurants that the members think will be most likely to succeed. Each group member should be as innovative and creative as possible, and no suggestions should be criticized.

2. Appoint one group member to write down the alternatives as they are identified.

3. Spend the next 10–15 minutes debating the pros and cons of the alternatives. As a group, try to reach a consensus on which alternative is most likely to succeed.

After making your decision, discuss the pros and cons of the brainstorming method, and decide whether any production blocking occurred.

When called on by the instructor, the spokesperson should be prepared to share your group's decision with the class, as well as the reasons for the group's decision.

Exploring the World Wide Web [LO7-4]

Go to www.brainstorming.co.uk. This website contains "Training on Creative Techniques" and "Creativity Puzzles." Spend at least 30 minutes on the training and/or puzzles. Think about what you have learned. Come up with specific ways in which you can be more creative in your thinking and decision making based on what you have learned.

Be the Manager [LO7-1, 7-2, 7-3, 7-4, 7-5]

You are a top manager who was recently hired by an oil field services company in Oklahoma to help it respond more quickly and proactively to potential opportunities in its market. You report to the chief operating officer (COO), who reports to the CEO, and you have been on the job for eight months. Thus far you have come up with three initiatives you carefully studied, thought were noteworthy, and proposed and justified to the COO. The COO seemed cautiously interested when you presented the proposals, and each time he indicated he would think about them and discuss them with the CEO because considerable resources were involved. Each time you never heard back from the COO, and after a few weeks elapsed, you casually asked the COO if there was any news on the proposal in question. For the first proposal, the COO said, "We think it's a good idea, but the timing is off. Let's shelve it for the time being and reconsider it next year." For the second proposal, the COO said, "Mike [the CEO] reminded me that we tried that two years ago and it wasn't well received in the market. I am surprised I didn't remember it myself when you first described the proposal, but it came right back to me once Mike mentioned it." For the third proposal, the COO simply said, "We're not convinced it will work."

You believe your three proposed initiatives are viable ways to seize opportunities in the marketplace, yet you cannot proceed with any of them. Moreover, for each proposal, you invested considerable time and even worked to bring others on board to support the proposal, only to have it shot down by the CEO. When you interviewed for the position, both the COO and the CEO claimed they wanted "an outsider to help them step out of the box and innovate." Yet your experience to date has been just the opposite. What are you going to do?

The New York Times Case in the News [LO7-1, 7-2, 7-4, 7-5]

For Many Older Americans, an Enterprising Path

When Marilyn Arnold was 9 years old, her mother, a skilled seamstress, patiently taught her to sew on a vintage Singer treadle sewing machine.

As her feet pumped away at the machine in her family's farmhouse near Paris, Missouri, she was smitten. "I was in love with sewing, even when I stuck my finger and it bled," Arnold said.

Soon she was whirling the thread for crisp white blouses with bright red sailor collars, gathered skirts, and, in time, her entire school wardrobe. She even competed in sewing contests at the Missouri State Fair.

But she never dreamed that now, at the age of 66, she would be running her own small business, Marilyn Arnold Designs, in Lee's Summit, Missouri.

Her specialty is custom designing and sewing 18-inch square pillows, christening dresses, and blankets as mementos made from cherished wedding gowns that had been relegated to the back of a closet.

She also stitches quilts big enough for a queen-size bed assembled from beloved T-shirts, and patches together vests from timeworn scarves. "Everything I make is from repurposed materials," she said.

The idea for her venture took root three years ago, shortly before she retired from her position as a managing partner at the New York Life Insurance Company, after 29 years in the insurance business.

That was when her accountant asked her what she planned to do in retirement. She acknowledged that she knew she had to do something, but had no idea what. The accountant asked a second question: "What did you want to do when you were a little girl?"

While her childhood dream was to become a dress designer, that endeavor seemed too lofty a goal at her age. The idea to design and sew custom pillows from a wedding dress was inspired by a friend's request.

That was the manageable beginning of a new career. Her start-up costs to buy equipment and supplies and to devise a marketing plan tallied $12,000, financed from personal savings, Arnold said.

First she sewed as a side job for several months before she retired to see if there was really enough interest to introduce a full-fledged business. In time she created a website, opened an online web storefront on Etsy, and began posting her designs on Pinterest.

Today she handles all the sewing duties herself, easily clocking 12-hour days. "My biggest challenge has been balancing my time in order to work on all aspects of my business," Ms. Arnold said. "I have to guard against spending too much time working in my business and not enough time working on my business."

Older American entrepreneurs like Arnold are on a roll.

Kimberly Palmer, author of *The Economy of You: Discover Your Inner Entrepreneur and Recession-Proof Your Life,* said she had noticed that the most eager audience for the book was often people approaching retirement or already in it. "They want to leverage their skills and experience into something entrepreneurial," she said.

According to a recent study published by the Kauffman Foundation and Legal Zoom, in 2013 about 20 percent of all new businesses were started by entrepreneurs aged 50 to 59 years, and 15 percent were 60 and over.

And in fact, over the last decade, the highest rate of entrepreneurial activity belongs to those in the 55–64 age group, according to the Kauffman Index of Entrepreneurial Activity.

A desire to work for oneself and create a business that is meaningful and has social impact at this stage of life, combined with a job market that makes it tough for workers over 50 to get hired, has clearly pushed more people to pursue the entrepreneurial path.

"For the longest time we've assumed that social entrepreneurship was the exclusive provenance of young people," said Marc Freedman, founder and chief executive of Encore.org, the nonprofit research center dedicated to second acts for the greater good. "Now we're realizing an undiscovered continent of innovation in the growing population over 50."

But it is not an easy road. Money is the biggest stumbling block. Most start-ups like Arnold's are underwritten with personal savings.

If someone does not have a nice stockpile of savings to tap, or a partner who is still bringing home a paycheck, it is tough to get going. And many entrepreneurs do not pay themselves for a year or so to allow their businesses to gain traction.

To finance the more than $100,000 it took to start Well Read New & Used Books in Hawthorne, New Jersey, about three years ago, for example, Bill Skees, then 56, asked his six siblings for a loan, and he and his wife, Mary Ann, were able to dip into savings for the rest. The banks he contacted were not enthusiastic.

"There's lots of red tape, and most banks aren't interested in financing a senior business start-up, which generally runs between $10,000 to $25,000, because it's too small," said Elizabeth Isele, 71, cofounder of SeniorEntrepreneurshipWorks.org, a nonprofit venture geared to helping workers over age 50 start their own businesses. "And age bias can be a big factor."

That said, many small and microbusinesses, particularly freelance, home-based and online e-commerce businesses, require only a fraction of that to get going, sometimes less than $1,000.

Where there's a will, there's a way. Determined older entrepreneurs have tapped retirement accounts, tracked down hard-to-get economic development loans in their communities, and turned to crowdfunding sites.

A Senate hearing titled "In Search of a Second Act: The Challenges and Advantages of Senior Entrepreneurship," offered a chance to air issues like age bias from lending organizations and the need to develop tax incentives for training and start-ups.

"In order to continue our economic recovery, we need to change how we view the terms 'start-up' or 'entrepreneur,'" said Senator Mary L. Landrieu, Democrat of Louisiana, chairwoman of the Committee on Small Business and Entrepreneurship.

"Most people associate those terms with a tech business and a young computer whiz, not a home business in a rural town and a seasoned executive with 30 years of management experience," Senator Landrieu said. "Senior entrepreneurs are especially critical to creating jobs and growing the economy because they have the right experience and resources to be successful."

Isele, who plans to testify at the hearing, said she and others would argue that this growing demographic group would not cause a crisis. "We need to help people in policy and private industry to understand, this isn't a silver tsunami," she said. "It's a silver lining, yielding golden dividends. Senior entrepreneurs contribute to the economy, paying taxes, creating jobs, paying people, and underwriting entitlement programs."

Senator Landrieu said she hoped the hearing would showcase successful initiatives and discuss whether they could be replicated elsewhere.

One innovative initiative is the eProv Studio, which will officially start this weekend at the Institute for the Ages' Conference on Positive Aging in Sarasota, Florida.

These new workshops, created by Isele and Cheryl Kiser, executive director of the Lewis Institute at Babson College, combine the methodology of entrepreneurial thought and action and the techniques of improvisational theater.

"Each participant comes to the workshop with a desire, an itch, an idea of what they might want to do," Kiser added. "The method we teach in these groups of 20 is to look at who you are, what you know, who you know, what you can do, and the resources you have at hand to create something of value."

Using the improvisation process can help decode someone's entrepreneurial history. "We help them understand decade by decade what they have accomplished and see a pattern of these accomplishments and

entrepreneurial skills they have had throughout their entire life," Isele said.

Other resources include a free, online, open-source entrepreneurship curriculum, hosted at the Lawrence N. Field Center for Entrepreneurship at the Zicklin School of Business at Baruch College. It is intended for people over 50 and includes help with developing business plans, obtaining loans, gaining and access to business start-up incubators, and meeting mentors to serve as sounding boards.

Then there is the Kauffman Foundation's FastTrac Boomer Entrepreneur program.

In collaboration with AARP and FastTrac affiliates in select American cities, Kauffman is piloting specialized 10-week courses in both English and Spanish. Up to 20 applicants will be accepted in each course. The cost is $200.

And while many older Americans are new to learning business skills, some cherish the personal rewards discovered along the way. "My business has given me so many things, but what I love the most is that I'm my own boss," Arnold said. "I manage my time."

Questions for Discussion

1. To what extent are the decisions would-be entrepreneurs and actual entrepreneurs make nonprogrammed decisions?

2. To what extent are the decisions they make characterized by risk and uncertainty?

3. Why is entrepreneurship and social entrepreneurship appealing to some Americans over 50 years of age?

4. What role does creativity and learning from feedback play in entrepreneurial success?

CHAPTER 8

The Manager as a Planner and Strategist

Learning Objectives

After studying this chapter, you should be able to:

LO8-1 Identify the three main steps of the planning process and explain the relationship between planning and strategy.

LO8-2 Describe some techniques managers can use to improve the planning process so they can better predict the future and mobilize organizational resources to meet future contingencies.

LO8-3 Differentiate between the main types of business-level strategies and explain how they give an organization a competitive advantage that may lead to superior performance.

LO8-4 Differentiate between the main types of corporate-level strategies and explain how they are used to strengthen a company's business-level strategy and competitive advantage.

LO8-5 Describe the vital role managers play in implementing strategies to achieve an organization's mission and goals.

How can identifying corporate strengths and weaknesses lead to better planning and strategy?

Toys"R"Us, Inc., with its mascot Geoffrey the Giraffe, is a well-known brand. The toy retailer was founded in 1948 as Children's Supermart and later rebranded as Toys"R"Us after adding toys to its baby furniture business. By 2014 the company had grown to 872 stores in the United States, and more than 700 stores outside the United States.[1]

Despite its growth, 2013 was not a good year for Toys"R"Us. Net sales in stores were down, and the company's net loss was $1 billion. Chairman and CEO Antonio Urcelay and President Hank Mullany announced Toy"R"Us' "TRU Transformation" plan.

"Our 'TRU Transformation' strategy is grounded in consumer research and customer insights, and is anchored by three guiding principles—Easy, Expert, Fair," Mullany said. "Among our highest priorities will be to deepen our focus on the customer, build meaningful relationships through loyalty and targeted marketing programs, and improve the shopping experience both in-store and online."[2]

First, Urcelay and Mullany recognize that external factors affect sales at Toys"R"Us. The factors identified by Urcelay and Mullany are opportunities and threats, over which Toys"R"Us has no control. They include falling birthrates, changes in the play patterns of children, and the growth of online shopping. While it might be easy for Urcelay and Mullany to blame falling sales on these factors, the two company leaders also looked at internal factors that hurt the business. They are the factors over which the company does have control. "We are encouraged that all of these . . . issues are firmly within our own control to fix," Urcelay said. "And our strategy will address these to improve the business over the short-term and put the company on track for the future."[3]

Urcelay and Mullany described four categories of weaknesses at Toys"R"Us and discussed how they could be turned into strengths. First, the retailer said it has provided a weak customer experience in-store and online. Customers complain that the checkout process in stores is slow and that the stores are cluttered and disorganized. The apps for Toys"R"Us' online stores are out of date and frustrating to customers.

President Hank Mullany (left) and CEO Antonio Urcelay (right) of Toys"R"Us, Inc. In 2013, Mullany and Urcelay announced a new business strategy grounded in consumer research and satisfaction, which is designed to help the company play to its strengths and address its weaknesses.

When customers do buy a product online, they often encounter shipping problems. Toys"R"Us would like to turn this weakness into a strength by making its stores easy, uncluttered places at which to shop with sales associates who have been trained and are perceived as experts on the products. It also plans to better staff its store and to expedite its checkout process.

Second, there is a perception that prices at Toys"R"Us are higher than at other retailers. Toys"R"Us would like to turn this weakness into a strength by making sure its prices are perceived as fair and by reducing the many exclusions to its price-matching policy. The company also plans to better use data from its loyalty program to send targeted offers to customers and to communicate more simplified offers to customers.

Third, the retailer has struggled with inventory management. Customers often find that sought-after items are out of stock. Toys"R"Us had already begun to work on this before the 2013 financial returns were in. The company expanded its ability to ship online orders from stores and distribution centers, resulting in a much more flexible inventory system. It also is using a "product life cycle management" system to get the right goods into stores at the right times. Further, clearance events will move out merchandise that has been around the store for too long.[4]

Finally, the retailer plans to right-size its cost structure. The company is working on an assessment of its business structure and operations to increase efficiency and effectiveness. As a part of this assessment, the company found 500 positions to eliminate. "As we look to the future, our strategy will establish a path to sustainable business growth, building upon the company's unique strengths," Urcelay said. "Toys'R'Us is one of the most recognized brands in the world with a strong international presence and a large and loyal customer base."[5]

Having identified the organization's strengths, weaknesses, opportunities, and threats is an important step in the planning process discussed in this chapter. This analysis gives Toys"R"Us the information it needs to turn weaknesses into strengths, to take advantage of opportunities, and to avoid damage from threats. Such planning will help Toys"R"Us hold onto and improve its market position.

As Mullany said: "We are committed to delivering on our mission to bring joy into the lives of our customers by being the toy and juvenile products authority and definitive destination for kid fun, gift-giving solutions, and parenting services."[6]

Overview

In a fast-changing competitive environment managers must continually evaluate how well their products are meeting customer needs, and they must engage in thorough, systematic planning to find new strategies to tailor their products to better meet those needs. This chapter explores the manager's role both as planner and as strategist. First, we discuss the nature and importance of planning, the kinds of plans managers develop, and the levels at which planning takes place. Second, we discuss the three major steps in the planning process: (1) determining an organization's mission and major goals, (2) choosing or formulating strategies to realize the mission and goals, and (3) selecting the most effective ways to implement and put these strategies into action. We also examine several techniques, such as scenario planning and SWOT analysis, that can help managers improve the quality of their planning; and we discuss a range of strategies managers

LO8-1

Identify the three main steps of the planning process and explain the relationship between planning and strategy.

Figure 8.1

Three Steps in Planning

DETERMINING THE ORGANIZATION'S
MISSION AND GOALS

Define the business.
Establish major goals.

FORMULATING STRATEGY

Analyze current situation and develop strategies.

IMPLEMENTING STRATEGY

Allocate resources and responsibilities to achieve strategies.

can use to give their companies a competitive advantage over their rivals. By the end of this chapter, you will understand the vital role managers carry out when they plan, develop, and implement strategies to create a high-performing organization.

Planning and Strategy

planning Identifying and selecting appropriate goals and courses of action; one of the four principal tasks of management.

strategy A cluster of decisions about what goals to pursue, what actions to take, and how to use resources to achieve goals.

mission statement A broad declaration of an organization's purpose that identifies the organization's products and customers and distinguishes the organization from its competitors.

Planning, as we noted in Chapter 1, is a process managers use to identify and select appropriate goals and courses of action for an organization.[7] The organizational plan that results from the planning process details the goals of the organization and the specific strategies managers will implement to attain those goals. Recall from Chapter 1 that a **strategy** is a cluster of related managerial decisions and actions to help an organization attain one of its goals. Thus planning is both a goal-making and a strategy-making process.

In most organizations, planning is a three-step activity (see Figure 8.1). The first step is determining the organization's mission and goals. A **mission statement** is a broad declaration of an organization's overriding purpose, what it is seeking to achieve from its activities; this statement also identifies what is *unique or important* about its products to its employees and customers; finally it *distinguishes or differentiates* the organization in some ways from its competitors. (For example, the mission statement of Nike is "to bring inspiration and innovation to every athlete in the world."[8])

The second step is formulating strategy. Managers analyze the organization's current situation and then conceive and develop the strategies necessary to attain the organization's mission and goals. The third step is implementing strategy. Managers decide how to allocate the resources and responsibilities required to implement the strategies among people and groups within the organization.[9] In subsequent sections of this chapter we look in detail at the specifics of these steps. But first we examine the general nature and purpose of planning.

The Nature of the Planning Process

Essentially, to perform the planning task, managers (1) establish and discover where an organization is at the *present time;* (2) determine where it should be in the future, its *desired future state;* and (3) decide how to *move it forward* to reach that future state. When managers plan, they must forecast what may happen in the future to decide what to do in the present. The better their predictions, the more effective will be the strategies they formulate to take advantage of future opportunities and counter emerging competitive threats in the environment. As previous chapters noted, however, the external environment is uncertain and complex, and managers typically must deal with incomplete information and "limitations on time, cognitive capacity, and data." This is why planning and strategy making are so difficult and risky; and if managers' predictions are wrong and strategies fail, organizational performance falls.

Why Planning Is Important

Almost all managers participate in some kind of planning because they must try to predict future opportunities and threats and develop a plan and strategies that will result in a high-performing organization. Moreover, the absence of a plan often results in hesitations, false steps, and mistaken changes of direction that can hurt an organization or even lead to disaster. Planning is important for four main reasons:

1. *Planning is necessary to give the organization a sense of direction and purpose.*[10] A plan states what goals an organization is trying to achieve and what strategies it intends to use to achieve them. Without the sense of direction and purpose that a formal plan provides, managers may interpret their own specific tasks and jobs in ways that best suit them-selves. The result will be an organization that is pursuing multiple and often conflicting goals and a set of managers who do not cooperate and work well together. By stating which organizational goals and strategies are important, a plan keeps managers on track so they use the resources under their control efficiently and effectively.

2. *Planning is a useful way of getting managers to participate in decision making about the appropriate goals and strategies for an organization.* Effective planning gives all managers the opportunity to participate in decision making. At Intel, for example, top managers, as part of their annual planning process, regularly request input from lower-level managers to determine what the organization's goals and strategies should be.

3. *A plan helps coordinate managers of the different functions and divisions of an organization to ensure that they all pull in the same direction and work to achieve its desired future state.* Without a well-thought-out plan, for example, it is possible that the manufacturing function will make more products than the sales function can sell, resulting in a mass of unsold inventory. In fact, this happened when harsh winter storms in 2013–2014 slowed car sales and left carmakers with unsold inventory. To sell the extra cars, many carmakers had to offer deep discounts to sell off their excess stock.

4. *A plan can be used as a device for controlling managers within an organization.* A good plan specifies not only which goals and strategies the organization is committed to but also *who* bears the responsibility for putting the strategies into action to attain the goals. When managers know they will be held accountable for attaining a goal, they are motivated to do their best to make sure the goal is achieved.

Henri Fayol, the originator of the model of management we discussed in Chapter 1, said that effective plans should have four qualities: unity, continuity, accuracy, and flexibility.[11] *Unity* means that at any time only one central, guiding plan is put into operation to achieve an organizational goal; more than one plan to achieve a goal would cause confusion and disorder. *Continuity* means that planning is an ongoing process in which managers build and refine previous plans and continually modify plans at all levels—corporate, business, and functional—so they fit together into one broad framework. *Accuracy* means that managers need to make every attempt to collect and use all available information in the planning process. Of course managers must recognize that uncertainty exists and that information is almost always incomplete (for reasons we discussed in Chapter 7). Despite the need for continuity and accuracy, however, Fayol emphasized that the planning process should be *flexible* enough so plans can be altered and changed if the situation changes; managers must not be bound to a static plan.

Levels of Planning

In large organizations planning usually takes place at three levels of management: corporate, business or division, and department or functional. Consider how General Electric (GE) operates. One of the world's largest global organizations, GE competes in over 150 different

Figure 8.2

Levels of Planning at General Electric

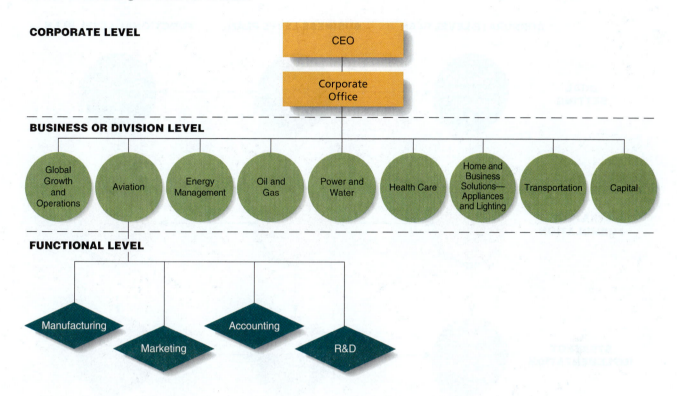

businesses or industries.[12] GE has three main levels of management: corporate level, business or divisional level, and functional level (see Figure 8.2). At the corporate level are CEO and Chairman Jeffrey Immelt, his top management team, and their corporate support staff. Together they are responsible for planning and strategy making for the organization as a whole.

Below the corporate level is the business level. At the business level are the different *divisions* or *business units* of the company that compete in distinct industries; GE has over 150 divisions, including Global Growth and Operations, Aviation, Energy Management, Oil and Gas, Power and Water, Health Care, and Transportation. Each division or business unit has its own set of *divisional managers* who control planning and strategy for their particular division or unit. So, for example, GE Aviations' divisional managers plan how to operate globally to reduce costs while meeting the needs of customers in different countries.

Going down one more level, each division has its own set of *functions* or *departments,* such as manufacturing, marketing, human resource management (HRM), and research and development (R&D). For example, Aviation has its own marketing function, as does GE Energy and Health Care. Each division's *functional managers* are responsible for the planning and strategy making necessary to increase the efficiency and effectiveness of their particular function. So, for example, GE Lighting's marketing managers are responsible for increasing the effectiveness of its advertising and sales campaigns in different countries to improve lightbulb sales.

Levels and Types of Planning

As just discussed, planning at GE, as at all other large organizations, takes place at each level. Figure 8.3 shows the link between these three levels and the three steps in the planning and strategy-making process illustrated in Figure 8.1.

The **corporate-level plan** contains top management's decisions concerning the organization's mission and goals, overall (corporate-level) strategy, and structure (see Figure 8.3). **Corporate-level strategy** specifies in which industries and national markets an organization

corporate-level plan Top management's decisions pertaining to the organization's mission, overall strategy, and structure.

corporate-level strategy A plan that indicates in which industries and national markets an organization intends to compete.

Figure 8.3

Levels and Types of Planning

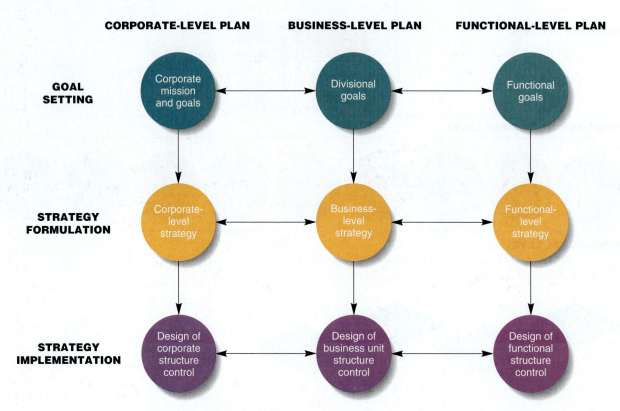

intends to compete and why. One of the goals stated in GE's corporate-level plan is that GE should be first or second in market share in every industry in which it competes. A division that cannot attain this goal may be sold to another company. GE Medical Systems was sold to Thompson of France for this reason. Another GE goal is to acquire other companies that can help a division build its market share to reach its corporate goal of being first or second in an industry.

In general, corporate-level planning and strategy are the primary responsibility of top or corporate managers.[13] The corporate-level goal of GE is to be the first or second leading company in every industry in which it competes. Jeffrey Immelt and his top management team decide which industries GE should compete in to achieve this goal. The corporate-level plan provides the framework within which divisional managers create their business-level plans. At the business level, the managers of each division create a **business-level plan** that details (1) the long-term divisional goals that will allow the division to meet corporate goals and (2) the division's business-level strategy and structure necessary to achieve divisional goals. **Business-level strategy** outlines the specific methods a division, business unit, or organization will use to compete effectively against its rivals in an industry. Managers at GE's Appliances and Lighting division (currently number two in the global lighting industry, behind the Dutch company Philips NV) develop strategies designed to help their division take over the number one spot and better contribute to GE's corporate goals. The division's specific strategies might focus on ways to reduce costs in all departments to lower prices and so gain market share from Philips. For example, GE has expanded its European lighting operations in Hungary, which is a low-cost location.[14]

At the functional level, the business-level plan provides the framework within which functional managers devise their plans. A **functional-level plan** states the goals that the managers of each function will pursue to help their division attain its business-level goals, which, in turn, will allow the entire company to achieve its corporate goals. **Functional-level strategy** is a plan of action that managers of individual functions (such as manufacturing or marketing) can follow to improve the ability of each function to perform its task-specific activities

business-level plan Divisional managers' decisions pertaining to divisions' long-term goals, overall strategy, and structure.

business-level strategy A plan that indicates how a division intends to compete against its rivals in an industry.

functional-level plan Functional managers' decisions pertaining to the goals that they propose to pursue to help the division attain its business-level goals.

functional-level strategy A plan of action to improve the ability of each of an organization's functions to perform its task-specific activities in ways that add value to an organization's goods and services.

in ways that add value to an organization's goods and services and thereby increase the value customers receive. Thus, for example, consistent with the lighting division's strategy of driving down costs, its manufacturing function might adopt the goal "To reduce production costs by 20 percent over the next three years," and functional strategies to achieve this goal might include (1) investing in state-of-the-art European production facilities and (2) developing an electronic global business-to-business network to reduce the costs of inputs and inventory holding. The many ways in which managers can use functional-level strategy to strengthen business-level strategy are discussed in detail in Chapter 9.

In the planning process, it is important to ensure that planning across the three different levels is *consistent*—functional goals and strategies should be consistent with divisional goals and strategies, which, in turn, should be consistent with corporate goals and strategies, and vice versa. When consistency is achieved, the whole company operates in harmony; activities at one level reinforce and strengthen those at the other levels, increasing efficiency and effectiveness. To help accomplish this, each function's plan is linked to its division's business-level plan, which, in turn, is linked to the corporate plan. Although few organizations are as large and complex as GE, most plan in the same way as GE and have written plans, which are frequently updated, to guide managerial decision making.

Time Horizons of Plans

time horizon The intended duration of a plan.

Plans differ in their **time horizons**, the periods of time over which they are intended to apply or endure. Managers usually distinguish among *long-term plans,* with a time horizon of five years or more; *intermediate-term plans,* with a horizon between one and five years; and *short-term plans,* with a horizon of one year or less.[15] Typically corporate- and business-level goals and strategies require long- and intermediate-term plans, and functional-level goals and strategies require intermediate- and short-term plans.

Although most companies operate with planning horizons of five years or more, this does not mean that managers undertake major planning exercises only once every five years and then "lock in" a specific set of goals and strategies for that period. Most organizations have an annual planning cycle that is usually linked to the annual financial budget (although a major planning effort may be undertaken only every few years). So a corporate- or business-level plan that extends over several years is typically treated as a *rolling plan*—a plan that is updated and amended every year to take account of changing conditions in the external environment. Thus the time horizon for an organization's 2015 corporate-level plan might be 2020; for the 2016 plan it might be 2021; and so on. The use of rolling plans is essential because of the high rate of change in the environment and the difficulty of predicting competitive conditions five years in the future. Rolling plans enable managers to make midcourse corrections if environmental changes warrant or to change the thrust of the plan altogether if it no longer seems appropriate. The use of rolling plans allows managers to plan flexibly without losing sight of the need to plan for the long term.

Standing Plans and Single-Use Plans

Another distinction often made between plans is whether they are standing plans or single-use plans. Managers create standing and single-use plans to help achieve an organization's specific goals. *Standing plans* are used in situations in which programmed decision making is appropriate. When the same situations occur repeatedly, managers develop policies, rules, and standard operating procedures (SOPs) to control the way employees perform their tasks. A policy is a general guide to action; a rule is a formal, written guide to action; and a standing operating procedure is a written instruction describing the exact series of actions that should be followed in a specific situation. For example, an organization may have a standing plan about ethical behavior by employees. This plan includes a policy that all employees are expected to behave ethically in their dealings with suppliers and customers; a rule that requires any employee who receives from a supplier or customer a gift worth more than $20 to report the gift; and an SOP that obliges the recipient of the gift to make the disclosure in writing within 30 days.

LO8-2

Describe some techniques managers can use to improve the planning process so they can better predict the future and mobilize organizational resources to meet future contingencies.

As we know all too well, oil and gas prices are unpredictable. Oil industry managers therefore sometimes use scenario planning to deal with this chaotic market.

In contrast, *single-use plans* are developed to handle non-programmed decision making in unusual or one-of-a-kind situations. Examples of single-use plans include *programs,* which are integrated sets of plans for achieving certain goals, and *projects,* which are specific action plans created to complete various aspects of a program. For instance, NASA is working on a major program to launch a rover in 2020 to investigate a specific environment on the surface of Mars. One project in this program is to develop the scientific instruments to bring samples back from Mars.[16]

Scenario Planning

Earlier we noted that effective plans have four qualities: unity, continuity, accuracy, and flexibility. One of the most widely used planning methods or techniques that can help managers create plans that have these qualities is scenario planning. **Scenario planning** (also known as *contingency planning*) is the generation of multiple forecasts of future conditions followed by an analysis of how to respond effectively to each of those conditions.

As noted previously, planning is about trying to forecast and predict the future in order to be able to anticipate future opportunities and threats. The future, however, is inherently unpredictable. How can managers best deal with this unpredictability? This question preoccupied managers at Royal Dutch Shell, the third largest global oil company, in the 1980s. In 1984 oil was $30 a barrel, and most analysts and managers, including Shell's, believed it would hit $50 per barrel by 1990. Although these high prices guaranteed high profits, Shell's top managers decided to conduct a scenario-planning exercise. Shell's corporate and divisional managers were told to use scenario planning to generate different future scenarios of conditions in the oil market and then to develop a set of plans that detailed how they would respond to these opportunities and threats if any such scenario occurred.

One scenario assumed that oil prices would fall to $15 per barrel, and managers had to decide what they should do to remain profitable in such a case. Managers went to work with the goal of creating a plan consisting of a series of recommendations. The final plan included proposals to cut oil exploration costs by investing in new technologies, to accelerate investments in cost-efficient oil-refining facilities, and to weed out unprofitable gas stations.[17] In reviewing these proposals, top management came to the conclusion that even if oil prices continued to rise, all of these actions would benefit Shell and increase its profit margin. So they decided to put the cost-cutting plan into action. As it happened, in the mid-1980s oil prices did not rise; they collapsed to $15 a barrel, but Shell, unlike its competitors, had already taken steps to be profitable in a low-oil-price world. Consequently, by 1990 the company was twice as profitable as its major competitors.

As this example suggests, because the future is unpredictable—the $30-a-barrel oil level was not reached again until the early 2000s, for example—the best way to improve planning is first to generate "multiple futures," or scenarios of the future, based on different assumptions about conditions that *might prevail* in the future and then to develop different plans that detail what a company should do if one of these scenarios occurs. Scenario planning is a learning tool that raises the quality of the planning process and can bring real benefits to an organization.[18] Over the years Shell scenario planners have generated more than 30 rounds of scenarios, including one in 2013 that involved governments having a role in developing more compact cities.[19] By 2011, 65 percent of *Fortune* 500 companies planned to use some version of scenario planning.[20] A major advantage of scenario planning is its ability not only to anticipate the challenges of an uncertain future but also to educate managers to think about the future—*to think strategically.*[21]

Figure 8.4

Three Mission Statements

COMPANY	MISSION STATEMENT
Tumblr:	"To empower creators to make their best work and get it in front of the audience they deserve."[i]
Pinterest:	"To help people discover the things they love and inspire them to do those things in their real life."[ii]
Google:	"To organize the world's information and make it universally accessible and useful."[iii]

Sources:

i. David, "News!" May 20, 2013, staff.tumblr.com/post/50902268806/news.
ii. about.pinterest.com, 2013.
iii. www.google.com/about/company/

Determining the Organization's Mission and Goals

As we discussed earlier, determining the organization's mission and goals is the first step of the planning process. Once the mission and goals are agreed upon and formally stated in the corporate plan, they guide the next steps by defining which strategies are appropriate.[22] Figure 8.4 presents the mission statements of seven similar but different Internet-based companies.

Defining the Business

To determine an organization's *mission*—the overriding reason it exists to provide customers with goods or services they value—managers must first *define its business* so they can identify what kinds of value customers are receiving. To define the business, managers must ask three related questions about a company's products: (1) *Who* are our customers? (2) *What* customer needs are being satisfied? (3) *How* are we satisfying customer needs?[23] Managers ask these questions to identify the customer needs that the organization satisfies and how the organization satisfies those needs. Answering these questions helps managers identify not only the customer needs they are satisfying now but also the needs they should try to satisfy in the future and who their true competitors are. All this information helps managers plan and establish appropriate goals.

Establishing Major Goals

Once the business is defined, managers must establish a set of primary goals to which the organization is committed. Developing these goals gives the organization a sense of direction or purpose. In most organizations, articulating major goals is the job of the CEO, although other managers have input into the process. Thus, at GE, CEO Immelt's primary goal is still to be one of the two best performers in every industry in which the company competes, even though this is highly challenging. However, the best statements of organizational goals are ambitious—that is, they *stretch* the organization and require that each of its members work to improve company performance.[24] The role of **strategic leadership**, the ability of the CEO and top managers to convey a compelling vision of what they want to achieve to their subordinates, is important here. If subordinates buy into the vision and model their behaviors on their leaders, they develop a willingness to undertake the hard, stressful work that is necessary for creative, risk-taking strategy making.[25] Many popular books such as *Built to Last* provide lucid accounts of strategic leaders establishing "big, hairy, audacious goals (BHAGs)" that serve as rallying points to unite their subordinates.[26]

Although goals should be challenging, they should also be realistic. Challenging goals give managers at all levels an incentive to look for ways to improve organizational performance, but a goal that is clearly unrealistic and impossible to attain may prompt managers to give up.[27] Jeff Immelt has to be careful not to set unrealistic sales targets for GE's divisions that might discourage their top managers, for example.

strategic leadership The ability of the CEO and top managers to convey a compelling vision of what they want the organization to achieve to their subordinates.

Finally, the time period in which a goal is expected to be achieved should be stated. Time constraints are important because they emphasize that a goal must be attained within a reasonable period; they inject a sense of urgency into goal attainment and act as a motivator. GE's managers committed themselves to reviving the fortunes of its appliance division in the 2010s and to significantly increase sales; the division is once again profitable and is no longer for sale.[28] In 2014 the appliance division hosted a "hackathon" to generate ideas for innovative products. Among the top finds were an in-sink dishwasher and an oven that sets the proper temperature for a product after the cook scans the product's bar code.[29]

Formulating Strategy

strategy formulation The development of a set of corporate, business, and functional strategies that allow an organization to accomplish its mission and achieve its goals.

SWOT analysis A planning exercise in which managers identify organizational strengths (S) and weaknesses (W) and environmental opportunities (O) and threats (T).

Once the mission and goals of the organization have been set, a strategy to achieve them needs to be formulated. In **strategy formulation** managers work to develop the set of strategies (corporate, divisional, and functional) that will allow an organization to accomplish its mission and achieve its goals.[30] Strategy formulation begins with managers' systematically analyzing the factors or forces inside an organization and outside in the global environment that affect the organization's ability to meet its goals now and in the future. SWOT analysis and the five forces model are two handy techniques managers can use to analyze these factors.

SWOT Analysis

SWOT analysis is a planning exercise in which managers identify *internal* organizational strengths (S) and weaknesses (W) and *external* environmental opportunities (O) and threats (T). Based on a SWOT analysis, managers at the different levels of the organization select the corporate, business, and functional strategies to best position the organization to achieve its mission and goals (see Figure 8.5). In Chapter 6 we discussed forces in the task and general environments that have the potential to affect an organization. We noted that changes in these forces can produce opportunities that an organization might take advantage of and threats that may harm its current situation.

The first step in SWOT analysis is to identify an organization's strengths and weaknesses. Table 8.1 lists many important strengths (such as high-quality skills in marketing and in research and development) and weaknesses (such as rising manufacturing costs and outdated technology). The task facing managers is to identify the strengths and weaknesses that characterize the present state of their organization.

The second step in SWOT analysis begins when managers embark on a full-scale SWOT planning exercise to identify potential opportunities and threats in the environment that affect the organization now or may affect it in the future. Examples of possible opportunities and threats that must be anticipated (many of which were discussed in Chapter 6) are listed in Table 8.1. Scenario planning is often used to strengthen this analysis.

Figure 8.5

Planning and Strategy Formulation

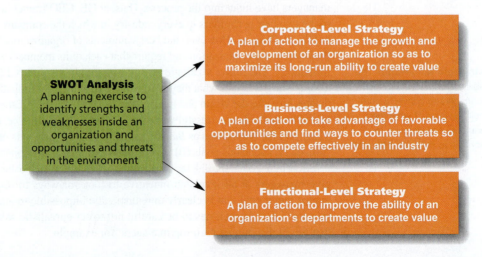

Table 8.1

Questions for SWOT Analysis

Potential Strengths	Potential Opportunities	Potential Weaknesses	Potential Threats
Well-developed strategy?	Expand core business(es)?	Poorly developed strategy?	Attacks on core business(es)?
Strong product lines?	Exploit new market segments?	Obsolete, narrow product lines?	Increase in domestic competition?
Broad market coverage?	Widen product range?	Rising manufacturing costs?	Increase in foreign competition?
Manufacturing competence?	Extend cost or differentiation advantage?	Decline in R&D innovations?	Change in consumer tastes?
Good marketing skills?	Diversify into new growth businesses?	Poor marketing plan?	Fall in barriers to entry?
Good materials management systems?	Expand into foreign markets?	Poor materials management systems?	Rise in new or substitute products?
R&D skills and leadership?	Apply R&D skills in new areas?	Loss of customer goodwill?	Increase in industry rivalry?
Human resource competencies?	Enter new related businesses?	Inadequate human resources?	New forms of industry competition?
Brand-name reputation?	Vertically integrate forward?	Loss of brand name?	Potential for takeover?
Cost of differentiation advantage?	Vertically integrate backward?	Growth without direction?	Changes in demographic factors?
Appropriate management style?	Overcome barriers to entry?	Loss of corporate direction?	Changes in economic factors?
Appropriate organizational structure?	Reduce rivalry among competitors?	Infighting among divisions?	Downturn in economy?
Appropriate control systems?	Apply brand-name capital in new areas?	Loss of corporate control?	Rising labor costs?
Ability to manage strategic change?	Seek fast market growth?	Inappropriate organizational structure and control systems?	Slower market growth?
Others?	Others?	High conflict and politics?	Others?
		Others?	

With the SWOT analysis completed, and strengths, weaknesses, opportunities, and threats identified, managers can continue the planning process and determine specific strategies for achieving the organization's mission and goals. The resulting strategies should enable the organization to attain its goals by taking advantage of opportunities, countering threats, building strengths, and correcting organizational weaknesses. To appreciate how managers can use SWOT analysis to formulate strategy, consider the example of General Motors. When Mary Barra became CEO in January 2014, the company was recovering from bankruptcy and profits were down. Yet those were not the biggest strategic challenges Barra would face in her first few weeks as CEO. For more details, see the discussion in the accompanying "Manager as a Person" feature.

**Manager as
a Person**

Mary Barra Faces GM's Problems

When Mary Barra took over as chief executive officer of General Motors in January 2014, it was a challenging time for the automaker. It had declared bankruptcy in 2009 and was still on the mend. Its net profit for 2013 was low due to several one-time costs, including restructuring in Europe. But even more important was that within weeks of taking the job, Barra began the recall of 1.6 million General Motors cars made between 2003 and 2007. The cars recalled were the Cobalt, the HHR, the G5, the Solstice, the Ion, and the Sky.

The cars had faulty ignition switches that would turn off the car while it was being driven, causing accidents and preventing the air bags from deploying. The company said the faulty switches caused at least 31 accidents and at least 12 deaths. More

Marry Barra, CEO of General Motors at the 2014 New York International Auto Show. Despite challenges at GM, Barra has decided not to change the company's basic strategy.

accidents and deaths could come to light as the investigation of the problem continues.

As part of the investigation, it was revealed that problems with the ignition switch emerged as early as 2001 during pre-production tests on the Ion. General Motors documents indicate that the problem was fixed at that time. However, in 2003, a General Motors service technician observed the problem in an Ion. At the time, the technician suggested that having several other keys on the key ring had worn out the ignition switch. In 2004, in a test of the Cobalt that used the same ignition switch, an engineer bumped the key and the car turned off. Despite these indicators, the switch was used for several more years and installed in several more car models.

This is the General Motors that Barra inherited: recovering from bankruptcy, down in net profit, and dealing with a significant scandal around why it took more than a decade to recall cars that were causing accidents and deaths. One might expect that Barra would seek to avoid responsibility for the recall, given that the problems occurred before she became CEO. However, she has taken ownership of the recall and company's failings.[31]

"We are putting the customer first, and that is guiding every decision we make. That is how we want today's GM to be judged. How we handle the recall will be an important test of that commitment," she said. "But it cannot stop there. We need to continue on the path of putting the customer first in everything we do. It's not something that only gets decided by senior leadership. We all have to own it . . . and we're using this opportunity to change much more about our business."[32]

Barra has publicly stated that problems within General Motors allowed the ignition switch to reach the market and vowed to make the development process much faster in the future. She also released a series of videos to answer consumer questions about the recall and whether the cars are safe to drive. She created the position of vice president for global vehicle safety and gave the position a more direct link to company leadership than past safety officers were given. She plans to testify before Congress when hearings are held about the recall.

Despite all the challenges she has been given, Barra does not seem inclined to change the company's strategy. She was quoted in February 2014 as saying, "There's no right turn or left turn in our strategy. We have a sound strategy. We need to accelerate the implementation of it. I want to make sure that employees around the globe understand the plan is the plan. Because I don't want to lose a minute."[33]

Barra's decision not to change the strategy of General Motors does not ignore the company's strengths, weaknesses, opportunities, and threats. In strengths, she perceives that General Motors has a strong lineup of vehicles to bring to the market. However, she notes a weakness in that some of the General Motors brands, specifically Cadillac and Chevrolet, need to be renewed.

She sees an opportunity for General Motors to grow in China and to become more global in general. While General Motors is already a leader in China, Barra believes there is still room for growth. In fact, she wants to create a new position of president of international operations to take the company's global strategy to the next level. She also plans to have General Motors pursue trends in the car industry such as fuel efficiency and autonomous driving. Also important, Bara said, will be finding ways to integrate smartphones and other consumer electronic devices into cars in a manner that will allow for their safe use while driving.

In threats, she has noted the costs of materials and competition from brands like the Opel in Europe.[34] The U.S. Department of Justice's ongoing investigation of the ignition switch and the timing of the recall is certainly a threat, but one for which Barra's handling has received much praise. One business writer listed Barra's strong communication skills as strength that will help the company as it deals with the recall and the investigation.[35]

The analysis of General Motors strengths, weaknesses, opportunities, and threats finds the company with much to do: "We clearly have a lot of work ahead to make all of our regions solidly and consistently profitable," Barra said. "It's going to be a multi-year journey that will include brand building, significant reductions in material and logistics cost and overall lower fixed cost."[36]

The Five Forces Model

A well-known model that helps managers focus on the five most important competitive forces, or potential threats, in the external environment is Michael Porter's five forces model.[37] We discussed the first four forces in the following list in Chapter 6. Porter identified these five factors as major threats because they affect how much profit organizations competing within the same industry can expect to make:

- *The level of rivalry among organizations in an industry:* The more that companies compete against one another for customers—for example, by lowering the prices of their products or by increasing advertising—the lower is the level of industry profits (low prices mean less profit).

- *The potential for entry into an industry:* The easier it is for companies to enter an industry—because, for example, barriers to entry, such as brand loyalty, are low—the more likely it is for industry prices and therefore industry profits to be low.

- *The power of large suppliers:* If there are only a few large suppliers of an important input, then suppliers can drive up the price of that input, and expensive inputs result in lower profits for companies in an industry.

- *The power of large customers:* If only a few large customers are available to buy an industry's output, they can bargain to drive down the price of that output. As a result, industry producers make lower profits.

- *The threat of substitute products:* Often the output of one industry is a substitute for the output of another industry (plastic may be a substitute for steel in some applications, for example; similarly, bottled water is a substitute for cola). When a substitute for their product exists, companies cannot demand high prices for it or customers will switch to the substitute, and this constraint keeps their profits low.

Porter argued that when managers analyze opportunities and threats, they should pay particular attention to these five forces because they are the major threats an organization will encounter. It is the job of managers at the corporate, business, and functional levels to formulate strategies to counter these threats so an organization can manage its task and general environments, perform at a high level, and generate high profits. At GM, Mary Barra performed such analysis to identify the opportunities and threats the company faces.

hypercompetition Permanent, ongoing, intense competition brought about in an industry by advancing technology or changing customer tastes.

Today competition is tough in most industries, whether companies make cars, soup, computers, or dolls. The term **hypercompetition** applies to industries that are characterized by permanent, ongoing, intense competition brought about by advancing technology or changing customer tastes and fads and fashions.[38] Clearly, planning and strategy formulation are much more difficult and risky when hypercompetition prevails in an industry.

Formulating Business-Level Strategies

Michael Porter, the researcher who developed the five forces model, also developed a theory of how managers can select a business-level strategy—a plan to gain a competitive advantage in a particular market or industry.[39] Porter argued that business-level strategy creates a competitive advantage because it allows an organization (or a division of a company) to *counter and reduce* the threat of the five industry forces. That is, successful business-level strategy reduces rivalry, prevents new competitors from entering the industry, reduces the power of suppliers or buyers, and lowers the threat of substitutes—and this raises prices and profits.

According to Porter, to obtain these higher profits managers must choose between two basic ways of increasing the value of an organization's products: *differentiating the product* to increase its value to customers or *lowering the costs* of making the product. Porter also argues that managers must choose between serving the whole market or serving just one segment or part of a market. Based on those choices, managers choose to pursue one of four business-level strategies: low cost, differentiation, focused low cost, or focused differentiation (see Table 8.2).

Low-Cost Strategy

low-cost strategy Driving the organization's costs down below the costs of its rivals.

With a **low-cost strategy**, managers try to gain a competitive advantage by focusing the energy of all the organization's departments or functions on driving the company's costs down below the costs of its industry rivals. This strategy, for example, would require that manufacturing managers search for new ways to reduce production costs, R&D managers focus on developing new products that can be manufactured more cheaply, and marketing managers find ways to lower the costs of attracting customers. According to Porter, companies pursuing a low-cost strategy can sell a product for less than their rivals sell it and yet still make a good profit because of their lower costs. Thus such organizations enjoy a competitive advantage based on their low prices. For example, BIC pursues a low-cost strategy: It offers customers razor blades priced lower than Gillette's and ballpoint pens less expensive than those offered by Cross or Waterman. Also, when existing companies have low costs and can charge low prices, it is difficult for new companies to enter the industry because entering is always an expensive process.

Differentiation Strategy

differentiation strategy Distinguishing an organization's products from the products of competitors on dimensions such as product design, quality, or after-sales service.

With a **differentiation strategy**, managers try to gain a competitive advantage by focusing all the energies of the organization's departments or functions on *distinguishing* the organization's products from those of competitors on one or more important dimensions, such as product design, quality, or after-sales service and support. Often the process of making products unique and different is expensive. This strategy, for example, frequently requires that managers increase spending on product design or R&D to differentiate products, and costs rise as a result. Organizations that successfully pursue a differentiation strategy may be able to charge a *premium price* for their products; the premium price lets organizations pursuing a differentiation strategy recoup their higher costs. Coca-Cola, PepsiCo, and Procter & Gamble are some of the many well-known companies that pursue a strategy of differentiation. They spend enormous amounts of money on advertising to differentiate, and create a unique image for, their products. Also, differentiation makes industry entry difficult because new companies have no brand name to help them compete and customers don't perceive other products to be close substitutes, so this also allows premium pricing and results in high profits.

"Stuck in the Middle"

According to Porter's theory, managers cannot simultaneously pursue both a low-cost strategy and a differentiation strategy. Porter identified a simple correlation: Differentiation raises costs and thus necessitates premium pricing to recoup those high costs. For example, if BIC suddenly began to advertise heavily to try to build a strong global brand image for its products, BIC's costs would rise. BIC then could no longer make a profit simply by pricing its blades

Table 8.2

Porter's Business-Level Strategies

Strategy	Number of Market Segments Served	
	Many	Few
Low cost	√	
Focused low cost		√
Differentiation	√	
Focused differentiation		√

or pens lower than Gillette or Cross. According to Porter, managers must choose between a low-cost strategy and a differentiation strategy. He refers to managers and organizations that have not made this choice as being "stuck in the middle."

Organizations stuck in the middle tend to have lower levels of performance than do those that pursue a low-cost or a differentiation strategy. To avoid being stuck in the middle, top managers must instruct departmental managers to take actions that will result in either low cost or differentiation.

However, exceptions to this rule can be found. For example, Southwest Airlines has written its mission statement to say "dedication to the highest quality of customer service delivered with a sense of warmth, friendliness, individual pride, and company spirit."[40] Based on this statement, the company seems to be pursuing a differentiation strategy based on customer service. Yet the average price of a one-way ticket on a Southwest flight in 2013 was $154.72, which suggests a cost leadership strategy. Likewise, Apple has a story that mixes cost leadership with differentiation. Apple CEO Tim Cook emphasizes that Apple's strategy is to focus on making great products—a differentiation strategy. He said the company never had the goal of selling a low-cost phone.[41] However, he said, the company did find a way to reach its goal of providing a great experience with a phone while reducing its cost. Cook emphasizes that differentiation was the goal, but low cost also became possible. These examples suggest that although Porter's ideas may be valid in most cases, very well-managed companies such as Southwest Airlines and Apple may pursue both low costs and differentiated products.

Focused Low-Cost and Focused Differentiation Strategies

Both the differentiation strategy and the low-cost strategy are aimed at serving many or most segments of a particular market, such as for cars, toys, foods, or computers. Porter identified two other business-level strategies that aim to serve the needs of customers in only one or a few market segments.[42] Managers pursuing a **focused low-cost strategy** serve one or a few segments of the overall market and aim to make their organization the lowest-cost company serving that segment. By contrast, managers pursuing a **focused differentiation strategy** serve just one or a few segments of the market and aim to make their organization the most differentiated company serving that segment.

focused low-cost strategy Serving only one segment of the overall market and trying to be the lowest-cost organization serving that segment.

focused differentiation strategy Serving only one segment of the overall market and trying to be the most differentiated organization serving that segment.

Companies pursuing either of these strategies have chosen to *specialize* in some way by directing their efforts at a particular kind of customer (such as serving the needs of babies or affluent customers) or even the needs of customers in a specific geographic region (customers on the East or West Coast). BMW, for example, pursues a focused differentiation strategy, producing cars exclusively for higher-income customers. By contrast, Toyota pursues a differentiation strategy and produces cars that appeal to consumers in almost all segments of the car market, from basic transportation (Toyota Corolla) through the middle of the market (Toyota Camry) to the high-income end of the market (Lexus). An interesting example of how companies pursuing a focused low-cost strategy, by specializing in one market segment, can compete with a large, established organization is profiled in the accompanying "Management Insight" feature.

Management Insight

Redbox and Netflix versus Blockbuster

Rent a DVD for $1.20 or a video game for $2? How about all the movies and television episodes you can watch for $7.99 a month? Redbox and Netflix, the two companies that supply these services, typify the low-cost leadership strategy.

Redbox is an automated kiosk store that rents DVDs, Blu-ray disks, and video games to consumers. The bright red kiosks are stores located inside or outside other stores, such as grocery stores, pharmacies, and convenience stores. Users can make their rental selections at the kiosks, online, or on the Redbox mobile app. Once the selection is made, either at the kiosk or otherwise, the consumer only has to swipe a credit card at the kiosk and the product will be automatically delivered within seconds. With about 35,900 kiosks nationwide, Redbox estimates that 68 percent of Americans can drive to one of its kiosks in five minutes or less.[43] Redbox also has on-demand Internet streaming service that allows consumers to watch films and television programs on different Internet-capable devices.

Netflix is a provider of films and television episodes through the mail and on-demand Internet streaming. Consumers can choose different levels of service, including streaming only, DVD mail order only, or a combination of the two. Netflix was founded in 1997 after Reed Hastings, a former math teacher and founder of a software company, paid $40 in late fees when returning a copy of the film *Apollo 13* well past its due date.[44] Hastings had just sold his software company and used the money to co-found Netflix with Marc Randolph, a former co-worker who had co-founded a computer mail order company. The business model for Netflix avoids problems like $40 late fees by charging a flat fee for unlimited rentals without due dates, shipping charges, or other types of per-rental fees. At the end of 2013, Netflix reported having 33.1 million subscribers in the United States.

Before Redbox and Netflix, companies like Blockbuster rented videos and games from large store locations. In 2004 Blockbuster had over 9,000 stores in the United States.[45] However, it filed for bankruptcy in 2010,[46] sold its assets to Dish Network in 2011,[47] and closed its last U.S. store in 2013.[48] What happened? Cost leaders like Redbox and Netflix entered the market, and Blockbuster found it could not compete.

It did have the opportunity to compete. In 2000 Netflix offered to sell Blockbuster a 49 percent stake in the company and to change the name from Netflix to Blockbuster .com. In other words, Netflix offered to provide an online subscription service for Blockbuster. Blockbuster declined the offer and started its own online subscription service in 2004. But by then Netflix had a foothold. Hastings said that the timing of Blockbuster's launch of online subscriptions allowed Netflix to survive. In 2000, when Netflix offered to sell Blockbuster a stake, Netflix was not yet profitable. "If they had launched two years earlier," Hastings said, "they would have killed us."[49]

But timing was not the only thing on the side of Redbox and Netflix. The low prices the companies offer to consumers are a big part of their success. Both companies are low-cost leaders who revolutionized the pricing structure for renting movies. While companies like Blockbuster charged customers to rent movies and then charged late fees if the movies were not returned on time, neither Redbox nor Netflix have late charges. Redbox simply charges customers by the day. Each day of rental is the same set low price. Netflix allows customers to keep DVDs for as long as the customer would like. When a customer returns a DVD, another one is sent. These pricing strategies mean customers know exactly how much their movie rentals cost.

Not every price leader drives competitors out of business, but Redbox and Netflix, as well as other streaming services, are responsible for the demise of an organization like Blockbuster.

Increasingly, smaller companies are finding it easier to pursue a focused strategy and compete successfully against large, powerful, low-cost and differentiated companies because of advances in IT that lower costs and enable them to reach and attract customers. By establishing a storefront on the web, thousands of small, specialized companies have been able to carve out a profitable niche against large bricks-and-mortar and virtual competitors. Zara, a Spanish manufacturer of fashionable clothing whose sales have soared in recent years, provides an excellent example of the way even a small bricks-and-mortar company can use IT to pursue a focused strategy and compete globally.[50] Zara has managed to position itself as the low-price, low-cost leader in the fashion segment of the clothing market, against differentiators like Gucci, Dior, and Armani, because it has applied IT to its specific needs. Zara has created IT that allows it to manage its design and manufacturing process in a way that minimizes the inventory it has to carry—the major cost borne by a clothing retailer. However, its IT also gives its designers instantaneous feedback on which clothes are selling well and in which countries, and this gives Zara a competitive advantage from differentiation. Specifically, Zara

Zara models an incredibly successful strategy in jumping on trends and turning out new fashion lines in record time, while its smart store layout allows shoppers to quickly find which styles appeal to them.

can manufacture more of a particular kind of dress or suit to meet high customer demand, decide which clothing should be sold in its rapidly expanding network of global stores, and constantly change the mix of clothes it offers customers to keep up with fashion—at low cost.

Zara's IT also lets it efficiently manage the interface between its design and manufacturing operations. Zara takes only five weeks to design a new collection and then a week to make it. Fashion houses like Chanel and Armani, by contrast, can take six or more months to design a collection and then three more months to make it available in stores.[51] This short time to market gives Zara great flexibility and allows the company to respond quickly to the rapidly changing fashion market, in which fashions can change several times a year. Because of the quick manufacturing-to-sales cycle and just-in-time fashion, Zara offers its clothes collections at relatively low prices and still makes profits that are the envy of the fashion clothing industry.[52]

Zara has been able to pursue a focused strategy that is simultaneously low-cost and differentiated because it has developed many strengths in functions such as clothing design, marketing, and IT that have given it a competitive advantage. Developing functional-level strategies that strengthen business-level strategy and increase competitive advantage is a vital managerial task. Discussion of this important issue is left until the next chapter. First, we need to go up one planning level and examine how corporate strategy helps an organization achieve its mission and goals.

Formulating Corporate-Level Strategies

LO8-4

Differentiate between the main types of corporate-level strategies and explain how they are used to strengthen a company's business-level strategy and competitive advantage.

Once managers have formulated the business-level strategies that will best position a company, or a division of a company, to compete in an industry and outperform its rivals, they must look to the future. If their planning has been successful, the company will be generating high profits, and their task now is to plan how to invest these profits to increase performance over time.

Recall that *corporate-level strategy* is a plan of action that involves choosing in which industries and countries a company should invest its resources to achieve its mission and goals. In choosing a corporate-level strategy, managers ask, How should the growth and development of our company be managed to increase its ability to create value for customers (and thus increase its performance) over the long run? Managers of effective organizations actively seek new opportunities to use a company's resources to create new and improved goods and services for customers. Examples of organizations whose product lines are growing rapidly are Google, Intel, Apple, and Toyota, whose managers pursue any feasible opportunity to use their companies' skills to provide customers with new products.

In addition, some managers must help their organizations respond to threats due to changing forces in the task or general environment that have made their business-level strategies less effective and reduced profits. For example, customers may no longer be buying the kinds of goods and services a company is producing (high-salt soup, bulky CRT televisions, or gas-guzzling SUVs), or other organizations may have entered the market and attracted away customers (this happened to Sony in the 2000s after Apple and Samsung began to produce better MP3 players, laptops, and smartphones). Top managers aim to find corporate strategies that can help the organization strengthen its business-level strategies and thus respond to these changes and improve performance.

The principal corporate-level strategies that managers use to help a company grow and keep it at the top of its industry, or to help it retrench and reorganize to stop its decline, are (1) concentration on a single industry, (2) vertical integration, (3) diversification, and (4) international expansion. An organization will benefit from pursuing any of these strategies only when the strategy helps further increase the value of the organization's goods and services so that more customers buy them. Specifically, to increase the value of goods and services, a corporate-level strategy must help a company, or one of its divisions, either (1) lower the costs of developing and making products or (2) increase product differentiation so that more customers want to buy the products even at high or premium prices. Both of these outcomes strengthen a company's competitive advantage and increase its performance.

Concentration on a Single Industry

concentration on a single industry Reinvesting a company's profits to strengthen its competitive position in its current industry.

Most growing companies reinvest their profits to strengthen their competitive position in the industry in which they are currently operating; in doing so, they pursue the corporate-level strategy of **concentration on a single industry**. Most commonly, an organization uses its functional skills to develop new kinds of products, or it expands the number of locations in which it uses those skills. For example, Apple continuously introduces improved mobile wireless digital devices such as the iPhone and iPad, whereas McDonald's, which began as one restaurant in California, focused all its efforts on using its resources to quickly expand across the globe to become the biggest and most profitable U.S. fast-food company. The way in which Crocs focuses on the shoe business is discussed in the accompanying "Management Insight" feature.

Management Insight

Getting Walked All Over in the Shoe Business

Crocs is one company that has stuck to its product. The company makes shoes. Not just any shoes: the company makes shoes from something called Croslite, a trademarked resin that makes Crocs comfortable, soft, and lightweight. The company was founded in 2002[53] and hit its popularity peak in 2007, when it sold 50 million pairs.[54] The best-known product of the company is its clog, a chunky and sometimes brightly colored shoe. The company has expanded its product line slightly to include accessories and apparel, but its main business remains shoes made of its special resin. Yet by 2009 the company was struggling. Sales were hurt by the recession that began in 2008 and by knockoff shoes that cut into sales of Crocs and helped saturate the market. As if that was not bad enough, there also was a backlash from consumers.

Some people hated the footwear enough to start a social media campaign against Crocs. One blog, called I Hate Crocs Dot Com, lamented that "blaringly, violently distasteful and while most trends of such an obviously unfashionable nature don't tend to survive for exceptionally long, Crocs have."[55] There also were videos posted to YouTube of people destroying the shoes and a Facebook page with more than 1.5 million likes that described Crocs as "like shoes . . . only well, repulsive."[56]

By the end of 2008 the company posted a $200 million loss, paralleling the $200 million profit it made in 2007. To recover, the company expanded its shoe line to include more fashionable—but still comfortable—shoes.[57] Then in 2013 the company fired its CEO and secured a $200 million investment from the private equity firm Blackstone.

In reporting on the financials for the last quarter of 2013, the chairman of the board, Thomas J. Smach, said, "As we look forward, 2014 will be a significant transition period for the company. We will recruit a new CEO who will work with the reconstituted board to refine the company's short-term and long-term strategic plans."[58] Clearly, Crocs is planning to stay in the shoe business for a long time.

On the other hand, when organizations are performing effectively, they often decide to enter *new industries* in which they can use their growing profits to establish new operating divisions to create and make a wider range of more valuable products. Thus they begin to pursue vertical integration or diversification—such as Coca-Cola, PepsiCo, and Campbell's Soup.

Vertical Integration

When an organization is performing well in its industry, managers often see new opportunities to create value either by producing the inputs it uses to make its products or by distributing and selling its products to customers. For example, as Tesla Motors works toward its goal of mass-producing an electric car that will sell for $35,000 by 2017, it recognizes that it will need batteries. To meet that need, Tesla will become its own battery supplier by building a large battery factory. Not only does Tesla expect that the factory will supply its needs, it also expects the factory to lower the costs of the batteries.[59] **Vertical integration** is a corporate-level strategy in which a company expands its business operations either backward into a new industry that produces inputs for the company's products (*backward vertical integration*) or forward into a new industry that uses, distributes, or sells the company's products (*forward vertical integration*).[60] A steel company that buys iron ore mines and enters the raw materials industry to supply the ore needed to make steel is engaging in backward vertical integration. A PC maker that decides to enter the retail industry and open a chain of company-owned retail outlets to sell its PCs is engaging in forward integration. For example, Apple entered the retail industry when it set up a chain of Apple stores to sell its computers and other electronic devices.

Figure 8.6 illustrates the four main stages in a typical raw material to customer value chain; value is added to the product at each stage by the activities involved in each industry. For a company based in the assembly stage, backward integration would involve establishing a new division in the intermediate manufacturing or raw material production industries; and forward integration would involve establishing a new division to distribute its products to wholesalers or a retail division to sell directly to customers. A division at one stage or one industry receives the product produced by the division in the previous stage or industry, transforms it in some way—adding value—and then transfers the output at a higher price to the division at the next stage in the chain.

As an example of how this industry value chain works, consider the cola segment of the soft drink industry. In the raw material industry, suppliers include sugar companies and manufacturers of artificial sweeteners such as NutraSweet and Splenda, which are used in diet colas. These companies sell their products to companies in the soft drink industry that make concentrate—such as Coca-Cola and PepsiCo, which mix these inputs with others to produce the cola concentrate. In the process, they add value to these inputs. The concentrate producers then sell the concentrate to companies in the bottling and distribution industry, which add carbonated water to the concentrate and package the resulting drinks—again adding value to the concentrate. Next the bottlers distribute and sell the soft drinks to retailers, including stores such as Costco and Walmart and fast-food chains such as McDonald's. Companies in the retail industry add value by making the product accessible to customers, and they profit from direct sales to customers. Thus value and profit are added by companies at each stage in the raw material to consumer chain.

vertical integration
Expanding a company's operations either backward into an industry that produces inputs for its products or forward into an industry that uses, distributes, or sells its products.

Figure 8.6

Stages in a Vertical Value Chain

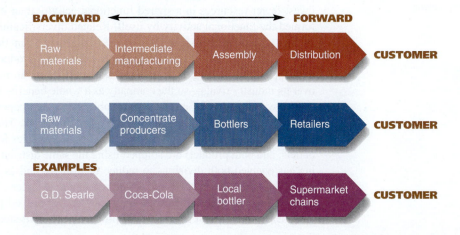

Managers pursue vertical integration because it allows them either to add value to their products by making them special or unique or to lower the costs of making and selling them. An example of using forward vertical integration to increase differentiation is Apple's decision to open its own stores to make its unique products more accessible to customers who could try them out before they bought them. An example of using forward vertical integration to lower costs is Matsushita's decision to open company-owned stores to sell its Panasonic and JVC products and thus keep the profit that otherwise would be earned by independent retailers.[61] So too is Coca-Cola's and PepsiCo's decision to buy their bottlers so they can better differentiate their products and lower costs in the future.

Although vertical integration can strengthen an organization's competitive advantage and increase its performance, it can also reduce its flexibility to respond to changing environmental conditions and create threats that must be countered by changing the organization's strategy. For example, GE acquired the television network NBC Universal in 1986 when it purchased Radio Corporation of America. However, in the 2010s, GE CEO Jeff Immelt wanted to refocus the company on its industrial roots. Selling NBC, Immelt suggested, would free up capital that GE could reinvest in businesses that use the company's core strengths. The company began selling NBC to Comcast Corp in 2010 and completed the sale in 2013. A similar story may play out at Procter and Gamble. P&G acquired the Gillette Company in 2005. Duracell batteries, a vertical integration for Gillette, came with it. However, Duracell stands out as an oddball among the other products in P&G's portfolio, and some analysts have suggested that P&G sell off Duracell.[62]

Thus, when considering vertical integration as a strategy to add value, managers must be careful because sometimes it may *reduce* a company's ability to create value when the environment changes. This is why so many companies have divested themselves of units that draw attention and resources away from an organization's primary purpose.

Diversification

diversification Expanding a company's business operations into a new industry in order to produce new kinds of valuable goods or services.

Diversification is the corporate-level strategy of expanding a company's business operations into a new industry in order to produce new kinds of valuable goods or services.[63] Examples include PepsiCo's diversification into the snack food business with the purchase of Frito Lay, and Cisco's diversification into consumer electronics when it purchased Linksys. There are two main kinds of diversification: related and unrelated.

related diversification Entering a new business or industry to create a competitive advantage in one or more of an organization's existing divisions or businesses.

RELATED DIVERSIFICATION   **Related diversification** is the strategy of entering a new business or industry to create a competitive advantage in one or more of an organization's existing divisions or businesses. Related diversification can add value to an organization's products if managers can find ways for its various divisions or business units to share their valuable skills or resources so that synergy is created.[64] **Synergy** is obtained when the value created by two divisions cooperating is greater than the value that would be created if the two divisions operated separately and independently. For example, suppose two or more divisions of a diversified company can use the same manufacturing facilities, distribution channels, or advertising campaigns—that is, share functional activities. Each division has to invest fewer resources in a shared functional activity than it would have to invest if it performed the functional activity by itself. Related diversification can be a major source of cost savings when divisions share the costs of performing a functional activity.[65] Similarly, if one division's R&D skills can improve another division's products and increase their differentiated appeal, this synergy can give the second division an important competitive advantage over its industry rivals—so the company as a whole benefits from diversification.

synergy Performance gains that result when individuals and departments coordinate their actions.

The way Procter & Gamble's disposable diaper and paper towel divisions cooperate is a good example of the successful production of synergies. These divisions share the costs of procuring inputs such as paper and packaging; a joint sales force sells both products to retail outlets; and both products are shipped using the same distribution system. This resource sharing has enabled both divisions to reduce their costs, and as a result, they can charge lower prices than their competitors and so attract more customers.[66] In addition, the divisions can share the research costs of developing new and improved products, such as finding more absorbent material, that increase both products' differentiated appeal. This is something that is also at the heart of 3M's corporate strategy.[67] From the beginning, 3M has pursued related diversification and created new businesses by leveraging its skills in research and development. Today the company has five business groups that share resources such as technology and marketing. The five groups are industrial, consumer, safety and graphics, health care, and electronics and energy. In 2011 the company spent 5.3 percent of revenue on research and development. In 2012 the company increased that amount to 5.5 percent. By 2017 3M expects to spend 6 percent of revenue on research and development and see about 40 percent of revenue come from products launched between 2012 and 2017.[68]

How does 3M do it? First, the company is a science-based enterprise with a strong tradition of innovation and risk taking. Risk taking is encouraged, and failure is not punished but is seen as a natural part of the process of creating new products and business.[69] Second, 3M's management is relentlessly focused on the company's customers and the problems they face. Many of 3M's products have come from helping customers to solve difficult problems. Third, managers set stretch goals that require the company to create new products and businesses at a rapid rate. Fourth, employees are given considerable autonomy to pursue their own ideas; indeed, 15 percent of employees' time can be spent working on projects of their own choosing without management approval. Many products have resulted from this autonomy, including the ubiquitous Post-it Notes. Fifth, while products belong to business units and business units are responsible for generating profits, the technologies belong to every unit within the company. Anyone at 3M is free to try to develop new applications for a technology developed by its business units. Finally, 3M organizes many companywide meetings where researchers from its different divisions are brought together to share the results of their work. Whether a company like PepsiCo should keep its acquisitions or split is discussed in the accompanying "Management Insight" feature.

Management Insight

PepsiCo: Would You Like a Snack with That Beverage?

The story of PepsiCo is a bit fizzy. The company's history tells a tale of related and unrelated diversification. Best known for the soda from which it gets its name, it was founded as the Pepsi-Cola Company in 1902. It merged with Frito-Lay, Inc., in 1965 to become PepsiCo. Along the way, it has diversified into many products related and unrelated to its beverage and packaged snack food businesses. For example, in unrelated diversification, the company once owned several restaurant chains like Pizza Hut, Taco Bell, and KFC. The company divested itself of its fast food division in 1997. Two examples of related diversification include the 1998 purchase of Tropicana and the 2001 purchase of Quaker Oats. The purchase of Tropicana diversified PepsiCo's beverage portfolio to include juices. The purchase of the Quaker Oats company was mainly to obtain the sports drink Gatorade, which Quaker owned. This purchase further diversified PepsiCo's beverage portfolio to include sports drinks. Also, the acquisition of Quaker's breakfast cereal, pasta, and rice business was not completely unrelated to the Frito-Lay snack food division.[70]

However, not everyone feels the products in PepsiCo's current portfolio are closely related. Activist investor Nelson Peltz would like to see PepsiCo split its beverage and food units apart. His argument is that the two units would be stronger apart than they are together. "A stand-alone snacks business would offer investors strong growth in sales, margins and free cash flow generation," he said. "And a stand-alone beverage business would provide strong, stable, free cash flow that may be optimized through an effective balance sheet and capital return program."[71] A *Wall Street Journal* survey released in 2014 indicated that the majority of institutional investors support splitting the company.[72]

However, at least two powerful voices do not want to see the company split. First, Warren Buffet, who is the chairman and chief executive officer of Berkshire Hathaway and someone to whom many investors will listen, said: "I think that Frito-Lay is an extremely good business. It's a better business than the soft drink business, but I think the soft drink business is a good business too, and I don't see any reason to split them up."[73]

The second powerful voice is that of PepsiCo CEO Indira Nooyi. Nooyi has been leading the company since 2006. In her previous roles with the company, she directed the divestment of the restaurant businesses as well as the acquisitions of Tropicana and Quaker Oats. Nooyi has insisted that beverages and snacks go together, both for consumers and for business logistics. "Decoupling our beverage and snack businesses in North America would significantly reduce our relevance to our customers," Nooyi said. "Within most of our largest grocery channel customers, we would fall from being the top supplier to a top 4-or-below supplier, and in the mass merchandise and drug channels, we would drop below the top 10."[74]

The company is keeping its beverage and food units together for now. But the arguments about whether these units are related or unrelated will likely continue for a long time.

In sum, to pursue related diversification successfully, managers search for new businesses where they can use the existing skills and resources in their departments and divisions to create synergies, add value to new products and businesses, and improve their competitive position and that of the entire company. In addition, managers may try to acquire a company in a new industry because they believe it possesses skills and resources that will improve the performance of one or more of their existing divisions. If successful, such skill transfers can help an organization to lower its costs or better differentiate its products because they create synergies between divisions.

unrelated diversification
Entering a new industry or buying a company in a new industry that is not related in any way to an organization's current businesses or industries.

UNRELATED DIVERSIFICATION   Managers pursue **unrelated diversification** when they establish divisions or buy companies in new industries that are *not* linked in any way to their current businesses or industries. One main reason for pursuing unrelated diversification is that sometimes managers can buy a poorly performing company, transfer their management skills to that company, turn around its business, and increase its performance—all of which create value.

Another reason for pursuing unrelated diversification is that purchasing businesses in different industries lets managers engage in *portfolio strategy,* which is apportioning financial resources among divisions to increase financial returns or spread risks among different businesses, much as individual investors do with their own portfolios. For example, managers may transfer funds from a rich division (a "cash cow") to a new and promising division (a "star") and, by appropriately allocating money between divisions, create value. Though used as a popular explanation in the 1980s for unrelated diversification, portfolio strategy ran into increasing criticism in the 1990s because it simply does not work.[75] Why? As managers expand the scope of their organization's operations and enter more and more industries, it becomes increasingly difficult for top managers to be knowledgeable about all of the organization's diverse businesses. Managers do not have the time to process all of the information required to adequately assess the strategy and performance of each division, and so the performance of the entire company often falls.

This problem has occurred at GE, as its then CEO Reg Jones commented: "I tried to review each business unit plan in great detail. This effort took untold hours and placed a tremendous burden on the corporate executive office. After a while I began to realize that no matter how hard we would work, we could not achieve the necessary in-depth understanding of the 40-odd business unit plans."[76] Unable to handle so much information, top managers are overwhelmed and eventually make important resource allocation decisions on the basis of only a superficial analysis of the competitive position of each division. This usually results in value being lost rather than created.[77]

Thus, although unrelated diversification can potentially create value for a company, research evidence suggests that *too much* diversification can cause managers to lose control of their organization's core business. As a result, diversification can reduce value rather than create it.[78] Because of this, during the last decade there has been an increasing trend for diversified companies to divest many of their unrelated, and sometimes related, divisions. Managers in companies like Tyco, Dial, and Textron have sold off many or most of their divisions and focused on increasing the performance of the core division that remained—in other words, they went back to a strategy of concentrating on a single industry.[79] In 2014 Honeywell International announced that it would divest its brake pads and braking system components business to better focus its corporate objectives around its core technologies. Before the announcement, Honeywell's outlook for 2014 was tepid at best. After the announcement, the company said it expected earnings growth of 8–12 percent.[80]

International Expansion

As if planning whether to vertically integrate, diversify, or concentrate on the core business were not a difficult enough task, corporate-level managers also must decide on the appropriate way to compete internationally. A basic question confronts the managers of any organization that needs to sell its products abroad and compete in more than one national market: To what extent should the organization customize features of its products and marketing campaign to different national conditions?[81]

global strategy Selling the same standardized product and using the same basic marketing approach in each national market.

multidomestic strategy Customizing products and marketing strategies to specific national conditions.

If managers decide that their organization should sell the same standardized product in each national market in which it competes, and use the same basic marketing approach, they adopt a **global strategy**.[82] Such companies undertake little, if any, customization to suit the specific needs of customers in different countries. But if managers decide to customize products and marketing strategies to specific national conditions, they adopt a **multidomestic strategy**. Matsushita, with its Panasonic and JVC brands, has traditionally pursued a global strategy, selling the same basic TVs, camcorders, and DVD and MP3 players in every country in which it does business and often using the same basic marketing approach. Unilever, the European food and household products company, has pursued a multidomestic strategy. Thus, to appeal to German customers, Unilever's German division sells a different range of food products and uses a different marketing approach than its North American division.

Both global and multidomestic strategies have advantages and disadvantages. The major advantage of a global strategy is the significant cost savings associated with not having to customize products and marketing approaches to different national conditions. For example, Rolex watches, Ralph Lauren or Tommy Hilfiger clothing, Chanel or Armani clothing or accessories or perfume, Dell computers, Chinese-made plastic toys and buckets, and U.S.-grown rice and wheat are all products that can be sold using the same marketing across many countries by simply changing the language. Thus companies can save a significant amount of money. The major disadvantage of pursuing a global strategy is that by ignoring national differences, managers may leave themselves vulnerable to local competitors that differentiate their products to suit local tastes.

Global food makers Kellogg's and Nestlé learned this when they entered the Indian processed food market, which is worth over $100 billion a year. These companies did not understand how to customize their products to the tastes of the Indian market and initially suffered large losses. When Kellogg's launched its breakfast cereals in India, for example, it failed to understand that most Indians eat cooked breakfasts because milk is normally not pasteurized. Today, with the growing availability of pasteurized or canned milk, it offers exotic cereals made from basmati rice and flavored with mango to appeal to customers. Similarly, Nestlé's Maggi noodles failed to please Indian customers until it gave them a "marsala" or mixed curry spice flavor; today its noodles have become a staple in Indian school lunches.[83]

The advantages and disadvantages of a multidomestic strategy are the opposite of those of a global strategy. The major advantage of a multidomestic strategy is that by customizing product offerings and marketing approaches to local conditions, managers may be able to gain market share or charge higher prices for their products. The major disadvantage is that customization raises production costs and puts the multidomestic company at a price disadvantage because it often has to charge prices higher than the prices charged by competitors pursuing a global strategy. Obviously the choice between these two strategies calls for trade-offs.

Managers at Gillette, the well-known razor blade maker that is now part of Procter & Gamble (P&G), created a strategy that combined the best features of both international strategies. Like P&G, Gillette has always been a global organization because its managers quickly saw the advantages of selling its core product, razor blades, in as many countries as possible. Gillette's strategy over the years has been pretty constant: Find a new country with a growing market for razor blades, form a strategic alliance with a local razor blade company and take

The offices of Hindustan Lever Limited in Mumbai, India. Unilever uses a multidomestic strategy to market its products globally.

a majority stake in it, invest in a large marketing campaign, and then build a modern factory to make razor blades and other products for the local market. For example, when Gillette entered Russia after the breakup of the Soviet Union, it saw a huge opportunity to increase sales. It formed a joint venture with a local company called Leninets Concern, which made a razor known as the Sputnik, and then with this base began to import its own brands into Russia. When sales grew sharply, Gillette decided to offer more products in the market and built a new plant in St. Petersburg.[84]

In establishing factories in countries where labor and other costs are low and then distributing and marketing its products to countries in that region of the world, Gillette pursued a global strategy. However, all of Gillette's research and development and design activities are located in the United States. As it develops new kinds of razors, it equips its foreign factories to manufacture them when it decides that local customers are ready to trade up to the new product. So, for example, Gillette's latest razor may be introduced in a country abroad years later than in the United States. Thus Gillette customizes its products to the needs of different countries and pursues a multidomestic strategy.

By pursuing this kind of international strategy, Gillette achieves low costs and still differentiates and customizes its product range to suit the needs of each country or world region.[85] P&G pursues a similar international strategy, and the merger between them to create the world's largest consumer products company came about because of the value that could be realized by pursuing related diversification at a global level. For example, P&G's corporate managers realized that substantial global synergies could be obtained by combining their global manufacturing, distribution, and sales operations across countries and world regions. These synergies have saved billions of dollars.[86] At the same time, by pooling their knowledge of the needs of customers in different countries, the combined companies can better differentiate and position products throughout the world. P&G's strategy is working; in 2013 *Fortune* named it 15th in its World's Most Admired Companies list.

CHOOSING A WAY TO EXPAND INTERNATIONALLY   As we have discussed, a more competitive global environment has proved to be both an opportunity and a threat for organizations and managers. The opportunity is that organizations that expand globally can open new markets, reach more customers, and gain access to new sources of raw materials and to low-cost suppliers of inputs. The threat is that organizations that expand globally are likely to encounter new competitors in the foreign countries they enter and must respond to new political, economic, and cultural conditions.

Before setting up foreign operations, managers of companies such as Amazon.com, Lands' End, GE, P&G, and Boeing needed to analyze the forces in the environment of a particular country (such as Korea or Brazil) to choose the right method to expand and respond to those forces in the most appropriate way. In general, four basic ways to operate in the global environment are importing and exporting, licensing and franchising, strategic alliances, and wholly owned foreign subsidiaries, Gillette's preferred approach. We briefly discuss each one, moving from the lowest level of foreign involvement and investment required of a global organization and its managers, and the least amount of risk, to the high end of the spectrum (see Figure 8.7).[87]

IMPORTING AND EXPORTING   The least complex global operations are exporting and importing. A company engaged in **exporting** makes products at home and sells them abroad. An organization might sell its own products abroad or allow a local organization in the foreign country to distribute its products. Few risks are associated with exporting because a company does not have to invest in developing manufacturing facilities abroad. It can further reduce its investment abroad if it allows a local company to distribute its products.

A company engaged in **importing** sells products at home that are made abroad (products it makes itself or buys from other companies). For example, most of the products that Pier 1 Imports and The Limited sell to their customers are made abroad. In many cases the appeal

exporting Making products at home and selling them abroad.

importing Selling products at home that are made abroad.

Figure 8.7
Four Ways to Expand Internationally

Level of foreign involvement and investment
and degree of risk

of a product—Irish crystal, French wine, Italian furniture, or Indian silk—is that it is made abroad. The Internet has made it much easier for companies to tell potential foreign buyers about their products; detailed product specifications and features are available online, and informed buyers can communicate easily with prospective sellers.

licensing Allowing a foreign organization to take charge of manufacturing and distributing a product in its country or world region in return for a negotiated fee.

LICENSING AND FRANCHISING In **licensing**, a company (the licenser) allows a foreign organization (the licensee) to take charge of both manufacturing and distributing one or more of its products in the licensee's country or world region in return for a negotiated fee. Chemical maker DuPont might license a local factory in India to produce nylon or Teflon. The advantage of licensing is that the licenser does not have to bear the development costs associated with opening up in a foreign country; the licensee bears the costs. The risks associated with this strategy are that the company granting the license has to give its foreign partner access to its technological know-how and so risks losing control of its secrets.

franchising Selling to a foreign organization the rights to use a brand name and operating know-how in return for a lump-sum payment and a share of the profits.

Whereas licensing is pursued primarily by manufacturing companies, franchising is pursued primarily by service organizations. In **franchising**, a company (the franchiser) sells to a foreign organization (the franchisee) the rights to use its brand name and operating know-how in return for a lump-sum payment and share of the franchiser's profits. Hilton Hotels might sell a franchise to a local company in Chile to operate hotels under the Hilton name in return for a franchise payment. The advantage of franchising is that the franchiser does not have to bear the development costs of overseas expansion and avoids the many problems associated with setting up foreign operations. The downside is that the organization that grants the franchise may lose control over how the franchisee operates, and product quality may fall. In this way franchisers, such as Hilton, Avis, and McDonald's, risk losing their good names. American customers who buy McDonald's hamburgers in Korea may reasonably expect those burgers to be as good as the ones they get at home. If they are not, McDonald's reputation will suffer over time. Once again, the Internet facilitates communication between partners and allows them to better meet each other's expectations.

strategic alliance An agreement in which managers pool or share their organization's resources and know-how with a foreign company, and the two organizations share the rewards and risks of starting a new venture.

STRATEGIC ALLIANCES One way to overcome the loss-of-control problems associated with exporting, licensing, and franchising is to expand globally by means of a strategic alliance. In a **strategic alliance**, managers pool or share their organization's resources and know-how with those of a foreign company, and the two organizations share the rewards or risks of starting a new venture in a foreign country. Sharing resources allows a U.S. company, for example, to take advantage of the high-quality skills of foreign manufacturers and the specialized knowledge of foreign managers about the needs of local customers and to reduce the risks involved in a venture. At the same time, the terms of the alliance give the U.S. company more control over how the good or service is produced or sold in the foreign country than it would have as a franchiser or licenser.

joint venture A strategic alliance among two or more companies that agree to jointly establish and share the ownership of a new business.

A strategic alliance can take the form of a written contract between two or more companies to exchange resources, or it can result in the creation of a new organization. A **joint venture** is a strategic alliance among two or more companies that agree to jointly establish and share the ownership of a new business.[88] An organization's level of involvement abroad increases in a joint venture because the alliance normally involves a capital investment in production facilities abroad in order to produce goods or services outside the home country. Risk, however, is reduced. The Internet and global teleconferencing provide the increased communication and coordination necessary for global partners to work together. For example, Coca-Cola and Nestlé formed a joint venture to market their teas, coffees, and health-oriented beverages in more than 50 countries.[89] And in 2014 Avon and KORRES, a Greek natural skin care company, entered a long-term strategic alliance in which Avon will manufacture and market KORRES products in Latin America. Avon is already established in Latin America, but adding KORRES products will allow Avon to pursue the natural and organic beauty market.[90]

wholly owned foreign subsidiary Production operations established in a foreign country independent of any local direct involvement.

WHOLLY OWNED FOREIGN SUBSIDIARIES   When managers decide to establish a **wholly owned foreign subsidiary**, they invest in establishing production operations in a foreign country independent of any local direct involvement. Many Japanese car component companies, for example, have established their own operations in the United States to supply U.S.-based Japanese carmakers such as Toyota and Honda with high-quality car components.

Operating alone, without any direct involvement from foreign companies, an organization receives all of the rewards and bears all of the risks associated with operating abroad.[91] This method of international expansion is much more expensive than the others because it requires a higher level of foreign investment and presents managers with many more threats. However, investment in a foreign subsidiary or division offers significant advantages: It gives an organization high potential returns because the organization does not have to share its profits with a foreign organization, and it reduces the level of risk because the organization's managers have full control over all aspects of their foreign subsidiary's operations. Moreover, this type of investment allows managers to protect their technology and know-how from foreign organizations. Large well-known companies like DuPont, GM, and P&G, which have plenty of resources, make extensive use of wholly owned subsidiaries.

Obviously global companies can use many of these different corporate strategies simultaneously to create the most value and strengthen their competitive position. We discussed earlier how P&G pursues related diversification at the global level while it pursues an international strategy that is a mixture of global and multidomestic. P&G also pursues vertical integration: It operates factories that make many of the specialized chemicals used in its products; it operates in the container industry and makes the thousands of different glass and plastic bottles and jars that contain its products; it prints its own product labels; and it distributes its products using its own fleet of trucks. Although P&G is highly diversified, it still puts the focus on its core individual product lines because it is famous for pursuing brand management—it concentrates resources around each brand, which in effect is managed as a "separate company." So P&G is trying to add value in every way it can from its corporate and business strategies. At the business level, for example, P&G aggressively pursues differentiation and charges premium prices for its products. However, it also strives to lower its costs and pursues the corporate-level strategies just discussed to achieve this.

One example of a joint venture is the new company formed from two established companies, Cargill of the United States and Copersucar of Brazil, discussed in the accompanying "Managing Globally" feature.

Managing Globally

Joint Venture Is a Sweet Deal for Sugar Production and Distribution

Two international companies sweetened the sugar market in 2014 with a joint venture. Each of the two companies brought different strengths to the venture, which aided the effectiveness of the global sugar supply chain.

The first company, Cargill, brought trading and logistics expertise to the venture along with a large global network of customers. Cargill began as a grain storage company in Minnesota in 1865 and has grown into a multinational corporation that trades, buys, and distributes agricultural commodities and produces animal feed and food ingredients. The company is the largest privately held corporation in terms of revenue in the United States. Cargill is "committed to feeding the world in a responsible way, reducing environmental impact and improving the communities where we live and work."[92]

Copersucar sponsors a racing car at the Masters Historic Racing Festival F1 race near Longfield, United Kingdom. Copersucar is leveraging its strengths by entering into a joint venture with Cargill.

The second company, Copersucar, brought mills that produce 10 percent of the world's sugar exports to the venture. Copersucar was founded in 2008 as a capital company. It is now Brazil's biggest trader and exporter of sugar. The mission of Copersucar is "to generate value through the vertical integration of the sugar and ethanol business chain."[93]

The joint venture will create a third entity and will operate out of Geneva, Switzerland.[94] The joint venture is expected to be completed in the second half of 2014. The ownership of the facilities will not change. Each company will continue to own its own assets. However, the assets will be pooled to serve the joint venture. Both companies also have assets that will not be a part of the venture.

What motivated these two companies to come together in a joint venture? Both have faced setbacks in recent years. Cargill was once a leader in sugar trading. However, in 2011 Cargill suffered its worst quarterly losses in a decade. The joint venture with Copersucar will allow it to regain its former status as a dominant force in sugar trading.

For its part, Copersucar had been dealing with losses from a prolonged dip in sugar prices and was further set back when its vital Santos port terminal and warehouses were destroyed in a fire in October 2013. The fire caused a 40 percent drop in sugar shipments from the port. With the joint venture, Copersucar will be able to refocus on sugar production.[95]

Working together, Cargill and Copersucar can better compete against other major traders. The two companies appear to have similar business values. Both mention ethical standards and social responsibility.

Planning and Implementing Strategy

After identifying appropriate business and corporate strategies to attain an organization's mission and goals, managers confront the challenge of putting those strategies into action. Strategy implementation is a five-step process:

1. Allocating responsibility for implementation to the appropriate individuals or groups.
2. Drafting detailed action plans that specify how a strategy is to be implemented.
3. Establishing a timetable for implementation that includes precise, measurable goals linked to the attainment of the action plan.
4. Allocating appropriate resources to the responsible individuals or groups.
5. Holding specific individuals or groups responsible for the attainment of corporate, divisional, and functional goals.

The planning process goes beyond just identifying effective strategies; it also includes plans to ensure that these strategies are put into action. Normally the plan for implementing a new strategy requires the development of new functional strategies, the redesign of an organization's structure, and the development of new control systems; it might also require a new program to change an organization's culture. These are issues we address in the next three chapters.

Summary and Review

LO8-1, 8-2

PLANNING Planning is a three-step process: (1) determining an organization's mission and goals; (2) formulating strategy; and (3) implementing strategy. Managers use planning to identify and select appropriate goals and courses of action for an organization and to decide how to allocate the resources they need to attain those goals and carry out those actions. A good plan builds commitment for the organization's goals, gives the organization a sense of direction and purpose, coordinates the different functions and divisions of the organization, and controls managers by making them accountable for specific goals. In large organizations planning takes place at three levels: corporate, business or divisional, and functional or departmental. Long-term plans have a time horizon of five years or more; intermediate-term plans, between one and five years; and short-term plans, one year or less.

LO8-1, 8-2, 8-3, 8-4   **DETERMINING MISSION AND GOALS AND FORMULATING STRATEGY**   Determining the organization's mission requires that managers define the business of the organization and establish major goals. Strategy formulation requires that managers perform a SWOT analysis and then choose appropriate strategies at the corporate, business, and functional levels. At the business level, managers are responsible for developing a successful low-cost and/or differentiation strategy, either for the whole market or a particular segment of it. At the functional level, departmental managers develop strategies to help the organization either add value to its products by differentiating them or lower the costs of value creation. At the corporate level, organizations use strategies such as concentration on a single industry, vertical integration, related and unrelated diversification, and international expansion to strengthen their competitive advantage by increasing the value of the goods and services provided to customers.

LO8-5   **IMPLEMENTING STRATEGY**   Strategy implementation requires that managers allocate responsibilities to appropriate individuals or groups; draft detailed action plans that specify how a strategy is to be implemented; establish a timetable for implementation that includes precise, measurable goals linked to the attainment of the action plan; allocate appropriate resources to the responsible individuals or groups; and hold individuals or groups accountable for the attainment of goals.

Management in Action

Topics for Discussion and Action

Discussion

1. Describe the three steps of planning. Explain how they are related. [LO8-1]

2. How can scenario planning help managers predict the future? [LO8-2]

3. What is the relationship among corporate-, business-, and functional-level strategies, and how do they create value for an organization? [LO8-3, 8-4]

4. Pick an industry and identify four companies in the industry that pursue one of the four main business-level strategies (low-cost, focused low-cost, and so on). [LO8-2, 8-3]

5. What is the difference between vertical integration and related diversification? [LO8-4]

Action

6. Ask a manager about the kinds of planning exercises he or she regularly uses. What are the purposes of these exercises, and what are their advantages or disadvantages? [LO8-1, 8-2]

7. Ask a manager to identify the corporate- and business-level strategies used by his or her organization. [LO8-3, 8-4]

Building Management Skills

How to Analyze a Company's Strategy [LO8-3, 8-4]

Pick a well-known business organization that has received recent press coverage and that provides annual reports at its website. From the information in the articles and annual reports, answer these questions:

1. What is (are) the main industry(ies) in which the company competes?

2. What business-level strategy does the company seem to be pursuing in this industry? Why?

3. What corporate-level strategies is the company pursuing? Why?

4. Have there been any major changes in its strategy recently? Why?

Managing Ethically [LO8-2, 8-5]

A few years ago, IBM announced that it had fired the three top managers of its Argentine division because of their involvement in a scheme to secure a $250 million contract for IBM to provide and service the computers of one of Argentina's largest state-owned banks. The three executives paid $14 million of the contract money to a third company, CCR, which paid nearly $6 million to phantom companies. This $6 million was then used to bribe the bank executives who agreed to give IBM the contract.

These bribes are not necessarily illegal under Argentine law. Moreover, the three managers argued that all companies have to pay bribes to get new business contracts, and they were not doing anything that managers in other companies were not.

Questions

1. Either by yourself or in a group decide if the business practice of paying bribes is ethical or unethical.

2. Should IBM allow its foreign divisions to pay bribes if all other companies are doing so?

3. If bribery is common in a particular country, what effect would this likely have on the nation's economy and culture?

Small Group Breakout Exercise

Low Cost or Differentiation? [LO8-2, 8-3]

Form groups of three or four people, and appoint one member as the spokesperson who will communicate your findings to the class when called on by the instructor. Then discuss the following scenario:

You are a team of managers of a major national clothing chain, and you have been charged with finding a way to restore your organization's competitive advantage. Recently your organization has been experiencing increasing competition from two sources. First, discount stores such as Walmart and Target have been undercutting your prices because they buy their clothes from low-cost foreign manufacturers, whereas you buy most of yours from high-quality domestic suppliers. Discount stores have been attracting your customers who buy at the low end of the price range. Second, small boutiques opening in malls provide high-price designer clothing and are attracting your customers at the high end of the market. Your company has become stuck in the middle, and you have to decide what to do: Should you start to buy abroad so you can lower your prices and pursue a low-cost strategy? Should you focus on the high end of the market and become more of a differentiator? Or should you try to pursue both a low-cost strategy and a differentiation strategy?

1. Using scenario planning, analyze the pros and cons of each alternative.

2. Think about the various clothing retailers in your local malls and city, and analyze the choices they have made about how to compete along the low-cost and differentiation dimensions.

Exploring the World Wide Web [LO8-1, 8-3, 8-4]

Go to Chipotle's webpage (www.chipotle.com) and click on "Company." Then click on "Development." Return to the main page and click on "Food with Integrity." Watch one (or more) of the videos posted to this page. Flip through the notebook on the page.

1. Which corporate-level strategy is Chipotle using?

2. What plans does Chipotle have for the future?

3. What makes Chipotle different from other restaurants?

Be the Manager [LO8-2, 8-3]

A group of investors in your city is considering opening a new upscale supermarket to compete with the major supermarket chains that are currently dominating the city's marketplace. They have called you in to help them determine what kind of upscale supermarket they should open. In other words, how can they best develop a competitive advantage against existing supermarket chains?

Questions

1. List the supermarket chains in your city, and identify their strengths and weaknesses.

2. What business-level strategies are these supermarkets currently pursuing?

3. What kind of supermarket would do best against the competition? What kind of business-level strategy should it pursue?

Bloomberg Businessweek Case in the News [LO 8-2, 8-3]

How the Average McDonald's Makes Twice as Much as Burger King

McDonald's may recently have struggled to lure customers, but it still does far more business at each location than rival burger chains. The average McDonald's restaurant in the U.S. drew $2.6 million in revenue last year. Average sales for No. 2 chain Burger King: $1.2 million, according to data from its largest franchisee, Carrols Restaurant Group.

What accounts for this more-than-a-million gap? "Everything from marketing and site selection to product initiatives and franchisee selection have been historical factors," said Nick Setyan, vice president in charge of equity research at Wedbush Securities, in an e-mail. Here are four factors that drive higher sales volumes at McDonald's:

1. **McDonald's gets more customers during off-peak hours.** Look no further than the strength of its breakfast business relative to that of Burger King, says Darren Tristano, executive vice president at restaurant consultancy Technomic. Egg McMuffin is part of the fast-food vocabulary in a way Burger King can't match. And beverage and snack offerings such as McCafe and wraps have helped increase McDonald's sales between meals. The dramatic impact from off-peak business explains why chains like Taco Bell are entering the battle for morning customers, while others such

as Starbucks are seeking more afternoon and evening business.

2. **The power of the Happy Meal.** McDonald's has the largest share of kids' meal sales in the fast-food industry and gets about 10 percent of total sales from Happy Meals, the most commonly advertised child-oriented fast-food item on television. Burger King, meanwhile, is still trying to win back "parties with kids and seniors and women," said Josh Kobza, Burger King's chief financial officer, at a conference last year. One way to do that: "We got rid of the creepy king character that tended to scare away women and children."

3. **McDonald's has an edge on efficiency.** Despite recent operational challenges at McDonald's, which have slowed down service, it is still more efficient. Its drive-through service can handle more cars at peak times, Tristano says, and McDonald's restaurants are adding a third service window to get customers through even faster. The average service time at McDonald's drive-throughs is 189.49 seconds, compared to 198.48 at Burger King, according to *QSR Magazine.* Drive-through service is important: Burger King franchisee Carrols gets 65 percent of its sales from the drive-through.

4. **More marketing dollars.** McDonald's spends a lot more on marketing than competitors, as Tristano points out. Its advertising costs in 2012 were $787.5 million vs. Burger King's $48.3 million, and the gap widened last year when Burger King itself spent only a few million on advertising in order to focus on equipment updates. In its 10-K submission, Burger King said it expects to spend less on advertising until 2016; the company declined to comment for this story.

Source: Venessa Wong, "How the Average McDonald's Makes Twice as Much as Burger King," *Bloomberg Business Week,* March 25, 2014. Used with permission of Bloomberg L.P. Copyright © 2014. All rights reserved.

Questions for Discussion

1. McDonald's uses a cost leadership strategy. However, what aspects of a differentiation strategy does this story suggest McDonald's uses?

2. What core strengths could Burger King use to catch up with McDonald's?

3. If you had to choose between eating at a McDonald's or a Burger King, which one would you choose and why? Does your answer have anything to do with the different strategies of the two companies?

CHAPTER 9

Value Chain Management: Functional Strategies for Competitive Advantage

Learning Objectives

After studying this chapter, you should be able to:

LO9-1 Explain the role of functional strategy and value chain management in achieving superior quality, efficiency, innovation, and responsiveness to customers.

LO9-2 Describe what customers want, and explain why it is so important for managers to be responsive to their needs.

LO9-3 Explain why achieving superior quality is so important, and understand the challenges facing managers and organizations that seek to implement total quality management.

LO9-4 Explain why achieving superior efficiency is so important, and understand the different kinds of techniques that need to be employed to increase efficiency.

LO9-5 Differentiate between two forms of innovation, and explain why innovation and product development are crucial components of the search for competitive advantage.

A MANAGER'S CHALLENGE

Ready for Takeoff? Increasing Airlines' Boarding Efficiency

Why is efficiency important? Is it faster to board the back of the plane first? Or should airlines file in passengers with window seats first, followed by those with middle seats, followed by those with aisle seats? What about just assigning passengers to random groups and boarding that way? Or how about not assigning seats and just allowing passengers to sit wherever they want?

These were the questions some major airlines were asking themselves recently in an effort to improve their punctuality ratings. Late departures and arrivals cost airlines dearly in more ways than reputation, so making sure boarding occurs in a timely manner is of great concern to the industry, as well as to passengers needing to make connecting flights.

Certainly the first two options sound like they would be faster than the free-for-all of allowing random groups to board at the same time or allowing passengers to sit wherever they like. Yet two recent studies found that random boarding does work a little quicker than the other options, believe it or not.

One study was conducted by American Airlines. It spent two years studying ways to speed up the boarding process and landed on randomized group boarding for most passengers. The airline still gives families, military personnel, and travelers with elite status priority boarding. It also allows passengers the option of paying for early boarding if they choose.

Part of American's study had observers watch thousands of boarding processes to see where things bogged down. Carry-on bags were a big problem. Passengers were bringing large bags on board to avoid baggage fees. When the plane was boarded back to front, those waiting in the aisles to get to their seats would put their bags in overhead

Airlines are always looking for ways to board passengers faster and more efficiently. What slows down boarding and departures? Both passengers who jump the line and those who pay for early boarding may be in the aisles as others try to board.

bins at the front of the plane, leaving no space for the bags of passengers who boarded later.

Using computer simulations, American not only found that the back-to-front boarding method was slower than the window-middle-aisle seat method, it surprisingly discovered that putting passengers into random boarding groups allowed the plane to fill up faster. Using the random method, more passengers got to their seats at the same time than the two-at-a-time rate of the back-to-front method. Also, passengers were more likely to stow their bags in overhead bins closer to their seats than at the front of the plane. The new method even reduced the number of bags American checked at the gate by 20 percent.[1] More recently, American tweaked the system to add passengers without carry-ons to the list of priority boarders.[2]

Another study was done by MythBusters, the Discovery Channel television show that applies scientific methods to test various accepted ideas. In the episode on plane boarding, the MythBusters team sought to confirm the myth that "when boarding an airplane, boarding back-to-front is the slowest method."[3] On the program, the hosts built a plane replica, complete with seats and overhead bins. Volunteers tested the various boarding methods. To further simulate reality, 5 percent of the volunteers were told to disrupt boarding by such actions as sitting in the wrong seat or standing in the aisle for longer than needed. Professional flight attendants were hired to help with the process. The program measured two outcomes of each method tested: how long it took to board the plane and how satisfied the volunteer passengers were with each experience.

The method with the highest satisfaction rating was the "reverse pyramid" in which elite passengers boarded first followed by

a complex set of zones that began with the rear window seats. That method allowed the plane to board in 15 minutes and 10 seconds. The method that allowed for fastest boarding was the one with no assigned seats. When used, the plane was boarded in 14 minutes and 7 seconds. Yet this method had the lowest satisfaction rating of all the methods attempted on the show.

The second fastest method was boarding elite passengers first, followed by the window-middle-aisle seat method. This method received high marks for passenger satisfaction. This method is similar to one called the "Steffen Method," named for astrophysicist Jason Steffen who wrote a research paper with a mathematical approach to efficient boarding. In that method, passengers board in the window-middle-aisle seat method, but in assigned zones that keep them in different parts of the plane and allow simultaneous boarding.[4]

What slows down boarding? Many industry analysts and bloggers have listed the reasons. For one, many passengers board outside their "zone" or whatever method the airline is using, which makes the system less efficient. Some passengers may do this purposefully and count on gate agents to look the other way.[5] Second, other passengers pay for early boarding or are given early boarding as part of their frequent flier reward program, which has the same effect as those who jumped the line. Both the passengers who boarded with the wrong group on purpose and those who paid for the privilege may be in the aisle as others try to board or may be strapped into middle or aisle seats and will need to stand when the window seat passengers arrive.[6] Third, sometimes after stowing a carry-on bag in the overhead bin, a passenger remembers something needed from the bag, stands up, and blocks the aisle while rummaging through the bag to find it.[7]

Probably the most mentioned culprit for slow boarding is baggage issues. Airlines started charging for checked luggage in 2008 when fuel prices went up.[8] To avoid the fees, more passengers began using carry-on luggage. The extra luggage slows the boarding process by leaving passengers in the aisle longer. The extra luggage also frequently fills up the bins, requiring extra time and effort for airline personnel to gate-check the bags.[9]

Why is the speed of boarding an airplane important? Airlines save $30 for every minute shaved off boarding times.[10] However, airlines appear to be making some of this money back in fees. In 2014 U.S.-based airlines planned to increase their fees, despite making over $6 billion from fees in 2013. United Continental,

which collected almost $650 million in checked bags fees in 2013, increased its fee charged to passengers flying with more than two bags by $25 per bag. Oversized bags cost $200 to check, and bags weighing more than 70 pounds cost $400 to check.[11] Delta Airlines collected about $1 billion in fees in 2013.[12]

Fees vary at different airlines, as do methods for boarding planes. Southwest Airlines uses the unassigned seat method of boarding. The airline assigns passengers to boarding groups and gives each passenger a boarding number within the group. Passengers line up in groups and in numerical order. Since seats are not assigned, each passenger selects a seat when on the plane.[13] Like American Airlines, most airlines use assigned seating and some type of boarding group system to put passengers on the planes.

Overview

As "A Manager's Challenge" suggests, organizations don't always agree on the best way to conduct business. Even organizations in the same industry can vary widely on business practices. Some organizations may adopt the latest research and methods, while others find different ways to stay competitive.

In this chapter we focus on the functional-level strategies managers can use to achieve superior efficiency, quality, innovation, and responsiveness to customers and so build competitive advantage. We also examine the nature of an organization's value chain and discuss how the combined or cooperative efforts of managers across the value chain are required if an organization is to achieve its mission and goal of maximizing the amount of value its products provide customers. By the end of this chapter, you will understand the vital role value chain management plays in creating competitive advantage and a high-performing organization.

Functional Strategies, the Value Chain, and Competitive Advantage

As we noted in Chapter 8, managers can use two basic business-level strategies to add value to an organization's products and achieve a competitive advantage over industry rivals. First, managers can pursue a *low-cost strategy* and lower the costs of creating value to attract customers by keeping product prices as low as or lower than competitors' prices. Second, managers can pursue a *differentiation strategy* and add value to a product by finding ways to make it superior in some way to the products of other companies. If they are successful and customers see greater value in the product, then like Apple they can charge a premium or higher price for the product. The four specific ways in which managers can lower costs and/or increase differentiation to obtain a competitive advantage were mentioned in Chapter 1 and are reviewed here; how organizations seek to achieve them is the topic of this chapter. (See Figure 9.1.)

Figure 9.1
Four Ways to Create a Competitive Advantage

1. *Achieve superior efficiency.* Efficiency is a measure of the amount of inputs required to produce a given amount of outputs. The fewer the inputs required to produce a given output, the higher is efficiency and the lower the cost of outputs. For example, in Gartner's annual ranking of the world's supply chains, Apple was ranked number one for six years in a row. Part of Apple's strength has been its focus on simplicity. Yet the company has begun to expand its product portfolio, which will increase the need for complexity management in its supply chain.[14]

2. *Achieve superior quality.* Quality means producing goods and services that have attributes—such as design, styling, performance, and reliability—that customers perceive as being superior to those found in competing products.[15] Providing high-quality products creates a brand-name reputation for an organization's products, and this enhanced reputation allows it to charge higher prices. In the car industry, for example, Toyota's reputation for making reliable vehicles allowed it to outperform rival carmakers and gives it a competitive advantage.

3. *Achieve superior innovation, speed, and flexibility.* Anything new or better about the way an organization operates or the goods and services it produces is the result of innovation. Successful innovation gives an organization something *unique* or different about its products that rivals lack—more attractive, useful, sophisticated products or superior production processes that strengthen its competitive advantage. Innovation adds value to products and allows the organization to further differentiate itself from rivals and attract customers who are often willing to pay a premium price for unique products. For example, Nintendo's former competitive advantage in handheld video game devices like the 3DS has been eroded as more games are available on smartphones and tablets.[16]

4. *Attain superior responsiveness to customers.* An organization that is responsive to customers tries to satisfy their needs and give them *exactly* what they want. An organization that treats customers better than its rivals do also provides a valuable service some customers may be willing to pay a higher price for. Managers can increase responsiveness by providing excellent after-sales service and support and by working to provide improved products or services to customers in the future. Today smartphone companies such as Samsung, Apple, and Nokia are searching for ways to better satisfy changing customer needs for higher-quality video, sound, and Internet connection speed.

Functional Strategies and Value Chain Management

Functional-level strategy is a plan of action to improve the ability of each of an organization's functions or departments (such as manufacturing or marketing) to perform its task-specific activities in ways that add value to an organization's goods and services.

value chain The coordinated series or sequence of functional activities necessary to transform inputs such as new product concepts, raw materials, component parts, or professional skills into the finished goods or services customers value and want to buy.

value chain management The development of a set of functional-level strategies that support a company's business-level strategy and strengthen its competitive advantage.

A company's **value chain** is the coordinated series or sequence of functional activities necessary to transform inputs such as new product concepts, raw materials, component parts, or professional skills into the finished goods or services customers value and want to buy (see Figure 9.2). Each functional activity along the chain *adds value* to the product when it lowers costs or gives the product differentiated qualities that increase the price a company can charge for it.

Value chain management is the development of a set of functional-level strategies that support a company's business-level strategy and strengthen its competitive advantage. Functional managers develop the strategies that increase efficiency, quality, innovation, and/or responsiveness to customers and thus strengthen an organization's competitive advantage. So the better the fit between functional- and business-level strategies, the greater will be the organization's competitive advantage, and the better able the organization is to achieve its mission and goal of maximizing the amount of value it gives customers. Each function along the value chain has an important role to play in value creation.

As Figure 9.2 suggests, the starting point of the value chain is often the search for new and improved products that will better appeal to customers, so the activities of the product development and marketing functions become important. *Product development* is the engineering and scientific research activities involved in innovating new or improved products that add value to a product. For example, Apple has been a leader in developing new kinds of mobile digital devices that have become so popular among buyers that its products are rapidly imitated by its competitors. Once a new product has been developed, the *marketing function's* task is to persuade customers that the product meets their needs and convince them to buy it. Marketing can help create value through brand positioning and advertising that increase customer perceptions of the utility of a company's product. For example, moviegoers appear willing to pay more to watch a movie in 3D. In 2014, 28 films were slated to be released in 3D.[17] Even filmmaker Steven Spielberg doubted the value of paying extra for 3D. In an interview, he said he hoped 3D ticket prices would get in line with 2D prices. However, he did indicate that IMAX movies would continue to be worth extra for "a premium experience in a premium environment."[18]

Even the best-designed product can fail if the marketing function hasn't devised a careful plan to persuade people to buy it and try it out—or to make sure customers really want it. For this reason, marketing often conducts consumer research to discover unmet customer product needs and to find better ways to tailor existing products to satisfy customer needs. Marketing then presents its suggestions to product development, which performs its own research to discover how best to design and make the new or improved products.

At the next stage of the value chain, the *materials management function* controls the movement of physical materials from the procurement of inputs through production and to distribution and delivery to the customer. The efficiency with which this is carried out can significantly lower costs and create more value. Walmart has the most efficient materials management function in the retail industry. By tightly controlling the flow of goods from its suppliers through its stores and into the hands of customers, Walmart has eliminated the need

Figure 9.2

Functional Activities and the Value Chain

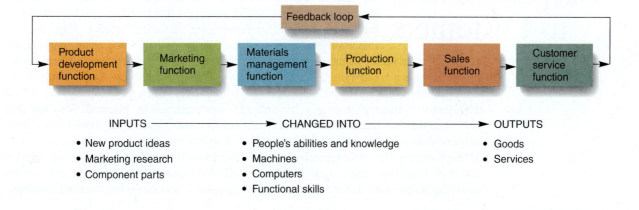

to hold large inventories of goods. Lower inventories mean lower costs and hence greater value creation.

The *production function* is responsible for creating, assembling, or providing a good or service—for transforming inputs into outputs. For physical products, when we talk about production, we generally mean manufacturing and assembly. For services such as banking or retailing, production takes place when the service is actually provided or delivered to the customer (for example, when a bank originates a loan for a customer, it is engaged in "production" of the loan). By performing its activities efficiently, the production function helps to lower costs. For example, the efficient production operations of Honda and Toyota have made them more profitable than competitors such as Renault, Volkswagen, and Chrysler. The production function can also perform its activities in a way that is consistent with high product quality, which leads to differentiation (and higher value) and to lower costs.

At the next stage in the value chain, the *sales function* plays a crucial role in locating customers and then informing and persuading them to buy the company's products. Personal selling—that is, direct face-to-face communication by salespeople with existing and potential customers to promote a company's products—is a crucial value chain activity. Which products retailers choose to stock, for example, or which drugs doctors choose to prescribe often depends on the salesperson's ability to inform and persuade customers that his or her company's product is superior and thus the best choice.

Finally, the role of the *customer service function* is to provide after-sales service and support. This function can create a perception of superior value in the minds of customers by solving customer problems and supporting customers after they have purchased the product. For example, FedEx can get its customers' parcels to any point in the world within 24 hours, creating value and support for customers' businesses. Customer service controls the electronic systems for tracking sales and inventory, pricing products, selling products, dealing with customer inquiries, and so on, all of which can greatly increase responsiveness to customers. Indeed, an important activity of sales and customer service is to tell product development and marketing why a product is meeting or not meeting customers' needs so the product can be redesigned or improved. Hence a feedback loop links the end of the value chain to its beginning (see Figure 9.2).

In the rest of this chapter, we examine the functional strategies used to manage the value chain to improve quality, efficiency, innovation, and responsiveness to customers. Notice, however, that achieving superior quality, efficiency, and innovation is *part* of attaining superior responsiveness to customers. Customers want value for their money, and managers who develop functional strategies that result in a value chain capable of creating innovative, high-quality, low-cost products best deliver this value to customers. For this reason, we begin by discussing how functional managers can increase responsiveness to customers.

Improving Responsiveness to Customers

All organizations produce outputs—goods or services—that are consumed by customers, who, in buying these products, provide the monetary resources most organizations need to survive. Because customers are vital to organizational survival, managers must correctly identify their customers and pursue strategies that result in products that best meet their needs. This is why the marketing function plays such an important part in the value chain, and good value chain management requires that marketing managers focus on defining their company's business in terms of the customer *needs* it is satisfying and not by the *type of products* it makes—or the result can be disaster.[19] For example, Kodak's managers said "no thanks" when the company was offered the rights to "instant photography," which was later marketed by Polaroid. Why did they make this mistake? Because the managers adopted a product-oriented approach to their business that didn't put the needs of customers first. Kodak's managers believed their job was to sell high-quality glossy photographs to people. Why would they want to become involved in instant photography, which results in inferior-quality photographs? In reality, Kodak was not satisfying people's needs for high-quality photographs; it was satisfying the need customers had to *capture and record the images of their lives*—their birthday parties, weddings, graduations, and so on. And people wanted those images quickly so they could share them right away with other people—which is why today digital photography has taken off and Kodak filed for bankruptcy in 2012.

LO9-2

Describe what customers want, and explain why it is so important for managers to be responsive to their needs.

What Do Customers Want?

Given that satisfying customer demand is central to the survival of an organization, an important question is "What do customers want?" Although specifying *exactly* what customers want is not possible because their needs vary from product to product, most customers prefer

1. A lower price to a higher price.
2. High-quality products to low-quality products.
3. Quick service and good after-sales service to slow service and poor after-sales support.
4. Products with many useful or valuable features to products with few features.
5. Products that are, as far as possible, customized or tailored to their unique needs.

Managers know that the more desired product attributes a company's value chain builds into its products, the higher the price that must be charged to cover the costs of developing and making the product. So what do managers of a customer-responsive organization do? They try to develop functional strategies that allow the organization's value chain to deliver to customers either *more* desired product attributes for the *same price* or the *same* product attributes for a *lower price*.[20] For example, in 2014 Walmart announced that it had made a deal to be the only national retailer to sell the Wild Oats brand organic foods and that it would do so at prices lower than those usually charged for organic products. Wild Oats was a well-known organic food brand in the late 1980s but has been struggling since the late 2000s. Walmart's massive size allows it the organizational efficiencies to offer the organic brand at a more affordable price for consumers.[21]

Managing the Value Chain to Increase Responsiveness to Customers

Because satisfying customers is so important, managers try to design and improve the way their value chains operate so they can supply products that have the desired attributes—quality, cost, and features. For example, the need to respond to customer demand for competitively priced, quality cars drove U.S. carmakers like Ford and GM to imitate Japanese companies and copy how Toyota and Honda perform their value chain activities. Today the imperative of satisfying customer needs shapes the activities of U.S. carmakers' materials management and manufacturing functions. As an example of the link between responsiveness to customers and an organization's value chain, consider how Southwest Airlines, the most profitable U.S. airline, operates.[22]

The major reason for Southwest's success is that it has pursued functional strategies that improve how its value chain operates to give customers what they want. Southwest commands high customer loyalty precisely because it can deliver products, such as flights from Houston to Dallas, that have all the desired attributes: reliability, convenience, and low price. In each of its functions, Southwest's strategies revolve around finding ways to lower costs. For example, Southwest offers a no-frills approach to in-flight customer service: no meals are served onboard, and there are no first-class seats. Southwest does not subscribe to the big reservation computers used by travel agents because the booking fees are too costly. Also, the airline flies only one aircraft, the fuel-efficient Boeing 737, which keeps training and maintenance costs down. All this translates into low

A Southwest ticket agent may assist a customer and then turn around to load her or his baggage as part of the organization's emphasis on cross-training workers for multiple tasks. Southwest's operating system is geared toward satisfying customer demand for low-priced, reliable, and convenient air travel, making it one of the most consistently successful airlines in recent years.

prices for customers. Additionally, Southwest is one of the few airlines that does not charge baggage fees. Passengers can check two bags for free.[23]

Southwest's reliability derives from the fact that it has the quickest aircraft turnaround time in the industry. A Southwest ground crew needs only 15 minutes to turn around an incoming aircraft and prepare it for departure. This speedy operation helps keep flights on time. Southwest has such a quick turnaround because it has a flexible workforce that has been cross-trained to perform multiple tasks. Thus the person who checks tickets might also help with baggage loading if time is short.

Southwest's convenience comes from its scheduling multiple flights every day between its popular locations, such as Dallas and Houston, and its use of airports that are close to downtown areas (Hobby at Houston and Love Field at Dallas) instead of using more distant major airports.[24] In sum, Southwest's excellent value chain management has given it a competitive advantage in the airline industry. Another company that has found a way to be responsive to customers by offering them faster service is Panera, which is profiled in the accompanying "Management Insight" feature.

Management Insight

Bread in the e-Commerce Fast Lane

Panera is a 1,777 bakery–café chain located in both the United States and Canada. The chain is made up of three companies: Saint Louis Bread Co., Paradise Bakery & Café, and Panera Bread.[25] Until recent years, the bakeries had been operating successfully with a traditional bakery–café model of offerings and service. That's until the company's CEO, Ron Shaich, had an epiphany. Always running late when driving his son to school in the mornings, Shaich would arrange for breakfast and lunch for his son by calling ahead to one of his stores and ordering. When he arrived at the store, his son would run in with his credit card, skip the line, and pick up the food. While the system worked for the Shaichs, it was not one that was available to everyone.

That's what gave Shaich the idea for Panera 2.0. Now customers can place orders via computer or mobile app. When the customer arrives at the restaurant, he or she can skip the line, pay for the ordered food, and either eat in or carry out. There also are touch-screen kiosks at the restaurants for customers who did not order ahead but who want to get through the line faster. And of course customers can still go to the register and place an order.[26]

One advantage of the new system is that it syncs with the MyPanera rewards program. The program remembers all orders that the customer places. If a customer ordered a custom sandwich at one visit, the system remembers it and offers to place the same order at the next visit.

Panera began testing the system in 2011 and hopes to have it rolled out to all restaurants by 2016. And it has already seen users of Panera 2.0 and kiosk users increase the frequency of their visits. At one location, sales were up more than 50 percent.[27]

The new system also has improved the order accuracy rates. The industry average is one in seven incorrectly fulfilled orders, many of the errors occurring during input at the register. "If we're in the to-go business, we have to be 100 percent accurate," Shaich says.[28] In addition to depending on the customer to enter the order correctly, employees double-check each order before it leaves the store.

Of course adding the system has meant changes for the employees at Panera. The information technology team has doubled. Operations have been affected as well. When customers place orders online or at a kiosk, it saves employees at the register from having to do so. Those employees can be redeployed to the kitchen to help keep up with the demand of incoming orders. Once the system is in place at every Panera location, Shaich believes Panera will be one of the 10 largest e-commerce operators in the United States.

Until recently, Panera Bread had been operating its bakery-cafés in a traditional manner. Now, after CEO Ron Shaich got the idea for Panera 2.0, customers can place orders online, skip the store line, pay for the order, and eat in or carry out. The new system allows Panera to increase their efficiency and customer service satisfaction.

Although managers must seek to improve their responsiveness to customers by improving how the value chain operates, they should not offer a level of responsiveness to customers that results in costs becoming *too high*—something that threatens an organization's future performance and survival. For example, a company that customizes every product to the unique demands of individual customers is likely to see its costs grow out of control.

Customer Relationship Management

One functional strategy managers can use to get close to customers and understand their needs is **customer relationship management (CRM)**. CRM is a technique that uses IT to develop an ongoing relationship with customers to maximize the value an organization can deliver to them over time. By the 2000s most large companies had installed sophisticated CRM IT to track customers' changing demands for a company's products; this became a vital tool to maximize responsiveness to customers. CRM IT monitors, controls, and links each of the functional activities involved in marketing, selling, and delivering products to customers, such as monitoring the delivery of products through the distribution channel, monitoring salespeople's selling activities, setting product pricing, and coordinating after-sales service. CRM systems have three interconnected components: sales and selling, after-sales service and support, and marketing.

customer relationship management (CRM) A technique that uses IT to develop an ongoing relationship with customers to maximize the value an organization can deliver to them over time.

Suppose a sales manager has access only to sales data that show the total sales revenue each salesperson generated in the last 30 days. This information does not break down how much revenue came from sales to existing customers versus sales to new customers. What important knowledge is being lost? First, if most revenues are earned from sales to existing customers, this suggests that the money being spent by a company to advertise and promote its products is not attracting new customers and so is being wasted. Second, important dimensions involved in sales are pricing, financing, and order processing. In many companies, to close a deal, a salesperson has to send the paperwork to a central sales office that handles matters such as approving the customer for special financing and determining specific shipping and delivery dates. In some companies, different departments handle these activities, and it can take a long time to get a response from them; this keeps customers waiting—something that often leads to lost sales. Until CRM systems were introduced, these kinds of problems were widespread and resulted in missed sales and higher operating costs. Today the sales and selling CRM software contains *best sales practices* that analyze this information and then recommend ways to improve how the sales process operates.

One company that has improved its sales and after-sales practices by implementing CRM is Empire HealthChoice Inc., the largest health insurance provider in New York, which sells its policies through 1,800 sales agents. For years these agents were responsible for collecting all the customer-specific information needed to determine the price of each policy. Once they had collected the necessary information, the agents called Empire to get price quotes. After waiting days for these quotes, the agents relayed them back to customers, who often then modified their requests to reduce the cost of their policies. When this occurred, the agents had to telephone Empire again to get revised price quotes. Because this frequently happened several times with each transaction, it often took more than 20 days to close a sale and another 10 days for customers to get their insurance cards.[29]

Recognizing that these delays were causing lost sales, Empire decided to examine how a CRM system could improve the sales process. Its managers chose a web-based system so agents themselves could calculate the insurance quotes online. Once an agent enters a customer's data, a quote is generated in just a few seconds. The agent can continually modify a policy while sitting face-to-face with the customer until the policy and price are agreed upon. As a result, the sales process can now be completed in a few hours, and customers receive their insurance cards in 2 to 3 days rather than 10.[30]

When a company implements after-sales service and support CRM software, salespeople are required to input detailed information about their follow-up visits to customers. Because the system tracks and documents every customer's case history, salespeople have instant access to a record of everything that occurred during previous phone calls or visits. They are in a much better position to respond to customers' needs and build customer loyalty, so a company's after-sales service improves. Cell phone companies like T-Mobile and Sprint, for example, require that telephone sales reps collect information about all customers' inquiries, complaints, and requests, and this is recorded electronically in customer logs. The CRM module can analyze the information in these logs to evaluate whether the customer service reps are meeting or exceeding the company's required service standards.

A CRM system can also identify the top 10 reasons for customer complaints. Sales managers can then work to eliminate the sources of these problems and improve after-sales support procedures. The CRM system also identifies the top 10 best service and support practices, which can then be taught to all sales reps.

Finally, as a CRM system processes information about changing customer needs, this improves marketing in many ways. Marketing managers, for example, have access to detailed customer profiles, including data about purchases and the reasons why individuals were or were not attracted to a company's products. Armed with this knowledge, marketing can better identify customers and the specific product attributes they desire. Traditional CRM systems were organized by having salespeople input customer information. Now social CRM systems can track customers on social media and put them on a company's radar. For example, if a Twitter user posts frequently about a topic relevant to the company or about the company's product, a CRM system can bring the user to the attention of the company as an important connection or a potential customer.[31] In sum, a CRM system is a comprehensive method of gathering crucial information about how customers respond to a company's products. It is a powerful functional strategy used to align a company's products with customer needs.

Improving Quality

As noted earlier, high-quality products possess attributes such as superior design, features, reliability, and after-sales support; these products are designed to better meet customer requirements.[32] Quality is a concept that can be applied to the products of both manufacturing and service organizations—goods such as an Apple computer or services such as Southwest Airlines flight service or customer service in a Citibank branch. Why do managers seek to control and improve the quality of their organizations' products?[33] There are two reasons (see Figure 9.3).

First, customers usually prefer a higher-quality product to a lower-quality product. So an organization able to provide, *for the same price,* a product of higher quality than a competitor's product is serving its customers better—it is being more responsive to its customers. Often providing high-quality products creates a brand-name reputation for an organization's products. This enhanced reputation may allow the organization to charge more for its products than its competitors can charge, and thus it makes greater profits. For example, in 2014 Lexus was ranked number one on the J.D. Power list of the 10 most reliable carmakers for the third year in a row.[34] The high quality of Lexus vehicles enables the company to charge higher prices for its cars than the prices charged by rival carmakers.

The second reason for trying to boost product quality is that higher product quality can increase efficiency and thereby lower operating costs and boost profits. Achieving high product quality lowers operating costs because of the effect of quality on employee productivity:

Figure 9.3

The Impact of Increased Quality on Organizational Performance

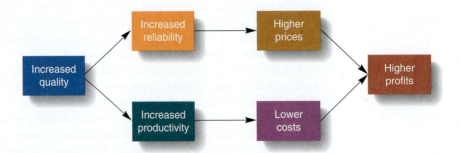

Higher product quality means less employee time is wasted in making defective products that must be discarded or in providing substandard services, and thus less time has to be spent fixing mistakes. This translates into higher employee productivity, which also means lower costs. The way each manager can have an impact on quality and cost is discussed in the accompanying "Management Insight" feature.

Management Insight

Vendor Relationships Key to TJX's Store Offerings

The TJX Companies Inc. sell clothes, shoes, handbags, and other fashions along with home decorating items at discounted prices. Its U.S. stores are T.J. Maxx, Marshalls, Sierra Trading Post, and HomeGoods. The company was founded in 1919 as the New England Trading Company and expanded into a chain of women's clothing stores. The sons of the founders built the Zayre department store in the 1950s; then came T.J. Maxx in 1976, which was created under the Zayre name. In a major restructuring in the late 1980s, the Zayre stores were sold and the company changed its name to TJX Companies. It later acquired Marshalls, HomeGoods, and Sierra Trading Post.

The company states its mission as delivering "a rapidly changing assortment of fashionable, quality, brand name and designer merchandise at prices generally 20–60 percent below department and specialty store regular prices, every day."[35] Aside from the savings, the main appeal of the stores is the "treasure-hunt shopping experience"[36] in which the stores have different items and a different look—often a somewhat opposite experience to perusing the more static seasonal product lines found in traditional department stores.[37]

The company's business model allows it to perform well in almost any economic environment. TJX is able to sell high-quality name-brand merchandise at a discount by purchasing overstocks and canceled orders from other retailers. TJX buys up excess inventory at a steep discount, which it then passes on to the customer.[38]

TJX stores have no walls or physical dividers between departments. This allows the merchandise categories to expand or contract according to supply and demand. Inventory turns rapidly, which keeps stores fresh and allows the company to buy as it needs.[39] "Our universe of over 16,000 vendors affords us tremendous flexibility, and we continue to strengthen our vendor relationships and build new ones to offer consumers even more exciting brands," said TJX CEO Carol Meyrowitz. "While we drive our top line, we expect to also drive our profitability through even better inventory management and a further improved supply chain."[40]

The supply chain is important to TJX's ability to deliver value and to properly stock each store. The retailer has more than 3,000 stores and plans to grow through new and remodeled stores, a new home office and data center, new distribution centers, and systems and supply chain improvements.[41] The company recently opened a new distribution center in Arizona, its first in about 10 years despite a 40 percent increased store base. Meyrowitz said the company will continue to invest in its supply chain in fiscal 2015.[42]

Total Quality Management

total quality management (TQM) A management technique that focuses on improving the quality of an organization's products and services.

At the forefront of the drive to improve product quality is a functional strategy known as total quality management.[43] **Total quality management (TQM)** focuses on improving the quality of an organization's products and stresses that *all* of an organization's value chain activities should be directed toward this goal. TQM requires the cooperation of managers in every function of an organization and across functions.[44] To show how TQM works, we next describe the way that Citibank used the technique. Then, using Citibank as an example, we look at the 10 steps that are necessary for managers to implement a successful TQM program.

In the 2000s Citibank's top managers decided the bank could retain and expand its customer base only if it could increase customer loyalty, so they decided to implement a TQM program to better satisfy customer needs. As the first step in its TQM effort, Citibank identified the factors that dissatisfy its customers. When analyzing the complaints, it found that most concerned the time it took to complete a customer's request, such as responding to an account problem or getting a loan. So Citibank's managers began to examine how they handled each kind of customer request. For each distinct request, they formed a cross-functional team that broke down the request into the steps required, between people and departments, to complete the response. In analyzing the steps, teams found that many of them were unnecessary and could be replaced by using the right information systems. They also found that delays often occurred because employees did not know how to handle a request. They were not being given the right kind of training, and when they couldn't handle a request, they simply put it aside until a supervisor could deal with it.

Citibank's second step to increase its responsiveness was to implement an organization-wide TQM program. Managers and supervisors were charged with reducing the complexity of the work process and finding the most effective way to process each particular request, such as a request for a loan. Managers were also charged with training employees to answer each specific request. The results were remarkable. For example, in the loan department the TQM program reduced by 75 percent the number of handoffs necessary to process a request. The department's average response time dropped from several hours to 30 minutes. What are the 10 steps in TQM that made this possible?

1. *Build organizational commitment to quality.* TQM will do little to improve the performance of an organization unless all employees embrace it, and this often requires a change in an organization's culture.[45] At Citibank the process of changing culture began at the top. First a group of top managers, including the CEO, received training in TQM from consultants from Motorola, where Six Sigma was founded (Six Sigma is trademarked by Motorola).[46] Each member of the top management group was then given the responsibility of training a group at the next level in the hierarchy, and so on down through the organization until all 100,000 employees had received basic TQM training.

2. *Focus on the customer.* TQM practitioners see a focus on the customer as the starting point.[47] According to TQM philosophy, the customer, not managers in quality control or engineering, defines what quality is. The challenge is fourfold: (1) to identify what customers want from the good or service that the company provides; (2) to identify what the company actually provides to customers; (3) to identify any gap between what customers want and what they actually get (the quality gap); and (4) to formulate a plan for closing the quality gap. The efforts of Citibank managers to increase responsiveness to customers illustrate this aspect of TQM well.

3. *Find ways to measure quality.* Another crucial element of TQM is the development of a measuring system that managers can use to evaluate quality. Devising appropriate measures is relatively easy in manufacturing companies, where quality can be measured by criteria such as defects per million parts. It is more difficult in service companies, where outputs are less tangible. However, with a little creativity, suitable quality measures can be devised as they were by managers at Citibank. Citibank used customer satisfaction surveys as quality measures and defined a defect as any rating below the two highest ratings.[48]

4. *Set goals and create incentives.* Once a measure has been devised, managers' next step is to set a challenging quality goal and to create incentives for reaching that goal. At Citibank the CEO set an initial goal of reducing customer complaints by 50 percent. One way of creating incentives to attain a goal is to link rewards, such as bonus pay and promotional opportunities, to the goal.

5. *Solicit input from employees.* Employees are a major source of information about the causes of poor quality, so it is important that managers establish a system for soliciting employee suggestions about improvements that can be made. At most companies, like Citibank, this is an ongoing endeavor—the process never stops.

6. *Identify defects and trace them to their source.* A major source of product defects is the production system; a major source of service defects is poor customer service procedures. TQM preaches the need for managers to identify defects in the work process, trace

inventory The stock of raw materials, inputs, and component parts that an organization has on hand at a particular time.

just-in-time (JIT) inventory system A system in which parts or supplies arrive at an organization when they are needed, not before.

those defects back to their source, find out why they occurred, and make corrections so they do not occur again. Today IT makes quality measurement much easier.

7. *Introduce just-in-time inventory systems.* **Inventory** is the stock of raw materials, inputs, and component parts that an organization has on hand at a particular time. When the materials management function designs a **just-in-time (JIT) inventory system**, parts or supplies arrive at the organization when they are needed, not before. Also, under a JIT inventory system, defective parts enter an organization's operating system immediately; they are not warehoused for months before use. This means defective inputs can be quickly spotted. JIT is discussed more later in the chapter.

8. *Work closely with suppliers.* A major cause of poor-quality finished goods is poor-quality component parts. To decrease product defects, materials managers must work closely with suppliers to improve the quality of the parts they supply. Managers at Xerox worked closely with suppliers to get them to adopt TQM programs, and the result was a huge reduction in the defect rate of component parts. Managers also need to work closely with suppliers to get them to adopt a JIT inventory system, also required for high quality.

9. *Design for ease of production.* The more steps required to assemble a product or provide a service, the more opportunities there are for making a mistake. It follows that designing products that have fewer parts or finding ways to simplify providing a service should be linked to fewer defects or customer complaints. For example, Apple continually redesigns the way it assembles its mobile digital devices to reduce the number of assembly steps required, and it constantly searches for new ways to reduce the number of components that have to be linked together. The consequence of these redesign efforts was a continuous fall in assembly costs and marked improvement in product quality during the 2000s. At Citibank, defect detection and resolution lead to better performance in process time, cash management, and customer satisfaction.[49]

10. *Break down barriers between functions.* Successful implementation of TQM requires substantial cooperation between the different value chain functions. Materials managers have to cooperate with manufacturing managers to find high-quality inputs that reduce manufacturing costs; marketing managers have to cooperate with manufacturing so that customer problems identified by marketing can be acted on; information systems have to cooperate with all other functions of the company to devise suitable IT training programs; and so on. At Citibank, a cross-functional process mapping method was used to describe the functions involved in each step of a process flow.[50]

In essence, to increase quality, all functional managers need to cooperate to develop goals and spell out exactly how they will be achieved. Managers should embrace the philosophy that mistakes, defects, and poor-quality materials are not acceptable and should be eliminated. Functional managers should spend more time working with employees and providing them with the tools they need to do the job. Managers should create an environment in which employees will not be afraid to report problems or recommend improvements. Output goals and targets need to include not only numbers or quotas but also some indicators of quality to promote the production of defect-free output. Functional managers also need to train employees in new skills to keep pace with changes in the workplace. Finally, achieving better quality requires that managers develop organizational values and norms centered on improving quality.

Six Sigma A technique used to improve quality by systematically improving how value chain activities are performed and then using statistical methods to measure the improvement.

SIX SIGMA   One TQM technique called **Six Sigma** has gained increasing popularity in the last decade, particularly because of the well-publicized success GE enjoyed as a result of implementing it across its operating divisions. The goal of Six Sigma is to improve a company's quality to only three defects per million by systematically altering the way all the processes involved in value chain activities are performed, and then carefully measuring how much improvement has been made using statistical methods. Six Sigma shares with TQM its focus on improving value chain processes to increase quality; but it differs because TQM emphasizes top-down organizationwide employee involvement, whereas the Six Sigma approach is to create teams of expert change agents, known as "green belts and black belts," to take control of the problem-finding and problem-solving process and then to train other employees in implementing solutions. The accompanying "Management Insight" feature shows how Six Sigma works for the city of Tyler, Texas.

Everything's Coming up Roses in One Texas Town

Tyler is a city of more than 107,000 people in the northeast quadrant of Texas.[51] It has the largest rose garden in the United States and a large rose-growing industry, earning it the nickname "Rose Capital of America."[52] Tyler Rose Garden has more than 500 varieties of roses. Each year the city hosts a rose festival when hundreds of thousands of roses are in bloom. Visitors can tour the Rose Museum and attend the Rose Parade.

But lately the city has also been noted for a quality control initiative that has saved it from some thorny issues. In 2009, facing reduced revenues from sales taxes and sluggish property values, the city hired a Six Sigma Master Black Belt and began training city employees in Lean Six Sigma, a branch of Six Sigma that focuses on eliminating waste in manufacturing and other areas. By 2014, when it was announced that Lean Six Sigma programs had saved more than $5 million for the city, almost 27 percent of city employees had been trained in Lean Six Sigma and worked on Lean Six Sigma projects as part of their regular workloads.

"In five short years, we've changed the culture of how we look at our jobs at city hall," Mayor Barbara Bass said. "For whichever department you're in, you're . . . looking with new eyes on how to improve your departments, and your friends from other departments are stepping up and helping you with that process."[53]

The city has completed more than 90 Lean Six Sigma projects and still has 35 more in process, according to City Manager Mark McDaniel. One project entailed developing and implementing inventory control. Before the Lean Six Sigma project, Tyler Purchasing Manager Sherry Pettit said no inventory was being done at the water utilities service center meter shop. "It was kind of a mess. We really didn't know what was in there or anything. So . . . we went in and cleaned it all up."[54]

Another project involved cleaning up the filing protocols and systems in the city attorney's office. A legal assistant commented, "It was taking us on average about 25 minutes to find our documents and everything, and after our project it saved about $10,000 in salary costs and got it down to four minutes."[55]

These and other projects led to reductions in overtime and improved waste collection. While the city population has grown by 30 percent since the mid-1980s, the Lean Six Sigma projects made it possible for the city services to work with roughly the same number of employees it had in the mid-1980s.

The city posts a list of its Lean Six Sigma Green Belts and Black Belts on its web page. Green Belts require 80 hours of training and are then assigned projects within the scope of the Green Belt's current job. Traditionally, a Green Belt would be trained in full-day, weeklong increments over two months. However, Tyler changed the format to four weeks of half-day training over four months. To be fully certified, a Green Belt must complete a Lean Six Sigma project within a year. Candidates for Black Belts are selected from the pool of Green Belts and attend an additional 80 hours of training. In Tyler, Black Belts participate in multiple projects across the city. As part of the certification, Black Belts must complete two Lean Six Sigma projects within a year, mentor Green Belts, and work to spread Lean Six Sigma throughout the organization.[56]

Barbara Bass, the mayor, said: "All of our Green Belts and Black Belts have completed projects that are focused on improving a city process, saving either time or money. Many other city employees have participated on project teams that put improvement into the hands of those most familiar with the process—our frontline employees."[57]

In Tyler style, the announcement of the savings accrued from Lean Six Sigma was made in the city's Rose Garden.

Improving Efficiency

The third goal of value chain management is to increase the efficiency of the various functional activities. The fewer the input resources required to produce a given volume of output, the higher will be the efficiency of the operating system. So efficiency is a useful measure of how well an organization uses all its resources—such as labor, capital, materials, or energy—to produce its outputs, or goods and services. Developing functional strategies to improve efficiency is an extremely important issue for managers because increased efficiency lowers production costs, which lets an organization make a greater profit or attract more customers by lowering its price. Several important functional strategies are discussed here.

LO9-4

Explain why achieving superior efficiency is so important, and understand the different kinds of techniques that need to be employed to increase efficiency.

Facilities Layout, Flexible Manufacturing, and Efficiency

The strategies managers use to lay out or design an organization's physical work facilities also determine its efficiency. First, the way in which machines and workers are organized or grouped together into workstations affects the efficiency of the operating system. Second, a major determinant of efficiency is the cost associated with setting up the equipment needed to make a particular product. **Facilities layout** is the strategy of designing the machine–worker interface to increase operating system efficiency. **Flexible manufacturing** is a strategy based on the use of IT to reduce the costs associated with the product assembly process or the way services are delivered to customers. For example, this might be how computers are made on a production line or how patients are routed through a hospital.

facilities layout The strategy of designing the machine–worker interface to increase operating system efficiency.

flexible manufacturing The set of techniques that attempt to reduce the costs associated with the product assembly process or the way services are delivered to customers.

FACILITIES LAYOUT The way in which machines, robots, and people are grouped together affects how productive they can be. Figure 9.4 shows three basic ways of arranging workstations: product layout, process layout, and fixed-position layout.

In a *product layout,* machines are organized so that each operation needed to manufacture a product or process a patient is performed at workstations arranged in a fixed sequence. In manufacturing, workers are stationary in this arrangement, and a moving conveyor belt takes the product being worked on to the next workstation so that it is progressively assembled. Mass production is the familiar name for this layout; car assembly lines are probably the best-known example. It used to be that product layout was efficient only when products were

Figure 9.4
Three Facilities Layouts

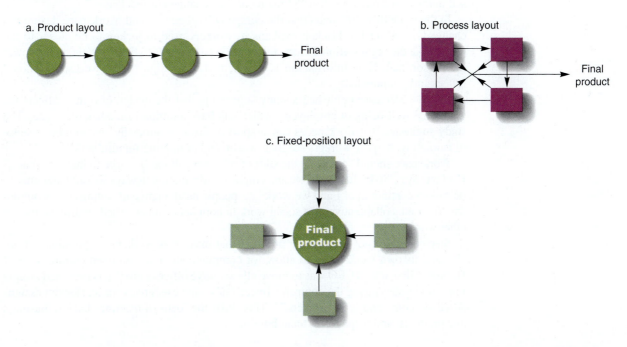

a. Product layout

Final product

b. Process layout

Final product

c. Fixed-position layout

Final product

created in large quantities; however, the introduction of modular assembly lines controlled by computers is making it efficient to make products in small batches.

In a *process layout,* workstations are not organized in a fixed sequence. Rather, each workstation is relatively self-contained, and a product goes to whichever workstation is needed to perform the next operation to complete the product. Process layout is often suited to manufacturing settings that produce a variety of custom-made products, each tailored to the needs of a different kind of customer. For example, a custom furniture manufacturer might use a process layout so different teams of workers can produce different styles of chairs or tables made from different kinds of woods and finishes. Such a layout also describes how a patient might go through a hospital from emergency room to X-ray room, to operating room, and so on. A process layout provides the flexibility needed to change a product, whether it is a PC or a patient's treatment. Such flexibility, however, often reduces efficiency because it is expensive.

In a *fixed-position layout,* the product stays in a fixed position. Its component parts are produced in remote workstations and brought to the production area for final assembly. Increasingly, self-managed teams are using fixed-position layouts. Different teams assemble each component part and then send the parts to the final assembly team, which makes the final product. A fixed-position layout is commonly used for products such as jet airliners, mainframe computers, and gas turbines—products that are complex and difficult to assemble or so large that moving them from one workstation to another would be difficult. Even companies that specialize in office architecture have rethought their workspaces, as the accompanying "Management Insight" feature discusses.

Management Insight

Workspace Company Redefines Its Own Workspace Philosophy, Putting Its Money Where Its Mouth Is

Steelcase develops and manufactures office furniture, technology, and other office architecture. The Michigan-based company was founded in 1912 as the Metal Office Furniture Company. Its first patent was in 1914 on a metal wastebasket—an important item in an era when straw wastebaskets were fire hazards. The company went on to develop and sell many office products. In 1954 the name was changed to Steelcase.[58]

In the more than 100 years that the company has been around, workspace design has changed. As CEO Jim Hackett explains it, workers used to jockey to be closer to the CEO. Like the organizational chart, the closer a person was to the CEO, the more power the person had. Now information is power, and the design of the workspace should reflect and promote that.

In 2014 Steelcase published a study suggesting that the design of offices affects the emotional well-being of employees, which can have an impact on business results. The study suggested that workspaces can support positive emotions by encouraging a sense of belonging, helping workers see their worth, and promoting mindfulness.[59]

Workspace should "celebrate the shift of what we call the 'I' space to the 'we' space," Hackett says. "Space has to enable and empower information in ways we only imagine . . . (across) a continuum of I and we work . . . people need a range of settings to accommodate focused, collaborative, and social work in both open and enclosed environments—in other words, a palette of place."[60]

Steelcase does not just sell the products that make new workspaces possible—it has changed its own workspaces to allow for communication and an open culture. One of Hackett's first acts as CEO was to move all executive offices onto floors designed around important issues facing the company. Instead of giving executives space, Hackett assigns space to "command-level projects."[61] This shifts the focus of meetings back to business and products, and helps foster team building.

"Innovation requires collective 'we' work," Hackett says. "To this end, it's critical to design spaces that not only support collaboration, but augment it (with) spaces that promote eye-to-eye contact, provide everyone with equal access to information, and allow people to move around and participate freely."[62]

FLEXIBLE MANUFACTURING In a manufacturing company, a major source of costs is setting up the equipment needed to make a particular product. One of these costs is that of production forgone because nothing is produced while the equipment is being set up. For example, components manufacturers often need as much as half a day to set up automated production equipment when switching from production of one component part (such as a washer ring for the steering column of a car) to another (such as a washer ring for the steering column of a truck). During this half-day, a manufacturing plant is not producing anything, but employees are paid for this "nonproductive" time.

It follows that if setup times for complex production equipment can be reduced, so can setup costs, and efficiency will rise; that is, the time that plant and employees spend in actually producing something will increase. This simple insight has been the driving force behind the development of flexible manufacturing techniques.

Flexible manufacturing aims to reduce the time required to set up production equipment.[63] By redesigning the manufacturing process so production equipment geared for manufacturing one product can be quickly replaced with equipment geared to make another product, setup times and costs can be reduced dramatically. Another favorable outcome from flexible manufacturing is that a company can produce many more varieties of a product than before in the same amount of time. Thus flexible manufacturing increases a company's ability to be responsive to its customers.

Housing units move on the production line as employees of Toyota Motor Corporation work during the installation process at the company's Kasugai Housing Works, one of the plants of Toyota home-brand houses on Kasugai, Aichi Prefecture, Japan. Toyota entered the housing industry 30 years ago applying the plant technology and experience it gained through producing cars.

To obtain the benefits from flexible manufacturing, General Motors built a plant in Lansing, Michigan, in 2001 that can expand as the company sees fit. When it was first built, the company's Grand River Assembly plant was already more flexible than its other plants.[64] It was modeled after GM's innovative overseas facilities. While some GM executives expressed concern that the site was too small to work well, the plant has received praise for its capacity to manufacture a variety of car models, as well as for the collaborative team management style it facilitates and its automation capabilities. And GM plans to add on to the plant. In 2013 GM announced that it would build a $44.5 million Logistics Optimization Center. The expansion will include a building in which parts will be sorted and delivered for the assembly line. In 2014 GM announced that a $162 million stamping plant would be added to the site. Stamping plants make parts for auto assembly lines.[65]

Just-in-Time Inventory and Efficiency

As noted earlier, a just-in-time inventory system gets components to the assembly line just as they are needed and thus drives down costs. In a JIT inventory system, component parts travel from suppliers to the assembly line in a small wheeled container known as a *kanban*. Assembly-line workers empty the kanbans, which are sent back to the suppliers as the signal to produce another small batch of component parts, and so the process repeats itself. This system can be contrasted with a just-in-case view of inventory, which leads an organization to stockpile excess inputs in a warehouse in case it needs them to meet sudden upturns in demand.

JIT inventory systems have major implications for efficiency. Great cost savings can result from increasing inventory turnover and reducing inventory holding costs, such as warehousing and storage costs and the cost of capital tied up in inventory. Although companies that manufacture and assemble products can obviously use JIT to great advantage, so can service organizations.[66] Walmart, the biggest retailer in the United States, uses JIT systems to replenish the stock in its stores at least twice a week. Many Walmart stores receive daily deliveries. As soon as goods are purchased, new ones are ordered through Walmart's sophisticated supply chain. However, while the supply chain does a good job of getting the goods to stores, Walmart recently ran into some problems with stores that were so leanly staffed, there were not enough people to move the goods from the storage area to the shelves. To maintain its efficiency-based competitive advantage, Walmart will need to bring staffing up to optimal levels as well.[67]

Even a small company can benefit from a kanban system, as the experience of United Electric Controls, headquartered in Watertown, Massachusetts, suggests. United Electric is the market leader in the manufacture of alarm and shutdown switches for industrial plant safety. At one time the company simply stored all its inputs in a warehouse and dispensed them as needed. Then it decided to reduce costs by storing the inputs closer to their point of use in the production system. This led to inaccurate part counts and caused production stoppages due to a lack of inputs.

So managers decided to experiment with a supplier kanban system even though United Electric had fewer than 40 suppliers and they were up to date with its input requirements. Managers decided to store a three-week supply of parts in a central storeroom—a supply large enough to avoid unexpected shortages.[68] They began by asking their casting supplier to deliver inputs in kanbans and bins. Once a week, this supplier checks the bins to determine how much stock needs to be delivered the following week. Other suppliers were then asked to participate in this system, and now more than 35 major suppliers operate some form of the kanban system.

By all measures of performance, the kanban system has succeeded. Inventory holding costs have fallen sharply. Products are delivered to all customers on time. And new products' design-to-production cycles have dropped by 50 percent because suppliers are now involved much earlier in the design process so they can supply new inputs as needed.

Self-Managed Work Teams and Efficiency

Another functional strategy to increase efficiency is the use of self-managed work teams.[69] A typical self-managed team consists of 5 to 15 employees who produce an entire product instead of just parts of it.[70] Team members learn all team tasks and move from job to job. The result is a flexible workforce because team members can fill in for absent coworkers. The members of each team also assume responsibility for scheduling work and vacations, ordering materials, and hiring new members—previously all responsibilities of first-line managers. Because people often respond well to greater autonomy and responsibility, the use of empowered self-managed teams can increase productivity and efficiency. Moreover, cost savings arise from eliminating supervisors and creating a flatter organizational hierarchy, which further increase efficiency.

The effect of introducing self-managed teams is often an increase in efficiency of 30 percent or sometimes much more. After the introduction of flexible manufacturing technology and self-managed teams, a GE plant in Salisbury, North Carolina, increased efficiency by 250 percent compared with other GE plants producing the same products.[71]

Process Reengineering and Efficiency

process reengineering
The fundamental rethinking and radical redesign of business processes to achieve dramatic improvement in critical measures of performance such as cost, quality, service, and speed.

The value chain is a collection of functional activities or business processes that transforms one or more kinds of inputs to create an output that is of value to the customer.[72] **Process reengineering** involves the fundamental rethinking and radical redesign of business processes (and thus the *value chain*) to achieve dramatic improvements in critical measures of performance such as cost, quality, service, and speed.[73] Order fulfillment, for example, can be thought of as a business process: When a customer's order is received (the input), many different functional tasks must be performed as necessary to process the order, and then the ordered goods are delivered to the customer (the output). Process reengineering boosts efficiency when it reduces the number of order fulfillment tasks that must be performed, or reduces the time they take, and so reduces operating costs.

For an example of process reengineering in practice, consider how Ford used it. One day a manager from Ford was working at its Japanese partner Mazda and discovered that Mazda had only five people in its accounts payable department. The Ford manager was shocked because Ford's U.S. operation had 500 employees in accounts payable. He reported his discovery to Ford's U.S. managers, who decided to form a task force to study this difference.

Ford managers discovered that procurement began when the purchasing department sent a purchase order to a supplier and sent a copy of the purchase order to Ford's accounts payable department. When the supplier shipped the goods and they arrived at Ford, a clerk at the receiving dock completed a form describing the goods and sent the form to accounts payable. The supplier, meanwhile, sent accounts payable an invoice. Thus accounts payable received three documents relating to these goods: a copy of the original purchase order, the receiving document, and the invoice. If the information in all three was in agreement (most of the time it was), a clerk in accounts payable issued payment. Occasionally, however, all three documents did not agree. And Ford discovered that accounts payable clerks spent most of their time straightening out the 1 percent of instances in which the purchase order, receiving document, and invoice contained conflicting information.[74]

Ford managers decided to reengineer the procurement process to simplify it. Now when a buyer in the purchasing department issues a purchase order to a supplier, that buyer also enters the order into an online database. As before, suppliers send goods to the receiving dock. When the goods arrive, the clerk at the receiving dock checks a computer terminal to see whether the received shipment matches the description on the purchase order. If it does, the clerk accepts the goods and pushes a button on the terminal keyboard that tells the database the goods have arrived. Receipt of the goods is recorded in the database, and a computer automatically issues and sends a check to the supplier. If the goods do not correspond to the description on the purchase order in the database, the clerk at the dock refuses the shipment and sends it back to the supplier.

Payment authorization, which used to be performed by accounts payable, is now accomplished at the receiving dock. The new process has come close to eliminating the need for an accounts payable department. In some parts of Ford, the size of the accounts payable department has been cut by 95 percent. By reducing the head count in accounts payable, the reengineering effort reduced the amount of time wasted on unproductive activities, thereby increasing the efficiency of the total organization.

Information Systems, the Internet, and Efficiency

With the rapid spread of computers, the explosive growth of the Internet and corporate intranets, and high-speed digital Internet technology, the information systems function is moving to center stage in the quest for operating efficiencies and a lower cost structure. The impact of information systems on productivity is wide-ranging and potentially affects all other activities of a company. For example, Cisco Systems has been able to realize significant cost savings by moving its ordering and customer service functions online. Cisco Systems designs, manufactures, and sells networking equipment. The company has just 300 service agents handling all its customer accounts, compared to the 900 it would need if sales were not handled online. The difference represents an annual savings of $30 million a year. Moreover, without automated customer service functions, Cisco calculates that it would need at least 1,000 additional service engineers, which would cost around $100 million.

All large companies today use the Internet to manage the value chain, feeding real-time information about order flow to suppliers, which use this information to schedule their own production to provide components on a just-in-time basis. This approach reduces the costs of coordination both between the company and its customers and between the company and its suppliers. Using the Internet to automate customer and supplier interactions substantially reduces the number of employees required to manage these interfaces, which significantly reduces costs. This trend extends beyond high-tech companies. Banks and financial service companies are finding that they can substantially reduce costs by moving customer accounts and support functions online. Such a move reduces the need for customer service representatives, bank tellers, stockbrokers, insurance agents, and others. For example, it costs about $1 when a customer executes a transaction at a bank, such as shifting money from one account to another; over the Internet the same transaction costs about $0.01.

Improving Innovation

As discussed in Chapter 6, *technology* comprises the skills, know-how, experience, body of scientific knowledge, tools, machines, computers, and equipment used in the design, production, and distribution of goods and services. Technology is involved in all functional activities, and the rapid advance of technology today is a significant factor in managers' attempts to improve how their value chains innovate new kinds of goods and services or ways to provide them.

LO9-5

Differentiate between two forms of innovation, and explain why innovation and product development are crucial components of the search for competitive advantage.

Two Kinds of Innovation

Two principal kinds of innovation can be identified based on the nature of the technological change that brings them about. **Quantum product innovation** results in the development of new, often radically different, kinds of goods and services because of fundamental shifts in technology brought about by pioneering discoveries. Examples are the creation of the Internet and the World Wide Web that have revolutionized the computer, cell phone, and media/music industries, and biotechnology, which has transformed the treatment of illness by creating new, genetically engineered medicines. Chipotle started a restaurant trend called "fast casual" that offers rapidly prepared but high-quality food in an upscale dining environment. Prices are higher than typical fast-food chains.[75]

quantum product innovation The development of new, often radically different, kinds of goods and services because of fundamental shifts in technology brought about by pioneering discoveries.

Incremental product innovation results in gradual improvements and refinements of products over time as existing technologies are perfected and functional managers, like those at Apple, Toyota, and McDonald's, learn how to perform value chain activities in better ways—ways that add more value to products. For example, since their debut, Google's staffers have made thousands of incremental improvements to the company's search engine, Chrome Internet browser, and Android operating system—changes that have enhanced their capabilities enormously such as giving them the ability to work on all kinds of mobile devices and making them available in many different languages.

incremental product innovation The gradual improvement and refinement of existing products that occur over time as existing technologies are perfected.

Quantum product innovations are relatively rare; most managers' activities focus on incremental product innovations that result from ongoing technological advances. For example, every time Dell or HP puts a new, faster Intel or AMD chip into a PC, or Google improves its search engine's capability, the company is making incremental product innovations. Similarly, every time car engineers redesign a car model, and every time McDonald's managers work to improve the flavor and texture of burgers, fries, and salads, their product development efforts are intended to lead to incremental product innovations. Incremental innovation is frequently as important as—or even more important than—quantum innovation in raising a company's performance. Indeed, as discussed next, it is often managers' ability to successfully manage incremental product development that results in success or failure in an industry—as Dell found out to its cost.

The need to speed innovation and quickly develop new and improved products becomes especially important when the technology behind the product is advancing rapidly. This is because the first companies in an industry to adopt the new technology will be able to develop products that better meet customer needs and gain a "first-mover" advantage over their rivals. Indeed, managers who do not quickly adopt and apply new technologies to innovate products may soon find they have no customers for their products—and destroy their organizations. In sum, the greater the rate of technological change in an industry, the more important it is for managers to innovate.

product development The management of the value chain activities involved in bringing new or improved goods and services to the market.

Strategies to Promote Innovation and Speed Product Development

There are several ways in which managers can promote innovation and encourage the development of new products. **Product development** is the management of the value chain activities involved in bringing new or improved goods and services to the market. The steps that Monte Peterson, former CEO of Thermos, took to develop a new barbecue grill show how good product development should proceed. Peterson had no doubt about how to increase Thermos's sales of barbecue grills: motivate Thermos's functional managers to create new and improved models. So Peterson assembled a cross-functional product development team of five functional managers (from marketing, engineering, manufacturing, sales, and finance) and told them to develop a new barbecue grill within 18 months. To ensure that they were not spread too thin, he assigned them to this team only. Peterson also arranged for leadership of the team to rotate. Initially, to focus on what customers wanted, the marketing manager would take the lead; then, when technical developments became the main consideration, leadership would switch to engineering; and so on.

Team members christened the group the "lifestyle team." To find out what people really wanted in a grill, the marketing manager and nine subordinates spent a month on the road, visiting customers. What they found surprised them. The stereotype of Dad slaving over a smoky barbecue grill was wrong—more women were barbecuing. Many cooks were tired of messy charcoal, and many homeowners did not like rusty grills that spoiled the appearance of their decks. Moreover, environmental and safety issues were increasing in importance. In California charcoal starter fluid is considered a pollutant and is banned; in New Jersey the use of charcoal and gas grills on the balconies of condos and apartments has been prohibited to avoid fires. Based on these findings, the team decided Thermos had to produce a barbecue grill that not only made the food taste good but also looked attractive, used no pollutants, and was safe for balcony use (which meant it had to be electric).

Within one year the basic attributes of the product were defined, and leadership of the team moved to engineering. The critical task for engineering was to design a grill that gave food the cookout taste that conventional electric grills could not provide because they did not get hot enough. To raise the cooking temperature, Thermos's engineers designed a domed vacuum top that trapped heat inside the grill, and they built electric heat rods directly into the surface of the grill. These features made the grill hot enough to sear meat and give it brown barbecue lines and a barbecue taste.

Manufacturing had been active from the early days of the development process, making sure any proposed design could be produced economically. Because manufacturing was involved from the beginning, the team avoided some costly mistakes. At one critical team meeting the engineers said they wanted tapered legs on the grill. Manufacturing explained that tapered legs would have to be custom-made—and would raise manufacturing costs—and persuaded the team to go with straight legs.

When the new grill was introduced on schedule, it was an immediate success. The study of many product development successes, such as that of Thermos's lifestyle team, suggests three strategies managers can implement to increase the likelihood that their product development efforts will result in innovative and successful new products.

INVOLVE BOTH CUSTOMERS AND SUPPLIERS Many new products fail when they reach the marketplace because they were designed with scant attention to customer needs. Successful product development requires inputs from more than just an organization's members; also needed are inputs from customers and suppliers. Thermos team members spent a month on the road, visiting customers to identify their needs. The revolutionary electric barbecue grill was a direct result of this process. In other cases companies have found it worthwhile to include customer representatives as peripheral members of their product development teams. Boeing, for example, has included its customers, the major airlines, in the design of its most recent commercial jet aircraft, the 787 Dreamliner. Boeing builds a mockup of the aircraft's cabin and then, over a period of months, allows each airline's representatives to experiment with repositioning the galleys, seating, aisles, and bathrooms to best meet the needs of their particular airline. Boeing has learned a great deal from this process.

ESTABLISH A STAGE–GATE DEVELOPMENT FUNNEL One of the most common mistakes managers make in product development is trying to fund too many new projects at any one time. This approach spreads the activities of the different value chain functions too thinly over too many different projects. As a consequence, no single project is given the functional resources and attention required.

stage–gate development funnel A planning model that forces managers to choose among competing projects so organizational resources are not spread thinly over too many projects.

One strategy for solving this problem is for managers to develop a structured process for evaluating product development proposals and deciding which to support and which to reject. A common solution is to establish a **stage–gate development funnel**, a technique that forces managers to choose among competing projects so functional resources are not spread thinly over too many projects. The funnel gives functional managers control over product development and allows them to intervene and take corrective action quickly and appropriately (see Figure 9.5).

At stage 1 the development funnel has a wide mouth, so top managers initially can encourage employees to come up with as many new product ideas as possible. Managers can create incentives for employees to come up with ideas. Many organizations run "bright-idea programs" that reward employees whose ideas eventually make it through the development process. Other organizations allow research scientists to devote a certain amount of work time to their own projects. Top managers at 3M, for example, have a 15 percent rule: They expect a research scientist to spend 15 percent of the workweek working on a project of his or her own choosing. Ideas may be submitted by individuals or by groups. Brainstorming (see Chapter 7) is a technique that managers frequently use to encourage new ideas.

New product ideas are written up as brief proposals. The proposals are submitted to a cross-functional team of managers, who evaluate each proposal at gate 1. The cross-functional team considers a proposal's fit with the organization's strategy and its technical feasibility. Proposals that are consistent with the strategy of the organization and are judged technically feasible pass through gate 1 and into stage 2. Other proposals are turned down (although the door is often left open for reconsidering a proposal later).

product development plan A plan that specifies all of the relevant information that managers need in order to decide whether to proceed with a full-blown product development effort.

The primary goal in stage 2 is to draft a detailed product development plan. The **product development plan** specifies all of the relevant information that managers need to decide whether to go ahead with a full-blown product development effort. The product development plan should include strategic and financial objectives, an analysis of the product's market potential, a list of desired product features, a list of technological requirements, a list of financial and human resource requirements, a detailed development budget, and a time line that contains specific milestones (for example, dates for prototype completion and final launch).

A cross-functional team of managers normally drafts this plan. Good planning requires a good strategic analysis (see Chapter 8), and team members must be prepared to spend considerable time in the field with customers, trying to understand their needs. Drafting a product development plan generally takes about three months. Once completed, the plan is reviewed by a senior management committee at gate 2 (see Figure 9.5). These managers focus on the details of the plan to see whether the proposal is attractive (given its market potential) and viable (given the technological, financial, and human resources that would be needed to develop the product). Senior managers making this review keep in mind all other product

Figure 9.5

A Stage–Gate Development Funnel

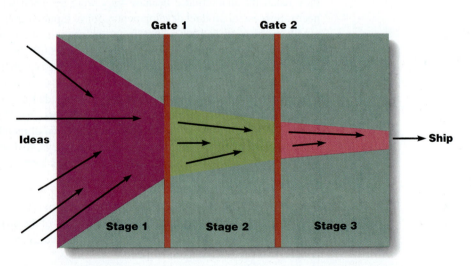

development efforts currently being undertaken by the organization. One goal at this point is to ensure that limited organizational resources are used to their maximum effect.

At gate 2 projects are rejected, sent back for revision, or allowed to pass through to stage 3, the development phase. Product development starts with the formation of a cross-functional team that is given primary responsibility for developing the product. In some companies, at the beginning of stage 3 top managers and cross-functional team members sign a **contract book**, a written agreement that details factors such as responsibilities, resource commitments, budgets, time lines, and development milestones. Signing the contract book is viewed as the symbolic launch of a product development effort. The contract book is also a document against which actual development progress can be measured. At 3M, for example, team members and top management negotiate a contract and sign a contract book at the launch of a development effort, thereby signaling their commitment to the objectives contained in the contract.

The stage 3 development effort can last anywhere from six months to 10 years, depending on the industry and type of product. Some electronics products have development cycles of six months, but it takes from three to five years to develop a new car, about five years to develop a new jet aircraft, and as long as 10 years to develop a new medical drug.

ESTABLISH CROSS-FUNCTIONAL TEAMS   A smooth-running cross-functional team also seems to be a critical component of successful product development, as the experience of Thermos suggests. Marketing, engineering, and manufacturing personnel are **core members** of a successful product development team—the people who have primary responsibility for the product development effort. Other people besides core members work on the project when the need arises, but the core members (generally from three to six individuals) stay with the project from inception to completion of the development effort (see Figure 9.6).

The reason for using a cross-functional team is to ensure a high level of coordination and communication among managers in different functions. Input from both marketing and manufacturing members of Thermos's lifestyle team determined the characteristics of the barbecue that the engineers on the team ended up designing.

If a cross-functional team is to succeed, it must have the right kind of leadership and it must be managed effectively. To be successful, a product development team needs a team leader who can rise above a functional background and take a cross-functional view. In addition

contract book A written agreement that details product development factors such as responsibilities, resource commitments, budgets, time lines, and development milestones.

core members The members of a team who bear primary responsibility for the success of a project and who stay with a project from inception to completion.

Figure 9.6

Members of a Cross-Functional Product Development Team

to having effective leadership, successful cross-functional product development teams have several other key characteristics. Often core members of successful teams are located close to one another, in the same office space, to foster a sense of shared mission and commitment to a development program. Successful teams develop a clear sense of their objectives and how they will be achieved, the purpose again being to create a sense of shared mission. Thermos eventually sold its grill business to the Char-Broil Division of W.C. Bradley Co. But its story demonstrates the three strategies that help ventures succeed: involving customers and suppliers, establishing a stage-gate development funnel, and establishing cross-functional teams. The way in which the Lego Group manages its product quality is discussed in the accompanying "Management Insight" feature.

Management Insight

Legos Doesn't Play Around When It Comes to Quality

"Lego" is an abbreviation of two Danish words: "leg" meaning play and "godt" meaning well.[76] The company, based in Denmark, was founded by Ole Kirk Kristiansen and has been passed from father to son over the years. It is now owned by Kjeld Kirk Kristiansen, a grandchild of the founder.[77]

The company is known for high-quality manufacturing. The LEGO Group, founded in 1932,[78] has made more than 560 billion of those colorful interlocking plastic parts kids (and even adults) have been building with for decades.[79] While the company also has launched supporting movies, video games, and themed amusement parks, its interlocking bricks remain its flagship product.

On its web page, the company touts its position on quality: "From a reputation for manufacturing excellence to becoming trusted by all—we believe in quality that speaks for itself and earns us the recommendation of all. For us quality means the challenge of continuous improvement to be the best toy, the best for children and their development and the best to our community and partners."[80]

Anyone who has played with Legos knows that the pieces (bricks, mostly) have to snap together. This leaves little room in the Lego manufacturing process for error. If the manufacturing process were to produce bricks that did not connect, the play sets would get a big thumbs down from children.

The company has several plants around the world making Lego bricks. Every plant must have the same specifications so that bricks created in one plant will lock with bricks created in another plant. Quality control is so high that only 18 out of 1 million pieces are found to be defective. The company's molds have a precision tolerance of 0.002 millimeters.[81]

To keep quality and specifications identical around the world, Lego provides the same training at different plants. Also, the equipment at all plants is standardized, so quality workers in different plants can share knowledge with one another.

Lego is also concerned with safety. John Hansen, senior vice president for engineering and quality at Lego's headquarters in Denmark, defines "a safe element" as one "that won't hurt anybody. But also that works as we expect it, that the appearance of the element and the dimensions are as expected."[82] Every Lego brick has its own numeric ID. The company also is considering

Lego is known for its interlocking brick pieces. To maintain its high quality control standards, Lego standardizes its equipment and trains its employees in the same way.

new materials for the bricks. The company is researching new material that is better for the environment than polymers. Lego also has reduced the size of packaging by making boxes smaller, which saves on cardboard and on shipping costs.

In 2014, Lego was No. 9 on the "Global RepTrak 100: The World's Most Reputable Companies" list.[83]

"The reason for this honor comes down to this. Lego delivers what it promises in its advertising," Hansen said. "It stands by its toys with a deeply rooted corporate philosophy of how the power of constructive play can drive the development of intellectual competencies—spatial, mathematical, and scientific inquiry. And, significantly, children (and adults, who are we kidding) develop and build on the habits of mind to develop and promote STEM [science, technology, engineering, and math] learning."[84]

In reference to the Lego Group's results, Henrik Strøier, managing partner of the Reputation Institute, agreed with Hansen. "Support is driven by who you are as a company; how fair you are when doing business, how you support the community, how sustainable your operation is, and how compelling your vision for the future is," he said. "What Lego does so well in these years is to engage with its customers, consumers, suppliers, partners, and opinion leaders on issues that matter to them; workplace, governance, and citizenship while producing amazing products."[85]

Managing innovation is an increasingly important aspect of a manager's job in an era of dramatic changes in advanced IT. Promoting successful new product development is difficult and challenging, and some product development efforts are much more successful than others. In sum, managers need to recognize that successful innovation and product development cut across roles and functions and require a high level of cooperation. They should recognize the importance of common values and norms in promoting the high levels of cooperation and cohesiveness necessary to build a culture for innovation. They also should reward successful innovators and make heroes of the employees and teams who develop successful new products. Finally, managers should fully utilize the product development techniques just discussed to guide the process.

Summary and Review

LO9-1 **VALUE CHAIN MANAGEMENT AND COMPETITIVE ADVANTAGE** To achieve high performance, managers try to improve their responsiveness to customers, the quality of their products, and the efficiency of their organization. To achieve these goals, managers can use a number of value chain management techniques to improve the way an organization operates.

LO9-2 **IMPROVING RESPONSIVENESS TO CUSTOMERS** To achieve high performance in a competitive environment, it is imperative that the organization's value chain be managed to produce outputs that have the attributes customers desire. A central task of value chain management is to develop new and improved operating systems that enhance the ability of the organization to economically deliver more of the product attributes that customers desire for the same price. Techniques such as CRM and TQM, JIT, flexible manufacturing, and process reengineering are popular because they promise to do this. As important as responsiveness to customers is, however, managers need to recognize that there are limits to how responsive an organization can be and still cover its costs.

LO9-3 **IMPROVING QUALITY** Managers seek to improve the quality of their organization's output because doing so enables them to better serve customers, to raise prices, and to lower production costs. Total quality management focuses on improving the quality of an organization's products and services and stresses that all of an organization's operations should be directed toward this goal. Putting TQM into practice requires having an organization-wide commitment to TQM, having a strong customer focus, finding ways to measure quality, setting quality improvement goals, soliciting input from employees about how to improve product quality, identifying defects and tracing them to their source, introducing just-in-time inventory systems, getting suppliers to adopt TQM practices, designing products for ease of manufacture, and breaking down barriers between functional departments.

LO9-4 **IMPROVING EFFICIENCY** Improving efficiency requires one or more of the following: the introduction of a TQM program, the adoption of flexible manufacturing technologies, the introduction of just-in-time inventory systems, the establishment of self-managed work teams, and the application of process reengineering. Top management is responsible for setting the context within which efficiency improvements can take place by, for example, emphasizing the need for continuous improvement. Functional-level managers bear prime responsibility for identifying and implementing efficiency-enhancing improvements in operating systems.

LO9-5 **IMPROVING PRODUCT INNOVATION** When technology is changing, managers must quickly innovate new and improved products to protect their competitive advantage. Some value chain strategies managers can use to achieve this are (1) involving both customers and suppliers in the development process; (2) establishing a stage–gate development funnel for evaluating and controlling different product development efforts; and (3) establishing cross-functional teams composed of individuals from different functional departments, and giving each team a leader who can rise above his or her functional background.

Management in Action

Topics for Discussion and Action

Discussion

1. What is CRM, and how can it help improve responsiveness to customers? **[LO9-2]**

2. What are the main challenges in implementing a successful total quality management program? **[LO9-3]**

3. What is efficiency, and what are some strategies managers can use to increase it? **[LO9-4]**

4. Why is it important for managers to pay close attention to value chain management if they wish to be responsive to their customers? **[LO9-1, 9-2]**

5. What is innovation, and what are some strategies managers can use to develop successful new products? **[LO9-5]**

Action

6. Ask a manager how responsiveness to customers, quality, efficiency, and innovation are defined and measured in his or her organization. **[LO9-1, 9-2]**

7. Go to a local store, restaurant, or supermarket; observe how customers are treated; and list the ways in which you think the organization is being responsive or unresponsive to the needs of its customers. How could this business improve its responsiveness to customers? **[LO9-1, 9-2]**

Building Management Skills

Managing the Value Chain [LO9-1, 9-2]

Choose an organization with which you are familiar—one that you have worked in or patronized or one that has received extensive coverage in the popular press. The organization should be involved in only one industry or business. Answer these questions about the organization:

1. What is the output of the organization?

2. Describe the value chain activities that the organization uses to produce this output.

3. What product attributes do customers of the organization desire?

4. Try to identify improvements that might be made to the organization's value chain to boost its responsiveness to customers, quality, efficiency, and innovation.

Managing Ethically [LO9-1, 9-4]

After implementing efficiency-improving techniques, many companies commonly lay off hundreds or thousands of employees whose services are no longer required. And frequently remaining employees must perform more tasks more quickly—a situation that can generate employee stress and other work-related problems. Also, these employees may experience guilt because they stayed while many of their colleagues and friends were fired.

Questions

1. Either by yourself or in a group, think through the ethical implications of using a new functionalstrategy to improve organizational performance.

2. What criteria would you use to decide which kind of strategy is ethical to adopt and how far to push employees to raise the level of their performance?

3. How big a layoff, if any, is acceptable? If layoffs are acceptable, what could be done to reduce their harm to employees?

Small Group Breakout Exercise

How to Compete in the Sandwich Business [LO9-1, 9-2]

Form groups of three or four people, and appoint one member as the spokesperson who will communicate your findings to the class when called on by the instructor. Then discuss the following scenario:

You and your partners are thinking about opening a new kind of sandwich shop that will compete head-to-head with Subway and Thundercloud Subs. Because these chains have good brand-name recognition, it is vital that you find some source of competitive advantage for your new sandwich shop, and you are meeting to brainstorm ways of obtaining one.

1. Identify the product attributes that a typical sandwich shop customer wants the most.

2. In what ways do you think you will be able to improve on the operations and processes of existing sandwich shops and increase responsiveness to customers through better product quality, efficiency, or innovation?

Exploring the World Wide Web [LO9-3, 9-4]

Go to the website for the Container Store (www.containerstore.com). You can click around on the various products available for storage. Find the page with tips for organizing your workspace. Click through the various categories of compartmentalize, de-clutterize, categorize, utilize, and minimize.

1. What tips about improving your personal work flow do you want to try out after reading the tips, and why?

2. What products would be most helpful to your new organization system, and why?

Be the Manager [LO9-1, 9-3, 9-4, 9-5]

How to Build Flatscreen Displays

You are the top manager of a start-up company that will produce innovative new flatscreen displays for PC makers like Apple and HP. The flatscreen display market is highly competitive, so there is considerable pressure to reduce costs. Also, PC makers are demanding ever-higher quality and better features to please customers. In addition, they demand that delivery of your product meets their production schedule needs. Functional managers want your advice on how to best meet these requirements, especially because they are in the process of recruiting new workers and building a production facility.

Questions

1. What kinds of techniques discussed in the chapter can help your functional managers to increase efficiency?

2. In what ways can these managers develop a program to increase quality and innovation?

3. What critical lessons do these managers need to learn about value chain management?

Bloomberg Businessweek Case in the News [LO9-1, 9-4]

Maybe March Madness Boosts (Rather Than Kills) U.S. Productivity

In 2006 an innovation was unleashed on the teeming, college-basketball-hungry masses that promised to unshackle us from the fear of watching NCAA March Madness tournament games at work. The Boss Button allowed basketball fans at work to switch between the live stream of a game and a phony financial statement or innocuous spreadsheet.

Most of us don't get paid to watch basketball. This year workers in the United States have so far spent 10.5 million hours watching NCAA tournament games while on the clock. If, as many have argued, all this time is completely unproductive and costs the U.S. economy $1.7 billion a year, bosses should rightfully crack down on tournament viewing at work.

These productivity analyses, however, are not based on hard data about how the tournament actually affects people's behavior. They're just multiplying the time spent watching games and picking brackets by the average hourly rate paid to workers. But let's think about the March Madness effect more broadly. What if, rather than employees just sitting at their desks glued to their monitors, March Madness gets people talking to their colleagues, walking around the office, and generally creating the kind of camaraderie and information flow that companies need to flourish?

Communication is the most important thing that happens at work, even if it's not work related. At a major pharmaceutical company, for example, our research showed that a 10 percent increase in face-to-face communication with people on other teams increased sales more than 10 percent, which translates into hundreds of millions of dollars.

To give this question a proper examination, then, I'll dig into data collected at my own early-stage tech company, Sociometric Solutions. We're still relatively small, with fewer than 10 people, but this is a good sample to start with. We collected data on ourselves using Sociometric Badges (wearable sensor ID badges) to measure how our interaction time changed during the first two days of the NCAA tournament. Then we compared these two days with data from earlier in the week, as well as a representative Thursday and Friday from previous weeks. To recap, the Sociometric Badges measure who talks to whom, how people talk to each other, how they move around, and where people spend time. Data on individuals are never shared with employers, and the badges are used on an opt-in basis, with dummy badges that don't collect data provided to people who don't want to participate.

OK, now let's get to the data:

I must admit, I was quite surprised when I saw these numbers. While the results are not statistically significant, more interaction actually occurred the first day of the tournament (March 20) than every other day that week. The second day of the tournament (March 21) saw a similar level of interaction. We can also see that the first two days of March Madness have much higher interaction levels than the typical Thursday and Friday.

This increased interaction is important. Rather than indicating we're being unproductive, these results argue that we're more productive in the long term thanks to March Madness. As we've seen in many organizations, more interaction within a tightly knit group yields higher performance and higher job satisfaction through increased trust and the development of a shared language.

So there you have it: March Madness does not reduce productivity. In fact, it may increase it.

In that spirit, I'd like to propose an updated Boss Button for 2015. Instead of hiding the live stream, this Boss Button will call your boss over to your desk to watch the game with you. Because, as the data show, we all should be getting paid to watch basketball.

Source: Ben Weber, "Maybe March Madness Boosts (Rather Than Kills) U.S. Productivity, *Bloomberg Business Week,* March 27, 2014. Used with permission of Bloomberg L.P. Copyright © 2014. All rights reserved.

Questions for Discussion

1. Besides March Madness, what other events might disrupt work at the office?

2. How can organizations control the disruptive effects of such events?

3. If disruptive events also have the positive side effect of increasing communication, how can organizations create a culture in which these events are appreciated for their positive effects?

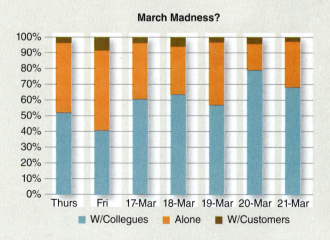

March Madness?

Legend: W/Collegues, Alone, W/Customers
(X-axis: Thurs, Fri, 17-Mar, 18-Mar, 19-Mar, 20-Mar, 21-Mar)

CHAPTER 10

Managing Organizational Structure and Culture

Learning Objectives

After studying this chapter, you should be able to:

LO10-1 Identify the factors that influence managers' choice of an organizational structure.

LO10-2 Explain how managers group tasks into jobs that are motivating and satisfying for employees.

LO10-3 Describe the types of organizational structures managers can design, and explain why they choose one structure over another.

LO10-4 Explain why managers must coordinate jobs, functions, and divisions using the hierarchy of authority and integrating mechanisms.

LO10-5 List the four sources of organizational culture, and explain why and how a company's culture can lead to competitive advantage.

A MANAGER'S CHALLENGE

Three Studios, Three Cultures, One Company

How can organizational structure influence employee creativity? What do Snow White, Buzz Lightyear, and Iron Man have in common? The studios that produced their movies are all owned by the Walt Disney Company. Disney owns several organizations, including Walt Disney Animation Studios, Pixar Animation Studios, and Marvel Studios.

While these three studios are owned by the same company and all do roughly the same thing (produce movies), they have different stories and different organization cultures. Walt Disney Animation Studios is the oldest of the three, established by Walt and Roy Disney under the name Disney Brothers Cartoon Studio in 1923. Its first feature film was *Snow White and the Seven Dwarfs* in 1937. In 2013 it released its 53rd animated film, *Frozen,* which became the No. 1 animated film of all time.[1]

Marvel was founded in 1939 as Timely Publications. In 1941 it introduced the comic book *Captain America* with a cover picture of the hero punching Adolf Hitler.[2] In 1991 Marvel Studios was established as a film production unit.[3] Marvel has more than 8,000 characters, including the *Avengers, Green Goblin, Iron Man, Spider-Man,* and the *X-Men.* Most of these characters live in the Marvel universe, in fictional cities similar to New York and Los Angeles. The Walt Disney Company bought Marvel in 2009.

In 2002 investor and then-owner of Marvel Ronald Perelman said, "It is a mini-Disney in terms of intellectual property. Disney's got much more highly recognized characters and softer characters, whereas our characters are termed action heroes. But at Marvel we are now in the business of the creation and marketing of characters."[4]

Pixar Animation Studios was founded in 1979 as Graphics Group. It was originally the computer division of Lucasfilm, and became

Ed Catmull, co-found of Pixar followed a different strategy when Disney and Pixar merged. Instead of consolidating, Catmull was adamant that the two not be integrated, that each studio retain its own unique culture. He is following the same policy with another acquisition, Marvel Studios.

its own corporation in 1986 with funding from Apple cofounder Steve Jobs. Its first feature film was *Toy Story* in 1995, which eventually was nominated for awards by the Academy of Motion Pictures Arts and Sciences.[5] The Walt Disney Company bought Pixar in 2006.

However, while *Toy Story* was a success, Pixar cofounder Ed Catmull found there were structural issues within the company. Pixar had insisted that communication happen through proper hierarchical channels. This led to hard feelings between the creative and production departments. While working on *A Bug's Life*, the film that followed *Toy Story*, Pixar created a rule that anyone could talk to anyone else, regardless of level. The resulting communication structure helped Pixar foster a more creative culture.[6]

In his recently published book *Creativity, Inc.: Overcoming the Unseen Forces That Stand in the Way of True Inspiration,* Catmull, now president of Walt Disney Animation Studios and Pixar, discussed the merger of Disney and Pixar. He said that when two organizations merge, there is typically a push to consolidate workflows and to reduce redundancies. However, when Disney and Pixar came together, they did something different.

"We took the exact opposite approach, which was to say to each studio, 'You may look at the tools that the other has, you may use them if you want, but the choice is entirely yours.' They each have a development group that's coming up with different ideas, but because we said, 'You don't have to take ideas from anybody else,' they felt freer to talk with each other."[7]

Yet some lessons from Pixar were applied at Disney, according to Catmull. When Pixar joined Disney in 2006, Disney employees were demoralized by a few lackluster film projects, including *Chicken Little* and *Home on the Range.* Pixar practices, such as creating an environment where workers can be candid and where innovative ideas can move forward, were applied at Disney. After the ideas took hold, the studio produced several big hits, including *Tangled* and *Frozen.*[8]

"The one thing we were really adamant about was that the two studios not be integrated together. We established an absolute rule, which we still adhere to, that neither studio can do any production work for the other. For me, the local ownership is really important. We put in place mechanisms to keep each studio's culture unique," Catmull said. "It's a model that Bob's using at Marvel. Marvel has a completely different culture than Pixar does, or Disney Animation, and he lets them run it their way. You want to have mechanisms to bridge between them, but you don't interfere with that local culture."[9]

Overview

As the examples of Disney Animation, Pixar, and Marvel Studios suggest, organizational culture is a powerful influence on how employees work. How an organization's structure is designed also affects employees' behavior and how well an organization operates, so in a quickly changing global environment it is important for managers to identify the best way to organize people and resources to increase efficiency and effectiveness.

In Part 4 of this book, we examine how managers can organize and control human and other resources to create high-performing organizations. To organize and control (two of the four tasks of management identified in Chapter 1), managers must design an organizational

organizational architecture
The organizational structure, control systems, culture, and human resource management systems that together determine how efficiently and effectively organizational resources are used.

architecture that makes the best use of resources to produce the goods and services customers want. **Organizational architecture** is the combination of organizational structure, culture, control systems, and human resource management (HRM) systems that together determine how efficiently and effectively organizational resources are used.

By the end of this chapter, you will be familiar not only with various forms of organizational structures and cultures but also with various factors that determine the organizational design choices that managers make. Then, in Chapters 11 and 12, we examine issues surrounding the design of an organization's control systems and HRM systems.

Designing Organizational Structure

LO10-1

Identify the factors that influence managers' choice of an organizational structure.

organizational structure
A formal system of task and reporting relationships that coordinates and motivates organizational members so they work together to achieve an organization's goals.

organizational design The process by which managers make specific organizing choices that result in a particular kind of organizational structure.

Organizing is the process by which managers establish the structure of working relationships among employees to allow them to achieve an organization's goals efficiently and effectively. **Organizational structure** is the formal system of task and job reporting relationships that determines how employees use resources to achieve an organization's goals.[10] *Organizational culture,* discussed in Chapter 3, is the shared set of beliefs, values, and norms that influence how people and groups work together to achieve an organization's goals. **Organizational design** is the process by which managers create a specific type of organizational structure and culture so a company can operate in the most efficient and effective way.[11]

Once a company decides what kind of work attitudes and behaviors it wants from its employees, managers create a particular arrangement of task and authority relationships, and promote specific cultural values and norms, to obtain these desired attitudes and behaviors. The challenge facing all companies is to design a structure and a culture that (1) *motivate* managers and employees to work hard and to develop supportive job behaviors and attitudes and (2) *coordinate* the actions of employees, groups, functions, and divisions to ensure they work together efficiently and effectively.

As noted in Chapter 2, according to contingency theory, managers design organizational structures to fit the factors or circumstances that are affecting the company the most and causing the most uncertainty.[12] Thus there is no one best way to design an organization: Design reflects each organization's specific situation, and researchers have argued that in some situations stable, mechanistic structures may be most appropriate while in others flexible, organic structures might be the most effective. Four factors are important determinants of the type of organizational structure or culture managers select: the nature of the organizational environment, the type of strategy the organization pursues, the technology (and particularly information technology) the organization uses, and the characteristics of the organization's human resources (see Figure 10.1).[13]

The Organizational Environment

In general, the more quickly the external environment is changing and the greater the uncertainty within it, the greater are the problems managers face in trying to gain access to scarce resources. In this situation, to speed decision making and communication and make it easier to obtain resources, managers typically make organizing choices that result in more flexible structures and entrepreneurial cultures.[14] They are likely to decentralize authority, empower lower-level employees to make important operating decisions, and encourage values and norms that emphasize change and innovation—a more organic form of organizing.

In contrast, if the external environment is stable, resources are readily available, and uncertainty is low, then less coordination and communication among people and functions are needed to obtain resources. Managers can make organizing choices that bring more stability or formality to the organizational structure and can establish values and norms that emphasize obedience and being a team player. Managers in this situation prefer to make decisions within a clearly defined hierarchy of authority and to use detailed rules, standard operating procedures (SOPs), and restrictive norms to guide and govern employees' activities—a more mechanistic form of organizing.

Figure 10.1

Factors Affecting Organizational Structure

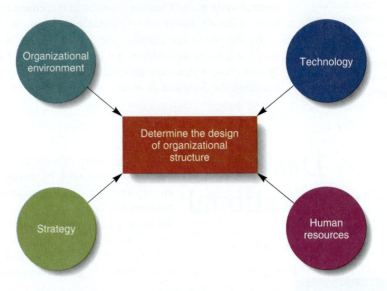

As we discussed in Chapter 6, change is rapid in today's marketplace, and increasing competition both at home and abroad is putting greater pressure on managers to attract customers and increase efficiency and effectiveness. Consequently, interest in finding ways to structure organizations—such as through empowerment and self-managed teams—to allow people and departments to behave flexibly has been increasing.

Strategy

Chapter 8 suggests that once managers decide on a strategy, they must choose the right means to implement it. Different strategies often call for the use of different organizational structures and cultures. For example, a differentiation strategy aimed at increasing the value customers perceive in an organization's goods and services usually succeeds best in a flexible structure with a culture that values innovation; flexibility facilitates a differentiation strategy because managers can develop new or innovative products quickly—an activity that requires extensive cooperation among functions or departments. In contrast, a low-cost strategy that is aimed at driving down costs in all functions usually fares best in a more formal structure with more conservative norms, which gives managers greater control over the activities of an organization's various departments.[15]

In addition, at the corporate level, when managers decide to expand the scope of organizational activities by vertical integration or diversification, for example, they need to design a flexible structure to provide sufficient coordination among the different business divisions.[16] As discussed in Chapter 8, many companies have been divesting businesses because managers have been unable to create a competitive advantage to keep them up to speed in fast-changing industries. By moving to a more flexible structure, managers gain more control over their different businesses. Finally, expanding internationally and operating in many different countries challenges managers to create organizational structures that allow organizations to be flexible on a global level.[17] As we discuss later, managers can group their departments or divisions in several ways to allow them to effectively pursue an international strategy.

Technology

Recall that technology is the combination of skills, knowledge, machines, and computers that are used to design, make, and distribute goods and services. As a rule, the more complicated the technology that an organization uses, the more difficult it is to regulate or control it because more unexpected events can arise. Thus the more complicated the technology, the greater is the need for a flexible structure and progressive culture to enhance managers' ability to respond to unexpected situations—and give them the freedom and desire to work out new solutions to the problems they encounter. In contrast, the more routine the technology, the more appropriate is a formal structure because tasks are simple and the steps needed to produce goods and services have been worked out in advance.

What makes a technology routine or complicated? One researcher who investigated this issue, Charles Perrow, argued that two factors determine how complicated or nonroutine technology is: task variety and task analyzability.[18] *Task variety* is the number of new or unexpected problems or situations that a person or function encounters in performing tasks or jobs. *Task analyzability* is the degree to which programmed solutions are available to people or functions to solve the problems they encounter. Nonroutine or complicated technologies are characterized by high task variety and low task analyzability; this means many varied problems occur and solving these problems requires significant nonprogrammed decision making. In contrast, routine technologies are characterized by low task variety and high task analyzability; this means the problems encountered do not vary much and are easily resolved through programmed decision making.

Examples of nonroutine technology are found in the work of scientists in an R&D laboratory who develop new products or discover new drugs, and they are seen in the planning exercises an organization's top management team uses to chart future strategy. Examples of routine technology include typical mass production or assembly operations, where workers perform the same task repeatedly and where managers have already identified the programmed solutions necessary to perform a task efficiently. Similarly, in service organizations such as fast-food restaurants, the tasks that crew members perform in making and serving fast food are routine.

LO10-2

Explain how managers group tasks into jobs that are motivating and satisfying for employees.

Human Resources

A final important factor affecting an organization's choice of structure and culture is the characteristics of the human resources it employs. In general, the more highly skilled its workforce, and the greater the number of employees who work together in groups or teams, the more likely an organization is to use a flexible, decentralized structure and a professional culture based on values and norms that foster employee autonomy and self-control. Highly skilled employees, or employees who have internalized strong professional values and norms of behavior as part of their training, usually desire greater freedom and autonomy and dislike close supervision.

Flexible structures, characterized by decentralized authority and empowered employees, are well suited to the needs of highly skilled people. Similarly, when people work in teams, they must be allowed to interact freely and develop norms to guide their own work interactions, which also is possible in a flexible organizational structure. Thus, when designing organizational structure and culture, managers must pay close attention to the needs of the workforce and to the complexity and kind of work employees perform.

In summary, an organization's external environment, strategy, technology, and human resources are the factors to be considered by managers seeking to design the best structure and culture for an organization. The greater the level of uncertainty in the organization's environment, the more complex its strategy and technologies, and the more highly qualified and skilled its workforce, the more likely managers are to design a structure and a culture that are flexible, can change quickly, and allow employees to be innovative in their responses to problems, customer needs, and so on. The more stable the organization's environment, the less complex and more well understood its strategy or technology, and the less skilled its workforce, the more likely managers are to design an organizational structure that is formal and controlling and a culture whose values and norms prescribe how employees should act in particular situations.

Later in the chapter we discuss how managers can create different kinds of organizational cultures. First, however, we discuss how managers can design flexible or formal organizational structures. The way an organization's structure works depends on the organizing choices managers make about three issues:

- How to group tasks into individual jobs.

- How to group jobs into functions and divisions.

- How to allocate authority and coordinate or integrate functions and divisions.

Grouping Tasks into Jobs: Job Design

The first step in organizational design is **job design**, the process by which managers decide how to divide into specific jobs the tasks that have to be performed to provide customers with goods and services. Managers at McDonald's, for example, have decided how best to divide the tasks required to provide customers with fast, cheap food in each McDonald's restaurant. After experimenting with different job arrangements, McDonald's managers decided on a basic division of labor among chefs and food servers. Managers allocated all the tasks involved in actually cooking the food (putting oil in the fat fryers, opening packages of frozen french fries, putting beef patties on the grill, making salads, and so on) to the job of chef. They allocated all the tasks involved in giving the food to customers (such as greeting customers, taking orders, putting fries and burgers into bags, adding salt, pepper, and napkins, and taking money) to food servers. In addition, they created other jobs—the job of dealing with drive-through customers, the job of keeping the restaurant clean, and the job of overseeing employees and responding to unexpected events. The result of the job design process is a *division of labor* among employees, one that McDonald's managers have discovered through experience is most efficient.

job design The process by which managers decide how to divide tasks into specific jobs.

At Subway, the roles of chef and server are combined into one, making the job "larger" than the jobs of McDonald's more specialized food servers. The idea behind job enlargement is that increasing the range of tasks performed by the worker will reduce boredom.

Establishing an appropriate division of labor among employees is a critical part of the organizing process, one that is vital to increasing efficiency and effectiveness. At McDonald's, the tasks associated with chef and food server were split into different jobs because managers found that, for the kind of food McDonald's serves, this approach was most efficient. It is efficient because when each employee is given fewer tasks to perform (so that each job becomes more specialized), employees become more productive at performing the tasks that constitute each job.

At Subway sandwich shops, however, managers chose a different kind of job design. At Subway there is no division of labor among the people who make the sandwiches, wrap the sandwiches, give them to customers, and take the money. The roles of chef and food server are combined into one. This different division of tasks and jobs is efficient for Subway and not for McDonald's because Subway serves a limited menu of mostly submarine-style sandwiches that are prepared to order. Subway's production system is far simpler than McDonald's; McDonald's menu is much more varied, and its chefs must cook many different kinds of foods. In 2014 Subway changed its children's menu to promote healthful options and trained its employees to encourage children to choose apples as part of their meals.[19]

Managers of every organization must analyze the range of tasks to be performed and then create jobs that best allow the organization to give customers the goods and services they want. In deciding how to assign tasks to individual jobs, however, managers must be careful not to take **job simplification**, the process of reducing the number of tasks that each worker performs, too far.[20] Too much job simplification may reduce efficiency rather than increase it if workers find their simplified jobs boring and monotonous, become demotivated and unhappy, and, as a result, perform at a low level.

job simplification The process of reducing the number of tasks that each worker performs.

Job Enlargement and Job Enrichment

In an attempt to create a division of labor and design individual jobs to encourage workers to perform at a higher level and be more satisfied with their work, several researchers have proposed ways other than job simplification to group tasks into jobs: job enlargement and job enrichment.

Job enlargement is increasing the number of different tasks in a given job by changing the division of labor.[21] For example, because Subway food servers make the food as well as serve it, their jobs are "larger" than the jobs of McDonald's food servers. The idea behind job enlargement is that increasing the range of tasks performed by a worker will reduce boredom and fatigue and may increase motivation to perform at a high level—increasing both the quantity and the quality of goods and services provided. The accompanying "Management Insight" feature describes how one Wendy's franchise tried to improve service by enlarging jobs through training.

job enlargement Increasing the number of different tasks in a given job by changing the division of labor.

Management Insight

Giving Wendy's a New Image

Wendy's is changing its image. It has redesigned its corporate logo and chosen a new look for its restaurants that includes new employee uniforms, WiFi, and flat-screen televisions. It also added lounge areas with fireplaces and faux leather chairs.[22]

What is the idea behind having a living room area at a fast food restaurant? "The hearth at home is a gathering place," said Tré Musco, who is the chief executive of Tesser, the design firm hired to oversee Wendy's remodeling efforts. "It's warm, it's comfortable, it says stay and relax, as opposed to, this is fast food, get in and get out as quickly as possible."[23]

Customers who dine in tend to spend a little more money, so having a welcoming environment can increase sales. Wendy's reported a 25 percent jump in sales at the renovated restaurants.[24]

The company plans to remodel over 600 of its restaurants in the more modern design by the end of 2015. The company also has a schedule for when franchise-owned restaurants will be updated. But at least one franchise owner is innovating in a way that has a similar effect, without the remodel.

Meritage Hospitality Group, which owns 121 Wendy's locations,[25] is improving customer service through training. First, the company committed to bringing on board 10 well-trained workers to each of its 48 stores in Michigan. That's almost 500 new workers. The company held a job fair and looked for friendly, caring people. Then the company provided extensive training for all employees. In fact, they hired the new position of corporate trainer to do one-on-one training with cashiers.[26] Employees are encouraged to look for ways to initiate a conversation with customers and create a personal connection. They also are encouraged to have a regular customer's order prepared before the customer asks. Finally, the franchise group instituted contests among the staff in the restaurants. One contest between the day shift and the night shift was to see who could get the most customer names in a given day.

As a result of the effort, sales went up, customer complaints went down, and customer compliments went up. "Our biggest tip is to invest the time in training," said Al Pruitt, president of Wendy's for Meritage. "If you spend time on your people, you will always get a return on your investment."[27]

---

job enrichment Increasing the degree of responsibility a worker has over his or her job.

Job enrichment is increasing the degree of responsibility a worker has over a job by, for example, (1) empowering workers to experiment to find new or better ways of doing the job, (2) encouraging workers to develop new skills, (3) allowing workers to decide how to do the work and giving them the responsibility for deciding how to respond to unexpected situations, and (4) allowing workers to monitor and measure their own performance.[28] The idea behind job enrichment is that increasing workers' responsibility increases their involvement in their jobs and thus improves their interest in the quality of the goods they make or the services they provide.

In general, managers who make design choices that increase job enrichment and job enlargement are likely to increase the degree to which people behave flexibly rather than rigidly or mechanically. Narrow, specialized jobs are likely to lead people to behave in predictable ways; workers who perform a variety of tasks and who are allowed and encouraged to discover new and better ways to perform their jobs are likely to act flexibly and creatively. Thus managers who enlarge and enrich jobs create a flexible organizational structure, and those who simplify jobs create a more formal structure. If workers are grouped into self-managed work teams, the organization is likely to be flexible because team members provide support for each other and can learn from one another.

The Job Characteristics Model

LO10-3

Describe the types of organizational structures managers can design, and explain why they choose one structure over another.

J. R. Hackman and G. R. Oldham's job characteristics model is an influential model of job design that explains in detail how managers can make jobs more interesting and motivating.[29]

Hackman and Oldham's model (see Figure 10.2) also describes the likely personal and organizational outcomes that will result from enriched and enlarged jobs.

According to Hackman and Oldham, every job has five characteristics that determine how motivating the job is. These characteristics determine how employees react to their work and lead to outcomes such as high performance and satisfaction and low absenteeism and turnover:

- *Skill variety:* The extent to which a job requires that an employee use a wide range of different skills, abilities, or knowledge. Example: The skill variety required by the job of a research scientist is higher than that called for by the job of a McDonald's food server.

- *Task identity:* The extent to which a job requires that a worker perform all the tasks necessary to complete the job, from the beginning to the end of the production process. Example: A craftsworker who takes a piece of wood and transforms it into a custom-made desk has higher task identity than does a worker who performs only one of the numerous operations required to assemble a flat-screen TV.

- *Task significance:* The degree to which a worker feels his or her job is meaningful because of its effect on people inside the organization, such as coworkers, or on people outside the organization, such as customers. Example: A teacher who sees the effect of his or her efforts in a well-educated and well-adjusted student enjoys high task significance compared to a dishwasher who monotonously washes dishes as they come to the kitchen.

- *Autonomy:* The degree to which a job gives an employee the freedom and discretion needed to schedule different tasks and decide how to carry them out. Example: Salespeople who have to plan their schedules and decide how to allocate their time among different customers have relatively high autonomy compared to assembly-line workers, whose actions are determined by the speed of the production line.

- *Feedback:* The extent to which actually doing a job provides a worker with clear and direct information about how well he or she has performed the job. Example: An air traffic controller whose mistakes may result in a midair collision receives immediate feedback on job performance; a person who compiles statistics for a business magazine often has little idea of when he or she makes a mistake or does a particularly good job.

Hackman and Oldham argue that these five job characteristics affect an employee's motivation because they affect three critical psychological states (see Figure 10.2). The more employees feel that their work is *meaningful* and that they are *responsible for work outcomes and responsible for knowing how those outcomes affect others,* the more motivating work becomes and the more likely employees are to be satisfied and to perform at a high level. Moreover, employees who have jobs that are highly motivating are called on to use their skills more and to perform more tasks, and they are given more responsibility for doing the

Figure 10.2

The Job Characteristics Model

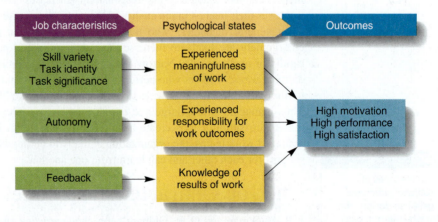

Source: From J. Richard Hackman and Greg R. Oldham, Work Redesign, 1st. Copyright © 1980. Reproduced by permission of Pearson Education, Inc., Upper Saddle River, New Jersey.

job. All of the foregoing are characteristic of jobs and employees in flexible structures where authority is decentralized and where employees commonly work with others and must learn new skills to complete the range of tasks for which their group is responsible.

Grouping Jobs into Functions and Divisions: Designing Organizational Structure

Once managers have decided which tasks to allocate to which jobs, they face the next organizing decision: how to group jobs together to best match the needs of the organization's environment, strategy, technology, and human resources. Typically managers first decide to group jobs into departments and then design a *functional structure* to use organizational resources effectively. As an organization grows and becomes more difficult to control, managers must choose a more complex organizational design, such as a divisional structure or a matrix or product team structure. The different ways in which managers can design organizational structure are discussed next. Selecting and designing an organizational structure to increase efficiency and effectiveness is a significant challenge. As noted in Chapter 8, managers reap the rewards of a well-thought-out strategy only if they choose the right type of structure to implement the strategy. The ability to make the right kinds of organizing choices is often what differentiates effective from ineffective managers and creates a high-performing organization.

Functional Structure

functional structure An organizational structure composed of all the departments that an organization requires to produce its goods or services.

A *function* is a group of people, working together, who possess similar skills or use the same kind of knowledge, tools, or techniques to perform their jobs. Manufacturing, sales, and research and development are often organized into functional departments. A **functional structure** is an organizational structure composed of all the departments that an organization requires to produce its goods or services. Figure 10.3 shows the functional structure that Pier 1 Imports, the home furnishings company, uses to supply its customers with a range of goods from around the world to satisfy their desires for new and innovative products.

Pier 1's main functions are finance and administration, merchandising (purchasing the goods), sales and customer experience (managing the retail outlets), marketing, planning and allocations (managing credit and product distribution), and human resources. Each job inside a function exists because it helps the function perform the activities necessary for high organizational performance. Thus within the marketing function are all the jobs necessary to efficiently advertise Pier 1's products to increase their appeal to customers (such as promotion, photography, and visual communication).

Figure 10.3

The Functional Structure of Pier 1 Imports

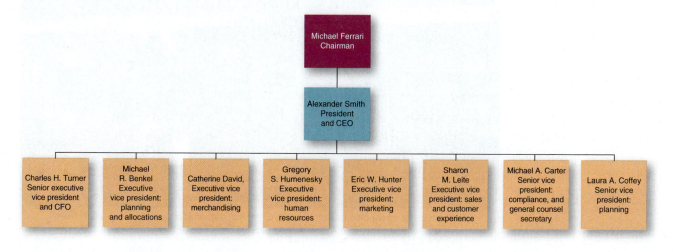

There are several advantages to grouping jobs according to function. First, when people who perform similar jobs are grouped together, they can learn from observing one another and thus become more specialized and can perform at a higher level. The tasks associated with one job often are related to the tasks associated with another job, which encourages cooperation within a function. In Pier 1's marketing department, for example, the person designing the photography program for an ad campaign works closely with the person responsible for designing store layouts and with visual communication experts. As a result, Pier 1 can develop a strong, focused marketing campaign to differentiate its products.

Second, when people who perform similar jobs are grouped together, it is easier for managers to monitor and evaluate their performance.[30] Imagine if marketing experts, purchasing experts, and real estate experts were grouped together in one function and supervised by a manager from merchandising. Obviously the merchandising manager would not have the expertise to evaluate all these different people appropriately. A functional structure allows workers to evaluate how well co-workers are performing their jobs, and if some workers are performing poorly, more experienced workers can help them develop new skills.

Finally, managers appreciate functional structure because it lets them create the set of functions they need to scan and monitor the competitive environment and obtain information about how it is changing.[31] With the right set of functions in place, managers are in a good position to develop a strategy that allows the organization to respond to its changing situation. Employees in the marketing group can specialize in monitoring new marketing developments that will allow Pier 1 to better target its customers. Employees in merchandising can monitor all potential suppliers of home furnishings both at home and abroad to find the goods most likely to appeal to Pier 1's customers and manage Pier 1's global supply chain.

As an organization grows, and particularly as its task environment and strategy change because it is beginning to produce a wider range of goods and services for different kinds of customers, several problems can make a functional structure less efficient and effective.[32] First, managers in different functions may find it more difficult to communicate and coordinate with one another when they are responsible for several different kinds of products, especially as the organization grows both domestically and internationally. Second, functional managers may become so preoccupied with supervising their own specific departments and achieving their departmental goals that they lose sight of the organization's goals. If that happens, organizational effectiveness will suffer because managers will be viewing issues and problems facing the organization only from their own, relatively narrow, departmental perspectives.[33] Both of these problems can reduce efficiency and effectiveness.

Pier 1 organizes its operations by function, which means that employees can more easily learn from one another and improve the service they provide to its customers.

Divisional Structures: Product, Market, and Geographic

divisional structure An organizational structure composed of separate business units within which are the functions that work together to produce a specific product for a specific customer.

As the problems associated with growth and diversification increase over time, managers must search for new ways to organize their activities to overcome the problems associated with a functional structure. Most managers of large organizations choose a **divisional structure** and create a series of business units to produce a specific kind of product for a specific kind of customer. Each *division* is a collection of functions or departments that work together to produce the product. The goal behind the change to a divisional structure is to create smaller, more manageable units within the organization. There are three forms of divisional structure (see Figure 10.4).[34] When managers organize divisions according to the *type of good or service* they provide, they adopt a product structure. When managers organize divisions according to the *area of the country or world* they operate in, they adopt a geographic structure. When managers organize divisions according to *the type of customer* they focus on, they adopt a market structure.

PRODUCT STRUCTURE   Imagine the problems that managers at Pier 1 would encounter if they decided to diversify into producing and selling cars, fast food, and health insurance—in addition to home furnishings—and tried to use their existing set of functional managers to oversee the production of all four kinds of products. No manager would have the

Figure 10.4

Product, Market, and Geographic Structures

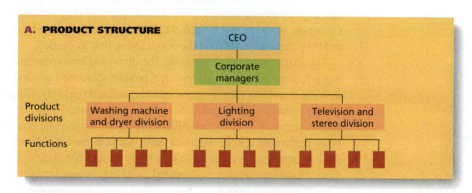

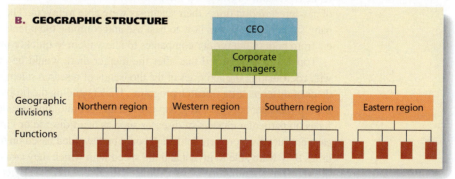

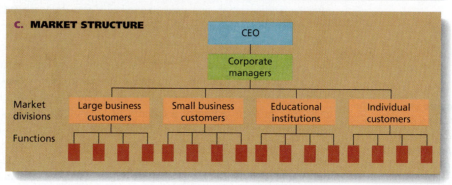

necessary skills or abilities to oversee those four products. No individual marketing manager, for example, could effectively market cars, fast food, health insurance, and home furnishings at the same time. To perform a functional activity successfully, managers must have experience in specific markets or industries. Consequently, if managers decide to diversify into new industries or to expand their range of products, they commonly design a product structure to organize their operations (see Figure 10.4a).

product structure An organizational structure in which each product line or business is handled by a self-contained division.

Using a **product structure**, managers place each distinct product line or business in its own self-contained division and give divisional managers the responsibility for devising an appropriate business-level strategy to allow the division to compete effectively in its industry or market.[35] Each division is self-contained because it has a complete set of all the functions— marketing, R&D, finance, and so on—that it needs to produce or provide goods or services efficiently and effectively. Functional managers report to divisional managers, and divisional managers report to top or corporate managers.

Grouping functions into divisions focused on particular products has several advantages for managers at all levels in the organization. First, a product structure allows functional managers to specialize in only one product area, so they can build expertise and fine-tune their skills in this particular area. Second, each division's managers can become experts in their industry; this expertise helps them choose and develop a business-level strategy to differentiate their products or lower their costs while meeting the needs of customers. Third, a product structure frees corporate managers from the need to supervise directly each division's day-to-day operations; this latitude lets corporate managers create the best corporate-level strategy to maximize the organization's future growth and ability to create value. Corporate managers are likely to make fewer mistakes about which businesses to diversify into or how to best expand internationally, for example, because they can take an organizationwide view.[36] Corporate managers also are likely to evaluate better how well divisional managers are doing, and they can intervene and take corrective action as needed.

The extra layer of management, the divisional management layer, can improve the use of organizational resources. Moreover, a product structure puts divisional managers close to their customers and lets them respond quickly and appropriately to the changing task environment. One pharmaceutical company that successfully adopted a new product structure to better organize its activities is GlaxoSmithKline. The need to innovate new kinds of prescription drugs to boost performance is a contivnual battle for pharmaceutical companies. In the 2000s many of these companies have been merging to try to increase their research productivity, and one of them, GlaxoSmithKline, was created from the merger between Glaxo Wellcome and Smith-Kline Beecham.[37] Prior to the merger, both companies experienced a steep decline in the number of new prescription drugs their scientists were able to invent. The problem facing the new company's top managers was how to best use and combine the talents of the scientists and researchers from both of the former companies to allow them to quickly innovate exciting new drugs.

Top managers realized that after the merger there would be enormous problems associated with coordinating the activities of the thousands of research scientists who were working on hundreds of different drug research programs. Understanding the problems associated with large size, the top managers decided to group the researchers into eight product divisions to allow them to focus on particular clusters of diseases such as heart disease or viral infections. The members of each product division were told they would be rewarded based on the number of new prescription drugs they were able to invent and the speed with which they could bring these new drugs to the market. GlaxoSmithKline's new product structure worked well; its research productivity doubled after the reorganization, and a record number of new drugs moved into clinical trials.[38] However, the need to innovate remains, and GlaxoSmithKline plans more restructuring before 2016.[39]

GEOGRAPHIC STRUCTURE   When organizations expand rapidly both at home and abroad, functional structures can create special problems because managers in one central location may find it increasingly difficult to deal with the different problems and issues that may arise in each region of a country or area of the world. In these cases, a **geographic structure**, in which divisions are broken down by geographic location, is often chosen (see Figure 10.4b). To achieve the corporate mission of providing next-day mail service, Fred Smith, CEO of FedEx, chose a geographic structure and divided up operations by creating a division in each region. Large retailers such as Macy's, Neiman Marcus, and Brooks Brothers

geographic structure An organizational structure in which each region of a country or area of the world is served by a self-contained division.

also use a geographic structure. Because the needs of retail customers differ by region—for example, shorts in California and down parkas in the Midwest—a geographic structure gives retail regional managers the flexibility they need to choose the range of products that best meets the needs of regional customers.

In adopting a *global geographic structure,* such as shown in Figure 10.5a, managers locate different divisions in each of the world regions where the organization operates. Managers are most likely to do this when they pursue a multidomestic strategy because customer needs vary widely by country or world region. If products that appeal to U.S. customers do not sell in Europe, the Pacific Rim, or South America, managers must customize the products to meet the needs of customers in those different world regions; a global geographic structure with global divisions will allow them to do this. For example, food and beverage companies need to customize the taste of their products to closely match the desires of customers in different countries and world regions. The accompanying "Managing Globally" feature describes how one company reorganized itself to be able to offer more services to customers in each region it serves.

Managing Globally

Engineering across the World

The Michael Baker Corporation has worked on some high-profile engineering projects. The company had a role in building the 789-mile Trans-Alaska Pipeline in North America, the 135-mile KHMR-American Friendship Highway in Cambodia, the New River Gorge Bridge in West Virginia, the Midfield Terminal Complex at the Pittsburgh International Airport, and a 2,600-mile fiber optic telecommunications network in Mexico.[40] More recently the company was selected to rehabilitate the Pulaski Skyway, the bridge that connects Newark and Jersey City in New Jersey.[41]

As the need for engineering, construction management, and other services expands nationally and internationally, the company launched a national and global expansion program.[42] Michael Baker Corporation merged with Integrated Mission Solutions in 2013 to create Michael Baker International.

The purpose statement of the organization reads, "Creating value by delivering innovative and sustainable solutions for infrastructure and the environment."[43] Its services include architectural, environmental, construction, planning, and program management. The company has worked with U.S. and foreign allied governments and with commercial customers.

The engineering and consulting firm has more than 6,000 employees in 90 national and international offices. In 2014 it decided to reorganize into an operations-centric structure in seven regions. In its announcement of the reorganization, the company suggested that its new structure would allow it to offer more services to customers in each region. The reorganization also would allow more local leadership of projects.

"This reorganization is a result of extensive review, market analysis, client demand, and discussion with personnel at all levels of the company identifying and highlighting opportunities for building a balanced business in each of our regions," stated Kurt Bergman, chief executive officer. "The new organization promotes empowered business leaders at the office and regional levels, supported by national market and practice leads, to build and manage well-balanced portfolios reflective of the complete continuum of services provided by the Michael Baker International enterprise."[44]

The renovation of the Pulaski Skyway in New Jersey is one of Michael Baker International's projects. The engineering and consulting firm has recently reorganized its operation to offer more services and allow for more local project leadership.

Figure 10.5
Global Geographic and Global Product Structures

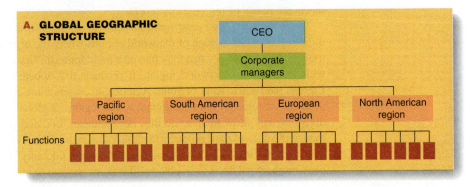

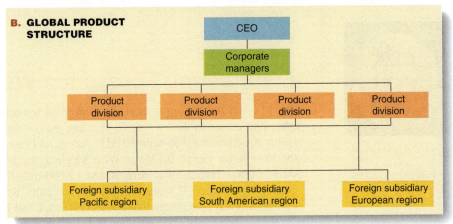

In contrast, to the degree that customers abroad are willing to buy the same kind of product or slight variations thereof, managers are more likely to pursue a global strategy. In this case they are more likely to use a global product structure. In a *global product structure*, each product division, not the country and regional managers, takes responsibility for deciding where to manufacture its products and how to market them in countries worldwide (see Figure 10.5b). Product division managers manage their own global value chains and decide where to establish foreign subsidiaries to distribute and sell their products to customers in foreign countries.

MARKET STRUCTURE   Sometimes the pressing issue facing managers is to group functions according to the type of customer buying the product in order to tailor the products the organization offers to each customer's unique demands. A PC maker such as Dell, for example, has several kinds of customers, including large businesses (which might demand networks of computers linked to a mainframe computer), small companies (which may need just a few PCs linked together), educational users in schools and universities (which might want thousands of independent PCs for their students), and individual users (who may want a high-quality multimedia PC so they can play the latest video games).

market structure An organizational structure in which each kind of customer is served by a self-contained division; also called *customer structure.*

To satisfy the needs of diverse customers, a company might adopt a **market structure**, which groups divisions according to the particular kinds of customers they serve (see Figure 10.4c). A market structure lets managers respond to the needs of their customers and allows them to act flexibly in making decisions in response to customers' changing needs. To spearhead its turnaround, for example, Dell created four streamlined market divisions that each focus on being responsive to one particular type of customer: individual consumers, small businesses, large companies, and government and state agencies. Organizations need to continually evaluate their structures and make sure that operations are working according to plan. The accompanying "Management Insight" feature provides an example of what can happen in an organization when leaders do not know what is happening.

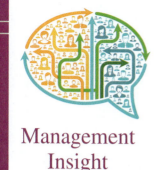

Management Insight

The Miami Dolphins' Team-First Culture

In the middle of the 2013 professional football season, Miami Dolphins offensive lineman Jonathan Martin abruptly quit and entered a hospital to get psychiatric help.[45] He said he had been bullied by three of his teammates.

The National Football League investigated the team and found Martin had been subjected to daily harassment by Richie Incognito, a guard for the Miami Dolphins, as well as John Jerry and Mike Pouncey, both offensive linemen who also played for the Miami Dolphins. The harassment included racial slurs about Martin being African American, sexual taunts about his mother and sister, and jokes that Martin was gay.

The owner of the Miami Dolphins, Stephen Ross, said, "When we asked the NFL to conduct this independent review, we felt it was important to take a step back and thoroughly research these serious allegations. As an organization, we are committed to a culture of team-first accountability and respect for one another."[46]

The investigation and subsequent report identified Incognito as the main instigator of the harassment.[47] After the report was released, Jim Turner, who was the coach of the offensive line, was fired for not stopping the harassment and for taking part in some taunting. Additionally, Kevin O'Neill, who was the head athletic trainer at the time, was fired for not cooperating with the investigation.[48] However, the investigation concluded that Joe Philbin, the coach for the Miami Dolphins, did not take part in or know of the harassment that Martin was subjugated to.

"After interviewing Coach Philbin at length, we were impressed with his commitment to promoting integrity and accountability throughout the Dolphins organization—a point echoed by many players," the report said. "We are convinced that had Coach Philbin learned of the underlying misconduct, he would have intervened promptly to ensure that Martin and others were treated with dignity."[49]

Philbin said that the information contained in the report about vulgar language and behavior was disappointing and violated the team's fundamental values. He also indicated that he would be responsible for making sure such events do not happen again. "That ultimately rests on my shoulders," he said. "And I will be accountable moving forward for making sure that we emphasize a team-first culture of respect toward one another."[50]

Matrix and Product Team Designs

Moving to a product, market, or geographic divisional structure allows managers to respond more quickly and flexibly to the particular circumstances they confront. However, when information technology or customer needs are changing rapidly and the environment is uncertain, even a divisional structure may not give managers enough flexibility to respond to the environment quickly. To operate effectively under these conditions, managers must design the most flexible kind of organizational structure available: a matrix structure or a product team structure (see Figure 10.6).

matrix structure An organizational structure that simultaneously groups people and resources by function and by product.

MATRIX STRUCTURE   In a **matrix structure**, managers group people and resources in two ways simultaneously: by function and by product.[51] Employees are grouped by *functions* to allow them to learn from one another and become more skilled and productive. In addition, employees are grouped into *product teams* in which members of different functions work together to develop a specific product. The result is a complex network of reporting relationships among product teams and functions that makes the matrix structure very flexible (see Figure 10.6a). Each person in a product team reports to two managers: (1) a functional boss, who assigns individuals to a team and evaluates their performance from a functional perspective, and (2) the boss of the product team, who evaluates their performance on the team. Thus team members are known as *two-boss employees*. The functional employees assigned to product teams change over time as the specific skills that the team needs change. At the

Figure 10.6
Matrix and Product Team Structures

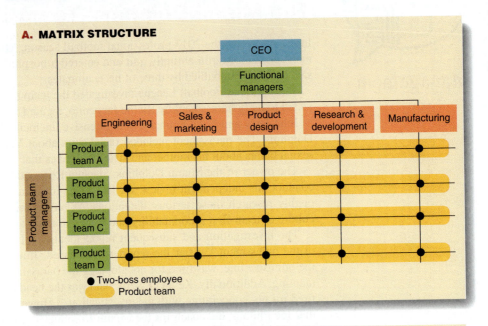

A. MATRIX STRUCTURE

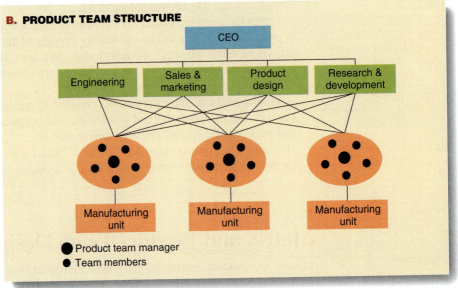

B. PRODUCT TEAM STRUCTURE

beginning of the product development process, for example, engineers and R&D specialists are assigned to a product team because their skills are needed to develop new products. When a provisional design has been established, marketing experts are assigned to the team to gauge how customers will respond to the new product. Manufacturing personnel join when it is time to find the most efficient way to produce the product. As their specific jobs are completed, team members leave and are reassigned to new teams. In this way the matrix structure makes the most use of human resources.

To keep the matrix structure flexible, product teams are empowered and team members are responsible for making most of the important decisions involved in product development.[52] The product team manager acts as a facilitator, controlling the financial resources and trying to keep the project on time and within budget. The functional managers try to ensure that the product is the best it can be to maximize its differentiated appeal.

High-tech companies that operate in environments where new product development takes place monthly or yearly have used matrix structures successfully for many years, and the need to innovate quickly is vital to the organization's survival. The flexibility afforded by a matrix structure lets managers keep pace with a changing and increasingly complex environment.[53]

PRODUCT TEAM STRUCTURE   The dual reporting relationships that are at the heart of a matrix structure have always been difficult for managers and employees to deal with. Often the functional boss and the product boss make conflicting demands on team members, who do not know which boss to satisfy first. Also, functional and product team bosses may come into conflict over precisely who is in charge of which team members and for how long. To avoid these problems, managers have devised a way of organizing people and resources that still allows an organization to be flexible but makes its structure easier to operate: a product team structure.

The **product team structure** differs from a matrix structure in two ways: (1) It does away with dual reporting relationships and two-boss employees, and (2) functional employees are permanently assigned to a cross-functional team that is empowered to bring a new or redesigned product to market. A **cross-functional team** is a group of managers brought together from different departments to perform organizational tasks. When managers are grouped into cross-functional teams, the artificial boundaries between departments disappear, and a narrow focus on departmental goals is replaced with a general interest in working together to achieve the organization's goals. For example, when mattress company Sealy saw its sales slipping, it pulled together a cross-functional team that was allowed to work outside the organization's hierarchy and quickly design a new mattress. With everyone focused on the goal, team members created a mattress that broke previous sales records.[54]

Members of a cross-functional team report only to the product team manager or to one of his or her direct subordinates. The heads of the functions have only an informal advisory relationship with members of the product teams—the role of functional managers is only to counsel and help team members, share knowledge among teams, and provide new technological developments that can help improve each team's performance (see Figure 10.6b).[55]

Increasingly, organizations are making empowered cross-functional teams an essential part of their organizational architecture to help them gain a competitive advantage in fast-changing organizational environments. For example, Newell Rubbermaid, the well-known maker of more than 5,000 household products, moved to a product team structure because its managers wanted to speed up the rate of product innovation. Managers created 20 cross-functional teams composed of five to seven people from marketing, manufacturing, R&D, and other functions.[56] Each team focuses its energies on a particular product line, such as garden products, bathroom products, or kitchen products. These teams develop more than 365 new products a year.[57]

cross-functional team A group of managers brought together from different departments to perform organizational tasks.

product team structure An organizational structure in which employees are permanently assigned to a cross-functional team and report only to the product team manager or to one of his or her direct subordinates.

Coordinating Functions and Divisions

The more complex the structure a company uses to group its activities, the greater are the problems of *linking and coordinating* its different functions and divisions. Coordination becomes a problem because each function or division develops a different orientation toward the other groups that affects how it interacts with them. Each function or division comes to view the problems facing the company from its own perspective; for example, they may develop different views about the major goals, problems, or issues facing a company.

At the functional level, the manufacturing function typically has a short-term view; its major goal is to keep costs under control and get the product out the factory door on time. By contrast, the product development function has a long-term viewpoint because developing a new product is a relatively slow process and high product quality is seen as more important than low costs. Such differences in viewpoint may make manufacturing and product development managers reluctant to cooperate and coordinate their activities to meet company goals. At the divisional level, in a company with a product structure, employees may become concerned more with making *their* division's products a success than with the profitability of the entire company. They may refuse, or simply not see, the need to cooperate and share information or knowledge with other divisions.

The problem of linking and coordinating the activities of different functions and divisions becomes more acute as the number of functions and divisions increases. We look first at how managers design the hierarchy of authority to coordinate functions and divisions so that they work together effectively. Then we focus on integration and examine the different integrating mechanisms managers can use to coordinate functions and divisions.

Allocating Authority

authority The power to hold people accountable for their actions and to make decisions concerning the use of organizational resources.

hierarchy of authority An organization's chain of command, specifying the relative authority of each manager.

span of control The number of subordinates who report directly to a manager.

As organizations grow and produce a wider range of goods and services, the size and number of their functions and divisions increase. To coordinate the activities of people, functions, and divisions and to allow them to work together effectively, managers must develop a clear hierarchy of authority.[58] **Authority** is the power vested in a manager to make decisions and use resources to achieve the organization's goals by virtue of his or her position in an organization. The **hierarchy of authority** is an organization's *chain of command*—the relative authority that each manager has—extending from the CEO at the top, down through the middle managers and first-line managers, to the nonmanagerial employees who actually make goods or provide services. Every manager, at every level of the hierarchy, supervises one or more subordinates. The term **span of control** refers to the number of subordinates who report directly to a manager.

Figure 10.7 shows a simplified picture of the restructured hierarchy of authority at McDonald's in 2015, after the retirement of COO Tim Fenton. At the top of the hierarchy is Don Thompson, CEO and president since 2012. Thompson is the manager who has ultimate responsibility for McDonald's performance, and he has the authority to decide how to use organizational resources to benefit McDonald's stakeholders. Tim Fenton, next in line, is chief operating officer and is responsible for overseeing 35,000 restaurants across the globe. Fenton, who reports directly to Thompson, will retire from McDonald's in late 2014. When he is gone, the board of directors has decided not to replace him, but to do some restructuring. McDonald's area of the world presidents, including the presidents of McDonald's Europe and McDonald's Latin America, will be directly accountable to Thompson. In place of Fenton's COO role, Executive Vice President and Chief Financial Officer Pete Bensen will be responsible for the development and franchising functions as well as the worldwide supply chain, and Steve Easterbrook, who is the executive vice president and global chief brand officer, will be responsible for the global corporate social responsibility department, the restaurant solutions group, corporate strategy, and the sustainability and philanthropy department. Also in the top management hierarchy is Bridget Coffing, who is the senior vice president and chief communications officer. Unlike the other managers, Coffing is not a **line manager**, someone in the direct line or chain of command who has formal authority over people and resources. Rather, Coffing is a **staff manager**, responsible for one of McDonald's specialist functions, communications. She reports directly to Thompson.[59]

line manager Someone in the direct line or chain of command who has formal authority over people and resources at lower levels.

staff manager Someone responsible for managing a specialist function, such as finance or marketing.

Managers at each level of the hierarchy confer on managers at the next level down the authority to decide how to use organizational resources. Accepting this authority, those lower-level managers are accountable for how well they make those decisions. Managers who

Figure 10.7

The Hierarchy of Authority and Span of Control at McDonald's Corporation

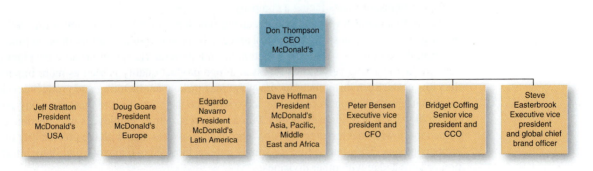

make the right decisions are typically promoted, and organizations motivate managers with the prospects of promotion and increased responsibility within the chain of command.

Below Thompson are the other main levels or layers in the McDonald's domestic chain of command—executive vice presidents of its West, Central, and East regions, zone managers, regional managers, and supervisors. A hierarchy is also evident in each company-owned McDonald's restaurant. At the top is the store manager; at lower levels are the first assistant, shift managers, and crew personnel. McDonald's managers have decided that this hierarchy of authority best allows the company to pursue its business-level strategy of providing fast food at reasonable prices—and its stock price was steadily climbing in the 2010s as performance has increased.

TALL AND FLAT ORGANIZATIONS   As an organization grows in size (normally measured by the number of its managers and employees), its hierarchy of authority normally lengthens, making the organizational structure taller. A *tall* organization has many levels of authority relative to company size; a *flat* organization has fewer levels relative to company size (see Figure 10.8).[60] As a hierarchy becomes taller, problems that make the organization's structure less flexible and slow managers' response to changes in the organizational environment may result.

Figure 10.8

Tall and Flat Organizations

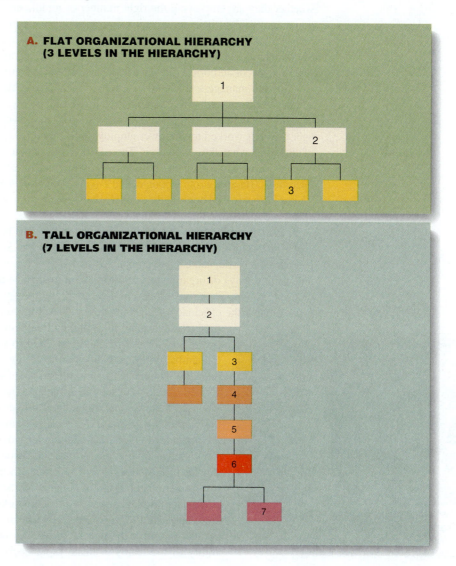

A. FLAT ORGANIZATIONAL HIERARCHY (3 LEVELS IN THE HIERARCHY)

B. TALL ORGANIZATIONAL HIERARCHY (7 LEVELS IN THE HIERARCHY)

Communication problems may arise when an organization has many levels in the hierarchy. It can take a long time for the decisions and orders of upper-level managers to reach managers further down in the hierarchy, and it can take a long time for top managers to learn how well their decisions worked. Feeling out of touch, top managers may want to verify that lower-level managers are following orders and may require written confirmation from them. Middle managers, who know they will be held strictly accountable for their actions, start devoting too much time to the process of making decisions to improve their chances of being right. They might even try to avoid responsibility by making top managers decide what actions to take.

Another communication problem that can result is the distortion of commands and messages being transmitted up and down the hierarchy, which causes managers at different levels to interpret what is happening differently. Distortion of orders and messages can be accidental, occurring because different managers interpret messages from their own narrow functional perspectives. Or distortion can be intentional, occurring because managers low in the hierarchy decide to interpret information in a way that increases their own personal advantage.

Another problem with tall hierarchies is that they usually indicate that an organization is employing many managers, and managers are expensive. Managerial salaries, benefits, offices, and secretaries are a huge expense for organizations. Large companies such as IBM and GM pay their managers millions of dollars a year. During the current recession, hundreds of thousands of managers were laid off as companies restructured and downsized their workforces to reduce costs. But in 2014 a gradual recovery was underway.[61]

THE MINIMUM CHAIN OF COMMAND   To ward off the problems that result when an organization becomes too tall and employs too many managers, top managers need to ascertain whether they are employing the right number of middle and first-line managers and whether they can redesign their organizational architecture to reduce the number of managers. Top managers might well follow a basic organizing principle—the principle of the minimum chain of command—which states that top managers should always construct a hierarchy with the fewest levels of authority necessary to efficiently and effectively use organizational resources.

Effective managers constantly scrutinize their hierarchies to see whether the number of levels can be reduced—for example, by eliminating one level and giving the responsibilities of managers at that level to managers above and by empowering employees below. One manager who has worked to empower employees is David Novak, CEO of Yum Brands. Instead of dictating what the company's Taco Bell, KFC, Pizza Hut, and WingStreet restaurants should do, Novak turned the corporate headquarters into the support center for worldwide operations. He also wrote a book called *Taking People with You: The Only Way to Make BIG Things Happen.* The book outlines the leadership program that Novak developed to motivate employees and align them with the organization's goals.[62]

In the United States over 5 million manufacturing jobs have been lost to factories in low-cost countries abroad in the 2000s. While many large U.S. manufacturing companies have given up the battle, some small companies such as electronics maker Plexus Corp. have been able to find ways of organizing that allow them to survive and prosper in a low-cost manufacturing world. They have done this by creating empowered work teams. U.S. companies cannot match the efficiency of manufacturers abroad in producing high volumes of a single product, such as millions of a particular circuit board used in a laptop computer. So Plexus's managers decided to focus their efforts on developing a manufacturing technology called "low–high" that could efficiently produce low volumes of many different kinds of products. Plexus's managers formed a team to design an organizational structure based on creating four "focused factories" in which control over production decisions is given to the workers, whose managers cross-trained them so they can perform all the operations involved in making a product in their "factory." Now, when work slows down at any point in the production of a particular product, a worker further along the production process can move back to help solve the problem that has arisen at the earlier stage.[63]

Furthermore, managers organized workers into self-managed teams that are empowered to make all the decisions necessary to make a particular product in one of the four factories. Because each product is different, the ability of the teams to make rapid decisions and respond to unexpected

Two employees working in the circuit board manufacturing area at Jabil Circuit Inc. illustrate cross-functional empowerment that can keep production lines moving.

contingencies is vital on a production line, where time is money. At Plexus, managers, by allowing teams to experiment, have reduced changeover time from hours to as little as 30 minutes so the line is making products over 80 percent of the time.[64] The flexibility brought about by self-managed teams is why Plexus is so efficient and can compete against low-cost manufacturers abroad.

CENTRALIZATION AND DECENTRALIZATION OF AUTHORITY Another way in which managers can keep the organizational hierarchy flat is by **decentralizing authority**— that is, by giving lower-level managers and nonmanagerial employees the right to make important decisions about how to use organizational resources.[65] If managers at higher levels give lower-level employees the responsibility of making important decisions and only *manage by exception,* then the problems of slow and distorted communication noted previously are kept to a minimum. Moreover, fewer managers are needed because their role is not to make decisions but to act as coach and facilitator and to help other employees make the best decisions. In addition, when decision-making authority is low in the organization and near the customer, employees are better able to recognize and respond to customer needs.

Decentralizing authority allows an organization and its employees to behave in a flexible way even as the organization grows and becomes taller. This is why managers are so interested in empowering employees, creating self-managed work teams, establishing cross-functional teams, and even moving to a product team structure. These design innovations help keep the organizational architecture flexible and responsive to complex task and general environments, complex technologies, and complex strategies.

Although more and more organizations are taking steps to decentralize authority, *too much* decentralization has certain disadvantages. If divisions, functions, or teams are given too much decision-making authority, they may begin to pursue their own goals at the expense of the organization's goals. Managers in engineering design or R&D, for example, may become so focused on making the best possible product that they fail to realize that the best product may be so expensive few people are willing or able to buy it. Also, too much decentralization can cause lack of communication among functions or divisions; this prevents the synergies of cooperation from ever materializing, and organizational performance suffers.

Top managers must seek the balance between centralization and decentralization of authority that best meets the four major contingencies an organization faces (see Figure 10.1). If managers are in a stable environment, are using well-understood technology, and are producing stable kinds of products (such as cereal, canned soup, or books), there is no pressing need to decentralize authority, and managers at the top can maintain control of much of organizational decision making.[66] However, in uncertain, changing environments where high-tech companies are producing state-of-the-art products, top managers must often empower employees and allow teams to make important strategic decisions so the organization can keep up with the changes taking place. No matter what its environment, a company that fails to control the balance between centralization and decentralization will find its performance suffering. The accompanying "Manager as a Person" feature describes how Microsoft's new CEO is using elements of both centralization and decentralization.

decentralizing authority
Giving lower-level managers and nonmanagerial employees the right to make important decisions about how to use organizational resources.

Manager as a Person

Satya Nadella, Microsoft's New CEO

In February 2014 Microsoft hired its third CEO in the company's almost 40 years. Satya Nadella was formerly the executive vice president of Microsoft's cloud and enterprise group.

Former Microsoft CEO Steve Ballmer retired in 2013. On the day Nadella was appointed CEO, Ballmer sent an email message to the employees of Microsoft announcing Nadella's appointment and touting Nadella's business, technical, and leadership skills. He also praised the strength of the leadership team, saying that together they would drive the company forward.[67]

In his first interview as CEO, Nadella discussed elements of centralization and decentralization at Microsoft. First, he said the effectiveness of the leadership team was his top priority, suggesting a focus on centralization. However, he also discussed the need for everyone in the organization to be innovating, suggesting a focus on decentralization.

On centralization, Nadella wants the leadership team "to commit and engage in an authentic way, and for us to feel that energy as a team."[68] Since he has worked with everyone on the team before, he has confidence in their ability to perform. However, he wants to see them come together as a team and lead the organization. The job of the leadership team, according to Nadella, is to clarify what needs to be done, make sure the organization is aligned to be able to do it, and pursue the work with intensity.[69]

On decentralization, Nadella said that the boundaries within the organization are crumbling and the company structure is changing. He wants to create a self-organizing organization in which employees own the innovation agenda and share implementation. An organization chart or structure is not helpful in creating such a company structure, Nadella said, but a change in organizational culture could achieve such a shift.[70]

In his first email message to Microsoft employees after being named CEO, Nadella stressed the need for innovation. He also called on all employees to pitch in and help lead change in the organizational culture.[71]

On the Microsoft web page, Nadella lists his hobbies as poetry and cricket.[72] In fact, in his first interview as CEO, he described a leadership lesson from his days on the cricket ground. His team captain once took him out of a match because he was not playing well. However, the team captain also put him back in the match before it was over. "I never asked him why he did that, but my impression is that he knew he would destroy my confidence if he didn't put me back in. And I went on to take a lot more wickets after that. It was a subtle, important leadership lesson about when to intervene and when to build the confidence of the team. I think that is perhaps the No. 1 thing that leaders have to do: to bolster the confidence of the people you're leading."[73]

Integrating and Coordinating Mechanisms

Much coordination takes place through the hierarchy of authority. However, several problems are associated with establishing contact among managers in different functions or divisions. As discussed earlier, managers from different functions and divisions may have different views about what must be done to achieve the organization's goals. But if the managers have equal authority (as functional managers typically do), the only manager who can tell them what to do is the CEO, who has the ultimate authority to resolve conflicts. The need to solve everyday conflicts, however, wastes top management time and slows strategic decision making; indeed, one sign of a poorly performing structure is the number of problems sent up the hierarchy for top managers to solve.

integrating mechanisms
Organizing tools that managers can use to increase communication and coordination among functions and divisions.

To increase communication and coordination among functions or between divisions and to prevent these problems from emerging, top managers incorporate various **integrating mechanisms** into their organizational architecture. The greater the complexity of an organization's structure, the greater is the need for coordination among people, functions, and divisions to make the organizational structure work efficiently and effectively.[74] Thus when managers adopt a divisional, matrix, or product team structure, they must use complex integrating mechanisms to achieve the organization's goals. Several integrating mechanisms are available to managers to increase communication and coordination.[75] Figure 10.9 lists these mechanisms, as well as examples of the individuals or groups who might use them.

LIAISON ROLES Managers can increase coordination among functions and divisions by establishing liaison roles. When the volume of contacts between two functions increases, one way to improve coordination is to give one manager in each function or division the responsibility for coordinating with the other. These managers may meet daily, weekly, monthly, or as needed. A liaison role is illustrated in Figure 10.9; the small dot represents the person within a function who has responsibility for coordinating with the other function. Coordinating is part of the liaison's full-time job, and usually an informal relationship develops between the people involved, greatly easing strains between functions. Furthermore, liaison roles provide a way of transmitting information across an organization, which is important in large organizations whose employees may know no one outside their immediate function or division.

TASK FORCES   When more than two functions or divisions share many common problems, direct contact and liaison roles may not provide sufficient coordination. In these cases, a more complex integrating mechanism, a **task force**, may be appropriate (see Figure 10.9). One manager from each relevant function or division is assigned to a task force that meets to solve a specific, mutual problem; members are responsible for reporting to their departments on the issues addressed and the solutions recommended. Task forces are often called *ad hoc committees* because they are temporary; they may meet on a regular basis or only a few times. When the problem or issue is solved, the task force is no longer needed; members return to their normal roles in their departments or are assigned to other task forces. Typically task force members also perform many of their normal duties while serving on the task force.

task force A committee of managers from various functions or divisions who meet to solve a specific, mutual problem; also called *ad hoc committee.*

CROSS-FUNCTIONAL TEAMS   In many cases the issues addressed by a task force are recurring problems, such as the need to develop new products or find new kinds of customers. To address recurring problems effectively, managers are increasingly using permanent integrating mechanisms such as cross-functional teams. An example of a cross-functional team is a new product development committee that is responsible for the choice, design, manufacturing, and marketing of a new product. Such an activity obviously requires a great deal of integration among functions if new products are to be successfully introduced, and using a complex integrating mechanism such as a cross-functional team accomplishes this. As discussed earlier, in a product team structure people and resources are grouped into permanent cross-functional teams to speed products to market. These teams assume long-term responsibility for all aspects of development and making the product.

INTEGRATING ROLES   An integrating role is a role whose only function is to increase coordination and integration among functions or divisions to achieve performance gains from synergies. Usually managers who perform integrating roles are experienced senior managers

Figure 10.9

Types and Examples of Integrating Mechanisms

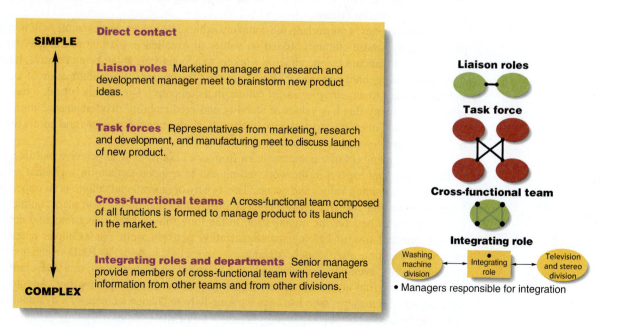

SIMPLE

Direct contact

Liaison roles Marketing manager and research and development manager meet to brainstorm new product ideas.

Task forces Representatives from marketing, research and development, and manufacturing meet to discuss launch of new product.

Cross-functional teams A cross-functional team composed of all functions is formed to manage product to its launch in the market.

Integrating roles and departments Senior managers provide members of cross-functional team with relevant information from other teams and from other divisions.

COMPLEX

Liaison roles

Task force

Cross-functional team

Integrating role

Washing machine division → Integrating role → Television and stereo division

• Managers responsible for integration

who can envisage how to use the resources of the functions or divisions to obtain new synergies. At PepsiCo, Amy Chen, now director of sales, coordinated with several divisions to help create a program that would deliver meals during the summer months to children from low-income families. The resulting program, Food for Good, delivers meals to children who would not normally receive a lunch at school.[76] The more complex an organization and the greater the number of its divisions, the more important integrating roles are.

In summary, to keep an organization responsive to changes in its task and general environments as it grows and becomes more complex, managers must increase coordination among functions and divisions by using complex integrating mechanisms. Managers must decide on the best way to organize their structures—that is, choose the structure that allows them to make the best use of organizational resources.

Organizational Culture

organizational culture
The shared set of beliefs, expectations, values, and norms that influence how members of an organization relate to one another and cooperate to achieve the organization's goals.

The second principal issue in organizational design is to create, develop, and maintain an organization's culture. As we discussed in Chapter 3, **organizational culture** is the shared set of beliefs, expectations, values, and norms that influence how members of an organization relate to one another and cooperate to achieve the organization's goals. Culture influences the work behaviors and attitudes of individuals and groups in an organization because its members adhere to shared values, norms, and expected standards of behavior. Employees *internalize* organizational values and norms and then let these values and norms guide their decisions and actions.[77]

A company's culture is a result of its pivotal or guiding values and norms. A company's *values* are the shared standards that its members use to evaluate whether they have helped the company achieve its vision and goals. The values a company might adopt include any or all of the following standards: excellence, stability, predictability, profitability, economy, creativity, morality, and usefulness. A company's *norms* specify or prescribe the kinds of shared beliefs, attitudes, and behaviors that its members should observe and follow. Norms are informal, but powerful, rules about how employees should behave or conduct themselves in a company if they are to be accepted and help it to achieve its goals. Norms can be equally as constraining as the formal written rules contained in a company's handbook. Companies might encourage workers to adopt norms such as working hard, respecting traditions and authority, and being courteous to others; being conservative, cautious, and a "team player"; being creative and courageous and taking risks; or being honest and frugal and maintaining high personal standards. Norms may also prescribe certain specific behaviors such as keeping one's desk tidy, cleaning up at the end of the day, taking one's turn to bring doughnuts, and even wearing jeans on Fridays.

Ideally a company's norms help the company achieve its values. For example, a new computer company whose culture is based on values of excellence and innovation may try to attain this high standard by encouraging workers to adopt norms about being creative, taking risks, and working hard now and looking long-term for rewards (this combination of values and norms leads to an *entrepreneurial* culture in a company). On the other hand, a bank or insurance company that has values of stability and predictability may emphasize norms of cautiousness and obedience to authority (the result of adopting these values and norms would be a *stable, conservative* culture in a company).

Over time, members of a company learn from one another how to perceive and interpret various events that happen in the work setting and to respond to them in ways that reflect the company's guiding values and norms. This is why organizational culture is so important: When a strong and cohesive set of organizational values and norms is in place, employees focus on what is best for the organization in the long run—all their decisions and actions become oriented toward helping the organization perform well. For example, a teacher spends personal time after school coaching and counseling students; an R&D scientist works 80 hours a week, evenings, and weekends to help speed up a late project; or a salesclerk at a department store runs after a customer who left a credit card at the cash register. An interesting example of a manager who has been working hard to change a company's dysfunctional culture is profiled in the accompanying "Manager as a Person" feature.

Marissa Mayer Shakes Up Yahoo!

When Marissa Mayer took the job of Yahoo! CEO in 2012, she inherited a company that needed a turnaround. Its revenues were down, and its image was stale.[78] In her time at Yahoo!, Mayer has made several bold moves. She has introduced dozens of new apps[79] and purchased 37 companies, including blogging service Tumblr.[80] However, her most infamous move was one that would change Yahoo!'s culture. She ended the company policy of allowing workers to telecommute. The memo ending the policy was leaked to the press and included this explanation from Jackie Reses, who is the head of HR:

"To become the absolute best place to work, communication and collaboration will be important, so we need to be working side-by-side. That is why it is critical that we are all present in our offices. Some of the best decisions and insights come from hallway and cafeteria discussions, meeting new people, and impromptu team meetings. Speed and quality are often sacrificed when we work from home. We need to be one Yahoo!, and that starts with physically being together."[81]

The reaction from employees, journalists, and other critics was mostly negative. There was some speculation that perhaps the real intent of the policy was to get unproductive workers to quit without having to hold layoffs.[82] Others lamented the change in routine: "The tone and tactics have infuriated some at the company. Even if that was what was previously agreed to with managers and HR, or was a part of the package to take a position, tough . . . It's outrageous and a morale killer."[83]

Under the headline "4 Reasons Marissa Mayer's No-At-Home-Work Policy Is an Epic Fail," business journalist Peter Cohan called the blanket rule on telecommuting a "meat-ax policy" and outlined reasons why the move was bad for Yahoo!.[84] The first reason was that the best employees would quit, leaving Yahoo! with only the mediocre employees who could not find other jobs that allowed them to telecommute. The second reason was that working from home creates less stress for employees and increases productivity. Bringing people to the office could raise stress and reduce productivity. The third reason was that bringing employees to the office would require Yahoo! to spend money on cubicles and other employee-related items to house the former telecommuters. The final reason was that requiring people to come to work would increase traffic and air pollution.

Founder of Virgin Group Richard Branson dedicated a blog post to Mayer's decision, writing "We like to give people the freedom to work where they want, safe in the knowledge that they have the drive and expertise to perform excellently, whether they at their desk or in their kitchen. Yours truly has never worked out of an office, and never will. So it was perplexing to see Yahoo! CEO Marissa Mayer tell employees who work remotely to relocate to company facilities. This seems a backwards step in an age when remote working is easier and more effective than ever."[85]

These criticisms were a far cry from the good wishes that greeted Mayer when she first accepted the job in 2012.[86] Headlines read "Marissa Mayer: Yahoo!'s Best Hope"[87] and "Google's First Lady Marissa Mayer Jumps Ship to Yahoo!"[88]

It may still be too early to determine whether Mayer's policy will change the company's fortunes. However, there are indicators that people are coming around. After Mayer had been in the job for one year, her team asked Yahoo! workers to click on a link that read "yo/thxmarissa" and leave a note of gratitude to Mayer regarding her work for Yahoo!. Some of the notes included "Thank you for epitomizing the values of a Yahoo! superstar" and "Best CEO I ever worked for." The messages were put into a book titled "Yahoo! Thanks You Marissa."[89] In 2013 the company received twice as many job applications—340,000—as it did in 2012. After the first quarter of 2014, there was good financial news as well. Yahoo!'s 2014 first quarter results were better than expected. While emphasizing that the company's turnaround still had a long way to go, Mayer told investors that the era of decline was over.[90]

"She deserves the credit relative to changing the attitude and morale and the desire, if you will, to . . . attract new folks as well as to retain folks we have," said Yahoo! CFO Ken Goldman in early 2014. "So I think—I'm very confident. If you talk to anybody at Yahoo! today you would find them, whether they've been here for a year or five years, they're very, very pleased with what they see in working at Yahoo!. I'm absolutely, very confident in that relative to attrition and our ability to hire all points to that."[91]

LO10-5

List the four sources of organizational culture, and explain why and how a company's culture can lead to competitive advantage.

Where Does Organizational Culture Come From?

In managing organizational architecture, some important questions that arise are these: Where does organizational culture come from? Why do different companies have different cultures? Why might a culture that for many years helped an organization achieve its goals suddenly harm the organization?

Organizational culture is shaped by the interaction of four main factors: the personal and professional characteristics of people within the organization, organizational ethics, the nature of the employment relationship, and the design of its organizational structure (see Figure 10.10). These factors work together to produce different cultures in different organizations and cause changes in culture over time.

CHARACTERISTICS OF ORGANIZATIONAL MEMBERS   The ultimate source of organizational culture is the people who make up the organization. If you want to know why organizational cultures differ, look at how the characteristics of their members differ. Organizations A, B, and C develop distinctly different cultures because they attract, select, and retain people who have different values, personalities, and ethics.[92] Recall the attraction–selection–attrition model from Chapter 3. People may be attracted to an organization whose values match theirs; similarly, an organization selects people who share its values. Over time, people who do not fit in leave. The result is that people inside the organization become more

Figure 10.10
Sources of an Organization's Culture

similar, the values of the organization become more pronounced and clear-cut, and the culture becomes distinct from those of similar organizations.[93]

The fact that an organization's members become similar over time and come to share the same values may actually hinder their ability to adapt and respond to changes in the environment.[94] This happens when the organization's values and norms become so strong and promote so much cohesiveness in members' attitudes that the members begin to misperceive the environment.[95] Companies such as Ford, Google, Apple, and Microsoft need a strong set of values that emphasize innovation and hard work; they also need to be careful their success doesn't lead members to believe their company is the best in the business. Companies frequently make this mistake. One famous example is the CEO of Digital Equipment, who in the 1990s laughed off the potential threat posed by PCs to his powerful minicomputers, claiming, "Personal computers are just toys." This company no longer exists.

organizational ethics The moral values, beliefs, and rules that establish the appropriate way for an organization and its members to deal with each other and with people outside the organization.

ORGANIZATIONAL ETHICS The managers of an organization can set out purposefully to develop specific cultural values and norms to control how its members behave. One important class of values in this category stems from **organizational ethics**, which are the moral values, beliefs, and rules that establish the appropriate way for an organization and its members to deal with each other and with people outside the organization. Recall from Chapter 4 that ethical values rest on principles stressing the importance of treating organizational stakeholders fairly and equitably. Managers and employees are constantly making choices about the right, or ethical, thing to do; and to help them make ethical decisions, top managers purposefully implant ethical values into an organization's culture.[96] Consequently ethical values, and the rules and norms that embody them, become an integral part of an organization's culture and determine how its members will manage situations and make decisions.

THE EMPLOYMENT RELATIONSHIP A third factor shaping organizational culture is the nature of the employment relationship a company establishes with its employees via its human resource policies and practices. Recall from Chapter 1 our discussion of the changing relationship between organizations and their employees due to the growth of outsourcing and employment of contingent workers. Like a company's hiring, promotion, and layoff policies, human resource policies, along with pay and benefits, can influence how hard employees will work to achieve the organization's goals, how attached they will be to the organization, and whether they will buy into its values and norms.[97] As we discuss in Chapter 12, an organization's human resource policies are a good indicator of the values in its culture concerning its responsibilities to employees. Consider the effects of a company's promotion policy, for example: A company with a policy of promoting from within will fill higher-level positions with employees who already work for the organization. On the other hand, a company with a policy of promotion from without will fill its open positions with qualified outsiders. What does this say about each organization's culture?

Promoting from within will bolster strong values and norms that build loyalty, align employees' goals with the organization, and encourage employees to work hard to advance within the organization. If employees see no prospect of being promoted from within, they are likely to look for better opportunities elsewhere, cultural values and norms result in self-interested behavior, and cooperation and cohesiveness fall. The tech sector has gone through great turmoil in recent years, and over 2 million U.S. tech employees lost their jobs during the 2000s because of outsourcing and the recession. Apple, HP, and IBM—known for their strong employee-oriented values that emphasized long-term employment and respect for employees—were among the many companies forced to lay off employees, and their cultures have changed as a result. To rebuild their cultures and make their remaining employees feel like "owners," many companies have HRM pay policies that reward superior performance with bonuses and stock options.[98] For example, Southwest Airlines and Google established companywide stock option systems that encourage their employees to be innovative and responsive to customers. Other companies offered different perks, such as Johnson & Johnson's concierge service and Cisco's acupuncture.[99]

ORGANIZATIONAL STRUCTURE We have seen how the values and norms that shape employee work attitudes and behaviors derive from an organization's people, ethics, and HRM policies. A fourth source of cultural values comes from the organization's structure. *Different kinds of structure give rise to different kinds of culture;* so to create a certain culture, managers often need to design a particular type of structure. Tall and highly centralized structures give rise to totally different sets of norms, rules, and cultural values than do structures that are flat and decentralized. In a tall, centralized organization people have little personal autonomy, and norms that focus on being cautious, obeying authority, and respecting traditions emerge because predictability and stability are desired goals. In a flat, decentralized structure people have more freedom to choose and control their own activities, and norms that focus on being creative and courageous and taking risks appear, giving rise to a culture in which innovation and flexibility are desired goals.

Whether a company is centralized or decentralized also leads to the development of different kinds of cultural values. By decentralizing authority and empowering employees, an organization can establish values that encourage and reward creativity or innovation. In doing this, an organization signals employees that it's okay to be innovative and do things their own way—as long as their actions are consistent with the good of the organization. Conversely, in some organizations it is important that employees do not make decisions on their own and that their actions be open to the scrutiny of superiors. In cases like this, centralization can be used to create cultural values that reinforce obedience and accountability. For example, in nuclear power plants, values that promote stability, predictability, and obedience to authority are deliberately fostered to prevent disasters.[100] Through norms and rules, employees are taught the importance of behaving consistently and honestly, and they learn that sharing information with supervisors, especially information about mistakes or errors, is the only acceptable form of behavior.[101]

An organization that seeks to manage and change its culture must take a hard look at all four factors that shape culture: the characteristics of its members, its ethical values, its human resource policies, and its organizational structure. However, changing a culture can be difficult because of the way these factors interact and affect one another.[102] Often a major reorganization is necessary for a cultural change to occur, as we discuss in the next chapter.

Strong, Adaptive Cultures versus Weak, Inert Cultures

Many researchers and managers believe that employees of some organizations go out of their way to help the organization because it has a strong and cohesive organizational culture—an adaptive culture that controls employee attitudes and behaviors. *Adaptive cultures* are those whose values and norms help an organization to build momentum and to grow and change as needed to achieve its goals and be effective. By contrast, *inert cultures* are those whose values and norms fail to motivate or inspire employees; they lead to stagnation and, often, failure over time. What leads to a strong adaptive culture or one that is inert and hard to change?

Researchers have found that organizations with strong adaptive cultures, like 3M, UPS, Microsoft, and IBM, invest in their employees. They demonstrate their commitment to their members by, for example, emphasizing the long-term nature of the employment relationship and trying to avoid layoffs. These companies develop long-term career paths for their employees and spend a lot of money on training and development to increase employees' value to the organization. In these ways, terminal and instrumental values pertaining to the worth of human resources encourage the development of supportive work attitudes and behaviors.

In adaptive cultures employees often receive rewards linked directly to their performance and to the performance of the company as a whole. Sometimes employee stock ownership plans (ESOPs) are developed in which workers as a group are allowed to buy a significant percentage of their company's stock. Workers who are owners of the company have additional incentive to develop skills that allow them to perform highly and search actively for ways to improve quality, efficiency, and performance.

Some organizations, however, develop cultures with values that do not include protecting and increasing the worth of their human resources as a major goal. Their employment practices are based on short-term employment according to the needs of the organization and on minimal investment in employees who perform simple, routine tasks. Moreover, employees are not often rewarded on the basis of their performance and thus have little incentive to improve their skills or otherwise invest in the organization to help it achieve goals. If a company has an inert culture, poor working relationships frequently develop between the organization and its employees, and instrumental values of noncooperation, laziness, and loafing and work norms of output restriction are common.

Moreover, an adaptive culture develops an emphasis on entrepreneurship and respect for the employee and allows the use of organizational structures, such as the cross-functional team structure, that empower employees to make decisions and motivate them to succeed. By contrast, in an inert culture, employees are content to be told what to do and have little incentive or motivation to perform beyond minimum work requirements. As you might expect, the emphasis is on close supervision and hierarchical authority, which result in a culture that makes it difficult to adapt to a changing environment.

Google is a good example of a company in which managers strive to create an adaptive culture that is based on values that emphasize creativity and innovation and where decision making is pushed right down to the bottom line to teams of employees who take up the challenge of developing the advanced software and hardware for which the company is known. Bureaucracy is kept to a minimum at Google; its adaptive culture is based on informal and personal relationships and norms of cooperation and teamwork. To help strengthen its culture, Google built a futuristic open-plan campus in which its engineers can work together to innovate ever more advanced products such as its new Nexus tablet that it announced in 2012.[103] Google's cultural values and norms can't be written down but are present in the work routines that cement people together and in the language and stories its members use to orient themselves to the company.

Another company with an adaptive culture is GlaxoSmithKline, the prescription drug maker. Much of GSK's success can be attributed to its ability to recruit the best research scientists because its adaptive culture nurtures scientists and emphasizes values and norms of innovation. Scientists are given great freedom to pursue intriguing ideas even if the commercial payoff is questionable. Moreover, researchers are inspired to think of their work as a quest to alleviate human disease and suffering worldwide, and GSK has a reputation as an ethical company whose values put people above profits.

Although the experience of Google and GSK suggests that organizational culture can give rise to managerial actions that ultimately benefit the organization, this is not always the case. The cultures of some organizations become dysfunctional, encouraging managerial actions that harm the organization and discouraging actions that might improve performance.[104] For example, when Trace Devanny joined health care information technology company TriZetto as CEO in 2010, he saw that employees had a "comfortable mentality." Devanny's solution was to focus on attitudes and insist that employees listen to clients and then act on their needs. He made changes that created a culture of accountability for outcomes by turning the company from being market-focused to being customer-focused. Devanny left the company in 2013, the same year it recorded record earnings.[105] Clearly managers can influence how their organizational culture develops over time.

Summary and Review

LO10-1 **DESIGNING ORGANIZATIONAL STRUCTURE**   The four main determinants of organizational structure are the external environment, strategy, technology, and human resources. In general, the higher the level of uncertainty associated with these factors, the more appropriate is a flexible, adaptable structure as opposed to a formal, rigid one.

LO10-2 **GROUPING TASKS INTO JOBS**   Job design is the process by which managers group tasks into jobs. To create more interesting jobs, and to get workers to act flexibly, managers can enlarge and enrich jobs. The job characteristics model is a tool that managers can use to measure how motivating or satisfying a particular job is.

LO10-3 **ORGANIZATIONAL STRUCTURE: GROUPING JOBS INTO FUNCTIONS AND DIVISIONS**   Managers can choose from many kinds of organizational structures to make the best use of organizational resources. Depending on the specific organizing problems they face, managers can choose from functional, product, geographic, market, matrix, product team, and hybrid structures.

LO10-4   **COORDINATING FUNCTIONS AND DIVISIONS**   No matter which structure managers choose, they must decide how to distribute authority in the organization, how many levels to have in the hierarchy of authority, and what balance to strike between centralization and decentralization to keep the number of levels in the hierarchy to a minimum. As organizations grow, managers must increase integration and coordination among functions and divisions. Four integrating mechanisms that facilitate this are liaison roles, task forces, cross-functional teams, and integrating roles.

LO10-5   **ORGANIZATIONAL CULTURE**   Organizational culture is the set of values, norms, and standards of behavior that control how individuals and groups in an organization interact with one another and work to achieve the organization's goals. The four main sources of organizational culture are member characteristics, organizational ethics, the nature of the employment relationship, and the design of organizational structure. How managers work to influence these four factors determines whether an organization's culture is strong and adaptive or inert and difficult to change.

Management in Action

Topics for Discussion and Action

Discussion

1. Would a flexible or a more formal structure be appropriate for these organizations? (a) A large department store, (b) a Big Five accounting firm, (c) a biotechnology company. Explain your reasoning. **[LO10-1, 10-2]**

2. Using the job characteristics model as a guide, discuss how a manager can enrich or enlarge subordinates' jobs. **[LO10-2]**

3. How might a salesperson's job or a secretary's job be enlarged or enriched to make it more motivating? **[LO10-2, 10-3]**

4. When and under what conditions might managers change from a functional to (a) a product, (b) a geographic, or (c) a market structure? **[LO10-1, 10-3]**

5. How do matrix structure and product team structure differ? Why is product team structure more widely used? **[LO10-1, 10-3, 10-4]**

6. What is organizational culture, and how does it affect the way employees behave? **[LO10-5]**

Action

7. Find and interview a manager and identify the kind of organizational structure that his or her organization uses to coordinate its people and resources. Why is the organization using that structure? Do you think a different structure would be more appropriate? Which one? **[LO10-1, 10-3, 10-4]**

8. With the same or another manager, discuss the distribution of authority in the organization. Does the manager think that decentralizing authority and empowering employees are appropriate? **[LO10-1, 10-3]**

9. Interview some employees of an organization and ask them about the organization's values and norms, the typical characteristics of employees, and the organization's ethical values and socialization practices. Using this information, try to describe the organization's culture and the way it affects how people and groups behave. **[LO10-1, 10-5]**

Building Management Skills

Understanding Organizing **[LO10-1, 10-2, 10-3]**

Think of an organization with which you are familiar, perhaps one you have worked for—such as a store, restaurant, office, church, or school. Then answer the following questions:

1. Which contingencies are most important in explaining how the organization is organized? Do you think it is organized in the best way?

2. Using the job characteristics model, how motivating do you think the job of a typical employee is in this organization?

3. Can you think of any ways in which a typical job could be enlarged or enriched?

4. What kind of organizational structure does the organization use? If it is part of a chain, what kind of structure does the entire organization use? What other structures discussed in the chapter might allow the organization to operate more effectively? For

example, would the move to a product team structure lead to greater efficiency or effectiveness? Why or why not?

5. How many levels are there in the organization's hierarchy? Is authority centralized or decentralized? Describe the span of control of the top manager and of middle or first-line managers.

6. Is the distribution of authority appropriate for the organization and its activities? Would it be possible to flatten the hierarchy by decentralizing authority and empowering employees?

7. What are the principal integrating mechanisms used in the organization? Do they provide sufficient coordination among individuals and functions? How might they be improved?

8. Now that you have analyzed the way this organization is structured, what advice would you give its managers to help them improve how it operates?

Managing Ethically [LO10-1, 10-3, 10-5]

Suppose an organization is downsizing and laying off many of its middle managers. Some top managers charged with deciding whom to terminate might decide to keep the subordinates they like, and who are obedient to them, rather than the ones who are difficult or the best performers. They might also decide to lay off the most highly paid subordinates even if they are high performers. Think of the ethical issues involved in designing a hierarchy, and discuss the following issues.

Questions

1. What ethical rules (see Chapter 4) should managers use to decide which employees to terminate when redesigning their hierarchy?

2. Some people argue that employees who have worked for an organization for many years have a claim on the organization at least as strong as that of its shareholders. What do you think of the ethics of this position—can employees claim to "own" their jobs if they have contributed significantly to the organization's past success? How does a socially responsible organization behave in this situation?

Small Group Breakout Exercise

Bob's Appliances [LO10-1, 10-3]

Form groups of three or four people, and appoint one member as the spokesperson who will communicate your findings to the class when called on by the instructor. Then discuss the following scenario:

Bob's Appliances sells and services household appliances such as washing machines, dishwashers, ranges, and refrigerators. Over the years, the company has developed a good reputation for the quality of its customer service, and many local builders patronize the store. However, large retailers such as Best Buy, Walmart, and Costco are also providing an increasing range of appliances. Moreover, to attract more customers these stores also carry a complete range of consumer electronics products—LCD TVs, computers, and digital devices. Bob Lange, the owner of Bob's Appliances, has decided that if he is to stay in business, he must widen his product range and compete directly with the chains.

In 2007 he decided to build a 20,000-square-foot store and service center, and he is now hiring new employees to sell and service the new line of consumer electronics. Because of his company's increased size, Lange is not sure of the best way to organize the employees. Currently he uses a functional structure; employees are divided into sales, purchasing and accounting, and repair. Bob is wondering whether selling and servicing consumer electronics is so different from selling and servicing appliances that he should move to a product structure (see the accompanying figure) and create separate sets of functions for each of his two lines of business.[106]

You are a team of local consultants whom Bob has called in to advise him as he makes this crucial choice. Which structure do you recommend? Why?

FUNCTIONAL STRUCTURE

Bob Lange

Sales | Purchasing and accounting | Repair

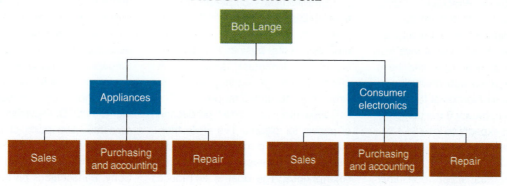

PRODUCT STRUCTURE

Bob Lange

Appliances

Sales | Purchasing and accounting | Repair

Consumer electronics

Sales | Purchasing and accounting | Repair

Exploring the World Wide Web [LO10-3]

Go to the website of Hitachi, a Japanese multinational engineering and electronics conglomerate (http://www.hitachi.com/about/corporate/organization/).

1. Look at the organizational chart. What type of structure does Hitachi have?

2. Click on the message from top management. What does this information tell you about how the structure might change or stay the same in the future?

3. Find the Hitachi Vision Book. How will the journey toward its vision affect the structure of Hitachi?

Be the Manager [LO10-1, 10-3, 10-5]

Speeding Up Website Design

You have been hired by a website design, production, and hosting company whose new animated website designs are attracting a lot of attention and many customers. Currently employees are organized into different functions such as hardware, software design, graphic art, and website hosting, as well as functions such as marketing and human resources. Each function takes its turn to work on a new project from initial customer request to final online website hosting.

The problem the company is experiencing is that it typically takes one year from the initial idea stage to the time a website is up and running; the company wants to shorten this time by half to protect and expand its market niche. In talking to other managers, you discover that they believe the company's current functional structure is the source of the problem—it is not allowing employees to develop websites fast enough to satisfy customers' demands. They want you to design a better structure.

Questions

1. Discuss how you can improve the way the current functional structure operates so it speeds website development.

2. Discuss the pros and cons of moving to a (a) multidivisional, (b) matrix, and (c) product team structure to reduce website development time.

3. Which of these structures do you think is most appropriate, and why?

4. What kind of culture would you help create to make the company's structure work more effectively?

Bloomberg Businessweek Case in the News [LO10-1, 10-3]

Panasonic Revives as Other Japanese Tech Giants Falter

These are trying times for the men running Japan's electronics giants. Nintendo President Satoru Iwata is taking a 50 percent pay cut after the company forecast a surprise 25 billion yen ($244 million) loss last month. Kazuo Hirai took the helm at Sony two years ago promising to stem a decade of losses at the television unit. On February 6 the company announced it expects to lose $1.1 billion in the current fiscal year ending March 31.

Like many Japanese consumer electronics companies, Panasonic has tried to be all things to all customers, making everything from smartphones to solar panels. And like its domestic rivals, it faces competition from lower-cost manufacturers in South Korea and China. Panasonic lost a combined 1.5 trillion yen in the two years ended in March 2013.

Over the past year, however, Chief Executive Officer Kazuhiro Tsuga has engineered a revamp of the Osaka-based company. By getting out of such money-losing businesses and focusing on new ventures, Panasonic is pushing through "essential structural reforms," says Chief Financial Officer Hideaki Kawai. Tsuga has said that he plans to eliminate unprofitable divisions by March 2016.

The strategy is beginning to pay off. Operating profit at Panasonic's automotive and industrial systems unit, which makes batteries and car entertainment systems, jumped to 28.2 billion yen in the last quarter of 2013, compared with a loss of 800 million yen the year before. Earnings in the appliances unit increased 60 percent, to 9.8 billion yen, while profits for the company as a whole increased 20 percent in the quarter, to 73.7 billion yen—68 percent higher than analysts' estimates. "The company has been making significant progress in its business restructuring," Maki Hanatate, senior credit officer at ratings agency Moody's, wrote in a February 6 report.

Tsuga has suspended production of panels for plasma TVs while trimming circuit board manufacturing and giving up on developing consumer smartphones. The goal is to reduce reliance on consumer electronics, where Panasonic has lagged behind Samsung Electronics and Apple. Instead Tsuga is building partnerships with companies such as Tesla Motors, the electric car maker that agreed in October to buy 2 billion battery cells from Panasonic over four years. In addition to making batteries for electric cars and car entertainment systems, Panasonic is focusing on auto safety devices such as cameras with 360-degree views. By 2019 the company plans to double revenue from auto-related products to 2 trillion yen.

One of Tsuga's biggest challenges is Panasonic's semiconductor operation, which has lost money for seven consecutive quarters. Panasonic is suffering because of the high cost of production in its home country. "It's really hard to compete in chips" against cheaper rivals in Taiwan and South Korea, says David Motozo Rubenstein, senior analyst and managing director with Advanced Research Japan in Tokyo. "So it's tough on both sides for the Japanese."

Last year Panasonic moved to reduce its exposure in chips by merging two operations into joint ventures, one with Fujitsu and another with Israel's Tower Semiconductor. On February 4 Panasonic said it would sell three semiconductor assembly plants in Southeast Asia to Singapore-based UTAC Manufacturing Services for $116.5 million.

For now, the company is sticking with LCD televisions and digital cameras—two parts of the business that have yet to be restructured. Still, compared with the problems at Sony, Panasonic is on the right track, Fitch Ratings analysts Shelley Jang, Kelvin Ho, and Steve Durose wrote in a February 12 report. "Panasonic made earlier decisions than Sony to get out of unprofitable businesses," they said. The result is a "slimmer, nimbler organization [that] gives Panasonic the opportunity to continue its recovery."

Source: Bruce Einhordn, Mariko Yasu, and Takashi Amano, "Panasonic Revives as Other Japanese Tech Giants Falter," *Bloomberg Business Week,* February 13, 2014. Used with permission of Bloomberg L.P. Copyright © 2014. All rights reserved.

Questions for Discussion

1. Using the information in the article alone, how do you believe Panasonic is organized?

2. What aspects of Panasonic's change do you believe Sony and Nintendo should imitate?

3. The article suggests that Panasonic was smart to move faster than Sony and Nintendo. What other moves do you believe it should make to stay in business?

CHAPTER 11

Organizational Control and Change

Learning Objectives

After studying this chapter, you should be able to:

LO11-1   Define organizational control and explain how it increases organizational effectiveness.

LO11-2   Describe the four steps in the control process and the way it operates over time.

LO11-3   Identify the main output controls, and discuss their advantages and disadvantages as means of coordinating and motivating employees.

LO11-4   Identify the main behavior controls, and discuss their advantages and disadvantages as a means of coordinating and motivating employees.

LO11-5   Discuss the relationship between organizational control and change, and explain why managing change is a vital management task.

A MANAGER'S CHALLENGE

The Zappos Holacracy

How can a company be controlled without becoming rigid? Zappos has always been a zany place to work. Before an employee even starts, the Las Vegas–based company offers the employee $2,000 to leave.[1] The company believes it saves money if an employee takes the offer because the company gets rid of someone who would be there only for the paycheck. The CEO wrote a book called *Delivering Happiness* about how concepts from happiness can be applied to business.[2] Then there's the call center. Rather than running a lean call center, Zappos encourages its employees to spend lots of time talking to customers and going the extra mile to resolve their issues. There are stories of the great lengths to which customer service representatives will go. For example, one employee went to a rival shoe store, bought a pair of shoes that Zappos did not have in stock, and delivered the shoes to the customer's Las Vegas hotel.[3]

This different way of doing things is reflected in the Zappos core values, like "deliver WOW through service," "embrace and drive change," "create fun and a little weirdness," "pursue growth and learning," "be adventurous, creative, and open-minded," "build a positive team and family spirit," "build open and honest relationships with communication," "be passionate and determined," and "be humble."[4]

And while the book and the active call center do not sound like trappings of a traditional lean company, another of the Zappos core values is "do more with less." The company claims that while it may have an informal culture, it is serious about operating efficiently. On its web page the company states, "We believe in operational excellence and realize that there is always room for improvement in everything we do.

Zappos CEO Tony Hsieh promotes core values and is now switching the company from a traditional hierarchical structure to a system called holacracy, which organizes employees around work to be done instead of the workers who do it.

This means that our work is never done. In order to stay ahead of the competition (or would-be competition), we need to continuously innovate as well as make incremental improvements to our operations, always striving to make ourselves more efficient, always trying to figure out how to do something better. We use mistakes as learning opportunities."[5]

Now the company is getting even leaner by removing the traditional chain of command, job titles, and managers.[6] The change is designed to prevent the company from becoming too rigid as it grows. "Research shows that every time the size of a city doubles, innovation or productivity per resident increases by 15 percent. But when companies get bigger, innovation or productivity per employee generally goes down," said CEO Tony Hsieh. "So we're trying to figure out how to structure Zappos more like a city, and less like a bureaucratic corporation. In a city, people and businesses are self-organizing. We're trying to do the same thing by switching from a normal hierarchical structure to a system called holacracy, which enables employees to act more like entrepreneurs and self-direct their work instead of reporting to a manager who tells them what to do."[7]

A holacracy is different from a traditional organization in three important ways. First, the former hierarchy is replaced with overlapping and self-governing circles of employees.[8] Second, employees are assigned several roles in different circles where they perform different functions. There are no job titles because holacracy organizes around the work to be done instead of the workers who do it. Decisions about what each role involves are made within the circle. Third, managers are redefined as "lead links" who assign employees to roles but do not tell them what to do. Despite this lack of formal structure, Zappos says employees will still be appraised. The constitution of holacracy begins with roles, which it defines as "an organizational entity with a 'purpose' to express, 'domains' to control, and 'accountabilities' to perform."[9] From this definition of roles, the constitution builds to include a circle structure that contains and integrates roles; a governance process that defines roles and policies, and an operational process in which members of the circles rely on one another to do operational work.[10]

John Bunch, who is leading the change for Zappos, was quoted in *The New York Times* as saying that people see the holacracy as removing managers. However, Bunch explains that they are "decoupling the professional development side of the business from the technical getting-the-work-done side."[11]

Zappos was acquired by Amazon in 2009 but is run as a mostly independent unit. Zappos expects to transition to holacracy by the end of 2014.

Overview

As we discussed in Chapter 10, the first task facing managers is to establish a structure of task and job reporting relationships that allows organizational members to use resources most efficiently and effectively. Structure alone, however, does not provide the incentive or motivation for people to behave in ways that help achieve organizational goals. When managers choose how to influence, shape, and regulate the activities of organizational divisions, functions, and employees to achieve the organization's mission and goals, they establish the second foundation of organizational architecture: organizational control. An organization's structure provides the organization with a skeleton, but its control systems give it the muscles, sinews, nerves, and sensations that allow managers to regulate and govern its activities. The control systems also give managers specific feedback on how well the organization and its members are performing. The managerial functions of organizing and controlling are inseparable, and effective managers must learn to make them work together in a harmonious way.

In this chapter, we look in detail at the nature of organizational control and describe the main steps in the control process. We also discuss the different types of control systems that are available to managers to shape and influence organizational activities—*output control, behavior control,* and *clan control.*[12] Finally, we discuss the important issue of organizational change, which is possible only when managers have put in place a control system that allows them to adjust the way people and groups behave and alter or transform the way the organization operates. Control is the essential ingredient that is needed to bring about and manage organizational change efficiently and effectively. By the end of this chapter, you will appreciate the different forms of control available to managers and understand why developing an appropriate control system is vital to increasing organizational performance.

What Is Organizational Control?

> **LO11-1**
> Define organizational control and explain how it increases organizational effectiveness.

As noted in Chapter 1, *controlling* is the process whereby managers monitor and regulate how efficiently and effectively an organization and its members are performing the activities necessary to achieve organizational goals. As discussed in previous chapters, when planning and organizing, managers develop the organizational strategy and structure that they hope will allow the organization to use resources most effectively to create value for customers. In controlling, managers monitor and evaluate whether the organization's strategy and structure are working as intended, how they could be improved, and how they might be changed if they are not working.

Control, however, does not mean just reacting to events after they have occurred. It also means keeping an organization on track, anticipating events that might occur, and then changing the organization to respond to whatever opportunities or threats have been identified. Control is concerned with keeping employees motivated, focused on the important problems confronting the organization, and working together to make the changes that will help an organization improve its performance over time.

The Importance of Organizational Control

To understand the importance of organizational control, consider how it helps managers obtain superior efficiency, quality, responsiveness to customers, and innovation—the four building blocks of competitive advantage.

To determine how efficiently they are using their resources, managers must be able to accurately measure how many units of inputs (raw materials, human resources, and so on) are being used to produce a unit of output, such as a Toyota vehicle. Managers also must be able to measure how many units of outputs (goods and services) are being produced. A control system contains the measures or yardsticks that let managers assess how efficiently the organization is producing goods and services. Moreover, if managers experiment with changing how the organization produces goods and services to find a more efficient way of producing them, these measures tell managers how successful they have been. For example, when Kimberly-Clark, maker of Kleenex and other products, outsourced logistics at a U.K. plant to a leading lean organization, it reduced long shifts and overtime for its workers. Absenteeism dropped and productivity improved as staff morale went up. Without a control system in place, managers have no idea how well their organization is performing and how its performance can be improved—information that is becoming increasingly important in today's highly competitive environment.

Today much of the competition among organizations centers on increasing the quality of goods and services. In the car industry, for example, cars within each price range compete in features, design, and reliability. Thus whether a customer buys a Ford Focus, GM Cruze,

Chrysler 200, Toyota Avalon, or Honda CRV depends significantly on the design and quality of each car. Organizational control is important in determining the quality of goods and services because it gives managers feedback on product quality. If the managers of carmakers consistently measure the number of customer complaints and the number of new cars returned for repairs, or if school principals measure how many students drop out of school or how achievement scores on nationally based tests vary over time, they have a good indication of how much quality they have built into their product—whether it is an educated student or a car that does not break down. Effective managers create a control system that consistently monitors the quality of goods and services so they can continuously improve quality—an approach to change that gives them a competitive advantage. These control systems include personal systems such as email, as the accompanying "Management Insight" feature suggests.

Management Insight

Email at Work

In terms of problems in the modern workplace, email may be number one.[13] Overuse of this communication medium and the problems surrounding it are hindering effectiveness in the workplace. The average worker spends about 13 hours per week on email.[14] How can managers help their employees handle email so that quality does not suffer? Three experts offer the following tips on handling email.

Marsha Egan, CEO of InboxDetox.com, shares the following advice for handling email:[15]

Marsha Egan, CEO of InboxDetox.com, is one CEO who has a system to help employees handle email efficiently and without wasting time.

1. Turn off notifications so you are not distracted by every message that arrives. "If you're interrupted, even if you handle it in one minute, it takes another four minutes to get back to what you were doing before."[16]

2. Don't check email more than three times a day, and choose when you do it. Egan recommends a morning, after lunch, and right before the end of the workday check.

3. If you need something in less than three hours, use a different mode of communication such as a phone call. Egan points out two benefits to the behavior. First, it allows co-workers to work on other tasks without dreading an email notification. Second, it models behavior that co-workers might adapt, resulting in fewer email messages.

4. Treat email in one of three ways: Respond to simple and urgent messages, file those that do not require a response, and flag any that require more thought and follow-up.

5. Do not open your inbox when you do not have time to send responses. "Check your email only when you have time to respond, not just react."[17]

Jill Duffy, a software analyst who writes a weekly column called "Get Organized," provides the following advice:

1. Delete unnecessary messages before reading the necessary ones. Move any items that you can to the trash. The email will still be there later if you decide you need them.

2. Write short email messages to save time.

3. Reuse standard sent email. For routine email that you send more than once, just remove the "Re:" in the subject line, update the message if needed, and send.

4. Reuse standard subject lines. This makes writing easier and allows you to sort by subject line.

5. Use groups. If you email the same group of people over and over, put them in a group so you do not have to type everyone's email addresses each time. This also allows you to sort messages to and from the group for easy archiving or deleting.

6. To maximize space in your mailbox, sort your sent items by file size or attachment and delete what you can. Working in your sent items is recommended because you likely have the attachments in your local files.

7. Turn off notifications of incoming email. These are distractions.

8. Turn off email when you need to focus on work.

9. Use auto-replies if you are concerned someone will try to contact you while you have your email turned off. You can write an auto-reply asking anyone with an urgent matter to call you instead.

10. Delete or refile messages. If you can, delete messages on which you will not act. If you feel you must hold on to some messages, create folders in which to store them so they are not in your inbox.

11. Empty the trash at the end of the day. Sometimes you will need to retrieve an email from trash, so make this the last thing you do each day (or each week if you prefer).[18]

Sarah Green, a senior associate editor at *Harvard Business Review,* shared the following tips that worked for her. Instead of telling readers what she recommends doing, she lists the things she stopped doing:

1. She stopped seeing email as separate from "real work." Building relationships is part of work, and email is one way to accomplish that. Making this mind shift from email not being real work to it being part of the job made it easier for her to make time for it.

2. She stopped using email to manage a to-do list and started using a project management app.

3. She stopped scheduling meetings back-to-back with no time for email. Now she places two hours of fake meeting times on the calendar each day so that she has time for email.

4. She stopped sending a mass email message that she was going on vacation and started putting the dates she would be away in her email signature for two weeks before she left. This helps people remember that she is leaving and helps her deal with last-minute requests. The result is that she can disconnect better when she is away.

5. She stopped relying on herself to sort email and got a filtering system that uses an algorithm to decide which messages are the most important and which can go into separate folders to be reviewed later. She also got an app that combines newsletter subscriptions into digest form and un-enrolls her from the ones she no longer wants.

6. She stopped listening to advice about avoiding reliance on her smartphone, finding that it allowed her to be brief and to the point in her responses.[19]

The advice on taming email is varied among the three experts, indicating that each user should look for a system of controlling email that works for him or her.

Effective organizational control can also increase responsiveness to customers. Managers can help make their organizations more responsive to customers, for example, if they develop a control system, such as a CRM system, that allows them to evaluate how well customer contact employees perform their jobs. Monitoring employee behavior can help managers find ways to increase employees' performance levels, perhaps by revealing areas in which skill training or new procedures can allow employees to perform their jobs better. Also, when employees know their behaviors are being monitored, they have more incentive to be helpful and consistent in how they act toward customers. For example, Caterpillar has a lean initiative to bring employees closer to customers so the employees can provide products and services that match customers' needs. Before Caterpillar introduced its lean manufacturing principle at its Aurora, Illinois facility in 2013, discovering defects on its medium wheel loader value stream was considered normal. Because the defects were discovered, they were fixed before being passed on to the customer. However, the defects were still costing the company lost time and other costs. After the company introduced its lean program at the plant and made it clear that the company was dedicated to eliminating defects, average internal defects fell by 60 percent.[20]

Finally, controlling can raise the level of innovation in an organization. Successful innovation takes place when managers create an organizational setting in which employees feel empowered to be creative and in which authority is decentralized to employees so they feel free to experiment and take control of their work activities. Deciding on the appropriate control systems to encourage risk taking is an important management challenge; organizational culture is vital in this regard. At Caterpillar the lean initiative extends beyond manufacturing to all functional areas and has been embraced by leaders at all levels. The standard across the company is that no defect, no matter how small, be passed on to another stage in the process. Every person at Caterpillar is expected to perform high-quality work.[21]

Control Systems and IT

control systems Formal target-setting, monitoring, evaluation, and feedback systems that provide managers with information about how well the organization's strategy and structure are working.

Control systems are formal target-setting, monitoring, evaluation, and feedback systems that provide managers with information about whether the organization's strategy and structure are working efficiently and effectively.[22] Effective control systems alert managers when something is going wrong and give them time to respond to opportunities and threats. An effective control system has three characteristics: It is flexible enough to allow managers to respond as necessary to unexpected events; it provides accurate information about organizational performance; and it gives managers information in a timely manner because making decisions on the basis of outdated information is a recipe for failure.

New forms of IT have revolutionized control systems because they facilitate the flow of accurate and timely information up and down the organizational hierarchy and between functions and divisions. Today employees at all levels of the organization routinely feed information into a company's information system or network and start the chain of events that affect decision making in some other part of the organization. This could be the department store clerk whose scanning of purchased clothing tells merchandise managers what kinds of clothing need to be reordered or the salesperson in the field who feeds into a tablet computer the CRM information necessary to inform marketing about customers' changing needs.

feedforward control
Control that allows managers to anticipate problems before they arise.

Control and information systems are developed to measure performance at each stage in the process of transforming inputs into finished goods and services (see Figure 11.1). At the input stage, managers use **feedforward control** to anticipate problems before they arise so problems do not occur later during the conversion process.[23] For example, by giving stringent

Figure 11.1

Three Types of Control

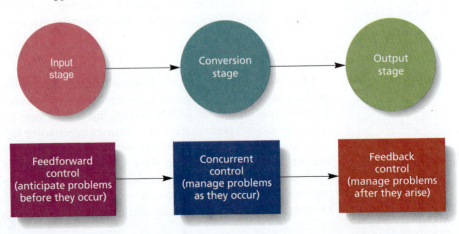

product specifications to suppliers in advance (a form of performance target), an organization can control the quality of the inputs it receives from its suppliers and thus avoid potential problems during the conversion process. Also, IT can be used to keep in contact with suppliers and to monitor their progress. Similarly, by screening job applicants, often by viewing their résumés electronically and using several interviews to select the most highly skilled people, managers can lessen the chance that they will hire people who lack the necessary skills or experience to perform effectively. In general, the development of management information systems promotes feedforward control that gives managers timely information about changes in the task and general environments that may impact their organization later on. Effective managers always monitor trends and changes in the external environment to try to anticipate problems. (We discuss management information systems in detail in Chapter 18.)

At the conversion stage, **concurrent control** gives managers immediate feedback on how efficiently inputs are being transformed into outputs so managers can correct problems as they arise. Concurrent control through IT alerts managers to the need to react quickly to whatever is the source of the problem, whether it is a defective batch of inputs, a machine that is out of alignment, or a worker who lacks the skills necessary to perform a task efficiently. Concurrent control is at the heart of total quality management programs (discussed in Chapter 9), in which workers are expected to constantly monitor the quality of the goods or services they provide at every step of the production process and inform managers as soon as they discover problems. For example, United Technologies Corporation uses a system called Achieving Competitive Excellence (ACE) to get employees involved in identifying and solving design and quality problems and finding better ways to assemble its products to increase quality and reduce costs. When problems are corrected on an ongoing basis, the result is finished products that are more valuable to customers and command higher prices.

At the output stage, managers use **feedback control** to provide information about customers' reactions to goods and services so corrective action can be taken if necessary. For example, a feedback control system that monitors the number of customer returns alerts managers when defective products are being produced, and a management information system (MIS) that measures increases or decreases in relative sales of different products alerts managers to changes in customer tastes so they can increase or reduce the production of specific products.

The Control Process

The control process, whether at the input, conversion, or output stage, can be broken down into four steps: establishing standards of performance and then measuring, comparing, and evaluating actual performance (see Figure 11.2).[24]

- Step 1: *Establish the standards of performance, goals, or targets against which performance is to be evaluated.*

Figure 11.2

Four Steps in Organizational Control

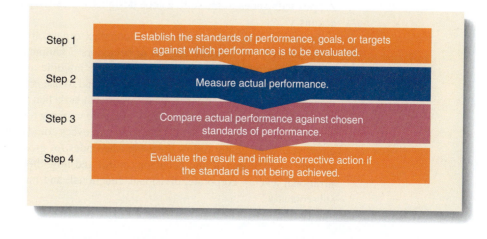

At step 1 in the control process managers decide on the standards of performance, goals, or targets that they will use in the future to evaluate the performance of the entire organization or part of it (such as a division, a function, or an individual). The standards of performance that managers select measure efficiency, quality, responsiveness to customers, and innovation.[25] If managers decide to pursue a low-cost strategy, for example, they need to measure efficiency at all levels in the organization.

At the corporate level, a standard of performance that measures efficiency is operating costs, the actual costs associated with producing goods and services, including all employee-related costs. Top managers might set a corporate goal of "reducing operating costs by 10% for the next three years" to increase efficiency. Corporate managers might then evaluate divisional managers for their ability to reduce operating costs within their respective divisions, and divisional managers might set cost-saving targets for functional managers. Thus performance standards selected at one level affect those at the other levels, and ultimately the performance of individual managers is evaluated in terms of their ability to reduce costs.

The number of standards or indicators of performance that an organization's managers use to evaluate efficiency, quality, and so on can run into the thousands or hundreds of thousands. Managers at each level are responsible for selecting standards that will best allow them to evaluate how well the part of the organization they are responsible for is performing.[26] Managers must be careful to choose standards of performance that let them assess how well they are doing with all four building blocks of competitive advantage. If managers focus on just one standard (such as efficiency) and ignore others (such as determining what customers really want and innovating a new line of products to satisfy them), managers may end up hurting their organization's performance.

- Step 2: *Measure actual performance.*

Once managers have decided which standards or targets they will use to evaluate performance, the next step in the control process is to measure actual performance. In practice, managers can measure or evaluate two things: (1) the actual *outputs* that result from the behavior of their members and (2) the *behaviors* themselves (hence the terms *output control* and *behavior control* used in this chapter).[27]

Sometimes both outputs and behaviors can be easily measured. Measuring outputs and evaluating behavior is relatively easy in a fast-food restaurant, for example, because employees are performing routine tasks. Managers at Home Depot are rigorous in using output control to measure how fast inventory flows through stores. Similarly, managers of a fast-food restaurant can easily measure outputs by counting how many customers their employees serve, the time each transaction takes, and how much money each customer spends. Managers can easily observe each employee's behavior and quickly take action to solve any problems that may arise.

When an organization and its members perform complex, nonroutine activities that are intrinsically hard to measure, it is more challenging for managers to measure outputs or behavior.[28] For example, it might be simple for a manager at Zappos to measure a customer service representative's effectiveness by examining sales figures and customer satisfaction reports. However, it would be difficult for the managers at the companies that supply Zappos with shoes to measure a shoe designer's creativity just by watching the designer's actions.

In general, the more nonroutine or complex organizational activities are, the harder it is for managers to measure outputs or behaviors.[29] Outputs, however, are usually easier to measure than behaviors because they are more tangible and objective. Therefore, the first kind of performance measures that managers tend to use is those that measure outputs. Then managers develop performance measures or standards that allow them to evaluate behaviors to determine whether employees at all levels are working toward organizational goals. Some simple behavior measures are (1) whether employees come to work on time and (2) whether employees consistently follow the established rules for greeting and serving customers. The various types of output and behavior control and how they are used at the different organizational levels—corporate, divisional, functional, and individual—are discussed in detail subsequently.

- Step 3: *Compare actual performance against chosen standards of performance.*

During step 3, managers evaluate whether—and to what extent—performance deviates from the standards of performance chosen in step 1. If performance is higher than expected, managers might decide they set performance standards too low and may raise them for the next period to challenge their subordinates.[30] Managers at successful companies are well known for the way they try to improve performance in manufacturing settings by constantly raising performance standards to motivate managers and workers to find new ways to reduce costs or increase quality.

However, if performance is too low and standards were not reached, or if standards were set so high that employees could not achieve them, managers must decide whether to take corrective action.[31] It is easy to take corrective action when the reasons for poor performance can be identified—for instance, high labor costs. To reduce costs, managers can search for low-cost overseas suppliers, invest more in technology, or implement cross-functional teams. More often, however, the reasons for poor performance are hard to identify. Changes in the environment, such as the emergence of a new global competitor, a recession, or an increase in interest rates, might be the source of the problem. Within an organization, perhaps the R&D function underestimated the problems it would encounter in developing a new product or the extra costs of doing unforeseen research or perhaps the faulty design of just one component in thousands slipped through the cracks. If managers are to take any form of corrective action, step 4 is necessary.

- Step 4: *Evaluate the result and initiate corrective action (that is, make changes) if the standard is not being achieved.*

The final step in the control process is to evaluate the results and bring about change as appropriate. Whether or not performance standards have been met, managers can learn a great deal during this step. If managers decide the level of performance is unacceptable, they must try to change how work activities are performed to solve the problem. Sometimes performance problems occur because the work standard was too high—for example, a sales target was too optimistic and impossible to achieve. In this case, adopting more realistic standards can reduce the gap between actual performance and desired performance.

However, if managers determine that something in the situation is causing the problem, then to raise performance they will need to change how resources are being utilized or shared.[32] Perhaps the latest technology is not being used; perhaps workers lack the advanced training needed to perform at a higher level; perhaps the organization needs to buy its inputs or assemble its products abroad to compete against low-cost rivals; perhaps it needs to restructure itself or reengineer its work processes using Six Sigma to increase efficiency. A recent case among forward-deployed troops throughout Afghanistan demonstrates the four steps of the control process (see the accompanying "Management Insight" feature).

Management Insight

The Four Control Steps in Afghanistan

The U.S. Army's research and development team seeks to increase efficiency and performance of power and energy. The Department of Defense's Project Manager Mobile Electric Power is the energy behind modern warfare.[33] Two electrical engineers from the army's Communications-Electronics Research, Development and Engineering Center (CERDEC) deployed to Afghanistan to support the project. The mission of Project Manager Mobile Electric Power is to manage the department's mobile electric power generators. In combat zones, power is mainly provided by mobile generators. It is the department's policy that all armed forces use the same

U.S. Army mobile power generator. The mission of Project Manager Mobile Electric Power is to manage the mobile electric power generators used by the army to power modern warfare using the four steps of the control process.

generator sets to the extent possible. Having everyone use the same generator sets reduces costs and enhances logistics support and interoperability.[34]

The job of the two engineers deployed to Afghanistan was to assess and improve the energy stability of forward-deployed troops. Their work followed the four steps of the control process.

Step 1: Establish the standards of performance, goals, or targets against which performance is to be evaluated. The two engineers on the project, Noel Pleta and Jennifer Whitmore, both outlined the need to know each soldier's energy needs, in addition to figuring out how much energy use could be reduced.

Step 2: Measure actual performance. The engineers began with collecting data that determined a power profile by surveying all equipment and combining the information with manufacturer data. The data were compiled into a database that can be used to make decisions. A separate planning tool allowed commanders to plan efficient power grids by generating virtual layouts of outposts and bases, along with how much energy would be needed based on the number of tents and other energy-using devices.

Step 3: Compare actual performance against chosen standards of performance. The engineers found that much of the current energy and power infrastructure was in bad condition and that the basics needed to be established as well. "Many of the COPs [combat outposts] were on their last leg of generator power, causing them to shut down their sustainment of life support systems and focus on the tactical support systems," Pleta said. "We found that backup power for tactical operation centers wasn't consistent. If the TOC [tactical operation center] goes down, the mission is compromised as well as the soldiers' safety, and that's priority. That's why it's so important to do it right the first time."[35]

Step 4: Evaluate the result and initiate corrective action if the standard is not being achieved. The engineers did initiate corrective action. More than 30 combat outposts and 35 village stability platforms were rebuilt. Electrical problems that were causing safety concerns were fixed, and new energy plans that improved key facilities for the soldiers, such as dining halls and latrines, were implemented. In 2014 it was reported that the work of the CERDEC engineers under Project Manager Mobile Electric Power lowered fuel consumption by 21 percent across the fleet. Also, units are now set up to do their own quality control by noting trends based on the tracking of energy/fuel consumption and maintenance frequency.[36]

"You just don't get the same experience behind a desk. With each deployment, we increase knowledge regarding the latest challenges," Pleta said. "Most importantly, it allows us to customize user-friendly solutions that will improve safety, reliability, and quality of life for the soldier."[37]

The next step is to extend the power assessments to the individual soldier. This process will apply the control process to the individual as well as to the squad requirements. In other words, the analysis will begin by establishing the goal for energy consumption by soldiers, then measure the actual energy consumption and consider the gap between the two. Engineers will then look to improve energy use by soldiers and squads by eliminating redundancies and finding ways to reduce energy use.

The simplest example of a control system is the thermostat in a home. By setting the thermostat, you establish the standard of performance with which actual temperature is to be compared. The thermostat contains a sensing or monitoring device, which measures the actual temperature against the desired temperature. Whenever there is a difference between them, the furnace or air-conditioning unit is activated to bring the temperature back to the standard. In other words, corrective action is initiated. This is a simple control system: It is entirely self-contained and the target (temperature) is easy to measure.

Establishing targets and designing measurement systems are much more difficult for managers because the high level of uncertainty in the organizational environment means managers rarely know what might happen in the future. Thus it is vital for managers to design control systems to alert them to problems quickly so they can be dealt with before they become threatening. Another issue is that managers are not just concerned about bringing the organization's performance up to some predetermined standard; they want to push that standard forward to

Figure 11.3

Three Organizational Control Systems

Type of Control	Mechanisms of Control
Output control	Financial measures of performance Organizational goals Operating budgets
Behavior control	Direct supervision Management by objectives Rules and standard operating procedures
Clan control	Values Norms Socialization

encourage employees at all levels to find new ways to raise performance. In 2014 Toyota was hit with a $1.2 billion fine by the U.S. Justice Department for not reporting a problem with accelerators in many of its vehicles. In addition to accepting the fine, the company vowed to make changes to its global operations to be more responsive to problems.[38]

In the following sections, we consider three important types of control systems that managers use to coordinate and motivate employees to ensure that they pursue superior efficiency, quality, innovation, and responsiveness to customers: output control, behavior control, and clan control (see Figure 11.3). Managers use all three to shape, regulate, and govern organizational activities, no matter what specific organizational structure is in place. However, as Figure 11.3 suggests, an important element of control is embedded in organizational culture, which is discussed later.

Output Control

All managers develop a system of output control for their organizations. First they choose the goals or output performance standards or targets that they think will best measure efficiency, quality, innovation, and responsiveness to customers. Then they measure to see whether the performance goals and standards are being achieved at the corporate, divisional, functional, and individual employee levels of the organization. The three main mechanisms that managers use to assess output or performance are financial measures, organizational goals, and operating budgets.

LO11-3

Identify the main output controls, and discuss their advantages and disadvantages as means of coordinating and motivating employees.

Financial Measures of Performance

Top managers are most concerned with overall organizational performance and use various financial measures to evaluate it. The most common are profit ratios, liquidity ratios, leverage ratios, and activity ratios. They are discussed here and summarized in Table 11.1.[39]

- *Profit ratios* measure how efficiently managers are using the organization's resources to generate profits. *Return on investment (ROI),* an organization's net income before taxes divided by its total assets, is the most commonly used financial performance measure because it allows managers of one organization to compare performance with that of other organizations. ROI lets managers assess an organization's competitive advantage. *Operating margin* is calculated by dividing a company's operating profit (the amount it has left after all the costs of making the product and running the business have been deducted) by sales revenues. This measure tells managers how efficiently an organization is using its resources; every successful attempt to reduce costs will be reflected in increased operating profit, for example. Also, operating margin is a means of comparing one year's performance to another; for example, if managers discover operating margin has improved by 5 percent from one year to the next, they know their organization is building a competitive advantage.

Table 11.1
Four Measures of Financial Performance

Profit Ratios

$$\text{Return on investment} = \frac{\text{Net profit before taxes}}{\text{Total assets}}$$

Measures how well managers are using the organization's resources to generate profits.

$$\text{Operating margin} = \frac{\text{Total operating profit}}{\text{Sales revenues}}$$

A measure of how much percentage profit a company is earning on sales; the higher the percentage, the better a company is using its resources to make and sell the product.

Liquidity Ratios

$$\text{Current ratio} = \frac{\text{Current assets}}{\text{Current liabilities}}$$

Do managers have resources available to meet claims of short-term creditors?

$$\text{Quick ratio} = \frac{\text{Current assets} - \text{Inventory}}{\text{Current liabilities}}$$

Can managers pay off claims of short-term creditors without selling inventory?

Leverage Ratios

$$\text{Debt-to-assets ratio} = \frac{\text{Total debt}}{\text{Total assets}}$$

To what extent have managers used borrowed funds to finance investments?

$$\text{Times-covered ratio} = \frac{\text{Profit before interest and taxes}}{\text{Total interest charges}}$$

Measures how far profits can decline before managers cannot meet interest charges. If this ratio declines to less than 1, the organization is technically insolvent.

Activity Ratios

$$\text{Inventory turnover} = \frac{\text{Cost of good sold}}{\text{Inventory}}$$

Measures how efficiently managers are turning inventory over so that excess inventory is not carried.

$$\text{Days sales outstanding} = \frac{\text{Current accounts receivable}}{\text{Sales for period divided by days in period}}$$

Measures how efficiently managers are collecting revenues from customers to pay expenses.

- *Liquidity ratios* measure how well managers have protected organizational resources to be able to meet short-term obligations. The *current ratio* (current assets divided by current liabilities) tells managers whether they have the resources available to meet the claims of short-term creditors. The *quick ratio* shows whether they can pay these claims without selling inventory.

- *Leverage ratios,* such as the *debt-to-assets ratio* and the *times-covered ratio,* measure the degree to which managers use debt (borrow money) or equity (issue new shares) to finance ongoing operations. An organization is highly leveraged if it uses more debt than equity. Debt can be risky when net income or profit fails to cover the interest on the debt—as some people learn too late when their paychecks do not allow them to pay off their credit cards.

- *Activity ratios* show how well managers are creating value from organizational assets. *Inventory turnover* measures how efficiently managers are turning inventory over so excess inventory is not carried. *Days sales outstanding* reveals how efficiently managers are collecting revenue from customers to pay expenses.

The objectivity of financial measures of performance is the reason why so many managers use them to assess the efficiency and effectiveness of their organizations. When an organization fails to meet performance standards such as ROI, revenue, or stock price targets, managers know they must take corrective action. Thus financial controls tell managers when a corporate reorganization might be necessary, when they should sell off divisions and exit businesses, or when they should rethink their corporate-level strategies.[40] Today, quantitative skills are needed by many job candidates and employees, as the accompanying "Management Insight" feature describes.

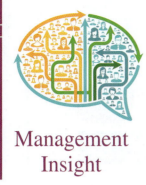

Quantitative Skills in the Job Market

In today's job market, quantitative skills are important for college graduates. The National Association of Colleges and Employers *Job Outlook 2014* survey reported that employers highly value an employee's or candidate's "ability to analyze quantitative information."[41] Other top skills included "ability to work in a team structure," "ability to make decisions and solve problems," "ability to plan, organize, and prioritize work," and "ability to verbally communicate with persons inside and outside the organization," and "ability to obtain and process information."[42]

These skills will be needed to cope with the flood of data being collected in the global economy. Data are being collected from all types of sources. In addition to collecting information on their own operations, companies are collecting data on their customers and suppliers. Mobile phones and other smart devices are creating and communicating data. There are even "exhaust data"—data that are by-products of other activities. All this information is being dubbed "big data." It is creating datasets so large that typical database software cannot store or analyze it. So data analysis is no longer the concern of a few well-trained data "geeks," according to McKinsey Global Institute. Big data are now relevant in every sector of the economy.[43]

A study by the McKinsey Global Institute predicts that there will be more jobs for people with strong data analysis skills than there will be people to fill them. There could be as many as 140,00 to 190,000 unfilled positions in the United States by the year 2018. The study also expects a lack of 1.5 million managers who can understand big data well enough to make decisions using them.[44] The gap is so big that the McKinsey report points out it cannot be filled through hiring. Organizations may need to send existing employees back to school to get needed training in data analysis.

That's not to say that soft skills are not in demand as well. Refer back to the list from the National Association of Colleges and Employers *Job Outlook 2014*. Many of the top skills include teamwork and communication.

Although financial information is an important output control, financial information by itself does not tell managers all they need to know about the four building blocks of competitive advantage. Financial results inform managers about the results of decisions they have already made; they do not tell managers how to find new opportunities to build competitive advantage in the future. To encourage a future-oriented approach, top managers must establish organizational goals that encourage middle and first-line managers to achieve superior efficiency, quality, innovation, and responsiveness to customers.

Organizational Goals

Once top managers consult with lower-level managers and set the organization's overall goals, they establish performance standards for the divisions and functions. These standards specify for divisional and functional managers the level at which their units must perform if the organization is to achieve its overall goals.[45] Each division is given a set of specific goals to achieve (see Figure 11.4). For example, Jeffrey Immelt, CEO of GE, has established the goal of having each GE division be first or second in its industry in profit. Divisional managers then develop a business-level strategy (based on achieving superior efficiency or innovation) that they hope will allow them to achieve that goal.[46] In consultation with functional managers, they specify the functional goals that the managers of different functions need to achieve to allow the division to achieve its goals. For example, sales managers might be evaluated for their ability to increase sales; materials management managers, for their ability to increase the quality of inputs or lower their costs; R&D managers, for the number of products they innovate or the number of patents they receive. In turn, functional managers establish goals that first-line managers and nonmanagerial employees need to achieve to allow the function to achieve its goals.

Figure 11.4

Organizationwide Goal Setting

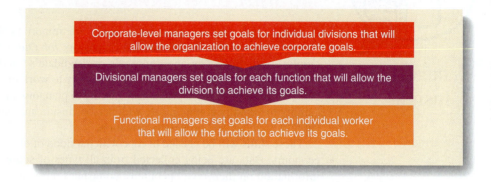

Corporate-level managers set goals for individual divisions that will allow the organization to achieve corporate goals.

Divisional managers set goals for each function that will allow the division to achieve its goals.

Functional managers set goals for each individual worker that will allow the function to achieve its goals.

Output control is used at every level of the organization, and it is vital that the goals set at each level harmonize with the goals set at other levels so managers and other employees throughout the organization work together to attain the corporate goals that top managers have set.[47] It is also important that goals be set appropriately so managers are motivated to accomplish them. If goals are set at an impossibly high level, managers might work only half-heartedly to achieve them because they are certain they will fail. In contrast, if goals are set so low that they are too easy to achieve, managers will not be motivated to use all their resources as efficiently and effectively as possible. Research suggests that the best goals are specific, difficult goals—goals that challenge and stretch managers' ability but are not out of reach and do not require an impossibly high expenditure of managerial time and energy. Such goals are often called *stretch goals.*

Deciding what is a specific difficult goal and what is a goal that is too difficult or too easy is a skill that managers must develop. Based on their own judgment and work experience, managers at all levels must assess how difficult a certain task is, and they must assess the ability of a particular subordinate manager to achieve the goal. If they do so successfully, challenging, interrelated goals—goals that reinforce one another and focus on achieving overall corporate objectives—will energize the organization.

Operating Budgets

operating budget A budget that states how managers intend to use organizational resources to achieve organizational goals.

Once managers at each level have been given a goal or target to achieve, the next step in developing an output control system is to establish operating budgets that regulate how managers and workers attain their goals. An **operating budget** is a blueprint that states how managers intend to use organizational resources to achieve organizational goals efficiently. Typically managers at one level allocate to subordinate managers a specific amount of resources to produce goods and services. Once they have been given a budget, these lower-level managers must decide how to allocate money for different organizational activities. They are then evaluated for their ability to stay within the budget and to make the best use of available resources. For example, managers at GE's washing machine division might have a budget of $50 million to spend on developing and selling a new line of washing machines. They must decide how much money to allocate to the various functions such as R&D, engineering, and sales so the division generates the most customer revenue and makes the biggest profit.

Large organizations often treat each division as a singular or stand-alone responsibility center. Corporate managers then evaluate each division's contribution to corporate performance. Managers of a division may be given a fixed budget for resources and be evaluated on the amount of goods or services they can produce using those resources (this is a cost or expense budget approach). Alternatively, managers may be asked to maximize the revenues from the sales of goods and services produced (a revenue budget approach). Or managers may be evaluated on the difference between the revenues generated by the sales of goods and services and the budgeted cost of making those goods and services (a profit budget approach). Japanese companies' use of operating budgets and challenging goals to increase efficiency is instructive in this context.

In summary, three components—objective financial measures, challenging goals and performance standards, and appropriate operating budgets—are the essence of effective output control. Most organizations develop sophisticated output control systems to allow managers at all levels to keep accurate account of the organization so they can move quickly to take corrective action as needed.[48] Output control is an essential part of management.

Problems with Output Control

When designing an output control system, managers must be careful to avoid some pitfalls. For example, they must be sure the output standards they create motivate managers at all levels and do not cause managers to behave in inappropriate ways to achieve organizational goals.

Suppose top managers give divisional managers the goal of doubling profits over a three-year period. This goal seems challenging and reachable when it is jointly agreed upon, and in the first two years profits go up by 70 percent. In the third year, however, an economic recession hits and sales plummet. Divisional managers think it is increasingly unlikely that they will meet their profit goal. Failure will mean losing the substantial monetary bonus tied to achieving the goal. How might managers behave to try to preserve their bonuses?

Perhaps they might find ways to reduce costs because profit can be increased either by raising sales revenues or reducing costs. Thus divisional managers might cut back on expensive research activities, delay machinery maintenance, reduce marketing expenditures, and lay off middle managers and workers to reduce costs so that at the end of the year they will make their target of doubling profits and receive their bonuses. This tactic might help them achieve a short-run goal—doubling profits—but such actions could hurt long-term profitability or ROI (because a cutback in R&D can reduce the rate of product innovation, a cutback in marketing will lead to the loss of customers, and so on).

The message is clear: Although output control is a useful tool for keeping managers and employees at all levels motivated and the organization on track, it is only a guide to appropriate action. Managers must be sensitive in how they use output control and must constantly monitor its effects at all levels in the organization—and on customers and other stakeholders.

Behavior Control

Organizational structure by itself does not provide any mechanism that motivates managers and nonmanagerial employees to behave in ways that make the structure work—or even improve how it works; hence the need for control. Put another way, managers can develop an organizational structure that has the right grouping of divisions and functions, and an effective chain of command, but it will work as designed *only* if managers also establish control systems that motivate and shape employee behavior in ways that *match* this structure.[49] Output control is one method of motivating employees; behavior control is another method. This section examines three mechanisms of behavior control that managers can use to keep subordinates on track and make organizational structures work as they are designed to work: direct supervision, management by objectives, and rules and standard operating procedures (see Figure 11.3).

LO11-4

Identify the main behavior controls, and discuss their advantages and disadvantages as a means of coordinating and motivating employees.

Direct Supervision

The most immediate and potent form of behavior control is direct supervision by managers who actively monitor and observe the behavior of their subordinates, teach subordinates the behaviors that are appropriate and inappropriate, and intervene to take corrective action as needed. Moreover, when managers personally supervise subordinates, they lead by example and in this way can help subordinates develop and increase their own skill levels. (Leadership is the subject of Chapter 14.)

Direct supervision allows managers at all levels to become personally involved with their subordinates and allows them to mentor subordinates and develop their management skills. Thus control through personal supervision can be an effective way of motivating employees and promoting behaviors that increase efficiency and effectiveness.[50]

Nevertheless, certain problems are associated with direct supervision. First, it is expensive because a manager can personally manage only a relatively small number of subordinates effectively. Therefore, if direct supervision is the main kind of control being used in an organization, a lot of managers will be needed and costs will increase. For this reason, output control is usually preferred to behavior control; indeed, output control tends to be the first type of control that managers at all levels use to evaluate performance. Second, direct supervision can *demotivate* subordinates. This occurs if employees feel they are under such close scrutiny that they are not free to make their own decisions or if they feel they are not being evaluated in an accurate and impartial way. Team members and other employees may start to pass the buck, avoid responsibility, and cease to cooperate with other team members if they feel their manager is not accurately evaluating their performance and is favoring some people over others.

Third, as noted previously, for many jobs personal control through direct supervision is simply not feasible. The more complex a job is, the more difficult it is for a manager to evaluate how well a subordinate is performing. The performance of divisional and functional managers, for example, can be evaluated only over relatively long periods (this is why an output control system is developed), so it makes little sense for top managers to continually monitor their performance. However, managers can still communicate the organization's mission and goals to their subordinates and reinforce the values and norms in the organization's culture through their own personal style.

Management by Objectives

management by objectives (MBO) A goal-setting process in which a manager and each of his or her subordinates negotiate specific goals and objectives for the subordinate to achieve and then periodically evaluate the extent to which the subordinate is achieving those goals.

To provide a framework within which to evaluate subordinates' behavior and, in particular, to allow managers to monitor progress toward achieving goals, many organizations implement some version of management by objectives. **Management by objectives (MBO)** is a formal system of evaluating subordinates on their ability to achieve specific organizational goals or performance standards and to meet operating budgets.[51] Most organizations use some form of MBO system because it is pointless to establish goals and then fail to evaluate whether they are being achieved. Management by objectives involves three specific steps:

- Step 1: *Specific goals and objectives are established at each level of the organization.*

MBO starts when top managers establish overall organizational objectives, such as specific financial performance goals or targets. Then, objective setting cascades down throughout the organization as managers at the divisional and functional levels set their goals to achieve corporate objectives.[52] Finally, first-level managers and employees jointly set goals that will contribute to achieving functional objectives.

- Step 2: *Managers and their subordinates together determine the subordinates' goals.*

An important characteristic of management by objectives is its participatory nature. Managers at every level sit down with each of the subordinate managers who report directly to them, and together they determine appropriate and feasible goals for the subordinate and bargain over the budget that the subordinate will need to achieve his or her goals. The participation of subordinates in the objective-setting process is a way of strengthening their commitment to achieving their goals and meeting their budgets.[53] Another reason why it is so important for subordinates (both individuals and teams) to participate in goal setting is that doing so enables them to tell managers what they think they can realistically achieve.[54]

- Step 3: *Managers and their subordinates periodically review the subordinates' progress toward meeting goals.*

Once specific objectives have been agreed on for managers at each level, managers are accountable for meeting those objectives. Periodically they sit down with their subordinates to evaluate their progress. Normally salary raises and promotions are linked to the goal-setting process, and managers who achieve their goals receive greater rewards than those who fall short. (The issue of how to design reward systems to motivate managers and other organizational employees is discussed in Chapter 13.)

In companies that have decentralized responsibility for the production of goods and services to empowered teams and cross-functional teams, management by objectives works somewhat differently. Managers ask each team to develop a set of goals and performance targets that the team hopes to achieve—goals consistent with organizational objectives. Managers then negotiate with each team to establish its final goals and the budget the team will need to achieve them. The reward system is linked to team performance, not to the performance of any one team member.

Cypress Semiconductor offers an interesting example of how IT can be used to manage the MBO process quickly and effectively. In the fast-moving semiconductor business, a premium is placed on organizational adaptability. At Cypress, CEO T. J. Rodgers was facing a problem: How could he control his growing 1,500-employee organization without developing a bureaucratic management hierarchy? Rodgers believed that a tall hierarchy hinders the ability of an organization to adapt to changing conditions. He was committed to maintaining a flat and decentralized organizational structure with a minimum of management layers. At the same time, he needed to control his employees to ensure that they performed in a manner consistent with the goals of the company.[55] How could he achieve this without resorting to direct supervision and the lengthy management hierarchy that it implies?

To solve this problem, Rodgers implemented an online information system through which he can monitor what every employee and team is doing in his fast-moving and decentralized organization. Each employee maintains a list of 10 to 15 goals, such as "Meet with marketing for new product launch" or "Make sure to check with customer X." Noted next to each goal are when it was agreed upon, when it is due to be finished, and whether it has been finished. All this information is stored on a central computer. Rodgers claims that he can review the goals of all employees in about four hours and that he does so each week.[56] How is this possible? He *manages by exception* and looks only for employees who are falling behind. He then calls them, not to scold but to ask whether there is anything he can do to help them get the job done. It takes only about half an hour each week for employees to review and update their lists. This system allows Rodgers to exercise control over his organization without resorting to the expensive layers of a management hierarchy and direct supervision.

MBO does not always work out as planned, however. Managers and their subordinates at all levels must believe that performance evaluations are accurate and fair. Any suggestion that personal biases and political objectives play a part in the evaluation process can lower or even destroy MBO's effectiveness as a control system. This is why many organizations work so hard to protect the integrity of their systems.

Also, when people work in teams, each member's contribution to the team and each team's contribution to the goals of the organization must be fairly evaluated. This is not easy to do. It depends on managers' ability to create an organizational control system that measures performance accurately and fairly and links performance evaluations to rewards so that employees stay motivated and coordinate their activities to achieve the organization's mission and goals.

Bureaucratic Control

bureaucratic control

Control of behavior by means of a comprehensive system of rules and standard operating procedures.

When direct supervision is too expensive and management by objectives is inappropriate, managers might turn to another mechanism to shape and motivate employee behavior: bureaucratic control. **Bureaucratic control** is control by means of a comprehensive system of rules and standard operating procedures (SOPs) that shapes and regulates the behavior of divisions, functions, and individuals. In Chapter 2 we discussed Weber's theory of bureaucracy and noted that all organizations use bureaucratic rules and procedures but some use them more than others.[57] Recall that rules and SOPs are formal, written instructions that specify a series of actions that employees should follow to achieve a given end; in other words, if *A* happens, then do *B* and *C*. For example, a simple set of rules developed by the supervisor of some custodial workers (Crew G) at a Texas A&M University building clearly established task responsibilities and clarified expectations (see Table 11.2).

Rules and SOPs guide behavior and specify what employees are to do when they confront a problem that needs a solution. It is the responsibility of a manager to develop rules that allow employees to perform their activities efficiently and effectively. Rules and SOPs also clarify people's expectations about one another and prevent misunderstandings over responsibility or the use of power. Such guidelines can prevent a supervisor from arbitrarily increasing a subordinate's workload and prevent a subordinate from ignoring tasks that are a legitimate part of the job.

Table 11.2

Team Rules of Conduct

1. All employees must call their supervisor or leader before 5:55 a.m. to notify of absence or tardiness.
2. Disciplinary action will be issued to any employee who abuses sick leave policy.
3. Disciplinary action will be issued to any employee whose assigned area is not up to custodial standards.
4. If a door is locked when you go in to clean an office, it's your responsibility to lock it back up.
5. Name tags and uniforms must be worn daily.
6. Each employee is responsible for buffing hallways and offices. Hallways must be buffed weekly, offices periodically.
7. All equipment must be put in closets during 9:00 a.m. and 11 a.m. breaks.
8. Do not use the elevator to move trash or equipment from 8:50 to 9:05, 9:50 to 10:05, 11:50 to 12:05, or 1:50 to 2:05 to avoid breaks between classes.
9. Try to mop hallways when students are in classrooms, or mop floors as you go down to each office.
10. Closets must be kept clean and all equipment must be clean and operative.
11. Each employee is expected to greet building occupants with "Good morning."
12. Always knock before entering offices and conference rooms.
13. Loud talking, profanity, and horseplay will not be tolerated inside buildings.
14. All custodial carts must be kept uniform and cleaned daily.
15. You must have excellent "public relations" with occupants at all times.

When employees follow the rules that managers have developed, their behavior is *standardized*—actions are performed the same way time and time again—and the outcomes of their work are predictable. And to the degree that managers can make employees' behavior predictable, there is no need to monitor the outputs of behavior because *standardized behavior leads to standardized outputs,* such as goods and services of the same uniform quality. Suppose a worker at Toyota comes up with a way to attach exhaust pipes that reduces the number of steps in the assembly process and increases efficiency. Always on the lookout for ways to standardize and improve procedures, managers make this idea the basis of a new rule that says, "From now on, the procedure for attaching the exhaust pipe to the car is as follows." If all workers follow the rule to the letter, every car will come off the assembly line with its exhaust pipe attached in the new way, and there will be no need to check exhaust pipes at the end of the line.

In practice, mistakes and lapses of attention happen, so output control is used at the end of the line, and each car's exhaust system is given a routine inspection. However, the number of quality problems with the exhaust system is minimized because the rule (bureaucratic control) is being followed. Service organizations such as retail stores, fast-food restaurants, and home improvement stores also attempt to standardize employee behavior, such as customer service quality, by instructing employees in the correct way to greet customers or the appropriate way to serve and bag food. Employees are trained to follow the rules that have proved to be most effective in a particular situation, and the better trained the employees are, the more standardized is their behavior and the more trust managers can have that outputs (such as food quality) will be consistent.

Not following rules is one of the reasons often given for the high death toll (158 people) of the 2011 tornado that swept through Joplin, Missouri. Tornado warnings were issued and residents were advised to seek shelter. However, many failed to do so. The reasons why were examined by the National Weather Service. The service performs a service assessment to review its performance after severe weather events. In the Joplin tornados, the National Weather Service concluded that initial siren warnings had lost their credibility due to many false alarms. Residents were waiting for more conclusive evidence that a severe weather event was actually happening. The report suggested ways to improve responses to warnings, noting that response to severe weather situations like tornados is a complex, nonlinear process. To improve responses to the warning and overcome complacency among residents, the report suggested a new structure for warnings that would be more credible and allow residents to make better decisions.[58]

Two years later, in May 2013, a series of tornados and related weather events like flash flooding killed 47 people in Oklahoma City, Oklahoma. Again the National Weather Service's service assessment concluded that sirens were not taken seriously. Some interpreted the sirens to mean that they should seek further information.[59] The Oklahoma City report drew on the knowledge gained from the Joplin report that previous experience with tornadoes influences how residents responded to warnings. What the reports on these two devastating weather events indicate is that the simple rule that when residents hear a warning they should take shelter is not enough. Severe weather events are complex situations, and better rules are needed to protect lives.[60]

The goal is simple: Use the rules to achieve a quick resolution of a complex issue. If the existing rules don't work, employees must experiment; and when they find a solution, it is turned into a new rule to be included in the procedures book to aid the future decision making of all employees in the organization.

Problems with Bureaucratic Control

All organizations, make extensive use of bureaucratic control because rules and SOPs effectively control routine organizational activities. With a bureaucratic control system in place, managers can manage by exception and intervene and take corrective action only when necessary. However, managers need to be aware of a number of problems associated with bureaucratic control because such problems can reduce organizational effectiveness.[61]

First, establishing rules is always easier than discarding them. Organizations tend to become overly bureaucratic over time as managers do everything according to the rule book. If the amount of red tape becomes too great, decision making slows and managers react sluggishly to changing conditions. This can imperil an organization's survival if agile new competitors emerge.

Looks like even Mickey Mouse approves! Bob Iger's redesign of Disney's methods of innovation and planning lets employees move faster on new ideas.

Second, because rules constrain and standardize behavior and lead people to behave in predictable ways, people might become so used to automatically following rules that they stop thinking for themselves. Thus too much standardization can actually *reduce* the level of learning taking place in an organization and get the organization off track if managers and workers focus on the wrong issues. An organization thrives when its members are constantly thinking of new ways to increase efficiency, quality, and customer responsiveness. By definition, new ideas do not come from blindly following standardized procedures. Similarly, the pursuit of innovation implies a commitment by managers to discover new ways of doing things; innovation, however, is incompatible with extensive bureaucratic control.

Consider, for example, what happened at Walt Disney when Bob Iger became CEO of the troubled company. Bob Iger had been COO of Disney under CEO Michael Eisner, and he had noticed that Disney was plagued by slow decision making that had led to many mistakes in putting its new strategies into action. Its Disney stores were losing money; its Internet properties were flops; and even its theme parks seemed to have lost their luster as few new rides or attractions were introduced. Iger believed one of the main reasons for Disney's declining performance was that it had become too tall and bureaucratic and its top managers were following financial rules that did not lead to innovative strategies.

One of Iger's first moves to turn around performance was to dismantle Disney's central strategic planning office. In this office several levels of managers were responsible for sifting through all the new ideas and innovations sent up by Disney's different business divisions, such as theme parks, movies, and gaming, and then deciding which ones to present to the CEO. Iger saw the strategic planning office as a bureaucratic bottleneck that reduced the number of ideas coming from below. So he dissolved the office and reassigned its managers back to the different business units.[62]

The result of cutting an unnecessary layer in Disney's hierarchy has been that more new ideas are generated by its different business units. The level of innovation has increased because managers are more willing to speak out and champion their ideas when they know they are dealing directly with the CEO and a top management team searching for innovative ways to improve performance—rather than a layer of strategic planning bureaucrats concerned only with the bottom line.[63] Disney continues to thrive. Captain America had the largest April opening of all time. The company's portfolio includes movies, theme parks, children's retailing, and cruise ships.[64]

Managers must always be sensitive about the way they use bureaucratic control. It is most useful when organizational activities are routine and well understood and when employees are making programmed decisions—for example, in mass-production settings such as Ford or in routine service settings such as stores like Target or Midas Muffler. Bureaucratic control is much less useful in situations where nonprogrammed decisions have to be made and managers have to react quickly to changes in the task environment. The accompanying "Ethics in Action" feature describes how one company has thrived without many bureaucratic rules.

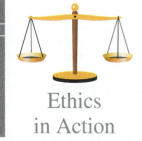

Ethics
in Action

Netflix: Freedom and Responsibility

Netflix, an organization that provides on-demand Internet streaming of movies and television shows as well as a DVD-by-mail service, uses little bureaucratic control. There are no traditional performance appraisals, no formal tracking of vacation time for managers, and no performance-based bonuses. On its web page the company describes itself this way: "At Netflix we value high performance, freedom, and responsibility. We don't focus on rules, processes, or procedures. We are candid and transparent and seek excellence in all that we do."[65]

Much of this lack of bureaucratic control is captured in a presentation called Freedom & Responsibility Culture available on the Netflix website.[66] Sheryl Sandberg, the chief operating officer at Facebook, is quoted as saying the slideshow "may well be the most important document ever to come out of [Silicon] Valley."[67] The presentation's name comes from the Netflix philosophy of allowing employees to make decisions rather than having a strong command and control environment.[68]

Patty McCord, the former chief talent officer at Netflix, outlined five ideas that defined Netflix's philosophy in a 2014 *Harvard Business Review* article.

1. "Hire, Reward, and Tolerate Only Fully Formed Adults":[69] Netflix asks employees to rely on their own judgment rather than corporate policies when making decisions. Thus it is important that Netflix hire people who understand how their actions affect others and who put the best interests of the company first.

2. "Tell the Truth about Performance":[70] The company did away with performance appraisals. It felt they were too infrequent and ritualistic and did not improve performance. Instead they encourage employees and managers to talk frequently. They also hold informal 360-degree reviews by asking employees to critique each other.

3. "Managers Own the Job of Creating Great Teams":[71] Netflix focuses its energies on making sure the right people are doing the right job for their skill set. The company places great importance on team building.

4. "Leaders Own the Job of Creating the Company Culture":[72] McCord makes three points about this: (1) There should not be a difference between how

culture and values are described and how they are carried out in the company. (2) Employees need to understand how the business works so they can support it. (3) There should be awareness that within the culture there will be subcultures to manage.

5. "Good Talent Managers Think Like Businesspeople and Innovators First, and Like HR People Last":[73] She thinks HR is better served to innovate and think of themselves like businesspeople, rather than focus on implementing morale improvement plans that don't usually work.[74]

Netflix was founded in 1997, launched its subscription service in 1999, and introduced streaming in 2007. It went from 857,000 members in 2002 to more than 40 million members in 2013.[75] It has been successful despite having little bureaucratic control.

To use output control and behavior control, managers must be able to identify the outcomes they want to achieve and the behaviors they want employees to perform to achieve those outcomes. For many of the most important and significant organizational activities, however, output control and behavior control are inappropriate for several reasons:

- A manager cannot evaluate the performance of workers such as doctors, research scientists, or engineers by observing their daily behavior.

- Rules and SOPs are of little use in telling a doctor how to respond to an emergency situation or a scientist how to discover something new.

- Output controls such as the amount of time a surgeon takes for each operation or the costs of making a discovery are crude measures of the quality of performance.

How can managers attempt to control and regulate the behavior of their subordinates when personal supervision is of little use, when rules cannot be developed to tell employees what to do, and when outputs and goals cannot be measured at all or can be measured usefully only over long periods?

Clan Control

clan control The control exerted on individuals and groups in an organization by shared values, norms, standards of behavior, and expectations.

One source of control increasingly being used by organizations is **clan control**, which takes advantage of the power of internalized values and norms to guide and constrain employee attitudes and behavior in ways that increase organizational performance.[76] The first function of a control system is to shape the behavior of organizational members to ensure that they are working toward organizational goals and to take corrective action if those goals are not being met. The second function of control, however, is to keep organizational members focused on thinking about what is best for their organization in the future and to keep them looking for new opportunities to use organizational resources to create value. Clan control serves this dual function of keeping organizational members goal-directed while open to new opportunities because it takes advantage of the power of organizational culture, discussed in the previous chapter.

Organizational culture functions as a kind of control system because managers can deliberately try to influence the kind of values and norms that develop in an organization—values and norms that specify appropriate and inappropriate behaviors and so determine the way its members behave.[77] We discussed the sources of organizational culture and the way managers can help create different kinds of cultures in Chapter 10, so there is no need to repeat this discussion here. Another example of using internalized values and norms to guide behavior is described in the accompanying "Management Insight" feature.

How Philanthrofits Help Users Help Charities

The popularity of a new category of fitness apps provides an example of how a control system can use internalized values and norms. Philanthrofits[78] are apps that donate money to charities based on the behaviors of the users. For example, the app Charity Miles donates 25 cents per mile for walkers and runners to charities including Habitat for Humanity, Feeding America, and Autism Speaks.[79] With a $1 million sponsorship pool, the company hopes that as the number of athletes using the app increase, so will the corporate sponsors, thus providing more money for athletes to donate to charity.[80] Users must share their activity on Facebook for their designated charity to receive the money raised.

On its web page, a Charity Miles user who lost 50 pounds by running wrote, "Charity Miles helped me get started with running because I knew with each run, I was doing something bigger. It helped me get to where I am today, and I would like others to get the same experience from it that I have."[81]

Another app, stickK, was developed by Yale University economists based on research of the effectiveness of people making contracts to achieve their goals. The standard objectives offered by the app include losing weight, exercising regularly, quitting smoking, preparing for a race, and maintaining weight. The user can also choose a custom goal, such as raising one's grade point average. Next the user can enter credit card information to wager money on whether the user will achieve the set goals. This step is optional. If the goal is achieved, the credit card is not charged. If the goal is not achieved, the money the user wagered will go to a charity of the user's choice. The chosen charity can be one the user supports or one the user would prefer not to support. To hold the user accountable, the user chooses a referee to monitor progress. The referee verifies the accuracy of the user's reports. Finally, the user can ask friends and family who also are registered for the app to act as supporters. These supporters can send the user encouraging messages on the app.[82]

There are too many Philanthrofit apps on the market to mention them all here. But Charity Miles and stickK represent two ways of leveraging users' internalized values and norms to influence behavior. Charity Miles allows the user to donate a sponsor's money. StickK has users donate their own money. Charity Miles donates money when users perform their activities and stickK donates when they do not. But perhaps the biggest difference is that stickK also allows users to donate to either a charity or an "anti-charity" if the user does not live up to the contract.

If a stickK user chooses to send money to a charity, stickK does not inform the user which charity receives the money. The idea is that if the user knew what good cause received the money, he or she might feel OK about breaking the contract. Instead the stickK web page lists a few reputable charities such as the Red Cross and Doctors without Borders. Users who chose the charity option are told that their money went to such a charity without providing the charity name.

However, if the user chooses an anti-charity, the user is told which charity got their money. An anti-charity is one with views the user opposes. The stickK website provides a choice of anti-charities from either side of controversial issues, including the political action committees supporting both the Republican and Democratic parties.

Organizational Change

As we have discussed, many problems can arise if an organization's control systems are not designed correctly. One of these problems is that an organization cannot change or adapt in response to a changing environment unless it has effective control over its activities. Companies can lose this control over time, or they can change in ways that make them more effective. **Organizational change** is the movement of an organization away from its present state toward some preferred future state to increase its efficiency and effectiveness.

organizational change
The movement of an organization away from its present state and toward some preferred future state to increase its efficiency and effectiveness.

LO11-5
Discuss the relationship between organizational control and change, and explain why managing change is a vital management task.

Interestingly enough, there is a fundamental tension or need to balance two opposing forces in the control process that influences how organizations change. As just noted, organizations and their managers need to be able to control their activities and make their operations routine and predictable. At the same time, however, organizations have to be responsive to the need to change, and managers and employees have to "think on their feet" and realize when they need to depart from routines to be responsive to unpredictable events. In other words, even though adopting the right set of output and behavior controls is essential for improving efficiency, because the environment is dynamic and uncertain, employees also need to feel that they have the autonomy to depart from routines as necessary to increase effectiveness. (See Figure 11.5.)

For this reason many researchers believe that the highest-performing organizations are those that are constantly changing—and thus become experienced at doing so—in their search to become more efficient and effective. Companies like UPS, Toyota, and Walmart are constantly changing the mix of their activities to move forward even as they seek to make their existing operations more efficient. For example, UPS entered the air express parcel market, bought a chain of mailbox stores, and began offering a consulting service. At the same time it has been increasing the efficiency of its ground and global air transport network, including 2,864 alternative fuel and technology vehicles.[83]

Lewin's Force-Field Theory of Change

Researcher Kurt Lewin developed a theory about organizational change. According to his *force-field theory,* a wide variety of forces arise from the way an organization operates—from its structure, culture, and control systems—that make organizations resistant to change. At the same time a wide variety of forces arise from changing task and general environments that push organizations toward change. These two sets of forces are always in opposition in an organization.[84] When the forces are evenly balanced, the organization is in a state of inertia and does not change. To get an organization to change, managers must find a way to *increase* the forces for change, *reduce* resistance to change, or do *both* simultaneously. Any of these strategies will overcome inertia and cause an organization to change.

Figure 11.6 illustrates Lewin's theory. An organization at performance level P1 is in balance: Forces for change and resistance to change are equal. Management, however, decides that the organization should strive to achieve performance level P2. To get to level P2, managers must *increase* the forces for change (the increase is represented by the lengthening of the up arrows), *reduce* resistance to change (the reduction is represented by the shortening of the down arrows), or both. If managers pursue any of the three strategies successfully,

Figure 11.5

Organizational Control and Change

Managers must balance the need for an organization to improve the way it currently operates and the need for it to change in response to new, unanticipated events.

Figure 11.6

Lewin's Force-Field Model of Change

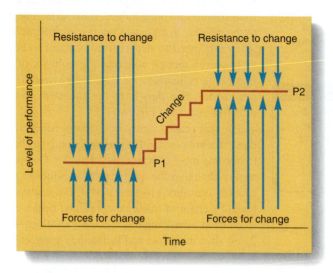

the organization will change and reach performance level P2. Before we look in more detail at the techniques managers can use to overcome resistance and facilitate change, we need to look at the types of change they can implement to increase organizational effectiveness.

Evolutionary and Revolutionary Change

Managers continually face choices about how best to respond to the forces for change. There are several types of change that managers can adopt to help their organizations achieve desired future states.[85] In general, types of change fall into two broad categories: evolutionary change and revolutionary change.[86]

evolutionary change
Change that is gradual, incremental, and narrowly focused.

Evolutionary change is gradual, incremental, and narrowly focused. Evolutionary change is not drastic or sudden but, rather, is a constant attempt to improve, adapt, and adjust strategy and structure incrementally to accommodate changes taking place in the environment.[87] Sociotechnical systems theory and total quality management, or kaizen, are two instruments of evolutionary change. Such improvements might entail using technology in a better way or reorganizing the work process.

Some organizations, however, need to make major changes quickly. Faced with drastic, unexpected changes in the environment (for example, a new technological breakthrough) or with an impending disaster resulting from mismanagement, an organization might need to act quickly and decisively. In this case, revolutionary change is called for.

revolutionary change
Change that is rapid, dramatic, and broadly focused.

Revolutionary change is rapid, dramatic, and broadly focused. Revolutionary change involves a bold attempt to quickly find new ways to be effective. It is likely to result in a radical shift in ways of doing things, new goals, and a new structure for the organization. The process has repercussions at all levels in the organization—corporate, divisional, functional, group, and individual. Reengineering, restructuring, and innovation are three important instruments of revolutionary change.

Managing Change

The need to constantly search for ways to improve efficiency and effectiveness makes it vital that managers develop the skills necessary to manage change effectively. Several experts have proposed a model of change that managers can follow to implement change successfully— that is, to move an organization away from its present state and toward some desired future state to increase its efficiency and effectiveness.[88] Figure 11.7 outlines the steps in this process. In the rest of this section we examine each one.

ASSESSING THE NEED FOR CHANGE   Organizational change can affect practically all aspects of organizational functioning, including organizational structure, culture, strategies, control systems, and groups and teams, as well as the human resource management

Figure 11.7

Four Steps in the Organizational Change Process

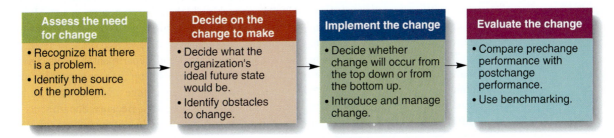

Assess the need for change	Decide on the change to make	Implement the change	Evaluate the change
• Recognize that there is a problem. • Identify the source of the problem.	• Decide what the organization's ideal future state would be. • Identify obstacles to change.	• Decide whether change will occur from the top down or from the bottom up. • Introduce and manage change.	• Compare prechange performance with postchange performance. • Use benchmarking.

system and critical organizational processes such as communication, motivation, and leadership. Organizational change can alter how managers carry out the critical tasks of planning, organizing, leading, and controlling and the ways they perform their managerial roles.

Deciding how to change an organization is a complex matter because change disrupts the status quo and poses a threat, prompting employees to resist attempts to alter work relationships and procedures. Organizational learning—the process through which managers try to increase organizational members' abilities to understand and appropriately respond to changing conditions—can be an important impetus for change and can help all members of an organization, including managers, effectively make decisions about needed changes.

Assessing the need for change calls for two important activities: recognizing that there is a problem and identifying its source. Sometimes the need for change is obvious, such as when an organization's performance is suffering. Often, however, managers have trouble determining that something is going wrong because problems develop gradually; organizational performance may slip for a number of years before a problem becomes obvious. Thus during the first step in the change process, managers need to recognize that there is a problem that requires change.

Often the problems that managers detect have produced a gap between desired performance and actual performance. To detect such a gap, managers need to look at performance measures—such as falling market share or profits, rising costs, or employees' failure to meet their established goals or stay within budgets—that indicate whether change is needed. These measures are provided by organizational control systems, discussed earlier in the chapter.

To discover the source of the problem, managers need to look both inside and outside the organization. Outside the organization, they must examine how changing environmental forces may be creating opportunities and threats that are affecting internal work relationships. Perhaps the emergence of low-cost competitors abroad has led to conflict among different departments that are trying to find new ways to gain a competitive advantage. Managers also need to look within the organization to see whether its structure is causing problems between departments. Perhaps a company does not have integrating mechanisms in place to allow different departments to respond to low-cost competition.

DECIDING ON THE CHANGE TO MAKE Once managers have identified the source of the problem, they must decide what they think the organization's ideal future state would be. In other words, they must decide where they would like their organization to be in the future—what kinds of goods and services it should be making, what its business-level strategy should be, how the organizational structure should be changed, and so on. During this step, managers also must plan how to attain the organization's ideal future state.

This step in the change process also includes identifying obstacles or sources of resistance to change. Managers must analyze the factors that may prevent the company from reaching its ideal future state. Obstacles to change are found at the corporate, divisional, departmental, and individual levels of the organization.

Corporate-level changes in an organization's strategy or structure, even seemingly trivial changes, may significantly affect how divisional and departmental managers behave. Suppose that to compete with low-cost foreign competitors, top managers decide to increase the resources spent on state-of-the-art machinery and reduce the resources spent on marketing or R&D. The power of manufacturing managers would increase, and the power of marketing and R&D managers would fall. This decision would alter the balance of power among departments and might increase conflict as departments fight to retain their status in the organization. An organization's present strategy and structure are powerful obstacles to change.

Whether a company's culture is adaptive or inert facilitates or obstructs change. Organizations with entrepreneurial, flexible cultures, such as high-tech companies, are much easier to change than are organizations with more rigid cultures, such as those sometimes found in large, bureaucratic organizations like the military or GM.

The same obstacles to change exist at the divisional and departmental levels. Division managers may differ in their attitudes toward the changes that top managers propose and, if their interests and power seem threatened, will resist those changes. Managers at all levels usually fight to protect their power and control over resources. Because departments have different goals and time horizons, they may also react differently to the changes other managers propose. When top managers are trying to reduce costs, for example, sales managers may resist attempts to cut back on sales expenditures if they believe that problems stem from manufacturing managers' inefficiencies.

At the individual level, too, people often resist change because it brings uncertainty and stress. For example, individuals may resist the introduction of a new technology because they are uncertain about their abilities to learn it and effectively use it.

These obstacles make organizational change a slow process. Managers must recognize the potential obstacles to change and take them into consideration. Some obstacles can be overcome by improving communication so all organizational members are aware of the need for change and of the nature of the changes being made. Empowering employees and inviting them to participate in planning for change also can help overcome resistance and allay employees' fears. In addition, managers can sometimes overcome resistance by emphasizing group or shared goals such as increased organizational efficiency and effectiveness. The larger and more complex an organization is, the more complex is the change process.

top-down change A fast, revolutionary approach to change in which top managers identify what needs to be changed and then move quickly to implement the changes throughout the organization.

bottom-up change A gradual or evolutionary approach to change in which managers at all levels work together to develop a detailed plan for change.

IMPLEMENTING THE CHANGE   Generally, managers implement—that is, introduce and manage—change from the top down or from the bottom up.[89] **Top-down change** is implemented quickly: Top managers identify the need for change, decide what to do, and then move quickly to implement the changes throughout the organization. For example, top managers may decide to restructure and downsize the organization and then give divisional and departmental managers specific goals to achieve. With top-down change, the emphasis is on making the changes quickly and dealing with problems as they arise; it is revolutionary in nature.

Bottom-up change is typically more gradual or evolutionary. Top managers consult with middle and first-line managers about the need for change. Then, over time, managers at all levels work to develop a detailed plan for change. A major advantage of bottom-up change is that it can co-opt resistance to change from employees. Because the emphasis in bottom-up change is on participation and on keeping people informed about what is going on, uncertainty and resistance are minimized. The accompanying "Managing Globally" feature provides an example of a change that leads to other changes.

Managing Globally

Changing Online Retailing with Virtusize

Sometimes an organization can make one small change that cascades throughout the organization, cutting costs and reallocating resources to important projects. In the online apparel industry, one such small change could be a reduction in merchandise returns. A company called Virtusize claims to reduce fit-related returns by 50 percent.[90]

Before the Zappos policy of free returns, online shoppers paid to return ill-fitting clothing and shoes. Then Zappos provided free returns and told customers to order in multiple sizes and return the ones that did not fit. To compete, other online retailers followed suit. Online shoppers now return between 20 and 30 percent of apparel orders.[91]

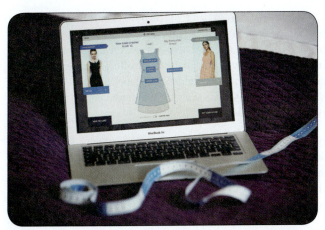

A page from the Virtusize website. The company helps online retailers show the size and fit of clothing by comparing an item silhouette to a reference silhouette with the shopper's own measurements.

Virtusize's vision is to be "a global standard for illustrating size and fit of clothes sold online".[92] The company helps online retailers show the size and fit of clothing to online shoppers by illustrating the silhouette of the garment, so there are fewer fit-related returns. Virtusize is a web widget that lets the online shoppers insert reference garments for different categories of clothing, such as pants, jackets, shirts and dresses.

To insert a reference garment, there are two options. The online shopper can enter measurements of a garment they already own or tag a previous purchase made at one of the Virtusize connected stores. Virtusize will then overlay the two silhouettes to help the online shopper to clearly see the difference in size and fit of the garment they want to buy compared to the garment they already own.

By decreasing the need for fit-related returns, companies like Virtusize can save money for organizations in at least two ways.[93] First, decreasing both the volume of returns and the volume of re-ships to customers can save the organization shipping costs. Nick Robertson, CEO of the global online fashion and beauty retailer ASOS, estimates that a 1 percent reduction in returns would add $16 million to the company's bottom line.[94] Second, fewer fit-related returns mean fewer customer support calls, reducing staff time in call centers.

But the savings to online retailers go beyond shipping and customer calls. If an online retailer has fewer returns to handle, the retailer can carry less necessary inventory, which saves on warehousing and delivery logistics costs.[95] Also, more intangibly, when customers do not have to return their online orders, their satisfaction increases and they may be more willing to buy from the retailer again.[96]

With the monetary savings provided by reduced fit-related returns, organizations can shift their focus to other efforts, such as improving customer service or developing new products. Just one small change in the supply chain can mean big change throughout the organization.

benchmarking The process of comparing one company's performance on specific dimensions with the performance of other high-performing organizations.

EVALUATING THE CHANGE The last step in the change process is to evaluate how successful the change effort has been in improving organizational performance.[97] Using measures such as changes in market share, in profits, or the ability of scientists to innovate new drugs, managers compare how well an organization is performing after the change with how well it was performing before. Managers also can use **benchmarking**, comparing their performance on specific dimensions with the performance of high-performing organizations to decide how successful a change effort has been. For example, when Xerox was performing poorly in the 1980s, it benchmarked the efficiency of its distribution operations against that of L.L.Bean, the efficiency of its central computer operations against that of John Deere, and the efficiency of its marketing abilities against that of Procter & Gamble. Those three companies are renowned for their skills in these different areas, and by studying how they performed, Xerox was able to dramatically increase its own performance. Benchmarking is a key tool in total quality management, an important change program discussed in Chapter 9.

In summary, organizational control and change are closely linked because organizations operate in environments that are constantly changing; so managers must be alert to the need to change their strategies and structures. Managers of high-performing organizations are attuned to the need to continually modify the way they operate, and they adopt techniques like empowered work groups and teams, benchmarking, and global outsourcing to remain competitive in a global world.

Summary and Review

LO11-1, 11-2

WHAT IS ORGANIZATIONAL CONTROL?   Controlling is the process whereby managers monitor and regulate how efficiently and effectively an organization and its members are performing the activities necessary to achieve organizational goals. Controlling is a four-step process: (1) establishing performance standards, (2) measuring actual performance, (3) comparing actual performance against performance standards, and (4) evaluating the results and initiating corrective action if needed.

LO11-3   **OUTPUT CONTROL**   To monitor output or performance, managers choose goals or performance standards that they think will best measure efficiency, quality, innovation, and responsiveness to customers at the corporate, divisional, departmental or functional, and individual levels. The main mechanisms that managers use to monitor output are financial measures of performance, organizational goals, and operating budgets.

LO11-4   **BEHAVIOR CONTROL**   In an attempt to shape behavior and induce employees to work toward achieving organizational goals, managers use direct supervision, management by objectives, and bureaucratic control by means of rules and standard operating procedures.

CLAN CONTROL   Clan control is the control exerted on individuals and groups by shared values, norms, and prescribed standards of behavior. An organization's culture is deliberately fashioned to emphasize the values and norms top managers believe will lead to high performance.

LO11-5   **ORGANIZATIONAL CHANGE**   There is a need to balance two opposing forces in the control process that influences the way organizations change. On one hand, managers need to be able to control organizational activities and make their operations routine and predictable. On the other hand, organizations have to be responsive to the need to change, and managers must understand when they need to depart from routines to be responsive to unpredictable events. The four steps in managing change are (1) assessing the need for change, (2) deciding on the changes to make, (3) implementing change, and (4) evaluating the results of change.

Management in Action

Topics for Discussion and Action

Discussion

1. What is the relationship between organizing and controlling? **[LO11-1]**

2. How do output control and behavior control differ? **[LO11-2, 11-3]**

3. Why is it important for managers to involve subordinates in the control process? **[LO11-3, 11-4]**

4. What kind of controls would you expect to find most used in (a) a hospital, (b) the Navy, and (c) a city police force? Why? **[LO11-2, 11-3, 11-4]**

5. What are the main obstacles to organizational change? What techniques can managers use to overcome these obstacles? **[LO11-1, 11-5]**

Action

6. Ask a manager to list the main performance measures that he or she uses to evaluate how well the organization is achieving its goals. **[LO11-1, 11-3, 11-4]**

7. Ask the same or a different manager to list the main forms of output control and behavior control that he or she uses to monitor and evaluate employee behavior. **[LO11-3, 11-4]**

Building Management Skills

Understanding Controlling **[LO11-1, 11-3, 11-4]**

For this exercise you will analyze the control systems used by a real organization such as a department store, restaurant, hospital, police department, or small business. It can be the organization that you investigated in Chapter 10 or a different one. Your objective is to uncover all the different ways in which managers monitor and evaluate the performance of the organization and employees.

1. At what levels does control take place in this organization?

2. Which output performance standards (such as financial measures and organizational goals) do managers use most often to evaluate performance at each level?

3. Does the organization have a management by objectives system in place? If it does, describe it. If it does not, speculate about why not.

4. How important is behavior control in this organization? For example, how much of managers' time is spent directly supervising employees? How formalized is the organization? Do employees receive a book of rules to teach them how to perform their jobs?

5. What kind of culture does the organization have? What are the values and norms? What effect does the organizational culture have on the way employees behave or treat customers?

6. Based on this analysis, do you think there is a fit between the organization's control systems and its culture? What is the nature of this fit? How could it be improved?

Managing Ethically **[LO11-1, 11-5]**

Some managers and organizations go to great lengths to monitor their employees' behavior, and they keep extensive records about employees' behavior and performance. Some organizations also seem to possess norms and values that cause their employees to behave in certain ways.

Questions

1. Either by yourself or in a group, think about the ethical implications of organizations' monitoring and collecting information about their employees.

What kinds of information is it ethical or unethical to collect? Why? Should managers and organizations tell subordinates they are collecting such information?

2. Similarly, some organizations' cultures seem to develop norms and values that cause their members

to behave in unethical ways. When and why does a strong norm that encourages high performance become one that can cause people to act unethically? How can organizations keep their values and norms from becoming "too strong"?

Small Group Breakout Exercise

How Best to Control the Sales Force? [LO11-1, 11-3, 11-5]

Form groups of three or four people, and appoint one member as the spokesperson who will communicate your findings to the class when called on by the instructor. Then discuss the following scenario:

You are the regional sales managers of an organization that supplies high-quality windows and doors to building supply centers nationwide. Over the last three years, the rate of sales growth has slackened. There is increasing evidence that, to make their jobs easier, salespeople are primarily servicing large customer accounts and ignoring small accounts. In addition, the salespeople are not dealing promptly with customer questions and complaints, and this inattention has resulted in poor after-sales service. You

have talked about these problems, and you are meeting to design a control system to increase both the amount of sales and the quality of customer service.

1. Design a control system that you think will best motivate salespeople to achieve these goals.

2. What relative importance do you put on (a) output control, (b) behavior control, and (c) organizational culture in this design?

Exploring the World Wide Web [LO11-1, 11-5]

Go to the website of *Fortune*'s 100 Best Companies to Work For. Check out a few of the different companies on the list. Read a few of the "What makes it so great?" profiles.

1. Do you notice any common values and norms in the top companies?

2. Is there anything about a particular company's culture or structure that would make you want to work there?

Be the Manager

You have been asked by your company's CEO to find a way to improve the performance of its teams of web design and web hosting specialists and programmers. Each team works on a different aspect of website production; and while each is responsible for the quality of its own performance, its performance also depends on how well the other teams perform. Your task is to create a control system that will help to increase the performance of each team separately and facilitate cooperation among the teams. This is necessary because the various projects are interlinked and affect one another just as the different parts of a car must fit together. Because competition in the website production market is intense, it is imperative that each website be up and running

as quickly as possible and incorporate all the latest advances in website software technology.

Questions

1. What kind of output controls will best facilitate positive interactions both within the teams and among the teams?

2. What kind of behavior controls will best facilitate positive interactions both within the teams and among the teams?

3. How would you help managers develop a culture to promote high team performance?

Bloomberg Businessweek Case in the News [LO11-1, 11-2, 11-5]

How Chick-fil-A Spent $50 Million to Change Its Grilled Chicken

Chick-fil-A wants a healthier image to go along with its emblematic fried chicken sandwiches. To that end, next week the country's largest chicken chain by sales will replace its old chargrilled menu options with a new recipe used for three new items: a grilled chicken sandwich, a grilled chicken club with bacon, and grilled chicken tenders. The new grilled recipe also replaces the chicken in its salads and wraps.

It's a small gamble for the company: the chargrilled sandwich accounted for 7 percent of Chick-fil-A's sales in 2013. "I never thought of it as being craveable," says David Farmer, vice president of product strategy and development. People ate it because they *should,* he theorizes, not because they looked forward to it. As consumers become more health conscious, Farmer says, having an enticing grilled option is necessary: "Taste is king, but it increasingly has to be healthy, natural, and sustainable."

Chick-fil-A claims it spent more than $50 million figuring out its new approach to grilling, which included developing new automated grills that wouldn't dry out the meat and installing them at all 1,775 restaurants. After trying more than a thousand recipe iterations, it settled on one that involved not just marinating the fillets

in "a blend of sea salt, lemon, garlic, and savory herbs," but also basting the chicken.

The result of all that testing, according to Chick-fil-A's marketing, is "a tender, juicy filet with just the right amount of smoky flavor." Add gluten-free to the list of promotional terms. Coming up with a new recipe would seem like an obvious place to start. But Chick-fil-A found otherwise: "The trick," Farmer explains, "was more on the equipment side." The old grill applied too much pressure on the meat, which produced dry sandwiches.

Like its predecessor, the new grill has a clamshell shape to cook the chicken on both sides—envision an industrial-scale George Foreman Grill—and slash the cooking time. The new version, developed by Garland Grills after Chick-fil-A's in-house prototype failed to make the cut, has cast-iron grates and is programmed to automatically lower and lift the upper part to apply the right amount of pressure on the meat.

It was also made the same size as the old grills, about one foot across and four feet deep—big enough to cook 10 fillets at a time—to make replacement at every restaurant relatively easy. "When we came up with a new cooking platform," Farmer says,

"that was the breakthrough that helped the most." The recipe was then tailored for the new grill.

If the new chicken items do well enough, the company will consider swapping out a fryer—most stores have three or four—to add a second grill. That would be a huge change for a brand built on fried chicken. "That's OK," Farmer says. "I could see that."

Source: Venessa Wong, "How Chick-fil-A Spent $50 Million to Change Its Grilled Chicken," *Bloomberg Business Week,* April 11, 2014. Used with permission of Bloomberg L.P. Copyright © 2014. All rights reserved.

Questions for Discussion

1. Describe how Chick-fil-A's timeline to new grilled chicken followed the four-step control process outlined in the chapter.

2. The goal of Chick-fil-A's new chicken items is to improve the company's image for healthful food. How can the company use clan control to help its employees further its goal?

3. Apply the first three steps of the four steps to managing change to this case. How should the company carry out the fourth step?

CHAPTER 12

Human Resource Management

Learning Objectives

After studying this chapter, you should be able to:

LO12-1 Explain why strategic human resource management can help an organization gain a competitive advantage.

LO12-2 Describe the steps managers take to recruit and select organizational members.

LO12-3 Discuss the training and development options that ensure organizational members can effectively perform their jobs.

LO12-4 Explain why performance appraisal and feedback are such crucial activities, and list the choices managers must make in designing effective performance appraisal and feedback procedures.

LO12-5 Explain the issues managers face in determining levels of pay and benefits.

LO12-6 Understand the role that labor relations play in the effective management of human resources.

Treating Employees Well Leads to Satisfied Customers and Low Turnover at the Four Seasons

How can managers promote high levels of personalized customer service in an industry known for high employee turnover? Four Seasons Hotels and Resorts is one of only 13 companies to be ranked one of the "100 Best Companies to Work For" every year since *Fortune* magazine started this annual ranking of companies (from 1998 to 2014).[1] And the Four Seasons often receives other awards and recognition such as having some of its properties included on the *Condé Nast Traveler* Gold List, the *Travel + Leisure* T + L 500 list, and Robb Report's World's Top 100 Hotels.[2] In 2013 the Four Seasons was awarded Best Hotel Group in the Travel Awards of the *Telegraph.*[3] In an industry in which annual turnover rates are relatively high, the Four Seasons' turnover rate for full-time employees is 12.7 percent, which is among the lowest in the industry.[4] Evidently employees and customers alike are satisfied with how they are treated at the Four Seasons. Understanding that the two are causally linked is perhaps the key to the Four Seasons' success. As the Four Seasons' founder and Chairman of the Board Isadore Sharp[5] suggested, "How you treat your employees is how you expect them to treat the customer."[6]

The Four Seasons was founded by Sharp in 1961 when he opened his first hotel called the Four Seasons Motor Hotel in a less-than-desirable area outside downtown Toronto. Whereas his first hotel had 125 inexpensively priced rooms appealing to the individual traveler, his fourth hotel was built to appeal to business travelers and conventions with 1,600 rooms, conference facilities, several restaurants, banquet halls, and shops in an arcade. Both these hotels were successful, but Sharp decided he could provide customers with a different kind of hotel experience by combining the best features of both kinds of hotel experiences—the sense of closeness and personal attention that a small hotel brings with the amenities of a big hotel to suit the needs of business travelers.[7]

Sharp sought to provide the kind of personal service that would really help business travelers on the road—giving them the amenities they have at home and in the office and miss when traveling on business. Thus the Four Seasons was the first hotel chain to provide bathrobes, shampoo, round-the-clock room service, laundry and dry cleaning services, large desks in every room, two-line phones, and round-the-clock secretarial

At the Four Seasons, treating employees well leads to satisfied customers. Everyone wins!

assistance.[8] While these are relatively concrete ways of personalizing the hotel experience, Sharp realized that how employees treat customers is just as, or perhaps even more, important. When employees view each customer as an individual with his or her own needs and desires, and empathetically try to meet these needs and desires and help customers both overcome any problems or challenges they face and truly enjoy their hotel experience, a hotel can indeed serve the purposes of a home away from home (and an office away from the office), and customers are likely to be both loyal and highly satisfied.[9]

Sharp always realized that for employees to treat customers well, the Four Seasons needs to treat its employees well. Salaries are relatively high at the Four Seasons by industry standards (between the 75th and 90th percentiles); employees participate in a profit-sharing plan; and the company contributes to their 401(k) plans. Four Seasons pays 78 percent of employees' health insurance premiums and provides free dental insurance.[10] All employees get free meals in the hotel cafeteria, have access to staff showers and a locker room, and receive an additional highly attractive benefit—once a new employee has worked for the Four Seasons for six months, he or she can stay for three nights free at any Four Seasons hotel or resort in the world. After a year of employment, this benefit increases to six free nights, and it continues to grow as tenure with the company increases. Employees like waitress Michelle De Rochemont loved this benefit. As she indicated, "You're never treated like just an employee. You're a guest. . . . You come back from those trips on fire. You want to do so much for the guest."[11]

All aspects of human resource management at the Four Seasons are oriented around ensuring that the guiding principle behind all Four Seasons operations is upheld.[12] As Nick Mutton, executive vice president for human resources, indicates, "Our strong culture has always been based on the Golden Rule—the simple idea of treating others as you would have them treat you."[13]

All job applicants to the Four Seasons, regardless of level or area, have a minimum of four interviews, one of which is with the general manager of the property.[14] The human resources department interviews many of the applicants because the philosophy at the Four Seasons is that employees need to be helpful and have a positive approach or perspective; the specific requirements for each job can be taught, but a helpful, positive attitude is something the Four Seasons looks for potential hires to bring with them to a new job. Given the reputation that the Four Seasons has for treating employees well and providing them with great benefits, it often has many applicants for job openings. For example, when the Four Seasons opened a new hotel in Baltimore, 4,000 people applied for 250 open positions. The Four Seasons devotes so much attention to hiring the right people because of the importance of each and every employee providing a consistently high level of empathetic and responsive customer service.[15]

New hires participate in a three-month training program that includes improvisation activities to help new hires learn how to anticipate guests' needs, requirements, and actions and appropriately respond to them.[16] The aim of training is to help ensure that all employees, regardless of area or function, provide consistently high quality and highly responsive customer service. Since customer service is everyone's responsibility, the Four Seasons has no separate customer service department per se. Training is ongoing at the Four Seasons and never really stops.[17]

The Four Seasons also tends to promote from within.[18] For example, while recent college graduates may start out as assistant managers, those who do well and have high aspirations could potentially become general managers in less than 15 years.

This helps to ensure that managers have empathy and respect for those in lower-level positions as well as the ingrained ethos of treating others (employees, subordinates, coworkers, and customers) as they would like to be treated. All in all, treating employees well leads to satisfied customers at the Four Seasons.[19]

Overview

LO12-1

Explain why strategic human resource management can help an organization gain a competitive advantage.

Managers are responsible for acquiring, developing, protecting, and utilizing the resources an organization needs to be efficient and effective. One of the most important resources in all organizations is human resources—the people involved in producing and distributing goods and services. Human resources include all members of an organization, ranging from top managers to entry-level employees. Effective managers like Isadore Sharp and Nick Mutton in "A Manager's Challenge" realize how valuable human resources are and take active steps to make sure their organizations build and fully utilize their human resources to gain a competitive advantage.

This chapter examines how managers can tailor their human resource management system to their organization's strategy and structure. We discuss in particular the major components of human resource management: recruitment and selection, training and development, performance appraisal, pay and benefits, and labor relations. By the end of this chapter you will understand the central role human resource management plays in creating a high-performing organization.

Strategic Human Resource Management

human resource management (HRM)
Activities that managers engage in to attract and retain employees and to ensure that they perform at a high level and contribute to the accomplishment of organizational goals.

strategic human resource management The process by which managers design the components of an HRM system to be consistent with each other, with other elements of organizational architecture, and with the organization's strategy and goals.

Organizational architecture (see Chapter 10) is the combination of organizational structure, control systems, culture, and a human resource management system that managers develop to use resources efficiently and effectively. **Human resource management (HRM)** includes all the activities managers engage in to attract and retain employees and to ensure that they perform at a high level and contribute to the accomplishment of organizational goals. These activities make up an organization's human resource management system, which has five major components: recruitment and selection, training and development, performance appraisal and feedback, pay and benefits, and labor relations (see Figure 12.1).

Strategic human resource management is the process by which managers design the components of an HRM system to be consistent with each other, with other elements of organizational architecture, and with the organization's strategy and goals.[20] The objective of strategic HRM is the development of an HRM system that enhances an organization's efficiency, quality, innovation, and responsiveness to customers—the four building blocks of competitive advantage. At the Four Seasons in "A Manager's Challenge," HRM practices ensure that all employees provide excellent customer service.

As part of strategic human resource management, some managers have adopted Six Sigma quality improvement plans. These plans ensure that an organization's products and services are as free of errors or defects as possible through a variety of human resource–related initiatives. Jack Welch, former CEO of General Electric Company (GE), indicated that these initiatives saved GE millions of dollars; and other companies, such as Whirlpool and Motorola, also have implemented Six Sigma initiatives. For such initiatives to be effective, however, top

Figure 12.1

Components of a Human Resource Management System

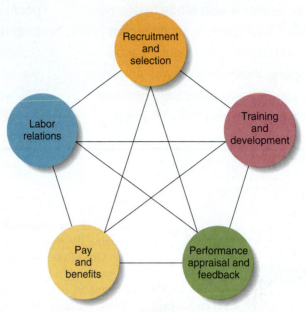

Each component of an HRM system influences
the others, and all five must fit together.

managers have to be committed to Six Sigma, employees must be motivated, and there must
be demand for the products or services of the organization in the first place. David Fitzpatrick, former head of Deloitte Consulting's Lean Enterprise Practice and currently a managing
director at AlixPartners Professionals,[21] estimated that most Six Sigma plans are not effective
because the conditions for effective Six Sigma are not in place. For example, if top managers are not committed to the quality initiative, they may not devote the necessary time and
resources to make it work and may lose interest in it prematurely.[22]

Overview of the Components of HRM

Managers use *recruitment and selection,* the first component of an HRM system, to attract
and hire new employees who have the abilities, skills, and experiences that will help an organization achieve its goals. Microsoft Corporation, for example, has the goal of remaining the
premier computer software company in the world. To achieve this goal, managers at Microsoft realize the importance of hiring only the best software designers: hundreds of highly
qualified candidates are interviewed and rigorously tested. This careful attention to selection
has contributed to Microsoft's competitive advantage. Microsoft has little trouble recruiting
top programmers because candidates know they will be at the forefront of the industry if they
work for Microsoft.[23]

After recruiting and selecting employees, managers use the second component, *training
and development,* to ensure that organizational members develop the skills and abilities that
will enable them to perform their jobs effectively in the present and the future. Training and
development are an ongoing process; changes in technology and the environment, as well
as in an organization's goals and strategies, often require that organizational members learn
new techniques and ways of working. At Microsoft, newly hired program designers receive
on-the-job training by joining small teams that include experienced employees who serve as
mentors or advisers. New recruits learn firsthand from team members how to develop computer systems that are responsive to customers' programming needs.[24]

Recruiting and selecting employees and providing training and development often go hand-
in-hand, as is true at Zappos, profiled in the accompanying "Management Insight" feature.

Management Insight

Recruitment and Selection and Training and Development at Zappos

Nothing is conventional about the online retailer Zappos, headquartered in Henderson, Nevada.[25] Think accountants running Pinewood Derby car races during the workday, a conference room that a team decorated to simulate a log cabin, employees ringing cowbells and blowing horns during visitor tours, costume parades, and managers spending 10–20 percent of their time socializing with their subordinates.[26] And the list could go on. Yet Zappos, founded in 1999 as a struggling online shoe shop, rode out the dot-com bust to earn over $1.6 billion in annual revenues in 2010 and be ranked 38th on *Fortune* magazine's list of the One Hundred Best Companies to Work For in 2014.[27] In 2009 Amazon.com purchased Zappos for shares worth $1.2 billion.[28] As a wholly owned subsidiary of Amazon, Zappos continues to be led by its long-standing CEO Tony Hsieh; Hsieh was the initial primary investor who kept Zappos afloat as a start-up and became its CEO in 2000.[29]

Training at Zappos for new employees of the Customer Loyalty Team. Zappos' careful attention to recruitment, selection, and training have contributed to the company's success, as has a work environment geared toward making employees happy.

Zappos has expanded from selling shoes to selling a wide range of products ranging from clothing and handbags to housewares, watches, and jewelry.[30] What is distinctive about Zappos is not so much the products it sells but rather the exceptional service it provides customers.[31] In fact, central to the guiding philosophy at Zappos is having a happy workforce of satisfied employees who actually want to come to work each day and have fun on and off the job.[32] Thus Hsieh and other managers at Zappos go to great lengths to ensure that the Zappos core values and unique culture are maintained and strengthened. The core values of Zappos are these: "1. Deliver WOW through Service; 2. Embrace and Drive Change; 3. Create Fun and a Little Weirdness; 4. Be Adventurous, Creative, and Open-Minded; 5. Pursue Growth and Learning; 6. Build Open and Honest Relationships with Communication; 7. Build a Positive Team and Family Spirit; 8. Do More with Less; 9. Be Passionate and Determined; 10. Be Humble."[33]

Because of the importance of having happy employees, Zappos goes to great lengths to effectively manage human resources. Potential new hires are interviewed by human resources, to make sure they will work well in Zappos's culture and support its values, as well as by the department doing the hiring, to determine their suitability for the position they are interviewing for. If human resources and the hiring manager disagree in their assessments of an applicant, Hsieh interviews the applicant himself and makes the final decision.[34]

Newly hired employees receive extensive training. For example, the Customer Loyalty Team (CLT) new hires who answer calls have two weeks of classroom training followed by two weeks of training in answering calls. Once the training is completed, they are given the opportunity to receive $2,000 and pay for the time they spent in training if they want to quit.[35] This way only new hires who want to stay with the company remain.

Experienced employees are encouraged to continue to grow and develop on the job. For example, employees who have worked at Zappos for two or fewer years have over 200 hours of classroom training and development during their work hours and are required to read nine books about business. More experienced employees receive training and development in such areas as financial planning and speaking in public. Zappos has a company library well stocked with multiple copies of business books and books about personal growth and development for employees to borrow and read. Training and development at Zappos not only help to keep employees happy but also help them gain the skills and abilities needed to advance to higher-level positions in the company.[36] All in all, careful attention to recruitment and selection and training and development have certainly contributed to Zappo's ongoing success story.

The third component, *performance appraisal and feedback,* serves two different purposes in HRM. First, performance appraisal can give managers the information they need to make good human resources decisions—decisions about how to train, motivate, and reward organizational members.[37] Thus the performance appraisal and feedback component is a kind of *control system* that can be used with management by objectives (discussed in Chapter 11). Second, feedback from performance appraisal serves a developmental purpose for members of an organization. When managers regularly evaluate their subordinates' performance, they can give employees valuable information about their strengths and weaknesses and the areas in which they need to concentrate.

On the basis of performance appraisals, managers distribute *pay* to employees, which is part of the fourth component of an HRM system. By rewarding high-performing organizational members with pay raises, bonuses, and the like, managers increase the likelihood that an organization's most valued human resources will be motivated to continue their high levels of contribution to the organization. Moreover, if pay is linked to performance, high-performing employees are more likely to stay with the organization, and managers are more likely to fill positions that become open with highly talented individuals. *Benefits* such as health insurance are important outcomes that employees receive by virtue of their membership in an organization.

Last but not least, *labor relations* encompass the steps that managers take to develop and maintain good working relationships with the labor unions that may represent their employees' interests. For example, an organization's labor relations component can help managers establish safe working conditions and fair labor practices in their offices and plants.

Managers must ensure that all five of these components fit together and complement their company's structure and control systems.[38] For example, if managers decide to decentralize authority and empower employees, they need to invest in training and development to ensure that lower-level employees have the knowledge and expertise they need to make the decisions that top managers would make in a more centralized structure.

Each of the five components of HRM influences the others (see Figure 12.1).[39] The kinds of people that the organization attracts and hires through recruitment and selection, for example, determine (1) the kinds of training and development that are necessary, (2) the way performance is appraised, and (3) the appropriate levels of pay and benefits. Managers at Microsoft ensure that their organization has highly qualified program designers by (1) recruiting and selecting the best candidates, (2) guiding new hires with experienced team members, (3) appraising program designers' performance in terms of their individual contributions and their teams' performance, and (4) basing programmers' pay on individual and team performance.

Effectively managing human resources helps ensure that both customers and employees are satisfied and loyal, as illustrated in the accompanying "Managing Globally" feature.

Managing Globally

Managing Human Resources at Semco

Ricardo Semler was 21 years old (and one of the youngest graduates from the Harvard Business School MBA program) when he took his father's place as head of the family business, Semco, based in São Paolo, Brazil, in 1984.[40] His father Antonio had founded Semco in 1954 as a machine shop; the company went on to become a manufacturer of marine pumps for the shipbuilding industry, with $4 million a year in revenues when Ricardo Semler took over. Today Semco's revenues are over $200 million a year from a diverse set of businesses ranging from the development and manufacture of industrial mixing and refrigeration equipment to the provision of systems to manage communication, correspondence, and goods exchanges between an organization and its suppliers, customers, and partners.[41] Semco prides itself on being a premier provider of goods and services in its markets and has loyal customers.[42]

Semler is the first to admit that Semco's track record of success is due to its human resources—its employees. In fact, Semler so firmly believes in Semco's employees that he and the other top managers are reluctant to tell employees what to do. Semco has no rules, regulations, or organizational charts; hierarchy is eschewed; and workplace democracy rules the day. Employees have levels of autonomy unheard of in other companies, and flexibility and trust are built into every aspect of human resource management at Semco.[43]

Human resource practices at Semco revolve around maximizing the contributions employees make to the company, and this begins by hiring individuals who want to, can, and will contribute. Semco strives to ensure that all selection decisions are based on relevant and complete information. Job candidates are first interviewed as a group; the candidates meet many employees, receive a tour of the company, and interact with potential coworkers. This gives Semco a chance to size up candidates in ways more likely to reveal their true natures, and it gives the candidates a chance to learn about Semco. When finalists are identified from the pool, multiple Semco employees interview each finalist five or six more times to choose the best person(s) to be hired. The result is that both Semco and new hires make informed decisions and are mutually committed to making the relationship a success.[44]

Once hired, entry-level employees participate in the Lost in Space program, in which they rotate through different positions and units of their own choosing for about a year.[45] In this way, the new hires learn about their options and can decide where their interests lie, and the units they work in learn about the new hires. At the end of the year, the new employees may be offered a job in one of the units in which they worked, or they may seek a position elsewhere in Semco. Seasoned Semco employees are also encouraged to rotate positions and work in different parts of the company to keep them fresh, energized, and motivated and to give them the opportunity to contribute in new ways as their interests change.[46]

Performance is appraised at Semco in terms of results; all employees and managers must demonstrate that they are making valuable contributions and deserve to be "rehired." For example, each manager's performance is anonymously appraised by all the employees who report to him or her, and the appraisals are made publicly available in Semco. Employees also can choose how they are paid from a combination of 11 different compensation options, ranging from fixed salaries, bonuses, and profit sharing to royalties on sales or profits and arrangements based on meeting annual self-set goals. Flexibility in compensation promotes risk taking and innovation, according to Semler, and maximizes returns to employees in terms of their pay and to the company in terms of revenues and profitability.[47] Flexibility, autonomy, the ability to change jobs often, and control of working hours and even compensation are some of the ways by which Semler strives to ensure that employees are loyal and involved in their work because they *want* to be; turnover at Semco is less than 1 percent annually.[48] And with human resource practices geared toward maximizing contributions and performance, Semco is well poised to continue to provide value to its customers.

The Legal Environment of HRM

In the rest of this chapter we focus in detail on the choices managers must make in strategically managing human resources to attain organizational goals and gain a competitive advantage. Effectively managing human resources is a complex undertaking for managers, and we provide an overview of some major issues they face. First, however, we need to look at how the legal environment affects human resource management.

The local, state, and national laws and regulations that managers and organizations must abide by add to the complexity of HRM. For example, the U.S. government's commitment

Table 12.1

Major Equal Employment Opportunity Laws Affecting HRM

Year	Law	Description
1963	Equal Pay Act	Requires that men and women be paid equally if they are performing equal work.
1964	Title VII of the Civil Rights Act	Prohibits employment discrimination on the basis of race, religion, sex, color, or national origin; covers a wide range of employment decisions, including hiring, firing, pay, promotion, and working conditions.
1967	Age Discrimination in Employment Act	Prohibits discrimination against workers over the age of 40 and restricts mandatory retirement.
1978	Pregnancy Discrimination Act	Prohibits employment discrimination against women on the basis of pregnancy, childbirth, and related medical decisions.
1990	Americans with Disabilities Act	Prohibits employment discrimination against individuals with disabilities and requires that employers make accommodations for such workers to enable them to perform their jobs.
1991	Civil Rights Act	Prohibits discrimination (as does Title VII) and allows the awarding of punitive and compensatory damages, in addition to back pay, in cases of intentional discrimination.
1993	Family and Medical Leave Act	Requires that employers provide 12 weeks of unpaid leave for medical and family reasons, including paternity and illness of a family member.

equal employment opportunity (EEO) The equal right of all citizens to the opportunity to obtain employment regardless of their gender, age, race, country of origin, religion, or disabilities.

to **equal employment opportunity (EEO)** has resulted in the creation and enforcement of a number of laws that managers must abide by. The goal of EEO is to ensure that all citizens have an equal opportunity to obtain employment regardless of their gender, race, country of origin, religion, age, or disabilities. Table 12.1 summarizes some of the major EEO laws affecting HRM. Other laws, such as the Occupational Safety and Health Act of 1970, require that managers ensure that employees are protected from workplace hazards and safety standards are met.

In Chapter 5 we explained how effectively managing diversity is an ethical and business imperative, and we discussed the many issues surrounding diversity. EEO laws and their enforcement make the effective management of diversity a legal imperative as well. The Equal Employment Opportunity Commission (EEOC) is the division of the Department of Justice that enforces most EEO laws and handles discrimination complaints. In addition, the EEOC issues guidelines for managers to follow to ensure that they are abiding by EEO laws. For example, the Uniform Guidelines on Employee Selection Procedures issued by the EEOC (in conjunction with the Departments of Labor and Justice and the Civil Service Commission) guide managers on how to ensure that the recruitment and selection component of human resource management complies with Title VII of the Civil Rights Act (which prohibits discrimination based on gender, race, color, religion, and national origin).[49]

Contemporary challenges that managers face related to the legal environment include how to eliminate sexual harassment (see Chapter 5 for an in-depth discussion of sexual harassment), how to accommodate employees with disabilities, how to deal with employees who have substance abuse problems, and how to manage HIV-positive employees and employees with AIDS.[50] HIV-positive employees are infected with the virus that causes AIDS but may show no AIDS symptoms and may not develop AIDS in the near future. Often such employees are able to perform their jobs effectively, and managers must take steps to ensure that they are allowed to do so and are not discriminated against in the workplace.[51] Employees with AIDS may or may not be able to perform their jobs effectively, and, once again, managers need to ensure that they are not unfairly discriminated against.[52] Many organizations have

LO12-2

Describe the steps managers take to recruit and select organizational members.

instituted AIDS awareness training programs to educate organizational members about HIV and AIDS, dispel myths about how HIV is spread, and ensure that individuals infected with the HIV virus are treated fairly and are able to be productive as long as they can be while not putting others at risk.[53]

Recruitment and Selection

recruitment Activities that managers engage in to develop a pool of qualified candidates for open positions.

selection The process that managers use to determine the relative qualifications of job applicants and their potential for performing well in a particular job.

human resource planning Activities that managers engage in to forecast their current and future needs for human resources.

outsource To use outside suppliers and manufacturers to produce goods and services.

Recruitment includes all the activities managers engage in to develop a pool of qualified candidates for open positions.[54] **Selection** is the process by which managers determine the relative qualifications of job applicants and their potential for performing well in a particular job. Before actually recruiting and selecting employees, managers need to engage in two important activities: human resource planning and job analysis (Figure 12.2).

Human Resource Planning

Human resource planning includes all the activities managers engage in to forecast their current and future human resource needs. Current human resources are the employees an organization needs today to provide high-quality goods and services to customers. Future human resource needs are the employees the organization will need at some later date to achieve its longer-term goals.

As part of human resource planning, managers must make both demand forecasts and supply forecasts. *Demand forecasts* estimate the qualifications and numbers of employees an organization will need given its goals and strategies. *Supply forecasts* estimate the availability and qualifications of current employees now and in the future, as well as the supply of qualified workers in the external labor market.

As a result of their human resource planning, managers sometimes decide to **outsource** to fill some of their human resource needs. Instead of recruiting and selecting employees to produce goods and services, managers contract with people who are not members of their organization to produce goods and services. Managers in publishing companies, for example, frequently contract with freelance editors to copyedit books that they intend to publish. Kelly Services is an organization that provides the services of technical and professional employees to managers who want to use outsourcing to fill some of their human resource requirements in these areas.[55]

Two reasons why human resource planning sometimes leads managers to outsource are flexibility and cost. First, outsourcing can give managers increased flexibility, especially when accurately forecasting human resource needs is difficult, human resource needs fluctuate over time, or finding skilled workers in a particular area is difficult. Second, outsourcing can sometimes allow managers to use human resources at a lower cost. When work is outsourced, costs can be lower for a number of reasons: The organization does not have to provide benefits to workers; managers can contract for work only when the work is needed; and managers do not have to invest in training. Outsourcing can be used for functional activities

Figure 12.2
The Recruitment and Selection System

such as after-sales service on appliances and equipment, legal work, and the management of information systems.[56]

Outsourcing has disadvantages, however.[57] When work is outsourced, managers may lose some control over the quality of goods and services. Also, individuals performing outsourced work may have less knowledge of organizational practices, procedures, and goals and less commitment to an organization than regular employees. In addition, unions resist outsourcing because it has the potential to eliminate some of their members. To gain some of the flexibility and cost savings of outsourcing and avoid some of its disadvantages, a number of organizations, such as Microsoft and IBM, rely on a pool of temporary employees to, for example, debug programs.

A major trend reflecting the increasing globalization of business is the outsourcing of office work, computer programming, and technical jobs from the United States and countries in western Europe, with high labor costs, to countries like India and China, with low labor costs.[58] For example, computer programmers in India and China earn a fraction of what their U.S. counterparts earn. Outsourcing (or *offshoring,* as it is also called when work is outsourced to other countries) has also expanded into knowledge-intensive work such as engineering, research and development, and the development of computer software. According to a study conducted by The Conference Board and Duke University's Offshoring Research Network, more than half of U.S. companies surveyed have some kind of offshoring strategy related to knowledge-intensive work and innovation.[59] Why are so many companies engaged in offshoring, and why are companies that already offshore work planning to increase the extent of offshoring? While cost savings continue to be a major motivation for offshoring, managers also want to take advantage of an increasingly talented global workforce and be closer to the growing global marketplace for goods and services.[60]

Major U.S. companies often earn a substantial portion of their revenues overseas. For example, Hewlett-Packard, Caterpillar, and IBM earn over 60 percent of their revenues from overseas markets. And many large companies employ thousands of workers overseas. For example, IBM employs close to 100,000 workers in India and Hewlett-Packard, over 25,000.[61] Managers at some smaller companies have offshored work to Sri Lanka, Russia, and Egypt.[62] Key challenges for managers who offshore are retaining sufficient managerial control over activities and employee turnover.[63] In recent times, there have been some interesting developments in outsourcing to other countries, as profiled in the accompanying "Managing Globally" feature.

Managing
Globally

Recent Trends in Outsourcing

Countries in Latin America and Eastern Europe are becoming increasingly popular outsourcing destinations for skilled professional workers in the areas of finance, accounting, research, and procurement. For example, São Paulo, Brazil, has a sizable population of engineering and business school graduates who speak English and can perform a diverse set of tasks ranging from financial analysis to video game development.[64] A Brazilian trade group for technology, Brasscom,[65] indicates that there are more Java programmers in Brazil than in any other country and Brazil has the second highest number of COBOL programmers. Thus perhaps it is not surprising that IBM's ninth research center is located in São Paulo.[66]

It typically costs more to outsource work to Latin American countries than to India. For example, outsourcing an entry-level accounting job to India costs around 51 percent less than hiring a worker in the United States; outsourcing the same job to Argentina costs about 13 percent less than hiring a U.S. worker.[67] However, if the Argentinian has a better understanding of business and is more skilled at interacting with clients, bearing the added costs might make sense. Additionally, if client interaction levels are high, it is advantageous for outsourcing countries and home countries to be in similar time zones. The time difference between New York and Argentina,

Indian office workers face a downswing in the amount of outsourced jobs from the United States. Argentina offers stiff competition with skilled workers whose hours are more closely aligned to the U.S. time zones but who can still be paid less than their U.S. counterparts.

for example, is much smaller than the time difference between New York and India.[68]

Copal Amba, an outsourcing/offshoring company that provides research and analytic services for global corporations and financial institutions, has offices in West Chester, Pennsylvania, Beijing, China, Gurgaon and Bangalore, India, Argentina, San Jose, Costa Rica, Prague, Czech Republic, and Colombo, Sri Lanka, in part because of the benefits of being in a closer time zone with clients.[69] As Rishi Khosla, the chairman and CEO of Copal Amba[70] put it, "If you're working with a hedge fund manager where you have to interact 10 to 15 times a day, having someone in about the same time zone is important."[71] Tata Consultancy Services, the Indian outsourcing giant, has over 8,000 employees in South American countries, including Peru and Paraguay.[72]

Countries in Eastern Europe are also seeing surges in outsourcing. For example, Microsoft, Ernst & Young, and IBM have all opened outsourcing facilities in Wroclaw, Poland. Ernst & Young actually has six outsourcing centers in cities in Poland that together have around 1,300 employees.[73] Young people in Poland are more likely to be college educated than in India, and they tend to be multilingual. Jacek Levernes, who managed outsourcing to Europe, Africa, and the Middle East for Hewlett-Packard's Wroclaw, Poland, facility indicated that having 26 different languages spoken in the center was advantageous for interacting with clients in different countries in these regions. Guatemala is also an outsourcing destination for companies like Capgemini Consulting and Coca-Cola enterprises. Evidently the trend toward "near-shoring" to countries closer to home has advantages.[74]

Job Analysis

job analysis Identifying the tasks, duties, and responsibilities that make up a job and the knowledge, skills, and abilities needed to perform the job.

Job analysis is a second important activity that managers need to undertake prior to recruitment and selection.[75] **Job analysis** is the process of identifying (1) the tasks, duties, and responsibilities that make up a job (the *job description*) and (2) the knowledge, skills, and abilities needed to perform the job (the *job specifications*).[76] For each job in an organization, a job analysis needs to be done.

Job analysis can be done in a number of ways, including observing current employees as they perform the job or interviewing them. Often managers rely on questionnaires compiled by jobholders and their managers. The questionnaires ask about the skills and abilities needed to perform the job, job tasks and the amount of time spent on them, responsibilities, supervisory activities, equipment used, reports prepared, and decisions made.[77] The Position Analysis Questionnaire (PAQ) is a comprehensive standardized questionnaire that many managers rely on to conduct job analyses.[78] It focuses on behaviors jobholders perform, working conditions, and job characteristics and can be used for a variety of jobs.[79] The PAQ contains 194 items organized into six divisions: (1) information input (where and how the jobholder acquires information to perform the job), (2) mental processes (reasoning, decision making, planning, and information processing activities that are part of the job), (3) work output (physical activities performed on the job and machines and devices used), (4) relationships with others (interactions with other people that are necessary to perform the job), (5) job context (the physical and social environment of the job), and (6) other job characteristics (such as work pace).[80] A trend, in some organizations, is toward more flexible jobs in which tasks and responsibilities change and cannot be clearly specified in advance. For these kinds of jobs, job analysis focuses more on determining the skills and knowledge workers need to be effective and less on specific duties.

After managers have completed human resource planning and job analyses for all jobs in an organization, they will know their human resource needs and the jobs they need to fill. They will also know what knowledge, skills, and abilities potential employees need to perform those jobs. At this point, recruitment and selection can begin.

External and Internal Recruitment

As noted earlier, recruitment is what managers do to develop a pool of qualified candidates for open positions.[81] They traditionally have used two main types of recruiting, external and internal, which are now supplemented by recruiting over the Internet.

EXTERNAL RECRUITING   When managers recruit externally to fill open positions, they look outside the organization for people who have not worked for the organization previously. There are multiple means through which managers can recruit externally: advertisements in newspapers and magazines, open houses for students and career counselors at high schools and colleges or on-site at the organization, career fairs at colleges, and recruitment meetings with groups in the local community.

Many large organizations send teams of interviewers to college campuses to recruit new employees. External recruitment can also take place through informal networks, as occurs when current employees inform friends about open positions in their companies or recommend people they know to fill vacant spots. Some organizations use employment agencies for external recruitment, and some external recruitment takes place simply through walk-ins—job hunters coming to an organization and inquiring about employment possibilities.

With all the downsizing and corporate layoffs that have taken place in recent years, you might think external recruiting would be a relatively easy task for managers. However, it often is not, because even though many people may be looking for jobs, many jobs that are open require skills and abilities that these job hunters do not have. Managers needing to fill vacant positions and job hunters seeking employment opportunities are increasingly relying on the Internet to connect with each other through employment websites such as Monster. com[82] and JobLine International.[83] Major corporations such as Coca-Cola, Cisco, Ernst & Young, Canon, and Telia have relied on JobLine to fill global positions.[84]

External recruiting has both advantages and disadvantages for managers. Advantages include having access to a potentially large applicant pool, being able to attract people who have the skills, knowledge, and abilities that an organization needs to achieve its goals, and being able to bring in newcomers who may have a fresh approach to problems and be up to date on the latest technology. These advantages have to be weighed against the disadvantages, including the relatively high costs of external recruitment. Employees recruited externally lack knowledge about the inner workings of the organization and may need to receive more training than those recruited internally. Finally, when employees are recruited externally, there is always uncertainty concerning whether they will actually be good performers. Nonetheless, managers can take steps to reduce some of the uncertainty surrounding external recruitment, as profiled in the accompanying "Information Technology Byte" feature.

Information Technology Byte

Fog Creek Software's Approach to Recruiting

Fog Creek Software is a small, privately owned software company founded in 2000 by Joel Spolsky and Michael Pryor in a renovated loft in the Fashion District of New York City.[85] Fog Creek has earned a profit each year since its founding.[86] Hiring great computer software developers is essential for a company like Fog Creek; according to Spolsky, the top 1 percent of software developers outperform average developers by a ratio of around 10:1. And the top 1 percent are the inventive types who can successfully develop new products while also being highly efficient.[87]

Fog Creek Software uses paid summer internships to help identify and attract promising software developers.

Finding, never mind recruiting, the top 1 percent is a real challenge for a small company like Fog Creek because many of these people already have great jobs and are not looking to switch employers. Realizing that the top 1 percent of developers might rarely apply for positions with Fog Creek (or any other company), Fog Creek uses paid summer internships to recruit over 50 percent of its developers while they are still in college; they are hired full-time after graduation.[88]

In the fall of every year, Fog Creek sends personalized letters to computer science majors across the country who have the potential to be top developers in the future, contacts professors at leading computer science programs for recommendations, and also seeks applications through its website.[89] This process yields hundreds of applicants for internships, the best of whom are then given a phone interview. During the interview, the candidates describe themselves and their classes, are asked how they would go about solving a software development problem or challenge, and then can ask anything they want about the company or living in New York City.[90]

Those who do well in the phone interview are flown to New York for an all-expense paid visit to Fog Creek—they are met at the airport in a limousine, stay in a hip hotel, receive welcoming gifts in their rooms, have a full day of interviews at Fog Creek, and then are given the option of staying two extra nights (at no cost to themselves) to get a feel for New York City. Typically only one out of every three recruits who has an on-site visit receives an internship offer.[91]

Interns perform real software development work—several summers ago, a team of four interns developed a new successful technology support product called Fog Creek Copilot.[92] This both motivates the interns and helps managers decide which interns they would like to hire. The interns are treated well—in addition to being paid, they receive free housing and are invited to outings, parties, and cultural events in New York City. At the conclusion of the internships, managers have a good sense of which interns are great programmers. These top programmers are offered jobs upon graduation with generous salaries, excellent working conditions, and great benefits. Although Fog Creek's approach to external recruitment is lengthy and expensive, it more than pays for itself by identifying and attracting top programmers. As Spolsky indicates, "An internship program creates a pipeline for great employees. It's a pretty long pipeline, so you need to have a long-term perspective, but it pays off in spades."[93]

lateral move A job change that entails no major changes in responsibility or authority levels.

INTERNAL RECRUITING   When recruiting is internal, managers turn to existing employees to fill open positions. Employees recruited internally are either seeking **lateral moves** (job changes that entail no major changes in responsibility or authority levels) or promotions. Internal recruiting has several advantages. First, internal applicants are already familiar with the organization (including its goals, structure, culture, rules, and norms). Second, managers already know the candidates; they have considerable information about their skills and abilities and actual behavior on the job. Third, internal recruiting can help boost levels of employee motivation and morale, both for the employee who gets the job and for other workers. Those who are not seeking a promotion or who may not be ready for one can see that promotion is a possibility in the future; or a lateral move can alleviate boredom once a job has been fully mastered and can also be a useful way to learn new skills. Finally, internal recruiting is normally less time-consuming and expensive than external recruiting.

Given the advantages of internal recruiting, why do managers rely on external recruiting as much as they do? The answer lies in the disadvantages of internal recruiting—among them, a limited pool of candidates and a tendency among those candidates to be set in the organization's ways. Often the organization simply does not have suitable internal candidates. Sometimes, even when suitable internal applicants are available, managers may rely on external recruiting to find the very best candidate or to help bring new ideas and approaches into their organization. When organizations are in trouble and performing poorly, external recruiting is often relied on to bring in managerial talent with a fresh approach.

HONESTY IN RECRUITING   At times, when trying to recruit the most qualified applicants, managers may be tempted to paint rosy pictures of both the open positions and the organization as a whole. They may worry that if they are honest about advantages and disadvantages, they either will not be able to fill positions or will have fewer or less qualified applicants. A manager trying to fill a secretarial position, for example, may emphasize the high level of pay and benefits the job offers and fail to mention the fact that the position is usually a dead-end job offering few opportunities for promotion.

Research suggests that painting a rosy picture of a job and the organization is not a wise recruiting strategy. Recruitment is more likely to be effective when managers give potential applicants an honest assessment of both the advantages and the disadvantages of the job and organization. Such an assessment is called a **realistic job preview (RJP)**.[94] RJPs can reduce the number of new hires who quit when their jobs and organizations fail to meet their unrealistic expectations, and they help applicants decide for themselves whether a job is right for them.

Take the earlier example of the manager trying to recruit a secretary. The manager who paints a rosy picture of the job might have an easy time filling it but might hire a secretary who expects to be promoted quickly to an administrative assistant position. After a few weeks on the job, the secretary may realize that a promotion is unlikely no matter how good his or her performance, become dissatisfied, and look for and accept another job. The manager then has to recruit, select, and train another new secretary. The manager could have avoided this waste of valuable organizational resources by using a realistic job preview. The RJP would have increased the likelihood of hiring a secretary who was comfortable with few promotional opportunities and subsequently would have been satisfied to remain on the job.

realistic job preview (RJP) An honest assessment of the advantages and disadvantages of a job and organization.

The Selection Process

Once managers develop a pool of applicants for open positions through the recruitment process, they need to find out whether each applicant is qualified for the position and likely to be a good performer. If more than one applicant meets these two conditions, managers must further determine which applicants are likely to be better performers than others. They have several selection tools to help them sort out the relative qualifications of job applicants and appraise their potential for being good performers in a particular job. These tools include background information, interviews, paper-and-pencil tests, physical ability tests, performance tests, and references (see Figure 12.3).[95]

BACKGROUND INFORMATION   To aid in the selection process, managers obtain background information from job applications and from résumés. Such information might include the highest levels of education obtained, college majors and minors, type of college or university attended, years and type of work experience, and mastery of foreign languages. Background information can be helpful both to screen out applicants who are lacking key qualifications (such as a college degree) and to determine which qualified applicants are more promising than others. For example, applicants with a BS may be acceptable, but those who also have an MBA may be preferable.

Increasing numbers of organizations are performing background checks to verify the background information prospective employees provide (and also to uncover any negative information such as crime convictions).[96] According to Automatic Data Processing, Inc. (ADP), an outsourcing company that performs payroll and human resource functions for organizations, more and more companies are performing background checks on prospective employees and are uncovering inaccuracies, inconsistencies, and negative information not reported on applications.[97] According to ADP, about 30 percent of applicants provide some form of false information about their employment history.[98] And in some cases, background checks reveal prior convictions.[99]

Figure 12.3
Selection Tools

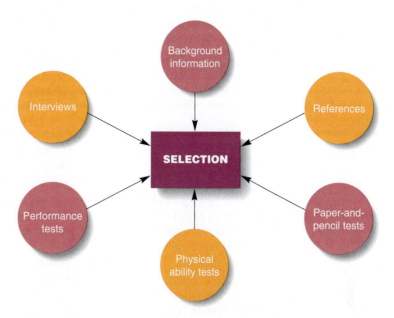

INTERVIEWS Virtually all organizations use interviews during the selection process, as is true at the Four Seasons in "A Manager's Challenge." Interviews may be structured or unstructured. In a *structured interview,* managers ask each applicant the same standard questions (such as "What are your unique qualifications for this position?" and "What characteristics of a job are most important to you?"). Particularly informative questions may be those that prompt an interviewee to demonstrate skills and abilities needed for the job by answering the question. Sometimes called *situational interview questions,* these often present interviewees with a scenario they would likely encounter on the job and ask them to indicate how they would handle it.[100] For example, applicants for a sales job may be asked to indicate how they would respond to a customer who complains about waiting too long for service, a customer who is indecisive, and a customer whose order is lost.

An *unstructured interview* proceeds more like an ordinary conversation. The interviewer feels free to ask probing questions to discover what the applicant is like and does not ask a fixed set of questions determined in advance. In general, structured interviews are superior to unstructured interviews because they are more likely to yield information that will help identify qualified candidates, are less subjective, and may be less influenced by the interviewer's biases.

Even when structured interviews are used, however, the potential exists for the interviewer's biases to influence his or her judgment. Recall from Chapter 5 how the similar-to-me effect can cause people to perceive others who are similar to themselves more positively than those who are different and how stereotypes can result in inaccurate perceptions. Interviewers must be trained to avoid these biases and sources of inaccurate perceptions as much as possible. Many of the approaches to increasing diversity awareness and diversity skills described in Chapter 5 are used to train interviewers to avoid the effects of biases and stereotypes. In addition, using multiple interviewers can be advantageous because their individual biases and idiosyncrasies may cancel one another out.[101]

When conducting interviews, managers cannot ask questions that are irrelevant to the job in question; otherwise their organizations run the risk of costly lawsuits. It is inappropriate and illegal, for example, to inquire about an interviewee's spouse or to ask questions about whether an interviewee plans to have children. Because questions such as these are irrelevant to job performance, they are discriminatory and violate EEO laws (see Table 12.1). Thus interviewers need to be instructed in EEO laws and informed about questions that may violate those laws.

Managers can use interviews at various stages in the selection process. Some use interviews as initial screening devices; others use them as a final hurdle that applicants must jump. Regardless of when they are used, managers typically use other selection tools in conjunction with interviews because of the potential for bias and for inaccurate assessments of interviewees. Even though training and structured interviews can eliminate the effects of some biases, interviewers can still come to erroneous conclusions about interviewees' qualifications. Interviewees, for example, who make a bad initial impression or are overly nervous in the first minute or two of an interview tend to be judged more harshly than less nervous candidates, even if the rest of the interview goes well.

PAPER-AND-PENCIL TESTS   The two main kinds of paper-and-pencil tests used for selection purposes are ability tests and personality tests; both kinds of tests can be administered in hard copy or electronic form. *Ability tests* assess the extent to which applicants possess the skills necessary for job performance, such as verbal comprehension or numerical skills. Autoworkers hired by General Motors, Chrysler, and Ford, for example, are typically tested for their ability to read and to do mathematics.[102]

Personality tests measure personality traits and characteristics relevant to job performance. Some retail organizations, for example, give job applicants honesty tests to determine how trustworthy they are. The use of personality tests (including honesty tests) for hiring purposes is controversial. Some critics maintain that honesty tests do not really measure honesty (that is, they are not valid) and can be faked by job applicants. Before using any paper-and-pencil tests for selection purposes, managers must have sound evidence that the tests are actually good predictors of performance on the job in question. Managers who use tests without such evidence may be subject to costly discrimination lawsuits.

PHYSICAL ABILITY TESTS   For jobs requiring physical abilities, such as firefighting, garbage collecting, and package delivery, managers use physical ability tests that measure physical strength and stamina as selection tools. Autoworkers are typically tested for mechanical dexterity because this physical ability is an important skill for high job performance in many auto plants.[103]

PERFORMANCE TESTS   *Performance tests* measure job applicants' performance on actual job tasks. Applicants for secretarial positions, for example, typically are required to complete a keyboarding test that measures how quickly and accurately they type. Applicants for middle and top management positions are sometimes given short-term projects to complete—projects that mirror the kinds of situations that arise in the job being filled—to assess their knowledge and problem-solving capabilities.[104]

Assessment centers, first used by AT&T, take performance tests one step further. In a typical assessment center, about 10 to 15 candidates for managerial positions participate in a variety of activities over a few days. During this time they are assessed for the skills an effective manager needs—problem-solving, organizational, communication, and conflict resolution skills. Some of the activities are performed individually; others are performed in groups. Throughout the process, current managers observe the candidates' behavior and measure performance. Summary evaluations are then used as a selection tool.

REFERENCES   Applicants for many jobs are required to provide references from former employers or other knowledgeable sources (such as a college instructor or adviser) who know the applicants' skills, abilities, and other personal characteristics. These individuals are asked to provide candid information about the applicant. References are often used at the end of the selection process to confirm a decision to hire. Yet the fact that many former employers are reluctant to provide negative information in references sometimes makes it difficult to interpret what a reference is really saying about an applicant.

In fact, several recent lawsuits filed by applicants who felt that they were unfairly denigrated or had their privacy invaded by unfavorable references from former employers have caused managers to be increasingly wary of providing any negative information in a reference, even if it is accurate. For jobs in which the jobholder is responsible for the safety and lives of other people, however, failing to provide accurate negative information in a reference does not just mean that the wrong person might get hired; it may also mean that other people's lives will be at stake.

reliability The degree to which a tool or test measures the same thing each time it is used.

validity The degree to which a tool or test measures what it purports to measure.

THE IMPORTANCE OF RELIABILITY AND VALIDITY Whatever selection tools a manager uses need to be both reliable and valid. **Reliability** is the degree to which a tool or test measures the same thing each time it is administered. Scores on a selection test should be similar if the same person is assessed with the same tool on two different days; if there is quite a bit of variability, the tool is unreliable. For interviews, determining reliability is more complex because the dynamic is personal interpretation. That is why the reliability of interviews can be increased if two or more different qualified interviewers interview the same candidate. If the interviews are reliable, the interviewers should come to similar conclusions about the interviewee's qualifications.

Validity is the degree to which a tool measures what it purports to measure—for selection tools, it is the degree to which the test predicts performance on the tasks or job in question. Does a physical ability test used to select firefighters, for example, actually predict on-the-job performance? Do assessment center ratings actually predict managerial performance? Do keyboarding tests predict secretarial performance? These are all questions of validity. Honesty tests, for example, are controversial because it is not clear that they validly predict honesty in such jobs as retailing and banking.

Managers have an ethical and legal obligation to use reliable and valid selection tools. Yet reliability and validity are matters of degree rather than all-or-nothing characteristics. Thus managers should strive to use selection tools in such a way that they can achieve the greatest degree of reliability and validity. For ability tests of a particular skill, managers should keep up to date on the latest advances in the development of valid paper-and-pencil tests and use the test with the highest reliability and validity ratings for their purposes. Regarding interviews, managers can improve reliability by having more than one person interview job candidates.

LO12-3

Discuss the training and development options that ensure organizational members can effectively perform their jobs.

Training and Development

training Teaching organizational members how to perform their current jobs and helping them acquire the knowledge and skills they need to be effective performers.

development Building the knowledge and skills of organizational members so they are prepared to take on new responsibilities and challenges.

needs assessment An assessment of which employees need training or development and what type of skills or knowledge they need to acquire.

Training and development help to ensure that organizational members have the knowledge and skills needed to perform jobs effectively, take on new responsibilities, and adapt to changing conditions. **Training** focuses primarily on teaching organizational members how to perform their current jobs and helping them acquire the knowledge and skills they need to be effective performers. **Development** focuses on building the knowledge and skills of organizational members so they are prepared to take on new responsibilities and challenges. Training tends to be used more frequently at lower levels of an organization; development tends to be used more frequently with professionals and managers.

Before creating training and development programs, managers should perform a **needs assessment** to determine which employees need training or development and what type of skills or knowledge they need to acquire (see Figure 12.4).[105]

Types of Training

There are two types of training: classroom instruction and on-the-job training.

CLASSROOM INSTRUCTION Through classroom instruction, employees acquire knowledge and skills in a classroom setting. This instruction may take place within the organization or outside it, such as through courses at local colleges and universities. Many organizations establish their own formal instructional divisions—some are even called "colleges"—to provide needed classroom instruction. For example, at Disney, classroom instruction and other forms of training and developing are provided to employees at Disney University.[106]

Classroom instruction frequently uses videos and role playing in addition to traditional written materials, lectures, and group discussions. *Videos* can demonstrate appropriate and inappropriate job behaviors. For example, by watching an experienced salesperson effectively deal with a loud and angry customer, inexperienced salespeople can develop skills in handling similar situations. During *role playing*, trainees either directly participate in or watch others perform actual job activities in a simulated setting. At McDonald's Hamburger University, for example, role playing helps franchisees acquire the knowledge and skills they need to manage their restaurants.

Simulations also can be part of classroom instruction, particularly for complicated jobs that require an extensive amount of learning and in which errors carry a high cost. In a simulation, key aspects of the work situation and job tasks are duplicated as closely as possible in an

Figure 12.4
Training and Development

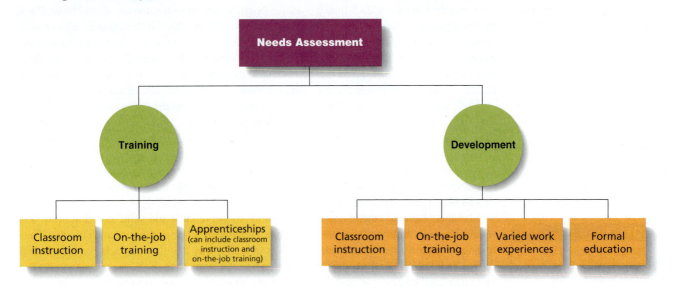

artificial setting. For example, air traffic controllers are trained by simulations because of the complicated nature of the work, the extensive amount of learning involved, and the very high costs of air traffic control errors.

on-the-job training Training that takes place in the work setting as employees perform their job tasks.

ON-THE-JOB TRAINING   In **on-the-job training,** learning occurs in the work setting as employees perform their job tasks. On-the-job training can be provided by coworkers or supervisors or can occur simply as jobholders gain experience and knowledge from doing the work. Newly hired waiters and waitresses in chains such as Red Lobster or the Olive Garden often receive on-the-job training from experienced employees. The supervisor of a new bus driver for a campus bus system may ride the bus for a week to ensure that the driver has learned the routes and follows safety procedures. Chefs learn to create new and innovative dishes by experimenting with different combinations of ingredients and cooking techniques. For all on-the-job training, employees learn by doing.

Managers often use on-the-job training on a continuing basis to ensure that their subordinates keep up to date with changes in goals, technology, products, or customer needs and desires. For example, sales representatives at Mary Kay Cosmetics Inc. receive ongoing training so they not only know about new cosmetic products and currently popular colors but also are reminded of Mary Kay's guiding principles. Mary Kay's expansion into Russia has succeeded in part because of the ongoing training that Mary Kay's Russian salespeople receive.[107]

At many restaurants, new employees receive on-the-job training by shadowing more experienced waiters and waitresses as they go about their work.

Types of Development

Although both classroom instruction and on-the-job training can be used for development as well as training, development often includes additional activities such as varied work experiences and formal education.

VARIED WORK EXPERIENCES   Top managers need to develop an understanding of, and expertise in, a variety of functions, products and services, and markets. To develop executives who will have this expertise, managers frequently make sure that employees with high potential have a wide variety of different job experiences, some in line positions and some in staff positions. Varied work experiences broaden employees' horizons and help them think about the big picture. For example, one- to three-year stints overseas are being used increasingly to provide managers with international work experiences. With organizations becoming more global, managers need to understand the different values, beliefs, cultures, regions, and ways of doing business in different countries.

Another development approach is mentoring. (Recall from Chapter 5 that a *mentor* is an experienced member of an organization who provides advice and guidance to a less experienced member, called a *protégé*.) Having a mentor can help managers seek out work experiences and assignments that will contribute to their development and can enable them to gain the most possible from varied work experiences.[108] Although some mentors and protégés hook up informally, organizations have found that formal mentoring programs can be valuable ways to contribute to the development of managers and all employees. For example, Goldman Sachs, Deloitte, and Time Inc. all have formal (and mandatory) mentoring programs.[109]

Formal mentoring programs ensure that mentoring takes place in an organization and structure the process. Participants receive training, efforts are focused on matching mentors and protégés so meaningful developmental relationships ensue, and organizations can track reactions and assess the potential benefits of mentoring. Formal mentoring programs can also ensure that diverse members of an organization receive the benefits of mentoring. A study conducted by David A. Thomas, a professor at the Harvard Business School, found that members of racial minority groups at three large corporations who were very successful in their careers had the benefit of mentors. Formal mentoring programs help organizations make this valuable development tool available to all employees.[110]

When diverse members of an organization lack mentors, their progress in the organization and advancement to high-level positions can be hampered. Ida Abott, a lawyer and consultant on work-related issues, presented a paper to the Minority Corporate Counsel Association in which she concluded, "The lack of adequate mentoring has held women and minority lawyers back from achieving professional success and has led to high rates of career dissatisfaction and attrition."[111]

Mentoring can benefit all kinds of employees in all kinds of work.[112] John Washko, a manager at the Four Seasons hotel chain, benefited from the mentoring he received from Stan Bromley on interpersonal relations and how to deal with employees; mentor Bromley, in turn, found that participating in the Four Seasons' mentoring program helped him develop his own management style.[113] More generally, development is an ongoing process for all managers, and mentors often find that mentoring contributes to their own personal development.

FORMAL EDUCATION   Many large corporations reimburse employees for tuition expenses they incur while taking college courses and obtaining advanced degrees. This is not just benevolence on the part of the employer or even a simple reward given to the employee; it is an effective way to develop employees who can take on new responsibilities and more challenging positions. For similar reasons, corporations spend thousands of dollars sending managers to executive development programs such as executive MBA programs. In these programs, experts teach managers the latest in business and management techniques and practices.

To save time and travel costs, some managers rely on *long-distance learning* to formally educate and develop employees. Using videoconferencing technologies, business schools such as the Harvard Business School, the University of Michigan, and Babson College teach courses on video screens in corporate conference rooms. Business schools also customize courses and degrees to fit the development needs of employees in a particular company and/or a particular geographic region.[114] Moreover, some employees and managers seek to advance their educations though online degree programs.[115]

Transfer of Training and Development

Whenever training and development take place off the job or in a classroom setting, it is vital for managers to promote the transfer of the knowledge and skills acquired *to the actual work situation*. Trainees should be encouraged and expected to use their newfound expertise on the job.

Performance Appraisal and Feedback

LO12-4

Explain why performance appraisal and feedback are such crucial activities, and list the choices managers must make in designing effective performance appraisal and feedback procedures.

performance appraisal
The evaluation of employees' job performance and contributions to their organization.

performance feedback
The process through which managers share performance appraisal information with subordinates, give subordinates an opportunity to reflect on their own performance, and develop, with subordinates, plans for the future.

The recruitment/selection and training/development components of a human resource management system ensure that employees have the knowledge and skills needed to be effective now and in the future. Performance appraisal and feedback complement recruitment, selection, training, and development. **Performance appraisal** is the evaluation of employees' job performance and contributions to the organization. **Performance feedback** is the process through which managers share performance appraisal information with their subordinates, give subordinates an opportunity to reflect on their own performance, and develop, with subordinates, plans for the future. Before performance feedback, performance appraisal must take place. Performance appraisal could take place without providing performance feedback, but wise managers are careful to provide feedback because it can contribute to employee motivation and performance.

Performance appraisal and feedback contribute to the effective management of human resources in several ways. Performance appraisal gives managers important information on which to base human resource decisions.[116] Decisions about pay raises, bonuses, promotions, and job moves all hinge on the accurate appraisal of performance. Performance appraisal can also help managers determine which workers are candidates for training and development and in what areas. Performance feedback encourages high levels of employee motivation and performance. It lets good performers know that their efforts are valued and appreciated. It also lets poor performers know that their lackluster performance needs improvement. Performance feedback can give both good and poor performers insight on their strengths and weaknesses and ways in which they can improve their performance in the future.

Types of Performance Appraisal

Performance appraisal focuses on the evaluation of traits, behaviors, and results.[117]

TRAIT APPRAISALS   When trait appraisals are used, managers assess subordinates on personal characteristics that are relevant to job performance, such as skills, abilities, or personality. A factory worker, for example, may be evaluated based on her ability to use computerized equipment and perform numerical calculations. A social worker may be appraised based on his empathy and communication skills.

Three disadvantages of trait appraisals often lead managers to rely on other appraisal methods. First, possessing a certain personal characteristic does not ensure that the personal characteristic will actually be used on the job and result in high performance. For example, a factory worker may possess superior computer and numerical skills but be a poor performer due to low motivation. The second disadvantage of trait appraisals is linked to the first. Because traits do not always show a direct association with performance, workers and courts of law may view them as unfair and potentially discriminatory. The third disadvantage of trait appraisals is that they often do not enable managers to give employees feedback they can use to improve performance. Because trait appraisals focus on relatively enduring human characteristics that change only over the long term, employees can do little to change their behavior in response to performance feedback from a trait appraisal. Telling a social worker that he lacks empathy says little about how he can improve his interactions with clients, for example. These disadvantages suggest that managers should use trait appraisals only when they can demonstrate that the assessed traits are accurate and important indicators of job performance.

BEHAVIOR APPRAISALS   Through behavior appraisals, managers assess how workers perform their jobs—the actual actions and behaviors that workers exhibit on the job. Whereas trait appraisals assess what workers *are like,* behavior appraisals assess what workers *do.* For example, with a behavior appraisal, a manager might evaluate a social worker on the extent to which he looks clients in the eye when talking with them, expresses sympathy when they are upset, and refers them to community counseling and support groups geared toward the specific problems they are encountering. Behavior appraisals are especially useful when *how* workers perform their jobs is important. In educational organizations such as high schools, for example, the numbers of classes and students taught are important, but also important is how they are taught or the methods teachers use to ensure that learning takes place.

Behavior appraisals have the advantage of giving employees clear information about what they are doing right and wrong and how they can improve their performance. And because behaviors are much easier for employees to change than traits, performance feedback from behavior appraisals is more likely to lead to improved performance.

RESULTS APPRAISALS   For some jobs, *how* people perform the job is not as important as *what* they accomplish or the results they obtain. With results appraisals, managers appraise performance by the results or the actual outcomes of work behaviors. Take the case of two new car salespeople. One salesperson strives to develop personal relationships with her customers. She spends hours talking to them and frequently calls them to see how their decision-making process is going. The other salesperson has a much more hands-off approach. He is very knowledgeable, answers customers' questions, and then waits for them to come to him. Both salespersons sell, on average, the same number of cars, and the customers of both are satisfied with the service they receive, according to postcards the dealership mails to customers asking for an assessment of their satisfaction. The manager of the dealership appropriately uses results appraisals (sales and customer satisfaction) to evaluate the salespeople's performance because it does not matter which behavior salespeople use to sell cars as long as they sell the desired number and satisfy customers. If one salesperson sells too few cars, however, the manager can give that person performance feedback about his or her low sales.

OBJECTIVE AND SUBJECTIVE APPRAISALS   Whether managers appraise performance in terms of traits, behaviors, or results, the information they assess is either *objective* or *subjective*. **Objective appraisals** are based on facts and are likely to be numerical—the number of cars sold, the number of meals prepared, the number of times late, the number of audits completed. Managers often use objective appraisals when results are being appraised because results tend to be easier to quantify than traits or behaviors. When *how* workers perform their jobs is important, however, subjective behavior appraisals are more appropriate than results appraisals.

Subjective appraisals are based on managers' perceptions of traits, behaviors, or results. Because subjective appraisals rest on managers' perceptions, there is always the chance that they are inaccurate (see Chapter 5). This is why both researchers and managers have spent considerable time and effort on determining the best way to develop reliable and valid subjective measures of performance.

Some of the more popular subjective measures such as the graphic rating scale, the behaviorally anchored rating scale (BARS), and the behavior observation scale (BOS) are illustrated in Figure 12.5.[118] When graphic rating scales are used, performance is assessed along a continuum with specified intervals. With a BARS, performance is assessed along a scale with clearly defined scale points containing examples of specific behaviors. A BOS assesses performance by how often specific behaviors are performed. Many managers may use both objective and subjective appraisals. For example, a salesperson may be appraised both on the dollar value of sales (objective) and the quality of customer service (subjective).

In addition to subjective appraisals, some organizations employ *forced rankings* whereby supervisors must rank their subordinates and assign them to different categories according to their performance (which is subjectively appraised). For example, at LendingTree, managers and employees are ranked by their superiors as a "1" (top 15 percent based on individual performance and goals), "2" (middle 75 percent), or "3" (bottom 10 percent).[119] Although the forced ranking system was originally adopted at LendingTree to reward high performers and make it less likely that they would seek positions elsewhere, in tough times when housing and mortgage sales are down, the "3's" are the ones mostly likely to be laid off if layoffs take place.[120] Some managers are proponents of forced rankings, but others strongly oppose the practice. Proponents believe that forced rankings help ensure that human resource decisions are made based on merit, top performers are recognized, and all employees know where they stand relative to others. Opponents of forced ranking believe that forced rankings can be demoralizing, lead to a competitive environment unsupportive of cooperation and teamwork, and also result in favoritism. And forced rankings schemes that force managers to group percentages of employees in certain predetermined categories might not make sense if the predetermined categories do not match the distribution of performance across the employees. For

---

objective appraisal An appraisal that is based on facts and is likely to be numerical.

subjective appraisal An appraisal that is based on perceptions of traits, behaviors, or results.

Figure 12.5

Subjective Measures of Performance

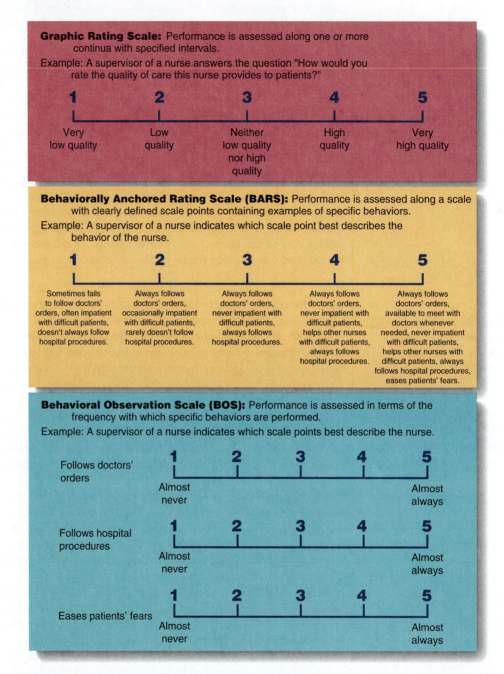

Graphic Rating Scale: Performance is assessed along one or more continua with specified intervals.

Example: A supervisor of a nurse answers the question "How would you rate the quality of care this nurse provides to patients?"

1	2	3	4	5
Very low quality	Low quality	Neither low quality nor high quality	High quality	Very high quality

Behaviorally Anchored Rating Scale (BARS): Performance is assessed along a scale with clearly defined scale points containing examples of specific behaviors.

Example: A supervisor of a nurse indicates which scale point best describes the behavior of the nurse.

1	2	3	4	5
Sometimes fails to follow doctors' orders, often impatient with difficult patients, doesn't always follow hospital procedures.	Always follows doctors' orders, occasionally impatient with difficult patients, rarely doesn't follow hospital procedures.	Always follows doctors' orders, never impatient with difficult patients, always follows hospital procedures.	Always follows doctors' orders, never impatient with difficult patients, helps other nurses with difficult patients, always follows hospital procedures.	Always follows doctors' orders, available to meet with doctors whenever needed, never impatient with difficult patients, helps other nurses with difficult patients, always follows hospital procedures, eases patients' fears.

Behavioral Observation Scale (BOS): Performance is assessed in terms of the frequency with which specific behaviors are performed.

Example: A supervisor of a nurse indicates which scale points best describe the nurse.

Follows doctors' orders

1	2	3	4	5
Almost never				Almost always

Follows hospital procedures

1	2	3	4	5
Almost never				Almost always

Eases patients' fears

1	2	3	4	5
Almost never				Almost always

example, a forced ranking system might require a manager to "force" 20 percent of his or her subordinates into the bottom ranking designation when in fact most of the subordinates' performance is average or above average and only 5 to 10 percent of employees are poor performers. When forced rankings are applied on a regional basis, they can cause conflict and political maneuvering among managers, each of whom wants to ensure that his or her subordinates are ranked in the better categories. Interestingly enough, while forced rankings were popularized, in part, by their use at General Electric under the leadership of Jack Welch, GE no longer uses a forced ranking system.

Who Appraises Performance?

We have been assuming that managers or the supervisors of employees evaluate performance. This is a reasonable assumption: supervisors are the most common appraisers of performance.[121] Performance appraisal is an important part of most managers' job duties. Managers are responsible for not only motivating their subordinates to perform at a high level but also making many decisions hinging on performance appraisals, such as pay raises or promotions. Appraisals by managers can be usefully augmented by appraisals from other sources (see Figure 12.6).

SELF, PEERS, SUBORDINATES, AND CLIENTS   When self-appraisals are used, managers supplement their evaluations with an employee's assessment of his or her own performance. Peer appraisals are provided by an employee's coworkers. Especially when subordinates work in groups or teams, feedback from peer appraisals can motivate team members while giving managers important information for decision making. A growing number of companies are having subordinates appraise their managers' performance and leadership as well. And sometimes customers or clients assess employee performance in terms of responsiveness to customers and quality of service. Although appraisals from these sources can be useful, managers need to be aware of potential issues that may arise when they are used. Subordinates sometimes may be inclined to inflate self-appraisals, especially if organizations are downsizing and they are worried about job security. Managers who are appraised by their subordinates may fail to take needed but unpopular actions out of fear that their subordinates will appraise them negatively. Some of these potential issues can be mitigated to the extent that there are high levels of trust in an organization.

360-DEGREE PERFORMANCE APPRAISALS   To improve motivation and performance, some organizations include 360-degree appraisals and feedback in their performance appraisal systems, especially for managers. In a **360-degree appraisal** a variety of people, beginning with the manager and including peers or coworkers, subordinates, superiors, and sometimes even customers or clients, appraise a manager's performance. The manager receives feedback based on evaluations from these multiple sources.

Companies in a variety of industries rely on 360-degree appraisals and feedback.[122] For 360-degree appraisals and feedback to be effective, there has to be trust throughout an organization. More generally, trust is a critical ingredient in any performance appraisal and feedback procedure. In addition, research suggests that 360-degree appraisals should focus on behaviors rather than traits or results and that managers need to carefully select appropriate raters. Moreover, appraisals tend to be more honest when made anonymously and when raters have been trained in how to use 360-degree appraisal forms.[123] Additionally, managers need

360-degree appraisal A performance appraisal by peers, subordinates, superiors, and sometimes clients who are in a position to evaluate a manager's performance.

Figure 12.6
Who Appraises Performance?

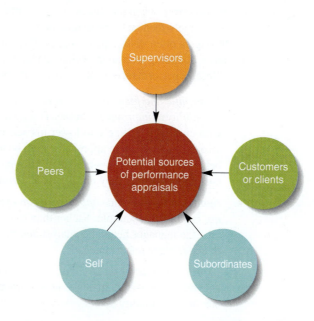

to think carefully about the extent to which 360-degree appraisals are appropriate for certain jobs and be willing to modify any appraisal system they implement if they become aware of unintended problems it creates.[124]

Even when 360-degree appraisals are used, it is sometimes difficult to design an effective process by which subordinates' feedback can be communicated to their managers; but advances in information technology can solve this problem. For example, ImproveNow. com has online questionnaires that subordinates fill out to evaluate the performance of their managers and give the managers feedback. Each subordinate of a particular manager completes the questionnaire independently, all responses are tabulated, and the manager is given specific feedback on behaviors in a variety of areas, such as rewarding good performance, looking out for subordinates' best interests and being supportive, and having a vision for the future.[125]

Effective Performance Feedback

formal appraisal An appraisal conducted at a set time during the year and based on performance dimensions and measures that were specified in advance.

For the appraisal and feedback component of a human resource management system to encourage and motivate high performance, managers must give their subordinates feedback. To generate useful information to feed back to their subordinates, managers can use both formal and informal appraisals. **Formal appraisals** are conducted at set times during the year and are based on performance dimensions and measures that have been specified in advance. A salesperson, for example, may be evaluated by his or her manager twice a year on the performance dimensions of sales and customer service, sales being objectively measured from sales reports, and customer service being measured with a BARS (see Figure 12.5).

Managers in most large organizations use formal performance appraisals on a fixed schedule dictated by company policy, such as every six months or every year. An integral part of a formal appraisal is a meeting between the manager and the subordinate in which the subordinate is given feedback on performance. Performance feedback lets subordinates know which areas they are excelling in and which areas need improvement; it should also tell them *how* they can improve their performance. Realizing the value of formal appraisals, managers in many large corporations have committed substantial resources to updating their performance appraisal procedures and training low-level managers in how to use them and provide accurate feedback to employees.[126]

Formal performance appraisals supply both managers and subordinates with valuable information; but subordinates often want more frequent feedback, and managers often want to motivate subordinates as the need arises. For these reasons many companies supplement formal performance appraisal with frequent **informal appraisals**, for which managers and their subordinates meet as the need arises to discuss ongoing progress and areas for improvement. Moreover, when job duties, assignments, or goals change, informal appraisals can give workers timely feedback concerning how they are handling their new responsibilities.

informal appraisal An unscheduled appraisal of ongoing progress and areas for improvement.

Managers often dislike providing performance feedback, especially when the feedback is negative, but doing so is an important managerial activity.[127] Here are some guidelines for giving effective performance feedback that contributes to employee motivation and performance:

- *Be specific and focus on behaviors or outcomes that are correctable and within a worker's ability to improve.* Example: Telling a salesperson that he is too shy when interacting with customers is likely to lower his self-confidence and prompt him to become defensive. A more effective approach would be to give the salesperson feedback about specific behaviors to engage in—greeting customers as soon as they enter the department, asking customers whether they need help, and volunteering to help customers find items.

- *Approach performance appraisal as an exercise in problem solving and solution finding, not criticizing.* Example: Rather than criticizing a financial analyst for turning in reports late, the manager helps the analyst determine why the reports are late and identify ways to better manage her time.

- *Express confidence in a subordinate's ability to improve.* Example: Instead of being skeptical, a first-level manager tells a subordinate that he is confident that the subordinate can increase quality levels.

- *Provide performance feedback both formally and informally.* Example: The staff of a preschool receives feedback from formal performance appraisals twice a year. The school director also provides frequent informal feedback such as complimenting staff members on creative ideas for special projects, noticing when they do a particularly good job handling a difficult child, and pointing out when they provide inadequate supervision.

- *Praise instances of high performance and areas of a job in which a worker excels.* Example: Rather than focusing on just the negative, a manager discusses the areas her subordinate excels in as well as the areas in need of improvement.

- *Avoid personal criticisms and treat subordinates with respect.* Example: An engineering manager acknowledges her subordinates' expertise and treats them as professionals. Even when the manager points out performance problems to subordinates, she refrains from criticizing them personally.

- *Agree to a timetable for performance improvements.* Example: A first-level manager and his subordinate decide to meet again in one month to determine whether quality levels have improved.

In following these guidelines, managers need to remember *why* they are giving performance feedback: to encourage high levels of motivation and performance. Moreover, the information that managers gather through performance appraisal and feedback helps them determine how to distribute pay raises and bonuses.

LO12-5

Explain the issues managers face in determining levels of pay and benefits.

Pay and Benefits

Pay includes employees' base salaries, pay raises, and bonuses and is determined by a number of factors such as characteristics of the organization and the job and levels of performance. Employee *benefits* are based on membership in an organization (not necessarily on the particular job held) and include sick days, vacation days, and medical and life insurance. In Chapter 13 we discuss how pay can motivate organizational members to perform at a high level, as well as the different kinds of pay plans managers can use to help an organization achieve its goals and gain a competitive advantage. As you will learn, it is important to link pay to behaviors or results that contribute to organizational effectiveness. Next we focus on establishing an organization's pay level and pay structure.

Pay Level

pay level The relative position of an organization's pay incentives in comparison with those of other organizations in the same industry employing similar kinds of workers.

Pay level is a broad comparative concept that refers to how an organization's pay incentives compare, in general, to those of other organizations in the same industry employing similar kinds of workers. Managers must decide if they want to offer relatively high wages, average wages, or relatively low wages. High wages help ensure that an organization is going to be able to recruit, select, and retain high performers, but high wages also raise costs. Low wages give an organization a cost advantage but may undermine the organization's ability to select and recruit high performers and to motivate current employees to perform at a high level. Either of these situations may lead to inferior quality or inadequate customer service.

In determining pay levels, managers should take into account their organization's strategy. A high pay level may prohibit managers from effectively pursuing a low-cost strategy. But a high pay level may be worth the added costs in an organization whose competitive advantage lies in superior quality and excellent customer service. As one might expect, hotel and motel chains with a low-cost strategy, such as Days Inn and Hampton Inns, have lower pay levels than chains striving to provide high-quality rooms and services, such as the Four Seasons profiled in "A Manager's Challenge."

Pay Structure

pay structure The arrangement of jobs into categories reflecting their relative importance to the organization and its goals, levels of skill required, and other characteristics.

After deciding on a pay level, managers have to establish a pay structure for the different jobs in the organization. A **pay structure** clusters jobs into categories reflecting their relative importance to the organization and its goals, levels of skill required, and other characteristics managers consider important. Pay ranges are established for each job category. Individual jobholders' pay within job categories is then determined by factors such as performance, seniority, and skill levels.

There are some interesting global differences in pay structures. Large corporations based in the United States tend to pay their CEOs and top managers higher salaries than do their European or Japanese counterparts. Also, the pay differential between employees at the bottom of the corporate hierarchy and those higher up is much greater in U.S. companies than in European or Japanese companies.[128]

Concerns have been raised over whether it is equitable or fair for CEOs of large companies in the United States to be making millions of dollars in years when their companies are restructuring and laying off a large portion of their workforces.[129] Additionally, the average CEO in the United States typically earns over 360 times what the average hourly worker earns.[130] Is a pay structure with such a huge pay differential ethical? Shareholders and the public are increasingly asking this very question and asking large corporations to rethink their pay structures.[131] Also troubling are the millions of dollars in severance packages that some CEOs receive when they leave their organizations. When many workers are struggling to find and keep jobs and make ends meet, people are questioning whether it is ethical for some top managers to be making so much money.[132]

Benefits

Organizations are legally required to provide certain benefits to their employees, including workers' compensation, Social Security, and unemployment insurance. Workers' compensation helps employees financially if they become unable to work due to a work-related injury or illness. Social Security provides financial assistance to retirees and disabled former employees. Unemployment insurance provides financial assistance to workers who lose their jobs due to no fault of their own. The legal system in the United States views these three benefits as ethical requirements for organizations and thus mandates that they be provided.

Other benefits such as health insurance, dental insurance, vacation time, pension plans, life insurance, flexible working hours, company-provided day care, and employee assistance and wellness programs have traditionally been provided at the option of employers. The Health Care Reform Bill signed by President Barack Obama in March 2010 contains provisions whereby, starting in 2014, employers with 50 or more employees may face fines if they don't provide their employees with health insurance coverage.[133] Benefits enabling workers to balance the demands of their jobs and of their lives away from the office or factory are of growing importance for many workers who have competing demands on their scarce time and energy.

cafeteria-style benefit plan A plan from which employees can choose the benefits they want.

In some organizations, top managers determine which benefits might best suit the employees and organization and offer the same benefit package to all employees. Other organizations, realizing that employees' needs and desires might differ, offer **cafeteria-style benefit plans** that let employees choose the benefits they want. Cafeteria-style benefit plans sometimes help managers deal with employees who feel unfairly treated because they are unable to take advantage of certain benefits available to other employees who, for example, have children. Some organizations have success with cafeteria-style benefit plans; others find them difficult to manage.

As health care costs escalate and overstretched employees find it hard to take time to exercise and take care of their health, more companies are providing benefits and incentives to promote employee wellness. According to a survey conducted by Fidelity Investments and the National Business Group on Health, close to 90 percent of organizations provide some kind of incentive, prize, or reward to employees who take steps to improve their health.[134] For working parents, family-friendly benefits are especially attractive. For example, access to on-site child care, being able to

Guerra DeBerry Coody offers family-friendly benefits such as child care.

telecommute and take time off to care for sick children, and provisions for emergency back-up child care can be valued benefits for working parents with young children.

Same-sex domestic partner benefits are also being used to attract and retain valued employees. Gay and lesbian workers are reluctant to work for companies that do not provide the same kinds of benefits for their partners as those provided for partners of the opposite sex.[135]

Labor Relations

labor relations The activities managers engage in to ensure that they have effective working relationships with the labor unions that represent their employees' interests.

Labor relations are the activities managers engage in to ensure that they have effective working relationships with the labor unions that represent their employees' interests. Although the U.S. government has responded to the potential for unethical and unfair treatment of workers by creating and enforcing laws regulating employment (including the EEO laws listed in Table 12.1), some workers believe a union will ensure that their interests are fairly represented in their organizations.

Before we describe unions in more detail, let's take a look at some examples of important employment legislation. In 1938 the government passed the Fair Labor Standards Act, which prohibited child labor and provided for minimum wages, overtime pay, and maximum working hours to protect workers' rights. In 1963 the Equal Pay Act mandated that men and women performing equal work (work requiring the same levels of skill, responsibility, and effort performed in the same kind of working conditions) receive equal pay (see Table 12.1). In 1970 the Occupational Safety and Health Act mandated procedures for managers to follow to ensure workplace safety. These are just a few of the U.S. government's efforts to protect workers' rights. State legislatures also have been active in promoting safe, ethical, and fair workplaces.

Unions

Unions exist to represent workers' interests in organizations. Given that managers have more power than rank-and-file workers and that organizations have multiple stakeholders, there is always the potential that managers might take steps that benefit one set of stakeholders such as shareholders while hurting another such as employees. For example, managers may decide to speed up a production line to lower costs and increase production in the hopes of increasing returns to shareholders. Speeding up the line, however, could hurt employees forced to work at a rapid pace and may increase the risk of injuries. Also, employees receive no additional pay for the extra work they are performing. Unions would represent workers' interests in a scenario such as this one.

Congress acknowledged the role that unions could play in ensuring safe and fair workplaces when it passed the National Labor Relations Act of 1935. This act made it legal for workers to organize into unions to protect their rights and interests and declared certain unfair or unethical organizational practices to be illegal. The act also established the National Labor Relations Board (NLRB) to oversee union activity. Currently the NLRB conducts certification elections, which are held among the employees of an organization to determine whether they want a union to represent their interests. The NLRB also makes judgments concerning unfair labor practices and specifies practices that managers must refrain from.

Employees might vote to have a union represent them for any number of reasons.[136] They may think their wages and working conditions need improvement. They may believe managers are not treating them with respect. They may think their working hours are unfair or they need more job security or a safer work environment. Or they may be dissatisfied with management and find it difficult to communicate their concerns to their bosses. Regardless of the specific reason, one overriding reason is power: A united group inevitably wields more power than an individual, and this type of power may be especially helpful to employees in some organizations.

Although these would seem to be potent forces for unionization, some workers are reluctant to join unions. Sometimes this reluctance is due to the perception that union leaders are corrupt. Some workers may simply believe that belonging to a union might not do them much good while costing them money in membership dues. Employees also might not want to be forced into doing something they do not want to, such as striking because the union thinks it is in their best interest. Moreover, although unions can be a positive force in organizations, sometimes they also can be a negative force, impairing organizational effectiveness.

For example, when union leaders resist needed changes in an organization or are corrupt, organizational performance can suffer.

The percentage of U.S. workers represented by unions today is smaller than it was in the 1950s, an era when unions were especially strong.[137] In the 1950s, around 35 percent of U.S. workers were union members; in 2013, 11.3 percent of workers were members of unions.[138] The American Federation of Labor–Congress of Industrial Organizations (AFL-CIO) includes 56 voluntary member unions representing over 12 million workers.[139] Overall, approximately 14.5 million workers in the United States belong to unions.[140] Union influence in manufacturing and heavy industries has been on the decline; more generally, approximately 6.7 percent of private sector workers are union members.[141] However, around 35.3 percent of government workers belong to unions.[142] Unions have made inroads in other segments of the workforce, particularly the low-wage end. Garbage collectors in New Jersey, poultry plant workers in North Carolina, and janitors in Baltimore are among the growing numbers of low-paid workers who are currently finding union membership attractive. North Carolina poultry workers voted in a union partly because they thought it was unfair that they had to buy their own gloves and hairnets used on the job and had to ask their supervisors' permission to go to the restroom.[143]

Union membership and leadership, traditionally dominated by white men, are becoming increasingly diverse. For example, Linda Chavez-Thompson was the executive vice president of the AFL-CIO from 1995 to 2007 and was the first woman and Hispanic to hold a top management position in the federation.[144] Labor officials in Washington, DC, also are becoming increasingly diverse. Elaine L. Chao, the 24th U.S. Secretary of Labor,[145] was the first Asian-American woman to hold an appointment in a U.S. president's cabinet.[146] In terms of union membership, women now make up over 45 percent of unionized workers.[147]

Collective Bargaining

collective bargaining
Negotiations between labor unions and managers to resolve conflicts and disputes about issues such as working hours, wages, benefits, working conditions, and job security.

Collective bargaining is negotiation between labor unions and managers to resolve conflicts and disputes about important issues such as working hours, wages, working conditions, and job security. Sometimes union members go on strike to drive home their concerns to managers. Once an agreement that union members support has been reached (sometimes with the help of a neutral third party called a *mediator*), union leaders and managers sign a contract spelling out the terms of the collective bargaining agreement. We discuss conflict and negotiation in depth in Chapter 17, but some brief observations are in order here because collective bargaining is an ongoing consideration in labor relations.

The signing of a contract, for example, does not finish the collective bargaining process. Disagreement and conflicts can arise over the interpretation of the contract. In such cases, a neutral third party called an *arbitrator* is usually called in to resolve the conflict. An important component of a collective bargaining agreement is a *grievance procedure* through which workers who believe they are not being fairly treated are allowed to voice their concerns and have their interests represented by the union. Workers who think they were unjustly fired in violation of a union contract, for example, may file a grievance, have the union represent them, and get their jobs back if an arbitrator agrees with them. Union members sometimes go on strike when managers make decisions that the members think will hurt them and are not in their best interests.

Summary and Review

STRATEGIC HUMAN RESOURCE MANAGEMENT Human resource management (HRM) includes all the activities managers engage in to ensure that their organizations can attract, retain, and effectively use human resources. Strategic HRM is the process by which managers design the components of a human resource management system to be **LO12-1** consistent with each other, with other elements of organizational architecture, and with the organization's strategies and goals.

LO12-2 **RECRUITMENT AND SELECTION** Before recruiting and selecting employees, managers must engage in human resource planning and job analysis. Human resource planning includes all the activities managers engage in to forecast their current and future needs for human resources. Job analysis is the process of identifying (1) the tasks, duties, and responsibilities that make up a job and (2) the knowledge, skills, and abilities needed to perform the job. Recruitment includes all the activities managers engage in to develop a pool of qualified applicants for open positions. Selection is the process by which managers determine the relative qualifications of job applicants and their potential for performing well in a particular job.

LO12-3 **TRAINING AND DEVELOPMENT** Training focuses on teaching organizational members how to perform effectively in their current jobs. Development focuses on broadening organizational members' knowledge and skills so they are prepared to take on new responsibilities and challenges.

LO12-4 **PERFORMANCE APPRAISAL AND FEEDBACK** Performance appraisal is the evaluation of employees' job performance and contributions to the organization. Performance feedback is the process through which managers share performance appraisal information with their subordinates, give them an opportunity to reflect on their own performance, and develop with them plans for the future. Performance appraisal gives managers useful information for decision making. Performance feedback can encourage high levels of motivation and performance.

LO12-5 **PAY AND BENEFITS** Pay level is the relative position of an organization's pay incentives in comparison with those of other organizations in the same industry employing similar workers. A pay structure clusters jobs into categories according to their relative importance to the organization and its goals, the levels of skill required, and other characteristics. Pay ranges are then established for each job category. Organizations are legally required to provide certain benefits to their employees; other benefits are provided at the discretion of employers.

LO12-6 **LABOR RELATIONS** Labor relations include all the activities managers engage in to ensure that they have effective working relationships with the labor unions that represent their employees' interests. The National Labor Relations Board oversees union activity. Collective bargaining is the process through which labor unions and managers resolve conflicts and disputes and negotiate agreements.

Management in Action

Topics for Discussion and Action

Discussion

1. Discuss why it is important for human resource management systems to be in sync with an organization's strategy and goals and with each other. **[LO12-1]**

2. Discuss why training and development are ongoing activities for all organizations. **[LO12-3]**

3. Describe the type of development activities you think middle managers are most in need of. **[LO12-3]**

4. Evaluate the pros and cons of 360-degree performance appraisals and feedback. Would you like your performance to be appraised in this manner? Why or why not? **[LO12-4]**

5. Discuss why two restaurants in the same community might have different pay levels. **[LO12-5]**

6. Explain why union membership is becoming more diverse. **[LO12-6]**

Action

7. Interview a manager in a local organization to determine how that organization recruits and selects employees. **[LO12-2]**

Building Management Skills

Analyzing Human Resource Management Systems [LO12-1, 12-2, 12-3, 12-4, 12-5]

Think about your current job or a job you have had in the past. If you have never had a job, interview a friend or family member who is currently working. Answer the following questions about the job you have chosen:

1. How are people recruited and selected for this job? Are the recruitment and selection procedures the organization uses effective or ineffective? Why?

2. What training and development do people who hold this job receive? Are the training and development appropriate? Why or why not?

3. How is performance of this job appraised? Does performance feedback contribute to motivation and high performance on this job?

4. What levels of pay and benefits are provided on this job? Are these levels appropriate? Why or why not?

Managing Ethically [LO12-4, 12-5]

Some managers do not want to become overly friendly with their subordinates because they are afraid that if they do so their objectivity when conducting performance appraisals and making decisions about pay raises and promotions will be impaired. Some subordinates resent it when they see one or more of their coworkers being very friendly with the boss; they are concerned about the potential for favoritism. Their reasoning runs something like this: If two subordinates are equally qualified for a promotion and one is a good friend of the boss and the other is a mere acquaintance, who is more likely to receive the promotion?

Questions

1. Either individually or in a group, think about the ethical implications of managers' becoming friendly with their subordinates.

2. Do you think managers should feel free to socialize and become good friends with their subordinates outside the workplace if they so desire? Why or why not?

Small Group Breakout Exercise

Building a Human Resource Management System [LO12-1, 12-2, 12-3, 12-4, 12-5]

Form groups of three or four people, and appoint one group member as the spokesperson who will communicate your findings to the class when called on by the instructor. Then discuss the following scenario:

You and your three partners are engineers who minored in business at college and have decided to start a consulting business. Your goal is to provide manufacturing process engineering and other engineering services to large and small organizations. You forecast that there will be an increased use of outsourcing for these activities. You discussed with managers in several large organizations the services you plan to offer, and they expressed considerable interest. You have secured funding to start your business and now are building the HRM system. Your human resource planning suggests that you need to hire between five and eight experienced engineers with good communication skills, two clerical/secretarial workers, and two MBAs who between them have financial, accounting, and human resource skills. You are striving to develop your human resources in a way that will enable your new business to prosper.

1. Describe the steps you will take to recruit and select (a) the engineers, (b) the clerical/secretarial workers, and (c) the MBAs.

2. Describe the training and development the engineers, the clerical/secretarial workers, and the MBAs will receive.

3. Describe how you will appraise the performance of each group of employees and how you will provide feedback.

4. Describe the pay level and pay structure of your consulting firm.

Exploring the World Wide Web [LO12-2]

Go to www.net-temps.com, a website geared toward temporary employment. Imagine that you have to take a year off from college and are seeking a one-year position. Guided by your own interests, use this website to learn about your options and possible employment opportunities.

1. What are the potential advantages of online job searching and recruiting? What are the potential disadvantages?

2. Would you ever rely on a website like this to help you find a position? Why or why not?

Be the Manager [LO12-4]

You are Walter Michaels and have just received some disturbing feedback. You are the director of human resources for Maxi Vision Inc., a medium-size window and glass door manufacturer. You recently initiated a 360-degree performance appraisal system for all middle and upper managers at Maxi Vision, including yourself, but excluding the most senior executives and the top management team.

You were eagerly awaiting the feedback you would receive from the managers who report to you; you had recently implemented several important initiatives that affected them and their subordinates, including a complete overhaul of the organization's performance appraisal system. While the managers who report to you were evaluated based on 360-degree appraisals, their subordinates were evaluated using a 20-question BARS scale you recently created that focuses on behaviors. Conducted annually, appraisals are an important input into pay raise and bonus decisions.

You were so convinced that the new performance appraisal procedures were highly effective that you hoped your own subordinates would mention them in their feedback to you. And boy did they! You were amazed to learn that the managers *and* their subordinates thought the new BARS scales were unfair, inappropriate, and a waste of time. In fact, the managers' feedback to you was that their own performance was suffering, based on the 360-degree appraisals they received, because their subordinates hated the new appraisal system and partially blamed their bosses, who were part of management. Some managers even admitted giving all their subordinates approximately the same scores on the scales so their pay raises and bonuses would not be affected by their performance appraisals.

You couldn't believe your eyes when you read these comments. You spent so much time developing what you thought was the ideal rating scale for this group of employees. Evidently, for some unknown reason, they wouldn't give it a chance. Your own supervisor is aware of these complaints and said that it was a top priority for you to fix "this mess" (with the implication that you were responsible for creating it). What are you going to do?

Amazon Recruits Face "Bar Raisers"

In fulfilling online orders, Amazon.com Inc. is all about expediency. The fewer people involved the better.

But when it comes to filling higher-level jobs, the e-commerce giant is in no rush—and it has a gantlet of people, dubbed "bar raisers," who must sign off on would-be hires.

Bar raisers are skilled evaluators who, while holding full-time jobs at the company in a range of departments, play a crucial role in Amazon's hiring process, interviewing job candidates in other parts of the company. With a word, they can veto any candidate, even if their expertise is in an area that has nothing to do with the prospective employee's.

Amazon believes the program, created in the company's infancy and honed by founder and Chief Executive Jeff Bezos, screens out cultural misfits and helps make the e-commerce giant a feared competitor in fields as diverse as logistics, tablet manufacturing and television production.

"There is no company that sticks to its process like Amazon does," says Valerie Frederickson, whose eponymous Menlo Park, Calif., human-resources consultancy works with Silicon Valley companies including Facebook Inc. and Twitter Inc. "They don't just hire the best of what they see; they're willing to keep looking and looking for the right talent."

As Amazon's payroll has swelled to 110,000 employees, however, the program is exacting a toll, current and former employees say.

There are several hundred bar raisers today across the company, according to former employees, though Amazon won't confirm a total.

Some employees shun the bar raiser designation, a voluntary program that comes with no extra pay, even though it reportedly can lead to speedier promotions because of the time demands. Bar raisers may be asked to assess as many as 10 candidates a week, for between two and three hours each, including paperwork and meetings—all while doing their regular full-time job, be it in finance, marketing or product development.

That has led to a crunch of bar raisers at times, some managers say. Andy Jassy, head of the fast-growing Amazon Web Services cloud-computing unit, said in an interview in November there seemed not to be enough bar raisers to go around and he was looking for more.

Not every Amazon applicant faces a bar raiser. Current and former employees say the company uses a streamlined process for warehouse employees, estimated to be three-fourths of its workforce.

Most others, though, must endure an obstacle course of phone interviews and one-on-one sessions. The interviewers then write evaluations and then meet to discuss the candidate. Inside Amazon, evaluating an applicant typically takes five or six employees at least two hours each.

"We want to be as objective and scientific in our hiring as possible," said Susan Harker, Amazon's vice president of global talent acquisition, noting the process extends even to C-level executives. "The point is to optimize our chances of having long-term employees."

Other tech companies have their own systems for identifying the best and brightest. For a time, Google Inc. asked candidates their I.Q's, and posed brain teasers.

Microsoft Corp. calls in senior executives known as "as-appropriates" in the late stages of considering some applicants. Facebook Inc. asks some job hopefuls tricky coding questions or solutions to business challenges.

The bar raiser is Amazon's distinction. To become a bar raiser, a worker generally must have conducted dozens or hundreds of interviews, and gained a reputation for asking tough questions and identifying candidates who go on to be stars.

Bar raisers typically interview candidates in another part of the company, posing unexpected or challenging questions to gauge an applicant's analytical skills. Current and former bar raisers say the designation is both an honor and a burden.

Sailesh Rachabathuni, who developed software for Kindle devices before leaving Amazon in 2012, says he once vetoed a candidate for a programming job because the candidate didn't know much about a specific programming language, a detail others missed.

"It's an enormous time commitment," Mr. Rachabathuni says. "I had to limit myself to six interviews a week."

One of Mr. Rachabathuni's former colleagues in Lab126, Amazon's secretive Silicon Valley hardware laboratory, says he conducted more than 700 interviews over eight years at Amazon. But this ex-employee declined to become a bar raiser for fear of devoting more time to hiring.

In cultivating the program, Mr. Bezos wanted to create a consistent corporate culture. Amazon executives say the approach reduces hiring mistakes by forcing several people to sign off on a candidate. The program is "something the broader team is very proud of," Mr. Bezos said in an interview last year.

John Vlastelica, an early Amazon human-resources employee who helped design the program, said the tough review process was meant to weed out job hopefuls who aren't adaptable and may be skilled at only one task.

"You want someone who can adapt to new roles in the company, not just someone who can fill the role that's vacant," said Mr. Vlastelica, who now runs HR consultancy Recruiting Toolbox and counted Amazon among his former clients. "It can be an expensive process because it takes longer, but think of how expensive it is to hire the wrong person."

The burden is likely to grow as Amazon extends its torrid hiring pace, needed to staff its ambitious efforts to expand same-day delivery, and to build Kindle tablets, as well as smartphones and set-top boxes. In the 12 months ended Sept. 30, Amazon added close to 30,000 employees, roughly as many as eBay Inc.'s total payroll. The retail giant's workforce has more than tripled in the past three years.

Google contracted to 46,421 employees as of the end of September 2013, from 53,546 a year earlier, due in part to cuts at its Motorola Mobility division. Apple Inc. grew by 10% to 80,300 in the fiscal year ended Sept. 28, and Microsoft Corp. increased its staff by 5% to 99,000 in the year ended June 30.

Dave Clark, vice president of Amazon's world-wide operations, said the company typically will conduct more than 75,000 interviews to hire 30,000 new workers. Bar raisers "help bring a consistency of the types of skill sets and perspectives that we're looking for," said Mr. Clark.

John Sullivan, a San Francisco State University management professor, said Amazon's protracted hiring process is an important signal for applicants that Amazon is a tough place to work, with a lot of pressure.

"If a job seeker feels like they want to run away from the building screaming after the interview, that's a probably a good sign that they don't belong there," he said.

Source: Greg Bensinger, "Amazon Recruits Face 'Bar Raisers'" *The Wall Street Journal,* January 8, 2014. Copyright © 2014 Dow Jones & Company, Inc. Reproduced with permission via Copyright Clearance Center.

Questions for Discussion

1. Why does Amazon use "bar raisers" in the hiring process?

2. What are the potential advantages of using bar raisers for Amazon?

3. What are the potential disadvantages of using bar raisers for Amazon?

4. What are the potential advantages and disadvantages for job applicants of bar raisers being used?

CHAPTER 13

Motivation and Performance

Learning Objectives

After studying this chapter, you should be able to:

LO13-1 Explain what motivation is and why managers need to be concerned about it.

LO13-2 Describe from the perspectives of expectancy theory and equity theory what managers should do to have a highly motivated workforce.

LO13-3 Explain how goals and needs motivate people and what kinds of goals are especially likely to result in high performance.

LO13-4 Identify the motivation lessons that managers can learn from operant conditioning theory and social learning theory.

LO13-5 Explain why and how managers can use pay as a major motivation tool.

How can managers ensure that employees are, and stay, highly motivated? The SAS Institute is in the enviable position of being listed on *Fortune* magazine's annual ranking of the "100 Best Companies to Work For" for 17 years in a row; in 2014 the SAS Institute was ranked second.[1] The SAS Institute is the world's largest privately owned software company, with over 13,700 employees worldwide and over $3 billion in revenues.[2] In fact, revenues have increased at SAS every year since the company was founded in 1976. SAS software is used at over 70,000 locations in more than 130 countries; over 90 of the top 100 companies on the *Fortune Global 500* list of largest companies use SAS software. Headquartered in Cary, North Carolina, SAS also has offices in Europe, the Middle East, Africa, Asia Pacific, Latin America, and Canada.[3]

Every indicator suggests that SAS employees are highly motivated and perform well while also working 35-hour weeks. Since its founding, the SAS Institute has strived to ensure that employees enjoy and are motivated by the work they perform. Managers approach motivation from the perspective that all employees should be interested and involved in the work that they are performing and have the sense that they are making meaningful contributions to SAS and SAS' customers. While some software companies that seek to develop new products buy companies that are already making these products, SAS develops its new products internally, and employees can perform interesting work at the forefront of technology.[4] Creativity is encouraged at SAS, and employees experience the excitement of developing a new product and seeing it succeed.[5] Overall, employees exert high levels of effort and persist in the face of setbacks to develop and provide the outstanding software solutions for businesses that SAS is renowned for.

Over 20 percent of annual revenues are committed to research and development at SAS, consistent with its long-term focus.[6] This long-term focus also helps ensure that SAS can weather economic downturns. For example, as a result of the recession that started in 2007, many technology companies laid off employees in 2009, which was not the case at SAS. As SAS cofounder and CEO James Goodnight puts it, "I've got a

Running into your boss's boss in the cafeteria isn't quite so daunting when the food is good, your pay is reasonable, and you know your kids are happily playing in the awesome day care just up the road! SAS knows how to keep its employees engaged in their work by recognizing a broad range of worker needs.

two-year pipeline of projects in R&D . . . Why would I lay anyone off?"[7]

Recognizing that sometimes employees might lose interest in the type of work they are doing or just need a change of pace, SAS allows employees to change jobs to prevent becoming bored with their work. SAS gives employees any additional training they might need when they change jobs. By encouraging these kinds of lateral moves, managers help to ensure that high levels of motivation at SAS are sustained over time.[8] While annual turnover rates in the software industry are around 15 percent, SAS's turnover rate in 2013 was 3.6 percent and average tenure at SAS is around 10 years.[9]

Managers at SAS fairly and equitably reward employees for a job well done. Moreover, Goodnight and other managers recognize that SAS's employees are its biggest asset and go to great lengths to satisfy their needs and create a work environment that will be conducive to creativity, high motivation, and well-being for employees and their families. At headquarters in North Carolina, employees have access to two child care centers that SAS subsidizes, a summer camp, three subsidized cafeterias, a 66,000-square-foot fitness and recreation center including an Olympic-size pool, and all kinds of services ranging from dry cleaning and car detailing to massages and a book exchange. Google (one of SAS's customers) actually used SAS as a prototype when Google was developing its own suite of employee benefits and perks.[10]

An on-campus health care center with an annual budget of $4.5 million and staff of 53 provides SAS employees and their families with free basic care clinic services.[11] The center is open 10 hours most days and has three physicians, 11 nurse practitioners, physical therapists, nurses, dietitians, lab technicians, and a psychologist on hand to attend to health needs and problems. In 2009 about 90 percent of headquarters' employees and their families had 40,000 appointments at the center. SAS estimates that the center saves the company about $5 million per year because employees are not losing valuable time traveling to doctors' offices and waiting a long time to see them. Moreover, employees are more likely to get care when they need it, and SAS can provide the care they need at lower costs.[12]

Wellness and work/life centers offer a variety of programs to help employees achieve a sense of balance in their lives and days. Programs range from Pilates, Zumba, and partner yoga to weight management, salsa aerobics, cooking classes, harmonic sound healing, and movies that employees can watch while floating in the pool. Employees with children are encouraged to have lunch with their kids in the subsidized cafeterias complete with high chairs, and of course they can bring their kids to the health center when they get sick.[13]

Employees have their own offices, and the work environment is rich in pleasant vistas, whether they be artwork on the walls or views of the rolling hills of Cary, North Carolina, at company headquarters. SAS keeps two artists on its staff in the belief that exposure to beautiful artwork and surroundings can spur creativity.[14] Employees and their families are encouraged to use the 200 acres that surround company headquarters for family walks and picnics.[15]

SAS trusts its employees to do what is right for the company. Thus many employees are able to determine their own work schedules and there are unlimited sick days.[16] Due to having so many benefits and facilities, employees do not have to interrupt their workdays or leave the campus for a doctor's appointment or to run an errand. And SAS realizes that to maintain high levels of motivation over time, employees need to have a balanced life—hence the 35-hour workweek. Of course, because SAS is a truly global company, sometimes employees on global teams with a tight new product development schedule need to work long hours and some employees check work email at home. Nonetheless, employees at SAS are not expected to work excessive hours as is common at some other companies.[17]

Since the company was founded, CEO James Goodnight has been committed to motivating employees to develop creative and high-quality products that meet customers' needs. Today hundreds of companies use SAS products for a wide variety of purposes including risk management, monitoring and measuring performance, managing relations with suppliers and customers, and detecting fraud.[18] SAS also provides educational software for schools and teachers through SAS in School.[19] Clearly, motivating employees and helping to satisfy their needs is a win–win situation for SAS. And by trusting employees and treating them well, SAS motivates employees to do what is best for SAS. As Bev Brown, a SAS employee in external communications put it, "Some may think that because SAS is family-friendly and has great benefits that we don't work hard . . . But people do work hard here, because they're motivated to take care of a company that takes care of them."[20]

Overview

Even with the best strategy in place and an appropriate organizational architecture, an organization will be effective only if its members are motivated to perform at a high level. James Goodnight of SAS in "A Manager's Challenge" clearly realizes this. One reason why leading is such an important managerial activity is that it entails ensuring that each member of an organization is motivated to perform highly and help the organization achieve its goals. When managers are effective, the outcome of the leading process is a highly motivated workforce. A key challenge for managers of organizations both large and small is to encourage employees to perform at a high level.

In this chapter we describe what motivation is, where it comes from, and why managers need to promote high levels of it for an organization to be effective and achieve its goals. We examine important theories of motivation: expectancy theory, need theories, equity theory, goal-setting theory, and learning theories. Each gives managers important insights about how to motivate organizational members. The theories are complementary in that each focuses on a different aspect of motivation. Considering all the theories together helps managers gain a rich understanding of the many issues and problems involved in encouraging high levels of motivation throughout an organization. Last, we consider the use of pay as a motivation tool. By the end of this chapter you will understand what it takes to have a highly motivated workforce.

motivation Psychological forces that determine the direction of a person's behavior in an organization, a person's level of effort, and a person's level of persistence.

The Nature of Motivation

Motivation may be defined as psychological forces that determine the direction of a person's behavior in an organization, a person's level of effort, and a person's level of persistence in the face of obstacles.[21] The *direction of a person's behavior* refers to the many possible behaviors a person could engage in. For example, employees at the SAS Institute are encouraged to be creative and develop new software that will meet customers' future needs. *Effort* refers to how hard people work. Employees at the SAS Institute exert high levels of effort to provide superior software solutions for business customers. *Persistence* refers to whether, when faced with roadblocks and obstacles, people keep trying or give up. Setbacks and obstacles are part and parcel of research and development work; at the SAS Institute, employees persist in the face of these difficulties to develop new sophisticated software.

Motivation is central to management because it explains *why* people behave the way they do in organizations[22]—why employees at the SAS Institute continue to develop software that is used by SAS customers around the world. Motivation also explains why a waiter is polite or rude and why a kindergarten teacher really tries to get children to enjoy learning or just goes through the motions. It explains why some managers truly put their organizations' best interests first, whereas others are more concerned with maximizing their salaries and why—more generally—some workers put forth twice as much effort as others.

intrinsically motivated behavior Behavior that is performed for its own sake.

Motivation can come from *intrinsic* or *extrinsic* sources. **Intrinsically motivated behavior** is behavior that is performed for its own sake; the source of motivation is actually performing the behavior, and motivation comes from doing the work itself. Many managers are intrinsically motivated; they derive a sense of accomplishment and achievement from helping the organization achieve its goals and gain competitive advantages. Jobs that are interesting and challenging or high on the five characteristics described by the job characteristics model (see Chapter 10) are more likely to lead to intrinsic motivation than are jobs that are boring or do not use a person's skills and abilities. An elementary school teacher who really enjoys teaching children, a computer programmer who loves solving programming problems, and a commercial photographer who relishes taking creative photographs are all intrinsically motivated. For these individuals, motivation comes from performing their jobs—teaching children, finding bugs in computer programs, and taking pictures.

A lack of intrinsic motivation at work sometimes propels people to make major changes in their lives, as illustrated in the accompanying "Managing Globally" feature.

Managing Globally

Seeking Intrinsic Motivation in Far-Flung Places

Dom Jackman and Rob Symington, then in their late 20s, were doing financial consulting work for Ernst & Young in London when they were both struck by how lacking their jobs felt in terms of intrinsic motivation. As Symington put it, "It felt like the work we did, crunching spreadsheets, just didn't matter to anyone, including to our customers or employers."[23] Realizing that they were probably not the only young workers in the finance field who didn't enjoy the work they were doing, Jackman and Symington decided to do something about it. They quit their jobs and created Escape the City, a website devoted to assisting bankers, financiers, and professionals find interesting and exciting work in far-flung places.[24] "The City" refers to the financial district in London, and hence Escape the City is a fitting name for a website oriented toward "escaping unfulfilling corporate jobs."[25]

Employers pay to list positions on the site that entail initiative and adventure, while job seekers can sign up for free.[26] Weekly email messages inform job seekers of interesting opportunities they might want to pursue, ranging from African charity work and employment with venture capital firms in Mongolia to microfinance work in India and surf camps in Morocco. Escape the City earned profits its first year in operation and has expanded to the United States with a New York office.[27]

Asia Pacific Investment Partners hired an operations manager and a communications manager from posting listings on the site.[28] Will Tindall landed the latter position, and as chief communications officer for Asia Pacific he works out of Hong Kong, Ulan Bator, and London. Harry Minter found a position as the manager of

Guludo Beach Lodge in Mozambique—he used to work in the hedge fund field at Headstart Advisers.[29] He has since moved on to another opportunity.[30] Of course not all professionals in finance and the corporate world find their work to be uninteresting and demotivating; some are intrinsically motivated by the work they do. Nonetheless, for those who are not motivated and desire more exciting, interesting, and meaningful work, Escape the City expands the set of options they might want to consider.

extrinsically motivated behavior Behavior that is performed to acquire material or social rewards or to avoid punishment.

Extrinsically motivated behavior is behavior that is performed to acquire material or social rewards or to avoid punishment; the source of motivation is the consequences of the behavior, not the behavior itself. A car salesperson who is motivated by receiving a commission on all cars sold, a lawyer who is motivated by the high salary and status that go along with the job, and a factory worker who is motivated by the opportunity to earn a secure income are all extrinsically motivated. Their motivation comes from the consequences they receive as a result of their work behaviors.

People can be intrinsically motivated, extrinsically motivated, or both intrinsically and extrinsically motivated.[31] A top manager who derives a sense of accomplishment and achievement from managing a large corporation and strives to reach year-end targets to obtain a hefty bonus is both intrinsically and extrinsically motivated. Similarly, a nurse who enjoys helping and taking care of patients and is motivated by having a secure job with good benefits is both intrinsically and extrinsically motivated. At the SAS Institute, employees are both extrinsically motivated, because of equitable pay and outstanding benefits, and intrinsically motivated, because of the opportunity to do interesting work. Whether workers are intrinsically motivated, extrinsically motivated, or both depends on a wide variety of factors: (1) workers' own personal characteristics (such as their personalities, abilities, values, attitudes, and needs), (2) the nature of their jobs (such as whether they have been enriched or where they are on the five core characteristics of the job characteristics model), and (3) the nature of the organization (such as its structure, its culture, its control systems, its human resource management system, and the ways in which rewards such as pay are distributed to employees).

prosocially motivated behavior Behavior that is performed to benefit or help others.

Where are you more likely to find prosocial motivation? Here in the classroom as a teacher walks her student through that tricky math problem. Getting companies to foster this type of motivation is a bit trickier!

In addition to being intrinsically or extrinsically motivated, some people are prosocially motivated by their work.[32] **Prosocially motivated behavior** is behavior that is performed to benefit or help others.[33] Behavior can be prosocially motivated in addition to being extrinsically and/or intrinsically motivated. An elementary school teacher who not only enjoys the process of teaching young children (has high intrinsic motivation) but also has a strong desire to give children the best learning experience possible and help those with learning disabilities overcome their challenges, and who keeps up with the latest research on child development and teaching methods in an effort to continually improve the effectiveness of his teaching, has high prosocial motivation in addition to high intrinsic motivation. A surgeon who specializes in organ transplants, enjoys the challenge of performing complex operations, has a strong desire to help her patients regain their health and extend their lives through successful organ transplants, and is also motivated by the relatively high income she earns has high intrinsic, prosocial, and extrinsic motivation. Recent preliminary research suggests that when workers have high prosocial motivation, also having high intrinsic motivation can be especially beneficial for job performance.[34]

outcome Anything a person gets from a job or organization.

Regardless of whether people are intrinsically, extrinsically, or prosocially motivated, they join and are motivated to work in organizations to obtain certain outcomes. An **outcome** is anything a person gets from a job or organization. Some outcomes, such as autonomy, responsibility, a feeling of accomplishment, and the pleasure of doing interesting or enjoyable work, result in intrinsically motivated behavior. Outcomes such as improving the lives or well-being of other people and doing good by helping others result in prosocially motivated

Figure 13.1
The Motivation Equation

INPUTS FROM ORGANIZATIONAL MEMBERS	PERFORMANCE	OUTCOMES RECEIVED BY ORGANIZATIONAL MEMBERS
Time Effort Education Experience Skills Knowledge Work behaviors	Contributes to organizational efficiency, organizational effectiveness, and the attainment of organizational goals	Pay Job security Benefits Vacation time Job satisfaction Autonomy Responsibility A feeling of accomplishment The pleasure of doing interesting work Improving the lives or well-being of others

behavior. Other outcomes, such as pay, job security, benefits, and vacation time, result in extrinsically motivated behavior.

input Anything a person contributes to his or her job or organization.

Organizations hire people to obtain important inputs. An **input** is anything a person contributes to the job or organization, such as time, effort, education, experience, skills, knowledge, and actual work behaviors. Inputs such as these are necessary for an organization to achieve its goals. Managers strive to motivate members of an organization to contribute inputs—through their behavior, effort, and persistence—that help the organization achieve its goals. How do managers do this? They ensure that members of an organization obtain the outcomes they desire when they make valuable contributions to the organization. Managers use outcomes to motivate people to contribute their inputs to the organization. Giving people outcomes when they contribute inputs and perform well aligns the interests of employees with the goals of the organization as a whole because when employees do what is good for the organization, they personally benefit.

LO13-2

Describe from the perspectives of expectancy theory and equity theory what managers should do to have a highly motivated workforce.

This alignment between employees and organizational goals as a whole can be described by the motivation equation depicted in Figure 13.1. Managers seek to ensure that people are motivated to contribute important inputs to the organization, that these inputs are put to good use or focused in the direction of high performance, and that high performance results in workers' obtaining the outcomes they desire.

expectancy theory The theory that motivation will be high when workers believe that high levels of effort lead to high performance and high performance leads to the attainment of desired outcomes.

Each of the theories of motivation discussed in this chapter focuses on one or more aspects of this equation. Each theory focuses on a different set of issues that managers need to address to have a highly motivated workforce. Together the theories provide a comprehensive set of guidelines for managers to follow to promote high levels of employee motivation. Effective managers, such as James Goodnight in "A Manager's Challenge," tend to follow many of these guidelines, whereas ineffective managers often fail to follow them and seem to have trouble motivating organizational members.

Expectancy Theory

Expectancy theory, formulated by Victor H. Vroom in the 1960s, posits that motivation is high when workers believe that high levels of effort lead to high performance and high performance leads to the attainment of desired outcomes. Expectancy theory is one of the most popular theories of work motivation because it focuses on all three parts of the motivation equation: inputs, performance, and outcomes. Expectancy theory identifies three major factors that determine a person's motivation: *expectancy, instrumentality,* and *valence* (see Figure 13.2).[35]

Figure 13.2

Expectancy, Instrumentality, and Valence

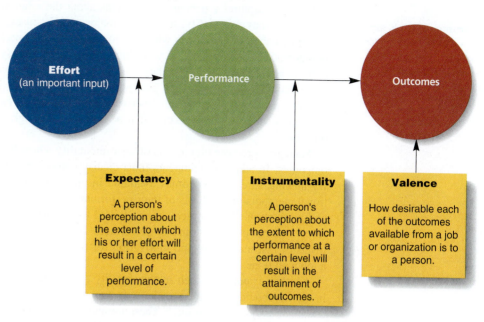

Effect (an important input)

Performance

Outcomes

Expectancy

A person's perception about the extent to which his or her effort will result in a certain level of performance.

Instrumentality

A person's perception about the extent to which performance at a certain level will result in the attainment of outcomes.

Valence

How desirable each of the outcomes available from a job or organization is to a person.

Expectancy

expectancy In expectancy theory, a perception about the extent to which effort results in a certain level of performance.

Expectancy is a person's perception about the extent to which effort (an input) results in a certain level of performance. A person's level of expectancy determines whether he or she believes that a high level of effort results in a high level of performance. People are motivated to put forth a lot of effort on their jobs only if they think that their effort will pay off in high performance—that is, if they have high expectancy. Think about how motivated you would be to study for a test if you thought that no matter how hard you tried, you would get a D. Think about how motivated a marketing manager would be who thought that no matter how hard he or she worked, there was no way to increase sales of an unpopular product. In these cases, expectancy is low, so overall motivation is also low.

Members of an organization are motivated to put forth a high level of effort only if they think that doing so leads to high performance.[36] In other words, in order for people's motivation to be high, expectancy must be high. Thus, in attempting to influence motivation, managers need to make sure their subordinates believe that if they do try hard, they can actually succeed. One way managers can boost expectancies is through expressing confidence in their subordinates' capabilities. Managers at The Container Store, for example, express high levels of confidence in their subordinates. As Container Store cofounder Garrett Boone put it, "Everybody we hire, we hire as a leader. Anybody in our store can take an action that you might think of typically being a manager's action."[37]

In addition to expressing confidence in subordinates, other ways for managers to boost subordinates' expectancy levels and motivation are by providing training so people have the expertise needed for high performance and increasing their levels of autonomy and responsibility as they gain experience so they have the freedom to do what it takes to perform at a high level. For example, the Best Buy chain of stores selling electronics, computers, music and movies, and gadgets of all sorts boosts salespeople's expectancies by giving them extensive training in on-site meetings and online. Electronic learning terminals in each department not only help salespeople learn how different systems work and can be sold as an integrated package but also enable them to keep up to date with the latest advances in technology and products. Salespeople also receive extensive training in how to determine customers' needs.[38] At the SAS Institute in "A Manager's Challenge," employees who change jobs receive any additional training they might need to be effective in their new positions, which boosts their expectancy.

Instrumentality

instrumentality In expectancy theory, a perception about the extent to which performance results in the attainment of outcomes.

Expectancy captures a person's perceptions about the relationship between effort and performance. **Instrumentality**, the second major concept in expectancy theory, is a person's perception about the extent to which performance at a certain level results in the attainment of outcomes (see Figure 13.2). According to expectancy theory, employees are motivated to perform at a high level only if they think high performance will lead to (or is *instrumental* for attaining) outcomes such as pay, job security, interesting job assignments, bonuses, or a feeling of accomplishment. In other words, instrumentalities must be high for motivation to be high—people must perceive that because of their high performance they will receive outcomes.[39]

Managers promote high levels of instrumentality when they link performance to desired outcomes. In addition, managers must clearly communicate this linkage to subordinates. By making sure that outcomes available in an organization are distributed to organizational members on the basis of their performance, managers promote high instrumentality and motivation. When outcomes are linked to performance in this way, high performers receive more outcomes than low performers. In "A Manager's Challenge," managers raise levels of instrumentality and motivation for SAS employees by rewarding employees for a job well done.

Another example of high instrumentality contributing to high motivation can be found in the Cambodian immigrants who own, manage, and work in more than 80 percent of the doughnut shops in California.[40] These immigrants see high performance as leading to many important outcomes such as income, a comfortable existence, family security, and the autonomy provided by working in a small business. Their high instrumentality contributes to their high motivation to succeed.

Valence

valence In expectancy theory, how desirable each of the outcomes available from a job or organization is to a person.

Although all members of an organization must have high expectancies and instrumentalities, expectancy theory acknowledges that people differ in their preferences for outcomes. For many people, pay is the most important outcome of working. For others, a feeling of accomplishment or enjoying one's work is more important than pay. The term **valence** refers to how desirable each of the outcomes available from a job or organization is to a person. To motivate organizational members, managers need to determine which outcomes have high valence for them—are highly desired—and make sure that those outcomes are provided when members perform at a high level.

Providing employees with highly valent outcomes not only can contribute to high levels of motivation but also has the potential to reduce turnover, as indicated in the accompanying "Management Insight" feature.

Management Insight

Motivating and Retaining Employees at The Container Store

Kip Tindell and Garrett Boone founded The Container Store in Dallas, Texas, in 1978, and Tindell currently serves as CEO and chairman (Boone is chairman emeritus).[41] When they opened their first store, they were out on the floor trying to sell customers their storage and organization products that would economize on space and time and make purchasers' lives a little less complicated. The Container Store has grown to include 65 stores in 23 U.S. markets from coast to coast; although the original

Kip Tindell, founder, CEO, and chairman of the Container Store. The Container Store has seen growth throughout its history which could be attributed to the way their managers actively assist customers on the shop floor.

store in Dallas had only 1,600 square feet, the stores today average around 25,000 square feet.[42] The phenomenal growth in the size of the stores has been matched by impressive growth rates in sales and profits.[43] Managers at The Container Store are often found on the shop floor tidying shelves and helping customers carry out their purchases.[44] And that, perhaps, is an important clue to the secret of their success. The Container Store has been consistently ranked among *Fortune* magazine's "100 Best Companies to Work For" for 15 years running.[45] In 2014 The Container Store was 28th on this list.[46]

Early on, Tindell and Boone recognized that people are The Container Store's most valuable asset and that after hiring great people, one of the most important managerial tasks is motivating them. One would think motivating employees might be especially challenging in the retail industry, which has an average annual turnover rate of 100 percent or more.[47] At The Container Store annual voluntary turnover is around 11 percent, a testament to Tindell's and other managers' ability to motivate.[48]

Tindell and Boone have long recognized the importance of rewarding employees for a job well done with highly valent outcomes. For example, the average annual pay for salespeople is around $48,000, which is significantly higher than retail averages; and employees receive merit pay increases for superior sales performance.[49] To encourage high individual performance as well as teamwork and cooperation, both individual and team-based rewards are given at The Container Store. Some high-performing salespeople earn more than their store managers, which suits the store managers fine as long as equitable procedures are used and rewards are distributed fairly.[50]

Professional development is another valent outcome employees obtain from working at The Container Store. Full-time salespeople receive over 240 hours of training their first year, and all employees have ongoing opportunities for additional training and development.[51] Employees also have flexible work options and flexible benefits; medical, dental, and 401(k) retirement plans; job security; a casual dress code; and access to a variety of wellness programs ranging from yoga classes and chair massages to a personalized web-based nutrition and exercise planner.[52] Another valent outcome is the opportunity to work with other highly motivated individuals in an environment that exudes enthusiasm and excitement. Not only are The Container Store's employees motivated, but they also look forward to coming to work and feel as if their coworkers and managers are part of their family. Employees feel pride in what they do—helping customers organize their lives, save space and time, and have a better sense of well-being. Hence they not only personally benefit from high performance by receiving highly valent outcomes but also feel good about the products they sell and the help they give customers.[53] Tindell and other managers at The Container Store evidently have never lost sight of the importance of motivation for both organizations and their members.

Bringing It All Together

According to expectancy theory, high motivation results from high levels of expectancy, instrumentality, and valence (see Figure 13.3). If any one of these factors is low, motivation is likely to be low. No matter how tightly desired outcomes are linked to performance, if a person thinks it is practically impossible to perform at a high level, motivation to perform at a high level will be low. Similarly, if a person does not think outcomes are linked to high performance, or if a person does not desire the outcomes that are linked to high performance, motivation to perform at a high level will be low. Effective managers realize the importance of high levels of expectancy, instrumentality, and valence and take concrete steps to ensure that their employees are highly motivated, as is true at Enterprise Rent-A-Car profiled in the accompanying "Management Insight" feature.

Management Insight

How Enterprise Rent-A-Car Motivates Employees

Enterprise Rent-A-Car was founded by Jack Taylor in 1957 in St. Louis, Missouri, as a very small auto leasing business.[54] Today Enterprise Holdings, which owns and operates Enterprise Rent-A-Car, is the biggest car rental company in the world with over $16 billion in revenues and over 78,000 employees. Enterprise has over 8,000 locations in the United States, Canada, the United Kingdom, Ireland, and Germany.[55] One of the biggest employers of new college graduates in the United States, Enterprise typically hires over 8,000 college graduates each year.[56] While starting salaries tend to be low and the work can be hard (e.g., four assistant managers once sued the company claiming that they should receive overtime pay), Enterprise has been ranked among the top 50 best companies for new college graduates to launch their careers by *Bloomberg Businessweek* magazine.[57]

One of the keys to Enterprise's success is the way it motivates its employees to provide excellent customer service.[58] Practically all entry-level hires participate in Enterprise's Management Training Program.[59] As part of the program, new hires learn all aspects of the company business, and how to provide excellent customer service. Management trainees first have a four-day training session focused primarily on Enterprise's culture. They are then assigned to a branch office for around 8 to 12 months where they learn all aspects of the business, from negotiating with body shops to helping customers to washing cars. As part of this training, they learn how important high-quality customer service is to Enterprise and how they can personally provide great service, increasing their confidence levels.[60]

All those who do well in the program are promoted after about a year to the position of management assistant. Management assistants who do well are promoted to become assistant branch managers with responsibility for mentoring and supervising employees. Assistant managers who do well can be promoted to become branch managers who are responsible for managing a branch's employees and provision of customer service, rental car fleet, and financial performance. Branch managers with about five years of experience in the position often move on to take up management positions at headquarters or assume the position of area manager overseeing all the branches in a certain geographic region.[61] By training all new hires in all aspects of the business including the provision of excellent customer service, by providing them with valuable experience with increasing levels of responsibility and empowerment, and by providing all new hires who perform well with the opportunity to advance in the company, Enterprise has developed a highly motivated workforce.[62]

In addition to motivating high performance and excellent customer service through training and promotional opportunities, Enterprise also uses financial incentives to motivate employees. Essentially each branch is considered a profit center, and the managers overseeing the branch and in charge of all aspects of its functioning have the autonomy and responsibility for the branch's profitability almost as if the branch was their own small business or franchise.[63] All branch employees at the rank of assistant manager and higher earn incentive compensation whereby their monthly pay depends on the profitability of their branch. Managers at higher levels, such as area managers, have their monthly pay linked to the profitability of the region they oversee. Thus managers at all levels know that their pay is linked to the profitability of the parts of Enterprise for which they are responsible. And they have the autonomy to make decisions ranging from buying and selling cars to opening new branches.[64]

All in all Enterprise's employees are highly motivated because of their high levels of expectancy, instrumentality, and valence. Contributing to high levels of expectancy is the training all new hires receive in all aspects of the business, including the provision of excellent customer service and the ongoing valuable experiences employees receive with increasing levels of responsibility and empowerment. Linking two highly valent outcomes, pay and promotions, to performance leads to high instrumentality. And highly motivated employees at Enterprise do provide excellent service to their customers.

Figure 13.3
Expectancy Theory

Expectancy is high:
People perceive that if they try hard, they can perform at a high level.

Instrumentality is high:
People perceive that high performance leads to the receipt of certain outcomes.

Valence is high:
People desire the outcomes that result from high performance.

HIGH MOTIVATION

Need Theories

LO13-3
Explain how goals and needs motivate people and what kinds of goals are especially likely to result in high performance.

need A requirement or necessity for survival and well-being.

need theories Theories of motivation that focus on what needs people are trying to satisfy at work and what outcomes will satisfy those needs.

Maslow's hierarchy of needs An arrangement of five basic needs that, according to Maslow, motivate behavior. Maslow proposed that the lowest level of unmet needs is the prime motivator and that only one level of needs is motivational at a time.

A **need** is a requirement or necessity for survival and well-being. The basic premise of **need theories** is that people are motivated to obtain outcomes at work that will satisfy their needs. Need theory complements expectancy theory by exploring in depth which outcomes motivate people to perform at a high level. Need theories suggest that to motivate a person to contribute valuable inputs to a job and perform at a high level, a manager must determine what needs the person is trying to satisfy at work and ensure that the person receives outcomes that help to satisfy those needs when the person performs at a high level and helps the organization achieve its goals.

There are several need theories. Here we discuss Abraham Maslow's hierarchy of needs, Clayton Alderfer's ERG theory, Frederick Herzberg's motivator-hygiene theory, and David McClelland's needs for achievement, affiliation, and power. These theories describe needs that people try to satisfy at work. In doing so, they give managers insights about what outcomes motivate members of an organization to perform at a high level and contribute inputs to help the organization achieve its goals.

Maslow's Hierarchy of Needs

Psychologist Abraham Maslow proposed that all people seek to satisfy five basic kinds of needs: physiological needs, safety needs, belongingness needs, esteem needs, and self-actualization needs (see Table 13.1).[65] He suggested that these needs constitute a **hierarchy of needs**, with the most basic or compelling needs—physiological and safety needs—at the bottom. Maslow argued that these lowest-level needs must be met before a person strives to satisfy needs higher up in the hierarchy, such as self-esteem needs. Once a need is satisfied, Maslow proposed, it ceases to operate as a source of motivation. The lowest level of *unmet* needs in the hierarchy is the prime motivator of behavior; if and when this level is satisfied, needs at the next highest level in the hierarchy motivate behavior.

Although this theory identifies needs that are likely to be important sources of motivation for many people, research does not support Maslow's contention that there is a need hierarchy or his notion that only one level of needs is motivational at a time.[66] Nevertheless, a key conclusion can be drawn from Maslow's theory: People try to satisfy different needs at work. To have a motivated workforce, managers must determine which needs employees are trying to satisfy in organizations and then make sure that individuals receive outcomes that satisfy their needs when they perform at a high level and contribute to organizational effectiveness. By doing this, managers align the interests of individual members with the interests of the

Table 13.1

Maslow's Hierarchy of Needs

	Needs	Description	Examples of How Managers Can Help People Satisfy These Needs at Work
Highest-level needs	**Self-actualization needs**	The needs to realize one's full potential as a human being.	By giving people the opportunity to use their skills and abilities to the fullest extent possible.
	Esteem needs	The needs to feel good about oneself and one's capabilities, to be respected by others, and to receive recognition and appreciation.	By granting promotions and recognizing accomplishments.
	Belongingness needs	Needs for social interaction, friendship, affection, and love.	By promoting good interpersonal relations and organizing social functions such as company picnics and holiday parties.
	Safety needs	Needs for security, stability, and a safe environment.	By providing job security, adequate medical benefits, and safe working conditions.
Lowest-level needs (most basic or compelling)	**Physiological needs**	Basic needs for things such as food, water, and shelter that must be met in order for a person to survive.	By providing a level of pay that enables a person to buy food and clothing and have adequate housing.

The lowest level of unsatisfied needs motivates behavior; once this level of needs is satisfied, a person tries to satisfy the needs at the next level.

Alderfer's ERG theory The theory that three universal needs—for existence, relatedness, and growth—constitute a hierarchy of needs and motivate behavior. Alderfer proposed that needs at more than one level can be motivational at the same time.

organization as a whole. By doing what is good for the organization (that is, performing at a high level), employees receive outcomes that satisfy their needs.

In our increasingly global economy, managers must realize that citizens of different countries might differ in the needs they seek to satisfy through work.[67] Some research suggests, for example, that people in Greece and Japan are especially motivated by safety needs and that people in Sweden, Norway, and Denmark are motivated by belongingness needs.[68] In less developed countries with low standards of living, physiological and safety needs are likely to be the prime motivators of behavior. As countries become wealthier and have higher standards of living, needs related to personal growth and accomplishment (such as esteem and self-actualization) become important motivators of behavior.

Alderfer's ERG Theory

Clayton **Alderfer's ERG theory** collapsed the five categories of needs in Maslow's hierarchy into three universal categories—existence, relatedness, and growth—also arranged in a hierarchy (see Table 13.2). Alderfer agreed with Maslow that as lower-level needs become satisfied, a person seeks to satisfy higher-level needs. Unlike Maslow, however, Alderfer believed that a person can be motivated by needs at more than one level at the same time. A cashier in a supermarket, for example, may be motivated by both existence needs and relatedness needs. The existence needs motivate the cashier to come to work regularly and not make mistakes so his job will be secure and he will be able to pay his rent and buy food. The relatedness needs

No one pumps their fist over their laptop unless it's for a good reason! Clearly, whipping an obnoxious spreadsheet into shape and sending out a calmly worded press release makes for satisfied self-actualization needs.

Table 13.2

Alderfer's ERG Theory

	Needs	Description	Examples of How Managers Can Help People Satisfy These Needs at Work
Highest-level needs ↑ ↓ **Lowest-level needs**	**Growth needs**	The needs for self-development and creative and productive work.	By allowing people to continually improve their skills and abilities and engage in meaningful work.
	Relatedness needs	The needs to have good interpersonal relations, to share thoughts and feelings, and to have open two-way communication.	By promoting good interpersonal relations and by providing accurate feedback.
	Existence needs	Basic needs for food, water, clothing, shelter, and a secure and safe environment.	By providing enough pay for the basic necessities of life and safe working conditions.

**As lower-level needs are satisfied, a person is motivated to satisfy higher-level needs.
When a person is unable to satisfy higher-level needs (or is frustrated),
motivation to satisfy lower-level needs increases.**

motivate the cashier to become friends with some of the other cashiers and have a good relationship with the store manager. Alderfer also suggested that when people experience *need frustration* or are unable to satisfy needs at a certain level, they will focus more intently on satisfying the needs at the next lowest level in the hierarchy.[69]

As with Maslow's theory, research does not support some of the specific ideas outlined in ERG theory, such as the existence of the three-level need hierarchy that Alderfer proposed.[70] However, for managers, the important message from ERG theory is the same as that from Maslow's theory: Determine what needs your subordinates are trying to satisfy at work, and make sure they receive outcomes that satisfy these needs when they perform at a high level to help the organization achieve its goals.

Herzberg's Motivator-Hygiene Theory

Herzberg's motivator-hygiene theory A need theory that distinguishes between motivator needs (related to the nature of the work itself) and hygiene needs (related to the physical and psychological context in which the work is performed) and proposes that motivator needs must be met for motivation and job satisfaction to be high.

Adopting an approach different from Maslow's and Alderfer's, Frederick Herzberg focused on two factors: (1) outcomes that can lead to high levels of motivation and job satisfaction and (2) outcomes that can prevent people from being dissatisfied. According to **Herzberg's motivator-hygiene theory**, people have two sets of needs or requirements: motivator needs and hygiene needs.[71] *Motivator needs* are related to the nature of the work itself and how challenging it is. Outcomes such as interesting work, autonomy, responsibility, being able to grow and develop on the job, and a sense of accomplishment and achievement help to satisfy motivator needs. To have a highly motivated and satisfied workforce, Herzberg suggested, managers should take steps to ensure that employees' motivator needs are being met.

Hygiene needs are related to the physical and psychological context in which the work is performed. Hygiene needs are satisfied by outcomes such as pleasant and comfortable working conditions, pay, job security, good relationships with coworkers, and effective supervision. According to Herzberg, when hygiene needs are not met, workers are dissatisfied, and when hygiene needs are met, workers are not dissatisfied. Satisfying hygiene needs, however, does not result in high levels of motivation or even high levels of job satisfaction. For motivation and job satisfaction to be high, motivator needs must be met.

Many research studies have tested Herzberg's propositions, and, by and large, the theory fails to receive support.[72] Nevertheless, Herzberg's formulations have contributed to our understanding of motivation in at least two ways. First, Herzberg helped to focus researchers' and managers' attention on the important distinction between intrinsic motivation (related to motivator needs) and extrinsic motivation (related to hygiene needs), covered earlier in the chapter. Second, his theory prompted researchers and managers to study how jobs could be designed or redesigned so they are intrinsically motivating.

McClelland's Needs for Achievement, Affiliation, and Power

need for achievement The extent to which an individual has a strong desire to perform challenging tasks well and to meet personal standards for excellence.

need for affiliation The extent to which an individual is concerned about establishing and maintaining good interpersonal relations, being liked, and having the people around him or her get along with each other.

need for power The extent to which an individual desires to control or influence others.

Psychologist David McClelland extensively researched the needs for achievement, affiliation, and power.[73] The **need for achievement** is the extent to which an individual has a strong desire to perform challenging tasks well and to meet personal standards for excellence. People with a high need for achievement often set clear goals for themselves and like to receive performance feedback. The **need for affiliation** is the extent to which an individual is concerned about establishing and maintaining good interpersonal relations, being liked, and having the people around him or her get along with each other. The **need for power** is the extent to which an individual desires to control or influence others.[74]

Although each of these needs is present in each of us to some degree, their importance in the workplace depends on the position one occupies. For example, research suggests that high needs for achievement and for power are assets for first-line and middle managers and that a high need for power is especially important for upper managers.[75] One study found that U.S. presidents with a relatively high need for power tended to be especially effective during their terms of office.[76] A high need for affiliation may not always be desirable in managers and other leaders because it might lead them to try too hard to be liked by others (including subordinates) rather than doing all they can to ensure that performance is as high as it can and should be. Although most research on these needs has been done in the United States, some studies suggest that the findings may be applicable to people in other countries as well, such as India and New Zealand.[77]

Other Needs

LO13-2

Describe from the perspectives of expectancy theory and equity theory what managers should do to have a highly motivated workforce.

Clearly, more needs motivate workers than the needs described by these four theories. For example, more and more workers are feeling the need for work–life balance and time to take care of their loved ones while simultaneously being highly motivated at work. Recall how the SAS Institute recognizes and seeks to satisfy these needs from "A Manager's Challenge." Interestingly enough, recent research suggests that being exposed to nature (even just being able to see some trees from an office window) has many salutary effects, and a lack of such exposure can impair well-being and performance.[78] Thus having some time during the day when one can at least see nature may be another important need. Managers of successful companies often strive to ensure that as many of their valued employees' needs as possible are satisfied in the workplace.

Equity Theory

equity theory A theory of motivation that focuses on people's perceptions of the fairness of their work outcomes relative to their work inputs.

Equity theory is a theory of motivation that concentrates on people's perceptions of the fairness of their work *outcomes* relative to, or in proportion to, their work *inputs*. Equity theory complements expectancy and need theories by focusing on how people perceive the relationship between the outcomes they receive from their jobs and organizations and the inputs they contribute. Equity theory was formulated in the 1960s by J. Stacy Adams, who stressed that what is important in determining motivation is the *relative* rather than the *absolute* levels of outcomes a person receives and inputs a person contributes. Specifically, motivation is influenced by the comparison of one's own outcome–input ratio with the outcome–input ratio of a referent.[79] The *referent* could be another person or a group of people who are perceived to be similar to oneself; the referent also could be oneself in a previous job or one's expectations about what outcome–input ratios

Table 13.3

Equity Theory

Condition	Person		Referent	Example
Equity	$\dfrac{\text{Outcomes}}{\text{Inputs}}$	$=$	$\dfrac{\text{Outcomes}}{\text{Inputs}}$	An engineer perceives that he contributes more inputs (time and effort) and receives proportionally more outcomes (a higher salary and choice job assignments) than his referent.
Underpayment inequity	$\dfrac{\text{Outcomes}}{\text{Inputs}}$	$<$ (less than)	$\dfrac{\text{Outcomes}}{\text{Inputs}}$	An engineer perceives that he contributes more inputs but receives the same outcomes as his referent.
Overpayment inequity	$\dfrac{\text{Outcomes}}{\text{Inputs}}$	$>$ (greater than)	$\dfrac{\text{Outcomes}}{\text{Inputs}}$	An engineer perceives that he contributes the same inputs but receives more outcomes than his referent.

should be. In a comparison of one's own outcome–input ratio to a referent's ratio, one's *perceptions* of outcomes and inputs (not any objective indicator of them) are key.

Equity

equity The justice, impartiality, and fairness to which all organizational members are entitled.

Equity exists when a person perceives his or her own outcome–input ratio to be equal to a referent's outcome–input ratio. Under conditions of equity (see Table 13.3), if a referent receives more outcomes than you receive, the referent contributes proportionally more inputs to the organization, so his or her outcome–input ratio still equals your ratio. Maria Sanchez and Claudia King, for example, both work in a shoe store in a large mall. Sanchez is paid more per hour than King but also contributes more inputs, including being responsible for some of the store's bookkeeping, closing the store, and periodically depositing cash in the bank. When King compares her outcome–input ratio to Sanchez's (her referent's), she perceives the ratios to be equitable because Sanchez's higher level of pay (an outcome) is proportional to her higher level of inputs (bookkeeping, closing the store, and going to the bank).

Similarly, under conditions of equity, if you receive more outcomes than a referent, your inputs are perceived to be proportionally higher. Continuing with our example, when Sanchez compares her outcome–input ratio to King's (her referent's) ratio, she perceives them to be equitable because her higher level of pay is proportional to her higher level of inputs.

When equity exists, people are motivated to continue contributing their current levels of inputs to their organizations to receive their current levels of outcomes. If people wish to increase their outcomes under conditions of equity, they are motivated to increase their inputs.

Inequity

inequity Lack of fairness.

Inequity, or lack of fairness, exists when a person's outcome–input ratio is not perceived to be equal to a referent's. Inequity creates pressure or tension inside people and motivates them to restore equity by bringing the two ratios back into balance.

There are two types of inequity: underpayment inequity and overpayment inequity (see Table 13.3). **Underpayment inequity** exists when a person's own outcome–input ratio is perceived to be *less* than that of a referent. In comparing yourself to a referent, you think you are *not* receiving the outcomes you should be, given your inputs. **Overpayment inequity** exists when a person perceives that his or her own outcome–input ratio is *greater* than that of a referent. In comparing yourself to a referent, you think you are receiving *more* outcomes than you should be, given your inputs.

underpayment inequity The inequity that exists when a person perceives that his or her own outcome–input ratio is less than the ratio of a referent.

overpayment inequity The inequity that exists when a person perceives that his or her own outcome–input ratio is greater than the ratio of a referent.

Ways to Restore Equity

According to equity theory, both underpayment inequity and overpayment inequity create tension that motivates most people to restore equity by bringing the ratios back into balance.[80] When people experience *underpayment* inequity, they may be motivated to lower their inputs by reducing their working hours, putting forth less effort on the job, or being absent; or they may be motivated to increase their outcomes by asking for a raise or a promotion. Susan Richie, a financial analyst at a large corporation, noticed that she was working longer hours and getting more work accomplished than a coworker who had the same position, yet they both received the exact same pay and other outcomes. To restore equity, Richie decided to stop coming in early and staying late. Alternatively, she could have tried to restore equity by trying to increase her outcomes, perhaps by asking her boss for a raise.

When people experience underpayment inequity and other means of equity restoration fail, they can change their perceptions of their own or the referent's inputs or outcomes. For example, they may realize that their referent is really working on more difficult projects than they are or that they really take more time off from work than their referent does. Alternatively, if people who feel they are underpaid have other employment options, they may leave the organization. As an example, John Steinberg, an assistant principal in a high school, experienced underpayment inequity when he realized all the other assistant principals of high schools in his school district had received promotions to the position of principal even though they had been in their jobs for a shorter time than he had. Steinberg's performance had always been appraised as being high, so after his repeated requests for a promotion went unheeded, he found a job as a principal in a different school district.

When people experience *overpayment* inequity, they may try to restore equity by changing their perceptions of their own or their referent's inputs or outcomes. Equity can be restored when people realize they are contributing more inputs than they originally thought. Equity also can be restored by perceiving the referent's inputs to be lower or the referent's outcomes to be higher than one originally thought. When equity is restored in this way, actual inputs and outcomes are unchanged, and the person being overpaid takes no real action. What is changed is how people think about or view their or the referent's inputs and outcomes. For instance, Mary McMann experienced overpayment inequity when she realized she was being paid $2 an hour more than a coworker who had the same job as she did in a health food store and who contributed the same amount of inputs. McMann restored equity by changing her perceptions of her inputs. She realized she worked harder than her coworker and solved more problems that came up in the store.

Experiencing either overpayment or underpayment inequity, you might decide that your referent is not appropriate because, for example, the referent is too different from your-self. Choosing a more appropriate referent may bring the ratios back into balance. Angela Martinez, a middle manager in the engineering department of a chemical company, experi-enced overpayment inequity when she realized she was being paid quite a bit more than her friend, who was a middle manager in the marketing department of the same company. After thinking about the discrepancy for a while, Martinez decided that engineering and marketing were so different that she should not be comparing her job to her friend's job even though they were both middle managers. Martinez restored equity by changing her referent; she picked a middle manager in the engineering department as a new referent.

Motivation is highest when as many people as possible in an organization perceive that they are being equitably treated—their outcomes and inputs are in balance. Top contribu-tors and performers are motivated to continue contributing a high level of inputs because they are receiving the outcomes they deserve. Mediocre contributors and performers realize that if they want to increase their outcomes, they have to increase their inputs. Managers of effective organizations, like the SAS Institute, realize the importance of equity for motiva-tion and performance and continually strive to ensure that employees believe they are being equitably treated.

The dot-com boom, its subsequent bust, and two recessions, along with increased global competition, have resulted in some workers putting in longer and longer working hours (increasing their inputs) without any increase in their outcomes. For those whose referents are not experiencing a similar change, perceptions of inequity are likely. According to Jill Andresky Fraser, author of *White Collar Sweatshop,* over 25 million U.S. workers work more than 49 hours per week in the office, almost 11 million work more than 60 hours per week in the office, and many also put in additional work hours at home. Moreover, advances in infor-mation technology, such as email and cell phones, have resulted in work intruding on home time, vacation time, and even special occasions.[81]

Equity and Justice in Organizations

distributive justice A person's perception of the fairness of the distribution of outcomes in an organization

Equity theory, given its focus on the fair distribution of outcomes in organizations to foster high motivation, is often labeled a theory of distributive justice.[82] **Distributive justice** refers to an employee's perception of the fairness of the distribution of outcomes (such as promotions, pay, job assignments, and working conditions) in an organization.[83] Employees are more likely to be highly motivated when they perceive distributive justice to be high rather than low.

procedural justice A person's perception of the fairness of the procedures that are used to determine how to distribute outcomes in an organization.

interpersonal justice A person's perception of the fairness of the interpersonal treatment he or she receives from whoever distributes outcomes to him or her.

informational justice A person's perception of the extent to which his or her manager provides explanations for decisions and the procedures used to arrive at them.

Three other forms of justice are important for high motivation. **Procedural justice** refers to an employee's perception of the fairness of the procedures used to determine how to distribute outcomes in an organization.[84] For example, if important outcomes such as pay and promotions are distributed based on performance appraisals (see Chapter 12) and an employee perceives that the procedure that is used (i.e., the performance appraisal system) is unfair, then procedural justice is low and motivation is likely to suffer. More generally, motivation is higher when procedural justice is high rather than low.[85] **Interpersonal justice** refers to an employee's perception of the fairness of the interpersonal treatment he or she receives from whoever distributes outcomes to him or her (typically his or her manager).[86] Interpersonal justice is high when managers treat subordinates with dignity and respect and are polite and courteous.[87] Motivation is higher when interpersonal justice is high rather than low. **Informational justice** refers to an employee's perception of the extent to which his or her manager provides explanations for decisions and the procedures used to arrive at them.[88] For example, if a manager explains how performance is appraised and how decisions about the distribution of outcomes are made, informational justice (and motivation) are more likely to be high than if the manager does not do this.[89] All in all, it is most advantageous for distributive, procedural, interpersonal, and informational justice all to be high.

Goal-Setting Theory

Goal-setting theory focuses on motivating workers to contribute their inputs to their jobs and organizations; in this way it is similar to expectancy theory and equity theory. But goal-setting theory takes this focus a step further by considering as well how managers can ensure that organizational members focus their inputs in the direction of high performance and the achievement of organizational goals.

LO13-3

Explain how goals and needs motivate people and what kinds of goals are especially likely to result in high performance.

goal-setting theory A theory that focuses on identifying the types of goals that are most effective in producing high levels of motivation and performance and explaining why goals have these effects.

Ed Locke and Gary Latham, the leading researchers for goal-setting theory, suggested that the goals organizational members strive to attain are prime determinants of their motivation and subsequent performance. A *goal* is what a person is trying to accomplish through his or her efforts and behaviors.[90] Just as you may have a goal to get a good grade in this course, so do members of an organization have goals they strive to meet. For example, salespeople at Neiman Marcus strive to meet sales goals, while top managers pursue market share and profitability goals.

Goal-setting theory suggests that to stimulate high motivation and performance, goals must be *specific* and *difficult*.[91] Specific goals are often quantitative—a salesperson's goal to sell $500 worth of merchandise per day, a scientist's goal to finish a project in one year, a CEO's goal to reduce debt by 40 percent and increase revenues by 20 percent, a restaurant manager's goal to serve 150 customers per evening. In contrast to specific goals, vague goals such as "doing your best" or "selling as much as you can" do not have much motivational impact.

Difficult goals are hard but not impossible to attain. In contrast to difficult goals, easy goals are those that practically everyone can attain, and moderate goals are goals that about one-half of the people can attain. Both easy and moderate goals have less motivational power than difficult goals.

Regardless of whether specific, difficult goals are set by managers, workers, or teams of managers and workers, they lead to high levels of motivation and performance. When managers set goals for their subordinates, their subordinates must accept the goals or agree to work toward them; also, they should be committed to them or really want to

Specific, difficult goals can encourage people to exert high levels of effort and to focus efforts in the right direction.

attain them. Some managers find that having subordinates participate in the actual setting of goals boosts their acceptance of and commitment to the goals. In addition, organizational members need to receive *feedback* about how they are doing; feedback can often be provided by the performance appraisal and feedback component of an organization's human resource management system (see Chapter 12). More generally, goals and feedback are integral components of performance management systems such as management by objectives (see Chapter 11).

Specific, difficult goals affect motivation in two ways. First, they motivate people to contribute more inputs to their jobs. Specific, difficult goals cause people to put forth high levels of effort, for example. Just as you would study harder if you were trying to get an A in a course instead of a C, so too will a salesperson work harder to reach a $500 sales goal instead of a $200 sales goal. Specific, difficult goals also cause people to be more persistent than easy, moderate, or vague goals when they run into difficulties. Salespeople who are told to sell as much as possible might stop trying on a slow day, whereas having a specific, difficult goal to reach causes them to keep trying.

A second way in which specific, difficult goals affect motivation is by helping people focus their inputs in the right direction. These goals let people know what they should be focusing their attention on, whether it is increasing the quality of customer service or sales or lowering new product development times. The fact that the goals are specific and difficult also frequently causes people to develop *action plans* for reaching them.[92] Action plans can include the strategies to attain the goals and timetables or schedules for the completion of different activities crucial to goal attainment. Like the goals themselves, action plans also help ensure that efforts are focused in the right direction and that people do not get sidetracked along the way.

Although specific, difficult goals have been found to increase motivation and performance in a wide variety of jobs and organizations both in the United States and abroad, recent research suggests that they may detract from performance under certain conditions. When people are performing complicated and challenging tasks that require them to focus on a considerable amount of learning, specific, difficult goals may actually impair performance.[93] Striving to reach such goals may direct some of a person's attention away from learning about the task and toward trying to figure out how to achieve the goal. Once a person has learned the task and it no longer seems complicated or difficult, then the assignment of specific, difficult goals is likely to have its usual effects. Additionally, for work that is very creative and uncertain, specific, difficult goals may be detrimental.

LO13-4

Identify the motivation lessons that managers can learn from operant conditioning theory and social learning theory.

Learning Theories

The basic premise of **learning theories** as applied to organizations is that managers can increase employee motivation and performance by how they link the outcomes that employees receive to the performance of desired behaviors and the attainment of goals. Thus learning theory focuses on the linkage between performance and outcomes in the motivation equation (see Figure 13.1).

learning theories
Theories that focus on increasing employee motivation and performance by linking the outcomes that employees receive to the performance of desired behaviors and the attainment of goals.

learning A relatively permanent change in knowledge or behavior that results from practice or experience.

Learning can be defined as a relatively permanent change in a person's knowledge or behavior that results from practice or experience.[94] Learning takes place in organizations when people learn to perform certain behaviors to receive certain outcomes. For example, a person learns to perform at a higher level than in the past or to come to work earlier because he or she is motivated to obtain the outcomes that result from these behaviors, such as a pay raise or praise from a supervisor.

Training can spur learning in all kinds of jobs and organizations, even ones where a good portion of the workforce is working freelance, at home, and part-time, as indicated in the accompanying "Management Insight" feature.

Management Insight

Training Spurs Learning at Stella & Dot

Stella & Dot, based in San Francisco, is a social selling company that sells jewelry and accessories exclusively through independent stylists who host trunk shows in their homes and online. Founded by Jessica Herrin, who started the firm by designing jewelry, is its current CEO, and was a cofounder of the WeddingChannel.com, Stella & Dot has grown to have over $200 million in sales.[95] Stella & Dot has approximately 10,000 stylists who work out of their homes, many of them part-time. According to Herrin, one of the keys to their success is the training they provide to stylists.[96]

CEO and founder of Stella & Dot, Jessica Herrin, whose company sells jewelry and accessories exclusively through independent stylists who host trunk shows in their homes and online. Its stylists are given training at its own online learning center, Stella & Dot University.

The company has its own online learning center, called Stella & Dot University, where stylists have access to interactive videos, guidebooks, tutorials, and audio training. Online quizzes ensure that learning takes place, and stylists receive immediate feedback when they master a content area. Weekly phone calls with headquarters also focus on coaching and training stylists to learn how best to market and sell products.[97] Herrin herself makes it a point to send personal email messages, and she calls at least 10 stylists a day to see how they are doing and to congratulate them when things go well.[98]

There are also many opportunities for stylists to learn from each other. High-performing stylists relate the keys to their own success in webcams in their homes, how they managed the process, and the obstacles they were able to overcome.[99] A national annual conference also enables stylists to learn from each other by providing networking opportunities and training sessions led by high-performing stylists. Regional training also is provided by local high-performing stylists.[100]

In all of its training efforts, Stella & Dot emphasizes treating stylists with respect as the professionals that they are and celebrating successes.[101] All in all, facilitating learning through training has certainly paid off for Stella & Dot.

Of the different learning theories, operant conditioning theory and social learning theory provide the most guidance to managers in their efforts to have a highly motivated workforce.

Operant Conditioning Theory

operant conditioning theory The theory that people learn to perform behaviors that lead to desired consequences and learn not to perform behaviors that lead to undesired consequences.

According to **operant conditioning theory**, developed by psychologist B. F. Skinner, people learn to perform behaviors that lead to desired consequences and learn not to perform behaviors that lead to undesired consequences.[102] Translated into motivation terms, Skinner's theory means that people will be motivated to perform at a high level and attain their work goals to the extent that high performance and goal attainment allow them to obtain outcomes they desire. Similarly, people avoid performing behaviors that lead to outcomes they do not desire. By linking the performance of *specific behaviors* to the attainment of *specific outcomes,* managers can motivate organizational members to perform in ways that help an organization achieve its goals.

Operant conditioning theory provides four tools that managers can use to motivate high performance and prevent workers from engaging in absenteeism and other behaviors that detract from organizational effectiveness. These tools are positive reinforcement, negative reinforcement, extinction, and punishment.[103]

positive reinforcement
Giving people outcomes they desire when they perform organizationally functional behaviors.

POSITIVE REINFORCEMENT   Positive reinforcement gives people outcomes they desire when they perform organizationally functional behaviors. These desired outcomes, called *positive reinforcers,* include any outcomes that a person desires, such as pay, praise, or a promotion. Organizationally functional behaviors are behaviors that contribute to organizational effectiveness; they can include producing high-quality goods and services, providing high-quality customer service, and meeting deadlines. By linking positive reinforcers to the performance of functional behaviors, managers motivate people to perform the desired behaviors.

negative reinforcement
Eliminating or removing undesired outcomes when people perform organizationally functional behaviors.

NEGATIVE REINFORCEMENT   Negative reinforcement also can encourage members of an organization to perform desired or organizationally functional behaviors. Managers using negative reinforcement actually eliminate or remove undesired outcomes once the functional behavior is performed. These undesired outcomes, called *negative reinforcers,* can range from a manager's constant nagging or criticism to unpleasant assignments or the ever-present threat of losing one's job. When negative reinforcement is used, people are motivated to perform behaviors because they want to stop receiving or avoid undesired outcomes. Managers who try to encourage salespeople to sell more by threatening them with being fired are using negative reinforcement. In this case, the negative reinforcer is the threat of job loss, which is removed once the functional behavior is performed.

Whenever possible, managers should try to use positive reinforcement. Negative reinforcement can create a very unpleasant work environment and even a negative culture in an organization. No one likes to be nagged, threatened, or exposed to other kinds of negative outcomes. The use of negative reinforcement sometimes causes subordinates to resent managers and try to get back at them.

IDENTIFYING THE RIGHT BEHAVIORS FOR REINFORCEMENT   Even managers who use positive reinforcement (and refrain from using negative reinforcement) can get into trouble if they are not careful to identify the right behaviors to reinforce—behaviors that are truly functional for the organization. Doing this is not always as straightforward as it might seem. First, it is crucial for managers to choose behaviors over which subordinates have control; in other words, subordinates must have the freedom and opportunity to perform the behaviors that are being reinforced. Second, it is crucial that these behaviors contribute to organizational effectiveness.

extinction Curtailing the performance of dysfunctional behaviors by eliminating whatever is reinforcing them.

EXTINCTION   Sometimes members of an organization are motivated to perform behaviors that detract from organizational effectiveness. According to operant conditioning theory, all behavior is controlled or determined by its consequences; one way for managers to curtail the performance of dysfunctional behaviors is to eliminate whatever is reinforcing the behaviors. This process is called extinction.

Suppose a manager has a subordinate who frequently stops by his office to chat—sometimes about work-related matters but at other times about various topics ranging from politics to last night's football game. The manager and the subordinate share certain interests and views, so these conversations can get quite involved, and both seem to enjoy them. The manager, however, realizes that these frequent and sometimes lengthy conversations are causing him to stay at work later in the evenings to make up for the time he loses during the day. The manager also realizes that he is reinforcing his subordinate's behavior by acting interested in the topics the subordinate brings up and responding at length to them. To extinguish this behavior, the manager stops acting interested in these non-work-related conversations and keeps his responses polite and friendly but brief. No longer being reinforced with a pleasurable conversation, the subordinate eventually ceases to be motivated to interrupt the manager during working hours to discuss non-work-related issues.

punishment Administering an undesired or negative consequence when dysfunctional behavior occurs.

PUNISHMENT   Sometimes managers cannot rely on extinction to eliminate dysfunctional behaviors because they do not have control over whatever is reinforcing the behavior or because they cannot afford the time needed for extinction to work. When employees are performing dangerous behaviors or behaviors that are illegal or unethical, the behavior needs to be eliminated immediately. Sexual harassment, for example, is an organizationally dysfunctional behavior that cannot be tolerated. In such cases managers often rely on punishment, which is administering an undesired or negative consequence to subordinates when they perform the dysfunctional behavior. Punishments used by organizations range from verbal reprimands to pay cuts, temporary suspensions, demotions, and firings. Punishment, however, can have some unintended side effects—resentment, loss of self-respect, a desire for retaliation—and should be used only when necessary.

To avoid the unintended side effects of punishment, managers should keep in mind these guidelines:

- Downplay the emotional element involved in punishment. Make it clear that you are punishing a person's performance of a dysfunctional behavior, not the person himself or herself.

- Try to punish dysfunctional behaviors as soon as possible after they occur and make sure the negative consequence is a source of punishment for the individuals involved. Be certain that organizational members know exactly why they are being punished.

- Try to avoid punishing someone in front of others because this can hurt a person's self-respect and lower esteem in the eyes of coworkers as well as make coworkers feel uncomfortable.[104] Even so, making organizational members aware that an individual who has committed a serious infraction has been punished can sometimes be effective in preventing future infractions and teaching all members of the organization that certain behaviors are unacceptable. For example, when organizational members are informed that a manager who has sexually harassed subordinates has been punished, they learn or are reminded of the fact that sexual harassment is not tolerated in the organization.

Managers and students alike often confuse negative reinforcement and punishment. To avoid such confusion, keep in mind the two major differences between them. First, negative reinforcement is used to promote the performance of functional behaviors in organizations; punishment is used to stop the performance of dysfunctional behaviors. Second, negative reinforcement entails the *removal* of a negative consequence when functional behaviors are performed; punishment entails the *administration* of negative consequences when dysfunctional behaviors are performed.

ORGANIZATIONAL BEHAVIOR MODIFICATION   When managers systematically apply operant conditioning techniques to promote the performance of organizationally functional behaviors and discourage the performance of dysfunctional behaviors, they are engaging in **organizational behavior modification (OB MOD)**.[105] OB MOD has been successfully used to improve productivity, efficiency, attendance, punctuality, safe work practices, customer service, and other important behaviors in a wide variety of organizations such as banks, department stores, factories, hospitals, and construction sites.[106] The five basic steps in OB MOD are described in Figure 13.4.

OB MOD works best for behaviors that are specific, objective, and countable, such as attendance and punctuality, making sales, or putting telephones together, all of which lend themselves to careful scrutiny and control. OB MOD may be questioned because of its lack of relevance to certain work behaviors (for example, the many work behaviors that are not specific, objective, and countable). Some people also have questioned it on ethical grounds. Critics of OB MOD suggest that it is overly controlling and robs workers of their dignity, individuality, freedom of choice, and even creativity. Supporters counter that OB MOD is a highly effective means of promoting organizational efficiency. There is some merit to both sides of this argument. What is clear, however, is that when used appropriately, OB MOD gives managers a technique to motivate the performance of at least some organizationally functional behaviors.[107]

Social Learning Theory

Social learning theory proposes that motivation results not only from direct experience of rewards and punishments but also from a person's thoughts and beliefs. Social learning theory extends operant conditioning's contribution to managers' understanding of motivation by explaining (1) how people can be motivated by observing other people performing a behavior and being reinforced for doing so (*vicarious learning*), (2) how people can be motivated to control their behavior themselves (*self-reinforcement*), and (3) how people's beliefs about their ability to successfully perform a behavior affect motivation (*self-efficacy*).[108] We look briefly at each of these motivators.

organizational behavior modification (OB MOD) The systematic application of operant conditioning techniques to promote the performance of organizationally functional behaviors and discourage the performance of dysfunctional behaviors.

social learning theory A theory that takes into account how learning and motivation are influenced by people's thoughts and beliefs and their observations of other people's behavior.

Figure 13.4

Five Steps in OB MOD

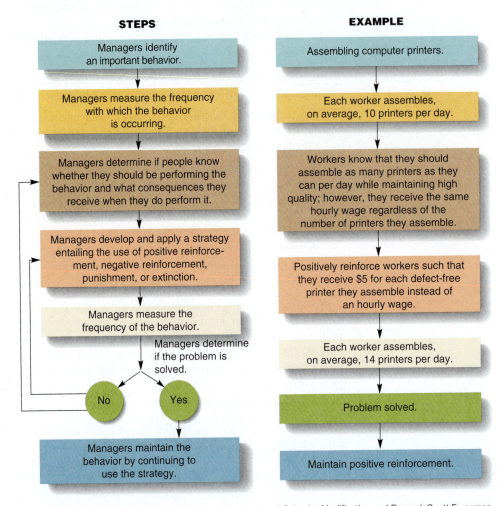

Source: Adapted from F. Luthans and R. Kreitner, Organizational Behavior Modification and Beyond, Scott Foresman, 1985. Copyright © 1985. Reprinted with permission of the authors.

vicarious learning Learning that occurs when the learner becomes motivated to perform a behavior by watching another person performing it and being reinforced for doing so; also called *observational learning.*

VICARIOUS LEARNING Vicarious learning, often called *observational learning,* occurs when a person (the learner) becomes motivated to perform a behavior by watching another person (the model) performing the behavior and being positively reinforced for doing so. Vicarious learning is a powerful source of motivation on many jobs in which people learn to perform functional behaviors by watching others. Salespeople learn how to help customers, medical school students learn how to treat patients, law clerks learn how to practice law, and nonmanagers learn how to be managers, in part, by observing experienced members of an organization perform these behaviors properly and be reinforced for them. In general, people are more likely to be motivated to imitate the behavior of models who are highly competent, are (to some extent) experts in the behavior, have high status, receive attractive reinforcers, and are friendly or approachable.[109]

To promote vicarious learning, managers should strive to have the learner meet the following conditions:

- The learner observes the model performing the behavior.
- The learner accurately perceives the model's behavior.
- The learner remembers the behavior.
- The learner has the skills and abilities needed to perform the behavior.
- The learner sees or knows that the model is positively reinforced for the behavior.[110]

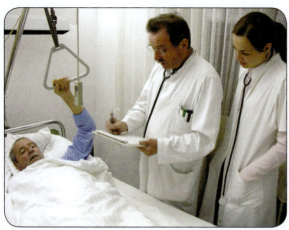

How do you treat that? When medical students enter residency, they learn vicariously by shadowing a full physician on his or her rounds.

self-reinforcer Any desired or attractive outcome or reward that a person gives to himself or herself for good performance.

self-efficacy A person's belief about his or her ability to perform a behavior successfully.

SELF-REINFORCEMENT Although managers are often the providers of reinforcement in organizations, sometimes people motivate themselves through self-reinforcement. People can control their own behavior by setting goals for themselves and then reinforcing themselves when they achieve the goals.[111] **Self-reinforcers** are any desired or attractive outcomes or rewards that people can give to themselves for good performance, such as a feeling of accomplishment, going to a movie, having dinner out, buying a new CD, or taking time out for a golf game. When members of an organization control their own behavior through self-reinforcement, managers do not need to spend as much time as they ordinarily would trying to motivate and control behavior through the administration of consequences because subordinates are controlling and motivating themselves. In fact, this self-control is often referred to as the *self-management of behavior.*

When employees are highly skilled and are responsible for creating new goods and services, managers typically rely on self-control and self-management of behavior, as is the case at Google. Employees at Google are given the flexibility and autonomy to experiment, take risks, and sometimes fail as they work on new projects. They are encouraged to learn from their failures and apply what they learn to subsequent projects.[112] Google's engineers are given one day a week to work on their own projects that they are highly involved with, and new products such as Google News often emerge from these projects.[113]

SELF-EFFICACY **Self-efficacy** is a person's belief about his or her ability to perform a behavior successfully.[114] Even with all the most attractive consequences or reinforcers hinging on high performance, people are not going to be motivated if they do not think they can actually perform at a high level. Similarly, when people control their own behavior, they are likely to set for themselves difficult goals that will lead to outstanding accomplishments only if they think they can reach those goals. Thus self-efficacy influences motivation both when managers provide reinforcement and when workers themselves provide it.[115] The greater the self-efficacy, the greater is the motivation and performance. Verbal persuasion such as a manager expressing confidence in an employee's ability to reach a challenging goal, as well as a person's own past performance and accomplishments and the accomplishments of other people, plays a role in determining a person's self-efficacy.

Pay and Motivation

LO13-5

Explain why and how managers can use pay as a major motivation tool.

In Chapter 12 we discussed how managers establish a pay level and structure for an organization as a whole. Here we focus on how, once a pay level and structure are in place, managers can use pay to motivate employees to perform at a high level and attain their work goals. Pay is used to motivate entry-level workers, first-line and middle managers, and even top managers such as CEOs. Pay can motivate people to perform behaviors that help an organization achieve its goals, and it can motivate people to join and remain with an organization.

Each of the theories described in this chapter alludes to the importance of pay and suggests that pay should be based on performance:

- *Expectancy theory:* Instrumentality, the association between performance and outcomes such as pay, must be high for motivation to be high. In addition, pay is an outcome that has high valence for many people.

- *Need theories:* People should be able to satisfy their needs by performing at a high level; pay can be used to satisfy several different kinds of needs.

- *Equity theory:* Outcomes such as pay should be distributed in proportion to inputs (including performance levels).

- *Goal-setting theory:* Outcomes such as pay should be linked to the attainment of goals.

- *Learning theories:* The distribution of outcomes, such as pay, should be contingent on the performance of organizationally functional behaviors.

merit pay plan A compensation plan that bases pay on performance.

As these theories suggest, to promote high motivation, managers should base the distribution of pay to organizational members on performance levels so that high performers receive more pay than low performers (other things being equal).[116] A compensation plan basing pay on performance is often called a **merit pay plan**.

In tough economic times, when organizations lay off employees and pay levels and benefits of those who are at least able to keep their jobs may be cut while their responsibilities are often increased,[117] managers are often limited in the extent to which they can use merit pay, if at all.[118] Nonetheless, in such times, managers can still try to recognize top performers. Jenny Miller, manager of 170 engineers in the commercial systems engineering department at Rockwell Collins, an aerospace electronics company in Cedar Rapids, Iowa, experienced firsthand the challenge of not being able to recognize top performers with merit pay during tough economic times.[119] Rockwell Collins laid off 8 percent of its workforce, and the workloads for the engineers Miller managed increased by about 15 percent. The engineers were working longer hours without receiving any additional pay; there was a salary freeze, so they knew raises were not in store. With a deadline approaching for flight deck software for a customer, she needed some engineers to work over the Thanksgiving holiday and so sent out an email request for volunteers. Approximately 20 employees volunteered. In recognition of their contributions, Miller gave them each a $100 gift card.[120]

A $100 gift card might not seem like much for an employee who is already working long hours to come to work over the Thanksgiving holiday for no additional pay or time off. Yet Steve Nieuwsma, division vice president at Rockwell Collins, indicates that the gift cards at least signaled that managers recognized and appreciated employees' efforts and sought to thank them for it. Not being able to give his employees raises at that time, Nieuwsma also gave gift cards to recognize contributions and top performers in amounts varying between $25 and $500.[121]

Once managers have decided to use a merit pay plan, they face two important choices: whether to base pay on individual, group, or organizational performance and whether to use salary increases or bonuses.

Basing Merit Pay on Individual, Group, or Organizational Performance

Managers can base merit pay on individual, group, or organizational performance. When individual performance (such as the dollar value of merchandise a salesperson sells, the number of loudspeakers a factory worker assembles, and a lawyer's billable hours) can be accurately determined, individual motivation is likely to be highest when pay is based on individual performance.[122] When members of an organization work closely together and individual performance cannot be accurately determined (as in a team of computer programmers developing a single software package), pay cannot be based on individual performance, and a group- or organization-based plan must be used. When the attainment of organizational goals hinges on members' working closely together and cooperating with each other (as in a small construction company that builds custom homes), group- or organization-based plans may be more appropriate than individual-based plans.[123]

It is possible to combine elements of an individual-based plan with a group- or organization-based plan to motivate each individual to perform highly and, at the same time, motivate all individuals to work well together, cooperate with one another, and help one another as needed. Lincoln Electric, a very successful company and a leading manufacturer of welding machines, uses a combination individual- and organization-based plan.[124] Pay is based on individual performance. In addition, each year the size of a bonus fund depends on organizational performance. Money from the bonus fund is distributed to people on the basis of their contributions to the organization, attendance, levels of cooperation, and other indications of performance. Employees of Lincoln Electric are motivated to cooperate and help one another because when the firm as a whole performs well, everybody benefits by having a larger bonus fund. Employees also are motivated to contribute their inputs to the organization because their contributions determine their share of the bonus fund.

Salary Increase or Bonus?

Managers can distribute merit pay to people in the form of a salary increase or a bonus on top of regular salaries. Although the dollar amount of a salary increase or bonus might be identical, bonuses tend to have more motivational impact for at least three reasons. First, salary levels are typically based on performance levels, cost-of-living increases, and so forth, from the day people start working in an organization, which means the absolute level of the salary is based largely on factors unrelated to *current* performance. A 5 percent merit increase in salary, for example, may seem relatively small in comparison to one's total salary. Second, a current salary increase may be affected by other factors in addition to performance, such as cost-of-living increases or across-the-board market adjustments. Third, because organizations rarely reduce salaries, salary levels tend to vary less than performance levels do. Related to this point is the fact that bonuses give managers more flexibility in distributing outcomes. If an organization is doing well, bonuses can be relatively high to reward employees for their contributions. However, unlike salary increases, bonus levels can be reduced when an organization's performance lags. All in all, bonus plans have more motivational impact than salary increases because the amount of the bonus can be directly and exclusively based on performance.[125]

Consistent with the lessons from motivation theories, bonuses can be linked directly to performance and vary from year to year and employee to employee, as at Gradient Corporation, a Cambridge, Massachusetts, environmental consulting firm.[126] Another organization that successfully uses bonuses is Nucor Corporation. Steelworkers at Nucor tend to be much more productive than steelworkers in other companies—probably because they can receive bonuses tied to performance and quality that can range from 130 percent to 150 percent of their regular base pay.[127] During the economic downturn in 2007–2009, Nucor struggled as did many other companies, and bonus pay for steelworkers dropped considerably. However, managers at Nucor avoided having to lay off employees by finding ways to cut costs and having employees work on maintenance activities and safety manuals, along with taking on tasks that used to be performed by independent contractors, such as producing specialty parts and mowing the grass.[128]

In addition to receiving pay raises and bonuses, high-level managers and executives are sometimes granted employee stock options. **Employee stock options** are financial instruments that entitle the bearer to buy shares of an organization's stock at a certain price during a certain period or under certain conditions.[129] For example, in addition to salaries, stock options are sometimes used to attract high-level managers. The exercise price is the stock price at which the bearer can buy the stock, and the vesting conditions specify when the bearer can actually buy the stock at the exercise price. The option's exercise price is generally set equal to the market price of the stock on the date it is granted, and the vesting conditions might specify that the manager has to have worked at the organization for 12 months or perhaps met some performance target (perhaps an increase in profits) before being able to exercise the option. In high-technology firms and start-ups, options are sometimes used in a similar fashion for employees at various levels in the organization.[130]

From a motivation standpoint, stock options are used not so much to reward past individual performance but, rather, to motivate employees to work in the future for the good of the company as a whole. This is true because stock options issued at current stock prices have value in the future only if an organization does well and its stock price appreciates; thus giving employees stock options should encourage them to help the organization improve its performance over time.[131] At high-technology start-ups and dot-coms, stock options have often motivated potential employees to leave promising jobs in larger companies and work for the start-ups. In the late 1990s and early 2000s, many dot-commers were devastated to learn not only that their stock options were worthless, because their companies went out of business or were doing poorly, but also that they were unemployed. Unfortunately stock options have also led to unethical behavior; for example, sometimes individuals seek to artificially inflate the value of a company's stock to increase the value of stock options.

employee stock option

A financial instrument that entitles the bearer to buy shares of an organization's stock at a certain price during a certain period or under certain conditions.

Examples of Merit Pay Plans

Managers can choose among several merit pay plans, depending on the work that employees perform and other considerations. Using *piece-rate pay,* an individual-based merit plan, managers base employees' pay on the number of units each employee produces, whether televisions, computer components, or welded auto parts. Managers at Lincoln Electric use piece-rate pay to determine individual pay levels. Advances in information technology have dramatically simplified the administration of piece-rate pay in a variety of industries.

Using *commission pay,* another individual-based merit pay plan, managers base pay on a percentage of sales. Managers at the successful real estate company Re/Max International Inc. use commission pay for their agents, who are paid a percentage of their sales. Some department stores, such as Neiman Marcus, use commission pay for their salespeople.

Examples of organizational-based merit pay plans include the Scanlon plan and profit sharing. The *Scanlon plan* (developed by Joseph Scanlon, a union leader in a steel and tin plant in the 1920s) focuses on reducing expenses or cutting costs; members of an organization are motivated to propose and implement cost-cutting strategies because a percentage of the cost savings achieved during a specified time is distributed to the employees.[132] Under *profit sharing,* employees receive a share of an organization's profits. Regardless of the specific kind of plan that is used, managers should always strive to link pay to the performance of behaviors that help an organization achieve its goals.

Japanese managers in large corporations have long shunned merit pay plans in favor of plans that reward seniority. However, more and more Japanese companies are adopting merit-based pay due to its motivational benefits; among such companies are SiteDesign,[133] Tokio Marine and Fire Insurance, and Hissho Iwai, a trading organization.[134]

Summary and Review

THE NATURE OF MOTIVATION Motivation encompasses the psychological forces within a person that determine the direction of the person's behavior in an organization, the person's level of effort, and the person's level of persistence in the face of obstacles. Managers strive to motivate people to contribute their inputs to an organization, to focus

LO13-1 these inputs in the direction of high performance, and to ensure that people receive the outcomes they desire when they perform at a high level.

LO13-2 EXPECTANCY THEORY According to expectancy theory, managers can promote high levels of motivation in their organizations by taking steps to ensure that expectancy is high (people think that if they try, they can perform at a high level), instrumentality is high (people think that if they perform at a high level, they will receive certain outcomes), and valence is high (people desire these outcomes).

LO13-3 NEED THEORIES Need theories suggest that to motivate their workforces, managers should determine what needs people are trying to satisfy in organizations and then ensure that people receive outcomes that satisfy these needs when they perform at a high level and contribute to organizational effectiveness.

LO13-2 EQUITY THEORY According to equity theory, managers can promote high levels of motivation by ensuring that people perceive that there is equity in the organization or that outcomes are distributed in proportion to inputs. Equity exists when a person perceives that his or her own outcome–input ratio equals the outcome–input ratio of a referent. Inequity motivates people to try to restore equity. Equity theory is a theory of distributive justice. It is most advantageous for distributive, procedural, interpersonal, and informational justice all to be high.

LO13-3 GOAL-SETTING THEORY Goal-setting theory suggests that managers can promote high motivation and performance by ensuring that people are striving to achieve specific, difficult goals. It is important for people to accept the goals, be committed to them, and receive feedback about how they are doing.

LO13-4   **LEARNING THEORIES**   Operant conditioning theory suggests that managers can motivate people to perform highly by using positive reinforcement or negative reinforcement (positive reinforcement being the preferred strategy). Managers can motivate people to avoid performing dysfunctional behaviors by using extinction or punishment. Social learning theory suggests that people can also be motivated by observing how others perform behaviors and receive rewards, by engaging in self-reinforcement, and by having high levels of self-efficacy.

LO13-5   **PAY AND MOTIVATION**   Each of the motivation theories discussed in this chapter alludes to the importance of pay and suggests that pay should be based on performance. Merit pay plans can be individual-, group-, or organization-based and can entail the use of salary increases or bonuses.

Management in Action

Topics for Discussion and Action

Discussion

1. Discuss why two people with similar abilities may have very different expectancies for performing at a high level. [LO13-2]

2. Describe why some people have low instrumentalities even when their managers distribute outcomes based on performance. [LO13-2]

3. Analyze how professors try to promote equity to motivate students. [LO13-2]

4. Describe three techniques or procedures that managers can use to determine whether a goal is difficult. [LO13-3]

5. Discuss why managers should always try to use positive reinforcement instead of negative reinforcement. [LO13-4]

Action

6. Interview three people who have the same kind of job (such as salesperson, waiter/waitress, or teacher), and determine what kinds of needs each is trying to satisfy at work. [LO13-3]

7. Interview a manager in an organization in your community to determine the extent to which the manager takes advantage of vicarious learning to promote high motivation among subordinates. [LO13-3]

Building Management Skills

Diagnosing Motivation [LO13-1, 13-2, 13-3, 13-4]

Think about the ideal job that you would like to obtain after graduation. Describe this job, the kind of manager you would like to report to, and the kind of organization you would be working in. Then answer the following questions:

1. What would be your levels of expectancy and instrumentality on this job? Which outcomes would have high valence for you on this job? What steps would your manager take to influence your levels of expectancy, instrumentality, and valence?

2. Whom would you choose as a referent on this job? What steps would your manager take to make you feel that you were being equitably treated? What would you do if, after a year on the job, you experienced underpayment inequity?

3. What goals would you strive to achieve on this job? Why? What role would your manager play in determining your goals?

4. What needs would you strive to satisfy on this job? Why? What role would your manager play in helping you satisfy these needs?

5. What behaviors would your manager positively reinforce on this job? Why? What positive reinforcers would your manager use?

6. Would there be any vicarious learning on this job? Why or why not?

7. To what extent would you be motivated by self-control on this job? Why?

8. What would be your level of self-efficacy on this job? Why would your self-efficacy be at this level? Should your manager take steps to boost your self-efficacy? If not, why not? If so, what would these steps be?

Managing Ethically [LO13-5]

Sometimes pay is so contingent upon performance that it creates stress for employees. Imagine a salesperson who knows that if sales targets are not met, she or he will not be able to make a house mortgage payment or pay the rent.

Questions

1. Either individually or in a group, think about the ethical implications of closely linking pay to performance.

2. Under what conditions might contingent pay be most stressful, and what steps can managers take to try to help their subordinates perform effectively and not experience excessive amounts of stress?

Small Group Breakout Exercise

Increasing Motivation [LO13-1, 13-2, 13-3, 13-4, 13-5]

Form groups of three or four people, and appoint one member as the spokesperson who will communicate your findings to the class when called on by the instructor. Then discuss the following scenario:

You and your partners own a chain of 15 dry-cleaning stores in a medium-size town. All of you are concerned about a problem in customer service that has surfaced recently. When any one of you spends the day, or even part of the day, in a particular store, clerks seem to provide excellent customer service, spotters make sure all stains are removed from garments, and pressers do a good job of pressing difficult items such as silk blouses. Yet during those same visits customers complain to you about such things as stains not being removed and items being poorly pressed in some of their previous orders; indeed, several customers have brought garments in to be redone. Customers also sometimes comment on having waited too long for service on previous visits. You and your partners are meeting today to address this problem.

1. Discuss the extent to which you believe that you have a motivation problem in your stores.

2. Given what you have learned in this chapter, design a plan to increase the motivation of clerks to provide prompt service to customers even when they are not being watched by a partner.

3. Design a plan to increase the motivation of spotters to remove as many stains as possible even when they are not being watched by a partner.

4. Design a plan to increase the motivation of pressers to do a top-notch job on all clothes they press, no matter how difficult.

Exploring the World Wide Web [LO13-1, 13-2, 13-3, 13-4, 13-5]

If you had the chance to choose which well-known corporation you would work for, which would it be? Now go to the website of that company and find out as much as you can about how it motivates employees. Also, using Google and other search engines, try to find articles in the news about this company. Based on what you have learned, would this company still be your top choice? Why or why not?

Be the Manager [LO13-1, 13-2, 13-3, 13-4, 13-5]

You supervise a team of marketing analysts who work on different snack products in a large food products company. The marketing analysts have recently received undergraduate degrees in business or liberal arts and have been on the job between one and three years. Their responsibilities include analyzing the market for their respective products, including competitors; tracking current marketing initiatives; and planning future marketing campaigns. They also need to prepare quarterly sales and expense reports for their products and estimated budgets for the next three quarters; to prepare these reports, they need to obtain data from financial and accounting analysts assigned to their products.

When they first started on the job, you took each marketing analyst through the reporting cycle, explaining what needs to be done and how to accomplish it and emphasizing the need for timely reports. Although preparing the reports can be tedious, you think the task is pretty straightforward and easily accomplished if the analysts plan ahead and allocate sufficient time for it. When reporting time approaches, you remind the analysts through email messages and emphasize the need for accurate and timely reports in team meetings.

You believe this element of the analysts' jobs couldn't be more straightforward. However, at the end of each quarter, the majority of the analysts submit their reports a day or two late, and, worse yet, your own supervisor (to whom the reports are eventually given) has indicated that information is often missing and sometimes the reports contain errors. Once you started getting flak from your supervisor about this problem, you decided you had better fix things quickly. You met with the marketing analysts, explained the problem, told them to submit the reports to you a day or two early so you could look them over, and more generally emphasized that they really needed to get their act together. Unfortunately, things have not improved much and you are spending more and more of your own time doing the reports. What are you going to do?

INC. Case in the News (LO13-1, 13-2, 13-3)

You Can Buy Employee Happiness. But Should You?

Companies that offer lavish benefits believe there is a return on their investment. The challenge: figuring out how to calculate it.

Employees don't pay a dime for health insurance. A registered dietitian is on hand to help workers create nutrition plans. If employees require time off to handle a family emergency, they get it, no questions asked. They get bonuses and profit sharing.

What kind of employer are we talking about? Some perk-laden tech start-up embroiled in a perpetual war for talent? Nope.

In fact, the company in question is Diamond Pet Foods, a manufacturer of, yes, pet food based in Meta, Missouri. The company, founded in 1970, has 535 employees at facilities in three states. Most of them are the kinds of factory workers and manual laborers who would be happy to have the most modest of benefits packages, let alone the lavish one supplied by Diamond.

Why go to such lengths when many of its peers do precisely the opposite? The answer: a substantial ROB, or return on benefits.

Wages at Diamond are no higher than those at similar manufacturers. But voluntary turnover is at a mere 3 percent, compared with an industry average of almost 11 percent. And people don't just stick around—they produce. "When employees don't have to worry about health care or financial issues, they can focus on success and growing our business," says Andrew Brondel, the company's director of administration. "They have the mental clarity to see areas for improvement and to take the initiative to offer and implement new ideas."

In an age of outsourcing, declining real wages, and ever-rising contributions for health care (assuming insurance is offered at all), you don't hear about this kind of thing very often. But some companies still go to extraordinary lengths and expense to attract, develop, and retain their employees. They treat benefits less as a cost of doing business than as an investment in their most important resource. More entrepreneurs would be wise to adopt such practices, says Kevin Lynch, leadership executive-in-residence at Benedictine University's Center for Values-Driven Leadership. "When I was a CFO, I tended to regard benefits as a burden," Lynch says. "I'm now confident that they do pay off—in the form of attracting good employees, retaining them, and making them more productive. When you have happy, satisfied employees, that creates value that does find its way into traditionally calculated ROI."

That's the thinking at Diamond. Benefits at the company account for about 35 percent of total compensation costs, compared with about 30 percent for a typical private employer, according to the Bureau of Labor Statistics. Many managers might see the greater expense as a threat to margins. But not Brondel. Robust benefits, he says, boost morale and well-being, and that translates into higher productivity. Diamond's workers, Brondel says, are willing to dig in when demand spikes, which gives Diamond a competitive advantage. Pet food is a cyclical business: demand rises in winter as animals consume more food. So everyone needs to step it up as temperatures drop. "I've literally heard people say, 'I know the company has my back,'" Brondel says, "'so I'm giving them everything I've got.'"

How to Get a Better Return on Benefits

Tailor your offerings to your specific workforce. Survey your workers about what they want, whether it's flextime, financial planning, or training and development. "Smaller companies have a big advantage here, because the decision makers are closer to the employees," says Kevin Lynch, of Benedictine University. "Plus, it's easier for small companies to be flexible in accommodating different preferences." When Integrated Project Management Company of Burr Ridge, Illinois, surveyed its employees, for example, it found they were indifferent to a long-term care policy it had been planning to offer. But they were very keen on training programs, so the company focused its efforts in that direction.

Communicate the value of what you offer. Diamond Pet Foods makes sure that every new employee understands the inner workings of its self-insured health plan. As a result, says Andrew Brondel, the director of administration, employees understand that every insurance claim is being paid for with, in essence, the same pool of "Diamond dollars" that also funds the company's 401(k) matching

contribution. That makes employees unusually disciplined about the medical services they use. Along those lines, entrepreneur Paul Spiegelman advises that you create an internal team that understands your benefits and educates employees about them continuously; an internal PR campaign ensures that employees don't lose sight of what they have.

Once you offer a benefit, don't rescind it. If employees see benefits taken away at the first sign of trouble, they will assume that the company simply offers them as gravy during good times but has no real commitment to them.

Get the right help. "Employee benefits are complex and getting more so," Lynch says. "There are many legal and financial issues that require technical competence from a dedicated expert. The key is to find one who understands your business and can apply his or her technical competence in a way that provides value to your company." If the person is not willing to take the time to truly get to know your organization, move on.

That logic is taken to another level at Aurora Electric, a Jamaica, New York–based electrical contractor that works on large, complicated projects, including the World Trade Center in Lower Manhattan. At its core, the company has just four employees, but that number rises to as many as 50 depending on how many projects the company has under way. And all of them get lavish benefits—even though many are union electricians who join the workforce on a project basis. (Under union contracts, employers provide coverage; they are required to meet certain minimum requirements but are free to go above and beyond.) Aurora's perks include complete funding of what founder Veronica Rose describes as a "Cadillac health plan that covers everything, including wellness programs and even a 30-day drug or alcohol rehab program." The company also offers a tuition reimbursement program that employees can use to build skills in

any field, not just construction or electronics.

Rose's union electricians are not payrolled employees. So why invest in the kinds of benefits that most companies justify in large part for the impact such perks have on retention? "It creates a much better work environment," Rose says. "Everyone is much more engaged. Instead of running to me with every little thing, they help each other."

Rose admits that she views treating workers well as an end in itself. But the practice also has a serious business rationale. "We only do very specific kinds of electrical work," she says. "We need electricians who have the highest security clearances, who have years of training in fiber optics and related technologies, and have pursued credentials on their own time. I need the cream of the crop, and they are hard to find. So I create an environment in which everyone wants to come and work for me."

Rose's instincts—that a well-designed benefits package can yield real, bottom-line results—are echoed by a number of business leaders. "Not enough company leaders try to quantify the results of providing both a good company culture and a good benefits package," says Paul Spiegelman, founder of BerylHealth and The Beryl Institute and chief culture officer of Stericycle, a medical services company with 13,000 employees."Historically, companies have relied on their financials as leading indicators. But employee satisfaction, customer satisfaction, attrition rates, and similar metrics should serve as your leading indicators, with financials becoming your lagging indicators."

When managers begin correlating one metric to another, Spiegelman says, they "begin to see the relationship between investing in your employees and financial results." Spiegelman's own experience provides a case in point. A few years ago, his companies began offering a new health benefit—the opportunity to see a registered nurse within two hours, either at work or at home. There was

LEADERS OF THE PACK

Company	Industry	Employees	Notable
The American Institute of Certified Public Accountants Durham, NC	Nonprofit	660	A health and wellness program that includes biometric screening and cooking classes.
Aurora Electric Jamaica, NY	Contracting	Varies	Pays tuition for nearly any degree program.
Capital District Physicians' Health Plan Albany, NY	Health insurer	700	Offers monthly one-on-one financial planning workshops.
CORE Engineering and Construction Winter Park, FL	Construction	28	Since 2004, only two employees have left voluntarily.
Diamond Pet Foods Meta, MO	Manufacturing	523	Offers free annual wellness exams; a registered dietitian helps employees create nutrition plans.
Groupware Technology Campbell, CA	IT services	80	Offers free gym memberships to employees and family members.
Integrated Project Management Burr Ridge, IL	Risk mitigation	115	Provides mentoring and a $10,000 tuition reimbursement program.
Medicus Solutions Alpharetta, GA	IT services	10	Offers resources to help workers with parenting, elder care, and work–life balance issues.
Nyhart Indianapolis	Consulting	100	Uses its actuarial expertise to help employees set and achieve retirement savings targets.
The Starr Conspiracy Fort Worth	Marketing	32	Offers unlimited vacation time.

HOW THE WINNERS WERE CHOSEN: More than 240 applicants were judged on a weighted scale that encompassed health care (35 percent), retirement (25 percent), insurance (15 percent), and company culture (25 percent). To qualify, applicants were required to have been in business for at least five years, employ from five to 1,000 people, and be based in the United States. Winners were chosen by a panel of judges consisting of Paul Spiegelman, founder of BerylHealth and chief culture officer of Stericycle; Dallas Salisbury, president and CEO of the Employee Benefits Research Institute; Lisa Kottler, senior vice president of NFP Retirement Services; Kevin Lynch, executive-in-residence at Benedictine University; and George Gendron, the former editor in chief of *Inc.*

an almost immediate payback: In just four months at Beryl, for example, 71 insurance claims were avoided and 246 work hours were saved (equating to an estimated $18,000 in wages) as employees got immediate care rather than having to visit a doctor.

Benedictine University's Kevin Lynch believes smart leaders are evolving toward a broader view of what constitutes compensation. To some degree, he says, they may have no choice. Younger workers increasingly regard work as being about something more than just a paycheck. "They expect to be treated with more respect," he says, "and that includes accommodating their external commitments, career goals, and other factors. All benefits programs are expensive propositions, but you can maximize the impact by offering the benefits that matter most to your workers."

Questions for Discussion

1. What motivation lessons can be learned from Diamond Pet Foods?

2. What motivation lessons can be learned from Aurora Electric?

3. How might providing employees with excellent benefits contribute to motivation from an expectancy theory perspective?

4. How might providing employees with excellent benefits contribute to motivation from an equity theory perspective and from a need theory perspective?

CHAPTER 14

Leadership

Learning Objectives

After studying this chapter, you should be able to:

LO14-1 Explain what leadership is, when leaders are effective and ineffective, and the sources of power that enable managers to be effective leaders.

LO14-2 Identify the traits that show the strongest relationship to leadership, the behaviors leaders engage in, and the limitations of the trait and behavior models of leadership.

LO14-3 Explain how contingency models of leadership enhance our understanding of effective leadership and management in organizations.

LO14-4 Describe what transformational leadership is, and explain how managers can engage in it.

LO14-5 Characterize the relationship between gender and leadership and explain how emotional intelligence may contribute to leadership effectiveness.

Jim Whitehurst Leads Red Hat

How can a leader foster creativity in a rapidly changing environment? Jim Whitehurst, president and CEO of Red Hat, Inc., the world's largest open-source software company with over $1 billion in revenues,[1] recognizes the vital role that creativity plays in organizations in rapidly changing arenas like open-source software. As he puts it, "In today's workforce, creativity is a critical skill. I strive every day at Red Hat to be a catalyst with our associates to fuel and spark their creativity and not stifle it by simply telling people what to do."[2]

Red Hat, headquartered in Raleigh, North Carolina, fully embraces the open source development model, which relies on global communities of contributors to develop, service, and improve software. Red Hat earns revenues through a variety of sources from its business and organizational customers. For example, software is provided via subscriptions (annual or multiyear) that include software support, new editions and updates of software, security upgrades, improvements and solutions to problems, advances in technology, functionality upgrades, and other services.[3] Red Hat also offers paid technical support to help clients most effectively utilize software as well as keep up-to-date with latest developments and integrate software offerings with other applications. Consulting services are also offered by Red Hat. Thus Red Hat provides its customers with the benefits of having a global community develop and improve open-source software while at the same time having expert software support and assistance to fully utilize the software to meet business needs while keeping up-to-date with the latest developments and improvements.[4] Red Hat's software includes Red Hat Enterprise Linux (an operating system that can be used on servers, work stations, and mainframes), Red Hat Enterprise Virtualization (which enables businesses to use multiple applications and operating systems on the same hardware foundation), Red Hat cloud offerings (to enable businesses to use cloud computing), Red Had Storage Server (which enables customers to use their physical

Jim Whitehurst, president and CEO of Red Hat, Inc., has a broad base of experience to draw upon in his leadership role at Red Hat. He has been COO of Delta Airlines, managing director and partner at Boston Consulting Group, and has degrees in computer science and economics as well as an MBA from Harvard.

storage as virtual storage), and Red Hat J Boss Middleware (to develop, manage, and use business applications).[5]

Jim Whitehurst has been CEO and president of Red Hat for over seven years. Prior to joining Red Hat, he was the chief operating officer for Delta Airlines and also served as senior vice president and chief network and planning officer at Delta.[6] Before joining Delta, he was a managing director and partner at the Boston Consulting Group. He has a bachelor's degree from Rice University in economics and computer science, a general course degree from the London School of Economics (from Friedrich-Alexander University in Germany), and an MBA from the Harvard Business School.[7] Thus his prior education and work experience have given him a broad base of expertise to draw upon in his leadership role at Red Hat.

At Red Hat, Whitehurst emphasizes that respect is earned by everyone (including top managers like himself) by what they do and how they contribute. In fact, Whitehurst believes that in order for leaders to be effective, they need to be respected by organizational members for their words and deeds and not just their titles. According to Whitehurst, three important means by which leaders like himself can gain the respect of organizational members is by being passionate about their mission and vision, being confident, and engaging other organizational members.[8] At Red Hat, Whitehurst is passionate about creatively developing better technology and software in an open-source manner involving communities of contributors, partners, and customers. Whitehurst is very competent and confident both in his own abilities and in the capabilities of teams at Red Hat. Whitehurst engages Red Hat employees by encouraging and supporting

their creative ideas and perspectives and being inspirational, open, and honest. Mutual trust and respect are important to Whitehurst (and at Red Hat) as are honesty, integrity, and open communication.[9]

A strong believer in empowerment and trusting employees to do what they think is right, Whitehurst also thinks that leaders and all employees must feel accountable to each other. In fact, when Red Hat has its annual big party for employees and their families, Whitehurst is personally reminded that he is partly responsible for the well-being of all those present. Whitehurst holds himself accountable to employees by his performance, by the ways in which he provides explanations for his decisions and for Red Hat's performance, and for his sincere apologies when things don't go as planned.[10] In fact, Whitehurst often asks employees for feedback before he makes decisions so as to make the best decisions possible. Whitehurst strives to create an environment in which employees will be creative, motivated, energetic, inspired, enthusiastic, and excited and use these sentiments to help Red Hat achieve its mission. Importantly, Whitehurst and other managers at Red Hat empower employees and give them the freedom to be creative in the ways in which they contribute to Red Hat's mission.[11]

Red Hat has performed well under Whitehurst's leadership. Thus it's not surprising that he has received recognition for his accomplishments. For example, in April 2014 Whitehurst gave the keynote address at The Cloud Factory conference in Banff, Alberta, Canada.[12] The Cloud Factory is a major enterprise technology conference.[13] And in March 2014 Whitehurst was awarded the William C. Friday Award by the Park Scholars at North Carolina State University.[14] This is an annual award named in honor of the former president of North Carolina State University and recognizing the recipient's leadership, character, service, and scholarship. The Park Scholars is a merit scholarship program, and the senior Park Scholars gave the award to Whitehurst.[15] All in all, Whitehurst certainly seems to be effectively leading Red Hat.

Overview

Jim Whitehurst exemplifies the many facets of effective leadership. In Chapter 1 we explained that one of the four primary tasks of managers is leading. Thus it should come as no surprise that leadership is a key ingredient in effective management. When leaders are effective, their subordinates or followers are highly motivated, committed, and high-performing. When leaders are ineffective, chances are good that their subordinates do not perform up to their capabilities, are demotivated, and may be dissatisfied as well. Jim Whitehurst is a leader at the top of an organization, but leadership is an important ingredient for managerial success at all levels of organizations: top management, middle management, and first-line management. Moreover, leadership is a key ingredient of managerial success for organizations large and small.

In this chapter we describe what leadership is and examine the major leadership models that shed light on the factors that contribute to a manager being an effective leader. We look at trait and behavior models, which focus on what leaders are like and what they do, and contingency models—Fiedler's contingency model, path–goal theory, and the leader substitutes model—each of which takes into account the complexity surrounding leadership and the role of the situation in leader effectiveness. We also describe how managers can use transformational leadership to dramatically affect their organizations. By the end of this chapter, you will appreciate the many factors and issues that managers face in their quest to be effective leaders.

> **LO14-1**
>
> Explain what leadership is, when leaders are effective and ineffective, and the sources of power that enable managers to be effective leaders.

The Nature of Leadership

Leadership is the process by which a person exerts influence over other people and inspires, motivates, and directs their activities to help achieve group or organizational goals.[16] The person who exerts such influence is a **leader**. When leaders are effective, the influence they exert over others helps a group or organization achieve its performance goals. When leaders are ineffective, their influence does not contribute to, and often detracts from, goal attainment. As "A Manager's Challenge" makes clear, Jim Whitehurst is taking multiple steps to inspire and motivate Red Hat's employees so they help Red Hat achieve its goals.

Beyond facilitating the attainment of performance goals, effective leadership increases an organization's ability to meet all the contemporary challenges discussed throughout this book, including the need to obtain a competitive advantage, the need to foster ethical behavior, and the need to manage a diverse workforce fairly and equitably. Leaders who exert influence over organizational members to help meet these goals increase their organizations' chances of success.

In considering the nature of leadership, we first look at leadership styles and how they affect managerial tasks and at the influence of culture on leadership styles. We then focus on the key to leadership, *power,* which can come from a variety of sources. Finally we consider the contemporary dynamic of empowerment and how it relates to effective leadership.

leadership The process by which an individual exerts influence over other people and inspires, motivates, and directs their activities to help achieve group or organizational goals.

leader An individual who is able to exert influence over other people to help achieve group or organizational goals.

Personal Leadership Style and Managerial Tasks

A manager's *personal leadership style*—that is, the specific ways in which a manager chooses to influence other people—shapes how that manager approaches planning, organizing, and controlling (the other principal tasks of managing). Consider Jim Whitehouse's personal leadership style in "A Manager's Challenge": He empowers employees, emphasizes being open and honest, and really cares about the well-being of employees and fostering their creativity and passion.

Managers at all levels and in all kinds of organizations have their own personal leadership styles that determine not only how they lead their subordinates but also how they perform the other management tasks. Michael Kraus, owner and manager of a dry cleaning store in the northeastern United States, for example, takes a hands-on approach to leadership. He has the sole authority for determining work schedules and job assignments for the 15 employees in his store (an organizing task), makes all important decisions by himself (a planning task), and closely monitors his employees' performance and rewards top performers with pay increases (a control task). Kraus's personal leadership style is effective in his organization. His employees generally are motivated, perform highly, and are satisfied; and his store is highly profitable.

Developing an effective personal leadership style often is a challenge for managers at all levels in an organization. This challenge is often exacerbated when times are tough, due, for example, to an economic downturn or a decline in customer demand. The recession in the late 2000s provided many managers with just such a challenge.

Although leading is one of the four principal tasks of managing, a distinction is often made between managers and leaders. When this distinction is made, managers are thought of as those organizational members who establish and implement procedures and processes to ensure smooth functioning and are accountable for goal accomplishment.[17] Leaders look to the future, chart the course for the organization, and attract, retain, motivate, inspire, and develop relationships with employees based on trust and mutual respect.[18] Leaders provide meaning and purpose, seek innovation rather than stability, and impassion employees to work together to achieve the leaders' vision.[19]

As part of their personal leadership style, some leaders strive to truly serve others. Robert Greenleaf, who was director of management research at AT&T and upon his retirement in 1964 embarked on a second career focused on writing, speaking, and consulting, came up with the term *servant leadership* to describe these leaders.[20] **Servant leaders**, above all else, have a strong desire to serve and work for the benefit of others.[21] Servant leaders share power with followers and strive to ensure that followers' most important needs are met, that they are able to develop as individuals, and that their well-being is enhanced, and that attention is paid to those who are least well-off in a society.[22] Greenleaf founded a nonprofit organization called the Greenleaf Center for Servant Leadership (formerly called the Center for Applied Ethics) to foster leadership focused on service to others, power sharing, and a sense of community between organizations and their multiple stakeholders.[23] Some entrepreneurs strive to incorporate servant leadership into their personal leadership styles, as profiled in the accompanying "Ethics in Action" feature.

servant leader A leader who has a strong desire to serve and work for the benefit of others.

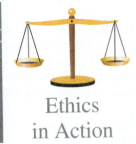

Ethics
in Action

Servant Leadership at Zingerman's

Ari Weinzweig and Paul Saginaw founded Zingerman's Delicatessen in Ann Arbor, Michigan, in 1982.[24] Food lovers at heart, Weinzweig and Saginaw delighted in finding both traditional and exotic foods from around the world, making delicious sandwiches to order, and having extensive selections of food items ranging from olives, oils, and vinegars to cheeses, smoked fish, and salami. As their business grew, and to maintain an intimate atmosphere with excellent customer service, Weinzweig and Saginaw expanded from their original deli into a community of related businesses called Zingerman's Community of Businesses. In addition to the original deli, Zingerman's Community of Businesses now includes a mail-order business, a bakery, a catering business, a creamery, a restaurant, a wholesale coffee business, and a training business, and has combined annual sales of around $45 million.[25] From the start, Weinzweig and Saginaw have been devoted to excellent customer service, great food, and a commitment to people and community.[26]

Paul Saginaw (left) and Ari Weinzweig have incorporated servant leadership into their personal leadership styles at Zingerman's.

As part of their commitment to people and community, Weinzweig and Saginaw have incorporated servant leadership into their personal leadership styles. As their business has grown and prospered, they have realized that increasing success means greater responsibility to serve others. They strive to treat their employees as well as they treat their customers and give their employees opportunities for growth and development on the job. They have also realized that when their own needs or desires differ from what is best for their company, they should do what is best for the company.[27]

To this day, the cofounders encourage their employees to let them know how they can help them and what they can do for them. And given Zingerman's culture of mutual respect and trust, employees do not hesitate to communicate how their leaders can serve them in many and varied ways. For example, when Weinzweig visits the Zingerman's Roadhouse restaurant and the staff is very busy, they may ask him to help out by serving customers or cleaning off tables. As he indicates, "People give me assignments all the time. Sometimes I'm the note-taker. Sometimes I'm the cleaner-upper. . . . Sometimes I'm on my hands and knees wiping up what people spilled."[28]

Weinzweig and Saginaw also have a strong sense of commitment to serving the local community; Zingerman's founded the nonprofit organization Food Gatherers to eliminate hunger and distribute food to the needy, and Food Gatherers is now an independent nonprofit responsible for the Washtenaw County Food Bank with over 5,000 volunteers and a 24-member staff.[29] On Zingerman's 20th anniversary, 13 nonprofit community organizations in Ann Arbor erected a plaque next to Zingerman's Delicatessen with a dedication that read, "Thank you for feeding, sheltering, educating, uplifting, and inspiring an entire community."[30] Clearly, for Weinzweig and Saginaw, leadership entails being of service to others.[31]

Leadership Styles across Cultures

Some evidence suggests that leadership styles vary not only among individuals but also among countries or cultures. Some research indicates that European managers tend to be more humanistic or people-oriented than both Japanese and American managers. The collectivistic culture in Japan places prime emphasis on the group rather than the individual, so the importance of individuals' own personalities, needs, and desires is minimized. Organizations in the United States tend to be very profit-oriented and thus tend to downplay the importance of individual employees' needs and desires. Many countries in Europe have a more individualistic perspective than Japan and a more humanistic perspective than the United States, and this may result in some European managers' being more people-oriented than their Japanese or American counterparts. European managers, for example, tend to be reluctant to lay off employees, and when a layoff is absolutely necessary, they take careful steps to make it as painless as possible.[32]

Another cross-cultural difference occurs in time horizons. While managers in any one country often differ in their time horizons, there are also national differences. For example, U.S. organizations tend to have a short-term profit orientation, and thus U.S. managers' personal leadership styles emphasize short-term performance. Japanese organizations tend to have a long-term growth orientation, so Japanese managers' personal leadership styles emphasize long-term performance. Justus Mische, a personnel manager at the European organization Hoechst, suggested that "Europe, at least the big international firms in Europe, have a philosophy between the Japanese, long term, and the United States, short term."[33] Research on these and other global aspects of leadership is ongoing; as it continues, more cultural differences in managers' personal leadership styles may be discovered.

Power: The Key to Leadership

No matter what one's leadership style, a key component of effective leadership is found in the *power* the leader has to affect other people's behavior and get them to act in certain ways.[34] There are several types of power: legitimate, reward, coercive, expert, and referent power (see Figure 14.1).[35] Effective leaders take steps to ensure that they have sufficient levels of each type and that they use the power they have in beneficial ways.

legitimate power The authority that a manager has by virtue of his or her position in an organization's hierarchy.

LEGITIMATE POWER   **Legitimate power** is the authority a manager has by virtue of his or her position in an organization's hierarchy. Personal leadership style often influences how a manager exercises legitimate power. Take the case of Carol Loray, who is a first-line manager in a greeting card company and leads a group of 15 artists and designers. Loray has the legitimate power to hire new employees, assign projects to the artists

Figure 14.1
Source of Managerial Power

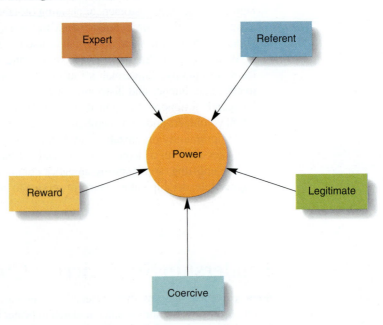

and designers, monitor their work, and appraise their performance. She uses this power effectively. She always makes sure her project assignments match the interests of her subordinates as much as possible so they will enjoy their work. She monitors their work to make sure they are on track but does not engage in close supervision, which can hamper creativity. She makes sure her performance appraisals are developmental, providing concrete advice for areas where improvements could be made. Recently Loray negotiated with her manager to increase her legitimate power so she can now initiate and develop proposals for new card lines.

reward power The ability of a manager to give or withhold tangible and intangible rewards.

REWARD POWER   **Reward power** is the ability of a manager to give or withhold tangible rewards (pay raises, bonuses, choice job assignments) and intangible rewards (verbal praise, a pat on the back, respect). As you learned in Chapter 13, members of an organization are motivated to perform at a high level by a variety of rewards. Being able to give or withhold rewards based on performance is a major source of power that allows managers to have a highly motivated workforce. Managers of salespeople in retail organizations like Neiman Marcus, Nordstrom, and Macy's[36] and in car dealerships such as Mazda, Ford, and Volvo often use their reward power to motivate their subordinates. Subordinates in organizations such as these often receive commissions on whatever they sell and rewards for the quality of their customer service, which motivate them to do the best they can.

Effective managers use their reward power to show appreciation for subordinates' good work and efforts. Ineffective managers use rewards in a more controlling manner (wielding the "stick" instead of offering the "carrot") that signals to subordinates that the manager has the upper hand. Managers also can take steps to increase their reward power. Carol Loray had the legitimate power to appraise her subordinates' performance, but she lacked the reward power to distribute raises and end-of-year bonuses until she discussed with her own manager why this would be a valuable motivational tool for her to use. Loray now receives a pool of money each year for salary increases and bonuses and has the reward power to distribute them as she sees fit.

coercive power The ability of a manager to punish others.

COERCIVE POWER   **Coercive power** is the ability of a manager to punish others. Punishment can range from verbal reprimands to reductions in pay or working hours to actual dismissal. In the previous chapter we discussed how punishment can have negative side effects, such as resentment and retaliation, and should be used only when necessary (for example, to curtail a dangerous behavior). Managers who rely heavily on coercive power tend to be ineffective as leaders and sometimes even get fired themselves. William J. Fife is one example; he was fired from his position as CEO of Giddings and Lewis Inc., a manufacturer of factory equipment, because of his overreliance on coercive power. In meetings Fife often verbally criticized, attacked, and embarrassed top managers. Realizing how destructive Fife's use of punishment was for them and the company, these managers complained to the board of directors, who, after a careful consideration of the issues, asked Fife to resign.[37]

Excessive use of coercive power seldom produces high performance and is questionable ethically. Sometimes it amounts to a form of mental abuse, robbing workers of their dignity and causing excessive levels of stress. Overuse of coercive power can even result in dangerous working conditions. Better results and, importantly, an ethical workplace that respects employee dignity can be obtained by using reward power.

expert power Power that is based on the special knowledge, skills, and expertise that a leader possesses.

EXPERT POWER   **Expert power** is based on the special knowledge, skills, and expertise that a leader possesses. The nature of expert power varies, depending on the leader's level in the hierarchy. First-level and middle managers often have technical expertise relevant to the tasks their subordinates perform. Their expert power gives them considerable influence over subordinates. Carol Loray has expert power: She is an artist herself and has drawn and designed some of her company's top-selling greeting cards. Jim Whitehurst in "A Manager's Challenge" has expert power from the prior leadership positions he has had and from his educational background. As indicated in the accompanying "Manager as a Person" feature, managers with expert power nonetheless need to recognize that they are not always right and seek and encourage input from others.

Manager as a Person

Gregory Maffei and Expert Power

Gregory Maffei is the president and chief executive officer of Liberty Media Corporation, which has operations in the communications, e-commerce, media, technology, and entertainment industries.[38] Liberty owns or has interests in a variety of companies in these industries, such as SiriusXM, Live Nation, True Position, Inc., Expedia, QVC, HSN, Starz, Red Envelope, Evite, ProFlowers, backcountry.com, Barnes & Noble, bodybuilding.com, and the Atlanta National League Baseball Club, Inc.[39]

Judging from his background and experience, Maffei would certainly appear to possess considerable amounts of expert power. With a bachelor's degree from Dartmouth College and an MBA from the Harvard Business School, Maffei held a number of important leadership positions before joining Liberty.[40] For example, he worked with Bill Gates as the chief financial officer of Microsoft and was the chairman of Expedia, the chairman and CEO of 360networks, and the president and chief financial officer for Oracle.[41] He is active in serving on boards of directors and also in the community. For example, he was the president of the Seattle Public Library and currently heads up the budget task force for the governor of Colorado.[42]

Interestingly enough, Maffei is the first to admit that he often doesn't have all the answers.[43] In fact, when he worked with Bill Gates, he realized that Gates often sought input from others and never thought that his ideas were necessarily the right ideas just because he had them.[44] Rather, Gates would ask other managers what they thought about his ideas. Maffei realizes the value of getting multiple inputs on ideas and having two-way conversations in which everyone feels free to speak their minds and ask probing questions, even of the CEO. The first manager Maffei promoted at Liberty was a colleague who would consistently question and sometimes critique his ideas; having valuable insights, Maffei recognized how constructive the exchanges of ideas were with this manager. And he strives to have all employees feel comfortable asking him questions and having a two-way conversation with him.[45] While expert power has certainly helped Maffei as CEO of Liberty, so too has his recognition that he is not always right just because he is CEO.[46]

Some top managers derive expert power from their technical expertise. Other top-level managers lack technical expertise and derive their expert power from their abilities as decision makers, planners, and strategists. Jack Welch, the former well-known leader and CEO of General Electric, summed it up this way: "The basic thing that we at the top of the company know is that we don't know the business. What we have, I hope, is the ability to allocate resources, people, and dollars."[47]

Effective leaders take steps to ensure that they have an adequate amount of expert power to perform their leadership roles. They may obtain additional training or education in their fields, make sure they keep up with the latest developments and changes in technology, stay abreast of changes in their fields through involvement in professional associations, and read widely to be aware of momentous changes in the organization's task and general environments. Expert power tends to be best used in a guiding or coaching manner rather than in an arrogant, high-handed manner.

REFERENT POWER   **Referent power** is more informal than the other kinds of power. Referent power is a function of the personal characteristics of a leader; it is the power that comes from subordinates' and coworkers' respect, admiration, and loyalty. Leaders who are likable and whom subordinates wish to use as a role model are especially likely to possess referent power, as is true of Jim Whitehurst in "A Manager's Challenge."

In addition to being a valuable asset for top managers like Whitehurst, referent power can help first-line and middle managers be effective leaders as well. Sally Carruthers, for example, is the first-level manager of a group of secretaries in the finance department of a

referent power Power that comes from subordinates' and coworkers' respect, admiration, and loyalty.

The Chrysler Jefferson North Assembly plant in Detroit. Empowered employees make some decisions that managers or other leaders used to make.

empowerment The expansion of employees' knowledge, tasks, and decision-making responsibilities.

large state university. Carruthers's secretaries are known to be among the best in the university. Much of their willingness to go above and beyond the call of duty has been attributed to Carruthers's warm and caring nature, which makes each of them feel important and valued. Managers can take steps to increase their referent power, such as taking time to get to know their subordinates and showing interest in and concern for them.

Empowerment: An Ingredient in Modern Management

More and more managers today are incorporating into their personal leadership styles an aspect that at first glance seems to be the opposite of being a leader. In Chapter 1 we described how empowerment—the process of giving employees at all levels the authority to make decisions, be responsible for their outcomes, improve quality, and cut costs—is becoming increasingly popular in organizations. When leaders empower their subordinates, the subordinates typically take over some responsibilities and authority that used to reside with the leader or manager, such as the right to reject parts that do not meet quality standards, the right to check one's own work, and the right to schedule work activities. Empowered subordinates are given the power to make some decisions that their leaders or supervisors used to make.

Empowerment might seem to be the opposite of effective leadership because managers are allowing subordinates to take a more active role in leading themselves. In actuality, however, empowerment can contribute to effective leadership for several reasons:

- Empowerment increases a manager's ability to get things done because the manager has the support and help of subordinates who may have special knowledge of work tasks.

- Empowerment often increases workers' involvement, motivation, and commitment; and this helps ensure that they are working toward organizational goals.

- Empowerment gives managers more time to concentrate on their pressing concerns because they spend less time on day-to-day supervision.

Effective managers like Jim Whitehurst realize the benefits of empowerment. The personal leadership style of managers who empower subordinates often entails developing subordinates' ability to make good decisions as well as being their guide, coach, and source of inspiration. Empowerment is a popular trend in the United States and is a part of servant leadership. Empowerment is also taking off around the world.[48] For instance, companies in South Korea (such as Samsung, Hyundai, and Daewoo), in which decision making typically was centralized with the founding families, are now empowering managers at lower levels to make decisions.[49]

Trait and Behavior Models of Leadership

Leading is such an important process in all organizations—nonprofit organizations, government agencies, and schools, as well as for-profit corporations—that it has been researched for decades. Early approaches to leadership, called the *trait model* and the *behavior model,* sought to determine what effective leaders are like as people and what they do that makes them so effective.

LO14-2

Identify the traits that show the strongest relationship to leadership, the behaviors leaders engage in, and the limitations of the trait and behavior models of leadership.

The Trait Model

The trait model of leadership focused on identifying the personal characteristics that cause effective leadership. Researchers thought effective leaders must have certain personal qualities that set them apart from ineffective leaders and from people who never become leaders. Decades of research (beginning in the 1930s) and hundreds of studies indicate that certain personal characteristics do appear to be associated with effective leadership. (See Table 14.1

Table 14.1

Traits and Personal Characteristics Related to Effective Leadership

Trait	Description
Intelligence	Helps managers understand complex issues and solve problems.
Knowledge and expertise	Help managers make good decisions and discover ways to increase efficiency and effectiveness.
Dominance	Helps managers influence their subordinates to achieve organizational goals.
Self-confidence	Contributes to managers' effectively influencing subordinates and persisting when faced with obstacles or difficulties.
High energy	Helps managers deal with the many demands they face.
Tolerance for stress	Helps managers deal with uncertainty and make difficult decisions.
Integrity and honesty	Help managers behave ethically and earn their subordinates' trust and confidence.
Maturity	Helps managers avoid acting selfishly, control their feelings, and admit when they have made a mistake.

for a list of these.)[50] Notice that although this model is called the "trait" model, some of the personal characteristics that it identifies are not personality traits per se but, rather, are concerned with a leader's skills, abilities, knowledge, and expertise. As "A Manager's Challenge" shows, Jim Whitehurst certainly appears to possess many of these characteristics (such as intelligence, knowledge and expertise, self-confidence, high energy, and integrity and honesty). Leaders who do not possess these traits may be ineffective.

Traits alone are not the key to understanding leader effectiveness, however. Some effective leaders do not possess all these traits, and some leaders who possess them are not effective in their leadership roles. This lack of a consistent relationship between leader traits and leader effectiveness led researchers to shift their attention away from traits and to search for new explanations for effective leadership. Rather than focusing on what leaders are like (the traits they possess), researchers began looking at what effective leaders actually do—in other words, at the behaviors that allow effective leaders to influence their subordinates to achieve group and organizational goals.

The Behavior Model

After extensive study in the 1940s and 1950s, researchers at The Ohio State University identified two basic kinds of leader behaviors that many leaders in the United States, Germany, and other countries engaged in to influence their subordinates: *consideration* and *initiating structure*.[51]

consideration Behavior indicating that a manager trusts, respects, and cares about subordinates.

CONSIDERATION Leaders engage in **consideration** when they show their subordinates that they trust, respect, and care about them. Managers who truly look out for the well-being of their subordinates, and do what they can to help subordinates feel good and enjoy their work, perform consideration behaviors. In "A Manager's Challenge," Jim Whitehurst engages in consideration when he looks out for the well-being of his employees, shows them that he trusts them, and fosters an environment in which they will be engaged and passionate about their work.

At Costco Wholesale Corporation, cofounder and director Jim Senegal believes that consideration not only is an ethical imperative but also makes good business sense,[52] as indicated in the accompanying "Management Insight" feature.

Consideration at Costco

Managers at Costco, including cofounder and director Jim Senegal and CEO Craig Jelinek, believe consideration is so important that one of the principles in Costco's code of ethics is "Take Care of Our Employees."[53] Costco Wholesale Corporation is the third largest retailer and the top warehouse retailer in the United States.[54] Wages at Costco are an average of $17 per hour—over 40 percent higher than the average hourly wage at Walmart, Costco's major competitor.[55] Costco pays the majority of health insurance costs for its employees (employees pay around 8 percent of health insurance costs compared to an industry average of around 25 percent), and part-time employees receive health insurance after they have been with the company six months. Overall, about 85 percent of Costco employees are covered by health insurance, compared with fewer than 45 percent of employees at Target and Walmart.[56]

Loyal Costco customers like these know that their bargains don't come at the expense of employees' paychecks and benefits.

Jim Senegal and Craig Jelinek believe that caring about the well-being of employees is a win–win proposition because Costco's employees are satisfied, committed, loyal, and motivated. Additionally, turnover and employee theft rates at Costco are much lower than industry averages.[57] In the retail industry, turnover tends to be high and costly because for every employee who quits, a new hire needs to be recruited, tested, interviewed, and trained. Even though pay and benefits are higher at Costco than at rival Walmart, Costco actually has lower labor costs as a percentage of sales and higher sales per square foot of store space than Walmart.[58]

Additionally, treating employees well helps build customer loyalty at Costco. Surely customers enjoy the bargains and low prices that come from shopping in a warehouse store, the relatively high quality of the goods Costco stocks, and Costco's policy of not marking up prices by more than 14–15 percent (relatively low markups for retail) even if the goods would sell with higher markups. However, customers are also loyal to Costco because they know the company treats its employees well and their bargains are not coming at the expense of employees' paychecks and benefits.[59]

Costco started out as a single warehouse store in Seattle, Washington, in 1983. Now the company has 652 stores (including stores in Puerto Rico, South Korea, Taiwan, Japan, Australia, Mexico, Canada, and Britain) and tens of millions of members who pay an annual fee to shop at Costco stores.[60] Costco's growth and financial performance are enviable.[61] For example, net sales for the first half of the 2014 fiscal year were $50.22 billion.[62] Clearly consideration has paid off for Costco and for its employees.[63]

True to caring for the well-being of employees, Costco did not lay off any employees during the recession in the late 2000s.[64] However, some female employees filed a class action lawsuit alleging gender discrimination at Costco.[65] The lawsuit started when Shirley Ellis filed a discrimination complaint and a later lawsuit in the early 2000s.[66] In December 2013 the lawsuit was tentatively settled for $8 million to compensate women who were inappropriately blocked from promotions to positions of assistant general manager and general manager.[67] The settlement also entails Costco having its promotion procedures for assistant general managers and general managers reviewed by an industrial organizational psychologist. Additionally, Costco will post assistant general manager openings and have a system for employees to indicate their interest in general manager positions. In terms of the settlement, Ellis indicated that, "I believe this to be a fair settlement to both parties. . . . Even though this process has taken much longer than anticipated initially, I'm encouraged by Costco's efforts to welcome women and all they have to offer in the ranks of GM and AGM companywide."[68]

initiating structure Behavior that managers engage in to ensure that work gets done, subordinates perform their jobs acceptably, and the organization is efficient and effective.

INITIATING STRUCTURE   Leaders engage in **initiating structure** when they take steps to make sure that work gets done, subordinates perform their jobs acceptably, and the organization is efficient and effective. Assigning tasks to individuals or work groups, letting subordinates know what is expected of them, deciding how work should be done, making schedules, encouraging adherence to rules and regulations, and motivating subordinates to do a good job are all examples of initiating structure.[69]

Michael Teckel, the manager of an upscale store selling imported men's and women's shoes in a Midwestern city, engages in initiating structure when he establishes weekly work, lunch, and break schedules to ensure that the store has enough salespeople on the floor. Teckel also initiates structure when he discusses the latest shoe designs with his subordinates so they are knowledgeable with customers, when he encourages adherence to the store's refund and exchange policies, and when he encourages his staff to provide high-quality customer service and to avoid a hard-sell approach.

Initiating structure and consideration are independent leader behaviors. Leaders can be high on both, low on both, or high on one and low on the other. Many effective leaders, like Jim Whitehurst of Red Hat, engage in both of these behaviors.

Leadership researchers have identified leader behaviors similar to consideration and initiating structure. Researchers at the University of Michigan, for example, identified two categories of leadership behaviors, *employee-centered behaviors* and *job-oriented behaviors,* that correspond roughly to consideration and initiating structure, respectively.[70] Models of leadership popular with consultants also tend to zero in on these two kinds of behaviors. For example, Robert Blake and Jane Mouton's Managerial Grid focuses on *concern for people* (similar to consideration) and *concern for production* (similar to initiating structure). Blake and Mouton advise that effective leadership often requires both a high level of concern for people and a high level of concern for production.[71] As another example, Paul Hersey and Kenneth Blanchard's model focuses on *supportive behaviors* (similar to consideration) and *task-oriented behaviors* (similar to initiating structure). According to Hersey and Blanchard, leaders need to consider the nature of their subordinates when trying to determine the extent to which they should perform these two behaviors.[72]

You might expect that effective leaders and managers would perform both kinds of behaviors, but research has found that this is not necessarily the case. The relationship between performance of consideration and initiating-structure behaviors and leader effectiveness is not clear-cut. Some leaders are effective even when they do not perform consideration or initiating-structure behaviors, and some leaders are ineffective even when they perform both kinds of behaviors. Like the trait model of leadership, the behavior model alone cannot explain leader effectiveness. Realizing this, researchers began building more complicated models of leadership, focused not only on the leader and what he or she does but also on the situation or context in which leadership occurs.

LO14-3

Explain how contingency models of leadership enhance our understanding of effective leadership and management in organizations.

Contingency Models of Leadership

Simply possessing certain traits or performing certain behaviors does not ensure that a manager will be an effective leader in all situations calling for leadership. Some managers who seem to possess the right traits and perform the right behaviors turn out to be ineffective leaders. Managers lead in a wide variety of situations and organizations and have various kinds of subordinates performing diverse tasks in a multiplicity of environmental contexts. Given the wide variety of situations in which leadership occurs, what makes a manager an effective leader in one situation (such as certain traits or behaviors) is not necessarily what that manager needs to be equally effective in a different situation. An effective army general might not be an effective university president; an effective restaurant manager might not be an effective clothing store manager; an effective football team coach might not be an effective fitness center manager; and an effective first-line manager in a manufacturing company might not be an effective middle manager. The traits or behaviors that may contribute to a manager's being an effective leader in one situation might actually result in the same manager being an ineffective leader in another situation.

Contingency models of leadership take into account the situation or context within which leadership occurs. According to contingency models, whether or not a manager is an effective leader is the result of the interplay between what the manager is like, what he or she does, and the situation in which leadership takes place. Contingency models propose that whether a leader who possesses certain traits or performs certain behaviors is effective depends on, or is contingent on, the situation or context. In this section we discuss three prominent contingency models developed to shed light on what makes managers effective leaders: Fred Fiedler's contingency model, Robert House's path–goal theory, and the leader substitutes model. As you will see, these leadership models are complementary; each focuses on a somewhat different aspect of effective leadership in organizations.

Fiedler's Contingency Model

Fred E. Fiedler was among the first leadership researchers to acknowledge that effective leadership is contingent on, or depends on, the characteristics of the leader *and* of the situation. Fiedler's contingency model helps explain why a manager may be an effective leader in one situation and ineffective in another; it also suggests which kinds of managers are likely to be most effective in which situations.[73]

LEADER STYLE   As with the trait approach, Fiedler hypothesized that personal characteristics can influence leader effectiveness. He used the term *leader style* to refer to a manager's characteristic approach to leadership and identified two basic leader styles: *relationship-oriented* and *task-oriented*. All managers can be described as having one style or the other.

Relationship-oriented leaders are primarily concerned with developing good relationships with their subordinates and being liked by them. Relationship-oriented managers focus on having high-quality interpersonal relationships with subordinates. This does not mean, however, that the job does not get done when such leaders are at the helm. But it does mean that the quality of interpersonal relationships with subordinates is a prime concern for relationship-oriented leaders.

Task-oriented leaders are primarily concerned with ensuring that subordinates perform at a high level and focus on task accomplishment. While task-oriented leaders also may be concerned about having good interpersonal relationships with their subordinates, task accomplishment is their prime concern.

In his research, Fiedler measured leader style by asking leaders to rate the coworker with whom they have had the most difficulty working (called the least preferred coworker or LPC) on a number of dimensions, such as whether the person is boring or interesting, gloomy or cheerful, enthusiastic or unenthusiastic, cooperative or uncooperative. Relationship-oriented leaders tend to describe the LPC in relatively positive terms; their concern for good relationships leads them to think well of others. Task-oriented leaders tend to describe the LPC in negative terms; their concern for task accomplishment causes them to think badly about others who make getting the job done difficult. Thus relationship-oriented and task-oriented leaders are sometimes referred to as high-LPC and low-LPC leaders, respectively.

SITUATIONAL CHARACTERISTICS   According to Fiedler, leadership style is an enduring characteristic; managers cannot change their style, nor can they adopt different styles in different kinds of situations. With this in mind, Fiedler identified three situational characteristics that are important determinants of how favorable a situation is for leading: leader–member relations, task structure, and position power. When a situation is favorable for leading, it is relatively easy for a manager to influence subordinates so they perform at a high level and contribute to organizational efficiency and effectiveness. In a situation unfavorable for leading, it is much more difficult for a manager to exert influence.

LEADER–MEMBER RELATIONS   The first situational characteristic Fiedler described, **leader–member relations**, is the extent to which followers like, trust, and are loyal to their leader. Situations are more favorable for leading when leader–member relations are good.

TASK STRUCTURE   The second situational characteristic Fiedler described, **task structure**, is the extent to which the work to be performed is clear-cut so that a leader's subordinates know what needs to be accomplished and how to go about doing it. When task structure is high, the situation is favorable for leading. When task structure is low, goals may be vague,

relationship-oriented leaders Leaders whose primary concern is to develop good relationships with their subordinates and to be liked by them.

task-oriented leaders Leaders whose primary concern is to ensure that subordinates perform at a high level.

leader–member relations The extent to which followers like, trust, and are loyal to their leader; a determinant of how favorable a situation is for leading.

task structure The extent to which the work to be performed is clear-cut so that a leader's subordinates know what needs to be accomplished and how to go about doing it; a determinant of how favorable a situation is for leading.

subordinates may be unsure of what they should be doing or how they should do it, and the situation is unfavorable for leading.

Task structure was low for Geraldine Laybourne when she was a top manager at Nickelodeon, the children's television network. It was never precisely clear what would appeal to her young viewers, whose tastes can change dramatically, or how to motivate her subordinates to come up with creative and novel ideas.[74] In contrast, Herman Mashaba, founder of Black Like Me, a hair care products company based in South Africa, seemed to have relatively high task structure when he started his company. His company's goals were to produce and sell inexpensive hair care products to native Africans, and managers accomplished these goals by using simple yet appealing packaging and distributing the products through neighborhood beauty salons.[75]

position power The amount of legitimate, reward, and coercive power that a leader has by virtue of his or her position in an organization; a determinant of how favorable a situation is for leading.

POSITION POWER   The third situational characteristic Fiedler described, **position power**, is the amount of legitimate, reward, and coercive power a leader has by virtue of his or her position in an organization. Leadership situations are more favorable for leading when position power is strong.

COMBINING LEADER STYLE AND THE SITUATION   By considering all possible combinations of good and poor leader–member relations, high and low task structure, and strong and weak position power, Fiedler identified eight leadership situations, which vary in their favorability for leading (see Figure 14.2). After extensive research, he determined that relationship-oriented leaders are most effective in moderately favorable situations (IV, V, VI, and VII in Figure 14.2) and task-oriented leaders are most effective in situations that are either very favorable (I, II, and III) or very unfavorable (VIII).

PUTTING THE CONTINGENCY MODEL INTO PRACTICE   Recall that, according to Fiedler, leader style is an enduring characteristic that managers cannot change. This suggests that for managers to be effective, either managers need to be placed in leadership situations that fit their style or situations need to be changed to suit the managers. Situations can be changed, for example, by giving a manager more position power or taking steps to increase task structure, such as by clarifying goals.

Take the case of Mark Compton, a relationship-oriented leader employed by a small construction company, who was in a very unfavorable situation and was having a rough time leading his construction crew. His subordinates did not trust him to look out for their well-being (poor leader–member relations); the construction jobs he supervised tended to be novel and complex (low task structure); and he had no control over the rewards and disciplinary actions his subordinates received (weak position power). Recognizing the need to improve matters, Compton's supervisor gave him the power to reward crew members with bonuses

Figure 14.2

Fiedler's Contingency Theory of Leadership

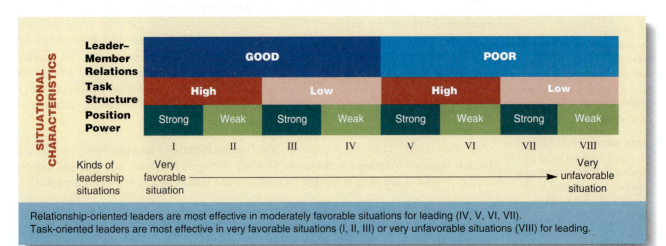

Relationship-oriented leaders are most effective in moderately favorable situations for leading (IV, V, VI, VII).
Task-oriented leaders are most effective in very favorable situations (I, II, III) or very unfavorable situations (VIII) for leading.

and overtime work as he saw fit and to discipline crew members for poor-quality work and unsafe on-the-job behavior. As his leadership situation improved to moderately favorable, so too did Compton's effectiveness as a leader and the performance of his crew.

Research studies tend to support some aspects of Fiedler's model but also suggest that, like most theories, it needs some modifications.[76] Some researchers have questioned what the LPC scale really measures. Others find fault with the model's premise that leaders cannot alter their styles. That is, it is likely that at least some leaders can diagnose the situation they are in and, when their style is inappropriate for the situation, modify their style so that it is more in line with what the leadership situation calls for.

House's Path–Goal Theory

path–goal theory
A contingency model of leadership proposing that leaders can motivate subordinates by identifying their desired outcomes, rewarding them for high performance and the attainment of work goals with these desired outcomes, and clarifying for them the paths leading to the attainment of work goals.

In what he called **path–goal theory**, leadership researcher Robert House focused on what leaders can do to motivate their subordinates to achieve group and organizational goals.[77] The premise of path–goal theory is that effective leaders motivate subordinates to achieve goals by (1) clearly identifying the outcomes that subordinates are trying to obtain from the workplace, (2) rewarding subordinates with these outcomes for high performance and the attainment of work goals, and (3) clarifying for subordinates the *paths* leading to the attainment of work *goals*. Path–goal theory is a contingency model because it proposes that the steps managers should take to motivate subordinates depend on both the nature of the subordinates and the type of work they do.

Based on the expectancy theory of motivation (see Chapter 13), path–goal theory gives managers three guidelines to being effective leaders:

1. *Find out what outcomes your subordinates are trying to obtain from their jobs and the organization.* These outcomes can range from satisfactory pay and job security to reasonable working hours and interesting and challenging job assignments. After identifying these outcomes, the manager should have the *reward power* needed to distribute or withhold the outcomes. Mark Crane, for example, is the vice principal of a large elementary school. Crane determined that the teachers he leads are trying to obtain the following outcomes from their jobs: pay raises, autonomy in the classroom, and the choice of which grades they teach. Crane had reward power for the latter two outcomes, but the school's principal determined how the pool of money for raises was to be distributed each year. Because Crane was the first-line manager who led the teachers and was most familiar with their performance, he asked the principal (his boss) to give him some say in determining pay raises. Realizing that this made a lot of sense, his principal gave Crane full power to distribute raises and requested only that Crane review his decisions with him before informing the teachers about them.

2. *Reward subordinates for high performance and goal attainment with the outcomes they desire.* The teachers and administrators at Crane's school considered several dimensions of teacher performance to be critical to achieving their goal of providing high-quality education: excellent in-class instruction, special programs to enhance student interest and learning (such as science and computer projects), and availability for meetings with parents to discuss their children's progress and special needs. Crane distributed pay raises to the teachers based on the extent to which they performed highly on each of these dimensions. The top-performing teachers were given first choice of grade assignments and also had practically complete autonomy in their classrooms.

3. *Clarify the paths to goal attainment for subordinates, remove any obstacles to high performance, and express confidence in subordinates' capabilities.* This does not mean that a manager needs to tell subordinates what to do. Rather, it means that a manager needs to make sure subordinates are clear about what they should be trying to accomplish and have the capabilities, resources, and confidence levels needed to be successful. Crane made sure all the teachers understood the importance of the three targeted goals and asked them whether, to reach them, they needed any special resources or supplies for their classes. Crane also gave additional coaching and guidance to teachers who seemed to be struggling. For example, Patrick Conolly, in his first year of teaching after graduate school, was unsure how to use special projects in a third grade class and how to react to

parents who were critical. Conolly's teaching was excellent, but he felt insecure about how he was doing on this dimension. To help build Conolly's confidence, Crane told Conolly that he thought he could be one of the school's top teachers (which was true). He gave Conolly some ideas about special projects that worked particularly well with the third grade, such as a writing project. Crane also role-played teacher–parent interactions with Conolly. Conolly played the role of a particularly dissatisfied or troubled parent, while Crane played the role of a teacher trying to solve the underlying problem while making the parent feel that his or her child's needs were being met. Crane's efforts to clarify the paths to goal attainment for Conolly paid off: Within two years the local PTS voted Conolly teacher of the year.

Path–goal theory identifies four kinds of leadership behaviors that motivate subordinates:

You could stand over your subordinate and berate him or you could empower him to find the solution by working to see where the issue developed. Supportive managers make a world of difference in retaining and motivating employees.

- *Directive behaviors* are similar to initiating structure and include setting goals, assigning tasks, showing subordinates how to complete tasks, and taking concrete steps to improve performance.

- *Supportive behaviors* are similar to consideration and include expressing concern for subordinates and looking out for their best interests.

- *Participative behaviors* give subordinates a say in matters and decisions that affect them.

- *Achievement-oriented behaviors* motivate subordinates to perform at the highest level possible by, for example, setting challenging goals, expecting that they be met, and believing in subordinates' capabilities.

Which of these behaviors should managers use to lead effectively? The answer to this question depends, or is contingent on, the nature of the subordinates and the kind of work they do.

Directive behaviors may be beneficial when subordinates are having difficulty completing assigned tasks, but they might be detrimental when subordinates are independent thinkers who work best when left alone. *Supportive* behaviors are often advisable when subordinates are experiencing high levels of stress. *Participative* behaviors can be particularly effective when subordinates' support of a decision is required. *Achievement-oriented* behaviors may increase motivation levels of highly capable subordinates who are bored from having too few challenges, but they might backfire if used with subordinates who are already pushed to their limit.

The Leader Substitutes Model

leadership substitute A characteristic of a subordinate or of a situation or context that acts in place of the influence of a leader and makes leadership unnecessary.

The leader substitutes model suggests that leadership is sometimes unnecessary because substitutes for leadership are present. A **leadership substitute** is something that acts in place of the influence of a leader and makes leadership unnecessary. This model suggests that under certain conditions managers do not have to play a leadership role—members of an organization sometimes can perform at a high level without a manager exerting influence over them.[78] The leader substitutes model is a contingency model because it suggests that in some situations leadership is unnecessary.

Take the case of David Cotsonas, who teaches English at a foreign language school in Cyprus, an island in the Mediterranean Sea. Cotsonas is fluent in Greek, English, and French; is an excellent teacher; and is highly motivated. Many of his students are businesspeople who have some rudimentary English skills and wish to increase their fluency to be able to conduct more of their business in English. He enjoys not only teaching them English but also learning about the work they do, and he often keeps in touch with his students after they finish his classes. Cotsonas meets with the director of the school twice a year to discuss semiannual class schedules and enrollments.

With practically no influence from a leader, Cotsonas is a highly motivated top performer at the school. In his situation, leadership is unnecessary because substitutes for leadership are present. Cotsonas's teaching expertise, his motivation, and his enjoyment of his work are substitutes for the influence of a leader—in this case the school's director. If the school's director were to try to influence how Cotsonas performs his job, Cotsonas would probably resent this infringement on his autonomy, and it is unlikely that his performance would improve because he is already one of the school's best teachers.

As in Cotsonas's case, *characteristics of subordinates*—such as their skills, abilities, experience, knowledge, and motivation—can be substitutes for leadership.[79] *Characteristics of the situation or context*—such as the extent to which the work is interesting and enjoyable—also can be substitutes. When work is interesting and enjoyable, as it is for Cotsonas, jobholders do not need to be coaxed into performing because performing is rewarding in its own right. Similarly, when managers *empower* their subordinates or use *self-managed work teams* (discussed in detail in Chapter 15), the need for leadership influence from a manager is decreased because team members manage themselves.

Substitutes for leadership can increase organizational efficiency and effectiveness because they free up some of managers' valuable time and allow managers to focus their efforts on discovering new ways to improve organizational effectiveness. The director of the language school, for example, was able to spend much of his time making arrangements to open a second school in Rhodes, an island in the Aegean Sea, because of the presence of leadership substitutes, not only for Cotsonas but for most other teachers at the school as well.

Bringing It All Together

Effective leadership in organizations occurs when managers take steps to lead in a way that is appropriate for the situation or context in which leadership occurs and for the subordinates who are being led. The three contingency models of leadership just discussed help managers focus on the necessary ingredients for effective leadership. They are complementary in that each one looks at the leadership question from a different angle. Fiedler's contingency model explores how a manager's leadership style needs to be matched to that person's leadership situation for maximum effectiveness. House's path–goal theory focuses on how managers should motivate subordinates and describes the specific kinds of behaviors managers can engage in to have a highly motivated workforce. The leadership substitutes model alerts managers to the fact that sometimes they do not need to exert influence over subordinates and thus can free up their time for other important activities. Table 14.2 recaps these three contingency models of leadership.

Table 14.2

Contingency Models of Leadership

Model	Focus	Key Contingencies
Fiedler's contingency model	Describes two leader styles, relationship-oriented and task-oriented, and the kinds of situations in which each kind of leader will be most effective.	Whether a relationship-oriented or a task-oriented leader is effective is contingent on the situation.
House's path–goal theory	Describes how effective leaders motivate their followers.	The behaviors that managers should engage in to be effective leaders are contingent on the nature of the subordinates and the work they do.
Leader substitutes model	Describes when leadership is unnecessary.	Whether leadership is necessary for subordinates to perform highly is contingent on characteristics of the subordinates and the situation.

Transformational Leadership

Time and time again, throughout business history, certain leaders seem to literally transform their organizations, making sweeping changes to revitalize and renew operations. For example, when Sue Nokes became senior vice president of sales and customer service at T-Mobile USA in 2002, the quality of T-Mobile's customer service was lower than that of its major competitors; on average, 12 percent of employees were absent on any day; and annual employee turnover was over 100 percent.[80] T-Mobile USA is a subsidiary of Deutsche Telekom; has approximately 38,000 employees; and provides wireless voice, messaging, and data services.[81] When Nokes arrived at T-Mobile, valuable employees were quitting their jobs and customers weren't receiving high-quality service; neither employees nor customers were satisfied with their experience with the company.[82] However, by the late 2000s T-Mobile was regularly receiving highest rankings for customer care and satisfaction in the wireless category by J. D. Power and Associates, absence and turnover rates substantially declined, and around 80 percent of employees indicated that they were satisfied with their jobs.[83] In fact, when Nokes visited call centers, it was not uncommon for employees to greet her with cheers and accolades.[84]

Nokes transformed T-Mobile into a company in which satisfied employees provide excellent service to customers.[85] When managers have such dramatic effects on their subordinates and on an organization as a whole, they are engaging in transformational leadership. **Transformational leadership** occurs when managers change (or transform) their subordinates in three important ways:[86]

1. *Transformational managers make subordinates aware of how important their jobs are for the organization and how necessary it is for them to perform those jobs as best they can so the organization can attain its goals.* At T-Mobile, Nokes visited call centers, conducted focus groups, and had town hall meetings to find out what employees and customers were unhappy with and what steps she could take to improve matters.[87] Her philosophy was that when employees are satisfied with their jobs and view their work as important, they are much more likely to provide high-quality customer service. She made employees aware of how important their jobs were by the many steps she took to improve their working conditions, ranging from providing them with their own workspaces to substantially raising their salaries.[88] She emphasized the importance of providing excellent customer service by periodically asking employees what was working well and what was not working well, asking them what steps could be taken to improve problem areas, and taking actions to ensure that employees were able to provide excellent customer service. Nokes also instituted a performance measurement system to track performance in key areas such as quality of service and speed of problem resolution.[89] She sincerely told employees, "You are No. 1, and the customer is why."[90]

2. *Transformational managers make their subordinates aware of the subordinates' own needs for personal growth, development, and accomplishment.* Nokes made T-Mobile's employees aware of their own needs in this regard by transforming training and development at T-Mobile and increasing opportunities for promotions to more responsible positions. Employees now spend over 130 hours per year in training and development programs and team meetings. Nokes also instituted a promote-from-within policy, and around 80 percent of promotions are given to current employees.[91]

3. *Transformational managers motivate their subordinates to work for the good of the organization as a whole, not just for their own personal gain or benefit.* Nokes emphasized that employees should focus on what matters to customers, coworkers, and T-Mobile as a whole. She let employees know that when they were unnecessarily absent from their jobs, they were not doing right by their coworkers. And she emphasized the need to try to resolve customer problems in a single phone call so customers can get on with their busy lives.[92]

When managers transform their subordinates in these three ways, subordinates trust the managers, are highly motivated, and help the organization achieve its goals. How do managers such as Nokes transform subordinates and produce dramatic effects in their organizations? There are at least three ways in which transformational leaders can influence their followers: by being a charismatic leader, by intellectually stimulating subordinates, and by engaging in developmental consideration (see Table 14.3).

Sue Nokes exhibited transformational leadership at T-Mobile.

transformational leadership Leadership that makes subordinates aware of the importance of their jobs and performance to the organization and aware of their own needs for personal growth and that motivates subordinates to work for the good of the organization.

Table 14.3
Transformational Leadership

Transformational managers

- Are charismatic.
- Intellectually stimulate subordinates.
- Engage in developmental consideration.

Subordinates of transformational managers

- Have increased awareness of the importance of their jobs and high performance.
- Are aware of their own needs for growth, development, and accomplishment.
- Work for the good of the organization and not just their own personal benefit.

Being a Charismatic Leader

charismatic leader An enthusiastic, self-confident leader who is able to clearly communicate his or her vision of how good things could be.

Transformational managers such as Nokes are **charismatic leaders**. They have a vision of how good things could be in their work groups and organizations that is in contrast with the status quo. Their vision usually entails dramatic improvements in group and organizational performance as a result of changes in the organization's structure, culture, strategy, decision making, and other critical processes and factors. This vision paves the way for gaining a competitive advantage.

Charismatic leaders are excited and enthusiastic about their vision and clearly communicate it to their subordinates. The excitement, enthusiasm, and self-confidence of a charismatic leader contribute to the leader's being able to inspire followers to enthusiastically support his or her vision.[93] People often think of charismatic leaders or managers as being "larger than life." The essence of charisma, however, is having a vision and enthusiastically communicating it to others. Thus managers who appear to be quiet and earnest can also be charismatic.

Stimulating Subordinates Intellectually

intellectual stimulation Behavior a leader engages in to make followers aware of problems and view these problems in new ways, consistent with the leader's vision.

Transformational managers openly share information with their subordinates so they are aware of problems and the need for change. The manager causes subordinates to view problems in their groups and throughout the organization from a different perspective, consistent with the manager's vision. Whereas in the past subordinates might not have been aware of some problems, may have viewed problems as a "management issue" beyond their concern, or may have viewed problems as insurmountable, the transformational manager's **intellectual stimulation** leads subordinates to view problems as challenges that they can and will meet and conquer. The manager engages and empowers subordinates to take personal responsibility for helping to solve problems, as did Nokes at T-Mobile.[94]

Engaging in Developmental Consideration

developmental consideration Behavior a leader engages in to support and encourage followers and help them develop and grow on the job.

When managers engage in **developmental consideration**, they not only perform the consideration behaviors described earlier, such as demonstrating true concern for the well-being of subordinates, but go one step further. The manager goes out of his or her way to support and encourage subordinates, giving them opportunities to enhance their skills and capabilities and to grow and excel on the job.[95] As mentioned earlier, Nokes did this in numerous ways. In fact, after she first met with employees in a call center in Albuquerque, New Mexico, Karen Viola, the manager of the call center, said, "Everyone came out crying. The people said that they had never felt so inspired in their lives, and that they had never met with any leader at that level who [they felt] cared."[96]

All organizations, no matter how large or small, successful or unsuccessful, can benefit when their managers engage in transformational leadership. Moreover, while the benefits of transformational leadership are often most apparent when an organization is in trouble, transformational leadership can be an enduring approach to leadership, leading to long-term organizational effectiveness.

The Distinction between Transformational and Transactional Leadership

Transformational leadership is often contrasted with transactional leadership. In **transactional leadership**, managers use their reward and coercive powers to encourage high performance. When managers reward high performers, reprimand or otherwise punish low performers, and motivate subordinates by reinforcing desired behaviors and extinguishing or punishing undesired ones, they are engaging in transactional leadership.[97] Managers who effectively influence their subordinates to achieve goals, yet do not seem to be making the kind of dramatic changes that are part of transformational leadership, are engaging in transactional leadership.

Many transformational leaders engage in transactional leadership. They reward subordinates for a job well done and notice and respond to substandard performance. But they also have their eyes on the bigger picture of how much better things could be in their organizations, how much more their subordinates are capable of achieving, and how important it is to treat their subordinates with respect and help them reach their full potential.

Research has found that when leaders engage in transformational leadership, their subordinates tend to have higher levels of job satisfaction and performance.[98] Additionally, subordinates of transformational leaders may be more likely to trust their leaders and their organizations and feel that they are being fairly treated, and this, in turn, may positively influence their work motivation (see Chapter 13).[99]

transactional leadership
Leadership that motivates subordinates by rewarding them for high performance and reprimanding them for low performance.

Gender and Leadership

LO14-5
Characterize the relationship between gender and leadership and explain how emotional intelligence may contribute to leadership effectiveness.

The increasing number of women entering the ranks of management, as well as the problems some women face in their efforts to be hired as managers or promoted into management positions, has prompted researchers to explore the relationship between gender and leadership. Although there are relatively more women in management positions today than there were 10 years ago, there are still relatively few women in top management and, in some organizations, even in middle management.

When women do advance to top management positions, special attention often is focused on them and the fact that they are women. For example, women CEOs of large companies are still rare; those who make it to the top post, such as Indra Nooyi of PepsiCo[100] and Meg Whitman of Hewlett-Packard, are salient. As business writer Linda Tischler puts it, "In a workplace where women CEOs of major companies are so scarce . . . they can be identified, like rock stars, by first name only."[101] Although women have certainly made inroads into leadership positions in organizations, they continue to be underrepresented in top leadership posts. For example, as was indicated in Chapter 5, while around 51.5 percent of the employees in managerial and professional jobs in the United States are women, only about 14.6 percent of corporate officers in the *Fortune* 500 are women, and only 8.1 percent of the top earners are women.[102]

A widespread stereotype of women is that they are nurturing, supportive, and concerned with interpersonal relations. Men are stereotypically viewed as being directive and focused on task accomplishment. Such stereotypes suggest that women tend to be more relationship-oriented as managers and engage in more consideration behaviors, whereas men are more task-oriented and engage in more initiating-structure behaviors. Does the behavior of actual male and female managers bear out these stereotypes? Do women managers lead in different ways than men do? Are male or female managers more effective as leaders?

Research suggests that male and female managers who have leadership positions in organizations behave in similar ways.[103] Women do not engage in more consideration than men, and men do not engage in more initiating structure than women. Research does suggest, however, that leadership style may vary between women and men. Women tend to be somewhat more participative as leaders than are men, involving subordinates in decision making and seeking their input.[104] Male managers tend to be less participative than are female managers, making more decisions on their own and wanting to do things their own way. Moreover, research suggests that men tend to be harsher when they punish their subordinates than do women.[105]

There are at least two reasons why female managers may be more participative as leaders than are male managers.[106] First, subordinates may try to resist the influence of female managers more than they do the influence of male managers. Some subordinates may never have reported to a woman before; some may incorrectly see a management role as being more appropriate for a man than for a woman; and some may just resist being led by a woman. To overcome this resistance and encourage subordinates' trust and respect, women managers may adopt a participative approach.

A second reason why female managers may be more participative is that they sometimes have better interpersonal skills than male managers.[107] A participative approach to leadership requires high levels of interaction and involvement between a manager and his or her subordinates, sensitivity to subordinates' feelings, and the ability to make decisions that may be unpopular with subordinates but necessary for goal attainment. Good interpersonal skills may help female managers have the effective interactions with their subordinates that are crucial to a participative approach.[108] To the extent that male managers have more difficulty managing interpersonal relationships, they may shy away from the high levels of interaction with subordinates necessary for true participation.

The key finding from research on leader behaviors, however, is that male and female managers do *not* differ significantly in their propensities to perform different leader behaviors. Even though they may be more participative, female managers do not engage in more consideration or less initiating structure than male managers.

Perhaps a question even more important than whether male and female managers differ in the leadership behaviors they perform is whether they differ in effectiveness. Consistent with the findings for leader behaviors, research suggests that across different kinds of organizational settings, male and female managers tend to be *equally effective* as leaders.[109] Thus there is no logical basis for stereotypes favoring male managers and leaders or for the existence of the "glass ceiling" (an invisible barrier that seems to prevent women from advancing as far as they should in some organizations). Because women and men are equally effective as leaders, the increasing number of women in the workforce should result in a larger pool of highly qualified candidates for management positions in organizations, ultimately enhancing organizational effectiveness.[110]

Emotional Intelligence and Leadership

Do the moods and emotions leaders experience on the job influence their behavior and effectiveness as leaders? Research suggests this is likely to be the case. For example, one study found that when store managers experienced positive moods at work, salespeople in their stores provided high-quality customer service and were less likely to quit.[111] Another study found that groups whose leaders experienced positive moods had better coordination, whereas groups whose leaders experienced negative moods exerted more effort; members of groups with leaders in positive moods also tended to experience more positive moods themselves; and members of groups with leaders in negative moods tended to experience more negative moods.[112]

A leader's level of emotional intelligence (see Chapter 3) may play a particularly important role in leadership effectiveness.[113] For example, emotional intelligence may help leaders develop a vision for their organizations, motivate their subordinates to commit to this vision, and energize them to enthusiastically work to achieve this vision. Moreover, emotional intelligence may enable leaders to develop a significant identity for their organization and instill high levels of trust and cooperation throughout the organization while maintaining the flexibility needed to respond to changing conditions.[114]

Emotional intelligence also plays a crucial role in how leaders relate to and deal with their followers, particularly when it comes to encouraging followers to be creative.[115] Creativity in organizations is an emotion-laden process; it often entails challenging the status quo, being willing to take risks and accept and learn from failures, and doing much hard work to bring creative ideas to fruition in terms of new products, services, or procedures and processes when uncertainty is bound to be high.[116] Leaders who are high on emotional intelligence are more likely to understand all the emotions surrounding creative endeavors, to be able to awaken and support the creative pursuits of their followers, and to provide the kind of support that enables creativity to flourish in organizations.[117]

Leaders, like people everywhere, sometimes make mistakes. Emotional intelligence may also help leaders respond appropriately when they realize they have made a mistake. Recognizing, admitting, and learning from mistakes can be especially important for entrepreneurs who start their own businesses, as profiled in the accompanying "Focus on Diversity" feature.

Focus on Diversity

Admitting a Mistake Helps Small Business Leader

Things seemed to be going well for Maureen Borzacchiello, CEO of Creative Display Solutions, located in Garden City, New York.[118] She founded her small business in 2001 to provide displays, graphics, and exhibits for use in trade shows and at events for companies ranging from American Express, FedEx, and General Electric to Jet-Blue Airways, AIG, and The Weather Channel.[119] Her company was growing, and she had received an award from the nonprofit organization, Count Me In for Women's Economic Independence.[120]

However, in 2006 she realized she had overextended her business financially. A large investment in inventory coupled with a sizable lease commitment, the need for office space renovations, the purchase of new furniture, and the addition of three new employees brought her to the point where she lacked the cash to pay her employees their regular salaries. When she had made these decisions, she thought she and her husband (who also works in the company) would be able to generate the revenues to cover the expenditures. But her brother-in-law unexpectedly passed away, and their involvement in family matters meant they weren't able to get new accounts as quickly as she had thought they would.[121]

Still confident that if she could get through this tough period, she would be able to get her business back on track, Borzacchiello decided to be honest with her employees about the company's current financial problems, why they occurred, and how she would strive to prevent such problems in the future. She met with her employees and told them, "All I can tell you is that I apologize. . . . We were so focused on accelerating growth that I didn't see it coming."[122] She admitted she needed to better understand her company's financial situation and daily cash flow, reassured employees that the company would be back on square footing in two to three months, and promised she would pay much more attention to ongoing financial performance and cash flow in the future.[123]

Borzacchiello also told employees that she and her husband would take no money out of the business for their own salaries until the financial problems were resolved. By being honest and open with employees, Borzacchiello gained their commitment and support. All employees decided to work shorter hours, and two employees were willing to have their hourly pay rates cut.[124] True to her promise, within two months all employees were able to return to their regular work hours; and by the beginning of 2007, Creative Display Solutions had over $1 million in revenues (which was more than double its revenues at the time of the financial problems).[125] Today, Creative Display Solutions is a profitable multimillion-dollar business with hundreds of clients.[126] Clearly Borzacchiello effectively handled the temporary crisis her company faced by admitting and apologizing for her mistake and being open and honest with employees about her company's future prospects.[127]

Summary and Review

LO14-1 **THE NATURE OF LEADERSHIP** Leadership is the process by which a person exerts influence over other people and inspires, motivates, and directs their activities to help achieve group or organizational goals. Leaders can influence others because they possess power. The five types of power available to managers are legitimate power, reward power, coercive power, expert power, and referent power. Many managers are using empowerment as a tool to increase their effectiveness as leaders.

LO14-2 **TRAIT AND BEHAVIOR MODELS OF LEADERSHIP** The trait model of leadership describes personal characteristics or traits that contribute to effective leadership. However, some managers who possess these traits are not effective leaders, and some managers who do not possess all the traits are nevertheless effective leaders. The behavior model of leadership describes two kinds of behavior that most leaders engage in: consideration and initiating structure.

LO14-3 **CONTINGENCY MODELS OF LEADERSHIP** Contingency models take into account the complexity surrounding leadership and the role of the situation in determining whether a manager is an effective leader. Fiedler's contingency model explains why managers may be effective leaders in one situation and ineffective in another. According to Fiedler's model, relationship-oriented leaders are most effective in situations that are moderately favorable for leading, and task-oriented leaders are most effective in situations that are very favorable or very unfavorable for leading. House's path–goal theory describes how effective managers motivate their subordinates by determining what outcomes their subordinates want, rewarding subordinates with these outcomes when they achieve their goals and perform at a high level, and clarifying the paths to goal attainment. Managers can engage in four kinds of behaviors to motivate subordinates: directive, supportive, participative, and achievement-oriented behaviors. The leader substitutes model suggests that sometimes managers do not have to play a leadership role because their subordinates perform at a high level without the manager having to exert influence over them.

LO14-4 **TRANSFORMATIONAL LEADERSHIP** Transformational leadership occurs when managers have dramatic effects on their subordinates and on the organization as a whole, and inspire and energize subordinates to solve problems and improve performance. These effects include making subordinates aware of the importance of their own jobs and high performance; making subordinates aware of their own needs for personal growth, development, and accomplishment; and motivating subordinates to work for the good of the organization and not just their own personal gain. Managers can engage in transformational leadership by being charismatic leaders, by intellectually stimulating subordinates, and by engaging in developmental consideration. Transformational managers also often engage in transactional leadership by using their reward and coercive powers to encourage high performance.

LO14-5 **GENDER AND LEADERSHIP** Female and male managers do not differ in the leadership behaviors they perform, contrary to stereotypes suggesting that women are more relationship-oriented and men more task-oriented. Female managers sometimes are more participative than male managers, however. Research has found that women and men are equally effective as managers and leaders.

LO14-5 **EMOTIONAL INTELLIGENCE AND LEADERSHIP** The moods and emotions leaders experience on the job, and their ability to effectively manage these feelings, can influence their effectiveness as leaders. Moreover, emotional intelligence can contribute to leadership effectiveness in multiple ways, including encouraging and supporting creativity among followers.

Management in Action

Topics for Discussion and Action

Discussion

1. Describe the steps managers can take to increase their power and ability to be effective leaders. [LO14-1]

2. Think of specific situations in which it might be especially important for a manager to engage in consideration and in initiating structure. [LO14-2]

3. For your current job or for a future job you expect to hold, describe what your supervisor could do to strongly motivate you to be a top performer. [LO14-3]

4. Discuss why managers might want to change the behaviors they engage in, given their situation, their subordinates, and the nature of the work being done. Do you think managers can readily change their leadership behaviors? Why or why not? [LO14-3]

5. Discuss why substitutes for leadership can contribute to organizational effectiveness. [LO14-3]

6. Describe what transformational leadership is, and explain how managers can engage in it. [LO14-4]

7. Discuss why some people still think men make better managers than women even though research indicates that men and women are equally effective as managers and leaders. [LO14-5]

8. Imagine that you are working in an organization in an entry-level position after graduation and have come up with what you think is a great idea for improving a critical process in the organization that relates to your job. In what ways might your supervisor encourage you to implement your idea? How might your supervisor discourage you from even sharing your idea with others? [LO14-4, 14-5]

Action

9. Interview a manager to find out how the three situational characteristics that Fiedler identified affect his or her ability to provide leadership. [LO14-3]

10. Find a company that has dramatically turned around its fortunes and improved its performance. Determine whether a transformational manager was behind the turnaround and, if one was, what this manager did. [LO14-4]

Building Management Skills

Analyzing Failures of Leadership [LO14-1, 14-2, 14-3, 14-4]

Think about a situation you are familiar with in which a leader was very ineffective. Then answer the following questions:

1. What sources of power did this leader have? Did the leader have enough power to influence his or her followers?

2. What kinds of behaviors did this leader engage in? Were they appropriate for the situation? Why or why not?

3. From what you know, do you think this leader was a task-oriented leader or a relationship-oriented leader? How favorable was this leader's situation for leading?

4. What steps did this leader take to motivate his or her followers? Were these steps appropriate or inappropriate? Why?

5. What signs, if any, did this leader show of being a transformational leader?

Managing Ethically [LO14-1]

Managers who verbally criticize their subordinates, put them down in front of their coworkers, or use the threat of job loss to influence behavior are exercising coercive power. Some employees subject to coercive power believe that using it is unethical.

Questions

1. Either alone or in a group, think about the ethical implications of the use of coercive power.

2. To what extent do managers and organizations have an ethical obligation to put limits on the amount of coercive power that is exercised?

Small Group Breakout Exercise

Improving Leadership Effectiveness [LO14-1, 14-2, 14-3, 14-4]

Form groups of three to five people, and appoint one member as the spokesperson who will communicate your findings and conclusions to the class when called on by the instructor. Then discuss the following scenario:

You are a team of human resource consultants who have been hired by Carla Caruso, an entrepreneur who has started her own interior decorating business. A highly competent and creative interior decorator, Caruso has established a working relationship with most of the major home builders in her community. At first she worked on her own as an independent contractor. Then because of a dramatic increase in the number of new homes being built, she became swamped with requests for her services and decided to start her own company.

She hired a secretary–bookkeeper and four interior decorators, all of whom are highly competent. Caruso still does decorating jobs herself and has adopted a hands-off approach to leading the four decorators who report to her because she feels that interior design is a very personal, creative endeavor. Rather than pay the decorators on some kind of commission basis (such as a percentage of their customers' total billings), she pays them a premium salary, higher than average, so they are motivated to do what's best for a customer's needs and not what will result in higher billings and commissions.

Caruso thought everything was going smoothly until customer complaints started coming in. The complaints ranged from the decorators' being hard to reach, promising unrealistic delivery times, and being late for or failing to keep appointments to their being impatient and rude when customers had trouble making up their minds. Caruso knows her decorators are competent and is concerned that she is not effectively leading and managing them. She wonders, in particular, if her hands-off approach is to blame and if she should change the manner in which she rewards or pays her decorators. She has asked for your advice.

1. Analyze the sources of power that Caruso has available to her to influence the decorators. What advice can you give her to either increase her power base or use her existing power more effectively?

2. Given what you have learned in this chapter (for example, from the behavior model and path–goal theory), does Caruso seem to be performing appropriate leader behaviors in this situation? What advice can you give her about the kinds of behaviors she should perform?

3. What steps would you advise Caruso to take to increase the decorators' motivation to deliver high-quality customer service?

4. Would you advise Caruso to try to engage in transformational leadership in this situation? If not, why not? If so, what steps would you advise her to take?

Exploring the World Wide Web [LO14-1, 14-2, 14-3, 14-4, 14-5]

Go to the website of the Center for Creative Leadership (www.ccl.org). Spend some time browsing through the site to learn more about this organization, which specializes in leadership. Then click on "Customized Services" and then "Leadership Coaching" (both located under "Quick Links"). Read about the different coaching programs and options the center provides. How do you think leaders might benefit from coaching? What kinds of leaders/managers may find coaching especially beneficial? Do you think coaching services such as those provided by the Center for Creative Leadership can help leaders become more effective? Why or why not?

Be the Manager [LO14-1, 14-2, 14-3, 14-4, 14-5]

You are the CEO of a medium-size company that makes window coverings similar to Hunter Douglas blinds and duettes. Your company has a real cost advantage in terms of being able to make custom window coverings at costs that are relatively low in the industry. However, the performance of your company has been lackluster. To make needed changes and improve performance, you met with the eight other top managers in your company and charged them with identifying problems and missed opportunities in each of their areas and coming up with an action plan to address the problems and take advantage of opportunities.

Once you gave the managers the okay, they were charged with implementing their action plans in a timely fashion and monitoring the effects of their initiatives monthly for the next 8 to 12 months.

You approved each of the managers' action plans, and a year later most of the managers were reporting that their initiatives had been successful in addressing the problems and opportunities they had identified a year ago. However, overall company performance continues to be lackluster and shows no signs of improvement. You are confused and starting to question your leadership capabilities and approach to change. What are you going to do to improve the performance and effectiveness of your company?

Bloomberg Businessweek Case in the News [LO14-1, 14-2, 14-4]

"Don't Mess This Up." How Lego Finally Trusted Warner Bros. to Bring Its Minifigs to the Big Screen

Kissing was a point of contention. "We had some kissing in the movie," says Dan Lin, the producer of *The Lego Movie.* "It wasn't lusty. When two minifigs kiss, there's no tongue or anything. It's just plastic kissing plastic, which we just thought was hilarious."

The Lego brand managers were less amused. "They warned us that parents don't like it when minifigs kiss," says Lin. "We tested the movie several times. They were right. Parents didn't like it." In the end (spoiler alert), the kisses got cut. Instead there are several romantic moments in the movie, featuring close-ups of amorous minifigures attempting to lock together their fingerless, cup-shaped hands. The effect is equally absurd.

On February 7 *The Lego Movie,* a feature-length animated film and the first theatrical release based on the ubiquitous toy, will open around the country. It's voiced by an ensemble cast of comedic actors (Will Arnett, Elizabeth Banks, Chris Pratt), Hollywood dignitaries (Morgan Freeman, Liam Neeson), and American celebrities at large (Shaquille O'Neal).

Produced by Lin, co-financed by Village Roadshow (VRL:AU), and distributed by Warner Bros. (TWX), *The Lego Movie* took more than five years to make. It's directed by Chris Miller and Phil Lord, whose credits include the animated hit *Cloudy with a Chance of Meatballs.* The Hollywood Reporter estimates it cost $60 million to $65 million to make.

Since the 2007 release of *Transformers,* when Paramount Pictures (VIAB) created a multibillion-dollar entertainment franchise out of a moribund toy line, Hollywood has been awash in toy-inspired media. From the outset, the filmmakers' goal was to create a Lego-infused movie that would amount to something more interesting than a 100-minute advertisement.

"A lot of people might think, 'OK, this is all about them trying to sell the most toys,'" says Jill Wilfert, Lego vice president for global licensing and entertainment. "For us, this was always about building the Lego brand." Which, of course, is about selling toys, and an avalanche will accompany the film's release, including 17 Lego building sets, a line of collectible minifigures, a video game, a theme park exhibit, a soundtrack album, children's books, and tons of lunchboxes, sticker books, T-shirts, hoodies, pajamas, backpacks, and Lego-branded undergarments.

At a time when Hollywood filmmakers are increasingly reliant on money from overseas audiences for survival, a movie based on a toy with such broad, cross-cultural appeal would seem like a no-brainer. "I can't tell you how many people come up to me now and say, 'Oh, a Lego movie? No duh. It's so obvious,'" says Lin, whose job it was to persuade Lego to seize this opportunity. "It was absolutely not obvious five years ago."

These days the 80-year-old company is flying high. In 2012 Lego generated a $969 million profit on revenue of $4 billion and, buoyed by a 24 percent increase in sales, passed Hasbro (HAS) to become the second-largest toymaker in the world. It's a big turnaround from 2003–04, when an ill-fated period of product experimentation resulted in big losses. The key lesson the company took away from its dark years: Focus on toys, proceed cautiously when experimenting, and find good

partners. In previous forays outside the toy business, the privately held company tried to do it all by itself and frequently stumbled.

Earning Lego's confidence, says Lin, was the biggest challenge. "My big pitch to them was, 'This is a way for you to get into the storytelling universe,'" says Lin, 40, a former Warner Bros. executive whose eponymous production company has a first-look deal with the studio. "It's up to us to meet your motto that 'Only the best is good enough.' If we tell a great story, it can have a halo effect for your brand."

Lin's ambitions for *The Lego Movie* went beyond simply enhancing the company's reputation. "What I've told Warner Bros.," says Lin, "is that if this movie works, in the future you'll have live-action movies, you'll have animated movies, and you'll have Lego movies. It will be a new class of films that look photo real, that are very funny, and have a very specific tone. It's a look you've never seen before."

On the way to the première, there was plenty of friction between toymaker and filmmaker. "I'm not saying it was an easy five years," says Lin. "There was a lot of great creative push and pull. We made different versions of this movie three times. The biggest thing was, how edgy can the movie be?"

Wilfert, 48, speaks in measured sentences and emits a calm vibe, absent the manic elation that typifies Hollywood salesmen. She says that since joining Lego a quarter century ago she's traveled to the company's headquarters in Billund, Denmark, so many times she "practically feels like a Dane." From her home base in Carlsbad, California (home also to one of the company's licensed Legoland theme parks), she serves as liaison to the movie, TV, and video game industries. She buys entertainment licenses for Lego to turn into toy lines, and she sells Lego licenses for others to turn into entertainment. Wilfert's job is not only to make sure Hollywood storytellers are happily playing with Lego but also to ensure they're playing well and in an un-profane manner.

She oversees a small group that's integrated into Lego's overall marketing and product development process. She doesn't have any distinct revenue targets to hit. "The focus is first and foremost on the brand and delivering quality content that is communicating our values," Wilfert says. "One of the great messages of the movie is that everybody can be creative and that there's no wrong way to build with Lego. For us, that's a really important message."

The middle of three siblings, Wilfert grew up in Richardson, Texas, on the outskirts of Dallas. Her father worked in retail. She attended Liberty University in Lynchburg, Virginia, a school founded by Christian televangelist Jerry Falwell. After graduating in 1988 with a degree in business administration and a minor in marketing, she moved back in with her parents, who had relocated to suburban Connecticut. Her parents' new house wasn't far from Lego's U.S. headquarters in Enfield. Proximity motivated her to apply for an entry-level position at the company, which she got.

Wilfert began her Lego career in the customer service department responding to fan letters and talking down frustrated kids who got stuck while building a Lego kit. Eventually Wilfert transferred to the marketing department. Over the next 15 years she worked in a variety of brand management roles. In 2003 Wilfert moved to Southern California and became Lego's woman in Hollywood.

When people in the movie business come to Lego, they're usually hoping to sell lucrative licensing rights to their new movie or television series. Each year Lego retires products to make room on the shelves for new ones. In a typical year newly launched lines account for roughly 60 percent of consumer sales, according to Lego's 2012 annual report. Wilfert says she usually makes one or two big purchases a year. "We get pitched everything," says Wilfert. "We say 'no,' a hundred times more than we say 'yes.'"

Throughout most of Lego's history, its toys were a superstar-free zone. Then in 1999, Lego acquired the rights from Lucasfilm to manufacture toys based on the Star Wars universe. Star Wars Lego was an overnight sensation. Fifteen years later it remains a top seller. "That was the beginning of our relationship with Hollywood," says Wilfert.

The company has since made dozens of building sets inspired by TV shows and movies, including Harry Potter, Spider-Man, Jurassic Park, SpongeBob SquarePants, Indiana Jones, Toy Story, Pirates of the Caribbean, and The Simpsons. "Licenses bring us relevance, stories, and characters," says Wilfert. "We can do that on our own. But kids are fickle today, especially in our business. They want what's new."

Wilfert's other mission is to extend the Lego brand into other kinds of entertainment. Over the years, Lego's efforts have grown incrementally. They've created Web trailers for Star Wars movies rendered in Legos; a Lego Atlantis movie for the Cartoon Network; a handful of direct-to-DVD movies based on the Lego Bionicle toys, a science fantasy theme introduced in 2000; and a series of video games. The company's biggest hits have been Ninjago: Masters of Spinjitzu and Legends of Chima, a pair of highly rated animated series on the Cartoon Network.

Kerry Phelan, who worked with Wilfert at Lego for more than a decade and who has since gone on to licensing jobs with Lucasfilm, Pixar, and DreamWorks (DWA), says Wilfert deserves credit for pushing Lego into new media while also being fiercely protective. "She's an amazing brand guardian and steward for Lego," says Phelan. "She's dedicated her entire career to it. She understands that on the entertainment side, the story has to be great. If you get the art right, the commerce will follow."

On a Saturday morning in late January, Lin sits down for an interview inside a pirate-themed room with a Jolly Roger bedspread at the Legoland Hotel in Carlsbad. He says that unlike movie-based Legos, a Lego movie wasn't an easy sell.

Lego's core audience tends to be 5- to 12-year-olds. At around 13, most kids age out. That's a red flag for studios that rely on teenagers to help drive opening-weekend box office. There were also questions about how Lego would translate into a narrative. The company has thrived by creating distinct, colorful wonderlands occupied for the most part by nameless, indistinct characters. The minifigures are essentially blank slates onto which kids can project their own stories and characters. That's great for inspiring creative play, less effective for winning over studio executives.

Lin says negotiating the rights to the Lego brand required a marathon courtship. To win over its executives, Lin and his handpicked film directors attended several BrickCons—massive gatherings of AFOLs, or adult fans of Lego. They visited Legoland in California. They went to Lego stores. They took part in Lego competitions.

In his proposal to the company, Lin emphasized that Warner Bros. had created global franchises around Harry Potter, Batman, and Sherlock Holmes while managing to protect the integrity of the intellectual property. For a toy company like Lego, which enjoys near market saturation in some countries (such as the United States and Germany) and is seeking more growth in places such as China and India, a big-budget movie offers a unique opportunity to introduce its brand to consumers in developing markets. Eventually, Lin's persistence paid off, and Lego and Warner Bros. struck a deal in August 2009.

The movie tells the story of Emmet, an ordinary construction worker who battles with a maniacal business mogul hell-bent on stamping out creativity in the Lego universe by super-gluing every brick into a permanent place. Emmet joins forces with an underground class of Lego master builders and discovers the untapped powers of his imagination. A creative rebellion ensues.

The Lego Movie is chock-full of cameos. Various characters Wilfert licensed over the years, from companies including Disney (DIS), DC Comics, and Mirage Studios, merrily comingle. The final mix has appearances by Superman, the Green Lantern, Han Solo, Chewbacca, Wonder Woman, Robin Hood, the Teenage Mutant Ninja Turtles, and Abraham Lincoln. Batman plays a starring role. "We have some great relationships with the various studios in town," says Wilfert. "They know that's how kids actually play with Lego. Kids will take Dumbledore and Batman and put them together in the same scenario."

Throughout the moviemaking process, Wilfert's team was invited to weigh in on almost every aspect of the film. "My pitch to them was, 'There is the contract, and then there is reality,'" says Lin. "You guys may not have certain approvals per the contract. But I'm working with your baby, and I want to treat it right. I want to make you partners."

At one point, Lin and his directors flew to Billund to participate in a "boost session," where the filmmakers tossed out concepts from the screenplay—such as a steampunk pirate ship—and then Lego's designers competed to build the best possible version. "A lot of that made it into the film," says Wilfert.

"They were very influential on story, script, every major casting decision, every director decision," says Lin. "It's a hybrid movie made out of [computer graphics] and real bricks. They co-built the movie."

Occasionally disputes arose. Appealing to teenagers often requires things like outlandish dialogue, potty jokes, and gunplay. "That required us going outside the Lego boundaries at times," says Lin. "So there was a lot of negotiation."

The Lego overseers made concessions, too. "I was like, 'Could we take out some of these butt jokes?'" says Wilfert. "They felt really strongly that it was adding to the humor and gestalt of the movie. We did a lot of screening, and moms were fine with it, so we left them in there."

Questions for Discussion

1. How would you characterize Dan Lin's personal leadership style? What are his sources of power, and what traits do you think he is high on?

2. Do you think Dan Lin is a transformational leader? If so, in what ways has he been a transformational leader? If not, why not?

3. How would you characterize Jill Willfert's personal leadership style, what are her sources of power, and what traits do you think she is high on?

4. Do you think Jill Willfert is a transformational leader? If so, in what ways has she been a transformational leader? If not, why not?

CHAPTER 15

Effective Groups and Teams

Learning Objectives

After studying this chapter, you should be able to:

LO15-1 Explain why groups and teams are key contributors to organizational effectiveness.

LO15-2 Identify the different types of groups and teams that help managers and organizations achieve their goals.

LO15-3 Explain how different elements of group dynamics influence the functioning and effectiveness of groups and teams.

LO15-4 Explain why it is important for groups and teams to have a balance of conformity and deviance and a moderate level of cohesiveness.

LO15-5 Describe how managers can motivate group members to achieve organizational goals and reduce social loafing in groups and teams.

A MANAGER'S CHALLENGE

Teams Innovate at W.L. Gore

How can managers promote innovation and high performance? W. L. Gore & Associates was founded by Wilbert ("Bill") Gore and his wife Genevieve ("Vieve") in the basement of their house in 1958, and the rest has literally been history.[1] Widely recognized for its diverse and innovative products, in 2013 Gore had over $3 billion in annual sales and over 10,000 employees (who are called associates) worldwide. Headquartered in Newark, Delaware, Gore's most widely recognized product is the waterproof fabric Gore-Tex. Gore makes a wide array of products including fabrics for outerwear, medical products used in surgeries, fibers for astronauts' space suits, and Elexir strings for acoustic guitars. While Gore has thousands of products and over 2,000 worldwide patents, most of Gore's products are based on a very adaptable material, expanded polytetrafluoroethylene (ePTFE), a polymer invented by the Gores' son in 1969.[2] A key ingredient to Gore's enduring success is its use of teams to innovate and motivate rather than relying on a hierarchy of managers.[3]

The Gores were 45 years old and the parents of five children when they took the plunge.[4] Prior to starting his own company, Bill Gore worked at DuPont, which helped him realize how teams can be powerful sources of innovation and high performance. As a member of small R&D teams at DuPont, Gore experienced firsthand how inspiring and motivating it can be to work on a self-managed team with the objective to create and innovate and having high levels of autonomy to do so. He reasoned that innovation and high motivation and performance would likely result when as many people as possible in an organization were members of self-managed teams tasked to be innovative with high levels of autonomy.

Gore uses teams to develop new products rather than a hierarchy of managers. Its best-known product is the waterproof fabric Gore-Tex.

And that is what he set out to accomplish by founding W. L. Gore. Thus many teams at Gore have the goal of developing innovative new products.[5]

While Gore has a CEO (Terri Kelly) and four divisions (electronics, fabrics, industrial, and medical), there are few managers, and associates do not have supervisors. Gore is structured around a lattice of self-managed teams in which associates and their teams communicate directly with each other whenever the need or desire arises and are tasked with the mission to innovate, perform highly, and to enjoy their work.[6] Personal initiative and high motivation are greatly valued at Gore, and working in self-managed teams with high levels of autonomy fuels new product innovations.[7]

Associates working in manufacturing are also empowered to work in self-managed teams. For example, a team of manufacturing associates realized that new manufacturing equipment was needed to produce work in the United States that had been produced overseas, leading to inefficiencies. The team gathered information from other teams to develop the specifications for the machinery. Teams of associates negotiated to have an outside supplier build the $2 million machinery. And all went well when the equipment was installed and used.[8]

At Gore, associates recognize leaders who are especially proficient at building great teams and accomplishing goals and willingly become their followers.[9] New hires at Gore are assigned into broad areas—such as R&D, engineering, sales and marketing, information technology, operations management, and human resources—and assigned a sponsor.[10] Sponsors are experienced associates who help newcomers learn the

ropes, meet other associates, and acclimatize to Gore's unique culture and values centered around high trust and motivation. When Jim Grigsby, an electrical engineer, was hired by Gore around 15 years ago, his sponsor told him to spend some time meeting other associates and gave him a list of associates it would be good for him to talk with.[11] Having worked for more traditional and hierarchical companies, Grigsby was surprised by this advice. His thinking: "Am I really getting paid just to meet people?" After gaining an appreciation for Gore's collaborative lattice structure and extensive use of self-managed teams weeks later, Grigsby realized that he had received good advice. As he put it, "It becomes apparent that you need these people to get project work done."[12] Ultimately sponsors help newcomers find a team for which they are a good fit. Teams are truly self-managing, so it is up to the team to decide if they want to have newcomers join them, and the newcomers are responsible to the teams they join. Experienced associates are typically members of multiple self-managed teams.[13]

One of the largest 200 privately held companies in the United States, Gore is owned by the Gore family and associates.[14] Associates are awarded a percentage of their salary in shares of the company and also participate in a profit-sharing program. The shares become vested after a certain time period elapses, and associates who leave the company can sell their shares back for cash payouts.[15]

At Gore, associates are accountable to each other and the teams they are members of. Thus perhaps it is not surprising that associates are reviewed by their peers. Each year information is gathered from around 20 colleagues of each associate and given to a compensation committee in their work unit that determines relative contributions and compensation levels for members of the unit.[16]

Associates thrive in Gore's collaborative and team-based structure. Thus it is not surprising that Gore has received recognition for being a top employer. For example, Gore has been on *Fortune* magazine's list of the "100 Best Companies to Work For" for 17 years in a row; in 2014 Gore was 22nd on the list.[17] As another example, in 2013 Gore was ranked 5th on a listing of the 25 "World's Best Multinational Workplaces" by the Great Places to Work Institute.[18] Gore has also been recognized as a best workplace in the United Kingdom, France, Germany, Sweden, Italy, Korea, and China.[19] As Gore CEO Terri Kelly indicates, ". . . we take great pride in our continued recognition as a top workplace in the United States and around the world, and we also continue to focus on cultivating an environment where creativity and innovation thrive."[20]

Overview

W. L. Gore is not alone in using groups and teams to innovate and improve organizational effectiveness. Managers in companies large and small are using groups and teams to enhance performance, increase responsiveness to customers, spur innovation, and motivate employees. In this chapter we look in detail at how groups and teams can contribute to organizational effectiveness and the types of groups and teams used in organizations. We discuss how different elements of group dynamics influence the functioning and effectiveness of groups, and we describe how managers can motivate group members to achieve organizational goals and reduce social loafing in groups and teams. By the end of this chapter you will appreciate why the effective management of groups and teams is a key ingredient for organizational performance and effectiveness.

Groups, Teams, and Organizational Effectiveness

group Two or more people who interact with each other to accomplish certain goals or meet certain needs.

team A group whose members work intensely with one another to achieve a specific common goal or objective.

A **group** may be defined as two or more people who interact with each other to accomplish certain goals or meet certain needs.[21] A **team** is a group whose members work *intensely* with one another to achieve a specific common goal or objective. As these definitions imply, all teams are groups, but not all groups are teams. The two characteristics that distinguish teams from groups are the *intensity* with which team members work together and the presence of a *specific, overriding team goal or objective.*

Recall from "A Manager's Challenge" how teams at Gore have the goal of developing innovative new products. In contrast, the accountants who work in a small CPA firm are a group: They may interact with one another to achieve goals such as keeping up-to-date on the latest changes in accounting rules and regulations, maintaining a smoothly functioning office, satisfying clients, and attracting new clients. But they are not a team because they do not work intensely with one another. Each accountant concentrates on serving the needs of his or her own clients.

Because all teams are also groups, whenever we use the term *group* in this chapter, we are referring to both groups *and* teams. As you might imagine, because members of teams work intensely together, teams can sometimes be difficult to form, and it may take time for members to learn how to effectively work together. Groups and teams can help an organization gain a competitive advantage because they can (1) enhance its performance, (2) increase its responsiveness to customers, (3) increase innovation, and (4) increase employees' motivation and satisfaction (see Figure 15.1). In this section we look at each of these contributions in turn.

Figure 15.1

Groups' and Teams' Contributions to Organizational Effectiveness

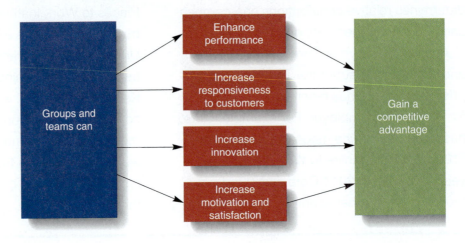

Groups and Teams as Performance Enhancers

synergy Performance gains that result when individuals and departments coordinate their actions.

One of the main advantages of using groups is the opportunity to obtain a type of **synergy**: People working in a group can produce more or higher-quality outputs than would have been produced if each person had worked separately and all their individual efforts were later combined. The essence of synergy is captured in the saying "The whole is more than the sum of its parts." Factors that can contribute to synergy in groups include the ability of group members to bounce ideas off one another, to correct one another's mistakes, to solve problems immediately as they arise, to bring a diverse knowledge base to bear on a problem or goal, and to accomplish work that is too vast or all-encompassing for any individual to achieve on his or her own.

To take advantage of the potential for synergy in groups, managers need to make sure that groups are composed of members who have complementary skills and knowledge relevant to the group's work. For example, at Hallmark Cards, synergies are created by bringing together all the different functions needed to create and produce a greeting card in a cross-functional team (a team composed of members from different departments or functions; see Chapter 10). For instance, artists, writers, designers, and marketing experts work together as team members to develop new cards.[22]

At Hallmark the skills and expertise of the artists complement the contributions of the writers and vice versa. Managers also need to give groups enough autonomy so that the groups, rather than the manager, are solving problems and determining how to achieve goals and objectives, as is true in the cross-functional teams at Hallmark and the teams at Gore in "A Manager's Challenge." To promote synergy, managers need to empower their subordinates and to be coaches, guides, and resources for groups while refraining from playing a more directive or supervisory role. The potential for synergy in groups may be why more and more managers are incorporating empowerment into their personal leadership styles (see Chapter 14).

When tasks are complex and involve highly sophisticated and rapidly changing technologies, achieving synergies in teams often hinges on having the appropriate mix of backgrounds and areas of expertise represented on the team. In large organizations with operations in many states and countries, managers can rely on databases and software applications to determine which employees might have the expertise needed on a particular team or for a certain project.

Groups, Teams, and Responsiveness to Customers

Being responsive to customers is not always easy. In manufacturing organizations, for example, customers' needs and desires for new and improved products have to be balanced against engineering constraints, production costs and feasibilities, government safety regulations, and marketing challenges. In service organizations such as health maintenance organizations (HMOs), being responsive to patients' needs and desires for prompt, high-quality medical care and treatment has to be balanced against meeting physicians' needs and desires and keeping health care costs under control. Being responsive to customers often requires the wide variety of skills and expertise found in different departments and at different levels in an organization's hierarchy. Sometimes, for example, employees at lower levels in an organization's hierarchy, such as sales representatives for a computer company, are closest to its customers and the most attuned to their needs. However, lower-level employees like salespeople often lack the technical expertise needed for new product ideas; such expertise is found in the research and development department. Bringing salespeople, research and development experts, and members of other departments together in a group or cross-functional team can enhance responsiveness to customers. Consequently, when managers form a team, they must make sure the diversity of expertise and knowledge needed to be responsive to customers exists within the team; this is why cross-functional teams are so popular.

In a cross-functional team, the expertise and knowledge in different organizational departments are brought together in the skills and knowledge of the team members. Managers of high-performing organizations are careful to determine which types of expertise and knowledge are required for teams to be responsive to customers, and they use this information in forming teams.

Teams and Innovation

Innovation—the creative development of new products, new technologies, new services, or even new organizational structures—is a topic we introduced in Chapter 1. Often an individual working alone does not possess the extensive and diverse skills, knowledge, and expertise required for successful innovation. Managers can better encourage innovation by creating teams of diverse individuals who together have the knowledge relevant to a particular type of innovation, as has been the case at Gore, rather than by relying on individuals working alone.

Using teams to innovate has other advantages. First, team members can often uncover one another's errors or false assumptions; an individual acting alone would not be able to do this. Second, team members can critique one another's approaches and build off one another's strengths while compensating for weaknesses—an advantage of devil's advocacy and dialectical inquiry, discussed in Chapter 7.

To further promote innovation, managers can empower teams and make their members fully responsible and accountable for the innovation process. The manager's role is to provide guidance, assistance, coaching, and the resources that team members need and *not* to closely direct or supervise their activities. To speed innovation, managers also need to form teams in which each member brings some unique resource to the team, such as engineering prowess, knowledge of production, marketing expertise, or financial savvy. Successful innovation sometimes requires that managers form teams with members from different countries and cultures.

Amazon uses teams to spur innovation, and many of the unique features on its website that enable it to be responsive to customers and meet their needs have been developed by teams, as indicated in the accompanying "Information Technology Byte" feature.

Information Technology Byte

Pizza Teams Innovate at Amazon

Jeff Bezos, founder, CEO, and chairman of the board of Amazon, is a firm believer in the power of teams to spur innovation.[23] At Amazon, teams have considerable autonomy to develop their ideas and experiment without interference from managers or other groups. And teams are kept deliberately small. According to Bezos, no team should need more than two pizzas to feed its members.[24] If more than two pizzas are needed to nourish a team, the team is too large. Thus teams at Amazon typically have no more than about five to seven members.[25]

Pepperoni or plain cheese? At Amazon, pizza teams are small enough to need just one of each.

"Pizza teams" have come up with unique and popular innovations that individuals working alone might never have thought of. A team developed the "Gold Box" deals that customers can click on to receive special offers that expire within a certain time period. Another team developed "Search Inside the Book," which allows customers to search and read content from millions of pages of books.[26] And a team developed the Amazon Kindle, a wireless reader that weighs less than 8 ounces, can hold over thousands of titles, can receive automatic delivery of major newspapers and blogs, and has a high-resolution screen that looks like and can be read like paper.[27]

While Bezos gives teams autonomy to develop and run with their ideas, he also believes in careful analysis and testing of ideas. A great advocate of the power of facts, data, and analysis, Bezos feels that whenever an idea can be tested through analysis, analysis should rule the day. When an undertaking is just too large or too uncertain or when data are lacking, Bezos and other experienced top managers make the final call.[28] But to make such judgment calls about implementing new ideas (either by data analysis or expert judgment), truly creative ideas are needed. To date, teams have played a very important role in generating ideas that have helped Amazon to be responsive to its customers, to have a widely known Internet brand name, and to be the highly successful and innovative company it is today.[29]

Groups and Teams as Motivators

Managers often form groups and teams to accomplish organizational goals and then find that using groups and teams brings additional benefits. Members of groups, and especially members of teams (because of the higher intensity of interaction in teams), are likely to be more satisfied than they would have been if they were working on their own. The experience of working alongside other highly charged and motivated people can be stimulating and motivating: Team members can see how their efforts and expertise directly contribute to the achievement of team and organizational goals, and they feel personally responsible for the outcomes or results of their work. This has been the case at Hallmark Cards.

The increased motivation and satisfaction that can accompany the use of teams can also lead to other outcomes, such as lower turnover. This has been Frank B. Day's experience as founder and chairman of the board of Rock Bottom Restaurants Inc.[30] To provide high-quality customer service, Day has organized the restaurants' employees into waitstaff teams, whose members work together to refill beers, take orders, bring hot chicken enchiladas to the tables, or clear off the tables. Team members share the burden of undesirable activities and unpopular shift times, and customers no longer have to wait until a particular waitress or waiter is available. Motivation and satisfaction levels in Rock Bottom restaurants seem to be higher than in other restaurants, and turnover is about half that experienced in other U.S. restaurant chains.[31]

Working in a group or team can also satisfy organizational members' needs for engaging in social interaction and feeling connected to other people. For workers who perform highly stressful jobs, such as hospital emergency and operating room staff, group membership can be an important source of social support and motivation. Family members or friends may not be able to fully understand or appreciate some sources of work stress that these group members experience firsthand. Moreover, group members may cope better with work stressors when they can share them with other members of their group. In addition, groups often devise techniques to relieve stress, such as the telling of jokes among hospital operating room staff.

Why do managers in all kinds of organizations rely so heavily on groups and teams? Effectively managed groups and teams can help managers in their quest for high performance, responsiveness to customers, and employee motivation. Before explaining how managers can effectively manage groups, however, we will describe the types of groups that are formed in organizations.

LO15-2

Identify the different types of groups and teams that help managers and organizations achieve their goals.

Types of Groups and Teams

To achieve their goals of high performance, responsiveness to customers, innovation, and employee motivation, managers can form various types of groups and teams (see Figure 15.2). **Formal groups** are those that managers establish to achieve organizational goals. The formal work groups are *cross-functional* teams composed of members from different departments, such as those at Hallmark Cards, and *cross-cultural* teams composed of members from different cultures or countries, such as the teams at global carmakers. As you will see, some of the groups discussed in this section also can be considered to be cross-functional (if they are composed of members from different departments) or cross-cultural (if they are composed of members from different countries or cultures).

Sometimes organizational members, managers or nonmanagers, form groups because they feel that groups will help them achieve their own goals or meet their own needs (for example, the need for social interaction). Groups formed in this way are **informal groups**. Four nurses who work in a hospital and have lunch together twice a week constitute an informal group.

formal group A group that managers establish to achieve organizational goals.

informal group A group that managers or nonmanagerial employees form to help achieve their own goals or meet their own needs.

top management team A group composed of the CEO, the president, and the heads of the most important departments.

The Top Management Team

A central concern of the CEO and president of a company is to form a **top management team** to help the organization achieve its mission and goals. Top management teams are responsible for developing the strategies that result in an organization's competitive advantage; most have between five and seven members. In forming their top management teams, CEOs are well advised to stress diversity in expertise, skills, knowledge, and experience. Thus many top management teams are also cross-functional teams: They are composed of members from different departments, such as finance, marketing, production, and engineering. Diversity helps ensure that the top management team will have all the background and resources it needs to make good decisions. Diversity also helps guard against *groupthink*—faulty group decision making that results when group members strive for agreement at the expense of an accurate assessment of the situation (see Chapter 7).

Research and Development Teams

research and development team A team whose members have the expertise and experience needed to develop new products.

Managers in pharmaceuticals, computers, electronics, electronic imaging, and other high-tech industries often create **research and development teams** to develop new products. Managers select R&D team members on the basis of their expertise and experience in a certain area. Sometimes R&D teams are cross-functional teams with members from departments such as engineering, marketing, and production in addition to members from the research and development department.

Figure 15.2

Types of Groups and Teams in Organizations

Command Groups

command group A group composed of subordinates who report to the same supervisor; also called *department* or *unit*.

Subordinates who report to the same supervisor compose a **command group**. When top managers design an organization's structure and establish reporting relationships and a chain of command, they are essentially creating command groups. Command groups, often called *departments* or *units,* perform a significant amount of the work in many organizations. In order to have command groups that help an organization gain a competitive advantage, managers not only need to motivate group members to perform at a high level but also need to be effective leaders. Examples of command groups include the salespeople in a large department store in New York who report to the same supervisor, the employees of a small swimming pool sales and maintenance company in Florida who report to a general manager, the telephone operators at the MetLife insurance company who report to the same supervisor, and workers on an automobile assembly line in the Ford Motor Company who report to the same first-line manager.

Task Forces

task force A committee of managers or nonmanagerial employees from various departments or divisions who meet to solve a specific, mutual problem; also called an *ad hoc committee.*

Managers form **task forces** to accomplish specific goals or solve problems in a certain time period; task forces are sometimes called *ad hoc committees.* For example, Michael Rider, owner and top manager of a chain of six gyms and fitness centers in the Midwest, created a task force composed of the general managers of the six gyms to determine whether the fitness centers should institute a separate fee schedule for customers who wanted to use the centers only for aerobics classes (and not use other facilities such as weights, steps, tracks, and swimming pools). The task force was given three months to prepare a report summarizing the pros and cons of the proposed change in fee schedules. After the task force completed its report and reached the conclusion that the change in fee structure probably would reduce revenues rather than increase them and thus should not be implemented, it was disbanded. As in Rider's case, task forces can be a valuable tool for busy managers who do not have the time to personally explore an important issue in depth.

Sometimes managers need to form task forces whose work, so to speak, is never done. The task force may be addressing a long-term or enduring problem or issue facing an organization, such as how to most usefully contribute to the local community or how to make sure the organization provides opportunities for potential employees with disabilities. Task forces that are relatively permanent are often referred to as *standing committees.* Membership in standing committees changes over time. Members may have, for example, a two- or three-year term on the committee, and memberships expire at varying times so there are always some members with experience on the committee. Managers often form and maintain standing committees to make sure important issues continue to be addressed.

Self-Managed Work Teams

self-managed work team A group of employees who supervise their own activities and monitor the quality of the goods and services they provide.

Self-managed work teams are teams in which members are empowered and have the responsibility and autonomy to complete identifiable pieces of work, as is true at W. L. Gore in "A Manager's Challenge." On a day-to-day basis, team members decide what the team will do, how it will do it, and which members will perform which specific tasks.[32] Managers can assign self-managed work teams' overall goals (such as assembling defect-free computer keyboards) but let team members decide how to meet those goals. Managers usually form self-managed work teams to improve quality, increase motivation and satisfaction, and lower costs. Often, by creating self-managed work teams, they combine tasks that individuals working separately used to perform, so the team is responsible for the whole set of tasks that yields an identifiable output or end product.

Managers can take a number of steps to ensure that self-managed work teams are effective and help an organization achieve its goals:[33]

- Give teams enough responsibility and autonomy to be truly self-managing. Refrain from telling team members what to do or solving problems for them even if you (as a manager) know what should be done.

- Make sure a team's work is sufficiently complex so that it entails a number of different steps or procedures that must be performed and results in some kind of finished end product.

- Carefully select members of self-managed work teams. Team members should have the diversity of skills needed to complete the team's work, have the ability to work with others, and want to be part of a team.

- As a manager, realize that your role with self-managed work teams calls for guidance, coaching, and supporting, not supervising. You are a resource for teams to turn to when needed.

- Analyze what type of training team members need and provide it. Working in a self-managed work team often requires that employees have more extensive technical and interpersonal skills.

Managers in a wide variety of organizations have found that self-managed work teams help the organization achieve its goals,[34] as profiled in the accompanying "Management Insight" feature.

Management Insight

Self-Managed Teams at Louis Vuitton and Nucor Corporation

Managers at Louis Vuitton, the most valuable luxury brand in the world, and managers at Nucor Corporation, the largest producer of steel and biggest recycler in the United States, have succeeded in effectively using self-managed teams to produce luxury accessories and steel, respectively. Self-managed teams at both companies not only are effective but truly excel and have helped make the companies leaders in their respective industries.[35]

Teams with between 20 and 30 members make Vuitton handbags and accessories. The teams work on only one product at a time; a team with 24 members might produce about 120 handbags per day. Team members are empowered to take ownership of the goods they produce, are encouraged to suggest improvements, and are kept up-to-date on key facts such as products' selling prices and popularity. As Thierry Nogues, a team leader at a Vuitton factory in Ducey, France, put it, "Our goal is to make everyone as multiskilled and autonomous as possible."[36]

Production workers at Nucor are organized into teams ranging in size from 8 to 40 members based on the kind of work the team is responsible for, such as rolling steel or operating a furnace. Team members have considerable autonomy to make decisions and creatively respond to problems and opportunities, and there are relatively few layers in the corporate hierarchy, supporting the empowerment of teams.[37] Teams develop their own informal rules for behavior and make their own decisions. As long as team members follow organizational rules and policies (such as those for safety) and meet quality standards, they are free to govern themselves. Managers act as coaches or advisers rather than supervisors, helping teams when needed.[38]

A team member assembles classic Louis Vuitton bags at the company's fine leather goods factory in the Normandy town of Ducey in France.

To ensure that production teams are motivated to help Nucor achieve its goals, team members are eligible for weekly bonuses based on the team's performance. Essentially, these production workers receive base pay that does not vary and are eligible to receive weekly bonus pay that can average from 80 percent to 150 percent of their regular pay.[39] The bonus rate is predetermined by the work a team performs and the capabilities of the machinery they use. Given the immediacy of the bonus and its potential magnitude, team members are motivated to perform at a high level, develop informal rules that support high performance, and strive to help Nucor reach its goals. Moreover, because all members of a team receive the same amount of weekly bonus money, they are motivated to do their best for the team, cooperate, and help one another out.[40] Of course, in tough economic times such as the recession in the late 2000s, Nucor's production workers' bonuses fall as demand for Nucor's products drops. Nonetheless, Nucor was able to avoid laying off employees, unlike a lot of other large corporations.[41]

Crafting a luxury handbag and making steel joists couldn't be more different from each other in certain ways. Yet the highly effective self-managed teams at Louis Vuitton and Nucor share some fundamental qualities. These teams really do take ownership of their work and are highly motivated to perform effectively. Team members have the skills and knowledge they need to be effective, they are empowered to make decisions about their work, and they know their teams are making vital contributions to their organizations.[42]

Sometimes employees have individual jobs but also are part of a self-managed team that is formed to accomplish a specific goal or work on an important project. Employees need to perform their own individual job tasks and also actively contribute to the self-managed team so that the team achieves its goal.

Sometimes self-managed work teams can run into trouble. Members may be reluctant to discipline one another by withholding bonuses from members who are not performing up to par or by firing members.[43] Buster Jarrell, a manager who oversaw self-managed work teams in AES Corporation's Houston plant, found that although the self-managed work teams were highly effective, they had a difficult time firing team members who were performing poorly.[44]

The Dallas office of the New York Life Insurance Company experimented with having members of self-managed teams evaluate one another's performance and determine pay levels. Team members did not feel comfortable assuming this role, however, and managers ended up handling these tasks.[45] One reason for team members' discomfort may be the close personal relationships they sometimes develop with one another. In addition, members of self-managed work teams may sometimes take longer to accomplish tasks, such as when team members have difficulties coordinating their efforts.

Virtual Teams

virtual team A team whose members rarely or never meet face-to-face but, rather, interact by using various forms of information technology such as e-mail, computer networks, telephone, fax, and videoconferences.

Virtual teams are teams whose members rarely or never meet face-to-face but, rather, interact by using various forms of information technology such as email, text messaging, computer networks, telephone, fax, and videoconferences. As organizations become increasingly global, and as the need for specialized knowledge increases due to advances in technology, managers can create virtual teams to solve problems or explore opportunities without being limited by team members needing to work in the same geographic location.[46]

Take the case of an organization that has manufacturing facilities in Australia, Canada, the United States, and Mexico and is encountering a quality problem in a complex manufacturing process. Each of its facilities has a quality control team headed by a quality control manager. The vice president for production does not try to solve the problem by forming and leading a team at one of the four manufacturing facilities; instead she forms and leads a virtual team composed of the quality control managers of the four plants and the plants' general managers. When these team members communicate via email, the company's networking site, and videoconferencing, a wide array of knowledge and experience is brought to solve the problem.

The principal advantage of virtual teams is that they enable managers to disregard geographic distances and form teams whose members have the knowledge, expertise, and experience to tackle a particular problem or take advantage of a specific opportunity.[47] Virtual teams also can include members who are not actually employees of the organization itself; a virtual team might include members of a company that is used for outsourcing. More and more companies, including BP PLC, Nokia Corporation, and Ogilvy & Mather, are using virtual teams.[48]

Members of virtual teams rely on two forms of information technology: synchronous technologies and asynchronous technologies.[49] *Synchronous technologies* let virtual team members communicate and interact with one another in real time simultaneously and include videoconferencing, teleconferencing, and electronic meetings. *Asynchronous technologies* delay communication and include email, electronic bulletin boards, and Internet websites. Many virtual teams use both kinds of technology depending on what projects they are working on.

Increasing globalization is likely to result in more organizations relying on virtual teams to a greater extent.[50] One challenge members of virtual teams face is building a sense of camaraderie and trust among team members who rarely, if ever, meet face-to-face. To address this challenge, some organizations schedule recreational activities, such as ski trips, so virtual team members can get together. Other organizations make sure virtual team members have a chance to meet in person soon after the team is formed and then schedule periodic face-to-face meetings to promote trust, understanding, and cooperation in the teams.[51] The need for such meetings is underscored by research suggesting that while some virtual teams can be as effective as teams that meet face-to-face, virtual team members might be less satisfied with teamwork efforts and have fewer feelings of camaraderie or cohesion. (Group cohesiveness is discussed in more detail later in the chapter.)[52]

Research also suggests that it is important for managers to keep track of virtual teams and intervene when necessary by, for example, encouraging members of teams who do not communicate often enough to monitor their team's progress and making sure team members actually have the time, and are recognized for, their virtual teamwork.[53] Additionally, when virtual teams are experiencing downtime or rough spots, managers might try to schedule face-to-face team time to bring team members together and help them focus on their goals.[54]

Researchers at the London Business School, including Professor Lynda Gratton, studied global virtual teams to try to identify factors that might help such teams be effective.[55] Based on their research, Gratton suggests that when forming virtual teams, it is helpful to include a few members who already know each other, other members who are well connected to people outside the team, and when possible, members who have volunteered to be a part of the team.[56] It is also advantageous for companies to have some kind of online site where team members can learn more about each other and the kinds of work they are engaged in, and in particular, a shared online workspace that team members can access around the clock.[57] Frequent communication is beneficial. Additionally, virtual team projects should be perceived as meaningful, interesting, and important by their members to promote and sustain their motivation.[58]

Friendship Groups

friendship group An informal group composed of employees who enjoy one another's company and socialize with one another.

The groups described so far are formal groups created by managers. **Friendship groups** are informal groups composed of employees who enjoy one another's company and socialize with one another. Members of friendship groups may have lunch together, take breaks together, or meet after work for meals, sports, or other activities. Friendship groups help satisfy employees' needs for interpersonal interaction, can provide needed social support in times of stress, and can contribute to people's feeling good at work and being satisfied with their jobs. Managers themselves often form friendship groups. The informal relationships that managers build in friendship groups can often help them solve work-related problems because members of these groups typically discuss work-related matters and offer advice.

Interest Groups

interest group An informal group composed of employees seeking to achieve a common goal related to their membership in an organization.

Employees form informal **interest groups** when they seek to achieve a common goal related to their membership in an organization. Employees may form interest groups, for example, to encourage managers to consider instituting flexible working hours, providing on-site child care, improving working conditions, or more proactively supporting environmental protection. Interest groups can give managers valuable insights into the issues and concerns that are foremost in employees' minds. They also can signal the need for change.

Group Dynamics

How groups function and, ultimately, their effectiveness hinge on group characteristics and processes known collectively as *group dynamics.* In this section we discuss five key elements of group dynamics: group size, tasks, and roles; group leadership; group development; group norms; and group cohesiveness.

LO15-3

Explain how different elements of group dynamics influence the functioning and effectiveness of groups and teams.

Group Size, Tasks, and Roles

Managers need to take group size, group tasks, and group roles into account as they create and maintain high-performing groups and teams.

GROUP SIZE The number of members in a group can be an important determinant of members' motivation and commitment and group performance. There are several advantages to keeping a group relatively small—between two and nine members. Compared with members of large groups, members of small groups tend to (1) interact more with each other and find it easier to coordinate their efforts, (2) be more motivated, satisfied, and committed, (3) find it easier to share information, and (4) be better able to see the importance of their personal contributions for group success. A disadvantage of small rather than large groups is that members of small groups have fewer resources available to accomplish their goals.

Large groups—with 10 or more members—also offer some advantages. They have more resources at their disposal to achieve group goals than small groups do. These resources include the knowledge, experience, skills, and abilities of group members as well as their actual time and effort. Large groups also let managers obtain the advantages stemming from the **division of labor**—splitting the work to be performed into particular tasks and assigning tasks to individual workers. Workers who specialize in particular tasks are likely to become skilled at performing those tasks and contribute significantly to high group performance.

division of labor Splitting the work to be performed into particular tasks and assigning tasks to individual workers.

The disadvantages of large groups include the problems of communication and coordination and the lower levels of motivation, satisfaction, and commitment that members of large groups sometimes experience. It is clearly more difficult to share information with, and coordinate the activities of, 16 people rather than 8 people. Moreover, members of large groups might not think their efforts are really needed and sometimes might not even feel a part of the group.

In deciding on the appropriate size for any group, managers attempt to gain the advantages of small group size and, at the same time, form groups with sufficient resources to accomplish their goals and have a well-developed division of labor. As a general rule of thumb, groups should have no more members than necessary to achieve a division of labor and provide the resources needed to achieve group goals. In R&D teams, for example, group size is too large when (1) members spend more time communicating what they know to others than applying what they know to solve problems and create new products, (2) individual productivity decreases, and (3) group performance suffers.[59]

GROUP TASKS The appropriate size of a high-performing group is affected by the kind of tasks the group is to perform. An important characteristic of group tasks that affects performance is **task interdependence**—the degree to which the work performed by one member of a group influences the work performed by other members.[60] As task interdependence increases, group members need to interact more frequently and intensely with one another, and their efforts have to be more closely coordinated if they are to perform at a high level. Management expert James D. Thompson identified three types of task interdependence: pooled, sequential, and reciprocal (see Figure 15.3).[61]

task interdependence The degree to which the work performed by one member of a group influences the work performed by other members.

pooled task interdependence The task interdependence that exists when group members make separate and independent contributions to group performance.

POOLED TASK INTERDEPENDENCE **Pooled task interdependence** exists when group members make separate and independent contributions to group performance; overall group performance is the sum of the performance of the individual members

Figure 15.3

Types of Task Interdependence

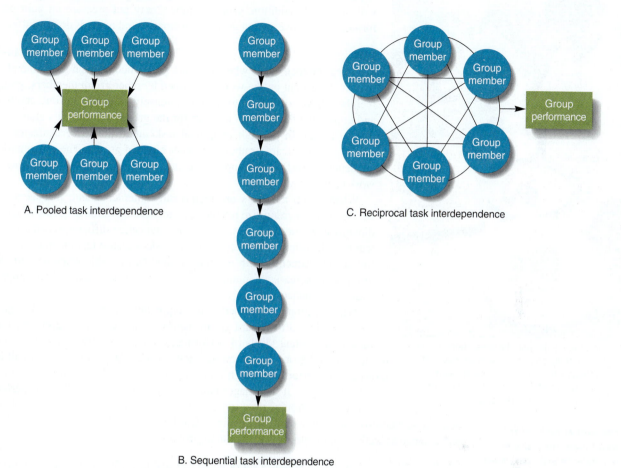

A. Pooled task interdependence

B. Sequential task interdependence

C. Reciprocal task interdependence

(see Figure 15.3a). Examples of groups that have pooled task interdependence include a group of teachers in an elementary school, a group of salespeople in a department store, a group of secretaries in an office, and a group of custodians in an office building. In these examples, group performance, whether it is the number of children who are taught and the quality of their education, the dollar value of sales, the amount of secretarial work completed, or the number of offices cleaned, is determined by summing the individual contributions of group members.

For groups with pooled interdependence, managers should determine the appropriate group size primarily from the amount of work to be accomplished. Large groups can be effective because group members work independently and do not have to interact frequently with one another. Motivation in groups with pooled interdependence will be highest when managers reward group members based on individual performance.

sequential task interdependence The task interdependence that exists when group members must perform specific tasks in a predetermined order.

SEQUENTIAL TASK INTERDEPENDENCE Sequential task interdependence exists when group members must perform specific tasks in a predetermined order; certain tasks have to be performed before others, and what one worker does affects the work of others (see Figure 15.3b). Assembly lines and mass-production processes are characterized by sequential task interdependence.

When group members are sequentially interdependent, group size is usually dictated by the needs of the production process—for example, the number of steps needed in an assembly line to efficiently produce a DVD player. With sequential interdependence, it is difficult to identify individual performance because one group member's performance depends on how well others perform their tasks. A slow worker at the start of an assembly line, for example, causes all workers further down to work slowly. Thus managers are often advised to reward

First the steak, then the green beans, then the carefully drizzled béarnaise; gourmet kitchens where the presentation is an integral part of the experience exemplify sequential task interdependence.

reciprocal task interdependence The task interdependence that exists when the work performed by each group member is fully dependent on the work performed by other group members.

group role A set of behaviors and tasks that a member of a group is expected to perform because of his or her position in the group.

role making Taking the initiative to modify an assigned role by assuming additional responsibilities.

group members for group performance. Group members will be motivated to perform at a high level because if the group performs well, each member will benefit. In addition, group members may put pressure on poor performers to improve so that group performance and rewards do not suffer.

RECIPROCAL TASK INTERDEPENDENCE Reciprocal task interdependence exists when the work performed by each group member is fully dependent on the work performed by other group members; group members have to share information, intensely interact with one another, and coordinate their efforts in order for the group to achieve its goals (see Figure 15.3c). In general, reciprocal task interdependence characterizes the operation of teams, rather than other kinds of groups. The task interdependence of R&D teams, top management teams, and many self-managed work teams is reciprocal.

When group members are reciprocally interdependent, managers are advised to keep group size relatively small because of the necessity of coordinating team members' activities. Communication difficulties can arise in teams with reciprocally interdependent tasks because team members need to interact frequently with one another and be available when needed. As group size increases, communication difficulties increase and can impair team performance.

When a group's members are reciprocally interdependent, managers also are advised to reward group members on the basis of group performance. Individual levels of performance are often difficult for managers to identify, and group-based rewards help ensure that group members will be motivated to perform at a high level and make valuable contributions to the group. Of course, if a manager can identify instances of individual performance in such groups, they too can be rewarded to maintain high levels of motivation. Microsoft and many other companies reward group members for their individual performance as well as for the performance of their group.

GROUP ROLES A group role is a set of behaviors and tasks that a member of a group is expected to perform because of his or her position in the group. Members of cross-functional teams, for example, are expected to perform roles relevant to their special areas of expertise. In our earlier example of cross-functional teams at Hallmark Cards, it is the role of writers on the teams to create verses for new cards, the role of artists to draw illustrations, and the role of designers to put verse and artwork together in an attractive and appealing card design. The roles of members of top management teams are shaped primarily by their areas of expertise—production, marketing, finance, research and development—but members of top management teams also typically draw on their broad expertise as planners and strategists.

In forming groups and teams, managers need to clearly communicate to group members the expectations for their roles in the group, what is required of them, and how the different roles in the group fit together to accomplish group goals. Managers also need to realize that group roles often change and evolve as a group's tasks and goals change and as group members gain experience and knowledge. Thus, to get the performance gains that come from experience or "learning by doing," managers should encourage group members to take the initiative to assume additional responsibilities as they see fit and modify their assigned roles. This process, called role making, can enhance individual and group performance.

In self-managed work teams and some other groups, group members themselves are responsible for creating and assigning roles. Many self-managed work teams also pick their own team leaders. When group members create their own roles, managers should be available to group members in an advisory capacity, helping them effectively settle conflicts and disagreements. At Johnsonville Foods, for example, the position titles of first-line managers were changed to "advisory coach" to reflect the managers' role with the self-managed work teams they oversaw.[62]

Group Leadership

All groups and teams need leadership. Indeed, as we discussed in detail in Chapter 14, effective leadership is a key ingredient for high-performing groups, teams, and organizations. Sometimes managers assume the leadership role in groups and teams, as is the case in many command groups and top management teams. Or a manager may appoint a member of a group who is not a manager to be group leader or chairperson, as is the case in a task force or standing committee. In other cases, group or team members may choose their own leaders, or a leader may emerge naturally as group members work together to achieve group goals. When managers empower members of self-managed work teams, they often let group members choose their own leaders. Some self-managed work teams find it effective to rotate the leadership role among their members. Whether or not leaders of groups and teams are managers, and whether they are appointed by managers (often referred to as *formal leaders*) or emerge naturally in a group (often referred to as *informal leaders*), they play an important role in ensuring that groups and teams perform up to their potential.

When teams do not live up to their promise, sometimes the problem is a lack of team leadership, as illustrated in the accompanying "Ethics in Action" feature.

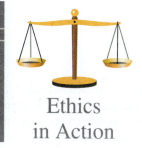

Ethics in Action

Leadership in Teams at ICU Medical

Dr. George Lopez, an internal medicine physician, founded ICU Medical in San Clemente, California, in 1984 after a patient of his accidentally died when an intravenous (IV) line became inadvertently disconnected.[63] Lopez thought there must be a better way to design components of IV lines so that these kinds of tragic accidents don't happen. He developed a product called the Click Lock, which has both a locking mechanism for IV systems and also a protected needle so that health care workers are protected from accidental needle pricks.[64] Today ICU Medical has over 2,260 employees and revenues over $313 million.[65] Lopez is a member of the board of directors, and ICU Medical made *Forbes* magazine's list of "The 200 Best Small Companies."[66] ICU Medical continues to focus on the development and manufacture of products that improve the functioning of IV lines and systems while protecting health care workers from accidental needle pricks.[67] For example, the CLAVE NeedleFree Connector for IV lines is one of ICU Medical's top-selling products.[68]

In the early 1990s Lopez experienced something not uncommon to successful entrepreneurs as their businesses grow. As the entrepreneur–CEO, he continued to make the majority of important decisions himself; yet he had close to 100 employees, demand for the CLAVE was very high, and he was starting to feel overloaded to the point where he would often sleep at nights in the office.[69] After watching one of his son's hockey games, he realized that a well-functioning team could work wonders; in the case of the hockey game, although the opposing team had an outstanding player, his son's team really pulled together as a team and was able to win the game despite the rival team's outstanding member. Lopez decided to empower employees to form teams to work on a pressing goal for ICU Medical: increasing production.[70] While employees did form teams and spent a lot of time in team interactions, the teams did not seem to come up with any real tangible results, perhaps because there were no team leaders in place and the teams had no guidelines to help them accomplish their goals.[71]

In an effort to improve team effectiveness, Lopez told employees that teams should elect team leaders. And together with Jim Reitz, ICU Medical's director of human resources at the time, Lopez came up with rules or guidelines teams should follow, such as "challenge the issue, not the person" and "stand up for your position, but never argue against the facts."[72] ICU Medical also started to reward team members for their team's contributions to organizational effectiveness. With these changes, Reitz and Lopez were striving to ensure that teams had leaders, had some guidelines for team member behavior, and were rewarded for their contributions to organizational effectiveness but, at the same time, were not bogged down by unnecessary constraints and structures and were truly self-managing.[73]

With these changes in place, teams at ICU Medical began to live up to their promise. Today any ICU Medical employee can create a team to address a problem, seize an opportunity, or work on a project ranging from developing a new product to making improvements in the physical work environment.[74] The teams have leaders and are self-managing.

Recognizing that self-managed teams still need rules, guidelines, leadership, and structure, a team of employees developed a 25-page guidebook for effective team functioning. And to ensure that teams learn from each other as well as get feedback, teams are required to put up notes from each of their meetings on ICU Medical's intranet, and any employee can provide feedback to any of the teams.[75] All in all, effectively led teams have helped ICU Medical prosper in its efforts to develop and manufacture products that protect the safety of both patients and health care workers.

Group Development over Time

As many managers overseeing self-managed teams have learned, it sometimes takes a self-managed work team two or three years to perform up to its true capabilities.[76] As their experience suggests, what a group is capable of achieving depends in part on its stage of development. Knowing that it takes considerable time for self-managed work teams to get up and running has helped managers have realistic expectations for new teams and know that they need to give new team members considerable training and guidance.

Although every group's development over time is unique, researchers have identified five stages of group development that many groups seem to pass through (see Figure 15.4).[77] In the first stage, *forming*, members try to get to know one another and reach a common understanding of what the group is trying to accomplish and how group members should behave. During this stage, managers should strive to make each member feel that he or she is a valued part of the group.

In the second stage, *storming*, group members experience conflict and disagreements because some members do not wish to submit to the demands of other group members. Disputes may arise over who should lead the group. Self-managed work teams can be particularly vulnerable during the storming stage. Managers need to keep an eye on groups at this stage to make sure conflict does not get out of hand.

During the third stage, *norming*, close ties between group members develop, and feelings of friendship and camaraderie emerge. Group members arrive at a consensus about what goals they should seek to achieve and how group members should behave toward one another. In the fourth stage, *performing*, the real work of the group gets accomplished. Depending on the type of group in question, managers need to take different steps at this stage to help ensure that groups are effective. Managers of command groups need to make sure that group members are motivated and that they are effectively leading group members. Managers overseeing

Figure 15.4

Five Stages of Group Development

self-managed work teams have to empower team members and make sure teams are given enough responsibility and autonomy at the performing stage.

The last stage, *adjourning,* applies only to groups that eventually are disbanded, such as task forces. During adjourning a group is dispersed. Sometimes adjourning takes place when a group completes a finished product, such as when a task force evaluating the pros and cons of providing on-site child care produces a report supporting its recommendation.

Managers should have a flexible approach to group development and should keep attuned to the different needs and requirements of groups at the various stages.[78] Above all else, and regardless of the stage of development, managers need to think of themselves as *resources* for groups. Thus managers always should strive to find ways to help groups and teams function more effectively.

LO15-4

Explain why it is important for groups and teams to have a balance of conformity and deviance and a moderate level of cohesiveness.

Group Norms

All groups, whether top management teams, self-managed work teams, or command groups, need to control their members' behaviors to ensure that the group performs at a high level and meets its goals. Assigning roles to each group member is one way to control behavior in groups. Another important way in which groups influence members' behavior is through the development and enforcement of group norms.[79] **Group norms** are shared guidelines or rules for behavior that most group members follow. Groups develop norms concerning a wide variety of behaviors, including working hours, the sharing of information among group members, how certain group tasks should be performed, and even how members of a group should dress.

group norms Shared guidelines or rules for behavior that most group members follow.

Managers should encourage members of a group to develop norms that contribute to group performance and the attainment of group goals. For example, group norms dictating that each member of a cross-functional team should always be available for the rest of the team when his or her input is needed, return phone calls as soon as possible, inform other team members of travel plans, and give team members a phone number at which he or she can be reached when traveling on business help to ensure that the team is efficient, performs at a high level, and achieves its goals. A norm in a command group of secretaries that dictates that secretaries who happen to have a light workload in any given week should help out secretaries with heavier workloads helps to ensure that the group completes all assignments in a timely and efficient manner. And a norm in a top management team that dictates that team members should always consult with one another before making major decisions helps to ensure that good decisions are made with a minimum of errors.

CONFORMITY AND DEVIANCE   Group members conform to norms for three reasons: (1) They want to obtain rewards and avoid punishments. (2) They want to imitate group members whom they like and admire. (3) They have internalized the norm and believe it is the right and proper way to behave.[80] Consider the case of Robert King, who conformed to his department's norm of attending a fund-raiser for a community food bank. King's conformity could be due to (1) his desire to be a member of the group in good standing and to have friendly relationships with other group members (rewards), (2) his copying the behavior of other members of the department whom he respects and who always attend the fund-raiser (imitating other group members), or (3) his belief in the merits of supporting the activities of the food bank (believing that is the right and proper way to behave).

Failure to conform, or deviance, occurs when a member of a group violates a group norm. Deviance signals that a group is not controlling one of its member's behaviors. Groups generally respond to members who behave defiantly in one of three ways:[81]

1. The group might try to get the member to change his or her deviant ways and conform to the norm. Group members might try to convince the member of the need to conform, or they might ignore or even punish the deviant. For example, in a Jacksonville Foods plant, Liz Senkbiel, a member of a self-managed work team responsible for weighing sausages, failed to conform to a group norm dictating that group members should periodically clean up an untidy interview room. Because Senkbiel refused to take part in the team's cleanup efforts, team members reduced her monthly bonus by

about \$225 for a two-month period.[82] Senkbiel clearly learned the costs of deviant behavior in her team.

2. The group might expel the member.

3. The group might change the norm to be consistent with the member's behavior.

This last alternative suggests that some deviant behavior can be functional for groups. Deviance is functional for a group when it causes group members to evaluate norms that may be dysfunctional but are taken for granted by the group. Often group members do not think about why they behave in a certain way or why they follow certain norms. Deviance can cause group members to reflect on their norms and change them when appropriate.

Consider a group of receptionists in a beauty salon who followed the norm that all appointments would be handwritten in an appointment book and, at the end of each day, the receptionist on duty would enter the appointments into the salon's computer system, which printed out the hairdressers' daily schedules. One day a receptionist decided to enter appointments directly into the computer system when they were being made, bypassing the appointment book. This deviant behavior caused the other receptionists to think about why they were using the appointment book at all. After consulting with the owner of the salon, the group changed its norm. Now appointments are entered directly into the computer, which saves time and reduces scheduling errors.

ENCOURAGING A BALANCE OF CONFORMITY AND DEVIANCE   To effectively help an organization gain a competitive advantage, groups and teams need the right balance of conformity and deviance (see Figure 15.5). A group needs a certain level of conformity to ensure that it can control members' behavior and channel it in

Figure 15.5
Balancing Conformity and Deviance in Groups

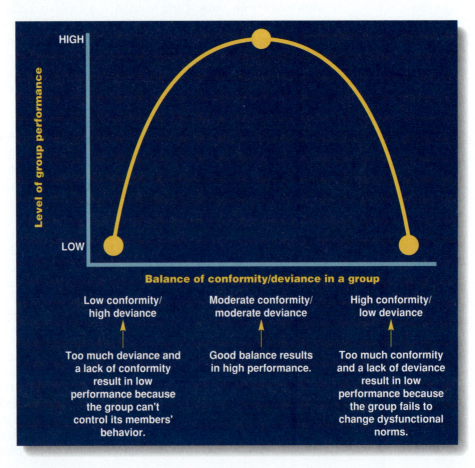

the direction of high performance and group goal accomplishment. A group also needs a certain level of deviance to ensure that dysfunctional norms are discarded and replaced with functional ones. Balancing conformity and deviance is a pressing concern for all groups, whether they are top management teams, R&D teams, command groups, or self-managed work teams.

The extent of conformity and reactions to deviance within groups are determined by group members themselves. The three bases for conformity just described are powerful forces that more often than not result in group members' conforming to norms. Sometimes these forces are so strong that deviance rarely occurs in groups, and when it does, it is stamped out.

Managers can take several steps to ensure adequate tolerance of deviance in groups so that group members are willing to deviate from dysfunctional norms and, when deviance occurs in their group, reflect on the appropriateness of the violated norm and change the norm if necessary. First, managers can be role models for the groups and teams they oversee. When managers encourage and accept employees' suggestions for changes in procedures, do not rigidly insist that tasks be accomplished in a certain way, and admit when a norm they once supported is no longer functional, they signal to group members that conformity should not come at the expense of needed changes and improvements. Second, managers should let employees know that there are always ways to improve group processes and performance levels and thus opportunities to replace existing norms with norms that will better enable a group to achieve its goals and perform at a high level. Third, managers should encourage members of groups and teams to periodically assess the appropriateness of their norms.

Managers in the innovative design firm IDEO, based in Palo Alto, California (IDEO's culture is described in Chapter 3), have excelled at ensuring that design teams have the right mix of conformity and deviance, resulting in IDEO's designing products in fields ranging from medicine to space travel to computing and personal hygiene, as indicated in the accompanying "Management Insight" feature.

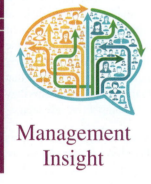

Management Insight

Teams Benefit from Deviance and Conformity at IDEO

IDEO has designed many products we now take for granted: the first Apple mouse, stand-up toothpaste containers, flexible shelving for offices, self-sealing drink bottles for sports, blood analyzers, and even equipment used in space travel.[83] Managers and designers at IDEO take pride in being experts at the process of innovation in general, rather than in any particular domain. Of course the company has technical design experts, such as mechanical and electrical engineers, who work on products requiring specialized knowledge; but on the same teams with the engineers might be an anthropologist, a biologist, and a social scientist.[84]

A guiding principle at IDEO is that innovation comes in many shapes and sizes, and it is only through diversity in thought that people can recognize opportunities for innovation. To promote such diversity in thought, new product development at IDEO is a team effort.[85] Moreover, both conformity and deviance are encouraged on IDEO teams.

Deviance, thinking differently, and not conforming to expected ways of doing things and mind-sets are encouraged at IDEO. In fact, innovative ideas often flow when designers try to see things as they really are and are not blinded by thoughts of what is appropriate, what is possible, or how things should be. Often constraints on new product design are created by designers themselves conforming to a certain mind-set about the nature of a product or what a product can or should do and look like. IDEO designers are encouraged to actively break down these constraints in their design teams.[86]

An IDEO team at work. Both conformity and deviance are encouraged at IDEO which makes it easier to recognize opportunities for innovation. IDEO has developed many products including the first Apple mouse.

Managers at IDEO realize the need for a certain amount of conformity so members of design teams can work effectively together and achieve their goals. Thus conformity to a few central norms is emphasized in IDEO teams. These norms include understanding what the team is working on (the product, market, or client need), observing real people in their natural environments, visualizing how new products might work and be used, evaluating and refining product prototypes, encouraging wild ideas, and never rejecting an idea simply because it sounds too crazy.[87] As long as these norms are followed, diversity of thought and even deviance promote innovation at IDEO. In fact, another norm at IDEO is to study "rule breakers"—people who don't follow instructions for products, for example, or who try to put products to different uses—because these individuals might help designers identify problems with existing products and unmet consumer needs.[88] All in all, IDEO's focus on encouraging both deviance and conformity in design teams has benefited all of us—we use IDEO-designed products that seem so familiar we take them for granted. We forget that these products did not exist until a design team at IDEO was called on by a client to develop a new product or improve an existing one.[89]

Group Cohesiveness

group cohesiveness The degree to which members are attracted to or loyal to their group.

Another important element of group dynamics that affects group performance and effectiveness is **group cohesiveness**, which is the degree to which members are attracted to or loyal to their group or team.[90] When group cohesiveness is high, individuals strongly value their group membership, find the group appealing, and have strong desires to remain a part of the group. When group cohesiveness is low, group members do not find their group particularly appealing and have little desire to retain their group membership. Research suggests that managers should strive to have a moderate level of cohesiveness in the groups and teams they manage because that is most likely to contribute to an organization's competitive advantage.

CONSEQUENCES OF GROUP COHESIVENESS   There are three major consequences of group cohesiveness: level of participation within a group, level of conformity to group norms, and emphasis on group goal accomplishment (see Figure 15.6).[91]

LEVEL OF PARTICIPATION WITHIN A GROUP   As group cohesiveness increases, the extent of group members' participation within the group increases. Participation contributes to group effectiveness because group members are actively involved in the group, ensure that group tasks get accomplished, readily share information with each other, and have frequent and open communication (the important topic of communication is covered in depth in Chapter 16).

A moderate level of group cohesiveness helps ensure that group members actively participate in the group and communicate effectively with one another. The reason why managers may not want to encourage high levels of cohesiveness is illustrated by the example of two cross-functional teams responsible for developing new toys. Members of the highly cohesive Team Alpha often have lengthy meetings that usually start with nonwork-related conversations and jokes, meet more often than most of the other cross-functional teams in the company, and spend a good portion of their time communicating the ins and outs of their department's contribution to toy development to other team members. Members of the

Figure 15.6

Sources and Consequences of Group Cohesiveness

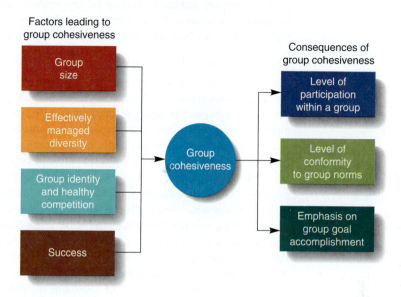

Factors leading to group cohesiveness

- Group size
- Effectively managed diversity
- Group identity and healthy competition
- Success

Group cohesiveness

Consequences of group cohesiveness

- Level of participation within a group
- Level of conformity to group norms
- Emphasis on group goal accomplishment

moderately cohesive Team Beta generally have efficient meetings in which ideas are communicated and discussed as needed, do not meet more often than necessary, and share the ins and outs of their expertise with one another to the extent needed for the development process. Teams Alpha and Beta have both developed some top-selling toys. However, it generally takes Team Alpha 30 percent longer to do so than Team Beta. This is why too much cohesiveness can be too much of a good thing.

LEVEL OF CONFORMITY TO GROUP NORMS   Increasing levels of group cohesiveness result in increasing levels of conformity to group norms, and when cohesiveness becomes high, there may be so little deviance in groups that group members conform to norms even when they are dysfunctional. In contrast, low cohesiveness can result in too much deviance and undermine the ability of a group to control its members' behaviors to get things done.

How much cohesiveness is too much? You can answer that question when you evaluate whether a group actually gets something done in its meetings or whether most of the conversation drifting out of the room consists of jokes, life experiences, or comparisons of the last company dinner's entrees.

Teams Alpha and Beta in the toy company both had the same norm for toy development. It dictated that members of each team would discuss potential ideas for new toys, decide on a line of toys to pursue, and then have the team member from R&D design a prototype. Recently a new animated movie featuring a family of rabbits produced by a small film company was an unexpected hit, and major toy companies were scrambling to reach licensing agreements to produce toy lines featuring the rabbits. The top management team in the toy company assigned Teams Alpha and Beta to develop the new toy lines quickly to beat the competition.

Members of Team Alpha followed their usual toy development norm even though the marketing expert on the team believed the process could have been streamlined to save time. The marketing expert on Team Beta urged the team to deviate from its toy development norm. She suggested that the team not have R&D develop prototypes but, instead, modify top-selling toys the company already made to feature rabbits and then reach a licensing agreement with the film company based on the high sales potential (given the company's prior success). Once the licensing agreement was signed, the company could take the time needed to develop innovative and unique rabbit toys with more input from R&D.

As a result of the willingness of the marketing expert on Team Beta to deviate from the norm for toy development, the toy company obtained an exclusive licensing agreement with the film company and had its first rabbit toys on the shelves of stores in a record three months. Groups need a balance of conformity and deviance, so a moderate level of cohesiveness often yields the best outcome, as it did in the case of Team Beta.

EMPHASIS ON GROUP GOAL ACCOMPLISHMENT   As group cohesiveness increases, the emphasis placed on group goal accomplishment also increases within a group. A strong emphasis on group goal accomplishment, however, does not always lead to organizational effectiveness. For an organization to be effective and gain a competitive advantage, the different groups and teams in the organization must cooperate with one another and be motivated to achieve *organizational goals,* even if doing so sometimes comes at the expense of the achievement of group goals. A moderate level of cohesiveness motivates group members to accomplish both group and organizational goals. High levels of cohesiveness can cause group members to be so focused on group goal accomplishment that they may strive to achieve group goals no matter what—even when doing so jeopardizes organizational performance.

At the toy company, the major goal of the cross-functional teams was to develop new toy lines that were truly innovative, utilized the latest in technology, and were in some way fundamentally distinct from other toys on the market. When it came to the rabbit project, Team Alpha's high level of cohesiveness contributed to its continued emphasis on its group goal of developing an innovative line of toys; thus the team stuck with its usual design process. Team Beta, in contrast, realized that developing the new line of toys quickly was an important organizational goal that should take precedence over the group's goal of developing groundbreaking new toys, at least in the short term. Team Beta's moderate level of cohesiveness contributed to team members' doing what was best for the toy company in this case.

FACTORS LEADING TO GROUP COHESIVENESS   Four factors contribute to the level of group cohesiveness (see Figure 15.6).[92] By influencing these *determinants of group cohesiveness,* managers can raise or lower the level of cohesiveness to promote moderate levels of cohesiveness in groups and teams.

GROUP SIZE   As we mentioned earlier, members of small groups tend to be more motivated and committed than members of large groups. Thus to promote cohesiveness in groups, when feasible, managers should form groups that are small to medium in size (about 2 to 15 members). If a group is low in cohesiveness and large in size, managers might want to consider dividing the group in half and assigning different tasks and goals to the two newly formed groups.

EFFECTIVELY MANAGED DIVERSITY   In general, people tend to like and get along with others who are similar to themselves. It is easier to communicate with someone, for example, who shares your values, has a similar background, and has had similar experiences. However, as discussed in Chapter 5, diversity in groups, teams, and organizations can help an organization gain a competitive advantage. Diverse groups often come up with more innovative and creative ideas. One reason why cross-functional teams are so popular in organizations like Hallmark Cards is that the diverse expertise represented in the teams results in higher levels of team performance.

In forming groups and teams, managers need to make sure the diversity in knowledge, experience, expertise, and other characteristics necessary for group goal accomplishment is represented in the new groups. Managers then have to make sure this diversity in group membership is effectively managed so groups will be cohesive (see Chapter 5).

GROUP IDENTITY AND HEALTHY COMPETITION   When group cohesiveness is low, managers can often increase it by encouraging groups to develop their own identities or personalities and engage in healthy competition. This is precisely what managers at Eaton Corporation's manufacturing facility in Lincoln, Illinois, did. Eaton's employees manufacture products such as engine valves, gears, truck axles, and circuit breakers. Managers at Eaton created self-managed work teams to cut costs and improve performance. They realized, however, that the teams would have to be cohesive to ensure that they would strive to achieve their goals. Managers promoted group identity by having the teams give themselves names such as "The Hoods," "The Worms," and "Scrap Attack" (a team striving to reduce costly scrap metal waste by 50 percent). Healthy competition among groups was promoted by displaying measures of each team's performance and the extent to which teams met their goals on a large TV screen in the cafeteria and by rewarding team members for team performance.[93]

If groups are too cohesive, managers can try to decrease cohesiveness by promoting organizational (rather than group) identity and making the organization as a whole the focus of the group's efforts. Organizational identity can be promoted by making group members feel that they are valued members of the organization and by stressing cooperation across groups to promote the achievement of organizational goals. Excessive levels of cohesiveness also can be reduced by reducing or eliminating competition among groups and rewarding cooperation.

SUCCESS   When it comes to promoting group cohesiveness, there is more than a grain of truth to the saying "Nothing succeeds like success." As groups become more successful, they become increasingly attractive to their members, and their cohesiveness tends to increase. When cohesiveness is low, managers can increase cohesiveness by making sure a group can achieve some noticeable and visible successes.

Consider a group of salespeople in the housewares department of a medium-size department store. The housewares department was recently moved to a corner of the store's basement. Its remote location resulted in low sales because of infrequent customer traffic in that part of the store. The salespeople, who were generally evaluated favorably by their supervisors and were valued members of the store, tried various initiatives to boost sales, but to no avail. As a result of this lack of success and the poor performance of their department, their cohesiveness started to plummet. To increase and preserve the cohesiveness of the group, the store manager implemented a group-based incentive across the store. In any month, members of the group with the best attendance and punctuality records would have their names and pictures posted on a bulletin board in the cafeteria and would each receive a $50 gift certificate. The housewares group frequently had the best records, and their success on this dimension helped to build and maintain their cohesiveness. Moreover, this initiative boosted attendance and discouraged lateness throughout the store.

Managing Groups and Teams for High Performance

Now that you understand why groups and teams are so important for organizations, the types of groups managers create, and group dynamics, we consider some additional steps managers can take to make sure groups and teams perform at a high level and contribute to organizational effectiveness. Managers striving to have top-performing groups and teams need to (1) motivate group members to work toward the achievement of organizational goals, (2) reduce social loafing, and (3) help groups manage conflict effectively.

LO15-5

Describe how managers can motivate group members to achieve organizational goals and reduce social loafing in groups and teams.

Motivating Group Members to Achieve Organizational Goals

When work is difficult, tedious, or requires a high level of commitment and energy, managers cannot assume group members will always be motivated to work toward the achievement of organizational goals. Consider a group of house painters who paint the interiors and exteriors of new homes for a construction company and are paid on an hourly basis. Why should they strive to complete painting jobs quickly and efficiently if doing so will just make them feel more tired at the end of the day and they will not receive any tangible benefits? It makes more sense for the painters to adopt a relaxed approach, to take frequent breaks, and to work at a leisurely pace. This relaxed approach, however, impairs the construction company's ability to gain a competitive advantage because it raises costs and increases the time needed to complete a new home.

Managers can motivate members of groups and teams to achieve organizational goals by making sure the members themselves benefit when the group or team performs highly. For example, if members of a self-managed work team know they will receive a weekly bonus based on team performance, they will be motivated to perform at a high level.

Managers often rely on some combination of individual and group-based incentives to motivate members of groups and teams to work toward the achievement of organizational goals. When individual performance within a group can be assessed, pay is often determined by individual performance or by both individual and group performance. When individual performance within a group cannot be accurately assessed, group performance should be the key determinant of pay levels. Many companies, that use self-managed work teams, base team members' pay in part on team performance.[94] A major challenge for managers is to develop a fair pay system that will lead to both high individual motivation and high group or team performance.

Other benefits managers can make available to high-performing group members—in addition to monetary rewards—include extra resources such as equipment and computer software, awards and other forms of recognition, and choice of future work assignments. For example, members of self-managed work teams that develop new software at companies such as Microsoft often value working on interesting and important projects; members of teams that have performed at a high level are rewarded by being assigned to interesting and important new projects.

At IDEO (profiled earlier in a "Management Insight" feature), managers motivate team members by making them feel important. As Tom Kelley, a partner at IDEO, put it, "When people feel special, they'll perform beyond your wildest dreams."[95] To make IDEO team members feel special, IDEO managers plan unique and fun year-end parties, give teams the opportunity to take time off if they feel they need or want to, encourage teams to take field trips, and see pranks as a way to incorporate fun into the workplace.[96]

Reducing Social Loafing in Groups

We have been focusing on the steps managers can take to encourage high levels of performance in groups. Managers, however, need to be aware of an important downside to group and team work: the potential for social loafing, which reduces group performance. **Social loafing** is the tendency of individuals to put forth less effort when they work in groups than when they work alone.[97] Have you ever worked on a group project in which one or two group members never seemed to be pulling their weight? Have you ever worked in a student club or committee in which some members always seemed to be missing meetings and never volunteered for activities? Have you ever had a job in which one or two of your coworkers seemed to be slacking off because they knew you or other members of your work group would make up for their low levels of effort? If so, you have witnessed social loafing in action.

Social loafing can occur in all kinds of groups and teams and in all kinds of organizations. It can result in lower group performance and may even prevent a group from attaining its goals. Fortunately managers can take steps to reduce social loafing and sometimes completely eliminate it; we will look at three (see Figure 15.7):

1. *Make individual contributions to a group identifiable.* Some people may engage in social loafing when they work in groups because they think they can hide in the crowd—no one will notice if they put forth less effort than they should. Other people may think if they put forth high levels of effort and make substantial contributions to the group, their contributions will not be noticed and they will receive no rewards for their work—so why bother?[98]

One way that managers can effectively eliminate social loafing is by making individual contributions to a group identifiable so that group members perceive that low and high levels of effort will be noticed and individual contributions evaluated.[99] Managers can accomplish this by assigning specific tasks to group members and holding them accountable for their completion. Take the case of a group of eight employees responsible for reshelving returned books in a large public library in New York. The head librarian was concerned that there was always a backlog of seven or eight carts of books to be reshelved, even though the employees

social loafing The tendency of individuals to put forth less effort when they work in groups than when they work alone.

Figure 15.7

Three Ways to Reduce Social Loafing

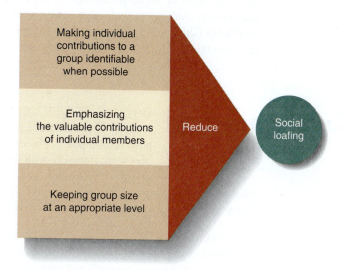

never seemed to be particularly busy and some even found time to sit down and read newspapers and magazines. The librarian decided to try to eliminate the apparent social loafing by assigning each employee sole responsibility for reshelving a particular section of the library. Because the library's front desk employees sorted the books by section on the carts as they were returned, holding the shelvers responsible for particular sections was easily accomplished. Once the shelvers knew the librarian could identify their effort or lack thereof, there were rarely any backlogs of books to be reshelved.

Sometimes the members of a group can cooperate to eliminate social loafing by making individual contributions identifiable. For example, in a small security company, members of a self-managed work team who assemble control boxes for home alarm systems start each day by deciding who will perform which tasks that day and how much work each member and the group as a whole should strive to accomplish. Each team member knows that, at the end of the day, the other team members will know exactly how much he or she has accomplished. With this system in place, social loafing never occurs in the team. Remember, however, that in some teams, individual contributions cannot be made identifiable, as in teams whose members are reciprocally interdependent.

2. *Emphasize the valuable contributions of individual members.* Another reason why social loafing may occur is that people sometimes think their efforts are unnecessary or unimportant when they work in a group. They feel the group will accomplish its goals and perform at an acceptable level whether or not they personally perform at a high level. To counteract this belief, when managers form groups, they should assign individuals to a group on the basis of the valuable contributions that *each* person can make to the group as a whole. Clearly communicating to group members why each person's contributions are valuable to the group is an effective means by which managers and group members themselves can reduce or eliminate social loafing.[100] This is most clearly illustrated in cross-functional teams, where each member's valuable contribution to the team derives from a personal area of expertise. By emphasizing why each member's skills are important, managers can reduce social loafing in such teams.

3. *Keep group size at an appropriate level.* Group size is related to the causes of social loafing we just described. As size increases, identifying individual contributions becomes increasingly difficult, and members are increasingly likely to think their individual contributions are not important. To overcome this, managers should form groups with no more members than are needed to accomplish group goals and perform at a high level.[101]

Helping Groups to Manage Conflict Effectively

At some point or other, practically all groups experience conflict either within the group (*intragroup* conflict) or with other groups (*intergroup* conflict). In Chapter 17 we discuss conflict in depth and explore ways to manage it effectively. As you will learn, managers can take several steps to help groups manage conflict and disagreements.

Summary and Review

GROUPS, TEAMS, AND ORGANIZATIONAL EFFECTIVENESS
A group is two or more people who interact with each other to accomplish certain goals or meet certain needs. A team is a group whose members work intensely with one another to achieve a specific common goal or objective. Groups and teams can contribute to organizational effectiveness by enhancing performance, increasing responsiveness to customers, increasing innovation, and being a source of motivation for their members.

LO15-1

LO15-2 **TYPES OF GROUPS AND TEAMS** Formal groups are groups that managers establish to achieve organizational goals; they include cross-functional teams, cross-cultural teams, top management teams, research and development teams, command groups, task forces, self-managed work teams, and virtual teams. Informal groups are groups that employees form because they believe the groups will help them achieve their own goals or meet their needs; they include friendship groups and interest groups.

LO15-3 **GROUP DYNAMICS** Key elements of group dynamics are group size, tasks, and roles; group leadership; group development; group norms; and group cohesiveness. The advantages and disadvantages of large and small groups suggest that managers should form groups with no more members than are needed to provide the group with the human resources it needs to achieve its goals and use a division of labor. The type of task interdependence that characterizes a group's work gives managers a clue about the appropriate size of the group. A group role is a set of behaviors and tasks that a member of a group is expected to perform because of his or her position in the group. All groups and teams need leadership.

LO15-3, 15-4 Five stages of development that many groups pass through are forming, storming, norming, performing, and adjourning. Group norms are shared rules for behavior that most group members follow. To be effective, groups need a balance of conformity and deviance. Conformity allows a group to control its members' behavior to achieve group goals; deviance provides the impetus for needed change.

LO15-4 Group cohesiveness is the attractiveness of a group or team to its members. As group cohesiveness increases, so do the level of participation and communication within a group, the level of conformity to group norms, and the emphasis on group goal accomplishment. Managers should strive to achieve a moderate level of group cohesiveness in the groups and teams they manage.

LO15-5 **MANAGING GROUPS AND TEAMS FOR HIGH PERFORMANCE** To make sure groups and teams perform at a high level, managers need to motivate group members to work toward the achievement of organizational goals, reduce social loafing, and help groups to effectively manage conflict. Managers can motivate members of groups and teams to work toward the achievement of organizational goals by making sure members personally benefit when the group or team performs at a high level.

Management in Action

Topics for Discussion and Action

Discussion

1. Why do all organizations need to rely on groups and teams to achieve their goals and gain a competitive advantage? [LO15-1]

2. What kinds of employees would prefer to work in a virtual team? What kinds of employees would prefer to work in a team that meets face-to-face? [LO15-2]

3. Think about a group that you are a member of, and describe that group's current stage of development. Does the development of this group seem to be following the forming, storming, norming, performing, and adjourning stages described in the chapter? [LO15-3]

4. Think about a group of employees who work in a McDonald's restaurant. What type of task interdependence characterizes this group? What potential problems in the group should the restaurant manager be aware of and take steps to avoid? [LO15-3]

5. Discuss the reasons why too much conformity can hurt groups and their organizations. [LO15-4]

6. Why do some groups have very low levels of cohesiveness? [LO15-4]

7. Imagine that you are the manager of a hotel. What steps will you take to reduce social loafing by members of the cleaning staff who are responsible for keeping all common areas and guest rooms spotless? [LO15-5]

Action

8. Interview one or more managers in an organization in your local community to identify the types of groups and teams that the organization uses to achieve its goals. What challenges do these groups and teams face? [LO15-2]

Building Management Skills

Diagnosing Group Failures [LO15-1, 15-2, 15-3, 15-4, 15-5]

Think about the last dissatisfying or discouraging experience you had as a member of a group or team. Perhaps the group did not accomplish its goals, perhaps group members could agree about nothing, or perhaps there was too much social loafing. Now answer the following questions:

1. What type of group was this?

2. Were group members motivated to achieve group goals? Why or why not?

3. How large was the group, what type of task interdependence existed in the group, and what group roles did members play?

4. What were the group's norms? How much conformity and deviance existed in the group?

5. How cohesive was the group? Why do you think the group's cohesiveness was at this level? What consequences did this level of group cohesiveness have for the group and its members?

6. Was social loafing a problem in this group? Why or why not?

7. What could the group's leader or manager have done differently to increase group effectiveness?

8. What could group members have done differently to increase group effectiveness?

Managing Ethically [LO15-1, 15-2, 15-3, 15-4, 15-5]

Some self-managed teams encounter a vexing problem: One or more members engage in social loafing, and other members are reluctant to try to rectify the situation. Social loafing can be especially troubling if team members' pay is based on team performance and social loafing reduces the team's performance and thus the pay of all members (even the highest performers). Even if managers are aware of the problem, they may be reluctant to take action because the team is supposedly self-managing.

Questions

1. Either individually or in a group, think about the ethical implications of social loafing in a self-managed team.

2. Do managers have an ethical obligation to step in when they are aware of social loafing in a self-managed team? Why or why not? Do other team members have an obligation to try to curtail the social loafing? Why or why not?

Small Group Breakout Exercise

Creating a Cross-Functional Team [LO15-1, 15-2, 15-3, 15-4, 15-5]

Form groups of three or four people, and appoint one member as the spokesperson who will communicate your findings to the class when called on by the instructor. Then discuss the following scenario:

You are a group of managers in charge of food services for a large state university in the Midwest. Recently a survey of students, faculty, and staff was conducted to evaluate customer satisfaction with the food services provided by the university's eight cafeterias. The results were disappointing, to put it mildly. Complaints ranged from dissatisfaction with the type and range of meals and snacks provided, operating hours, and food temperature to frustration about unresponsiveness to current concerns about healthful diets and the needs of vegetarians. You have decided to form a cross-functional team that will further evaluate reactions to the food services and will develop a proposal for changes to be made to increase customer satisfaction.

1. Indicate who should be on this important cross-functional team, and explain why.

2. Describe the goals the team should strive to achieve.

3. Describe the different roles that will need to be performed on this team.

4. Describe the steps you will take to help ensure that the team has a good balance between conformity and deviance and has a moderate level of cohesiveness.

Exploring the World Wide Web [LO15-1, 15-2, 15-3, 15-4, 15-5]

Many consultants and organizations provide team-building services to organizations. Although some managers and teams have found these services to be helpful, others have found them to be a waste of time and money—another consulting fad that provides no real performance benefits. Search online for team-building services, and examine the websites of a few consultants/companies. Based on what you have read, what might be some advantages and disadvantages of team-building services? For what kinds of problems/issues might these services be beneficial, and when might they have little benefit or perhaps even do more harm than good?

Be the Manager [LO15-1, 15-2, 15-3, 15-4, 15-5]

You were recently hired in a boundary-spanning role for the global unit of an educational and professional publishing company. The company is headquartered in New York (where you work) and has divisions in multiple countries. Each division is responsible for translating, manufacturing, marketing, and selling a set of books in its country. Your responsibilities include interfacing with managers in each of the divisions in your region (Central and South America), overseeing their budgeting and financial reporting to headquarters, and leading a virtual team consisting of the top managers in charge of each of the divisions in your region. The virtual team's mission is to promote global learning, explore new potential opportunities and markets, and address ongoing problems. You communicate directly with division managers via telephone and email, as well as written reports, memos, and faxes. When virtual team meetings are convened, video-conferencing is often used.

After your first few virtual team meetings, you noticed that the managers seemed to be reticent about speaking up. Interestingly enough, when each manager communicates with you individually, primarily in telephone conversations and e-mails, she or he tends to be forthcoming and frank, and you feel you have a good rapport with each of them. However, getting the managers to communicate with one another as a virtual team has been a real challenge. At the last meeting you tried to prompt some of the managers to raise issues relevant to the agenda that you knew were on their minds from your individual conversations with them. Surprisingly, the managers skillfully avoided informing their teammates about the heart of the issues in question. You are confused and troubled. Although you feel your other responsibilities are going well, you know your virtual team is not operating like a team at all; and no matter what you try, discussions in virtual team meetings are forced and generally unproductive. What are you going to do to address this problem?

The Wall Street Journal Case in the News

[LO15-1, 15-2, 15-3, 15-4, 15-5]

The Team Can See You Now

A visit to the doctor may mean seeing someone else instead.

An increasing number of practices are scrapping the traditional one-on-one doctor–patient relationship. Instead, patients are receiving care from a group of health professionals who divide up responsibilities that once would have largely been handled by the doctor in charge. While the supervising doctor still directly oversees patient care, other medical professionals—nurse practitioners, physician assistants and clinical pharmacists—are performing more functions. These include adjusting medication dosage, ensuring that patients receive tests and helping them to manage chronic diseases.

"I can't possibly do everything that needs to be done for our patients as a single human being," says Kirsten Meisinger, supervising physician for a team of between 9 and 11 medical professionals at the Union Square Family Health Center in Somerville, Mass., one of 15 primary-care centers run by Harvard Medical School-affiliated Cambridge Health Alliance. For example, Dr. Meisinger says she may see a diabetic patient once every three months. But nurses on her team generally see the patient more frequently and for longer visits. And patients are likely to feel more comfortable telling a nurse than a doctor if, for instance, they haven't been taking their medication, she says.

The new approach, called team-based care, comes amid a shortage in many parts of the U.S. of primary-care physicians, a situation expected to worsen as the number of new patients obtaining insurance under the federal Affordable Care Act rises. Pervasive chronic diseases such as diabetes also are straining the health-care system.

"In many primary-care practices today, physicians are doing a great deal of work that could be done by others on the team," says Don Goldmann, chief medical officer of the Institute for Healthcare Improvement, in Cambridge, Mass., a nonprofit that works with medical practices to improve delivery of health care. Dr. Goldmann expects that within 10 years team-based care "will be the norm."

Team-based care is also becoming more common as large health-care providers increasingly purchase private physician practices and shift from traditional fee-for-service payments to other models, such as those that provide fixed payments to care for patients over a set time.

Lucas Calixto, a 24-year-old software-implementation engineer, ended up in the emergency room with a pulmonary embolism, a blockage in a lung artery caused by a blood clot last summer. He is now on blood-thinning medication and needs close monitoring to prevent a recurrence. On his regular visits to the Union Square clinic, he often doesn't see the doctor. Instead, another member of the medical team, clinical pharmacist Joseph Falinski, who has a doctor of pharmacy degree, monitors the levels of medication in his system and adjusts the dose as needed. Mr. Calixto also meets with registered nurse Amberly Killmer, who talks to him about how his condition is affecting his life and whether he is adhering to his diet and exercise regimen.

Dr. Meisinger says she diagnoses and treats patients like Mr. Calixto initially, then gives guidance to the team for follow-up. Mr. Calixto feels confident in the care he receives from other team members. "To be honest, unless it is an emergency, they can address whatever issue I'm having and they always seem to do a good job," he says.

The idea of team-based care is to allow the team members to practice at the highest level allowed by their training and medical license. Physician assistants, for example, complete graduate-level programs lasting on average 27 months and do clinical rotations in different specialties. They can examine patients, diagnose injuries and illnesses, provide treatment, prescribe medications and perform some surgical procedures. But they must be under the supervision of physicians, and the care they can provide varies widely by state and by health-care provider.

Studies have shown that team-based care can improve patient outcomes and reduce costs. A 2012 study looked at 214 adults with depression, combined with either diabetes or heart disease or both. It found that after two years, patients

overseen by a team of nurses, working under primary-care-doctor supervision, were significantly less depressed and had improved levels of blood sugar, cholesterol and blood pressure, compared with patients who didn't receive nurse coaching and monitoring.

The study, conducted by the University of Washington and the research arm of Group Health, a non-profit health-care provider in Seattle, also found that for patients, whose care cost $11,000 annually on average, team-based care was associated with nearly $300 in yearly savings at Group Health, which charges a fixed monthly rate for unlimited care.

Winning over patients to team-based care can be a challenge. A 2012 survey of more than 1,000 low-income people in California by the Blue Shield of California Foundation found that the majority preferred to be seen by doctors. About 1 in 4 of the respondents already had team-based care, and 94% of them said they liked it. Among those who didn't have team-based care, 81% said they were willing to try it.

Doctors may resist being part of a team and ceding care of their patients, studies have found. Experts in health-care delivery also caution that team members must coordinate care and delegate clearly to avoid anything falling through the cracks.

At the Somerville Union Square clinic, team members meet in "huddles" usually twice a day to review incoming patients and decide who needs to see them. The meetings also aim to identify which patients may need extra attention. Patients who are chronically late, for instance, may get assistance from Paula Coutinho, a clinical social worker, who might arrange transportation or child care.

Physician assistant Juliane Liberus is often the first practitioner new patients see. She will take medical histories, review medications and perform physical exams. "I do well-child visits, geriatric care, the whole gamut

of things," she says. If needed, Ms. Liberus will refer cases to Dr. Meisinger for follow-up.

Dr. Meisinger says the team helps her with countless behind-the-scenes tasks, like the medical assistants and receptionists who follow up on abnormal mammogram results and chase down patients to come in for colonoscopy tests. "We literally have lists of the lives they've saved," Dr. Meisinger says. Medical assistant Fabiola Marcelin, who is also a phlebotomist, does blood work and explains to patients how to do certain tests, such as fecal occult blood tests for colon cancer.

Ms. Killmer, the registered nurse, says she sometimes has to educate patients about the team members' different roles and explain to patients that they may not need the doctor for certain things. Sometimes if a patient insists on seeing the doctor, Dr. Meisinger will look into the room and assure the patient that Ms. Killmer's plan is a good one. "That little bit of interaction makes patients feel like, hey, I saw the doctor, but I have a pretty smart nurse," says Ms. Killmer.

Source: Sue Shellenbarger, "Help! I'm on a Conference Call," *The Wall Street Journal,* February 26, 2014. Copyright © 2014 Dow Jones & Company, Inc. Reproduced with permission via Copyright Clearance Center.

Questions for Discussion

1. How might using teams in health care settings enhance performance, responsiveness to patients, and health care provider motivation?

2. What kind of interdependence do you think exists in teams in health care settings?

3. What kinds of norms do you think it would be important for these teams to have?

4. Why might it be important for teams in health care settings to have a moderate level of cohesiveness?

CHAPTER 16

Promoting Effective Communication

Learning Objectives

After studying this chapter, you should be able to:

LO16-1 Explain why effective communication helps an organization gain a competitive advantage.

LO16-2 Describe the communication process, and explain the role of perception in communication.

LO16-3 Define information richness, and describe the information richness of communication media available to managers.

LO16-4 Describe the communication networks that exist in groups and teams.

LO16-5 Explain how advances in technology have given managers new options for managing communication.

LO16-6 Describe important communication skills that managers need as senders and as receivers of messages and why it is important to understand differences in linguistic styles.

A MANAGER'S CHALLENGE

Encouraging Effective Communication and Collaboration at Salesforce.com

How can managers encourage effective communication and collaboration? Not only does Marc Benioff, cofounder, chairman of the board of directors, and chief executive officer of Salesforce.com, foster effective communication and collaboration in his company, but his company also gives its customers the tools to promote effective communication in their own organizations and with their own customers. An effective communicator himself, Benioff well knows the importance of building a common understanding, trust, and a collaborative atmosphere for effective communication.[1]

Salesforce.com was founded in 1999 and provides its subscribing companies with customer relationship management software and applications via cloud computing (cloud computing entails the delivery of software, services, data management, and storage over the Internet).[2] Thus, through cloud computing, Salesforce.com gives companies tools to effectively manage sales and relations with their own customers, accounting and data management and storage, and communications within their companies. Salesforce.com has over 100,000 subscribers ranging from Dell, Cisco, and Google to NBCUniversal, Bank of America, and the Japanese government.[3] Rather than subscribers having to purchase, install, upgrade, and maintain software to manage communications and business activities, Salesforce.com enables them to access software, communication tools, and data management and storage over the Internet through

cloud computing. Salesforce.com's growth trajectory has been remarkable.[4] For fiscal 2014, Salesforce.com had revenues of $4.07 billion—33 percent higher than its revenues were in fiscal 2013.[5]

With over 10,000 employees globally and more than 100,000 customers, Salesforce.com is a leader in the move toward social enterprises that use mobile, social, and cloud technology to better serve customers.[6] Salesforce.com offers its subscribers (or customers) access to different kinds of social networks to facilitate the sharing of information, communication, and coordination both internally among employees and externally with customers. For example, Salesforce.com's Chatter is

Marc Benioff, chairman and CEO of Salesforce.com, Inc. Benioff promotes communication and collaboration within his company with such devices as Chatter, a social networking app for internal use by Salesforce employees.

a social networking application (or "app"),[7] similar to Facebook, for internal use by a company's employees. On computers and mobile devices like smartphones and tablets, and in news feeds and groups open to all employees, employees can communicate with each other, work on drafts, collaborate, get feedback on new ideas, and perform data analyses in real time. Inside Salesforce.com, some groups bring together employees from different functions and hierarchical ranks to share thoughts and ideas about their own work experiences, such as the groups named Airing of Grievances and Tribal Knowledge.[8]

Each day, employees at Salesforce.com post approximately 3,000 entries on Chatter, with their identities known to all.[9] Thus, while posts cannot get out of hand, this open forum for real-time communication certainly seems to facilitate collaboration and shared understandings. After salesforce.com developed and adopted Chatter, managers found that around 30 percent fewer internal email messages were being sent among employees. Chatter seems to keep both employees and managers more informed about what is going on in the company. Benioff himself indicated that "I learned more about my company in a few months through using Chatter than I had in the last three years."[10] Chatter is used by the vast majority of Salesforce.com customers without any extra charge.[11]

While Saleforce.com excels in the arena of electronic communication and social networking, Benioff, a consummate salesperson, nonetheless recognizes the importance of face-to-face communication as well. As a case in point, consider how he managed the acquisition of Rypple, a Canadian start-up that develops human resources applications.[12] Rypple was founded by Daniel Debow and David Stein, who were speaking at the same conference as Benioff in New York City. Even though Benioff already had had several discussions with the pair about Salesforce.com's potentially acquiring Rypple, the night before the meeting, Benioff took Debow and Stein to one of his favorite Italian restaurants in midtown Manhattan. The next day after the conference events were finished, Benioff took Debow (Stein had a flight back home to catch) to the 2nd Avenue Deli for a tasty deli spread at the counter. Rather than talk business, the two just had a casual conversation. Building a good sense of rapport and a common understanding with the CEO of the company that was going to acquire their company evidently meant a lot to Debow and Stein. Even though they had a better offer to acquire their company from one of Salesforce.com's competitors, they decided to accept Salesforce.com's $60 million bid for Rypple. As Debow puts it, "It wasn't only about deal terms, but corporate culture. . . . We barely met the other CEO . . . we entrepreneurs could be part of their family. Nobody can keep up the artifice over a couple of hours of sharing pickles."[13]

On May 29, 2014, Salesforce.com and Microsoft declared that they had entered into a strategic partnership such that Salesforce.com's customers would be able to access Salesforce.com applications and customer relationship management software through Microsoft Windows and Office.[14] This partnership has the potential to improve performance and communication for Salesforce.com's customers. As Benioff put it, "Today is about putting the customer first. . . . Together with Microsoft, we are building bridges that allow customers to be more productive."[15]

Importantly, Benioff is also concerned about giving back to the community and doing volunteer work. Salesforce.com originated the "1/1/1" system of philanthropy that other companies like Google are modeling their approaches after.[16] Essentially, Salesforce.com donates 1 percent of its employees' paid workdays to volunteer work (six workdays per year per employee) and also donates 1 percent of its services to small nonprofits. Moreover, when Salesforce.com became a public company, it set aside 1 percent of its stock for the Salesforce.com Foundation. The foundation focuses on giving grants to programs and initiatives oriented around poverty, education, young people, innovation, and other arenas in which employees are interested in volunteering. The foundation also helps large nonprofits and institutions of higher education improve their communication efforts by selling them Salesforce.com subscriptions at an 80 percent discount with the foundation keeping the proceeds from the subscriptions.[17] Interestingly enough, when employees volunteer for projects, they not only have a sense of fulfillment from doing something worthwhile, but they also increase their sense of camaraderie and collaboration with their coworkers. As Julie Trell, who worked at the foundation, put it, "You bring your whole self to work. . . . Employees bring in their causes, others join in, and it teaches team building."[18] All in all, Salesforce.com appears to be helping many people and organizations be better communicators.[19]

Overview

Even with all the advances in information technology provided by companies like Salesforce.com that are available to managers, ineffective communication continues to take place in organizations. Ineffective communication is detrimental for managers, employees, and organizations; it can lead to poor performance, strained interpersonal relations, poor service, and dissatisfied customers. For an organization to be effective and gain a competitive advantage, managers at all levels need to be good communicators.

In this chapter we describe the nature of communication and the communication process and explain why all managers and their subordinates need to be effective communicators. We describe the communication media available to managers and the factors they need to consider in selecting a communication medium for each message they send. We consider the communication networks organizational members rely on, and we explore how advances in information technology have expanded managers' range of communication options. We describe the communication skills that help managers to be effective senders and receivers of messages. By the end of this chapter, you will appreciate the nature of communication and the steps managers can take to ensure that they are effective communicators.

communication The sharing of information between two or more individuals or groups to reach a common understanding.

Communication and Management

Communication is the sharing of information between two or more individuals or groups to reach a common understanding.[20] First and foremost, no matter how electronically based, communication is a human endeavor and involves individuals and groups. Second, communication does not take place unless a common understanding is reached. Thus when you call a business to speak to a person in customer service or billing and are bounced between endless automated messages and menu options and eventually hang up in frustration, communication has not taken place.

The Importance of Good Communication

In Chapter 1 we described how an organization can gain a competitive advantage when managers strive to increase efficiency, quality, responsiveness to customers, and innovation. Good communication is essential for attaining each of these four goals and thus is a necessity for gaining a competitive advantage.

Managers can *increase efficiency* by updating the production process to take advantage of new and more efficient technologies and by training workers to operate the new technologies and to expand their skills. Good communication is necessary for managers to learn about new technologies, implement them in their organizations, and train workers in how to use them. Similarly, *improving quality* hinges on effective communication. Managers need to communicate to all members of an organization the meaning and importance of high quality and the routes to attaining it. Subordinates need to communicate quality problems and suggestions for increasing quality to their superiors, and members of self-managed work teams need to share their ideas on improving quality with one another.

Good communication can also help increase *responsiveness to customers*. When the organizational members who are closest to customers, such as department store salespeople and bank tellers, are empowered to communicate customers' needs and desires to managers, managers can better respond to these needs. Managers, in turn, must communicate with other organizational members to determine how best to respond to changing customer preferences.

Innovation, which often takes place in cross-functional teams, also requires effective communication. Members of a cross-functional team developing a new electronic game, for example, must effectively communicate with one another to develop a game that customers will want to play; that will be engaging, interesting, and fun; and that can potentially lead to sequels. Members of the team also must communicate with managers to secure the resources they need for developing the game and to keep managers informed of progress on the project. Innovation in organizations is increasingly taking place on a global level, making effective communication all the more important, as illustrated in the accompanying "Managing Globally" feature.

Managing Globally

Global Communication for Global Innovation at GE Healthcare

GE Healthcare (headquartered in the United Kingdom) is a provider of medical technology and services and makes medical imaging, diagnostic, and monitoring systems such as CT scanners. With over 52,000 employees around the world, GE Healthcare has approximately $18 billion in revenues.[21] To make the best scanners that meet the needs of doctors and patients around the world with next-generation technology, new product development and manufacture are truly global endeavors at GE Healthcare Technologies. Consider the development of the LightSpeed VCT scanner series (*VCT* stands for "volume controlled tomography"), which can perform a full-body scan in under 10 seconds and yields a three-dimensional picture of patients' hearts within five heartbeats.[22]

The LightSpeed was developed through global collaboration. GE managers not only spoke with doctors (including cardiologists and radiologists) around the world to find out what their needs were and what kinds of tests they would perform with the LightSpeed but also gathered information about differences among patients in various countries. Engineers in Hino (Japan), Buc (France), and Waukesha, Wisconsin, developed the electronics for the LightSpeed. Other parts, such as the automated table that patients lie on,

As GE Healthcare learned, conference calls and email are beneficial, but nothing replaces getting managers together for face-to-face conversations and problem solving.

were made in Beijing (China) and Hino. Software for the LightSpeed was written in Haifa (Israel), Bangalore (India), Buc, and Waukesha.[23]

Effective global communication was a challenge and a necessity to successfully develop the LightSpeed series. As Brian Duchinsky, who was GE's general manager for global CT at the time, put it, "If we sat around in this cornfield west of Milwaukee, we wouldn't come up with the same breadth of good ideas. But yet, getting six countries on the phone to make a decision can be a pain."[24]

GE managers facilitated effective communication in a number of ways—participating in daily conference calls, making sure teams in different countries depended on one another, developing an internal website devoted to the LightSpeed, encouraging teams to ask one another for help, and holding face-to-face meetings in different locations. Although much communication took place electronically, such as through conference calls, face-to-face meetings were also important. As Bob Armstrong, who was GE's general manager for engineering at the time, indicated, "You need to get your people together in one place if you want them to really appreciate how good everyone is, and how good you are as a team."[25]

LO16-2

Describe the communication process, and explain the role of perception in communication.

sender The person or group wishing to share information.

message The information that a sender wants to share.

encoding Translating a message into understandable symbols or language.

noise Anything that hampers any stage of the communication process.

receiver The person or group for which a message is intended.

medium The pathway through which an encoded message is transmitted to a receiver.

Effective communication is necessary for managers and all members of an organization to increase efficiency, quality, responsiveness to customers, and innovation and thus gain a competitive advantage for the organization. Managers therefore must understand the communication process well if they are to perform effectively.

The Communication Process

The communication process consists of two phases. In the *transmission phase*, information is shared between two or more individuals or groups. In the *feedback phase*, a common understanding is ensured. In both phases, a number of distinct stages must occur for communication to take place (see Figure 16.1).[26]

Starting the transmission phase, the **sender**, the person or group wishing to share information with some other person or group, decides on the **message**, what information to communicate. Then the sender translates the message into symbols or language, a process called **encoding**; often messages are encoded into words. **Noise** is a general term that refers to anything that hampers any stage of the communication process.

Once encoded, a message is transmitted through a medium to the **receiver**, the person or group for which the message is intended. A **medium** is simply the pathway, such as a phone call, a letter, a memo, or face-to-face communication in a meeting, through which an encoded message is transmitted to a receiver. At the next stage, the receiver interprets

Figure 16.1

The Communication Process

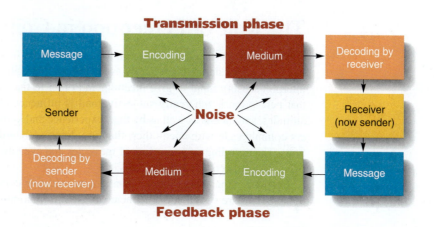

decoding Interpreting and trying to make sense of a message.

If a picture is worth a thousand words, so too is nonverbal communication; facial expressions, body language, posture, and eye contact all send powerful messages.

verbal communication
The encoding of messages into words, either written or spoken.

nonverbal communication
The encoding of messages by means of facial expressions, body language, and styles of dress.

and tries to make sense of the message, a process called **decoding**. This is a critical point in communication.

The feedback phase is initiated by the receiver (who becomes a sender). The receiver decides what message to send to the original sender (who becomes a receiver), encodes it, and transmits it through a chosen medium (see Figure 16.1). The message might contain a confirmation that the original message was received and understood or a restatement of the original message to make sure it has been correctly interpreted, or it might include a request for more information. The original sender decodes the message and makes sure a common understanding has been reached. If the original sender determines that a common understanding has not been reached, sender and receiver cycle through the whole process as many times as needed to reach a common understanding. Feedback eliminates misunderstandings, ensures that messages are correctly interpreted, and enables senders and receivers to reach a common understanding.

The encoding of messages into words, written or spoken, is **verbal communication**. We can also encode messages without using written or spoken language.

Nonverbal communication shares information by means of facial expressions (smiling, raising an eyebrow, frowning, dropping one's jaw), body language (posture, gestures, nods, and shrugs), and even style of dress (casual, formal, conservative, trendy). The trend toward increasing empowerment of the workforce has led some managers to dress informally to communicate that all employees of an organization are team members, working together to create value for customers.

Nonverbal communication can be used to back up or reinforce verbal communication. Just as a warm and genuine smile can back up words of appreciation for a job well done, a concerned facial expression can back up words of sympathy for a personal problem. In such cases, the congruence between the verbal and the nonverbal communication helps to ensure that a common understanding is reached.

Sometimes when members of an organization decide not to express a message verbally, they inadvertently do so nonverbally. People tend to have less control over nonverbal communication, and often a verbal message that is withheld gets expressed through body language or facial expressions. A manager who agrees to a proposal that she or he actually does not like may unintentionally communicate her or his disfavor by grimacing.

Sometimes nonverbal communication is used to send messages that cannot be sent through verbal channels. Many lawyers are well aware of this communication tactic. Lawyers are often schooled in techniques of nonverbal communication, such as choosing where to stand in the courtroom for maximum effect and using eye contact during different stages of a trial. Lawyers sometimes get into trouble for using inappropriate nonverbal communication in an attempt to influence juries. In a Louisiana court, prosecuting attorney Thomas Pirtle was admonished and fined $2,500 by Judge Yada Magee for shaking his head in an expression of doubt, waving his arms indicating disfavor, and chuckling when the attorneys for the defense were stating their case.[27]

The Role of Perception in Communication

Perception plays a central role in communication and affects both transmission and feedback. In Chapter 5 we defined *perception* as the process through which people select, organize, and interpret sensory input to give meaning and order to the world around them. We mentioned that perception is inherently subjective and is influenced by people's personalities, values, attitudes, and moods as well as by their experience and knowledge. When senders and receivers communicate with each other, they are doing so based on their own subjective perceptions. The encoding and decoding of messages and even the choice of a medium hinge on the perceptions of senders and receivers.

In addition, perceptual biases can hamper effective communication. Recall from Chapter 5 that *biases* are systematic tendencies to use information about others in ways that result in inaccurate perceptions. In Chapter 5 we described a number of biases that can cause unfair treatment of diverse members of an organization. The same biases also can lead to ineffective communication. For example, *stereotypes*—simplified and often inaccurate beliefs about the characteristics of particular groups of people—can interfere with the encoding and decoding of messages.

Suppose a manager stereotypes older workers as being fearful of change. When this manager encodes a message to an older worker about an upcoming change in the organization, she may downplay the extent of the change so as not to make the older worker feel stressed. The older worker, however, fears change no more than do his younger colleagues and thus decodes the message to mean that only a minor change is going to be made. The older worker fails to adequately prepare for the change, and his performance subsequently suffers because of his lack of preparation for the change. Clearly this ineffective communication was due to the manager's inaccurate assumptions about older workers. Instead of relying on stereotypes, effective managers strive to perceive other people accurately by focusing on their actual behaviors, knowledge, skills, and abilities. Accurate perceptions, in turn, contribute to effective communication.

The Dangers of Ineffective Communication

Because managers must communicate with others to perform their various roles and tasks, managers spend most of their time communicating, whether in meetings, in telephone conversations, through email, or in face-to-face interactions. Indeed, some experts estimate that managers spend approximately 85 percent of their time engaged in some form of communication.[28]

Effective communication is so important that managers cannot just be concerned that they themselves are effective communicators; they also have to help their subordinates be effective communicators. When all members of an organization can communicate effectively with one another and with people outside the organization, the organization is much more likely to perform highly and gain a competitive advantage.

When managers and other members of an organization are ineffective communicators, organizational performance suffers and any competitive advantage the organization might have is likely to be lost. Moreover, poor communication sometimes can be downright dangerous and even lead to tragic and unnecessary loss of human life. For example, researchers from Harvard University studied the causes of mistakes, such as a patient receiving the wrong medication, in two large hospitals in the Boston area. They discovered that some mistakes in hospitals occur because of communication problems—physicians not having the information they need to correctly order medications for their patients or nurses not having the information they need to correctly administer medications. The researchers concluded that some of the responsibility for these mistakes lies with hospital management, which has not taken active steps to improve communication.[29]

Communication problems in airplane cockpits and between flying crews and air traffic controllers are unfortunately all too common, sometimes with deadly consequences. In the late 1970s two jets collided in Tenerife (one of the Canary Islands) because of miscommunication between a pilot and the control tower, and 600 people were killed. The tower radioed to the pilot, "Clipper 1736 report clear of runway." The pilot mistakenly interpreted this message to mean that he was cleared for takeoff.[30] Unfortunately communication problems persist in the airline industry. In 2009 a Northwest Airlines Airbus A320 flew 150 miles past its Minneapolis destination while the crew of the airplane was out of contact with air traffic controllers for over an hour.[31] A safety group at NASA tracked more than 6,000 unsafe flying incidents and found that communication difficulties caused approximately 529 of them.[32] And NASA has its own communication difficulties.[33] In 2004 NASA released a report detailing communication problems at the International Space Station jointly managed and staffed by NASA and the Russian space agency; the problems included inadequate record keeping, missing information, and failure to keep data current.[34]

Information Richness and Communication Media

information richness The amount of information that a communication medium can carry and the extent to which the medium enables the sender and receiver to reach a common understanding.

To be effective communicators, managers (and other members of an organization) need to select an appropriate communication medium for each message they send. Should a change in procedures be communicated to subordinates in a memo sent through email? Should a congratulatory message about a major accomplishment be communicated in a letter, in a phone call, or over lunch? Should a layoff announcement be made in a memo or at a plant meeting? Should the members of a purchasing team travel to Europe to cement a major agreement with a new supplier, or should they do so through conference calls and email messages? Managers deal with these questions day in and day out.

There is no one best communication medium for managers to rely on. In choosing a communication medium for any message, managers need to consider three factors. The first and most important is the level of information richness that is needed. **Information richness** is the amount of information a communication medium can carry and the extent to which the medium enables the sender and receiver to reach a common understanding.[35] The communication media that managers use vary in their information richness (see Figure 16.2).[36] Media high in information richness can carry an extensive amount of information and generally enable receivers and senders to come to a common understanding.

The second factor that managers need to take into account in selecting a communication medium is the *time* needed for communication because managers' and other organizational members' time is valuable. Managers at United Parcel Service, for example, dramatically reduced the amount of time they spent on communicating by using videoconferences instead of face-to-face communication, which required that managers travel overseas.[37]

The third factor that affects the choice of a communication medium is the *need for a paper or electronic trail* or some kind of written documentation that a message was sent and received. A manager may wish to document in writing, for example, that a subordinate was given a formal warning about excessive lateness.

In the remainder of this section we examine four types of communication media that vary along these three dimensions (information richness, time, and paper or electronic trail).[38]

Face-to-Face Communication

Face-to-face communication is the medium that is highest in information richness. When managers communicate face-to-face, they not only can take advantage of verbal communication but also can interpret each other's nonverbal signals such as facial expressions and body

Figure 16.2

The Information Richness of Communication Media

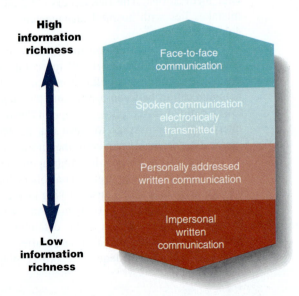

High information richness

Low information richness

Face-to-face communication

Spoken communication electronically transmitted

Personally addressed written communication

Impersonal written communication

language. A look of concern or puzzlement can sometimes say more than a thousand words, and managers can respond to such nonverbal signals on the spot. Face-to-face communication also enables managers to receive instant feedback. Points of confusion, ambiguity, or misunderstanding can be resolved, and managers can cycle through the communication process as many times as needed to reach a common understanding.

With the growing proliferation of electronic forms of communication, such as email, some managers fear that face-to-face communication is being shortchanged to the detriment of building common understandings and rapport.[39] Moreover, some messages that really should be communicated face-to-face or at least in a phone conversation, and messages that are more efficiently communicated in this manner, are nonetheless sent electronically.[40] As indicated in the accompanying "Management Insight" feature, managers need to carefully consider whether face-to-face communication is being shortchanged in their organizations and, if it is, take steps to rectify the situation.

Management Insight

Knowing When Face-to-Face Communication Is Called For

Anyone who has participated in one of those frustrating email exchanges where messages shoot back and forth and it seems to take forever to resolve a problem or reach a common understanding knows there must be a better way. In such cases a face-to-face conversation (or if that is not possible, a phone conversation) often will lead to better outcomes all around.

"No Email Friday" bolsters in-person conversations and strengthens employee ties.

According to Ron McMillan, a consultant to managers at all ranks and coauthor of best-selling books on communication, email should not be relied on to communicate information that is complex, important, or sensitive.[41] In such cases face-to-face communication (or even a phone conversation) can convey more information than email can, and it is much more effective at generating a common understanding. Research conducted by Albert Mehrabian, professor emeritus of psychology at UCLA, suggests that more meaning is conveyed by nonverbal communication from facial expressions and body language and from tone of voice and vocal inflection than is conveyed by the actual words that are used when communicating.[42] And of course nonverbal communication, tone of voice, and vocal inflection are all missing when email is used. JoAnne Yates, a professor at the Sloan School of Management at MIT, suggests that email is best for simple information that will be readily understood.[43]

Sara Roberts, founder and chief executive officer of Roberts Golden Consulting in San Francisco, recognizes the value of face-to-face communication.[44] Although consultants in her firm regularly communicate with each other, clients, and suppliers via email and this is often efficient and effective, Roberts believes rapport and collaboration can suffer when email is used extensively. So she instituted "No Email Fridays" at her firm. On Fridays employees are not to use email unless it is clearly necessary (such as to reply to a client who wants an urgent email response).[45] As Roberts put it, "No Email Friday helps us to remember we really could go over to that person sitting right over there and collaborate more."[46] In fact a growing number of organizations are experimenting with "no email Fridays" to encourage more face-to-face communication and phone conversations.[47]

Allowing opportunities for face-to-face communication can be especially important when trying to effectively communicate with employees located in other countries. For example, Greg Caltabiano, CEO of Teknovus Inc., which is based in Petaluma, California, and has offices in Asia, arranges for U.S. employees to go to Asia and Asian employees to come to the United States to engage in face-to-face communication to build mutual understanding.[48]

management by wandering around is a face-to-face communication technique that is effective for many managers at all levels in an organization.[49] Rather than scheduling formal meetings with subordinates, managers walk around work areas and talk informally with employees about issues and concerns that both employees and managers may have. These informal conversations give managers and subordinates important information and at the same time foster the development of positive relationships. William Hewlett and David Packard, founders and former top managers of Hewlett-Packard, found management by wandering around to be a highly effective way of communicating with their employees.

Because face-to-face communication is highest in information richness, you might think it should always be the medium of choice for managers. This is not the case, however, because of the amount of time it can take and the lack of a paper or electronic trail resulting from it. For messages that are important, personal, or likely to be misunderstood, it is often well worth managers' time to use face-to-face communication and, if need be, supplement it with some form of written communication documenting the message.

Advances in information technology are giving managers new communication media that are close substitutes for face-to-face communication. Many organizations, such as American Greetings Corp. and Hewlett-Packard, are using *videoconferences* to capture some of the advantages of face-to-face communication (such as access to facial expressions) while saving time and money because managers in different locations do not have to travel to meet with one another. During a videoconference, managers in two or more locations communicate with each other over large TV or video screens; they not only hear each other but also see each other throughout the meeting.

In addition to saving travel costs, videoconferences sometimes have other advantages. Managers at American Greetings have found that decisions get made more quickly when videoconferences are used because more managers can be involved in the decision-making process and therefore fewer managers have to be consulted outside the meeting itself. Managers at Hewlett-Packard have found that videoconferences have shortened new product development time by 30 percent for similar reasons. Videoconferences also seem to lead to more efficient meetings. Some managers have found that their meetings are 20–30 percent shorter when videoconferences are used instead of face-to-face meetings.[50]

Taking videoconferences a leap forward, Cisco Systems has developed its TelePresence line of products, enabling individuals and teams in different locations to communicate live and in real time over the Internet with high-definition life-size video and excellent audio that make it feel like all participants, no matter where they are, are in the same room.[51] One morning Cisco CEO John Chambers was able to participate in meetings with employees and teams in India, Japan, Cleveland, and London in less than four hours by using TelePresence.[52] Other companies, such as HP, have developed similar products. What distinguishes these products from older videoconferencing systems is the lack of transmission delay and the sharp, clear, life-size video quality.[53]

Spoken Communication Electronically Transmitted

After face-to-face communication, spoken communication electronically transmitted over phone lines (and the World Wide Web and the Internet) is second highest in information richness (see Figure 16.2). Although managers communicating over the telephone do not have access to body language and facial expressions, they do have access to the tone of voice in which a message is delivered, the parts of the message the sender emphasizes, and the general manner in which the message is spoken, in addition to the actual words themselves. Thus telephone conversations can convey extensive amounts of information. Managers can ensure that mutual understanding is reached because they can get quick feedback over the phone and answer questions. When Greg Caltabiano, CEO of Teknovus Inc., wanted to improve

---

management by wandering around A face-to-face communication technique in which a manager walks around a work area and talks informally with employees about issues and concerns.

communication between engineers in California who design semiconductors for fiber optic networks and employees and customers in Asia, he encouraged the engineers to communicate via the telephone instead of by email.[54]

Skype enables people to communicate using voice and video over the Internet.[55] Thus Skype enables access to nonverbal forms of communication, and video conferences and interviews can be conducted over the Internet with Skype. For example, some business schools who interview top applicants for their PhD programs require an in-person interview prior to making admission decisions. Given the high costs of airline tickets for top overseas candidates, some schools arrange for interviews with these applicants to be conducted via Skype.

Voice mail systems and answering machines also allow managers to send and receive verbal electronic messages over telephone lines. Voice mail systems are companywide systems that let senders record messages for members of an organization who are away from their desks and allow receivers to access their messages even when hundreds of miles away from the office. Such systems are obviously a necessity when managers are frequently out of the office, and managers on the road are well advised to periodically check their voice mail.

Personally Addressed Written Communication

Lower in information richness than electronically transmitted verbal communication is personally addressed written communication (see Figure 16.2). One advantage of face-to-face communication and electronically transmitted verbal communication is that they both tend to demand attention, which helps ensure that receivers pay attention. Personally addressed written communications, such as memos and letters, also have this advantage. Because they are addressed to a particular person, the chances are good that the person will actually pay attention to (and read) them. Moreover, the sender can write the message in a way that the receiver is most likely to understand. Like voice mail, written communication does not enable a receiver to have his or her questions answered immediately; but when messages are clearly written and feedback is provided, common understandings can still be reached.

Even if managers use face-to-face communication, sending a follow-up in writing is often necessary for messages that are important or complicated and need to be referred to later on. This is precisely what Karen Stracker, a hospital administrator, did when she needed to tell one of her subordinates about an important change in how the hospital would be handling denials of insurance benefits. Stracker met with the subordinate and described the changes face-to-face. Once she was sure the subordinate understood them, she handed her a sheet of instructions to follow, which essentially summarized the information they had discussed.

Email and text messages also fit into this category of communication media because senders and receivers are communicating through personally addressed written words. The words, however, appear on their computer screens or smartphones rather than on paper. Email is so widespread in the business world that some managers find they have to deliberately take time out from managing their email to get their work done, think about pressing concerns, and come up with new and innovative ideas.[56] According to the Radacati Group, an independent market research firm, the average email account in corporations today receives about 18 megabytes of email and attachments per workday; the volume of email is expected to increase over time.[57] To help their employees effectively manage email, a growing number of organizations are instituting training programs to help employees learn how to more effectively use email by sending clearer messages, avoiding email copies to multiple parties who do not really need to see it, and writing clear and informative subject lines.[58] For example, Capital One trains employees to (1) write clear subject lines so recipients know why they are receiving a message and can easily search for it and retrieve it later, and (2) convey information clearly and effectively in the email body.[59]

Ultimately, for messages that are sensitive or potentially misunderstood, or that require the give-and-take of a face-to-face or telephone conversation, relying on email can take considerably more time to reach a common understanding.[60] Additionally, given the lack of nonverbal cues, tone of voice, and intonation in email, senders need to be aware of the potential for misunderstandings.[61] Based on her research, Kristin Byron, a professor of management at Syracuse University, suggests that recipients may have a tendency to perceive some of the email they receive as more negative than the senders intended.[62] Senders who are rushed, for example, may send short, curt messages lacking greeting and closing lines because they are so busy.[63] Recipients, however, might read something more negative into messages like these.[64]

The growing popularity of email has also enabled many workers and managers to become *telecommuters*—people who are employed by organizations and work out of offices in their own homes. It is estimated that there are around 30 million telecommuters in the United States.[65] Many telecommuters indicate that the flexibility of working at home lets them be more productive and, at the same time, be closer to their families and not waste time traveling to and from the office.[66] In a study conducted by Georgetown University, 75 percent of the telecommuters surveyed said their productivity increased, and 83 percent said their home life improved once they started telecommuting.[67]

Unfortunately the widespread use of email has been accompanied by growing abuse of email. There have been cases of employees sexually harassing coworkers through email, sending pornographic content via email, and sending messages that disparage certain employees or groups.[68] To counter disparaging remarks making their way to employees' in-boxes (and being copied to coworkers), Mark Stevens, CEO of MSCO, a 40-person marketing firm in Purchase, New York, instituted a policy that forbade employees from using email or Blackberries to communicate messages that criticized someone else.[69]

Managers need to develop a clear, written policy specifying what company email can and should be used for and what is out of bounds. Managers also should clearly communicate this policy to all members of the organization, as well as tell them what procedures will be used when email abuse is suspected and what consequences will result if the abuse is confirmed. According to a survey conducted by the ePolicy Institute, of the 79 percent of companies that have an email policy, only about 54 percent actually give employees training and education to ensure that they understand it.[70] Training and education are important to ensure that employees know not only what the policy is but also what it means for their own email use.

Additionally, email policies should specify how much personal email is appropriate and when the bounds of appropriateness have been overstepped. Just as employees make personal phone calls while on the job (and sometimes have to), so too do they send and receive personal email. In fact, according to Waterford Technologies, a provider of email management and archive services based in Irvine, California, about one-third of email to and from companies is personal or not work-related.[71] Clearly, banning all personal email is impractical and likely to have negative consequences for employees and their organizations (such as lower levels of job satisfaction and increased personal phone conversations). Some companies limit personal email to certain times of the day or a certain amount of time per day; others have employees create lists of contacts from whom they want to receive email at work (family members, children, baby-sitters); still others want personal email to be sent and received through web-based systems like Gmail and Hotmail rather than the corporate email system.[72]

According to the American Management Association, while the majority of organizations have a written policy about email use, some do not have written guidelines for instant messaging.[73] *Instant messaging* allows people who are online and linked through a buddy or contact list to send instant messages back and forth through a small window on their computer screens without having to go through the steps of sending and receiving email.[74]

What about surfing the Internet on company time? According to a study conducted by Websense, approximately half of the employees surveyed indicated that they surfed the web at work, averaging about two hours per week.[75] Most visited news and travel sites, but about 22 percent of the male respondents and 12 percent of the female respondents indicated that they visited pornographic websites.[76] Of all those surveyed, 56 percent said they sent personal email at work. The majority of those surveyed felt that sending personal email and surfing the web had no effect on their performance, and 27 percent thought that doing so improved their productivity.[77] Other statistics suggest that while overall there is more Internet use at home than at work, individuals who use the Internet at work spend more time on it and visit more sites than do those who use it at home.[78] As indicated in the accompanying "Ethics in Action" feature, personal email and Internet surfing at work present managers with some challenging ethical dilemmas.

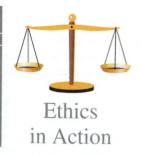

Ethics in Action

Monitoring Email and Internet Use

A growing number of companies provide managers and organizations with tools to track the websites their employees visit and the email and instant messages they send.[79] For example, network forensic software enables managers to record and replay everything that takes place on employees' computer monitors and can also track keystrokes.[80] Currently a majority of large corporations in the United States monitor their employees' email and Internet usage; the percentage is higher among organizations in certain industries.[81] Most of the organizations that monitor email tell their employees about the monitoring.[82] However, the means by which they let employees know are not necessarily effective. For example, putting information about email monitoring in an employee handbook might be ineffective if most employees do not read the handbook.[83]

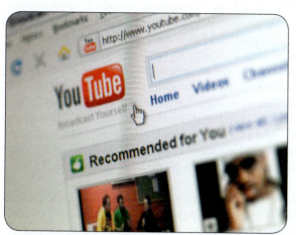

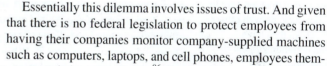

Intrusive monitoring policies may have unintended negative consequences in organizations.

Monitoring employees raises concerns about privacy.[84] Most employees would not like to have their bosses listening to their phone conversations; similarly, some believe that monitoring email and tracking Internet use are an invasion of privacy.[85] Given the increasingly long working hours of many employees, should personal email and Internet use be closely scrutinized? Clearly, when illegal and unethical email use is suspected, such as sexually harassing coworkers or divulging confidential company information, monitoring may be called for. But should it be a normal part of organizational life, even when there are no indications of a real problem?

Essentially this dilemma involves issues of trust. And given that there is no federal legislation to protect employees from having their companies monitor company-supplied machines such as computers, laptops, and cell phones, employees themselves can take steps to protect their own privacy.[86] Lewis Maltby, founder of the National Workrights Institute, which is devoted to safeguarding privacy at work, suggests that when sending sensitive or personal information, employees can use their own equipment (e.g., private cell phone or laptop) and an outside Wi-Fi provider so that their employing organization cannot access the information.[87] Employees also need to be careful about what email messages they send and avoid sending private and sensitive email on workplace systems. Once email messages are sent, they live on in the recipients' computers and systems and can potentially come back to haunt senders or be subpoenaed in a court of law.[88]

Impersonal Written Communication

Impersonal written communication is lowest in information richness but is well suited for messages that need to reach many receivers. Because such messages are not addressed to particular receivers, feedback is unlikely, so managers must make sure messages sent by this medium are written clearly in language that all receivers will understand.

Managers often find company newsletters useful vehicles for reaching large numbers of employees. Many managers give their newsletters catchy names to spark employee interest and also to inject a bit of humor into the workplace.[89] Increasing numbers of companies are distributing their newsletters online. For example, IBM's employee newsletter w3 is distributed to employees online and is updated daily.[90]

Managers can use impersonal written communication for various messages, including announcements of rules, regulations, policies, newsworthy information, changes in procedures, and the arrival of new organizational members. Impersonal written communication also can convey instructions about how to use machinery or how to process work orders or customer requests. For these kinds of messages, the paper or electronic trail left by this communication medium can be valuable for employees.

Just as with personal written communication, impersonal written communication can be delivered and retrieved electronically, and this is increasingly the case in companies large and small. Unfortunately the ease with which electronic messages can spread has led to their proliferation. Many managers' and workers' electronic in-boxes are so backlogged that often they do not have time to read all the electronic work-related information available to them. The problem with such **information overload** is the potential for important information to be ignored or overlooked (even that which is personally addressed) while tangential information receives attention. Moreover, information overload can result in thousands of hours and millions of dollars in lost productivity.

Some managers and organizations use blogs to communicate with employees, investors, customers, and the general public.[91] A **blog** is a website on which an individual, group, or organization posts information, commentary, and opinions and to which readers can often respond with their own commentary and opinions.[92] Some top managers write their own blogs, and some companies such as Cisco Systems and Oracle have corporate blogs.[93] Just as organizations have rules and guidelines about employee email and Internet use, a growing number of organizations are instituting employee guidelines for blogs.[94] At IBM over 25,000 employees have blogs on IBM's internal computer network.[95] Guidelines for the use of blogs include following IBM's code of conduct (especially with regard to confidentiality, respect, and privacy), refraining from criticizing competitors, and refraining from mentioning customers' names without obtaining prior permission; bloggers must also reveal their own identity on their blogs (anonymous blogs are not permitted).[96]

A **social networking site** such as Facebook or Twitter is a website that enables people to communicate with others with whom they might have some common interest or connection. Participants in these sites create customized profiles and communicate with networks of other participants.[97] Millions of people in the United States and other countries communicate via social networking sites.[98] While communication through social networking sites can be work-related, some managers are concerned that their employees are wasting valuable time at work communicating with their friends through these sites. According to a recent study sponsored by Robert Half Technology, over 50 percent of the U.S. companies included in the study prohibit employees from accessing social networking sites such as Twitter, MySpace, LinkedIn, and Facebook while at work.[99] Around 19 percent of the companies permit communicating through social networking sites for work-related reasons, and 16 percent permit some personal communication through these sites. Just 10 percent of the companies surveyed permit full use of social networking sites while on the job.[100]

information overload The potential for important information to be ignored or overlooked while tangential information receives attention.

blog A website on which an individual, group, or organization posts information, commentary, and opinions and to which readers can often respond with their own commentary and opinions.

social networking site A website that enables people to communicate with others with whom they have some common interest or connection.

LO16-4
Describe the communication networks that exist in groups and teams.

Communication Networks

Although various communication media are used, communication in organizations tends to flow in certain patterns. The pathways along which information flows in groups and teams and throughout an organization are called **communication networks**. The type of communication network that exists in a group depends on the nature of the group's tasks and the extent to which group members need to communicate with one another to achieve group goals.

communication networks The pathways along which information flows in groups and teams and throughout the organization.

Communication Networks in Groups and Teams

As you learned in Chapter 15, groups and teams, whether they are cross-functional teams, top management teams, command groups, self-managed work teams, or task forces, are the building blocks of organizations. Four kinds of communication networks can develop in groups and teams: the wheel, the chain, the circle, and the all-channel network (see Figure 16.3).

Figure 16.3

Communication Networks in Groups and Teams

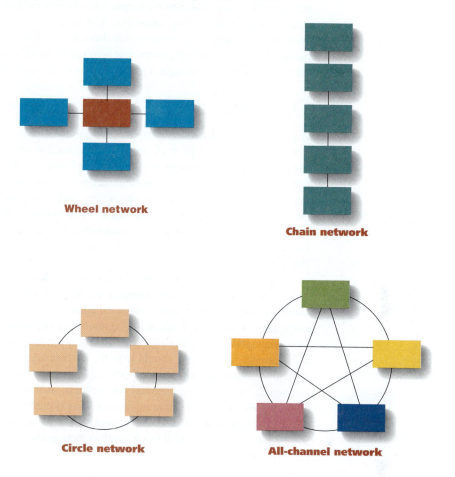

Wheel network

Chain network

Circle network

All-channel network

WHEEL NETWORK   In a wheel network, information flows to and from one central member of the group. Other group members do not need to communicate with one another to perform at a high level, so the group can accomplish its goals by directing all communication to and from the central member. Wheel networks are often found in command groups with pooled task interdependence. Picture a group of taxi drivers who report to the same dispatcher, who is also their supervisor. Each driver needs to communicate with the dispatcher, but the drivers do not need to communicate with one another. In groups such as this, the wheel network results in efficient communication, saving time without compromising performance. Although found in groups, wheel networks are not found in teams because they do not allow the intense interactions characteristic of teamwork.

CHAIN NETWORK   In a chain network, members communicate with one another in a predetermined sequence. Chain networks are found in groups with sequential task interdependence, such as in assembly-line groups. When group work has to be performed in a predetermined order, the chain network is often found because group members need to communicate with those whose work directly precedes and follows their own. Like wheel networks, chain networks tend not to exist in teams because of the limited amount of interaction among group members.

CIRCLE NETWORK   In a circle network, group members communicate with others who are similar to them in experiences, beliefs, areas of expertise, background, office location, or even where they sit when the group meets. Members of task forces and standing committees, for example, tend to communicate with others who have similar experiences or backgrounds. People also tend to communicate with people whose offices are next to their own. Like wheel and chain networks, circle networks are most often found in groups that are not teams.

ALL-CHANNEL NETWORK   An all-channel network is found in teams. It is characterized by high levels of communication: every team member communicates with every other team member. Top management teams, cross-functional teams, and self-managed work teams frequently have all-channel networks. The reciprocal task interdependence often found in such teams requires that information flows in all directions. Computer software specially designed for use by work groups can help maintain effective communication in teams with all-channel networks because it gives team members an efficient way to share information.

Organizational Communication Networks

An organization chart may seem to be a good summary of an organization's communication network, but often it is not. An organization chart summarizes the *formal* reporting relationships in an organization and the formal pathways along which communication takes place. Often, however, communication is *informal* and flows around issues, goals, projects, and ideas instead of moving up and down the organizational hierarchy in an orderly fashion. Thus an organization's communication network includes not only the formal communication pathways summarized in an organization chart but also informal communication pathways along which a great deal of communication takes place (see Figure 16.4).

Communication can and should occur across departments and groups as well as within them and up and down and sideways in the corporate hierarchy. Communication up and down the corporate hierarchy is often called *vertical* communication. Communication among employees at the same level in the hierarchy, or sideways, is called *horizontal* communication. Managers obviously cannot determine in advance what an organization's communication network will be, nor should they try to. Instead, to accomplish goals and perform at a high level, organizational members should be free to communicate with whomever they need to contact. Because organizational goals change over time, so do organizational communication networks. Informal communication networks can contribute to an organization's competitive advantage because they help ensure that organizational members have the information they need when they need it to accomplish their goals.

Figure 16.4

Formal and Informal Communication Networks in an Organization

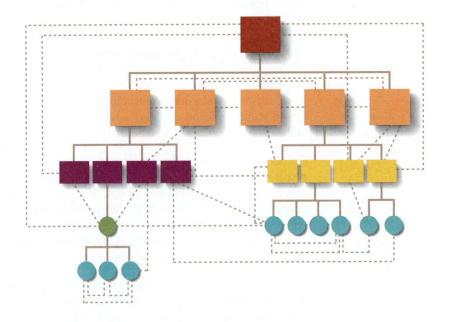

——— Formal pathways of communication summarized in an organization chart.

----- Informal pathways along which a great deal of communication takes place.

grapevine An informal communication network along which unofficial information flows.

The **grapevine** is an informal organizational communication network along which unofficial information flows quickly, if not always accurately.[101] People in an organization who seem to know everything about everyone are prominent in the grapevine. Information spread over the grapevine can be about issues of either a business nature (an impending takeover) or a personal nature (the CEO's separation from his wife).

External Networks

In addition to participating in networks within an organization, managers, professional employees, and those with work-related ties outside their employing organization often are part of external networks whose members span a variety of companies. For example, scientists working in universities and in corporations often communicate in networks formed around common underlying interests in a particular topic or subfield. As another example, physicians working throughout the country belong to specialty professional associations that help them keep up-to-date on the latest advances in their fields. For some managers and professionals, participation in such interest-oriented networks is as important as, or even more important than, participation in internal company networks. Networks of contacts who are working in the same discipline or field or who have similar expertise and knowledge can be very helpful, for example, when an individual wants to change jobs or find a job after a layoff. Unfortunately, as a result of discrimination and stereotypes, some of these networks are off-limits to certain individuals due to gender or race. For example, the term *old boys' network* alludes to the fact that networks of contacts for job leads, government contracts, or venture capital funding have sometimes been dominated by men and less welcoming of women.[102]

Information Technology and Communication

Advances in information technology have dramatically increased managers' abilities to communicate with others as well as to quickly access information to make decisions. Advances that are having major impacts on managerial communication include the Internet, intranets, groupware, and collaboration software. However, managers must not forget that communication is essentially a human endeavor, no matter how much it may be facilitated by information technology.

LO16-5

Explain how advances in technology have given managers new options for managing communication.

Internet A global system of computer networks.

The Internet

The **Internet** is a global system of computer networks that is easy to join and is used by employees of organizations around the world to communicate inside and outside their companies. Over 245 million people in the United States alone use the Internet, and Internet use has dramatically increased around the world.[103] Table 16.1 lists the 20 countries with the most Internet users.[104]

On the Internet, the World Wide Web is the "business district" with multimedia capabilities. Companies' home pages on the web are like offices that potential customers can visit. In attractive graphic displays on home pages, managers communicate information about the goods and services they offer, why customers should want to purchase them, how to purchase them, and where to purchase them. By surfing the web and visiting competitors' home pages, managers can see what their competitors are doing.[105] Each day hundreds of new companies add themselves to the growing number of organizations on the World Wide Web.[106] According to one study, the six "web-savviest" nations (taking into account use of broadband connections) in descending order are Denmark, Great Britain, Sweden, Norway, Finland, and the United States.[107] By all counts, use of the Internet for communication is burgeoning.

Intranets

Growing numbers of managers are finding that the technology on which the World Wide Web and the Internet are based has enabled them to improve communication within their own companies. These managers use this technology to share information within their own companies

Table 16.1
Top 20 Countries in Internet Usage as of June 30, 2012

Country	Internet Users
China	538,000,000
United States	245,203,319
India	137,000,000
Japan	101,228,736
Brazil	88,494,756
Russia	67,982,547
Germany	67,483,860
Indonesia	55,000,000
United Kingdom	52,731,209
France	52,228,905
Nigeria	48,366,179
Mexico	42,000,000
Iran	42,000,000
Korea	40,329,660
Turkey	36,455,000
Italy	35,800,000
Philippines	33,600,000
Spain	31,606,233
Vietnam	31,034,900
Egypt	29,809,724

Source: "Top 20 Countries with the Highest Number of Internet Users," *Internet World Stats Usage and Population Statistics*, www.internetworldstats.com/top20.htm, June 2, 2014. Used by permission.

intranet A company-wide system of computer networks.

through company networks called **intranets**. Intranets are being used at many companies including Chevron, Goodyear, Levi Strauss, IBM, Pfizer, Chrysler, Motorola, and Ford.[108]

Intranets allow employees to have many kinds of information at their fingertips. Directories, manuals, inventory figures, product specifications, information about customers, biographies of top managers and the board of directors, global sales figures, meeting minutes, annual reports, delivery schedules, and up-to-the-minute revenue, cost, and profit figures are just a few examples of the information that can be shared through intranets. Intranets can be accessed with different kinds of computers so that all members of an organization can be linked together. Intranets are protected from unwanted intrusions, by hackers or by competitors, by firewall security systems that ask users to provide passwords and other identification before they are allowed access.[109]

The advantage of intranets lies in their versatility as a communication medium. They can be used for a number of different purposes by people who may have little expertise in computer software and programming. While some managers complain that the Internet is too crowded and the World Wide Web too glitzy, informed managers are realizing that using the Internet's technology to create their own computer networks may be one of the Internet's biggest contributions to organizational effectiveness.

Groupware and Collaboration Software

groupware Computer software that enables members of groups and teams to share information with one another.

Groupware is computer software that enables members of groups and teams to share information with one another to improve their communication and performance. In some organizations, such as the Bank of Montreal, managers have had success in introducing groupware into the organization; in other organizations, such as the advertising agency Young & Rubicam, managers have encountered considerable resistance to groupware.[110] Even in companies where the introduction of groupware has been successful, some employees resist using it. Some clerical and secretarial workers at the Bank of Montreal, for example, were dismayed to find that their neat and accurate files were being consolidated into computer files that would be accessible to many of their coworkers.

Managers are most likely to be able to successfully use groupware as a communication medium in their organizations when certain conditions are met:[111]

1. The work is group- or team-based, and members are rewarded, at least in part, for group performance.
2. Groupware has the full support of top management.
3. The culture of the organization stresses flexibility and knowledge sharing, and the organization does not have a rigid hierarchy of authority.
4. Groupware is used for a specific purpose and is viewed as a tool that enables group or team members to work more effectively together, not as a personal source of power or advantage.
5. Employees receive adequate training in the use of computers and groupware.[112]

Employees are likely to resist using groupware and managers are likely to have a difficult time implementing it when people are working primarily on their own and are rewarded for individual performance.[113] Under these circumstances, information is often viewed as a source of power, and people are reluctant to share information with others by means of groupware.

Consider three salespeople who sell insurance policies in the same geographic area; each is paid based on the number of policies he or she sells and on his or her retention of customers. Their supervisor invested in groupware and encouraged them to use it to share information about their sales, sales tactics, customers, insurance providers, and claim histories. The supervisor told the salespeople that having all this information at their fingertips would allow them to be more efficient as well as sell more policies and provide better service to customers.

Even though they received extensive training in how to use the groupware, the salespeople never got around to using it. Why? They all were afraid that giving away their secrets to their coworkers might reduce their own commissions. In this situation, the salespeople were essentially competing with one another and thus had no incentive to share information. Under such circumstances, a groupware system may not be a wise choice of communication medium. Conversely, had the salespeople been working as a team and had they received bonuses based on team performance, groupware might have been an effective communication medium.

For an organization to gain a competitive advantage, managers need to keep up-to-date on advances in information technology such as groupware. But managers should not adopt these or other advances without first considering carefully how the advance in question might improve communication and performance in their particular groups, teams, or whole organization. Moreover, managers need to keep in mind that all of these advances in IT are tools for people to use to facilitate effective communication; they are not replacements for face-to-face communication.

collaboration software Groupware that promotes and facilitates collaborative, highly interdependent interactions and provides an electronic meeting site for communication among team members.

Collaboration software is groupware that aims to promote collaborative, highly interdependent interactions among members of a team and to provide the team with an electronic meeting site for communication.[114] Collaboration software gives members of a team an online work site where they can post, share, and save data, reports, sketches, and other documents; keep calendars; have team-based online conferences; and send and receive messages. The software can also keep and update progress reports, survey team members about different issues, forward documents to managers, and let users know which of their team members are also online and at the site.[115] Having an integrated online work area can help organize and centralize the work of a team, help ensure that information is readily available as needed, and also help team members make sure important information is not overlooked. Collaboration software can be much more efficient than email or instant messaging for managing ongoing team collaboration and interaction that is not face-to-face. Moreover, when a team does meet face-to-face, all documents the team might need in the meeting are just a click away.[116]

For work that is truly team-based, entails a number of highly interdependent yet distinct components, and involves team members with distinct areas of expertise who need to closely coordinate their efforts, collaboration software can be a powerful communication tool. The

New York–based public relations company Ketchum Inc. uses collaboration software for some of its projects. For example, Ketchum managed public relations, marketing, and advertising for a charitable program of Fireman's Fund Insurance Co. By using the eRoom software provided by Documentum (a part of EMC Corporation), Ketchum employees working on the project at six different locations, employee representatives from Fireman's, and a graphics company that was designing a website for the program were able to share plans, documents, graphic designs, and calendars at an online work site.[117] Members of the Ketchum–Fireman team got email alerts when something had been modified or added to the site. As Ketchum's chief information officer Andy Roach put it, "The fact that everyone has access to the same document means Ketchum isn't going to waste time on the logistics and can focus on the creative side."[118]

Another company taking advantage of collaboration software is Honeywell International Inc. Managers at Honeywell decided to use the SharePoint collaboration software provided by Microsoft, in part because it can be integrated with other Microsoft software such as Outlook.[119] For example, if a team using SharePoint makes a change to the team's calendar, that change will be automatically made in team members' Outlook calendars.[120] Clearly, collaboration software has the potential to enhance communication efficiency and effectiveness in teams.

Wikis, a result of the open-source software movement, are a free or very low-cost form of collaboration software that a growing number of organizations are using. Wikis enable the organizations not only to promote collaboration and better communication but also to cut back on the use of email,[121] as indicated in the accompanying "Information Technology Byte" feature.

Information Technology Byte

Collaborating with Wikis

According to Websense, a company that provides World Wide Web, email, and other communications security solutions in San Diego, California, approximately 20 percent of all email sent and received is legitimate.[122] And while many organizations have invested in filtering software to keep spam from flooding employees' in-boxes, according to Websense, 76 percent of messages that make their way into employees' in-boxes are spam.[123] Darren Lennard, a managing director at Dresdner Kleinwort Wasserstein, an investment bank in London, was receiving approximately 250 email messages a day, of which only 15 percent were relevant to his job. Every day Lennard's first and last activities were to clear out his in-box on his BlackBerry—until frustration got the better of him, after a long and grueling workday, and he smashed his BlackBerry on the kitchen countertop in his home.[124]

In particular, wikis (in Hawaiian, the word *wiki* means "fast"), which are relatively easy to use and low-cost or free, are becoming increasingly popular as collaborative communication tools.[125] A wiki uses server software to enable users to create and revise web pages quickly on a company intranet or through a hosted Internet site. Users who are authorized to access a wiki can log onto it and edit and update data, as well as see what other authorized users have contributed. Wikis enable collaboration in real time, and they keep a history so that users can see what changes were made, for example, to a spreadsheet or a proposal.[126] Some web-based collaboration software providers, such as Basecamp, provide customers with wikis as part of their services.[127]

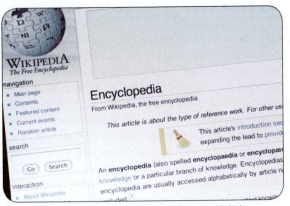

Wikis allow a wide range of people from multiple locations to contribute their specific skills and knowledge to the same task, resulting in a truly collaborative process.

Soar Technology Inc., an artificial intelligence company in Ann Arbor, Michigan, that does work for the U.S. Office of Naval Research, has found that relying on wikis for collaboration has reduced the time it takes to complete projects by 50 percent.[128] According to Jacob Crossman, an engineer at Soar, wikis save time because they do away with the need for multiple email messages with attachments and eliminate the typical confusion that surrounds multiple iterations of the same document.[129] Lennard created a wiki to figure out how to increase profits on a certain kind of trade. In the past he would send email messages with attachments to multiple colleagues, have to integrate and make sense of all the responses he received back from them, and then perhaps follow up with subsequent email. Instead, on the wiki page he created, colleagues contributed ideas, commented on each others' ideas, and revised and edited in real time. Lennard estimates that what would have taken about two weeks to accomplish through email took about two days using a wiki.[130]

Even though IBM has its own collaboration software, Lotus Notes, IBM employees rely on wikis for collaboration to such a great extent that IBM created Wiki Central to manage the wikis. Wiki Central manages over 20,000 IBM wikis and has over 100,000 users.[131] For example, some teams use wikis to coordinate the development of computer software. Wiki Central also gives employees tools to improve and enhance the functioning of their wikis, such as the "polling widget" (used for electronic voting) and the "rating widget" (used to evaluate proposals).[132] Clearly, managers have multiple options to ensure efficient, effective, and collaborative communication.[133]

Communication Skills for Managers

LO16-6

Describe important communication skills that managers need as senders and as receivers of messages and why it is important to understand differences in linguistic styles.

Some of the barriers to effective communication in organizations have their origins in senders. When messages are unclear, incomplete, or difficult to understand, when they are sent over an inappropriate medium, or when no provision for feedback is made, communication suffers. Other communication barriers have their origins in receivers. When receivers pay no attention to or do not listen to messages or when they make no effort to understand the meaning of a message, communication is likely to be ineffective. Sometimes advanced information technology, such as automated phone systems, can hamper effective communication to the extent that the human element is missing.

To overcome these barriers and effectively communicate with others, managers (as well as other organizational members) must possess or develop certain communication skills. Some of these skills are particularly important when managers *send* messages; others are critical when managers *receive* messages. These skills help ensure that managers will be able to share information, will have the information they need to make good decisions and take action, and will be able to reach a common understanding with others.

Communication Skills for Managers as Senders

Organizational effectiveness depends on the ability of managers (as well as other organizational members) to effectively send messages to people both inside and outside the organization. Table 16.2 summarizes seven communication skills that help ensure that when managers send messages, they are properly understood and the transmission phase of the communication process is effective. Let's see what each skill entails.

SEND CLEAR AND COMPLETE MESSAGES   Managers need to learn how to send a message that is clear and complete. A message is clear when it is easy for the receiver to understand and interpret, and it is complete when it contains all the information that the sender and receiver need to reach a common understanding. In striving to send messages that are both clear and complete, managers must learn to anticipate how receivers will interpret messages and must adjust messages to eliminate sources of misunderstanding or confusion.

ENCODE MESSAGES IN SYMBOLS THE RECEIVER UNDERSTANDS   Managers need to appreciate that when they encode messages, they should use symbols or language that the receiver understands. When sending messages in English to receivers whose

Table 16.2

Seven Communication Skills for Managers as Senders of Messages

- Send messages that are clear and complete.
- Encode messages in symbols that the receiver understands.
- Select a medium that is appropriate for the message.
- Select a medium that the receiver monitors.
- Avoid filtering and information distortion.
- Ensure that a feedback mechanism is built into messages.
- Provide accurate information to ensure that misleading rumors are not spread.

native language is not English, for example, it is important to use common vocabulary and to avoid using clichés that, when translated, may make little sense and sometimes are either comical or insulting. **Jargon,** specialized language that members of an occupation, group, or organization develop to facilitate communication among themselves, should never be used when communicating with people outside the occupation, group, or organization.

SELECT A MEDIUM APPROPRIATE FOR THE MESSAGE   As you have learned, when relying on verbal communication, managers can choose from a variety of communication media, including face-to-face communication in person, written letters, memos, newsletters, phone conversations, email, voice mail, faxes, and videoconferences. When choosing among these media, managers need to take into account the level of information richness required, time constraints, and the need for a paper or electronic trail. A primary concern in choosing an appropriate medium is the nature of the message. Is it personal, important, nonroutine, or likely to be misunderstood and in need of further clarification? If it is, face-to-face communication is likely to be in order.

SELECT A MEDIUM THE RECEIVER MONITORS   Another factor that managers need to take into account when selecting a communication medium is whether the medium is one that the receiver monitors. Managers differ in the communication media they pay attention to. Many managers simply select the medium that they themselves use the most and are most comfortable with, but doing this can often lead to ineffective communication. Managers who dislike telephone conversations and too many face-to-face interactions may prefer to use email, send many email messages per day, and check their own email often. Managers who prefer to communicate with people in person or over the phone may have email addresses but may be less likely to respond to email messages. No matter how much a manager likes email, sending email to someone who does not respond to email may be futile. Learning which managers like things in writing and which prefer face-to-face interactions and then using the appropriate medium enhances the chance that receivers will actually receive and pay attention to messages.

A related consideration is whether receivers have disabilities that hamper their ability to decode certain messages. A blind receiver, for example, cannot read a written message. Managers should ensure that employees with disabilities have resources available to communicate effectively with others. For example, deaf employees can effectively communicate over the telephone by using text-typewriters that have a screen and a keyboard on which senders can type messages. The message travels along the phone lines to special operators called *communication assistants,* who translate the typed message into words that the receiver can listen to. The receiver's spoken replies are translated into typewritten text by the communication assistants and appear on the sender's screen. The communication assistants relay messages back and forth to each sender and receiver.[134] Additionally, use of fax and email instead of phone conversations can aid deaf employees.

AVOID FILTERING AND INFORMATION DISTORTION   **Filtering** occurs when a sender withholds part of a message because she or he (mistakenly) thinks the receiver does not need the information or will not want to receive it. Filtering can occur at all levels in an organization and in both vertical and horizontal communication. Rank-and-file workers may

jargon Specialized language that members of an occupation, group, or organization develop to facilitate communication among themselves.

filtering Withholding part of a message because of the mistaken belief that the receiver does not need or will not want the information.

filter messages they send to first-line managers, first-line managers may filter messages to middle managers, and middle managers may filter messages to top managers. Such filtering is most likely to take place when messages contain bad news or problems that subordinates are afraid they will be blamed for. Managers need to hear bad news and be aware of problems as soon as they occur so they can take swift steps to rectify the problem and limit the damage it may have caused.

Some filtering takes place because of internal competition in organizations or because organizational members fear their power and influence will be diminished if others have access to some of their specialized knowledge. By increasing levels of trust in an organization, taking steps to motivate all employees (and the groups and teams they belong to) to work together to achieve organizational goals, and ensuring that employees realize that when the organization reaches its goals and performs effectively, they too will benefit, this kind of filtering can be reduced.

information distortion Changes in the meaning of a message as the message passes through a series of senders and receivers.

Information distortion occurs when the meaning of a message changes as the message passes through a series of senders and receivers. Some information distortion is accidental— due to faulty encoding and decoding or to a lack of feedback. Other information distortion is deliberate. Senders may alter a message to make themselves or their groups look good and to receive special treatment.

Managers themselves should avoid filtering and distorting information. But how can they eliminate these barriers to effective communication throughout their organization? They need to establish trust throughout the organization. Subordinates who trust their managers believe they will not be blamed for things beyond their control and will be treated fairly. Managers who trust their subordinates give them clear and complete information and do not hold things back.

INCLUDE A FEEDBACK MECHANISM IN MESSAGES   Because feedback is essential for effective communication, managers should build a feedback mechanism into the messages they send. They either should include a request for feedback or indicate when and how they will follow up on the message to make sure it was received and understood. When managers write letters and memos or send faxes, they can request that the receiver respond with comments and suggestions in a letter, memo, or fax; schedule a meeting to discuss the issue; or follow up with a phone call. By building feedback mechanisms such as these into their messages, managers ensure that they get heard and are understood.

rumors Unofficial pieces of information of interest to organizational members but with no identifiable source.

PROVIDE ACCURATE INFORMATION   **Rumors** are unofficial pieces of information of interest to organizational members but with no identifiable source. Rumors spread quickly once they are started, and usually they concern topics that organizational members think are important, interesting, or amusing. Rumors, however, can be misleading and can harm individual employees and their organizations when they are false, malicious, or unfounded. Managers can halt the spread of misleading rumors by giving organizational members accurate information about matters that concern them.

Providing accurate information is especially important in tough economic times like the recession in the late 2000s.[135] During a recession, employees are sometimes laid off or find their working hours or pay levels cut back and often experience high levels of stress. When managers give employees accurate information, this can help reduce their stress levels as well as motivate them to find ways to help their companies weather the tough times.[136] Moreover, when the economy does turn around, employees who received accurate information from their bosses may be more likely to remain with their organizations rather than pursue other opportunities.

Table 16.3

Three Communication Skills for Managers as Receivers of Messages

- Pay attention.
- Be a good listener.
- Be empathetic.

Communication Skills for Managers as Receivers

Managers receive as many messages as they send. Thus managers must possess or develop communication skills that allow them to be effective receivers of messages. Table 16.3 summarizes three of these important skills, which we examine here in greater detail.

PAY ATTENTION   Because of their multiple roles and tasks, managers often are overloaded and forced to think about several things at once. Pulled in many different directions, they sometimes do not pay sufficient attention to the messages they receive. To be effective, however, managers should always pay attention to messages they receive, no matter how busy they are. When discussing a project with a subordinate, an effective manager focuses on the project and not on an upcoming meeting with his or her own boss. Similarly, when managers are reading written communication, they should focus on understanding what they are reading; they should not be sidetracked into thinking about other issues.

BE A GOOD LISTENER   Managers (and all other members of an organization) can do several things to be good listeners. First, managers should refrain from interrupting senders in the middle of a message so that senders do not lose their train of thought and managers do not jump to erroneous conclusions based on incomplete information. Second, managers should maintain eye contact with senders so that senders feel their listeners are paying attention; doing this also helps managers focus on what they are hearing. Third, after receiving a message, managers should ask questions to clarify points of ambiguity or confusion. Fourth, managers should paraphrase, or restate in their own words, points senders make that are important, complex, or open to alternative interpretations; this is the feedback component so critical to successful communication.

Managers, like most people, often like to hear themselves talk rather than listen to others. Part of being a good communicator, however, is being a good listener—an essential communication skill for managers as receivers of messages transmitted face-to-face and over the telephone.

BE EMPATHETIC   Receivers are empathetic when they try to understand how the sender feels and try to interpret a message from the sender's perspective, rather than viewing the message from only their own point of view. Marcia Mazulo, the chief psychologist in a public school system in the Northwest, recently learned this lesson after interacting with Karen Sanchez, a new psychologist on her staff. Sanchez was distraught after meeting with the parent of a child she had been working with extensively. The parent was difficult to talk to and argumentative and was not supportive of her own child. Sanchez told Mazulo how upset she was, and Mazulo responded by reminding Sanchez that she was a professional and that dealing with such a situation was part of her job. This feedback upset Sanchez further and caused her to storm out of the room.

In hindsight, Mazulo realized that her response had been inappropriate. She had failed to empathize with Sanchez, who had spent so much time with the child and was deeply concerned about the child's well-being. Rather than dismissing Sanchez's concerns, Mazulo realized, she should have tried to understand how Sanchez felt and given her some support and advice for dealing positively with the situation.

Understanding Linguistic Styles

Consider the following scenarios:

- A manager from New York is having a conversation with a manager from Iowa City. The Iowa City manager never seems to get a chance to talk. He keeps waiting for a pause to signal his turn to talk, but the New York manager never pauses long enough. The New York manager wonders why the Iowa City manager does not say much. He feels uncomfortable when he pauses and the Iowa City manager says nothing, so he starts talking again.

- Elizabeth compliments Bob on his presentation to upper management and asks Bob what he thought of her presentation. Bob launches into a lengthy critique of Elizabeth's presentation and describes how he would have handled it differently. This is hardly the response Elizabeth expected.

- Catherine shares with co-members of a self-managed work team a new way to cut costs. Michael, another team member, thinks her idea is a good one and encourages the rest of the team to support it. Catherine is quietly pleased by Michael's support. The group implements "Michael's" suggestion, and it is written up as such in the company newsletter.

• Robert was recently promoted and transferred from his company's Oklahoma office to its headquarters in New Jersey. Robert is perplexed because he never seems to get a chance to talk in management meetings; someone else always seems to get the floor. Robert's new boss wonders whether Robert's new responsibilities are too much for him, although Robert's supervisor in Oklahoma rated him highly and said he is a real "go-getter." Robert is timid in management meetings and rarely says a word.

linguistic style A person's characteristic way of speaking.

What do these scenarios have in common? Essentially, they all describe situations in which a misunderstanding of linguistic styles leads to a breakdown in communication. The scenarios are based on the research of linguist Deborah Tannen, who describes **linguistic style** as a person's characteristic way of speaking. Elements of linguistic style include tone of voice, speed, volume, use of pauses, directness or indirectness, choice of words, credit taking, and use of questions, jokes, and other manners of speech.[137] When people's linguistic styles differ and these differences are not understood, ineffective communication is likely.

The first and last scenarios illustrate regional differences in linguistic style.[138] The Iowa City manager and Robert from Oklahoma expect the pauses that signal turn taking in conversations to be longer than the pauses made by their colleagues in New York and New Jersey. This difference causes communication problems. The Iowan and transplanted Oklahoman think their Eastern colleagues never let them get a word in edgewise, and the Easterners cannot figure out why their colleagues from the Midwest and South do not get more actively involved in conversations.

Differences in linguistic style can be a particularly insidious source of communication problems because linguistic style is often taken for granted. People rarely think about their own linguistic styles and often are unaware of how linguistic styles can differ. In the example here, Robert did not realize that when dealing with his New Jersey colleagues, he could and should jump into conversations more quickly than he used to do in Oklahoma, and his boss never realized that Robert felt he was not being given a chance to speak in meetings.

The aspect of linguistic style just described, length of pauses, differs by region in the United States. Much more dramatic differences in linguistic style occur cross-culturally.

Cross-cultural differences in linguistic style can lead to misunderstandings.

CROSS-CULTURAL DIFFERENCES   Managers from Japan tend to be more formal in their conversations and more deferential toward upper-level managers and people with high status than are managers from the United States. Japanese managers do not mind extensive pauses in conversations when they are thinking things through or when they think further conversation might be detrimental. In contrast, U.S. managers (even managers from regions of the United States where pauses tend to be long) find lengthy pauses disconcerting and feel obligated to talk to fill the silence.[139]

Another cross-cultural difference in linguistic style concerns the appropriate physical distance separating speakers and listeners in business-oriented conversations.[140] The distance between speakers and listeners is greater in the United States, for example, than it is in Brazil or Saudi Arabia. Citizens of different countries also vary in how direct or indirect they are in conversations and the extent to which they take individual credit for accomplishments. Japanese culture, with its collectivist or group orientation, tends to encourage linguistic styles in which group rather than individual accomplishments are emphasized. The opposite tends to be true in the United States.

These and other cross-cultural differences in linguistic style can and often do lead to misunderstandings. For example, when a team of American managers presented a proposal for a joint venture to Japanese managers, the Japanese managers were silent as they thought about the implications of what they had just heard. The American managers took this silence as a sign that the Japanese managers wanted more information, so they went into more detail about the proposal. When they finished, the Japanese were silent again, not only frustrating the Americans but also making them wonder whether the Japanese were interested in the project. The American managers suggested that if the Japanese already had decided they did not want to pursue the project, there was no reason for the meeting to continue. The Japanese were bewildered. They were trying to carefully think out the proposal, yet the Americans thought they were not interested!

Communication misunderstandings and problems like this can be overcome if managers learn about cross-cultural differences in linguistic styles. If the American managers and the Japanese managers had realized that periods of silence are viewed differently in Japan and in the United States, their different linguistic styles might have been less troublesome barriers to communication. Before managers communicate with people from abroad, they should try to find out as much as they can about the aspects of linguistic style that are specific to the country or culture in question. Expatriate managers who have lived in the country in question for an extended time can be good sources of information about linguistic styles because they are likely to have experienced firsthand some of the differences that citizens of a country are not aware of. Finding out as much as possible about cultural differences also can help managers learn about differences in linguistic styles because the two are often closely linked.

GENDER DIFFERENCES   Referring again to the four scenarios that open this section, you may be wondering why Bob launched into a lengthy critique of Elizabeth's presentation after she paid him a routine compliment on his presentation, or you may be wondering why Michael got the credit for Catherine's idea in the self-managed work team. Research conducted by Tannen and other linguists has found that the linguistic styles of men and women differ in practically every culture or language.[141] Men and women take their own linguistic styles for granted and thus do not realize when they are talking with someone of a different gender that differences in their styles may lead to ineffective communication.

In the United States, women tend to downplay differences between people, are not overly concerned about receiving credit for their own accomplishments, and want to make everyone feel more or less on an equal footing so that even poor performers or low-status individuals feel valued. Men, in contrast, tend to emphasize their own superiority and are not reluctant to acknowledge differences in status. These differences in linguistic style led Elizabeth to routinely compliment Bob on his presentation even though she thought he had not done a particularly good job. She asked him how her presentation was so he could reciprocate and give her a routine compliment, putting them on an equal footing. Bob took Elizabeth's compliment and question about her own presentation as an opportunity to confirm his superiority, never realizing that all she was expecting was a routine compliment. Similarly, Michael's enthusiastic support for Catherine's cost-cutting idea and her apparent surrender of ownership of the idea after she described it led team members to assume incorrectly that the idea was Michael's.[142]

Do some women try to prove they are better than everyone else, and are some men unconcerned about taking credit for ideas and accomplishments? Of course. The gender differences in linguistic style that Tannen and other linguists have uncovered are general tendencies evident in *many* women and men, not in *all* women and men.

Where do gender differences in linguistic style come from? Tannen suggests they begin developing in early childhood. Girls and boys tend to play with children of their own gender, and the ways in which girls and boys play are quite different. Girls play in small groups, engage in a lot of close conversation, emphasize how similar they are to one another, and view boastfulness negatively. Boys play in large groups, emphasize status differences, expect leaders to emerge who boss others around, and give one another challenges to try to meet. These differences in styles of play and interaction result in different linguistic styles when boys and girls grow up and communicate as adults. The ways in which men communicate emphasize status differences and play up relative strengths; the ways in which women communicate emphasize similarities and downplay individual strengths.[143]

Interestingly, gender differences are also turning up in how women and men use email and electronic forms of communication. For example, Susan Herring, a researcher at Indiana University, has found that in public electronic forums such as message boards and chat rooms, men tend to make stronger assertions, be more sarcastic, and be more likely to use insults and profanity than women, whereas women are more likely to be supportive, agreeable, and polite.[144] David Silver, a researcher at the University of Washington, has found that women are more expressive electronic communicators and encourage others to express their thoughts and feelings, while men are briefer and more to the point.[145] Interestingly enough, some men find email to be a welcome way to express their feelings to people they care about. For example, real estate broker Mike Murname finds it easier to communicate with, and express his love for, his grown children via email.[146]

MANAGING DIFFERENCES IN LINGUISTIC STYLES Managers should not expect to change people's linguistic styles and should not try to. To be effective, managers need to understand differences in linguistic styles. Knowing, for example, that some women are reluctant to speak up in meetings, not because they have nothing to contribute but because of their linguistic style, should lead managers to ensure that these women have a chance to talk. And a manager who knows certain people are reluctant to take credit for ideas can be careful to give credit where it is deserved. As Tannen points out, "Talk is the lifeblood of managerial work, and understanding that different people have different ways of saying what they mean will make it possible to take advantage of the talents of people with a broad range of linguistic styles."[147]

Summary and Review

LO16-1, 16-2

COMMUNICATION AND MANAGEMENT Communication is the sharing of information between two or more individuals or groups to reach a common understanding. Good communication is necessary for an organization to gain a competitive advantage. Communication occurs in a cyclical process that entails two phases: transmission and feedback.

LO16-3 **INFORMATION RICHNESS AND COMMUNICATION MEDIA** Information richness is the amount of information a communication medium can carry and the extent to which the medium enables the sender and receiver to reach a common understanding. Four categories of communication media, in descending order of information richness, are face-to-face communication (includes videoconferences), electronically transmitted spoken communication (includes voice mail), personally addressed written communication (includes email), and impersonal written communication.

LO16-4 **COMMUNICATION NETWORKS** Communication networks are the pathways along which information flows in an organization. Four communication networks found in groups and teams are the wheel, the chain, the circle, and the all-channel network. An organization chart summarizes formal pathways of communication, but communication in organizations is often informal, as is true of communication through the grapevine.

LO16-5   INFORMATION TECHNOLOGY AND COMMUNICATION   The Internet is a global system of computer networks that managers around the world use to communicate within and outside their companies. The World Wide Web is the multimedia business district on the Internet. Intranets are internal communication networks that managers can create to improve communication, performance, and customer service. Intranets use the same technology that the Internet and World Wide Web are based on. Groupware is computer software that enables members of groups and teams to share information with one another to improve their communication and performance.

LO16-6   COMMUNICATION SKILLS FOR MANAGERS   There are various barriers to effective communication in organizations. To overcome these barriers and effectively communicate with others, managers must possess or develop certain communication skills. As senders of messages, managers should send messages that are clear and complete, encode messages in symbols the receiver understands, choose a medium appropriate for the message and monitored by the receiver, avoid filtering and information distortion, include a feedback mechanism in the message, and provide accurate information to ensure that misleading rumors are not spread. Communication skills for managers as receivers of messages include paying attention, being a good listener, and being empathetic. Understanding linguistic styles is also an essential communication skill for managers. Linguistic styles can vary by geographic region, gender, and country or culture. When these differences are not understood, ineffective communication can occur.

Management in Action

Topics for Discussion and Action

Discussion

1. Which medium (or media) do you think would be appropriate for each of the following kinds of messages that a subordinate could receive from his or her boss: (a) a raise, (b) not receiving a promotion, (c) an error in a report prepared by the subordinate, (d) additional job responsibilities, and (e) the schedule for company holidays for the upcoming year? Explain your choices. **[LO16-3]**

2. Discuss the pros and cons of using the Internet and World Wide Web for communication within and between organizations. **[LO16-1, 16-2, 16-3, 16-5]**

3. Why do some organizational members resist using groupware? **[LO16-5]**

4. Why do some managers find it difficult to be good listeners? **[LO16-6]**

5. Explain why subordinates might filter and distort information about problems and performance shortfalls when communicating with their bosses. What steps can managers take to eliminate filtering and information distortion? **[LO16-6]**

6. Explain why differences in linguistic style, when not understood by senders and receivers of messages, can lead to ineffective communication. **[LO16-6]**

Action

7. Interview a manager in an organization in your community to determine with whom he or she communicates on a typical day, what communication media he or she uses, and which typical communication problems the manager experiences. **[LO16-1, 16-2, 16-3, 16-4, 16-5, 16-6]**

Building Management Skills

Diagnosing Ineffective Communication [LO16-1, 16-2, 16-3, 16-4, 16-5, 16-6]

Think about the last time you experienced very ineffective communication with another person—someone you work with, a classmate, a friend, a member of your family. Describe the incident. Then answer the following questions:

1. Why was your communication ineffective in this incident?

2. What stages of the communication process were particularly problematic and why?

3. Describe any filtering or information distortion that occurred.

4. Do you think differences in linguistic styles adversely affected the communication that took place? Why or why not?

5. How could you have handled this situation differently so communication would have been effective?

Managing Ethically [LO16-3, 16-5]

Many employees use their company's Internet connections and email systems to visit websites and send personal email and instant messages.

Questions

1. Either individually or in a group, explore the ethics of using an organization's Internet connection and email system for personal purposes at work and while away from the office. Should employees have some rights to use this resource? When does their behavior become unethical?

2. Some companies track how their employees use the company's Internet connection and email system. Is it ethical for managers to read employees' personal email or to record websites that employees visit? Why or why not?

Small Group Breakout Exercise

Reducing Resistance to Advances in Information Technology [LO16-5]

Form groups of three or four people, and appoint one member as the spokesperson who will communicate your findings to the class when called on by the instructor. Then discuss the following scenario:

You are a team of managers in charge of information and communication in a large consumer products corporation. Your company has already implemented many advances in information technology. Managers and workers have access to email, the Internet, your company's own intranet, groupware, and collaboration software.

Many employees use the technology, but the resistance of some is causing communication problems. A case in point is the use of groupware and collaboration software. Many teams in your organization have access to groupware and are encouraged to use it. While some teams welcome this communication tool and actually have made suggestions for improvements, others are highly resistant to sharing documents in their teams' online workspaces.

Although you do not want to force people to use the technology, you want them to at least try it and give it a chance. You are meeting today to develop strategies for reducing resistance to the new technologies.

1. One resistant group of employees is made up of top managers. Some of them seem computer-phobic and are highly resistant to sharing information online, even with sophisticated security precautions in place. What steps will you take to get these managers to have more confidence in electronic communication?

2. A second group of resistant employees consists of middle managers. Some middle managers resist using your company's intranet. Although these managers do not resist the technology per se and do use electronic communication for multiple purposes, they seem to distrust the intranet as a viable way to communicate and get things done. What steps will you take to get these managers to take advantage of the intranet?

3. A third group of resistant employees is made up of members of groups and teams who do not want to use the groupware that has been provided to them. You think the groupware could improve their communication and performance, but they seem to think otherwise. What steps will you take to get these members of groups and teams to start using groupware?

Exploring the World Wide Web [LO16-5]

Atos SE is a global information technology company that provides IT services to major corporations to improve, facilitate, integrate, and manage operations, information, and communication across multiple locations. Visit Atos's website at http://atos.net/en-us/home/we-are .html and read about this company and the services it provides to improve communication. How can companies like Atos help managers improve communication effectiveness in their organizations? What kinds of organizations and groups are most likely to benefit from services provided by Atos? Why is it beneficial for some organizations to contract with firms like Atos for their IT and communication needs rather than meet these needs internally with their own employees?

Be the Manager [LO16-1, 16-2, 16-3, 16-6]

You supervise support staff for an Internet merchandising organization that sells furniture over the Internet. You always thought that you needed to expand your staff, and just when you were about to approach your boss with such a request, business slowed. Thus your plan to try to add new employees to your staff is on hold.

However, you have noticed a troubling pattern of communication with your staff. Ordinarily, when you want a staff member to work on a task, you email that subordinate the pertinent information. For the last few months, your email requests have gone unheeded, and your subordinates seem to respond to your requests only after you visit them in person and give them a specific deadline. Each time they apologize for not getting to the task sooner but say they are so overloaded with requests that they sometimes even stop answering their phones. Unless someone asks for something more than once, your staff seems to feel the request is not that urgent and can be put on hold. You think this state of affairs is dysfunctional and could lead to serious problems down the road. Also, you are starting to realize that your subordinates seem to have no way of prioritizing tasks—hence some very important projects you asked them to complete were put on hold until you followed up with them about the tasks. Knowing you cannot add employees to your staff in the short term, what are you going to do to improve communication with your overloaded staff?

The Wall Street Journal Case in the News [LO16-1, 16-2, 16-3, 16-5, 16-6]

"Help! I'm on a Conference Call"

The conference call is one of the most familiar rituals of office life—and one of the most hated.

Abuses are rife. People on the line interrupt others, zone out or multitask, forgetting to hit "mute" while talking to kids or slurping drinks.

Sales executive Erica Pearce has seen teleconferences interrupted by home FedEx deliveries, crying children and the sound of a co-worker vacuuming his house. "Nobody could hear," she says of the cleaning. As leader of the meeting, she said into the phone, "If you're vacuuming, I appreciate that, and you're welcome to come to my house afterward. But you need to be on mute."

Another conference call ended when a participant put his line on hold, starting a stream of elevator music, says Ms. Pearce of Scottsdale, Ariz., a global account executive for a software company. Conference-call complaints are so widespread that a recent comedy video showing how ridiculous conference-call behavior such as secretly playing solitaire would look "in real life" has drawn more than 6 million views.

But conference calls aren't going anywhere; they are too useful for businesses dealing with far-flung workplaces, flexible schedules and a clampdown on business-travel expenses. Time spent in audio conferences in the U.S. is expected to grow 9.6% a year through 2017, according to Wainhouse Research, a Boston market-research firm; about 65% of all conferencing is still done by audio calls.

There are ways to fix the problems. For instance, meeting leaders must set firmer ground rules than they do for face-to-face meetings and tighter, more explicit agendas. Leaders also have to work harder to get participants talking, both by asking more questions and by listening more.

Many conference calls are split between people in a conference room and others on a muddy-sounding call-in line. This often makes remote participants "feel like second-class citizens, like, 'The cool kids are here,'" says Laura Stack, author of "Execution Is the Strategy."

She advises leaders to have all participants say their names when they speak so remote callers know what's going on. If someone cracks a joke and the room bursts into laughter, the leader should "let the others know who said what and repeat the joke," says Ms. Stack, a Denver productivity consultant and trainer.

One of the biggest problems with virtual meetings is that it is hard for participants to build rapport with each other, a hurdle cited by 75% of 3,301 businesspeople surveyed in 2012 by RW3, a New York culture and leadership training company. The absence of nonverbal cues such as facial expressions makes many people hesitant to speak up and makes it harder to pay attention. In the survey, 71% of participants cited a lack of participation by others as a problem with virtual meetings.

To build relationships, Ms. Pearce takes time during the teleconferences she leads to have participants who don't know each other introduce themselves, explain their roles in the project at hand and tell what they want out of the meeting, she says.

For teleconferences, agendas and goals should be clearer and more explicit than for face-to-face meetings. "You need to script them more tightly" to keep people's attention from wandering, says Daniel Mittleman, an associate professor in computing and digital media at DePaul University, Chicago. Teleconferences requiring interaction should be no larger than seven to nine people, experts say.

Meeting leaders should talk less than in face-to-face meetings and listen more, says Paul Donehue, president of Paul Charles & Associates, a Londonderry, N.H., sales-management consulting firm. For a problem-solving teleconference, for example, a leader might talk 40% of the time and listen 60%, compared with a 55%-to-45% ratio when meeting face-to-face for the same purpose, Mr. Donehue says.

Leaders should spend as much time on preparing questions to ask participants as on writing the agenda, Mr. Donehue says. He advises leaders to use a form with spaces to note comments by individual participants during the meeting. This helps leaders listen closely and hold participants' attention by citing their earlier input.

Managing conflicts is harder in teleconferences. Not everyone can sense when a silent participant is frustrated or angry. "There's sometimes a little passive-aggressiveness in that silence," Ms. Stack says. "Some people just check out, thinking, 'OK, you dummies, go ahead and do that. I'm going to sit here on mute.'" She suggests posing a question: " 'Jane, you're kind of quiet. What are your thoughts?' You sometimes get an explosion," but this can get important issues out in the open, Ms. Stack says.

Participants can help meetings run more smoothly by volunteering to serve as moderator, keeping people on-topic and sticking to time limits. Divvying up moderating and note-taking duties can free meeting leaders to participate and keep people engaged, Ms. Stack says. Some managers encourage any participant to moderate, breaking in if a speaker wanders off-topic and asking that everyone stick to the agenda, says Steven M. Smith, senior consultant in Seattle for SolutionsIQ, a management consulting and training firm.

Time-zone differences can irritate people who have to rise at midnight to meet with colleagues in the U.S., says Michael Schell, chief executive officer of RW3. "It's important to move the meeting times around" to be fair, he says. Also, meetings should start promptly; taking 10 minutes to get coffee might seem normal at 9 a.m. in New York, but it can seem disrespectful to a colleague in Australia who got out of bed to join the call, Mr. Schell says.

Videoconferencing can solve some of the problems. The technology is increasingly inexpensive and easy to use, and a growing number of applications, such as Vidyo and Blue Jeans Network, can connect users on a variety of devices, including webcams, laptops, tablets or smartphones, says David Coleman, founder and managing director of Collaborative Strategies Inc., San Mateo, Calif.

The technology can create other challenges, though. Mr. Smith says participants who aren't tech-savvy often consume valuable meeting time getting used to unfamiliar systems.

Videoconferencing also can make people self-conscious. Many people avoid video, Ms. Stack says, because they don't want to put on makeup or change their workout clothes. "I cannot tell you how many times I've heard people say, 'I don't know what's wrong with my webcam. I can't get it to work, so I'm just going to be here in voice,'" she says.

Questions for Discussion

1. How and why can conference calls facilitate effective communication in organizations?

2. How and why might conference calls have the potential to lead to ineffective communication in organizations?

3. What are some potential sources of noise in the communication process during conference calls?

4. When are conference calls likely to be most and least effective in organizations?

CHAPTER 17

Managing Conflict, Politics, and Negotiation

Learning Objectives

After studying this chapter, you should be able to:

LO17-1 Explain why conflict arises, and identify the types and sources of conflict in organizations.

LO17-2 Describe conflict management strategies that managers can use to resolve conflict effectively.

LO17-3 Understand the nature of negotiation and why integrative bargaining is more effective than distributive negotiation.

LO17-4 Describe ways in which managers can promote integrative bargaining in organizations.

LO17-5 Explain why managers need to be attuned to organizational politics, and describe the political strategies that managers can use to become politically skilled.

A MANAGER'S CHALLENGE

Indra Nooyi Collaborates and Builds Alliances at PepsiCo

How can managers effectively collaborate and build alliances? By all accounts, Indra Nooyi is a powerful business leader.[1] As CEO and chairman of PepsiCo, she oversees a company with over $66 billion in net revenues and around 274,000 employees; Pepsi-Cola, Lay's, Doritos, Tropicana, Mountain Dew, Gatorade, and Quaker are among Pepsi's many well-known brands.[2] She effectively uses her vision for PepsiCo, "Performance with Purpose," to both motivate and guide Pepsi employees and communicate PepsiCo's stance on important issues such as health, obesity, and protecting the natural environment around the world.[3] In 2014 she was ranked 13th on *Forbes* magazine's list of "The 25 Most Powerful Women in the World."[4]

Nooyi, born and raised in India, was senior vice president of strategic planning at PepsiCo before assuming the top post on October 1, 2006.[5] When the PepsiCo's board of directors was deciding who would be the next CEO of the company, two senior executives at PepsiCo were under consideration, Nooyi and Michael White, vice chairman.[6] When Nooyi found out that the board had chosen her, one of her top priorities was to ensure that White would stay at PepsiCo, the two would maintain the great relationship they had with each other that had evolved from years of working together, and she would have his support and advice.[7] At the time, White was on vacation at his beach house in Cape Cod, Massachusetts. Nooyi flew to Cape Cod and the two walked on the beach, had ice cream together, and

even played a duet (Nooyi and White both are fond of music and in this case, he played the piano and she sang). Prior to leaving Cape Cod, she told White, "Tell me whatever I need to do to keep you, and I will."[8] Ultimately White decided to remain at PepsiCo as CEO of PepsiCo International as well as vice chairman of PepsiCo.[9] At a meeting announcing Nooyi's appointment, Nooyi told employees, "I treat Mike as my partner. He could easily have been CEO." White said, "I play the piano and Indra sings."[10] Nooyi was named Chairman of PepsiCo in 2007. In 2009 White retired from PepsiCo.[11]

Nooyi excels at building alliances both inside and outside of PepsiCo. Given the breadth of her responsibilities, she decided to increase the team of top managers she works closely with. She has good relations with key decision makers around the world in both government and business.[12]

Indra Nooyi, CEO and chairman of PepsiCo, excels at building alliances both inside and outside of PepsiCo.

Her philosophy is that leaders of top global companies like PepsiCo need to work hard to build and maintain collaborative relationships with the countries they operate in and their governments and other organizations and people that have a stake in their operations such as customers, communities, suppliers, nongovernmental organizations, and shareholders. She adopts a long-term approach to do what it takes to build alliances that will enable PepsiCo to achieve its goals and effectively meet the needs of its stakeholders.[13]

Nooyi also excels at gaining the support of PepsiCo's employees (a very important group of stakeholders at PepsiCo).[14] She is down-to-earth, sincere, and genuine in her interactions with employees and also comfortable just being herself; she has been known to walk barefoot in the halls of PepsiCo on occasion and sometimes sings at gatherings. Celebrations for employees' birthdays include a cake. As a mother of two daughters, Nooyi also recognizes how employees' families are affected by their work and what a great source of support families can be.[15]

In fact, when Nooyi was named CEO of PepsiCo and she visited her mother in India, her mother had many of their relatives come by to visit.[16] After saying hello to Nooyi, they all went up to her mother to congratulate her for doing such a good job raising Nooyi. This experience got Nooyi thinking. She decided to write to the parents of all the executives that reported to her relaying what happened in India and thanking them for their (adult) children who were doing such a great job at PepsiCo. And so relations were developed not only with her subordinates but with their parents.[17]

Nooyi also picked around 200 people in the company from those around 35 years old to very senior employees who she thought could be key contributors to the future direction of Pepsi-Co.[18] She built alliances with them by dividing them into groups of around 15 people and spending a few days with them to get to know them. When she was trying to hire a potentially valuable employee who had an offer from another company, she called his mother and introduced herself and told her why she thought her son should join PepsiCo. When the son came home and told his mother he was thinking of accepting the other offer, she told him he should work for PepsiCo and that Nooyi had called her. And he ended up joining PepsiCo.[19]

Nooyi effectively developed and maintained alliances and built support to transform PepsiCo in some fundamental ways. For example, PepsiCo traditionally focused on products that the company calls "fun for you" such as Pepsi, Doritos, Tostitos, and Lays. Nooyi recognized that people around the world were seeking to eat more healthful foods, have more balance in their diets, and looking to prevent disease by decreasing their intake of sugar, salt, and fat.[20] Thus, in addition to eating "fun for you" products, consumers also wanted "better for you" products like Diet Pepsi and Baked Lay's and "good for you" products like Tropicana orange juice and Quaker Oats. Nooyi built alliances to try to make each of these three categories of products more healthful for consumers while not sacrificing on taste or making the products hard to find or too costly.[21]

As another example, PepsiCo traditionally was very much a U.S. company with a big footprint in developed economies. Nooyi built alliances to help PepsiCo expand into emerging markets.[22] Importantly, she realized that to successfully grow its global presence in emerging markets, PepsiCo needed to develop employees with global experience and knowledge in emerging markets in the Middle East, Asia, and Latin America.[23]

As a final example, Nooyi built alliances to help protect the natural environment and contribute to sustainability in the communities and countries in which PepsiCo operates. Initiatives to reduce PepsiCo's water consumption, reduce waste, and lower the use of plastic help communities and local governments.[24] Her exceptional skills at building alliances and gaining support continue to help her as she leads PepsiCo forward on these and other initiatives.[25] As she indicated, ". . . you give the team of people a set of objectives and goals and get them all to buy into it, and they can move mountains."[26]

Overview

Successful leaders such as Indra Nooyi in "A Manager's Challenge" can effectively use their power to influence others and to manage conflict to achieve win–win solutions. In Chapter 14 we described how managers, as leaders, influence other people to achieve group and organizational goals and how managers' sources of power enable them to exert such influence. In this chapter we describe why managers need to develop the skills necessary to manage organizational conflict, politics, and negotiation if they are going to be effective and achieve their goals.

We describe conflict and the strategies managers can use to resolve it effectively. We discuss one major conflict resolution technique, negotiation, in detail, outlining the steps managers can take to be good negotiators. Then we discuss the nature of organizational politics and the political strategies managers can use to maintain and expand their power and use it effectively. By the end of this chapter, you will appreciate why managers must develop the skills necessary to manage these important organizational processes if they are to be effective and achieve organizational goals.

Organizational Conflict

LO17-1

Explain why conflict arises, and identify the types and sources of conflict in organizations.

organizational conflict
The discord that arises when the goals, interests, or values of different individuals or groups are incompatible and those individuals or groups block or thwart one another's attempts to achieve their objectives.

Organizational conflict is the discord that arises when the goals, interests, or values of different individuals or groups are incompatible and those individuals or groups block or thwart one another's attempts to achieve their objectives.[27] Conflict is an inevitable part of organizational life because the goals of different stakeholders such as managers and workers are often incompatible. Organizational conflict also can exist between departments and divisions that compete for resources or even between managers who may be competing for promotion to the next level in the organizational hierarchy.

It is important for managers to develop the skills necessary to manage conflict effectively. In addition, the level of conflict present in an organization has important implications for organizational performance. Figure 17.1 illustrates the relationship between organizational conflict and performance. At point A there is little or no conflict, and organizational performance suffers. Lack of conflict in an organization often signals that managers emphasize conformity at the expense of new ideas, resist change, and strive for agreement rather than effective decision making. As the level of conflict increases from point A to point B, organizational effectiveness is likely to increase. When an organization has an optimum level of conflict, managers are likely to be open to, and encourage, a variety of perspectives; look for ways to improve organizational functioning and effectiveness; and view debates and disagreements as a necessary ingredient of effective decision making and innovation. As the level of conflict increases from point B to point C, conflict escalates to the point where organizational performance suffers. When an organization has a dysfunctionally high level of

Figure 17.1

The Effect of Conflict on Organizational Performance

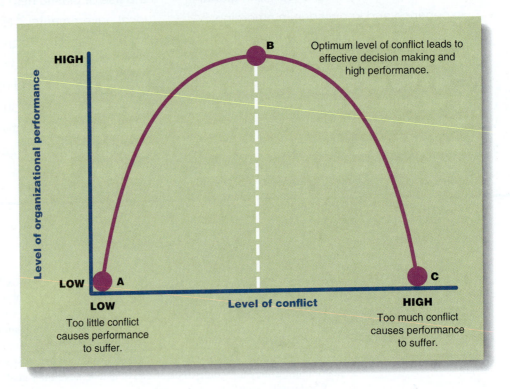

conflict, managers are likely to waste organizational resources to achieve their own ends, to be more concerned about winning political battles than about doing what will lead to a competitive advantage for their organization, and to try to get even with their opponents rather than make good decisions.

Conflict is a force that needs to be managed rather than eliminated.[28] Managers should never try to eliminate all conflict but, rather, should try to keep conflict at a moderate and functional level to promote change efforts that benefit the organization. Additionally, managers should strive to keep conflict focused on substantive, task-based issues and minimize conflict based on personal disagreements and animosities. To manage conflict,[29] managers must understand the types and sources of conflict and be familiar with strategies that can be effective in dealing with it.

Types of Conflict

There are several types of conflict in organizations: interpersonal, intragroup, intergroup, and interorganizational (see Figure 17.2).[30] Understanding how these types differ can help managers deal with conflict.

INTERPERSONAL CONFLICT Interpersonal conflict is conflict between individual members of an organization, occurring because of differences in their goals or values. Two managers may experience interpersonal conflict when their values concerning protection of the environment differ. One manager may argue that the organization should do only what is required by law. The other manager may counter that the organization should invest in equipment to reduce emissions even though the organization's current level of emissions is below the legal limit.

INTRAGROUP CONFLICT Intragroup conflict arises within a group, team, or department. When members of the marketing department in a clothing company disagree about how they should spend budgeted advertising dollars for a new line of men's designer jeans, they are experiencing intragroup conflict. Some of the members want to spend all the money on

Figure 17.2

Types of Conflict in Organizations

advertisements in magazines. Others want to devote half of the money to billboards and ads in city buses and subways.

INTERGROUP CONFLICT Intergroup conflict occurs between groups, teams, or departments. R&D departments, for example, sometimes experience intergroup conflict with production departments. Members of the R&D department may develop a new product that they think production can make inexpensively by using existing manufacturing capabilities. Members of the production department, however, may disagree and believe that the costs of making the product will be much higher. Managers of departments usually play a key role in managing intergroup conflicts such as this.

INTERORGANIZATIONAL CONFLICT Interorganizational conflict arises across organizations. Sometimes interorganizational conflict occurs when managers in one organization feel that another organization is not behaving ethically and is threatening the well-being of certain stakeholder groups. Interorganizational conflict also can occur between government agencies and corporations, as illustrated in the accompanying "Ethics in Action" feature.

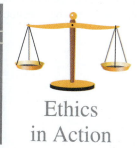

Ethics in Action

The U.S. Labor Department and Big Home Builders Clash

In 2011 the U.S. Labor Department sent letters to big home-building companies, including Pulte Group, Inc., D. R. Horton Inc., KB Home, and Lennar Corp., asking them to provide information regarding the names, social security numbers, addresses, hours worked, and pay rates for all their employees for the past two years and also the names of all their contractors.[31] The investigation falls under the rubric of the Fair Labor Standards Act, which pertains to the federal minimum wage, overtime pay, and youth employment.[32]

And in 2012 the Labor Department petitioned the Federal District Court in Michigan to require Pulte Group, based in Bloomfield Hills, Michigan,[33] to give the department thousands of documents pertaining to its employees and subcontractors.[34] It appears that Pulte did provide the department with records for its own employees. However, Pulte has told the court that it thinks the request for payroll records for building projects from late 2009 to early 2012 in eight states is too all-encompassing.[35]

Apparently part of the conflict arises from the fact that, although large building companies like Pulte buy land for homes and market them, they ordinarily rely on

Conflict management hits a wall: Pulte Group's stand-off with the Labor Department's request for comprehensive records of its subcontractors' practices, like how much this worker gets paid, embodies a negotiation failure.

contractors to actually build the houses rather than doing it themselves.[36] Unions and other labor groups have griped that the big home builders have lowered wages in the industry by relying on subcontractors who don't pay employees the minimum wage, don't pay overtime pay, and/or don't provide benefits such as health care. In this current case, it appears that the Labor Department wants to make sure that carpenters, roofers, bricklayers, laborers, and other subcontractors are receiving the federal minimum wage, overtime pay, and benefits stipulated by the Fair Labor Standards Act.[37]

Managers at Pulte think that the Labor Department is requiring too much from them in the investigation and subpoena.[38] Some of the other information the department requested includes records pertaining to contracts it has with suppliers and contractors for the subsequent 12-month period. James Zeumer, vice president for investor communications,[39] indicated that "while the skilled labor crews building our homes are not Pulte employees, our vendor agreements state that contractors are required to comply with all applicable labor laws and wage practices."[40] With the Labor Department and Pulte engaged in conflict, this is one for the courts to decide.

Sources of Conflict

Conflict in organizations springs from a variety of sources. The ones we examine here are different goals and time horizons, overlapping authority, task interdependencies, different evaluation or reward systems, scarce resources, and status inconsistencies (see Figure 17.3).[41]

DIFFERENT GOALS AND TIME HORIZONS Recall from Chapter 10 that an important managerial activity is organizing people and tasks into departments and divisions to accomplish an organization's goals. Almost inevitably this grouping creates departments and divisions that have different goals and time horizons, and the result can be conflict.

Figure 17.3
Sources of Conflict in Organizations

Production managers, for example, usually concentrate on efficiency and cost cutting; they have a relatively short time horizon and focus on producing quality goods or services in a timely and efficient manner. In contrast, marketing managers focus on sales and responsiveness to customers. Their time horizon is longer than that of production because they are trying to be responsive not only to customers' needs today but also to their changing needs in the future to build long-term customer loyalty. These fundamental differences between marketing and production often breed conflict.

Suppose production is behind schedule in its plan to produce a specialized product for a key customer. The marketing manager believes the delay will reduce sales of the product and therefore insists that the product be delivered on time even if saving the production schedule means increasing costs by paying production workers overtime. The production manager says that she will happily schedule overtime if marketing will pay for it. Both managers' positions are reasonable from the perspective of their own departments, and conflict is likely.

OVERLAPPING AUTHORITY   When two or more managers, departments, or functions claim authority for the same activities or tasks, conflict is likely.[42] This is precisely what happened when heirs of the Forman liquor distribution company, based in Washington, DC, inherited the company from their parents. One of the heirs, Barry Forman, wanted to control the company and was reluctant to share power with the other heirs. Several of the heirs felt they had authority over certain tasks crucial to Forman's success (such as maintaining good relationships with the top managers of liquor companies). What emerged was a battle of wills and considerable conflict, which escalated to the point of being dysfunctional, requiring that the family hire a consulting firm to help resolve it.[43]

TASK INTERDEPENDENCIES   Have you ever been assigned a group project for one of your classes and had one group member who consistently failed to get things done on time? This probably created some conflict in your group because other group members were dependent on the late member's contributions to complete the project. Whenever individuals, groups, teams, or departments are interdependent, the potential for conflict exists.[44] With differing goals and time horizons, the managers of marketing and production come into conflict precisely because the departments are interdependent. Marketing is dependent on production for the goods it markets and sells, and production is dependent on marketing to create demand for the things it makes.

DIFFERENT EVALUATION OR REWARD SYSTEMS   How interdependent groups, teams, or departments are evaluated and rewarded can be another source of conflict.[45] Production managers, for example, are evaluated and rewarded for their success in staying within budget or lowering costs while maintaining quality. So they are reluctant to take any steps that will increase costs, such as paying workers high overtime rates to finish a late order for an important customer. Marketing managers, in contrast, are evaluated and rewarded for their success in generating sales and satisfying customers. So they often think overtime pay is a small price to pay for responsiveness to customers. Thus conflict between production and marketing is rarely unexpected.

SCARCE RESOURCES   Management is the process of acquiring, developing, protecting, and using the resources that allow an organization to be efficient and effective (see Chapter 1). When resources are scarce, management is more difficult and conflict is likely.[46] For example, divisional managers may be in conflict over who has access to financial capital, and organizational members at all levels may be in conflict over who gets raises and promotions.

STATUS INCONSISTENCIES   The fact that some individuals, groups, teams, or departments within an organization are more highly regarded than others in the organization can also create conflict. In some restaurants, for example, the chefs have relatively higher status than the people who wait on tables. Nevertheless, the chefs receive customers' orders from the waitstaff, and the waitstaff can return to the chefs food that their customers or they think is not acceptable. This status inconsistency—high-status chefs taking orders from low-status waitstaff—can be the source of considerable conflict between chefs and the waitstaff. For this reason, some restaurants require that the waitstaff put orders on a spindle, thereby reducing the amount of direct order giving from the waitstaff to the chefs.[47]

LO17-2

Describe conflict management strategies that managers can use to resolve conflict effectively.

compromise A way of managing conflict in which each party is concerned about not only its own goal accomplishment but also the goal accomplishment of the other party and is willing to engage in a give-and-take exchange and make concessions.

collaboration A way of managing conflict in which both parties try to satisfy their goals by coming up with an approach that leaves them better off and does not require concessions on issues that are important to either party.

accommodation An ineffective conflict-handling approach in which one party, typically with weaker power, gives in to the demands of the other, typically more powerful, party.

avoidance An ineffective conflict-handling approach in which the parties try to ignore the problem and do nothing to resolve their differences.

competition An ineffective conflict-handling approach in which each party tries to maximize its own gain and has little interest in understanding the other party's position and arriving at a solution that will allow both parties to achieve their goals.

Conflict Management Strategies

If an organization is to achieve its goals, managers must be able to resolve conflicts in a functional manner. *Functional conflict resolution* means the conflict is settled by compromise or by collaboration between the parties in conflict (later in the chapter we discuss other typically less functional ways in which conflicts are sometimes resolved).[48] **Compromise** is possible when each party is concerned about not only its own goal accomplishment but also the goal accomplishment of the other party and is willing to engage in a give-and-take exchange and to make concessions until a reasonable resolution of the conflict is reached. **Collaboration** is a way of handling conflict in which the parties try to satisfy their goals without making any concessions but, instead, come up with a way to resolve their differences that leaves them both better off.[49]

In addition to compromise and collaboration, there are three other ways in which conflicts are sometimes handled: accommodation, avoidance, and competition.[50] When **accommodation** takes place, one party to the conflict simply gives in to the demands of the other party. Accommodation typically takes place when one party has more power than the other and can pursue its goal attainment at the expense of the weaker party. From an organizational perspective, accommodation is often ineffective: The two parties are not cooperating with each other, they are unlikely to want to cooperate in the future, and the weaker party who gives in or accommodates the more powerful party might look for ways to get back at the stronger party in the future.

When conflicts are handled by **avoidance**, the parties to a conflict try to ignore the problem and do nothing to resolve the disagreement. Avoidance is often ineffective because the real source of the disagreement has not been addressed, conflict is likely to continue, and communication and cooperation are hindered.

Competition occurs when each party to a conflict tries to maximize its own gain and has little interest in understanding the other party's position and arriving at a solution that will allow both parties to achieve their goals. Competition can actually escalate levels of conflict as each party tries to outmaneuver the other. As a way of handling conflict, competition is ineffective for the organization because the two sides to a conflict are more concerned about winning the battle than cooperating to arrive at a solution that is best for the organization and acceptable to both sides. Handling conflicts through accommodation, avoidance, or competition is ineffective from an organizational point of view because the parties do not cooperate with each other and work toward a mutually acceptable solution to their differences.

When the parties to a conflict are willing to cooperate with each other and, through compromise or collaboration, devise a solution that each finds acceptable, an organization is more likely to achieve its goals.[51] Conflict management strategies that managers can use to ensure that conflicts are resolved in a functional manner focus on individuals and on the organization as a whole. Next we describe four strategies that focus on individuals: increasing awareness of the sources of conflict, increasing diversity awareness and skills, practicing job rotation or temporary assignments, and using permanent transfers or dismissals when necessary. We also describe two strategies that focus on the organization as a whole: changing an organization's structure or culture and directly altering the source of conflict.

STRATEGIES FOCUSED ON INDIVIDUALS

INCREASING AWARENESS OF THE SOURCES OF CONFLICT   Sometimes conflict arises because of communication problems and interpersonal misunderstandings. For example, different linguistic styles (see Chapter 16) may lead some men in work teams to talk more and take more credit for ideas than women in those teams. These communication differences can cause conflict when the men incorrectly assume that the women are uninterested or less capable because they participate less and the women incorrectly assume that the men are bossy and are not interested in their ideas because they seem to do all the talking. By increasing people's awareness of this source of conflict, managers can help resolve conflict functionally. Once men and women realize that the source of their conflict is different linguistic styles, they can take steps to interact with each other more effectively. The men can give the women more chances to provide input, and the women can be more proactive in providing this input.

Sometimes personalities clash in an organization. In these situations, too, managers can help resolve conflicts functionally by increasing organizational members' awareness of the source of their difficulties. For example, some people who are not inclined to take risks may come into conflict with those who are prone to taking risks. The non–risk takers might complain that those who welcome risk propose outlandish ideas without justification, whereas the risk takers might complain that their innovative ideas are always getting shot down. When both types of people are made aware that their conflicts are due to fundamental differences in their ways of approaching problems, they will likely be better able to cooperate in coming up with innovative ideas that entail only moderate levels of risk.

INCREASING DIVERSITY AWARENESS AND SKILLS   Interpersonal conflicts also can arise because of diversity. Older workers may feel uncomfortable or resentful about reporting to a younger supervisor, a Hispanic may feel singled out in a group of non-Hispanic workers, or a female top manager may feel that members of her predominantly male top management team band together whenever one of them disagrees with one of her proposals. Whether or not these feelings are justified, they are likely to cause recurring conflicts. Many of the techniques we described in Chapter 5 for increasing diversity awareness and skills can help managers effectively manage diversity and resolve conflicts that originate in differences among organizational members.

Increasing diversity awareness and skills can be especially important when interacting with people, groups, and organizations in other countries, as indicated in the accompanying "Managing Globally" feature.

Managing Globally

Understanding Other Cultures

When interacting with people, groups, and organizations from other cultures, it is particularly important to try to gain an appreciation of their culture to avoid potential misunderstandings and effectively manage conflict. For example, decades ago when Scott McKain, who often travels abroad on business, was at a welcome dinner for a trade delegation to Brazil with the mayor of a local community, the mayor asked McKain how he liked his first Brazilian dinner.[52] Since his mouth was full, McKain gave the mayor an OK gesture with this index finger and thumb. The mayor was shocked—the okay gesture in Brazil has a similar connotation to putting up a middle finger in the United States. McKain was young and inexperienced at the time, but other more experienced members of the trade delegation were able to smooth things over with the mayor.[53]

Think they're outdated? Think again: the business card, the fancier the better, continues to reign in triumph in China. Best to brush up those paper squares when headed there on business, just as it is wise to check out local customs anywhere you go.

In China, business cards remain an important part of business etiquette. Business cards should always be professionally made, and when a person receives a business card, it is important to be impressed with it.[54] More generally, the Chinese are very attuned to and respectful of status differences and positions in networks. For instance, a lower-status person such as a subordinate should always reach first to shake the hand of a higher-status person such as a superior. Brian Su, CEO of a global consulting firm called Artisan Business Group,[55] indicates that "a high-ranking person in the company should never, ever initiate a handshake."[56]

When communicating in a group in China, it is important to maintain harmony, even if this harmony is superficial.[57] Rather than strongly expressing an emotion, it is better to be indirect. Exuberant praise can embarrass a group member because this may elevate his or her status and disturb harmony in the group. Complaints and criticisms should be handled with care, and expressions of negative emotions should be avoided if possible, with messages being expressed in a more indirect manner.[58] For example, Neng Zhao, a Chinese senior associate at private equity company Blue Oak Capital in[59] Beijing, China, once had an American boss and she felt mortified by his directness. Zhao says, "I remember I was so embarrassed when my American boss told me he didn't like something I was doing, right in front of me . . . The Chinese way would have been much more indirect."[60]

Before brand consultant Karen Post when to Jeddah, Saudi Arabia, to deliver a lecture on branding to around 400 managers and employees in marketing at Saudi Arabian Airlines, she bought an abaya, a long black robe/dress that some Muslim women wear.[61] Post indicated that on the Saudi Airline flight to Jeddah from New York's Kennedy Airport, some women were wearing the clothes they normally would wear in New York City. However, once the plane was about an hour away from landing and was in Saudi airspace, the women changed into abayas in the restrooms on the planes. Saudi Arabia has many restrictions on what women can and cannot do, and U.S. State Department Guidelines indicate that the religious police can compel women to wear abayas.[62] All in all, when working and traveling in other countries, it is important to understand the local culture.

PRACTICING JOB ROTATION OR TEMPORARY ASSIGNMENTS   Sometimes conflicts arise because individual organizational members simply do not understand the work activities and demands that others in an organization face. A financial analyst, for example, may be required to submit monthly reports to a member of the accounting department. These reports have a low priority for the analyst, who typically turns them in a couple of days late. On each due date the accountant calls the financial analyst, and conflict ensues as the accountant describes in detail why she must have the reports on time and the financial analyst describes everything else he needs to do. In situations such as this, job rotation or temporary assignments, which expand organizational members' knowledge base and appreciation of other departments, can be a useful way of resolving the conflict. If the financial analyst spends some time working in the accounting department, he may appreciate better the need for timely reports. Similarly, a temporary assignment in the finance department may help the accountant realize the demands a financial analyst faces and the need to streamline unnecessary aspects of reporting.

USING PERMANENT TRANSFERS OR DISMISSALS WHEN NECESSARY   Sometimes when other conflict resolution strategies do not work, managers may need to take more drastic steps, including permanent transfers or dismissals.

Suppose two first-line managers who work in the same department are always at each other's throats; frequent bitter conflicts arise between them even though they both seem to get along well with other employees. No matter what their supervisor does to increase their understanding of each other, the conflicts keep occurring. In this case the supervisor may want to transfer one or both managers so they do not have to interact as frequently.

When dysfunctionally high levels of conflict occur among top managers who cannot resolve their differences and understand each other, it may be necessary for one of them to leave the company. This is how Gerald Levin managed such conflict among top managers when he was chairman of Time Warner. Robert Daly and Terry Semel, one of the most respected management teams in Hollywood at the time and top managers in the Warner Brothers film company, had been in conflict with Michael Fuchs, a long-time veteran of Time Warner and head of the music division, for two years. As Semel described it, the company "was running like a dysfunctional family, and it needed one management team to run it."[63] Levin realized that Time Warner's future success rested on resolving this conflict, that it was unlikely that Fuchs would ever be able to work effectively with Daly and Semel, and that he risked losing Daly and Semel to another company if he did not resolve the conflict. Faced with that scenario, Levin asked Fuchs to resign.[64]

STRATEGIES FOCUSED ON THE WHOLE ORGANIZATION

CHANGING AN ORGANIZATION'S STRUCTURE OR CULTURE   Conflict can signal the need for changes in an organization's structure or culture. Sometimes managers can effectively resolve conflict by changing the organizational structure they use to group people and tasks.[65]

As an organization grows, for example, the *functional structure* (composed of departments such as marketing, finance, and production) that was effective when the organization was small may cease to be effective, and a shift to a *product structure* might effectively resolve conflicts (see Chapter 10).

Managers also can effectively resolve conflicts by increasing levels of integration in an organization. Recall from Chapter 15 that Hallmark Cards increased integration by using cross-functional teams to produce new cards. The use of cross-functional teams sped new card development and helped resolve conflicts between different departments. Now when a writer and an artist have a conflict over the appropriateness of the artist's illustrations, they do not pass criticisms back and forth from one department to another because they are on the same team and can directly resolve the issue on the spot.

Sometimes managers may need to take steps to change an organization's culture to resolve conflict (see Chapter 3). Norms and values in an organizational culture might inadvertently promote dysfunctionally high levels of conflict that are difficult to resolve. For instance, norms that stress respect for formal authority may create conflict that is difficult to resolve when an organization creates self-managed work teams and managers' roles and the structure of authority in the organization change. Values stressing individual competition may make it difficult to resolve conflicts when organizational members need to put others' interests ahead of their own. In circumstances such as these, taking steps to change norms and values can be an effective conflict resolution strategy.

ALTERING THE SOURCE OF CONFLICT   When the source of conflict is overlapping authority, different evaluation or reward systems, or status inconsistencies, managers can sometimes effectively resolve the conflict by directly altering its source. For example, managers can clarify the chain of command and reassign tasks and responsibilities to resolve conflicts due to overlapping authority.

LO17-3

Understand the nature of negotiation and why integrative bargaining is more effective than distributive negotiation.

negotiation A method of conflict resolution in which the parties consider various alternative ways to allocate resources to come up with a solution acceptable to all of them.

Negotiation

Negotiation is a particularly important conflict resolution technique for managers and other organizational members in situations where the parties to a conflict have approximately equal levels of power. During **negotiation** the parties to a conflict try to come up with a solution acceptable to themselves by considering various alternative ways to allocate resources to each other.[66] Sometimes the sides involved in a conflict negotiate directly with each other. Other times a **third-party negotiator** is relied on. Third-party negotiators are impartial individuals who are not directly involved in the conflict and have special expertise in handling conflicts and negotiations;[67] they are relied on to help the two negotiating parties reach an acceptable resolution of their conflict.[68] When a third-party negotiator acts as a **mediator**, his or her role in the negotiation process is to facilitate an effective negotiation between the two parties; mediators do not force either party to make concessions, nor can they force an agreement to resolve a conflict. **Arbitrators**, on the other hand, are third-party negotiators who can impose what they believe is a fair solution to a dispute that both parties are obligated to abide by.[69]

third-party negotiator An impartial individual with expertise in handling conflicts and negotiations who helps parties in conflict reach an acceptable solution.

mediator A third-party negotiator who facilitates negotiations but has no authority to impose a solution.

arbitrator A third-party negotiator who can impose what he or she thinks is a fair solution to a conflict that both parties are obligated to abide by.

distributive negotiation Adversarial negotiation in which the parties in conflict compete to win the most resources while conceding as little as possible.

integrative bargaining Cooperative negotiation in which the parties in conflict work together to achieve a resolution that is good for them both.

Distributive Negotiation and Integrative Bargaining

There are two major types of negotiation—distributive negotiation and integrative bargaining.[70] In **distributive negotiation**, the two parties perceive that they have a "fixed pie" of resources that they need to divide.[71] They take a competitive, adversarial stance. Each party realizes that he or she must concede something but is out to get the lion's share of the resources.[72] The parties see no need to interact with each other in the future and do not care if their interpersonal relationship is damaged or destroyed by their competitive negotiation.[73] In distributive negotiations, conflicts are handled by competition.

In **integrative bargaining**, the parties perceive that they might be able to increase the resource pie by trying to come up with a creative solution to the conflict. They do not view the conflict competitively as a win-or-lose situation; instead they view it cooperatively, as a win–win situation in which both parties can gain. Trust, information sharing, and the desire of both

In integrative bargaining, conflicts are handled by avoiding a win–lose competitive mindset, and creating a win–win situation for both parties.

parties to achieve a good resolution of the conflict characterize integrative bargaining.[74] In integrative bargaining, conflicts are handled through collaboration and/or compromise.

Consider how Adrian Hofbeck and Joseph Steinberg, partners in a successful German restaurant in the Midwest, resolved their recent conflict. Hofbeck and Steinberg founded the restaurant 15 years ago, share management responsibilities, and share equally in the restaurant's profits. Hofbeck recently decided that he wanted to retire and sell the restaurant, but retirement was the last thing Steinberg had in mind; he wanted to continue to own and manage the restaurant. Distributive negotiation was out of the question because Hofbeck and Steinberg were close friends and valued their friendship; neither wanted to do something that would hurt the other or their continuing relationship. So they opted for integrative bargaining, which they thought would help them resolve their conflict so both could achieve their goals and maintain their friendship.

Strategies to Encourage Integrative Bargaining

Managers in all kinds of organizations can rely on five strategies to facilitate integrative bargaining and avoid distributive negotiation: emphasizing superordinate goals; focusing on the problem, not the people; focusing on interests, not demands; creating new options for joint gain; and focusing on what is fair (see Table 17.1).[75] Hofbeck and Steinberg used each of these strategies to resolve their conflict.

EMPHASIZING SUPERORDINATE GOALS   *Superordinate goals* are goals that both parties agree to regardless of the source of their conflict. Increasing organizational effectiveness, increasing responsiveness to customers, and gaining a competitive advantage are just a few of the many superordinate goals that members of an organization can emphasize during integrative bargaining. Superordinate goals help parties in conflict to keep in mind the big picture and the fact that they are working together for a larger purpose or goal despite their disagreements. Hofbeck and Steinberg emphasized three superordinate goals during their bargaining: ensuring that the restaurant continued to survive and prosper, allowing Hofbeck to retire, and allowing Steinberg to remain an owner and manager as long as he wished.

FOCUSING ON THE PROBLEM, NOT THE PEOPLE   People who are in conflict may not be able to resist the temptation to focus on the other party's shortcomings and weaknesses, thereby personalizing the conflict. Instead of attacking the problem, the parties to the conflict attack each other. This approach is inconsistent with integrative bargaining and can easily lead both parties into a distributive negotiation mode. All parties to a conflict need to keep focused on the problem or on the source of the conflict and avoid the temptation to discredit one another.

Given their strong friendship, this was not much of an issue for Hofbeck and Steinberg, but they still had to be on their guard to avoid personalizing the conflict. Steinberg recalls that when they were having a hard time coming up with a solution, he started thinking that Hofbeck, a healthy 57-year-old, was lazy to want to retire so young: "If only he wasn't so lazy, we would never be in the mess we're in right now." Steinberg never mentioned these thoughts

Table 17.1

Negotiation Strategies for Integrative Bargaining

- Emphasize superordinate goals.
- Focus on the problem, not the people.
- Focus on interests, not demands.
- Create new options for joint gain.
- Focus on what is fair.

to Hofbeck (who later admitted that sometimes he was annoyed with Steinberg for being such a workaholic) because he realized that doing so would hurt their chances for reaching an integrative solution.

FOCUSING ON INTERESTS, NOT DEMANDS   Demands are *what* a person wants; interests are *why* the person wants them. When two people are in conflict, it is unlikely that the demands of both can be met. Their underlying interests, however, can be met, and meeting them is what integrative bargaining is all about.

Hofbeck's demand was that they sell the restaurant and split the proceeds. Steinberg's demand was that they keep the restaurant and maintain the status quo. Obviously both demands could not be met, but perhaps their interests could be. Hofbeck wanted to be able to retire, invest his share of the money from the restaurant, and live off the returns on the investment. Steinberg wanted to continue managing, owning, and deriving income from the restaurant.

CREATING NEW OPTIONS FOR JOINT GAIN   Once two parties to a conflict focus on their interests, they are on the road to achieving creative solutions to the conflict that will benefit them both. This win–win scenario means that rather than having a fixed set of alternatives from which to choose, the two parties can come up with new alternatives that might even expand the resource pie.

Hofbeck and Steinberg came up with three such alternatives. First, even though Steinberg did not have the capital, he could buy out Hofbeck's share of the restaurant. Hofbeck would provide the financing for the purchase, and in return Steinberg would pay him a reasonable return on his investment (the same kind of return he could have obtained had he taken his money out of the restaurant and invested it). Second, the partners could seek to sell Hofbeck's share in the restaurant to a third party under the stipulation that Steinberg would continue to manage the restaurant and receive income for his services. Third, the partners could continue to jointly own the restaurant. Steinberg would manage it and receive a proportionally greater share of its profits than Hofbeck, who would be an absentee owner not involved in day-to-day operations but would still receive a return on his investment in the restaurant.

FOCUSING ON WHAT IS FAIR   Focusing on what is fair is consistent with the principle of distributive justice, which emphasizes the fair distribution of outcomes based on the meaningful contributions that people make to organizations (see Chapter 5). It is likely that two parties in conflict will disagree on certain points and prefer different alternatives that each party believes may better serve his or her own interests or maximize his or her own outcomes. Emphasizing fairness and distributive justice will help the two parties come to a mutual agreement about what the best solution is to the problem.

Steinberg and Hofbeck agreed that Hofbeck should be able to cut his ties with the restaurant if he chose to do so. They decided to pursue the second alternative described and seek a suitable buyer for Hofbeck's share. They were successful in finding an investor who was willing to buy out Hofbeck's share and let Steinberg continue managing the restaurant. And they remained good friends.

When managers pursue these five strategies and encourage other organizational members to do so, they are more likely to be able to effectively resolve their conflicts through integrative bargaining. In addition, throughout the negotiation process, managers and other organizational members need to be aware of, and on their guard against, the biases that can lead to faulty decision making (see Chapter 7).[76]

LO17-5

Explain why managers need to be attuned to organizational politics, and describe the political strategies that managers can use to become politically skilled.

Organizational Politics

Managers must develop the skills necessary to manage organizational conflict for an organization to be effective. Suppose, however, that top managers are in conflict over the best strategy for an organization to pursue or the best structure to adopt to use organizational resources efficiently. In such situations resolving conflict is often difficult, and the parties to the conflict resort to organizational politics and political strategies to try to resolve the conflict in their favor.

organizational politics
Activities that managers engage in to increase their power and to use power effectively to achieve their goals and overcome resistance or opposition.

political strategies Tactics that managers use to increase their power and to use power effectively to influence and gain the support of other people while overcoming resistance or opposition.

Organizational politics are the activities that managers (and other members of an organization) engage in to increase their power and to use power effectively to achieve their goals and overcome resistance or opposition.[77] Managers often engage in organizational politics to resolve conflicts in their favor.

Political strategies are the specific tactics that managers (and other members of an organization) use to increase their power and to use power effectively to influence and gain the support of other people while overcoming resistance or opposition. Political strategies are especially important when managers are planning and implementing major changes in an organization: Managers need not only to gain support for their change initiatives and influence organizational members to behave in new ways but also to overcome often strong opposition from people who feel threatened by the change and prefer the status quo. By increasing their power, managers are better able to make needed changes. In addition to increasing their power, managers also must make sure they use their power in a way that actually enables them to influence others.

The Importance of Organizational Politics

The term *politics* has a negative connotation for many people. Some may think that managers who are political have risen to the top not because of their own merit and capabilities but because of whom they know. Or people may think that political managers are self-interested and wield power to benefit themselves, not their organization. There is a grain of truth to this negative connotation. Some managers do appear to misuse their power for personal benefit at the expense of their organization's effectiveness.

Nevertheless, organizational politics are often a positive force. Managers striving to make needed changes often encounter resistance from individuals and groups who feel threatened and wish to preserve the status quo. Effective managers engage in politics to gain support for and implement needed changes. Similarly, managers often face resistance from other managers who disagree with their goals for a group or for the organization and with what they are trying to accomplish. Engaging in organizational politics can help managers overcome this resistance and achieve their goals.

Indeed, managers cannot afford to ignore organizational politics. Everyone engages in politics to a degree—other managers, coworkers, and subordinates, as well as people outside an organization, such as suppliers. Those who try to ignore politics might as well bury their heads in the sand because in all likelihood they will be unable to gain support for their initiatives and goals.

Political Strategies for Gaining and Maintaining Power

Managers who use political strategies to increase and maintain their power are better able to influence others to work toward the achievement of group and organizational goals. (Recall from Chapter 14 that legitimate, reward, coercive, expert, and referent powers help managers influence others as leaders.) By controlling uncertainty, making themselves irreplaceable, being in a central position, generating resources, and building alliances, managers can increase their power (see Figure 17.4).[78] We next look at each of these strategies.

CONTROLLING UNCERTAINTY   Uncertainty is a threat for individuals, groups, and whole organizations and can interfere with effective performance and goal attainment. For example, uncertainty about job security is threatening for many workers and may cause top performers (who have the best chance of finding another job) to quit and take a more secure position with another organization. When an R&D department faces uncertainty about customer preferences, its members may waste valuable resources to develop a product, such as smokeless cigarettes, that customers do not want. When top managers face uncertainty about global demand, they may fail to export products to countries that want them and thus may lose a source of competitive advantage.

Managers who can control and reduce uncertainty for other managers, teams, departments, and the organization as a whole are likely to see their power increase.[79] Managers of labor unions gain power when they can eliminate uncertainty over job security for workers.

Figure 17.4

Political Strategies for Increasing Power

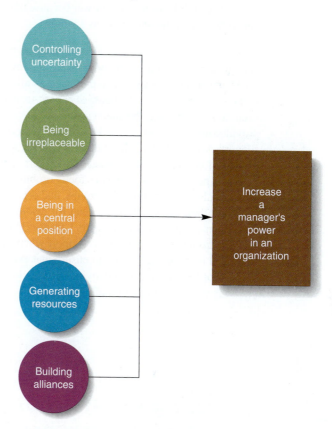

Marketing and sales managers gain power when they can eliminate uncertainty for other departments such as R&D by accurately forecasting customers' changing preferences. Top managers gain power when they are knowledgeable about global demand for an organization's products. Managers who can control uncertainty are likely to be in demand and be sought after by other organizations.

MAKING ONESELF IRREPLACEABLE   Managers gain power when they have valuable knowledge and expertise that allow them to perform activities no one else can handle. This is the essence of being irreplaceable.[80] The more central these activities are to organizational effectiveness, the more power managers gain from being irreplaceable.

BEING IN A CENTRAL POSITION   Managers in central positions are responsible for activities that are directly connected to an organization's goals and sources of competitive advantage and often are located in central positions in important communication networks in an organization.[81] Managers in key positions have control over crucial organizational activities and initiatives and have access to important information. Other organizational members depend on them for their knowledge, expertise, advice, and support, and the success of the organization as a whole is seen as riding on these managers. These consequences of being in a central position are likely to increase managers' power.

Managers who are outstanding performers, have a wide knowledge base, and have made important and visible contributions to their organizations are likely to be offered central positions that will increase their power.

GENERATING RESOURCES   Organizations need three kinds of resources to be effective: (1) input resources such as raw materials, skilled workers, and financial capital; (2) technical resources such as machinery and computers; and (3) knowledge resources such as marketing, information technology, or engineering expertise. To the extent that a manager can generate one or more of these kinds of resources for an organization, that manager's power is likely to increase.[82] In universities, for example, professors who win large grants to fund their research, from associations such as the National Science Foundation and the Army Research Institute, gain power because of the financial resources they generate for their departments and the university as a whole.

BUILDING ALLIANCES When managers build alliances, they develop mutually beneficial relationships with people both inside and outside the organization, as does Indra Nooyi in "A Manager's Challenge." The parties to an alliance support one another because doing so is in their best interests, and all parties benefit from the alliance. Alliances give managers power because they provide the managers with support for their initiatives. Partners to alliances provide support because they know the managers will reciprocate when their partners need support. Alliances can help managers achieve their goals and implement needed changes in organizations because they increase managers' levels of power.

Many powerful top managers focus on building alliances not only inside their organizations but also with individuals, groups, and organizations in the task and general environments on which their organizations depend for resources. These individuals, groups, and organizations enter alliances with managers because doing so is in their best interests and they know they can count on the managers' support when they need it. When managers build alliances, they need to be on their guard to ensure that everything is aboveboard, ethical, and legal.

As profiled in the accompanying "Ethics in Action" feature, sometimes managers build alliances with seemingly unlikely partners.

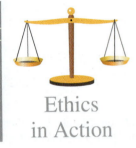

Ethics
in Action

Building Alliances at The Nature Conservancy

A large chemical company or individual fishermen would seem to have not that much in common with a large conservation organization devoted to protecting nature, land, forests, and dwindling fish populations.[83] In fact, it is not difficult to imagine that the conservation organization would be in conflict with such individuals and groups, and some conservation organizations have had heated conflicts with groups and organizations that they felt were threatening the natural environment.

This is definitely not the case, though, with The Nature Conservancy. The Nature Conservancy is the biggest conservation organization in the world.[84] A nonprofit organization, the conservancy has chapters in over 30 countries and every state within the United States. With over 1 million members and assets valued at more than $5 billion, the conservancy's annual income is around $1 billion.[85] The conservancy has either purchased or received as a donation over 177 million acres of land with environmental value. Government agencies often buy this land from the conservancy to create natural preserves and parks. While continuing with this legacy of acquiring lands at risk and ensuring that they are preserved, the conservancy has branched out to collaborate with groups and organizations to conserve and protect nature for people and the groups and organizations that provide them with goods and services.[86]

Leading these efforts is a dedicated group of scientists, managers, and leaders at the conservancy. Mark Tercek is the president and chief executive officer of The Nature Conservancy.[87] With a BA in English from Williams College and an MBA from Harvard, Tercek previously worked as the director of the Environmental Strategy Group at Goldman Sachs. Importantly, the initiatives and efforts that Tercek leads to protect nature and the environment at the conservancy are informed by a strong appreciation for ecology and conservation science and research. Peter Kareiva, chief scientist on The Nature Conservancy Leadership Team, leads some 600 scientists who work at the conservancy and is always involved in major decisions that Tercek makes. In fact, Tercek refers to Kareiva as his "closest intellectual advisor."[88] With an MS in

Trailhead at The Nature Conservancy Disney Wilderness Preserve in Florida. The Nature Conservancy has formed alliances with unlikely partners like Dow Chemical to conserve and protect nature.

environmental biology from the University of California at Irvine and a PhD in ecology and evolutionary biology from Cornell, Kareiva has worked as a professor, taught at eight universities, directed the Northwest Fisheries Science Center Conservation Biology Division of the National Oceanic and Atmospheric Administration, has published over 100 scientific articles, and was elected to the prestigious American Academy of Arts and Sciences.[89]

While one would think that a chemical company and a conservation organization would never be able to partner together, Tercek, Kareiva, and other leaders and scientists at The Nature Conservancy are in the midst of a five-year alliance with Dow Chemical.[90] Dow has periodically faced pollution allegations. For instance, citizens in Saginaw County, Michigan, filed suits against Dow, claiming that Dow polluted a river with dioxin. Why, then, would The Nature Conservancy engage in an alliance with Dow? Part of the reason is to assist Dow with inventorying and valuing its vast land and water resources around the globe. By assessing these natural resources and their "natural capital" value, Dow may be better equipped to figure out how to protect and improve the natural resources it controls.[91]

Nonetheless, critics argue that a conservation organization should not be receiving funding from a huge corporation like Dow. For example, Anne Rolfes, a founding director of the Louisiana Bucket Brigade,[92] which has had run-ins with Dow over alleged pollution, suggests that ". . . Dow is awful. . . . We would never take money from them or partner with them."[93] The Bucket Brigade is a nonprofit organization in Louisiana that helps neighborhoods bordering chemical plants and oil refineries keep their lands pollution-free.[94] Kareiva acknowledges that while things might not always go smoothly or as planned, on a global level, the alliance has the potential to yield a net benefit for the environment and conservancy. As Tercek puts it, "I know there's a lot of skepticism about these corporate initiatives, but for Dow to agree with us philosophically that it relies on nature for business reasons and to begin to put a business value on its natural assets, that's huge."[95]

The Nature Conservancy has also formed alliances with fishermen, resulting in the fishermen being able to sustain their livelihoods while meeting more stringent government regulations to protect shrinking fish populations and endangered habitats.[96] The conservancy's approach here and on other initiatives is both to protect nature and the environment and also forge alliances with the people who depend on the environment for their living and well-being—helping those individuals protect the resources that sustain them.

The Nature Conservancy has formed alliances with Latin American countries to protect their water supplies. For example, rather than creating water treatment plants, the conservancy helped Columbia to buy land near Bogota's watershed and pay soda plants and sugar farmers to run their businesses in a sustainable fashion.[97] Relying on research and science, Tercek, Kareiva, and other managers and leaders at The Nature Conservancy focus on building alliances with many different kinds of groups and organizations for mutual benefit.[98]

Political Strategies for Exercising Power

Politically skilled managers not only understand, and can use, the five strategies to increase their power; they also appreciate strategies for exercising their power. These strategies generally focus on how managers can use their power *unobtrusively*.[99] When managers exercise power unobtrusively, other members of an organization may not be aware that the managers are using their power to influence them. They may think they support these managers for a

Figure 17.5
Political Strategies for Exercising Power

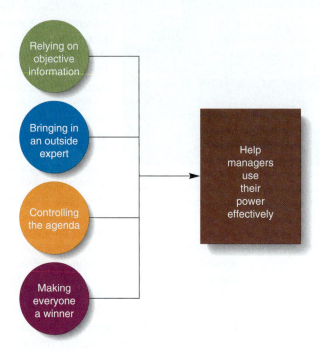

variety of reasons: because they believe it is the rational or logical thing to do, because they believe doing so is in their own best interests, or because they believe the position or decision the managers are advocating is legitimate or appropriate.

The unobtrusive use of power may sound devious, but managers typically use this strategy to bring about change and achieve organizational goals. Political strategies for exercising power to gain the support and concurrence of others include relying on objective information, bringing in an outside expert, controlling the agenda, and making everyone a winner (see Figure 17.5).[100]

RELYING ON OBJECTIVE INFORMATION Managers require the support of others to achieve their goals, implement changes, and overcome opposition. One way for a manager to gain this support and overcome opposition is to rely on objective information that supports the manager's initiatives. Reliance on objective information leads others to support the manager because of the facts; objective information causes others to believe that what the manager is proposing is the proper course of action. By relying on objective information, politically skilled managers unobtrusively exercise their power to influence others.

Take the case of Mary Callahan, vice president of Better Built Cabinets, a small cabinet company in the Southeast. Callahan is extremely influential in the company; practically every new initiative that she proposes to the president and owner of the company is implemented. Why is Callahan able to use her power in the company so effectively? Whenever she has an idea for a new initiative that she thinks the company might pursue, she and her subordinates begin by collecting objective information supporting the initiative. Recently Callahan decided that Better Built should develop a line of high-priced European-style kitchen cabinets. Before presenting her proposal to Better Built's president, she compiled objective information showing that (1) there was strong unmet demand for these kinds of cabinets, (2) Better Built could manufacture them in its existing production facilities, and (3) the new line had the potential to increase Better Built's sales by 20 percent while not detracting from sales of the company's other cabinets. Presented with this information, the president agreed to Callahan's proposal. Moreover, the president and other members of Better Built whose cooperation was needed to implement the proposal supported it because they thought it would help Better Built gain a competitive advantage. Using objective information to support her position enabled Callahan to unobtrusively exercise her power and influence others to support her proposal.

BRINGING IN AN OUTSIDE EXPERT   Bringing in an outside expert to support a proposal or decision can, at times, provide managers with some of the same benefits that the use of objective information does. It lends credibility to a manager's initiatives and causes others to believe that what the manager is proposing is the appropriate or rational thing to do. Suppose Callahan had hired a consultant to evaluate whether her idea was a good one. The consultant reports back to the president that the new European-style cabinets are likely to fulfill Callahan's promises and increase Better Built's sales and profits. As with objective information, this information provided by an objective expert can lend a sense of legitimacy to Callahan's proposal and allow her to unobtrusively exercise power to influence others.

Although you might think consultants and other outside experts are neutral or objective, they sometimes are hired by managers who want them to support a certain position or decision in an organization. For instance, when managers face strong opposition from others who fear that a decision will harm their interests, the managers may bring in an outside expert. They hope this expert will be perceived as a neutral observer to lend credibility and "objectivity" to their point of view. The support of an outside expert may cause others to believe that a decision is indeed the right one. Of course sometimes consultants and other outside experts actually are brought into organizations to be objective and guide managers on the appropriate course of action.

CONTROLLING THE AGENDA   Managers also can exercise power unobtrusively by controlling the agenda—influencing which alternatives are considered or even whether a decision is made.[101] When managers influence the alternatives that are considered, they can make sure that each considered alternative is acceptable to them and that undesirable alternatives are not in the feasible set. In a hiring context, for example, managers can exert their power unobtrusively by ensuring that job candidates whom they do not find acceptable do not make their way onto the list of finalists for an open position. They do this by making sure that these candidates' drawbacks or deficiencies are communicated to everyone involved in making the hiring decision. When three finalists for an open position are discussed and evaluated in a hiring meeting, a manager may seem to exert little power or influence and just go along with what the rest of the group wants. However, the manager may have exerted power in the hiring process unobtrusively by controlling which candidates made it to the final stage.

Sometimes managers can prevent a decision from being made. A manager in charge of a community relations committee, for example, may not favor a proposal for the organization to become more involved in local youth groups such as the Boy Scouts and the Girl Scouts. The manager can exert influence in this situation by not including the proposal on the agenda for the committee's next meeting. Alternatively, the manager could place the proposal at the end of the agenda for the meeting and feel confident that the committee will run out of time and not get to the last items on the agenda because that is what always happens. Either approach enables the manager to unobtrusively exercise power. Committee members do not perceive this manager as trying to influence them to turn down the proposal. Rather, the manager has made the proposal into a nonissue that is not even considered.

MAKING EVERYONE A WINNER   Often, politically skilled managers can exercise their power unobtrusively because they make sure that everyone whose support they need benefits personally from providing that support. By making everyone a winner, a manager can influence other organizational members because these members see supporting the manager as being in their best interest.

When top managers turn around troubled companies, some organizational members and parts of the organization are bound to suffer due to restructurings that often entail painful layoffs. However, the power of the turnaround CEO often accelerates as it becomes clear that the future of the company is on surer footing and the organization and its stakeholders are winners as a result of the change effort.

Making everyone a winner not only is an effective way of exercising power but, when used consistently and forthrightly, can increase managers' power and influence over time. That is, when a manager actually does make everyone a winner, all stakeholders will see it as in their best interests to support the manager and his or her initiatives. When managers who make everyone a winner have strong ethical values, everyone really is a winner, as profiled in the accompanying "Ethics in Action" feature.

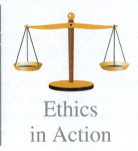

El Faro Estate Coffee Benefits Multiple Stakeholders

When Estuardo Porras was taking business classes at Pepperdine University in Malibu, California, in the 1990s, he was surprised to see the high prices that Starbucks charged for coffee.[102] In his native country of Guatemala, coffee used to be the major export until prices declined in the 1980s due to a large influx of low-cost coffee beans coming on the market from countries like Vietnam. Porras had a vision of returning to Guatemala, resurrecting an old coffee plantation, and operating it in a socially responsible way that protected the natural environment, looked out for and contributed to the well-being of the workers who operated it and the local community, and produced high-quality coffee beans that a socially responsible organization like Starbucks would be interested in purchasing.[103]

Fermenting coffee beans in recycled water is just one of the many areas in which Estuardo Porras has transformed El Faro into a productive, environmentally responsible enterprise.

Porras returned to Guatemala, borrowed $1.25 million from his father, who had recently sold a Coca-Cola bottling company, and transformed an abandoned plantation called El Faro into a marvel of environmental sustainability, social responsibility, and effectiveness.[104] El Faro Estate Coffee protects the natural environment, helps a poor community, and produces high-quality arabica coffee used by specialty coffee companies like Starbucks. And because of Starbucks' commitment to purchasing coffee beans from growers that abide by ethical, social, and environmental values, El Faro can sell all the coffee beans it grows that meet Starbucks' standards for more than the beans would sell for on the general commodity export market.[105]

El Faro is located near a volcano, and the ash from the volcano provides excellent soil for growing coffee. Coffee beans are fermented in recycled water, and the casings from the beans are eaten by earthworms, yielding an organic fertilizer. Much of the work on the plantation is done by hand.[106] El Faro supports a free elementary school for children in the local community and buses older children to a high school in the vicinity. Employees receive free health care after they have been with El Faro for three months; the care is provided in the plantation's medical office, staffed by a part-time doctor and full-time nurse. They also receive 15 days of paid vacation annually. Many of El Faro's full-time employees and their families live on the plantation; El Faro also has part-time employees.[107]

Porras initially sold El Faro's coffee beans on the commodity export market while persistently trying to make inroads at Starbucks by sending letters and coffee samples to no avail. Eventually an exporter who bought beans from El Faro persuaded two coffee buyers from Starbucks to visit the plantation. After a tour and coffee tasting, the buyers were so delighted with what they saw and tasted that they ordered coffee from El Faro that day and gave Porras the opportunity to participate in a program that gives long-term contracts to growers who are socially responsible.[108]

Today El Faro Estate Coffee is sold exclusively to Starbucks, and Finca El Faro is a Starbucks' C.A.F.E. Practices supplier.[109] Clearly Porras has made everyone a winner and, in the process, has created a sustainable and thriving business.[110]

Summary and Review

LO17-1, 17-2

ORGANIZATIONAL CONFLICT Organizational conflict is the discord that arises when the goals, interests, or values of different individuals or groups are incompatible and those individuals or groups block or thwart each other's attempts to achieve their objectives. Four types of conflict arising in organizations are interpersonal conflict, intragroup conflict, intergroup conflict, and interorganizational conflict. Sources of conflict in organizations include different goals and time horizons, overlapping authority, task interdependencies, different evaluation or reward systems, scarce resources, and status inconsistencies. Conflict management strategies focused on individuals include increasing awareness of the sources of conflict, increasing diversity awareness and skills, practicing job rotation or temporary assignments, and using permanent transfers or dismissals when necessary. Strategies focused on the whole organization include changing an organization's structure or culture and altering the source of conflict.

LO17-3, 17-4

NEGOTIATION Negotiation is a conflict resolution technique used when parties to a conflict have approximately equal levels of power and try to come up with an acceptable way to allocate resources to each other. In distributive negotiation, the parties perceive that there is a fixed level of resources for them to allocate, and they compete to receive as much as possible at the expense of the other party, not caring about their relationship in the future. In integrative bargaining, both parties perceive that they may be able to increase the resource pie by coming up with a creative solution to the conflict, trusting each other, and cooperating with each other to achieve a win–win resolution. Five strategies that managers can use to facilitate integrative bargaining are to emphasize superordinate goals; focus on the problem, not the people; focus on interests, not demands; create new options for joint gain; and focus on what is fair.

LO17-5

ORGANIZATIONAL POLITICS Organizational politics are the activities that managers (and other members of an organization) engage in to increase their power and to use power effectively to achieve their goals and overcome resistance or opposition. Effective managers realize that politics can be a positive force that enables them to make needed changes in an organization. Five important political strategies for gaining and maintaining power are controlling uncertainty, making oneself irreplaceable, being in a central position, generating resources, and building alliances. Political strategies for effectively exercising power focus on how to use power unobtrusively and include relying on objective information, bringing in an outside expert, controlling the agenda, and making everyone a winner.

Management in Action

Topics for Discussion and Action

Discussion

1. Discuss why too little conflict in an organization can be just as detrimental as too much conflict. **[LO17-1]**

2. Why are compromise and collaboration more effective ways of handling conflict than accommodation, avoidance, and competition? **[LO17-2]**

3. Why should managers promote integrative bargaining rather than distributive negotiation? **[LO17-3]**

4. How can managers promote integrative bargaining? **[LO17-4]**

5. Why do organizational politics affect practically every organization? **[LO17-5]**

6. Why do effective managers need good political skills? **[LO17-5]**

7. What steps can managers take to ensure that organizational politics are a positive force leading to a competitive advantage, not a negative force leading to personal advantage at the expense of organizational goal attainment? **[LO17-5]**

8. Think of a member of an organization whom you know and who is particularly powerful. What political strategies does this person use to increase his or her power? **[LO17-5]**

9. Why is it best to use power unobtrusively? How are people likely to react to power that is exercised obtrusively? **[LO17-5]**

Action

10. Interview a manager in a local organization to determine the kinds of conflicts that occur in his or her organization and the strategies that are used to manage them. **[LO17-1, 17-2]**

Building Management Skills

Effective and Ineffective Conflict Resolution
[LO17-1, 17-2]

Think about two recent conflicts that you had with other people—one conflict that you felt was effectively resolved (C1) and one that you felt was ineffectively resolved (C2). The other people involved could be coworkers, students, family members, friends, or members of an organization that you are a member of. Answer the following questions:

1. Briefly describe C1 and C2. What type of conflict was involved in each of these incidents?

2. What was the source of the conflict in C1 and in C2?

3. What conflict management strategies were used in C1 and in C2?

4. What could you have done differently to more effectively manage conflict in C2?

5. How was the conflict resolved in C1 and in C2?

Managing Ethically [LO17-5]

One political strategy managers can engage in is controlling the agenda by subtly influencing which alternatives are considered or even whether a decision is up for discussion. Some employees believe this can be unethical and can prevent important issues from being raised and points of view from being expressed.

Questions

1. Either individually or in a group, think about the ethical implications of controlling the agenda as a political strategy.

2. What steps can managers and organizations take to ensure that this strategy does not result in important issues and differing points of view being suppressed in an organization?

Small Group Breakout Exercise

Negotiating a Solution [LO17-3, 17-4]

Form groups of three or four people. One member of your group will play the role of Jane Rister, one member will play the role of Michael Schwartz, and one or two members will be observer(s) and spokesperson(s) for your group.

Jane Rister and Michael Schwartz are assistant managers in a large department store. They report directly to the store manager. Today they are meeting to discuss some important problems they need to solve but about which they disagree.

The first problem hinges on the fact that either Rister or Schwartz needs to be on duty whenever the store is open. For the last six months, Rister has taken most of the least desirable hours (nights and weekends). They are planning their schedules for the next six months. Rister thought Schwartz would take more of the undesirable times, but Schwartz has informed Rister that his wife has just gotten a nursing job that requires her to work weekends, so he needs to stay home weekends to take care of their infant daughter.

The second problem concerns a department manager who has had a hard time retaining salespeople in his department. The turnover rate in his department is twice that in the other store departments. Rister thinks the manager is ineffective and wants to fire him. Schwartz thinks the high turnover is just a fluke and the manager is effective.

The last problem concerns Rister's and Schwartz's vacation schedules. Both managers want to take off the week of July 4, but one of them needs to be in the store whenever it is open.

1. The group members playing Rister and Schwartz assume their roles and negotiate a solution to these three problems.

2. Observers take notes on how Rister and Schwartz negotiate solutions to their problems.

3. Observers determine the extent to which Rister and Schwartz use distributive negotiation or integrative bargaining to resolve their conflicts.

4. When called on by the instructor, observers communicate to the rest of the class how Rister and Schwartz resolved their conflicts, whether they used distributive negotiation or integrative bargaining, and their actual solutions.

Exploring the World Wide Web [LO17-1, 17-2]

Think of a major conflict in the business world that you have read about in the past few weeks. Then search on the web for magazine and newspaper articles presenting differing viewpoints and perspectives on the conflict.

Based on what you have read, how are the parties to this conflict handling it? Is their approach functional or dysfunctional, and why?

Be the Manager [LO17-1, 17-2, 17-3, 17-4, 17-5]

You are a middle manager in a large corporation, and lately you feel that you are caught between a rock and a hard place. Times are tough; your unit has experienced layoffs; your surviving subordinates are overworked and demoralized; and you feel that you have no meaningful rewards, such as the chance for a pay raise, bonus, or promotion, to motivate them with. Your boss keeps increasing the demands on your unit as well as the unit's

responsibilities. Moreover, you believe that you and your subordinates are being unfairly blamed for certain problems beyond your control. You believe that you have the expertise and skills to perform your job effectively and also that your subordinates are capable and effective in their jobs. Yet you feel that you are on shaky ground and powerless given the current state of affairs. What are you going to do?

The New York Times Case in the News

Advocates for Workers Raise the Ire of Business

As America's labor unions have lost members and clout, new types of worker advocacy groups have sprouted nationwide, and they have started to get on businesses' nerves—protesting low wages at Capital Grille restaurants, for instance, and demonstrating outside Austin City Hall in Texas against giving Apple tax breaks.

After ignoring these groups for years, business groups and powerful lobbyists, heavily backed by the restaurant industry, are mounting an aggressive campaign against them, maintaining that they are fronts for organized labor.

Business officials say these groups often demonize companies unfairly and inaccurately, while the groups question why corporations have attacked such fledgling organizations.

The United States Chamber of Commerce issued a detailed report in November criticizing what it calls "progressive activist foundations" that donate millions of dollars to these groups, which are often called worker centers. The business-backed Worker Center Watch has asked Florida's attorney general to investigate the finances of the Coalition of Immokalee Workers. That group sponsored a protest last March in which more than 100 workers marched 200 miles to the headquarters of Publix supermarkets to urge it to pay more for tomatoes so farmworkers could be paid more.

A prominent Washington lobbyist, Richard Berman, has run full-page ads attacking the Restaurant Opportunities Center, accusing it of intimidating opponents. He has even set up a separate website, ROCexposed. com, to attack the group.

The Restaurant Opportunities Center is one of the nation's largest worker centers, sponsoring repeated protests inside Capital Grille restaurants

and winning sizable settlements from famous chefs. The group even infiltrated the National Restaurant Association's lobbying day on Capitol Hill, learning about the association's goals and strategies.

Business groups argue that worker centers should face the same strictures as labor unions under federal law, including detailed financial disclosure, regular election of leaders and bans on certain types of picketing. Business groups say worker centers act like unions by targeting specific employers and pushing them to improve wages.

Regarding the Restaurant Opportunities Center, Scott DeFife, an executive vice president at the National Restaurant Association, said: "They're trying to have it both ways. They're a union and not a union. They're organizing workers but not organizing workers. They have a history of tactics unions couldn't get away with."

Business groups say they have grown far more concerned about these new organizations since Richard L. Trumka, the AFL–CIO's president, announced last March that organized labor would work closely with these groups, many of which were formed to help immigrant workers whom unions had long overlooked. "For the employer community, it's a question of what does this grow into," said Glenn Spencer, executive director of the Chamber's Workforce Freedom Initiative, which commissioned the study on foundation funding. "Judging from Trumka's remarks, organized labor sees a lot of potential in this model."

According to that study, millions of dollars have flowed to worker centers from 21 foundations. From 2009 to 2012, it found, the Marguerite Casey Foundation gave $300,000 to the Southwest Workers Union and

$300,000 to the Coalition of Immokalee Workers. The Ford Foundation gave $717,000 to the National Domestic Workers Alliance, $1.15 million to the New Orleans Workers Center for Racial Justice, and $2.4 million to the Restaurant Opportunities Center.

Mr. Berman, who receives millions of dollars from business to fight unions and oppose a higher minimum wage, acknowledges that he is using a hammer to prevent these groups from growing far more powerful and troublesome.

"There's quite a range of activity among worker centers," said Mr. Berman, whose lobbying firm has spawned numerous spinoff nonprofits, including the Center for Union Facts. "They have yet to reach the point of being a long-term problem. We're trying to stay ahead of the curve."

Saru Jayaraman, a co-founder of the Restaurant Opportunities Center, has repeatedly strategized to get under the industry's skin. Her group does an annual dining guide, giving a thumbs down to restaurants it says treats employees poorly by, for instance, avoiding paid sick days.

The group enraged one of New York's top chefs, Daniel Boulud, by demonstrating outside his Daniel restaurant with a 12-foot-tall inflatable cockroach, asserting that the restaurant's Hispanic and Bangladeshi employees faced discrimination when they applied to become waiters. Her group reached a confidential settlement with Mr. Boulud. After a similar protest against Mario Batali's Del Posto restaurant in Manhattan, he reached a settlement that called for paying $1.15 million over misappropriated tips and unpaid overtime and included new policies on promotions and paid sick days.

Because of its in-your-face tactics and numerous successes, the restaurant group has faced many attacks from business.

"It's flattering," Ms. Jayaraman said. "The fact that they're attacking us is a sign that they feel threatened. That's what happens when you challenge the industry to do the right thing."

Greg Asbed, co-founder of the Coalition of Immokalee Workers, noted that numerous companies had signed onto his group's far-reaching "Fair Food Program" to improve pay and working conditions. The group announced on Thursday that Walmart had joined the program, which calls for paying a penny more per pound for Florida tomatoes. But Mr. Asbed criticized some attacks leveled by business as "McCarthy-era tactics." "Attacking workers who are fighting poverty wages, sexual harassment and other problems in the food industry is doing a disservice to those companies that are working to prepare the industry for the challenges of the 21st century," he said.

The chamber questions not just the millions that foundations are giving worker centers but also the image that they run on a shoestring budget.

But worker center leaders say they need foundation funding to get off the ground and keep operating. Some foundations viewed the chamber's report as a brushback pitch intended to discourage them from giving.

In a statement, the Ford Foundation said: "Growing numbers of workers are finding themselves in low-wage jobs with limited resources to support a family and move up the economic ladder. The foundation's support for worker centers is one part of our effort to help more hard-working people climb out of poverty and achieve economic security."

Industry officials say that when the Restaurant Opportunities Center negotiated with Mr. Batali about promotions and other policies after suing him, those negotiations resembled collective bargaining. But in 2006, the general counsel's office of the National Labor Relations Board concluded that ROC was not a labor organization under federal law, finding that it was not engaged in a pattern of dealing with specific employers.

Ms. Jayaraman said her group was not bargaining, but instead seeking injunctive relief to settle a lawsuit. Mr. Berman, the lobbyist whom the CBS program *60 Minutes* once called "Dr. Evil," has mounted a multipronged offensive against worker centers. He is hitting not just ROC and the Immokalee coalition, but also the recent fast-food strikes and Black Friday protests at Walmart, which have strong union backing. "They put on a costume and call themselves something other than a union," Mr. Berman said. "They're doing Potemkin-village unionization." He declined to disclose his sources of funding.

Janice R. Fine, a labor relations professor at Rutgers, said one should distinguish between efforts like the Walmart protests, which were largely organized by a labor union, and worker centers, which are generally independent of unions.

"Business groups have this notion that unions have created worker centers as front groups, that they are creatures of these big institutions," Professor Fine said. "The idea that they are sort of offspring of organized labor is just wrong. They were often set up because of a vacuum left by the labor movement. There was often downright hostility between them."

Source: Steven Greenhouse, "Advocates for Workers Raise the Ire of Business," *The New York Times,* January 17, 2014. Copyright © 2014. Used with permission of The New York Times.

Questions for Discussion

1. What types of conflicts are described in this Case in the News?

2. What are some potential sources of the conflicts?

3. What conflict management strategies do you think are being used to manage the conflicts?

4. How might integrative bargaining be used to resolve some of the conflicts described in this case?

CHAPTER 18

Using Advanced Information Technology to Increase Performance

Learning Objectives

After studying this chapter, you should be able to:

LO18-1 Differentiate between data and information, and explain how the attributes of useful information allow managers to make better decisions.

LO18-2 Describe three reasons why managers must have access to information to perform their tasks and roles effectively.

LO18-3 Describe the computer hardware and software innovations that created the IT revolution and changed the way managers behave.

LO18-4 Differentiate among seven performance-enhancing kinds of management information systems.

LO18-5 Explain how IT is helping managers build strategic alliances and network structures to increase efficiency and effectiveness.

How can managers harness the latest technology to improve efficiency and performance? Imagine you are sitting at your desk writing a report on your computer. How will the boss know how productive you are? She could install a program that monitors the number of keystrokes you make on the computer, or watch you from another cubicle. But there's a new way for the boss to know everything you do. Imagine that while you are working, you are wearing a sensor, just like your employee ID badge, on a lanyard around your neck.

The sensor picks up your body movements, voice inflections, and environmental factors like lighting and temperature. It records that you are sitting at your desk busily typing your report. After 30 minutes, you start to feel a bit fatigued. The badge notes that your pace has slowed. After an hour, you decide to take a short break before your upcoming meeting. The badge records your movements from your desk to the break room. In the break room, you run into a colleague who asks about your fantasy football team. You speak animatedly about how well it is doing. The device records to whom you are speaking (if the other person is also wearing a sensor) and the enthusiasm in your voice. Then the badge tracks your movements from the break room to the conference room for your meeting. It then records who else is in the meeting. If you sit quietly at the meeting and do not contribute, the badge records that. If you nod your head or speak, the badge records that as well.

What is this sensor? It's a "wearable." Wearables allow companies to track where employees are, what they are doing, and how enthusiastically they are doing it. Wearables are somewhat like pedometers, but they do much more than measure steps. With wearables, companies can compare how animated a worker is around certain colleagues and how unanimated that worker is around others. It can tell in which meetings a worker participates and in which the worker prefers to keep quiet.

A smart wristband which has been synchronized with a smartphone. The wristband is a "wearable," a device that allows companies to keep track of workers and allows information to flow from one device to another.

Wearables can come in the form of smart watches, eyeglasses, earpieces, badges, and other devices.[1] For example, a small camera in a pair of "smart glasses" developed by Vizuix can be worn by distribution center workers to automatically scan bar codes and provide information to the worker in a visual display. The glasses can warn workers if an item is fragile or needs to be picked up a certain way. The glasses also connect to software that can track the flow of workers throughout the distribution center. They can feed back information about which item the workers should pick up next and the fastest route to the item.[2]

Another organization that has used wearables is the Buffalo Bills' football team. The team has embedded a wearable called OptimEye from Catapult Sports in the players' shirts. The device measures speed, acceleration, and distance. The data provided by the OptimEye gives the coaches a "Player-Load" statistic that allows them to consider whether a player is becoming fatigued. Fatigue is a common cause of injury. If the OptimEye shows that a player ran a lot in one practice, the coach might reduce the running requirement in the next practice to avoid injuring the player. Also, the data provided by the device allow different coaches on the team to see everything each player is doing. So if a player practices with the special teams coach and then with the defense coach, both coaches will know how hard the player worked. In the long term, the team

may be able to use all the data collected to gain new insights into training.[3]

Wearables can provide much valuable data that can be used to improve productivity. In fact, one study found the productivity of workers using wearables increased by 8.5 percent and their job satisfaction increased by 3.5 percent.[4] But there are problems as well. Workers can feel that wearables impinge upon their privacy, that they are never alone at work, even in the bathroom. Also, workers may feel that the only purpose of the wearable is to improve outcomes in efficiency or productivity for the company.[5] Research indicates that when new technologies are touted as improving efficiency, workers tend to resent the meddling of management.[6]

One organization that uses a wearable, Sociometric Solutions, suggests reassuring employees that their privacy is protected by letting them know what is being tracked, telling them that managers will see aggregate data, not each individual's data, and making participation voluntary. Companies also can present wearables as something that will help workers by making work safer or more interesting and autonomous.[7] Ben Waber, the president and CEO of Sociometric Solutions, says, "What we're trying to do is really quantify what people have always felt to be unquantifiable. Things like, how are people interacting with each other? How do you talk to customers? How engaged are you in a conversation? And how is information flowing in an organization?"[8]

Overview   In a world in which business activities of all kinds are increasingly conducted through the Internet, the challenge facing managers is to continually update and improve their use of advancing IT to increase organizational performance. Managers must utilize the most effective IT solutions such as social networking and cloud computing to assist their employees and customers, or risk being surpassed by more effective rivals who have developed superior IT competencies. Google and Apple have become two of the most valuable companies in the world because they provide advanced IT solutions that increase people's ability to access, search, and use the potential of the WWW and communicate with others. The most successful B&M and online companies, such as Walmart, Best Buy, Amazon.com, and eBay, excel in developing improved company-specific IT solutions. The implication is clear: There are enormous opportunities for managers of all kinds of organizations to find new ways to employ IT to use organizational resources more efficiently and effectively.

In this chapter we begin by looking at the relationship between information and the manager's job and then examine the ongoing IT revolution. Then we discuss six types of management information systems, each of which is based on a different sort of IT, which can help managers perform their jobs more efficiently and effectively. Next we examine the impact of rapidly evolving IT on managers' jobs and on an organization's competitive advantage. By the end of this chapter, you will understand how new developments in IT are profoundly shaping managers' tasks and roles and the way organizations operate.

Information and the Manager's Job

data Raw, unsummarized, and unanalyzed facts.

information Data that are organized in a meaningful fashion.

Managers cannot plan, organize, lead, and control effectively unless they have access to information. Information is the source of the knowledge and intelligence they need to make the right decisions. Information, however, is not the same as data.[9] **Data** are raw, unsummarized, and unanalyzed facts such as volume of sales, level of costs, or number of customers. **Information** is data that are organized in a meaningful fashion, such as in a graph showing the changes in sales volume or costs over time. Data alone do not tell managers anything; information, in contrast, can communicate a great deal of useful knowledge to the person who receives it—such as a manager who sees sales falling or costs rising. The distinction between data and information is important because one purpose of IT is to help managers transform data into information to make better managerial decisions.

To further clarify the difference between data and information, consider a supermarket manager who must decide how much shelf space to allocate to two breakfast cereal brands: Dentist's Delight and Sugar Supreme. Most supermarkets use checkout scanners to record individual sales and store the data on a computer. Accessing this computer, the manager might find that Dentist's Delight sells 50 boxes per day and Sugar Supreme sells 25 boxes per day. These raw data, however, are of little value in helping the manager decide how to allocate shelf space. The manager also needs to know how much shelf space each cereal currently occupies and how much profit each cereal generates for the supermarket.

LO18-1

Differentiate between data and information, and explain how the attributes of useful information allow managers to make better decisions.

Suppose the manager discovers that Dentist's Delight occupies 10 feet of shelf space and Sugar Supreme occupies 4 feet and that Dentist's Delight generates 20 cents of profit a box while Sugar Supreme generates 40 cents of profit a box. By putting these three bits of data together (number of boxes sold, amount of shelf space, and profit per box), the manager gets some useful information on which to base a decision: Dentist's Delight generates $1 of profit per foot of shelf space per day [(50 boxes $\times$ $.20)/10 feet], and Sugar Supreme generates $2.50 of profit per foot of shelf space per day [(25 boxes $\times$ $.40)/4 feet]. Armed with this information, the manager might decide to allocate less shelf space to Dentist's Delight and more to Sugar Supreme.

Attributes of Useful Information

Four factors determine the usefulness of information to a manager: quality, timeliness, completeness, and relevance (see Figure 18.1).

QUALITY Accuracy and reliability determine the quality of information.[10] The greater its accuracy and reliability, the higher is the quality of information. Modern IT gives managers access to high-quality real-time information that they can use to improve long-term decision

Figure 18.1

Factors Affecting the Usefulness of Information

making and alter short-term operating decisions, such as how much of a particular product to make daily or monthly. Supermarket managers, for example, use handheld bar code readers linked to a server to monitor and record how demand for particular products such as milk, chicken, or bread changes daily so they know how to restock their shelves to ensure the products are always available.

TIMELINESS   Information that is timely is available when it is required to allow managers to make the optimal decision—not after the decision has been made. In today's rapidly changing world, the need for timely information often means information must be available on a real-time basis—hence the enormous growth in the demand for PDAs such as smartphones.[11] **Real-time information** is information that reflects current changes in business conditions. In an industry that experiences rapid changes, real-time information may need to be updated frequently.

Airlines use real-time information about the number of flight bookings and competitors' prices to adjust their prices hourly to maximize their revenues. Thus, for example, the fare for flights from New York to Seattle might change from one hour to the next as fares are reduced to fill empty seats and raised when most seats have been sold. Airlines use real-time information about reservations to adjust fares at the last possible moment to fill planes and maximize revenues. U.S. airlines make more than 100,000 fare changes each day.[12] Obviously the managers who make such pricing decisions need real-time information about current market demand.

COMPLETENESS   Information that is complete gives managers all the information they need to exercise control, achieve coordination, or make an effective decision. Recall from Chapter 7, however, that managers rarely have access to complete information. Instead, because of uncertainty, ambiguity, and bounded rationality, they have to make do with incomplete information.[13] One function of IT is to increase the completeness of managers' information.

RELEVANCE   Information that is relevant is useful and suits a manager's particular needs and circumstances. Irrelevant information is useless and may actually hurt the performance of a busy manager who has to spend valuable time determining whether information is relevant. Given the massive amounts of information that managers are now exposed to and their limited information-processing capabilities, a company's information systems designers need to ensure that managers receive only relevant information.

What Is Information Technology?

Information technology (IT) is the set of methods or techniques for acquiring, organizing, storing, manipulating, and transmitting information.[14] A **management information system (MIS)** is a specific form of IT that managers select and use to generate the specific, detailed

real-time information
Frequently updated information that reflects current conditions.

information technology The set of methods or techniques for acquiring, organizing, storing, manipulating, and transmitting information.

management information system (MIS) A specific form of IT that managers utilize to generate the specific, detailed information they need to perform their roles effectively.

Charts and graphs may be clichés at managerial meetings, but the data they represent are key for making informed decisions.

information they need to perform their roles effectively. Management information systems have existed for as long as there have been organizations, which is a long time indeed—merchants in ancient Egypt used clay tablets to record their transactions. Before the computing age, most systems were paper-based: Clerks recorded important information on paper documents (often in duplicate or triplicate) in words and numbers; sent copies of the documents to superiors, customers, or suppliers; and stored other copies in filing cabinets for future reference.

Rapid advances in the power of IT—specifically the development of ever more powerful and sophisticated computer hardware and software— have had a fundamental impact on organizations and managers, as suggested by the developments in employee monitoring systems discussed in "A Manager's Challenge." Some recent IT developments, such as inventory management and customer relationship management (CRM) systems, contribute so much to performance that organizations that do *not* adopt it, or that implement it ineffectively, become uncompetitive compared with organizations that do adopt it.[15] Predictions for 2014 and beyond include having customer content and services driven by mobile applications and having big data and analytics improve customer service and loyalty.[16]

Managers need information for three reasons: to make effective decisions, to control the activities of the organization, and to coordinate the activities of the organization. Next we examine these uses of information in detail.

Information and Decisions

Much of management (planning, organizing, leading, and controlling) is about making decisions. For example, the marketing manager must decide what price to charge for a product, what distribution channels to use, and what promotional messages to emphasize to maximize sales. The manufacturing manager must decide how much of a product to make and how to make it. The purchasing manager must decide from whom to purchase inputs and what inventory of inputs to hold. The human relations manager must decide how much employees should be paid, how they should be trained, and what benefits they should be given. The engineering manager must make decisions about new product design. Top managers must decide how to allocate scarce financial resources among competing projects, how best to structure and control the organization, and what business-level strategy the organization should be pursuing. And regardless of their functional orientation, all managers have to make decisions about matters such as what performance evaluation to give to a subordinate.

To make effective decisions, managers need information both from inside the organization and from external stakeholders. When deciding how to price a product, for example, marketing managers need information about how consumers will react to different prices. They need information about unit costs because they do not want to set the price below the cost of production. And they need information about competitive strategy because pricing strategy should be consistent with an organization's competitive strategy. Some of this information will come from outside the organization (for example, from consumer surveys) and some from inside the organization (information about production costs comes from manufacturing). As this example suggests, managers' ability to make effective decisions rests on their ability to acquire and process information.

Information and Control

As discussed in Chapter 11, controlling is the process through which managers regulate how efficiently and effectively an organization and its members perform the activities necessary to achieve its stated goals.[17] Managers achieve control over organizational activities by taking four steps (see Figure 11.2): (1) They establish measurable standards of performance or goals; (2) they measure actual performance; (3) they compare actual performance against established goals; and (4) they evaluate the results and take corrective action if necessary.[18] The package delivery company UPS, for example, has a delivery goal: to deliver 95 percent of the overnight packages it picks up by noon the next day.[19] UPS has thousands of U.S. ground stations (branch offices that coordinate the pickup and delivery of packages in a particular area) that are responsible for the physical pickup and delivery of packages. UPS managers monitor the delivery performance of these stations regularly; if they find that the 95 percent goal is not being attained, they determine why and take corrective action if necessary.

To achieve control over any organizational activity, managers must have information. To control ground station activities, a UPS manager might need to know what percentage of packages each station delivers by noon. To obtain this information the manager uses UPS's own IT; UPS is also a leader in developing proprietary in-house IT. All packages to be shipped to the stations have been scanned with handheld scanners by the UPS drivers who pick them up; then all this information is sent wirelessly through UPS servers to its headquarters' mainframe computer. When the packages are scanned again at delivery, this information is also transmitted through its computer network. Managers can access this information to quickly discover what percentage of packages were delivered by noon of the day after they were picked up, and also how this information breaks down station by station so they can take corrective action if necessary.

Management information systems are used to control all divisional and functional operations. In accounting, for example, information systems are used to monitor expenditures and compare them against budgets.[20] To track expenditures against budgets, managers need information about current expenditures, broken down by relevant organizational units; accounting IT is designed to give managers this information. A twist on using IT to improve customer service is being used by Walt Disney World Resort. Instead of having employees use wearables (as described in "A Manager's Challenge"), Disney is giving the wearables to the guests in the form of a wristband that works as a hotel room key, parking ticket, and charge card. The data collected will help Disney provide better customer service. For example, in the future, if a guest is wearing a wristband, a Disney employee can greet a visitor by name. The Disney wristband can collect a lot of important information about a guest. From an employer's standpoint, there is a lot of information on the Internet about various employees. The accompanying "Management Insight" feature provides ideas on how that information can be used to make decisions.[21]

Management Insight

Using "Big Data"

How do you track the knowledge, skills, and abilities of every employee in an organization? This information was once stored in personnel files in the form of employee written profiles and lists of knowledge, skills, and abilities created to match the organization needs.[22] When a new project or a promotion came up requiring a new set of skills, the hiring manager would scan the current employees and check their profiles to see if the needed skills were available. If they were not in the organization's files, the organization might hire an outsider or bring in a contractor for the assignment.

Now there is software that can track the knowledge, skills, and abilities of employees without looking in the employee's file. This software looks at "big data" to find information about employees that is not formally listed in a file and may never have been mentioned to a manager. The software scans the Internet for information about each employee and compiles information from social media sites like Facebook and Twitter, blogs, comments on news stories, and other information input into the Internet by the employee.

IBM's Smarter Workforce Institute offers products to help organizations locate the talent hidden within their own networks. Jonathan Ferrar, vice president of IBM's Smarter Workforce talent and workforce management division, called the products "a different way of finding people."[23] When using the system, a hiring manager can input the knowledge, skills, and abilities desired for a new position or project. The software searches current employees who fit the profile. The software also provides searches to help with recruitment and selection of quality candidates for jobs and provides help with the

IBM's Smarter Workforce Institute offers products to help organizations locate the talent hidden within their own staff. Its software can track the knowledge, skills, and abilities of employees by scanning the Internet and compiling information about each employee from social media sites like Facebook and Twitter.

management of current employees, including on-boarding of new employees, compensation and rewards, training, performance appraisal, and employee engagement.[24]

Can a computer program do a better job of finding talent than a hiring manager with years of experience? Dr. Peter Cappelli, director of Wharton's Center for Human Resources, suggests that it can. A program can take different information into account than the average hiring manager can. "The industrial psychologists who've been working on this for a hundred years have their own sets of models. The great possibility of big data is in finding things that are outside these paradigms."[25]

Programs like those provided by the Smarter Workforce Institute help businesses to make sense of big data and leverage it for business success. Senior Vice President of the Information and Analytics Group at IBM Bob Picciano said, "Businesses and governments worldwide are being challenged to make sense of data and gather valuable insights from structured and unstructured data that are emerging from a variety of sources such as videos, blogs and social networking sites. We are helping clients tackle these big data challenges in virtually every industry—from public safety to healthcare, retail, automotive, telecommunications, and everything in between."[26]

Information and Coordination

Coordinating department and divisional activities to achieve organizational goals is another basic task of management. As an example of the size of the coordination task that managers face, consider the coordination effort necessary to prepare between 500,000 and 1 million meals for the people who visit Disney parks and resorts every day. Combine that type of volume with Disney's efforts to get food locally, and logistics get complicated fast. According to Executive Chef for Resorts Lenny DeGeorgeat, the supply chain for the restaurants at 18 Disney resorts in the United States and abroad depends on the location of the resort and what local growers and producers can provide. In Florida, for example, the company works with "Fresh from Florida" to find out what is in season and available. In Southern California, DeGeorgeat is pleased to have some local growers providing organic produce. The longer growing season in Southern California also is a bonus for the restaurants around the Disneyland resort there.[27]

Starbucks has a program called "Origin Experience" that allows its employees to get involved in the logistics of the supply chain. This experience allows associates to travel overseas and meet Starbucks partners where the coffee beans are grown. The trips provide associates with a new perspective on the supply chain and the coffee that ends up in their stores.

The supply chain at Starbucks runs from the field where the coffee beans are grown to the cup of coffee poured by a friendly barista at a local shop. The supply chain spans 19 countries. From the field, the beans travel to one of six roasting centers where they are prepared and then shipped to their final destination. The company makes more than 70,000 deliveries per day.[28]

In the Origin Experience, one store manager from Ohio flew to Costa Rica to see the process from "farm to cup." While there, the manager toured the fields where the coffee was grown and the mill where it was processed. She also sampled locally grown coffee and met local people. She traded email addresses with the farmer's children and they keep in touch to let her know how the growing season is going. In return, she tells them how sales are going in her store. Also as a result of the trip, she said she now thinks more like a farmer and works to make things sustainable in her store. Her new zeal for not wasting anything saves the store about 15 gallons of milk per week.[29]

Another associate traveled to Ecuador to visit a source of Starbucks coffee beans at a small farmer cooperative. The associate blogged about his impressions of the trip, such as the irrigation system used by one farmer who had applied the lessons of training. The associate also shared how thrilled the farmers were to taste the chocolate bars Starbucks sells that come from the cocoa pods they harvest.[30]

These visits help Starbucks employees learn about the supply chain and how to make it run more smoothly. The visits provide employees at the end of the supply chain with information about how things work at the beginning. Joseph Michelli, author of *Leading the Starbucks Way,* suggests that such trips can break down the silos in any organization and help employees understand their role in the supply chain.[31] Michelli suggests that such supply chain immersions and the subsequent stories told to customers strengthen the overall supply chain by improving the ties with vendors as well as making customers more comfortable with what the company is doing.

The IT Revolution

Advances in IT have enabled managers to make gigantic leaps in the way they can collect more timely, complete, relevant, and high-quality information and use it in more effective ways. To better understand the ongoing revolution in IT that has transformed companies, allowing them to improve their responsiveness to customers, minimize costs, and improve their competitive position, we need to examine several key aspects of advanced IT.

LO18-3

Describe the computer hardware and software innovations that created the IT revolution and changed the way managers behave.

The Effects of Advancing IT

The IT revolution began with the development of the first computers—the hardware of IT—in the 1950s. The language of computers is a digital language of zeros and ones. Words, numbers, images, and sound can all be expressed in zeros and ones. Each letter in the alphabet has its own unique code of zeros and ones, as does each number, each color, and each sound. For example, the digital code for the number 20 is 10100. In the language of computers it takes a lot of zeros and ones to express even a simple sentence, to say nothing of complex color graphics or moving video images. Nevertheless, modern computers can read, process, and store trillions of instructions per second (an *instruction* is a line of software code) and thus vast amounts of zeros and ones. This awesome number-crunching power forms the foundation of the ongoing IT revolution.

The products and services that result from advancing IT are all around us—ever more powerful microprocessors and PCs, high-bandwidth wireless smartphones, sophisticated word-processing software, ever-expanding computer networks, inexpensive digital cameras and camcorders, and more and more useful online information and retailing services that did not exist a generation ago. These products are commonplace and are being continuously improved. Many managers and companies that helped develop the new IT have reaped enormous gains.

However, while many companies have benefited from advancing IT, others have been threatened. Traditional landline telephone companies such as AT&T, Verizon, and other long-distance companies the world over have seen their market dominance threatened by new companies offering Internet, broadband, and wireless telephone technology. They have been forced to respond by buying wireless cell phone companies, building their own high-powered broadband networks, and forming alliances with companies such as Apple to make smartphones that will work on their networks. So advancing IT is both an opportunity and a threat, and managers have to move quickly to protect their companies and maintain their competitive advantage.[32]

On one hand, IT helps create new product opportunities that managers and their organizations can take advantage of—such as online travel and vacation booking. On the other hand, IT creates new and improved products that reduce or destroy demand for older, established products—such as the services provided by bricks-and-mortar travel agents. Walmart, by developing its own sophisticated proprietary IT, has been able to reduce retailing costs so much that it has put hundreds of thousands of small and medium-size stores out of business. Similarly, thousands of small, specialized U.S. bookstores have closed in the last decade as a result of advances in IT that made online bookselling possible.

IT and the Product Life Cycle

product life cycle The way demand for a product changes in a predictable pattern over time.

When IT is advancing, organizational survival requires that managers quickly adopt and apply it. One reason for this is how IT affects the length of the **product life cycle**, which is the way demand for a product changes in a predictable pattern over time.[33] In general, the product life cycle consists of four stages: the embryonic, growth, maturity, and decline stages (see Figure 18.2). In the embryonic stage, a product has yet to gain widespread acceptance; customers are unsure what a product, such as a new music player, has to offer, and demand for it is minimal.

As a product, like Apple's iPod, becomes accepted by customers (although many products do not, like Blackberry's tablet), demand takes off and the product enters its growth stage. In the growth stage many consumers are entering the market and buying the product for the first time, and demand increases rapidly. For example, iPod launched in 2001. It quickly entered the growth stage, selling 2 million units by the end of 2003 and 141 million by the end of 2007.[34] Between its launch and 2014, 26 devices were released, including the iPod Mini (released in 2004), the iPod Shuffle (released in 2005), the iPod Nano (released in 2005), and the iPod Touch (released in 2007).

The growth stage ends and the maturity stage begins when market demand peaks because most customers have already bought the product (there are relatively few first-time buyers left). At this stage, demand is typically replacement demand. The iPod transitioned to this stage after the launch of the iPod Touch. Its users had to decide whether to trade up to the more powerful version. In the iPod's maturity stage, the devices were still selling well. By the end of 2010, 275 million had been sold. Then in 2012, Apple made the last major upgrade to the iPod Touch.[35]

Once demand for a product starts to fall, the decline stage begins; this typically occurs when advancing IT leads to the development of a more advanced product, making the old one obsolete, such as when the iPod destroyed Sony's Walkman franchise. In the case of the decline of the iPod, it was another Apple product that put the iPod into decline: the iPhone. The iPhone had iPod capability built in. When it launched in 2007, the Apple CEO Steve Jobs joked that it was "the best iPod we've ever made."[36]

In general, demand for every generation of a digital device such as a PC, smartphone, or MP3 music player falls off when the current leaders' technology is superseded by new products that incorporate the most recent IT advances. One reason the IT revolution has been so important for managers is that advances in IT are one of the most significant determinants of the length of a product's life cycle, and therefore of competition in an industry.[37]

Figure 18.2

A Product Life Cycle

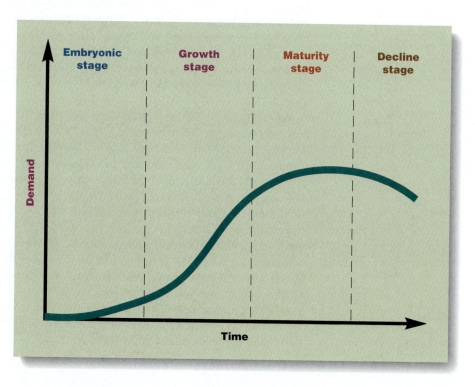

In more and more industries, advances in IT are shortening product life cycles as customers jump on the latest fad or fashion. For example, in the early 2010s, two products led the book downloading and reading market: Google's Kindle and Barnes and Noble's Nook. However, with the explosion of tablets and apps that allow tablet users to download and read books, the market for Kindle and Nook has shrunk.[38] But just because a product enters the decline phase of product development does not mean that everyone stops using it, as the accompanying "Information Technology Byte" feature discusses.

Information Technology Byte

What Happened to Windows XP?

Microsoft XP is an operating system at the end of its product cycle. The system was introduced in 2001 and enjoyed more than a decade of popularity. Its launch followed the flops of Windows 98 and Windows Me, both of which had problems with bugs and compatibility.[39] But Windows XP proved to be a hit. In its first five years on the market, more than 400 million copies were sold.[40] In 2013, one year before Microsoft ended support for the system, it was estimated that 500 million people were still using Windows XP.[41] It had a bigger share of the desktop market than all other versions of Windows combined until 2011, when Windows 7 overtook it.[42]

The system was designed more for business users than for consumers. Part of its success was that it was as user-friendly as a consumer product but as strong as an industrial product.[43] So why did Microsoft decide to stop supporting it? Because technology changed and Windows XP cannot keep up. "The world has changed an awful lot," said Tom Murphy, Microsoft's Windows Communications Director. "If you look at the security threats that PC users face today, they are fundamentally different to when Windows XP was designed. Windows XP just isn't designed—or any technology from that time—to address those threats. If you look at the more modern operating systems particularly Windows we've done a lot of work completely engineering the operating system from the ground up to address those security risks and make it safer for the users."[44]

In other words, Windows XP was developed before crimeware and other malware became a big problem.[45] The system allowed users to access settings to improve system performance for the user's needs. However, this ease of access left the user's computer more open to attacks from viruses and other problems. Microsoft issued patches and updates, but the system remained problematic. To overcome the problem, Microsoft launched a new operating system called Vista. However, the security in Vista made the system cumbersome and slow, so many users stuck with Windows XP rather than upgrade.[46]

While Microsoft did send out updates that made XP more secure over the years, it never did become completely secure.[47] Many users did move on to Windows 7 and Windows 8, but others remained loyal to Windows XP. Now that Microsoft does not support Windows XP at all, any computer using the operating system is vulnerable to attack. The firewalls and anti-virus software can only protect the system from known threats. If there is a previously unknown flaw in Windows XP that can be exploited by hackers, the old firewalls and anti-virus software will not work.

Before support ended, Microsoft began encouraging users to upgrade to a safer system.[48] At the time Microsoft stopped support, 36 percent of XP users said they would continue using XP.[49] The percentage of those keeping the old system was estimated to be even higher at small companies. Why are more companies not getting rid of Windows XP? For one, it takes years to upgrade a computer network. Second, upgrading is expensive. It's not just the cost of the new operating system either. Many organizations have created custom software that is critical to their operations. Changing to a new system will require a redevelopment of the software.[50]

The message for managers is clear: The shorter a product's life cycle because of advancing IT, the more important it is to innovate products quickly and continuously. A PC company that cannot develop a new and improved product line every three to six months will soon find itself in trouble. Increasingly managers are trying to outdo their rivals by being the first to market with a product that incorporates some advance in IT, such as advanced stability or steering control that prevents vehicle wrecks.[51] In sum, the tumbling price of information brought about by advances in IT is at the heart of the IT revolution. So how can managers use all this computing power to their advantage?

The Network of Computing Power

The tumbling price of computing power and applications has allowed all kinds of organizations, large and small, to invest more to develop networks of computer servers that are customized with the mix of hardware and software applications that best meets the needs of their current value chain management, as described in the accompanying "Management Insight" feature.

Management Insight

Accessing and Storing Data

Server computers (servers) are designed to provide powerful information-intensive computing solutions that in the past could have been executed only on huge, expensive mainframe computers. Servers also link networks of desktop and laptop PCs, and they link to wireless personal digital assistants (PDAs) such as netbooks, tablet computers, and smartphones. Using this array of computing devices, a company's employees can access its installed software applications and databases to obtain the real-time information they need to manage ongoing activities.

Blackbox server racks, such as this one created by Sun Microsystems, now part of Oracle, offer a significant safeguard to companies looking for cost- and space-conscious ways to back up their information.

Today servers can process staggering amounts of data to execute highly complex software applications, and they can access and store amazing amounts of information. Server sales have increased greatly over time (the server market was \$49.7 billion in 2013)[52] because of their ever-increasing computing power and low cost compared to mainframes—although most large companies still use a single mainframe as the "brain" that stores the most essential, secret, and important operating routines and that coordinates the companywide computing network.

In 2013 HP and IBM each held about 27 percent of the worldwide server market.[53] As large companies began to buy hundreds and then thousands of servers to meet their increasing need to process and store information, server makers such as HP and IBM designed rack servers that link individual servers to increase their joint power. For example, a rack server links an individual server into a rack of 10 connected servers; then 10 racks create a network of 100 servers; 100 racks create a network of a thousand servers, and so on.

Using software from specialized companies, such as IBM and Oracle, to link the operations of these server racks, large companies developed "server farms," which are brick and mortar (B&M) operating facilities that are remote and physically separate from company headquarters. Server farms are database centers composed of thousands of networked server racks that are constantly monitored, maintained, and upgraded by a company's IT engineers (or specialized outsourcers such as IBM) to protect a company's information and databases. IT storage and database storage are the lifeblood of a global company, which cannot function without them. Should a company lose such information, it would be helpless; it would have no record of its transactions with its employees, customers, suppliers, and so on.

A growing concern of managers today is how to reduce the cost of database storage, which is hundreds of millions of dollars for large companies. In the late 2000s, a new way to offer companies a quick, efficient system to enlarge and upgrade their database center capabilities to respond to the vast increase in Internet use was to house these server racks in standard-size storage containers—the same kind of containers hauled on trucks or stacked on cargo ships. The first U.S. server maker to offer such a mobile database solution was Sun (now part of Oracle), which launched its "Blackbox" data center containing its proprietary Solaris rack servers in a 20-foot shipping container. Each Blackbox contained a mobile data center that could deliver the computing capability of a 9,000-square-foot physical data center but would cost only about one-fifth as much.

Another company called SGI quickly announced its own new "Concentro" mobile server container—the first self-contained data center based on custom-designed, high-density server racks and data storage housed in a larger 40-foot shipping container.[54] Because SGI's space-saving rack servers are half as deep as standard servers, it could cram twice as many individual servers into a 40-foot container as could its competitors. The immense processing power of Concentro containers, equivalent to a 30,000-square-foot B&M data center, allowed companies to rethink their need for high-cost brick-and-mortar data centers, especially given the relatively low operating costs of SGI containers compared to physical data centers. Mobile data centers were soon snapped up by companies such as Google, Yahoo!, and Amazon.

In the late 2000s, the term "cloud computing" was popularized by companies like IBM, Microsoft, and Google to refer to a new way to offer companies computing and data storage service similar to how they used and paid for utilities like water or electricity. The strategy behind cloud computing was to create a cost-effective Internet-based global platform of hardware and software provided by a network of thousands of interlinked IT companies that had the capability to provide a full range of on-demand software applications, computing services, and database storage to millions of companies and individuals around the world. The advantage of cloud-based web services was that the cost of running applications or storing data through the Internet was much less than the cost of purchasing hardware and installing software on in-house servers.

Cloud computing was like an alliance in which IT companies pooled their resources to share processing power and applications that let them offer better prices to customers. For example, installing and managing the software and hardware to operate a specialized software application might cost $50,000 a year; in cloud computing the same service could be rented for $500 a month—which is why Amazon, Google, and Microsoft pushed cloud computing so vigorously. Cloud computing offered outsourced, pay-as-you-go, on-demand Internet software capabilities to companies for a fee.

Of course a major concern is information reliability and security. If cloud computing expands, even the largest companies may cease to operate their own database centers and outsource all their information and computing operations to web-based IT providers because they can perform these IT activities at a significantly lower cost. The problem facing managers is to choose the most efficient and effective method to manage their companywide computing networks and database storage operations to reduce operating costs by millions or billions of dollars a year.

network Interlinked computers that exchange information.

As the "Management Insight" feature discusses, the typical organizationwide computing **network** that has emerged over time is a four-tier network solution that consists of "external" PDAs such as netbooks, smartphones, and tablet computers, connected to desktops and laptops, and then through rack servers to a company's mainframe (see Figure 18.3). Through wireless and wired communication an employee with the necessary permissions can hook

Figure 18.3

A Four-Tier Information System with Cloud Computing

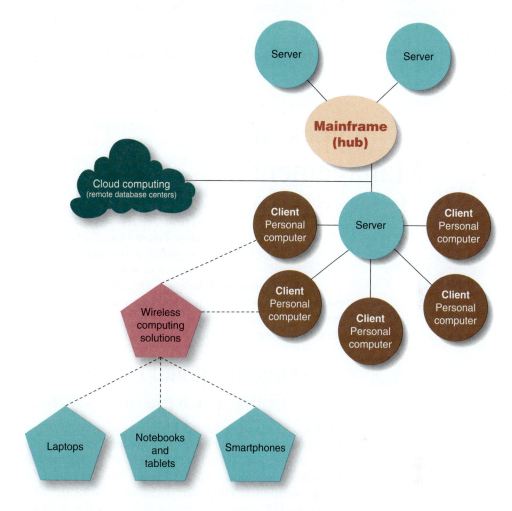

into a company's IT system from any location—in the office, at home, on a boat, on the beach, in the air—anywhere a wireless or wired link can be established.

The internal network is composed of "client" desktop and laptop PCs connected by Ethernet to the company's system of rack servers. The client computers that are linked directly to a server constitute a *local area network* (LAN), and most companies have many LANs—for example, one in every division and function. Large companies that need immense processing power have a mainframe computer at the center or hub of the network that can quickly process vast amounts of information, issue commands, and coordinate computing devices at the other levels. The mainframe can also handle electronic communications between servers and PCs situated in different LANs, and the mainframe can connect to the mainframes of other companies. The mainframe is the master computer that controls the operations of all the other types of computers and digital devices as needed and can link them into one integrated system. It also provides the connection to the *external* IT networks outside the organization; for example, it gives a user access to an organization's cloud computing services—but with high security and reliability and only from recognized and protected computing devices. For instance, a manager with a PDA or PC hooked into a four-tier system can access data and software stored in the local server, in the mainframe, or through the Internet to a cloud-based computing solution hosted by an outsourcer whose B&M database might be located anywhere in the world.

Just as computer hardware has been advancing rapidly, so has computer software. *Operating system software* tells the computer hardware how to run. *Applications software,* such as programs for word processing, spreadsheets, graphics, and database management, is developed for a specific task or use. The increase in the power of computer hardware has allowed software developers to write increasingly powerful programs that are also increasingly user-friendly. By harnessing the rapidly growing power of microprocessors, applications software has vastly increased the ability of managers to acquire, organize, and transmit information. In doing so, it also has improved the ability of managers to coordinate and control the activities of their organization and to make better decisions.

Types of Management Information Systems

Advances in IT have continuously increased managers' ability to obtain the information they need to make better decisions and coordinate and control organizational resources. Next we discuss six types of management information systems (MIS) that have been particularly helpful to managers as they perform their management tasks: transaction-processing systems, operations information systems, decision support systems, expert systems, enterprise resource planning systems, and e-commerce systems (see Figure 18.4). These MIS systems are arranged along a continuum according to the sophistication of the IT they are based on—IT that determines their ability to give managers the information they need to make nonprogrammed decisions. (Recall from Chapter 7 that nonprogrammed decision making occurs in response to unusual, unpredictable opportunities and threats.) We examine each of these systems after focusing on the management information system that preceded them all: the organizational hierarchy.

The Organizational Hierarchy: The Traditional Information System

Traditionally managers have used the organizational hierarchy as the main way to gather the information necessary to make decisions and coordinate and control organizational activities (see Chapter 10 for a detailed discussion of organizational structure and hierarchy). According to business historian Alfred Chandler, the use of the hierarchy as an information network was perfected by U.S. railroad companies in the 1850s.[55] At that time railroads were among the largest U.S. companies, and because of the size of their geographic footprint they faced unique problems of coordination and control. Railroad companies started to solve these problems by designing hierarchical management structures that gave top managers the information they needed to coordinate and control their nationwide operations.

Daniel McCallum, superintendent of the Erie Railroad, realized that the lines of authority and responsibility that defined Erie's management hierarchy also were channels of communication along which information traveled. McCallum established what was perhaps the first modern management information system when he ordered that regular daily and monthly reports should be sent up the hierarchy to top managers so that they

Figure 18.4

Six Computer-Based Management Information Systems

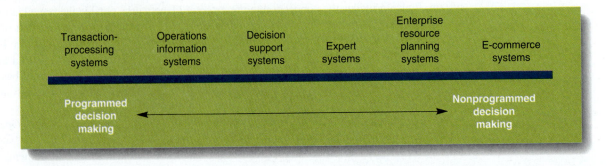

could make the best decisions about, for example, controlling costs and setting freight rates. Decisions were then sent back down the hierarchy to be carried out by lower-level managers. When the performance gains from this system were publicized, many organizations imitated the railroads by using their hierarchies to collect, channel, and process information.

Although hierarchy is a useful information system, it has several drawbacks, as we noted in Chapter 10. First, when too many layers of managers exist, it takes a long time for information and requests to travel up the hierarchy and for decisions and answers to travel back down. The slow communication can reduce the timeliness and usefulness of the information and prevent a quick response to changing market conditions.[56] Second, information can be distorted as it moves from one layer of management to another, and information distortion reduces the quality of information.[57] Third, managers have only a limited span of control; so as an organization grows larger and its hierarchy lengthens, more managers must be hired, and this makes the hierarchy an expensive information system. The popular idea that companies with tall management hierarchies are bureaucratic and unresponsive to the needs of their customers arises from the inability of tall hierarchies to effectively process data and give managers timely, complete, relevant, and high-quality information. The management hierarchy is still the best information system available today—the one that results in the best decisions—*if* managers have access to the other kinds of MIS systems discussed next.

Transaction-Processing Systems

A **transaction-processing system** is an MIS designed to handle large volumes of routine recurring transactions (see Figure 18.4). Transaction-processing systems began to appear in the early 1960s with the advent of commercially available mainframe computers. They were the first type of computer-based IT adopted by many organizations, and today they are commonplace. Bank managers use a transaction-processing system to record deposits into, and payments out of, bank accounts. Supermarket managers use a transaction-processing system to record the sale of items and to track inventory levels. More generally, most managers in large organizations use a transaction-processing system to handle tasks such as payroll preparation and payment, customer billing, and payment of suppliers.

Operations Information Systems

Many types of MIS followed hard on the heels of transaction-processing systems in the 1960s as companies like IBM advanced IT. An **operations information system** is an MIS that gathers comprehensive data, organizes them, and summarizes them in a form that is of value to managers. Whereas a transaction-processing system processes routine transactions, an operations information system gives managers information they can use in their nonroutine coordinating, controlling, and decision-making tasks. Most operations information systems are coupled with a transaction-processing system. An operations information system typically accesses data gathered by a transaction-processing system, processes those data into useful information, and organizes that information into a form accessible to managers. As described in the opening "Manager's Challenge," the data collected by wearables could be part of an operations information system.

UPS uses an operations information system to track the performance of its thousands of ground stations. Each ground station is evaluated according to four criteria: delivery (to deliver 95 percent of all packages within the agreed-upon time period), productivity (measured by the number of packages shipped per employee-hour), cost control and efficiency, and station profitability. Each ground station also has specific delivery, efficiency, cost, and profitability targets that it must attain. Every month UPS's operations information system gathers information about these four criteria and summarizes it for top managers, who can then compare the performance of each station against its previously established targets. The system quickly alerts senior managers to underperforming ground stations so they can intervene selectively to help solve any problems that may have given rise to the poor performance.

Decision Support Systems

A **decision support system** provides computer-built models that help managers make better nonprogrammed decisions.[58] Recall from Chapter 7 that nonprogrammed decisions are those that are relatively unusual or novel, such as decisions to invest in new productive capacity, develop a new product, launch a new promotional campaign, enter a new market, or expand internationally. Whereas an operations information system organizes important information for managers, a decision support system gives managers model-building capability and the chance to manipulate information in a variety of ways. Managers might use a decision support system to help them decide whether to cut prices for a product. The decision support system might contain models of how customers and competitors would respond to a price cut. Managers could run these models and use the results as an *aid* to decision making.

The stress on the word *aid* is important—in the final analysis a decision support system is not meant to make decisions for managers. Rather, its function is to give managers valuable information they can use to improve the quality of their decisions.

A good example of a sophisticated decision support system is one developed by Iteris, a software company that specializes in traffic management. Iteris develops technologies and information systems to manage aspects of the transportation industry, such as weather analytics, congestion, and safety. Its new decision support system, ClearPath Weather, helps government agencies develop road maintenance strategies that optimize the use of personnel, equipment, and chemicals to keep roadways clear in snowy conditions. The system uses proprietary algorithms and several prediction systems to give managers the information needed to make good decisions about when to plow, the quantity of chemicals to buy, and other key decisions.

The winter of 2013 was particularly snowy and a good pilot test for the system. It received kudos from at least one member of the Indiana Department of Transportation, who said that despite having one of the coldest and snowiest winters on record, road were efficiently managed and communications between garage units was improved.[59]

Most decision support systems are geared toward aiding middle managers in the decision-making process. For example, a loan manager at a bank might use a decision support system to evaluate the credit risk involved in lending money to a particular client. Rarely does a top manager use a decision support system. One reason for this is that most electronic management information systems have not yet become sophisticated enough to handle effectively the ambiguous types of problems facing top managers. To improve this situation, IT experts have been developing a variant of the decision support system: an executive support system.

An **executive support system** is a sophisticated version of a decision support system that is designed to meet the needs of top managers. One defining characteristic of executive support systems is user-friendliness. Many of them include simple pull-down menus to take a manager through a decision analysis problem. Moreover, they may contain stunning graphics and other visual and interactive features to encourage top managers to use them.[60] Increasingly, executive support systems are used to link top managers virtually so they can function as a team; this type of executive support system is called a **group decision support system**.

Ultimately top managers' intuition, judgment, and integrity will always be needed to decide whether to pursue the course of action suggested by an MIS. There are always many different issues to be factored into a decision, not least of which are its ethical implications.

Artificial Intelligence and Expert Systems

Artificial intelligence has been defined as behavior by a machine that, if performed by a human being, would be called "intelligent."[61] Artificial intelligence has already made it possible to write programs that can solve problems and perform simple tasks. For example, software programs variously called *software agents, softbots,* or *knowbots* can be used to perform simple managerial tasks such as sorting through reams of data or incoming email messages to look for important ones. The interesting feature of these programs is that from "watching" a manager sort through such data they can "learn" what his or her preferences are. Having done this, they can take over some of this work from the manager, freeing time for the manager to work on other tasks. Most of these programs are still in the development stage, but they may be commonplace within a decade.[62]

expert system A management information system that employs human knowledge, embedded in a computer, to solve problems that ordinarily require human expertise.

Expert systems, the most advanced management information systems available, incorporate artificial intelligence in their design.[63] An **expert system** is a system that employs human knowledge, embedded in computer software, to solve problems that ordinarily require human expertise.[64] Mimicking human expertise (and intelligence) requires IT that can at a minimum (1) recognize, formulate, and solve a problem; (2) explain the solution; and (3) learn from experience.

Recent developments in artificial intelligence that go by names such as "fuzzy logic" and "neural networks" have resulted in computer programs that, in a primitive way, try to mimic human thought processes. Although artificial intelligence is still at an early stage of development, an increasing number of business applications are beginning to emerge in the form of expert systems.

Enterprise Resource Planning Systems

To achieve high performance, it is not sufficient just to develop an MIS inside each of a company's functions or divisions to provide better information and knowledge. It is also vital that managers in the different functions and divisions have access to information about the activities of managers in other functions and divisions. The greater the flow of information and knowledge among functions and divisions, the more learning can take place, and this builds a company's stock of knowledge and expertise. This knowledge and expertise are the source of its competitive advantage and profitability.

enterprise resource planning (ERP) systems Multimodule application software packages that coordinate the functional activities necessary to move products from the design stage to the final customer stage.

In the last 25 years, another revolution has taken place in IT as software companies have worked to develop enterprise resource planning systems, which essentially incorporate most MIS aspects just discussed, as well as much more. **Enterprise resource planning (ERP) systems** are multimodule application software packages that allow a company to link and coordinate the entire set of functional activities and operations necessary to move products from the initial design stage to the final customer stage. Essentially ERP systems (1) help each individual function improve its functional-level skills and (2) improve integration among all functions so they work together to build a competitive advantage for the company. Today choosing and designing an ERP system to improve how a company operates is the biggest challenge facing the IT function inside a company. To understand why almost every large global company has installed an ERP system in the last few decades, it is necessary to return to the concept of the value chain, introduced in Chapter 8.

Recall that a company's value chain is composed of the sequence of functional activities that are necessary to make and sell a product. The value chain idea focuses attention on the fact that each function, in sequence, performs its activities to add or contribute value to a product. After one function has made its contribution, it hands the product over to the next function, which makes its own contribution, and so on down the line.

The primary activity of marketing, for example, is to uncover new or changing customer needs or new groups of customers and then decide what kinds of products should be developed to appeal to those customers. It shares or "hands off" its information to product development, where engineers and scientists work to develop and design the new products. In turn, manufacturing and materials management work to find ways to make the new products as efficiently as possible. Then sales is responsible for finding the best way to convince customers to buy these products.

The value chain is useful in demonstrating the sequence of activities necessary to bring products to the market successfully. In an IT context, however, it suggests the enormous amount of information and communication that needs to link and coordinate the activities of all the various functions. Installing an ERP system for a large company can cost tens of millions of dollars. The accompanying "Information Technology Byte" feature discusses the ERP system designed and sold by IQMS, which is meant specifically for manufacturers.

ERP Helps Custom Profile

Organizations are made up of departments, divisions, offices, and other units. How can all these areas communicate with one another so that everyone knows what everyone else is doing? One way is the enterprise resource planning system. One such system is EnterpriseIQ by IQMS. IQMS began in 1989 with the DOS-based product IQ/Genesis, which contained manufacturing and accounting modules. In 1993 it expanded the product with IQRealTime, which fed information to the software directly from work centers. In 1997 it released IQWin32, a Windows-based system. In 1999 it changed the name of its product to EnterpriseIQ and continues to update it to keep pace with the needs of the manufacturing industry.[65]

IQMS is an ERP specifically designed for the manufacturing industry. Its flagship product is EnterpriseIQ, which handles both manufacturing and financial systems. Within the EnterpriseIQ system is a complete manufacturing and shop-floor planning system, sales and distribution modules, and a financial management system. The ERP allows an organization to improve efficiency by eliminating unneeded downtime, minimizing inventory, and tracking products throughout the supply chain.[66] IQMS is an ERP software system that lays the groundwork for collaborative and ebusiness environments. It brings together all departments to ensure efficient and timely delivery of products. The manufacturing and shop-floor planning system allows the organization to manage production at multiple plants, to monitor production cycles, and to optimize scheduling. The sales and distribution modules allow the organization to quickly respond to customer questions through easy access to sales order status, tracking, and shipping. The financial management system connects information about sales, distribution, and manufacturing.

In 2002, a Michigan-based company called Custom Profile was expanding but was hindered by its use of four different software systems.[67] In addition to several system crashes per day, customer service did not have easy access to production data that would have allowed it to produce better sales orders. The company uses raw plastic material to manufacture specialized extruded plastic products for several industries. EnterpriseIQ was able to help Custom Profile by providing a structure in which data could be accessed by customer service representatives in response to customer questions. It also provided a scheduling and material requirements planning (MRP) system that optimized production time and materials. Finally, it supplied simplified budgeting for the organization and applied forecasting tools.[68] In other words, EnterpriseIQ connected the different systems of the business together and allowed Custom Profile to see its entire process through one system.

As an example of how an ERP system works, let's examine how SAP, the world's leading supplier of ERP software, helps management coordinate activities to speed product development. Suppose marketing has discovered some new unmet customer need, has suggested what kind of product needs to be developed, and forecasts that the demand for the product will be 40,000 units a year. With SAP's IT, engineers in product development use their expert system to work out how to design the new product in a way that builds in quality at the lowest possible cost. Manufacturing managers, watching product development's progress, work simultaneously to find the best way to make the product and thus use their expert system to find out how to keep operating costs at a minimum.

SAP's IT gives all the other functions access to this information; they can tap into what is going on between marketing and manufacturing in real time. So materials management managers, watching manufacturing make its plans, can simultaneously plan how to order supplies of inputs or components from global suppliers or how and when to ship the final product to customers to keep costs at a minimum. At the same time, HRM is tied into the ERP system and uses its expert system to forecast the type and cost of the labor that will be required to carry out the activities in the other functions—for example, the number of manufacturing employees who will be required to make the product or the number of salespeople who will be needed to sell the product to achieve the 40,000 sales forecast.

How does this build competitive advantage and profitability? First, it speeds up product development; companies can bring products to market much more quickly, thereby generating higher sales revenues. Second, SAP's IT focuses on how to drive down operating costs while keeping quality high. Third, SAP's IT is oriented toward the final customer; its CRM module watches how customers respond to the new product and then feeds back this information quickly to the other functions.

To see what this means in practice, let's jump ahead three months and suppose that the CRM component of SAP's ERP software reports that actual sales are 20% below target. Further, the software has reasoned that the problem is occurring because the product lacks a crucial feature that customers want. The product is a smartphone, for example, and customers demand a built-in digital camera. Sales decides this issue deserves major priority and alerts managers in all the other functions about the problem. Now managers can begin to decide how to manage this unexpected situation.

Engineers in product development, for example, use their expert system to work out how much it would cost, and how long it would take, to modify the product so that it includes the missing feature, the digital camera, that customers require. Managers in other functions watch the engineers' progress through the ERP system and can make suggestions for improvement. In the meantime, manufacturing managers know about the slow sales and have already cut back on production to avoid a buildup of the unsold product in the company's warehouse. They are also planning how to phase out this product and introduce the next version, with the digital camera, to keep costs as low as possible. Similarly, materials management managers are contacting digital camera makers to find out how much such a camera will cost and when it can be supplied. Meanwhile marketing managers are researching how they missed this crucial product feature and are developing new sales forecasts to estimate demand for the modified product. They announce a revised sales forecast of 75,000 units of the modified product.

It takes the engineers one month to modify the product; but because SAP's IT has been providing information about the modified product to managers in manufacturing and materials management, the product reaches the market only two months later. Within weeks, the sales function reports that early sales figures for the product have greatly exceeded even marketing's revised forecast. The company knows it has a winning product, and top managers give the go-ahead for manufacturing to build a second production line to double production of the product. All the other functions are expecting this decision; in fact, they have already been experimenting with their SAP modules to find out how long it will take them to respond to such a move. Each function gives the others its latest information so they can all adjust their functional activities accordingly.

This quick and responsive action is possible because of the ERP system that gives a company better control of its manufacturing and materials management activities. Quality is increased because a greater flow of information between functions allows a better-designed product. Innovation is speeded because a company can rapidly change its products to suit the needs of customers. Finally, responsiveness to customers improves because, using its CRM software module, sales can better manage and react to customers' changing needs and provide better service and support to back up the sales of the product. ERP's ability to promote competitive advantage is the reason why managers in so many companies, large and small, are moving to find the best ERP solution for their particular companies.

E-Commerce Systems

e-commerce Trade that takes place between companies, and between companies and individual customers, using IT and the Internet.

business-to-business (B2B) commerce Trade that takes place between companies using IT and the Internet to link and coordinate the value chains of different companies.

E-commerce is trade that takes place between companies, and between companies and individual customers, using IT and the Internet. **Business-to-business (B2B) commerce** is trade that takes place between companies using IT and the Internet to link and coordinate the value chains of different companies. (See Figure 18.5.) The goal of B2B commerce is to increase the profitability of making and selling goods and services. B2B commerce increases profitability because it lets companies reduce operating costs and may improve product quality. A

Figure 18.5

Types of E-Commerce

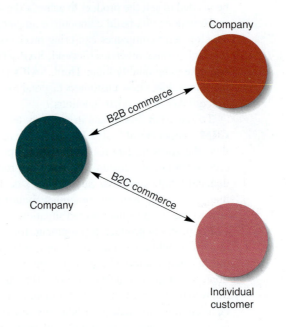

principal B2B software application is **B2B marketplaces**, which are Internet-based trading platforms that have been set up in many industries to connect buyers and sellers. To participate in a B2B marketplace, companies adopt a common software standard that allows them to search for and share information with one another. Then companies can work together over time to find ways to reduce costs or improve quality.

B2B marketplace An Internet-based trading platform set up to connect buyers and sellers in an industry.

business-to-customer (B2C) commerce Trade that takes place between a company and individual customers using IT and the Internet.

Business-to-customer (B2C) commerce is trade that takes place between a company and individual customers using IT and the Internet. Using IT to connect directly to the customer means companies can avoid having to use intermediaries, such as wholesalers and retailers, who capture a significant part of the profit in the value chain. The use of websites and online stores also lets companies give their customers much more information about the value of their products. This often allows them to attract more customers and thus generate higher sales revenues.

In the 2010s, computer software makers, including Microsoft, Oracle, SAP, and IBM, have rushed to use cloud computing to make their products work seamlessly with the Internet and thus respond to global companies' growing demand for e-commerce software. Previously their software was configured to work only on a particular company's intranet; today their software must be able to network a company's IT systems to other companies, such as their suppliers and distributors. At the same time, as we discussed earlier, companies also need to use social networking software to establish a secure platform their employees can use to share information inside their organizations.

The challenge facing managers now is to select e-commerce software that allows seamless exchange of information between companies anywhere in the world. The stakes are high because global competitive advantage goes to the company first with a major new technological advance. For example, SAP rushed to update its ERP modules to allow transactions over the Internet, and today all its modules have full cloud computing capability. However, Oracle, IBM, and many small specialist companies have also developed ways to provide advanced cloud computing and Internet applications at a lower price, so SAP faces increased global competition.

In summary, by using advanced types of MIS, managers have more control over a company's activities and operations and can work to improve its competitive advantage and profitability. Today the IT function is becoming increasingly important because IT managers select which kind of hardware and software a company will use and then train other functional managers and employees how to use it.

The Impact and Limitations of Information Technology

Advances in IT and management information systems are having important effects on managers and organizations. By improving the ability of managers to coordinate and control the activities of the organization and by helping managers make more effective decisions, modern IT has become a central component of any organization's structure. And evidence that IT can be a source of competitive advantage is growing; organizations that do not adopt leading-edge IT are likely to be at a competitive disadvantage. In this section we examine how the rapid advances in IT are affecting organizational structure and competitive advantage. We also examine problems associated with implementing management information systems effectively, as well as the limitations of MIS.

LO18-5

Explain how IT is helping managers build strategic alliances and network structures to increase efficiency and effectiveness.

---

strategic alliance An agreement in which managers pool or share their organization's resources and know-how with a foreign company, and the two organizations share the rewards and risks of starting a new venture.

B2B network structure A series of global strategic alliances that an organization creates with suppliers, manufacturers, and distributors to produce and market a product.

Strategic Alliances, B2B Network Structures, and IT

Recently, increasing globalization and the use of new IT have brought about two innovations that are sweeping through U.S. and European companies: electronically managed strategic alliances and B2B network structures. A **strategic alliance** is a formal agreement that commits two or more companies to exchange or share their resources in order to produce and market a product.[69] Most commonly, strategic alliances are formed because the companies share similar interests and believe they can benefit from cooperating. For example, in 2014, Coca-Cola entered a strategic alliance with InterContinental Hotels Group. As part of the alliance, the hotels will serve Coke products at the hotels. Both companies have well-known brands and both have headquarters in Atlanta, Ga.[70]

Throughout the 2000s, the growing sophistication of IT using global intranets, cloud computing, and teleconferencing made it much easier to manage strategic alliances and allow managers to share information and cooperate. One outcome of this has been the growth of strategic alliances into an IT-based network structure. A **B2B network structure** is a formal series of global strategic alliances that one or several organizations create with suppliers, manufacturers, and distributors to produce and market a product. Network structures allow an organization to manage its global value chain in order to find new ways to reduce costs and increase the quality of products—without incurring the high costs of operating a complex organizational structure (such as the costs of employing many managers). More and more U.S. and European companies are relying on global network structures to gain access to low-cost foreign sources of inputs, as discussed in Chapter 6. Shoemakers such as Nike and Adidas are two companies that have used this approach extensively.

Nike is the largest and most profitable sports shoe manufacturer in the world. The key to Nike's success is the network structure that Nike founder and CEO Philip Knight created to allow his company to produce and market shoes. As noted in Chapter 8, the most successful companies today are trying to pursue simultaneously a low-cost and a differentiation strategy. Knight decided early that to do this at Nike he needed to focus his company's efforts on the most important functional activities, such as product design and engineering, and leave the others, such as manufacturing, to other organizations.

By far the largest function at Nike's Oregon headquarters is the design and engineering function, whose members pioneered innovations in sports shoe design such as the air pump and Air Jordans that Nike introduced so successfully. Designers use computer-aided design (CAD) to design Nike shoes, and they electronically store all new product information, including manufacturing instructions. When the designers have finished their work, they electronically transmit the blueprints for the new products to a network of Southeast Asian suppliers and manufacturers with which Nike has formed strategic alliances.[71] Instructions for the design of a new sole may be sent to a supplier in Taiwan; instructions for the leather uppers, to a supplier in Malaysia. The suppliers produce the shoe parts and send them for final assembly to a manufacturer in China with which Nike has established another strategic alliance. From China the shoes are shipped to distributors throughout the world. 99% of the over 100 million pairs of shoes that Nike makes each year are made in Southeast Asia.

This network structure gives Nike two important advantages. First, Nike can quickly respond to changes in sports shoe fashion. Using its global IT system, Nike literally can change the instructions it gives each of its suppliers overnight, so that within a few weeks its foreign manufacturers are producing new kinds of shoes.[72] Any alliance partners that fail to perform up to Nike's standards are replaced with new partners through the regular B2B marketplace.

Second, Nike's costs are low because wages in Southeast Asia are a fraction of what they are in the United States, and this difference gives Nike a low-cost advantage. Also, Nike's ability to outsource and use foreign manufacturers to produce all its shoes abroad allows Knight to keep the organization's U.S. structure flat and flexible. Nike can use a relatively inexpensive functional structure to organize its activities.

The use of network structures is increasing rapidly as organizations recognize the many opportunities they offer to reduce costs and increase organizational flexibility. Supply chain spending by U.S. firms is expected to increase by more than 10 percent between 2014 and 2017.[73] The push to lower costs has led to the development of B2B marketplaces in which most or all of the companies in an industry (for example, carmakers) use the same software platform to link to each other and establish industry specifications and standards. Then these companies jointly list the quantity and specifications of the inputs they require and invite bids from the thousands of potential suppliers around the world. Suppliers also use the same software platform, so electronic bidding, auctions, and transactions are possible between buyers and sellers around the world. The idea is that high-volume standardized transactions can help drive down costs at the industry level. Also, quality will increase as these relationships become more stable as a B2B network structure develops.

Flatter Structures and Horizontal Information Flows

Rapid advances in IT have been associated with a "delayering" (flattening) of the organizational hierarchy, a move toward greater decentralization and horizontal information flows within organizations, and the concept of the boundaryless organization.[74] By electronically giving managers high-quality, timely, relevant, and relatively complete information, modern management information systems have reduced the need for tall management hierarchies.

Modern IT has reduced the need for a hierarchy to function as a means of coordinating and controlling organizational activities. Also, by reducing the need for hierarchy, modern IT can directly increase an organization's efficiency because fewer employees are required to perform organizational activities. At one time, for example, 13 layers of management separated Kodak's general manager of manufacturing and factory workers; with IT the number of layers has been cut to four. Similarly, Intel found that by increasing the sophistication of its own MIS, it could cut the number of hierarchical layers in the organization from 10 to 5.[75]

The ability of IT to flatten structure and facilitate the flow of horizontal information between employees has led many researchers and consultants to popularize the idea of a **boundaryless organization**. Such an organization is composed of people linked by IT—computers, faxes, computer-aided design systems, and video teleconferencing—who may rarely, if ever, see one another face-to-face. People are utilized when their services are needed, but they are not formal members of an organization; they are functional experts who form an alliance with an organization, fulfill their contractual obligations, and then move on to the next project.

Large consulting companies, such as Accenture, IBM, and McKinsey & Co., use their global consultants in this way. Consultants are connected by laptops to an organization's **knowledge management system**—its company-specific virtual information system that systematizes the knowledge of its employees and facilitates the sharing and integrating of expertise within and between functions and divisions through real-time interconnected IT. Knowledge management systems let employees share their knowledge and expertise and give them virtual access to other employees who have the expertise to solve the problems they encounter as they perform their jobs.

Some organizations, especially those that provide complex services and employ highly trained workers, have gone one step further and created what has been called a virtual

boundaryless organization An organization whose members are linked by computers, faxes, computer-aided design systems, and video teleconferencing and who rarely, if ever, see one another face-to-face.

knowledge management system A company-specific virtual information system that systematizes the knowledge of its employees and facilitates the sharing and integrating of their expertise.

virtual organization A company in which employees are linked to an organization's centralized databases by computers, faxes, and video-conferencing and rarely meet face-to-face.

organization. A **virtual organization** is one in which employees are linked to an organization's centralized databases by computers, faxes, and videoconferencing and rarely see one another face-to-face, if ever.[76] These employees might only infrequently visit the physical premises of their companies; they receive their assignments electronically, report back to their superiors electronically, and operate autonomously.[77] Almost all their employees are out in the field, working anywhere around the globe with clients to solve their problems. The number of teleworkers in the United States increased in the early 2010s, despite the recession. As the following "Information Technology Byte" box illustrates, organizations are finding benefits in allowing employees to work from home.

Information Technology Byte

PeopleG2 Goes Virtual

In 2008, as the recession began, PeopleG2 was outgrowing its office space. Chris Dyer, founder and CEO of the background screening organization, decided to send most of his workers home. In doing so, he turned his bricks and mortar organization into one that is almost completely virtual. The majority of his workers now have home offices from which they work for the company. But saving on office space rent and weathering the recession were not the only benefits of having all but three of the organization's 24 employees work from home. Dyer said that the move changed the company culture, provided more transparency, and improved performance.[78]

Even before the office space problem and the recession, Dyer felt the organization needed a culture change. In the beginning, the organization was a startup and Dyer hired a lot of people he already knew. As outsiders joined the organization, they were having a difficult time fitting in with the close-knit group. Dyer wanted to leave the start-up culture behind and move on. Changing the way everyone worked had the desired effect.[79]

Another benefit of being almost virtual for Dyer was that there is more transparency in who is doing the work. Dyer said he was better able to tell which of his remote workers were doing more work based on their output. He also was better able to determine which workers take the easy assignments and leave the more difficult background searches for others.[80] Finally, as is common when people telecommute, performance improved. Employees even talk about how much more productive they are now that they work from home. Tina Kalogeropoulos, a research manager, said, "I feel like I get so much more work done, there are so many less distractions. I also feel a greater sense of personal responsibility."[81]

The experience of Dyer and PeopleG2 is just an example of what is happening with telework in the United States. The number of teleworkers in the United States grew almost 80 percent between 2005 and 2012.[82] While some predicted that the recession would send people back to office desks, telecommuting actually grew by 16 percent between 2008 and 2012.[83] According to Global Workplace Analytics, 3.3 million people—about 2.6 percent of the U.S. workforce—work from home full time.[84] That number does not include those who are self-employed or working as unpaid volunteers.[85]

The agency also estimates that 25 million U.S. employees will work from home at least one day a month in 2014.[86] And Kalogeropoulos' observation that she is more productive at home is backed by research. In a controlled experiment, it was found that employees who were allowed to work at home were more productive, less likely to quit, and happier than employees who worked in the office.[87]

Despite their usefulness, IT, in general, and management information systems, in particular, have some limitations. A serious potential problem is that in all the enthusiasm for MIS, communication via computer networks might lose the vital human element of communication. There is a strong argument that electronic communication should support face-to-face communication rather than replacing it. For example, it would be wrong to make a judgment about an individual's performance merely by "reading the numbers" provided by an MIS. Instead the numbers should be used to alert managers to individuals who may have a performance problem. The nature of this problem should then be explored in a face-to-face meeting, during which more detailed information can be gathered. One drawback of using IT, such as e-mail and teleconferencing, is that employees may spend too much time watching their computer screens and communicating electronically—and little time interacting directly with other employees.[88] If this occurs, important and relevant information may not be obtained because of the lack of face-to-face contact, and the quality of decision making may fall.

Summary and Review

INFORMATION AND THE MANAGER'S JOB Computer-based IT is central to the operation of most organizations. By giving managers high-quality, timely, relevant, and relatively complete information, properly implemented IT can improve managers' ability to coordinate and control the operations of an organization and to make effective decisions.

LO18-1, 18-2 Moreover, IT can help the organization attain a competitive advantage through its beneficial impact on productivity, quality, innovation, and responsiveness to customers. Thus modern IT is an indispensable management tool.

LO18-3 **THE IT REVOLUTION** Over the last 30 years there have been rapid advances in the power and rapid declines in the cost of IT. Falling prices, wireless communication, computer networks, and software developments have all radically improved the power and efficacy of computer-based IT.

LO18-4 **TYPES OF MANAGEMENT INFORMATION SYSTEMS** Traditionally managers used the organizational hierarchy as the main system for gathering the information they needed to coordinate and control the organization and to make effective decisions. Today managers use six main types of computer-based information systems. Listed in ascending order of sophistication, they are transaction-processing systems, operations information systems, decision support systems, expert systems, enterprise resource planning systems, and e-commerce systems.

LO18-5 **THE IMPACT AND LIMITATIONS OF IT** Modern IT has changed organizational structure in many ways. Using IT, managers can create electronic strategic alliances and form a B2B network structure. A network structure, based on some shared form of IT, can be formed around one company, or a number of companies can join together to create an industry B2B network. Modern IT also makes organizations flatter and encourages more horizontal cross-functional communication. As this increasingly happens across the organizational boundary, the term *boundaryless organizations* has been coined to refer to virtual organizations whose members are linked electronically.

Management in Action

Topics for Discussion and Action

Discussion

1. To be useful, information must be of high quality, be timely, be relevant, and be as complete as possible. Why does a tall management hierarchy, when used as a management information system, have negative effects on these desirable attributes? **[LO18-1]**

2. What is the relationship between IT and competitive advantage? **[LO18-2]**

3. Because of the growth of high-powered, low-cost wireless communications and IT such as videoconferencing, many managers soon may not need to come into the office to do their jobs. They will be able to work at home. What are the pros and cons of such an arrangement? **[LO18-3, 18-4, 18-5]**

4. Many companies have reported that it is difficult to implement advanced management information systems such as ERP systems. Why do you think this is so? How might the roadblocks to implementation be removed? **[LO18-4]**

5. How can IT help in the new product development process? **[LO18-4]**

6. Why is face-to-face communication between managers still important in an organization? **[LO18-4, 18-5]**

Action

7. Ask a manager to describe the main kinds of IT that he or she uses on a routine basis at work. **[LO18-1, 18-4]**

8. Compare the pros and cons of using a network structure to perform organizational activities versus performing all activities in-house or within one organizational hierarchy. **[LO18-3, 18-4, 18-5]**

9. What are the advantages and disadvantages of business-to-business networks? **[LO18-5]**

Building Management Skills

Analyzing Management Information Systems [LO18-3, 18-4]

Pick an organization about which you have some direct knowledge. It may be an organization you worked for in the past or are in contact with now (such as the college or school you attend). For this organization, answer the following questions:

1. Describe the management information systems that are used to coordinate and control organizational activities and to help make decisions.

2. Do you think that the organization's existing MIS gives managers high-quality, timely, relevant, and relatively complete information? Why or why not?

3. How might advanced IT improve the competitive position of this organization? In particular, try to identify the impact that a new MIS might have on the organization's efficiency, quality, innovation, and responsiveness to customers.

Managing Ethically [LO18-1, 18-2]

The use of management information systems, such as ERPs, often gives employees access to confidential information from all functions and levels of an organization. Employees can see important information about the company's products that is of great value to competitors. As a result, many companies monitor employees' use of the intranet and Internet to prevent an employee from acting unethically, such as by selling this information to competitors. On the other hand, with access to this information employees might discover that their company has been engaging in unethical or even illegal practices.

Questions

1. Ethically speaking, how far should a company go to protect its proprietary information, given that it also needs to protect the privacy of its employees? What steps can it take?

2. When is it ethical for employees to give information about a company's unethical or illegal practices to a third party, such as a newspaper or government agency?

Small Group Breakout Exercise

Using New Management Information Systems [LO18-2, 18-4]

Form groups of three or four people, and appoint one member as the spokesperson who will communicate your findings to the class when called on by the instructor. Then discuss the following scenario:

You are a team of managing partners of a large management consulting company. You are responsible for auditing your firm's MIS to determine whether it is appropriate and up to date. To your surprise, you find that although your organization has a wireless email system in place and consultants are connected into a powerful local area network (LAN) at all times, most of the consultants (including partners) are not using this technology. It seems that most important decision making still takes place through the organizational hierarchy.

Given this situation, you are concerned that your organization is not exploiting the opportunities offered by new

IT to obtain a competitive advantage. You have discussed this issue and are meeting to develop an action plan to get consultants to appreciate the need to learn about and use the new IT.

1. What advantages can you tell consultants they will obtain when they use the new IT?

2. What problems do you think you may encounter in convincing consultants to use the new IT?

3. What steps might you take to motivate consultants to learn to use the new technology?

Exploring the World Wide Web [LO18-2, 18-5]

Go to the website for Samsung: http://www.samsung.com/us/. Click on the line that says "discover" and look at the various products, such as the Galaxy 5, the Galazy note, and the Gear Fit.

1. Where do you believe each product is in its life cycle?

2. How do the products overlap? In other words, might some products make others reach the decline stage of development?

Be the Manager [LO18-4]

You are one of the managers of a small specialty maker of custom tables, chairs, and cabinets. You have been charged with finding ways to use IT and the Internet to identify new business opportunities that can improve your company's competitive advantage, such as ways to reduce costs or attract customers.

Questions

1. What are the various forces in a specialty furniture maker's task environment that have the most effect on its performance?

2. What kinds of IT or MIS can help the company better manage these forces?

3. In what ways can the Internet help this organization improve its competitive position?

Bloomberg Businessweek Case in the News

Twitter and Amazon Go Hashtag Shopping and Solve a Problem No One Ever Had [LO18-3, 18-5]

Amazon.com's priority is to remove every barrier that might keep someone from buying something online. A particularly minuscule obstacle fell on Monday as Twitter made it possible for users to add items to their Amazon shopping carts with a tweet.

Just enable the service on your Twitter and Amazon accounts, and you can add a product discussed on Twitter by replying to the tweet and adding the hashtag #amazoncart. The next time you visit Amazon, the item will be in your cart, and you can then complete the purchase.

In theory, this will keep users from forgetting to purchase something seen in their Twitter timeline. Did this obstacle ever actually exist? Who knows. At one point this morning, only about 10 percent of the tweets that used #amazoncart even included a link to an Amazon product page, according to iTrendTV, a Twitter analytics firm. Many of the hashtag's early adopters seemed to be misunderstanding the service or spoofing it, judging from the traffic on @MyAmazon, the account that tweets out receipts to people who add items to their carts. Then again, maybe Bridget Carey from CNET actually saw a tweet advertising a horsehead mask and decided she couldn't let the moment pass.

The initial spike in attention was bound to come from Twittering cynics attempting to amuse one another. Perhaps the service will catch on. After all, the model for a successful advancement in online commerce goes like this: Technology companies make shopping easier, cynics scoff at the service—"Why would I ever give my credit card number to PayPal?" or "Why would I ever want to shop on my phone?"—and then people begin using the services. The model for unsuccessful advances in online commerce is the same, except for the last step.

If #amazoncart catches on, Amazon will presumably sell more horsehead masks, or banana slicers. Because users tweet their intentions to purchase things, it could also give some free social-media publicity to Amazon, Twitter, and the businesses using the services to sell their goods. There would have to be a lot of tweet-related shopping for Amazon to feel a difference. Its e-commerce business did $15.5 billion in sales last quarter, an increase of about 18 percent from the same period in 2013.

For Twitter, the deal presents only intangible benefits, since the service won't get a cut of any sales that originate with tweets. What it might get is an additional way to induce people to use Twitter at a time when the company is having trouble attracting new users and coaxing existing users to stay engaged, leading some critics to suspect the start of a serious decline. If people like using the hashtag, they could find themselves turning to Twitter as a shopping environment. It could also inspire businesses selling things on Amazon to use Twitter to get the word out. All those things would give the company a stronger position to find other ways to make money directly. Then again, why would anyone want to shop directly through Twitter when Amazon and hundreds of other websites designed for shopping are just a click away?

Source: Joshua Brustein, "Twitter and Amazon Go Hashtag Shopping and Solve a Problem No One Ever Had," *Bloomberg Business Week,* May 5, 2014. Used with permission of Bloomberg L.P. Copyright © 2014. All rights reserved.

Questions for Discussion

1. Do you believe hashtag ordering will be successful? Why or why not?

2. What are the advantage of hashtag ordering? What are the disadvantages?

3. Would you use hashtag ordering? Why or why not?

CREDITS

Notes

Chapter 1

1. www.alconent.com.
2. R. Abrams, "VOD 'Definitely Not Offsetting Decline on DVD,'" variety.com/2013/digital/news/vod-definitely-not-offsetting-decline-on-dvd-1200004637, 2014.
3. creativefuture.org.
4. G.R. Jones, *Organization Theory, Design, and Change* (Upper Saddle River, NJ: Pearson, 2011).
5. J.P. Campbell, "On the Nature of Organization Effectiveness," in P.S. Goodman, J.M. Pennings, et al., *New Perspectives on Organizational Effectiveness* (San Francisco: Jossey-Bass, 1977).
6. R. Abrams, "VOD 'Definitely Not Offsetting Decline on DVD,'" variety.com/2013/digital/news/vod-definitely-not-offsetting-decline-on-dvd-1200004637, 2014.
7. "Summary Report for: 11-1021.00–General and Operations Managers," www.onetonline.org/link/summary/11-1021.00.
8. H. Fayol, *General and Industrial Management* (New York: IEEE Press, 1984). Fayol actually identified five different managerial tasks, but most scholars today believe these four capture the essence of Fayol's ideas.
9. P.F. Drucker, *Management Tasks, Responsibilities, and Practices* (New York: Harper & Row, 1974).
10. "Alcon Entertainment [us]," www.imdb.com/company/co0054452, 2014.
11. Ibid.
12. Ibid.
13. armstrongconsultants.com/about/, 2014.
14. "Feature Local Business: Armstrong Consultants, Inc.," n.d., gjep.org/business-and-industry/featured-local-business.
15. "Airports Q&A," n.d., www.airlines.org/Pages/Airports-QA.aspx.
16. "Feature Local Business: Armstrong Consultants, Inc.," n.d., gjep.org/business-and-industry/featured-local-business.
17. "Airports Q&A," n.d., www.airlines.org/Pages/Airports-QA.aspx.
18. "Kenneth Chenault," *Forbes,* n.d., www.forbes.com/profile/kenneth-chenault-1.
19. R.H. Guest, "Of Time and the Foreman," *Personnel* 32 (1955), 478–86.
20. L. Hill, *Becoming a Manager: Mastery of a New Identity* (Boston: Harvard Business School Press, 1992)
21. Ibid.
22. H. Mintzberg, "The Manager's Job: Folklore and Fact," *Harvard Business Review,* July–August 1975, 56–62.
23. H. Mintzberg, *The Nature of Managerial Work* (New York: Harper & Row, 1973).
24. J. Kotter, *The General Managers* (New York: Free Press, 1992).
25. C.P. Hales, "What do Managers Do? A Critical Review of the Evidence," *Journal of Management Studies,* January 1986, 88–115; A.I. Kraul, P.R. Pedigo, D.D. McKenna, and M.D. Dunnett, "The Role of the Manager: What's Really Important in Different Management Jobs," *Academy of Management Executive,* November 1989, 286–93.
26. A.K. Gupta, "Contingency Perspectives on Strategic Leadership," in D.C. Hambrick, ed., *The Executive Effect: Concepts and Methods for Studying Top Managers* (Greenwich, CT: JAI Press, 1988), 147–78.
27. D.G. Ancona, "Tom Management Teams: Preparing for the Revolution," in J.S. Carroll, ed., *Applied Social Psychology and Organizational Settings* (Hilllsdale, NJ: Erlbaum, 1990); D.C. Hambrick and P.A. Mason, "Upper Echelons: The Organization as a Reflection of Its Top Managers," *Academy of Management Journal* 9 (1984), 193–206.
28. T.A. Mahony, T.H. Jerdee, and S.J. Carroll, "The Jobs of Management," *Industrial Relations* 4 (1965), 97–110; L. Gomez-Mejia, J. McCann, and R.C. Page, "The Structure of Managerial Behaviors and Rewards," *Industrial Relations* 24 (1985), 147–54.
29. W.R. Nord and M.J. Waller, "The Human Organization of Time: Temporal Realities and Experiences," *Academy of Management Review* 29 (January 2004), 137–40.
30. R.L. Katz, "Skills of an Effective Administrator," *Harvard Business Review,* September–October 1974, 90–102.
31. Ibid.
32. P. Tharenou, "Going Up? Do Traits and Informal Social Processes Predict Advancing in Management?" *Academy of Management Journal* 44 (October 2001), 1005–18.
33. C.J. Collins and K.D. Clark, "Strategic Human Resource Practices, Top Management Team Social Networks, and Firm Performance: The Role of Human Resource Practices in Creating Organizational Competitive Advantage," *Academy of Management Journal* 46 (December 2003), 740–52.
34. R. Stewart, "Middle Managers: Their Jobs and Behaviors," in J.W. Lorsch, ed., *Handbook of Organizational Behavior* (Englewood Cliffs, NJ: Prentice-Hall, 1987), 385–91.
35. S.C. de Janasz, S.E. Sullivan, and V. Whiting, "Mentor Networks and Career Success: Lessons for Turbulent Times," *Academy of Management Executive* 17 (November 2003), 78–92.
36. K. Labich, "Making Over Middle Managers," *Fortune,* May 8, 1989, 58–64.
37. B. Wysocki, "Some Companies Cut Costs Too Far, Suffer from Corporate Anorexia," *The Wall Street Journal,* July 5, 1995, A1.
38. "Job Outsourcing Statistics," January 1, 2014, www.statisticbrain.com/outsourcing-statistics-by-country.
39. www.dell.com, 2008, 2010, 2012.
40. S. Mallaby, "American Industry Is on the Move," *Financial Times,* January 9, 2013.
41. C. Fishman, "The Insourcing Boom," *The Atlantic,* November 28, 2012, www.theatlantic.com/magazine/archive/2012/12/the-insourcing-boom/309166/.
42. "Close to 10,000 Expected at GE Appliance Parks' 60th Birthday Celebration," press release, pressroom.geappliances.com/news/close-to-10-000-expected-at-ge-appliance-parks-60th-birthday-celebration.
43. V.U. Druskate and J.V. Wheeler, "Managing from the Boundary: The Effective Leadership of Self-Managing Work Teams," *Academy of Management Journal* 46 (August 2003), 435–58.
44. S.R. Parker, T.D. Wall, and P.R. Jackson, "That's Not My Job: Developing Flexible Work Orientations," *Academy of Management Journal* 40 (1997), 899–929.
45. B. Dumaine, "The New Non-Manager," *Fortune,* February 22, 1993, 80–84.
46. H.G. Baum, A.C. Joel, and E.A. Mannix, "Management Challenges in a New Time," *Academy of Management Journal* 45 (October 2002), 916–31.
47. A. Shama, "Management under Fire: The Transformation of Management in the Soviet Union and Eastern Europe," *Academy of Management Executive* 10 (1993), 22–35.
48. J. Kasperkevic, "Google Secretly Phases Out '20% Time,'" *Inc.,* August 13, 2013, www.inc.com/jana-kasperkevic/google-secretly-phases-out-20-percent-time.html.
49. K. Seiders and L.L. Berry, "Service Fairness: What It Is and Why It Matters,"

Academy of Management Executive 12 (1998), 8–20.

50. G.A. Fowler and N. Sheth, "Sony Opens New Chapter in Rivalry with Amazon over E-Book Readers," *The Wall Street Journal,* August 26, 2009, online.wsj.com/news/articles/SB125121418474557227.

51. T. Donaldson, "Editor's Comments: Taking Ethics Seriously–A Mission Now More Possible," *Academy of Management Review* 28 (July 2003), 363–67.

52. C. Anderson, "Values-Based Management," *Academy of Management Executive* 11(1997), 25–46.

53. W.H. Shaw and V. Barry, *Moral Issues in Business,* 6th ed. (Belmont, CA: Wadsworth, 1995); T. Donaldson, *Corporations and Morality* (Englewood Cliffs, NJ: Prentice-Hall, 1982).

54. www.apple.com, press releases, 2010, 2012.

55. P. Wahba, "Avon Bribery Probe Deal Could Hit $132 Million; Sales Continue Slide," *Reuters,* Febuary 13, 2014, http://www.reuters.com/article/2014/02/13/us-avon-results-idUSBREA1C0RP20140213.

56. B. Chen, "Apple Says Supplies Don't Come from War Zones," *The Economic Times,* February 14, 2014, articles.economictimes.indiatimes.com/2014-02-14/news/47336504_1_conflict-minerals-foxconn-suppliers.

57. "Apple to Track Suppliers' Sourcing of Conflict Minerals," *CBCNews,* February 13, 2014, www.cbc.ca/news/business/apple-to-track-suppliers-sourcing-of-conflict-minerals-1.2535784.

58. www.apple.com/supplier-responsibility.

59. S. Jackson et al., *Diversity in the Workplace: Human Resource Initiatives* (New York: Guilford Press, 1992).

60. G. Robinson and C.S. Daus, "Building a Case for Diversity," *Academy of Management Executive* 3 (1997), 21–31; S.J. Bunderson and K.M. Sutcliffe, "Comparing Alternative Conceptualizations of Functional Diversity in Management Teams: Process and Performance Effects," *Academy of Management Journal* 45 (October 2002) 875–94.

61. D. Jamieson and J. O'Mara, *Managing Workforce 2000: Gaining a Diversity Advantage* (San Francisco: Jossey-Bass, 1991).

62. http://digital.virtualmarketingpartners.com/vmp/accenture/diversity-inclusion/index.php, 2010.

63. "An Inclusive, Diverse Environment," http://www.accenture.com/microsites/corporate-citizenship-report-2012/our-people/Pages/inclusive-diverse-environment.aspx.

64. "Dell CEO Kevin Rollins Cites Workforce Diversity as Key to Gaining Competitive Advantages in Business," press release, March 6, 2006, www.dell.com.

65. "Union Bank of California Honored by U.S. Labor Department for Employment Practices," press release, September 11, 2000.

66. M. Wohlsen, "The Astronomical Math behind UPS's New Tool to Deliver Packages Faster," *Wired,* June 13, 2013.

67. "Upper Big Branch Mine–South Mine ID: 46-08436: April 5, 2010 Accident: Final Report: December 6, 2011," December 6, 2011, www.msha.gov/Fatals/2010/UBB/UBBSummary.pdf.

68. "Upper Big Branch Report," www.nttc.edu/ubb.

69. "Upper Big Branch Mine–South Mine ID: 46-08436: April 5, 2010 Accident: Final Report: December 6, 2011," December 6, 2011, www.msha.gov/Fatals/2010/UBB/UBBSummary.pdf.

70. S. Plummer, "Manchin Tells Company to Remove Him from UBB Film," April 1, 2014, abcnews.go.com/US/wireStory/manchin-tells-company-remove-ubb-film-23146355; J. Cable, "Blankenship Documentary Blames MSHA for Upper Big Branch Mine Disaster," April 2, 2014, ehstoday.com/safety/blankenship-documentary-blames-msha-upper-big-branch-mine-disaster.

71. "Upper Big Branch Report," www.nttc.edu/ubb.

72. "Injury Trends in Mining," www.msha.gov/MSHAINFO/FactSheets/MSHAFCT5.HTM.

73. J. Main, "Mining's Changing Culutre—4 Years after UBB," April 3, 2014, social.dol.gov/blog/mining%e2%80%99s-changing-culture-%e2%80%94-4-years-after-ubb.

Chapter 2

1. "Letter to Shareowners," *GE 2013 Annual Report,* n.d., www.ge.com/ar2013/pdf/GE_AR13_Letter.pdf.

2. "Letter to Shareowners," *GE 2013 Annual Report,* n.d., www.ge.com/ar2013/pdf/GE_AR13_Letter.pdf; W. Alden, "In Annual Letter, G.E. Chief Extols 'Simplification,'" *The New York Times,* March 10, 2014, dealbook.nytimes.com/2014/03/10/in-annual-letter-g-e-chief-extolls-simplification/.

3. S. Lohr, "G.E. Goes with What It Knows: Making Stuff," *The New York Times,* December 4, 2010, www.nytimes.com/2010/12/05/business/05ge.html?pagewanted=all.

4. A. Smith, *The Wealth of Nations* (London: Penguin, 1982).

5. Ibid., 110.

6. J.G. March and H.A. Simon, *Organizations* (New York: Wiley, 1958).

7. L.W. Fry, "The Maligned F.W. Taylor: A Reply to His Many Critics," *Academy of Management Review* 1 (1976), 124–29.

8. F.W. Taylor, *Shop Management* (New York: Harper, 1903); F.W. Taylor, *The Principles of Scientific Management* (New York: Harper, 1911).

9. J.A. Litterer, *The Emergence of Systematic Management as Shown by the Literature from 1870–1900* (New York: Garland, 1986).

10. H.R. Pollard, *Developments in Management Thought* (New York: Crane, 1974).

11. D. Wren, *The Evolution of Management Thought* (New York: Wiley, 1994), 134.

12. M.A. Johnson, "Pennsylvania McDonald's Franchisee Accused of Abusing Foreign Workers," *NBCNews,* March 8, 2013, usnews.nbcnews.com/_news/2013/03/08/17227684-pennsylvania-mcdonalds-franchisee-accused-of-abusing-foreign-workers?lite.

13. "Testimony of Rich Floersch–McDonald's Corporation," *McDonald's and Health Care/Senate Committee,* n.d., news.mcdonalds.com/Corporate/manual-releases/2010/McDonald-s-and-Health-Care-Senate-Committee.

14. J. Lawrence, "McDonald's Commitment to Building Trust and Unity," *Great Place to Work,* August 22, 2013, www.greatplacetowork.co.uk/publications-and-events/blogs-and-news/786-mcdonalds-commitment-to-building-trust-and-unity; "McDonald's USA National Employee Scholarship Program," n.d., www.scholarships.com/financial-aid/college-scholarships/scholarships-by-grade-level/high-school-scholarships/mcdonalds-usa-national-employee-scholarship-program/.

15. J. Lawrence, "McDonald's Commitment to Building Trust and Unity," *Great Place to Work,* August 22, 2013, www.greatplacetowork.co.uk/publications-and-events/blogs-and-news/786-mcdonalds-commitment-to-building-trust-and-unity.

16. F.B. Gilbreth, *Primer of Scientific Management* (New York: Van Nostrand Reinhold, 1912).

17. F.B. Gilbreth Jr. and E.G. Gilbreth, *Cheaper by the Dozen* (New York: Crowell, 1948).

18. D. Roy, "Efficiency and the Fix: Informal Intergroup Relations in a Piece Work Setting," *American Journal of Sociology* 60 (1954), 255–66.

19. K. Poole, "Biography of John D. Rockefeller, Senior," *Public Broadcasting Service,* n.d., www.pbs.org/wgbh/americanexperience/features/biography/rockefellers-john/.

20. Ibid.

21. R. Chernow, *Titan: The Life of John D. Rockefeller, Sr.* (New York: Random House, 2004).

22. K. Poole, "Biography of John D. Rockefeller, Senior," *Public Broadcasting Service,* n.d., www.pbs.org/wgbh/americanexperience/features/biography/rockefellers-john/.

23. E.G. Coffey and N. Shuker, *John D. Rockefeller, Empire Building* (Silver Burdett, 1989).

24. K. Poole, "Biography of John D. Rockefeller, Senior," *Public Broadcasting Service,* n.d., www.pbs.org/wgbh/

americanexperience/features/biography/
rockefellers-john/.

25. M. Weber, *From Max Weber: Essays in Sociology,* ed. H.H. Gerth and C.W. Mills (New York: Oxford University Press, 1946); M. Weber, *Economy and Society,* ed. G. Roth and C. Wittich (Berkeley: University of California Press, 1978).

26. C. Perrow, *Complex Organizations,* 2nd ed. (Glenview, IL: Scott, Foresman, 1979).

27. Weber, *From Max Weber,* 331.

28. B. Saporito, "The Trouble Lurking on Walmart's Empty Shelves," *Time,* April 9, 2013, business.time.com/2013/04/09/the-trouble-lurking-on-walmarts-empty-shelves/.

29. See Perrow, *Complex Organizations,* chap. 1, for a detailed discussion of these issues.

30. H. Fayol, *General and Industrial Management* (New York: IEEE Press, 1984).

31. "Innovative Technology Companies Rely on PayScale to Attract and Retain Talent: Impressive List of More Than 400 Technology Companies That Depend on Highly Skilled Professionals Use PayScale's Real-Time Market Data and Cloud Software to Get Pay Right," *Ein News,* March 31, 2014, www.einnews.com/pr_news/197824565/innovative-technology-companies-rely-on-payscale-to-attract-and-retain-talent.

32. Ibid.

33. Ibid.

34. H. Fayol, *General and Industrial Management* (New York: IEEE Press, 1984), 79.

35. "Innovative Technology Companies Rely on PayScale to Attract and Retain Talent: Impressive List of More Than 400 Technology Companies That Depend on Highly Skilled Professionals Use PayScale's Real-Time Market Data and Cloud Software to Get Pay Right," *Ein News,* March 31, 2014, www.einnews.com/pr_news/197824565/innovative-technology-companies-rely-on-payscale-to-attract-and-retain-talent.

36. J. Collins, "Good to Great," jimcollins.com, October 2001, www.jimcollins.com/article_topics/articles/good-to-great.html.

37. K. Weisul, "Jim Collins: Good to Great in 10 Steps," *Inc.,* May 7, 2012, www.inc.com/kimberly-weisul/jim-collins-good-to-great-in-ten-steps.html.

38. R.E. Eccles and N. Nohira, *Beyond the Hype: Rediscovering the Essence of Management* (Boston: Harvard Business School Press, 1992).

39. L.D. Parker, "Control in Organizational Life: The Contribution of Mary Parker Follett," *Academy of Management Review* 9 (1984), 736–45.

40. P. Graham, *M.P. Follett—Prophet of Management: A Celebration of Writings from the 1920s* (Boston: Harvard Business School Press, 1995).

41. M.P. Follett, *Creative Experience* (London: Longmans, 1924).

42. E. Mayo, *The Human Problems of Industrial Civilization* (New York: Macmillan, 1933); F.J. Roethlisberger and W.J. Dickson, *Management and the Worker* (Cambridge: Harvard University Press, 1947).

43. D.W. Organ, "Review of *Management and the Worker,* by F.J. Roethlisberger and W.J. Dickson," *Academy of Management Review* 13 (1986), 460–64.

44. D. Roy, "Banana Time: Job Satisfaction and Informal Interaction," *Human Organization* 19 (1960), 158–61.

45. For an analysis of the problems in distinguishing cause from effect in the Hawthorne studies and in social settings in general, see A. Carey, "The Hawthorne Studies: A Radical Criticism," *American Sociological Review* 33 (1967), 403–16.

46. D. McGregor, *The Human Side of Enterprise* (New York: McGraw-Hill, 1960).

47. Ibid., 48.

48. "Southwest Citizenship," southwest.com, n.d., www.southwest.com/citizenship/.

49. "Southwest Cares," southwest.com, n.d., www.southwest.com/assets/pdfs/corporate-commitments/southwestcares.pdf.

50. T. Dewett and G.R. Jones, "The Role of Information Technology in the Organization: A Review, Model, and Assessment," *Journal of Management* 27 (2001), 313–46.

51. W.E. Deming, *Out of the Crisis* (Cambridge: MIT Press, 1986).

52. "Toyota Production System," toyota-global.com, n.d., http://www.toyota-global.com/company/vision_philosophy/toyota_production_system/.

53. J.D. Thompson, *Organizations in Action* (New York: McGraw-Hill, 1967).

54. D. Katz and R.L. Kahn, *The Social Psychology of Organizations* (New York: Wiley, 1966); Thompson, *Organizations in Action.*

55. T. Burns and G.M. Stalker, *The Management of Innovation* (London: Tavistock, 1961); P.R. Lawrence and J.R. Lorsch, *Organization and Environment* (Boston: Graduate School of Business Administration, Harvard University, 1967).

56. Burns and Stalker, *The Management of Innovation.*

57. C.W.L. Hill and G.R. Jones, *Strategic Management: An Integrated Approach,* 8th ed. (Florence, KY: Cengage, 2010).

58. A. Lashinsky, "How Apple Works: Inside the World's Biggest Startup," *Fortune,* August 25, 2011, tech.fortune.cnn.com/2011/08/25/how-apple-works-inside-the-worlds-biggest-startup/.

59. E. Werner, "Slaughterhouse Owner Acknowledges Abuse," www.pasadenastarnews.com, March 13, 2008.

60. D. Bunis and N. Luna, "Sick Cows Never Made Food Supply, Meat Plant Owner Says," www.ocregister.com, March 12, 2008.

61. "Worker Sentenced in Slaughterhouse Abuse," www.yahoo.com, March 22, 2008.

Chapter 3

1. A. Bryant, "In a Corporate Culture, It's a Gift to Be Simple," *The New York Times,* November 22, 2013, B2; L. Dishman, "What's In Store: How Polyvore's Stylish Social Commerce Is Cracking Retail 3.0," *Forbes,* http://www.forbes.com/sites/lydiadishman/2012/12/21/whats-in-store-how-polyvores-stylish-social-commerce-is-cracking-retail-3-0/, February 21, 2014.; About—Polyvore, http://www.polyvore.com/cgi/about, February 21, 2014.; L. Orsini,"The Art of Technology and Vice Versa: Polyvore's Jess Lee," *ReadWrite,* http://readwrite.com/2013/09/16/polyvore-jess-lee-art-technology-fashion-design-builders#feed=/series/builders&awesm=~ozruSxdDwrOX2T, February 21, 2014.

2. A. Bryant, "In a Corporate Culture, It's a Gift to Be Simple," *The New York Times,* November 22, 2013, B2.

3. A. Bryant, "In a Corporate Culture, It's a Gift to Be Simple," *The New York Times,* November 22, 2013, B2; L. Dishman, "Polyvore's Jess Lee Turns Fashion Lovers into Style Trendsetters," *Fast Company,* http://www.fastcompany.com/1793703/polyvores-jess-lee-turns-fashion-lovers-style-trendsetters, February 21, 2014.

4. L. Orsini, "The Art of Technology and Vice Versa: Polyvore's Jess Lee," *ReadWrite,* http://readwrite.com/2013/09/16/polyvore-jess-lee-art-technology-fashion-design-builders#feed=/series/builders&awesm=~ozruSxdDwrOX2T, February 21, 2014.; L. Dishman, "Polyvore's Jess Lee Turns Fashion Lovers into Style Trendsetters," *Fast Company,* http://www.fastcompany.com/1793703/polyvores-jess-lee-turns-fashion-lovers-style-trendsetters, February 21, 2014; A. Preiser, "Polyvore Takes on the Home," *ELLE Decor,* http://www.elledecor.com/shopping/shop-talk/polyvore-home-decor, February 21, 2014.

5. L. Orsini, "The Art of Technology and Vice Versa: Polyvore's Jess Lee," *ReadWrite,* http://readwrite.com/2013/09/16/polyvore-jess-lee-art-technology-fashion-design-builders#feed=/series/builders&awesm=~ozruSxdDwrOX2T, February 21, 2014.

6. A. Bryant, "In a Corporate Culture, It's a Gift to Be Simple," *The New York Times,* November 22, 2013, B2.

7. A. Bryant, "In a Corporate Culture, It's a Gift to Be Simple," *The New York Times,* November 22, 2013, B2.

8. V.A. Kansara, "Founder Stories: Jess Lee's Journey from Polyvore Superuser to CEO," *Business of Fashion,* http://www.businessoffashion.com/2013/08/

founder-stories-jess-lees-journey-from-polyvore-superuser-to-ceo-marissa-mayer-google.html, February 21, 2014.

9. L. Dishman, "What's in Store: How Polyvore's Stylish Social Commerce Is Cracking Retail 3.0," *Forbes,* http://www.forbes.com/sites/lydiadishman/2012/12/21/whats-in-store-how-polyvores-stylish-social-commerce-is-cracking-retail-3-0/, February 21, 2014.; J. Graham, "Polyvore Releases iPad App," *USA Today,* http://www.usatoday.com/story/tech/columnist/talkingtech/2013/10/31/polyvore-releases-ipad-app/3296915/, February 21, 2014.

10. J. Xavier, "Hackers' Way Meets Runway: Silicon Valley Startups Take Aim at Fashion Industry," *Silicon Valley Business Journals,* http://www.bizjournals.com/sanjose/print-edition/2014/02/21/hackers-way-meets-runway-fashion.html, February 21, 2014.

11. K. Liyakasa, "Polyvore: Connecting Commerce to the Sphere of Social Data," *AdExchanger,* http://www.adexchanger.com/ecommerce-2/polyvore-connecting-commerce-to-the-sphere-of-social-data/, February 21, 2014.

12. About—Polyvore, http://www.polyvore.com/cgi/about, February 21, 2014.; C. Gregoire, "This CEO's Secret to a Happy, Productive Workplace—and Game-Changing Innovation," *Huffington Post,* http://www.huffingtonpost.com/2013/08/14/the-simple-trick-that-mad_n_3742942.html, February 21, 2014.

13. About—Polyvore, http://www.polyvore.com/cgi/about, February 21, 2014.

14. A. Bryant, "In a Corporate Culture, It's a Gift to Be Simple," *The New York Times,* November 22, 2013, B2.

15. About—Polyvore, http://www.polyvore.com/cgi/about, February 21, 2014.

16. A. Bryant, "In a Corporate Culture, It's a Gift to Be Simple," *The New York Times,* November 22, 2013, B2.

17. L. Orsini,"The Art of Technology and Vice Versa: Polyvore's Jess Lee," *ReadWrite,* http://readwrite.com/2013/09/16/polyvore-jess-lee-art-technology-fashion-design-builders#feed=/series/builders&awesm=~ozruSxdDwrOX2T, February 21, 2014.

18. Techlicious / E. Harper, "The 5 Best Sites for One-Stop Online Shopping," *Time,* http://techland.time.com/2013/12/03/the-5-best-sites-for-one-stop-online-shopping/, March 11, 2014.

19. A. Bryant, "In a Corporate Culture, It's a Gift to Be Simple," *The New York Times,* November 22, 2013, B2.

20. S. Carpenter, "Different Dispositions, Different Brains," *Monitor on Psychology,* February 2001, 66–68.

21. J.M. Digman, "Personality Structure: Emergence of the Five-Factor Model," *Annual Review of Psychology* 41 (1990), 417–40; R.R. McCrae and P.T. Costa, "Validation of the Five-Factor Model of Personality across Instruments and Observers," *Journal of Personality and Social Psychology* 52 (1987), 81–90; R.R. McCrae and P.T. Costa, "Discriminant Validity of NEO-PIR Facet Scales," *Educational and Psychological Measurement* 52 (1992), 229–37.

22. Digman, "Personality Structure"; McCrae and Costa, "Validation of the Five-Factor Model"; McCrae and Costa, "Discriminant Validity"; R.P. Tett and D.D. Burnett, "A Personality Trait-Based Interactionist Model of Job Performance," *Journal of Applied Psychology* 88, no. 3 (2003), 500–17; J.M. George, "Personality, Five-Factor Model," in S. Clegg and J.R. Bailey, eds., *International Encyclopedia of Organization Studies* (Thousand Oaks, CA: Sage, 2007).

23. L.A. Witt and G.R. Ferris, "Social Skills as Moderator of Conscientiousness–Performance Relationship: Convergent Results across Four Studies," *Journal of Applied Psychology* 88, no. 5 (2003), 809–20; M.J. Simmering, J.A. Colquitte, R.A. Noe, and C.O. L.H. Porter, "Conscientiousness, Autonomy Fit, and Development: A Longitudinal Study," *Journal of Applied Psychology* 88, no. 5 (2003), 954–63.

24. M.R. Barrick and M.K. Mount, "The Big Five Personality Dimensions and Job Performance: A Meta-Analysis," *Personnel Psychology* 44 (1991), 1–26; S. Komar, D.J. Brown, J.A. Komar, and C. Robie, "Faking and the Validity of Conscientiousness: A Monte Carlo Investigation," *Journal of Applied Psychology* 93 (2008), 140–54.

25. Digman, "Personality Structure"; McCrae and Costa, "Validation of the Five-Factor Model"; McCrae and Costa, "Discriminant Validity."

26. Under Armour, Inc.—Executive Team, http://investor.underarmour.com/management.cfm, March 12, 2014.

27. D. Roberts, "Under Armour Gets Serious," *Fortune,* November 7, 2011, 152–62; K. Plank, as told to Mark Hyman, "How I Did It: Kevin Plank: For the Founder of Apparel-Maker Under Armour, Entrepreneurship Is 99% Perspiration and 1% Polyester," *Inc.,* http://www.inc.com/magazine/20031201/howididit_Printer_Friendly.html, March 26, 2012.

28. Roberts, "Under Armour Gets Serious"; Plank, as told to Mark Hyman, "How I Did It"; "Under Armour's Kevin Plank: Creating the Biggest, Baddest Brand on the Planet," *Knowledge@Wharton,* January 5, 2011, http://knowledge.wharton.upenn.edu/printer_friendly.cfm?articleid=2665, March 26, 2012; "2011 Under Armour Annual Report," Under Armour, Inc.—Annual Report & Proxy, http://investor.underarmour.com/annuals.cfm?sh_print=yes&, March 30, 2012.

29. Roberts, "Under Armour Gets Serious."

30. "Under Armour Reports Fourth Quarter Net Revenues Growth of 35% and Full Year Net Revenues Growth of 27%; Raises Full Year 2014 Outlook," http://investor.underarmour.com/releasedetail.cfm?ReleaseID=821996, March 12, 2014.

31. Roberts, "Under Armour Gets Serious"; "Creating the Biggest, Baddest Brand on the Planet."

32. Roberts, "Under Armour Gets Serious."

33. Roberts, "Under Armour Gets Serious."

34. "2011 Under Armour Annual Report."

35. "2011 Under Armour Annual Report."

36. Roberts, "Under Armour Gets Serious."; M. Urger, "Shining Armour," baltimoremagazine.net, August 2013, 173-177, 244, 245.

37. Roberts, "Under Armour Gets Serious"; "Creating the Biggest, Baddest Brand on the Planet."

38. Roberts, "Under Armour Gets Serious."

39. J.B. Rotter, "Generalized Expectancies for Internal versus External Control of Reinforcement," *Psychological Monographs* 80 (1966), 1–28; P. Spector, "Behaviors in Organizations as a Function of Employees' Locus of Control," *Psychological Bulletin* 91 (1982), 482–97.

40. J. Brockner, *Self-Esteem at Work* (Lexington, MA: Lexington Books, 1988).

41. D.C. McClelland, *Human Motivation* (Glenview, IL: Scott, Foresman, 1985); D.C. McClelland, "How Motives, Skills, and Values Determine What People Do," *American Psychologist* 40 (1985), 812–25; D.C. McClelland, "Managing Motivation to Expand Human Freedom," *American Psychologist* 33 (1978), 201–10.

42. D.G. Winter, *The Power Motive* (New York: Free Press 1973).

43. M.J. Stahl, "Achievement, Power, and Managerial Motivation: Selecting Managerial Talent with the Job Choice Exercise," *Personnel Psychology* 36 (1983), 775–89; D.C. McClelland and D.H. Burnham, "Power Is the Great Motivator," *Harvard Business Review* 54 (1976), 100–110.

44. R.J. House, W.D. Spangler, and J. Woycke, "Personality and Charisma in the U.S. Presidency: A Psychological Theory of Leader Effectiveness," *Administrative Science Quarterly* 36 (1991), 364–96.

45. G.H. Hines, "Achievement, Motivation, Occupations and Labor Turnover in New Zealand," *Journal of Applied Psychology* 58 (1973), 313–17; P.S. Hundal, "A Study of Entrepreneurial Motivation: Comparison of Fast- and Slow-Progressing Small Scale Industrial Entrepreneurs in Punjab, India," *Journal of Applied Psychology* 55 (1971), 317–23.

46. M. Rokeach, *The Nature of Human Values* (New York: Free Press 1973).

47. Ibid.

48. Ibid.

49. M. Rokeach, *The Nature of Human Values* (New York: Free Press, 1973).

50. Ibid.

51. Ibid.

52. Ibid.

53. Ibid.

54. K.K. Spors, "Top Small Workplaces 2007: Gentle Giant Moving," *The Wall Street Journal,* October 1, 2007, R4–R5; "Gentle Giant Sees Revenue Boost, *Boston Business Journal,* January 15, 2008, www.gentlegiant.com/news-011508-1. htm, February 5, 2008; Company History: Gentle Giant Moving Company, "Company History," http://www .gentlegiant.com/history.php, February 3, 2010; "Massachusetts Moving Company Gentle Giant Moving Company Celebrates 30 Years in Operation," January 25, 2010, http://www.gentlegiant. com/press/press20100125.php, February 3, 2010.

55. Spors, "Top Small Workplaces 2007"; Full Service Moving Company—Gentle Giant History, http://www.gentlegiant. com/moving-companies/full-service-moving.aspx, March 13, 2014.; Chicago Movers—Gentle Giant Moving Company, http://www.gentlegiant.com/Locations/ Illinois.aspx, March 13, 2014.

56. Full Service Moving Company—Gentle Giant History, http://www.gentlegiant. com/moving-companies/full-service-moving.aspx, March 30, 2012; R. Libby, branch manager, Providence, RI, http:// www.gentlegiant.com/moving-companies/ furniture-movers/ryan-libby.aspx, March 13, 2014.

57. R. Libby, branch manager, Providence, RI, "Moving Services and Moving Tips from Gentle Giant Moving Company," http://www.gentlegiant.com/moving-companies/furniture-movers/ryan-libby. aspx.

58. Spors, "Top Small Workplaces 2007."

59. Ibid.

60. Spors, "Top Small Workplaces 2007"; "Gentle Giant Receives Top Small Workplace Award," www.gentlegiant. com/topsmallworkplace.htm, January 5, 2008; "Corporate Overview," http://www. gentlegiant.com/company.php, February 3, 2010.

61. Spors, "Top Small Workplaces 2007."

62. Ibid.

63. A.P. Brief, *Attitudes In and Around Organizations* (Thousand Oaks, CA: Sage, 1998).

64. P.S. Goodman, "U.S. Job Losses in December Dim Hopes for Quick Upswing," *The New York Times,* http:// www.nytimes.com/2010/01/09/business/ economy/09jobs.html?pagewanted=print, February 3, 2010; U.S. Bureau of Labor Statistics, "Economic News Release Employment Situations Summary," http://data.bls.gov/cgi-bin/print.pl/news. release/empsit.nr0.htm, February 3, 2010; B. Steverman, "Layoffs: Short-Term Profits, Long-Term Problems," *BusinessWeek,* http://www.businessweek. com/print/investor/content/jan2010/

pi20100113_133780.htm, February 3, 2010.

65. J. Aversa, "Americans' Job Satisfaction Falls to Record Low," http://news. yahoo.com/s/ap/20100105/ap_on_bi_ge/ us_unhappy_workers/print, February 3, 2010.

66. The Conference Board, press release/ news, "U.S. Job Satisfaction at Lowest Level in Two Decades," January 5, 2010, http://www.conference-board.org/utilities/ pressPrinterFriendly.cfm?press_ID=3820, February 3, 2010.

67. Aversa, "Americans' Job Satisfaction"; Conference Board, press release/news, "U.S. Job Satisfaction."

68. Aversa, "Americans' Job Satisfaction"; Conference Board, press release/news, "U.S. Job Satisfaction."

69. Aversa, "Americans' Job Satisfaction"; Conference Board, press release/news, "U.S. Job Satisfaction."

70. G. Levanon, "The Determinants of Job Satisfaction," http://hcexchange.conference-board.org/blog/post.cfm?post=1927, March 13, 2014.

71. Job Satisfaction: 2013 Edition—The Conference Board, http://www.conference-board.org/publications/publicationdetail. cfm?publicationid=2522, March 13, 2014.

72. G. Levanon, "The Determinants of Job Satisfaction," http://hcexchange .conference-board.org/blog/post. cfm?post=1927, March 13, 2014.

73. "Subaru of Indiana Automotive Welcomes New President," press release, March 26, 2012, Subaru of Indiana Automotive, Inc., (SIA), http://www.subaru-sia.com/news/ release/okawaraPR.pdf, April 2, 2012; "Outline of Production Facility," March 1, 2011, Subaru of Indiana Automotive, Inc., (SIA), http://www.subaru-sia.com/ company/sia.outline.english.pdf, April 12, 2012; "Outline of Production Facility," Subaru of Indiana Automotive, Inc., http://www.subaru-sia.com/company/sia. outline.english.pdf, March 13, 2014.

74. R. Farzad, "The Scrappiest Car Manufacturer in America," *Bloomberg Businessweek,* June 6, 12, 2011, 68–74.

75. Ibid.

76. Ibid.

77. Ibid.

78. Ibid.

79. Farzad, "Scrappiest Car Manufacturer"; "SIA and Wellfit Reward Weight-Loss Winners," press release, November 29, 2011, Subaru of Indiana Automotive, Inc., (SIA), http://www.subaru-sia.com/news/ release/20111129.pdf, April 1, 2012.

80. Farzad, "Scrappiest Car Manufacturer."

81. Ibid.

82. Ibid.

83. D.W. Organ, *Organizational Citizenship Behavior: The Good Soldier Syndrome* (Lexington, MA: Lexington Books, 1988).

84. J.M. George and A.P. Brief, "Feeling Good—Doing Good: A Conceptual Analysis of the Mood at Work—Organizational Spontaneity Relationship," *Psychological Bulletin* 112 (1992), 310–29.

85. W.H. Mobley, "Intermediate Linkages in the Relationship between Job Satisfaction and Employee Turnover," *Journal of Applied Psychology* 62 (1977), 237–40.

86. C. Hymowitz, "Though Now Routine, Bosses Still Stumble during Layoff Process," *The Wall Street Journal,* June 25, 2007, B1; J. Brockner, "The Effects of Work Layoffs on Survivors: Research, Theory and Practice," in B.M. Staw and L.L. Cummings, eds., *Research in Organizational Behavior,* vol. 10 (Greenwich, CT: JAI Press, 1988), 213–55.

87. Hymowitz, "Though Now Routine."

88. Ibid.

89. Ibid.

90. Goodman, "U.S. Job Losses in December Dim Hopes for Quick Upswing."

91. M. Luo, "For Small Employers, Rounds of Shedding Workers and Tears," *The New York Times,* May 7, 2009, A1, A3.

92. Luo, "Rounds of Shedding Workers and Tears."

93. Ibid.

94. N. Solinger, W. van Olffen, and R.A. Roe, "Beyond the Three-Component Model of Organizational Commitment," *Journal of Applied Psychology* 93 (2008), 70–83.

95. J.E. Mathieu and D.M. Zajac, "A Review and Meta-Analysis of the Antecedents, Correlates, and Consequences of Organizational Commitment," *Psychological Bulletin* 108 (1990), 171–94.

96. D. Watson and A. Tellegen, "Toward a Consensual Structure of Mood," *Psychological Bulletin* 98 (1985), 219–35.

97. Watson and Tellegen, "Toward a Consensual Structure of Mood."

98. J.M. George, "The Role of Personality in Organizational Life: Issues and Evidence," *Journal of Management* 18 (1992), 185–213.

99. H.A. Elfenbein, "Emotion in Organizations: A Review and Theoretical Integration," in J.P. Walsh and A.P. Brief, eds., *The Academy of Management Annals,* vol. 1 (New York: Lawrence Erlbaum Associates, 2008), 315–86.

100. J.P. Forgas, "Affect in Social Judgments and Decisions: A Multi-Process Model," in M. Zanna, ed., *Advances in Experimental and Social Psychology,* vol. 25 (San Diego, CA: Academic Press, 1992), 227–75; J.P. Forgas and J.M. George, "Affective Influences on Judgments and Behavior in Organizations: An Information Processing Perspective," *Organizational Behavior and Human Decision Processes* 86 (2001), 3–34; J.M. George, "Emotions and Leadership: The Role of

Emotional Intelligence," *Human Relations* 53 (2000), 1027–55; W.N. Morris, *Mood: The Frame of Mind* (New York: Springer-Verlag, 1989).

101. George, "Emotions and Leadership."

102. J.M. George and K. Bettenhausen, "Understanding Prosocial Behavior, Sales Performance, and Turnover: A Group Level Analysis in a Service Context," *Journal of Applied Psychology* 75 (1990), 698–709.

103. George and Brief, "Feeling Good—Doing Good"; J.M. George and J.Zhou, "Understanding When Bad Moods Foster Creativity and Good Ones Don't: The Role of Context and Clarity of Feelings," paper presented at the Academy of Management Annual Meeting, 2001; A.M. Isen and R.A. Baron, "Positive Affect as a Factor in Organizational Behavior," in B.M. Staw and L.L. Cummings, eds., *Research in Organizational Behavior,* vol. 13 (Greenwich, CT: JAI Press, 1991), 1–53.

104. J.M. George and J. Zhou, "Dual Tuning in a Supportive Context: Joint Contributions of Positive Mood, Negative Mood, and Supervisory Behaviors to Employee Creativity," *Academy of Management Journal* 50 (2007), 605–22; J.M. George, "Creativity in Organizations," in J.P. Walsh and A.P. Brief, eds., *The Academy of Management Annals,* vol. 1 (New York: Lawrence Erlbaum Associates, 2008), 439–77.

105. J.D. Greene, R.B. Sommerville, L.E. Nystrom, J.M. Darley, and J.D. Cohen, "An FMRI Investigation of Emotional Engagement in Moral Judgment," *Science,* September 14, 2001, 2105–08; L. Neergaard, "Brain Scans Show Emotions Key to Resolving Ethical Dilemmas," *Houston Chronicle,* September 14, 2001, 13A.

106. George and Zhou, "Dual Tuning in a Supportive Context."

107. George and Zhou, "Dual Tuning in a Supportive Context;" J.M. George, "Dual Tuning: A Minimum Condition for Understanding Affect in Organizations?" *Organizational Psychology Review,* no. 2 (2011), 147–64.

108. R.C. Sinclair, "Mood, Categorization Breadth, and Performance Appraisal: The Effects of Order of Information Acquisition and Affective State on Halo, Accuracy, Informational Retrieval, and Evaluations," *Organizational Behavior and Human Decision Processes* 42 (1988), 22–46.

109. D. Heath and C. Heath, "Passion Provokes Action," *Fast Company,* February 2011, 28–30; "Our Management Team," Our Management Team—North American Tool Corporation, North American Tool, http://www.natool.com/staff/our-management-team, April 3, 2012; Our Staff—North American Tool, http://www.natool.com/about-us/our-staff?tid=2, March 14, 2014.

110. Heath and Heath, "Passion Provokes Action."

111. Ibid.

112. Heath and Heath, "Passion Provokes Action"; "About Us," About Us, http://cedars-sinai.edu/About-Us/, April 3, 2012; Cedars-Sinai—A Non-Profit Hospital in Los Angeles, http://cedars-sinai.edu/, March 14, 2014.

113. Heath and Heath, "Passion Provokes Action."

114. Ibid.

115. Ibid.

116. Ibid.

117. D. Goleman, *Emotional Intelligence* (New York: Bantam Books, 1994); J.D. Mayer and P. Salovey, "The Intelligence of Emotional Intelligence," *Intelligence* 17 (1993), 433–42; J.D. Mayer and P. Salovey, "What Is Emotional Intelligence?" in P. Salovey and D. Sluyter, eds., *Emotional Development and Emotional Intelligence: Implications for Education* (New York: Basic Books, 1997); P. Salovey and J.D. Mayer, "Emotional Intelligence," *Imagination, Cognition, and Personality* 9 (1989–1990), 185–211.

118. S. Epstein, *Constructive Thinking* (Westport, CT: Praeger, 1998).

119. "Leading by Feel," *Inside the Mind of the Leader,* January 2004, 27–37.

120. P.C. Early and R.S. Peterson, "The Elusive Cultural Chameleon: Cultural Intelligence as a New Approach to Intercultural Training for the Global Manager," *Academy of Management Learning and Education* 3, no. 1 (2004), 100–15.

121. George, "Emotions and Leadership"; S. Begley, "The Boss Feels Your Pain," *Newsweek,* October 12, 1998, 74; D. Goleman, *Working with Emotional Intelligence* (New York: Bantam Books, 1998).

122. J. Bercovici, "Remembering Bernie Goldhirsh," www.medialifemagazine.com/news2003/jun03/jun30/4_thurs/news1thursday.html, April 15, 2004.

123. B. Burlingham, "Legacy: The Creative Spirit," *Inc.,* September 2003, 11–12.

124. Burlingham, "Legacy: The Creative Spirit"; "Inc. Magazine," www.inc.com/magazine, May 28, 2006.

125. Burlingham, "Legacy: The Creative Spirit"; "Inc. Magazine," www.inc.com, February 5, 2008.

126. "Leading by Feel," *Inside the Mind of the Leader,* January 2004, 27–37.

127. George, "Emotions and Leadership."

128. J. Zhou and J.M. George, "Awakening Employee Creativity: The Role of Leader Emotional Intelligence," *Leadership Quarterly* 14 (2003), 545–68.

129. H.M. Trice and J.M. Beyer, *The Cultures of Work Organizations* (Englewood Cliffs, NJ: Prentice-Hall, 1993).

130. J.B. Sørensen, "The Strength of Corporate Culture and the Reliability of Firm Performance," *Administrative Science Quarterly* 47 (2002), 70–91.

131. "Personality and Organizational Culture," in B. Schneider and D.B. Smith, eds., *Personality and Organizations* (Mahway, NJ: Lawrence Erlbaum, 2004), 347–69; J.E. Slaughter, M.J. Zickar, S. Highhouse, and D.C. Mohr, "Personality Trait Inferences about Organizations: Development of a Measure and Assessment of Construct Validity," *Journal of Applied Psychology* 89, no. 1 (2004), 85–103.

132. T. Kelley, *The Art of Innovation: Lessons in Creativity from IDEO, America's Leading Design Firm* (New York: Random House, 2001).

133. "Personality and Organizational Culture."

134. B. Schneider, "The People Make the Place," *Personnel Psychology* 40 (1987), 437–53.

135. "Personality and Organizational Culture."

136. Ibid.

137. B. Schneider, H.B. Goldstein, and D.B. Smith, "The ASA Framework: An Update," *Personnel Psychology* 48 (1995), 747–73; J. Schaubroeck, D.C. Ganster, and J.R. Jones, "Organizational and Occupational Influences in the Attraction–Selection–Attrition Process," *Journal of Applied Psychology* 83 (1998), 869–91.

138. Kelley, *The Art of Innovation.*

139. www.ideo.com, February 5, 2008.

140. Kelley, *The Art of Innovation.*

141. "Personality and Organizational Culture."

142. Kelley, *The Art of Innovation.*

143. George, "Emotions and Leadership."

144. Kelley, *The Art of Innovation.*

145. Ibid.

146. D.C. Feldman, "The Development and Enforcement of Group Norms," *Academy of Management Review* 9 (1984), 47–53.

147. G.R. Jones, *Organizational Theory, Design, and Change* (Upper Saddle River, NJ: Prentice-Hall, 2003).

148. H. Schein, "The Role of the Founder in Creating Organizational Culture," *Organizational Dynamics* 12 (1983), 13–28.

149. J.M. George, "Personality, Affect, and Behavior in Groups," *Journal of Applied Psychology* 75 (1990), 107–16.

150. J. Van Maanen, "Police Socialization: A Longitudinal Examination of Job Attitudes in an Urban Police Department," *Administrative Science Quarterly* 20 (1975), 207–28.

151. www.intercotwest.com/Disney; M.N. Martinez, "Disney Training Works Magic," *HRMagazine,* May 1992, 53–57.

152. P.L. Berger and T. Luckman, *The Social Construction of Reality* (Garden City, NY: Anchor Books, 1967).

153. H.M. Trice and J.M. Beyer, "Studying Organizational Culture through Rites and Ceremonials," *Academy of Management Review* 9 (1984), 653–69.

154. Kelley, *The Art of Innovation.*

155. H.M. Trice and J.M. Beyer, *The Cultures of Work Organizations* (Englewood Cliffs, NJ: Prentice-Hall, 1993).

156. B. Ortega, "Walmart's Meeting Is a Reason to Party," *The Wall Street Journal,* June 3, 1994, A1.

157. H.M. Trice and J.M. Beyer, "Studying Organizational Culture through Rites and Ceremonies," *Academy of Management Review* 9 (1984), 653–69.

158. Kelley, *The Art of Innovation.*

159. www.ibm.com; IBM Investor Relations—Corporate Governance, Executive Officers, "Executive Officers," http://www.ibm.com/investor/governance/executive-officers.wss, February 5, 2010; "Board of Directors," IBM Annual Report 2011—Board of Directors and Senior Leadership, http://www.ibm.com/annualreport/2011/board-of-directors.html, April 4, 2012.

160. K.E. Weick, *The Social Psychology of Organization* (Reading, MA: Addison Wesley, 1979).

161. B. McLean and P. Elkind, *The Smartest Guys in the Room: The Amazing Rise and Scandalous Fall of Enron* (New York: Penguin Books, 2003); R. Smith and J.R. Emshwiller, *24 Days: How Two Wall Street Journal Reporters Uncovered the Lies That Destroyed Faith in Corporate America* (New York: HarperCollins, 2003); M. Swartz and S. Watkins, *Power Failure: The Inside Story of the Collapse of ENRON* (New York: Doubleday, 2003).

Chapter 4

1. n.d., www.letsmove.gov/.

2. Ibid.

3. Ibid.

4. M. Fox, "First Lady Proposes Ban on Junk Food Marketing in Schools," February 25, 2014, www.nbcnews.com/health/kids-health/first-lady-proposes-ban-junk-food-marketing-schools-n38201.

5. U.S. Department of Agriculture, "Proposed Wellness Standards for a Healthy School Environment: Leaders Voice Their Support," www.fns.usda.gov/sites/default/files/LWP_final_508.pdf.

6. H. Cardello, "Better-for-You Foods: It's Just Good Business," October 13, 2011, www.hudson.org/research/8423-better-for-you-foods-it-s-just-good-business.

7. www.apple.com, press release, 2012.

8. D. Kravets, "Supreme Court to Hear Case on Medical Pot," www.yahoo.com, June 29, 2004; C. Lane, "A Defeat for Users of Medical Marijuana," www.washingtonpost.com, June 7, 2005.

9. M. Bruce, "Obama Says Wall St. Protests Voice Widespread Frustrations," October 6, 2011, abcnews.go.com/blogs/politics/2011/10/obama-says-wall-st-protests-voice-widespread-frustrations/.

10. R.E. Freeman, *Strategic Management: A Stakeholder Approach* (Marshfield, MA: Pitman, 1984).

11. S. Bianchi, "Bill Gates Seeks $1.5 Billion More to Eradicate Polio by 2018," *Bloomberg,* April 25, 2013, www.bloomberg.com/news/2013-04-25/bill-gates-seeks-1-5-billion-more-to-eradicate-polio-by-2018.html.

12. J.A. Pearce, "The Company Mission as a Strategic Tool," *Sloan Management Review,* Spring 1982, 15–24.

13. H. Bapuji and S. Riaz, "Occupy Wall Street: What Businesses Need to Know," *Harvard Business Review,* October 14, 2011, blogs.hbr.org/2011/10/occupy-wall-street-what-business/.

14. C.I. Barnard, *The Functions of the Executive* (Cambridge, MA: Harvard University Press, 1948).

15. Freeman, *Strategic Management.*

16. "Michelin Job Cuts at Granton Plant 'Devastating': Company Says Market for Small Car and Truck Tires Is Diminishing," March 3, 2014, www.cbc.ca/news/canada/nova-scotia/michelin-job-cuts-at-granton-plant-devastating-1.2557903.

17. P.S. Adler, "Corporate Scandals: It's Time for Reflection in Business Schools," *Academy of Management Executive* 16 (August 2002), 148–50.

18. C. Main, "Volcker Rule, EU Bank Deadlock, Deutsche Bank Risk: Compliance," *Bloomberg,* December 10, 2013, www.bloomberg.com/news/2013-12-10/volcker-rule-eu-bank-deadlock-deutsche-bank-risk-compliance.html.

19. R. Kerber, "Growth in Compensation for U.S. CEOs May Have Slowed," *Reuters,* March 17, 2014, www.reuters.com/article/2014/03/17/us-compensation-ceos-2013-insight-idUSBREA2G05520140317.

20. W.G. Sanders and D.C. Hambrick, "Swinging for the Fences: The Effects of CEO Stock Options on Company Risk Taking and Performance," *Academy of Management Journal* 53, no. 5 (2007), 1055–78.

21. R. Bowman, "Is This the Year When Supply Chains Become Socially Responsible?" *Forbes,* March 11, 2014, www.forbes.com/sites/robertbowman/2014/03/11/is-this-the-year-when-supply-chains-become-socially-responsible/.

22. S. Greenhouse, "Bangladesh Inspections Find Gaps in Safety," *The New York Times,* March 11, 2014, www.nytimes.com/2014/03/12/business/safety-flaws-found-in-new-inspections-of-factories-in-bangladesh.html?hpw8rref=business.

23. Ibid.

24. R. Cho, "What Happens to All That Plastic?" January 31, 2012, blogs.ei.columbia.edu/2012/01/31/what-happens-to-all-that-plastic/.

25. A.C. Steinemann, I.C. MacGregor, S.M. Gordon, L.G. Gallagher, A.L. Davis, D.S. Ribeiro, et al., "Fragranced Consumer Products: Chemicals Emitted, Ingredients Unlisted," *Environ Impact Review* 31 (2011), 328–33.

26. The Soap Dispensary, March 5, 2014, www.facebook.com/pages/The-Soap-Dispensary/266253066720178.

27. "Why Buy Locally Owned?" *Sustainable Connections,* n.d., sustainableconnections.org/thinklocal/why.

28. N. Burg, "How One Business Diverted 8,000 Plastic Bottles from Landfills," *Forbes,* March 16, 2014, www.forbes.com/sites/citi/2014/03/16/how-one-business-diverted-8000-plastic-bottles-from-landfills/.

29. T.L. Beauchamp and N.E. Bowie, eds., *Ethical Theory and Business* (Englewood Cliffs, NJ: Prentice-Hall, 1929); A. MacIntyre, *After Virtue* (South Bend, IN: University of Notre Dame Press, 1981).

30. R.E. Goodin, "How to Determine Who Should Get What," *Ethics,* July 1975, 310–21.

31. E.P. Kelly, "A Better Way to Think about Business" (book review), *Academy of Management Executive* 14 (May 2000), 127–29.

32. T.M. Jones, "Ethical Decision Making by Individuals in Organization: An Issue Contingent Model," *Academy of Management Journal* 16 (1991), 366–95; G.F. Cavanaugh, D.J. Moberg, and M. Velasquez, "The Ethics of Organizational Politics," *Academy of Management Review* 6 (1981), 363–74.

33. L.K. Trevino, "Ethical Decision Making in Organizations: A Person–Situation Interactionist Model," *Academy of Management Review* 11 (1986), 601–17; W.H. Shaw and V. Barry, *Moral Issues in Business,* 6th ed. (Belmont, CA: Wadsworth, 1995).

34. T.M. Jones, "Instrumental Stakeholder Theory: A Synthesis of Ethics and Economics," *Academy of Management Review* 20(195), 404–37.

35. B. Victor and J.B. Cullen, "The Organizational Bases of Ethical Work Climates," *Administrative Science Quarterly* 33 (1988), 101–25.

36. D. Collins, "Organizational Harm, Legal Consequences and Stakeholder Retaliation," *Journal of Business Ethics* 8 (1988), 1–13.

37. R.C. Solomon, *Ethics and Excellence* (New York: Oxford University Press, 1992).

38. T.E. Becker, "Integrity in Organizations: Beyond Honesty and Conscientiousness," *Academy of Management Review* 23 (January 1998), 154–62.

39. S.W. Gellerman, "Why Good Managers Make Bad Decisions," in K.R. Andrews, ed, *Ethics in Practice: Managing the Moral Corporation* (Boston: Harvard Business School Press, 1989).

40. J. Dobson, "Corporate Reputation: A Free Market Solution to Unethical Behavior," *Business and Society* 28 (1989), 1–5.

41. M.S. Baucus and J.P. Near, "Can Illegal Corporate Behavior Be Predicted? An Event History Analysis," *Academy of Management Journal* 34 (1991), 9–36.

42. Trevino, "Ethical Decision Making."

43. "GSK, Merck, and Bristol Myers Squibb Are the World's Most Ethical Companies Across All Sectors, Swiss Study," www.medicalnewstoday.com, January 8, 2006.

44. A.S. Waterman, "On the Uses of Psychological Theory and Research in the Process of Ethical Inquiry," *Psychological Bulletin* 103, no. 3 (1988), 283–98.

45. A. Knobloch, "Siemens Bribery Case Spreads to Brazilian Politics," *DW,* March 12, 2013, www.dw.de/siemens-bribery-case-spreads-to-brazilian-politics/a-17268276.

46. "Corruption by Country / Territory," *Transparency International,* n.d., www.transparency.org/country.

47. "Hard to Read," *The Economist,* January 29, 2014, www.economist.com/blogs/schumpeter/2014/01/brazil-s-new-anti-corruption-law.

48. R. Kanani, "CEO of Tiffany & Co. On Ethical Sourcing, Responsible Mining, and Leadership," *Forbes,* January 19, 2014, www.forbes.com/sites/rahimkanani/2014/01/19/ceo-of-tiffany-co-on-ethical-sourcing-responsible-mining-and-leadership/.

49. *Initiative for Responsible Mining Assurance,* www.responsiblemining.net/.

50. Ibid.

51. *Kimberly Process,* www.kimberleyprocess.com/.

52. R. Kanani, "CEO of Tiffany & Co. On Ethical Sourcing, Responsible Mining, and Leadership," *Forbes,* January 19, 2014, www.forbes.com/sites/rahimkanani/2014/01/19/ceo-of-tiffany-co-on-ethical-sourcing-responsible-mining-and-leadership/.

53. M.S. Frankel, "Professional Codes: Why, How, and with What Impact?" *Ethics* 8 (1989), 109–15.

54. J. Van Maanen and S.R. Barley, "Occupational Communities: Culture and Control in Organizations," in B. Staw and L. Cummings, eds., *Research in Organizational Behavior,* vol. 6 (Greenwich, CT: JAI Press, 1984), 287–365.

55. M. Maynard, "The Steep Cost of Toyota's Settlement with the U.S. Government," *Forbes,* March 19, 2014, www.forbes.com/sites/michelinemaynard/2014/03/19/the-steep-cost-of-toyotas-settlement-with-the-u-s-government/.

56. Ibid.

57. Jones, "Ethical Decision Making."

58. *Seva Canada,* www.seva.ca/wwa.htm.

59. "TOMS Introduces TOMS Eyewear, the Next One for One™ Product," *PRNewswire,* June 7, 2011, www.prnewswire.com/news-releases/toms-introduces-toms-eyewear-the-next-one-for-one-product-123372898.html.

60. "TOMS Is On a Mission to Brew Something Greater: TOMS Roasting Co. Launches as the Next One for One® Product," press release, *The Wall Street Journal,* March 12, 2014, online.wsj.com/article/PR-CO-20140312-908430.html,.

61. E. Gatewwod and A.B. Carroll, "The Anatomy of Corporate Social Response," *Business Horizons,* September–October 1981, 9–16.

62. J. Healey, "GM CEO Admits Recall Tardy, Won't Pledge Liability," *USA Today,* March 18, 2014, www.usatoday.com/story/money/cars/2014/03/18/gm-ceo-barra-president-reuss-recalls-safety/6557865/.

63. "Fitbit Force Skin Irritation FAQs," *fitbithelp,* February 26, 2014, https://help.fitbit.com/customer/portal/articles/1425569.

64. M. Friedman, "A Friedman Doctrine: The Social Responsibility of Business Is to Increase Its Profits," *New York Times Magazine,* September 13, 1970, 33.

65. L. Neumeister and M. Gordon, "Hedge Fund Giant SAC Captial to Pay $1.8B Penalty," *Associated Press,* November 4, 2013, bigstory.ap.org/article/hedge-giant-sac-capital-case-resolution-ny.

66. *The New York Times,* http://topics.nytimes.com/top/news/business/companies/nucor_corporation/.

67. P. Engardio and M. Arndt, "What Price Reputation?" July 9, 2007, www.businessweek.com,.

68. M. Conlin, "Where Layoffs Are a Last Resort," www.businessweek.com, October 8, 2001; Southwest Airlines Fact Sheet, www.southwest.com, 2004.

69. G.R. Jones, *Organizational Theory: Text and Cases* (Englewood Cliffs, NJ: Prentice-Hall, 2008).

70. P.E. Murphy, "Creating Ethical Corporate Structure," *Sloan Management Review,* Winter 1989, 81–87.

71. R. Johnson, "Ralston to Buy Beechnut, Gambling It Can Overcome Apple Juice Scandal," *The Wall Street Journal,* September 18, 1989, B11.

Chapter 5

1. "PricewaterhouseCoopers on the Forbes America's Largest Private Companies List," http://www.forbes.com/companies/pricewaterhousecoopers/, March 25, 2014.; "Facts and Figures: PwC," http://www.pwc.com/gx/en/about-pwc/facts-and-figures.jhtml, March 25, 2014.; "PwC: Business Services, Audit, Assurance, Tax and Advisory for the US and the Globe," http://www.pwc.com/us/en/about-us/index.jhtml, March 26, 2014.

2. "PricewaterhouseCoopers on the Forbes America's Largest Private Companies List," http://www.forbes.com/companies/pricewaterhousecoopers/, March 25, 2014.; "Facts and Figures: PwC," http://www.pwc.com/gx/en/about-pwc/facts-and-figures.jhtml, March 25, 2014.; "PwC: Business Services, Audit, Assurance, Tax and Advisory for the US and the Globe," http://www.pwc.com/us/en/about-us/index.jhtml, March 26, 2014.; "PwC History and Milestones," http://www.pwc.com/us/en/about-us/pwc-corporate-history.jhtml, March 26, 2014.

3. "PricewaterhouseCoopers on the Forbes America's Largest Private Companies List," http://www.forbes.com/companies/pricewaterhousecoopers/, March 25, 2014.; "PwC: Business Services, Audit, Assurance, Tax and Advisory for the US and the globe," http://www.pwc.com/us/en/about-us/index.jhtml, March 26, 2014.

4. "PwC—Bob Moritz," http://www.pwc.com/us/en/about-us/leadership/bob-moritz.jhtml, March 26, 2014.; A. Bryant, "Bob Moritz, on How to Learn about Diversity," *The New York Times,* September 14, 2013, http://www.nytimes.com/2013/09/15/business/bob-moritz-on-how-to-learn-about-diversity.html?_r=0, March 24, 2014.

5. "PwC—Bob Moritz," http://www.pwc.com/us/en/about-us/leadership/bob-moritz.jhtml, March 26, 2014.; A. Bryant, "Bob Moritz, on How to Learn about Diversity," *The New York Times,* September 14, 2013, http://www.nytimes.com/2013/09/15/business/bob-moritz-on-how-to-learn-about-diversity.html?_r=0, March 24, 2014.

6. "The 2012 DiversityInc Top 50 Companies for Diversity List," *DiversityInc,* June 2012, 44–74.

7. "The 2012 DiversityInc Top 50 Companies for Diversity List," *DiversityInc,* June 2012, 44–74; "The DiversityInc Top 50," *DiversityInc,* June 2013, 29–76.

8. "Leveraging the Power of Our Differences," PwC, May 2013, http://www.pwc.com/us/en/about-us/diversity.jhtml, March 27, 2014.

9. "The 2012 DiversityInc Top 50 Companies for Diversity List," *DiversityInc,* June 2012, 44–74; "The DiversityInc Top 50," *DiversityInc,* June 2013, 29–76.

10. "Leveraging the Power of Our Differences," PwC, May 2013, http://www.pwc.com/us/en/about-us/diversity.jhtml, March 27, 2014.

11. "Leveraging the Power of Our Differences."

12. "Leveraging the Power of Our Differences."

13. "Leveraging the Power of Our Differences."

14. "Leveraging the Power of Our Differences."

15. "The DiversityInc Top 50," *DiversityInc,* June 2013, 29–76.

16. "Leveraging the Power of Our Differences."

17. D. McCracken, "Winning the Talent War for Women," *Harvard Business Review,* November–December 2000, 159–67.

18. W.B. Swann, Jr., J.T. Polzer, D.C. Seyle, and S.J. Ko, "Finding Value in Diversity: Verification of Personal and Social Self-Views in Diverse Groups," *Academy of Management Review* 29, no. 1 (2004), 9–27.

19. "Usual Weekly Earnings Summary," *News: Bureau of Labor Statistics,* April 16, 2004 (www.bls.gov/news.release/whyeng.nr0.htm); "Facts on Affirmative Action in Employment and Contracting," *Americans for a Fair Chance,* January 28, 2004 (fair-chance.civilrights.org/research_center/details.cfm?id=18076); "Household Data Annual Averages," www.bls.gov, April 28, 2004.

20. "Prejudice: Still on the Menu," *Business-Week,* April 3, 1995, 42.

21. "She's a Woman, Offer Her Less," *BusinessWeek,* May 7, 2001, 34.

22. "Glass Ceiling Is a Heavy Barrier for Minorities, Blocking Them from Top Jobs," *The Wall Street Journal,* March 14, 1995, A1.

23. "Catalyst Report Outlines Unique Challenges Faced by African-American Women in Business," *Catalyst* news release, February 18, 2004.

24. C. Gibson, "Nation's Median Age Highest Ever, but 65-and-Over Population's Growth Lags, Census 2000 Shows," *U.S. Census Bureau News,* May 30, 2001 (www.census.gov); "U.S. Census Press Releases: Nation's Population One-Third Minority," *U.S. Census Bureau News,* May 10, 2006 (www.census.gov/Press-Release/www/releases/archives/population/006808.html); "The World Factbook," *Central Intelligence Agency,* https://www.cia.gov/library/publications/the-world-factbook/fields/2177.html, April 5, 2012.; "The World Factbook," Central Intelligence Agency, https://www.cia.gov/library/publications/the-world-factbook/fields/2177.html, April 1, 2014.

25. "Table 2: United States Population Projections by Age and Sex: 2000–2050," *U.S. Census Board, International Data Base, 94,* April 28, 2004 (www.census.gov/ipc/www.idbprint.html); "An Older and More Diverse Nation by Midcentury," August 14, 2008, Newsroom: Population, http://www.census.gov/newsroom/releases/archives/population/cb08-123.html, April 5, 2012.

26. U.S. Equal Employment Opportunity Commission, "Federal Laws Prohibiting Job Discrimination—Questions and Answers," www.eeoc.gov, June 20, 2001.

27. "Sex by Industry by Class of Worker for the Employed Civilian Population 16 Years and Over," *American FactFinder,* October 15, 2001 (factfinder.census.gov); "2002 Catalyst Census of Women Corporate Officers and Top Earners in the *Fortune* 500," www.catalystwomen.org, August 17, 2004; "WB—Statistics & Data," http://www.dol.gov/wb/stats/main.htm?PrinterFriendly=true&, February 9, 2010; "Statistical Overview of Women in the Workplace," *Catalyst,* December 2011, http://www.catalyst.org/publication/219/statistical-overview-of-women-in-the-workplace, April 4, 2012.; "Usual Weekly Earnings of Wage and Salary Workers Fourth Quarter 2013," Bureau of Labor Statistics U.S. Department of Labor, January 22, 2014, http://www.bls.gov/news.release/pdf/wkyemg.pdf, April 1, 2014.

28. "Profile of Selected Economic Characteristics: 2000," *American FactFinder,* October 15, 2001 (factfinder.census.gov); "Usual Weekly Earnings Summary," www.bls.gov/news.release, August 17, 2004; "WB—Statistics & Data," http://www.dol.gov/wb/stats/main.htm?PrinterFriendly=true&, February 9, 2010; "Usual Weekly Earnings of Wage and Salary Workers Fourth Quarter 2011," January 24, 2012, *Bureau of Labor Statistics, U.S. Department of Labor (BLS),* http://www.bls.gov/news.release/pdf/wkyeng.pdf, April 5, 2012.; "Usual Weekly Earnings of Wage and Salary Workers Fourth Quarter 2013," Bureau of Labor Statistics U.S. Department of Labor, January 22, 2014, http://www.bls.gov/news.release/pdf/wkyemg.pdf, April 1, 2014.

29. "Women in Management in the United States, 1960–Present," July 2011, *Catalyst,* http://www.catalyst.org/publication/207/women-in-management-in-the-united-states-1960-p, April 5, 2012.; "Statistical Overview of Women in the Workplace," Knowledge Center – Catalyst.org, March 3, 2014, http://www.catalyst.org/knowledge/statistical-overview-women-workplace, April 1, 2014.

30. "2000 Catalyst Census of Women Corporate Officers and Top Earners of the *Fortune* 500," www.catalystwomen.org, October 21, 2001; S. Wellington, M. Brumit Kropf, and P.R. Gerkovich, "What's Holding Women Back?" *Harvard Business Review,* June 2003, 18–19; D. Jones, "The Gender Factor," *USA Today.com,* December 30, 2003; "2002 Catalyst Census of Women Corporate Officers and Top Earners in the *Fortune* 500," www.catalystwomen.org, August 17, 2004; "2007 Catalyst Census of Women Corporate Officers and Top Earners of the *Fortune* 500," www.catalyst.org/knowledge/titles/title.php?page=cen_COTE_07, February 8, 2008; "No News Is Bad News: Women's Leadership Still Stalled in Corporate America," December 14, 2011, *Catalyst,* http://www.catalyst.org/press-release/199/no-news-is-bad-news-womens-leadership-still-sta . . . , April 5, 2012.; "Statistical Overview of Women in the Workplace," Knowledge Center – Catalyst.org, March 3, 2014, http://www.catalyst.org/knowledge/statistical-overview-women-workplace, April 1, 2014.; "Fortune 500 Executive Officer Top Earner Positions Held by Women," Knowledge Center—Catalyst.org, http://www.catalyst.org/knowledge/women-executive-officer-top-earners-fortune-500-0, April 1, 2014.

31. T. Gutner, "Wanted: More Diverse Directors," *BusinessWeek,* April 30, 2001, 134; "2003 Catalyst Census of Women Board Directors," www.catalyst-women.org, August 17, 2004; "2007 Catalyst Census of Women Board Directors of the *Fortune* 500," www.catalyst.org/knowledge/titles/title.php?page+cen_WBD_07, February 8, 2008; "Statistical Overview of Women in the Workplace," *Catalyst,* December 2011, http://www.catalyst.org/publication/219/statistical-overview-of-women-in-the-workplace, April 4, 2012.; "Statistical Overview of Women in the Workplace," Knowledge Center – Catalyst.org, March 3, 2014, http://www.catalyst.org/knowledge/statistical-overview-women-workplace, April 1, 2014.

32. Günter, "Wanted: More Diverse Directors"; "2003 Catalyst Census of Women Board Directors."

33. R. Sharpe, "As Leaders, Women Rule," *BusinessWeek,* November 20, 2000, 75–84.

34. R. Sharpe, "As Leaders, Women Rule," *BusinessWeek,* November 20, 2000, 75–84.

35. "New Catalyst Study Reveals Financial Performance Is Higher for Companies with More Women at the Top," *Catalyst* news release, January 26, 2004.

36. P. Sellers, "Women on Boards (NOT!)," *Fortune,* October 15, 2007, 105.

37. U.S. Census 2010, U.S. Department of Commerce, U.S. Census Bureau; K.R. Hums, N.A. Jones, and R.R. Ramirez, "Overview of Race and Hispanic Original: 2010," *2010 Census Briefs,* March 2011, *United States Census Bureau,* http://www.census.gov/prod/cen2010/briefs/c2010br-02.pdf, April 5, 2012.

38. U.S. Census 2010.

39. B. Guzman, "The Hispanic Population," U.S. Census Bureau, May 2001; U.S. Census Bureau, "Profiles of General Demographic Characteristics," May 2001; U.S. Census Bureau, "Revisions to the Standards for the Classification of Federal Data on Race and Ethnicity," November 2, 2000, 1–19.

40. L. Chavez, "Just Another Ethnic Group," *The Wall Street Journal,* May 14, 2001, A22.

41. Bureau of Labor Statistics, "Civilian Labor Force 16 and Older by Sex, Age, Race, and Hispanic Origin, 1978, 1988, 1998, and Projected 2008," stats.bls.gov/emp, October 16, 2001.

42. "An Older and More Diverse Nation by Midcentury," August 14, 2008, http://www.census.gov/newsroom/releases/archives/population/cb08-123.html,

April 5, 2012; Humes, Jones, and Ramirez, "Overview of Race and Hispanic Original: 2010."

43. Humes, Jones, and Ramirez, "Overview of Race and Hispanic Original: 2010."

44. "U.S. Census Bureau, Profile of General Demographic Characteristics: 2000," *Census 2000,* www.census.gov; "U.S. Census Press Releases: Nation's Population One-Third Minority," *U.S. Census Bureau News,* May 10, 2006 (www.census.gov/Press-Release/www/releases/archives/population/006808.html); Humes, Jones, and Ramirez, "Overview of Race and Hispanic Original: 2010."

45. "An Older and More Diverse Nation by Midcentury," August 14, 2008, http://www.census.gov/newsroom/releases/archives/population/cb08-123.html, April 5, 2012.

46. "Usual Weekly Earnings of Wage and Salary Workers Fourth Quarter 2011," January 24, 2012, Bureau of Labor Statistics U.S. Department of Labor (BLS), http://www.bls.gov/news.release/pdf/wkyeng.pdf, April 5, 2012.; "Usual Weekly Earnings of Wage and Salary Workers Fourth Quarter 2013," Bureau of Labor Statistics U.S. Department of Labor, January 22, 2014, http://www.bls.gov/news.release/pdf/wkyemg.pdf, April 1, 2014.

47. J. Flint, "NBC to Hire More Minorities on TV Shows," *The Wall Street Journal,* January 6, 2000, B13.

48. J. Poniewozik, "What's Wrong with This Picture?" *Time,* June 1, 2001 (www.Time.com); "Hispanic Heritage Month 2013: Sept. 15 – Oct. 15," U.S. Census Bureau News, https://www.census.gov/newsroom/releases/pdf/cb13ff-19-hispancheritage.pdf.

49. J. Poniewozik, "What's Wrong with This Picture?" *Time,* June 1, 2001 (www.Time.com).

50. National Association of Realtors, "Real Estate Industry Adapting to Increasing Cultural Diversity," *PR Newswire,* May 16, 2001.

51. "Toyota Apologizes to African Americans over Controversial Ad," *Kyodo News Service,* Japan, May 23, 2001.

52. J.H. Coplan, "Putting a Little Faith in Diversity," *BusinessWeek Online,* December 21, 2000.

53. Coplan, "Putting a Little Faith in Diversity."

54. Coplan, "Putting a Little Faith in Diversity."

55. K. Holland, "When Religious Needs Test Company," *The New York Times,* February 25, 2007, BU17.

56. J.N. Cleveland, J. Barnes-Farrell, and J.M. Ratz, "Accommodation in the Workplace," *Human Resource Management Review* 7 (1997), 77–108; A. Colella, "Coworker Distributive Fairness Judgments of the Workplace Accommodations of Employees with Disabilities," *Academy of Management Review* 26 (2001), 100–16.

57. Colella, "Coworker Distributive Fairness"; D. Stamps, "Just How Scary Is the

ADA," *Training* 32 (1995), 93–101; M.S. West and R.L. Cardy, "Accommodating Claims of Disability: The Potential Impact of Abuses," *Human Resource Management Review* 7 (1997), 233–46.

58. G. Koretz, "How to Enable the Disabled," *BusinessWeek,* November 6, 2000 (*BusinessWeek* Archives).

59. Colella, "Coworker Distributive Fairness."

60. "Notre Dame Disability Awareness Week 2004 Events," www.nd.edu/~bbuddies/daw.html, April 30, 2004.

61. P. Hewitt, "UH Highlights Abilities, Issues of the Disabled," *Houston Chronicle,* October 22, 2001, 24A.

62. Center for Students with DisAbilities (CSD)—University of Houston, http://www.uh.edu/csd/about_us/staff.html, April 1, 2014.

63. "Notre Dame Disability Awareness"; Hewitt, "UH Highlights Abilities, Issues of the Disabled."

64. J.M. George, "AIDS/AIDS-Related Complex," in L.H. Peters, C.R. Greer, and S.A. Youngblood, eds., *The Blackwell Encyclopedic Dictionary of Human Resource Management* (Oxford, UK: Blackwell, 1997), 6–7.

65. J.M. George, "AIDS Awareness Training," 6.

66. S. Armour, "Firms Juggle Stigma, Needs of More Workers with HIV," *USA Today,* September 7, 2000, B1.

67. Armour, "Firms Juggle Stigma."

68. Armour, "Firms Juggle Stigma"; S. Vaughn, "Career Challenge; Companies' Work Not Over in HIV and AIDS Education," *Los Angeles Times,* July 8, 2001.

69. R. Brownstein, "Honoring Work Is Key to Ending Poverty," *Detroit News,* October 2, 2001, 9; G. Koretz, "How Welfare to Work Worked," *BusinessWeek,* September 24, 2001 (*BusinessWeek* Archives).

70. "As Ex-Welfare Recipients Lose Jobs, Offer Safety Net," *The Atlanta Constitution,* October 10, 2001, A18.

71. C.S. Rugaber, "Job Openings in a Squeeze," *Houston Chronicle,* February 10, 2010, D1.

72. Press releases, U.S. Census Bureau, "Income, Poverty and Health Insurance Coverage in the United States: 2008," http://www.census.gov/Press-Release/www/releases/archives/income_wealth/014227.html, February 8, 2010; "The 2009 HHS Poverty Guidelines," http://aspe.hhs.gov/poverty/09poverty.shtml, February 8, 2010; "Income, Poverty and Health Insurance Coverage in the United States: 2010," September 13, 2011, http://www.census.gov/newsroom/releases/archives/income_wealth/cb11-157.html, April 5, 2012.; "About Poverty—Highlights—U.S. Census Bureau," http://www.census.gov/hhes/www/poverty/about/overview/index.html, April 1, 2014.

73. U.S. Census Bureau, "Poverty—How the Census Bureau Measures Poverty," *Census 2000,* September 25, 2001; "How the Census Bureau Measures Poverty," http://www.census.gov/hhes/www/poverty/about/overview/measure.html, April 1, 2014.

74. Press releases, U.S. Census Bureau, "Income, Poverty and Health Insurance Coverage in the United States: 2008," http://www.census.gov/Press-Release/www/releases/archives/income_wealth/014227.html, February 8, 2010; "The 2009 HHS Poverty Guidelines," http://aspe.hhs.gov/poverty/09poverty.html, February 8, 2010; "Income, Poverty and Health Insurance Coverage in the United States: 2010," September 13, 2011, http://www.census.gov/newsroom/releases/archives/income_wealth/cb11-157.html, April 5, 2012.; "Income, Poverty and Health Insurance Coverage in the United States: 2012," http://www.census.gov/newsroom/releases/archives/income_wealth/cb13-165.html, April 1, 2014.

75. I. Lelchuk, "Families Fear Hard Times Getting Worse/$30,000 in the Bay Area Won't Buy Necessities, Survey Says," *San Francisco Chronicle,* September 26, 2001, A13; S.R. Wheeler, "Activists: Welfare-to-Work Changes Needed," *Denver Post,* October 10, 2001, B6.

76. B. Carton, "Bedtime Stories: In 24-Hour Workplace, Day Care Is Moving to the Night Shift," *The Wall Street Journal,* July 6, 2001, A1, A4.

77. Carton, "Bedtime Stories"; "Mission, Core Values, and Philosophy," *Children's Choice Features,* http://childrenschoice.com/AboutUs/MissionCoreValuesandPhilosophy/tabid/59/Default.aspx, February 9, 2010.

78. Carton, "Bedtime Stories."

79. Carton, "Bedtime Stories."

80. G.J. Gates, "How Many People Are Lesbian, Gay, Bisexual, and Transgender?" April 2011, *The William Institute,* http://williamsinstitute.law.ucla.edu/wp-content/uploads/Gates-How-Many-People-LGBT-Apr-2011.pdf, April 5, 2012.

81. S.E. Needleman, "More Programs Move to Halt Bias against Gays," *The Wall Street Journal,* November 26, 2007, B3; "How the Census Bureau Measures Poverty," http://www.census.gov/hhes/www/poverty/about/overview/measure.html, April 1, 2014.

82. K. Fahim, "United Parcel Service Agrees to Benefits in Civil Unions," *The New York Times,* July 31, 2007, A19.

83. J. Hempel, "Coming Out in Corporate America," *BusinessWeek,* December 15, 2003, 64–72; "LGBT Equality at the Fortune 500," *Human Rights Campaign,* http://www.hrc.org/resources/entry/lgbt-equality-at-the-fortune-500, April 5, 2012.

84. Hempel, "Coming Out in Corporate America."

85. J. Files, "Study Says Discharges Continue under 'Don't Ask, Don't Tell,'" *The New York Times,* March 24, 2004, A14; J. Files, "Gay Ex-Officers Say 'Don't Ask' Doesn't Work," *The New York Times,* December 10, 2003, A14.

86. Hempel, "Coming Out in Corporate America"; "DreamWorks Animation SKG Company History," www.dreamworks-animation.com/dwa/opencms/company/history/index.html, May 29, 2006; J. Chng, "Allan Gilmour: Former Vice-Chairman of Ford Speaks on Diversity," www.harbus.org/media/storage/paper343/news/2006/04/18/News/Allan.Gilmour.Former.ViceChairman.Of.Ford.Speaks.On.Diversity-1859600.html?nore write 200606021800&sourcedomain=www.harbus.org, April 18, 2006; "Allan D. Gilmour Profile," Forbes.com, http://people.forbes.com/profile/print/allan-d-gilmour/27441, April 11, 2012.; Allan Gilmour—Forbes, http://www.forbes.com/profile/allan-gilmour/, April 1, 2014.

87. Needleman, "More Programs Move to Halt Bias"; "A History of Respect—Diversity and Inclusion at SC Johnson," https://www.scjohnson.com/en/commitment/diversity/17Years.aspx, April 1, 2014.

88. Hempel, "Coming Out in Corporate America."

89. D. Kopecki, "JPMorgan, Goldman Rank Among Best Workplaces for Gays, Lesbians," December 9, 2011, *Bloomberg BusinessWeek,* http://www.businessweek.com/news/2011-12-09/jpmorgan-goldman-rank-among-best-work. . . , April 5, 2012; "Best Places to Work 2012," http://www.hrc.org/resources/entry/best-places-to-work-2012, April 5, 2012; "Award for Workplace Equality Innovation," *Human Right Campaign,* http://www.hrc.org/resources/entry/award-for-workplace-equality-innovation, April 5, 2012.; "Best Places to Work 2014—Resources—Human Rights Campaign," http://hrc.org/resources/entry/best-places-to-work-2014, April 1, 2014.; "The 304 Best Places to Work for LGBT Equality in America – Human Rights Campaign," http://www.hrc.org/blog/entry/the-304-best-places-to-work-for-lgbt-equality-in-american, April 1, 2014.

90. Needleman, "More Programs Move to Halt Bias."

91. Needleman, "More Programs Move to Halt Bias."

92. "Best Places to Work 2012"; "Best Places to Work 2014—Resources—Human Rights Campaign," http://hrc.org/resources/entry/best-places-to-work-2014, April 1, 2014.

93. "For Women, Weight May Affect Pay," *Houston Chronicle,* March 4, 2004, 12A.

94. V. Valian, *Why So Slow? The Advancement of Women* (Cambridge, MA: MIT Press, 2000).

95. S.T. Fiske and S.E. Taylor, *Social Cognition,* 2nd ed. (New York: McGraw-Hill, 1991); Valian, *Why So Slow?*

96. P. Dvorak, "Firms Push New Methods to Promote Diversity," *The Wall Street Journal,* December 18, 2006, B3; www.sodexousa.com/, February 7, 2008, "About Us," http://www.sodexousa.com/usen/aboutus/aboutus.asp; February 8, 2010; "Catalyst Honors Initiatives at Sodexo and Commonwealth Bank of Australia with the 2012 Catalyst Award," January 24, 2012, http://www.sodexousa.com/usen/newsroom/press/press12/sodexo_catalyst_award.asp, April 5, 2012.; "Sodexo in USA," http://sodexousa.com/usen/about-us/About_us/sodexo-in-USA.aspx, March 28, 2014.

97. Dvorak, "Firms Push New Methods."

98. Dvorak, "Firms Push New Methods."

99. Dvorak, "Firms Push New Methods."

100. Dvorak, "Firms Push New Methods"; "Sodexo Executive Dr. Rohini Anand Honored with Mosaic Woman Leadership Award," November 17, 2011, http://www.sodexousa.com/usen/newsroom/press/press11/rohinianandmosaicaward.asp, April 5, 2012.

101. "Sodexho Named Large Employer of the Year by Pike Area (Alabama) Committee," www.sodexousa.com/press-releases/pr110907_2.asp, February 6, 2008; "No. 6 Sodexo—DiversityInc.com," http://www.diversityinc.com/content/1757/article/5454/?No_6_Sodexo, February 9, 2010; "Sodexo Tops 2009 HACR List of Most Inclusive Companies for Hispanics," http://www.sodexousa.com/usen/newsroom/press/press10/hacrcorporateinclusion.asp, February 8, 2010.

102. "Corporate Diversity," www.sodexousa.com/press-factsheets/press_fact_corporate.asp, February 6, 2008; "Sodexho Named to Atlanta Tribune's Top Companies for Minorities," www.sodexousa.com/-press-releases/pr111207_1.asp, February 6, 2008; "Sodexho Recognized as Leader in Corporate Social Responsibility by Montgomery County Chamber of Commerce," www.sodexousa.com/press-releases/pr111507.asp, February 6, 2008; "Catalyst Honors Initiatives at Sodexo and Commonwealth Bank of Australia with the 2012 Catalyst Award," January 24, 2012, http://www.sodexousa.com/usen/newsroom/press/press12/sodexo_catalyst_award.asp, April 5, 2012.; "The DiversityInc Top 50," *DiversityInc,* June 2013, 29–76.

103. "Principal.com—About the Principal," http://www.principal.com/about/index.htm?print, February 8, 2010; "Principal Financial Group Company Overview—Principal.com," http://www.principal.com/about/corporate.htm?print, March 28, 2014.

104. "100 Best Companies to Work for 2008: Principal Financial Group snapshot/FORTUNE," http://money.cnn.com/magazines/fortune/bestcompanies/2008/snapshots/21.html, February 8, 2010;

"100 Best Companies to Work For 2009: Principal Financial Group—PFG—from *Fortune,*" http://money.cnn.com/magazines/fortune/bestcompanies/2009/snapshots/17.html, February 8, 2010; J. Hempel, "In the Land of Women," *Fortune,* February 4, 2008, 68–69; "Diversity: The Principal Financial Group Earns High Marks in 2010 Corporate Equality . . . ," http://www.echelonmagazine.com/index.php?id=1123, February 8, 2010; "Human Rights Campaign Foundation, Corporate Equality Index, 2010"; "HRC/Corporate Equality Index," http://www.hrc.org/issues/workplace/cei.htm, February 22, 2010.

105. Hempel, "In the Land of Women."

106. Hempel, "In the Land of Women."

107. "Principal.com—Careers: Diversity," http://www.principal.com/careers/workinghere/diversity.htm?print, February 8, 2010; "Principal.com—Careers at The Principal." http://www.principal.com/careers/workinghere/benefits_main.htm?print, February 8, 2010.

108. "Principal.com—Careers: Diversity," http://www.principal.com/careers/workinghere/diversity.htm?print, February 8, 2010; "Principal.com—Careers at The Principal," http://www.principal.com/careers/workinghere/benefits_main.htm?print, February 8, 2010.

109. Valian, *Why So Slow?*

110. S. Rynes and B. Rosen, "A Field Survey of Factors Affecting the Adoption and Perceived Success of Diversity Training," *Personnel Psychology* 48 (1995), 247–70; Valian, *Why So Slow?*

111. V. Brown and F.L. Geis, "Turning Lead into Gold: Leadership by Men and Women and the Alchemy of Social Consensus," *Journal of Personality and Social Psychology* 46 (1984), 811–24; Valian, *Why So Slow?*

112. Valian, *Why So Slow?*

113. J. Cole and B. Singer, "A Theory of Limited Differences: Explaining the Productivity Puzzle in Science," in H. Zuckerman, J.R. Cole, and J.T. Bruer, eds., *The Outer Circle: Women in the Scientific Community* (New York: Norton, 1991), 277–310; M.F. Fox, "Sex, Salary, and Achievement: Reward Dualism in Academia," *Sociology of Education* 54 (1981), 71–84; J.S. Long, "The Origins of Sex Differences in Science," *Social Forces* 68 (1990), 1297–1315; R.F. Martell, D.M. Lane, and C. Emrich, "Male–Female Differences: A Computer Simulation," *American Psychologist* 51 (1996), 157–58; Valian, *Why So Slow?*

114. Cole and Singer, "A Theory of Limited Differences"; Fox, "Sex, Salary, and Achievement"; Long, "The Origins of Sex Differences"; Martell, Lane, and Emrich, "Male–Female Differences: A Computer Simulation"; Valian, *Why So Slow?*

115. R. Folger and M.A. Konovsky, "Effects of Procedural and Distributive Justice on Reactions to Pay Raise Decisions," *Academy of Management Journal* 32 (1989), 115–30; J. Greenberg, "Organizational Justice: Yesterday, Today, and Tomorrow," *Journal of Management* 16 (1990), 399–402; O. Janssen, "How Fairness Perceptions Make Innovative Behavior More or Less Stressful," *Journal of Organizational Behavior* 25 (2004), 201–15.

116. Catalyst, "The Glass Ceiling in 2000: Where Are Women Now?" www.catalystwomen.org, October 21, 2001; Bureau of Labor Statistics, 1999, www.bls.gov; Catalyst, "1999 Census of Women Corporate Officers and Top Earners," www.catalystwomen.org; "1999 Census of Women Board Directors of the *Fortune* 1000," www.catalystwomen.org; Catalyst, "Women of Color in Corporate Management: Opportunities and Barriers, 1999," www.catalystwomen.org, October 21, 2001.

117. "Household Data Annual Averages," www.bls.gov, April 28, 2004; U.S. Bureau of Labor Statistics, Economic News Release, Table 7. *Median Usual Weekly Earnings of Full-Time Wage and Salary Workers by Occupation and Sex, Annual Averages,* http://data.bls.gov/cgi-bin/print.pl/news.release/wkyeng.t07.htm, February 9, 2010; "Household Data Annual Averages: 39. Median Weekly Earnings of Full-Time Wage and Salary Workers by Detailed Occupation and Sex," http://www.bls.gov/cps/cpsaat39.pdf, April 11, 2012.; "Household Data Annual Averages 39. Median Weekly Earnings of Full-Time Wage Salary Workers by Detailed Occupation and Sex," http://www.bls.gov/cps/cpsaat39.htm, April 1, 2014.

118. "Household Data Annual Averages," www.bls.gov, April 28, 2004; "Household Data Annual Averages: 39"; "Household Data Annual Averages 39. Median Weekly Earnings of Full-Time Wage Salary Workers by Detailed Occupation and Sex," http://www.bls.gov/cps/cpsaat39.htm, April 1, 2014.

119. A.M. Jaffe, "At Texaco, the Diversity Skeleton Still Stalks the Halls," *The New York Times,* December 11, 1994, sec. 3, p. 5.

120. Greenberg, "Organizational Justice"; M.G. Ehrhart, "Leadership and Procedural Justice Climate as Antecedents of Unit-Level Organizational Citizenship Behavior," *Personnel Psychology* 57 (2004), 61–94; A. Colella, R.L. Paetzold, and M.A. Belliveau, "Factors Affecting Coworkers' Procedural Justice Inferences of the Workplace Accommodations of Employees with Disabilities," *Personnel Psychology* 57 (2004), 1–23.

121. G. Robinson and K. Dechant, "Building a Case for Business Diversity," *Academy of Management Executive* 3 (1997), 32–47.

122. A. Patterson, "Target 'Micromarkets' Its Way to Success; No 2 Stores Are Alike," *The Wall Street Journal,* May 31, 1995, A1, A9.

123. "The Business Case for Diversity: Experts Tell What Counts, What Works," DiversityInc.com, October 23, 2001.

124. B. Hetzer, "Find a Niche—and Start Scratching," *BusinessWeek,* September 14, 1998 (*BusinessWeek* Archives). B. Hetzer, "Find a Niche—and Start Scratching," *BusinessWeek,* September 14, 1998 (*BusinessWeek* Archives).

125. K. Aaron, "Woman Laments Lack of Diversity on Boards of Major Companies," *The Times Union,* May 16, 2001 (www.timesunion.com).

126. "The Business Case for Diversity."

127. B. Frankel, "Measuring Diversity Is One Sure Way of Convincing CEOs of Its Value," DiversityInc.com, October 5, 2001.

128. A. Stevens, "Lawyers and Clients," *The Wall Street Journal,* June 19, 1995, B7.

129. J. Kahn, "Diversity Trumps the Downturn," *Fortune,* July 9, 2001, 114–16.

130. K. Weise, "The Mann Who Took on Merrill," *Bloomberg Businessweek,* November 28, 2013, 56–61.

131. Weise, "The Mann Who Took on Merrill" *Bloomberg Businessweek,* November 28, 2013, 56-61.; P. McGeehan, "Merrill Lynch In Big Payout for Bias Case," *The New York Times,* August 28, 2013.

132. P. McGeehan, "Bank of America to Pay $39 Million in Gender Bias Case," *The New York Times,* September 6, 2013.

133. McGeehan, "Bank of America to Pay $39 Million in Gender Bias Case." *The New York Times,* September 6, 2013.

134. H.R. Schiffmann, *Sensation and Perception: An Integrated Approach* (New York: Wiley, 1990).

135. McDonald's Corporation, "2008 Annual Report"; "McDonald's 2013 Financial Information Workbook.xlsx," http://www.aboutmcdonalds.com/med/investors/financial_highlights.html, April 3, 2014.

136. A.E. Serwer, "McDonald's Conquers the World," *Fortune,* October 17, 1994, 103–16.

137. S.T. Fiske and S.E. Taylor, *Social Cognition* (Reading, MA: Addison-Wesley, 1984).

138. J.S. Bruner, "Going beyond the Information Given," in H. Gruber, G. Terrell, and M. Wertheimer, eds., *Contemporary Approaches to Cognition* (Cambridge, MA: Harvard University Press, 1957); Fiske and Taylor, *Social Cognition.*

139. Fiske and Taylor, *Social Cognition.*

140. Valian, *Why So Slow?*

141. D. Bakan, *The Duality of Human Existence* (Chicago: Rand McNally, 1966); J.T. Spence and R.L. Helmreich, *Masculinity and Femininity: Their Psychological Dimensions, Correlates, and Antecedents* (Austin: University of Texas Press, 1978); J.T. Spence and L.L. Sawin, "Images of Masculinity and Femininity: A Reconceptualization," in V.E. O'Leary, R.K. Unger, and B.B. Wallston, eds., *Women, Gender, and Social Psychology* (Hillsdale, NJ: Erlbaum, 1985), 35–66; Valian, *Why So Slow?*

142. Valian, *Why So Slow?*

143. Serwer, "McDonald's Conquers the World"; P.R. Sackett, C.M. Hardison, and M.J. Cullen, "On Interpreting Stereotype Threat as Accounting for African American–White Differences on Cognitive Tests," *American Psychologist* 59, no. 1 (January 2004), 7–13; C.M. Steele and J.A. Aronson, "Stereotype Threat Does Not Live by Steele and Aronson," *American Psychologist* 59, no. 1 (January 2004), 47–55; P.R. Sackett, C.M. Hardison, and M.J. Cullen, "On the Value of Correcting Mischaracterizations of Stereotype Threat Research," *American Psychologist* 59, no. 1 (January 2004), 47–49; D.M. Amodio, E. Harmon-Jones, P.G. Devine, J.J. Curtin, S.L. Hartley, and A.E. Covert, "Neural Signals for the Detection of Unintentional Race Bias," *Psychological Science* 15, no. 2 (2004), 88–93.

144. M. Loden and J.B. Rosener, *Workforce America! Managing Employee Diversity as a Vital Resource* (Burr Ridge, IL: Irwin, 1991).

145. M.E. Heilman and T.G. Okimoto, "Motherhood: A Potential Source of Bias in Employment Decisions," *Journal of Applied Psychology* 93, no. 1 (2008), 189–98.

146. L. Roberson, B.M. Galvin, and A.C. Charles, "Chapter 13, When Group Identities Matter: Bias in Performance Appraisal," in J.P. Walsh and A.P. Brief, eds., *The Academy of Management Annals* 1 (New York: Erlbaum, 2008, 617–50).

147. A. Stein Wellner, "The Disability Advantage," *Inc.,* October 2005, 29–31.

148. Ken's Krew Inc.—Home, http://kenskrew.org, April 3, 2014.

149. A. Merrick, "Erasing 'Un' from 'Unemployable,'" *The Wall Street Journal,* August 2, 2007, B6; "2012 Spirit of Social Work Awards Luncheon–Public Citizen of the Year Award / Online. . . ," http://www.event.com/events/2012-spirit-of-social-work-awards-luncheon/custom-19-a3be. . . , April 11, 2012.; http://kenskrew.org/partners.htm, April 3, 2014.

150. Merrick, "Erasing 'Un' from 'Unemployable.'"

151. Merrick, "Erasing 'Un' from 'Unemployable.'"

152. "Habitat International: Our Products," www.habitatint.com/products.htm, April 6, 2006; "Habitat International,

Inc. Home Page," www.habitatint.com, April 6, 2006; "Habitat International, Inc. Home Page," http://www.habitatint.com/, April 11, 2012; Habitat International, Inc. Home Page, http://www.habitatint.com/, April 3, 2014.

153. Wellner, "The Disability Advantage."

154. "Habitat International: Our People," Habitat International—Our People, http://www.habitatint.com/people.htm, February 10, 2010.

155. Wellner, "The Disability Advantage."

156. "Habitat International: Our People"; Wellner, "The Disability Advantage."

157. "Habitat International: Our People"; Wellner, "The Disability Advantage."

158. "Habitat International: Our People"; Wellner, "The Disability Advantage."

159. "Habitat International: Our People"; Wellner, "The Disability Advantage."

160. E.D. Pulakos and K.N. Wexley, "The Relationship among Perceptual Similarity, Sex, and Performance Ratings in Manager Subordinate Dyads," *Academy of Management Journal* 26 (1983), 129–39.

161. Fiske and Taylor, *Social Cognition.*

162. "Hotel to Pay $8 Million in Settlement," *The Houston Chronicle,* March 22, 2000, 3A; M. France and T. Smart, "The Ugly Talk on the Texaco Tape," *BusinessWeek,* November 18, 1996, 58; J.S. Lublin, "Texaco Case Causes a Stir in Boardrooms," *The Wall Street Journal,* November 22, 1996, B1, B6; T. Smart, "Texaco: Lessons from a Crisis-in-Progress," *BusinessWeek,* December 2, 1996, 44; "Ford Settling Bias Case, Will Hire More Women, Minorities," *The Houston Chronicle,* February 19, 2000, 8C; C. Salter, "A Reformer Who Means Business," *Fast Company,* April 2003, 102–11; A. Zimmerman, "Walmart Appeals Bias-Suit Ruling," *The Wall Street Journal,* August 8, 2005, B5; C.H. Deutsch, "Chief of Unit Files Lawsuit Accusing G.E. of Racial Bias," *The New York Times,* May 18, 2005, C3; "Nike Settles Discrimination Suit for $7.6 Million," *The Wall Street Journal,* July 31, 2007, B9; R. Parloff, "The War over Unconscious Bias," *Fortune,* October 15, 2007, 90–102.

163. N. Alster, "When Gray Heads Roll, Is Age Bias at Work?" *The New York Times,* January 30, 2005, BU3.

164. "Nike Settles Discrimination Suit for $7.6 Million," *The Wall Street Journal,* July 31, 2007, B9.

165. "Nike Settles Discrimination Suit for $7.6 Million."

166. "Nike Settles Discrimination Suit for $7.6 Million."

167. M. Fackler, "Career Women in Japan Find a Blocked Path," *The New York Times,* August 6, 2007, A6; "Japan Values Women Less—As It Needs Them

More," Inter Press Service, January 31, 2013, http://www.ipsnews.net/2013/01/japan-values-women-less-as-it-needs-them-more/ April 3, 2014.

168. Fackler, "Career Women in Japan"; www.un.org, February 11, 2008.

169. Fackler, "Career Women in Japan."

170. www.nissanusa.com.

171. Fackler, "Career Women in Japan."

172. Press releases, U.S. Census Bureau, "Income, Poverty and Health Insurance Coverage in the United States: 2008," http://www.census.gov/Press-Release/www/releases/archives/income_wealth/014227.html, February 8, 2010.

173. Jennifer Levitz, "More Workers Cite Age Bias during Layoffs," *The Wall Street Journal,* March 11, 2009, pp. D1–2; "Age Discrimination in Employment Act (ADEA) Charges," U.S. Equal Employment Opportunity Commission, http://www1.eeoc.gov/eeoc/statistics/enforcement/adea.cfm?renderforprint=1, April 12, 2012; "What It Takes to Win an Age Discrimination Suite." *Forbes,* http://www.forbes.com/sites/nextavenue/2013/04/30/what-it-takes-to-win-an-age-discrimination-suit/, April 3, 2014.

174. "EEOC Issues Final Rule on 'Reasonable Factors Other Than Age' under the ADEA," http://www1.eeoc.gov//eeoc/newsroom/release/3-29-12.cfm?renderforprint=1, April 12, 2012.

175. Levitz, "More Workers Cite Age Bias."

176. Levitz, "More Workers Cite Age Bias."

177. Levitz, "More Workers Cite Age Bias."

178. A. Raghavan, "Terminated: Why the Women of Wall Street Are Disappearing," Forbes.com—Magazine Article, *ForbesWoman,* March 16, 2009, http://forbes.com/forbes/2009/0316-072_terminated_women_print.html, February 10, 2010.

179. Raghavan, "Terminated: Why the Women of Wall Street Are Disappearing/."

180. G. Gross, "Dell Hit with Discrimination Class-Action Lawsuit," *The New York Times,* October 29, 2008, http://www.nytimes.com/external/idg/2008/10/29/29idg-Dell-hit-with-d.html?pagewanted . . . .

181. A. Shah, "Dell Settles Discrimination Suit for $9.1 Million," July 24, 2009, *PC World,* http://www.pcworld.com/printable/article/id,169046/printable.html, April 12, 2012; "Dell Settles Discrimination Lawsuit for $9.1M," July 27, 2009, http://www.bizjournals.com/austin/stories/2009/07/27/daily1.html?s=print, April 12, 2012.

182. A. Gonsalves, "Dell Denies Discrimination In Layoffs," *InformationWeek,* November 3, 2008, http://www.informationweek.com/shared/printableArticleSrc.jhtml;jsessionid=5RQQTNK . . . , February 11, 2010.

183. A.G. Greenwald and M. Banaji, "Implicit Social Cognition: Attitudes,

Self-Esteem, and Stereotypes," *Psychological Review* 102 (1995), 4–27.

184. A. Fisher, "Ask Annie: Five Ways to Promote Diversity in the Workplace," *Fortune,* April 23, 2004 (www.fortune.com/fortune/subs/print/0,15935,455997,00.html); E. Bonabeau, "Don't Trust Your Gut," *Harvard Business Review,* May 2003, 116–23.

185. A.P. Carnevale and S.C. Stone, "Diversity: Beyond the Golden Rule," *Training & Development,* October 1994, 22–39.

186. Fisher, "Ask Annie."

187. J.S. Lublin, "Top Brass Try Life in the Trenches," *The Wall Street Journal,* June 25, 2007, B1, B3; J.S. Lublin, "How to Be a Better Boss? Spend Time on the Front Lines," *The Wall Street Journal,* February 9, 2012, http://online.wsj.com/article/SB10001424052970203824904577212951446826014.html.

188. www.davita.com, February 11, 2008; "Company—About DaVita," http://www.davita.com/about/, February 11, 2010; Lublin, "How to Be a Better Boss? Spend Time on the Front Lines."

189. Lublin, "Top Brass Try Life in the Trenches"; "Developing Leaders—Community Care—DaVita," http://www.davita.com/community-care/helping-teammates/leadership-development, April 3, 2014.

190. Lublin, "Top Brass Try Life in the Trenches."

191. Lublin, "Top Brass Try Life in the Trenches."

192. Lublin, "Top Brass Try Life in the Trenches;" www.loews.com/loews.nsf/governance.htm, February 7, 2008; "Lowes Hotel—Resorts," http://www.loewshotels.com/en/default.aspx?cm_mmc=Google-_-National-_-Paid%20Sea . . . , February 11, 2010.

193. B. De Lollis, "Lowes Hotels' new CEO advised Virgin Hotels," USAToday.com, January 4, 2012, http://travel.usatoday.com/hotels/post/2012/01/virgin-hotels-director-to-become-ceo-loews. . . , April 12, 2012.; "Jonathan M. Tisch—Leadership & BOD at Loews Corporation," http://www.loews.com/leadership/jonathan-m-tisch/, April 3, 2014.

194. Lublin, "Top Brass Try Life in the Trenches."

195. B.A. Battaglia, "Skills for Managing Multicultural Teams," *Cultural Diversity at Work* 4 (1992); Carnevale and Stone, "Diversity: Beyond the Golden Rule."

196. Swann et al., "Finding Value in Diversity."

197. Valian, *Why So Slow?*

198. A.P. Brief, R.T. Buttram, R.M. Reizenstein, S.D. Pugh, J.D. Callahan, R.L. McCline, and J.B. Vaslow, "Beyond Good Intentions: The Next Steps toward Racial Equality in the American Workplace," *Academy of Management Executive,* November 1997, 59–72.

199. Brief, Buttram, et al., "Beyond Good Intentions."

200. Brief, Buttram, et al., "Beyond Good Intentions."

201. Brief, Buttram, et al., "Beyond Good Intentions."

202. Y. Cole, "Linking Diversity to Executive Compensation," *Diversity Inc.,* August–September 2003, 58–62.

203. B. Mandell and S. Kohler-Gray, "Management Development That Values Diversity," *Personnel,* March 1990, 41–47.

204. B. Leak, "Online Extra: UPS Delivers an Eye-Opener," *BusinessWeek,* October 10, 2005, http://www.businessweek.com/print/magazine/content/05_41/b3954012.htm?chan=gl, February 11, 2010; Community Internship Program—UPS Corporate Responsibility, "Community Internship Program," http://www.community.ups.com/Community/Community+Internship+Program, February 11, 2010.

205. B. Filipczak, "25 Years of Diversity at UPS," *Training,* August 1992, 42–46.

206. D.A. Thomas, "Race Matters: The Truth about Mentoring Minorities," *Harvard Business Review,* April 2001, 99–107.

207. Thomas, "Race Matters."

208. "Chevron Settles Claims of 4 Women at Unit as Part of Sex Bias Suit," *The Wall Street Journal,* January 22, 1995, B12.

209. D.K. Berman, "TWA Settles Harassment Claims at JFK Airport for $2.6 Million," *The Wall Street Journal,* June 25, 2001, B6.

210. A. Lambert, "Insurers Help Clients Take Steps to Reduce Sexual Harassment," *Houston Business Journal,* March 19, 2004 (Houston.bizjournals.com/Houston/stories/2004/03/22/focus4.html).

211. L.M. Holson, "Chief of American Apparel Faces Second Harassment Suit," *The New York Times,* March 24, 2011: B2.

212. T. Segal, "Getting Serious about Sexual Harassment," *BusinessWeek,* November 9, 1992, 78–82.

213. J. Green, "The Silencing of Sexual Harassment," *Bloomberg BusinessWeek,* November 21–27, 2011, 27–28.

214. U.S. Equal Employment Opportunity Commission, "Facts about Sexual Harassment," www.eeoc.gov/facts/fs-sex.html, May 1, 2004.

215. B. Carton, "Muscled Out? At Jenny Craig, Men Are Ones Who Claim Sex Discrimination," *The Wall Street Journal,* November 29, 1994, A1, A7.

216. R.L. Paetzold and A.M. O'Leary-Kelly, "Organizational Communication and the Legal Dimensions of Hostile Work Environment Sexual Harassment," in G.L. Kreps, ed., *Sexual Harassment: Communication Implications* (Cresskill, NJ: Hampton Press, 1993).

217. M. Galen, J. Weber, and A.Z. Cuneo, "Sexual Harassment: Out of the Shadows," *Fortune,* October 28, 1991, 30–31.

218. A.M. O'Leary-Kelly, R.L. Paetzold, and R.W. Griffin, "Sexual Harassment as Aggressive Action: A Framework for Understanding Sexual Harassment," paper presented at the annual meeting of the Academy of Management, Vancouver, August 1995.

219. B.S. Roberts and R.A. Mann, "Sexual Harassment in the Workplace: A Primer," www3.uakron.edu/lawrev/robert1.html, May 1, 2004.

220. "Former FedEx Driver Wins EEOC Lawsuit," *Houston Chronicle,* February 26, 2004, 9B.

221. "Former FedEx Driver Wins EEOC Lawsuit."

222. J. Robertson, "California Jury Awards $61M for Harassment," http://news.Yahoo.com, June 4, 2006.

223. S.J. Bresler and R. Thacker, "Four-Point Plan Helps Solve Harassment Problems," *HR Magazine,* May 1993, 117–24.

224. "Du Pont's Solution," *Training,* March 1992, 29.

225. "Du Pont's Solution."

226. "Du Pont's Solution."

Chapter 6

1. J. Yunker, "How to Improve Online Checkout for Global Markets," *Pitney Bowes Inc.,* December 30, 2013, blogs.pb.com/ecommerce/2013/12/30/improve-online-checkout-global-markets/#sht=6121b48ec35a9fe01250eb0ee96ff458.

2. Ibid.

3. Ibid.

4. J. Yunker, "The Authoritative Guide to Emerging Trends and Best Practices in Web Globalization," *The 2014 Web Globalization Report Card,* 10th ed., n.d., bytelevel.com/reportcard2014/.

5. J. Yunker, "The Worst Global Websites of the 2014 Web Globalization Report Card," *Global By Design,* March 10, 2014, www.globalbydesign.com/2014/03/10/the-worst-global-websites-of-the-2014-web-globalization-report-card/.

6. Ibid.

7. L.J. Bourgeois, "Strategy and Environment: A Conceptual Integration," *Academy of Management Review* 5 (1985), 25–39.

8. M.E. Porter, *Competitive Strategy* (New York: Free Press, 1980).

9. "Coca-Cola versus Pepsi-Cola and the Soft Drink Industry," Harvard Business School Case 9-391-179.

10. www.splenda.com, 2012.

11. D. Engber, "The Quest for a Natural Sugar Substitute," *The New York Times,* January 1, 2014, www.nytimes.com/2014/01/05/magazine/the-quest-for-a-natural-sugar-substitute.html?_r=0.

12. A.K. Gupta and V. Govindarajan, "Cultivating a Global Mind-Set," *Academy of Management Executive* 16 (February 2002), 116–27.

13. "Boeing's Worldwide Supplier Network," *Seattle Post-Intelligencer,* April 9, 1994, 13.

14. I. Metthee, "Playing a Large Part," *Seattle Post-Intelligencer,* April 9, 1994, 13.

15. "Business: Link in the Global Chain," *The Economist,* June 2, 2001, 62–63.

16. S. Denning, "Why Apple and GE Are Bringing Back Manufacturing," *Forbes,* December 7, 2012, www.forbes.com/sites/stevedenning/2012/12/07/why-apple-and-ge-are-bringing-manufacturing-back/.

17. D. Zehr, "Apple Confirms Mac Pro Production Has Started in Austin," *statesman.com,* December 18, 2013, www.statesman.com/news/business/apple-confirms-mac-pro-production-has-started-in-a/ncN3M/.

18. P. Ravasio, "How Can We Stop Water from Becoming a Fashion Victim?" *The Guardian,* March 7, 2012, www.theguardian.com/sustainable-business/water-scarcity-fashion-industry.

19. K. Drennan, "Reduce Your Wardrobe's Water Footprint," *GreenLiving,* n.d., www.greenlivingonline.com/article/reduce-your-wardrobes-water-footprint.

20. "Water Pollution," Eco360, n.d., www.sustainablecommunication.org/eco360/what-is-eco360s-causes/water-pollution.

21. Ravasio, "How Can We Stop Water from Becoming a Fashion Victim?"

22. "Water Pollution."

23. E. Hutchings, "Adidas Introduces T-Shirts Made Without Water," *psfk,* August 6, 2012, www.psfk.com/2012/08/adidas-waterless-tshirts.html#!CFKRH.

24. D. Ferris, "Nike, Adidas Want to Dye your Shirt With No Water," *Forbes,* August 30, 2012, www.forbes.com/sites/davidferris/2012/08/30/nike-adidas-want-to-color-your-shirt-with-no-water/.

25. "Water Pollution," Eco360, n.d., www.sustainablecommunication.org/eco360/what-is-eco360s-causes/water-pollution.

26. L. Kaye, "Clothing to Dye For: The Textile Sector Must Confront Water Risks," *The Guardian,* August 12, 2013, www.theguardian.com/sustainable-business/dyeing-textile-sector-water-risks-adidas.

27. R. Hosseini, "Recycling Water to Make Your Jeans," Levi Strauss & Co., February 19, 2014, www.levistrauss.com/unzipped-blog/2014/02/recycling-water-to-make-your-jeans-infographic/.

28. Sustainable Business News, "Nike Moves to Water-Free, Chemical-Free Dyeing," *GreenBiz.com,* December 17, 2013, www.greenbiz.com/blog/2013/12/17/nike-moves-water-free-chemical-free-dyeing.

29. A. Brettman, "6 Questions about Nike's Water-Less Fabric Dyeing Technology," *The Oregonian,* December 3, 2013, www.oregonlive.com/playbooks-profits/index.ssf/2013/12/6_questions_about_nikes_water-.html.

30. J.M. Chua, "Adidas Launches Water-Saving 'DryDye' Range of T-Shirts," *ecouterre,* August 8, 2012, www.ecouterre.com/adidas-launches-water-saving-drydye-range-of-t-shirts/adidas-dry-dye-3/.

31. "Nike, Inc. Unveils ColorDry Technology and High-Tech Taiwanese Facility to Eliminate Water and Chemicals in Dyeing," *BusinessWire,* December 2, 2013, www.businesswire.com/news/home/20131202006450/en/NIKE-Unveils-ColorDry-Technology-High-Tech-Taiwanese-Facility#.Uz3FaVdLsjU.

32. M.E. Porter, *Competitive Advantage* (New York: Free Press, 1985).

33. www.walmart.com, 2012.

34. J. Trop, "Bridgestone Admits Guilt in U.S. Price-Fixing Case," *The New York Times,* February 13, 2014, www.nytimes.com/2014/02/14/business/bridgestone-admits-guilt-in-us-price-fixing-case.html?_r=0.

35. "The Future of Computers: What Can We Expect?" *UniBlue,* August 21, 2013, www.uniblue.com/news/future-computers-what-can-we-expect/.

36. D. Kucera, "Amazon Surges to Record High on Global E-Commerce Growth," *Bloomberg,* January 7, 2013, www.bloomberg.com/news/2013-01-07/amazon-surges-to-record-high-on-global-e-commerce-growth.html.

37. T. Levitt, "The Globalization of Markets," *Harvard Business Review,* May–June 1983, 92–102.

38. "Dell CEO Would Like 40 Percent PC Market Share," www.dailynews.yahoo.com, June 20, 2001.

39. Press release, "Gartner Says Worldwide PC Shipments Declined 6.9 Percent in Fourth Quarter of 2013," *Gartner,* January 9, 2014, www.gartner.com/newsroom/id/2647517.

40. For views on barriers to entry from an economics perspective, see Porter, *Competitive Strategy.* For the sociological perspective, see J. Pfeffer and G. R. Salancik, *The External Control of Organization: A Resource Dependence Perspective* (New York: Harper & Row, 1978).

41. Porter, *Competitive Strategy;* J.E. Bain, *Barriers to New Competition* (Cambridge, MA: Harvard University Press, 1956); R.J. Gilbert, "Mobility Barriers and the Value of Incumbency," in R. Schmalensee and R.D. Willig, eds., *Handbook of Industrial Organization,* vol. 1 (Amsterdam: North Holland, 1989).

42. Press release, www.amazon.com, May 2001.

43. C.W.L. Hill, "The Computer Industry: The New Industry of Industries," in Hill and Jones, *Strategic Management: An Integrated Approach* (Boston: Houghton Mifflin, 2010).

44. J. Schumpeter, *Capitalism, Socialism and Democracy* (London: Macmillan, 1950), 68. Also see R.R. Winter and S.G. Winter, *An Evolutionary Theory of Economic Change* (Cambridge, MA: Harvard University Press, 1982).

45. D. Takahasi, "AMD Launches Kaveri Processors, Aimed at Starting a Computing Revolution," *VentureBeat,* January 14, 2014, enturebeat.com/2014/01/14/amd-launches-kaveri-processors-aimed-at-starting-a-computing-revolution/.

46. N. Goodman, *An Introduction to Sociology* (New York: HarperCollins, 1991); C. Nakane, *Japanese Society* (Berkeley: University of California Press, 1970).

47. D. Markham, "Green Business Ideas: Organic Food Delivery Service," *Ecoprenuerist,* n.d., ecopreneurist.com/2014/02/07/green-business-ideas-organic-food-delivery-service/.

48. M. Wilke, "Organic Delivery Services," *Public Radio Kitchen,* March 22, 2011, publicradiokitchen.wbur.org/2011/03/22/organic-delivery-services.

49. For a detailed discussion of the importance of the structure of law as a factor explaining economic change and growth, see D.C. North, *Institutions, Institutional Change, and Economic Performance* (Cambridge: Cambridge University Press, 1990).

50. P. Krugman, "This Age of Bubbles," *The New York Times,* August 22, 2013, www.nytimes.com/2013/08/23/opinion/krugman-this-age-of-bubbles.html?partner=rssnyt&emc=rss&_r=0.

51. R.B. Reich, *The Work of Nations* (New York: Knopf, 1991).

52. "What Is the Transatlantic Trade Investment Partnership?" European Commission, December 20, 2013, ec.europa.eu/trade/policy/in-focus/ttip/questions-and-answers/#what-is-ttip.

53. D. Lee, "The Trans-Pacific Partnership: Who Wins, Who Loses, Why It Matters," *Los Angeles Times,* February 19, 2014, articles.latimes.com/2014/feb/19/news/la-pn-trans-pacific-partnership-20140219.

54. "Trans-Pacific Partnership (TPP): Job Loss, Lower Wages and Higher Drug Prices," Public Citizen, n.d., www.citizen.org/TPP.

55. M.A. Carpenter and J.W. Fredrickson, "Top Management Teams, Global Strategic Posture, and the Moderating Role of Uncertainty," *Academy of Management Journal* 44 (June 2001), 533–46.

56. A. Glass, "Ernst & Young Launches Women Athletes Global Leadership Network," *Forbes,* March 12, 2013, www.forbes.com/sites/alanaglass/2013/03/12/ernst-young-launches-women-athletes-global-leadership-network/.

57. "Ernest & Young to Launch Leadership Network for Elite Female Athletes to address Unmet Global Need," PRWeb, March 8, 2013, www.prweb.com/releases/2013/3/prweb10505195.htm.

58. "Women Athletes Business Network: Perspectives on Sport and Teams," *EY,* May 2013, www.ey.com/BR/pt/About-us/Our-sponsorships-and-programs/Women-Athletes-Global-Leadership-Network—perspectives-on-sport-and-teams.

59. Ibid.

60. E. Kinlin, "From Athletics to Leadership," *Women Executives,* September 26, 2013, kinlin.com/blog/2013/09/from-athletics-to-leadership/.

61. Ibid.

62. "EY Women Athletes Global Leadership Network," *EY,* n.d., www.leadersmag.com/issues/2013.4_Oct/EY%20Women%20Athletes/LEADERS-Beth-Brooke-EY-Donna-de-Varona-DAMAR-Productions.html.

63. A. Glass, "Ernst & Young Launches Women Athletes Global Leadership Network," *Forbes,* March 12, 2013, www.forbes.com/sites/alanaglass/2013/03/12/ernst-young-launches-women-athletes-global-leadership-network/.

64. "Ernest & Young to Launch Leadership Network for Elite Female Athletes to address Unmet Global Need," PRWeb, March 8, 2013, www.prweb.com/releases/2013/3/prweb10505195.htm.

65. B. Davis, "Chinese Car Tire Imports to U.S. at an All-Time High," *tirebusiness.com,* March 18, 2014, www.tirebusiness.com/article/20140318/NEWS/140319890/chinese-car-tire-imports-to-u-s-at-an-all-time-high.

66. J. Bhagwati, *Protectionism* (Cambridge, MA: MIT Press, 1988).

67. For a summary of these theories, see P. Krugman and M. Obstfeld, *International Economics: Theory and Policy* (New York: HarperCollins, 1991). Also see C.W.L. Hill, *International Business* (New York: McGraw-Hill, 1997), chap. 4.

68. A.M. Rugman, "The Quest for Global Dominance," *Academy of Management Executive* 16 (August 2002), 157–60.

69. www.wto.org.com, 2004.

70. "Tariff Cuts," *World Trade Organization,* n.d., www.wto.org/english/thewto_e/whatis_e/tif_e/agrm2_e.htm.

71. www.wto.org.com, 2012.

72. C.A. Bartlett and S. Ghoshal, *Managing across Borders* (Boston: Harvard Business School Press, 1989).

73. C. Arnst and G. Edmondson, "The Global Free-for-All," *BusinessWeek,* September 26, 1994, 118–26.

74. "AU in a Nutshell," *African Union,* n.d., www.au.int/en/about/nutshell.

75. *Southern African Development Community,* n.d., www.sadc.int/.

76. "Areas of Cooperation Achievements," *The Cooperation Council for Arab States of the Gulf,* n.d., www.gcc-sg.org/eng/indexa3c2.html?action=Sec-Show&ID=47.

77. E.B. Tylor, *Primitive Culture* (London: Murray, 1971).

78. "A Quick Guide: What's Happening in Ukraine," *The Wall Street Journal,* January 28, 2014, online.wsj.com/news/articles/SB100014240527023037755045 79393324230970300.

79. "Timeline: What's Happened Since Egypt's Revolution," *Frontline,* September 17, 2013, www.pbs.org/wgbh/pages/frontline/foreign-affairs-defense/egypt-in-crisis/timeline-whats-happened-since-egypts-revolution/.

80. For details on the forces that shape culture, see Hill, *International Business,* chap. 2. G. Hofstede, B. Neuijen, D.D. Ohayv, and G. Sanders, "Measuring Organizational Cultures: A Qualitative and Quantitative Study across Twenty Cases," *Administrative Science Quarterly* 35 (1990), 286–316.

81. Hofstede et al., "Measuring Organizational Cultures."

82. M.H. Hoppe, "Introduction: Geert Hofstedes Culture's Consequences: International Difference in Work-Related Values," *Academy of Management Executive* 19 (February 2004), 73–75.

83. R. Bellah, *Habits of the Heart: Individualism and Commitment in American Life* (Berkeley: University of California Press, 1985).

84. R. Bellah, *The Tokugawa Religion* (New York: Free Press, 1957).

85. C. Nakane, *Japanese Society* (Berkeley: University of California Press, 1970).

86. Ibid.

87. G. Hofstede, "The Cultural Relativity of Organizational Practices and Theories," *Journal of International Business Studies,* Fall 1983, 75–89.

88. Hofstede et al., "Measuring Organizational Cultures."

89. J. Perlez, "GE Finds Tough Going in Hungary," *The New York Times,* July 25, 1994, C1, C3.

90. www.ge.com, 2004, 2010, 2012.

91. J.P. Fernandez and M. Barr, *The Diversity Advantage* (New York: Lexington Books, 1994).

92. www.ibm.com, 2012.

93. "Things to Do before Relocation to China," *Expat Life: Top 5 Lists,* n.d., expatexplorer.hsbc.com/hintsandtips/list/4463.

94. "Tips for Child Health Care in the Netherlands," *Expat Life: Top 5 Lists,* n.d., expatexplorer.hsbc.com/hintsandtips/list/4457.

95. M. Fisher, "Want to Move Abroad? This Map Shows the Best and Worst Countries to Be an Expatriate," *The Washington Post,* November 5, 2013, www.washingtonpost.com/blogs/worldviews/wp/2013/11/05/want-to-move-abroad-this-map-shows-the-best-and-worst-countries-to-be-an-expatriate/?tid=pm_pop.

96. "League Table," HSBC, n.d., www.expatexplorer.hsbc.com/#/countries.

97. "Expats in BRICs and Frontier Economies Are Upbeat about the Economy and Have Greater Disposable Income," HSBC, n.d., www.expatexplorer.hsbc.com/finding/59/expats-in-brics-and-frontier-economies-are-upbeat-about-the-economy-and-have-greater-disposable-income/criteria:00000000000000.

98. *Expat Life: Top 5 Lists* HSBC, n.d., expatexplorer.hsbc.com/hintsandtips/list/4217.

99. "League Table," HSBC, n.d., www.expatexplorer.hsbc.com/#/countries.

100. "Things No One Ever Tells You and Should," *Expat Life: Top 5 Lists,* n.d., expatexplorer.hsbc.com/hintsandtips/list/4248.

101. "Eating and Cooking in the USA," *Expat Life: Top 5 Lists,* n.d., expatexplorer.hsbc.com/hintsandtips/list/4416.

102. "Tips for Settling into Life in the USA," *Expat Life: Top 5 Lists,* n.d., expatexplorer.hsbc.com/hintsandtips/list/4232.

103. "Tips for German Speakers to Improve Communication with Americans," *Expat Life: Top 5 Lists,* n.d., expatexplorer.hsbc.com/hintsandtips/list/4493.

104. "Understanding the American Way of Working," *Expat Life: Top 5 Lists,* n.d., https://expatexplorer.hsbc.com/hintsandtips/list/4533.

105. D. Skariachan and S. Cavale, "Home Depot's Do-It-Yourself Model Fails In China's Do-It-For-Me Market," *The Huffington Post,* September 13, 2012, www.huffingtonpost.com/2012/09/13/home-depots-china_n_1882779.html.

106. L. Burkitt, "Home Depot Learns Chinese Prefer 'Do-It-For-Me,'" *The Wall Street Journal,* September 14, 2012, online.wsj.com/news/articles/SB100008723963904 44433504577651072911154602.

Chapter 7

1. "Planting the Seeds for 1-800-Flowers.com," *Fortune,* March, 17, 2014, 47–50; "James McCann: Executive Profile & Biography," *Businessweek,* http://investing.businessweek.com/research/stocks/people/person.asp?personId=234954&ticker=FLWS.

2. "Planting the Seeds for 1-800-Flowers.com." *Fortune,* March, 17, 2014, 47–50.

3. "Planting the Seeds for 1-800-Flowers.com."

4. "Planting the Seeds for 1-800-Flowers.com."

5. D. Schawbel, "Jim McCann: How He Turned 1-800-Flowers.com into a Household Name," *Forbes,* http://www.forbes.com/sites/danschawbel/2014/01/27/jim-mccann-how-he-turned-1-800-flowers-com-into-a-household-name/, April 14, 2014.

6. "Planting the Seeds for 1-800-Flowers.com"; "Jim McCann: From Bartender to 30 Million Clients—Off the Cuff," *Yahoo News,* http://news.yahoo.com/blogs/off-the-cuff/jim-mccann-bartender-30-million-clients-094417515.html.

7. "Planting the Seeds for 1-800-Flowers.com." Planting the Seeds for 1-800-Flowers.com, *Fortune,* March, 17, 2014, 47–50.

8. "Planting the Seeds for 1-800-Flowers.com."

9. "Planting the Seeds for 1-800-Flowers.com."

10. "Planting the Seeds for 1-800-Flowers.com."

11. "Planting the Seeds for 1-800-Flowers.com."

12. "Planting the Seeds for 1-800-Flowers.com."

13. "Planting the Seeds for 1-800-Flowers.com."

14. "Planting the Seeds for 1-800-Flowers.com."

15. "Planting the Seeds for 1-800-Flowers.com."

16. "Planting the Seeds for 1-800-Flowers.com."

17. "Planting the Seeds for 1-800-Flowers.com."

18. "1-800-Flowers.com, Inc.—Investor Overview," http://investor.1800flowers.com/index.cfm?pg=profile, April 16, 2014.; "SoLoMo—An Interview with Christopher G. McCann," http://files.shareholder.com/downloads/FLWS/3092623901x0x504093/5f089d9d-6e25-4fd2-9600-5dc331cd5292/LEADERS-Christopher-McCann-1-800-FLOWERS.pdf, April 14, 2014.

19. "Planting the Seeds for 1-800-Flowers.com."

20. "Planting the Seeds for 1-800-Flowers.com."

21. "Planting the Seeds for 1-800-Flowers.com."

22. G.P. Huber, *Managerial Decision Making* (Glenview, IL: Scott, Foresman, 1993).

23. "Martin Cooper—History of Cell Phone and Martin Cooper," http://inventors.about.com/cs/inventorsalphabet/a/martin_cooper.htm?p=1, February 16, 2010; "Motorola Demonstrates Portable Telephone to Be Available for Public Use by 1976," April 3, 1973, www.motorola.com, February 17, 2009; "The Cellular Telephone Concept—An Overview," September 10, 1984, www.motorola.com, February 17, 2009;" "iPod," http://www.apple.com/, February 16, 2010.

24. H.A. Simon, *The New Science of Management* (Englewood Cliffs, NJ: Prentice-Hall, 1977).

25. N.A. Hira, "The Making of a UPS Driver," *Fortune,* November 12, 2007, 118–29.

26. Hira, "The Making of a UPS Driver"; J. Lovell, "Left-Hand Turn Elimination," *The New York Times,* December 9, 2007,www.nytimes.com/2007/12/09/magazine/09left-handturn.html?_r=2&oref=slogin&r, February 20, 2008.

27. Hira, "The Making of a UPS Driver."

28. L. Osburn, "Expecting the World on a Silver Platter," *Houston Chronicle,* September 17, 2007, D1, D6.

29. Hira, "The Making of a UPS Driver"; UPS Integrad—UPS Corporate Responsibility, http://www.community.ups.com/

Safety/Training+For+Safety/UPS+ Integrad, April 18, 2012.

30. Hira, "The Making of a UPS Driver"; "Welcome to UPS Careers," https://ups .managehr.com/Home.htm, February 20, 2008; "UPS Integrad—UPS Corporate Responsibility," http://www.responsibility .ups.com/safety/Training+For+Safety/ UPS+Integrad, April 17, 2014.

31. "UPS Integrad—UPS Corporate Responsibility."

32. Hira, "The Making of a UPS Driver"; "UPS Integrad—UPS Corporate Responsibility."

33. "Best Webcast Series: Evolving the Leadership Development Culture at UPS," *American Society for Training & Development,* http://webcasts.astd.org/ webinar/811, April 17, 2014.

34. Hira, "The Making of a UPS Driver."

35. Hira, "The Making of a UPS Driver"; "UPS Integrad—UPS Corporate Responsibility."

36. D. Petersik, "Oxygen Learning," http:// oxygenlearning.com/who-we-are/ don-petersik/, April 17, 2014.

37. Hira, "The Making of a UPS Driver."

38. Hira, "The Making of a UPS Driver."

39. D. Kahneman, "Maps of Bounded Rationality: A Perspective on Intuitive Judgment and Choice," *Prize Lecture,* December 8, 2002; E. Jaffe, "What Was I Thinking? Kahneman Explains How Intuition Leads Us Astray," *American Psychological Society* 17, no. 5 (May 2004), 23–26; E. Dane and M. Pratt, "Exploring Intuition and Its Role in Managerial Decision Making," *Academy of Management Review* 32 (2007), 33–54.

40. One should be careful not to generalize too much here, however; for as Peter Senge has shown, programmed decisions rely on the implicit assumption that the environment is in a steady state. If environmental conditions change, sticking to a routine decision rule can produce disastrous results. See P. Senge, *The Fifth Discipline: The Art and Practice of the Learning Organization* (New York: Doubleday, 1990).

41. Kahneman, "Maps of Bounded Rationality"; Jaffe, "What Was I Thinking?"

42. Kahneman, "Maps of Bounded Rationality"; Jaffe, "What Was I Thinking?"

43. J. Lehrer, "The Science of Irrationality," *The Wall Street Journal,* October 15, 2011, C18.

44. J. Smutniak, "Freud, Finance and Folly: Human Intuition Is a Bad Guide to Handling Risk," *The Economist* 24 (January 2004), 5–6.

45. Kahneman, "Maps of Bounded Rationality"; Jaffe, "What Was I Thinking?"

46. Kahneman, "Maps of Bounded Rationality"; Jaffe, "What Was I Thinking?"

47. J. Pfeffer, "Curbing the Urge to Merge," *Business 2.0,* July 2003, 58; Smutniak, "Freud, Finance and Folly."

48. Kahneman, "Maps of Bounded Rationality"; Jaffe, "What Was I Thinking?"

49. Pfeffer, "Curbing the Urge to Merge"; Smutniak, "Freud, Finance and Folly."

50. M. Landler, "New Austerity for German Car Industry," *The New York Times,* September 29, 2005, C3; E. Taylor and C. Rauwald, "DaimlerChrysler to Cut 8,500 Jobs at Mercedes," *The Wall Street Journal,* September 29, 2005, A6; G. Edmondson, "On the Hot Seat at Daimler," *BusinessWeek Online,* February 17, 2006, www.businessweek.com/autos/ content/feb2006/bw20060217_187348. htm?campaign_id=search); "Daimler AG News," *The New York Times,* http:// topics.nytimes.com/topics/news/business/ companies/daimler_ag/index.html.

51. "Hiring Freeze and Cost Cuts at Time Inc.," *The New York Times,* August 2005, B13.

52. Pfeffer, "Curbing the Urge to Merge."

53. J. Lehrer, "The Science of Irrationality," *The Wall Street Journal,* October 15, 2011, C18.

54. Pfeffer, "Curbing the Urge to Merge."

55. H.A. Simon, *Administrative Behavior* (New York: Macmillan, 1947), 79.

56. H.A. Simon, *Models of Man* (New York: Wiley, 1957).

57. K.J. Arrow, *Aspects of the Theory of Risk Bearing* (Helsinki: Yrjo Johnssonis Saatio, 1965).

58. Arrow, *Aspects of the Theory of Risk Bearing.*

59. R.L. Daft and R.H. Lengel, "Organizational Information Requirements, Media Richness and Structural Design," *Management Science* 32 (1986), 554–71.

60. R. Cyert and J. March, *Behavioral Theory of the Firm* (Englewood Cliffs, NJ: Prentice-Hall, 1963).

61. J.G. March and H.A. Simon, *Organizations* (New York: Wiley, 1958).

62. H.A. Simon, "Making Management Decisions: The Role of Intuition and Emotion," *Academy of Management Executive* 1 (1987), 57–64.

63. M.H. Bazerman, *Judgment in Managerial Decision Making* (New York: Wiley, 1986). Also see Simon, *Administrative Behavior.*

64. "Scott G. McNealy Profile," *Forbes.com,* http://people.forbes.com/profile/scott- g-mcnealy/75347, February 16, 2010; Sun Oracle, "Overview and Frequently Asked Questions," www.oracle.com, February 16, 2010.

65. "Sun Microsystems—Investor Relations: Officers and Directors," www.sun .com/aboutsun/investor/sun_facts/ officers_directors.html, June 1, 2004; "How Sun Delivers Value to Customers," *Sun Microsystems—Investor Relations: Support & Training,* June 1, 2004 (www .sun.com/aboutsun/investor/sun_facts/ core_strategies.html); "Sun at a Glance," *Sun Microsystems—Investor Relations:*

Sun Facts, June 1, 2004 (www.sun.com/ aboutsun/investor/sun_facts/index.html); "Plug in the System, and Everything Just Works," *Sun Microsystems— Investor Relations: Product Portfolio,* June 1, 2004 (www.sun.com/aboutsun/ investor/sun_facts/portfolio/html).

66. N.J. Langowitz and S.C. Wheelright, "Sun Microsystems, Inc. (A)," Harvard Business School Case 686–133.

67. R.D. Hof, "How to Kick the Mainframe Habit," *BusinessWeek,* June 26, 1995, 102–104.

68. Bazerman, *Judgment in Managerial Decision Making;* Huber, *Managerial Decision Making;* J.E. Russo and P.J. Schoemaker, *Decision Traps* (New York: Simon & Schuster, 1989).

69. M.D. Cohen, J.G. March, and J.P. Olsen, "A Garbage Can Model of Organizational Choice," *Administrative Science Quarterly* 17 (1972), 1–25.

70. Cohen, March, and Olsen, "A Garbage Can Model."

71. Bazerman, *Judgment in Managerial Decision Making.*

72. Senge, *The Fifth Discipline.*

73. E. de Bono, *Lateral Thinking* (London: Penguin, 1968); Senge, *The Fifth Discipline.*

74. Russo and Schoemaker, *Decision Traps.*

75. Bazerman, *Judgment in Managerial Decision Making.*

76. B. Berger, "NASA: One Year after *Columbia*—Bush's New Vision Changes Agency's Course Midstream," *Space News Business Report,* January 26, 2004 (www.space.com/spacenews/ businessmonday_040126.html).

77. J. Glanz and J. Schwartz, "Dogged Engineer's Effort to Assess Shuttle Damage," *The New York Times,* September 26, 2003, A1.

78. M.L. Wald and J. Schwartz, "NASA Chief Promises a Shift in Attitude," *The New York Times,* August 28, 2003, A23.

79. J. Light, "Sustainability Jobs Get Green Light at Large Firms," *The Wall Street Journal,* July 11, 2011, B5.

80. Light, "Sustainability Jobs Get Green;" "Scott Wicker—UPS Pressroom," http:// www.pressroom.ups.com/Biography/ ci.Scott+Wicker.print, April 18, 2012.; "Executive Statement—Scott Wicker, Chief Sustainability Officer," http:// www.responsibility.ups.com/community/ static%20files/sustainability/ups_ csr2012_scott_wicker.pdf, April 17, 2014.

81. "Scott Wicker—UPS Pressroom."

82. L.J. Fisher, "DuPont.com: Meet the Executives," http://www2.dupont.com/ Our_Company/en_US/executives/fisher .html, April 18, 2012.; "Bio Linda J. Fisher, VP, DuPont SHE; Chief Sustainability Officer," http://www.dupont.com/ corporate-functions/our-company/

leadership/executive-leadership/articles/fisher.html, April 17, 2014.

83. "An Interview with Linda Fisher Chief Sustainability Officer, DuPont," February 13, 2012, http://www.globe.net.com/articles/2012/february/9/an-interview-with-linda-fisher-chief-su . . . , April 18, 2012.

84. "Coca-Cola—Press Center—Press Kits—Beatriz Perez Named Chief Sustainability Officer," May 19, 2011, http://www.thecoca-colacompany.com/dynamic/press_center/2011/05/new-chief-sustainab . . . , April 18, 2012.

85. M. Albanese, "How She Leads: Coca-Cola's Beatriz Perez," October 3, 2011, http://www.greenbiz.com/print/44395, April 18, 2012.; "Infographic: Coca-Cola at a Glance: The Coca-Cola Company," http://www.coca-colacompany.com/our-company/infographic-coca-cola-at-a-glance, April 17, 2014.

86. M. Albanese, "How She Leads."

87. Russo and Schoemaker, *Decision Traps.*

88. S. Clifford, "Marc Shuman Was Determined to Expand Fast," *Inc.,* March, 2006, 44–50; D. Kocieniewski, "After $12,000, There's Even Room to Park the Car," *The New York Times,* February 20, 2006; "The World's Cleanest Garage," www.garagetek.com, May 30, 2006 (www.garagetek.com/nav.asp); "What Is Garagetek?" www.garagetek.com, May 30, 2006 (www.garagetek.com/content_CNBC.asp); L. Christie, "7 Franchises: Riding the Housing Boom," CNNMoney.com, March 7, 2006 (http://money.cnn.com/2006/03/07/smbusiness/homefranchises/index.htm); "745 Businesses to Start Now!" *Entrepreneur,* January 2005, 88, 192, 193; "Franchise Opportunities Available," http://www.garagetek.com/FranchiseOpportunities/ February 16, 2010; "GarageTek Inc.: Private Company Information," *BusinessWeek,* http://investing.businessweek.com/research/stocks/private/snapshot.asp?privcapId=126174 . . . , February 15, 2010; "Garage Makeover," *Inc.,* July 2007, 53.; "About GarageTek—Garage Storage & Organizational Systems—Garag Solutions," http://www.garagetek.com/AboutUs/, April 15, 2014.

89. "About Us," *Garagetek,* http://www.garagetek.com/AboutUs/, April 17, 2012.

90. Clifford, "Marc Shuman Was Determined to Expand Fast."

91. Clifford, "Marc Shuman Was Determined to Expand Fast."

92. Clifford, "Marc Shuman Was Determined to Expand Fast;" "Franchise Opportunities," *GarageTek,* www.garagetek.com/FranchiseOpportunities/GarageTek-Opportunities.aspx, February 14, 2008.

93. Clifford, "Marc Shuman Was Determined to Expand Fast."

94. Clifford, "Marc Shuman Was Determined to Expand Fast."

95. "Franchise Opportunities Available," *Garagetek,* http://www.garagetek.com/FranchiseOpportunities/, April 17, 2012.

96. Clifford, "Marc Shuman Was Determined to Expand Fast."

97. "About Us," About GarageTek—Garage Storage & Organizational Systems—Garage Solutions, http://www.garagetek.com/AboutUs/, April 15, 2014.

98. Clifford, "Marc Shuman Was Determined to Expand Fast."

99. D. Kahneman and A. Tversky, "Judgment under Uncertainty: Heuristics and Biases," *Science* 185 (1974), 1124–31.

100. C.R. Schwenk, "Cognitive Simplification Processes in Strategic Decision Making," *Strategic Management Journal* 5 (1984), 111–28.

101. An interesting example of the illusion of control is Richard Roll's hubris hypothesis of takeovers. See R. Roll, "The Hubris Hypothesis of Corporate Takeovers," *Journal of Business* 59 (1986), 197–216.

102. J. Pfeffer and R.I. Sutton, *Hard Facts, Dangerous Half-Truths, and Total Nonsense: Profiting from Evidence-Based Management* (Boston: Harvard Business School Press, 2006).

103. B.M. Staw, "The Escalation of Commitment to a Course of Action," *Academy of Management Review* 6 (1981), 577–87.

104. Russo and Schoemaker, *Decision Traps.*

105. Russo and Schoemaker, *Decision Traps.*

106. I.L. Janis, *Groupthink: Psychological Studies of Policy Decisions and Disasters,* 2nd ed. (Boston: Houghton Mifflin, 1982).

107. C.R. Schwenk, *The Essence of Strategic Decision Making* (Lexington, MA: Lexington Books, 1988).

108. See R.O. Mason, "A Dialectic Approach to Strategic Planning," *Management Science* 13 (1969) 403–14; R.A. Cosier and J.C. Aplin, "A Critical View of Dialectic Inquiry in Strategic Planning," *Strategic Management Journal* 1 (1980), 343–56; I.I. Mitroff and R.O. Mason, "Structuring III—Structured Policy Issues: Further Explorations in a Methodology for Messy Problems," *Strategic Management Journal* 1 (1980), 331–42.

109. Mason, "A Dialectic Approach to Strategic Planning."

110. D.M. Schweiger and P.A. Finger, "The Comparative Effectiveness of Dialectic Inquiry and Devil's Advocacy," *Strategic Management Journal* 5 (1984), 335–50.

111. M.C. Gentile, *Differences That Work: Organizational Excellence through Diversity* (Boston: Harvard Business School Press, 1994); F. Rice, "How to Make Diversity Pay," *Fortune,* August 8, 1994, 78–86.

112. B. Hedberg, "How Organizations Learn and Unlearn," in W.H. Starbuck and P.C. Nystrom, eds., *Handbook of Organizational Design,* vol. 1 (New York: Oxford University Press, 1981), 1–27.

113. Senge, *The Fifth Discipline.*

114. Senge, *The Fifth Discipline.*

115. P.M. Senge, "The Leader's New Work: Building Learning Organizations," *Sloan Management Review,* Fall 1990, 7–23.

116. W. Zellner, K.A. Schmidt, M. Ihlwan, and H. Dawley, "How Well Does Walmart Travel?" *BusinessWeek,* September 3, 2001, 82–84.

117. J.M George, "Creativity in Organizations," in J.P. Walsh and A.P. Brief, eds., *The Academy of Management Annals,* Vol. 1 (New York: Erlbaum, 2008), 439–77.

118. George, "Creativity in Organizations."

119. C. Saltr, "FAST 50: The World's Most Innovative Companies," *Fast Company,* March 2008, 73–117.

120. R.W. Woodman, J.E. Sawyer, and R.W. Griffin, "Towards a Theory of Organizational Creativity," *Academy of Management Review* 18 (1993), 293–321.

121. T. Evans, "Entrepreneurs Seek to Elicit Workers' Ideas," *The Wall Street Journal,* December 22, 2009, B7; D. Dahl, "Rounding Up Staff Ideas," Inc.com, February 1, 2010, http://www.inc.com/magazine/20100201/rounding-up-staff-ideas_Printer_Friendly.html, February 12, 2010; "About Borrego Solar," http://www.borregosolar.com/solar-energy-company/solar-contractor.php, February 15, 2010.

122. T.J. Bouchard Jr., J. Barsaloux, and G. Drauden, "Brainstorming Procedure, Group Size, and Sex as Determinants of Problem Solving Effectiveness of Individuals and Groups," *Journal of Applied Psychology* 59 (1974), 135–38.

123. M. Diehl and W. Stroebe, "Productivity Loss in Brainstorming Groups: Towards the Solution of a Riddle," *Journal of Personality and Social Psychology* 53 (1987), 497–509.

124. D.H. Gustafson, R.K. Shulka, A. Delbecq, and W.G. Walster, "A Comparative Study of Differences in Subjective Likelihood Estimates Made by Individuals, Interacting Groups, Delphi Groups, and Nominal Groups," *Organizational Behavior and Human Performance* 9 (1973), 280–91.

125. N. Dalkey, *The Delphi Method: An Experimental Study of Group Decision Making* (Santa Monica, CA: Rand Corp., 1989).

126. T. Lonier, "Some Insights and Statistics on Working Solo," www.workingsolo.com.

127. I.N. Katsikis and L.P. Kyrgidou, "The Concept of Sustainable Entrepreneurship: A Conceptual Framework and Empirical Analysis," *Academy of Management Proceedings,* 2007, 1–6, web.ebscohost.com/ehost/delivery?vid=7&hid=102&sid=434afdf5-5ed9-45d4-993b-, January 24, 2008; "What Is a Social Entrepreneur?" http://ashoka.org/social_entrepreneur, February 20,

2008; C. Hsu, "Entrepreneur for Social Change," *U.S.News.com,* October 31, 2005, www.usnews.com/usnews/news/articles/051031/31drayton.htm; D.M. Sullivan, "Stimulating Social Entrepreneurship: Can Support from Cities Make a Difference?" *Academy of Management Perspectives,* February 2007, 78.

128. Katsikis and Kyrgidou, "The Concept of Sustainable Entrepreneurship"; "What Is a Social Entrepreneur?"; Hsu, "Entrepreneur for Social Change"; Sullivan, "Stimulating Social Entrepreneurship."

Chapter 8

1. Press release, "Toys'R'Us, Inc. Reports Results for Fourth Quarter and Full Year of Fiscal 2013," March 26, 2014, www.toysrusinc.com/press-room/releases/financial/2014/toysrus-inc.-reports-results-for-fourth-quarter-and-full-year-of-fisca/.

2. Press release, "Toys'R'US, Inc. Outlines 'TRU Transformation' Strategy," March 16, 2014, www.toysrusinc.com/press-room/releases/general/2014/toysrus-inc.-outlines-tru-transformation-strategy/.

3. Ibid.

4. B. Thau, "New Toys'R'Us CEO Reveals 'Diagnosis,' Treatment Plan for Ailing Chain," *Forbes,* March 27, 2014, www.forbes.com/sites/barbarathau/2014/03/27/new-toys-r-us-ceo-reveals-diagnosis-treatment-plan-for-ailing-chain/.

5. Press release, "Toys'R'US, Inc. Outlines 'TRU Transformation' Strategy."

6. Ibid.

7. A. Chandler, *Strategy and Structure: Chapters in the History of the American Enterprise* (Cambridge, MA: MIT Press, 1962).

8. "Nike Mission Statement," nike.com, n.d.help-en-us.nike.com/app/answers/detail/a_id/113/p/3897.

9. A. Chandler, *Strategy and Structure.*

10. H. Fayol, *General and Industrial Management* (1884; New York: IEEE Press, 1984).

11. Ibid., 18.

12. F.J. Aguilar, "General Electric: Reg Jones and Jack Welch," in *General Managers in Action* (Oxford: Oxford University Press, 1992).

13. Aguilar, "General Electric."

14. www.ge.com, 2012.

15. C.W. Hofer and D. Schendel, *Strategy Formulation: Analytical Concepts* (St. Paul, MN: West, 1978).

16. "Mars 2020," Jet Propulsion Laboratory, n.d., www.jpl.nasa.gov/missions/mars-2020.

17. P. De Geus, "Planning as Learning," *Harvard Business Review,* March–April 1988, 70–74.

18. P. Wack, "Scenarios: Shooting the Rapids," *Harvard Business Review,* November–December 1985, 139–50.

19. "New Lens Scenarios," shell.com, n.d., www.shell.com/global/future-energy/scenarios/new-lens-scenarios.html.

20. A. Wilkinson and R. Kupers, "Living in the Futures," *Harvard Business Review,* May 2013, hbr.org/2013/05/living-in-the-futures/ar/1.

21. R. Phelps, C. Chan, and S.C. Kapsalis, "Does Scenario Planning Affect Firm Performance?" *Journal of Business Research,* March 2001, 223–32.

22. J. A. Pearce, "The Company Mission as a Strategic Tool," *Sloan Management Review,* Spring 1992, 15–24.

23. D.F. Abell, *Defining the Business: The Starting Point of Strategic Planning* (Englewood Cliff s, NJ: Prentice-Hall, 1980).

24. G. Hamel and C.K. Prahalad, "Strategic Intent," *Harvard Business Review,* May–June 1989, 63–73.

25. D.I. Jung and B.J. Avolio, "Opening the Black Box: An Experimental Investigation of the Mediating Effects of Trust and Value Congruence on Transformational and Transactional Leadership," *Journal of Organizational Behavior,* December 2000, 949–64; B.M. Bass and B.J. Avolio, "Transformational and Transactional Leadership: 1992 and Beyond," *Journal of European Industrial Training,* January 1990, 20–35.

26. J. Porras and J. Collins, *Built to Last: Successful Habits of Visionary Companies* (New York: HarperCollins, 1994).

27. E.A. Locke, G.P. Latham, and M. Erez, "The Determinants of Goal Commitment," *Academy of Management Review* 13 (1988), 23–39.

28. www.ge.com, 2012.

29. Robinson, "Cracking the Code: GE Appliances Hosting Hackathon." *Louisville Business First,* February 7, 2014, www.bizjournals.com/louisville/news/2014/02/07/cracking-the-code-ge-appliances.html.

30. K.R. Andrews, *The Concept of Corporate Strategy* (Homewood, IL: Irwin, 1971).

31. M. Wolff, "Wolff: GM's Barra Shames Voiceless CEOs," *USAToday,* March 23, 2014, www.usatoday.com/story/money/columnist/wolff/2014/03/23/gms-mary-barra-takes-ownership-of-crisis/6656729/.

32. J. Jelter, "GM CEO Mary Barra on Recalls: 'We Have to Own It,'" *The Wall Street Journal,* March 17, 2014, blogs.marketwatch.com/thetell/2014/03/17/gm-ceo-mary-barra-on-recalls-we-have-to-own-it/.

33. P. Sellers, "Car Talk (and More!) with Mary Barra, GM's New Chief," *Fortune,* February 6, 2014, money.cnn.com/2014/02/06/leadership/global-mpw-mary-barra-gm.pr.fortune/.

34. Ibid.

35. N. Bomey, "GM's Mary Barra Earning High Marks for Response to Ignition-Recall Crisis," *Detroit Free Press,* March 26, 2014, www.freep.com/article/20140326/

BUSINESS0101/303260112/GM-Mary-Barra-General-Motors-recall.

36. "General Motors' CEO Discusses Q4 2013 Results—Earnings Call Transcript," *Yahoo Finance,* February 6, 2014, finance.yahoo.com/news/general-motors-ceo-discusses-q4-184101363.html.

37. M.E. Porter, "How Competititve Forces Shape Strategy," *Harvard Business Review,* March—April 1979.

38. R.D. Aveni, *Hypercompetition* (New York: Free Press, 1994).

39. M.E. Porter, *Competitive Strategy* (New York: Free Press, 1980).

40. "Operate with a Warrior Spirit, a Servant's Heart, and a Fun-LUVing Attitude," southwestonereport.com, n.d., www.southwestonereport.com/2011/#!/thirty-thousand-foot-view/mission-and-vision.

41. S. Grobart, "Tim Cooke: The Complete Interview," *Bloomberg Businessweek,* September 20, 2013, www.businessweek.com/articles/2013-09-20/apple-ceo-tim-cooks-complete-interview-with-bloomberg-businessweek#p1.

42. Porter, *Competitive Strategy.*

43. "Media Center: Redbox Fun Facts," redbox.com, n.d., www.redbox.com/facts.

44. "Netflix, Inc. History," Funding Universe, n.d., http://www.fundinguniverse.com/company-histories/netflix-inc-history/; "Netflix Us @netflix," Twitter, n.d., twitter.com/netflix/statuses/2746816142.

45. T. Leopold, "Your Late Fees Are Waived: Blockbuster Closes," cnn.com, November 6, 2013, www.cnn.com/2013/11/06/tech/gaming-gadgets/blockbuster-video-stores-impact/.

46. Dealbook, "Blockbuster Files for Bankruptcy," *The New York Times,* September 23, 2010, dealbook.nytimes.com/2010/09/23/blockbuster-files-for-bankruptcy/.

47. Leopold, "Your Late Fees Are Waived: Blockbuster Closes."

48. "Blockbuster Closing All of Its Remaining Retail Stores," *The Huffington Post,* November 6, 2013, http://www.huffingtonpost.com/2013/11/06/blockbuster-closing_n_4226735.html.

49. I. Mochari, "The History of Netflix and the Future of Television," *Inc.,* January 30, 2014, www.inc.com/ilan-mochari/netflix-history.html.

50. G. Petro, "The Future of Fashion Retailing: The Zara Approach (Part 2 of 3)" *Forbes,* October 25, 2010, http://www.forbes.com/sites/gregpetro/2012/10/25/the-future-of-fashion-retailing-the-zara-approach-part-2-of-3/.

51. C. Vitzthum, "Just-in-Time-Fashion," *The Wall Street Journal,* May 18, 2001, B1, B4.

52. www.zara.com, 2010.

53. "About Crocs," crocs.com, n.d., company.crocs.com/.

54. E. Volkman, "Are Crocs Coming Back in Style? Blackstone Group Thinks So," March 7, 2014, www.dailyfinance.com/2014/03/07/crocs-coming-back-blackstone-group-thinks-yes/.

55. V. Ravina, "I Hate Crocs dot com.," September 28, 2011, ihatecrocsblog.blogspot.com/.

56. "I Don't Care How Comfortable Crocs Are, You Look Like a Dumbass," Facebook, n.d., www.facebook.com/pages/I-Dont-Care-How-Comfortable-Crocs-Are-You-Look-Like-A-Dumbass/88367110762.

57. J. Spellman, "How a Trendy Show Nearly Lost Its Footing," *CNNLiving,* March 17, 2012, www.cnn.com/2012/03/16/living/american-comeback-crocs/?_ga=1.209043991.480445444.1395999381.

58. News release, "Crocs Inc. Reports Fourth Quarter and Full Year 2013 Financial Results," crocs.com, February 20, 2014, investors.crocs.com/phoenix.zhtml?c=193409&p=irol-newsArticle&ID=1901742&highlight=#sthash.ZqAOVCRv.dpuf.

59. M. Ramsey, "Will Tesla's $5 Billion Gigafactory Make a Battery Nobody Else Wants?" *The Wall Street Journal,* April 4, 2014, blogs.wsj.com/corporate-intelligence/2014/04/04/will-teslas-5-billion-gigafactory-make-a-battery-no-ne-else-wants/.

60. M.K. Perry, "Vertical Integration: Determinants and Effects," in R. Schmalensee and R.D. Willig, *Handbook of Industrial Organization,* vol. 1 (New York: Elsevier Science, 1989).

61. "Matsushita Electric Industrial (MEI) in 1987," Harvard Business School Case 388–144.

62. "Time to Switch Off Duracell for P&G?," *Forbes,* June 16, 2011, www.forbes.com/sites/greatspeculations/2011/06/16/time-to-switch-off-duracell-for-pg/.

63. E. Penrose, *The Theory of the Growth of the Firm* (Oxford: Oxford University Press, 1959).

64. M.E. Porter, "From Competitive Advantage to Corporate Strategy," *Harvard Business Review* 65 (1987), 43–59.

65. D.J. Teece, "Economies of Scope and the Scope of the Enterprise," *Journal of Economic Behavior and Organization* 3 (1980), 223–47.

66. M.E. Porter, *Competitive Advantage: Creating and Sustaining Superior Performance* (New York: Free Press, 1985).

67. www.3M.com, 2005, 2010, 2012.

68. www.3M.com, 2014.

69. C. Wyant, "Minnesota Companies Make *BusinessWeek*'s 'Most Innovative' List," *Minneapolis/St. Paul Business Journal,* April 18, 2008.

70. "Our History," pepsico.com, n.d., www.pepsico.com/Company/Our-History.

71. M. Rocco, "Nelson Peltz Renews Call to Split PepsiCo," *FoxBusiness,* February 20, 2014, www.foxbusiness.com/industries/2014/02/20/nelson-peltz-revives-campaign-to-split-up-pepsico/.

72. L. Baertlein, "Most Investors in Survey Back Pepsi Split; Buffett Opposes," *Reuters,* March 3, 2014, www.reuters.com/article/2014/03/03/us-pepsico-peltz-buffett-idUSBREA221PT20140303.

73. Ibid.

74. Ibid.

75. For a review of the evidence, see C.W.L. Hill and G.R. Jones, *Strategic Management: An Integrated Approach,* 5th ed. (Boston: Houghton Mifflin, 2011), chap.10.

76. C.R. Christensen et al., *Business Policy Text and Cases* (Homewood, IL: Irwin, 1987), 778.

77. C.W.L. Hill, "Conglomerate Performance over the Economic Cycle," *Journal of Industrial Economics* 32 (1983), 197–213.

78. V. Ramanujam and P. Varadarajan,"Research on Corporate Diversification: A Synthesis," *Strategic Management Journal* 10 (1989), 523–51. Also see A. Shleifer and R.W. Vishny, "Takeovers in the 1960s and 1980s: Evidence and Implications," in R.P. Rumelt, D.E. Schendel, and D.J. Teece, eds., *Fundamental Issues in Strategy* (Boston: Harvard Business School Press, 1994).

79. J.R. Williams, B.L. Paez, and L. Sanders, "Conglomerates Revisited," *Strategic Management Journal* 9 (1988), 403–14.

80. "Honeywell to Divest Friction Material Biz," *Yahoo Finance,* January 8, 2014, finance.yahoo.com/news/honeywell-divest-friction-material-biz-132004619.html.

81. C.A. Bartlett and S. Ghoshal, *Managing across Borders* (Boston: Harvard Business School Press, 1989).

82. C.K. Prahalad and Y.L. Doz, *The Multinational Mission* (New York: Free Press, 1987).

83. "Noodle in India," *Euromonitor International,* January 2014, www.euromonitor.com/noodles-in-india/report.

84. "Gillette Co.'s New $40 Million Razor Blade Factory in St. Petersburg, Russia," *Boston Globe,* June 7, 2000, C 6.

85. D. Sewell, "P & G Replaces Ex–Gillette CEO at Operations," www.yahoo.com, May 24, 2006.

86. www.pg.com, 2005, 2008, 2010.

87. R.E. Caves, *Multinational Enterprise and Economic Analysis* (Cambridge: Cambridge University Press, 1982).

88. B. Kogut, "Joint Ventures: Theoretical and Empirical Perspectives," *Strategic Management Journal* 9 (1988), 319–33.

89. "Venture with Nestlé SA Is Slated for Expansion," *The Wall Street Journal,* April 15, 2001, B2.

90. Press release, "Avon and KORRES Enter into Strategic Alliance in Latin America," avon.com, February 10, 2014, media.avoncompany.com/index.php?s=10922&item=126262.

91. N. Hood and S. Young, *The Economics of the Multinational Enterprise* (London: Longman, 1979).

92. "Cargill's AKEY Business Celebrates 50 years of Leadership in Animal Nutrition," cargill.com, November 13, 2013, www.cargill.com/news/releases/2013/NA3081187.jsp.

93. "Vision, Mission, Values," copersucar.com, n.d., www.copersucar.com.br/visao_en.html.

94. Press release, "Cargill & Copersucar Reach Agreement to Combine Global Sugar Trading Activities in New Joint Venture," cargill.com, March 27, 2014, www.cargill.com/news/releases/2014/NA31367201.jsp.

95. J. Bunge, "Cargill Exits Coal Trade, Plans Sugar Venture," *The Wall Street Journal,* March 27, 2014, online.wsj.com/news/articles/SB10001424052702303325204579465092624021818.

Chapter 9

1. S. McCartney, "Airlines Go Back to Boarding School to Move Fliers onto Planes Faster," *The Wall Street Journal,* July 21, 2011, online.wsj.com/news/articles/SB10001424053111904233404576457930970524522?mg=reno64-wsj&url=http%3A%2F%2Fonline.wsj.com%2Farticle%2FSB1000142405311190423340457645793097052452522.html.

2. E. Chemi, "The Dumb Way We Board Airplanes Remains Impervious to Good Data," *Bloomberg Businessweek,* April 23, 2014, www.businessweek.com/articles/2014-04-23/the-dumb-way-we-board-airplanes-remains-impervious-to-good-data#r=hp-ls.

3. "Episode 197: Airplane Boarding," *MythBusters Results,* December 16, 2012, mythbustersresults.com/airplane-boarding.

4. Center for Particle Astrophysics, n.d., home.fnal.gov/~jsteffen/airplanes.html.

5. C. Morran, "4 Things That Make Airline Boarding a Complete Mess," *Consumerist,* November 18, 2013, consumerist.com/2013/11/18/4-things-that-make-airline-boarding-a-complete-mess/.

6. Ibid.

7. Ibid.

8. M. Maynard, "Like American, More Airlines Add Fees for Checking Luggage," *The New York Times,* June 13, 2008, www.nytimes.com/2008/06/13/business/13bags.html?_r=0.

9. J. Peterson, "A Common Sense Solution to Slow Airplane Boarding," linkedin.com, August 27, 2013, www.linkedin.com/today/post/article/20130827063031-11846967-a-common-sense-solution-to-slow-airplane-boarding.

10. D. Koenig, "The Airlines' Endless Quest for Better Boarding Procedures," *The Huffington Post,* July 31, 2013, www.huffingtonpost.com/2013/07/31/airline-boarding-procedures_n_3683523.html.

11. "Changed Bag Rules and Optional Services," united.com, n.d., www.united.com/CMS/en-US/travel/Pages/ChangedBagRulesOptionalServices.aspx?v_ctrk=HHLN$0-772-5782-1-3907.

12. C. Harress, "Airlines Made $6 Billion in Baggage and Change Fees in 2013, but Increases Coming in 2014," *International Business Times,* December 31, 2013, www.ibtimes.com/airlines-made-6-billion-baggage-change-fees-2013-increases-coming-2014-1523896.

13. "Boarding the Plane," southwest.com, n.d., www.southwest.com/html/travel-experience/boarding-your-flight/index.html.

14. D. Hofman, S. Aronow, and K. Nilles, "The Gartner Supply Chain Top 25 for 2013," *Gartner,* May 22, 2013, www.gartner.com/doc/2493115/gartner-supply-chain-top-; D. Hofman, S. Aronow, and K. Nilles, "Gartner's 2013 Supply Chain Top 25: Learning from the Industry Leaders," *SupplyChain247,* September 10, 2013, www.supplychain247.com/article/gartners_2013_supply_chain_top_25_learning_from_the_industry_leaders.

15. See D. Garvin, "What Does Product Quality Really Mean?" *Sloan Management Review* 26 (Fall 1984), 25–44; P.B. Crosby, *Quality Is Free* (New York: Mentor Books, 1980); A. Gabor, *The Man Who Discovered Quality* (New York: Times Books, 1990).

16. M. Rogowsky, "Dismal Wii U Sales Move Nintendo Closer to 'Game Over,'" *Forbes,* January 17, 2014, www.forbes.com/sites/markrogowsky/2014/01/17/dismal-wii-u-sales-move-nintendo-closer-to-game-over/.

17. D. Lieberman, "2014 Box Office Will Be Hurt by Diminishing Popularity of 3D Movies: Analyst," *Deadline New York,* February 3, 2014, www.deadline.com/2014/02/2014-box-office-will-be-hurt-by-diminishing-popularity-of-3d-movies-analyst/.

18. M. Eisenberg, "Steven Spielberg & Peter Jackson Rant about 3D Ticket Prices," screenrant.com, updated February 15, 2014, screenrant.com/steven-spielberg-peter-jackson-rant-3d-ticket-prices-mikee-125010/.

19. D.F. Abell, *Defining the Business: The Starting Point of Strategic Planning* (Englewood Cliffs, NJ: Prentice-Hall, 1980).

20. According to Richard D'Aveni, the process of pushing price-attribute curves to the right is a characteristic of the competitive process. See R. D'Aveni, *Hypercompetition* (New York: Free Press, 1994).

21. "Walmart and Wild Oats Unveil Cheaper Organic Line," *Fox News,* April 10, 2014, www.foxnews.com/leisure/2014/04/10/wal-mart-teams-up-with-wild-oats-to-sell-lower-priced-organic-food-offering/.

22. www.southwest.com, 2012.

23. "Bags Fly Free," southwest.com, n.d., www.southwest.com/html/air/bags-fly-free.html.

24. B. O'Brian, "Flying on the Cheap," *The Wall Street Journal,* October 26, 1992, A1; B. O'Reilly, "Where Service Flies Right," *Fortune,* August 24, 1992, 116–17; A. Salukis, "Hurt in Expansion Airlines Cut Back and May Sell Hubs," *The Wall Street Journal,* April 1, 1993, A1, C8.

25. "Our History," panerabread.com, n.d., www.panerabread.com/en-us/company/about-panera/our-history.html.

26. B. Kowitt, "With Digital Ordering, Panera Makes a Big Bet on Tech," *Fortune,* March 27, 2014, tech.fortune.cnn.com/tag/food-tech/.

27. Ibid.

28. Ibid.

29. www.ciu.com, 2012.

30. www.crm.com, 2012.

31. n.d., www.nimble.com/product-tour/.

32. The view of quality as reliability goes back to the work of Deming and Juran; see Gabor, *The Man Who Discovered Quality.*

33. See Garvin, "What Does Product Quality Really Mean?"; Crosby, *Quality Is Free;* Gabor, *The Man Who Discovered Quality.*

34. www.jdpa.com, 2009, 2012, 2014.

35. "Our Company," tjx.com, June 2013, www.tjx.com/about-tjx.asp.

36. Ibid.

37. zacks.com, "Cheap Shirts and Suits Are Just Some of the Reasons to Like TJX Companies," *Forbes,* www.forbes.com/sites/zacks/2010/10/22/cheap-shirts-and-suits-are-just-some-of-the-reasons-to-like-tjx-companies/.

38. Ibid.

39. "Our Company," tjx.com, June 2013, www.tjx.com/about-tjx.asp.

40. Ibid.

41. "TJX CEO: 'We're Innovators, We Strive to Be Ahead of the Curve,'" *Retail Info Systems News,* October 28, 2013, risnews.edgl.com/retail-news/TJX-CEO—We-re-Innovators,-We-Strive-to-be-Ahead-of-the-Curve-89127.

42. Press release, "The TJX Companies, Inc. Reports Fiscal 2014 EPS Growth of 15% over 24% Increase Last Year on an Adjusted Basis; Announces New $2.0 Billion Stock Repurchase Program; Plans 21% Increase in Dividend," tjx.com, February 26, 2014, investor.tjx.com/phoenix.zhtml?c=118215&p=irol-newsArticle&ID=1903765&highlight=supply%20chain.

43. See J.W. Dean and D.E. Bowen, "Management Theory and Total Quality: Improving Research and Practice through Theory Development," *Academy of Management Review* 19 (1994), 392–418.

44. For general background information, see J.C. Anderson, M. Rungtusanatham, and R.G. Schroeder, "A Theory of Quality Management Underlying the Deming anagement Method," *Academy of Management Review* 19 (1994), 472–509; "How to Build Quality," *The Economist,* September 23, 1989, 91–92; Gabor, *The Man Who Discovered Quality;* Crosby, *Quality Is Free.*

45. Bowles, "Is American Management Really Committed to Quality?" *Management Review,* April 1992, 42–46.

46. n.d., www.isixsigma.com.

47. Gabor, *The Man Who Discovered Quality.*

48. J. Biolos, "Six Sigma Meets the Service Economy—Six Sigma: It's Not Just for Manufacturing," *Harvard Business School: Working Knowledge Archive,* January 27, 2003, hbswk.hbs.edu/archive/3278.html.

49. S. Kumar, "Six Sigma at Citibank," SigmaWay, April 2, 2014, www.gosigmaway.com/index.php/easyblog/entry/six-sigma-at-citibank#sthash.15OXtwLH.dpuf.

50. R. Rucker, "Six Sigma at Citibank," Quality Digest, n.d., www.qualitydigest.com/dec99/html/citibank.html.

51. "City Demographics," cityoftyler.org, January 1, 2014, www.cityoftyler.org/Departments/PlanningDepartment/CityDemographics.aspx.

52. "Step Away from the Hustle and Bustle to Enjoy the Natural Beauty and Amenities of the 'Rose Capital of America,'" tourtexas.com, n.d., www.tourtexas.com/content.cfm?id=104.

53. K. Gooch, "Lean Six Sigma: City of Tyler Celebrates over $5 Million in Savings with Program," *Tyler Morning Telegraph,* April 2, 2014, www.tylerpaper.com/TP-News+Local/197509/lean-six-sigma-city-of-tyler-celebrates-over-5-million-in-savings-with-program#.U1nR7VehQV5.

54. Ibid.

55. Ibid.

56. "Black Belts and Green Belts," cityoftyler.org, n.d., www.cityoftyler.org/Departments/Innovation/BlackBeltsandGreenBelts.aspx.

57. D. Bentley, "Lean Six Sigma Celebrates $5 Million In Savings," 19KYTX, April 2, 2014, www.cbs19.tv/story/25148071/lean-six-sigma-celebrates-5-million-in-savings.

58. "About Steelcase," steelcase.com, n.d., www.steelcase.com/en/company/who/about-steelcase/pages/aboutsteelcase.aspx.

59. B. Arantes, "How to Design Your Workspace to Encourage Positive Emotions at Work," *Fast Company,* April 23, 2014, www.fastcompany.com/3029384/work-smart/how-to-design-your-workspace-to-encourage-positive-emotions-at-work.

60. G. Bradt, "Steelcase CE on How Office Layout Impacts Corporate Culture," *Forbes*, August 7, 2012, http://www.forbes.com/sites/georgebradt/2012/08/07/steelcase-ceo-on-how-office-layout-impacts-corporate-culture/.

61. Ibid.

62. Ibid.

63. P. Nemetz and L. Fry, "Flexible Manufacturing Organization: Implication for Strategy Formulation," *Academy of Management Review* 13 (1988), 627–38; N. Greenwood, *Implementing Flexible Manufacturing Systems* (New York: Halstead Press, 1986).

64. L. VanHulle, "Lansing Grand River Plant's Milestone 'Means Confidence,'" *Lansing State Journal*, September 14, 2013, www.lansingstatejournal.com/article/20130915/BUSINESS01/309150083/Lansing-Grand-River-plant-s-milestone-means-confidence-.

65. L. VanHulle, "GM to Build $162M Stamping Plant at Lansing Grand River, Add 65 Jobs," *Lansing State Journal*, March 6, 2014, www.lansingstatejournal.com/article/20140306/BUSINESS/303060025/GM-build-162M-stamping-plant-Lansing-Grand-River-add-65-jobs.

66. For an interesting discussion of some other drawbacks of JIT and other "Japanese" manufacturing techniques, see S.M. Young, "A Framework for Successful Adoption and Performance of Japanese Manufacturing Practices in the United States," *Academy of Management Review* 17 (1992), 677–701.

67. B. Saporito, "The Trouble Lurking on Walmart's Empty Shelves," *Time*, April 9, 2013, business.time.com/2013/04/09/the-trouble-lurking-on-walmarts-empty-shelves/.

68. T. Stundza, "Massachusetts Switch Maker Switches to Kanban," *Purchasing*, November 16, 2000, 103.

69. B. Dumaine, "The Trouble with Teams," *Fortune*, September 5, 1994, 86–92.

70. See C.W.L. Hill, "Transaction Cost Economizing as a Source of National Competitive Advantage: The Case of Japan," *Organization Science*, 2 (1994); M. Aoki, *Information, Incentives, and Bargaining in the Japanese Economy* (Cambridge: Cambridge University Press, 1989).

71. J. Hoerr, "The Payoff from Teamwork," *BusinessWeek*, July 10, 1989, 56–62.

72. M. Hammer and J. Champy, *Reengineering the Corporation* (New York: Harper-Business, 1993), 35.

73. Ibid., 46.

74. Ibid.

75. D. Yohn, "How Chipotle Changes American Fast Food Forever," *Fast Company*, March 14, 2014, www.fastcompany.com/3027647/lessons-learned/how-chipotle-changed-american-fast-food-forever.

76. "LEGO History Timeline," lego.com, January 9, 2012, aboutus.lego.com/en-us/lego-group/the_lego_history.

77. Ibid.

78. Ibid.

79. B. Alexander, "'The Lego Movie' Hopes to Cement a Built-in Fan Base," *USA Today*, October 23, 2013, www.usatoday.com/story/life/movies/2013/10/23/lego-movie-peek-will-ferrell/2918385/.

80. "The LEGO Brand," lego.com, December 7, 2011, aboutus.lego.com/en-us/lego-group/the_lego_brand/.

81. M. Venables, "How Lego Makes Safe, Quality, Diverse and Irresistible Toys Everyone Wants: Part Two," *Forbes*, April 20, 2013, www.forbes.com/sites/michaelvenables/2013/04/20/how-lego-makes-the-safe-quality-diverse-and-irresistible-toys-we-all-want-part-two/.

82. Ibid.

83. S. Adams, "The World's Most Reputable Companies," *Forbes*, April 8, 2014, www.forbes.com/sites/susanadams/2014/04/08/the-worlds-most-reputable-companies/.

84. Venables, "How Lego Makes Safe, Quality, Diverse and Irresistible Toys."

85. Ibid.

Chapter 10

1. D. Price, "Managing Creativity: Lessons from Pixar and Disney Animation," *Harvard Business Review*, April 9, 2014, blogs.hbr.org/2014/04/managing-creativity-lessons-from-pixar-and-disney-animation/.

2. "Captain America Comics," marvel.com, n.d., marvel.com/comics/issue/7849/captain_america_comics_1941_1.

3. "Overview," marvel.disneycareers.com, n.d., marvel.disneycareers.com/en/about-marvel/overview/.

4. "Excerpt," randomhouse.com, n.d., www.randomhouse.com/features/comicwars/excerpt.html.

5. "The Pixar Timeline 1979 to Present," pixar.com, n.d., www.pixar.com/about/Our-Story.

6. E. Catmull, "Building a Sense of Purpose at Pixar," McKinsey & Company, April 2014, www.mckinsey.com/Insights/Media_Entertainment/Building_a_sense_of_purpose_at_Pixar?cid=other-eml-alt-mkq-mck-oth-1404.

7. D. Price, "Managing Creativity: Lessons from Pixar and Disney Animation," *Harvard Business Review*, April 9, 2014, blogs.hbr.org/2014/04/managing-creativity-lessons-from-pixar-and-disney-animation/.

8. "How Pixar Changed Disney Animation from Within," *CBC News*, April 11, 2014, www.cbc.ca/news/business/how-pixar-changed-disney-animation-from-within-1.2607439.

9. D. Price, "Managing Creativity: Lessons from Pixar and Disney Animation."

10. G. R. Jones, *Organizational Theory, Design, and Change: Text and Cases* (Upper Saddle River: Prentice-Hall, 2011).

11. J. Child, *Organization: A Guide for Managers and Administrators* (New York: Harper & Row, 1977).

12. P.R. Lawrence and J.W. Lorsch, *Organization and Environment* (Boston: Graduate School of Business Administration, Harvard University, 1967).

13. R. Duncan, "What Is the Right Organizational Design?" *Organizational Dynamics*, Winter 1979, 59–80.

14. T. Burns and G.R. Stalker, *The Management of Innovation* (London: Tavistock, 1966).

15. D. Miller, "Strategy Making and Structure: Analysis and Implications for Performance," *Academy of Management Journal* 30 (1987), 7–32.

16. A.D. Chandler, *Strategy and Structure* (Cambridge, MA: MIT Press, 1962).

17. J. Stopford and L. Wells, *Managing the Multinational Enterprise* (London: Longman, 1972).

18. C. Perrow, *Organizational Analysis: A Sociological View* (Belmont, CA: Wadsworth, 1970).

19. "First Lady Michelle Obama Announces Commitment by Subway® Restaurants to Promote Healthier Choices to Kids," The White House: Office of the First Lady, January 23, 2014, www.whitehouse.gov/the-press-office/2014/01/23/first-lady-michelle-obama-announces-commitment-subway-restaurants-promot.

20. F.W. Taylor, *The Principles of Scientific Management* (New York: Harper, 1911).

21. R.W. Griffin, *Task Design: An Integrative Approach* (Glenview, IL: Scott, Foresman, 1982).

22. V. Wong, "Let's Go to Wendy's and Cuddle by the Fireplace," *Bloomberg Businessweek*, February 28, 2013, www.businessweek.com/articles/2013-02-28/lets-go-to-wendys-and-cuddle-by-the-fireplace.

23. Ibid.

24. Ibid.

25. "Meritage Announces Opening of Atlanta Wendy's Restaurant; Company's 121st Restaurant," bloomberg.com, March 26, 2014, www.bloomberg.com/article/2014-03-26/aaETOk8Or0zA.html.

26. J. Daley, "Wendy's Franchise Owner Launches a Big Training Initiative," *Entrepreneur*, September 27, 2013, www.entrepreneur.com/article/227968#.

27. Ibid.

28. Ibid.

29. J.R. Hackman and G.R. Oldham, *Work Redesign* (Reading, MA: Addison-Wesley, 1980).

30. J.R. Galbraith and R.K. Kazanjian, *Strategy Implementation: Structure,*

System, and Process, 2nd ed. (St. Paul, MN: West, 1986).

31. Lawrence and Lorsch, *Organization and Environment.*

32. Jones, *Organizational Theory.*

33. Lawrence and Lorsch, *Organization and Environment.*

34. R.H. Hall, *Organizations: Structure and Process* (Englewood Cliffs, NJ: Prentice-Hall, 1972); R. Miles, *Macro Organizational Behavior* (Santa Monica, CA: Goodyear, 1980).

35. Chandler, *Strategy and Structure.*

36. G.R. Jones and C.W.L. Hill, "Transaction Cost Analysis of Strategy–Structure Choice," *Strategic Management Journal* 9 (1988), 159–72.

37. www.gsk.com, 2006.

38. www.gsk.com, 2012.

39. J. Hodgson, "Glaxo Plans More Restructuring as Profit Sinks," *The Wall Street Journal,* February 6, 2013, online. wsj.com/news/articles/SB1000142412788 73245909045782876206004804 36.

40. "Michael Baker International Selected for Pulaski Skyway Bridge Project," mbakercorp.com, March 13, 2014, www.mbakercorp.com/index.php? option=com_content&task=view&id= 2577&Itemid=203.

41. E. Bader, "Michael Baker International Selected for Pulaski Skyway Bridge Project," NJBIZ, March 14, 2014, www.njbiz.com/article/20140314/ NJBIZ01/140319874/Michael-Baker-International-selected-for-Pulaski-Skyway-Bridge-project.

42. "Michael Baker International Unveils New Organizational Structure for National and International Expansion," *Business Wire,* April 15, 2014, www.businesswire .com/news/home/20140415006475/en/ Michael-Baker-International-Unveils-Organizational-Structure-National#. U1D5b1ehQV4.

43. "Purpose/Vision/Values," mbakercorp .com, n.d., www.mbakercorp.com/index .php?option=com_content&task=category &sectionid=9&id=165&Itemid=336.

44. "Michael Baker International Unveils New Organizational Structure for National and International Expansion," *Business Wire.*

45. C. Mortensen, "Jonathan Martin Went to Hospital," espn.go.com, November 8, 2013, espn.go.com/nfl/story/_/id/ 9936309/jonathan-martin-checked-hospital-leaving-miami-dolphins.

46. "Incognito, Others Tormented Martin," espn.go.com, February 15, 2014, espn .go.com/nfl/story/_/id/10455447/miami-dolphins-bullying-report-released-richie-incognito-others-responsible-harassment.

47. Ibid.

48. "Heads Roll Following Report on Miami Dolphins Bullying Scandal," *The Blaze,* February 19, 2014, www.theblaze.com/

stories/2014/02/19/heads-roll-following-report-on-miami-dolphins-bullying-scandal/.

49. "Incognito, Others Tormented Martin," espn.go.com.

50. "Heads Roll Following Report on Miami Dolphins bullying Scandal," *The Blaze.*

51. S.M. Davis and P.R. Lawrence, *Matrix* (Reading, MA: Addison-Wesley, 1977); J.R. Galbraith, "Matrix Organization Designs: How to Combine Functional and Project Forms," *Business Horizons* 14 (1971), 29–40.

52. L.R. Burns, "Matrix Management in Hospitals: Testing Theories of Matrix Structure and Development," *Administrative Science Quarterly* 34 (1989), 349–68.

53. C.W.L. Hill, *International Business* (Homewood, IL: Irwin, 2003).

54. Kotter International, "5 Innovation Secrets from Sealy," *Forbes,* October 10, 2012, www.forbes.com/sites/ johnkotter/2012/10/10/5-innovation-secrets-from-sealy/.

55. Jones, *Organizational Theory.*

56. A. Farnham, "America's Most Admired Company," *Fortune,* February 7, 1994, 50–54.

57. "Newell Rubbermaid," jobs. newellrubbermaid.com, n.d., jobs. newellrubbermaid.com/huntersville/ research-%EF%B9%A0-development_ engineering/jobid4936844-principal-engineer-advanced-technology-jobs.

58. P. Blau, "A Formal Theory of Differentiation in Organizations," *American Sociological Review* 35 (1970), 684–95.

59. "Leadership," aboutmcdonalds.com, n.d., www.aboutmcdonalds.com/mcd/our_ company/leadership.html; "McDonald's Announces Chief Operating Officer Tim Fenton to Retire and Global Management Restructure," news.mcdonalds.com, March 20, 2014, news.mcdonalds.com/ Corporate/news-stories/McDonald-s-Announces-Chief-Operating-Officer-Tim-F.

60. Child, *Organization.*

61. J. Schoen, "Many Feel Like Recession Still Hasn't Ended," *USA Today,* January 1, 2014, www.usatoday.com/story/ money/personalfinance/2014/01/01/ cnbc-recovery-slowed-economy/4222929/.

62. "Yum! Brands Chariman and CEO David Novak Shares Break-Through Leadership Strategies in New Book, *Taking People with You: The Only Way to Make Big Things Happen,*" yum.com, January 3, 2012, www.yum.com/company/ inthenews/pressreleases/010312.asp; G. Bradt, "IBM, Ritz-Carlton and Yum! Brands Empower Front Line Employees, Do You?" *Forbes,* April 17, 2013, www .forbes.com/sites/georgebradt/2013/04/17/ ibm-ritz-carlton-and-yum-brands-empower-front-line-employees-do-you/.

63. www.plexus.com, 2012.

64. W.M. Bulkeley, "Plexus Strategy: Smaller Runs of More Things," *The Wall Street Journal,* October 8, 2003, B1, B12.

65. P.M. Blau and R.A. Schoenherr, *The Structure of Organizations* (New York: Basic Books, 1971).

66. Jones, *Organizational Theory.*

67. S. Ballmer, "Steve Ballmer Email to Employees on New CEO," Microsoft News Center, February 4, 2014, www .microsoft.com/en-us/news/press/2014/ feb14/02-04mail1.aspx.

68. "Satya Nadella, Chief of Microsoft, on His New Role," *The New York Times,* February 20, 2014, www.nytimes. com/2014/02/21/business/satya-nadella-chief-of-microsoft-on-his-new-role.html.

69. Ibid.

70. Ibid.

71. "Satya Nadella, Chief of Microsoft, on His New Role."

72. "Satya Nadella," Microsoft CEO, n.d., www .microsoft.com/en-us/news/ceo/index.html.

73. "Satya Nadella, Chief of Microsoft, on His New Role," *The New York Times,* February 20, 2014, www.nytimes. com/2014/02/21/business/satya-nadella-chief-of-microsoft-on-his-new-role.html.

74. Lawrence and Lorsch, *Organization and Environment,* 50–55.

75. J.R. Galbraith, *Designing Complex Organizations* (Reading, MA: Addison-Wesley, 1977), chap. 1; Galbraith and Kazanjian, *Strategy Implementation,* chap. 7.

76. J. Townsend, "How Intrapreneurs Are Building Better Businesses from the Inside," *Fast Company,* December 10, 2012, www.fastcoexist.com/1680995/ how-intrapreneurs-are-building-better-businesses-from-the-inside.

77. S.D.N. Cook and D. Yanow, "Culture and Organizational Learning." *Journal of Management Inquiry* 2 (1993), 373–90.

78. Cathy, "Time for Mayer to Step Down at Walmart?" *Who's Minding the Store,* April 3, 2014, whosmindingthestore.org/ category/mm/.

79. Kotter International, "5 Ways Mayer's Trying to Kick-Start The Yahoo! Culture," *Forbes,* July 18, 2013, www.forbes.com/ sites/johnkotter/2013/07/18/the-marissa-mayer-method-5-steps-to-kick-starting-the-yahoo-culture/.

80. J. McDuling, "Yahoo Says Marissa Mayer Has Fixed Its Biggest Problem," *Quartz,* March 5, 2014, qz.com/184046/yahoo-says-marissa-mayer-has-fixed-its-biggest-problem/.

81. K. Swisher, "'Physically Together': Here's the Internal Yahoo No-Work-from-Home Memo for Remote Workers and Maybe More," *All Things D,* February 22, 2013, allthingsd.com/20130222/ physically-together-heres-the-internal-yahoo-no-work-from-home-memo-which-extends-beyond-remote-workers/.

82. J. Guynn, "Yahoo CEO Marissa Mayer Causes Uproar with Telecommuting Ban," *Los Angeles Times,* February 26, 2013, articles.latimes.com/2013/feb/26/business/la-fi-yahoo-telecommuting-20130226.

83. Swisher, "'Physically Together.'"

84. P. Cohan, "4 Reasons Marissa Mayer's No-at-Home-Work Policy Is an Epic Fail," *Forbes,* February 26, 2013, www.forbes.com/sites/petercohan/2013/02/26/4-reasons-marissa-mayers-no-at-hme-work-policy-is-an-epic-fail/.

85. R. Branson, "Give People the Freedom of Where to Work," virgini.com, n.d., www.virgin.com/richard-branson/give-people-the-freedom-of-where-to-work.

86. D. Frommer, "Marissa Mayer: Yahoo's Best Hope," *Salon,* July 16, 2012, www.salon.com/2012/07/16/marissa_mayer_yahoos_best_hope/

87. Ibid.

88. J. Prynn, "Google's First Lady Marissa Mayer Jumps Ship to Yahoo . . . and She's Six Months Pregnant," *London Evening Standard,* July 17, 2012, www.standard.co.uk/business/business-news/googles-first-lady-marissa-mayer-jumps-ship-to-yahoo--and-shes-six-months-pregnant-7952407.html.

89. J. Edwards, "Silicon Valley Is Living inside a Bubble of Tone-Deaf Arrogance," *Business Insider,* December 15, 2013, www.businessinsider.com/silicon-valley-arrogance-bubble-2013-12.

90. H. Tsukayama, "Yahoo Earnings: Marissa Mayer's Strategy May Be Starting to Pay Off," *The Washington Post,* April 15, 2014, www.washingtonpost.com/blogs/the-switch/wp/2014/04/15/yahoo-earnings-marissa-mayers-strategy-may-be-starting-to-pay-off/.

91. J. McDuling, "Yahoo Says Marissa Mayer Has Fixed Its Biggest Problem."

92. B. Schneider, "The People Make the Place," *Personnel Psychology* 40 (1987), 437–53.

93. J.E. Sheriden, "Organizational Culture and Employee Retention," *Academy of Management Journal* 35 (1992), 657–92.

94. M. Hannan and J. Freeman, "Structural Inertia and Organizational Change," *American Sociological Review* 49 (1984), 149–64.

95. C.A. O'Reilly, J. Chatman, and D.F. Caldwell, "People and Organizational Culture: Assessing Person–Organizational Fit," *Academy of Management Journal* 34 (1991), 487–517.

96. T.L. Beauchamp and N.E. Bowie, eds., *Ethical Theory and Business* (Englewood Cliffs, NJ: Prentice-Hall, 1979); A. MacIntyre, *After Virtue* (Notre Dame, IN: University of Notre Dame Press, 1981).

97. A. Sagie and D. Elizur, "Work Values: A Theoretical Overview and a Model of Their Effects," *Journal of Organizational Behavior* 17 (1996), 503–14.

98. G.R. Jones, "Transaction Costs, Property Rights, and Organizational Culture: An Exchange Perspective," *Administrative Science Quarterly* 28 (1983), 454–67.

99. M. Stanger, "18 of The Best Perks at Top Employers," *Business Insider,* February 11, 2013, www.businessinsider.com/companies-with-awesome-perks-payscale-2013-1?op=1#ixzz2zGoNrOoG.

100. C. Perrow, *Normal Accidents* (New York: Basic Books, 1984).

101. H. Mintzberg, *The Structuring of Organizational Structures* (Englewood Cliffs, NJ: Prentice-Hall, 1979).

102. G. Kunda, *Engineering Culture* (Philadelphia: Temple University Press, 1992).

103. www.google.com, 2012.

104. K.E. Weick, *The Social Psychology of Organization* (Reading, MA: Addison-Wesley, 1979).

105. G. Bradt, "How TriZetto's CEO Changes Its Culture by Changing Its Attitude," *Forbes,* August 29, 2012, www.forbes.com/sites/georgebradt/2012/08/29/how-trizettos-ceo-changed-its-culture-by-changing-its-attitude/; E. Sealover, "TriZetto Corp. Hires New CEO After 10-Month Search," *Denver Business Journal,* March 18,2014, www.bizjournals.com/denver/news/2014/03/18/trizetto-corp-hires-new-ceo-after-10-month-search.html.

106. Copyright © 2006, Gareth R. Jones.

Chapter 11

1. S. Rosenbaum, "The Happiness Culture: Zappos Isn't a Company—It's a Mission," *Fast Company,* June 4, 2010, www.fastcompany.com/1657030/happiness-culture-zappos-isnt-company-its-mission.

2. "About the Book," deliveringhappiness.com, n.d., www.deliveringhappiness.com/about-us/about-2/.

3. J. Edwards, "Check Out the Insane Lengths Zappos Customer Service Reps Will Go to," *Business Insider,* January 9, 2012, www.businessinsider.com/zappos-customer-service-crm-2012-1.

4. "Zappos Family Core Values," zappos.com, n.d., about.zappos.com/our-unique-culture/zappos-core-values.

5. "Zappos Family Core Value #8," zappos.com, n.d., about.zappos.com/our-unique-culture/zappos-core-values/do-more-less.

6. J. McGregor, "Zappos Says Goodbye to Bosses," January, 4, 2014, www.washingtonpost.com/blogs/on-leadership/wp/2014/01/03/zappos-gets-rid-of-all-managers/.

7. "Holacracy," zapposinsights.com, n.d., www.zapposinsights.com/training/Holacracy.

8. J. McGregor, "Zappos Says Goodbye to Bosses."

9. "Holacracy Constitution in Plain English," holacracy.org, n.d., Holacracy.org/constitution.

10. Ibid.

11. McGregor, "Zappos Says Goodbye to Bosses."

12. W. G. Ouchi, "Markets, Bureaucracies, and Clans," *Administrative Science Quarterly* 25 (1980), 129–41.

13. J. Brustein, "How to Cope with E-mail Overload at Work," *Bloomberg Businessweek,* December 19, 2013, www.businessweek.com/articles/2013-12-19/asanas-justin-rosenstein-on-e-mail-overload.

14. D. Bates, "You've Got (More) Mail: The Average Office Worker Now Spends Over a Quarters of Their Day Dealing with Email," July 31, 2012, www.dailymail.co.uk/sciencetech/article-2181680/Youve-got-mail-The-average-office-worker-spend-half-hours-writing-emails.html.

15. C. Ericson, "5 Ways to Keep Email from Taking over Your Life," *LearnVest,* March 14, 2014, www.learnvest.com/2014/03/manage-email-tips/.

16. Ibid.

17. Ibid.

18. J. Duffy, "Get Organized: 11 Tips for Managing Email," PCMag.com, March 5, 2012, www.pcmag.com/article2/0,2817,2401081,00.asp.

19. S. Green, "8 Ways Not to Manage Your Email (and 5 and a Half Tactics That Work)," *Harvard Business Review,* April 11, 2014, blogs.hbr.org/2014/04/8-ways-not-to-manage-your-email-and-5-tactics-that-work/.

20. "Caterpillar Enterprise System Group: Lean: A Journey That Delivers Significant Results," caterpillar.com, n.d., reports.caterpillar.com/yir/segments_enterpriseResource_story2.html.

21. Ibid.

22. P. Lorange, M. Morton, and S. Ghoshal, *Strategic Control* (St. Paul, MN: West, 1986).

23. H. Koontz and R.W. Bradspies, "Managing through Feedforward Control," *Business Horizons,* June 1972, 25–36.

24. E.E. Lawler III and J.G. Rhode, *Information and Control in Organizations* (Pacific Palisades, CA: Goodyear, 1976).

25. C.W.L. Hill and G.R. Jones, *Strategic Management: An Integrated Approach,* 6th ed. (Boston: Houghton Mifflin, 2011).

26. E. Flamholtz, "Organizational Control Systems as a Management Tool," *California Management Review,* Winter 1979, 50–58.

27. W.G. Ouchi, "The Transmission of Control through Organizational Hierarchy," *Academy of Management Journal* 21 (1978), 173–92.

28. W.G. Ouchi, "The Relationship between Organizational Structure and Organizational Control," *Administrative Science Quarterly* 22 (1977), 95–113.

29. Ouchi, "Markets, Bureaucracies, and Clans."

30. W.H. Newman, *Constructive Control* (Englewood Cliffs, NJ: Prentice-Hall, 1975).

31. J.D. Thompson, *Organizations in Action* (New York: McGraw-Hill, 1967).

32. R.N. Anthony, *The Management Control Function* (Boston: Harvard Business School Press, 1988).

33. "PM Mobile Electric Power," peocscss .army.mil, April 23, 2014, www.peocscss .army.mil/PMMEP.html.

34. Ibid.

35. T. Clements, "Knowledge Is Power," Assistant Secretary of Defense for Operational Energy Plans and Programs, February 14, 2014, energy.defense.gov/ Blog/tabid/2569/Article/8056/knowledge- is-power.aspx.

36. Ibid.

37. Ibid.

38. D. Douglas and M. Fletcher, "Toyota Reaches $1.2 Billion Settlement to End Probe of Accelerator Problems," *The Washington Post,* March 19, 2014, www.washingtonpost.com/ business/economy/toyota-reaches- 12-billion-settlement-to-end-criminal- probe/2014/03/19/5738a3c4-af69- 11e3-9627-c65021d6d572_story.html.

39. Ouchi, "Markets, Bureaucracies, and Clans."

40. Hill and Jones, *Strategic Management.*

41. K. Gray and A. Koncz, "The Candi- date Skills/Qualities Employers Want," *National Association of College and Employers,* October 10, 2013, www .naceweb.org/about-us/press/skills- qualities-employers-want.aspx.

42. Ibid.

43. "Big Data: The Next Frontier for Inno- vation, Competition, and Productivity," McKinsey & Company, June 2011, www .mckinsey.com/~/media/mckinsey/ dotcom/insights and pubs/mgi/research/ technology and innovation/big data/ mgi_big_data_full_report.ashx.

44. Ibid.

45. R. Simons, "Strategic Orientation and Top Management Attention to Control Sys- tems," *Strategic Management Journal* 12 (1991), 49–62.

46. G. Schreyogg and H. Steinmann, "Strategic Control: A New Perspective," *Academy of Management Review* 12 (1987), 91–103.

47. B. Woolridge and S.W. Floyd, "The Strat- egy Process, Middle Management Involve- ment, and Organizational Performance," *Strategic Management Journal* 11 (1990), 231–41.

48. J.A. Alexander, "Adaptive Changes in Corporate Control Practices," *Academy of Management Journal* 34 (1991), 162–93.

49. Hill and Jones, *Strategic Management.*

50. G.H.B. Ross, "Revolution in Management Control," *Management Accounting* 72 (1992), 23–27.

51. P.F. Drucker, *The Practice of Management* (New York: Harper & Row, 1954).

52. S.J. Carroll and H.L. Tosi, *Management by Objectives: Applications and Research* (New York: Macmillan, 1973).

53. R. Rodgers and J.E. Hunter, "Impact of Management by Objectives on Organiza- tional Productivity," *Journal of Applied Psychology* 76 (1991), 322–26.

54. M.B. Gavin, S.G. Green, and G.T. Fairhurst, "Managerial Control— Strategies for Poor Performance over Time and the Impact on Subordinate Reactions," *Organizational Behavior and Human Decision Processes* 63 (1995), 207–21.

55. www.cypress.com, 2001, 2005, 2012.

56. B. Dumaine, "The Bureaucracy Busters," *Fortune,* June 17, 1991, 46.

57. D.S. Pugh, D.J. Hickson, C.R. Hinings, and C. Turner, "Dimensions of Organiza- tional Structure," *Administrative Science Quarterly* 13 (1968), 65–91.

58. "NWS Central Region Service Assess- ment: Joplin, Missouri, Tornado—May 22, 2011," U.S. Department of Commerce, July 2011, www.nws.noaa.gov/os/assess- ments/pdfs/Joplin_tornado.pdf.

59. "Service Assessments," National Weather Service, March 19, 2014, www.nws.noaa .gov/om/assessments/index.shtml.

60. "Service Assessments: May 2013 Okla- homa Tornadoes and Flash Flooding," U.S. Department of Commerce, March 2014, www.nws.noaa.gov/om/assessments/ pdfs/13Oklahoma_tornadoes.pdf.

61. P.M. Blau, *The Dynamics of Bureaucracy* (Chicago: University of Chicago Press, 1955).

62. J. McGregor, "The World's Most Innova- tive Companies," www.businessweek .com, May 4, 2007.

63. www.waltdisney.com, 2010, 2012.

64. "Disney's Captain America Rules the Box Office with Best April Opening of All Time," *Forbes,* April 9, 2014, www.forbes .com/sites/greatspeculations/2014/04/09/ disneys-captain-america-rules-the- box-office-with-best-april-opening- of-all-time/; K. Favaro, "How IKEA, Disney, and Berkshire Hathaway Succeed with Adjacencies," *Forbes,* March 31, 2014, www.forbes.com/sites/ boozandcompany/2014/03/31/how-ikea- disney-and-berkshire-hathaway-succeed- with-adjacencies/.

65. "Who We Are," netflix.com, n.d., jobs .netflix.com/who-we-are.html.

66. Ibid.

67. A. Shontell, "Sheryl Sandberg: 'The Most Important Document Ever to Come Out of the Valley,'" *Business Insider,* February 4, 2013, www.businessinsider.com/netflixs- management-and-culture-presentation- 2013-2.

68. Ibid.

69. P. McCord, "How Netflix Reinvented HR," *Harvard Business Review,* January–February 2014, hbr.org/2014/01/ how-netflix-reinvented-hr/ar/1.

70. Ibid.

71. Ibid.

72. Ibid.

73. Ibid.

74. Ibid.

75. "A Brief History of the Company That Revolutionized Watching of Movies and TV Shows," netflix.com, n.d., pr.netflix. com/WebClient/loginPageSalesNetWorks Action.do?contentGroupId=10477&cont entGroup=Company+Timeline.

76. Ouchi, "Markets, Bureaucracies, and Clans."

77. Ibid.

78. J. Herman, "The Latest Fitness Fat (That WE Really Like): Philanthrofits," *Cosmopolitan,* March 11, 2013, www .cosmopolitan.com/celebrity/news/ charity-fitness-apps.

79. n.d., charitymiles.org.

80. J. Pan, "Fitness App Lets Charities Cash in on Your Exercise Routine," *Mashable,* June 11, 2012, mashable.com/2012/06/11/ charity-miles-app/.

81. "Charity Miles," tumblr.com, n.d., charitymiles.tumblr.com/.

82. "FAQ—Commitment Contracts— Charities," stick.com, n.d., www.stickk .com/faq.php#charities.

83. "Worldwide," ups.com, n.d., www.ups .com/content/us/en/about/facts/worldwide .html.

84. This section draws heavily on K. Lewin, *Field Theory in Social Science* (New York: Harper & Row, 1951).

85. L. Chung-Ming and R.W. Woodman, "Understanding Organizational Change: A Schematic Perspective," *Academy of Management Journal* 38, no. 2 (1995), 537–55.

86. D. Miller, "Evolution and Revolution: A Quantum View of Structural Change in Organizations," *Journal of Manage- ment Studies* 19 (1982), 11–151; D. Miller, "Momentum and Revolution in Organizational Adaptation," *Acad- emy of Management Journal* 2 (1980), 591–614.

87. C.E. Lindblom, "The Science of Mud- dling Through," *Public Administration Review* 19 (1959), 79–88; P.C. Nystrom and W.H. Starbuck, "To Avoid Organiza- tional Crises, Unlearn," *Organizational Dynamics* 12 (1984), 53–65.

88. L. Brown, "Research Action: Organi- zational Feedback, Understanding, and Change," *Journal of Applied Behavioral Research* 8 (1972), 697–711; P.A. Clark, *Action Research and Organizational Change* (New York: Harper & Row, 1972); N. Margulies and A.P. Raia, eds., *Conceptual Foundations of Orga- nizational Development* (New York: McGraw-Hill, 1978).

89. W.L. French and C.H. Bell, *Organizational Development* (Englewood Cliffs, NJ: Prentice-Hall, 1990).

90. R. Shah, "Fixing How Clothes Fit You Can Reshape Online Retail Logistics," *Forbes,* April 11, 2014, www.forbes.com/sites/rawnshah/2014/04/11/fixing-how-clothes-fit-you-can-reshape-online-retail-logistics/2/.

91. M. Brohan, "Reducing the Rate of Returns," *Internet Retailer,* May 29, 2013, www.internetretailer.com/2013/05/29/reducing-rate-returns.

92. "Our Story," virtusize.com, n.d., www.virtusize.com/company.

93. Shah, "Fixing How Clothes Fit You Can Reshape Online Retail Logistics."

94. Ibid.

95. Ibid.

96. Ibid.

97. W.L. French, "A Checklist for Organizing and Implementing an OD Effort," in W.L. French, C.H. Bell, and R.A. Zawacki, eds., *Organizational Development and Transformation* (Homewood, IL: Irwin, 1994), 484–95.

Chapter 12

1. J.M. O'Brien, "100 Best Companies to Work For—A Perfect Season," *Fortune,* February 4, 2008, 64–66; "Four Seasons Employees Name Company to *Fortune* '100 Best Companies to Work For' List," www.fourseasons.com/about_us/press_release_280.html, February 22, 2008; "Four Seasons Hotels and Resort Named to *Fortune* List of the '100 Best Companies to Work For,'" http://press.fourseasons.com/news-releases/four-seasons-hotels-and-resorts-named-to-fortu . . . , February 24, 2010; "Four Seasons Hotels & Resorts—Best Companies to Work For 2012," *Fortune,* http://money.cnn.com/magazines/fortune/best-companies/2012/snapshots/85.html, April 23, 2012.; "Employer of Choice: Four Seasons Hotels and Resorts Named to FORTUNE List of the '100 Best Companies to Work For' for 17th Consecutive Year," employer-of-choice-four-seasons-hotels-and-resorts-named-to-fortune-list-of-the-100-best-companies-to-work-for-fo-17th-consecutive-year, April 23, 2014.; M. Moskowitz and R. Levering, "The 100 Best Companies to Work For," *Fortune,* February 3, 2014, 108–20.

2. "Four Seasons Employees Name Company to *Fortune* '100 Best Companies to Work For' List"; "Employer of Choice: Four Seasons Hotels and Resorts Named to FORTUNE List of the '100 Best Companies to Work For' for 17th Consecutive Year."

3. "Employer of Choice: Four Seasons Hotels and Resorts Named to FORTUNE List of the '100 Best Companies to Work For' for 17th Consecutive Year."

4. O'Brien, "100 Best Companies to Work For—A Perfect Season"; "Four Seasons Hotels & Resorts—Best Companies to Work For 2012"; "Four Seasons Hotels—100 Best Companies to Work For 2014—Fortune, http://money.cnn.com/magazines/fortune/best-companies/2014/snapshots/91.html.

5. "Four Seasons Hotels and Resorts—About Us: Corporate Bios," http://www.fourseasons.com/about_us/corporate_bios/, February 24, 2010; "Four Seasons Hotels and Resorts Jobs / Hotel and Resort Career Search Site," http://jobs.fourseasons.com/Pages/Home.aspx, April 26, 2012.; "Four Seasons Holdings Inc.: Private Company Information," *Businessweek,* http://investing.businessweek.com/research/stocks/private/snapshot.asp?privcapId=357114, April 23, 2014.

6. O'Brien, "100 Best Companies to Work For—A Perfect Season."

7. O'Brien, "100 Best Companies to Work For—A Perfect Season"; "Creating the Four Seasons Difference," www.businessweek.com/print/innovate/content/jan2008/id20080122_671354.htm, February 22, 2008.

8. O'Brien, "100 Best Companies to Work For—A Perfect Season"; "Creating the Four Seasons Difference."

9. "Creating the Four Seasons Difference"; "Four Seasons Employees Name Company to *Fortune* '100 Best Companies to Work For' List."

10. M. Moskowitz, R. Levering, and C. Tkaczyk, "The List," *Fortune,* February 8, 2010, 75–88.

11. O'Brien, "100 Best Companies to Work For—A Perfect Season."

12. "Creating the Four Seasons Difference."

13. "Employer of Choice: Four Seasons Hotels and Resorts Named to FORTUNE List of the '100 Best Companies to Work For' for 17th Consecutive Year."

14. O'Brien, "100 Best Companies to Work For—A Perfect Season."

15. O'Brien, "100 Best Companies to Work For—A Perfect Season."

16. O'Brien, "100 Best Companies to Work For—A Perfect Season."

17. O'Brien, "100 Best Companies to Work For—A Perfect Season."

18. O'Brien, "100 Best Companies to Work For—A Perfect Season."

19. O'Brien, "100 Best Companies to Work For—A Perfect Season"; "Creating the Four Seasons Difference"; "Four Seasons Employees Name Company to *Fortune* '100 Best Companies to Work For' List"; "Employer of Choice: Four Seasons Hotels and Resorts Named to FORTUNE List of the '100 Best Companies to Work For' for 17th Consecutive Year."

20. J.E. Butler, G.R. Ferris, and N.K. Napier, *Strategy and Human Resource Management* (Cincinnati: Southwestern Publishing, 1991); P.M. Wright and G.C. McMahan, "Theoretical Perspectives for Strategic Human Resource Management," *Journal of Management* 18 (1992), 295–320.

21. AlixPartners Professionals, "Fitzpatrick, David A.," http://www.alixpartners.com/en/Professionals/tabid/670/EmployeeBio/FitzpatrickDavidA/Id/1709/Default.aspx, April 23, 2014.

22. L. Clifford, "Why You Can Safely Ignore Six Sigma," *Fortune,* January 22, 2001, 140.

23. J.B. Quinn, P. Anderson, and S. Finkelstein, "Managing Professional Intellect: Making the Most of the Best," *Harvard Business Review,* March–April 1996, 71–80.

24. Quinn et al., "Managing Professional Intellect."

25. "Looking for Ideas in Shared Workspaces. Established Companies Hope Interaction with Others Will Spark Collaboration," *The Wall Street Journal* (http://www.zappos.com/streetwear), March 20, 2012, http://about.zappos.com/press-center/media-coverage/looking-ideas-shared-workspaces-est. . ., April 23, 2012.

26. D. Garnick, "CEO Takes a Walk on the Whimsical Side," *Boston Herald,* Wednesday, May 20, 2009, http://about.zappos.com/press-center/media-coverage/ceo-takes-walk-whimsical-side, February 22, 2010; C. Palmeri, "Zappos Retails Its Culture," *BusinessWeek,* December 30, 2009, http://www.businessweek.com/print/magazine/content/10_02/b4162057120453.htm, February 22, 2010; "On a Scale of 1 to 10, How Weird Are You?" *The New York Times,* January 10, 2010, http://www.nytimes.com/2010/01/10/business/10corner.html?pagewanted=print, February 22, 2010; M. Chafkin, "Get Happy," *Inc.,* May 2009, 66–73; "Keeper of the Flame," *The Economist,* April 18, 2009, 75; M. Rich, "Why Is This Man Smiling," *The New York Times,* April 8, 2011.

27. 100 Best Companies to Work For 2010: Zappos.com—AMZN—from FORTUNE, "15. Zappos.com," http://money.cnn.com/magazines/fortune/bestcompanies/2010/snapshots/15.html, February 22, 2010; "Zappos.com, Best Companies to Work For 2012," *Fortune,* http://money.cnn.com/magazines/fortune/best-companies/2012/snapshots/11.html, April 23, 2012.; Moskowitz and Levering, "The 100 Best Companies to Work For." Fortune, February 3, 2014, pp. 108-120.

28. R. Wauters, "Amazon Closes Zappos Deal, Ends Up Paying $1.2 Billion," *TechCrunch,* November 2, 2009, http://techcrunch.com/2009/11/02/amazon-closes-zappos-deal-ends-up-paying-1-2-billion/, February 22, 2010.

29. J. McGregor, "Zappo's Secret: It's an Open Book," *BusinessWeek,* March 23 & 30, 2009, 62; "About.zappos.com,"

Tony Hsieh—CEO, http://about.zappos
.com/meet-our-monkeys/tony-hsieh-ceo,
February 22, 2010; Chafkin, "Get Happy."

30. Chafkin, "Get Happy"; "Keeper of the
Flame."

31. "In The Beginning—Let There Be
Shoes," about.zappos.com, http://
about.zappos.com/zappos-story/in-the-
beginning-let-there-be-shoes, February 22,
2010; Looking Ahead—Let There Be
Anything and Everything," about
.zappos.com, http://about.zappos.com/
zappos-story/looking-ahead-let-there-be-
anything-and-everything, February 22,
2010; J.B. Darin, "Curing Customer
Service," *Fortune,* May 20, 2009, http://
about.zappos.com/press-center/media-
coverage/curing-customer-service,
February 22, 2010.

32. Chafkin, "Get Happy"; "Keeper of the
Flame."

33. "Zappos Core Values," about.zappos.
com, http://about.zappos.com/our-unique-
culture/zappos-core-values, February
22, 2010; "Zappos Family Core Values,"
about.zappos.com, http://about.zappos.
com/our-unique-culture/zappos-core-
values, April 23, 2012.

34. "From Upstart to $1 Billion Behemoth,
Zappos Marks 10 Years," *Las Vegas Sun,*
June 16, 2009, http://about.zappos.com/
press-center/media-coverage/upstart-1-
billion-behemoth-zappos- . . . , February
22, 2010; Chafkin, "Get Happy"; "Keeper
of the Flame."

35. Chafkin, "'Get Happy"; "Keeper of the
Flame."

36. Chafkin, "Get Happy."

37. C.D. Fisher, L.F. Schoenfeldt, and J.B.
Shaw, *Human Resource Management*
(Boston: Houghton Mifflin, 1990).

38. Wright and McMahan, "Theoretical
Perspectives."

39. L. Baird and I. Meshoulam, "Managing
Two Fits for Strategic Human Resource
Management," *Academy of Management
Review* 14, 116–28; J. Milliman, M. Von
Glinow, and M. Nathan, "Organizational
Life Cycles and Strategic International
Human Resource Management in Mul-
tinational Companies: Implications for
Congruence Theory," *Academy of Man-
agement Review* 16 (1991), 318–39; R.S.
Schuler and S.E. Jackson, "Linking Com-
petitive Strategies with Human Resource
Management Practices," *Academy of
Management Executive* 1 (1987), 207–19;
P.M. Wright and S.A. Snell, "Toward
an Integrative View of Strategic Human
Resource Management," *Human Resource
Management Review* 1 (1991), 203–225.

40. "Who's in Charge Here? No One,"
The Observer, April 27, 2003 (http://
observer.guardian.co.uk/business/
story/0,6903,944138,00.html); "Ricardo
Semler, CEO, Semco SA," cnn.com, June
29, 2004 (http://cnn.worldnews.printthis.
clickability.com/pt/cpt&title=cnn.com);

D. Kirkpatrick, "The Future of Work: An
'Apprentice' Style Office?" *Fortune,* April
14, 2004 (www.fortune.com/fortune/
subs/print/0,15935,611068,00.html); A.
Strutt and R. Van Der Beek, "Report from
HR2004," www.mce.be/hr2004/reportd2.
htm, July 2, 2004; R. Semler, "Seven-Day
Weekend Returns Power to Employees,"
workopolis.com, May 26, 2004 (http://
globeandmail.workopolis.com/servlet/
content/qprinter/20040526/cabooks26);
"SEMCO," http://semco.locaweb.com.br/
ingles, May 31, 2006; "Ricardo Semler,
Semco SA: What Are You Reading?" cnn.
com, May 31, 2006. (www.cnn.com/2004/
BUSINESS/06/29/semler.profile/index.
html); "About the Semco Group, *SEMCO,*
http://www.semco.com.br/en/content.
asp?content=1&contentID=610., April
24, 2012.

41. "Group Companies: Semco Capital Goods
Division," *SEMCO,* http://www.semco
.com.br/en/content.asp?content=7&
contentID=611, April 24, 2012; "Group
Companies: Pitney Bowes Semco,"
SEMCO, http://www.semco.com.br/en/
content.asp?content=7&contentID=612,
April 24, 2012.

42. R. Semler, *The Seven-Day Weekend:
Changing the Way Work Works* (New
York: Penguin, 2003); "SEMCO";
Semco Partners, http://semco.com.br/en/,
April 23, 2014.

43. Semler, *The Seven-Day Weekend;*
"SEMCO"; G. Hamel, *The Future of
Management* (Cambridge, MA: Harvard
Business Press, 2007).

44. A. Strutt, "Interview with Ricardo Semler," *Management Centre Europe,* April
2004 (www.mce.be/knowledge/392/35).

45. Semler, *The Seven-Day Weekend.*

46. Semler, *The Seven-Day Weekend.*

47. R. Semler, "How We Went *Digital* without
a *Strategy,*" *Harvard Business Review* 78,
no. 5 (September–October 2000), 51–56.

48. Semler, *The Seven-Day Weekend.*

49. Equal Employment Opportunity Commission, "Uniform Guidelines on Employee
Selection Procedures," *Federal Register*
43 (1978), 38290–315.

50. R. Stogdill II, R. Mitchell, K. Thurston,
and C. Del Valle, "Why AIDS Policy
Must Be a Special Policy," *BusinessWeek,*
February 1, 1993, 53–54.

51. J.M. George, "AIDS/AIDS-Related
Complex," in L. Peters, B. Greer, and S.
Youngblood, eds., *The Blackwell Ency-
clopedic Dictionary of Human Resource
Management* (Oxford, England: Black-
well Publishers, 1997).

52. George, "AIDS/AIDS-Related Complex."

53. George, "AIDS/AIDS-Related Complex";
Stogdill et al., "Why AIDS Policy Must
Be a Special Policy"; K. Holland, "Out
of Retirement and into Uncertainty," *The
New York Times,* May 27, 2007, BU17.

54. S.L. Rynes, "Recruitment, Job Choice,
and Post-Hire Consequences: A Call for

New Research Directions," in M.D. Dunnette and L.M. Hough, eds., *Handbook of
Industrial and Organizational Psychology,* vol. 2 (Palo Alto, CA: Consulting
Psychologists Press, 1991), 399–444.

55. "Kelly Services—Background," http://
www.kellyservices.com/web/global/
services/en/pages/background.html,
April 24, 2012.

56. R.L. Sullivan, "Lawyers a la Carte,"
Forbes, September 11, 1995, 44.

57. E. Porter, "Send Jobs to India? U.S. Companies Say It's Not Always Best," *The
New York Times,* April 28, 2004, A1, A7.

58. D. Wessel, "The Future of Jobs: New
Ones Arise; Wage Gap Widens," *The Wall
Street Journal,* April 2, 2004, A1, A5;
"Relocating the Back Office," *The Econo-
mist,* December 13, 2003, 67–69.

59. The Conference Board, "Offshoring Evolving at a Rapid Pace, Report Duke University
and The Conference Board," August 3,
2009, http://www.conference-board.org/
utilities/pressPrinterFriendly.cfm?press_
ID=3709, February 24, 2010; S. Minter,
"Offshoring by U.S. Companies Doubles,"
Industry Week, August 19, 2009, http://
www.industryweek.com/PrintArticle.aspx?
ArticleID=19772&SectionID=3, February
24, 2010; AFP, "Offshoring by U.S. Companies Surges: Survey," August 3, 2009,
http://www.google.com/hostednews/afp/
article/ALeqM5iDaq1D2KZU16YfbKrM
PdborD7. . ., February 24, 2010; V. Wad-
hwa, "The Global Innovation Migration,"
BusinessWeek, November 9, 2009, http://
www.businessweek.com/print/technology/
content/nov2009/tc2009119_331698.htm,
February 24, 2010; T. Heijmen, A.Y. Lewin,
S. Manning, N. Perm-Ajchariyawong, and
J.W. Russell, "Offshoring Research the
C-Suite," 2007–2008 ORN Survey Report,
The Conference Board, in collaboration
with Duke University Offshoring Research
Network.

60. The Conference Board, "Offshoring
Evolving at a Rapid Pace"; Minter, "Offshoring by U.S. Companies Doubles";
AFP, "Offshoring by U.S. Companies
Surges"; V. Wadhwa, "The Global Innovation Migration"; Heijmen et al., "Offshoring Research the C-Suite."

61. V. Wadhwa, "The Global Innovation
Migration."

62. The Conference Board, "Offshoring
Evolving at a Rapid Pace."

63. The Conference Board, "Offshoring
Evolvingat a Rapid Pace"; Minter, "Off-
shoring by U.S. Companies Doubles";
AFP, "Offshoring by U.S. Companies
Surges"; Heijmen et al., "Offshoring
Research the C-Suite."

64. "Outsourcing: A Passage Out of India,"
Bloomberg Businessweek, March 19–25,
2012.

65. BRASSCOM – Brazilian Association
of Information Technology and Communication Companies, http://www.

brasscomglobalitforum.com/index.php, April 24, 2014.

66. "Outsourcing: A Passage Out of India"; "IBM Research—Brazil," http://www. research.ibm.com/brazil/, April 25, 2012.

67. "Outsourcing: A Passage Out of India."

68. "Outsourcing: A Passage Out of India."

69. KPO Services, "'Knowledge Process Outsourcing—Copal Amba," http://www .copalamba.com/about-us; "Copal Amba," Wikipedia, the free encyclopedia, http:// en.wikipedia.org/wiki/Copal_Amba.

70. KPO Services, "Knowledge Process Outsourcing."

71. "Outsourcing: A Passage Out of India"; "Senior Management—Copal Partners," http://www.copalpartners.com/Senior%20 Management, April 25, 2012.

72. "Outsourcing: A Passage Out of India."

73. "Outsourcing: A Passage Out of India."

74. "Outsourcing: A Passage Out of India."

75. R.J. Harvey, "Job Analysis," in Dunnette and Hough, *Handbook of Industrial and Organizational Psychology,* 71–163.

76. E.L. Levine, *Everything You Always Wanted to Know about Job Analysis: A Job Analysis Primer* (Tampa, FL: Mariner Publishing, 1983).

77. R.L. Mathis and J.H. Jackson, *Human Resource Management,* 7th ed. (Minneapolis: West, 1994).

78. E.J. McCormick, P.R. Jeannerette, and R.C. Mecham, *Position Analysis Questionnaire* (West Lafayette, IN: Occupational Research Center, Department of Psychological Sciences, Purdue University, 1969).

79. Fisher et al., *Human Resource Management;* Mathis and Jackson, *Human Resource Management;* R.A. Noe, J.R. Hollenbeck, B. Gerhart, and P.M. Wright, *Human Resource Management: Gaining a Competitive Advantage* (Burr Ridge, IL: Irwin, 1994).

80. Fisher et al., *Human Resource Management;* E.J. McCormick, *Job Analysis: Methods and Applications* (New York: American Management Association, 1979); E.J. McCormick and P.R. Jeannerette, "The Position Analysis Questionnaire," in S. Gael, ed., *The Job Analysis Handbook for Business, Industry, and Government* (New York: Wiley, 1988); Noe et al., *Human Resource Management.*

81. Rynes, "Recruitment, Job Choice, and Post-Hire Consequences."

82. R. Sharpe, "The Life of the Party? Can Jeff Taylor Keep the Good Times Rolling at Monster.com?" *BusinessWeek,* June 4, 2001 (*BusinessWeek* Archives); D.H. Freedman, "The Monster Dilemma," *Inc.,* May 2007, 77–78; P. Korkki, "So Easy to Apply, So Hard to Be Noticed," *The New York Times,* July 1, 2007, BU16.

83. Jobline International, "Resume Vacancy Posting, Employment Resources, Job Searches," http://www.jobline.net, February 25, 2010.

84. www.jobline.org, Jobline press releases, May 8, 2001, accessed June 20, 2001.

85. J. Spolsky, "There Is a Better Way to Find and Hire the Very Best Employees," *Inc.,* May 2007, 81–82; "About the Company," www.fogcreek.com, March 5, 2008; "Fog Creek Software," www.fogcreek .com, March 5, 2008; Fog Creek Software, "About the Company," http:// fogcreek.com/About.html, February 25, 2010.; "About Us—Fog Creek Software," http://www.fogcreek.com/about/, April 24, 2014.

86. Spolsky, "Better Way to Find and Hire"; "Fog Creek Software"; "Careers and Internships—Fog Creek Software," http:// www.fogcreek.com/careers/, April 24, 2014.

87. Spolsky, "Better Way to Find and Hire"; "Fog Creek Software."

88. Spolsky, "Better Way to Find and Hire"; "Fog Creek Software"; "Intern in Software Development—Fog Creek Software," http://www.fogcreek.com/jobs/ summerintern.

89. Spolsky, "Better Way to Find and Hire"; "Intern in Software Development."

90. Spolsky, "Better Way to Find and Hire."

91. Spolsky, "Better Way to Find and Hire"; "Fog Creek Software."

92. Spolsky, "Better Way to Find and Hire"; "About the Company"; "Fog Creek Software."

93. Spolsky, "Better Way to Find and Hire."

94. S.L. Premack and J.P. Wanous, "A Meta-Analysis of Realistic Job Preview Experiments," *Journal of Applied Psychology* 70 (1985), 706–19; J.P. Wanous, "Realistic Job Previews: Can a Procedure to Reduce Turnover also Influence the Relationship between Abilities and Performance?" *Personnel Psychology* 31 (1978), 249–58; J.P. Wanous, *Organizational Entry: Recruitment, Selection, and Socialization of Newcomers* (Reading, MA: Addison-Wesley, 1980).

95. R.M. Guion, "Personnel Assessment, Selection, and Placement," in Dunnette and Hough, *Handbook of Industrial and Organizational Psychology,* 327–97.

96. T. Joyner, "Job Background Checks Surge," *Houston Chronicle,* May 2, 2005, D6.

97. Joyner, "Job Background Checks Surge"; "ADP News Releases: Employer Services: ADP Hiring Index Reveals Background Checks Performed More Than Tripled since 1997," *Automatic Data Processing, Inc.,* June 3, 2006 (www.investquest.com/iq/a/aud/ne/news/ adp042505background.htm); "Employee Benefits Administration," *ADP,* http:// www.adp.com/, April 25, 2012.

98. "Background Checks and Employment Screening from ADP," http://www.adp-es.co.uk/employment-screening/? printpreview=1, April 25, 2012.

99. "ADP News Releases."

100. Noe et al., *Human Resource Management;* J.A. Wheeler and J.A. Gier, "Reliability and Validity of the Situational Interview for a Sales Position," *Journal of Applied Psychology* 2 (1987), 484–87.

101. Noe et al., *Human Resource Management.*

102. J. Flint, "Can You Tell Applesauce from Pickles?" *Forbes,* October 9, 1995, 106–8.

103. Flint, "Can You Tell Applesauce from Pickles?"

104. "Wanted: Middle Managers, Audition Required," *The Wall Street Journal,* December 28, 1995, A1.

105. I.L. Goldstein, "Training in Work Organizations," in Dunnette and Hough, *Handbook of Industrial and Organizational Psychology,* 507–619.

106. "Disney Workplaces: Training & Development," *The Walt Disney Company,* 2010 Corporate Citizenship Report, http://corporate.disney.go.com/citizenship2010/disneyworkplaces/overview/ trainingandde . . . , April 25, 2012.

107. N. Banerjee, "For Mary Kay Sales Reps in Russia, Hottest Shade Is the Color of Money," *The Wall Street Journal,* August 30, 1995, A8.

108. T.D. Allen, L.T. Eby, M.L. Poteet, E. Lentz, and L. Lima, "Career Benefits Associated with Mentoring for Protégés: A Meta-Analysis," *Journal of Applied Psychology* 89, no. 1 (2004), 127–36.

109. M. Khidekel, "The Misery of Mentoring Millennials," *Bloomberg Businessweek,* http://www.businessweek.com/printer/ articles/102262-the-misery-of-mentoring-millennials, April 24, 2014.

110. P. Garfinkel, "Putting a Formal Stamp on Mentoring," *The New York Times,* January 18, 2004, BU10.

111. Garfinkel, "Putting a Formal Stamp on Mentoring."

112. Allen et al., "Career Benefits Associated with Mentoring"; L. Levin, "Lesson Learned: Know Your Limits. Get Outside Help Sooner Rather Than Later," *BusinessWeek Online,* July 5, 2004 (www.businessweek.com); "Family, Inc.," *BusinessWeek Online,* November 10, 2003 (www.businessweek.com); J. Salamon, "A Year with a Mentor. Now Comes the Test," *The New York Times,* September 30, 2003, B1, B5; E. White, "Making Mentorships Work," *The Wall Street Journal,* October 23, 2007, B11.

113. Garfinkel, "Putting a Formal Stamp on Mentoring."

114. J.A. Byrne, "Virtual B-Schools," *BusinessWeek,* October 23, 1995, 64–68; "Michigan Executive Education Locations around the Globe," http://exceed .bus.umich.edu/InternationalFacilities/ default.aspx, February 25, 2010.

115. "Top Distance Learning & Online MBA Programs," *Businessweek,* http:// www.businessweek.com/bschools/ rankings/distance_mba_profiles, April 24, 2014.

116. Fisher et al., *Human Resource Management.*

117. Fisher et al., *Human Resource Management;* G.P. Latham and K.N. Wexley, *Increasing Productivity through Performance Appraisal* (Reading, MA: Addison-Wesley, 1982).

118. T.A. DeCotiis, "An Analysis of the External Validity and Applied Relevance of Three Rating Formats," *Organizational Behavior and Human Performance* 19 (1977), 247–66; Fisher et al., *Human Resource Management.*

119. L. Kwoh, "Rank and Yank," *The Wall Street Journal,* January 31, 2012: B6.

120. Kwoh, "Rank and Yank."

121. J.S. Lublin, "It's Shape-Up Time for Performance Reviews," *The Wall Street Journal,* October 3, 1994, B1, B2.

122. J.S. Lublin, "Turning the Tables: Underlings Evaluate Bosses," *The Wall Street Journal,* October 4, 1994, B1, B14; S. Shellenbarger, "Reviews from Peers Instruct—and Sting," *The Wall Street Journal,* October 4, 1994, B1, B4.

123. C. Borman and D.W. Bracken, "360 Degree Appraisals," in C.L. Cooper and C. Argyris, eds., *The Concise Blackwell Encyclopedia of Management* (Oxford, England: Blackwell Publishers, 1998), 17; D.W. Bracken, "Straight Talk about Multi-Rater Feedback," *Training and Development* 48 (1994), 44–51; M.R. Edwards, W.C. Borman, and J.R. Sproul, "Solving the Double Bind in Performance Appraisal: A Saga of Solves, Sloths, and Eagles," *Business Horizons* 85 (1985), 59–68.

124. M.A. Peiperl, "Getting 360 Degree Feedback Right," *Harvard Business Review,* January 2001, 142–47.

125. A. Harrington, "Workers of the World, Rate Your Boss!" *Fortune,* September 18, 2000, 340, 342; www.ImproveNow.com, June 2001.

126. Lublin, "It's Shape-Up Time for Performance Reviews."

127. S.E. Moss and J.I. Sanchez, "Are Your Employees Avoiding You? Managerial Strategies for Closing the Feedback Gap," *Academy of Management Executive* 18, no. 1 (2004), 32–46.

128. J. Flynn and F. Nayeri, "Continental Divide over Executive Pay," *BusinessWeek,* July 3, 1995, 40–41.

129. J.A. Byrne, "How High Can CEO Pay Go?" *BusinessWeek,* April 22, 1996, 100–106.

130. A. Borrus, "A Battle Royal against Regal Paychecks," *BusinessWeek,* February 24, 2003, 127; "Too Many Turkeys," *The Economist,* November 26, 2005, 75–76; G. Morgenson, "How to Slow Runaway Executive Pay," *The New York Times,* October 23, 2005, 1, 4; S. Greenhouse, *The Big Squeeze: Tough Times for the American Worker* (New York: Alfred A. Knopf, 2008); "Trends in CEO Pay," *AFL-CIO,* http://www.aflcio.org/Corporate-Watch/CEO-Pay-and-the-99/Trends-in-CEO-Pay, April 26, 2012.

131. "Executive Pay," *BusinessWeek,* April 19, 2004, 106–110.

132. "Home Depot Chief's Pay in 2007 Could Reach $8.9m," *The New York Times,* Bloomberg News, January 25, 2007, C7; E. Carr, "The Stockpot," *The Economist, A Special Report on Executive Pay,* January 20, 2007, 6–10; E. Porter, "More Than Ever, It Pays to Be the Top Executive," *The New York Times,* May 25, 2007, A1, C7.

133. K. Garber, "What Is (and Isn't) in the Healthcare Bill," *U.S. News & World Report,* March 22, 2010, http://www.usnews.com/articles/news/politics/2010/02/22/what-is-and-isnt-in-the-healthca . . ., March 29, 2010; S. Condon, "Health Care Bill Signed by Obama," Political Hotsheet—CBS News, http://www.cbsnews.com/8301-503544_162-20000981-503544.html; T.S. Bernard, "For Consumers, Clarity on Health Care Changes," *The New York Times,* March 21, 2010, http://www.nytimes.com/2010/03/22/your-money/health-insurance/22consumer.html?sq=h. . .; CBSNews.com, "Health Care Reform Bill Summary: A Look At What's in the Bill," March 23, 2009, http://www.cbsnews.com/8301-503544_162-20000846-503544.html; Reuters, "Factbox: Details of final healthcare bill", March 21, 2010, http://www.reuters.com/article/idUSTRE62K11V20100321.

134. J. Wieczner, "Your Company Wants to Make You Healthy," "Pros and Cons of Company Wellness Program Incentives," WSJ.com, http://online.wsj.com/news/articles/SB10001424127887323393304578360252284151378, April 24, 2014.

135. S. Shellenbarger, "Amid Gay Marriage Debate, Companies Offer More Benefits to Same-Sex Couples," *The Wall Street Journal,* March 18, 2004, D1.

136. S. Premack and J.E. Hunter, "Individual Unionization Decisions," *Psychological Bulletin* 103 (1988), 223–34.

137. M.B. Regan, "Shattering the AFL-CIO's Glass Ceiling," *BusinessWeek,* November 13, 1995, 46; S. Greenhouse, "The Hard Work of Reviving Labor," *The New York Times,* September 16, 2009, B1, B7.

138. S. Greenhouse, "Survey Finds Deep Shift in the Makeup of Unions," *The New York Times,* November 11, 2009, B5; "Union Members—2011," Union Members Summary, January 27, 2012, http://www.bls.gov/news.release/union2.nr0.htm; "Union Members Summary, Economic New Release," http://www.bls.gov/news.release/union2.nr0.htm.

139. www.aflcio.org, June 2001; "About Us," AFL-CIO, http://www.aflcio.org/aboutus; S. Greenhouse, "Most U.S. Union Members Are Working for the Government, New Data Shows," *The New York Times,* January 23, 2010, http://www.nytimes.com/2010/01/23/business/23labor.html?pagewanted=print; "About the AFL-CIO," http://www.aflcio.org/About; About the AFL-CIO, http://www.aflcio.org/About.

140. Greenhouse, "Most U.S. Union Members Are Working for the Government"; "Union Members—2011," Union Members Summary, January 27, 2012, http://www.bls.gov/news.release/union2.nr0.htm; Union Members Summary, Economic New Release, http://www.bls.gov/news.release/union2.nr0.htm.

141. Greenhouse, "Survey Finds Deep Shift in the Makeup of Unions"; "Union Members—2011," Union Members Summary, January 27, 2012, http://www.bls.gov/news.release/union2.nr0.htm; Union Members Summary, Economic New Release, http://www.bls.gov/news.release/union2.nr0.htm.

142. Greenhouse, "Most U.S. Union Members Are Working for the Government."

143. G.P. Zachary, "Some Unions Step Up Organizing Campaigns and Get New Members," *The Wall Street Journal,* September 1, 1995, A1, A2; "Union Members Summary, Economic New Release," http://www.bls.gov/news.release/union2.nr0.htm, April 24, 2014.

144. Regan, "Shattering the AFL-CIO's Glass Ceiling"; www.aflcio.org, June 2001; R.S. Dunham, "Big Labor: So Out It's Off the Radar Screen," *BusinessWeek,* March 26, 2001 (*BusinessWeek* Archives); "Chavez-Thompson to Retire as Executive Vice President," *AFL-CIO Weblog,* http://blog.aflcio.org/2007/09/13/chavez-thompson-to-retire-as-executive-vice-president/print/, March 6, 2008.

145. "Secretary of Labor Elaine L. Chao," U.S. Department of Labor—Office of the Secretary of Labor Elaine L. Chao (OSEC), www.dol.gov/_sec/welcome.htm, March 6, 2008; S. Greenhouse, "Departing Secretary of Labor Fends Off Critics," *The New York Times,* January 10, 2009, http://www.nytimes.com/2009/01/10/washington/10chao.html?_r=1&pagewanted=print, February 25, 2010; "Biography," http://www.elainechao.com/index.php/biography/Print.html, April 27, 2012.

146. "The Honorable Elaine L. Chao, United States Secretary of Labor," www.dol.gov/dol/sec/public/aboutosec/chao.htm, June 25, 2001.

147. Greenhouse, "Survey Finds Deep Shift in the Makeup of Unions"; "Union Members—2011," news release, Bureau of Labor Statistics (BLS), U.S. Department of Labor, January 27, 2012, www.bls.gov/news.release/pdf/union2.pdf, April 27, 2012.; "'Table 1. Union Affiliation of Employed Wage and Salary Workers by Selected Characteristics, Economic News Release," http://www.bls.gov/news.release/union2.t01.htm, April 24, 2014.

Chapter 13

1. J. Schlosser and J. Sung, "The 100 Best Companies to Work For," *Fortune,* January 8, 2001, 148-68; R. Levering, M. Moskowitz, and S. Adams,"The 100 Best Companies to Work For," *Fortune* 149, no. 1 (2004), 56-78; "*Fortune* 100 Best Companies to Work For 2006, CNNMoney.com, June 5, 2006 (www.money.cnn.com/magazines/fortune/bestcompanies/snapshots/1181.html; "Awards," *SAS,* http://www.sas.com/awards/index.html, April 1, 2008; R. Levering and M. Moskowitz, "100 Best Companies to Work For: The Rankings," *Fortune,* February 4, 2008, 75–94; "100 Best Companies to Work For 2012 : Full List," *Fortune,* http://money.cnn.com/magazines/fortune/best-companies/2012/full_list/, April 30, 2012.; "Inside Story at SAS Institute Inc.—Great Rated!" http://us.greatrated.com/sas, April 29, 2014.; "Best Companies to Work For 2014," *Fortune,* http://www.cnn.com/magazines/fortune/best-companies/, April 29, 2014.; "SAS Ranks No. 2 on 2014 Fortune List of Best Companies to Work For in the US," January 16, 2014, http://www.sas.com/en_us/news/press-releases/2014/january/great-workplace-US-Fortune-2014.html, April 29, 2014.; "SAF—100 Best Companies to Work For 2014," *Fortune,* http://money.cnn.com/magazines/fortune/best-companies/2014/snapshots/2.html?iid=BC14_sp_list, April 29, 2014.

2. E.P. Dalesio, "Quiet Giant Ready to Raise Its Profits," *Houston Chronicle,* May 6, 2001, 4D; Levering et al., "The 100 Best Companies to Work For"; J. Goodnight, "Welcome to SAS," www.sas.com/corporate/index.html, August 26, 2003; "SAS Press Center: SAS Corporate Statistics," www.sas.com/bin/pfp.pl?=fi, April 18, 2006; "SAS Continues Annual Revenue Growth Streak," www.sas.com/news/prelease/031003/newsl.html, August 28, 2003; R. Levering and M. Moskowitz, "100 Best Companies to Work For: The Rankings"; L. Buchanan, "No Doubt about It," *Inc.,* September 2011, 104–110; 'SAS Institute—Best Companies to Work For 2012," *Fortune,* http://money.cnn.com/magazines/fortune/best-companies/2012/snapshots/3.html, April 30, 2012.; "SAS Surpasses $3 Billion in 2013 Revenue, Growing 5.2% Over 2012 Results," January 23, 2014, http://www.sas.com/en_us/news/press-release/2014/january/2013-financials.html, April 29, 2014.; "SAS Overview and Annual Report – 2013," http://www.sas.com/content/dam/SAS/en_us/doc/other1/2013-annual-report.pdf, April 29, 2014.

3. "About SAS," SAS, http://www.sas.com/corporate/overview/index.html, March 1, 2010; "Corporate Statistics," SAS, Updated February 2010, http://www.sas.com/presscenter/bgndr_statistics.html,

March 1, 2010.; "About SAS," SAS, http://www.sas.com/en_us/company-information.html, April 29, 2014.; M. Crowley, "How SAS Became the World's Best Place to Work," http://www.fastcompany.com/3004953/how-sas-became-worlds-best-place-work, April 29, 2014.

4. J. Pfeffer, "SAS Institute: A Different Approach to Incentives and People Management Practices in the Software Industry," (January 1998), *Harvard Business School* Case HR-6.

5. "Saluting the Global Awards Recipients of Arthur Andersen's Best Practices Awards 2000," www.fortune.com, September 6, 2000; N. Stein, "Winning the War to Keep Top Talent," www.fortune.com, September 6, 2000.

6. S. Lahr, "At a Software Powerhouse, the Good Life Is Under Siege," *The New York Times,* 22 November 2009, BU1, BU6; "SAS Overview and Annual Report—2013," http://www.sas.com/content/dam/SAS/en_us/doc/other1/2013-annual-report.pdf, April 29, 2014.

7. Lahr, "At a Software Powerhouse, the Good Life Is Under Siege."

8. J. Pfeffer, "SAS Institute: A Different Approach to Incentives and People Management Practices in the Software Industry," January 1998, *Harvard Business School* Case HR-6; D.A. Kaplan, "The Best Company to Work For," *FORTUNE,* February 8, 2010, 57–64.

9. Kaplan, "The Best Company to Work For"; "SAS Ranks No. 2 on 2014 Fortune List of Best Companies to Work For in the US," January 16, 2014, http://www.sas.com/en_us/news/press-releases/2014/january/great-workplace-US-Fortune-2014.html, April 29, 2014.

10. Kaplan, "The Best Company to Work For"; Lahr, "At a Software Powerhouse, the Good Life Is Under Siege."

11. Kaplan, "The Best Company to Work For"; Lahr, "At a Software Powerhouse, the Good Life Is Under Siege"; "SAF—100 Best Companies to Work For 2014," *Fortune,* http://money.cnn.com/magazines/fortune/best-companies/2014/snapshots/2.html?iid=BC14_sp_list, April 29, 2014.

12. Kaplan,"The Best Company to Work For"; Lahr, "At a Software Powerhouse, the Good Life Is Under Siege"; "SAF—100 Best Companies to Work For 2014," *Fortune,* http://money.cnn.com/magazines/fortune/best-companies/2014/snapshots/2.html?iid=BC14_sp_list, April 29, 2014.

13. Kaplan, "The Best Company to Work For."

14. Ibid.

15. "Saluting the Global Awards Recipients of Arthur Andersen's Best Practices Awards 2000," www.fortune.com, September 6, 2000; N. Stein, "Winning the War to Keep Top Talent," www.fortune.com, September 6, 2000.

16. Kaplan, "The Best Company to Work For"; Lahr, "At a Software Powerhouse, the Good Life Is Under Siege"; J. Pfeffer, "SAS Institute: A Different Approach to Incentives and People Management Practices in the Software Industry," January 1998, *Harvard Business School* Case HR-6.

17. Kaplan, "The Best Company to Work For"; Lahr, "At a Software Powerhouse, the Good Life Is Under Siege."

18. Goodnight, "Welcome to SAS"; "By Solution," www.sas.com/success/solution.html, August 26, 2003; www.sas.com, June 8, 2006.

19. S.H. Wildstrom, "Do Your Homework, Microsoft," *BusinessWeek Online,* August 8, 2005 (www.businessweek.com/print/magazine/content/05-b3946033-mz006.htm?chan); www.sas.com, June 8, 2006.

20. Kaplan, "The Best Company to Work For." by David A. Kaplan, *FORTUNE,* February 8, 2010, pp. 57–64.

21. R. Kanfer, "Motivation Theory and Industrial and Organizational Psychology," in M.D. Dunnette and L.M. Hough, eds., *Handbook of Industrial and Organizational Psychology,* 2nd ed., vol. 1 (Palo Alto, CA: Consulting Psychologists Press, 1990), 75–170.

22. G.P. Latham and M.H. Budworth, "The Study of Work Motivation in the 20th Century," in L.L. Koppes, ed., *Historical Perspectives in Industrial and Organizational Psychology* (Hillsdale, NJ: Laurence Erlbaum, 2006).

23. S. Clark, "Finding Daring Jobs for Bored Bankers," *Bloomberg Businessweek,* June 6–12, 2011.

24. Clark, "Finding Daring Jobs for Bored Bankers"; S. Clark, "Ex-Banker Wants You to Trade Wall Street 'Misery' for Mongolia," *Bloomberg,* May 26, 2011, http://www.bloomberg.com/news/print/2011-05-26/ex-banker-wants-you-to-trade-wall-stree . . . , May 1, 2012; S. Clark, "Finding Adventurous Jobs for Bored Bankers," *BusinessWeek,* June 2, 2011, http://www.businessweek.com/print/magazine/content/11_24/b4232053145331.htm, May 1, 2012.; "Escape the City—Do Something Different," http://www.escapethecity.org/, May 1, 2014.

25. Team Esc, "How to Use Escape the City," November 24, 2011, http://blog.escapethecity.org/categories/how-to-use-escape-the-city/, May 1, 2012.

26. Clark, "Finding Daring Jobs for Bored Bankers."

27. Clark, "Finding Daring Jobs for Bored Bankers"; "The Team—Escape the City," http://escapethecity.org/pages/team, May 1, 2012.

28. Clark, "Finding Daring Jobs for Bored Bankers."

29. Clark, "Finding Daring Jobs for Bored Bankers."

30. "Harry Minter," LinkedIn, http://www.linkedin.com/pub/harry-minter/11/a10/505, May 1, 2014.

31. N. Nicholson, "How to Motivate Your Problem People," *Harvard Business Review,* January 2003, 57–65.

32. A.M. Grant, "Does Intrinsic Motivation Fuel the Prosocial Fire? Motivational Synergy in Predicting Persistence, Performance, and Productivity," *Journal of Applied Psychology* 93, no. 1 (2008), 48–58.

33. Grant, "Does Intrinsic Motivation Fuel the Prosocial Fire?"; C.D. Batson, "Prosocial Motivation: Is It Ever Truly Altruistic?" in L. Berkowitz, ed., *Advances in Experimental Social Psychology,* vol. 20 (New York: Academic Press, 1987), 65–122.

34. Grant, "Does Intrinsic Motivation Fuel the Prosocial Fire?"; Batson, "Prosocial Motivation: Is It Ever Truly Altruistic?"

35 J.P. Campbell and R.D. Pritchard, "Motivation Theory in Industrial and Organizational Psychology," in M.D. Dunnette, ed., *Handbook of Industrial and Organizational Psychology* (Chicago: Rand McNally, 1976), 63–130; T.R. Mitchell, "Expectancy Value Models in Organizational Psychology," in N.T. Feather, ed., *Expectations and Actions: Expectancy Value Models in Psychology* (Hillsdale, NJ: Erlbaum, 1982), 293–312; V.H. Vroom, *Work and Motivation* (New York: Wiley, 1964).

36. N. Shope Griffin, "Personalize Your Management Development," *Harvard Business Review* 8, no. 10 (2003), 113–119.

37. T.A. Stewart, "Just Think: No Permission Needed," *Fortune,* January 8, 2001 (www.fortune.com, June 26, 2001).

38. M. Copeland, "Best Buy's Selling Machine," *Business 2.0,* July 2004, 91–102; L. Heller, "Best Buy Still Turning on the Fun," *DSN Retailing Today* 43, no. 13 (July 5, 2004), 3; S. Pounds, "Big-Box Retailers Cash In on South Florida Demand for Home Computer Repair," *Knight Ridder Tribune Business News,* July 5, 2004 (gateway.proquest .com); J. Bloom, "Best Buy Reaps the Rewards of Risking Marketing Failure," *Advertising Age* 75, no. 25 (June 21, 2004), 16; L. Heller, "Discount Turns Up the Volume: PC Comeback, iPod Popularity Add Edge," *DSN Retailing Today* 43, no. 13 (July 5, 2004), 45; www.bestbuy.com, June 8, 2006.

39. T.J. Maurer, E.M. Weiss, and F.G. Barbeite, "A Model of Involvement in Work-Related Learning and Development Activity: The Effects of Individual, Situational, Motivational, and Age Variables," *Journal of Applied Psychology* 88, no. 4 (2003), 707–24.

40. J. Kaufman, "How Cambodians Came to Control California Doughnuts," *The Wall Street Journal,* February 22, 1995, A1, A8; H. Lee, "We Eat LA— Why There Are No Dunkin' Donuts in Los Angeles," December 2002, http://we-eat-la.com/post/267302770/why-there-are-no-dunkin-donuts-in-los-angeles, May 1, 2012.

41. "Learn about Us"; The Container Store, "Welcome from Kip Tindell, Chairman & CEO," http://standfor.containerstore.com, March 3, 2010.; "The Container Store—Corporate Governance—Management," http://investor.containerstore.com/corporate-governance/management/default.aspx, May 2, 2014.

42. M. Duff, "Top-Shelf Employees Keep Container Store on Track," www.looksmart.com, www.findarticles.com, March 8, 2004; M.K. Ammenheuser, "The Container Store Helps People Think inside the Box," www.icsc.org, May 2004; "The Container Store: Store Location," www.containerstore.com/find/index.jhtml, June 5, 2006; "Store Locations," *The Container Store,* www.containerstore.com/find/index.jhtml, April 1, 2008; "The Container Store—What We Stand For— Our Story," http://standfor.containerstore.com/our-story/, March 3, 2010; "CEO Maxine Clark, of Build-a-Bear, Traded in Her Kid-Filled Existence for a Day in the Orderly Aisles of the Container Store, Doing the 'Closet Dance,'" *Fortune,* February 8, 2010, 68–72; "Store Locator," *The Container Store,* http://www.containerstore.com/locations/index.htm, May 3, 2012.; "The Container Store Group, Inc. Announces Fourth Quarter and Full Fiscal 2013 Financial Results," April 28, 2014, http://investor.containerstore.com/press-releases/press-release-details/2014/The-Container-Store-Group-Inc-Announces-Fourth-Quarter-and-Full-Fiscal-2013-Financial-Results/default.aspx, May 2, 2014.

43. "Learn about Us," www.containerstore.com, June 26, 2001.

44. "Learn about Us," www.containerstore.com, June 26, 2001.

45. J. Schlosser and J. Sung, "The 100 Best Companies to Work For," *Fortune,* January 8, 2001, 148–168; "Fortune 100 Best Companies to Work For 2006," cnn.com, June 5, 2006 (http://money.cnn.com/magazines/fortune/bestcompanies/snapshots/359.html); "Learn about Us"; "A Career at The Container Store," *The Container Store,* http://www.containerstore.com/careers/index.html, May 3, 2012.; "The Container Store Organizes Stakeholders to Talk Conscious Capitalism in New Purpose-Focused Marketing Campaign," January 16, 2014, http://investor.containerstore.com/press-releases/press-release-details/2014/The-Container-Store-Organizes-Stakeholders-to-Talk-Conscious-Capitalism-in-New-Purpose-Focused-Marketing-Campaign/default.aspx, May 2, 2014.

46. "The Container Store," www.careerbuilder.com, July 13, 2004; "Tom Takes Re-imagineto PBS," Case Studies, www.tompeters.com, March 15, 2004; "2004 Best Companies to Work For," www.fortune.com, July 12, 2004; "*Fortune* 100 Best Companies to Work For 2006"; Levering and Moskowitz, "100 Best Companies to Work For: The Rankings"; Moskowitz, Levering, and Tkacyzk, "The List"; "100 Best Companies to Work for 2012," *Fortune,* http://money.cnn.com/magazines/fortune/best-companies/2012/snapshots/22.html, May 3, 2012.; "The Container Store—100 Best Companies to Work For 2014," *Fortune,* http://money.cnn.com/magazines/fortune/best-companies/2014/snapshots/28.html, May 2, 2014.

47. "The Container Store—What We Stand For."

48. D. Roth, "My Job at The Container Store," *Fortune,* January 10, 2000 (www.fortune.com, June 26, 2001); "*Fortune* 2004: 100 Best Companies to Work For," www.containerstore.com/careers/FortunePR_2004.jhtml?message=/repository/messages/fortuneCareer.jhtml, January 12, 2004; Levering, Moskowitz, and Adams, "The 100 Best Companies to Work For"; www.containerstore.com/careers/FortunePR_2004.jhtml?message=/repository/messages/fortuneCareer.jhtml, January 12, 2004.; "The Container Store—100 Best Companies to Work For 2014," *Fortune,* http://money.cnn.com/magazines/fortune/best-companies/2014/snapshots/28.html, May 2, 2014.

49. "The Container Store—100 Best Companies to Work For 2014," *Fortune,* http://money.cnn.com/magazines/fortune/best-companies/2014/snapshots/28.html, May 2, 2014.

50. Roth, "My Job at The Container Store."

51. "Learn about Us," www.containerstore.com, June 26, 2001.

52. R. Yu, "Some Texas Firms Start Wellness Programs to Encourage Healthier Workers," *Knight Ridder Tribune Business News,* July 7, 2004 (gateway.proquest.com); Levering et al., "The 100 Best Companies to Work For."

53. Roth, "My Job at The Container Store"; "The Foundation Is Organization," *The Container Store,* June 5, 2006 (www.containerstore.com/careers/foundation.html).

54. C.J. Loomis, "The Big Surprise Is Enterprise," *Fortune,* July 14, 2006, http://cnnmoney.printthis.clickability.com/pt/cpt?action=cpt&title=Fortune%3A+The+big. . ., March 31, 2008.

55. "Overview," *Enterprise Rent-A-Car Careers—Overview,* http://www.erac.com/recruit/about_enterprise.asp?navID=overview, March 27, 2008; "Enterprise Rent-A-Car Looks to Hire Student-Athletes, Partners with Career Athletes," April 25, 2012, http://www.enterpriseholdings.com/press-room/enterprise-rent-a-car-looks-to-hire-student-. . . , April 30, 2012.; EnterpriseHoldings, World Headquarters, Highlights, http://www.enterpriseholdings.com/, April 29, 2014.; Enterprise-Holdings – Alamo, Enterprise, National, Enterprise CarShare, http://www.enterpriseholdings.com/, April 29, 2014.

56. A. Fisher, "Who's Hiring New College Grads Now," *CNNMoney.com,* http://cnnmoney.printthis.clickability.com/pt/cpt?action=cpt&title=Who%27s+hiring+coll. . ., March 31, 2008; Francesca Di Meglio, "A Transcript for Soft Skills, Wisconsin Is Considering a Dual Transcript—One for Grades and One to Assess Critical Areas Such As Leadership and Communication," http://www.businessweek.com/print/bschools/content/feb2008/bs20080221_706663.htm, March 28, 2008; "Enterprise Rent-A-Car Career Site," http://www.erac.com/opportunities/default.aspx, May 1, 2012.

57. "Enterprise Ranked in Top 10 of Business Week's 'Customer Service Champs,'" February 22, 2007, *Enterprise Rent-A-Car Careers*—Enterprise in the News, http://www.erac.com/recruit/news_detail.asp?navID=frontpage&RID=211, March 27, 2008; L. Gerdes, "The Best Places to Launch a Career, *Business Week,* September 24, 2007, 49–60; P. Lehman, "A Clear Road to the Top," *Businessweek,* September 18, 2006, 72–82.

58. "Enterprise Ranked in Top 10"; L. Gerdes, "The Best Places to Launch a Career."

59. "It's Running a Business . . . Not Doing a Job," *Enterprise Rent-A-Car Careers—Opportunities,* http://www.erac.com/recruit/opportunities.asp, March 27, 2008.

60. Loomis, "The Big Surprise Is Enterprise"; Lehman, "A Clear Road to the Top."

61. Loomis, "The Big Surprise Is Enterprise"; Lehman, "A Clear Road to the Top."

62. Lehman, "A Clear Road to the Top."

63. Loomis, "The Big Surprise Is Enterprise."

64. Loomis, "The Big Surprise Is Enterprise"; Lehman, "A Clear Road to the Top."

65. A.H. Maslow, *Motivation and Personality* (New York: Harper & Row, 1954); Campbell and Pritchard, "Motivation Theory in Industrial and Organizational Psychology."

66. Kanfer, "Motivation Theory and Industrial and Organizational Psychology."

67. S. Ronen, "An Underlying Structure of Motivational Need Taxonomies: A Cross-Cultural Confirmation," in H.C. Triandis, M.D. Dunnette, and L.M. Hough, eds., *Handbook of Industrial and Organizational Psychology,* vol. 4 (Palo Alto, CA: Consulting Psychologists Press, 1994), 241–69.

68. N.J. Adler, *International Dimensions of Organizational Behavior,* 2nd ed. (Boston: P.W.S. Kent, 1991); G. Hofstede, "Motivation, Leadership, and Organization: Do American Theories Apply Abroad?" *Organizational Dynamics,* Summer 1980, 42–63.

69. C.P. Alderfer, "An Empirical Test of a New Theory of Human Needs," *Organizational Behavior and Human Performance* 4 (1969), 142–75; C.P. Alderfer, *Existence, Relatedness, and Growth: Human Needs in Organizational Settings* (New York: Free Press, 1972); Campbell and Pritchard, "Motivation Theory in Industrial and Organizational Psychology."

70. Kanfer, "Motivation Theory and Industrial and Organizational Psychology."

71. F. Herzberg, *Work and the Nature of Man* (Cleveland: World, 1966).

72. N. King, "Clarification and Evaluation of the Two-Factor Theory of Job Satisfaction," *Psychological Bulletin* 74 (1970), 18–31; E.A. Locke, "The Nature and Causes of Job Satisfaction," in Dunnette, *Handbook of Industrial and Organizational Psychology,* 1297–1349.

73. D.C. McClelland, *Human Motivation* (Glenview, IL: Scott, Foresman, 1985); D.C. McClelland, "How Motives, Skills, and Values Determine What People Do," *American Psychologist* 40 (1985), 812–25; D.C. McClelland, "Managing Motivation to Expand Human Freedom," *American Psychologist* 33 (1978), 201–10.

74. D.G. Winter, *The Power Motive* (New York: Free Press, 1973).

75. M.J. Stahl, "Achievement, Power, and Managerial Motivation: Selecting Managerial Talent with the Job Choice Exercise," *Personnel Psychology* 36 (1983), 775–89; D.C. McClelland and D.H. Burnham, "Power Is the Great Motivator," *Harvard Business Review* 54 (1976), 100–10.

76. R.J. House, W.D. Spangler, and J. Woycke, "Personality and Charisma in the U.S. Presidency: A Psychological Theory of Leader Effectiveness," *Administrative Science Quarterly* 36 (1991), 364–96.

77. G.H. Hines, "Achievement, Motivation, Occupations, and Labor Turnover in New Zealand," *Journal of Applied Psychology* 58 (1973), 313–17; P.S. Hundal, "A Study of Entrepreneurial Motivation: Comparison of Fast- and Slow-Progressing Small Scale Industrial Entrepreneurs in Punjab, India," *Journal of Applied Psychology* 55 (1971), 317–23.

78. R.A. Clay, "Green Is Good for You," *Monitor on Psychology,* April 2001, 40–42.

79. J.S. Adams, "Toward an Understanding of Inequity," *Journal of Abnormal and Social Psychology* 67 (1963), 422–36.

80. Adams, "Toward an Understanding of Inequity"; J. Greenberg, "Approaching Equity and Avoiding Inequity in Groups and Organizations," in J. Greenberg and R.L. Cohen, eds., *Equity and Justice in Social Behavior* (New York: Academic Press, 1982), 389–435; J. Greenberg, "Equity and Workplace Status: A Field Experiment," *Journal of Applied Psychology* 73 (1988), 606–13; R.T. Mowday, "Equity Theory Predictions of Behavior in Organizations," in R.M. Steers and L.W. Porter, eds., *Motivation and Work Behavior* (New York: McGraw-Hill, 1987), 89–110.

81. A. Goldwasser, "Inhuman Resources," Ecompany.com, March 2001, 154–55.

82. L.J. Skitka and F.J. Crosby, "Trends in the Social Psychological Study of Justice," *Personality and Social Psychology Review* 7 (April 2003), 282–85.

83. J.A. Colquitt, J. Greenbery, and C.P. Zapata-Phelan, "What Is Organizational Justice? A Historical Overview," in J. Greenberg and J.A. Colquitt (eds.), *Handbook of Organizational Justice* (Mahwah, NJ: Erlbaum, 2005), 12–45; J.A. Colquitt, "On the Dimensionality of Organizational Justice: A Construct Validation of a Measure," *Journal of Applied Psychology* 86 (March 2001), 386–400.

84. R. Folger and M.A. Konovsky, "Effects of Procedural and Distributive Justice on Reactions to Pay Raise Decisions," *Academy of Management Journal* 32 (1989), 115–30; J. Greenberg, "Organizational Justice: Yesterday, Today, and Tomorrow," *Journal of Management* 16 (1990), 339–432; M.L. Ambrose and A. Arnaud, "Are Procedural Justice and Distributive Justice Conceptually Distinct?" in J. Greenberg and J.A. Colquitt (eds.), *Handbook of Organizational Justice* (Mahwah, NJ: Erlbaum, 2005), 60–78.

85. M.L. Ambrose and M. Schminke, "Organization Structure as a Moderator of the Relationship Between Procedural Justice, Interactional Justice, Perceived Organizational Support, and Supervisory Trust," *Journal of Applied Psychology* 88 (February 2003), 295–305.

86. J.A. Colquitt, "On the Dimensionality of Organizational Justice: A Construct Validation of a Measure," *Journal of Applied Psychology* 86 (March 2001), 386–400.

87. Greenberg, "Organizational Justice: Yesterday, Today, and Tomorrow"; E.A. Lind and T. Tyler, *The Social Psychology of Procedural Justice* (New York: Plenum, 1988).

88. R.J. Bies, "The Predicament of Injustice: The Management of Moral Outrage," in L.L. Cummings and B.M. Staw (eds.), *Research in Organizational Behavior,* vol. 9 (Greenwich, CT: JAI Press, 1987), 289–319; R.J. Bies and D.L. Shapiro, "Interactional Fairness Judgments: The Influence of Casual Accounts," *Social Justice Research* 1 (1987), 199–218; J. Greenberg, "Looking Fair vs. Being Fair: Managing Impression of Organizational Justice," in B.M. Staw and L.L. Cummings (eds.), *Research in Organizational Behavior,* vol. 12 (Greenwich, CT: JAI Press, 1990), 111–57; T.R. Tyler and R. J. Bies, "Beyond Formal Procedures: The Interpersonal Context of Procedural Justice," in J. Carroll (ed.), *Advances in Applied Social Psychology: Business Settings* (Hillsdale, NJ: Erlbaum, 1989), 77–98; J.A. Colquitt, "On the Dimensionality of Organizational Justice: A Construct Validation of a Measure," *Journal of Applied Psychology* 86(March 2001), 386–400.

89. J.A. Colquitt, "On the Dimensionality of Organizational Justice: A Construct Validation of a Measures," *Journal of Applied Psychology* 86(March 2001), 386–400; J.A. Colquitt and J.C. Shaw, "How Should Organizational Justice Be Measured?" in J. Greenberg and J.A. Colquitt (eds.), *Handbook of Organizational Justice* (Mahwah, NJ: Erlbaum, 2005), 115–41.

90. E.A. Locke and G.P. Latham, *A Theory of Goal Setting and Task Performance* (Englewood Cliffs, NJ: Prentice-Hall, 1990).

91. Locke and Latham, *A Theory of Goal Setting and Task Performance;* J.J. Donovan and D.J. Radosevich, "The Moderating Role of Goal Commitment on the Goal Difficulty–Performance Relationship: A Meta-Analytic Review and Critical Analysis," *Journal of Applied Psychology* 83 (1998), 308–15; M.E. Tubbs, "Goal Setting: A Meta Analytic Examination of the Empirical Evidence," *Journal of Applied Psychology* 71 (1986), 474–83.

92. E.A. Locke, K.N. Shaw, L.M. Saari, and G.P. Latham, "Goal Setting and Task Performance: 1969–1980," *Psychological Bulletin* 90 (1981), 125–52.

93. P.C. Earley, T. Connolly, and G. Ekegren, "Goals, Strategy Development, and Task Performance: Some Limits on the Efficacy of Goal Setting," *Journal of Applied Psychology* 74 (1989), 24–33; R. Kanfer and P.L. Ackerman, "Motivation and Cognitive Abilities: An Integrative/Aptitude–Treatment Interaction Approach to Skill Acquisition," *Journal of Applied Psychology* 74 (1989), 657–90.

94. W.C. Hamner, "Reinforcement Theory and Contingency Management in Organizational Settings," in H. Tosi and W.C. Hamner, eds., *Organizational Behavior and Management: A Contingency Approach* (Chicago: St. Clair Press, 1974).

95. "Our Story / Stella & Dot," http://www.stelladot.com/about, May 2, 2012; "Our History / Stella & Dot," http://www.stelladot.com/about/our-history, May 2, 2012.; "Our Story—Stella & Dot," http://www.stelladot.com/about, May 2, 2014.; "Meet the Team—Stella & Dot," http://www.stelladot.com/about/meet-the-team, May 2, 2014.

96. B. Kowitt, "Full-Time Motivation for Part-Time Employees," *Fortune,* October 17, 2011, 58.

97. "Learn How to Be a Jewelry + Accessories Stylist/Stella & Dot," "Training Program," http://www.stelladot.com/stylist/training-program, May 2, 2012.

98. Kowitt, "Full-Time Motivation for Part-Time Employees."

99. Kowitt, "Full-Time Motivation for Part-Time Employees."

100. "How to Be a Jewelry + Accessories Stylist."

101. Kowitt, "Full-Time Motivation for Part-Time Employees."

102. B.F. Skinner, *Contingencies of Reinforcement* (New York: Appleton-Century-Crofts, 1969).

103. H.W. Weiss, "Learning Theory and Industrial and Organizational Psychology," in Dunnette and Hough, *Handbook of Industrial and Organizational Psychology,* 171–221.

104. Hamner, "Reinforcement Theory and Contingency Management."

105. F. Luthans and R. Kreitner, *Organizational Behavior Modification and Beyond* (Glenview, IL: Scott, Foresman, 1985); A.D. Stajkovic and F. Luthans, "A Meta-Analysis of the Effects of Organizational Behavior Modification on Task Performance, 1975–95," *Academy of Management Journal* 40 (1997), 1122–49.

106. A.D. Stajkovic and F. Luthans, "Behavioral Management and Task Performance in Organizations: Conceptual Background, Meta Analysis, and Test of Alternative Models," *Personnel Psychology* 56 (2003), 155–94.

107. Stajkovic and Luthans, "Behavioral Management and Task Performance"; Luthans and A.D. Stajkovic, "Reinforce for Performance: The Need to Go beyond Pay and Even Rewards," *Academy of Management Executive* 13, no. 2 (1999), 49–56; G. Billikopf Enciina and M.V. Norton, "Pay Method Affects Vineyard Pruner Performance,"www.cnr.berkeley.edu/ucce50/ag-labor/ 7research/7calag05.htm.

108. A. Bandura, *Principles of Behavior Modification* (New York: Holt, Rinehart and Winston, 1969); A. Bandura, *Social Learning Theory* (Englewood Cliffs, NJ: Prentice-Hall, 1977); T.R.V. Davis and F. Luthans, "A Social Learning Approach to Organizational Behavior," *Academy of Management Review* 5 (1980), 281–90.

109. A.P. Goldstein and M. Sorcher, *Changing Supervisor Behaviors* (New York: Pergamon Press, 1974); Luthans and Kreitner, *Organizational Behavior Modification and Beyond.*

110. Bandura, *Social Learning Theory;* Davis and Luthans, "A Social Learning Approach to Organizational Behavior"; Luthans and Kreitner, *Organizational Behavior Modification and Beyond.*

111. A. Bandura, "Self-Reinforcement: Theoretical and Methodological Considerations," *Behaviorism* 4 (1976), 135–55.

112. K.H. Hammonds, "Growth Search," *Fast Company,* April, 2003, 74–81.

113. B. Elgin, "Managing Google's Idea Factory," *BusinessWeek,* October 3, 2005, 88–90.

114. A. Bandura, *Self-Efficacy: The Exercise of Control* (New York: W.H. Freeman, 1997); J.B. Vancouver, K.M. More, and R.J. Yoder, "Self-Efficacy and Resource Allocation: Support for a Nonmonotonic, Discontinuous Model," *Journal of Applied Psychology* 93, no. 1 (2008), 35–47.

115. A. Bandura, "Self-Efficacy Mechanism in Human Agency," *American Psychologist* 37 (1982), 122–27; M.E. Gist and T.R. Mitchell, "Self-Efficacy: A Theoretical Analysis of Its Determinants and Malleability," *Academy of Management Review* 17 (1992), 183–211.

116. E.E. Lawler III, *Pay and Organization Development* (Reading, MA: Addison-Wesley, 1981).

117. P. Dvorak and S. Thurm, "Slump Prods Firms to Seek New Compact with Workers," *The Wall Street Journal,* October 19, 2009, A1, A18.

118. D. Mattioli, "Rewards for Extra Work Come Cheap in Lean Times," *The Wall Street Journal,* January 4, 2010, B7.

119. Mattioli, "Rewards for Extra Work Come Cheap"; http://www.rockwellcollins.com/, March 3, 2010.

120. Mattioli, "Rewards for Extra Work Come Cheap."

121. Mattioli, "Rewards for Extra Work Come Cheap."

122. Lawler, *Pay and Organization Development.*

123. Lawler, *Pay and Organization Development.*

124. J.F. Lincoln, *Incentive Management* (Cleveland: Lincoln Electric Company, 1951); R. Zager, "Managing Guaranteed Employment," *Harvard Business Review* 56 (1978), 103–15.

125. Lawler, *Pay and Organization Development.*

126. M. Gendron, "Gradient Named 'Small Business of Year,'" *Boston Herald,* May 11, 1994, 35; "Gradient—Environmental Consulting," http://www.gradientcorp.com/index.php, March 3, 2010.

127. W. Zeller, R.D. Hof, R. Brandt, S. Baker, and D. Greising, "Go-Go Goliaths," *BusinessWeek,* February 13, 1995, 64–70.

128. N. Byrnes, "A Steely Resolve" *Business-Week,* April 6, 2009, 54.

129. "Stock Option," *Encarta World English Dictionary,* June 28, 2001 (www.dictionary.msn.com); personal interview with Professor Bala Dharan, Jones Graduate School of Business, Rice University, June 28, 2001.

130. Personal interview with Professor Bala Dharan.

131. Personal interview with Professor Bala Dharan.

132. C.D. Fisher, L.F. Schoenfeldt, and J.B. Shaw, *Human Resource Management*

(Boston: Houghton Mifflin, 1990); B.E. Graham-Moore and T.L. Ross, *Productivity Gainsharing* (Englewood Cliffs, NJ: Prentice-Hall, 1983); A.J. Geare, "Productivity from Scanlon Type Plans," *Academy of Management Review* 1 (1976), 99–108.

133. K. Belson, "Japan's Net Generation," *BusinessWeek,* March 19, 2001 (*BusinessWeek* Archives, June 27, 2001).

134. K. Belson, "Taking a Hint from the Upstarts," *BusinessWeek,* March 19, 2001 (*BusinessWeek* Archives, June 27, 2001); "Going for the Gold," *BusinessWeek,* March 19, 2001 (*BusinessWeek* Archives, June 27, 2001); "What the Government Can Do to Promote a Flexible Workforce," *BusinessWeek,* March 19, 2001 (*BusinessWeek* Archives, June 27, 2001).

Chapter 14

1. I. Faletski, "Yes, You Can Make Money with Open Source," *Harvard Business Review,* http://blogs.hbr.org/2013/01/yes-you-can-make-money-with-op/, May 5, 2014; "The Open Source CEO: Jim Whitehurst," *TechCrunch,* http://techcrunch.com/2012/04/27/i-would-like-to-work-at-red-hat/, May 5, 2014.

2. "Great Leaders are Comfortable with Who They Are," Opensource.com, http://opensource.com/14/3/leadership-tips-red-hat-earn-respect, May 5, 2014.

3. Faletski, "Yes, You Can Make Money with Open Source."

4. Faletski, "Yes, You Can Make Money with Open Source"; "Red Hat——About Red Hat," http://www.redhat.com/about/, May 5, 2014; "Red Hat Inc—Form 10-K," EDGAR Online, http://files.shareholders.com/downloads/RHAT/3149726759x0x51193125-14157171/1087423/final.pdf, May 6, 2014.

5. "Red Hat Inc—Form 10-K," EDGAR Online, http://files.shareholders.com/downloads/RHAT/3149726759x0x51193125-14157171/1087423/final.pdf, May 6, 2014.

6. "James Whitehurst: Executive Profile & Biography," *Businessweek,* http://investing.businessweek.com/research/stocks/people/person.asp?personId=1474206&ticker=RHT, May 5, 2014; "Red Hat—Jim Whitehurst," http://www.red-hat.com/about/company/management/bios/management-team-jim-whitehurst-bio, May 5, 2014.

7. "James Whitehurst: Executive Profile & Biography."

8. J. Haden, "What's Your Mission?" *Inc.,* April 12, 2013; "Great Leaders Are Comfortable with Who They Are," Opensource.com, http://opensource.com/14/3/leadership-tips-red-hat-earn-respect, May 5, 2014; J. Bort, "Red Hat CEO: My Employees and I Cuss at Each Other," *Business Insider,* http://www.businessinsider.com/red-hat-ceo-cussing-at-employees-2013-9, May 5, 2014.

9. Haden, "What's Your Mission?"; "Great Leaders Are Comfortable with Who They Are"; Bort, "Red Hat CEO: My Employees and I Cuss at Each Other"; L.K. Ohnesorge, "Red Hat CEO Jim Whitehurst Doubles as a Cloud Computing Evangelist and Entrepreneur Advisor," http://upstart.bizjournals.com/entrepreneurs/hot-shots/2014/05/04/passion-drives-red-hat-jim-whitehurst.html?page=all, May 5, 2014.

10. Haden, "What's Your Mission?"; "Great Leaders Are Comfortable with Who They Are"; Bort, "Red Hat CEO: My Employees and I Cuss at Each Other."

11. Haden, "What's Your Mission?"; "Great Leaders Are Comfortable with Who They Are"; Bort, "Red Hat CEO: My Employees and I Cuss at Each Other"; P. High, "Red Hat CEO Jim Whitehurst Opens Up," *Forbes,* http://www.forbes.com/sites/peterhigh/2012/12/11/red-hat-ceo-jim-whitehurst-opens-up/, May 5, 2014.

12. "Red Hat CEO Jim Whitehurst to Deliver Keynote Address at the Cloud Factory," http://www.redhat.com/about/news/press-archive/2014/4/red-hat-ceo-jim-whitehurst-to-deliver-keynote-address-at-the-cloud-factory, May 5, 20104.

13. "Planet Earth's Premiere Enterprise Technology Conference," The Cloud Factory, http://thecloudfactory.io/story/, May 6, 2014.

14. "Red Hat CEO Jim Whitehurst Awarded William C. Friday Award," http://www.marketwatch.com/story/red-hat-ceo-jim-whitehurst-awarded-william-c-friday-award, May 5, 2014.

15. "Red Hat CEO Jim Whitehurst Awarded William C. Friday Award."

16. G. Yukl, *Leadership in Organizations,* 2nd ed. (New York: Academic Press, 1989); R.M. Stogdill, *Handbook of Leadership: A Survey of the Literature* (New York: Free Press, 1974).

17. W.D. Spangler, R.J. House, and R. Palrecha, "Personality and Leadership," in B. Schneider and D.B. Smith, eds., *Personality and Organizations* (Mahwah, NJ: Lawrence Erlbaum, 2004), 251–90.

18. Spangler, House, and Palrecha, "Personality and Leadership"; "Leaders vs. Managers: Leaders Master the Context of Their Mission, Managers Surrender to It," www.msue.msu.edu/msue/imp/modtd/visuals/tsld029.htm, July 28, 2004; "Leadership," Leadership Center at Washington State University; M. Maccoby, "Understanding the Difference between Management and Leadership," *Research Technology Management* 43, no. 1 (January–February2000), 57–59, www.maccoby.com/articles/UtDBMaL.html; P. Coutts, "Leadership vs. Management," www.telusplanet.net/public/pdcoutts/leadership/LdrVsMgnt.htm, October 1, 2000; S. Robbins, "The Difference between Managing and Leading," www.Entrepreneur.com/article/0,4621,304743,00.html, November 18, 2002; W. Bennis, "The Leadership Advantage," *Leader to Leader* 12 (Spring 1999), www.pfdf.org/leaderbooks/121/spring99/bennis/html.

19. Spangler et al., "Personality and Leadership"; "Leaders vs. Managers"; "Leadership"; Maccoby, "Understanding the Difference between Management and Leadership"; Coutts, "Leadership vs. Management"; Robbins, "The Difference between Managing and Leading"; Bennis, "The Leadership Advantage."

20. "Greenleaf: Center for Servant Leadership: History," *Greenleaf Center for Servant Leadership,* www.greenleaf.org/aboutus/history.html, April 7, 2008.

21. "What Is Servant Leadership?" *Greenleaf: Center for Servant Leadership,* http://www.greenleaf.org/whatissl/index.html, April 2, 2008.

22. "What Is Servant Leadership?"; Review by F. Hamilton of L. Spears and M. Lawrence, *Practicing Servant Leadership: Succeeding through Trust, Bravery, and Forgiveness* (San Francisco: Jossey-Bass, 2004), in *Academy of Management Review* 30 (October 2005), 875–87; R.R. Washington, "Empirical Relationships between Theories of Servant, Transformational, and Transactional Leadership," *Academy of Management,* Best Paper Proceedings, 2007, 1–6.

23. "Greenleaf: Center for Servant Leadership: History"; "What Is Servant Leadership?"; "Greenleaf: Center for Servant Leadership: Our Mission," *Greenleaf Center for Servant Leadership,* www.greenleaf.org/aboutus/mission.html, April 7, 2008.

24. B. Burlingham, "The Coolest Small Company in America," *Inc.,* January 2003, www.inc.com/magazine/20030101/25036_Printer_Friendly.html, April 7, 2008; A. Weinzweig, "Step into the Future," *Inc.,* February 2011: 85–91.

25. Burlingham, "The Coolest Small Company in America"; "Zingerman's Community of Businesses," *About Us,* www.zingermans.com/AboutUs.aspx, April 7, 2008; L. Buchanan, "In Praise of Selflessness," *Inc.,* May 2007, 33–35; Zingerman's Community of Businesses, http://www.zingermanscommunity.com, March 3, 2010; D. Walsh, "No secrets: Businesses find it pays to open books to employees," *Crain's Detroit Business,* January 28, 2010, http://www.crainsdetroit.com/article/20100117/FREE/301179994/no-secrets-businesses-fi. . ., May 17, 2012.; "Zingerman's Community," http://www.zingermanscommunity.com/about-us/, May 14, 2014.

26. Burlingham, "The Coolest Small Company in America"; "Zingerman's Community of Businesses"; Buchanan, "In Praise of Selflessness."

27. Buchanan, "In Praise of Selflessness."

28. Buchanan, "In Praise of Selflessness."

29. Burlingham, "The Coolest Small Company in America"; "In a Nutshell,"

food gatherers, www.foodgatherers.org/about.htm, April 7, 2008; Food Gatherers, "In a Nutshell," http://www.foodgatherers.org/about.htm, March 3, 2010; "About Us in a Nutshell," *Food Gatherers,* http://www.foodgatherers.org/?module=Page&sID=about-us, May 17, 2012; "About Us," *Food Gatherers,* http://foodgatherers.org/?module=Page&sID=about-us, May 14, 2014.

30. "In a Nutshell."

31. Buchanan, "In Praise of Selflessness."

32. R. Calori and B. Dufour, "Management European Style," *Academy of Management Executive* 9, no. 3 (1995), 61–70.

33. Calori and Dufour, "Management European Style."

34. H. Mintzberg, *Power in and around Organizations* (Englewood Cliffs, NJ: Prentice-Hall, 1983); J. Pfeffer, *Power in Organizations* (Marshfield, MA: Pitman, 1981).

35. R.P. French, Jr., and B. Raven, "The Bases of Social Power," in D. Cartwright and A.F. Zander, eds., *Group Dynamics* (Evanston, IL: Row, Peterson, 1960), 607–23.

36. C. Frey, "Nordstrom Salesman's Million-Dollar Secret Is in His Treasured Client List," *Seattle Post-Intelligencer,* Saturday, March 27, 2004, http://www.seattlepi.com/business/166571_retail27.html, March 5, 2010; "Macy's Herald Square, New York, NY: Retail Commission Sales Associate—Women's Shoes," http://jobview.monster.com/Macy's-Herald-Square-New-York-NY-Retail-Commission-Sale . . ., March 5, 2010.

37. R.L. Rose, "After Turning Around Giddings and Lewis, Fife Is Turned Out Himself," *The Wall Street Journal,* June 22, 1993, A1.

38. "Company Overview," *Liberty Media,* http://www.libertymedia.com/company-overview.aspx, May 17, 2012; "Management," *Liberty Media Corporation,* http://ir.libertymedia.com/management.cfm, May 17, 2012; "Gregory B. Maffei Profile," Forbes.com, http://people.forbes.com/profile/print/gregory-b-maffei/28822, May 17, 2012; "Liberty Media Corporation—Management," http://ir.libertymedia.com/management.cfm?sh_print=yes&, May 14, 2014.

39. "Company Overview"; "Management" *Liberty;* "Gregory B. Maffei Profile."

40. "Management"; "Gregory B. Maffei Profile."

41. A. Bryant, "Take Me On, You Might Get a Promotion," *The New York Times,* January 9, 2011, BU2.

42. "Management"; "Gregory B. Maffei Profile."

43. Bryant, "Take Me On."

44. Bryant, "Take Me On."

45. Bryant, "Take Me On."

46. Bryant, "Take Me On."

47. M. Loeb, "Jack Welch Lets Fly on Budgets, Bonuses, and Buddy Boards," *Fortune,* May 29, 1995, 146.

48. T.M. Burton, "Visionary's Reward: Combine 'Simple Ideas' and Some Failures; Result: Sweet Revenge," *The Wall Street Journal,* February 3, 1995, A1, A5.

49. L. Nakarmi, "A Flying Leap toward the 21st Century? Pressure from Competitors and Seoul May Transform the Chaebol," *BusinessWeek,* March 20, 1995, 78–80.

50. B.M. Bass, *Bass and Stogdill's Handbook of Leadership: Theory, Research, and Managerial Applications,* 3rd ed. (New York: Free Press, 1990); R.J. House and M.L. Baetz, "Leadership: Some Empirical Generalizations and New Research Directions," in B.M. Staw and L.L. Cummings, eds., *Research in Organizational Behavior,* vol. 1 (Greenwich, CT: JAI Press, 1979), 341–423; S. A. Kirpatrick and E.A. Locke, "Leadership: Do Traits Matter?" *Academy of Management Executive* 5, no. 2 (1991), 48–60; Yukl, *Leadership in Organizations;* G. Yukl and D.D. Van Fleet, "Theory and Research on Leadership in Organizations," in M.D. Dunnette and L.M. Hough, eds., *Handbook of Industrial and Organizational Psychology,* 2nd ed., vol. 3 (Palo Alto, CA: Consulting Psychologists Press, 1992), 147–97.

51. E.A. Fleishman, "Performance Assessment Based on an Empirically Derived Task Taxonomy," *Human Factors* 9 (1967), 349–66; E.A. Fleishman, "The Description of Supervisory Behavior," *Personnel Psychology* 37 (1953), 1–6; A.W. Halpin and B.J. Winer, "A Factorial Study of the Leader Behavior Descriptions," in R.M. Stogdill and A.I. Coons, eds., *Leader Behavior: Its Description and Measurement* (Columbus Bureau of Business Research, Ohio State University, 1957); D. Tscheulin, "Leader Behavior Measurement in German Industry," *Journal of Applied Psychology* 56 (1971), 28–31.

52. S. Greenhouse, "How Costco Became the Anti-Wal-Mart," *The New York Times,* July 17, 2005, BU1, BU8; "Directors," *Costco Wholesale, Investors Relations,* http://phx.corporate-ir.net/phoenix.zhtml?c=83830&p=irol-govBoard, April 8, 2008; "Company Profile," *Costco Wholesale, Investor Relations,* http://phx.corporate-ir.net/phoenix.zhtml?c=83830&p=irol-homeprofile, May 17, 2012.

53. "Corporate Governance," *Costco Wholesale, Investor Relations,* April 28, 2006, http://phx.corporate-ir.net/phoenix.zhtml?c=83830&p=irol-govhighlights; J. Wohl, "Costco CEO's Legacy Continues as He Steps Down," September 1, 2011, Business & Financial News, Breaking US & International News, *Reuters.com,* http://www.reuters.com/assets/print?aid=USTRE7805VW20110901, May 10, 2012.; A. Gonzalez, "Costco Cofounder Sinegal Honored with Top Retail Award," *The Seattle Times,* January 8, 2014, http://seattletimes.com/html/businesstechnology/2022616694_costcoawardxml.html, May 14, 2014; Costco—Biography," http://phx

corporate-ir.net/phoenix.zhtml?c=83830&p=irol-govBio&ID=202690, May 14, 2014; "Costco—Directors," http://phx.corporate-ir.net/phoenix.zhtml?c=8380&p=irol-govBoard, May 14, 2014.

54. Greenhouse, "How Costco Became the Anti-Wal-Mart;" M. Allison, "Costco's Colorful CEO, Cofounder Jim Sinegal to Retire," *The Seattle Times,* August 31, 2011, http://seattletimes.nwsource.com/html/businesstechnology/2016072309_costco01.html, May 10, 2012.

55. Greenhouse, "How Costco Became the Anti-Wal-Mart."

56. Greenhouse, "How Costco Became the Anti-Wal-Mart."

57. Greenhouse, "How Costco Became the Anti-Wal-Mart"; S. Clifford, "Because Who Knew a Big-Box Chain Could Have a Generous Soul," *Inc.,* April 2005, 88.

58. S. Holmes and W. Zellner, "Commentary: The Costco Way," *BusinessWeek Online,* April 12, 2004, www.businessweek.com/print/magazine/content/04_15/b3878084_mz021.htm? chan . . .; M. Herbst, "The Costco Challenge: An Alternative to Wal-Martization?" *LRA Online,* July 5, 2005, www.laborresearch.org/print.php?id=391.

59. Greenhouse, "How Costco Became the Anti-Wal-Mart."

60. Greenhouse, "How Costco Became the Anti-Wal-Mart"; "Company Profile," *Costco Wholesale, Investor Relations,* http://phx.corporate-ir.net/phoenix.zhtml?c=83830&p=irol-homeprofile, April 8, 2008; "Costco—Company Profile," http://phx.corporate-ir.net/phoenix.zhtml?c=83830&p=irol-homeprofile, March 5, 2010; "Company Profile," *Costco Wholesale, Investor Relations,* http://phx.corporate-ir.net/phoenix.zhtml?c=83830&p=irol-homeprofile, May 17, 2012; "Costco—News Release," Costco Wholesale Corporation Reports April Sales Results, http://phx.corporate-ir.net/phoenix.zhtml?c=83830&p=irol-newsArticle&ID=1928586&highlight=, May14, 2014.

61. A. Martinez and M. Allison, "Costco, Other Warehouse Clubs Holding Their Own during Recession," *The Seattle Times,* February 1, 2010, http://seattletimes.nwsource.com/cgi-bin/PrintStory.pl?document_id=2010922094&zsection . . ., March 3, 2010; S. Skidmore, "Wholesale Clubs' Profit Grows as Grocery Supermarkets Slide," *USA TODAY,* http://www.usatoday.com/cleanprint/?1267669249262, March 3, 2010.

62. Costco—Company Profile; "Company Profile," *Costco Wholesale, Investor Relations;* "Costco—News Release: Costco Wholesale Corporation Reports Second Quarter and Year-to-Date Operating Results for Fiscal 2014 and February Sales Results," http://phx.corporate-ir.net/phoenix.zhtml?c=83830&p=irol-newsArticle&ID=1906628&highlight=, May 14, 2014.

63. "Costco Wholesale Corporation Reports Second Quarter and Year-to-Date Operating Results Fiscal 2006 and February Sales Results," *Costco Wholesale, Investor Relations: News Release,* April 28, 2006, http://phx.corporate-ir.net/phoenix.zhtml?c=83830&p=irol-newsArticle&ID=824344&highlight=; "Costco Wholesale Corporation Reports March Sales Results and Plans for Membership Fee Increase," *Costco Wholesale, Investor Relations: News Release,* April 28, 2006, http://phx.corporate-ir.net/phoenix.zhtml?c=83830&p=irol-newsArticle&ID=839605&highlight=; "Wal-Mart Stores Post Higher January Sales," *BusinessWeek Online,* February 2, 2006, www.businessweek.com/print/investor/conent/feb2006/pi2006022_0732_pi004.htm.

64. Martinez and Allison, "Costco, Other Warehouse Clubs Holding Their Own"; M. Allison, "Costco's Colorful CEO, Co-Founder Jim Sinegal to Retire."

65. "Costco Class Action Discrimination Lawsuit: Women Sue Costco," http://genderclassactionagainstcostco.com/costco94.pl, March 3, 2010; M.C. Fisk and K. Gullo, "Costco Ignored Sex Bias Warnings, Employees Say," http://www.seattlepi.com/business/284317_costcobias08.html, March 3, 2010; "Costco Job-Bias Lawsuit Advances," *Los Angeles Times,* January 12, 2007, http://articles.latimes.com/2007/jan/12/business/fi-costco12, March 3, 2010.

66. A. Gonzalez, "Costco Settles Promotion Lawsuit for $8M, Vows Reforms," *The Seattle Times,* December 18, 2013, http://seattletimes.com/html/businesstechnology/2022479586_costcosettlementxml.html, May 14, 2014.

67. Gonzalez, "Costco Settles Promotion Lawsuit for $8M, Vows Reforms."

68. Gonzalez, "Costco Settles Promotion Lawsuit for $8M, Vows Reforms."

69. E.A. Fleishman and E.F. Harris, "Patterns of Leadership Behavior Related to Employee Grievances and Turnover," *Personnel Psychology* 15 (1962), 43–56.

70. R. Likert, *New Patterns of Management* (New York: McGraw-Hill, 1961); N.C. Morse and E. Reimer, "The Experimental Change of a Major Organizational Variable," *Journal of Abnormal and Social Psychology* 52 (1956), 120–29.

71. R.R. Blake and J.S. Mouton, *The New Managerial Grid* (Houston: Gulf, 1978).

72. P. Hersey and K. Blanchard, *Management of Organizational Behavior: Utilizing Human Resources* (Englewood Cliffs, NJ: Prentice-Hall, 1982).

73. F.E. Fiedler, *A Theory of Leadership Effectiveness* (New York: McGraw-Hill, 1967); F.E. Fiedler, "The Contingency Model and the Dynamics of the Leadership Process," in L. Berkowitz, ed., *Advances in Experimental Social Psychology* (New York: Academic Press, 1978).

74. J. Fierman, "Winning Ideas from Maverick Managers," *Fortune,* February 6, 1995, 66–80; "Laybourne, Geraldine, U.S. Media Executive," *Laybourne, Geraldine,* http://museum.tv/archives/etv/L/htmlL/laybournege/laybournege.htm, April 8, 2008.

75. M. Schuman, "Free to Be," *Forbes,* May 8, 1995, 78–80; "Profile—Herman Mashaba," *SAIE—Herman Mashaba,* www.entrepreneurship.co.za/page/herman_mashaba, April 8, 2008.

76. House and Baetz, "Leadership"; L.H. Peters, D.D. Hartke, and J.T. Pohlmann, "Fiedler's Contingency Theory of Leadership: An Application of the Meta-Analysis Procedures of Schmidt and Hunter," *Psychological Bulletin* 97 (1985), 274–85; C.A. Schriesheim, B.J. Tepper, and L.A. Tetrault, "Least Preferred Co-Worker Score, Situational Control, and Leadership Effectiveness: A Meta-Analysis of Contingency Model Performance Predictions," *Journal of Applied Psychology* 79 (1994), 561–73.

77. M.G. Evans, "The Effects of Supervisory Behavior on the Path–Goal Relationship," *Organizational Behavior and Human Performance* 5 (1970), 277–98; R.J. House, "A Path–Goal Theory of Leader Effectiveness," *Administrative Science Quarterly* 16 (1971), 321–38; J.C. Wofford and L.Z. Liska, "Path–Goal Theories of Leadership: A Meta-Analysis," *Journal of Management* 19 (1993), 857–76.

78. S. Kerr and J.M. Jermier, "Substitutes for Leadership: Their Meaning and Measurement," *Organizational Behavior and Human Performance* 22 (1978), 375–403; P.M. Podsakoff, B.P. Niehoff, S.B. MacKenzie, and M.L. Williams, "Do Substitutes for Leadership Really Substitute for Leadership? An Empirical Examination of Kerr and Jermier's Situational Leadership Model," *Organizational Behavior and Human Decision Processes* 54 (1993), 1–44.

79. Kerr and Jermier, "Substitutes for Leadership"; Podsakoff et al., "Do Substitutes for Leadership Really Substitute for Leadership?"

80. J. Reingold, "You Got Served," *Fortune,* October 1, 2007, 55–58; "News on Women," *News on Women: Sue Nokes SVP at T-Mobile,* http://newsonwomen.typepad.com/news_on_women/2007/09/sue-nokes-svp-a.html, April 8, 2008.

81. "Company Information," "T-Mobile Cell Phone Carrier Quick Facts," http://www.t-mobile/Company/CompanyInfo.aspx?tp=Abt_Tab_CompanyOverview, April 8, 2008; "T-Mobile Cell Phone Carrier Quick Facts," http://www.t-mobile.com/Company/CompanyInfo.aspx?tp=Abt_Tab_CompanyOverview, March 5, 2010; "T-Mobile Company Information / Quick Facts," http://www.t-mobile.com/Company/CompanyInfo.aspx?tp=Abt_Tab_CompanyOverview, May 17, 2012; T-Mobile Company Information – Quick Facts, http://www.t-mobile.com/Company/CompanyInfo.aspx?tp=Abt_Tab_CompanyOverview, May 15, 2014.

82. Reingold, "You Got Served."

83. Reingold, "You Got Served"; "Company Information," "Highest Customer Satisfaction & Wireless Call Quality—J.D. Power Awards," http://www.t-mobile.com/Company/CompanyInfo.aspx?tp=Abt_Tab_Awards, April 8, 2008.

84. Reingold, "You Got Served."

85. Reingold, "You Got Served."

86. B.M. Bass, *Leadership and Performance beyond Expectations* (New York: Free Press, 1985); Bass, *Bass and Stogdill's Handbook of Leadership;* Yukl and Van Fleet, "Theory and Research on Leadership."

87. Reingold, "You Got Served."

88. Reingold, "You Got Served."

89. Reingold, "You Got Served."

90. Reingold, "You Got Served."

91. Reingold, "You Got Served."

92. Reingold, "You Got Served."

93. J.A. Conger and R.N. Kanungo, "Behavioral Dimensions of Charismatic Leadership," in J.A. Conger, R.N. Kanungo, and Associates, *Charismatic Leadership* (San Francisco: Jossey-Bass, 1988).

94. Bass, *Leadership and Performance beyond Expectations;* Bass, *Bass and Stogdill's Handbook of Leadership;* Yukl and Van Fleet, "Theory and Research on Leadership;" Reingold, "You Got Served."

95. Bass, *Leadership and Performance beyond Expectations;* Bass, *Bass and Stogdill's Handbook of Leadership;* Yukl and Van Fleet, "Theory and Research on Leadership;" Reingold, "You Got Served."

96. Reingold, "You Got Served."

97. Bass, *Leadership and Performance beyond Expectations.*

98. Bass, *Bass and Stogdill's Handbook of Leadership;* B.M. Bass and B.J. Avolio, "Transformational Leadership: A Response to Critiques," in M.M. Chemers and R. Ayman, eds., *Leadership Theory and Research: Perspectives and Directions* (San Diego: Academic Press, 1993), 49–80; B.M. Bass, B.J. Avolio, and L. Goodheim, "Biography and the Assessment of Transformational Leadership at the World Class Level," *Journal of Management* 13 (1987), 7–20; J.J. Hater and B.M. Bass, "Supervisors' Evaluations and Subordinates' Perceptions of Transformational and Transactional Leadership," *Journal of Applied Psychology* 73 (1988), 695–702; R. Pillai, "Crisis and Emergence of Charismatic Leadership in Groups: An Experimental Investigation," *Journal of Applied Psychology* 26 (1996), 543–62; J. Seltzer and B.M. Bass, "Transformational Leadership: Beyond Initiation and Consideration," *Journal of Management* 16 (1990), 693–703; D.A. Waldman, B.M. Bass, and W.O. Einstein, "Effort, Performance, Transformational Leadership in Industrial and Military Service," *Journal of Occupation Psychology* 60 (1987), 1–10.

99. R. Pillai, C.A. Schriesheim, and E.S. Williams, "Fairness Perceptions and Trust as Mediators of Transformational and Transactional Leadership: A Two-Sample Study," *Journal of Management* 25 (1999), 897–933; "About Us," HP, http://www8.hp.com/us/en/hp-information/about-hp/index.html, May 14, 2012.

100. "50 Most Powerful Women—1. Indra Nooyi (1)—*Fortune*," http://money.cnn.com/galleries/2009/fortune/0909/gallery.most_powerful_ women.fortune/i . . ., March 5, 2010.

101. L. Tischler, "Where Are the Women?" *Fast Company,* February 2004, 52–60.

102. "2000 Catalyst Census of Women Corporate Officers and Top Earners of the *Fortune* 500," www.catalyst women.org, October 21, 2001; S. Wellington, M. Brumit Kropf, and P.R. Gerkovich, "What's Holding Women Back?" *Harvard Business Review,* June 2003, 18–19; D. Jones, "The Gender Factor," USA *Today.com,* December 30, 2003; "2002 Catalyst Census of Women Corporate Officers and Top Earners in the *Fortune* 500," www.catalystwomen.org, August 17, 2004; "2007 Catalyst Census of Women Corporate Officers and Top Earners of the *Fortune* 500," www.catalyst.org/knowledge/titles/title/php?page=cen_COTE_07, February 8, 2008; "No News Is Bad News: Women's Leadership Still Stalled in Corporate America," December 14, 2011, *Catalyst,* http://www.catalyst.org/press-release/199/no-news-is-bad-news-womens-leadership-still-sta. . ., April 5, 2012; Knowledge Center – Catalyst.org, Statistical Overview of Women in the Workplace, March 3, 2014, http://www.catalyst.org/knowledge/statistical-overview-women-workplace, April 1, 2014; "Knowledge Center—Catalyst.org, *Fortune* 500 Executive Officer Top Earner Positions Held by Women," http://www.catlyst.org/knowledge/women-executive-officer-top-earners-fortune-500-0, April 1, 2014.

103. A.H. Eagly and B.T. Johnson, "Gender and Leadership Style: A Meta-Analysis," *Psychological Bulletin* 108 (1990), 233–56.

104. Eagly and Johnson, "Gender and Leadership Style: A Meta-Analysis."

105. The Economist, "Workers Resent Scoldings from Female Bosses," *Houston Chronicle,* August 19, 2000, 1C.

106. The Economist, "Workers Resent Scoldings from Female Bosses."

107. The Economist, "Workers Resent Scoldings from Female Bosses."

108. The Economist, "Workers Resent Scoldings from Female Bosses."

109. A.H. Eagly, S.J. Karau, and M.G. Makhijani, "Gender and the Effectiveness of Leaders: A Meta-Analysis," *Psychological Bulletin* 117 (1995), 125–45.

110. Eagly, Karau, and Makhijani, "Gender and the Effectiveness of Leaders: A Meta-Analysis."

111. J.M. George and K. Bettenhausen, "Understanding Prosocial Behavior, Sales Performance, and Turnover: A Group-Level Analysis in a Service Context," *Journal of Applied Psychology* 75 (1990), 698–709.

112. T. Sy, S. Cote, and R. Saavedra, "The Contagious Leader: Impact of the Leader's Mood on the Mood of Group Members, Group Affective Tone, and Group Processes," *Journal of Applied Psychology* 90(2), (2005), 295–305.

113. J.M. George, "Emotions and Leadership: The Role of Emotional Intelligence," *Human Relations* 53 (2000), 1027–55.

114. George, "Emotions and Leadership."

115. J. Zhou and J.M. George, "Awakening Employee Creativity: The Role of Leader Emotional Intelligence," *The Leadership Quarterly* 14, no. 45 (August–October 2003), 545–68.

116. Zhou and George, "Awakening Employee Creativity."

117. Zhou and George, "Awakening Employee Creativity."

118. D. Fenn, "My Bad," *Inc.,* October 2007, 37–38; *Creative Display Solutions: About Us,* www.creativedisplaysolutions.com/pages/about/about.html, April 4, 2008; *Creative Display Solutions: About Us,* http://www.creativedisplaysolutions.com/pages/about/about.html, March 5, 2010; "Maureen Borzacchiello—Creative Display Solutions, Inc.," http://www.savorthesuccess.com/member/maureen-borzacchiello, May 15, 2014; "What We DoTrade Show Marketing Event Services," http://creativedisplaysolutions.com/what-we-do, May 15, 2014.

119. Fenn, "My Bad"; *Creative Display Solutions: About Us,* www.creativedisplaysolutions.com/pages/about/about.html, April 4, 2008.

120. Fenn, "My Bad."

121. Fenn, "My Bad."

122. Fenn, "My Bad."

123. Fenn, "My Bad."

124. Fenn, "My Bad."

125. Fenn, "My Bad"; C. Mason-Draffen, "Inside Stories," "Feeling Like a Million," *Creative Display Solutions: CDS News,* www.creativedisplaysolutions.com/pages/about/news6.html, April 4, 2008.

126. D. Sonnenberg, "Mother Load: How to Balance Career and Family," July 30, 2007, *Creative Display Solutions: CDS News,* www.creativedisplay solutions.com/pages/about/news8.html, April 4, 2008; C. Mason-Draffen, "Partnership at Work: Couples in Business Together Have Their Share of Sweet Rewards and Unique Challenges," February 13, 2007, *Creative Display Solutions, CDS News,* www.creativedisplaysolutions.com/pages/about/news7.html, April 4, 2008; "Client List," *Creative Display Solutions: About Us,* www.creativedisplaysolutions.com/pages/about/clients.html, April 8, 2008; Fenn, "My Bad;" "Client List," *Creative,* http://www.creativedisplaysolutions.com/pages/about/clients.html, March 5, 2010; "Creative Display Solutions—Who We Are," http://www.creativedisplaysolutions.com/who-we-are.shtml, May 17, 2012; "What We Do—Trade Show Marketing Event Services," http://creativedisplaysolutions.com/what-we-do, May 15, 2014.

127. Fenn, "My Bad."

Chapter 15

1. G. Hamel, *The Future of Management* (Boston, MA: Harvard Business School Press, 2007); "Our History," http://gore.com/en_xx/aboutus/timeline/index.html, May 20, 2014.

2. Hamel, *The Future of Management;* "Our History."

3. Hamel, *The Future of Management;* "Our History."

4. Hamel, *The Future of Management;* "Our History."

5. Hamel, *The Future of Management;* "Our History."

6. "Gore Culture," http://www.gore.com/en_xx/aboutus/culture/index.html, May 19, 2014.

7. Hamel, *The Future of Management;* "Our History."

8. R.E. Silverman, "Who's the Boss? There Isn't One," *The Wall Street Journal,* sec. Careers, June 20, 2012, B1, B8.

9. Hamel, *The Future of Management;* "Our History."

10. Hamel, *The Future of Management;* "Our History"; "Opportunities for Professionals at Gore," http://www.gore.com/en_xx/careers/professionals/index.html, May 20, 2014.

11. Silverman, "Who's the Boss? There Isn't One."

12. Silverman, "Who's the Boss? There Isn't One."

13. Hamel, *The Future of Management;* "Our History."

14. "Our History."

15. Hamel, *The Future of Management;* "Our History."

16. Hamel, *The Future of Management.*

17. "W.L. Gore & Associates Named a Top U.S. Workplace in 2014," http://www.gore.com/en_xx/news/FORTUNE-2014.html_May 19, 2014.

18. "Gore Recognized as One of the World's Best Multinational Workplaces by Great Place to Work," October 22, 2013, http://www.gore.com/en_xx/news/best-multinational-places-to-work-2013.html, May 19, 2014.

19. "Our History," http://gore.com/en_xx/aboutus/timeline/index.html, May 20, 2014.

20. "W.L. Gore & Associates Named a Top U.S. Workplace in 2014," http://www.gore.com/en_xx/news/FORTUNE-2014.html_May 19, 2014.

21. T.M. Mills, *The Sociology of Small Groups* (Englewood Cliffs, NJ: Prentice-Hall, 1967); M.E. Shaw, *Group Dynamics* (New York: McGraw-Hill, 1981).

22. R.S. Buday, "Reengineering One Firm's Product Development and Another's Service Delivery," *Planning Review,* March–April 1993, 14–19; J.M. Burcke, "Hallmark's Quest for Quality Is a Job Never Done," *Business Insurance,* April 26, 1993, 122; M. Hammer and J. Champy, *Reengineering the Corporation* (New York: HarperBusiness, 1993); T.A. Stewart, "The Search for the Organization of Tomorrow," *Fortune,* May 18, 1992, 92–98; "Hallmark Corporate Information/About Hallmark," http://corporate.hallmark.com/Company, March 15, 2010; "Hallmark Corporate Information / Hallmark Facts," http://corporate.hallmark.com/Company/Hallmark-Facts, May 24, 2012.

23. "Amazon.com Investor Relations: Officers & Directors," http://phx.corporate-ir.net/phoenix.zhtml?c=97664&p=irol-govManage, June 19, 2006; "Amazon.com Investor Relations: Press Release," http://phx.corporate-ir.net/phoenix.zhtml?c=97664&p=irol-newsArticle&ID=1102342&hi. . ., April 17, 2008; "Amazon.com Investor Relations: Officers & Directors," http://phx.corporate-ir.net/phoenix.zhtml?c=97664&p=irol-govmanage_pf, March 14, 2010; "Amazon.com Investor Relations: Officers & Directors," http://phx.corporate-ir.net/phoenix.zhtml?c=97664&p=irol.govmanage, May 24, 2012; "Amazon.com Investor Relations: Officers & Directors," http://phx.corporate-ir.net/phoenix.zhtml?c=97664&p=irol-govmanage_pf, May 21, 2014.

24. R.L. Brandt, "Birth of a Salesman," *The Wall Street Journal,* October 15, 2011, C1–2; "Jeff Bezos' 'Two Pizza Rule' for Productive Meetings," *Business Insider,* http://www.businessinsider.com/jeff-bezos-two-pizza-rule-for-productive-meetings-2013-10, May 21, 2014.

25. A. Deutschman, "Inside the Mind of Jeff Bezos," *Fast Company,* August 2004, 50–58.

26. Deutschman, "Inside the Mind of Jeff Bezos"; "Amazon.com Digital Media Technology," http://media-server.amazon.com/jobs/jobs.html, June 19, 2006; "Amazon.Com: Search Inside the Book," http://www.amazon.com/Search-Inside-Book-Books/b?node=10197021, May 21, 2014; "Amazon.com Help: About Gold Box Deals," http://www.amazon.com/gp/help/customer/display.html?nodeId=914590, May 21, 2014.

27. "Amazon.com: Kindle: Amazon's New Wireless Reading Device: Kindle Store," www.amazon.com/gp/product/B000F173MA/ref=amb_link_6369712_2?pf_rd_m=A. . ., April 17, 2008; "Amazon.com: Kindle Wireless Reading Device (6$$$" Display, U.S. Wireless): Kindle Store," http://www.amazon.com/Kindle-Wireless-Reading-Device-Display/dp/B00154JDAI, March 15, 2010; "Kindle Touch 3G: Touchscreen e-Reader with Free 3G + Wi-Fi, 6" E Ink Display, 3G Wo. . .," http://www.amazon.com/gp/product/B005890G8O/ref=famstripe_kt3g, May 24, 2012; "Kindle Paperwhite Touch Screen E-Reader with Light," http://www.amazon.com/Kindle-Paperwhite-Ereader/dp/B00AWH595M, May 21, 2014.

28. Deutschman, "Inside the Mind of Jeff Bezos."

29. "Online Extra: Jeff Bezos on Word-of-Mouth Power," *BusinessWeek Online,* August 2, 2004, www.businessweek.com; R.D. Hof, "Reprogramming Amazon," *BusinessWeek Online,* December 22, 2003, www.businessweek.com; "About Amazon.com: Company Information," www.amazon.com/exec/obidos/tg/browsw/-/574562/104-0138839-3693547, June 19, 2006; "Amazon.com Investor Relations: Press Release."

30. "RockBottom Restaurants," www.rockbottom.com/RockBottomWeb/RBR/index.aspx?PageName=/RockBottom. . ., April 15, 2008; "Craft Works Restaurants & Breweries Inc.," http://www.craftworksrestaurants.com/executive.html, May 24, 2012; "Rock Bottom Restaurants, Inc. – Franchising.com," http://www.franchising.com/rockbottom-restaurant/, May 21, 2014.

31. S. Dallas, "Rock Bottom Restaurants: Brewing Up Solid Profits," *BusinessWeek,* May 22, 1995, 74.

32. J.A. Pearce II and E.C. Ravlin, "The Design and Activation of Self-Regulating Work Groups," *Human Relations* 11 (1987), 751–82.

33. B. Dumaine, "Who Needs a Boss?" *Fortune,* May 7, 1990, 52–60; Pearce and Ravlin, "The Design and Activation of Self-Regulating Work Groups."

34. Dumaine, "Who Needs a Boss?"; A.R. Montebello and V.R. Buzzotta, "Work Teams That Work," *Training and Development,* March 1993, 59–64.

35. C. Matlack, R. Tiplady, D. Brady, R. Berner, and H. Tashiro, "The Vuitton Machine," *BusinessWeek,* March 22, 2004, 98–102; "America's Most Admired Companies," *Fortune.com,* August 18, 2004, www.fortune.com/fortune/mostadmired/snapshot/0,15020,383,00.html; "Art Samberg's Ode to Steel," *Big Money Weekly,* June 29, 2004, http://trading.sina/com/trading/rightside/bigmoney_weekly_040629.b5.shtml; "Nucor Reports Record Results for First Quarter of 2004," www.nucor.com/financials.asp?finpage=newsreleases, August 18, 2004; "Nucor Reports Results for First Half and Second Quarter of 2004," www.nucor.com/financials.asp?finpage=newsreleases; J.C. Cooper, "The Price of Efficiency," *BusinessWeek Online,* March 22, 2004, www.businessweek.com/magazine/content/04_12/b3875603.htm; "LVHM—Fashion & Leather Goods," www.lvmh.com, June 18, 2006; C. Matlack, "Rich Times for the Luxury Sector," *BusinessWeek Online,* March 6, 2006, www.businessweek.com/globalbiz/content/mar2006/gb20060306_296309.htm?campaign_id=search; N. Byrnes, "The Art of Motivation," *BusinessWeek,* May 1, 2006, 56–62; "Nucor Steel," http://www.nucor.com/indexinner.aspx?finpage=aboutus, April 16, 2008; "Annual General Meetings—Group Investor Relations—Corporate Governance," http://www.lvmh.com/comfi/pg_home.asp?rub=6&srub=0, March 16, 2008; B. Sowray, "Louis Vuitton: The World's Most Valuable Luxury Brand," *Telegraph,* May 24, 2012, http://fashion.telegraph.co.uk/news-features/TMG9287478/Louis-Vuitton-the-world-most. . ., May 24, 2012; "Nucor Corporation / Our Story / Chapter 1: Corporate Overview," http://www.nucor.com/story/chapter1/, May 24, 2012; "Nucor Corporation," http"//www.mucor.com/, May 21, 2014.

36. Matlack et al., "The Vuitton Machine."

37. M. Arndt, "Out of the Forge and into the Fire," *BusinessWeek,* June 18, 2001, *BusinessWeek* Archives; Byrnes, "The Art of Motivation."

38. S. Baker, "The Minimill That Acts Like a Biggie," *BusinessWeek,* September 30, 1996, 101–104; S. Baker, "Nucor," *BusinessWeek,* February 13, 1995, 70; S. Overman, "No-Frills at Nucor," *HRMagazine,* July 1994, 56–60.

39. www.nucor.com, November 21, 2001; "Nucor: About Us."

40. Baker, "The Minimill That Acts Like a Biggie"; Baker, "Nucor"; Overman, "No-Frills at Nucor"; www.nucor.com; Byrnes, "The Art of Motivation"; "Nucor: About Us."

41. N. Byrnes, "A Steely Resolve," *BusinessWeek,* April 6, 2009, 54; "Nucor Corporation," http"//www.mucor.com/, May 21, 2014.

42. Matlack et al., "The Vuitton Machine"; "About Nucor"; "America's Most Admired Companies"; "Art Samberg's Ode to Steel"; "Nucor Reports Record Results for First Quarter of 2004"; "Nucor Reports Results for First Half and Second Quarter of 2004"; Byrnes, "The Art of Motivation."

43. T.D. Wall, N.J. Kemp, P.R. Jackson, and C.W. Clegg, "Outcomes of Autonomous Work Groups: A Long-Term Field Experiment," *Academy of Management Journal* 29 (1986), 280–304.

44. A. Markels, "A Power Producer Is Intent on Giving Power to Its People," *The Wall Street Journal,* July 3, 1995, A1, A12; "AES Corporation/The Power of Being Global," www.aes.com/aes/index?page=home, April 15, 2008.

45. J.S. Lublin, "My Colleague, My Boss," *The Wall Street Journal,* April 12, 1995, R4, R12.

46. W.R. Pape, "Group Insurance," *Inc.* (Technology Supplement), June 17, 1997, 29–31; A.M. Townsend, S.M. DeMarie, and A.R. Hendrickson, "Are You Ready for Virtual Teams?" *HR Magazine,* September 1996, 122–126; A.M. Townsend, S.M. DeMarie, and A.M. Hendrickson, "Virtual Teams: Technology and the Workplace of the Future," *Academy of Management Executive* 12, no. 3 (1998), 17–29.

47. Townsend et al., "Virtual Teams."

48. Pape, "Group Insurance"; Townsend et al., "Are You Ready for Virtual Teams?"; L. Gratton, "Working Together . . .When Apart," *The Wall Street Journal,* June 16–17, 2007, R4.

49. D.L. Duarte and N.T. Snyder, *Mastering Virtual Teams* (San Francisco: Jossey-Bass, 1999); K A. Karl, "Book Reviews: *Mastering Virtual Teams," Academy of Management Executive,* August 1999, 118–19.

50. B. Geber, "Virtual Teams," *Training* 32, no. 4 (August 1995), 36–40; T. Finholt and L.S. Sproull, "Electronic Groups at Work," *Organization Science* 1 (1990), 41–64.

51. Geber, "Virtual Teams."

52. E.J. Hill, B.C. Miller, S.P. Weiner, and J. Colihan, "Influences of the Virtual Office on Aspects of Work and Work/Life Balance," *Personnel Psychology* 31 (1998), 667–83; S.G. Strauss, "Technology, Group Process, and Group Outcomes: Testing the Connections in Computer-Mediated and Face-to-Face Groups," *Human Computer Interaction,* 12 (1997), 227–66; M.E. Warkentin, L. Sayeed, and R. High-tower, "Virtual Teams versus Face-to-Face Teams: An Exploratory Study of a Web-Based Conference System," *Decision Sciences* 28, no. 4 (Fall 1997), 975–96.

53. S.A. Furst, M. Reeves, B. Rosen, and R.S. Blackburn, "Managing the Life Cycle of Virtual Teams," *Academy of Management Executive* 18, no. 2 (May 2004), 6–20.

54. Furst et al., "Managing the Life Cycle of Virtual Teams."

55. Gratton, "Working Together . . .When Apart."

56. Gratton, "Working Together . . .When Apart."

57. Gratton, "Working Together . . .When Apart."

58. Gratton, "Working Together . . .When Apart."

59. A. Deutschman, "The Managing Wisdom of High-Tech Superstars," *Fortune,* October 17, 1994, 197–206.

60. J.D. Thompson, *Organizations in Action* (New York: McGraw-Hill, 1967).

61. Thompson, *Organizations in Action.*

62. Lublin, "My Colleague, My Boss."

63. "About ICU Medical, Inc.," www.icumed.com/about.asp, April 11, 2008.

64. "About ICU Medical, Inc."

65. "ICU Medical, Inc.—Fundamentals," http://phx.corporate-ir.net/phoenix.zhtml?c=86695&p=irol-fundamentals, April 11, 2008; "ICU Medical Inc. (ICUI): Stock Quote & Company Profile—BusinessWeek," *Business-Week,* http://investing.businessweek.com/research/stocks/snapshot/snapshot_article.asp?symbol=. . ., April 11, 2008; "The 200 Best Small Companies \#80 ICU Medical," *Forbes.com,* http://www.forbes.com/lists/2009/23/small-companies-09_ICU-Medical_J1UO.html, March 14, 2010; "2011 Annual Report to Shareholders and Form 10-K," ICU Medical, http://files.shareholder.com/downloads/ICUI/0x0x563714/664702F0-84A0-41B4-B90B-B8204D2437EC/ICU_WEB_READY_PDF.pdf, May 24, 2012; "People at ICUI – Executives, Board, & Key Employees at ICU Medical Inc.—WSJ.com," http://quotes.wsj.com/ICUI/company-people, May 22, 2014.

66. "ICU Medical, Inc.—Investor Relations Home," http://phx.corporate-ir.net/phoenix.zhtml?c=86695&p=irol-IRHome, April 11, 2008; "The 200 Best Small Companies \#80 ICU Medical"; "People at ICUI – Executives, Board, & Key Employees at ICU Medical Inc.—WSJ.com," http://quotes.wsj.com/ICUI/company-people, May 22, 2014.

67. "About ICU Medical, Inc."

68. "Clave Connector," ICU Medical, Inc., www.icumend.com, April 11, 2008; "2011 Annual Report to Shareholders and Form 10-K," *ICU Medical,* http://files.shareholder.com/downloads/ICUI/0x0x563714/664702F0-84A0-41B4-B90B-B8204D2437EC/ICU_WEB_READY_PDF.pdf, May 24, 2012.

69. E. White, "How a Company Made Everyone a Team Player," *The Wall Street Journal,* August 13, 2007, B1, B7.

70. White, "How a Company Made Everyone a Team Player."

71. White, "How a Company Made Everyone a Team Player."

72. White, "How a Company Made Everyone a Team Player."

73. White, "How a Company Made Everyone a Team Player."

74. White, "How a Company Made Everyone a Team Player."

75. White, "How a Company Made Everyone a Team Player."

76. R.G. LeFauve and A.C. Hax, "Managerial and Technological Innovations at Saturn Corporation," *MIT Management,* Spring 1992, 8–19.

77. B.W. Tuckman, "Developmental Sequences in Small Groups," *Psychological Bulletin* 63 (1965), 384–99; B.W. Tuckman and M.C. Jensen, "Stages of Small Group Development," *Group and Organizational Studies* 2 (1977), 419–27.

78. C.J.G. Gersick, "Time and Transition in Work Teams: Toward a New Model of Group Development," *Academy of Management Journal* 31 (1988), 9–41; C.J.G. Gersick, "Marking Time: Predictable Transitions in Task Groups," *Academy of Management Journal* 32 (1989), 274–309.

79. J.R. Hackman, "Group Influences on Individuals in Organizations," in M.D. Dunnette and L.M. Hough, eds., *Handbook of Industrial and Organizational Psychology,* 2nd ed., vol. 3 (Palo Alto, CA: Consulting Psychologists Press, 1992), 199–267.

80. Hackman, "Group Influences on Individuals."

81. Hackman, "Group Influences on Individuals."

82. Lublin, "My Colleague, My Boss."

83. T. Kelley and J. Littman, *The Art of Innovation* (New York: Doubleday, 2001); "ideo.com: Our Work," www.ideo.com/portfolio, June 19, 2006; "About IDEO," *IDEO,* http://www.ideo.com/about/, May 24, 2012; "IDEO – A Design and Innovation Consulting Firm," http://www.ideo.com/, May 22, 2014.

84. B. Nussbaum, "The Power of Design," *BusinessWeek,* May 17, 2004, 86–94; "ideo.com: About Us: Teams," www.ideo.com/about/index.asp?x=1&y=1, June 19, 2006.

85. "ideo.com: About Us: Teams," www.ideo.com/about/index.asp?x=1&y=1, June 19, 2006; "ideo.com: About Us: Teams," www.ideo.com/about/index.asp?x=1&y=1, April 18, 2008; "Teams—IDEO," http://www.ideo.com/culture/teams/ March 15, 2010.

86. Nussbaum, "The Power of Design."

87. Kelley and Littman, *The Art of Innovation.*

88. Kelley and Littman, *The Art of Innovation;* www.ideo.com; "1999 Idea Winners," *BusinessWeek,* June 7, 1999, *BusinessWeek* Archives.

89. Nussbaum, "The Power of Design; "ideo.com: About Us: Teams;" "About IDEO," IDEO, http://www.ideo.com/about/, May 24, 2012.

90. L. Festinger, "Informal Social Communication," *Psychological Review* 57 (1950), 271–82; Shaw, *Group Dynamics.*

91. Hackman, "Group Influences on Individuals in Organizations"; Shaw, *Group Dynamics.*

92. D. Cartwright, "The Nature of Group Cohesiveness," in D. Cartwright and A. Zander, eds., *Group Dynamics,* 3rd ed. (New York: Harper & Row, 1968); L. Festinger, S. Schacter, and K. Black, *Social Pressures in Informal Groups* (New York: Harper & Row, 1950); Shaw, *Group Dynamics.*

93. T.F. O'Boyle, "A Manufacturer Grows Efficient by Soliciting Ideas from Employees," *The Wall Street Journal,* June 5, 1992, A1, A5.

94. Lublin, "My Colleague, My Boss."

95. Kelley and Littman, "The Art of Innovation," 93; "People—Tom Kelley—IDEO," http://www.ideo.com/people/tom-kelley, May 22, 2014.

96. Kelley and Littman, "The Art of Innovation."

97. P.C. Earley, "Social Loafing and Collectivism: A Comparison of the United States and the People's Republic of China," *Administrative Science Quarterly* 34 (1989), 565–81; J.M. George, "Extrinsic and Intrinsic Origins of Perceived Social Loafing in Organizations," *Academy of Management Journal* 35 (1992), 191–202; S.G. Harkins, B. Latane, and K. Williams, "Social Loafing: Allocating Effort or Taking It Easy," *Journal of Experimental Social Psychology* 16 (1980), 457–65; B. Latane, K.D. Williams, and S. Harkins, "Many Hands Make Light the Work: The Causes and Consequences of Social Loafing," *Journal of Personality and Social Psychology* 37 (1979), 822–32; J.A. Shepperd, "Productivity Loss in Performance Groups: A Motivation Analysis," *Psychological Bulletin* 113 (1993), 67–81.

98. George, "Extrinsic and Intrinsic Origins"; G.R. Jones, "Task Visibility, Free Riding, and Shirking: Explaining the Effect of Structure and Technology on Employee Behavior," *Academy of Management Review* 9 (1984), 684–95; K. Williams, S. Harkins, and B. Latane, "Identifiability as a Deterrent to Social Loafing: Two Cheering Experiments," *Journal of Personality and Social Psychology* 40 (1981), 303–11.

99. S. Harkins and J. Jackson, "The Role of Evaluation in Eliminating Social Loafing," *Personality and Social Psychology Bulletin* 11 (1985), 457–65; N.L. Kerr and S.E. Bruun, "Ringelman Revisited: Alternative Explanations for the Social Loafing Effect," *Personality and Social Psychology Bulletin* 7 (1981), 224–31; Williams et al., "Identifiability as a Deterrent to Social Loafing"; Harkins and Jackson, "The Role of Evaluation in Eliminating Social Loafing."

100. M.A. Brickner, S.G. Harkins, and T.M. Ostrom, "Effects of Personal Involvement: Thought-Provoking Implications for Social Loafing," *Journal of Personality and Social Psychology* 51 (1986), 763–69; S.G. Harkins and R.E. Petty, "The Effects of Task Difficulty and Task Uniqueness on Social Loafing," *Journal of Personality and Social Psychology* 43 (1982), 1214–29.

101. B. Latane, "Responsibility and Effort in Organizations," in P.S. Goodman, ed., *Designing Effective Work Groups* (San Francisco: Jossey-Bass, 1986); Latane et al., "Many Hands Make Light the Work"; I.D. Steiner, *Group Process and Productivity* (New York: Academic Press, 1972).

Chapter 16

1. D.A. Kaplan, "Salesforce's Happy Workforce," *Fortune,* February 6, 2012, 101–12; "Salesforce Software: Welcome to the Social Enterprise," 2012 Annual Report, http://www2.sfdcstatic.com/assets/pdf/investors/AnnualReport.pdf; "Salesforce.com Cloud Computing Leaders—Salesforce.com," Salesforce.com leadership, http://www.salesforce.com/company/leadership/, June 2, 2014.

2. Kaplan, "Salesforce's Happy Workforce"; "Salesforce Software"; "Trusted Clouds Apps and Platform for the Social Enterprise," http://www.salesforce.com/products/, May 30, 2012.

3. Kaplan, "Salesforce's Happy Workforce"; "Salesforce Service Cloud and Customers Take Home Four 2012 CRM Magazine Service Awards," http://www.salesforce.com/company/news-press/press-releases/2012/03/120319.jsp, May 30, 2012; "Salesforce Software: Welcome to the Social Enterprise," 2012 Annual Report, http://www2.sfdcstatic.com/assets/pdf/investors/AnnualReport.pdf.

4. "Salesforce Software."

5. "Salesforce.com Announces Fiscal 2014 Fourth Quarter and Full Year Results," February 27, 2014, http://www.salesforce.com/company/news-press/press-releases/2014/02/140227.jsp, June 2, 2014.

6. Kaplan, "Salesforce's Happy Workforce"; "Careers #dreamjob," *Salesforce.com,* http://www.salesforce.com/careers/main/, June 5, 2012; "Best Companies 2014 Salesforce.com," http://fortune.com/best-companies/salesforce-com-7/, June 2, 2014.

7. "What Does APP Mean?"—APP Definition—Meaning of APP—Internet Slang.com, http://www.internetslang.com/APP-meaning-definition.asp, June 1, 2012.

8. Kaplan, "Salesforce's Happy Workforce."

9. Kaplan, "Salesforce's Happy Workforce."

10. Kaplan, "Salesforce's Happy Workforce."

11. Kaplan, "Salesforce's Happy Workforce."

12. Kaplan, "Salesforce's Happy Workforce."

13. Kaplan, "Salesforce's Happy Workforce."

14. "Microsoft and Salesforce.com Announce Global Strategic Partnership," May 29, 2014, http://www.salesforce.com/company/news-press/press-releases/2014/05/140529.jsp, June 2, 2014.

15. "Microsoft and Salesforce.com Announce Global Strategic Partnership," May 29, 2014, http://www.salesforce.com/company/news-press/press-releases/2014/05/140529.jsp, June 2, 2014.

16. Kaplan, "Salesforce's Happy Workforce."; "Salesforce Foundation," http://www.salesforcefoundation.org/, June 2, 2014.

17. Kaplan, "Salesforce's Happy Workforce."

18. Kaplan, "Salesforce's Happy Workforce."

19. Kaplan, "Salesforce's Happy Workforce"; "Salesforce Software."

20. C.A. O'Reilly and L.R. Pondy, "Organizational Communication," in S. Kerr, ed., *Organizational Behavior* (Columbus, OH: Grid, 1979).

21. "World's First Volume Computed Tomography (VCT) System, Developed by GE Healthcare, Scanning Patients at Froedtert," www.gehealthcare.com/company/pressroom/releases/pr_release_9722.html, June 18, 2004; "GE Healthcare Fact Sheet," *GE Healthcare Worldwide,* June 20, 2006, www.gehealthcare.com/usen/about/ge_factsheet.html; WTN News, "GE Healthcare Names New CEO," *Wisconsin Technology Network,* January 25, 2006, http://wistechnology.com/printarticle.php?id=2639, June 20, 2006; "About GE Healthcare," *GE Healthcare-Brochure—About GE Healthcare,* www.gehealthcare.com/usen/about/about.html, April 25, 2008; "About GE Healthcare," *GE Healthcare-Brochure—About GE Healthcare,* http://www.gehealthcare.com/usen/about/about.html, March 15, 2010; "GE Healthcare-Company Information—about GE Healthcare," http://www.gehealthcare.com/eueu/msabout/msabout.html, June 5, 2012; "About Us—gehealthcare.com," http://www3.gehealthcare.com/en/About_Us, June 2, 2014; "GE Healthcare Fact Sheet—About Us—gehealthcare.com," http://www3.gehealthcare.com/en/About_Us/GE_Healthcare_Fact_Sheet, June 2, 2014; "GE Healthcare Careers—About Us—gehealthcare.com," http://www3.gehealthcare.com/en/About_Us/GE_Healthcare_Careers, June 2, 2014.

22. "New CT Scanner by GE Healthcare Advances Imaging Technology," *Wisconsin Technology Network,* June 21, 2004, www.wistechnology.com; S. Kirsner, "Time [Zone] Travelers," *Fast Company,* August 2004, 60–66; "LightSpeed VCT Series," *GE Healthcare Worldwide,* June 20, 2006, www.gehealthcare.com/usen/ct/products/vct.html.

23. Kirsner, "Time [Zone] Travelers."

24. Kirsner, "Time [Zone] Travelers."

25. Kirsner, "Time [Zone] Travelers."

26. E.M. Rogers and R. Agarwala-Rogers, *Communication in Organizations* (New York: Free Press, 1976).

27. R.B. Schmitt, "Judges Try Curbing Lawyers' Body Language Antics," *The Wall Street Journal,* September 11, 1997, B1, B7.

28. D.A. Adams, P.A. Todd, and R.R. Nelson, "A Comparative Evaluation of the Impact of Electronic and Voice Mail on Organizational Communication," *Information & Management* 24 (1993), 9–21.

29. R. Winslow, "Hospitals' Weak Systems Hurt Patients, Study Says," *The Wall Street Journal,* July 5, 1995, B1, B6.

30. B. Newman, "Global Chatter," *The Wall Street Journal,* March 22, 1995, A1, A15.

31. M.L. Wald, "Details Are Added on Pilots in Overflight," *The New York Times,* December 17, 2009, A34; "Pilots Who Missed Airport OK Deal," *Houston Chronicle,* Tuesday, March 16, 2010, A6.

32. "Miscommunications Plague Pilots and Air Traffic Controllers," *The Wall Street Journal,* August 22, 1995, A1.

33. P. Reinert, "Miscommunication Seen as Threat to Space Station," *Houston Chronicle,* September 24, 2003, 6A.

34. W.E. Leary, "NASA Report Says Problems Plague Space Station Program," *The New York Times,* February 28, 2004, A12.

35. R.L. Daft, R.H. Lengel, and L.K. Trevino, "Message Equivocality, Media Selection, and Manager Performance: Implications for Information Systems," *MIS Quarterly* 11 (1987), 355–66; R.L. Daft and R.H. Lengel, "Information Richness: A New Approach to Managerial Behavior and Organization Design," in B.M. Staw and L.L. Cummings, eds., *Research in Organizational Behavior* (Greenwich, CT: JAI Press, 1984).

36. R.L. Daft, *Organization Theory and Design* (St. Paul, MN: West, 1992).

37. "Lights, Camera, Meeting: Teleconferencing Becomes a Time-Saving Tool," *The Wall Street Journal,* February 21, 1995, A1.

38. Daft, *Organization Theory and Design.*

39. A.S. Wellner, "Lost in Translation," *Inc.,* September 2005, 37–38.

40. Wellner, "Lost in Translation."

41. Wellner, "Lost in Translation"; R. McMillan, "Business Communication Expert and *New York Times* Bestselling Author," www.vitalsmarts.com, June 20, 2006; "Ron McMillan," http://www.ronmcmillan.net/, June 2, 2014.

42. Wellner, "Lost in Translation"; "Faculty—UCLA Psychology Department: Home," Albert Mehrabian, http://www.psych.ucla.edu/faculty/faculty_page?id=181&area=7, June 2, 2014.

43. Wellner, "Lost in Translation"; "MIT Sloan Faculty Directory—MIT Sloan," JoAnne Yates, http://mitsloan.mit.edu/faculty/detail.php?in_spseqno=41395, June 2, 2014.

44. "Team," *Roberts Golden Consulting,* http://www.robertsgolden.com/about/team, June 5, 2012; "Roberts Golden—Our Team," http://www.robertsgolden.com/about/our-team/, June 2, 2014.

45. Wellner, "Lost in Translation"; S. Roberts, "Sara Roberts, President, Roberts Golden Consulting—Biographies," www.robertsgolden.com/bios.html, June 20, 2006; "Roberts Golden Consulting," www.robertsgolden.com, June 20, 2006; "Roberts Golden Consulting— About Us," "Management Team," http://www.robertsgolden.com/about_us/mgmt_team.html, March 15, 2010; "Roberts Golden Consulting—About Us," http://www.robertsgolden.com/about_us/index.html, March 15, 2010.

46. Wellner, "Lost in Translation."

47. S. Shellenbarger, "A Day without E-mail Is Like . . . ," *The Wall Street Journal,* October 11, 2007, D1, D2; D. Brady, "*!#?@ the E-Mail. Can We Talk?" *BusinessWeek,* December 4, 2006, 109; "No Email Friday Pays Off for Florida-based Bank," *Simply* Communicate.com, http://www.simply-communicate.com/news/simply-news/no-email-Friday-pays-florida-base . . . , June 5, 2012.

48. P. Dvorak, "Frequent Contact Helps Bridge International Divide," *The Wall Street Journal,* June 1, 2009, B4.

49. T.J. Peters and R.H. Waterman, Jr., *In Search of Excellence* (New York: Harper & Row, 1982); T. Peters and N. Austin, *A Passion for Excellence: The Leadership Difference* (New York: Random House, 1985).

50. "Lights, Camera, Meeting."

51. R. Kirkland, "Cisco's Display of Strength," *Fortune,* November 12, 2007, 90–100; "Cisco TelePresence Overview," Overview *(TelePresence)—Cisco Systems,* www.cisco.com/en/US/solutions/ns669/networking_solutions_ products_genericcont. . . , April 25, 2008.

52. R. Kirkland, "Cisco's Display of Strength"; "Cisco Systems—Corporate Governance," http://investor.cisco.com/governance.cfm, June 2, 2014.

53. Kirkland, "Cisco's Display of Strength"; "Cisco TelePresence Overview."

54. Dvorak, "Frequent Contact Helps Bridge International Divide"; "Greg Caltabiano—News, Articles, Biography, Photos—WSJ.com," http://topics.wsj.com/person/C/greg-caltabiano/1602, June 2, 2014.

55. "Skype Technologies S.A. News," *The New York Times,* http://topics.nytimes.com/top/news/business/companies/skype_technologies_sa/index.html, June 5, 2012.

56. C. Hymowitz, "Missing from Work: The Chance to Think, Even to Dream a Little," *The Wall Street Journal,* March 23, 2004, B1.

57. D. Beizer, "Email Is Dead . . . ," *Fast Company,* July–August 2007, 46; "The Radicati Group, Inc.," www.radicati.com, April 28, 2008; "The Radicati Group, Inc.," http://www.radicati.com/, June 2, 2014.

58. J. Sandberg, "Employees Forsake Dreaded E-mail for the Beloved Phone," *The Wall Street Journal,* September 26, 2006, B1.

59. Beizer, "Email Is Dead . . ."

60. Sandberg, "Employees Forsake Dreaded E-mail."

61. Sandberg, "Employees Forsake Dreaded E-mail."

62. K. Byron, "Carrying Too Heavy a Load? The Communication and Miscommunication of Emotion by E-mail," *Academy of Management Review* 33, no. 2 (2008), 309–27; "Whitman School of Management—Syracuse University," Kris Byron, http://whitman.syr.edu/Directory/showInfo.aspx?id=249, June 2, 2014.

63. "There's a Message in Every E-mail," *Fast Company,* September 2007, 43; Byron, "Carrying Too Heavy a Load?"

64. Byron, "Carrying Too Heavy a Load?"

65. "Telecommuters Bring Home Work and Broadband," www.emarketer.com/Article.aspx?1002943, July 20, 2004; "Annual Survey Shows Americans Are Working from Many Different Locations outside Their Employer's Office," *International Telework Association & Council,* May 10, 2006, www.workingfromanywhere.org/news; "Itac, the Telework Advisory Group for World at Work," www.workingfromanywhere.org, May 10, 2006; "Virtual Business Owners Community—FAQ Center: Telecommuting/Telework," www.vsscyberoffice.com/vfaq/25.html, May 10, 2006; T. Schadler, "US Telecommuting Forecast, 2009 to 2016: Telecommuting Will Rise to Include 43% of US Workers by 2016," March 11, 2009, http://www.forrester.com/rb/Research/us_telecommuting_forecast%2C_2009_to_2016/q/i. . . , March 15, 2010; "One In Five Americans Work From Home, Numbers Seen Rising Over 60%," Forbes, http://www.forbes.com/sites/kenrapoza/2013/02/18/one-in-five-americans-work-from-home-numbers-seen-rising-over-60/, June 2, 2014.

66. E. Baig, "Taking Care of Business—Without Leaving the House," *BusinessWeek,* April 17, 1995, 106–07.

67. "Life Is Good for Telecommuters, but Some Problems Persist," *The Wall Street Journal,* August 3, 1995, A1.

68. "E-Mail Abuse: Workers Discover High-Tech Ways to Cause Trouble in the Office," *The Wall Street Journal,* November 22, 1994, A1; "E-mail Alert: Companies Lag in Devising Policies on How It Should Be Used," *The Wall Street Journal,* December 29, 1994, A1.

69. Wellner, "Lost in Translation"; "Mark Stevens—Entrepreneur.com," http://www.entrepreneur.com/author/mark-stevens, June 2, 2014.

70. "The Most Important Part of an E-mail System Isn't the Software. It's the Rules You Make About Using It," *Inc. Magazine,* October 2005, 119–22.

71. "The Most Important Part of an E-mail System Isn't the Software."

72. "The Most Important Part of an E-mail System Isn't the Software."

73. American Management Association and the ePolicy Institute's N. Flynn, "2004 Workplace E-Mail and Instant Messaging Survey Summary," www.amanet.org, 2004; "2007 Electronic Monitoring & Surveillance Survey," *AMA/ePolicy Institute Research, American Management Association,* 2008.

74. J. Tyson, "How Instant Messaging Works," computer.howstuffworks.com, August 23, 2004.

75. "Study: Workers Are Surfing on Company Time," www.medialifemagazine.com/news2004/may04/may03/3_wed/news8wednesday.html, May 5, 2004; "Company Profile," *Websense,* www.websense.com/global/en/AboutWebsense/, April 25, 2008.

76. "Study: Workers Are Surfing on Company Time."

77. "Study: Workers Are Surfing on Company Time."

78. ClikZ Stats staff, "U.S. Web Usage and Traffic, July 2004," www.clickz.com/stats/big_picture/traffic_patterns/article.php/3395351, August 23, 2004.

79. L. Guernsey, "Technology; Keeping Watch Over Instant Messages," April 15, 2002, http://www.nytimes.com/2002/04/15/business/technology-keeping-watch-over-instant-mess. . . , June 6, 2012; "About Smarsh," *Smarsh,* http://www.smarsh.com/about-smarsh, June 6, 2012; L. Petrecca, "More Employers Use Tech to Track Workers," *USA Today.com,* http://www.usatoday.com/money/workplace/2010-03-17-workplaceprivacy15_CV_N.htm., June 6, 2012; "How to Monitor Your Employees' PCs without Going Too Far," *PCWorld,* http://www.pcworld.com/printable/article/id,222169/printable.html, June 5, 2012.

80. "Employers Spying on Staff: Big Brother Bosses," *The Economist,* http://www.economist.com/node/14413380/print, June 5, 2012.

81. "Is Your Employer Monitoring Your Internet Use? *World Law Direct,* August 14, 2011, http://www.worldlawdirect.com/article/451/your-employer-monitoring-your-internet-use.html, June 6, 2012.

82. Conley, "The Privacy Arms Race"; "2007 Electronic Monitoring & Surveillance Survey"; M. Villano, "The Risk Is All Yours in Office E-Mail," *The New York Times,* March 4, 2007, BU17.

83. "2007 Electronic Monitoring & Surveillance Survey."

84. J. Pfeffer, "It's Time to Start Trusting the Workforce," *Business 2.0,* December 2006, 68.

85. Conley, "The Privacy Arms Race."

86. S.E. Ante, "With Little on Law Books, Employers Have Latitude in Monitoring Workers," *The Wall Street Journal,* October 23, 2013, B6.

87. Ante, "With Little on Law Books, Employers Have Latitude in Monitoring Workers."

88. A. Tugend, "What to Think about before You Hit Send," *The New York Times,* April 21, 2012, B5.

89. "Employee-Newsletter Names Include the Good, the Bad, and the Boring," *The Wall Street Journal,* July 18, 1995, A1.

90. W.M. Bulkeley, "Playing Well with Others," *The Wall Street Journal,* June 18, 2007, R10.

91. E. White, J.S. Lublin, and D. Kesmodel, "Executives Get the Blogging Bug," *The Wall Street Journal,* July 13, 2007, B1, B2.

92. *Blog—Wikipedia, the free encyclopedia,* http://en.wikipedia.org/wiki/Blog, April 28, 2008; White et al., "Executives Get the Blogging Bug."

93. *Blog—Wikipedia, the free encyclopedia;* White et al., "Executives Get the Blogging Bug"; "GM FastLane Blog: Lutz Biography," http://fastlane.gmblogs.com/archives/2005/01/lutz_biography_1.html, April 28, 2008.

94. "2006 Workplace E-Mail, Instant Messaging & Blog Survey: Bosses Battle Risk by Firing E-Mail, IM & Blog Violators," New York, July 11, 2006, *AMA Press Room,* http://press.amanet.org/press-releases/28/2006-workplace-e-mail-instant-messaging-blogs. . . April 28, 2008.

95. Bulkeley, "Playing Well with Others."

96. Bulkeley, "Playing Well with Others."

97. D.M. Boyd and N.B. Ellison, "Social Network Sites: Definition, History, and Scholarship," *Journal of Computer-Mediated Communication* 13, no. 1 (2007), article 11, http://jcmc.indiana.edu/vol13/issue1/boyd.ellison.html, March 15, 2010; "Social Networking Site Definition from PC Magazine Encyclopedia," http://www.pcmag.com/encyclopedia_term/0,2542,t=social+networking&i=55316,00.asp, March 15, 2010; "Factsheet/Facebook," http://www.facebook.com/press/info.php?factsheet, March 15, 2010; "Statistics / Facebook," http://www.facebook.com/press/info.php?statistics, March 15, 2010; "Twitter News—*The New York Times,*" http://topics.nytimes.com/top/news/business/companies/twitter/index.html, March 15, 2010; "Twitter," http://twitter.com/about, March 15, 2010; "Facebook, Inc.: Private Company Information—*Business Week,*" http://investing.businessweek.com/research/stocks/private/snapshot.asp?privcapId=207654. . . , March 15, 2010.

98. J.E. Vascellaro, "Why E-mail No Longer Rules," *The Wall Street Journal,* October 12, 2009, R1–3.

99. "Study: 54 Percent of Companies Ban Facebook, Twitter at Work/Epicenter/Wired.com," October 9, 2009, http://www.wired.com/epicenter/2009/10/study-54-of-companies-ban-facebook-twitter-at-. . . March 16, 2010.

100. "Study: 54 Percent of Companies Ban Facebook, Twitter."

101. O.W. Baskin and C.E. Aronoff, *Interpersonal Communication in Organizations* (Santa Monica, CA: Goodyear, 1989).

102. T. Gutner, "Move Over, Bohemian Grove," *BusinessWeek,* February 19, 2001, 102.

103. "We've All Got Mail," *Newsweek,* May 15, 2001, 73K; "Diversity Deficit," *BusinessWeek Online,* May 14, 2001; "Dial-Up Users Converting to Broadband in Droves," www.emarketer.com/Article.aspx?1003009, August 23, 2004; "Top 20 Countries with the Highest Number of Internet Users," *Internet World Stats,* June 20, 2006, www.internetworldstats.com/top20.htm; "Top 20 Countries with the Highest Number of Internet Users," www.internetworldstats.com/top20.htm, April 29, 2008; "Top 20 Countries with the Highest Number of Internet Users," http://www.internetworldstats.com/top20.htm, March 15, 2010; "Internet Users—Top 20 Countries—Internet Usage," *Internet World Stats,* http://www.internetworldstats.com/top20.htm, June 6, 2012; "Top 20 Countries With The Highest Number of Internet Users," http://www.internetworldstats.com/top20.htm, June 2, 2014.

104. "Top 15 Countries in Internet Usage, 2002," www.infoplease.com/ipa/A0908185.html, August 25, 2004; "Top 20 Countries with the Highest Number of Internet Users," http://www.internetworldstats.com/top20.htm, April 29, 2008; "Top 20 Countries with the Highest Number of Internet Users," http://www.internetworldstats.com/top20.htm, March 15, 2010; "Internet Users—Top 20 Countries—Internet Usage," *Internet World Stats,* http://www.internetworldstats.com/top20.htm, June 6, 2012.

105. J. Sandberg, "Internet's Popularity in North America Appears to Be Soaring," *The Wall Street Journal,* October 30, 1995, B2.

106. "How to Research Companies," *Oxford Knowledge Company,* www.oxford-knowledge.co.uk, September 10, 2004.

107. "Survey: Denmark Is Web-Savviest Nation," MSNBC.com, April 19, 2004, www.msnbc.msn.com/id/4779944/1/displaymode/1098; L. Grinsven, "U.S. Drops on Lists of Internet Savvy," *Houston Chronicle,* April 20, 2004, 6B.

108. M.J. Cronin, "Ford's Intranet Success," *Fortune,* March 30, 1998, 158; M.J. Cronin, "Intranets Reach the

Factory Floor," *Fortune,* June 10, 1997; A.L. Sprout, "The Internet inside Your Company," *Fortune,* November 27, 1995, 161–68; J.B. White, "Chrysler's Intranet: Promise vs. Reality," *The Wall Street Journal,* May 13, 1997, B1, B6.

109. White, "Chrysler's Intranet: Promise vs. Reality."

110. G. Rifkin, "A Skeptic's Guide to Groupware," *Forbes ASAP,* 1995, 76–91.

111. Rifkin, "A Skeptic's Guide to Groupware."

112. Rifkin, "A Skeptic's Guide to Groupware."

113. "Groupware Requires a Group Effort," *BusinessWeek,* June 26, 1995, 154.

114. M. Totty, "The Path to Better Teamwork," *The Wall Street Journal,* May 20, 2004, R4; "Collaborative Software," *Wikipedia,* August 25, 2004, en.wikipedia.org/wiki/Collaborative_software; "Collaborative Groupware Software," www.svpal.org/~grantbow/groupware.html, August 25, 2004.

115. Totty, "The Path to Better Teamwork"; "Collaborative Software."

116. Totty, "The Path to Better Teamwork"; "Collaborative Software"; "Collaborative Groupware Software."

117. Totty, "The Path to Better Teamwork"; "Collaborative Software."

118. Totty, "The Path to Better Teamwork"; "Collaborative Software."

119. Microsoft Windows SharePoint Services Developer Center, "Windows SharePoint Service," http://msdn.microsoft.com/sharepoint, June 21, 2006.

120. Totty, "The Path to Better Teamwork"; "Collaborative Software."

121. M. Conlin, "E-mail Is So Five Minutes Ago," *BusinessWeek,* November 28, 2005, 111–12; D. Dahl, "The End of E-mail," *Inc.,* February 2006, 41–42; "Weaving a Secure Web around Education: A Guide to Technology Standards and Security," http://nces.ed.gov/pubs2003/secureweb/glossary.asp, June 21, 2006; "Wikis Make Collaboration Easier," *InformationWeek,* June 20, 2006, www.informationweek.com/shared/printableArticleSrc.jhtml?articleID=170100392.

122. "Websense 2013 Threat Report: Nearly 600 Percent Increase in Global Malicious Websites; 85 Percent on Legitimate Sites," February 13, 2013, http://community.websense.com/blogs/websense-news-releases/archive/2013/02/13/websense-2013-threat-report-nearly-600-percent-increase-in-global-malicious-websites-85-percent-on-legitimate-sites.aspx, June 3, 2014; "Company—Websense.com," http://www.websense.com/content/company.aspx, June 3, 2014.

123. "Websense 2013 Threat Report: Nearly 600 Percent Increase in Global Malicious Websites; 85 Percent on Legitimate

Sites," February 13, 2013, http://community.websense.com/blogs/websense-news-releases/archive/2013/02/13/websense-2013-threat-report-nearly-600-percent-increase-in-global-malicious-websites-85-percent-on-legitimate-sites.aspx, June 3, 2014.

124. Conlin, "E-mail Is So Five Minutes Ago."

125. Dahl, "The End of E-mail"; "Wikis Make Collaboration Easier"; V. Vara, "Wikis at Work," *The Wall Street Journal,* June 18, 2007, R11.

126. Dahl, "The End of E-mail."

127. D. Dahl, "Connecting the Dots," *Inc.,* June 2009, 103–4; "Project Management, Collaboration, and Task Software: Basecamp," http://basecamphq.com/, March 15, 2010; "Basecamp's Exclusive Single-Page Projects Keep Everything Organized," http://basecamp.com/one-page-project, June 6, 2012; "Get a Basecamp Wiki for Every Project—CBS News," July 31, 2008, http://www.cbsnews.com/news/get-a-basecamp-wiki-for-every-project/, June 3, 2014.

128. Conlin, "E-mail Is So Five Minutes Ago"; "Soar Technology, Thinking inside the Box," *Soar Technology, Inc.,* www.soartech.com/home.php, April 28, 2008; "SoarTech—About—History," http://www.soartech.com/about/history/, June 6, 2012; "SoarTech," http://www.soartech.com/, June 3, 2014.

129. Conlin, "E-mail Is So Five Minutes Ago."

130. Conlin, "E-mail Is So Five Minutes Ago."

131. Bulkeley, "Playing Well with Others."

132. Bulkeley, "Playing Well with Others."

133. Conlin, "E-mail Is So Five Minutes Ago"; Dahl, "The End of E-mail"; "Weaving a Secure Web around Education."

134. Wakizaka, "Faxes, E-Mail, Help the Deaf Get Office Jobs," *The Wall Street Journal,* October 3, 1995, B1, B5.

135. S.E. Needleman, "Business Owners Try to Motivate Employees," *The Wall Street Journal,* January 14, 2010, B5.

136. Needleman, "Business Owners Try to Motivate Employees."

137. D. Tannen, "The Power of Talk," *Harvard Business Review,* September–October 1995, 138–48; D. Tannen, *Talking from 9 to 5* (New York: Avon Books, 1995).

138. Tannen, "The Power of Talk."

139. Tannen, "The Power of Talk."

140. Tannen, "The Power of Talk."

141. Tannen, "The Power of Talk."

142. Tannen, "The Power of Talk"; Tannen, *Talking from 9 to 5.*

143. Tannen, *Talking from 9 to 5.*

144. J. Cohen, "He Writes, She Writes," *Houston Chronicle,* July 7, 2001, C1–C2.

145. Cohen, "He Writes, She Writes."

146. Cohen, "He Writes, She Writes."

147. Tannen, "The Power of Talk," 148.

Chapter 17

1. "The 100 Most Powerful Women #5 Indra K. Nooyi," *Forbes.com,* August 30, 2007, www.forbes.com/lists/2007/11/biz-07women_Indra-K-Nooyi_1S5D_print.html, April 23, 2008; "Indra K. Nooyi Profile," *Forbes.com,* http://people.forbes.com/profile/indra-k-nooyi/62917, March 17, 2010.

2. "PepsiCo—Investor Overview," http://phx.corporate-ir.net/phoenix.zhtml?c=78265&p=irol-irhome, May 2, 2008; "Indra Nooyi—News, Articles, Biography, Photos," *WSJ.com,* http://topics.wsj.com/person/n/indra-k-nooyi/247, March 17, 2010; "Pepsico—Indra K. Nooyi," http://www.pepsico.com/company/leadership, June 6, 2014; "PepsiCo on the Forbes Global 2000 List," http://www.forbes.com/companies/pepisco/, June 6, 2014.

3. Morris, "The Pepsi Challenge"; D. Brady, "Indra Nooyi: Keeping Cool in Hot Water," *BusinessWeek,* June 11, 2007, www.businessweek.com/print/magazine/content/07_24/b4038067.htm?chan=gl, April 30, 2008; P. Maidment, "Re-Thinking Social Responsibility," *Forbes.com,* January 25, 2008, www.forbes.com/2008/01/25/davos-corporate-responsibility-lead-cx_pm_0125notes . . . , April 23, 2008; B. Saporito, "Indra Nooyi," *TIME in Partnership with CNN,* Monday, April 30, 2007, www.time.com/time/specials/2007/printout/0,29239,1595326_1615737_1615996,00 . . . , April 23, 2008.

4. "Indra Nooyi—In Photos: The 25 Most Powerful Women In the World, 2014—Forbes," http://www.forbes.com/pictures/lmh45lfdj/indra-nooyi/, June 6, 2014.

5. Morris, "The Pepsi Challenge"; "PepsiCo's Board of Directors Appoints Indra K. Nooyi as Chief Executive Officer Effective October 1, 2006, Steve Reinemund to Retire as Chairman in May 2007," *PEPSICO,* news release, http://phx.corporate-ir.net/phoenix.zhtml?c=78265&p=irol-news Article_print&ID=895346 . . . , May 8, 2008.

6. Morris, "The Pepsi Challenge."

7. Morris, "The Pepsi Challenge."

8. Morris, "The Pepsi Challenge."

9. "PEPSICO Officers and Directors," *PepsiCo* http://www.pepsico.com/PEP_Company/OfficersDirectors/index.cfm, May 2, 2008.

10. Morris, "The Pepsi Challenge."

11. "PepsiCo Announces Upcoming Retirement of Michael White Chairman and PepsiCo International CEO," http://www.pepsico.com/PressRelease/PepsiCo-Announces-Upcoming-Retirement-of-mic . . . , March 17, 2010.

12. Morris, "The Pepsi Challenge."

13. C. Leaf, "Say Wha???) The CEO Who Writes Her Employees' Parents," *Fortune,* January 28, 2014, http://fortune.com/2014/01/28/

say-wha-the-ceo-who-writes-her-employees-parents/, 6/6/2014.

14. A. Moore, MarketWatch, "Indra Nooyi's Pepsi Challenge, CEO Puts Her Own Brand on New Products and Global Goals," December 6, 2007, www.marketwatch.com/news/story/indra-nooyi-puts-her-brand/story.aspx?guid=%7 . . . , April 23, 2008.

15. Morris, "The Pepsi Challenge."

16. Leaf, "Say Wha???) The CEO Who Writes Her Employees' Parents."

17. Leaf, "Say Wha???) The CEO Who Writes Her Employees' Parents."

18. Leaf, "Say Wha???) The CEO Who Writes Her Employees' Parents."

19. Leaf, "Say Wha???) The CEO Who Writes Her Employees' Parents."

20. Leaf, "Say Wha???) The CEO Who Writes Her Employees' Parents."

21. Leaf, "Say Wha???) The CEO Who Writes Her Employees' Parents."

22. Leaf, "Say Wha???) The CEO Who Writes Her Employees' Parents."

23. Leaf, "Say Wha???) The CEO Who Writes Her Employees' Parents."

24. C Leaf, "Say Wha???) The CEO Who Writes Her Employees' Parents."

25. Leaf, "Say Wha???) The CEO Who Writes Her Employees' Parents."

26. Morris, "The Pepsi Challenge."

27. J.A. Litterer, "Conflict in Organizations: A Reexamination," *Academy of Management Journal* 9 (1966), 178–86; S.M. Schmidt and T.A. Kochan, "Conflict: Towards Conceptual Clarity," *Administrative Science Quarterly* 13 (1972), 359–70; R.H. Miles, *Macro Organizational Behavior* (Santa Monica, CA: Goodyear, 1980).

28. S.P. Robbins, *Managing Organizational Conflict: A Nontraditional Approach* (Englewood Cliffs, NJ: Prentice-Hall, 1974); L. Coser, *The Functions of Social Conflict* (New York: Free Press, 1956).

29. K.A. Jehn, "A Qualitative Analysis of Conflict Types and Dimensions in Organizational Groups," Cornell University, 1997; K.A. Jehn, "A Multimethod Examination of the Benefits and Detriments of Intragroup Conflict," Cornell University, 1995.

30. L.L. Putnam and M.S. Poole, "Conflict and Negotiation," in F.M. Jablin, L.L. Putnam, K.H. Roberts, and L.W. Porter, eds., *Handbook of Organizational Communication: An Interdisciplinary Perspective* (Newbury Park, CA: Sage, 1987), 549–99.

31. M. Trottman and R. Whelan, "U.S. Hits Builders with Probe into Pay," *The Wall Street Journal,* September 12, 2011: B1, http://search.proquest.ezproxy.rice.edu/docprintview/887932566?accountid=7064, June 12, 2012.

32. Trottman and Whelan, "U.S. Hits Builders with Probe into Pay"; "Compliance Assistance—Fair Labor Standards Act (FLSA)," *U.S. Department of Labor,*

Wage and Hour Division (WHD), http://www.dol.gov/whd/flsa, June 12, 2012.

33. "Welcome," *PulteGroup, Inc.,* http://pultegroupinc.com/, June 12, 2012; "PULTEGROUP, Inc.," http://pultegroupinc.com/contact-us/default.aspx, June 6, 2014.

34. R. Whelan and M. Trottman, "U.S. Battles Home Builder over Pay Probe," *The Wall Street Journal,* March 23, 2012, B3.

35. Whelan and Trottman, "U.S. Battles Home Builder over Pay Probe."

36. Whelan and Trottman, "U.S. Battles Home Builder over Pay Probe."

37. Whelan and Trottman, "U.S. Battles Home Builder over Pay Probe."

38. Whelan and Trottman, "U.S. Battles Home Builder over Pay Probe."

39. "Directors & Officers," *PulteGroup, Inc.,* Pulte Homes, Investor Relations, http://phx.corporate-ir-net/phoenix.zhtml?c=77968&p=77968&p=irol-govmanage, June 12, 2012.

40. Whelan and Trottman, "U.S. Battles Home Builder over Pay Probe."

41. L.R. Pondy, "Organizational Conflict: Concepts and Models," *Administrative Science Quarterly* 2 (1967), 296–320; R.E. Walton and J.M. Dutton, "The Management of Interdepartmental Conflict: A Model and Review," *Administrative Science Quarterly* 14 (1969), 62–73.

42. G.R. Jones and J.E. Butler, "Managing Internal Corporate Entrepreneurship: An Agency Theory Perspective," *Journal of Management* 18 (1992), 733–49.

43. T. Petzinger, Jr., "All Happy Businesses Are Alike, but Heirs Bring Unique Conflicts," *The Wall Street Journal,* November 17, 1995, B1.

44. J.A. Wall, Jr., "Conflict and Its Management," *Journal of Management* 21 (1995), 515–58.

45. Walton and Dutton, "The Management of Interdepartmental Conflict."

46. Pondy, "Organizational Conflict."

47. W.F. White, *Human Relations in the Restaurant Industry* (New York: McGraw-Hill, 1948).

48. R.L. Pinkley and G.B. Northcraft, "Conflict Frames of Reference: Implications for Dispute Processes and Outcomes," *Academy of Management Journal* 37 (February 1994), 193–206.

49. K.W. Thomas, "Conflict and Negotiation Processes in Organizations," in M.D. Dunnette and L.M. Hough, eds., *Handbook of Industrial and Organizational Psychology,* 2nd ed., vol. 3 (Palo Alto, CA: Consulting Psychologists Press, 1992), 651–717.

50. Thomas, "Conflict and Negotiation Processes in Organizations."

51. Pinkley and Northcraft, "Conflict Frames of Reference."

52. G. Stoller, "Foreign Etiquette for Americans: A Guide to Dos and Don'ts Abroad," *USAToday,* March 29, 2011,

http://travel.usatoday.com/news/story/2011/03/Foreign-etiquette-for-Americans-A-guide-t . . . , June 12, 2012.

53. Stoller, "Foreign Etiquette for Americans: A Guide to Dos and Don'ts Abroad."

54. E. Spitznagel, "Impress Your Chinese Boss," *Bloomberg Businessweek,* January 9, 2012: 80–81.

55. "Artisan Business Group, Inc.," http://www.artisanbusinessgroup.com/about.html, June 6, 2014.

56. Spitznagel, "Impress Your Chinese Boss."

57. M-J. Chen, "Inside Chinese Business: A Guide for Managers Worldwide," MA: Harvard Business School Press, 2001.

58. Chen, "Inside Chinese Business: A Guide for Managers Worldwide."

59. "NengZhao—Blue Oak Capital Limited—ZoomInfo.com," http://www.zoominfo.com/p/Neng-Zhao/1430584918, June 6, 2014.

60. H. Seligson, "For American Workers in China, a Culture Clash, *The New York Times,* http://www.nytimes.com/2009/12/24/business/global/24chinawork.html?_r=1&pagewante . . . , June 12, 2012.

61. J. Sharkey, "On a Visit to Saudi Arabia, Doing What the Saudis Do," *The New York Times,* March 15, 2011: B8.

62. Sharkey, "On a Visit to Saudi Arabia, Doing What the Saudis Do."

63. E. Shapiro, J.A. Trachtenberg, and L. Landro, "Time Warner Settles Feud by Pushing Out Music Division's Fuchs," *The Wall Street Journal,* November 17, 1995, A1, A6.

64. Shapiro et al., "Time Warner Settles Feud."

65. P.R. Lawrence, L.B. Barnes, and J.W. Lorsch, *Organizational Behavior and Administration* (Homewood, IL: Irwin, 1976).

66. R.J. Lewicki and J.R. Litterer, *Negotiation* (Homewood, IL: Irwin, 1985); G.B. Northcraft and M.A. Neale, *Organizational Behavior* (Fort Worth, TX: Dryden, 1994); J.Z. Rubin and B.R. Brown, *The Social Psychology of Bargaining and Negotiation* (New York: Academic Press, 1975).

67. C. Bendersky, "Organizational Dispute Resolution Systems: A Complementarities Model," *Academy of Management Review* 28 (October 2003), 643–57.

68. R.E. Walton, "Third Party Roles in Interdepartmental Conflicts," *Industrial Relations* 7 (1967), 29–43.

69. "Meaning of Arbitrator," www.hyperdictionary.com, September 4, 2004; "Definitions of Arbitrator on the Web," www.google.com, September 4, 2004.

70. L. Thompson and R. Hastie, "Social Perception in Negotiation," *Organizational Behavior and Human Decision Processes* 47 (1990), 98–123.

71. Thomas, "Conflict and Negotiation Processes in Organizations."

72. R.J. Lewicki, S.E. Weiss, and D. Lewin, "Models of Conflict, Negotiation, and Third Party Intervention: A Review and Synthesis," *Journal of Organizational Behavior* 13 (1992), 209–52.

73. Northcraft and Neale, *Organizational Behavior.*

74. Lewicki et al., "Models of Conflict, Negotiation, and Third Party Intervention"; Northcraft and Neale, *Organizational Behavior;* D.G. Pruitt, "Integrative Agreements: Nature and Consequences," in M.H. Bazerman and R.J. Lewicki, eds., *Negotiating in Organizations* (Beverly Hills, CA: Sage, 1983).

75. R. Fischer and W. Ury, *Getting to Yes* (Boston: Houghton Mifflin, 1981); Northcraft and Neale, *Organizational Behavior.*

76. P.J. Carnevale and D.G. Pruitt, "Negotiation and Mediation," *Annual Review of Psychology* 43 (1992), 531–82.

77. A.M. Pettigrew, *The Politics of Organizational Decision Making* (London: Tavistock, 1973); Miles, *Macro Organizational Behavior.*

78. D.J. Hickson, C.R. Hinings, C.A. Lee, R.E. Schneck, and D.J. Pennings, "A Strategic Contingencies Theory of Intraorganizational Power," *Administrative Science Quarterly* 16 (1971), 216–27; C.R. Hinings, D.J. Hickson, J.M. Pennings, and R.E. Schneck, "Structural Conditions of Interorganizational Power," *Administrative Science Quarterly* 19 (1974), 22–44; J. Pfeffer, *Power in Organizations* (Boston: Pitman, 1981).

79. Pfeffer, *Power in Organizations.*

80. Pfeffer, *Power in Organizations.*

81. M. Crozier, "Sources of Power of Lower Level Participants in Complex Organizations," *Administrative Science Quarterly* 7 (1962), 349–64; A.M. Pettigrew, "Information Control as a Power Resource," *Sociology* 6 (1972), 187–204.

82. Pfeffer, *Power in Organizations;* G.R. Salancik and J. Pfeffer, "The Bases and Uses of Power in Organizational Decision Making," *Administrative Science Quarterly* 19 (1974), 453–73; J. Pfeffer and G.R. Salancik, *The External Control of Organizations: A Resource Dependence View* (New York: Harper & Row, 1978).

83. K. Wells, "Nature's Own Hedge Fund," *Bloomberg Businessweek,* June 4–June 10, 2012; B. Griscom, "New Study Finds That Loggers and Conservationists Can Be Allies," May 21, 2012, http:// thinkprogress.org/climate/2012/05/21/ 487604/new-study-finds-that-loggers-and-con . . . , June 11, 2012; L. Kaufman, "Partnership Preserves Livelihoods and Fish Stocks," *The New York Times,* http:// www.nytimes.com/2011/11/28/science/ earth/nature-conservancy-partners-with-califor . . . , June 8, 2012.

84. Wells, "Nature's Own Hedge Fund."

85. Wells, "Nature's Own Hedge Fund."

86. Wells, "Nature's Own Hedge Fund."

87. Wells, "Nature's Own Hedge Fund"; "Executive Team Members—The Nature Conservacncy," http://www.nature.org/ about-us/governance/executive-team/, June 6, 2014.

88. Wells, "Nature's Own Hedge Fund."

89. P. Kareiva, "Our Scientists," *The Nature Conservancy,* http://www.nature.org/ ourscience/ourscientists/conservation-science-at-the-nature-conserva . . . , June 8, 2012.

90. Wells, "Nature's Own Hedge Fund."

91. Wells, "Nature's Own Hedge Fund."

92. "Louisiana Bucket Brigade: Staff," http://www.labucketbrigade.org/article. php?list=type&type=138, June 11, 2012; "LA Bucket Brigade: Anne Rolfes," http://www.labucketbrigade. org/article.php?id=417, June 6, 2014.

93. Wells, "Nature's Own Hedge Fund."

94. "Louisiana Bucket Brigade: About Us," http://www.labucketbrigade.org/article. php?list=type&type=136, June 11, 2012.

95. Wells, "Nature's Own Hedge Fund."

96. L. Kaufman, "Partnership Preserves Livelihoods and Fish Stocks," *The New York Times,* http://www.nytimes. com/2011/11/28/science/earth/nature-conservancy-partners-with-califor . . . , June 8, 2012.

97. P. Voosen, E&E reporter, "Conservation: Myth-Busting Scientist Pushes Greens Past Reliance on 'Horror Stories,'" *Greenwire,* April 3, 2012, http://www.eenews.net/public/ Greenwire/2012/04/03/1?page_type=print, June 8, 2012.

98. Wells, "Nature's Own Hedge Fund"; Voosen, "Conservation: Myth-Busting Scientist Pushes Greens"; Griscom, "New Study Finds That Loggers and Conservationists Can Be Allies"; Kaufman, "Partnership Preserves Livelihoods and Fish Stocks."

99. Pfeffer, *Power in Organizations.*

100. Pfeffer, *Power in Organizations.*

101. Pfeffer, *Power in Organizations.*

102. L. Kramer, "Doing Well and Good: How Social Responsibility Helped One Coffee Grower Land a Deal with Starbucks," *Inc.,* June 2006, 55–56.

103. Kramer, "Doing Well and Good"; "Corporate Social Responsibility," www.star bucks.com/aboutus/csr.asp, June 25, 2006.

104. "The Exceptional Cup Participating Farms Finca El Faro," www.guatemalan coffees.com/GCContent/GCeng/ auction_tec_fincas/FincaElFaro.asp, June 25, 2006; "Coca-Cola Years," *El Faro Estate Coffee,* http://www .elfaroestate.com/history/coca-Cola-Years.php, June 13, 2012.

105. Kramer, "Doing Well and Good."

106. Kramer, "Doing Well and Good."

107. Kramer, "Doing Well and Good."

108. Kramer, "Doing Well and Good."

109. "Welcome to El Faro Estate Website," *El Faro Estate Coffee,* www.elfaroestate. com/default.htm, May 7, 2008; "El Faro Today," El Faro Estate Coffee, www .elfaroestate.com/history/elFaro/ ElFaroToday.htm, May 7, 2008; "C.A.F.E. Practices (Coffee and Farmer Equity Practices)," *Starbucks Coffee,* "The Business of Coffee," www. starbucks.com/aboutus/sourcingcoffee. asp, May 7, 2008; "Welcome to El Faro Estate Website," http://www.elfaroestate. com/default.php, March 18, 2010; "El Faro Today," *El Faro Estate Coffee,* http://www.elfaroestate.com/history/elFaro/elFaroToday.php, March 18, 2010; "El Faro Today," *El Faro Estate Coffee,* http://www.elfaroestate.com/history/ elFaro/elFaroToday.php, June 13, 2012; "Welcome to El Faro Estate Website," *El Faro Estate Coffee,* http://www .elfaroestate.com/default.php, June 13, 2012.; "El Faro Estate Coffee," http:// www.elfaroestate.com/history/elFaro/ elFaroToday.php, June 6, 2014.

110. Kramer, "Doing Well and Good."

Chapter 18

1. "How to Develop Employees Who Are Engaged At Work," *Forbes,* April 15, 2014, www.forbes.com/sites/unify/ 2014/04/15/how-to-develop-employees-who-are-engaged-at-work/.

2. H. J. Wilson, "The Hot New thing in Business Attire is Technology," *The Wall Street Journal,* October 20, 2013, online. wsj.com/news/articles/SB300014240527 02303796404579099203059125112.

3. Ibid.

4. C. Brauer, "Workplace Wearables: Yoru Boss Knows When You've Had a Good Night's Sleep?" cnn.com, May 7, 2014, edition.cnn.com/2014/05/01/ tech/innovation/workplace-wearables-your-boss-knows/.

5. B. Greene, "How Your Boss Can Keep You on a Leash," cnn.com, February 2, 2014, www.cnn.com/2014/02/02/ opinion/greene-corporate-surveillance/.

6. H. J. Wilson, "The Hot New thing in Business Attire is Technology," *The Wall Street Journal,* October 20, 2013, online .wsj.com/news/articles/SB30001424052 702303796404579099203059125112.

7. Ibid.

8. D. Gura, "If Your Company ID Badge was a Tracking Device . . . " *Marketplace Business,* April 28, 2014, www .marketplace.org/topics/business/if-your-company-id-badge-was-tracking-device.

9. N. B. Macintosh, *The Social Software of Accounting Information Systems* (New York: Wiley, 1995).

10. C. A. O'Reilly, "Variations in Decision Makers' Use of Information: The Impact of Quality and Accessibility," *Academy of Management Journal* 25 (1982), 756–71.

11. G. Stalk and T. H. Hout, *Competing against Time* (New York: Free Press, 1990).

12. www.iata.com, 2012.

13. R. Cyert and J. March, *Behavioral Theory of the Firm* (Englewood Cliff s, NJ: Prentice-Hall, 1963).

14. E. Turban, *Decision Support and Expert Systems* (New York: Macmillan, 1988).

15. W. H. Davidow and M. S. Malone, *The Virtual Corporation* (New York: Harper Business, 1992); M. E. Porter, *Competitive Advantage* (New York: Free Press, 1984).

16. S. Baghdassarian, B. Blau, J. Ekhold, S. Shen, "Predicts 2014: Apps, Personal cloud and Data Analytics Will Drive New Consumer Interactions," *Gartner,* November 22, 2013, www.gartner.com/doc/2628016.

17. S. M. Dornbusch and W. R. Scott, *Evaluation and the Exercise of Authority* (San Francisco: Jossey-Bass, 1975).

18. J. Child, *Organization: A Guide to Problems and Practice* (London: Harper & Row, 1984).

19. "Contract Logistics—Retail," ups-scs .com, n.d., www.ups-scs.com/logistics/industries/retail.html.

20. Macintosh, *The Social Soft ware of Accounting Information Systems.*

21. H. J. Wilson, "The Hot New Thing in Business Attire Is Technology," *The Wall Street Journal,* October 20, 2013, online. wsj.com/news/articles/SB4000142405270 2303796404579099203059125112.

22. T. Meek, "Bid Data in HR: Finding In-House Talent in the Digital Age," *Forbes,* April 29, 2014, http://www .forbes.com/sites/netapp/2014/04/29/big-data-in-hr/.

23. Ibid.

24. "Talent and Workforce Management," ibm.com, n.d., http://www-03.ibm.com/software/products/en/category/SW333.

25. E. Byrne, "Tomorrow's Recruitment: Big-Data Robots Bring Better Hires," *Forbes,* May 29, 2013, http://www .forbes.com/sites/netapp/2013/05/29/recruitment-big-data/.

26. C. Versace, "Talking Big Data and Analytics With IBM," *Forbes,* April 1, 2014, http://www.forbes.com/sites/chrisversace/2014/04/01/talking-big-data-and-analytics-with-ibm/.

27. J. Clampet, "Skift Q&A: The Man Who Feeds More Than 300,000 Disney Guests a Day," *Skift,* October 9, 2013, http://skift .com/2013/10/09/skift-qa-the-man-who-feeds-more-than-300000-disney-visitors-a-day/.

28. "Behind the Scenes at Starbucks Supply Chain Operations It's Plan, Source, Make & Deliver," *SupplyChain247,* September 20, 2013, www.supplychain247.com/article/

behind_the_scenes_at_starbucks_supply_chain_operations/green.

29. N. Cotiaux, "Starbucks Supply-Chain Program Holds Lessons for Small Businesses," intuit.com, March 14, 2014, blog.intuit.com/employees/starbucks-supply-chain-program-holds-lessons-for-small-businesses/.

30. "Cocoa Origin Trip Report—Ecuador," starbucks.com, January 10, 2011, www.starbucks.com/blog/cocoa-origin-trip-report-e28093-ecuador.

31. N. Cotiaux, "Starbucks Supply-Chain Program Holds Lessons for Small Businesses," intuit.com, March 14, 2014, blog .intuit.com/employees/starbucks-supply-chain-program-holds-lessons-for-small-businesses/.

32. J. A. Schumpeter, *Capitalism, Socialism, and Democracy* (New York: Harper, 1942).

33. V. P. Buell, *Marketing Management* (New York: McGraw-Hill, 1985).

34. "Apple Press Info", apple.com, n.d., www .apple.com/pr/products/ipodhistory/.

35. D. Lee, "Apple's iPod: Is the End Nigh?" *BBC,* January 28, 2014, www.bbc.com/news/technology-25927366.

36. Ibid.

37. See M. M. J. Berry and J. H. Taggart, "Managing Technology and Innovation: A Review," *R & D Management* 24 (1994), 341–53; K. B. Clark and S. C. Wheelwright, *Managing New Product and Process Development* (New York: Free Press, 1993).

38. D. Gross, "As Tablets Boom, E-readers Feel the Blast," cnn.com, February 28, 2013, www.cnn.com/2013/02/28/tech/gaming-gadgets/tablets-replacing-e-readers/.

39. D. Athow, "Windows XP End-of-Life: Thanks for All the Fish!" techradar .com, April 6, 2014, www.techradar .com/news/software/operating-systems/windows-xp-end-of-life-what-you-need-to-know-1240791.

40. Ibid.

41. "In A Year, Microsoft Is Going Abandon 500 Million Windows XP Users," *Business Insider,* April 15, 2013, www .businessinsider.com/microsoft-to-cut-windows-xp-2013-4#!Hv4jA.

42. D. Athow, "Windows XP End-of-Life: Thanks for All the Fish!" techradar .com, April 6, 2014, www.techradar .com/news/software/operating-systems/windows-xp-end-of-life-what-you-need-to-know-1240791.

43. "In A Year, Microsoft Is Going Abandon 500 Million Windows XP Users," *Business Insider,* April 15, 2013, www .businessinsider.com/microsoft-to-cut-windows-xp-2013-4#!Hv4jA.

44. "End of Windows XP Support—What It Means to Consumers and Businesses," CBS Radio News, April 8, 2014, soundcloud.com/cbs-radio-news/end-of-windows-xp-support-what.

45. "In A Year, Microsoft Is Going Abandon 500 Million Windows XP Users," *Business Insider,* April 15, 2013, www .businessinsider.com/microsoft-to-cut-windows-xp-2013-4#!Hv4jA.

46. Ibid.

47. Ibid.

48. microsoft.com, n.d., www.microsoft.com/en-us/windows/enterprise/end-of-support .aspx.

49. "Business Owners: 10 Things You Need to Do Before Migrating Off Windows XP," *Forbes,* April 8, 2014, www.forbes .com/sites/groupthink/2014/04/08/business-owners-10-things-you-need-to-do-before-migrating-off-windows-xp/.

50. "In A Year, Microsoft Is Going Abandon 500 Million Windows XP Users," *Business Insider,* April 15, 2013, www .businessinsider.com/microsoft-to-cut-windows-xp-2013-4#!Hv4jA.

51. See Berry and Taggart, "Managing Technology and Innovation"; M. Gort and J. Klepper, "Time Paths in the Diffusion of Product Innovations," *Economic Journal,* September 1982, 630–53. Looking at the history of 46 products, Gort and Klepper found that the length of time before other companies entered the markets created by a few inventive companies declined from an average of 14.4 years for products introduced before 1930 to 4.9 years for those introduced after 1949—implying that product life cycles were being compressed. Also see A. Griffin, "Metrics for Measuring Product Development Cycle Time," *Journal of Production and Innovation Management* 10 (1993), 112–25.

52. "Press Release: Worldwide Server Market Revenues Decline—4.4% in the Fourth Quarter as Weak Midrange and High-end Server Demand Weighs on the Market, According to IDC," idc.com, February 26, 2014, www.idc.com/getdoc.jsp?container Id=prUS24704714.

53. Ibid.

54. www.sgi.com, 2012.

55. A. D. Chandler, *The Visible Hand* (Cambridge, MA: Harvard University Press, 1977).

56. C. W. L. Hill and J. F. Pickering, "Divisionalization, Decentralization, and Performance of Large United Kingdom Companies," *Journal of Management Studies* 23 (1986), 26–50.

57. O. E. Williamson, *Markets and Hierarchies: Analysis and Antitrust Implications* (New York: Free Press, 1975).

58. Turban, *Decision Support and Expert Systems.*

59. "Iteris Launches ClearPath Weather™ Road Maintenance Decision Support System," *Fort Mill Times,* May 5, 2014, www.fortmilltimes.com/2014/05/05/3458761/iteris-launches-clearpath-weather.html.

60. Turban, *Decision Support and Expert Systems.*

61. E. Rich, *Artificial Intelligence* (New York: McGraw-Hill, 1983).

62. R. Brandt, "Agents and Artificial Life," *BusinessWeek,* June 13, 1994, 55–56.

63. Rich, *Artificial Intelligence.*

64. Ibid., 346.

65. "IQMS EnterpriseIQ ERP," erpshootout .com, n.d., www.erpshootout.com/iqms_ enterpriseiq_erp.html.

66. Ibid.

67. "From Four to One: Custom Profile's Success with Comprehensive ERP Software from IQMS," iqms.com, n.d., www .iqms.com/company/custom-profile/ index.html.

68. Ibid.

69. B. Kogut, "Joint Ventures: Theoretical and Empirical Perspectives," *Strategic Management Journal* 9 (1988), 319–32.

70. "IHG Announces Strategic Alliance with the Coca-Cola Company," ihgplc.com, April 17, 2014, www.ihgplc.com/index .asp?PageID=57&newsid=3200& rssfeed=tccportal.

71. G. S. Capowski, "Designing a Corporate Identity," *Management Review,* June 1993, 37–38.

72. J. Marcia, "Just Doing It," *Distribution,* January 1995, 36–40.

73. L. Columbus, "Gartner Predicts CRM Will Be A $36B Market by 2017," *Forbes,* June 18, 2013, www.forbes.com/sites/ louiscolumbus/2013/06/18/gartner-predicts- crm-will-be-a-36b-market-by-2017/.

74. Davidow and Malone, *The Virtual Corporation.*

75. Ibid., 168.

76. J. Fulk and G. Desanctis, "Electronic Communication and Changing Organi- zational Forms," *Organizational Science,* 1995, vol. 6, 337–49.

77. Y. P. Shao, S. Y. Liao, and H. Q. Wang, "A Model of Virtual Organizations," *Acad- emy of Management Executive,* 1998, 12, 120–28.

78. K. Gurchiek, "Teleworking Not Remotely a Problem for Some Companies," *Society for Human Resource Management,* March 31, 2014, www.shrm.org/ hrdisciplines/technology/articles/pages/ teleworking-not-a-problem.aspx.

79. M. Rafter, "Employees Told to Go Home— and Work," *Orange County Register,* March 3, 2014, www.ocregister.com/articles/ office-604071-says-work.html.

80. K. Gurchiek, "Teleworking Not Remotely a Problem for Some Companies," *Society for Human Resource Management,* March 31, 2014, www.shrm.org/ hrdisciplines/technology/articles/pages/ teleworking-not-a-problem.aspx.

81. M. Rafter, "Employees Told to Go Home—and Work," *Orange County Register,* March 3, 2014, www.ocregister. com/articles/office-604071-says-work. html.

82. "Latest Telecommuting Statistics," Global Workplace Analytics, n.d., www.globalworkplaceanalytics.com/ telecommuting-statistics.

83. Ibid.

84. Ibid.

85. Ibid.

86. Ibid.

87. N. Bloom, "To Raise Productivity, Let More Employees Work from Home," *Harvard Business Review,* January– February 2014, hbr.org/2014/01/to-raise- productivity-let-more-employees-work- from-home/ar/1.

88. T. Stewart, "Managing in a Wired Com- pany," *Fortune,* July 11, 1994, 44–56.

CREDITS

Photo Credits

Chapter 1

Opener: © Sam Edwards/age fotostock RF; p. 3: © Eric Charbonneau /Invision/AP Images; p. 10: © Mark Peterson/Redux; p. 19: © Scott Olson/Getty Images; p. 23: © Imaginechina via AP Images; p. 24: © India Today Group/Getty Images.

Chapter 2

Opener: © Fuse/Getty Images RF; p. 33: © *Bloomberg* via Getty Images; p. 37: © Bettmann/Corbis; p. 39: © © 20th Century Fox Film Corp. All rights reserved./courtesy Everett Collection; p. 41: © akg-images/ The Image Works; p. 47: Photo courtesy of Regina A. Greenwood, from the Ronald G. Greenwood Collection; p. 50: © Jon Freilich/ *Bloomberg* via Getty Images.

Chapter 3

Opener: © Sam Edwards/age fotostock RF; p. 61: © Bryan Bedder/Getty Images for *Lucky Magazine*; p. 66: © J. Meric/Getty Images; p. 70: Courtesy of Gentle Giant Moving Company; p. 72: © AP Photo/Rick Bowmer; p. 75: © Flying Colours Ltd/Getty Images RF; p. 79: Image courtesy of IDEO.

Chapter 4

Opener: © Chris Ryan/age fotostock RF; p. 91: © AP Photo/Evan Vucci; p. 95: © Hulton Archive/Getty Images; p. 97: © AP Photo/Craig Ruttle; p. 102: © Liang Sen/ Xinhua Press/Corbis; p. 113: © Stefanie Keenan/WireImage/Getty Images.

Chapter 5

Opener: © Sam Edwards/age fotostock RF; p. 123: © Joe Fox/Radharc Images/Alamy; p. 128: © ColorBlind Images/Blend Images LLC RF; p. 132: © Mikkel Bækhøj Christensen/De/Demotix/Corbis; p. 134: © PR NEWSWIRE/AP Images; p. 141: © Tannis Toohey/*Toronto Star*/ZUMA Press/Newscom; p. 145: © Digital Vision/Getty Images RF.

Chapter 6

Opener: © Polka Dot Images/Jupiterimages; p. 157: © Imaginechina/Corbis; p. 161: © John Van Hasselt/Corbis; p. 165: © Philip Game/ Lonely Planet Images/Getty Images; p. 171:

© Buda Mendes/Getty Images For Laureus; p. 177: © Comstock/Stockbyte/Getty Images RF.

Chapter 7

Opener: © Robert Nicholas/age fotostock RF; p. 185: © Bloomberg via Getty Images; p. 190: © AP Images RF; p. 199: Courtesy GarageTek; p. 203: © Morgan Lane Photography/Alamy RF.

Chapter 8

Opener: © Tom Merton/age fotostock RF; p. 215: © *Bloomberg* via Getty Images; p. 222: © AP Images/Tom Mihalek; p. 226: © AP Photo/Mark Lennihan; p. 231: © *Bloomberg* via Getty Images; p. 238: © Indranil Mukherjee/ AFP/Getty Images; p. 241: © Darrell Ingham/Getty Images.

Chapter 9

Opener: © Tom Merton/age fotostock RF; p. 247: © Image Source/Christopher Robbins RF; p. 253: © AP Images/Joseph Kaczmarek; p. 254: *Bloomberg* via Getty Images; p. 263: © Junko Kimura/Getty Images; p. 270: © Bloomberg via Getty Images.

Chapter 10

Opener: © Patrick Heagney/Getty Images RF; p. 277: © Alberto E. Rodriguez/WireImage/ Getty Images; p. 282: © Jeffrey Allan Salter/ Corbis; p. 286: © Tim Boyle/Getty Images; p. 289: © AP Photo/Mel Evans; p. 296: © Bloomberg via Getty Images.

Chapter 11

Opener: © Image Source/Getty Images RF; p. 313: © Charley Gallay/ Getty Images; p. 316: Courtesy Marsha Egan; p. 321: © U.S. Army Photo; p. 331: © AP Photo/Disney, Gene Duncan; p. 339: © Courtesy Virtusize.

Chapter 12

Opener: © David Lees/Getty Images RF; p. 345: © Mark Peterson/Redux; p. 349: © Jared McMillen/Aurora Photos/Corbis; p. 355: © david pearson/Alamy; p. 357: Courtesy of Fog Creek Software; p. 362: © Reza Estakhrian/Photographer's Choice/ Getty Images; p. 370: © Photo by Jess Haessler/Courtesy Guerra DeBerry Coody.

Chapter 13

Opener: © Yuri Arcurs/Cutcaster RF; p. 379: © Jeremy M. Lange/*The New York Times*/ Redux; p. 383: © LWA/Dann Tardif/Blend Images/Corbis RF; p. 387: © Brad Swonetz/ Redux; p. 390: © Jim Esposito/Getty Images RF; p. 396: © Stockbyte/Punchstock Images RF; p. 397: © Ari Perilstein/Getty Images; p. 401: © vario images GmbH & Co.KG/Alamy.

Chapter 14

Opener: © Joshua Hodge Photography/Getty Images RF; p. 413: © Tony Kurdzuk/Star Ledger/Corbis; p. 417: Courtesy Zingerman's Delicatessen; p. 421: © AP Photo/Paul Sancya; p. 423: © Tim Boyle/Getty Images; p. 428: © Stockbyte/Getty Images RF; p. 430: © IPON-BONESS/SIPA/Newscom.

Chapter 15

Opener: © Digital Vision/Getty Images RF; p. 443: © Ruaridh Stewart/ZUMA Press, Inc./ Alamy; p. 448: © Emmanuel Faure/Stone/ Getty Images; p. 451: © AP Images/Alexandra Boulat/VII; p. 456: © Digital Vision/Getty Images RF; p. 462: © OJO Images Ltd/Alamy RF; p. 463: © Associated Press RF.

Chapter 16

Opener: © Tom Merton/age fotostock RF; p. 475: © *Bloomberg* via Getty Images; p. 478: © Doug Menuez/Getty Images RF; p. 480: © Allan Danahar/Getty Images RF; p. 483: © 2009 Jupiterimages Corporation RF; p. 487: © David Lee/Alamy; p. 494: © NetPhotos/ Alamy; p. 499: © Photodisc/Alamy RF.

Chapter 17

Opener: © Chris Ryan/age fotostock RF; p. 509: © Bloomberg via Getty Images; p. 514: © Hugh Sitton/Corbis; p. 517: © Move Art Management/Corbis; p. 520: © moodboard/ SuperStock RF; p. 525: © Ian G Dagnall/Alamy; p. 528: Courtesy of El Faro Estate Coffee.

Chapter 18

Opener: © Sam Edwards/age fotostock RF; p. 535: © Haiyin Wang/Alamy RF; p. 539: © Jose Luis Pelaez Inc/Blend Images LLC RF; p. 541: © James Leynse/Corbis; p. 545: © George Frey/*Bloomberg* via Getty Images.

INDEX

Name Index

A

Aaron, K., 573
Abell, D. F., 580, 582
Abott, Ida, 116, 363
Abrams, R., 562
Ackerman, P. L., 594
Adams, D. A., 602
Adams, J. S., 392, 593
Adams, S., 583, 591
Adler, N. J., 593
Adler, P. S., 568
Agarwala-Rogers, R., 601
Aguilar, F. J., 580
Albanese, M., 579
Alden, W., 563
Alderfer, Clayton, 389, 390, 391
Alderfer, C. P., 593
Alexander, B., 583
Alexander, J. A., 586
Allen, T. D., 589
Allison, M., 596, 597
Alster, N., 574
Ambrose, M. L., 593
Ammenheuser, M. K., 592
Amodio, D. M., 573
Amoruso, Cheryl, 130
Anand, Rohini, 134
Ancona, D. G., 562
Anderson, C., 563
Anderson, J. C., 582
Anderson, P., 587
Andrews, K. R., 568, 580
Ante, S. E., 603
Anthony, R. N., 586
Aplin, J. C., 579
Arantes, B., 582
Argyris, C., 590
Ariishi, Takako, 143
Armour, S., 571
Armstrong, Bob, 479
Arnaud, A., 593
Arndt, M., 569, 599
Arnett, Will, 438
Arnold, Marilyn, 212, 213
Arnst, C., 576
Aronoff, C. E., 603
Aronow, S., 582
Aronson, J. A., 573
Arrow, K. J., 578
Asbed, Greg, 533
Athow, D., 607
Austin, N., 602
Aveni, R. D., 580
Aversa, J., 566
Avolio, B. J., 580, 597
Ayman, R., 597

B

Bader, E., 584
Baertlein, L., 581
Baetz, M. L., 596
Baghdassarian, S., 607
Baig, E., 602
Bailey, J. R., 565
—, J. E., 576
—, L., 588

Bakan, D., 573
Baker, S., 594, 599
Ballmer, S., 584
Ballmer, Steve, 297
Banaji, M., 574
Bandura, A., 594
Banerjee, N., 589
Banks, Elizabeth, 438
Bapuji, H., 568
Barbeite, F. G., 592
Barley, S. R., 569
Barnard, C. I., 568
Barnes, L. B., 605
Barnes-Farrell, J., 571
Baron, R. A., 567
Barr, M., 577
Barra, Mary, 114, 225–227
Barrick, M. R., 565
Barry, V., 563, 568
Barsaloux, J., 579
Bartlett, C. A., 576, 581
Baskin, O. W., 603
Bass, Barbara, 260
Bass, B. M., 580, 596, 597
Batali, Mario, 532, 533
Bates, D., 585
Batson, C. D., 592
Batstone, David, 88
Battaglia, B. A., 574
Baucus, M. S., 569
Baum, H. G., 562
Bazerman, M. H., 578, 606
Beauchamp, T. L., 568, 585
Becker, T. E., 568
Begley, S., 567
Beizer, D., 602
Bell, C. H., 586
Bellah, R., 577
Belliveau, M. A., 573
Belson, K., 595
Bender, Leon, 75
Bendersky, C., 605
Benioff, Marc, 475–477
Bennis, W., 595
Bensen, Pete, 294
Bentley, D., 582
Bercovici, J., 567
Berger, B., 578
Berger, P. L., 567
Bergman, Kurt, 289
Berkowitz, L., 597
Berman, D. K., 575
Berman, Richard, 532, 533
Bernard, T. S., 590
Berne, R., 599
Berry, L. L., 562
Berry, M. M. J., 607
Bettenhausen, K., 567, 598
Beyer, J. M., 567
Bezos, Jeff, 163, 376, 377, 447, 448
Bhagwati, J., 576
Bianchi, S., 568
Bies, R. J., 593
Biolos, J., 582
Black, K., 600
Blackburn, R. S., 600
Blake, Robert, 424
Blake, R. R., 597

Blanchard, K., 597
Blanchard, Kenneth, 424
Blankenship, Chip, 19
Blankenship, Don, 26
Blau, B., 607
Blau, P. M., 584, 586
Bloom, J., 592
Bloom, N., 608
Bloomberg, Michael, 91
Bomey, N., 580
Bonabeau, E., 574
Bond, Ron, 134
Boone, Garrett, 385, 386, 387
Borman, C., 590
Borman, W. C., 590
Borrus, A., 590
Bort, J., 595
Borzacchiello, Maureen, 434
Bouchard, T. J., Jr., 579
Boulud, Daniel, 532
Bourgeois, L. J., 575
Bowen, D. E., 582
Bowie, N. E., 568, 585
Bowman, R., 568
Bowman, Robert, 100
Boyd, D. M., 603
Boyle, Dennis, 82
Bracken, D. W., 590
Bradspies, R. W., 585
Bradt, G., 583, 585
Brady, D., 599, 602, 604
Brandt, R., 594, 608
Brandt, R. L., 599
Branson, R., 585
Branson, Richard, 301
Brauer, C., 606
Bresler, S. J., 575
Breteau, Sébastien, 99, 100
Brett, J. B., 71n
Brettman, A., 576
Brickner, M. A., 601
Brief, A. P., 76n, 566, 573, 574, 575, 579
Brockner, J., 565, 566
Brohan, M., 586
Bromley, Stan, 363
Brondel, Andrew, 408, 409
Brooke, Beth, 170, 171
Brown, Bev, 381
Brown, B. R., 605
Brown, D. J., 565
Brown, L., 586
Brown, Sherrod, 182
Brown, V., 572
Brownstein, R., 571
Bruce, M., 568
Bruer, J. T., 572
Bruner, J. S., 573
Brustein, J., 585
Bruun, S. E., 601
Bryant, A., 564, 569, 596
Buchanan, L., 591, 595, 596
Buday, R. S., 599
Budworth, M. H., 591
Buell, V. P., 607
Buffett, Warren, 96, 235
Bulkeley, W. M., 584, 603
Bunch, John, 314
Bunderson, S. J., 563

Bunge, J., 581
Bunis, D., 564
Burcke, J. M., 599
Burg, N., 568
Burke, M. J., 76n
Burkitt, L., 577
Burlingham, B., 567, 595
Burnett, D. D., 565
Burnham, D. H., 565, 593
Burns, L. R., 584
Burns, T., 564, 583
Burns, Tom, 52, 53
Burton, T. M., 596
Butler, J. E., 587, 605
Buttram, R. T., 574, 575
Buzzotta, V. R., 599
Byrne, E., 607
Byrne, J. A., 589, 590
Byrnes, N., 594, 599
Byron, K., 602
Byron, Kristin, 485

C

Cable, J., 563
Caldwell, D. F., 585
Calixto, Lucas, 472
Callahan, J. D., 574
Callahan, Mary, 526, 527
Calori, R., 596
Caltabiano, Greg, 484
Campbell, J. P., 562, 592
Campbell, Tracey, 137
Capowski, G. S., 608
Cappelli, Peter, 541
Cardello, H., 568
Cardy, R. L., 571
Carey, A., 564
Carey, Bridget, 561
Carnevale, A. P., 574
Carnevale, P. J., 606
Carpenter, M. A., 576
Carpenter, S., 565
Carr, E., 590
Carroll, A. B., 569
Carroll, J. S., 562
Carroll, S. J., 562, 586
Carruthers, Sally, 420–421
Carton, B., 571, 575
Cartwright, D., 596, 600
Case, Steve, 186
Casey, Jim, 189
Catmul, E., 583
Catmull, Ed, 277, 278
Cavale, S., 577
Cavanaugh, G. F., 568
Caves, R. E., 581
Chafkin, M., 587
Chambers, John, 484
Champy, J., 583, 599
Chan, C., 580
Chandler, Alfred D., 548, 580, 583, 607
Chang, J., 572
Chao, Elaine, 372, 590
Chaplin, Charlie, 38
Charles, A. C., 573
Charney, Dov, 148
Chatman, J., 585
Chavel, George, 134
Chavez, L., 570
Chavez-Thompson, Linda, 372
Cheema, Wasim Khalid, 110
Chemers, M. M., 597
Chemi, E., 581
Chen, Amy, 300
Chen, B., 563
Chen, M-J., 605
Chenault, Kenneth, 10, 562
Child, J., 583, 607

Cho, R., 568
Christensen, C. R., 581
Christie, L., 579
Chua, J. M., 576
Chung-Ming, L., 586
Clampet, J., 607
Clark, Dave, 377
Clark, K. B., 607
Clark, K. D., 562
Clark, Maurice, 40
Clark, P. A., 586
Clark, S., 591
Clay, R. A., 593
Clegg, C. W., 599
Clegg, S., 565
Clements, T., 586
Cleveland, J. N., 571
Clifford, L., 587
Clifford, S., 579, 596
Clinton, Hillary, 171
Coffey, E. G., 563
Coffin, Charles, 35
Coffing, Bridget, 294
Cohan, P., 585
Cohan, Peter, 301
Cohen, J., 604
Cohen, J. D., 567
Cohen, M. D., 578
Cohen, R. L., 593
Cole, J. R., 572
Cole, Y., 575
Colella, A., 571, 573
Coleman, David, 506
Colihan, J., 600
Collins, C. J., 562
Collins, D., 568
Collins, J., 564, 580
Collins, Jim, 42, 45, 46
Colquitt, J. A., 565, 593
Columbus, L., 608
Compton, Mark, 426–427
Condon, S., 590
Conger, J. A., 597
Conlin, M., 569, 604
Connolly, T., 594
Conolly, Patrick, 427–428
Conway, Ron, 88
Cook, S. D. N., 584
Cook, Tim, 229
Coons, A. I., 596
Cooper, C. L., 590
Cooper, J. C., 599
Cooper, Martin, 187
Cooper, William, 123
Copeland, M., 592
Coplan, J. H., 571
Coser, L., 605
Cosier, R. A., 579
Costa, P. T., 565
Cote, S., 598
Cotiaux, N., 607
Cotsonas, David, 428–429
Coutinho, Paula, 472
Coutts, P., 595
Covert, A. E., 573
Cox, Bill, 147
Crane, Mark, 427–428
Cronin, M. J., 603
Crosby, F. J., 593
Crosby, P. B., 582
Crossman, Jacob, 494
Crowley, M., 591
Crozier, M., 606
Cullen, J. B., 568
Cullen, M. J., 573
Cummings, L. L., 566, 567, 569, 593, 596, 602
Cuneo, A. Z., 575
Curb, Mike, 29

Curtin, J. J., 573
Cyert, R., 578, 607

D

Daft, R. L., 578, 602
Dahl, D., 579, 604
Dalesio, E. P., 591
Daley, J., 583
Dalkey, N., 579
Dallas, S., 599
Daly, Robert, 518
Dane, E., 578
Darin, J. B., 588
Darley, J. M., 567
Daruwala, Nikki, 137
Daus, C. S., 563
D'Aveni, Richard, 582
Davidow, W. H., 607
Davis, A. L., 568
Davis, B., 576
Davis, S. M., 584
Davis, T. R. V., 594
Dawley, H., 579
Day, Frank B., 448
Dean, J. W., 582
de Bono, E., 578
de Bono, Edward, 196
Debow, Daniel, 476
Dechant, K., 573
DeCotiis, T. A., 590
DeFife, Scott, 532
DeGeorgeat, Lenny, 541
De Geus, P., 580
Delbecq, A., 579
Dell, Michael, 207
De Lollis, B., 574
Del Valle, C., 588
DeMarie, S. M., 600
Deming, W. E., 564
Denning, S., 575
De Rochemont, Michelle, 346
Desanctis, G., 608
Deutsch, C. H., 574
Deutschman, A., 599, 600
Devanny, Trace, 305
Devine, P. G., 573
Dewett, T., 564
Dharan, Bala, 594
Dickson, W. J., 564
Diehl, M., 579
Digman, J. M., 565
Di Meglio, Francesca, 593
DiMicco, Daniel R., 116
Dishman, L., 564
Disney, Roy, 277
Disney, Walt, 81, 277
Dobson, J., 568
Donahue, Randy, 131
Donaldson, T., 563
Donatone, Lorna, 134
Donehue, Paul, 505
Donovan, J. J., 593
Dornbusch, S. M., 607
Douglas, D., 586
Doz, Y. L., 581
Drauden, G., 579
Drennan, K., 575
Drucker, P. F., 562, 586
Druskate, V. U., 562
Duarte, D. L., 600
Duchinsky, Brian, 479
Duff, M., 592
Duffy, J., 585
Duffy, Jill, 316
Dufour, B., 596
Dumaine, B., 562, 583, 586, 599
Duncan, R., 583

Dunham, R. B., 71n
Dunham, R. S., 590
Dunnette, M. D., 562, 588, 591, 592, 593, 596, 600, 605
Durose, Steve, 310
Dutton, J. M., 605
Dvorak, P., 572, 594, 602
Dyer, Chris, 557

E

Eagly, A. H., 598
Earley, P. C., 594, 601
Early, P. C., 567
Easterbrook, Steve, 294
Easterday, Tom, 72
Eberhardt, Pia, 182
Eby, L. T., 589
Eccles, R. E., 564
Edison, Thomas, 35
Edmondson, G., 576, 578
Edwards, J., 585
Edwards, M. R., 590
Egan, Marsha, 316
Ehrhart, M. G., 573
Einstein, W. O., 597
Eisenberg, M., 582
Eisner, Michael, 331
Ekegren, G., 594
Ekhold, J., 607
Elfenbein, H. A., 566
Elgin, B., 594
Elizur, D., 585
Elkind, P., 568
Ellis, Shirley, 423
Ellison, N. B., 603
Emrich, C., 572
Emshwiller, J. R., 568
Enciina, G. Billikopf, 594
Engardio, P., 569
Engber, D., 575
Epstein, S., 567
Erez, M., 580
Ericson, C., 585
Evans, M. G., 597
Evans, T., 579

F

Fackler, M., 574
Fahim, K., 571
Fairhurst, G. T., 586
Faletski, I., 595
Falinski, Joseph, 472
Falwell, Jerry, 439
Farmer, David, 343
Farnham, A., 584
Farzad, R., 566
Favaro, K., 586
Fayo, H., 580
Fayol, H., 562, 564
Fayol, Henri, 40, 42–46, 49, 53, 54, 218
Feather, N. T., 592
Feldman, D. C., 567
Fenn, D., 598
Fenton, Tim, 294
Fernandez, J. P., 577
Ferrar, Jonathan, 540
Ferris, D., 575
Ferris, G. R., 565, 587
Festinger, L., 600
Fiedler, F. E., 597
Fiedler, Fred, 425, 427, 429
Fierman, J., 597
Fife, William J., 419
Files, J., 572
Filipczak, B., 575
Filo, David, 206
Fine, Janice R., 533
Finger, P. A., 579
Finholt, T., 600

Finkelstein, S., 587
Fischer, R., 606
Fisher, A., 574, 593
Fisher, C. D., 588, 589, 590, 594
Fisher, Linda, 197
Fisher, L. J., 578
Fisher, M., 577
Fishman, C., 562
Fisk, M. C., 597
Fiske, S. T., 572, 573
Fitzpatrick, David, 348
Flamholtz, E., 585
Fleishman, E. A., 596, 597
Fleming, Denise Russell, 153, 154
Fletcher, M., 586
Flint, J., 571, 589
Floersch, Rich, 563
Floyd, S. W., 586
Flynn, J., 590
Folger, R., 573, 593
Follett, Mary Parker, 46–47, 53, 564
Ford, Henry, 38, 49
Forgas, J. P., 566
Forman, Barry, 515
Fowler, G. A., 563
Fox, M., 568
Fox, M. F., 572
France, M., 574
Frankel, M. S., 569
Fraser, Jill Andresky, 394
Frederickson, Valerie, 376
Fredrickson, J. W., 576
Freedman, D. H., 589
Freedman, Marc, 212
Freeman, J., 585
Freeman, Morgan, 438
Freeman, R. E., 568
French, R. P., Jr., 596
French, W. L., 586
Frey, C., 596
Friedman, M., 569
Frommer, D., 585
Fry, L., 563, 583
Fuchs, Michael, 518
Fulk, J., 608
Furst, S. A., 600

G

Gabor, A., 582
Galbraith, J. R., 583, 584
Galen, M., 575
Gallagher, L. G., 568
Galvin, B. M., 573
Ganster, D. C., 567
Garber, K., 590
Garfinkel, P., 589
Garnick, D., 587
Garvin, D., 582
Gates, Bill, 81, 96, 568
Gates, Gary, 131
Gates, G. J., 571
Gatewood, E., 569
Gavin, M. B., 586
Geare, A. J., 595
Geber, B., 600
Geffen, David, 132
Geis, F. L., 572
Gellerman, S. W., 568
Gendron, George, 410
Gendron, M., 594
Gentile, M. C., 579
George, J. M., 76n, 565, 566, 567, 571, 588, 598, 601
Gerdes, L., 593
Gerhart, B., 589
Gerkovich, P. R., 570, 598
Gersick, C. J. G., 600
Gerstner, Lou, 84
Gerth, H. H., 564
Ghoshal, S., 576, 581, 585
Gibson, C., 570

Gier, J. A., 589
Gilbert, R. J., 576
Gilbreth, E. G., 563
Gilbreth, F. B., Jr., 563
Gilbreth, Frank, 39, 563
Gilbreth, Lillian, 39
Gillettee, F., 440n
Gilmour, Allan, 132
Gist, M. E., 594
Glanz, J., 578
Glass, A., 576
Goldberg, L. R., 65n
Goldhirsh, Bernard, 76–77
Goldman, Ken, 302
Goldmann, Don, 471
Goldstein, A. P., 594
Goldstein, H. B., 567
Goldstein, I. L., 589
Goldwasser, A., 593
Goleman, D., 567
Gomez-Mejia, L., 562
Gonsalves, A., 574
Gonzalez, A., 596, 597
Gooch, K., 582
Goodheim, L., 597
Goodin, R. E., 568
Goodman, N., 576
Goodman, P. S., 562, 566, 601
Goodnight, James, 379–380, 381, 384
Gordon, M., 569
Gordon, S. M., 568
Gore, Genevieve, 443
Gore, Wilbert, 443
Gort, M., 607
Govindarajan, V., 575
Gracin, Mark, 201
Graham, J., 565
Graham, P., 564
Graham-Moore, B. E., 595
Grant, A. M., 592
Grasso, Richard A., 98
Gratton, L., 600
Gratton, Lynda, 453
Gray, K., 586
Green, J., 575
Green, Sarah, 317, 585
Green, S. G., 586
Greenberg, J., 573, 593
Greene, B., 606
Greene, J. D., 567
Greenhouse, S., 533n, 568, 590, 596
Greenleaf, Robert, 416
Greenwald, A. G., 574
Greenwald, Tony, 153
Greenwood, N., 583
Greer, B., 588
Greer, C. R., 571
Gregoire, C., 565
Greising, D., 594
Griffin, A., 607
Griffin, N. Shope, 592
Griffin, R. W., 575, 579, 583
Grigsby, Jim, 444
Grinberg, David, 143
Grinsven, L., 603
Griscom, B., 606
Grobart, S., 580
Gross, D., 607
Gross, G., 574
Gruber, H., 573
Guernsey, L., 603
Guest, R. H., 562
Guion, R. M., 589
Gullo, J., 597
Gupta, A. K., 562, 575
Gupta, Rajat Kumar, 97
Gura, D., 606
Gurchiek, K., 608
Gustafson, D. H., 579
Gutner, T., 570, 603
Guynn, J., 585
Guzman, B., 570

H

Hackett, Jim, 262–263
Hackman, J. R., 283–284, 583, 600
Haden, J., 595
Hales, C. P., 562
Hall, R. H., 584
Hall, Sharon, 8, 13
Halpin, A. W., 596
Hambrick, D. C., 562, 568
Hamel, G., 580, 598
Hamilton, F., 595
Hammer, Edward, 34
Hammer, M., 583, 599
Hammonds, K. H., 594
Hamner, W. C., 594
Hanatate, Maki, 310
Hannan, M., 585
Hannon, K., 213n
Hansen, John, 270, 271
Harden, Judy, 131
Hardison, C. M., 573
Harker, Susan, 376
Harkins, S., 601
Harkins, S. G., 601
Harmon-Jones, E., 573
Harper, E., 565
Harress, C., 582
Harrington, A., 590
Harris, E. F., 597
Hartke, D. D., 597
Hartley, S. L., 573
Harvey, R. J., 589
Hastie, R., 605
Hastings, Reed, 230
Hater, J. J., 597
Hax, A. C., 600
Heal, Jamie, 141
Healey, J., 569
Heath, C., 567
Heath, D., 567
Heather, Sean, 183
Hedberg, B., 579
Heijmen, T., 588
Heilman, M. E., 573
Heller, L., 592
Helmreich, R. L., 573
Hempel, J., 571, 572
Hendrickson, A. R., 600
Herbst, M., 596
Herman, J., 586
Herrin, Jessica, 397
Herring, Susan, 501
Hersey, P., 597
Hersey, Paul, 424
Herzberg, F., 593
Herzberg, Frederick, 389, 391–392
Hetzer, B., 573
Hewitt, P., 571
Hewlett, William, 484
Hickson, D. J., 586, 606
Higa, James, 88–89
High, P., 595
Highhouse, S., 567
Hightower, R., 600
Hill, C. W. L., 564, 576, 577, 581, 583, 584, 585, 607
Hill, E. J., 600
Hill, L., 562
Hines, G. H., 565, 593
Hinings, C. R., 586, 606
Hira, N. A., 577, 578
Hirai, Kazuo, 310
Hitler, Adolf, 277
Ho, Kelvin, 310
Ho, R. D., 599
Hodgson, J., 584
Hoerr, J., 583
Hof, R. D., 578, 594
Hofbeck, Adrian, 520–521
Hofer, C. W., 580
Hofman, D., 582
Hofstede, G., 577, 593

Hofstede, Geert, 175, 176
Hollan, K., 571
Holland, K., 588
Hollenbeck, J. R., 589
Holmes, S., 596
Holson, L. M., 575
Hood, N., 581
Hoppe, M. H., 577
Hosseini, R., 575
Hough, L. M., 588, 591, 593, 596, 600, 605
House, R. J., 565, 593, 595, 596, 597
House, Robert, 425, 427, 429
Hout, T. H., 607
Hsieh, Tony, 313, 314, 349, 588
Hsu, C., 580
Huber, G. P., 577
Hudson, Linda, 153
Humes, K. R., 570, 571
Hundal, P. S., 565, 593
Hunter, J. E., 586, 590
Hutchings, E., 575
Hyman, Mark, 565
Hymowitz, C., 566, 602

I

Iger, Bob, 331–332
Ihlwan, M., 579
Immelt, Jeffrey, 18, 34, 35, 219, 220, 223, 234, 325
ImproveNow.com, 368
Incognito, Richie, 291
Isele, Elizabeth, 213
Isen, A. M., 567
Ismail, Lobna, 129
Iverson, Ken, 116
Iwata, Satoru, 310

J

Jablin, F. M., 605
Jackman, Dom, 382
Jackson, J., 601
Jackson, Jesse, 129
Jackson, J. H., 589
Jackson, P. R., 562, 599
Jackson, S., 563
Jackson, S. E., 588
Jaffe, A. M., 573
Jaffe, E., 578
Jamieson, D., 563
Janasz, S. C. de, 562
Jang, Shelley, 310
Janis, I. L., 579
Janssen, O., 573
Jarrell, Buster, 452
Jassy, Andy, 376
Jayaraman, Saru, 532, 533
Jeannerette, P. R., 589
Jehn, K. A., 605
Jelinek, Craig, 423
Jelter, J., 580
Jensen, M. C., 600
Jerdee, T. H., 562
Jermier, J. M., 597
Jerry, John, 291
Jobs, Steve, 22, 88, 278, 543
Joel, A. C., 562
Johnson, Broderick, 3, 8, 13, 14
Johnson, B. T., 598
Johnson, Lyndon, 202
Johnson, M. A., 563
Johnson, Magic, 134
Johnson, R., 569
Jones, D., 570, 598
Jones, Gareth R., 585
Jones, G. R., 562, 564, 567, 569, 581, 583, 584, 585, 601, 605
Jones, J. R., 567
Jones, N. A., 570, 571
Jones, Reg, 236
Jones, Stephen, 189
Jones, T. M., 568, 569

Joyner, T., 589
Jung, D. I., 580

K

Kahn, J., 573
Kahn, R. L., 564
Kahn, Robert, 51
Kahneman, D., 578, 579
Kahneman, Daniel, 190, 200
Kalogeropoulos, Tina, 557
Kanani, R., 569
Kanfer, R., 591, 594
Kansara, V. A., 564
Kanungo, R. N., 597
Kaplan, David A., 591, 601
Kapsalis, S. C., 580
Karau, S. J., 598
Kareiva, P., 606
Kareiva, Peter, 524–525
Karl, K. A., 600
Kasperkevic, J., 562
Katsikis, I. N., 579
Katz, D., 564
Katz, Daniel, 51
Katz, R. L., 562
Kaufman, J., 592
Kaufman, L., 606
Kawai, Hideaki, 310
Kaye, L., 575
Kazanjian, R. K., 583
Kelleher, Herb, 50, 116
Kelley, David, 78–79, 80
Kelley, T., 567, 600
Kelley, Tom, 466
Kelly, E. P., 568
Kelly, Terri, 444, 445
Kemp, N. J., 599
Kennedy, John F., 202
Kerber, R., 568
Kerr, N. L., 601
Kerr, S., 597, 601
Kesmodel, D., 603
Khidekel, M., 589
Khosla, Rishi, 355
Kibler, Carolyn, 145–146
Kiledjian, Edward, 121
Killmer, Amberly, 472
King, Claudia, 393
King, N., 593
King, Robert, 459
Kinlin, E., 576
Kirkland, R., 602
Kirkpatrick, D., 588
Kirpatrick, S. A., 596
Kirsner, S., 601
Kirui, Abel, 162
Kiser, Cheryl, 213
Klepper, J., 607
Knight, Philip, 555, 556
Knobloch, A., 569
Ko, S. J., 570
Kochan, T. A., 605
Kocieniewski, D., 579
Koenig, D., 582
Kogut, B., 581, 608
Kohler-Gray, S., 575
Komar, J. A., 565
Komar, S., 565
Koncz, A., 586
Konovsky, M. A., 573, 593
Koontz, H., 585
Kopecki, D., 572
Koppes, L. L., 591
Koretz, G., 571
Korkki, P., 589
Kosove, Andrew, 3, 13
Kotter, J., 562
Kottler, Lisa, 410
Kowalski, Michael J., 108, 109
Kowitt, B., 582, 594
Kramer, L., 606

Kraul, A. I., 562
Kraus, Michael, 416
Kravets, D., 568
Kreitner, R., 400n, 594
Kreps, G. L., 575
Kristiansen, Kjeld Kirk, 270
Kristiansen, Ole Kirk, 270
Kroc, Ray, 81, 82–83
Kropf, M. Brumit, 570, 598
Krugman, P., 576
Krugman, Paul, 168
Kucera, D., 576
Kullman, Ellen, 171
Kumar, S., 582
Kunda, G., 585
Kupers, R., 580
Kwoh, L., 590
Kyrgidou, L. P., 579

L

Labich, K., 562
Lahr, S., 591
Lambert, A., 575
Lambert, Melissa, 153
Lampe, Stewart, 102
Landler, M., 578
Landrieu, Mary L., 213
Landro, L., 472n, 605
Lane, C., 568
Lane, D. M., 572
Langowitz, N. J., 578
Lansbery, Curt, 75
Lashinsky, A., 564
Latane, B., 601
Latham, G. P., 395, 580, 590, 591, 593, 594
Law, K., 77n
Lawler, E. E., III, 585, 594
Lawrence, J., 563
Lawrence, M., 595
Lawrence, P. R., 52, 564, 583, 584, 605
Laybourne, Geraldine, 426
Leaf, C., 604
Leak, B., 575
Leary, W. E., 602
Lee, C. A., 606
Lee, D., 576, 607
Lee, Ed, 88
Lee, H., 592
Lee, Jess, 61–63, 66, 68, 564
LeFauve, R. G., 600
Lehman, P., 593
Lehrer, J., 578
Leibs, S., 410n
Lelchuk, I., 571
Lengel, R. H., 578, 602
Lennard, Darren, 494, 495
Leno, Jay, 38
Lentz, E., 589
Leonsis, Ted, 186
Leopold, T., 580
Levanon, G., 566
Lever, William, 173
Levering, R., 586, 587, 591
Levernes, Jacek, 355
Levin, Gerald, 518
Levin, L., 589
Levine, E. L., 589
Levitt, T., 576
Levitz, Jennifer, 574
Lew, Kai, 57, 58
Lewicki, R. J., 605, 606
Lewin, A. Y., 588
Lewin, D., 606
Lewin, K., 586
Lewin, Kurt, 335
Lewis, Randy, 140–141
Liao, S. Y., 608
Libby, R., 566
Libby, Ryan, 70
Liberus, Juliane, 472
Lieberman, D., 582

Light, J., 578
Likert, R., 597
Lima, L., 589
Lin, Dan, 438, 439, 440
Lincoln, J. F., 594
Lind, E. A., 593
Lindblom, C. E., 586
Liska, L. Z., 597
Litterer, J. A., 563, 605
Litterer, J. R., 605
Littman, J., 600
Liyakasa, K., 565
Locke, E. A., 394, 395, 580, 593, 594, 596
Loden, M., 573
Loeb, M., 596
Lohr, S., 563
Long, J. S., 572
Lonier, T., 579
Loomis, C. J., 592
Lopez, George, 457–458
Lorange, P., 585
Loray, Carol, 418–419
Lord, Phil, 438
Lorsch, J. R., 564
Lorsch, J. W., 52, 562, 583, 584, 605
Lovell, J., 577
Lublin, J. S., 154n, 574, 590, 600, 603
Luckman, T., 567
Luna, N., 564
Luo, M., 566
Luthans, F., 400n, 594
Lynch, Kevin, 408, 409

M

Maanen, J. Van, 569
Maccoby, M., 595
MacGregor, I. C., 568
Macintosh, N. B., 606
MacIntyre, A., 568, 585
MacKenzie, S. B., 597
Maffei, Gregory, 420
Magee, Yada, 480
Mahony, T. A., 562
Maidment, P., 604
Main, C., 568
Main, J., 563
Main, Joseph A., 26
Makhijani, M. G., 598
Mallaby, S., 562
Malone, M. S., 607
Maltby, Lewis, 487
Manchin, Joe, III, 26
Mandell, B., 575
Mann, R. A., 575
Mann, Richard A., 150
Manning, S., 588
Mannix, E. A., 562
Marcelin, Fabiola, 472
March, James, 191–192, 193, 194, 563, 578, 607
Marcia, J., 608
Margulies, N., 586
Markels, A., 599
Markham, D., 576
Martell, R. F., 572
Martin, Jonathan, 291
Martinez, A., 596, 597
Martinez, Angela, 394
Martinez, M. N., 567
Mashaba, Herman, 426
Maslow, Abraham, 389, 390, 391
Maslow, A. H., 593
Mason, P. A., 562
Mason, R. O., 579
Mason-Draffen, C., 598
Mass-Mutual Financial Group, 171
Mathieu, J. E., 566
Mathis, R. L., 589
Matlack, C., 599
Mattioli, D., 594
Maurer, T. J., 592
Mayer, J. D., 567

Mayer, Marissa, 61, 301–302
Maynard, M., 569, 581
Mayo, E., 564
Mayo, Elton, 47, 48
Mazulo, Marcia, 498
McAdams, Rachel, 38
McCallum, Daniel, 548
McCann, Chris, 186
McCann, J., 562
McCann, James, 185–186, 187, 189
McCartney, S., 581
McClelland, David, 68, 389, 392
McClelland, D. C., 565, 593
McCline, R. L., 574
McCord, P., 586
McCord, Patty, 332
McCormick, E. J., 589
McCracken, D., 570
McCrae, R. R., 565
McDaniel, Mark, 260
McDuling, J., 584, 585
McGeehan, P., 573
McGregor, D., 564
McGregor, Douglas, 48–49
McGregor, J., 585, 586, 587
McKain, Scott, 517
McKenna, D. D., 562
McLean, B., 568
McMahan, G. C., 587
McMann, Mary, 394
McMillan, R., 602
McMillan, Ron, 483
McNealy, Scott, 194, 195, 197
Mecham, R. C., 589
Meek, T., 607
Mehrabian, Albert, 483
Meisinger, Kirsten, 471, 472
Mendell, Steven, 56
Merrick, A., 573
Meshoulam, I., 588
Metthee, I., 575
Meyrowitz, Carol, 257
Michelli, Joseph, 542
Miles, R. H., 605
Miller, B. C., 600
Miller, Chris, 438
Miller, D., 583, 586
Miller, Jenny, 402
Milliman, J., 588
Mills, C. W., 564
Mills, T. M., 599
Minter, Harry, 382
Minter, S., 588
Mintzberg, H., 562, 585, 596
Mintzberg, Henry, 10–11, 12
Mische, Justus, 418
Mitchell, R., 588
Mitchell, T. R., 592, 594
Mitroff, I. I., 579
Mittleman, Daniel, 505
Moats, Maria Castañón, 124
Moberg, D. J., 568
Mobley, W. H., 566
Mochari, I., 580
Mohr, D. C., 567
Montebello, A. R., 599
Moore, A., 605
More, K. M., 594
Morgenson, G., 590
Moriguchi, Takahiro, 24
Moritz, Bob, 123–124, 142, 569
Morran, C., 581
Morris, David, 141
Morris, Saul, 141
Morris, W. N., 567
Morse, N. C., 597
Mortensen, C., 584
Morton, M., 585
Moskowitz, M., 586, 587, 591
Moss, S. E., 590
Mount, M. K., 565
Mouton, Jane, 424

Mouton, J. S., 597
Mowday, R. T., 593
Mozilo, Angelo, 98
Mubarak, Hosni, 175
Mullany, Hank, 215, 216
Mullinax, Harrison, 140
Murname, Mike, 501
Murphy, P. E., 569
Murphy, Tom, 544
Musco, Tré, 283
Musk, Elon, 30–31
Mutton, Nick, 346, 347
Mycoskie, Blake, 113–114

N

Nadella, S., 584
Nadella, Satya, 297–298
Nader, Ralph, 182
Nakane, C., 577
Nakarmi, L., 596
Napier, N. K., 587
Nathan, M., 588
Nayeri, F., 590
Neale, M. A., 605
Near, J. P., 569
Needleman, S. E., 571, 572, 604
Neely, Susan, 92
Neergaard, L., 567
Neeson, Liam, 438
Nelson, R. R., 602
Nemetz, P., 583
Neuijen, B., 577
Neumeister, L., 569
Newman, B., 602
Newman, W. H., 586
Nicholson, N., 592
Niehoff, B. P., 597
Nieuwsma, Steve, 402
Nilles, K., 582
Nixon, Richard, 202
Noe, R. A., 565, 589
Nogues, Thierry, 451
Nohira, N., 564
Nokes, Sue, 430, 431
Nooyi, Indra, 127, 236, 432, 509–511, 524, 604
Nord, W. R., 562
North, D. C., 576
Northcraft, G. B., 605
Norton, M. V., 594
Nosek, Brian, 153
Novak, David, 296
Nussbaum, B., 600
Nystrom, L. E., 567
Nystrom, P. C., 579, 586

O

Obama, Barack, 95, 370
Obama, Michelle, 91–92
O'Boyle, T. F., 601
O'Brian, B., 582
O'Brien, J. M., 586, 587
Obstfeld, M., 576
Ohayv, D. D., 577
Ohnesorge, L. K., 595
Okimoto, T. G., 573
Oldham, G. R., 283–284, 583
O'Leary, V. E., 573
O'Leary-Kelly, A. M., 575
Olffen, W. van, 566
Olsen, J. P., 578
O'Mara, J., 563
O'Neal, Shaquille, 438
O'Neill, Kevin, 291
O'Reilly, B., 582
O'Reilly, C. A., 585, 601, 607
Organ, D. W., 564, 566
Orsini, L., 564
Ortega, B., 568
Osburn, L., 577
Ostrom, T. M., 601

O'Toole, Larry, 69–70
Ouchi, W. G., 585, 586

P

Packard, David, 484
Paetzold, R. L., 573, 575
Paez, B. L., 581
Page, R. C., 562
Palmer, Kimberly, 212
Palmeri, C., 587
Palmisano, Samuel, 84
Palrecha, R., 595
Pan, J., 586
Pape, W. R., 600
Parish, Scott, 3–4, 5–6, 9, 10, 14, 15
Parisi, Diane, 153
Parker, L. D., 564
Parker, S. R., 562
Parloff, R., 574
Patterson, A., 573
Pearce, Erica, 505
Pearce, J. A., 568, 580, 599
Pedigo, P. R., 562
Peiperl, M. A., 590
Peltz, Nelson, 235
Pennings, D. J., 606
Pennings, J. M., 562
Penrose, E., 581
Perelman, Ronald, 277
Perez, Beatriz, 197
Perlez, J., 577
Perm-Ajchariyawong, N., 588
Perrow, C., 564, 583, 585
Perrow, Charles, 281
Perry, M. K., 581
Peters, L. H., 571, 588, 597
Peters, Tom, 45, 602
Petersik, D., 578
Petersik, Don, 189
Peterson, J., 581
Peterson, Monte, 267
Peterson, R. S., 567
Petrecca, L., 603
Petro, G., 580
Pettigrew, A. M., 606
Pettit, Sherry, 260
Petty, R. E., 601
Petzinger, T., Jr., 605
Pfeffer, J., 45, 191, 576, 578, 579, 591, 596, 603, 606
Phelan, Kerry, 440
Phelps, R., 580
Philbin, Joe, 291
Picciano, Bob, 541
Pickering, J. F., 607
Pillai, R., 597, 598
Pink, 38
Pinkley, R. L., 605
Pirtle, Thomas, 480
Plank, K., 565
Plank, Kevin, 66–67
Pleta, Noel, 322
Plummer, S., 563
Podsakoff, P. M., 597
Pohlmann, J. T., 597
Pollard, H. R., 563
Polum, Shelly, 73
Polzer, J. T., 570
Pondy, L. R., 601, 605
Poniewozik, J., 571
Poole, K., 563
Poole, M. S., 605
Porras, Estuardo, 528
Porras, J., 580
Porter, C. O. L. H., 565
Porter, E., 588, 590
Porter, L. W., 593, 605
Porter, M. E., 227–228, 575, 576, 580, 581, 607
Post, Karen, 518
Poteet, M. L., 589
Pouncey, Mike, 291
Pounds, S., 592

Prahalad, C. K., 580, 581
Pratt, Chris, 438
Pratt, M., 578
Preiser, A., 564
Premack, S., 590
Premack, S. L., 589
Presnell, Connie, 141
Price, D., 583
Price, Lowell, 123
Pritchard, R. D., 592
Pruitt, Al, 283
Pruitt, D. G., 606
Prynn, J., 585
Pryor, Michael, 356
Pugh, D. S., 586
Pugh, S. D., 574
Pulakos, E. D., 574
Putnam, L. L., 605

Q

Quinn, J. B., 587

R

Rachabathuni, Sailesh, 376
Radosevich, D. J., 593
Rafter, M., 608
Raghavan, A., 574
Raia, A. P., 586
Ramanujam, V., 581
Ramirez, R. R., 570, 571
Ramsey, M., 581
Randolph, Marc, 230
Ratz, J. M., 571
Rauwald, C., 578
Ravasio, P., 575
Raven, B., 596
Ravina, V., 581
Ravlin, E. C., 599
Reeves, M., 600
Regan, M. B., 590
Reich, R. B., 576
Reimer, E., 597
Reinert, P., 602
Reingold, J., 597
Reitz, Jim, 457, 458
Reizenstein, R. M., 574
Rennert, Ira, 182
Reses, Jackie, 301
Rhode, J. G., 585
Riaz, S., 568
Ribeiro, D. S., 568
Rice, F., 579
Rich, E., 608
Rich, M., 587
Richie, Susan, 394
Rider, Michael, 450
Rifkin, G., 604
Rive, Peter, 30
Rivera, Carlos, 88–89
Roach, Andy, 494
Robbins, S., 595, 605
Roberson, L., 76n, 573
Roberts, Barry S., 150
Roberts, B. S., 575
Roberts, D., 565
Roberts, K. H., 605
Roberts, S., 602
Roberts, Sara, 483
Robertson, J., 575
Robertson, Nick, 339
Robie, C., 565
Robinson, B., 76n
Robinson, G., 563, 573
Rocco, M., 581
Rockefeller, John D., 40, 563
Rockefeller, William, 40
Rodgers, R., 586
Rodgers, T. J., 329
Roe, R. A., 566
Roethlisberger, F. J., 48, 564

Rogers, E. M., 601
Rogowsky, M., 582
Rokeach, M., 565
Rokeach, Milton, 69
Rolfes, Anne, 525
Roll, R., 579
Rollins, Kevin, 24, 563
Rometty, Virginia, 127
Ronen, S., 593
Rose, R. L., 596
Rose, Veronica, 409
Rosen, B., 572, 600
Rosenbaum, S., 585
Rosener, J. B., 573
Rosenfeld, Irene, 171
Ross, G. H. B., 586
Ross, Stephen, 291
Ross, T. L., 595
Roth, D., 592
Roth, G., 564
Rotter, J. B., 565
Rousseff, Dilma, 171
Roy, D., 563, 564
Rubenstein, David Motozo, 310
Rubin, J. Z., 605
Rucker, R., 582
Rugaber, C. S., 571
Rugman, A. M., 576
Rumelt, R. P., 581
Rungtusanatham, M., 582
Rusli, E. M., 89n
Russell, J. W., 588
Russo, J. E., 578
Rynes, S., 572
Rynes, S. L., 588

S

Saari, L. M., 594
Saavedra, R., 598
Sackett, P. R., 573
Sagie, A., 585
Saginaw, Paul, 416–417
Salamon, J., 589
Salancik, G. R., 606
Salisbury, Dallas, 410
Salovey, P., 567
Salter, C., 574
Saltr, C., 579
Salukis, A., 582
Sanchez, J. I., 590
Sanchez, Karen, 498
Sanchez, Maria, 393
Sandberg, J., 602, 603
Sandberg, Sheryl, 332
Sanders, G., 577
Sanders, L., 581
Sanders, W. G., 568
Saporito, B., 564, 583, 604
Sawin, L. L., 573
Sawyer, J. E., 579
Sayeed, L., 600
Scanlon, Joseph, 404
Schacter, S., 600
Schadler, T., 602
Schaubroeck, J., 567
Schawbel, D., 577
Schein, H., 567
Schell, Michael, 506
Schendel, D. E., 580, 581
Schiffmann, H. R., 573
Schlosser, J., 591, 592
Schmalensee, R., 576, 581
Schmidt, K. A., 579
Schmidt, S. M., 605
Schminke, M., 593
Schmitt, R. B., 602
Schneck, R. E., 606
Schneide, B., 585
Schneider, B., 567, 595
Schneider, Benjamin, 78
Schoemaker, P. J., 578

Schoen, J., 584
Schoenfeldt, L. F., 588, 594
Schoenherr, R. A., 584
Schreyogg, G., 586
Schriesheim, C. A., 597, 598
Schroeder, R. G., 582
Schuler, R. S., 588
Schuman, M., 597
Schumpeter, J., 576, 607
Schwab, Marion, 149
Schwartz, J., 578
Schweiger, D. M., 579
Schwenk, C. R., 579
Scott, W. R., 607
Sealover, E., 585
Segal, T., 575
Seiders, K., 562
Seligson, H., 605
Sellers, P., 570, 580
Seltzer, J., 597
Semel, Terry, 518
Semler, Antonio, 350
Semler, R., 588
Semler, Ricardo, 350–351
Senegal, Jim, 422, 423
Senge, Peter, 196, 204, 578, 579
Senkbiel, Liz, 459–460
Serwer, A. E., 573
Sewell, D., 581
Seyle, D. C., 570
Shah, A., 574
Shah, R., 586
Shaich, Ron, 253
Shama, A., 562
Shao, Y. P., 608
Shapiro, D. L., 594
Shapiro, E., 605
Sharkey, J., 605
Sharp, Isadore, 345–346, 347
Sharpe, R., 570, 589
Shaw, J. B., 588, 594
Shaw, J. C., 593
Shaw, K. N., 594
Shaw, M. E., 599
Shaw, W. H., 563, 568
Shellenberger, S., 506n, 590, 602
Shen, S., 607
Shepperd, J. A., 601
Sheriden, J. E., 585
Sheth, N., 563
Shleifer, A., 581
Shontell, A., 586
Shuker, N., 563
Shulka, R. K., 579
Shuman, Marc, 199
Silver, David, 501
Silverman, R. E., 598
Simmering, M. J., 565
Simon, H. A., 563, 577, 578
Simon, Herbert, 191–192, 193, 194
Simons, R., 586
Sinclair, R. C., 567
Singer, B., 572
Skariachan, D., 577
Skees, Bill, 213
Skees, Mary Ann, 213
Skidmore, S., 596
Skinner, B. F., 397, 594
Skitka, L. J., 593
Slaughter, J. E., 567
Sluyter, D., 567
Smach, Thomas J., 232
Smart, T., 574
Smith, A., 563
Smith, Adam, 36
Smith, D. B., 567, 595
Smith, Fred, 288
Smith, R., 568
Smith, Steven M., 506
Smutniak, J., 578
Snell, S. A., 588
Snyder, N. T., 600

Soderstrom, Johanna, 153
Solinger, N., 566
Solomon, R. C., 568
Sommerville, R. B., 567
Song, L., 77n
Sonnenberg, D., 598
Sorcher, M., 594
Sørensen, J. B., 567
Sowray, B., 599
Spangler, W. D., 565, 593, 595
Spears, L., 595
Spector, P., 565
Spellman, J., 581
Spence, J. T., 573
Spencer, Glenn, 532
Spiegelman, Paul, 409
Spielberg, Steven, 251
Spitznagel, E., 605
Spolsky, J., 589
Spolsky, Joel, 356, 357
Spors, K. K., 566
Sproul, J. R., 590
Sproull, L. S., 600
Sprout, A. L., 604
Sprunk, Eric, 162
Stack, Laura, 505, 506
Stahl, M. J., 565, 593
Stajkovic, A. D., 594
Stalk, G., 607
Stalker, G. M., 52, 53, 564
Stalker, G. R., 583
Stamps, D., 571
Stanger, M., 585
Stappaerts, Eddy, 143
Starbuck, W. H., 579, 586
Staw, B. M., 566, 567, 569, 579, 593, 596, 602
Steele, C. M., 573
Steers, R. M., 593
Steffen, Jason, 248
Stein, David, 476
Stein, N., 591
Steinberg, John, 394
Steinberg, Joseph, 520–521
Steinemann, A. C., 568
Steiner, I. D., 601
Steinhafel, Gregg, 121
Steinmann, H., 586
Stevens, A., 573
Stevens, Mark, 486
Steverman, B., 566
Stewart, R., 562
Stewart, T., 608
Stewart, T. A., 592, 599
Stogdill, R. M., 588, 596
Stoller, G., 605
Stone, S. C., 574
Stone, Sharon, 38
Stopford, J., 583
Stracker, Karen, 485
Strauss, S. G., 600
Stroebe, W., 579
Strøier, Henrik, 271
Strutt, A., 588
Stundza, T., 583
Su, Brian, 517
Suh, Sarah, 134
Sullivan, D. M., 580
Sullivan, John, 377
Sullivan, R. L., 588
Sullivan, S. E., 562
Sung, J., 591, 592
Sutcliffe, K. M., 563
Sutton, R. I., 579
Swann, W. B., Jr., 570
Swartz, M., 568
Swisher, K., 584, 585
Sy, T., 598
Symington, Rob, 382

T

Taggart, J. H., 607
Takahasi, D., 576

Tannen, D., 604
Tannen, Deborah, 499, 500, 501
Tashiro, H., 599
Taylor, E., 578
Taylor, Frederick, 37–38, 39, 46, 47
Taylor, F. W., 563, 583
Taylor, Jack, 388
Taylor, S. E., 572, 573
Teckel, Michael, 424
Teece, D. J., 581
Tellegen, A., 566
Tepper, B. J., 597
Tercek, Mark, 524, 525
Terrell, G., 573
Tetrault, L. A., 597
Tett, R. P., 565
Thacker, R., 575
Tharenou, P., 562
Thau, B., 580
Thomas, Charlie, 73
Thomas, D. A., 575
Thomas, David, 148, 363
Thomas, K. W., 605
Thomas, Ron, 73
Thompson, Don, 294
Thompson, James, 51, 454
Thompson, J. D., 564, 586, 600
Thompson, L., 605
Thurm, S., 594
Thurston, K., 588
Tindall, Will, 382
Tindell, Kip, 386, 387
Tiplady, R., 599
Tisch, Jonathan, 146
Tischler, L., 598
Tischler, Linda, 432
Tkaczyk, C., 587
Todd, P. A., 602
Tomblin, Earl Ray, 26
Tosi, H. L., 586, 594
Totty, M., 604
Townsend, A. M., 600
Townsend, J., 584
Trachtenberg, J. A., 605
Trell, Julie, 477
Trevino, L. K., 568, 602
Triandis, H. C., 593
Trice, H. M., 567
Trop, J., 576
Trottman, M., 605
Trumka, Richard L., 532
Truong, Linh, 102
Tsuda, Miiko, 143
Tsuga, Kazuhiro, 310
Tubbs, M. E., 593
Tuckman, B. W., 600
Tugend, A., 603
Turban, E., 607
Turner, C., 586
Turner, Jim, 291
Tversky, A., 579
Tversky, Amos, 190, 200
Twain, Shania, 38
Tyler, T., 593
Tylor, E. B., 577
Tyson, J., 603

U

Unger, R. K., 573
Urcelay, Antonio, 215, 216
Urger, M., 565
Ury, W., 606

V

Valian, V., 572
Valian, Virginia, 135, 139
Vancouver, J. B., 594
Van Der Beek, R., 588
Van Fleet, D. D., 596
Van Harten, Gus, 183

VanHulle, L., 583
Van Maanen, J., 567
Varadarajan, P., 581
Vascellaro, J. E., 603
Vaslow, J. B., 574
Vaughn, S., 571
Velasquez, M., 568
Venables, M., 583
Versace, C., 607
Vest, Valarie, 135
Victor, B., 568
Vilsack, Tom, 92
Viola, Karen, 431
Vishny, R. W., 581
Vitzthum, C., 580
Vlastelica, John, 377
Volkman, E., 581
Von Glinow, M., 588
Voosen, P., 606
Vroom, V. H., 592
Vroom, Victor H., 384

W

Waber, Ben, 536
Wack, P., 580
Wadhwa, V., 588
Wahba, P., 563
Wald, M. L., 578, 602
Waldman, D. A., 597
Wall, J. A., Jr., 605
Wall, T. D., 562, 599
Wallach, Lori, 182
Waller, M. J., 562
Wallston, B. B., 573
Walsh, D., 595
Walsh, J. P., 566, 573, 579
Walster, W. G., 579
Walton, R. E., 605
Wang, H. Q., 608
Wanous, J. P., 589
Warkentin, M. E., 600
Washington, R. R., 595
Washko, John, 363
Waterman, A. S., 569
Waterman, R. H., Jr., 602
Watkins, S., 568
Watson, D., 566
Wauters, R., 587
Weber, J., 575
Weber, M., 564
Weber, Max, 40–42, 43, 46, 53, 54
Webster, J., 76n
Weick, K. E., 568, 585
Weiner, S. P., 600
Weinzweig, A., 595
Weinzweig, Ari, 416–417
Weise, K., 573
Weiss, D. J., 71n
Weiss, E. M., 592
Weiss, H. W., 594
Weiss, S. E., 606
Weisul, K., 564
Weitzel, Bridgette A., 154
Welch, Jack, 347, 366, 420
Wellington, S., 570, 598
Wellington, Sheila, 127
Wellner, A. Stein, 573, 574, 602
Wells, K., 606
Wells, L., 583
Werner, E., 564
Wertheimer, M., 573
Wessel, D., 588
West , M. S., 571
Wexley, K. N., 574, 590
Wheeler, J. A., 589
Wheeler, J. V., 562
Wheeler, S. R., 571
Wheelright, S. C., 578
Wheelwright, S. C., 607
Whelan, R., 605
White, E., 589, 600, 603

White, J. B., 604
White, Michael, 509
White, W. F., 605
Whitehurst, Jim, 413–415, 419, 420, 421, 422, 424
Whiting, V., 562
Whitman, Meg, 432
Whitmore, Jennifer, 322
Wicker, Scott, 197
Wieczner, J., 590
Wildstrom, S. H., 591
Wilfert, Jill, 439
Wilke, M., 576
Wilkinson, A., 580
Williams, E. S., 598
Williams, J. R., 581
Williams, K. D., 601
Williams, M. L., 597
Williamson, O. E., 607
Willig, R. D., 576, 581
Wilson, H. J., 606, 607
Winer, B. J., 596
Winslow, R., 602
Winter, D. G., 565, 593
Winter, R. R., 576
Winter, S. G., 576
Witt, L. A., 565
Wittich, C., 564
Wofford, J. C., 597
Wohl, J., 596
Wohlsen, M., 563
Wolff, M., 580
Wong, C., 77n
Wong, V., 583
Woodman, R. W., 579, 586
Woolridge, B., 586
Woycke, J., 565, 593
Wren, D., 563
Wright, P. M., 587, 588, 589
Wyant, C., 581
Wysocki, B., 562

X

Xavier, J., 565

Y

Yang, Jerry, 206
Yanow, D., 584
Yanukovych, Viktor, 175
Yates, JoAnne, 483
Yoder, R. J., 594
Yohn, D., 583
Young, S., 581
Young, S. M., 583
Youngblood, S. A., 571, 588
Yu, R., 592
Yukl, G., 595, 596
Yunker, J., 575
Yunker, John, 158

Z

Zachary, G. P., 590
Zager, R., 594
Zajac, D. M., 566
Zander, A. F., 596, 600
Zanna, M., 566
Zapata-Phelan, C. P., 593
Zarin, Larry, 186
Zawacki, Joan, 143
Zawacki, R. A., 586
Zehr, D., 575
Zeller, W., 594
Zellner, W., 579, 596
Zeumer, James, 514
Zhao, Neng, 517–518
Zhou, J., 567, 598
Zickar, M. J., 567
Zimmerman, A., 574
Zuckerman, H., 572

Organizations Index

A

Abercrombie & Fitch, 3–4, 6, 99, 556
Accenture, 16, 24, 163
Acer, 163
Adam's Mark, 142
Adidas, 162, 555
Adobe, 160
Advanced Research Japan, 310
Advantica, 138
AES Corporation, 452
AFL–CIO, 532
African Union, 174
AIG, 434
Airbnb, 30–31
Airbus Industries, 20
Alcon Entertainment, 5–6, 6, 7, 8, 8–9, 9, 10, 11, 13, 21
AlixPartners Professionals, 348
Alpha Natural Resources, 26
Amazon, 3, 22, 157, 163, 164, 165, 238, 314, 349, 376–377, 447–448, 537, 546, 561
AMD, 160, 166, 266
American Academy of Arts and Sciences, 525
American Airlines, 247–248, 249
American Apparel, 148
American Beverage Association, 92
American Eagle Outfitters, 99
American Express, 10, 147, 434
American Greetings Corp., 484
American Institute of Certified Public Accountants, 410
American Management Association, 486
Ameritrade, 163
Amor Perfecto, 88
AOL, 186, 191
Apollo, 197
Apple, 6, 16, 22, 23, 49, 53–54, 79, 88, 89, 161, 164, 187, 193, 205, 229, 231, 232, 233, 234, 249, 250, 251, 256, 259, 266, 274, 278, 303, 310, 377, 461, 532, 537, 542, 543
Armani, 230, 231, 237
Army Research Institute, 524
Arthur Andersen, 111–112, 115
Artisan Business Group, 517
ASDA, 204–205
AsiaInspection, 99
Asia Pacific Investment Partners, 382
ASOS, 339
AT&T, 17, 360, 416, 542
Atlanta National Baseball League Club, 420
Atos, 504
Aurora Electric, 409, 410
Autism Speaks, 334
Automatic Data Processing, 358
Avis, 239
Avon, 23, 240

B

Babson College, 363
backcountry.com, 420
BAE Systems, 23, 153
Bank of America, 132, 138, 143, 475
Bank of Montreal, 492, 493
Bank of Tokyo, 143
Barclays, 95
Barnes & Noble, 420, 544
Bayer, 147
Beech-Nut, 119–120
Bell South, 142
Benedictine University, 408, 409, 410
Berkshire Hathaway, 235
BerylHealth, 409, 410
Best Buy, 164, 308, 385, 537
Better Built Cabinets, 526
BIC, 228

Bill and Melinda Gates Foundation, 96
Blackberry, 543
Black Like Me, 426
Blackstone, 232
Blockbuster, 229, 230
BloomNet, 186
Blue Bottle, 88
Blue Cross–Blue Shield, 107
Blue Oak Capital, 517
BMW, 229
bodybuilding.com, 420
Boeing, 132, 161, 238, 253, 267
Bombardier Aerospace, 121
Borrego Solar Systems, 205
Boston Consulting Group, 414
BP PLC, 453
Brainvisa, 189
Brasscom, 354
Bridgestone Corporation, 163
Bristol Myers Squibb, 107
Brooks Brothers, 288
Budweiser, 158
Bureau of Labor Statistics, 409
Burger King, 56, 138

C

Calvert Group, 137
Campbell's Soup, 232
Canon, 356
Capgemini Consulting, 163, 355
Capital District Physicians' Health Plan, 410
Capital Grille, 532
Capital One, 95, 485
Cargill, 240, 241
Catalyst, 127
Catapult Sports, 536
Caterpillar, 317–318, 354
Cedars-Sinai Medical Center, 75
Center for Applied Ethics, 416
Center for Union Facts, 532
Cessna, 9
Chanel, 231, 237
Charles Schwab, 163
Chevron, 132, 148, 492
Chick-fil-A, 343
Children Now, 128
Children's Choice Learning Center, 131
Chipotle, 266
Chrysler, 191, 252, 316, 360, 421, 492
Chubb Group, 132
Cisco Systems, 160, 163, 234, 265, 303, 356, 475, 484, 488
Citibank, 78, 256, 257–258, 259
Citigroup, 143
CNET, 561
Coalition of Immokalee Workers, 532, 533
Coca-Cola, 138, 142, 147, 160, 163, 167, 170, 197, 228, 232, 233, 234, 239–240, 355, 356, 528, 555
Colgate, 163
Collaborative Strategies, 506
Comambault Mining, 42
Comcast, 34, 234
Compaq, 191
Computer Associates, 115
Conference Board, 354
Container Store, 274, 385, 386–387
Cook Ross Inc., 153
Cooperation Council for the Arab States of the Gulf, 174
Coopers and Lybrand, 123
Copal Amba, 355
Copersucar, 241
CORE Engineering and Construction, 410
Cornell University, 525
Corporate Europe Observatory, 182
Costco, 174, 233, 308, 422, 423
Count Me In for Women's Economic Independence, 434

Countrywide Mortgage, 98
Creative Display Solutions, 434
Crocs, 232
Cross, 228, 229
Curb Records, 29
Custom Profile, 552
Cypress Semiconductor, 329

D

Daewoo, 421
Daimler, 191
Daniel restaurant, 532
Darden Restaurants, 92, 137
Dartmouth College, 420
DaVita Inc., 145
Days Inn, 369
DC Comics, 440
Dell, 15, 17, 24, 116, 143–144, 160, 161, 163, 164, 207, 237, 266, 290, 475
Deloitte & Touche, 125
Deloitte Consulting, 348, 363
Del Posto restaurant, 532
Delta Airlines, 414
DePaul University, 505
Deutsche Bank, 57–58
Deutsche Telekom, 430
DHL, 161
Dial, 236
Diamond Pet Foods, 408–409, 410
Digital Equipment, 303
Dior, 230
Dish Network, 230
Disney, 440
Doe Run Perú, 182
Dow Chemical, 153, 525
DreamWorks SKG, 132, 440
Dresdner Kleinwort Wasserstein, 494
D. R. Horton, 513
DTE Energy Holding Company, 132
Duke University, 354
DuPont, 17, 116, 149, 171, 197, 239, 240, 443
Duracell, 234
DyeCoo Textile Systems, 162

E

Eaton Corporation, 464
eBay, 165, 377, 537
Edison General Electric Company, 35
EEOC, 143, 148, 149, 152
El Faro Estate Coffee, 528
Embraer, 20
EMC Corporation, 494
Empire HealthChoice, 255
Employment Management Association, 137
Encore.org, 212
Enron, 84, 107, 115
Enterprise Holdings, 388
Enterprise Rent-A-Car, 387, 388
Equal Employment Opportunity Commission, 143, 148, 149, 152, 352
Erie Railroad, 548
Ernst & Young, 132, 137, 170–171, 355, 356, 382
Escape the City, 382, 383
E*Trade, 163
Etsy, 212
European Union, 168
Evite, 420
Expedia, 420
ExxonMobil, 78

F

Facebook, 88, 157, 205, 232, 332, 376, 488, 540
Factory Investigating Commission, 100
Federal Aviation Administration, 9

FedEx, 149, 161, 162, 186, 252, 288, 434, 505
FedEx Kinko's, 181
Feeding America, 334
Fidelity Investments, 370
Fireman's Fund Insurance Co., 494
Fitbit, 114
Fitch Ratings, 310
Fog Creek Software, 356–357
Food Gatherers, 417
Ford, 17, 51, 114, 132, 142, 160, 174, 193, 204, 253, 265, 303, 315, 332, 360, 419, 450, 492
Forman, 515
Four Seasons Hotels and Resorts, 345–347, 359, 363, 369
Foxconn Technology Group, 23, 161
Franklin Motor Company, 38
Friedrich-Alexander University, 414
Frito-Lay, 234, 235
Fruit of the Loom, 99
Fujitsu, 310
FutureWork Institute, 121

G

Gap, 100, 180
GarageTek, 199
Garland Grills, 343
Gartner, 250
Gates Foundation, 96
Gateway, 163, 164
G. D. Searle, 160
GE, 16, 18–19, 35–37, 51, 57, 142, 161, 177, 218–221, 223–224, 234, 236, 238, 259, 264, 325, 326, 347, 366, 420, 434
GE Capital, 34
GE Healthcare, 478–479
General Motors, 114, 116, 225–227, 240, 253, 263, 296, 315, 338, 360
Gentle Giant Moving Company, 69–70
Georgetown University, 486
Gerber Products, 119
Giddings and Lewis, 419
Gillette, 228, 229, 234, 237–238
GlaxoSmithKline, 107, 288, 305
Global by Design, 157
Global Trade Watch, 182
Goldman Sachs, 97, 132, 363, 524
Goodyear, 492
Google, 15–16, 21, 49, 53, 61, 62, 80, 116, 117, 132, 153, 157, 165, 168, 205, 208, 231, 266, 301, 303, 305, 376, 377, 401, 407, 475, 477, 537, 544, 546
Gradient Corporation, 403
Greenleaf Center for Servant Leadership, 416
Green Mountain Coffee, 116
Group Health, 472
Groupware Technology, 410
Gucci, 230
Guerra DeBerry Coody, 370

H

Habitat for Humanity, 334
Habitat International Inc., 141
Hallmark Cards, 446, 449, 456, 464, 519
Hammond's Candies, 205
Hampton Inns, 369
Harris Interactive, 131
Harvard Business School, 363, 414
Harvard University, 481, 524
Hasbro, 439
Headstart Advisers, 383
Healthy Weight Commitment Foundation, 92
Hewlett-Packard, 191, 266, 274, 303, 354, 355, 432, 484, 545
Hilton, 239
Hindustan Lever Limited, 238
Hissho Iwai, 404
Hitachi, 25, 309
Hoechst, 20, 418
Home Depot, 130, 140, 141, 180, 320

Honda, 170, 240, 252, 253, 316
Honeywell, 237, 494
Hotels.com, 157
HP, 17, 49, 163, 164
HSBC, 95, 178–179
HSN, 420
Hubbard & Hubbard, 137
Humane Society, 56
Human Rights Campaign, 132
Hunter College, 135
Hunter Douglas, 438
Hyundai, 421

I

IBM, 15, 16, 17, 25, 53, 84, 127, 132, 163, 164, 175, 177–178, 296, 303, 304, 354, 355, 487, 488, 492, 495, 540, 541, 545, 546, 554, 556
ICU Medical, 457–458
IDEO Product Development, 78, 78–79, 80, 82, 83, 84, 87, 461–462, 466
IKEA, 171, 173
ImproveNow.com, 368
InboxDetox.com, 316
Inc. magazine, 76–77
Indiana University, 501
Infosurv, 205
ING, 95
InnSeekers, 137
Institute for Healthcare Improvement, 471
Integrated Mission Solutions, 289
Integrated Project Management Company, 409, 410
Intel, 116, 160, 163, 218, 231, 266, 556
InterContinental Hotels Group, 555
Invention Hub, 88
IQMS, 551, 552
Iteris, 550

J

Jabil Circuit, 296
Jack-in-the-Box, 138
Jacksonville Foods, 459
J.D. Power, 256
Jenny Craig, 148
JetBlue Airways, 434
JFK International Airport, 148
JobLine International, 356
John Deere, 19, 339
Johnson & Johnson, 111, 112, 117, 142, 303
Johnsonville Foods, 456
JPMorgan Chase, 95, 132
Juniper, 88
Just Business, 88

K

Kauffman Foundation, 212
KB Home, 513
KBR/Halliburton, 23
Kellogg, 186, 237
Kelly Services, 353
Ken's Krew, 140
Kentucky Fried Chicken, 138
Ketchum, 494
KFC, 235
Kimberly-Clark, 315
Kodak, 252–253, 556
KORRES, 240
Kraft, 167
Krispy Kreme, 167

L

Lands' End, 238
Lawrence Livermore National Laboratory, 143
Lawrence N. Field Center for Entrepreneurship, 213
LEGO Group, 270–271, 438–440
Lehman Brothers, 115
LendingTree, 365

Leninets Concern, 238
Lennar Corp., 513
Lenovo, 163, 164
Levi Strauss, 114, 160, 162, 492
Lexus, 256
LG, 20
Li & Fung, 161, 173
Liberty Media Corporation, 420
Liberty University, 429
The Limited, 238
Lincoln Electric, 402, 404
LinkedIn, 488
Linksys, 234
Live Nation, 420
L.L. Bean, 339
Lockheed Corporation, 208
Lockheed Martin, 132
Loews Hotels, 146
London School of Economics, 414
Lone Pine Resources, 182
Louisiana Bucket Brigade, 525
Louis Vuitton, 451, 452
Lowe's, 141
Lucasfilm, 277, 440
Lucent Technologies, 132
Lundberg Family Farms, 165

M

Macy's, 180, 288, 419
Manville Corporation, 115
Marilyn Arnold Designs, 212
Martha Stewart Living Omnimedia, 73
Marvel, 277, 278
Mary Kay Cosmetics, 362
Massey Energy, 26
Matsushita, 234
Mazda, 265, 419
McDonald's, 5, 6, 38–39, 42, 53, 81, 82–83, 102–103, 116, 138, 140, 163, 232, 233, 239, 266, 282, 284, 294–295, 361
McGill University, 11
McKinsey & Co., 556
McKinsey Global Institute, 325
McNeil Nutritionals, 160
Medicus Solutions, 410
Medtronic, 69
Merck & Co., 132
Meritage Hospitality Group, 283
Merrill Lynch, 115, 138, 142, 143
Metal Office Furniture Company, 262
MetLife, 450
Michael Baker Corporation, 289
Michael Baker International, 289
Michelin North America, 97
Microsoft, 15, 16, 25, 80, 81, 96, 132, 153, 160, 168, 171, 208, 297–298, 303, 304, 348, 354, 355, 376, 377, 420, 456, 466, 476–477, 494, 544, 546, 554
Midas Muffler, 332
Mine Health and Safety Administration, 26
Minority Corporate Counsel Association, 363
Mirage Studios, 440
MIT, 189, 483
Mondolez International, 171
Monetary Authority of Singapore, 57–58
Monster.com, 356
Moody's, 310
Morton Thiokol, 187, 197, 202
Motorola, 168, 187, 194, 195, 258, 347, 377, 492
MSCO, 486
MySpace, 488

N

NAACP, 128
National Association for Female Executives, 148
National Association for the Advancement of Colored People, 128
National Association of Colleges and Employers, 325
National Electric Lamp Association, 34

National Football League, 142, 291
National Labor Relations Board, 371, 533
National Oceanic and Atmospheric
     Administration, 525
National Restaurant Association, 532
National Science Foundation, 524
National Workrights Institute, 487
Nature Conservancy, 524–525
Natuzzi, 20
NBC Universal, 35, 234, 475
Neiman Marcus, 288, 395, 404, 419
Nestlé, 120, 237, 240
Netflix, 3, 229–230, 332–333
Newell Rubbermaid, 293
New England Trading Company, 257
New Regency, 14
New York Life Insurance Company, 212, 452
New York Stock Exchange, 98
The New York Times, 111
NeXT Computer, 88
Nickelodeon, 426
Nike, 22, 66, 142–143, 162, 217, 555–556
Nintendo, 250, 310
Nippon Restaurant Enterprise Co., 165
Nissan, 143
Nokia, 17, 158, 250, 453
Nordstrom, 419
North American Tool, 75
North Carolina State University, 414, 415
Northwest Airlines, 481
Northwestern University, 134
Not for Sale, 88
Nucor, 116, 403, 451–452
Nyhart, 410

O

Ogilvy & Mather, 453
Ohio State University, 422
Olive Garden, 362
1-800-Flowers, 185, 186
Oppenheimer, 171
Oracle, 15, 160, 163, 194, 420, 488, 545, 546, 554

P

PAC, 107
Panasonic, 310
Panera, 253
Paramount Pictures, 439
Partnership for a Healthier America, 92
Paul Charles & Associates, 505
PayScale Incorporated, 45
PeopleG2, 557
Pepperdine University, 528
PepsiCo, 127, 160, 167, 170, 228, 232, 234,
     235–236, 300, 432, 509–511
Pfizer, 153, 492
Philanthropic Ventures Foundation, 88
Philip Morris, 182
Philips, 34, 220
Pier 1 Imports, 238, 286, 287
Pinterest, 212
Pixar, 277–278, 440
Pizza Hut, 138, 235
Plexus Corp., 296, 297
Polaroid, 252
Polyvore, 61–63, 66, 68
PricewaterhouseCoopers, 123–125, 153
Princeton University, 74
Principal Financial Group, 134, 135
Procter & Gamble, 67, 111, 163, 228, 234,
     237, 238, 339
ProFlowers, 420
Prudential, 66, 107, 111
Public Citizen, 169
Publix, 42, 532
Pulte Group, 513, 514
Purdue University, 72
PVH, 99

Q

Quaker Oats, 167, 235, 236
Quantum, 160
QVC, 420

R

Radacati Group, 485
Radio Corporation of America, 234
Rainbow Coalition, 129
Ralph Lauren, 174, 237
Ralston Purina, 120
Ram Tool, 73
Raytheon, 132
RCA, 34
Realogy Corp., 143
Recruiting Toolbox, 377
Redbox, 229–230
Red Cross, 98
Red Envelope, 420
Red Hat, 413–415, 424
Red Lobster, 362
Re/Max International, 404
Renault, 252
Republic Steel, 30
Reputation Institute, 271
Restaurant Opportunities Center, 532–533
Rice University, 414
Robert Half Technology, 488
Roberts Golden Consulting, 483
Rock Bottom Restaurants, 448
Rockwell Collins, 402
Rolex, 237
Royal Dutch Shell, 222
Rutgers University, 533
RW3, 505, 506
Rypple, 476

S

SAC Capital Advisors, 116
Salesforce.com, 88, 475–477
Salesforce.com Foundation, 477
Samsung, 20, 163, 231, 250, 310, 421, 560
San Francisco State University, 377
SAP, 163, 552–553, 554
SAS, 379–381, 383, 385, 386, 394
Saudi Arabian Airlines, 518
Schering, 20
S.C. Johnson & Sons, 132
Scottrade, 163
Seagate Technologies, 160
Sealy, 293
2nd Avenue Deli, 476
Securities and Exchange Commission, 23, 97
Semco, 350–351
SeniorEntrepreneurshipWorks. org, 213
Seva Foundation, 113
SGI, 546
Shell, 222
Shuqualak Lumber, 73
Siemens, 23, 107, 108, 163
Silevo, 30
Singer, 212
SiriusXM, 420
SiteDesign, 404
Skype, 485
Smarter Workforce Institute, 540–541
Smith-Kline Beecham, 288
Soap Dispensary, 100, 101–102
Soar Technology, 494
Sociometric Solutions, 275, 536
Sodexo, 134–135
SolarCity, 30–31
SolutionsIQ, 506
Sony, 22, 158, 160, 163, 166, 171, 231, 310, 543
Sony Pictures Television, 14
Southern African Development Community, 174

Southern California Edison, 132
Southwest Airlines, 50, 117, 229, 249,
     253–254, 256, 303
SpaceX, 30
Sprint, 255
Standard Chartered Bank, 95
Standard Oil, 39, 40
Stanford University, 61, 88, 143, 191
Starbucks, 528, 541–542
Starr Conspiracy, 410
Starz, 420
Steelcase, 262–263
Stella & Dot, 397
Stericycle, 409, 410
St. John's Home for Boys, 185
Subaru, 72–73
Subway, 274, 282
Sun Microsystems, 194, 195, 197, 198, 545, 546
SupplyChainBrain, 100
Syracuse University, 485

T

Taco Bell, 56, 235
Target, 114, 116, 121, 332, 423
Tata Consultancy Services, 355
Tate & Lyle, 160
Teknovus, 484
Telia, 356
Tesla Motors, 30, 31, 233, 310
Tesser, 283
Texaco, 142
Texas A&M University, 81, 329
Textron, 236
Thermos, 267, 269
Thomas-Houston Company, 35
3M, 16, 49, 208, 235, 268, 269, 304
360networks, 420
Thundercloud Subs, 274
Tiffany & Co., 108–109
Time, Inc., 363
Timely Publications, 277
Time Warner, 191, 518
Tipping Point, 88
TJX Companies, 257
T-Mobile, 255, 430, 431
Tokio Marine and Fire Insurance, 404
Tommy Hilfiger, 237
TOMS, 113–114
Toronto-Dominion Bank, 132
Toshiba, 163
Tower Semiconductor, 310
Toyota, 51, 109–110, 117, 129, 170, 171, 229, 231, 240,
     250, 252, 253, 263, 266, 315, 316, 323, 330, 335
Toys"R"Us, 215–216
Trans Pacific Partnership, 168–169, 182–183
TriZetto, 305
Tropicana, 235, 236
True Position, 420
Tumblr, 301
Tungsram, 177
TWA, 148
Twitter, 256, 376, 488, 540, 561
Tyco, 84, 107, 236

U

Uber, 30–31
Under Armour, 66–67
Unilever, 163, 173, 237
Union Bank of California, 24
United Continental, 249
United Electric Controls, 264
United Nations, 109
United States Chamber of Commerce, 183, 532
United Technologies, 319
University of California at Irvine, 525
University of Houston, 130
University of Maryland, 66, 67
University of Michigan, 363, 424

University of Notre Dame, 129–130
University of Washington, 153, 472, 501
UPS, 5, 25, 111, 117, 147, 162, 188–189, 197, 304, 335, 482, 539–540, 549
U.S. Air Force, 8
U.S. Department of Justice, 121, 226
U.S. Department of Labor, 26, 513, 514
U.S. Postal Service, 162
UTAC Manufacturing Services, 310

V

Vattenfall, 182
Verizon, 542
Village Roadshow, 438
Virgin Group, 301
Virginia Tech, 189
Virtusize, 338–339
Visa, 157
Vizuix, 536
Volkswagen, 252
Volvo, 419

W

Wainhouse Research, 505
Walgreens, 140–141

Walmart, 6, 22, 42, 82, 140, 142, 158, 160, 163, 174, 204–205, 233, 251–252, 253, 264, 308, 335, 423, 533, 537, 542
Walt Disney Company, 81, 277, 278, 331–332, 361, 540, 541
Warner Bros., 438, 439, 440
Washtenaw County Food Bank, 417
Waterford Technologies, 486
Water for People, 113
Waterman, 228
W.C. Bradley, 270
The Weather Channel, 434
Websense, 494
Well Read New & Used Books, 213
Wendy's, 138, 283
Western Electric Company, 47
Westland/Hallmark Meat Co., 56
WhatsApp, 88
Whirlpool, 347
Whole Foods, 107, 116
Wild Oats, 253
Williams College, 524
Winning Workplaces, 70
Witeck Communications, 131
W. L. Gore, 443–445, 446, 447, 450
Women Athletes Global Leadership Network, 171

WorldCom, 84, 107, 115
World Trade Organization, 173

X

Xerox, 17, 259, 339

Y

Yahoo! 61, 132, 206, 301–302, 546
Yale University, 137, 334
Yeh Group, 162
York University, 183
Young & Rubicam, 492
Yum Brands, 296

Z

Zales, 186
Zappos, 313–314, 320, 338, 348, 349
Zara, 230–231
Zayre, 257
Zen Desk, 88
Zingerman's Delicatessen, 416–417

Subject Glindex

A

Abayas, 319, 518
Ability tests, 360
Accommodation   An ineffective conflict-handling approach in which one party, typically with weaker power, gives in to the demands of the other, typically more powerful, party, 516
Accommodations for disabled workers, 129
Accommodative approach   Companies and their managers behave legally and ethically and try to balance the interests of different stakeholders as the need arises, 115
Accord on Fire and Building Safety, 99–100
Accounting, ethical failures, 110, 115
Accounts payable departments, 265
Accuracy of information, 497
Accuracy of planning, 218
Achievement, need for, 68, 207, 392
Achievement orientation   A worldview that values assertiveness, performance, success, and competition, 176
Achievement-oriented behaviors, 428
Acquired immune deficiency syndrome, 130
Acquisitions
    by GE, 33–34
    importance of personal relationships, 476
    preserving organizational structures after, 277–278
    synergies from, 236
Action plans, 396
Activity ratios, 324
Actors' compensation, 5–6
Adaptive cultures, 304–305, 338
Ad hoc committees, 299, 450
Adjourning stage, 459
Administrative management   The study of how to create an organizational structure and control system that leads to high efficiency and effectiveness, 40–46
Administrative model   An approach to decision making that explains why decision making is inherently uncertain and risky and why managers usually make satisfactory rather than optimum decisions, 191–194
Affiliation, need for, 68, 392
Affinity groups, 134
Afghanistan power project, 321–322
African Union, 174
Age discrimination, 126–127, 143
Age Discrimination in Employment Act (1967), 127, 128, 352
Age diversity, 126–127
Agenda, controlling, 527
Agile companies, 21
Aging populations, 168
Agreeableness   The tendency to get along well with other people, 64–65
AIDS awareness training, 130, 353
Airline industry
    communication problems, 481
    efficiency programs, 247–249
    global business impact, 173
    improving responsiveness to customers, 253–254
    information needs, 538
Airport management, 8–9
Alderfer's ERG theory   The theory that three universal needs—for existence, relatedness, and growth—constitute a hierarchy of needs and motivate behavior. Alderfer proposed that needs at more than one level can be motivational at the same time, 390–391
All-channel networks, 490
Alliances
    building, 524–525
    building at PepsiCo, 509–511
Alternatives, decision-making, 195–198

Ambiguous information   Information that can be interpreted in multiple and often conflicting ways, 193
Americans with Disabilities Act (1990), 127, 129–130, 140, 352
Analyzability of tasks, 281
Annual meetings, 82
Anti-charities, 334
Appliance manufacturing, 18–19
Appliance Park, 18–19
Applications software, 547–548
Arbitration, 182–183, 372
Arbitrators   Third-party negotiators who can impose what they think is a fair solution to a conflict that both parties are obligated to abide by, 519
Artificial intelligence   Behavior performed by a machine that, if performed by a human being, would be called "intelligent," 550–551
Artificial sweeteners, 160
Assessment centers, 360
Asynchronous technologies, 453
Athletics, leadership development and, 170–171
Attention, 47–48, 139, 498
Attitudes   Collections of feelings and beliefs, 70–74
Attraction–selection–attrition framework   A model that explains how personality may influence organizational culture, 78
Audits of workplace safety, 100
Authority   The power to hold people accountable for their actions and to make decisions concerning the use of organizational resources, 41, 294
    allocation in organizational structures, 294–298
    in Fayol's theory, 43
    knowledge based, 47
    overlapping, 515
    Weber's principles, 41–42
Automakers
    ethical failures, 109–110, 115
    flexible manufacturing, 263
    improving responsiveness to customers, 253
    process reengineering, 265
    SWOT analysis, 225–227
Autonomy of jobs, 284
Auto-replies, 317
Avoidance   An ineffective conflict-handling approach in which the parties try to ignore the problem and do nothing to resolve their differences, 516

B

Baby food, 119–120
Background information on job applicants, 358
Backward vertical integration, 233
Baggage fees, 249
Bangladesh building collapse, 99–100
Bank wiring room experiments, 48
Barbecue grills, 267
Bar raisers, 376–377
Barriers to entry   Factors that make it difficult and costly for an organization to enter a particular task environment or industry, 164, 227
Bay of Pigs invasion, 202
Behaviorally anchored rating scale, 365, 366
Behavioral management   The study of how managers should behave to motivate employees and encourage them to perform at high levels and be committed to the achievement of organizational goals, 46–50
Behavior appraisals, 364–365, 368, 369
Behavior observation scale, 365, 366
Behaviors. *See also* Motivation
    control systems, 327–333
    evaluating, 364–365, 368, 369
    leadership models based on, 422–424, 427–428
    measuring, 320
    theories of learning, 396–401

Belongingness needs, 390
Benchmarking   The process of comparing one company's performance on specific dimensions with the performance of other high-performing organizations, 339
Benefits. *See* Employee benefits
Bias   The systematic tendency to use information about others in ways that result in inaccurate perceptions, 141, 480–481
    avoiding in interviews, 359
    decision-making, 200–201
    effects over time, 135
    hidden, 153–154
Big, hairy, audacious goals, 223
Big data, 325, 540–541
Big Five personality traits, 63–68
Black Belts (Six Sigma), 260
Blackbox data centers, 545, 546
Blogs   Websites on which an individual, group, or organization posts information, commentary, and opinions and to which readers can often respond with their own commentary and opinions, 488
Boarding processes, 247–249
Boards of directors, women on, 127
Body language, 480
Boeing jet component suppliers, 161
Bonuses. *See also* Reward systems
    for innovation, 208
    motivational impact, 403, 452
    in scientific management, 37, 38
Book Days, 200
Boss Button, 275
Bottom-up change   A gradual or evolutionary approach to change in which managers at all levels work together to develop a detailed plan for change, 338
Boundaryless organizations   Organizations whose members are linked by computers, faxes, computer-aided design systems, and video teleconferencing and who rarely, if ever, see one another face-to-face, 556
Bounded rationality   Cognitive limitations that constrain one's ability to interpret, process, and act on information, 192
Brainstorming, 205–206
Brand loyalty   Customers' preference for the products of organizations currently existing in the task environment, 164–165
Brasscom, 354
Brazil, outsourcing to, 354
Breakfast, fast food, 245
Bribery, 22–23, 107–108
BRIC countries, 179
B2B marketplaces   Internet-based trading platforms set up to connect buyers and sellers in an industry, 554
B2B network structure   A series of global strategic alliances that an organization creates with suppliers, manufacturers, and distributors to produce and market a product, 555–556
Budgets, 326
Bullying, 291
Bureaucracy   A formal system of organization and administration designed to ensure efficiency and effectiveness, 41
    shortcomings, 34, 42, 331–332
    Weber's principles, 40–42
Bureaucratic control   Control of behavior by means of a comprehensive system of rules and standard operating procedures, 329–333
Bureau of Mines (U.S.), 26
Business cards, 517
Business-level plan   Divisional managers' decisions pertaining to divisions' long-term goals, overall strategy, and structure, 220

Business-level strategy A plan that indicates how a division intends to compete against its rivals in an industry, 220, 227–231, 325

Business-to-business commerce Trade that takes place between companies using IT and the Internet to link and coordinate the value chains of different companies, 553–554

Business-to-customer commerce Trade that takes place between a company and individual customers using IT and the Internet, 554

Business travelers, 345

Business units, planning in, 219

C

Cab driver fraud, 110–111

Cafeteria-style benefit plans Plans from which employees can choose the benefits they want, 370

CAFTA, 174

Call centers, 313

Cambodian immigrants, 386

Capital, forms of, 171–172

Capital punishment, 95

Carcinogens in soaps, 101

Career advancement, 124

Career planning, 44–45

Carrera workstation, 194

Case in the News boxes
    arbitration, 182–183
    bar raisers, 376–377
    Chick-fil-A menu changes, 343
    Deutsche Bank investigation, 57–58
    hashtag shopping, 558
    hidden biases, 153–154
    Higa, James, 88–89
    The Lego Movie, 438–440
    March Madness, 275
    McDonald's profitability, 245
    Musk's green energy investments, 30–31
    older entrepreneurs, 212–213
    Panasonic strategy, 310
    returns on employee benefits, 408–410
    Target hacking scandal, 121
    team-based health care, 471–472
    teleconferences, 505–506
    worker centers, 532–533

Cautious organizational cultures, 80

Cell phone concept, 187

Central American Free Trade Agreement, 174

Central banks, 57–58

Centralization
    authority, 297–298
    Fayol's principles, 44
    impact on organizational culture, 304

Centralization The concentration of authority at the top of the managerial hierarchy, 44

Central positions, 523

Ceremonies, 82

Chain networks, 489

Chain of command. *See also* Hierarchies; Organizational structure
    Fayol's principles, 43–44
    hierarchies of authority, 294
    minimizing, 296–297, 314

Challenger space shuttle, 187, 197, 202

Change
    challenges for firms, 334–335
    evolutionary versus revolutionary, 336
    force-field theory, 335–336
    influence on organizational structures, 279–280, 297
    managing, 336–339
    resistance to, 337–338
    role of emotion in, 75

Charismatic leaders Enthusiastic, self-confident leaders who are able to clearly communicate their vision of how good things could be, 431

Charitable donation apps, 334

Charity Miles app, 334

Chatter app, 475–476

Cheaper by the Dozen, 39

Cheating, 105–106

Checkout systems, 157

Chernobyl nuclear disaster, 25

Chief executive officers
    compensation, 97–98, 370
    defined, 13
    ethical example, 112–113
    self-interested actions, 97–98
    turnaround specialists, 22
    women as, 432

Chief operating officers, 13

Chief sustainability officers, 197–198

Child care, 131

Childhood obesity, 91–92

China
    business etiquette, 517–518
    concerns about product copying in, 18
    Home Depot's withdrawal, 180
    as leading outsourcing country, 17, 161, 162
    relocating to, 178
    worker abuses in, 23

Chiselers, 48

Circle networks, 489

City government quality initiatives, 260

Civil Rights Act (1991), 127, 352

Clan control The control exerted on individuals and groups in an organization by shared values, norms, standards of behavior, and expectations, 333

Classical decision-making model A prescriptive approach to decision making based on the assumption that the decision maker can identify and evaluate all possible alternatives and their consequences and rationally choose the most appropriate course of action, 191

Classroom instruction, 361–362

Clean water, 113

ClearPath Weather, 550

Closed system A system that is self-contained and thus not affected by changes occurring in its external environment, 51

Cloud computing, 546, 547, 554

Coal mining safety, 26–27

Codes of ethics, 111–112

Coercive power The ability of a manager to punish others, 419

Coffee business, 113–114, 528

Cohesiveness of groups, 462–465

Cola producers, 233

Coldbath Fields prison, 95

Collaboration A way of managing conflict in which both parties try to satisfy their goals by coming up with an approach that leaves them better off and does not require concessions on issues that are important to either party, 516

Collaboration software Groupware that promotes and facilitates collaborative, highly interdependent interactions and provides an electronic meeting site for communication among team members, 493–495

Collective bargaining Negotiations between labor unions and managers to resolve conflicts and disputes about issues such as working hours, wages, benefits, working conditions, and job security, 372

Collectivism A worldview that values subordination of the individual to the goals of the group and adherence to the principle that people should be judged by their contribution to the group, 167, 176

College basketball tournament, 275

Columbia space shuttle, 187, 197

Command, unity of, 43

Command groups Groups composed of subordinates who report to the same supervisor; also called *departments* or *units*, 450

Commission pay, 404

Commitment, 74, 201

Common interests, 45

Communication The sharing of information between two or more individuals or groups to reach a common understanding, 477. *See also* Information technology
    email management, 316–317
    enhancing in workplace, 275, 278
    importance for managers, 478–479
    ineffective, 481
    modes and media, 482–488, 496
    networks, 488–491
    perception in, 480–481
    problems in hierarchies, 296
    process overview, 479–480
    shortcomings of IT methods, 557–558
    skills for managers, 495–501
    technology, 491–495

Communication assistants, 496

Communication networks The pathways along which information flows in groups and teams and throughout the organization, 488–491

Communities as stakeholders, 102–103

Community service, 477

Compact fluorescent bulbs, 34

Company newsletters, 487

Compensation. *See also* Reward systems
    fairness in, 104–105
    Fayol's principles, 45
    for film actors, 5–6
    gender disparities, 127, 136
    major components, 369–371
    median for general managers, 7
    motivation and, 388, 401–404
    as part of human resource management, 350
    racial disparities, 128
    at Semco, 351
    Taylor's approach, 37, 38
    of top managers, 97–98, 115, 370

Competency centers, 177–178

Competition An ineffective conflict-handling approach in which each party tries to maximize its own gain and has little interest in understanding the other party's position and arriving at a solution that will allow both parties to achieve their goals, 516

Competitive advantage
    customer service as, 21–22, 250, 313, 349
    GE's efforts to maintain, 33–35
    global challenges, 20–22

Competitive advantage The ability of one organization to outperform other organizations because it produces desired goods or services more efficiently and effectively than they do, 20

Competitors
    impact on task environment, 163–165
    teams as, 464–465

Competitors Organizations that produce goods and services that are similar to a particular organization's goods and services, 163

Complaints, 256

Completeness of information, 538

Component suppliers, 160

Compromise A way of managing conflict in which each party is concerned about not only its own goal accomplishment but also the goal accomplishment of the other party and is willing to engage in a give-and-take exchange and make concessions, 516

Computer programmers, 354, 356–357

Computers. *See* Information technology

Concentration on a single industry Reinvesting a company's profits to strengthen its competitive position in its current industry, 232

Concentro containers, 546

Conceptual skills The ability to analyze and diagnose a situation and to distinguish between cause and effect, 14–15

Concurrent control Control that gives managers immediate feedback on how efficiently inputs are being transformed into outputs so managers can correct problems as they arise, 319

Conference calls, 505–506

Confidence, excessive, 190–191

Conflict
  Collins's view, 46
  helping groups to manage, 468
  levels of, 511–512
  management strategies, 516–519
  political strategies to address, 521–528
  sources, 514–515, 516–517
  in teleconferences, 505
  types, 512–514
Conflict minerals, 23, 109
Conformity, 459–462, 463–464
Conscientiousness The tendency to be careful, scrupulous, and persevering, 65–66
Conservative cultures, 300
Consideration Behavior indicating that a manager trusts, respects, and cares about subordinates, 422, 423
Consistency in planning process, 221
Contingency models of leadership, 424–429
Contingency planning, 222
Contingency theory The idea that the organizational structures and control systems managers choose depend on (are contingent on) characteristics of the external environment in which the organization operates, 52–54
Continuity in planning process, 218
Contract books Written agreements that detail product development factors such as responsibilities, resource commitments, budgets, time lines, and development milestones, 269
Control. *See also* Organizational control
  illusion of, 200
  locus of, 67–68, 207
Controlling Evaluating how well an organization is achieving its goals and taking action to maintain or improve performance; one of the four principal tasks of management, 10, 84
Controlling the agenda, 527
Control systems Formal target-setting, monitoring, evaluation, and feedback systems that provide managers with information about how well the organization's strategy and structure are working, 318
  applying, 319–323
  behavior control, 327–333
  clan control, 333–334
  information needs, 539–540
  output control, 323–327
  use of IT, 318–319, 329
Convenience, 254
Conversion stage, 51
Conveyor belts, 38
Cooperation Council for the Arab States of the Gulf, 174
Coordination
  of divisions and functions in firms, 293–300
  information needs, 541–542
  mechanisms, 298–300
Core competency The specific set of departmental skills, knowledge, and experience that allows one organization to outperform another, 15
Core members The members of a team who bear primary responsibility for the success of a project and who stay with a project from inception to completion, 269
Corporate-level plans Top management's decisions pertaining to the organization's mission, overall strategy, and structure, 219–220
Corporate-level strategies Plans that indicate in which industries and national markets organizations intend to compete, 219–220, 231–232
  diversification, 234–237
  industry concentration, 232
  international expansion, 237–241
  vertical integration, 233–234
Corporate social responsibility. *See* Social responsibility
Corrective actions, 321, 322
Cosmetics industry, 22–23

Cost controls in film production, 10
Cost of information, 193
Cotton production, 162
Crafts production, 35
Creativity A decision maker's ability to discover original and novel ideas that lead to feasible alternative courses of action, 203
  diversity's advantages, 137
  emotion in, 433–434
  entrepreneurship and, 206–208
  mood states and, 74
  in organizational cultures, 79, 84, 278
  promoting, 205–206, 413, 414
Credit card data theft, 121
Credos, 111–112
Crime, changing views about, 94–95
Crisis management, 25–27
Criticism, avoiding, 368, 369
Croslite resin, 232
Cross-departmental responsibility, 13
Cross-functional teams Groups of managers brought together from different departments to perform organizational tasks, 53, 293
  competitive advantage from, 293
  customer service, 447
  permanent, 299
  product development benefits, 269–270, 299
  synergies from, 446
  top management teams as, 449
Cross-functioning, 47, 259
Cross-training, 21
CT scanners, 478
Culture. *See* National culture; Organizational culture
Currency market manipulation, 57–58
Current ratio, 324
Customer Loyalty Teams, 349
Customer relationship management A technique that uses IT to develop an ongoing relationship with customers to maximize the value an organization can deliver to them over time, 255
  benefits of, 255–256
  software, 475, 553
Customers Individuals and groups that buy the goods and services an organization produces, 163
  basic wants of, 253
  divisional structures based on, 290
  impact on task environment, 163
  involving in product development, 267
  performance appraisals by, 367
  as stakeholders, 100–102
Customer service
  as benefit of treating workers well, 345–347
  as competitive advantage, 21–22, 250, 313, 349
  diversity's advantages, 137
  from groups and teams, 446–447
  improving quality, 256–260, 283, 430
  improving responsiveness, 252–256, 317–318
  motivation to provide, 388
  training, 283
  in value chain management, 252

D

Data Raw, unsummarized, and unanalyzed facts, 537
Data analysis skills, 325
Database systems, 545–546
Day care facilities, 131
Days sales outstanding, 324
Death penalty, 95
Debt-to-assets ratio, 324
Decentralization, 44, 173, 304
Decentralizing authority Giving lower-level managers and nonmanagerial employees the right to make important decisions about how to use organizational resources, 297–298
Decisional roles of managers, 12, 133
Decision making The process by which managers respond to opportunities and threats by analyzing

options and making determinations about specific organizational goals and courses of action, 187
  administrative model, 191–194
  biases, 200–201
  classical model, 191
  entrepreneurial, 206–208
  ethical rules for, 103–105
  in groups, 201–203
  information needs, 539
  learning from, 185–186, 203–206
  in organizational cultures, 78, 84
  in planning process, 218
  programmed versus nonprogrammed, 188–191
  steps in process, 194–199
  uncertainties in process, 10–11
Decision-making styles, 201
Decision rules, 103–105, 188
Decision support systems Interactive computer-based management information systems that managers can use to make nonroutine decisions, 550
Decline stage, 543
Decoding Interpreting and trying to make sense of a message, 480
Defects, identifying, 258–259, 318
Defensive approach Companies and their managers behave ethically to the degree that they stay within the law and strictly abide by legal requirements, 115
Defining the business, 223
Delayering, 556
Delphi technique A decision-making technique in which group members do not meet face-to-face but respond in writing to questions posed by the group leader, 206
Demand forecasts, 353
Demands, interests versus, 521
Demographic forces Outcomes of changes in, or changing attitudes toward, the characteristics of a population, such as age, gender, ethnic origin, race, sexual orientation, and social class, 167
Department of State (U.S.), 44
Departments Groups of people who work together and possess similar skills or use the same knowledge, tools, or techniques to perform their jobs, 11
  as command groups, 450
  cooperation between, 44
  hierarchies within, 15, 44
  organizational structures based on, 285–286
  planning in, 219
Deregulation, 168
Derivatives, 165
Design of products, 259
Development Building the knowledge and skills of organizational members so they are prepared to take on new responsibilities and challenges, 361
  approaches, 362–363
  of groups and teams, 458–459
  as part of human resource management, 348
  at Zappos, 349
Developmental consideration Behavior a leader engages in to support and encourage followers and help them develop and grow on the job, 431–432
Deviance in groups and teams, 459–462
Devil's advocacy Critical analysis of a preferred alternative, made in response to challenges raised by a group member who, playing the role of devil's advocate, defends unpopular or opposing alternatives for the sake of argument, 202–203
Dialectical inquiry Critical analysis of two preferred alternatives in order to find an even better alternative for the organization to adopt, 203
Dialysis clinics, 145–146
Differentiation strategy Distinguishing an organization's products from the products of competitors on dimensions such as product design, quality, or after-sales service, 8, 228–229
  influence on organizational structure, 280
  methods of achieving, 249–250

Difficult goals, 395–396
Digital piracy, 4, 105
Dilemmas, ethical, 93
Direction, from planning, 218
Directive behaviors, 428
Direct supervision, 327–328
Disabled employees, 129–130, 140–141, 496
Discipline Obedience, energy, application, and
other outward marks of respect for a superior's
authority, 45, 46
Discrimination
age-based, 126–127, 143
based on disability, 129–130
continuing problems, 126
Costco lawsuit, 423
gender-based, 126, 136, 143–144
in job interviews, 359
lawsuits, 138, 142–143
major laws against, 352
overt, 142–144
perceptual bias and, 140–142
recent trends, 136
religious, 129
sexual orientation, 131–132
Dismissals, 518
Disseminators, managers as, 12, 133
Distance, as declining barrier, 173
Distance learning, 363
Distorted messages, 296
Distributive justice A moral principle
calling for fair distribution of pay, promotions,
and other organizational resources based on
meaningful contributions that individuals have
made and not personal characteristics over
which they have no control, 136, 395
Distributive negotiation Adversarial
negotiation in which the parties in conflict
compete to win the most resources while
conceding as little as possible, 519, 520
Distributors Organizations that help other
organizations sell their goods or services to
customers, 99, 162–163
Disturbance handlers, managers as, 12, 133
Diversification Expanding a company's business
operations into a new industry in order to produce
new kinds of valuable goods or services, 234–237
Diversity Dissimilarities or differences among
people due to age, gender, race, ethnicity,
religion, sexual orientation, socioeconomic
background, education, experience, physical
appearance, capabilities/disabilities, and any
other characteristic that is used to distinguish
between people, 125
advantages in organizations, 79
cultural, 177
of decision makers, 203
effective management, 24, 133–138, 144–148
in groups and teams, 464
hidden biases and, 153–154
importance of awareness, 125–126
major types, 126–133
mentoring and, 363
perception and, 138–144
at PricewaterhouseCoopers, 123–125
sexual harassment and, 148–150
as source of conflict, 517
Diversity awareness programs, 145, 147, 153–154
Diversity circles, 124–125
Diversity education, 146, 147
Divestitures
to concentrate on core business, 236–237
by GE, 34–35, 234
by PepsiCo, 235
Divisional structure An organizational
structure composed of separate business units
within which are the functions that work
together to produce a specific product for a
specific customer, 287–290
Division of labor Splitting the work to be performed into particular tasks and assigning tasks to
individual workers, 454. *See also* Specialization

Divisions
coordinating within firms, 293–300
goals, 325, 327
planning in, 219, 220
Dodd-Frank Act, 23
Downsizing, 17, 73
Drive-through sales, 245
Dual command, 43
Dual reporting relationships, 291, 293
DVD rentals, 229–230
Dyeing processes, 162

E

E-book readers, 22
E-commerce Trade that takes place between
companies, and between companies and
individual customers, using IT and the Internet,
216, 553–554, 558. *See also* Online retailing
Economically feasible choices, 196
Economic conditions, 72, 166, 179
Economic forces Interest rates, inflation,
unemployment, economic growth, and other
factors that affect the general health and well-
being of a nation or the regional economy of an
organization, 166
Economies of scale Cost advantages
associated with large operations, 164
Education, 14–15, 16, 363
Effectiveness A measure of the appropriateness
of the goals an organization is pursuing and the
degree to which the organization achieves those
goals, 6
Efficiency A measure of how well or how
productively resources are used to achieve
a goal, 5
airline industry programs, 247–249
as competitive advantage, 21, 250, 313–314
in fast food business, 245
organizational controls, 320
quality and, 256–257
role of effective communication, 478
Taylor's emphasis, 37–38
in value chain management, 261–266
Effort, 381–382, 385, 386
Electronics industry changes, 310
Email
average volume, 485
gender differences in use, 501
management monitoring, 487
managing, 316–317
shortcomings, 483, 485–486
when to use, 496
Embryonic stage, 543
Emotional intelligence The ability to
understand and manage one's own moods and
emotions and the moods and emotions of other
people, 76–77, 433–434
Emotions Intense, relatively short-lived feelings,
74–75, 80
Empathy, 76, 498
Employee benefits
assessing motivational impact, 408–410
common types, 370–371
at Four Seasons, 346
Employee-centered behaviors, 424
Employees. *See also* Compensation
attitudes, 70–74
benefits of treating well, 116, 117, 304–305,
345–347, 423
diversity. *See* Diversity
encouraging ideas from, 47, 50, 258
Hawthorne effect, 47–48
resistance to scientific management, 38
as stakeholders, 99
as temporary salespersons, 19
Theory X and Y views of, 48–49
tracking activities, 535–536
unionized, 160, 371–372
Employee stock options A financial instrument that entitles the bearer to buy shares of an

organization's stock at a certain price during a
certain period or under certain conditions, 403
for top managers, 97, 98, 115
Employee stock ownership plans, 304
Employment relationships, 303
Empowerment The expansion of employees'
knowledge, tasks, and decision-making
responsibilities, 19
benefits of, 19, 296–297, 421
The expansion of employees' knowledge, tasks,
and decision- making responsibilities, 421
in learning organizations, 204
Encoding Translating a message into understandable
symbols or language, 479, 495–496
Engineering firms, 289
Enhancement, rites of, 82
EnterpriseIQ, 552
Enterprise resource planning systems
Multimodule application software packages that
coordinate the functional activities necessary to
move products from the design stage to the final
customer stage, 551–553
Entertainment industry, 3–4, 128–129
Entrepreneurial cultures, 300
Entrepreneurs Individuals who notice
opportunities and decide how to mobilize
the resources necessary to produce new and
improved goods and services, 206
creativity, 206–208
as managers, 207–208
managers as, 12, 133
needs of, 76–77
overconfidence, 191
role in creating organizational culture, 78–79, 81
Entrepreneurship The mobilization of
resources to take advantage of an opportunity to
provide customers with new or improved goods
and services, 207–208, 212–213
Entropy The tendency of a closed system to lose
its ability to control itself and thus to dissolve
and disintegrate, 51
Environmental factors
general environment, 165–169
global, 169–174
Hawthorne effect, 47–48
influence on organizational structures, 279–280
management theories focused on, 51–54
national cultures, 175–179
overview, 158–159
task environment, 159–165
Environmental protection. *See also* Sustainability
in mining activities, 109
Nature Conservancy alliances, 524–525
Soap Dispensary business, 101–102
Subaru's efforts, 72–73
eProv Studio, 213
Equal employment opportunity The equal
right of all citizens to the opportunity to obtain
employment regardless of their gender, age, race,
country of origin, religion, or disabilities, 352
Equal Employment Opportunity Commission, 352
Equal Pay Act (1963), 127, 352, 371
Equity The justice, impartiality, and fairness to
which all organizational members are entitled,
44, 393
Equity theory A theory of motivation that
focuses on people's perceptions of the fairness
of their work outcomes relative to their work
inputs, 392–395, 401
ERG theory The theory that three universal needs—
for existence, relatedness, and growth—constitute a
hierarchy of needs and motivate behavior. Alderfer
proposed that needs at more than one level can be
motivational at the same time, 390–391
eRoom software, 494
Errors, 198–199, 200, 434
Escalating commitment A source of
cognitive bias resulting from the tendency to
commit additional resources to a project even if
evidence shows that the project is failing, 201
Escape the City website, 382–383

Esprit de corps Shared feelings of comradeship, enthusiasm, or devotion to a common cause among members of a group, 45

Esteem needs, 390

Ethical dilemmas The quandaries people find themselves in when they have to decide if they should act in a way that might help another person or group even though doing so might go against their own self-interest, 93

Ethics The inner guiding moral principles, values, and beliefs that people use to analyze or interpret a situation and then decide what is the right or appropriate way to behave, 93
changing standards, 94–95
decision-making criteria, 103–105, 196
importance for managers, 22–23, 105–107
individual, 110–111
laws and dilemmas, 93–94
of managing diverse workforce, 136–137
in meatpacking industry, 56
occupational, 109–110
organizational, 111–114, 303
role of emotion in decisions, 74
social responsibility and, 114–117
societal, 107–109
stakeholders, 95–103
Ethics in Action boxes
Accord on Fire and Building Safety, 99–100
Apple supplier oversight, 23
disabled employees, 140–141
El Faro Estate Coffee, 528
email and Internet use, 487
employee treatment at McDonald's, 38–39
environmental protection by Subaru, 72–73
Gentle Giant Moving Company, 69–70
government conflict with builders, 513–514
mine worker safety, 26–27
Nature Conservancy alliances, 524–525
Netflix culture, 332–333
Soap Dispensary, 101–102
sustainable decisions, 197–198
team leadership, 457–458
Zingerman's servant leadership, 416–417

Ethics ombudspersons Managers responsible for communicating and teaching ethical standards to all employees and monitoring their conformity to those standards, 117

Ethnic diversity, 128–129

Ethnic minorities. *See* Minorities

European Union, 168

Evaluating changes, 339

Evolutionary change Change that is gradual, incremental, and narrowly focused, 336

Exception, managing by, 297, 329

Executive compensation, 97–98, 115, 370

Executive support systems Sophisticated versions of decision support systems that are designed to meet the needs of top managers, 550

Exercise price, 403

Exhaust data, 325

Existence needs, 391

Expat Explorer Survey, 178–179

Expatriates, 178–179

Expectancy In expectancy theory, a perception about the extent to which effort results in a certain level of performance, 385

Expectancy theory The theory that motivation will be high when workers believe that high levels of effort lead to high performance and high performance leads to the attainment of desired outcomes, 384–388, 401, 427

Experience
development via, 362–363
openness to, 65, 66–67

Expertise, 47, 190–191, 527

Expert power Power that is based on the special knowledge, skills, and expertise that a leader possesses, 419–420

Expert systems Management information systems that employ human knowledge,

embedded in a computer, to solve problems that ordinarily require human expertise, 551

Exporting Making products at home and selling them abroad, 238

External locus of control The tendency to locate responsibility for one's fate in outside forces and to believe one's own behavior has little impact on outcomes, 68, 207

External networks, 491

External recruiting, 356–357

Extinction Curtailing the performance of dysfunctional behaviors by eliminating whatever is reinforcing them, 398

Extraversion The tendency to experience positive emotions and moods and to feel good about oneself and the rest of the world, 64, 65

Extrinsically motivated behavior Behavior that is performed to acquire material or social rewards or to avoid punishment, 383

Eyeglasses, 113

F

Face-to-face communication, 482–484

Facilities layout The strategy of designing the machine–worker interface to increase operating system efficiency, 261–263

Fair Labor Standards Act (1938), 371

Fairness, 393, 521

Family and Medical Leave Act (1993), 127, 352

Family-friendly benefits, 370–371, 380

Fashion websites, 61–63

Fast foods
Chick-fil-A menu changes, 343
contribution to childhood obesity, 91
industry responses to ethical challenges, 102–103
job design, 282
sales volumes, 245

FastTrac Boomer program, 213

Fatigue, 39

Federal Aviation Administration, 9

Feedback
in communications model, 479, 480
effective, 368–369
in goal-setting theory, 396
in job design, 284
learning from, 198–199, 350
mechanisms for, 497
in performance appraisal, 350, 364

Feedback control Control that gives managers information about customers' reactions to goods and services so corrective action can be taken if necessary, 319

Feedback phase, 479, 480

Feedforward control Control that allows managers to anticipate problems before they arise, 318–319

Fiedler's contingency model, 425–427, 429

Figureheads, managers as, 12, 133

Film production companies
actor compensation, 5–6
Lego Movie challenges, 438–440
management challenges, 3–4
organizational structure, 277–278
planning by, 8

Filtering Withholding part of a message because of the mistaken belief that the receiver does not need or will not want the information, 496–497

Financial capital, 171

Financial industry
currency market manipulation, 57–58
ethical failures, 110, 115
factors in 2008 crisis, 165
protests against, 95
risks, 34

Financial performance measures, 323–325

Financial problems, candor about, 434

FireEye software, 121

First-line managers Managers who are responsible for the daily supervision of nonmanagerial employees, 11

Fitness apps, 334

Fitness trend, 167

Five forces model, 227

Fixed-position layouts, 262

Flat organizations, 295, 296–298, 304, 556

Flexibility
to accommodate diversity, 146
competitive advantage from, 21, 250
in job design, 355
in organizational cultures, 78
of organizational structure, 280, 297
in planning process, 218
via outsourcing, 353

Flexible manufacturing The set of techniques that attempt to reduce the costs associated with the product assembly process or the way services are delivered to customers, 261, 263

Flower stores, 185–186

Focused differentiation strategy Serving only one segment of the overall market and trying to be the most differentiated organization serving that segment, 229

Focused low-cost strategy Serving only one segment of the overall market and trying to be the lowest-cost organization serving that segment, 229

Focus on Diversity boxes
admitting mistakes, 434
sexual orientation, 131–132
Sodexo and Principal Financial, 134–135
UPS decision making, 188–189

Folkways The routine social conventions of everyday life, 175

Food for Good, 300

Football wearables, 536

Forced rankings, 365–366

Force-field theory, 335–336

Forecasting labor supply and demand, 353

Formal appraisals Appraisals conducted at a set time during the year and based on performance dimensions and measures that were specified in advance, 368, 369. *See also* Performance appraisal

Formal communications, 490

Formal groups Groups that managers establish to achieve organizational goals, 449

Formality, 78, 81, 83

Formal leaders, 457

Forming stage, 458

Forward vertical integration, 233, 234

Foundations, worker center funding from, 532, 533

Founders, 78–79, 81

Franchises, 199

Franchising Selling to a foreign organization the rights to use a brand name and operating know-how in return for a lump-sum payment and a share of the profits, 239

Free trade agreements, 168–169, 174, 182–183

Free-trade doctrine The idea that if each country specializes in the production of the goods and services that it can produce most efficiently, this will make the best use of global resources, 172

Friendship groups Informal groups composed of employees who enjoy one another's company and socialize with one another, 453

Functional conflict resolution, 516

Functional-level plan Functional managers' decisions pertaining to the goals that they propose to pursue to help the division attain its business-level goals, 220–221

Functional-level strategy A plan of action to improve the ability of each of an organization's functions to perform its task-specific activities in ways that add value to an organization's goods and services, 220–221, 250–252, 325

Functional structure An organizational structure composed of all the departments that an organization requires to produce its goods or services, 285–286

Functions, coordinating within firms, 293–300

G

Garage organizers, 199
Garment industry safety, 99–100
Gates Foundation, 96
Gay and lesbian workers, 124, 131–132
Gender and leadership, 432–433
Gender-based conflict, 516
Gender differences in communication, 500–501
Gender discrimination, 126, 136, 143–144, 423
Gender diversity, 127–128
Gender schemas Preconceived beliefs or
  ideas about the nature of men and women and
  their traits, attitudes, behaviors, and preferences,
  139, 140
General Agreement on Tariffs and Trade, 173
General and Industrial Management (Fayol), 7
General environment The wide-ranging
  global, economic, technological, sociocultural,
  demographic, political, and legal forces that
  affect an organization and its task environment,
  159, 165–169
Generation Y, 188–189
Geographic structure An organizational
  structure in which each region of a country or
  area of the world is served by a self-contained
  division, 288–290
Geopolitical tensions, 25
GeoSpring water heater, 18
Germany
  investments in training, 21
  opposition to arbitration clauses, 182
  reputation for ethics, 107
  reputation for social responsibility, 116
Gift cards, 402
Glass ceiling metaphor alluding to the
  invisible barriers that prevent minorities and
  women from being promoted to top corporate
  positions, 126
Global business ethics, 22–23
Global environment The set of global
  forces and conditions that operates beyond an
  organization's boundaries but affects a manager's ability to acquire and utilize resources,
  158, 169–174
Global geographic structures, 289, 290
Globalization The set of specific and general
  forces that work together to integrate and
  connect economic, political, and social systems
  across countries, cultures, or geographical
  regions so that nations become increasingly
  interdependent and similar, 170
  major effects, 170–174
  management challenges, 20–27
  outsourcing and, 17
  of websites, 157–158
  workplace safety and, 99–100
Global network structures, 555–556
Global organizations Organizations that
  operate and compete in more than one
  country, 20, 158
Global outsourcing The purchase or
  production of inputs or final products from
  overseas suppliers to lower costs and improve
  product quality or design, 161. *See also*
  Outsourcing
Global product structures, 290
Global strategy Selling the same standardized
  product and using the same basic marketing
  approach in each national market, 237–241
Global virtual teams, 453
Global warming, 25
Goals
  conflicts over, 514–515
  establishing for firms, 223–224
  of groups and teams, 445, 464, 465–466
  importance to managers, 5
  leading subordinates to achieve, 427–428
  for quality, 258
  superordinate, 520
  use in organizational control, 320, 325–326, 327

Goal-setting theory A theory that focuses
  on identifying the types of goals that are most
  effective in producing high levels of motivation
  and performance and explaining why goals have
  these effects, 395–396, 401
Gold Box deals, 448
Good to Great (Collins), 46
Gore-Tex, 443
Government quality initiatives, 260
Government subsidies to business, 30, 31
Grand River assembly plant, 263
Grapevine An informal communication network
  along which unofficial information flows, 491
Graphic rating scale, 365, 366
Green Belts (Six Sigma), 260
Grievance procedures, 372
Grilled chicken sandwiches, 343
Ground stations (UPS), 549
group cohesiveness The degree to which
  members are attracted to or loyal to their group, 462
Group creativity, 205–206
Group decision making, 201–203
Group decision support systems
  Executive support systems that link top
  managers so they can function as a team, 550
Group dynamics
  cohesiveness, 462–465
  group development, 458–459
  leadership, 457–458
  norms, 459–462
  size, tasks, and roles, 454–456
Group norms Shared guidelines or rules for
  behavior that most group members follow,
  459–462, 463–464
Group rewards, 402, 452
Group role A set of behaviors and tasks that
  a member of a group is expected to perform
  because of his or her position in the group, 456
Groups Collections of two or more people who
  interact with each other to accomplish certain
  goals or meet certain needs, 445. *See also* Teams
  communication networks, 488–490
  enhancing performance with, 446–447
  high performing, 465–468
  types, 449–454
Groupthink A pattern of faulty and biased
  decision making that occurs in groups whose
  members strive for agreement among themselves
  at the expense of accurately assessing
  information relevant to a decision, 202, 449
Groupware Computer software that enables
  members of groups and teams to share
  information with one another, 492–493
Growth needs, 391
Growth stage, 543

H

Hackers, 121
Haiyan (Typhoon), 25
Handshakes, 517
Hand-washing, 75
Happy Meals, 245
Hawthorne effect The finding that a manager's
  behavior or leadership approach can affect
  workers' level of performance, 48
Hawthorne studies, 47–48
Hazardous substances in soaps, 101
Health care
  insurance benefits, 370, 408, 409
  promoting infection control, 75
  on-site, 380
  team-based, 471–472
Health trend, 167
Healthy Weight Commitment Foundation, 92
Hedgehog Principle, 46
Herzberg's motivator-hygiene theory
  A need theory that distinguishes between motivator
  needs (related to the nature of the work itself) and
  hygiene needs (related to the physical and psychological context in which the work is performed)

and proposes that motivator needs must be met for
  motivation and job satisfaction to be high, 391–392
Heterogeneous System Architecture, 166
Heuristics Rules of thumb that simplify decision
  making, 200
Hidden work biases, 153–154
Hierarchies. *See also* Organizational structure
  departmental, 15, 44
  environments favoring, 53
  Fayol's principles, 43–44
  as information systems, 548–549
  minimizing, 296–297, 556
  shortcomings, 295–296
  in Weber's theory, 41
Hierarchy of authority An organization's
  chain of command, specifying the relative
  authority of each manager, 294
Hierarchy of needs An arrangement of five
  basic needs that, according to Maslow, motivate
  behavior. Maslow proposed that the lowest level
  of unmet needs is the prime motivator and that
  only one level of needs is motivational at a time,
  389–390
Hiring process. *See* Recruitment; Selection
Hispanics, 128
HIV-positive employees, 130, 352–353
Hofstede's model, 175–177
Holacracy, 314
Holidays, 129
Honesty in recruiting, 358
Honesty tests, 360
Horizontal communication, 490
Hospitals, infection control, 75
**Hostile work environment sexual
  harassment** Telling lewd jokes, displaying
  pornography, making sexually oriented remarks
  about someone's personal appearance, and
  other sex-related actions that make the work
  environment unpleasant, 149
Hotel industry, 345–347
House's path–goal theory, 427–428, 429
Human capital, 171
Human-created crises, 25
Human immunodeficiency virus, 130
Human relations movement A management
  approach that advocates the idea that supervisors
  should receive behavioral training to manage
  subordinates in ways that elicit their cooperation
  and increase their productivity, 48
Human resource management Activities
  that managers engage in to attract and retain
  employees and to ensure that they perform at a
  high level and contribute to the accomplishment
  of organizational goals, 347
  diversity programs, 24
  ethical failures, 110
  influence on organizational structures, 281
  legal environment, 351–353
  major components, 348–351
Human resource planning Activities that
  managers engage in to forecast their current and
  future needs for human resources, 353–354
Human rights, 38–39. *See also* Ethics
Human skills The ability to understand,
  alter, lead, and control the behavior of other
  individuals and groups, 15
Human trafficking, 88
Hygiene needs, 391
Hypercompetition Permanent, ongoing, intense
  competition brought about in an industry by
  advancing technology or changing customer
  tastes, 227

I

Ideas, soliciting, 267
Ideas for new products, 267
Ignition switch problem, 225–226
Illusion of control A source of cognitive bias
  resulting from the tendency to overestimate one's
  own ability to control activities and events, 200

Impersonal written communication, 487–488
Implementing changes, 338
Implementing decisions, 198
Implied Association Test, 153
Importing Selling products at home that are made abroad, 238–239
Incentives. *See also* Motivation; Reward systems
 Collins's view, 46
 organizational cultures and, 304
 for quality, 258
 in scientific management, 37, 38
Incomplete information, 192, 194
Incremental improvement, 46
Incremental product innovation The gradual improvement and refinement of existing products that occur over time as existing technologies are perfected, 266
India
 food maker challenges in, 237
 as leading outsourcing country, 17, 354–355
Individual ethics Personal standards and values that determine how people view their responsibilities to others and how they should act in situations when their own self-interests are at stake, 110
Individualism A worldview that values individual freedom and self-expression and adherence to the principle that people should be judged by their individual achievements rather than by their social background, 167, 175–176
Individual rewards, 402
Industrial revolution, 35–36
Industry concentration strategies, 232
Inequity Lack of fairness, 393
Inert cultures, 304–305, 338
Informal appraisals Unscheduled appraisal of ongoing progress and areas for improvement, 368, 369
Informal authority, 43
Informal communications, 490, 491
Informal groups Groups that managers or nonmanagerial employees form to help achieve their own goals or meet their own needs, 449
Informality, 79, 81, 83
Informal leaders, 457
Informal organization The system of behavioral rules and norms that emerge in a group, 48
Information
 major needs, 539–542
 useful, 537–538
Information Data that are organized in a meaningful fashion, 537
Informational justice A person's perception of the extent to which his or her manager provides explanations for decisions and the procedures used to arrive at them, 395
Informational roles of managers, 12, 133
Information costs, 193
Information distortion Changes in the meaning of a message as the message passes through a series of senders and receivers, 497
Information overload The potential for important information to be ignored or overlooked while tangential information receives attention, 488
Information richness The amount of information that a communication medium can carry and the extent to which the medium enables the sender and receiver to reach a common understanding, 482–488
Information technology The set of methods or techniques for acquiring, organizing, storing, manipulating, and transmitting information, 538–539
 for communication, 491–495
 for control systems, 318–319, 329, 537–538
 customer relationship management, 255–256, 475, 553
 efficiency gains from, 265–266
 as empowerment tool, 19

enabling virtual teams, 452–453
 as factor in restructuring, 17, 556–557
 IBM services, 177–178
 limitations, 557–558
 major effects on markets, 542–545
 MIS systems, 538–539, 548–554
 opportunities resulting from, 166, 230–231, 542, 545–548, 555–556
 outsourcing, 17
 seeking new ways to use, 25
 use in flexible manufacturing, 261, 263
Information Technology Byte boxes
 Amazon pizza teams, 447–448
 enterprise resource planning systems, 552
 Fog Creek Software, 356–357
 virtual organizations, 557
 wikis, 494–495
 Windows XP, 544
Initiating structure Behavior that managers engage in to ensure that work gets done, subordinates perform their jobs acceptably, and the organization is efficient and effective, 424
Initiative The ability to act on one's own without direction from a superior, 45
Initiative for Responsible Mining Assurance, 109
Innovation The process of creating new or improved goods and services or developing better ways to produce or provide them, 21
 competitive advantage from, 21, 250
 hindrances in large firms, 34, 331–332
 impact of control systems, 318
 impact on product life cycles, 18
 opportunities resulting from, 166
 in organizational cultures, 78, 79, 83–84
 promoting, 205–206, 208, 266–271, 461–462
 role of effective communication, 478
 synergies from, 235
 from teams, 443–445, 447–448
Inputs Anything a person contributes to his or her job or organization, 384
Input stage, 51
Insourcing, 18–19
Instant messaging, 486
Instant photography, 252–253
Instructions, software, 542
Instrumentality In expectancy theory, a perception about the extent to which performance results in the attainment of outcomes, 386
Instrumental values Modes of conduct that individuals seek to follow, 69, 80
Integrad (UPS), 189
Integrating mechanisms Organizing tools that managers can use to increase communication and coordination among functions and divisions, 298–300, 519
Integrating roles, 299–300
Integration, rites of, 82
Integrative bargaining Cooperative negotiation in which the parties in conflict work together to achieve a resolution that is good for them both, 519–521
Intellectual stimulation Behavior a leader engages in to make followers aware of problems and view these problems in new ways, consistent with the leader's vision, 431
Intelligence, emotional, 76–77
Interest groups Informal groups composed of employees seeking to achieve a common goal related to their membership in an organization, 453
Interests, demands versus, 521
Intergroup conflict, 513
Intermediate-term plans, 221
Internal locus of control The tendency to locate responsibility for one's fate within oneself, 67, 207
Internal recruiting, 357–358
International agreements, 168–169, 174, 182–183
International expansion strategies, 237–241
International Space Station, 481

Internet A global system of computer networks, 491
 data storage, 546
 efficiency gains from, 265–266
 elements of, 491
 global presence, 157–158
 meal ordering via, 254
 surfing on work time, 486, 487
Internships, 357
Interorganizational conflict, 513–514
Interpersonal conflict, 512
Interpersonal justice A person's perception of the fairness of the interpersonal treatment he or she receives from whoever distributes outcomes to him or her, 395
Interpersonal roles of managers, 12, 133
Interpersonal skills of women in leadership, 433
Interviews (employment)
 bar raisers role, 376–377
 at Semco, 351
 types, 359–360
Intragroup conflict, 512–513
Intranets Companywide systems of computer networks, 491–492
Intrapreneurs Managers, scientists, or researchers who work inside an organization and notice opportunities to develop new or improved products and better ways to make them, 207, 208
Intrinsically motivated behavior Behavior that is performed for its own sake, 382–383
Introverts, 64
Intuition Feelings, beliefs, and hunches that come readily to mind, require little effort and information gathering, and result in on-the-spot decisions, 189–190
Invention Hub, 88
Inventory The stock of raw materials, inputs, and component parts that an organization has on hand at a particular time, 259
Inventory management, 216, 259, 263–264
Inventory turnover, 324
Investors, 96
iPhone, 543
iPod, 187, 543
Irreplaceability, 523

J

Japan
 collectivism in, 176
 discrimination in, 143
 earthquake (2011), 73
 investments in training, 21
 linguistic style, 500
 Moritz's experience, 124
 reputation for ethics, 107
 reputation for social responsibility, 116
 trade barriers, 165
Jargon Specialized language that members of an occupation, group, or organization develop to facilitate communication among themselves, 83, 496
Jewelry industry, 108–109
Job analysis Identifying the tasks, duties, and responsibilities that make up a job and the knowledge, skills, and abilities needed to perform the job, 355–356
Job characteristics model, 283–285
Job descriptions, 355
Job design The process by which managers decide how to divide tasks into specific jobs, 282–285
Job enlargement Increasing the number of different tasks in a given job by changing the division of labor, 282
Job enrichment Increasing the degree of responsibility a worker has over his or her job, 283
Job-oriented behaviors, 424
Job rotation, 518
Job satisfaction The collection of feelings and beliefs that managers have about their current jobs, 70–73, 80

Job simplification The process of reducing the number of tasks that each worker performs, 282

Job specialization The process by which a division of labor occurs as different workers specialize in different tasks over time, 36

Job specifications, 355

Job titles, eliminating, 314

Joint ventures Strategic alliances among two or more companies that agree to jointly establish and share the ownership of new businesses, 239–240

Joplin (MO) tornado, 330–331

Judgment, 189–190

Justice, 136–137, 395

Justice rule An ethical decision distributes benefits and harms among people and groups in a fair, equitable, or impartial way, 104–105

Just-in-time inventory systems Systems in which parts or supplies arrive at an organization when they are needed, not before, 259, 263–264

K

Kanbans, 263, 264

Kidney dialysis clinics, 145–146

Kimberley Process Certification Scheme, 109

Kindle, 22, 448, 544

Knowbots, 550–551

Knowledge, 47, 540–541

Knowledge management systems Company-specific virtual information systems that systematize the knowledge of their employees and facilitate the sharing and integrating of their expertise, 556

Knowledge workers, 354–355

L

Labor relations The activities managers engage in to ensure that they have effective working relationships with the labor unions that represent their employees' interests, 350, 371–372

Labor suppliers, 160

Labor unions, 160, 371–372

Landline telephone service, 542

Language, organization-specific, 82–83

Large groups, 454

Lateral moves Job changes that entail no major changes in responsibility or authority levels, 357

Lawrence N. Field Center for Entrepreneurship, 213

Laws. *See also* Regulation

equal opportunity, 126–127, 351–353, 359

ethics enforcement via, 93–94

labor relations, 371

Lawsuits

discrimination, 138, 142–143

sexual harassment, 148, 149

Layoffs

impact on organizational cultures, 303

job satisfaction and, 73

overt discrimination in, 143

as stakeholder decision, 97

unions and, 160

Leader–member relations The extent to which followers like, trust, and are loyal to their leader; a determinant of how favorable a situation is for leading, 425

Leaders Individuals who can exert influence over other people to help achieve group or organizational goals, 415

Leadership The process by which an individual exerts influence over other people and inspires, motivates, and directs their activities to help achieve group or organizational goals, 415

behavior model, 422–424

contingency models, 424–429

cross-functional teams, 269

cultural influences, 417–418

emotional intelligence in, 433–434

gender and, 432–433

in groups, 457–458

personal styles, 415–417

power in, 418–421

trait model, 421–422

transformational, 430–432

Leadership substitute A characteristic of a subordinate or of a situation or context that acts in place of the influence of a leader and makes leadership unnecessary, 428–429

Leader substitutes model, 428–429

Leading Articulating a clear vision and energizing and enabling organizational members so they understand the part they play in achieving organizational goals; one of the four principal tasks of management, 10

influence of organizational culture, 84

as major management function, 12, 133

Lean manufacturing, 317–318

Lean Six Sigma, 260

Learning A relatively permanent change in knowledge or behavior that results from practice or experience, 396

Learning from decisions, 185–186

Learning organizations Organizations in which managers try to maximize the ability of individuals and groups to think and behave creatively and thus maximize the potential for organizational learning to take place, 203, 204–205

Learning theories Theories that focus on increasing employee motivation and performance by linking the outcomes that employees receive to the performance of desired behaviors and the attainment of goals, 396–401

Least preferred coworkers, 425

Legal environment. *See* Laws; Regulation

Legality of choices, 196

Legitimate power The authority that a manager has by virtue of his or her position in an organization's hierarchy, 418–419

The Lego Movie, 438–440

Lesbian, gay, bisexual, or transgender workers, 131–132

Let's Move! campaign, 91–92, 93

Level 5 leadership, 46

Levels of planning, 218–221

Leverage ratios, 324

Lewin's force-field theory, 335–336

Liaisons, managers as, 12, 133, 298–299

Librie, 22

Licensing Allowing a foreign organization to take charge of manufacturing and distributing a product in its country or world region in return for a negotiated fee, 239

Lightbulbs, 33, 34

LightSpeed scanner, 478–479

Line manager Someone in the direct line or chain of command who has formal authority over people and resources at lower levels, 294

Line of authority The chain of command extending from the top to the bottom of an organization, 43–44

Linguistic style A person's characteristic way of speaking, 498–501, 516

Liquidity ratios, 324

Listening, 498

Local area networks, 547

Locus of control, 67–68, 207

London Olympics, 170

Long-distance learning, 363

Long-term employment, 45

Long-term orientation A worldview that values thrift and persistence in achieving goals, 176–177

Long-term plans, 221

Low-cost strategy Driving the organization's costs down below the costs of its rivals, 8, 228–229, 230

influence on organizational structure, 280

methods of achieving, 249–250

Southwest Airlines, 253–254

Loyalty, 303

Luggage fees, 249

M

Mac Pro, 161

Mainframes, 545, 547

Malware, 121

Management The planning, organizing, leading, and controlling of human and other resources to achieve organizational goals efficiently and effectively, 5

benefits of studying, 6–7

entrepreneurship versus, 207–208

global challenges, 20–27

levels, 11–14

major functions, 7–11

organizational culture and, 78–80, 83–84

overview, 5–6

recent trends, 17–19

required skills, 14–16, 207–208

Management by objectives A goal-setting process in which a manager and each of his or her subordinates negotiate specific goals and objectives for the subordinate to achieve and then periodically evaluate the extent to which the subordinate is achieving those goals, 328–329

Management by wandering around A face-to-face communication technique in which a manager walks around a work area and talks informally with employees about issues and concerns, 484

Management information systems Specific form of IT that managers utilize to generate the specific, detailed information they need to perform their roles effectively, 50, 538–539

enhanced control from, 319

limitations, 557–558

types, 548–554

Management Insight boxes

Afghanistan power project, 321–322

big data, 540–541

Collins, Jim, 46

consideration at Costco, 423

Crocs strategy, 232

email, 316–317

emotions and change, 75

Enterprise Holdings, 388

expatriates, 178–179

face-to-face communication, 483

IDEO team innovation, 461–462

learning by GarageTek, 199

Miami Dolphins, 291

motivation at Container Store, 386–387

Panera 2.0, 254

PepsiCo strategy, 235–236

philanthrofits, 334

quality at Lego Group, 270–271

quantitative skills, 325

self-managed teams, 451–452

server computers, 545–546

Steelcase workspace design, 262–263

Stella & Dot training, 397

TJX strategy, 257

top managers in frontline jobs, 145–146

Tyler (TX) Six Sigma program, 260

video rental market changes, 229–230

Wendy's upgrades, 283

Zappos human resource management, 349

Management science theory An approach to management that uses rigorous quantitative techniques to help managers make maximum use of organizational resources, 50–51

Management theory

administrative management, 40–46

behavioral management, 46–50

management science, 50–51

organizational environments, 51–54

scientific management, 35–39

Manager as a Person boxes

Barra, Mary, 225–227

Corsi, Dennis, 8–9

Maffei, Gregory, 420

Mayer, Marissa, 301–302

Manager as a Person boxes—*Cont.*
  Nadella, Satya, 297–298
  overconfidence, 190–191
  Plank, Kevin, 66–67
  Rockefeller, John D., 40
Managerial Grid, 424
Managers
  personality traits, 63–69, 79
  as stakeholders, 96–98
Managing Globally boxes
  Ernst & Young women's initiative, 170–171
  Escape the City website, 382–383
  GE Healthcare, 478–479
  GE's insourcing, 18–19
  Michael Baker International, 289
  outsourcing trends, 354–355
  Semco human resource management, 350–351
  sweetener joint venture, 240–241
  understanding cultures, 517–518
  Virtusize, 338–339
  water use, 162
Manufacturing
  electronics industry changes, 310
  empowered work teams, 296–297
  ethical failures, 110, 115
  flexible, 261, 263
  GE's focus on, 35
  industrial revolution, 35–36
  insourcing, 18–19
  outsourcing, 555–556. *See also* Outsourcing
  sweatshops, 22
March Madness, 275
Marijuana, 94–95
Marketing function
  CRM system benefits, 256
  ethical failures, 110
  fast food, 245
  in value chain management, 251, 252
Market structure   An organizational structure
    in which each kind of customer is served by a
    self-contained division, 290
Maslow's hierarchy of needs   An arrange-
    ment of five basic needs that, according to
    Maslow, motivate behavior. Maslow proposed
    that the lowest level of unmet needs is the prime
    motivator and that only one level of needs is
    motivational at a time, 389–390
Materials management function, 251–252
Matrix structure   An organizational structure
    that simultaneously groups people and resources
    by function and by product, 291–293
"A Matter of Respect" program, 149–150
Maturity stage, 543
McClellan's need theory, 392
McGregor's Theory X and Y, 48–50
Meaningfulness of jobs, 284
Mechanistic structure   An organizational
    structure in which authority is centralized, tasks
    and rules are clearly specified, and employees
    are closely supervised, 53
Mediators   Third-party negotiators who facilitate
    negotiations but have no authority to impose a
    solution, 372, 519
Medical care. *See* Health care
Medical ethics, 109
Medication errors, 481
Medium   The pathway through which an
    encoded message is transmitted to a
    receiver, 479
Mental models, 195–196, 204
Mentoring   A process by which an experienced
    member of an organization (the mentor) provides
    advice and guidance to a less experienced
    member (the protégé) and helps the less
    experienced member learn how to advance in
    the organization and in his or her career, 148
  diversity and, 124, 148
  formal programs, 363
Mergers, 33–34, 191, 200
Merit pay plans   Compensation plans that base
    pay on performance, 402–404

Message   The information that a sender wants to
    share, 479
Miami Dolphins, 291
Middle managers   Managers who supervise
    first-line managers and are responsible for
    finding the best way to use resources to achieve
    organizational goals, 12–13
Millennials, 153
Mine Health and Safety Administration, 26–27
Minimum wages, 103
Mining
  in conflict zones, 23, 109
  ethical practices, 109
  safety violations, 26–27
Minnesota Satisfaction Questionnaire, 71
Minorities
  benefits of mentoring for, 363
  mentoring for, 148
  PricewaterhouseCoopers provisions for,
    124–125
  representation in U.S. workforce, 128–129
Mission, defining, 223
Mission statements   Broad declarations
    of organizations' purpose that identify the
    organizations' products and customers and dis-
    tinguish organizations from their competitors,
    217, 223, 229
Mistakes, 198–199, 200, 434
Mobile data centers, 546
Modern Times, 38
Monetary Authority of Singapore, 57–58
Monitoring email, 487
Monitors, managers as, 12, 133
Mood   A feeling or state of mind, 74–75, 80
Moral rights rule   An ethical decision is one
    that best maintains and protects the fundamental
    or inalienable rights and privileges of the people
    affected by it, 104
Mores   Norms that are considered to be central
    to the functioning of society and to social
    life, 175
Motivation   Psychological forces that determine
    the direction of a person's behavior in an organi-
    zation, a person's level of effort, and a person's
    level of persistence, 381. *See also* Incentives;
    Leadership
  Collins's view, 46
  compensation and, 401–404
  empowerment as, 19
  equity theory, 392–395, 401
  expectancy theory, 384–388, 401
  as factor in organizational structure, 279
  goal-setting theory, 395–396, 401
  of groups and teams, 465–466
  impact of centralization, 44
  impact of direct supervision, 328
  in job design, 284–285
  learning theories, 396–401
  nature of, 381–384
  need theories, 389–392, 401
  SAS Institute emphasis, 379–381
  in scientific management, 37, 38
  using groups and teams, 448
Motivator-hygiene theory   A need theory that
    distinguishes between motivator needs (related
    to the nature of the work itself) and hygiene
    needs (related to the physical and psychological
    context in which the work is performed) and
    proposes that motivator needs must be met
    for motivation and job satisfaction to be high,
    391–392
Motivator needs, 391
Movie production companies. *See* Film production
    companies
Movie rentals, 229–230
Multidomestic strategy   Customizing
    products and marketing strategies to specific
    national conditions, 237
Municipal government quality initiatives, 260
MyPanera rewards program, 254
MythBusters, 248

N

NAFTA, 174
National culture   The set of values that a
    society considers important and the norms of
    behavior that are approved or sanctioned in that
    society, 167
  as declining barrier, 173–174
  impact on communications, 500
  impact on global business, 175–179
  impact on leadership styles, 417–418
  shopping preferences in, 204
  as source of conflict, 517–518
National Labor Relations Act (1935), 371
National Labor Relations Board, 371
National Workrights Institute, 487
Nations as stakeholders, 102–103
Natural disasters, 25
Nature, exposure to, 392
Nature Conservancy alliances, 524–525
NCAA basketball tournament, 275
Need for achievement   The extent to which
    an individual has a strong desire to perform
    challenging tasks well and to meet personal
    standards for excellence, 68, 207, 392
Need for affiliation   The extent to which an
    individual is concerned about establishing
    and maintaining good interpersonal relations,
    being liked, and having other people get
    along, 68, 392
Need for change, assessing, 335, 336–337
Need for power   The extent to which an
    individual desires to control or influence
    others, 68, 392
Needs   Requirements or necessities for survival
    and well-being, 389
Needs assessment   An assessment of which
    employees need training or development and
    what type of skills or knowledge they need to
    acquire, 361
Need theories   Theories of motivation that
    focus on what needs people are trying to satisfy
    at work and what outcomes will satisfy those
    needs, 389–392, 401
Negative affectivity   The tendency to experience
    negative emotions and moods, to feel distressed,
    and to be critical of oneself and others, 64
Negative reinforcement   Eliminating or remov-
    ing undesired outcomes when people perform
    organizationally functional behaviors, 398, 399
Negotiation   A method of conflict resolution in
    which the parties consider various alternative
    ways to allocate resources to come up with a
    solution acceptable to all of them, 519–521
Negotiators, managers as, 12, 133
Netherlands, reputation for social responsibility, 116
Networks (communication), 488–491
Networks (computer)   Interlinked computers that
    exchange information, 545–548
Newsletters, 487
Newton PDA, 193
New York cab driver fraud, 110–111
No Email Fridays, 483
Noise   Anything that hampers any stage of the
    communication process, 479
Nominal group technique   A decision-making
    technique in which group members write down
    ideas and solutions, read their suggestions to
    the whole group, and discuss and then rank the
    alternatives, 206
Nonprofit organizations, unethical management, 98
Nonprogrammed decision making
    Nonroutine decision making that occurs in
    response to unusual, unpredictable opportunities
    and threats, 189–190, 550
Nonroutine technologies, 281
Nonverbal communication   The encoding of
    messages by means of facial expressions, body
    language, and styles of dress, 480, 482–483
Nook tablet, 544
Norming stage, 458

Norms Unwritten, informal codes of conduct that prescribe how people should act in particular situations and are considered important by most members of a group or organization, 42, 69, 175
of groups and teams, 459–462, 463–464
in organizational cultures, 80–83, 300
as sources of conflict, 519
North American Free Trade Agreement, 174
Not-for-profit organizations, globalization's impact, 20
Not for Sale, 88
Nurturing orientation A worldview that values the quality of life, warm personal friendships, and services and care for the weak, 176
NutraSweet, 160

O-bento lunches, 165
Obesity, 91–92, 133
Objective appraisals Appraisals that are based on facts and are likely to be numerical, 365
Objective information, 526
Objectives, 328–329. *See also* Goals
Observational learning, 400
Obstacles to change, 337–338
Obstructionist approach Companies and their managers choose *not* to behave in a socially responsible way and instead behave unethically and illegally, 115
Occupational ethics Standards that govern how members of a profession, trade, or craft should conduct themselves when performing work-related activities, 109
Occupational Safety and Health Act (1970), 352, 371
Occupy Wall Street, 95, 96
Offshoring, 354. *See also* Outsourcing
Old boys' network, 491
Olympics, 170
Ombudspersons, 117
One for One model, 113–114
Online retailing, 216, 254, 338–339. *See also* E-commerce
On-the-job training Training that takes place in the work setting as employees perform their job tasks, 362
Openness to experience The tendency to be original, have broad interests, be open to a wide range of stimuli, be daring, and take risks, 65, 66–67, 207
Open-source software, 413
Open system A system that takes in resources from its external environment and converts them into goods and services that are then sent back to that environment for purchase by customers, 51
Open-systems view, 51–52
Operant conditioning theory The theory that people learn to perform behaviors that lead to desired consequences and learn not to perform behaviors that lead to undesired consequences, 397–399
Operating budgets Budgets that state how managers intend to use organizational resources to achieve organizational goals, 326
Operating margin, 323, 324
Operating system software, 544, 547
Operations information systems Management information systems that gather, organize, and summarize comprehensive data in a form that managers can use in their nonroutine coordinating, controlling, and decision-making tasks, 549
Operations management, 50
Opportunities, identifying, 224–225
OptimEye, 536
Optimum decisions The most appropriate decisions in light of what managers believe to be the most desirable consequences for the organization, 191
Order The methodical arrangement of positions to provide the organization with the greatest benefit and to provide employees with career opportunities, 44

Order fulfillment, 264
Organic structure An organizational structure in which authority is decentralized to middle and first-line managers and tasks and roles are left ambiguous to encourage employees to cooperate and respond quickly to the unexpected, 53
Organizational architecture The organizational structure, control systems, culture, and human resource management systems that together determine how efficiently and effectively organizational resources are used, 279
Organizational behavior The study of the factors that have an impact on how individuals and groups respond to and act in organizations, 48
Organizational behavior modification The systematic application of operant conditioning techniques to promote the performance of organizationally functional behaviors and discourage the performance of dysfunctional behaviors, 399
Organizational change The movement of an organization away from its present state and toward some preferred future state to increase its efficiency and effectiveness, 334–339. *See also* Change
Organizational charts, 44–45
Organizational citizenship behaviors Behaviors that are not required of organizational members but that contribute to and are necessary for organizational efficiency, effectiveness, and competitive advantage, 73
Organizational commitment The collection of feelings and beliefs that managers have about their organization as a whole, 74
Organizational communications networks, 490–491
Organizational conflict The discord that arises when the goals, interests, or values of different individuals or groups are incompatible and those individuals or groups block or thwart one another's attempts to achieve their objectives, 511
levels of, 511–512
management strategies, 516–519
political strategies to address, 521–528
sources, 514–515, 516–517
types, 512–514
Organizational control
behavior control, 327–333
clan control, 333–334
importance, 315–318
information needs, 539–540
output control, 323–327
process overview, 319–323
systems, 318–319
Organizational culture The shared set of beliefs, expectations, values, norms, and work routines that influence how individuals, groups, and teams interact with one another and cooperate to achieve organizational goals, 78, 300
adaptive versus inert, 304–305, 338
dysfunctional, 84
in Fayol's theory, 45
as form of organizational control, 333
founders' influence, 78–79, 81
influence on managers, 83–84
as source of conflict, 518–519
sources, 302–304
values and norms in, 80–83, 116–117
Organizational design The process by which managers make specific organizing choices that result in a particular kind of organizational structure, 279–281
Organizational environment The set of forces and conditions that operate beyond an organization's boundaries but affect a manager's ability to acquire and utilize resources, 51–54. *See also* Environmental factors
Organizational ethics The guiding practices and beliefs through which a particular company

and its managers view their responsibility toward their stakeholders, 111, 303
Organizational goals, 464, 465–466
Organizational hierarchies, 548–549. *See also* Hierarchies
Organizational learning The process through which managers seek to improve employees' desire and ability to understand and manage the organization and its task environment, 203–206, 337
Organizational performance A measure of how efficiently and effectively a manager uses resources to satisfy customers and achieve organizational goals, 5
Organizational politics Activities that managers engage in to increase their power and to use power effectively to achieve their goals and overcome resistance or opposition, 521–528
Organizational socialization The process by which newcomers learn an organization's values and norms and acquire the work behaviors necessary to perform jobs effectively, 81
Organizational structure A formal system of task and reporting relationships that coordinates and motivates organizational members so they work together to achieve organizational goals, 9, 279
in administrative management approaches, 40–46
basic types, 285–293
coordinating divisions and functions, 293–300
environmental influences, 51–54
factors in creating, 279–281
impact on organizational culture, 303–304
as information system, 548–549
preserving after acquisitions, 277–278
as source of conflict, 518–519
team-based, 443–445
Organizations Collections of people who work together and coordinate their actions to achieve a wide variety of goals or desired future outcomes, 5
Organization-wide rewards, 402
Organizing Structuring working relationships in a way that allows organizational members to work together to achieve organizational goals; one of the four principal tasks of management, 9, 84
Origin Experience program, 541–542
ORION system, 25
Outcomes Anything a person gets from a job or organization, 383–384
Output restriction, 48
Outputs, 320, 323–327, 333
Output stage, 51
Outside experts, 527
Outsourcing Contracting with another company, usually abroad, to have it perform an activity the organization previously performed itself, 17, 353
advantages and disadvantages, 353–354
ethical challenges, 22–23
global approach, 161, 555–556
influences leading to, 17–19, 160–161
as utilitarian decision, 103–104
workplace safety and, 99–100
Overconfidence, 190–191
Overlapping authority, 515
Overpayment inequity The inequity that exists when a person perceives that his or her own outcome–input ratio is greater than the ratio of a referent, 393, 394
Overt discrimination Knowingly and willingly denying diverse individuals access to opportunities and outcomes in an organization, 142

Packaging, 72, 101–102
Paper-and-pencil tests, 360
Parents, support systems for, 124, 130–131
Participation levels in groups, 462–463
Participative behaviors, 428, 432–433
Partnership for a Healthier America, 92
Passage, rites of, 82

Path–goal theory A contingency model of leadership proposing that leaders can motivate subordinates by identifying their desired outcomes, rewarding them for high performance and the attainment of work goals with these desired outcomes, and clarifying for them the paths leading to the attainment of work goals, 427–428, 429

Pay. *See* Compensation

Pay level The relative position of an organization's pay incentives in comparison with those of other organizations in the same industry employing similar kinds of workers, 369

Pay structure The arrangement of jobs into categories reflecting their relative importance to the organization and its goals, levels of skill required, and other characteristics, 369–370

Peer appraisals, 367

Perception The process through which people select, organize, and interpret what they see, hear, touch, smell, and taste to give meaning and order to the world around them, 138
clarifying, 144
in communications, 480–481
discrimination based on, 140–142
factors in, 139

Performance appraisal The evaluation of employees' job performance and contributions to their organization, 364
approaches, 364–366
as component of human resource management, 350
diversity awareness in, 146–147
effective, 368–369
main purposes, 350
organizational structures and, 286
for organizations, 319–323
at Semco, 351
sources, 366–368

Performance feedback The process through which managers share performance appraisal information with subordinates, give subordinates an opportunity to reflect on their own performance, and develop, with subordinates, plans for the future, 350, 364, 368–369. *See also* Feedback

Performance standards, 320
Performance tests, 360
Performing stage, 458–459
Persistence, 382
Personal criticism, 520–521
Personal digital assistants, 193
Personality conflicts, 517
Personality tests, 360

Personality traits Enduring tendencies to feel, think, and act in certain ways, 63–68, 79

Personal leadership style, 415–417
Personally addressed written messages, 485–487
Personal mastery, 204
Personal relationships, 41
Peters Projection World Map, 169
Philanthrofits, 334
Philanthropic Ventures Foundation, 88
Physical ability tests, 360
Physician assistants, 472
Physiological needs, 390
Piece-rate pay, 404
Piracy, 4
Pizza teams, 447–448

Planning Identifying and selecting appropriate goals; one of the four principal tasks of management, 7, 217
elements of, 217–222
as major management function, 7–8
organizational culture's impact, 83–84
Toys"R"Us challenges, 215–216
Platform-only model, 30
Poland, outsourcing to, 355
Policies, 222, 486

Political and legal forces Outcomes of changes in laws and regulations, such as deregulation of industries, privatization of organizations, and increased emphasis on environmental protection, 168

Political capital, 172
Political integration, 168

Political strategies Tactics that managers use to increase their power and to use power effectively to influence and gain the support of other people while overcoming resistance or opposition, 522–528

Pollution, 25, 103
Polytetrafluoroethylene, 443

Pooled task interdependence The task interdependence that exists when group members make separate and independent contributions to group performance, 454–455

Porter's five forces model, 227
Portfolio strategy, 236
Position Analysis Questionnaire, 355

Position power The amount of legitimate, reward, and coercive power that a leader has by virtue of his or her position in an organization; a determinant of how favorable a situation is for leading, 426

Positive reinforcement Giving people outcomes they desire when they perform organizationally functional behaviors, 398

Potential competitors Organizations that presently are not in a task environment but could enter if they so choose, 164

Poverty rate, 130–131
Power
in leadership, 418–421
need for, 68, 392
strategies for exercising, 525–528
strategies to gain and maintain, 522–525

Power distance The degree to which societies accept the idea that inequalities in the power and well-being of their citizens are due to differences in individuals' physical and intellectual capabilities and heritage, 176

Practicality of choices, 196

Practical rule An ethical decision is one that a manager has no reluctance about communicating to people outside the company because the typical person in a society would think it is acceptable, 105

Pregnancy Discrimination Act (1978), 127, 352
Premium pricing, 228
Price fixing, 163
Pricing, quality and, 256

Prior hypothesis bias A cognitive bias resulting from the tendency to base decisions on strong prior beliefs even if evidence shows that those beliefs are wrong, 200

Proactive approach Companies and their managers actively embrace socially responsible behavior, going out of their way to learn about the needs of different stakeholder groups and using organizational resources to promote the interests of all stakeholders, 116

Problem recognition, 337
Problem solving, 205–206. *See also* Decision making

Procedural justice A moral principle calling for the use of fair procedures to determine how to distribute outcomes to organizational members, 136–137, 395

Process layouts, 262

Process reengineering The fundamental rethinking and radical redesign of business processes to achieve dramatic improvement in critical measures of performance such as cost, quality, service, and speed, 264–265

Procurement, 265

Product champions Managers who take "ownership" of a project and provide the leadership and vision that take a product from the idea stage to the final customer, 208

Product design for quality, 259

Product development
benefits of ERP for, 552–553
improving, 266–271

Product development The management of the value chain activities involved in bringing new

or improved goods and services to the market, 251, 266

Product development plan A plan that specifies all of the relevant information that managers need in order to decide whether to proceed with a full-blown product development effort, 268

Production blocking A loss of productivity in brainstorming sessions due to the unstructured nature of brainstorming, 206

Production function, 252
Productivity
Hawthorne effect, 47–48
specialization's impact, 36
of virtual organizations, 557
Product layouts, 261–262

Product life cycle The way demand for a product changes in a predictable pattern over time, 18, 542–545

Product obsolescence, 166

Product structure An organizational structure in which each product line or business is handled by a self-contained division, 287–288, 290

Product teams, 291–293

Product team structure An organizational structure in which employees are permanently assigned to a cross-functional team and report only to the product team manager or to one of his or her direct subordinates, 293

Professions, ethics in, 109, 110
Profitability, 137, 245
Profit ratios, 323, 324
Profit sharing, 404, 444

Programmed decision making Routine, virtually automatic decision making that follows established rules or guidelines, 188–189

Programs, 222
Project Manager Mobile Electric Power, 321–322
Projects, 222
Promotions, 303, 388

Prosocially motivated behavior Behavior that is performed to benefit or help others, 383

Pulaski Skyway, 289

Punishment Administering an undesired or negative consequence when dysfunctional behavior occurs, 398–399, 419

Purpose, 218

Q

Quality
for competitive advantage, 21, 250
of information, 537–538
at Lego Group, 270–271
reasons to improve, 256–257
role of effective communication, 478
role of organizational control in, 315–316
total quality management programs, 257–260, 347–348
Quantitative management, 50
Quantitative skills, 325

Quantum product innovation The development of new, often radically different, kinds of goods and services because of fundamental shifts in technology brought about by pioneering discoveries, 266

Quick ratio, 324

Quid pro quo sexual harassment Asking for or forcing an employee to perform sexual favors in exchange for receiving some reward or avoiding negative consequences, 148

R

Racial diversity, 128–129
Racial minorities. *See* Minorities
Rack servers, 545
Railroad companies, 548–549
Rana Plaza disaster, 99–100
Ranking choices, 198
Ratebusters, 48
Razor blades, 237–238

Realistic goals, 223

Realistic job preview An honest assessment of the advantages and disadvantages of a job and organization, 358

Real-time information Frequently updated information that reflects current conditions, 538

Reasoned judgment A decision that requires time and effort and results from careful information gathering, generation of alternatives, and evaluation of alternatives, 189–190

Recalls, 225–226

Receiver The person or group for which a message is intended, 479, 480, 497–498

Recession of 2008, 165

Reciprocal task interdependence The task interdependence that exists when the work performed by each group member is fully dependent on the work performed by other group members, 456

Recognition, 205

Recruitment Activities that managers engage in to develop a pool of qualified candidates for open positions, 353
    external and internal, 356–358
    honesty in, 358
    as part of human resource management, 348
    at Zappos, 349

References, 360

Referent power Power that comes from subordinates' and coworkers' respect, admiration, and loyalty, 420–421

Referents, 392–393

Refill stores, 102

Regional trade agreements, 168–169, 174, 182–183

Regulation. *See also* Laws
    airports, 9
    as barrier to entry, 165
    employee benefits, 370
    equal opportunity, 126–127, 351–353, 359
    ethics enforcement via, 93–94
    meatpacking, 56
    mining safety, 26
    to rein in top management abuses, 97–98

Reinforcement, 398, 401

Related diversification Entering a new business or industry to create a competitive advantage in one or more of an organization's existing divisions or businesses, 234–236

Relatedness needs, 391

Relationship-oriented leaders Leaders whose primary concern is to develop good relationships with their subordinates and to be liked by them, 425

Relevance of information, 538

Reliability The degree to which a tool or test measures the same thing each time it is used, 254, 361

Religious diversity, 129

Remuneration. *See* Compensation

Reporting structures, 291, 293

Representativeness bias A cognitive bias resulting from the tendency to generalize inappropriately from a small sample or from a single vivid event or episode, 200

Reputation The esteem or high repute that individuals or organizations gain when they behave ethically, 107

Research and development, 234–235, 379–380

Research and development teams Teams whose members have the expertise and experience needed to develop new products, 449

Resistance to change, 337–338

Resource allocators, managers as, 12, 133

Resource capital, 172

Resources
    conflicts over, 515
    control systems, 315
    generating, 523–524
    wasting, 106

Respect, earning in leadership, 414

Responsibility, increasing, 283

Responsiveness
    in customer service, 252–256, 317–318
    from groups and teams, 446–447
    role of effective communication, 478

Restructuring Downsizing an organization by eliminating the jobs of large numbers of top, middle, and first-line managers and nonmanagerial employees, 17, 73

Results appraisals, 365

Retirement, 212–213

Retirement plans, 75

Return of online purchases, 338–339

Return on investment, 323, 324

Revolutionary change Change that is rapid, dramatic, and broadly focused, 336

Reward power The ability of a manager to give or withhold tangible and intangible rewards, 419, 427

Rewards programs, 254

Reward systems. *See also* Compensation; Motivation
    conflicting, 515
    for innovation, 208
    with MBO, 328–329
    merit pay, 402–404
    organizational cultures and, 304
    for quality, 258
    in scientific management, 37, 38
    for teams, 402, 452, 466
    for top managers, 97–98, 115, 370

Rice markets, 165

Risk The degree of probability that the possible outcomes of a particular course of action will occur, 192–193

Risk taking
    in organizational cultures, 83, 84
    personality traits, 66, 67
    values and, 69, 80

Rites, 82

Role making Taking the initiative to modify an assigned role by assuming additional responsibilities, 456

Role playing, 361

Roles in groups, 456

Rolling plans, 221

Routine technologies, 281

Rules Formal written instructions that specify actions to be taken under different circumstances to achieve specific goals, 42
    decision-making, 103–105, 188, 200
    as standing plans, 222
    use in organizational control, 329–331

Rumors Unofficial pieces of information of interest to organizational members but with no identifiable source, 497

S

Safety
    disregard for, 197
    garment industry, 99–100
    as need, 390
    Subaru's efforts, 73

Salaries. *See* Compensation

Sales
    CRM system benefits, 255–256
    ethical failures, 110
    training production workers in, 19
    in value chain management, 252

Salesforce.com Foundation, 477

Salience effect, 142

Same-sex domestic partner benefits, 371

Sao Paolo Metro, 108

Satisficing Searching for and choosing an acceptable, or satisfactory, response to problems and opportunities, rather than trying to make the best decision, 193–194

Saudi Arabia, 518

Scanlon plans, 404

Scenario planning The generation of multiple forecasts of future conditions followed by an analysis of how to respond effectively to each of those conditions, 222

Schema An abstract knowledge structure that is stored in memory and makes possible the interpretation and organization of information about a person, event, or situation, 139

Scientific management The systematic study of relationships between people and tasks for the purpose of redesigning the work process to increase efficiency, 35–39, 37

Securities and Exchange Commission, 97

Selection The process that managers use to determine the relative qualifications of job applicants and their potential for performing well in a particular job, 353
    bar raisers, 376–377
    as part of human resource management, 348
    process overview, 358–361
    self-managed team members, 451
    at Zappos, 349

Self-actualization needs, 390

Self-appraisals, 367

Self-efficacy A person's belief about his or her ability to perform a behavior successfully, 401

Self-esteem The degree to which individuals feel good about themselves and their capabilities, 68, 207

Self-interest of top managers, 97–98

Self-managed teams Groups of employees who assume responsibility for organizing, controlling, and supervising their own activities and monitoring the quality of the goods and services they provide, 19, 450
    efficiency gains from, 264, 296–297
    ensuring effectiveness, 450–452
    at IBM, 177–178
    leadership, 457–458
    roles in, 456
    as sources of innovation, 443–445
    trend toward, 44
    weaknesses, 452

Self-reinforcers Any desired or attractive outcome or reward that a person gives to himself or herself for good performance, 401

Semiconductor makers, 310

Sender The person or group wishing to share information, 479, 480, 495–497

Sequential task interdependence The task interdependence that exists when group members must perform specific tasks in a predetermined order, 455–456

Servant leaders Leaders who have a strong desire to serve and work for the benefit of others, 416–417

Server computers, 545–546

Setup times, 263

Seva Foundation, 113

Severance packages, 370

Sexual harassment, 148–150

Sexual orientation, 131–132

Sf.citi, 88

Shared vision, 204

Shareholders. *See* Stockholders

SharePoint software, 494

Shoe sales, 113, 232, 555–556

Short-term orientation A worldview that values personal stability or happiness and living for the present, 176–177

Short-term plans, 221

Silence, cultural differences, 500

Similarity, 79

Similar-to-me effect, 141

Simulations, 361–362

Single-use plans, 222

Situational characteristics, in Fiedler's leadership model, 425–426

Situational interviews, 359

Six Sigma A technique used to improve quality by systematically improving how value chain activities are performed and then using statistical methods to measure the improvement, 258, 259
    examples, 260
    for human resource management, 347–348
    ineffective programs, 348

Sizes of groups, 454–456, 467
Skills
    communication, 495–501
    for competitive advantage, 21
    needed by managers, 14–16, 207–208
    quantitative, 325
    tracking in organizations, 540–541
    variety needed in jobs, 284
Skunkworks   A group of intrapreneurs who are
    deliberately separated from the normal operation
    of an organization to encourage them to devote all
    their attention to developing new products, 208
Skype, 485
Slavery, 94
Small groups, 454
Smarter Workforce Institute, 540–541
Smart glasses, 536
Social entrepreneurs   Individuals who pursue
    initiatives and opportunities and mobilize
    resources to address social problems and needs
    in order to improve society and well-being
    through creative solutions, 207
Socialization in organizations, 81
Social learning theory   A theory that takes
    into account how learning and motivation are
    influenced by people's thoughts and beliefs and
    their observations of other people's behavior,
    399–401
Social loafing   The tendency of individuals to
    put forth less effort when they work in groups
    than when they work alone, 466–468
Social networking sites   Websites that enable
    people to communicate with others with whom
    they have some common interest or connection,
    475–476, 488
Social responsibility   The way a company's
    managers and employees view their duty or
    obligation to make decisions that protect,
    enhance, and promote the welfare and well-
    being of stakeholders and society as a whole,
    23, 114–116
Social Security, 370
Social status effect, 142
Social structure   The traditional system of
    relationships established between people and
    groups in a society, 167
Societal ethics   Standards that govern how
    members of a society should deal with one
    another in matters involving issues such as
    fairness, justice, poverty, and the rights of the
    individual, 107
Societies
    ethical standards, 107–109
    as stakeholders, 102–103
Sociocultural forces   Pressures emanating
    from the social structure of a country or society
    or from the national culture, 167
Socioeconomic background, 130–131
Softbots, 550–551
Soft drink industry, 233, 235–236
Software advances, 547–548
Software agents, 550–551
Software companies
    communications, 475–477
    employee benefits, 379–381
    leadership of, 413–415
    need to upgrade products, 544
    organizational structures, 305
    recruitment, 348, 356–357
Solar panels, 30–31
Southern African Development Community, 174
Space shuttle disasters, 187, 197, 202
Spam email, 494
Span of control   The number of subordinates
    who report directly to a manager, 294
Specialization
    in business strategies, 229
    in Fayol's theory, 42
    impact on productivity, 36
    in scientific management, 37
Specific goals, 395–396

Speed, competitive advantage from, 21, 250
Splenda, 160
Spoken communications, 484–485
Spokespersons, managers as, 12, 133
Sports, leadership development and, 170–171
Sports apparel, 66–67
Stable, conservative cultures, 300
Staff managers   Someone responsible for
    managing a specialist function, such as finance
    or marketing, 294
Stage–gate development funnel
    A planning model that forces managers to
    choose among competing projects so organiza-
    tional resources are not spread thinly over too
    many projects, 267–269
Stakeholders
    considering impact of decisions on, 103–105
    main groups, 96–103
    varying commitments to, 93
Stakeholders   The people and groups that supply
    a company with its productive resources and so
    have a claim on and a stake in the company, 95
Standardization, 37, 330
Standard operating procedures   Spe-
    cific sets of written instructions about how
    to perform a certain aspect of a task, 42, 222,
    329–330, 331
Standards, 320, 329–330, 331
Standing committees, 450
Standing plans, 221
Start-up firms. *See also* Entrepreneurs
    creating organizational cultures, 78–79, 81
    as entrepreneurial ventures, 207–208
    in retirement, 212–213
Status inconsistencies, 515
Steffen method, 248
Stereotypes   Simplistic and often inaccurate
    beliefs about the typical characteristics of
    particular groups of people, 140, 359, 481
stickK app, 334
St. John's Home for Boys, 185
Stockholders, 96, 103–104, 304
Stock options, 97, 98, 115, 403
Stories, 82–83
Storming stage, 458
Strategic alliances   Agreements in which man-
    agers pool or share their organizations' resources
    and know-how with foreign companies, and
    the organizations share the rewards and risks of
    starting ventures, 239, 555
Strategic human resource management
    The process by which managers design the com-
    ponents of an HRM system to be consistent with
    each other, with other elements of organizational
    architecture, and with the organization's strategy
    and goals, 347
Strategic leadership   The ability of the CEO
    and top managers to convey a compelling vision
    of what they want the organization to achieve to
    their subordinates, 223
Strategy   A cluster of decisions about what goals
    to pursue, what actions to take, and how to use
    resources to achieve goals, 217
    influence on organizational structures, 280
    levels, 219–221
    steps in implementing, 241
Strategy formulation   The development of a
    set of corporate, business, and functional strate-
    gies that allow an organization to accomplish its
    mission and achieve its goals, 224
    business level, 227–231
    corporate level, 231–241
    five forces model, 227
    SWOT analysis, 224–227
Stratification, social, 167
Strengths and weaknesses, identifying, 224–225
Stretch goals, 223, 326
Structured interviews, 359
Subjective appraisals   Appraisals that are
    based on perceptions of traits, behaviors, or
    results, 365–366

Subordinate appraisals, 367, 368
Substitute products, 227
Substitutes for leadership, 428–429
Success, group cohesiveness and, 465
Sugar trading, 241
Supermarkets, 537, 538
Superordinate goals, 520
Supervisors, 11, 327–328
Suppliers   Individuals and organizations that
    provide an organization with the input resources
    it needs to produce goods and services, 159
    codes of conduct, 101
    ethical challenges, 22, 23, 108–109
    impact on task environment, 159–162
    involving in product development, 267
    as stakeholders, 99
    working closely with, 257, 259
    workplace safety, 99–100
Supply forecasts, 353
Supportive behaviors, 424, 428
Sustainability. *See also* Environmental protection
    in decision making, 197–198
    El Faro Estate Coffee, 528
    Nature Conservancy alliances, 524–525
    PepsiCo initiatives, 511
    Soap Dispensary business, 101–102
    in water use, 23, 162
Sweatshops, 22
Sweden, ethics and social responsibility in, 107, 116
Switzerland, ethics and social responsibility in,
    107, 116
SWOT analysis   A planning exercise in
    which managers identify organizational
    strengths (S) and weaknesses (W) and
    environmental opportunities (O) and threats (T),
    215–216, 224–227
Synchronous technologies, 453
Synergy   Performance gains that result when
    individuals and departments coordinate their
    actions, 52
    from acquisitions, 236
    from groups, 446
    from research and development, 234–235
Systematic errors   Errors that people make
    over and over and that result in poor decision
    making, 200
Systems thinking, 204

T

Tall organizations, 295–296, 304
Tantalum, 23
Tariffs   Taxes that a government imposes on
    imported or, occasionally, exported goods, 172
Task analyzability, 281
Task environment   The set of forces and condi-
    tions that originates with suppliers, distributors,
    customers, and competitors and affects an orga-
    nization's ability to obtain inputs and dispose of
    its outputs. These forces and conditions influ-
    ence managers daily, 159–165
Task forces   Committees of managers or non-
    managerial employees from various departments
    or divisions who meet to solve a specific, mutual
    problem; also called *ad hoc committees*, 299, 450
Task identity, 284
Task interdependence   The degree to which
    the work performed by one member of a group
    influences the work performed by other mem-
    bers, 454–456, 515
Task-oriented behaviors, 424
Task-oriented leaders   Leaders whose pri-
    mary concern is to ensure that subordinates
    perform at a high level, 425
Task significance, 284
Task structure   The extent to which the work to
    be performed is clear-cut so that a leader's sub-
    ordinates know what needs to be accomplished
    and how to go about doing it; a determinant of
    how favorable a situation is for leading, 425–426
Task variety, 281

Taxicab driver fraud, 110–111
Team-based care, 471–472
Team learning, 204
Teams Groups whose members work intensely with one another to achieve a specific common goal or objective, 445. *See also* Self-managed teams
  achieving synergy with, 52
  cohesiveness, 462–465
  communication networks, 488–490
  cross-functional, 53, 269–270, 293, 299. *See also* Cross-functional teams
  diversity on, 132
  enhancing performance with, 446–447
  global, 177
  group development, 458–459
  high performing, 465–468
  leadership, 457–458
  in matrix structures, 291–293
  norms, 459–462
  sizes, tasks, and roles, 454–456
  as sources of innovation, 443–445, 447–448
  types, 449–454
Technical skills The job-specific knowledge and techniques required to perform an organizational role, 15
Technological forces Outcomes of changes in the technology managers use to design, produce, or distribute goods and services, 166
Technology The combination of skills and equipment that managers use in designing, producing, and distributing goods and services, 166
  enabling virtual teams, 452–453
  influence on organizational structures, 280–281
  wearables, 535–536, 540
Telecommuting, 301, 486, 557
Teleconferences, 505–506
Telephone service, IT impacts, 542
TelePresence, 484
Television programs, 128–129
Temporary assignments, 518
Tenerife crash, 481
Tenure, 45
Terminal values Lifelong goals or objectives that individuals seek to achieve, 69, 80
Tests, 360–361
Texas A&M custodial team rules, 329, 330
Textile industry water use, 162
Theory X A set of negative assumptions about workers that leads to the conclusion that a manager's task is to supervise workers closely and control their behavior, 48–49
Theory Y A set of positive assumptions about workers that leads to the conclusion that a manager's task is to create a work setting that encourages commitment to organizational goals and provides opportunities for workers to be imaginative and to exercise initiative and self-direction, 49
Thermostats, 322
Third-party negotiator An impartial individual with expertise in handling conflicts and negotiations who helps parties in conflict reach an acceptable solution, 519
Threats, 224–225, 227. *See also* Environmental factors
3D movies, 251
360-degree appraisal Performance appraisal by peers, subordinates, superiors, and sometimes clients who are in a position to evaluate a manager's performance, 367–368
Time-and-motion studies, 37, 39
Time constraints, 193, 224
Time horizon The intended duration of a plan, 221, 418, 514–515
Timeliness of information, 538
Times-covered ratio, 324
Tipping Point, 88
Tire makers, 172
Title VII of the Civil Rights Act (1964), 127, 352
Tokugawa period, 176

Top-down change A fast, revolutionary approach to change in which top managers identify what needs to be changed and then move quickly to implement the changes throughout the organization, 338
Top management team A group composed of the CEO, the COO, the president, and the heads of the most important departments, 13, 449
Top managers Managers who establish organizational goals, decide how departments should interact, and monitor the performance of middle managers, 13
  commitment to diversity, 144
  compensation, 97–98, 115, 370
  ethical example, 112–113, 117
  main responsibilities, 13, 14, 220
  need for power, 68
  organizational change initiated by, 338
  self-interested actions, 97–98
  for sustainability, 197–198
  women as, 127–128, 225–227, 432–433, 509–511
Tornado warnings, 330–331
Total quality management A management technique that focuses on improving the quality of an organization's products and services, 257
  for competitive advantage, 21
  concurrent controls, 319
  elements of, 50, 258–259
  Six Sigma, 258, 259–260
Toyota Production System, 51
Tracking devices, 535–536
Trade agreements, 168–169, 174, 182–183
Trade barriers, 172–173
Training Teaching organizational members how to perform their current jobs and helping them acquire the knowledge and skills they need to be effective performers, 361
  about sexual orientation, 132
  basic types, 361–362
  for competitive advantage, 21
  in conceptual skills, 14–15, 16
  customer service, 283
  in decision making, 188–189
  diversity, 24, 145, 146, 147
  for franchisees, 199
  learning through, 397
  motivation via, 385, 387, 388
  as part of human resource management, 348
  for self-managed teams, 451
  sexual harassment, 149–150
  unconscious bias, 153–154
  at Zappos, 349
Trait appraisals, 364
Trait model of leadership, 421–422
Transactional leadership Leadership that motivates subordinates by rewarding them for high performance and reprimanding them for low performance, 432
Transaction-processing systems Management information systems designed to handle large volumes of routine recurring transactions, 549
Transatlantic Trade and Investment Partnership, 168, 182
Transfers, 518
Transformational leadership Leadership that makes subordinates aware of the importance of their jobs and performance to the organization and aware of their own needs for personal growth and that motivates subordinates to work for the good of the organization, 430–432
Transmission phase, 479–480
Trans Pacific Partnership, 168–169, 182–183
Transportation advances, 173
Treaties, 182
Triangle Shirtwaist fire, 99–100
Triclosan, 101
Trust The willingness of one person or group to have faith or confidence in the goodwill of another person, even though this puts them at risk, 105–106
"TRU Transformation" plan, 215

Truvia, 160
Tuition expenses, 363
Turnaround management The creation of a new vision for a struggling company based on a new approach to planning and organizing to make better use of a company's resources and allow it to survive and prosper, 22
Turnover, 73, 137
Two-boss employees, 291
Typhoon Haiyan, 25

U

Ukraine conflict, 175
Uncertainty Unpredictability, 193, 522–523
Uncertainty avoidance The degree to which societies are willing to tolerate uncertainty and risk, 176
Unconscious bias training, 153–154
Underemployment, 72
Underpayment inequity The inequity that exists when a person perceives that his or her own outcome–input ratio is less than the ratio of a referent, 393–394
Unemployment, 72
Unemployment insurance, 370
Uniform Guidelines on Employee Selection Procedures, 352
Unions, 160, 371–372, 532, 533
Unity in planning process, 218
Unity of command A reporting relationship in which an employee receives orders from, and reports to, only one superior, 43
Unity of direction The singleness of purpose that makes possible the creation of one plan of action to guide managers and workers as they use organizational resources, 44
Unobtrusive use of power, 525–526
Unpredictability of future conditions, 222
Unrelated diversification Entering a new industry or buying a company in a new industry that is not related in any way to an organization's current businesses or industries, 236
Unstructured interviews, 359
Upper Big Branch South Mine, 26
U.S. Army, 321–322
Utilitarian rule An ethical decision that produces the greatest good for the greatest number of people, 103–104

V

Valence In expectancy theory, how desirable each of the outcomes available from a job or organization is to a person, 386
Validity The degree to which a tool or test measures what it purports to measure, 361
Value chain The coordinated series or sequence of functional activities necessary to transform inputs such as new product concepts, raw materials, component parts, or professional skills into the finished goods or services customers value and want to buy, 251
  benefits of ERP for, 551–553
  improving responsiveness in, 253–255
  stages, 251–252
Value chain management The development of a set of functional-level strategies that support a company's business-level strategy and strengthen its competitive advantage, 251–252
Values Ideas about what a society believes to be good, right, desirable, or beautiful, 175, 300
  conflicts over, 519
  role in organizational cultures, 302–303, 304
Value systems The terminal and instrumental values that are guiding principles in individuals' lives, 69
  major types, 69–70
  in organizational cultures, 78, 79, 80–83
Varied work experiences, 362–363
VCT scanners, 478–479

Vendors, 99–100, 101. *See also* Suppliers
Verbal communication The encoding of messages into words, either written or spoken, 480
Vertical communication, 490
Vertical integration Expanding a company's operations either backward into an industry that produces inputs for its products or forward into an industry that uses, distributes, or sells its products, 233–234
Vesting conditions, 403
Vicarious learning Learning that occurs when the learner becomes motivated to perform a behavior by watching another person performing it and being reinforced for doing so; also called *observational learning*, 399, 400
Videoconferences, 484, 506
Video rentals, 229–230
Video training, 361
Vietnam War, 202
Virtual organizations Companies in which employees are linked to an organization's centralized databases by computers, faxes, and videoconferencing and rarely meet face-to-face, 557
Virtual teams Teams whose members rarely or never meet face-to-face but, rather, interact by using various forms of information technology such as e-mail, computer networks, telephone, fax, and videoconferences, 452–453

Vision, 10, 204, 223
Vista operating system, 544
VITM countries, 179
Voice mail, 485
Volcker Rule, 97
Volunteer work, 477

W

Wages. *See* Compensation
Waste reduction, 72–73, 101–102. *See also* Sustainability
Water conservation, 23, 162
Water for People, 113
Watergate break-in, 202
Weaknesses and strengths, identifying, 224–225
Wearables, 535–536, 540
Web Globalization Report Card, 157–158
Websites, 62, 157–158. *See also* Information technology; Internet
Welfare reform, 130
Wellness centers, 380
Wheel networks, 489
Wholly owned foreign subsidiaries Production operations established in foreign countries independent of any local direct involvement, 240
Wiki Central, 495

Wikis, 494–495
Windows XP, 544
Win–win scenarios, 521, 527
Women
  on boards of directors, 127, 128
  communication styles, 500–501
  disparate earnings, 127, 136
  foreign restrictions on, 518
  hidden biases against, 153–154
  leadership behavior, 432–433
  leadership development programs, 170–171
  sexual harassment, 148–149
  status in workplace, 135
  as top managers, 127–128, 225–227, 432–433, 509–511
Worker centers, 532–533
Workers. *See* Employees
Workers' compensation, 370
Work experience, 362–363
Workplace safety, 73, 99–100
Workstation layouts, 261–262
World Wide Web, 491
Written communications, 485–488

Z

Zero-tolerance policies, 147, 149